The Last Dance

The Last Dance

TENTH EDITION

Encountering Death and Dying

LYNNE ANN DeSPELDER
Cabrillo College

ALBERT LEE STRICKLAND

McGraw Hill Education

McGraw Hill Education

THE LAST DANCE: ENCOUNTERING DEATH AND DYING, TENTH EDITION

Published by McGraw-Hill Education, 2 Penn Plaza, New York, NY 10121.

This book is printed on acid-free paper.

1 2 3 4 5 6 7 8 9 0 DOC/DOC 1 0 9 8 7 6 5 4

ISBN: 978-0-07-803546-3
MHID: 0-07-803546-5

Senior Vice President, Products & Markets: *Kurt L. Strand*
Vice President, General Manager, Products & Markets: *Michael Ryan*
Vice President, Content Production & Technology Services: *Kimberly Meriwether David*
Senior Brand Manager: *Maureen E. Prado Roberts*
Managing Development Editor: *Penina Braffman*
Marketing Specialist: *Alexandra Schultz*
Director, Content Production: *Terri Schiesl*
Lead Content Project Manager: *Jane Mohr*
Buyer: *Nichole Birkenholz*
Cover Designer: *Studio Montage, St. Louis, MO.*
Cover Images: *Edvard Munch, The Dance of Life, 1889–1900. Oil on canvas. 49¼"× 74¾". National Gallery, Oslo.*
Media Project Manager: *Jennifer Bartell*
Compositor: *Laserwords Private Limited*
Typeface: *10/12 New Baskerville*
Printer: *R. R. Donnelley*

Library of Congress Cataloging-in-Publication Data

DeSpelder, Lynne Ann, 1944-
The last dance : encountering death and dying / Lynne Ann DeSpelder, Cabrillo College, Albert Lee Strickland.—Tenth edition.
pages cm
ISBN 978-0-07-803546-3 (alk. paper)
1. Death—Psychological aspects—Textbooks. 2. Death--Social aspects—Textbooks. I. Strickland, Albert Lee. II. Title.
BF789.D4D53 2014
155.9'37—dc23 2013041273

www.mhhe.com

In memory of
Coleen DeSpelder
who lived with lightness
through the shadows of terminal illness
April 2, 1954—May 17, 2001

and to our parents

Bruce Erwin DeSpelder
and
Dorothy Roediger DeSpelder

Luther Leander Strickland
and
Bertha Wittenburg Strickland

Brief Contents

Contents

CHAPTER *2*

Learning About Death: Socialization *49*

CHAPTER *3*

Perspectives on Death: Historical and Cultural *89*

CHAPTER *8*

Last Rites: Funerals and Body Disposition *295*

CHAPTER 9

Survivors: Understanding the Experience of Loss 341

CHAPTER *10*

Death in the Lives of Children and Adolescents *385*

CHAPTER *11*

Death in the Lives of Adults *417*

CHAPTER *12*

Suicide *447*

CHAPTER *13*

Risks, Perils, and Traumatic Death *489*

CHAPTER 14

Beyond Death / After Life 531

CHAPTER 15

The Path Ahead: Personal and Social Choices 569

Preface

In *The Last Dance: Encountering Death and Dying,* we offer a comprehensive and readable introduction to the study of death and dying, one that highlights the main issues and questions. The study of death—or thanatology, from the Greek *thanatos,* meaning "death"—is concerned with questions rooted at the core of our experience. Thus, the person who sets out to increase his or her knowledge of death and dying is embarking on an exploration that is partly a journey of personal discovery. This is a journey that has both cognitive (intellectual) and affective (emotional) components. Thus, *The Last Dance* embodies an approach to the study of death and dying that combines the intellectual and the emotional, the social and the psychological, the experiential and the scholarly.

The title *The Last Dance* relates to a book written by Carlos Castaneda about the warriors of the Yaqui Indian tribe in Central America. Because a warrior can die on any day, the warrior makes a dance of power in the face of death. Castaneda says that, to truly live, we must keep death over our left shoulder. In other words, death is part of life and, because we can die at any time, we should be dancing through life.

The painting on the cover, The *Dance of Life,* by Norwegian artist Edvard Munch, evokes thoughts of the inexorable, compelling cycle of life. It depicts a festival dance on the Asgaardstrand beach on a midsummer night. An indifferent moon sheds light on the water while the dancers dance a roundel, a ring dance. One woman is entering the dance, another is leaving. There is youth, innocent new life, and age.

We are sometimes asked how we came to write a college textbook on death and dying. Lynne says, "It's as simple as the realization that students hated buying the many books needed for studying all of the topics important to learning about death and dying. And I hated having to assign all those books. One day at the start of a new semester, after getting the usual complaints from students, I whined to Al, 'Why isn't there just *one* book that a student could pick up and put under his or her arm that would cover all of these topics?' Al's response was, 'Well, why don't we write one?'"

So, some years ago, after five years dedicated to research and writing, *The Last Dance: Encountering Death and Dying* was born. Each subsequent edition reflects the changes and transformations that have occurred in the field of death studies. This book provides a solid grounding in theory and research as well as in methods for applying what is learned to readers' own circumstances, both personal and professional. It encourages a constructive process of self-discovery. *The Last Dance* is not an indoctrination to any particular point of view but, rather, an introduction to diverse points of view. The values of compassion, listening, and tolerance for the views of others are emphasized. Readers may form their own opinions, but when they do we hope it is only after considering other possibilities in a spirit of open-mindedness. Unbiased investigation leads to choices that might otherwise be neglected or overlooked.

While retaining the popular features of earlier editions, this new edition of *The Last Dance* reflects the ongoing evolution of death studies. Although people sometimes think, "What changes about death?" the truth revealed in these pages is that much has changed in recent decades and continues to change in the present. Because of this fact, every chapter has been revised to integrate the latest research, practices, and ideas and to enhance clarity of presentation.

Throughout the text, we give attention to the ways cultural and ethnic viewpoints shape our relationship with death, and there is specific discussion of the viewpoints and traditions associated with people of African heritage, Hispanic heritage, Native American heritage, Jewish heritage, Celtic heritage, Arab heritage, Oceanian heritage, and Asian heritage, including the diverse cultures of Southeast Asia as well as the cultures of India, China, Taiwan, Japan, Korea, and the Philippines. In the pages of *The Last Dance,* you will also find coverage of

- Ongoing developments in care of the seriously ill and dying, especially as they pertain to hospice and palliative care
- Death through the life course, from infancy through later adulthood, including a new section on death and the college student
- New directions in mortuary services, including personalized funerals, "green burials," and innovative options for body disposition and memorialization
- A changing health care system and its impact on dying and death
- How the Internet is influencing our relationship to death, dying, and bereavement in the digital age
- Insights about grief gained through an appreciation of the dual process and two-track models of coping with bereavement, as well as other models that can aid in understanding bereavement, grief, and mourning, including discussion of working through grief, maintaining continuing bonds with the deceased, and "telling the story" or narrative approaches to coping with grief
- How achieving the "Care-Full Society" and striving toward the creation of "compassionate cities" could improve and enhance our encounters with death

In addition, this edition contains new and updated material on physician-assisted suicide, remembrance rituals and linking objects, grief counseling and grief therapy, horrendous death, the placebo effect, familicide, and the death of a companion animal.

The study of death is unavoidably multidisciplinary. Accordingly, contributions from medicine, the humanities, and the social sciences are all found here in their relevant contexts. Throughout the book, principles and concepts are made meaningful by use of examples and anecdotes. Boxed material, photographs, and other illustrative materials expand upon and provide counterpoint to the textual presentation. Specialized terms, when needed, are clearly defined. Accompanying this edition is a companion Online Learning Center, www.mhhe.com/despelder10e, designed to promote mastery of the material covered in the text itself. We urge readers to make use of these features.

Chapter-by-Chapter Tour

Before you begin using *The Last Dance,* please join us for a quick tour through the text.

- In Chapter 1, we look at expressions of attitudes toward death in mass media, language, music, literature, and the visual arts. We ask what it means to live with an awareness of death, and we explore death anxiety, or fear of death. We conclude by examining the reasons people tend to be unfamiliar with death in modern, cosmopolitan societies.
- In Chapter 2, we investigate how we learn about death throughout the life course.
- In Chapter 3, we explore historical and cultural factors that shape attitudes and practices relative to dying and death.
- Chapter 4 shows how public policy affects our dealings with dying and death by means of a society's "death systems." Certification of death, the role of coroners and medical examiners, the functions of autopsies, procedures for legally defining and making a determination of death, medicolegal views of homicide and capital punishment, and rules regarding organ donation and transplantation are important aspects of the death system. An instructive cross-cultural example describing how Japan has dealt with ethical, moral, and legal questions involving brain death and organ transplantation wraps up this discussion.
- Care of dying persons is the primary focus of Chapter 5. Topics include health care financing; rationing of health resources; the relationship between caregivers and the patient; hospice, palliative care, and home care; elder care; trauma and emergency care; death notification procedures; and caregiver stress and compassion fatigue.

- Chapter 6 deals with a variety of issues and decisions that pertain to the end of life. Some of these issues and decisions become important in the context of diagnosis and treatment—for example, informed consent. Others come to the fore when individuals face a more immediate prospect of dying. These include choices about withholding or withdrawing life-sustaining medical treatment, physician-assisted death, and euthanasia, as well as issues involving artificial nutrition and hydration. Also discussed is the rule of double effect, which may be invoked when a medical intervention that is intended to relieve suffering leads to death. Some issues regarding the end of life can be dealt with before the crisis of a life-limiting illness—for example, making a will, setting up a living trust, obtaining life insurance, and completing advance directives to express wishes about medical treatment in the event one becomes incapacitated.
- Chapter 7, with its focus on how people live with a life-threatening illness, gives attention to the psychological and social meanings associated with such illnesses and offers insight about the ways individuals and families cope with "living-dying," from the time of initial diagnosis to the final stages of the dying trajectory. Discussion includes treatment options and issues, as well as pain management and complementary therapies. The chapter concludes with sections on the social role of the dying patient and advice about being with someone who is dying.
- The ceremonies and rituals enacted by individuals and social groups after a death form the content of Chapter 8. Death rites and customs create opportunities for expressing grief and integrating loss. This chapter examines the nature and function of last rites, with particular attention to the history of mortuary services in the United States. Information about the options for funeral services and body disposition, as well as a discussion about making meaningful choices, completes the chapter.
- Chapter 9 is devoted to helping readers gain a comprehensive understanding of bereavement, grief, and mourning. A number of important models of grief are discussed, with the recognition that any notion that "one size fits all" is likely to be inadequate. An understanding of the ways people experience and express grief, and of the variables that influence grief, demonstrates that there are many ways to cope with grief and to provide support to the bereaved. The concluding section shows that, despite loss, bereavement can present opportunities for growth.
- Employing a life-span perspective, Chapters 10 and 11 deal with death-related issues associated with different stages of life, from early childhood through old age.
- Chapter 10 includes discussion of children with life-threatening illness and discussion of children as survivors of a close death. It provides guidelines for helping children cope with change and loss.
- Chapter 11 examines losses occurring in adulthood, such as miscarriage, stillbirth, and neonatal death, and the death of a child, a parent, a spouse,

or a close friend, as well as losses associated with aging. A new section on death in the lives of college students has been added for the tenth edition.

- Chapter 12 offers insights into suicide and its risk factors, including the social and psychological context of suicide and suicidal behavior; life-span perspectives on suicide; psychological autopsies; suicide notes; and suicide prevention, intervention, and postvention. The chapter concludes with advice about helping someone who is in a suicidal crisis.
- Chapter 13 broadens the scope of death-related risks and threats. These include accidents and injuries, disasters, violence, war, genocide, terrorism, emerging diseases, and other examples of horrendous and traumatic death.
- Questions about human mortality and its meaning are at the forefront in the final two chapters of the book. Chapter 14 describes a variety of both religious and secular viewpoints, as well as accounts of near-death experiences, to present a survey of concepts and beliefs concerning immortality and the afterlife. Whether death is viewed as a "wall" or as a "door" can have important consequences for how we live our lives.
- Chapter 15 emphasizes personal and social values that are enhanced by learning about death. Examples of new directions in thanatology include efforts to bridge research and practice, clarify the goals of death education, gain an international perspective, and create compassionate cities, as well as to improve cultural competence. What does it mean to live with death and dying? Bringing together a host of topics covered in earlier chapters, this final chapter presents food for thought that can stimulate consideration of how a "good death" might be defined.

For those who wish to pursue further study of particular topics, a list of recommended readings is provided at the end of each chapter, and citations given in the chapter notes provide guidance to additional sources and references. Thus, while the text serves as an introduction to a broad range of topics in death studies, readers are pointed to resources for investigating topics that evoke special interest.

Supplements

In addition to the textbook itself, there are a number of instructor and student resources available.

- The Online Learning Center at www.mhhe.com/despelder10e provides instructors with a Test Bank, Instructor's Guide, PowerPoint presentations, quizzes, and other premium instructor's content. This premium content contains numerous files ranging from instructor's resources on the Web to activities an instructor might use such as a questionnaire to examine attitudes and experiences.
- For students, the Online Learning Center, www.mhhe.com/despelder10e, offers a glossary, and each chapter has quizzes, Web activities, chapter objectives, key terms, and flashcards.

Acknowledgments

The Last Dance has been reviewed by professors in a broad range of academic disciplines. Their suggestions have helped to make this text an outstanding teaching tool. Formal reviews have been provided by Jennifer T. Aberle, Colorado State University; Susan Adams, University of Central Arkansas; Joel R. Ambelang, Concordia University, Wisconsin; Lisa Angermeier, Indiana University at Bloomington; Patrick Ashwood, Hawkeye Community College; Thomas Attig, Bowling Green State University; Ronald K. Barrett, Loyola Marymount University, Los Angeles; Michael Beechem, University of West Florida, Pensacola; Laura Billings, Southwestern Illinois College; John B. Bond, University of Manitoba; Tashel Bordere, University of Central Missouri; Sandor B. Brent, Wayne State University; Tom Bruce, Sacramento City College; John P. Colatch, Lafayette College, Easton, Pennsylvania; Elizabeth M. Collier, The College of New Jersey; Richard Cording, Sam Houston State University; Charles A. Corr, Southern Illinois University; Gerry R. Cox, Fort Hays State University; Illene N. Cupit, University of Wisconsin, Green Bay; Steven A. Dennis, Utah State University; Kenneth J. Doka, College of New Rochelle; Donald J. Ebel, Minnesota State University; Alishia Ferguson, University of Arkansas; Stephen J. Fleming, York University, Toronto; Audrey K. Gordon, Oakton Community College; Judy Green, Walsh University, Ohio; Debra Bence Grow, Pennsylvania State University; John Harvey, Western Illinois University; Russell G. Henke, Towson State University; Lorie Henley, Finger Lakes Community College; David D. Karnos, Eastern Montana College; Linda C. Kinrade, California State University, Hayward; Dennis Klass, Webster University; Anthony Lenzer, University of Hawaii at Manoa; Daniel Leviton, University of Maryland; Paul C. Luken, Arizona State University West, Phoenix; J. Davis Mannino, Santa Rosa Junior College; Coleman C. Markham, Barton College, North Carolina; Wendy Martyna, University of California, Santa Cruz; Samuel J. Marwit, University of Missouri; Debbie Mattison, University of Michigan School of Social Work; Marsha McGee, Northeast Louisiana University; Walter L. Moore, Florida State University, Tallahassee; Lachelle Norris, Tennessee Tech University; Tina Olson, Arizona State University; Leah Rogne, Minnesota State University; Vincent M. Rolletta, Erie Community College; Cheri Barton Ross, Santa Rosa Junior College; Lee Ross, Frostburg State University, Maryland; Rita S. Santanello, Belleville Area Community College, Illinois; Thomas W. Satre, Sam Houston State University; Edwin S. Shneidman, University of California, Los Angeles; Virginia Slaughter, The University of Queensland; Judith M. Stillion, Western Carolina University; Gordon Thornton, Indiana University of Pennsylvania; Jeffrey S. Turner, Mitchell College; Mary Warner, Northern State University, South Dakota; Hannelore Wass, University of Florida, Gainesville; Jack Borden Watson, Stephen F. Austin State University, Nacogdoches, Texas; John B. Williamson, Boston College; C. Ray Wingrove, University of Richmond;

Robert Wrenn, University of Arizona, Tucson; Joseph M. Yonder, Villa Maria College of Buffalo; Margaret H. Young, Washington State University; and Andrew Scott Ziner, University of North Dakota. In addition to those named, other colleagues and students have generously shared ideas for enhancing and improving the text. We thank all who have offered helpful suggestions about the book through its successive incarnations.

We also thank our collaborators who have helped prepare ancillary instructional materials over the course of various editions of *The Last Dance*. These include Barbara Jade Sironen, Patrick Vernon Dean, Robert James Baugher, Matt and Kelley Strickland, and Carol Berns, who deserves special thanks for her work on this edition's test bank and other resources for instructors, as well as on the Online Learning Center at www.mhhe.com/despelder10e. In addition, we are grateful to staff members at many museums, libraries, and governmental institutions who have assisted us in our research and in gathering both text and art resources over the years.

Over the course of ten editions of *The Last Dance,* we have had the pleasure of working with many talented people who exemplify excellence in publishing. At McGraw-Hill, among the many individuals who helped bring this book to press, we want to particularly thank Mike Sugarman, publisher *par excellence;* Terri Schiesl, production maven, who at the outset got the ball rolling down the right track; and Erin Guendelsberger, developmental editor, who guided the typescript into production with attention to detail, good cheer, and thorough professionalism. To all whose help was instrumental in bringing this edition of *The Last Dance* to readers, our heartfelt thanks.

L. A. D.
A. L. S.

Additional McGraw-Hill Resources

- Craft your teaching resources to match the way you teach! With McGraw-Hill Create™, www.create.mcgraw-hill.com, instructors can easily rearrange chapters, combine material from other content sources, and quickly upload personal content such as a course syllabus or teaching notes. Find the content you need in Create by searching through thousands of leading McGraw-Hill textbooks. Arrange your book to fit your teaching style. Create even allows you to personalize your book's appearance by selecting the cover and adding your name, school, and course information. Order a Create book and you'll receive a complimentary print review copy in three to five business days or a complimentary electronic review copy (eComp) via e-mail in minutes. Go to www.create.mcgraw-hill.com today and register to experience how McGraw-Hill Create™ empowers you to teach your students your way.
- With the CourseSmart eTextbook version of this title, students can save up to 50 percent off the cost of a print book, reduce their impact on the environment, and access powerful Web tools for learning. Faculty can also review and compare the full text online without having to wait for a print desk copy. CourseSmart is an online eTextbook, which means users need to be connected to the Internet in order to access it. Students can also print sections of the book for maximum portability. For further details, contact your sales representative or go to www.coursesmart.com.

P R O L O G U E

I don't know how much time I have left. I've spent my life dispensing salves and purgatives, potions and incantations—miracles of nature (though I admit that some were pure medicine-show snake oil). Actually, half the time all I offered was just plain common sense. Over the years, every kind of suffering person has made his or her way here. Some had broken limbs or broken bodies . . . or hearts. Often their sorrow was an ailing son or daughter. It was always so hard when they'd lose a child. I never did get used to that. And then there were the young lovers. Obtaining their heart's desire was so important to them. I had to smile. I always made them sweat and beg for their handful of bark, and for those willful tortures I'll probably go to hell . . . if there is one. My God, how long has it been since I had those feelings myself? The fever, the lump in the throat, the yearning. I can't remember. A long time . . . maybe never. Well, there have been other passions for me. There's my dusty legion of jars. Each one holds its little secret. Barks, roots, soils, leaves, flowers, mushrooms, bugs—magic dust, every bit of it. There's my book—my "rudder," a ship's pilot would call it. That's a good name for it. Every salve, every purgative . . . they're all in there. (Everything, that is, except my stained beard, scraggly hair, and flowing robes—they'll have to figure those out on their own.) And then there's my walking stick (always faithful) . . . and the ballerina. And ten thousand mornings, ten thousand afternoons, ten thousand nights. And the stars. Oh, I have had my loves.

It hurts to move. My shelf and jars seem so far away, though I know that, if I tried, I could reach them. But no. It's enough, and it's time . . . almost. I hope he makes it back in time. He burst through my door only two days ago. A young man, well spoken. Tears were streaming down his face. He looked so bent and beaten that I could not refuse him. He told me that his wife had died over a month ago and that he had been inconsolable since.

"Please help me," he pleaded, "or kill me." He covered his face with his hands. "Perhaps they're the same thing. I don't know anymore."

I let him cry a while so I could watch him, gauge him. When at last he looked up, with my good hand I motioned him to take a seat. Then, between coughing fits, I went to work. "Do you see that toy there?" I said. "The little ballerina . . . yes, that's it. Pick it up."

"Pick it up?"

"It won't bite. Pick it up." (He probably thought it was a trick—that's what they expect.) He grasped it carefully with one hand, then wiped his eyes with the other. "That's better," I continued. "That's just a toy to you. You don't know what meaning to put to it yet. So, I want you to look at that ballerina."

He was hesitant, but I waited stubbornly until he looked down and fixed his attention on the little toy dancer. I went on: "I knew a young man once who was very handsome—always had been. He not only turned every head, he was strong and smart, and his family was wealthy. His main concern each day was which girl he should court that evening. He had planned that, after several seasons of playing at love, he would marry a beautiful girl, have beautiful children, and settle down to spend the money his father had promised him. And he had plans for that money. He had already purchased the land he wanted to live on and was having built there the biggest house in the area. He was going to raise and race horses, I think. One morning, he got on his favorite horse and went for a ride. He whipped that horse into a gallop; it stepped in a hole and threw him. The young man broke his neck and died." I stared at my guest and waited.

"That's a tragedy," he finally croaked.

"For whom? For those he left behind, perhaps. But was it for him? When he opened his eyes that morning, he didn't know he would die that day. He had no intention *of dying for another sixty years, if then. None of us does." The young man looked confused. "His mistake was that he forgot that he* could *die that day."*

"That's a morbid thought," he replied, and he looked as though he had just smelled something putrid.

"Is it? A moment ago, you asked me to end your grieving by ending your own life. Suppose I oblige?" I stared at him for a few moments with my most practiced penetrating glare. "Suppose I did agree to kill you. How would you spend your last few minutes?"

He was still a little wary of me but relieved that I seemed to be suggesting a hypothetical situation rather than a serious course of action. He considered the possibilities for a while, then straightened in his chair. "Well, I guess I would step outside and take a last, best look at the sky, the clouds, the trees."

"Suppose you lived that way all the time?" He stared at me, then looked down at his hands, searching them. "That young man I told you about . . . perhaps the tragedy for him was not that he died, but that he failed to use the eventual certainty of his death to make himself live! *Did he woo each of those ladies as though it might be his last romance? Did he build that house as though it might be his last creation? Did he ride that horse as though it would be his last ride? I don't know; I hope so." My young guest nodded, but he was still sad. I pointed to the toy ballerina he was holding. "That was given to me by a young lady who understood these things."*

He looked at the figure closely. "Is she a dancer?"

"Yes, she is, and she is dead." The young man looked up, once again off balance. "She has been dead for, oh, a very long time." After all these years, a tear fell onto my cheek. I let it go. "She was many things. A child, a woman, a cook and a gardener, a friend, lover, daughter. . . . But what she really was—who she was—was a dancer. When she was dying, she gave that doll to me, smiled, and whispered, 'At the moment of my death, I will take all of my dancing and put it in there, so my dancing can live on.'"

Tears welled in my guest's eyes.

"I can help you," I said, "but first there is something that you must do." He became very attentive. "Go to town, and knock on the door of the first house you come to. Ask the people inside if their family has ever been touched by death. If so, go to the next house. When you find a family that has not been touched by death, bring them to me. Do you understand?" He nodded, and I sighed. "I'm tired now."

He got up, set the ballerina back on the table, and started for the door. I stopped him. "Young man!" He faced me from the doorway. "Come back as soon as you can."

David Gordon

In a Spanish village, neighbors and relatives peer through the doorway upon the deathbed scene of a villager.

CHAPTER 1

Attitudes Toward Death: A Climate of Change

Dead end. Dead on. Dead center. Dead heat. Deadwood. Deadbeat. Dead tired. Dead stop. Deadline. Dead reckoning. Deadlock. Dead ahead.

Look at some of the connotations of the word *dead* in the English language. Are they positive or negative? There is no place to go when you get to a dead end, and there are usually unpleasant consequences when you miss a deadline. In contrast, however, dead reckoning gives us direction to a place where we are going.

This bit of linguistic exploration points up a paradox involved in the study of death and dying. How is our social world, our culture, set up to deal with death and the dead? Do we, consciously or unconsciously, relate to death as something to avoid? Or does death capture our attention as a defining moment, worthy of reflection and deliberate thought?

Of all human experiences, none is more overwhelming in its implications than death. Yet, we tend to relegate death to the periphery of our lives, as if it can be kept "out of sight, out of mind."[1] A first step toward gaining new choices about death is to recognize that avoiding thinking about it estranges us from an integral aspect of human life. As one writer says, "The moment we begin to be we are old enough to die."[2]

The study of death can "lead us to take seriously our finitude, our mortality, as something that provides significance to our lives."[3] Formally, *thanatology* is defined as the study of the facts or events of death and the social and psychological mechanisms for dealing with them. The word is a linguistic heir of *Thantatos* from Greek mythology, where it is generally understood as a reference to "the personification of death." A practical definition of thanatology includes ethical and moral questions, as well as cultural considerations. It is concerned not only with medicine and philosophy, but also with many other disciplines: history, psychology, sociology, and comparative religion, to name a few. In a commencement address at Stanford University, Apple founder Steve Jobs said, "Death is very likely the single best invention of life." He called it "life's change agent."[4]

Expressions of Attitudes Toward Death

Direct, firsthand experience with death is rare. Nevertheless, death has a significant place in our social and cultural worlds. This is revealed through the manner in which death is portrayed by the mass media and in the language people use when talking about death, as well as in music, literature, and the visual arts. Notice how these varied expressions reveal thoughts and feelings about death, both individually and culturally.

Mass Media

Modern communication technology makes us all survivors of death as news of disasters, accidents, violence, and war is flashed around the world. When situations involve a perceived threat, people turn to the mass media for information. On September 11, 2001, for example, more than two billion people worldwide watched the attacks in real time or watched news reports about the attacks.[5] The Internet not only increases the speed at which news is reported, it also allows us to follow along with updates from international news agencies and comments from blogs giving further details and opinion.[6] What do these secondhand sources tell us about death and dying?

In the News

When you read the newspaper or an online news source, what kinds of encounters with death vie for your attention? You are likely to find an assortment of accidents, murders, suicides, and disasters involving sudden, violent deaths. A jetliner crashes, and the news is announced with banner headlines. You see a story describing how a family perished when trapped inside their burning home, or a story describing how a family's vacation came to an untimely end due to a fatal collision on the interstate.

Then there are the deaths of the famous, which are likely to be announced on the front pages, followed soon by feature-length *obituaries.* Prefaced by headlines, obituaries send a message about the newsworthiness editors attribute to the deaths of famous people. News organizations maintain files of pending obituaries for individuals whose deaths are considered newsworthy, and these obituaries are kept updated so they are ready when the occasion demands.

In contrast, the death of the average Joe or Jill is usually made known by a *death notice*—a brief, standardized statement printed in small type and listed alphabetically in a column of vital statistics "as uniform as a row of tiny

Herbert Johnson, Library of Congress

grave plots."[7] In some newspapers, obituaries for "ordinary Joes" are given more attention with "egalitarian obits," which aim to "nail down quickly what it is we're losing when a particular person dies."[8] Still, ordinary deaths—the kind most of us will experience—are usually mentioned only in routine fashion. The spectacular obscures the ordinary.

Whether routine or extraordinary, our encounters with death in the news media influence the way we think about and respond to death. Reports may have less to do with the *event* than with how that event is *perceived*. This point is illustrated by Jack Lule in his description of how black activist Huey Newton's death was reported in newspapers across the country.[9] Newton had a public career spanning two decades, yet most reports focused on the violent nature of Newton's death while ignoring other aspects of his life.

People look to the media not only for information about events but also for clues about their meaning. This can present problems in determining what is appropriate to report in stories that involve death and survivors' grief. Media coverage of horrific deaths sometimes leads to "revictimization" or "second trauma" after the initial trauma of the event itself. Reporters may seek to capture the experience of a tragedy at the expense of victims or their survivors. The journalistic stance "If it bleeds, it leads" often sets priorities. Do the media help us explore the meaning of death or merely seek to grab our attention with sensational news flashes? Robert Fulton and Greg Owen point out that the media may "submerge the human meaning of death while depersonalizing the event further by sandwiching actual reports of loss of life between commercials or other mundane items."[10] The distinction between *public* event and *private* loss sometimes blurs, and the grief experienced by survivors or the disruption of their lives is generally given little attention.

Deaths from cancer and heart disease don't seem to interest us as much as deaths from plane crashes, roller coaster mishaps, or mountain lion attacks. Bizarre or dramatic exits grab our attention. Although the odds of dying from a heart attack are about 1 in 5, we seem more fascinated by death from bee stings (1 in 62,950), lightning (1 in 81,701), or fireworks (1 in 479,992).[11]

Media experts say that the "reality violence" on TV news really began with coverage of the Vietnam War.[12] As a "living-room" war, replete with daily doses of violent images for more than a decade, it would exert a lasting influence on how news is presented. Viewers were given a succession of violent images: wartime casualties both friend and foe, the execution of a Viet Cong lieutenant by gunshot to the head on a Saigon street, pictures of napalmed children, and images of a burning monk. This is "action news," and it is a marketable format that flourishes with such events as school shootings and the public death of a man on a Los Angeles overpass who, retrieving a shotgun, "blasted half his head away as police and news choppers hovered above."[13] Allan Kellehear says, "There is no shortage of death reportage in the media . . . however, what passes for death is frequently merely violence."[14] He adds: "As long as death and loss appear in newspapers and TV programmes in the context of 'problems' and 'tragedies,' our understanding of these will be coloured by these terms and concepts."[15]

Media analyst George Gerbner observes that depictions of death in the mass media are often embedded in a structure of violence that conveys "a heightened sense of danger, insecurity, and mistrust."[16] Such depictions reflect what Gerbner and his colleagues call a "mean world syndrome," in which the symbolic use of death contributes to an "irrational dread of dying and thus to diminished vitality and self-direction in life."

According to Gerbner, the effect of violent images in the media is not to cause viewers to become more violent themselves; rather, viewers are likely to perceive the world as a frightening and scary place, a place of murder and mayhem, disease and plague, threats of war, a world populated by psychotic killers, child abductors, terrorists, and threatening animals. This perception of a mean world in which predators of every stripe—and every species—appear forever on the loose and in attack mode creates a sense of anxiety and fear that is out of proportion with reality.[17]

Entertaining Death

Television's influence on our lives is well established. Programs such as *Six Feet Under, Bones,* and *CSI* may challenge certain taboos surrounding death, but this interest in death and dying mainly serves to make the corpse what some commentators call the new "porn star" of popular culture.[18] Seldom do images portrayed in the mass media enhance our understanding of death by dealing with such real-life topics as how people cope with a loved one's death or confront their own dying.

Besides its appearance in movies of the week and on crime and adventure series, death is a staple of newscasts (typically, several stories involving death are featured in each broadcast), nature programs (death in the animal kingdom), children's cartoons (caricatures of death), soap operas (which seem always to have some character dying), sports (with descriptions such as "the ball is dead" and "the other team is killing them"), and religious programs (with theological and anecdotal mention of death). Despite this, the lack of stories depicting realistic themes portraying death, dying, and bereavement has been characterized as "an impoverishment of death symbolism" in the media.[19]

Turning to programming directed toward children, recall cartoon depictions of death. Daffy Duck is pressed to a thin sheet by a steamroller, only to pop up again a moment later. Elmer Fudd aims his shotgun at Bugs Bunny, pulls the trigger, bang! Bugs, unmarked by the rifle blast, clutches his throat, spins around several times, and mutters, "It's all getting dark now, Elmer. . . . I'm going. . . ." Bugs falls to the ground, both feet still in the air. As his eyes close, his feet finally hit the dirt. But wait! Now Bugs pops up, good as new. Reversible death!

Consider the western, which mutes the reality of death by describing the bad guy as "kicking the bucket"—relegated, no doubt, to Boot Hill at the edge of town, where the deceased "pushes up daisies." The camera pans from the dying person's face to a close-up of hands twitching—then all movement ceases as the person's breathing fades away in perfect harmony with the musical score. Or, more likely, the death is violent: the cowboy gunfight at the OK Corral, high noon. The gent with the slower draw is hit, reels, falls, his body convulsing into cold silence.

People who have been present as a person dies describe a very different picture. Many recall the gurgling, gasping sounds as the last breath rattles through the throat; the changes in body color as flesh tones tinge blue; the feeling of a once warm and flexible body growing cold and flaccid. Surprised by the reality, they say, "Death is not at all what I thought it would be like; it doesn't look or sound or feel like anything I see on television or in movies!"

Unrealistic portrayals of violent death fail to show real harm to victims, their pain, or appropriate punishment for perpetrators.

Thrillers featuring extreme violence and what has been called death porn have become a profitable genre for moviemakers. The road to more "blood and gore" in popular films was paved in part by the success of classic "slasher" or "dead teenager" movies, like *Nightmare on Elm Street* (1984), which included point-of-view shots from the killer's perspective. In traditional horror films, the audience viewed the action through the eyes of the victim and thus identified with his or her fate. In slasher films, however, viewers are asked

> One of the first things we teach to journalism students in the USA is to use "died" instead of "passed away" or "departed this life," which is how most people can tell the difference between an obituary written by the funeral director and one written by a newspaper staff member. Even in American English, it seems nearly disrespectful to go to such lengths to avoid saying the obvious; when my time comes, I hope to have pre-written my own obit, which will say something to the effect that "Old Man Wilcox is dead. He has ceased to be. He has expired and gone to meet his maker. He is a stiff. Bereft of life, he rests in peace. Services will be held on Wednesday; cocktails will be served."

to identify with the attacker. (A similar form of identification can be found in violent video games.) The depictions of violence in such movies suggest that residual tendencies from our evolutionary background may attract human beings to "exhibitions of brutality and terror."[20]

When told of his grandfather's death, one contemporary seven-year-old asked, "Who did it to him?" Death is generally portrayed on television or in movies as coming from outside, often violently, reinforcing the notion that dying is something that *happens to* us, rather than something we *do.* Death is an accidental rather than a natural process. As our firsthand *experiences* of death and violence have diminished, *representations* of death and violence in the media have increased in sensationalism.

Movies engage our psychological faculties in profound and unique ways.[21] In thinking about the films, DVDs, and television programs you've watched recently, what are your observations about the ratio of positive and negative images of dying and death?

Language

Listen to the language people use when talking about dying or death, and you are likely to discover that it is often indirect. The words *dead* and *dying* tend to be avoided; instead, loved ones "pass away," embalming is "preparation," the deceased is "laid to rest," burial becomes "interment," the corpse is "remains," the tombstone is a "monument," and the undertaker is transformed into a "funeral director." Such euphemisms—substitutions of indirect or vague words and phrases for ones considered harsh or blunt—tend to suggest a well-choreographed production surrounding the dead. Hannelore Wass, a pioneering death educator, notes that euphemisms substituting for plain-spoken "*D* words" turn up even in the language of death and dying experts as terminal care becomes "palliative care," and dying patients are described as "life threatened."[22] Death may be described as "a negative patient-care outcome" and an airline crash as an "involuntary conversion of a 727."[23]

When plain talk about death is subverted by substitutions, reality is devalued and depersonalized. For example, description of the horror of death in war is often cloaked by euphemisms—individuals killed in battle

TABLE 1-1 *Death Talk: Metaphors, Euphemisms, and Slang*

Croaked	No longer with us
Kicked the bucket	Taking the dirt nap
Gone	In the great beyond
Expired	On the other side
Succumbed	Asleep in Christ
Left us	Departed
Lost	Transcended
Wasted	Bought the farm
Checked out	With the angels
Laid to rest	Cashed in
Pushing up daisies	Crossed over Jordan
Called home	Perished
Was a goner	Ate it
Bit the dust	It was curtains
Annihilated	Out of his/her misery
Liquidated	Ended it all
Terminated	Resting in peace
Gave up the ghost	Dropped the body
Rubbed out	That was all she wrote
Snuffed	Joined the ancestors
Bit the grass	Subject just fataled
Took the last journey	Gone west

are described in terms of "body counts" and civilian deaths are termed "collateral damage." The language people use when talking about death often reflects a desire to avoid blunt reality. Euphemisms, metaphors, and slang make up a large part of death talk (see Table 1-1).

However, the use of euphemism and metaphor does not always imply an impulse to deny the reality of death or avoid talking about it. These linguistic devices are also used to communicate subtler or deeper meanings than those associated with plainer speech. For example, terms like *passing* or *passing on* may convey an understanding of death as a spiritual transition, especially among members of some religious and ethnic traditions.

Similarly, sympathy cards provide a way for people to express condolences to the bereaved without directly mentioning death.[24] Some cards refer to death metaphorically, as in sentiments like "What is death but a long sleep?" while others apparently deny it in verses like "He is not dead, he is just away." Images of sunsets and flowers create an impression of peace, quiet, and perhaps a return to nature. The fact of bereavement, losing a loved one by death, is generally mentioned within the context of memories or the healing process of time. It is interesting to check the greeting-card rack to see if you can find a card that plainly uses the word *dead* or *death.* By acknowledging loss in a gentle fashion, sympathy cards are intended to comfort the bereaved.

After someone dies, our conversations about that person usually move from present tense to past tense: "He *was* fond of music," "She *was* a leader in her field." Using this form of speech, which grammarians term the *indicative voice,* is a way of acknowledging the reality of death while distancing us from the dead. One way to continue to include the "voice" of the deceased in present circumstances lies in the use of the *subjunctive,* which has been described as the mode of "as if," of what "might be" or "could have been." It is a "zone of possibility," rather than certainty.[25] We hear examples of this when people say things like "He would have been proud of you" or "She would have enjoyed this gathering tonight."

Language usage also tells us something about the intensity and immediacy of a person's encounter with death, as in the form of "danger of death" narratives—stories about close calls with death. In such stories, a shift in tense typically occurs when the narrator reaches the crucial point in his or her story, the point when death seems imminent and unavoidable. Consider the following example: A man who had experienced a frightening incident while driving in a snowstorm began telling his story in the past tense as he described the circumstances. As he came to the point when his car went out of control on an icy curve and began to slide into the opposing lane of traffic, however, he abruptly switched to the present tense, as if he were *reliving* the experience of watching an oncoming car heading straight for him and believing in that moment that he was about to die.[26]

Word choices can also reflect changes in how a death event is experienced at different times. For example, after a disaster occurs, as the focus of rescue efforts changes, so does the language used to describe the work of emergency personnel and search-and-rescue teams. As hours stretch into days, *rescue* work becomes *recovery* work.

Scholars point out that language appears to influence many aspects of human thought. In fact, what we normally call "thinking" is a complex set of collaborations between linguistic and nonlinguistic representations and processes.[27] Look again at the words and phrases used in death talk (see Table 1-1). Notice how language offers clues about the manner of death and the speaker's attitude toward the death. Subtle distinctions may reflect different attitudes, sometimes involving cultural frameworks. Consider, for instance, the difference between *passed away* and *passed on.* Paying attention to the euphemisms, metaphors, slang, and other linguistic devices people use when talking about death is a way to appreciate the variety and range of attitudes toward dying and death.

Music

In *Music of the Soul,* Joy Berger writes, "Nearly every civilization, culture, and religion exemplifies the use of music at times of loss and grief."[28] Pipes and flutes were referred to by Euripedes in his play *Helen* as an aid to mourning. Leonard Bernstein's Symphony no. 3 (*Kaddish*) is based on the Jewish prayer for the dead. Richard Strauss's *Death and Transfiguration* depicts the death of an artist. Significant compositions written to commemorate the events of September 11, 2001 include John Adam's *On the Transmigration of Souls* and Steve Reich's *WTC 9/11*. Music scholar Ted Gioia reminds us that the potency and transformational power of music is enhanced by its ability to create a unity of purpose. He notes that the "deep faith in the transformational power of sound is so widespread in traditional cultures that we are perhaps justified in calling it a universal belief."[29]

The *dirge* (a hymn of grief) is a musical form associated with funeral processions and burials. The jazz funeral of New Orleans is a well-known example of a popular interpretation of the dirge. Beethoven, Schubert, Schumann, Strauss, Brahms, Mahler, and Stravinsky all wrote dirges. Related to dirges are *elegies*—musical settings for poems commemorating a person's death—and *laments.* Elegies are emotional acknowledgments that "all things are impermanent, which is itself a profound spiritual understanding."[30]

Laments are an expression of stylized or ritualized leave-taking found in many cultural settings, one example being Scottish clan funerals, where bagpipes are played. Vocally, the typical lament is an expression of mourning called *keening,* an emotional expression of loss and longing that is reminiscent of crying. For the ancient Greeks, lamentation was intended to both "praise the deceased and provide emotional release for the bereaved."[31] An audience, hearing the lament, were "enabled to use the expressions of loss and sorrow as their own, thereby diminishing the opportunity for explosive and spontaneous eruptions of anguish."[32]

Laments may help the bereaved identify their altered social status and seek sympathetic understanding from the community.[33] Italian philosopher Ernesto De Martino traced how the practice of lamentation—in word, gesture, and music—moderates the tendency toward collapse or breakdown that threatens persons in moments of extreme crisis, such as the aftermath of the death of a close relative.[34] In this way, laments promote the cultural reintegration of the mourner while simultaneously reestablishing bonds of alliance between the living and the dead. In a well-known Greek lament, a mother says that she will take her pain to the goldsmith and have it made into an amulet so that she can wear it forever.[35]

The *requiem,* a musical composition played at a mass for the dead, is related to the elegy. This musical form has attracted composers like Mozart, Berlioz, and Verdi, among others. One section of the Requiem Mass, the *Dies Irae* ("Day of Wrath"), is a musical symbol for death in works by many composers. In Berlioz's *Symphonie Fantastique* (1830), this theme is heard, first following an ominous tolling of bells and then, as the music reaches its climax, in counterpoint to the frenzied dancing of witches at a *sabbat.* Berlioz's *Symphonie* tells the story of a young musician who, spurned by his beloved, attempts suicide with an overdose of opium. In a narcotic coma, he experiences fantastic dreams that include a nightmarish march to the gallows. The *Dies Irae* is also heard in Camille Saint-Saëns's *Danse Macabre* (1874) and Franz Liszt's *Totentanz* (1849), two of the best-known musical renditions of the Dance of Death (discussed in its historical context in Chapter 3).

Tragedy and death are common in opera. This art form, which combines drama with music, has been characterized as obsessed with death, or at least a romanticized view of death prevalent in Western culture during the time frame of such classic compositions as *Aida, Carmen, La Bohème, Madame Butterfly, Tosca,* and *La Traviata.*[36]

As these examples attest, death themes are heard in both religious and secular compositions. Pink Floyd's "Time" is a musical reminder of the limits of a life span and how each day's passing brings us "closer to death." Eric Clapton's "Tears in Heaven" was written for his four-year-old son who died from a fall from a high-rise in Manhattan. Tim McGraw's "Live Like You Were Dying" celebrates life renewed after the death of his father.

The lyrics of Elvis Presley's early hit "Heartbreak Hotel" reportedly were inspired by a suicide note that contained the phrase "I walk the lonely street." The branch of heavy metal music known as death metal is partly defined by its lyrics, which convey images of homicide, catastrophic destruction, and suicide, performed by bands with names like Morbid Angel, Napalm Death, Carcass, and Entombed. Indeed, death imagery in rock music may have helped break the taboo against public mention of death. Support for this thesis is found in surveys of Top 40 songs.[37] Some authorities have traced the beginnings of the civil rights movement to a musical event that occurred sixteen years before Rosa Parks refused to yield her seat on a Montgomery, Alabama, bus: Billie Holiday's singing of "Strange Fruit," the lyrics of which describe horrific imagery of the lynching of African Americans.[38]

Music has been recruited to enlist patriotic support for war efforts, as in George M. Cohan's "Over There" during the First World War.[39] It has also been used to cast doubt on the legitimacy of war. During the Vietnam conflict, listeners heard Country Joe McDonald's "Fixin' to Die Rag," with its well-known refrain, "What are we fighting for?"

Mayhem and misery have long been staples of music. Folk ballads describe premonitions of death, deathbed scenes, last wishes of the dying, the sorrow and grief of mourners, and the afterlife. Consider such songs as "Where Have All the Flowers Gone?" (war), "Long Black Veil" (mourning), "Casey Jones" (accidental death), and "John Henry" (occupational hazards).

Themes of suicide are also common, especially in tales of love and death. Some songs, such as "The Ballad of Jesse James," glorify outlaws and other bad guys. Graeme Thomson observes that "Stagger Lee" is a close relative of "Jesse James," except "Stag has no great quest for justice to pursue; he is just plain *bad.*"[40] This musical genre is also found in Mexican popular culture in the form of *narcocorridos,* narrative songs or *corridos* that describe the careers of smugglers and drug lords.[41]

In American blues music, themes of loss, separation, tribulation, and death are commonly heard. Disasters have inspired blues lyrics, as with the sinking of the *Titanic* and the 1927 Mississippi River flood. The desire to be remembered after death is voiced in Blind Lemon Jefferson's "See That My Grave Is Kept Clean." In "I Feel Like Going Home," Muddy Waters tells us that death sometimes brings relief. Other examples of blues themes include

Bessie Smith's "Nobody Knows You When You're Down and Out" (economic reversal), T-Bone Walker's "Call It Stormy Monday" (lost love), John Mayall's "The Death of J. B. Lenoir" (death of friend in a car accident), and Otis Spann's "The Blues Never Die" (consolation in loss). In all, the blues express "a deep stoic grief and despair, a dark mood of lamentation, but also a wry and ribald humor."[42]

Sometimes characterized as the flip side of the blues, gospel music expresses a wealth of images of loss and grief. Examples include "Oh, Mary Don't You Weep" (mourning), "Known Only to Him" (facing one's own death), "When the Saints Go Marching In" (the afterlife), "If I Could Hear My Mother Pray Again" (a parent's death), and "Precious Memories" (adjustment to loss and sustaining bonds with the deceased).

Charles Reagan Wilson identifies six categories of death in country music: (1) the pervasiveness of death, (2) violent and tragic death, (3) songs of love and death, (4) death and the family, (5) celebrity death, and (6) religious influences on death.[43] "Will the Circle Be Unbroken," a song that can be classified as both gospel and country, describes a mother's death and a child's grief in precise imagery. The Appalachian dirge "O, Death" reflects the *memento mori* tradition, a reminder of the reality of death. Country songs, as Wilson says, "continue to embody the idea that death should not be segregated from the rest of life, but should be dealt with openly as a natural and profound human concern."[44]

In traditional Hawaiian culture, chants known as *mele kanikau* were used as laments for commemorating a person's death.[45] Some *kanikau* were carefully composed; others were chanted spontaneously during the funeral procession. Imagery of the natural world is called upon to portray the writer's experience of loss.[46] Memories of shared experiences amid natural surroundings are mentioned: "My companion in the chill of Manoa" or "My companion in the forest of Makiki." Such chants fondly recall the things that bind together the deceased and his or her survivors. The message was not "I am bereft without you" but, rather, "These are the things I cherish about you."

Think about how music provides solace in experiences of loss. As we cope with losses that beset us throughout life, certain songs and musical works bring to mind poignant memories that refresh our grief.[47] Whether Mozart's *Requiem* or a Top 40 tune, music can cue the recall of happy moments shared with loved ones whose death has left us bereft. At other times, a lyric or melody sets us reflecting on our own mortality.

Themes of loss and death are heard in all musical styles (see Table 1-2).[48] As you listen to various styles of music, notice the references to dying and death and ask yourself, What messages are being conveyed? What attitudes are being expressed? Whatever your musical taste, you will find a wealth of information about individual and cultural attitudes toward death.

Literature

From the epic poetry of Homer's *Iliad* and the classic drama of Sophocles' *Oedipus the King* and Shakespeare's *King Lear*, through modern classics like

TABLE 1-2 *Death Themes in Popular Music*

Performer	Song	Theme
Beatles	"Eleanor Rigby"	Aging and loss
Boyz II Men	"Say Goodbye to Yesterday"	Grief
Jackson Browne	"For a Dancer"	Eulogy
Mariah Carey	"One Sweet Day"	Missing a loved one
Johnny Cash	"The Man Comes Around"	Judgment Day
Eric Clapton	"Tears in Heaven"	Death of young son
Joe Diffie	"Almost Home"	Father's death
Dion	"Abraham, Martin, and John"	Assassination
Doors	"The End"	Homicide
Bob Dylan	"Knockin' on Heaven's Door"	Last words
Grateful Dead	"Black Peter"	Social support
Jimi Hendrix	"Mother Earth"	Inevitability of death
Elton John	"Candle in the Wind"	Deaths of Marilyn Monroe and Princess Diana
Patty Loveless	"How Can I Help You Say Goodbye"	Mother's death
Dave Matthews	"Gravedigger"	Anticipation of dying
Sinead O'Connor	"I Am Stretched on Your Grave"	Mourning
Pink Floyd	"Dogs of War"	Combat death
The Police	"Murder by Numbers"	Political deaths
Elvis Presley	"In the Ghetto"	Violent death
Snoop Dogg	"Murder Was the Case"	Urban homicide
Bruce Springstein	"Streets of Philadelphia"	AIDS
James Taylor	"Fire and Rain"	Friend's death
Stevie Wonder	"My Love Is With You"	Death of a child
Warren Zevon	"My Ride's Here"	Arrival of hearse and death

Leo Tolstoy's *The Death of Ivan Ilych,* James Agee's *A Death in the Family,* William Faulkner's *As I Lay Dying,* and Ernest J. Gaines's *A Lesson Before Dying,* death is treated as significant in human experience.[49] Ted Bowman observes that the language of bereavement and grief is enhanced by literary resources that help people give voice to their own stories of loss.[50]

Uncertainty about death is often found in poetry of mourning for the dead, which, Jahan Ramazani says, "assumes in the modern period an extraordinary diversity and range, incorporating more anger and skepticism, more conflict and anxiety than ever before."[51] Earlier in this chapter, we discussed elegies in the context of musical expressions of attitudes toward death. Elegies are also expressed in literature. Note that the elegy is not to be confused with a eulogy (oratory or praise in honor of the deceased) or epitaph (a brief statement commemorating the deceased, often inscribed as a memorial on a tomb).

The term *elegy* refers to a poem or song memorializing the dead.[52] It is usually pensive, reflective, or plaintive, an expression of suffering or woe. Elegies typically describe feelings of sorrow, sadness, mournfulness, melancholy, nostalgia, lamentation, or some blending of these qualities. Elegies have been characterized as "a way to say goodbye while celebrating who or what is gone."[53]

Early examples of the genre of elegy in English literature include John Milton's "Lycidas" (1637) and Thomas Gray's "Elegy Written in a Country Churchyard" (1750). Examples from American literature include "O Captain, My Captain" (1865), Walt Whitman's elegy on the death of President Abraham Lincoln, and "For the Union Dead" (1965), Robert Lowell's elegy based on the story of Colonel Robert Shaw, who led the first all-black brigade during the American Civil War.

Elegies have been written to express a personal sense of grief as well as out of a generalized feeling of loss and metaphysical sadness. Examples include the series of ten poems in *Duino Elegies* by the German poet Rainer Maria Rilke and poems by Czeslaw Milosz, which lament the cruelties of totalitarian government. Other examples are Wilfred Owen's poems of moral objection to the pain wrought by industrialized warfare; Allen Ginsberg's *Kaddish* after the death of his mother; Seamus Heaney's memorials to the suffering caused by political violence in Ireland; and the "parental elegies" in the poetry of Sylvia Plath, Anne Sexton, and Adrienne Rich. Poems give us insight into the universality of loss in ways that can be consoling and therapeutic.[54] Edward Hirsch tells us, "Implicit in poetry is the notion that we are deepened by heartbreaks, that we are not so much diminished as enlarged by grief, by our refusal to vanish—to let others vanish—without leaving a verbal record."[55]

In literature, the meaning of death is often explored as it relates to society as well as the individual. Novels about war depict how individuals and societies search for meaning in shattering experiences of trauma and loss. In *All Quiet on the Western Front,* a novel set in the time of World War I, Erich Maria Remarque described the pointlessness of modern warfare by telling the story of a youthful combatant who quickly moves from innocence to disillusionment. The technological horror of World War II, particularly devastation

John O'Hara's *Appointment in Samarra* reminds us that we cannot escape our mortality nor the pervasive angst that it arouses. In that story, a servant returns, profoundly shaken, from a trip to the market. His master asks what has caused the servant's terror. The servant replies that when someone in the crowd jostled him, he turned and noticed the Angel of Death beckoning him. The horror-stricken servant then asks his master for a horse so that he might ride to Samarra, some distance away, where the Angel of Death won't be able to find him. The master agrees, and the servant leaves for Samarra. Later that day, the master goes to the market. He, too, encounters the Angel of Death and asks why the Angel had made that threatening gesture to his servant. Death allegedly replies, "That was not a threatening gesture, simply one of surprise. I didn't expect to see him here today since I had an appointment to meet him tonight in Samarra."

Jean Lipman-Blumen,
"Our Existential Vulnerability to Toxic Leaders"

caused by the atomic bomb, is the focus of John Hersey's *Hiroshima.* The surreal aspects of the Vietnam War received attention in books like Michael Herr's *Dispatches* and Tim O'Brien's *Going After Cacciato,* and similar accounts are being published about the recent wars in Iraq and Afghanistan.

In Holocaust literature, devastating experiences of horror and mass death are dealt with in victims' diaries, as well as in novels and psychological studies.[56] Examples include Chaim Kaplan's *Warsaw Diary,* Charlotte Delbo's *None of Us Will Return,* Elie Wiesel's *Night,* and Anne Frank's *Diary of a Young Girl.*

Modern literature often explores the meaning of death in situations that are seemingly incomprehensible. The hero tries to come to terms with sudden and violent death in situations that allow no time or place for survivors to express their grief or mourn their dead.[57] Themes may focus on a "landscape of violence."[58] In "vigilante" stories, for example, such as detective novels and some westerns, the hero sets out to avenge evil but is often corrupted by a self-justifying morality that only perpetuates violence.[59] Finding meaning in death is problematic, as violence reduces persons to the status of *things.*

Cadets at the United States Military Academy (West Point) learn about the historical role of poetry in shaping culture, attitudes, and values, with the aim of "dispelling the illusion that prepackaged answers are always there for the taking in a world flush with ambiguities."[60]

Visual Arts

In the visual arts, death themes are revealed through symbols, signs, and images.[61] Edvard Munch's *The Dance of Life,* which appears on the cover of this text, represents the artist's summing up of human fate: "Love and death, beginnings and endings, are fused in a roundel that joins private lives and lusts to the larger, inexorable cycle of ongoing generations."[62]

Art is often a vehicle for expressing the impact of personal loss. When Pan Am Flight 103 was brought down by a terrorist bomb, Suse Lowenstein's son was among those killed. As a sculptor, she found a way to express her own grief and that of other women bereft by the crash by making a series of female nude figures that compose an exhibit titled *Dark Elegy.* In earth tones, the larger-than-life figures are shown in the throes of grief (see Figure 1-1). Some figures look mute. Others are obviously screaming. Some look as though they were eviscerated. Lowenstein expressed the hope that *Dark Elegy* will be "a reminder that life is fragile and that we can lose that which is most precious to us so easily and have to live with that loss for the remainder of our lives."[63]

Art gives us a window into the customs and beliefs of other ages and places. For example, Charles Willson Peale's *Rachel Weeping* (1772 and 1776) depicts a deathbed scene from the American colonial period in which the artist's wife is shown mourning their dead child. The child's jaw is wrapped with a fabric strap to keep it closed. Her arms are bound with cord to keep them at her sides. Medicines, all of which have proved ineffective, sit on a

Figure 1-1 *Dark Elegy*
About the women portrayed in her work *Dark Elegy,* the artist says, "One by one, they come into my studio, step onto a posing platform, close their eyes, and go back to December 21, 1988, to that horrible moment when they learned that their loved one had died. . . . This is the moment I freeze in time. This is the pose that I shape into sculpture."

bedside table. As the mother gazes heavenward, she holds a handkerchief to wipe away the tears streaming down her face, her grief in marked contrast to the dead child's peaceful countenance.

Francisco José de Goya's *Self-Portrait with Dr. Arrieta* exemplifies an artistic genre that depicts deathbed scenes and persons *in extremis*. Completed for the doctor who aided in Goya's recovery from a life-threatening illness, this painting shows the doctor holding medicine to Goya's lips while the figure of Death is depicted next to people who are thought to be Goya's priest and his housekeeper. Suicide is another theme dealt with by artists of virtually all eras and cultures. A well-known example is Rembrandt van Rijn's *The Suicide of Lucretia,* which portrays Lucretia with a tear in her eye, moments after she has stabbed herself with a dagger.

One of the most arresting expressions of dying and death ever to emerge in the graphic arts occurred in Western Europe during the Middle Ages. Growing out of widespread fears about the spread of plague, the images associated with the *Danse Macabre* (Dance of Death) display a concern with the stark features of mortality and fears of sudden, unexpected death. An example is found in the Bargello National Museum in Florence, where a series of three wax sculptures by Italian artist Gaetano Giulio Zumbo depicts the process of body dissolution from the fresh cadaver to one the worms have completely devoured. The morbid aspects of mortality have also evoked attention by more recent artists, as in Fritz Eichenberg's woodcuts depicting the fears of our era: annihilation caused by war, environmental catastrophe, and diseases such as AIDS.[64]

In some art, we find a whimsical attitude toward death, as in the engravings of Mexican artist José Guadalupe Posada, which contain skeletal figures from all walks of life engaged in daily routines, or in American sculptor Richard Shaw's *Walking Skeleton,* with the skeleton composed of twigs, bottles, playing cards, and similar found objects.

During the nineteenth century, people throughout the United States incorporated both classical and Christian symbols of death to memorialize public figures as well as family members.[65] Embroidered memorials to the dead were hung in the parlor, the most important room of the house, and elaborate quilts were sewn into designs that celebrated the life of the deceased. Such mourning art provided not only a way to perpetuate memories of a loved one but also a focus for physically coping with grief, an opportunity to actively grieve by doing something.

Similar motives led to the making of a massive quilt to commemorate persons who had died from AIDS: The Names Project AIDS Memorial Quilt.[66] In folk art, quilts represent family and community. As the largest ongoing community arts project in America, the AIDS Quilt affirms the value of creative expression as a means of coping with loss.

> The quilt symbolized individuals sharing their grief by sharing their continuing bonds with friends and lovers, and in doing so the survivors became a community of mourners.[67]

Smithsonian Institution

© Albert Lee Strickland

The making of a memorial quilt was among the elaborate personal and social mechanisms for dealing with grief widely practiced during the nineteenth century, as in this example memorializing a granddaughter who died in infancy. This traditional mourning custom was revived recently to commemorate and remember persons who died from AIDS; in the example shown here, words and symbols express beloved qualities of Joe's life. For survivors, the creation of such memorials provides not only a focus for physically working through grief but also a means of perpetualizing the memory of the loved one.

Maxine Junge points out,

> Creativity in the face of death offers a spectrum of life-enhancing possibilities. These possibilities can ward off a meaningless conclusion to a life, give meaning and hope to a life lived and to a future in which the dead, through memory, still exist.[68]

The urge to memorialize the dead and offer comfort to the bereaved through artistic means is also demonstrated by a variety of homemade condolences sent to relatives of military men and women killed in Iraq and Afghanistan.[69] Operation Gold Star Flag, formed by a group of military wives, revived a tradition of flag-making that began during World War I, when families with relatives in the military displayed in their windows small flags—white fields with red borders and in the middle a blue star, which was changed to gold if the serviceman was killed. Other groups, such as Marine Comfort Quilts and Operation Homemade Quilts, fashion quilts with center squares personalized in memory of each casualty.

A woman who had been given one of the Marine Comfort Quilts described how, when she finds herself missing her brother, she wraps herself in the quilt and cries until the wee hours of the morning: "It's called a 'comfort quilt,'" she said, "and that's exactly what it is; it has so much love from so many different people who never even met my brother." Another woman, a mother whose son was killed by friendly fire (that is, by his own comrades), said: "Your friends and family are there, but when you receive good deeds from people you don't even know, it makes you feel like you're not alone."[70]

Like the AIDS Memorial Quilt, the Vietnam Veterans Memorial Wall in Washington, D.C., designed by architect Maya Lin, is an example of contemporary mourning art that works to counter the anonymity of lives lost. It has been described as the "iconographic reversal of the Tomb of the Unknowns," with its "vast polished surface" serving as "the tombstone of the known."[71] On the wall, names of the dead are listed chronologically by the date of their death, rather than alphabetically, presenting a chronicle that vividly depicts the scale of losses. Mementos left by visitors are collected by the National Park Service, and items have been displayed at the Smithsonian's National Museum of American History.

Similarly, at Arlington National Cemetery, the graves of veterans killed in Iraq and Afghanistan are decorated with handwritten notes and items that poignantly celebrate personal connection. Before those wars, the expression of grief at Arlington was confined to wreaths and flowers. Now, personnel from the U.S. Army Center for Military History come each week to add to a collection that may one day become an exhibit in a museum devoted to telling the story of war and its cost. About the commemorative function of war museums, Andrew Whitmarsh says:

> Memory and commemoration are constructed according to the social, cultural, and political nature, as well as the needs and experiences, of the society and individuals producing them. War museums have often been accused of sanitizing

> or glamorizing war through their depiction of "heroes" and their portrayal of death, The commemorative aspect of war museums directly affects their style of interpretation.[72]

In Japan, a shrine honoring the "spirits" of war dead has stirred diplomatic and domestic controversy because of differing interpretations of its significance and purpose.[73]

As Carla Sofka points out, when handled with care and sensitivity, such museums can be healing spaces, honoring the memories and legacies of both victims and survivors.[74]

The importance of the arts in a comprehensive understanding of how people cope with loss is expressed in this statement by the International Work Group on Death, Dying, and Bereavement:

> The arts and humanities with their images, symbols, and sounds express themes of life, death, and transcendence. They are the language of the soul and can enable people to express and appreciate the universality as well as the particularity of each person's experience.[75]

In the visual arts, these themes and this language are evident in a broad range of works, from those formed out of the particulars of an individual's unique loss—as in the sculptures of Suse Lowenstein, which depict the grief of a parent following the death of a child—to those that function on a larger scale as *sites of memory* for losses that are both personal and communal—such as those commemorated by the AIDS Memorial Quilt and the Vietnam Veterans Memorial Wall. Whatever the scale, as Sandra Bertman points out, one of the main functions of art is to engage our awareness and "bring us closer to what language cannot reach."[76]

Humor

Humor defuses our anxiety about death. It puts fearful possibilities into manageable perspective. James Thorson says, "We make fun of that which threatens us."[77] Death-related humor comes in many different forms, from funny epitaphs to so-called black or gallows humor. Incongruity is one of the components of humor.[78] One joke, for example, describes a project manager who leaves a suicide note in the form of a PowerPoint presentation; the joke tells how his colleagues ignore the tragic content of the note while critiquing its presentation. Similarly, on a highway, motorists are taken aback by a gleaming white hearse with the cryptic license plates "Not Yett." Serious and somber matters can be easier to deal with when there is comedic relief.

There are "intimate connections between death and laughter."[79] Mary Hall observes that "what is humorous to each of us depends on our particular cultural set, our own experience, and our personal inclination."[80] Humor often functions as a kind of comment on incongruity or inconsistency relative to social norms or perspectives, as when a young girl wrote a letter to God asking, "Instead of letting people die and having to make new ones, why don't you just keep the ones You have now?"[81] As Thorson points out, "Taking potshots at the spectre that will destroy us may not in fact do away with the

Ultimate Problem, but satire at least makes us feel better in some small way about our common fate. This is the essence of coping."[82]

A joke that is shared gleefully by one group of people may be shocking to others; there are constraints on the kinds of humor that a particular person or group finds acceptable. Nevertheless, humor helps us cope with painful situations. Individuals held as prisoners of war during the Vietnam War considered humor so important to coping that they would "risk torture to tell a joke through the walls to another prisoner who needed to be cheered up."[83] Humor is an important aid in confronting our fears and gaining a sense of mastery over the unknown.

Humor functions in several ways relative to death: First, it raises our consciousness about a taboo subject and gives us a way to talk about it. Second, it presents an opportunity to rise above sadness, providing a release from pain and promoting a sense of control over a traumatic situation, even if we cannot change it. Third, humor is a great leveler; it treats everyone alike and sends the message that there are no exemptions from the human predicament. Thus, it binds us together and encourages a sense of intimacy, which helps us face what is unknown or distressing. Humor can be a "social glue" that helps us empathize with others. After a death has occurred, humor can comfort survivors as they recall the funny as well as the painful events of a loved one's life. A sense of humor can moderate the intensity of negative life events.

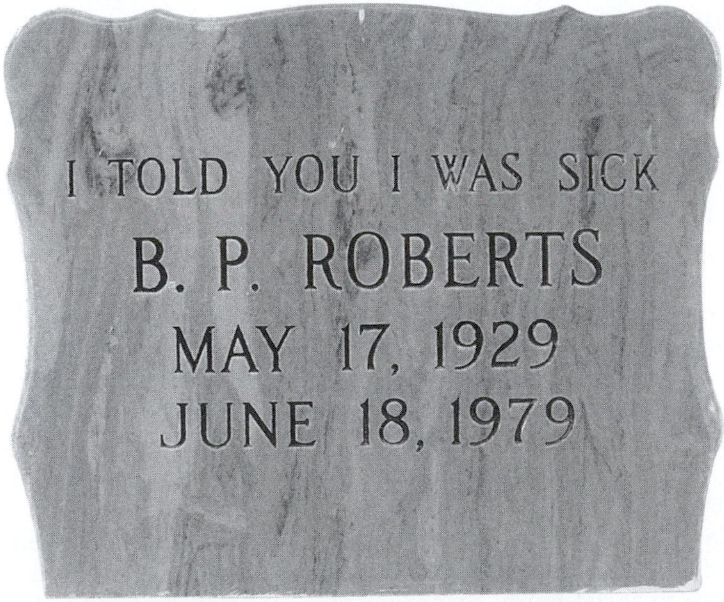

© Albert Lee Strickland

In place of the conventional sentiment usually engraved on tombstones, a touch of whimsy adorns this memorial to B. P. Roberts at a cemetery in Key West, Florida.

In situations involving interactions between patients and health care providers, humor is "one of the great tools of reassurance on the hospital ward."[84] For people who are seriously ill, humor offers a way to cope with the effects of a shattering diagnosis. It provides another perspective on a painful situation, as in the jest "Halitosis is better than no breath at all." When things are bad, humor can serve a protective psychological function and help people maintain their equilibrium.

Emergency services personnel and other individuals who encounter death on their jobs use humor to distance themselves from horrific death, as well as to rebond as a team rather than feeling isolated in their individual grief after traumatic incidents. A group of doctors at a medical center avoided using the word *death* when a patient died because of concern that it might alarm other patients. One day, as a medical team was examining a patient, an intern came to the door with information about the death of a patient. Knowing that the word *death* was taboo and finding no ready substitute, she announced, "Guess who's not going to shop at Walmart any more?" This phrase quickly became the standard way for staff members to convey the news of a patient's death among themselves when in a public setting. For caregivers, humor serves to communicate important messages, promote social relations, diminish discomfort, and manage delicate situations; it has been called the "oil of society."[85]

Living with Awareness of Death

It is said that "one of the most important and unique aspects of human experience is the awareness of our own mortality."[86] Ultimately, one cannot ignore or deny death. "Societies have traditionally taken tremendous care with the shared transformation of life into death because of their responsibility to preserve everyday life's continuity and stability in the face of death's many disruptions."[87] In our time, globalization exposes us to information about deaths far distant from the comfort of our own homes. We are confronted with death seemingly at every turn.

Threats of environmental destruction, nuclear catastrophe, violence, war, and terrorism have been joined by the specter of emerging pandemics. Today's global population has been described as *hibakusha,* a Japanese word meaning "explosion affected." Initially used to describe survivors of the

> Clearly, nobody was exempt from the life of life, which dictated that old age, disease, and death were our common lot. Krishnamurti himself had often talked about it, jokingly quoting an Italian saying, *"Tutti gli uomini debbeno morire, forse anch'io."* When I asked him what it meant, he translated it, "All men must die, perhaps I, too."
>
> Michael Krohnen, *The Kitchen Chronicles: 1001 Lunches with J. Krishnamurti*

atomic bombings of Hiroshima and Nagasaki, the term now connotes pervasive anxiety about the threat of annihilation in our "cosmopolitan era."

Contemplating Mortality

Why is there death? Looking at the big picture, we see that death promotes variety through the evolution of species. The normal human life span is long enough for us to reproduce ourselves and ensure that the lineage of our species continues. Yet it is brief enough to allow for new genetic combinations that provide a means of adaptation to changing conditions in the environment. From the perspective of species survival, death makes sense. But this explanation offers little comfort when death touches our own lives. Norman Wirzba observes:

> Life as we know it *depends* on death, *needs* death, which means that death is not simply the cessation of life but its precondition. . . . Eating involves us in a daily life and death drama in which, beyond all comprehension, some life is sacrificed so that other life can thrive.[88]

In an article titled "Human Existence as a Waltz of Eros and Thanatos," the authors suggest that

> the proper antidote for death is love, but until the ubiquitous and powerful role of death is accepted, until we learn to "dance with death," love will continue to be treated as something appropriate only for romance and Sunday School.[89]

To remedy this misapprehension and expand our understanding of the relationship between love and death, we need to step out of our fast-paced lives and take time to learn how to "waltz with death" by contemplating the basic questions of human existence.

Dimensions of Thanatology

As pioneering Italian thanatologist Francesco Campione points out, death is not only a topic for reflection, study, and research; it is also an "existential problem," which touches every aspect of human existence and every field of knowledge.[90] Existential questions—such as, Who am I? What am I doing here? Where do I fit in the world?—focus on the meaning of life. Such questions are "concerned with the nature of authenticity and the responsibility of choice," and they are "discovered via a person's perception of reality and meaning."[91]

Robert Kastenbaum says that, although the term *thanatology* is usually defined as "the study of death," it is perhaps better defined as "the study of life with death left in."[92] Thus, as a field of study, thanatology encompasses a variety of disciplines and areas of concern (see Table 1-3). Other dimensions and examples can be added to this listing. For instance, *religious* thanatology has concerns similar to those of philosophical thanatology, but specifically as they occur in the context of devotion to a set of beliefs about the nature of ultimate reality (usually involving a deity); issues such as what happens to a person's soul or spirit after death and the nature of the afterlife are important within this domain of thanatology.

TABLE 1-3 *Dimensions of Thanatology*

Focus	Major Areas of Concern	Example Issues
Philosophical and ethical	The meaning of death in human life; questions of values and ethics	"Good" vs. "bad" death; concept of death; suicide and euthanasia
Psychological	Mental and emotional effects of death on individuals	Grief; coping with terminal illness; death anxiety
Sociological	How groups organize themselves to deal with social needs and problems related to dying and death	Response to disaster; disposal of the dead; socialization of children
Anthropological	Role of culture and environment across time and space regarding how individuals and societies relate to death and dying	Funeral rites; memorialization; ancestor worship
Clinical	Management of dying and death in medical settings; diagnosis and prognosis; relationships among patients, doctors, nurses, other caregivers	Treatment options; hospice and palliative care; pain and symptom control
Political	Governmental actions and policies related to dying and death	Capital punishment; organ transfer rules; conduct of war
Educational	Death education; public awareness of death-related issues and concerns	Curricula for instruction in schools; community programs

Acquiring a core knowledge of thanatology involves becoming familiar with all of these dimensions and their aspects. Together, they constitute what might be called "Thanatology" with a capital *T.* Professionals who work with the dying or the bereaved need to establish a firm foundation in thanatology alongside their expertise in health care or counseling.

Reviewing the scope and mission of death studies, Kastenbaum notes that mainstream thanatology has devoted its efforts to improving the care of people faced with life-threatening illness or bereavement, and it may be time to broaden the focus to include "large-scale death" and "death that occurs through complex and multi-domain processes."[93] This perspective would include not only the "horrendous deaths" that human beings inflict on each other in war and other forms of violence but also human-caused activities that threaten or result in the extinction of other species.

Death Anxiety and Fear of Death

Our relationship with death has, as Herman Feifel observed, "a shaping power on thinking and behavior at all points in the life span."[94] The way in which we anticipate death, Feifel says, governs our "now" in an influential manner. This applies not only to people who are terminally ill, combatants in war, or people who fit other categories we tend to associate with an increased risk of death, such as those who are very old or suicidal. On the contrary, it is true for everyone and "for all seasons." Death challenges the idea that human life has meaning and purpose.[95]

The manner in which individuals respond to this challenge is "intertwined with the death ethos of the cultures in which they are embedded."[96] The distinctive stance toward death in a particular culture affects the behavior of its members as they go about their daily lives, influencing, for example, their willingness to engage in risky behaviors or their likelihood of taking out an insurance policy, as well as their attitudes toward such issues as organ donation, the death penalty, euthanasia, or the possibility of an afterlife. In a variety of ways, our culture helps us "deny, manipulate, distort, or camouflage death so that it is a less difficult threat with which to cope."[97] Consider, for example, the effect of a public health discourse that suggests death and misfortune can be avoided if people behave properly—eat the right things, exercise, stop smoking, and so on.[98] The paradox of our attitude toward death is highlighted by the writer Thomas McGuane in his remark that "everyone knows that they are going to die; yet nobody believes it."[99]

Avery Weisman pointed out that *realization* is critical in our efforts to understand death: "Most people concede that death is inevitable, a fact of nature. But they are not prepared to realize. We postpone, put aside, disavow, and deny its relevance to us."[100] Individuals and societies must, in fact, both accept and deny death. We must accept death if we wish to maintain a grasp on reality. Yet we must deny it if we are to go about our daily lives with a sense of commitment to a future that is inevitably limited by our mortality. According to Talcott Parsons, the characteristic attitude toward death in modern societies is less a matter of outright denial than it is "bringing to bear every possible resource to prolong active and healthful life" and accepting death only when "it is felt to be inevitable."[101]

The largest area of empirical research in thanatology is concerned with the measurement of attitudes toward death, and, more particularly, *death anxiety*.[102] In posing the question, What do we fear when we fear death? Robert Neimeyer and his colleagues suggest that the term *death anxiety* may be understood as "a shorthand designation for a cluster of death attitudes characterized by fear, threat, unease, discomfort, and similar negative emotional reactions, as well as anxiety in the psychodynamic sense as a kind of diffuse fear that has no clear object."[103]

Generally speaking, the findings from this research indicate that death anxiety tends to be higher among females than among males, higher among blacks than among whites, and higher among youth and middle-aged adults than among older people. People who describe themselves as religious tend to report less death anxiety than those who do not characterize themselves this way. Individuals who report a greater degree of self-actualization and sense of internal control also report less death anxiety than their counterparts. This summary gives a very broad-brush understanding of the overall picture of death anxiety research. It is important to understand, however, that the responses elicited by such research are "by no means a full representation of one's awareness of the advancing resoluteness of death or consciousness of being-in-the-world."[104]

Despite the accumulated data from numerous studies, there are significant questions, which Neimeyer summarizes as follows:[105] First, what definition of death is implied by the various testing instruments? Second, what are the strengths and limitations of the various instruments that have been used in death anxiety research? Third, based on answers to the first two questions, what are the implications for future research? And, finally, reviewing the data gathered up to now, what do we really know?

One conclusion reached by Neimeyer and his colleagues is that "persons who accept both the dying process and the prospect of being dead one day as a natural part of their lives express less intense fear of dying and death." In short, they are "probably more able than others to see meaning in death by putting it into an overarching context."[106]

Research into death anxiety has been characterized by Kastenbaum as "thanatology's own assembly line."[107] Part of the appeal of death anxiety research, he says, lies in the fact that it "allows the researcher (and the readers, if they so choose) to enjoy the illusion that death has really been studied." How data from such research can be applied to practical issues is uncertain. If, for example, it were possible to reliably state that doctors with high death anxiety relate poorly to dying patients, then that finding might be applied constructively in health care settings. However, we are mostly unable to adequately gauge the effect of death anxiety on real-world issues.

What shall we make of studies showing that women have higher death anxiety scores than men? Does this gender difference mean that women are *too anxious* about death or that men are *not anxious enough?* Reviewing the research in this area, Herman Feifel said:

> Fear of death is not a unitary or monolithic variable. . . . In the face of personal death, the human mind ostensibly operates simultaneously on various levels of reality, or finite provinces of meaning, each of which can be somewhat autonomous. We, therefore, need to be circumspect in accepting at face value the degree of fear of death affirmed at the conscious level.[108]

Terror Management

Terror management theory (TMT) states that human behavior is mostly motivated by an unconscious fear of mortality. In other words, awareness of one's own death affects the decision making of individuals and groups, a concept known as *mortality salience.*[109] Because death is always a possibility for us, fear of death is built into human life.[110] To cope with this fear, we erect defenses against death awareness, defenses that are based in denial and include an irrational belief in being "personally special" as well as an irrational belief in "an ultimate rescuer."[111]

Terror management theory suggests that people learn to assuage their fears of death by finding meaning in life and value in themselves, this meaning and value being provided by the culture into which people are socialized.[112] "The resulting perception that one is a *valuable* member of a *meaningful* universe constitutes self-esteem; and self-esteem is the primary psychological mechanism by which culture serves its death-denying function."[113] Although cultures differ in their specific beliefs, they "share claims that the universe is meaningful and orderly, and that immortality is attainable, be it literally, through concepts of soul and afterlife, or symbolically, through enduring accomplishments and identifications."[114]

In an interview days before his death, Ernest Becker, the initiator of terror management studies, addressed "four strands of emphasis" relevant to terror management theory:[115]

1. The world is a terrifying place.
2. The basic motivation for human behavior is the need to control our basic anxiety, to deny the terror of death.
3. Because the terror of death is so overwhelming, we conspire to keep it unconscious.
4. Our heroic projects aimed at destroying evil have the paradoxical effect of bringing more evil into the world. . . . We are able to focus on almost any perceived threat, whether of people, political or economic ideology, race, religion, and blow it up psychologically into a life and death struggle against ultimate evil. . . . This is the dynamic of spiralizing violence that characterizes so much of human history.

One of the common reactions to terror management theory is that it couldn't possibly be correct because people just don't think about death all that often.[116] However, studies show that "fear of death functions as a motivating force whether people are currently focused on this particular issue or not; it is the implicit knowledge of death rather than current focal awareness that is the motivating factor."[117] In a commentary on the TMT perspective, Robert Kastenbaum points out that we live with sorrow as well as anxiety, and that there are connections between anxiety and sorrow.[118] He says, "Much remains to be learned about the interweaving of sorrow and anxiety throughout human experience."[119] Summarizing the insights of TMT, Robert Solomon says, "Put in the least flattering way, we might say that my death is a bad thing because it deprives the universe of me."[120]

Studying Death and Dying

Take a death and dying course or read a book like this, and someone will probably ask, "Why would you want to take a class about death?" or "Why are you reading about death?" Despite public interest in death-related issues, individuals exhibit varying degrees of avoidance and acceptance when it comes to discussing death openly. A philosophy teacher tells how he was asked to lecture on a subject of his choosing, so he submitted the title "Facing Death." He reports that his hosts were shocked, forcing him to change to "Immortality: Pros and Cons."[121] Our relationship with death seems to be in a period of transition.

Ambivalent attitudes toward death are evident when one educator applauds the study of death as the "last of the old taboos to fall," while another contends that death is "not a fit subject for the curriculum." In response to this state of affairs, Patrick Dean observes that, if death education is criticized by some as a "bastard child of the curriculum, hidden in the closet," then those who value death education can be grateful to such critics because they are creating opportunities for highlighting the importance of death education as preparation for living.[122] In fact, Dean says, death education could appropriately be renamed "life and loss education," because "only through awareness of our lifelong losses and appreciation of our mortality are we free to be in the present, to live fully."

The Rise of Death Education

Informal death education occurs in the context of "teachable moments" that arise out of events in daily life. Such an event may be the death of a gerbil in an elementary school classroom, or it may be an event experienced widely, such as a school shooting, a terrorist attack, a devastating tsunami or hurricane, or the sudden death of a celebrity.

The first formal course in death education at an American university was initiated by Robert Fulton at the University of Minnesota in the spring of 1963.[123] The first conference on death education was held at Hamline University in Minnesota in 1970. From these beginnings, death education has embraced a wide range of issues and topics, from nuts-and-bolts issues such as selecting mortuary services or probating an estate to philosophical and ethical matters such as the definition of death and speculation about what happens after death.

Because death education addresses both objective facts and subjective concerns, it receives broad academic support, with courses offered in a variety of disciplines.[124] In most courses, mastery of facts is enhanced by personal narratives that describe the myriad ways human beings encounter and cope with death.[125] The arts and humanities serve to balance scientific and technical perspectives. Images, symbols, and sounds express themes of life, death, and transcendence that allow for many ways of knowing and learning.

In the broad picture, death education includes training for physicians, nurses, allied health personnel, funeral directors, and other professionals whose duties involve contact with dying and bereaved individuals. This includes police officers, firefighters, and emergency medical technicians (EMTs). As witnesses to human tragedy in the line of duty, they are called upon to comfort victims and survivors. The stoic image of the police officer, EMT, or firefighter who "keeps it all in" instead of expressing natural emotions is challenged by the recognition that such a strategy may be physically and psychologically harmful.

Pioneers in Death Studies

The establishment of death studies in modern times can be traced to explorations of death by Freud and others of the psychoanalytic school and to anthropological accounts of death customs in far-flung societies. Discourse about death and dying during the 1940s and 1950s is highlighted by, for example, Sylvia Anthony's studies of children (1940), Erich Lindemann's analysis of acute grief among survivors of a nightclub fire (1944), and Geoffrey Gorer's essay "The Pornography of Death" (1955; reprinted 1963).[126] Edgar Jackson wrote about grief for both lay and scholarly readerships in publications such as *Understanding Grief: Its Roots, Dynamics, and Treatment* (1957) and *You and Your Grief* (1961). The 1950s may have been the threshhold of a new era in which death and dying were "rediscovered." The question became "What does death mean to you?"[127]

The modern scientific approach to the study of death, or thanatology, is usually traced to a symposium organized by Herman Feifel at a 1956 meeting in Chicago of the American Psychological Association.[128] This symposium resulted in a book, edited by Feifel: *The Meaning of Death* (1959). This landmark book brought together experts from different disciplines whose essays encompassed theoretical approaches, cultural studies, and clinical insights. Death was shown to be an important topic for public and scholarly consideration. Given the prevailing resistance at that time to discussing death, this was no easy feat. About his early efforts in death studies, Feifel recalled that he was emphatically told that "the one thing you never do is to discuss death with a patient."[129]

The same message was communicated to Elisabeth Kübler-Ross, whose book *On Death and Dying* (1969) "caught the public's imagination" by "offering a vision of a natural death unburdened by technology."[130] Hospice pioneer Cicely Saunders had addressed similar issues in her earlier work, *Care of the Dying* (1959). Barney G. Glaser and Anselm L. Strauss applied the tools of sociological analysis to conduct studies focusing on the way awareness of dying affected patients, hospital staff, and family members and on how the "timing" of death occurred in hospital settings. These studies, published as *Awareness of Dying* (1965) and *Time for Dying* (1968), showed that caregivers were reluctant to discuss death and avoided telling patients they were dying. Jeanne Quint Benoliel, who collaborated with Glaser and Strauss, published *The Nurse and the Dying Patient* (1967), which called for systematic death education for nurses.

The 1960s were a fruitful period for death studies. John Hinton's *Dying* (1967) shed light on contemporary practices and suggested how care of the dying could be improved. In "Death in American Society" (1963), sociologist Talcott Parsons looked at the impact of technological advances in health and medicine on dying. Philosopher Jacques Choron traced the history of ideas and attitudes about death and investigated the fear of death and its meaning for human beings in *Death and Western Thought* (1963) and *Death and Modern Man* (1964). Robert Fulton gathered a group of scholars and practitioners to address both theoretical and practical issues in his compilation, *Death and Identity* (1965). During the same era, literary works such as C. S. Lewis's *A Grief Observed* (1961) brought attention to issues involving bereavement and mourning.

The progress of death studies during the 1960s continued into the 1970s with works like Avery D. Weisman's *On Dying and Denying: A Psychiatric Study of Terminality* (1972), which astutely combined research skills and clinical experience with dying patients, and Ernest Becker's *The Denial of Death* (1973), which drew upon a broad range of psychological and theological insights in order to better understand the "terror" of death in human life. Richard Kalish and David K. Reynolds initiated multicultural studies in *Death and Ethnicity: A Psychocultural Study* (1976). The early 1970s also witnessed the blossoming of the first peer-reviewed journal in the field of death studies, *Omega: Journal of Death and Dying,* which had begun its life as a newsletter in 1966 with an article in the first issue by Weisman titled "Birth of the Death-People."[131] This was a decade of collaboration and connection, as individuals recognized a mutual interest manifested in organizations like The Foundation of Thanatology, Ars Moriendi (a forerunner of the International Work Group on Death, Dying, and Bereavement, or IWG) and the Forum for Death Education and Counseling (now known as the Association for Death Education and Counseling, or ADEC).[132]

In the decades since these pioneering contributions, *Omega* has been joined by other scholarly journals, including *Death Studies; Journal of Personal and Interpersonal Loss; Illness, Crisis, and Loss;* and *Mortality* (an international journal published in the United Kingdom), and textbooks in thanatology have come on the scene.[133] Meanwhile, books written for a general readership, such as Mitch Albom's *Tuesdays with Morrie* and Joan Didion's *The Year of Magical Thinking,* have become bestsellers, and information about death and dying is now widely available on the Internet. In 1971, the *Psychology Today* questionnaire "You and Death" garnered a response from readers that exceeded the response to a previous sex questionnaire. A recent study of responses to the questionnaire concluded that "interest in death as a topic was not a passing fad but continues to be a topic of interest across the United States."[134]

The publication of several encyclopedic works covering death studies (including at least one on the Internet) is another sign of the maturing of the field.[135] Clearly, the seeds planted a few decades ago by pioneers have ripened into a thriving interest in dying, death, and bereavement that is evident in both the academic setting and the larger public arena.[136]

Tracing the emergence of thanatology, Luciana Fonseca and Ines Testoni write: "Thanatology *theory* took shape as death studies and research, whereas thanatology *practice* manifests primarily as formal death education, end-of-life care, and bereavement counseling."[137] Hannelore Wass observes that thanatology can help individuals and societies transcend self-interest in favor of concern for others.[138] Death studies "is about love, care, and compassion . . . about helping and healing."

Factors Affecting Familiarity with Death

The past hundred years have seen dramatic change in the size, shape, and distribution of the American population—that is, its *demographics.* These changes—the most notable of which involve increased life expectancy and lower mortality rates—significantly affect our expectations about death. In the past, a typical household would include parents, uncles, aunts, and aged grandparents, as well as children of varying ages. Such extended families, with several generations living together under the same roof, are rare today. One consequence is that most of us have fewer opportunities to experience our relatives' deaths firsthand.

Consider how experiences with dying and death have changed.[139] During the late 1800s and early 1900s, individuals typically died at home, often surrounded by an extended family that spanned several generations. As death drew near, relatives and friends gathered to maintain a vigil at the bedside. Afterward, they washed the body and prepared it for burial. A home-built coffin was placed in the parlor of the house, where friends and relatives participated in a wake and shared in mourning the deceased. Death was a domestic experience.

In close-knit communities, a death bell tolled the age of the deceased, giving notification of the death so that others in the community could join in the rites and ceremonies marking the deceased's passing (see Figure 1-2). Children were included in activities surrounding the dead, staying with adults and sometimes sleeping in the same room as the corpse. Later, in a

You can feel the silence pass over the community as all activity is stopped and the number of rings is counted. One, two, three—it must be the Myer's baby that has the fever. No, it's still tolling—four, five, six. There is another pause at twenty—could that be Molly Shields? Her baby is due at any time now—no, it's still tolling. Will it never stop? Thirty-eight, thirty-nine, another pause—who? It couldn't be Ben; he was here just yesterday; said he was feeling fit as a fiddle—no, it's starting again. Seventy, seventy-one, seventy-two. Silence. You listen, but there is no sound—only silence. Isaac Tipton. He has been ailing for two weeks now. It must be Isaac.

Figure 1-2 *Tolling the Bell*

family plot at the homeplace or a nearby churchyard cemetery, the coffin was lowered into the grave, and those closest to the deceased shoveled dirt over the coffin to fill in the grave. Throughout this process, from caring for the dying person through burial, death remained within the realm of the family.

If you were a person living in those times who was suddenly transported to the present, you would likely experience culture shock as you walked into the "slumber room" of a typical mortuary. There, in place of a simple wooden coffin, you view an elaborate casket. The corpse shows the mortician's skill in cosmetic restoration. At the funeral, you watch as relatives and friends eulogize the deceased. Ah, that's familiar, you say—but where is the dear departed? Off to the side a bit, the casket remains closed, death tastefully concealed. At the graveside, as the service concludes, you are amazed to see mourners leaving while the casket lies yet unburied; the cemetery crew will complete the actual burial. You may be most impressed by the fact that the deceased's family and friends are spectators rather than participants. The tasks of preparing the dead for burial and managing the rites of passage are carried out by hired professionals.

Our familiarity with death has also been powerfully influenced by sophisticated medical technologies, which have affected both the *place* where death most often occurs and the *manner* in which most people die. In contrast to earlier generations, who typically had major roles in the care of their dying and dead, we usually rely on professionals—from the cardiologist to the coroner to the cremator—to act as our go-betweens. The net result is that, for most of us, death is unfamiliar.

Life Expectancy and Mortality Rates

Since 1900, average life expectancy in the United States has increased from forty-seven to nearly seventy-nine years (see Figure 1-3).[140] Japan, at eighty-three years, has the longest life expectancy of countries worldwide.[141] These figures reflect what demographers call "cohort life expectancy," meaning the *average* number of years a specified group of infants would live if they were to experience throughout their lives the age-specific death rates prevailing in their birth year. Thus, for 2011, life expectancy at birth for the U.S. population as a whole was 78.7 years. When this overall U.S. cohort is

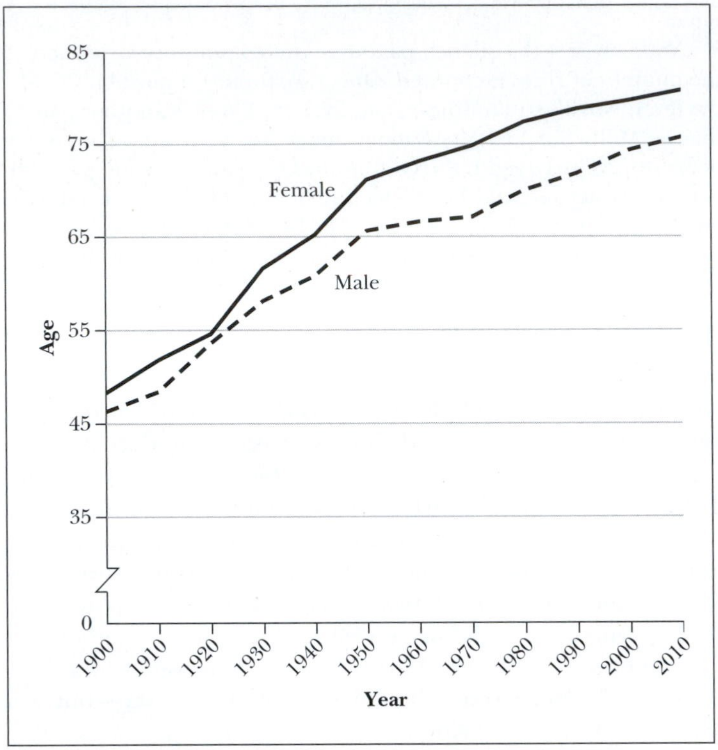

Figure 1-3 *Expectation of Life at Birth, 1900–2010*

broken out into population groups, however, we find that Hispanic females have the longest life expectancy (83.7 years), followed by non-Hispanic white females (81.1 years), Hispanic males (78.9 years), non-Hispanic black females (77.8 years), non-Hispanic white males (76.4 years), and non-Hispanic black males (71.6 years).[142] In addition to differences between birth cohorts, it should be recognized that such figures represent statistical life expectancies. The actual life span lived out by any particular individual may well be significantly shorter or longer than the average for his or her cohort.

Although there are certainly localized and regional variations, widespread human longevity is quite recent, occurring in the last century or so. As one writer said, "Despite what the fashion magazines tell you, 40 isn't the new 30. Seventy is."[143] Today, we tend to assume that a newborn child will live into his or her seventh or eighth decade, perhaps longer. This was not the case in 1900. Over half of the deaths in 1900 occurred among children age fourteen and younger; now, fewer than 2 percent of deaths occur among this age group.[144] This fact influences how we think (or don't think) about death.

Another way to appreciate the changing impact of death is to examine death rates (which are typically stated as the number of individuals dying per 1000 population in a given year). In 1900, the death rate in America was about 17 per 1000; today, it is about 7.4 per 1000, a record low (see Figure 1-4).[145]

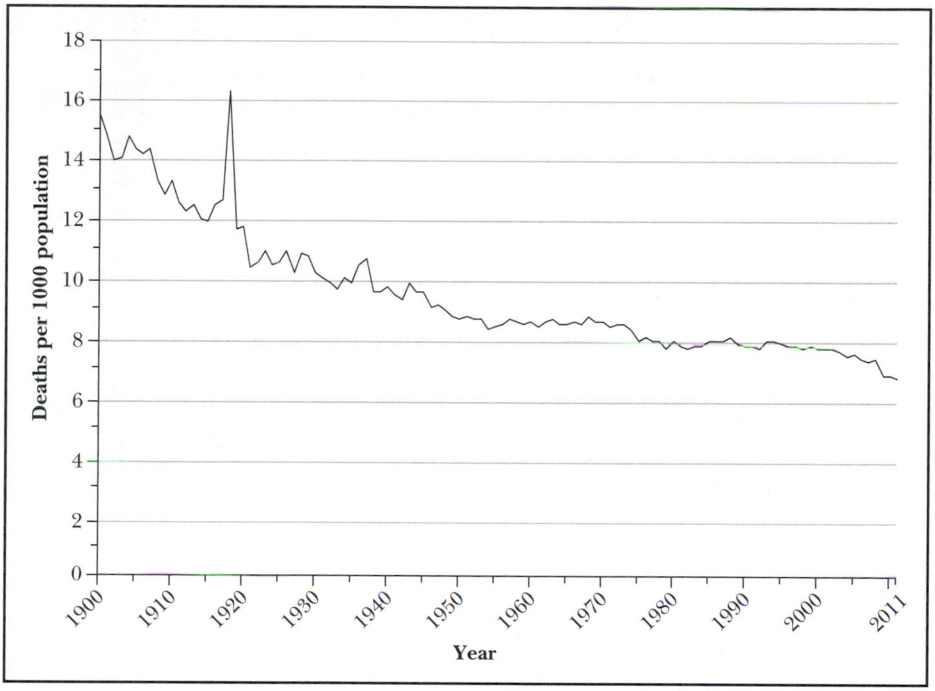

Figure 1-4 *Death Rates, 1900–2011*

Imagine yourself in an environment where death at an early age is common. Consider how different experiences of dying and death were at a time when the comparatively high percentage of infant deaths tended to be thought of as a matter of "fate" that could not be changed. Both young and old were familiar with death as a natural part of the human condition. In the 1870s, nine out of ten Americans over fifteen had lost a parent or sibling.[146] Mothers died in childbirth; babies were stillborn; one or both parents might die before their children had grown to adolescence. Surviving siblings often had a postmortem photograph of a dead brother or sister displayed, a memorial to the deceased and testament to the integrity of the family.[147] Living with a commonplace awareness of mortality, our ancestors could not avoid the fact of death. Ultimately, of course, none of us is exempt. Despite the increases in life expectancy and lowered death rates, the statistical odds of dying still finally add up to 100 percent.

Causes of Death

Changes in life expectancy and mortality rates are due largely to changes in the most common causes of death. In the early 1900s, the leading causes of death were related to acute infectious diseases such as tuberculosis, typhoid fever, diphtheria, streptococcal septicemia, syphilis, or pneumonia. Most such diseases came on suddenly, and death soon followed. Today, most deaths result from a chronic illness, such as heart disease, cancer, or stroke, and tend

TABLE 1-4 *Leading Causes of Death: United States*

Cause of Death	Deaths	% of Total Deaths
All causes	2,512,873	100.0
Heart disease	596,339	23.7
Cancer	575,313	22.9
Respiratory disease	143,382	5.7
Stroke	129,931	5.2
Accidents	122,777	4.9
Alzheimer's disease	84,691	3.4
Diabetes	73,282	2.9
Influenza and pneumonia	53,667	2.1
Kidney disease	45,731	1.8
Suicide	38,285	1.5

to follow a slow, progressive course that lasts weeks, months, or even years (see Table 1-4). The ten leading causes of death account for about 75 percent of all deaths in the United States, with the top two causes, heart disease and cancer, accounting for nearly half of all deaths.[148] (It is worth noting that, although heart disease and cancer are the two leading causes of death, accidental deaths result in slightly more lost years of potential life; that is, the number of dead is smaller, but the number of years of life lost is greater.)[149]

This historical shift in patterns of disease and causes of death—a shift that demographers call an *epidemiologic transition*—is characterized by a redistribution of deaths from the young to the old.[150] (Epidemiology is the study of the patterns of health and disease.) With a reduced risk of dying at a young age from infectious diseases, more people survive into older ages, where they tend to die from degenerative diseases. This results in a growing proportion of aged people in the population.

In 1900, people sixty-five and older made up 4 percent of the population in the United States; now they constitute just over 13 percent.[151] In other words, the proportion of aged people in the population has more than tripled since 1900, and adults aged sixty-five and over are expected to constitute one-fifth of the total U.S. population by the year 2030.[152] In 1900, people sixty-five and older accounted for about 17 percent of deaths; today, about 73 percent of the 2.5 million deaths each year in the United States occur among people in this age group.[153] In short, people are living longer and dying at older ages. One result is that we tend to associate death with the elderly when, in fact, it is not confined to any particular segment of the life span.

Geographic Mobility and Intergenerational Contact

Historically, relationships with friends, neighbors, and relatives were closely tied to place; today, they depend more on one's present role or function than on a lifetime of shared experiences. Children, once they are grown, rarely live in the same house with parents or, even more rarely, with their

Gordon Parks, FSA Collection, Library of Congress

Five generations of the Machado family form an extended family network rarely seen today. Firsthand experiences of death in such a family come through the closeness of multigenerational living.

brothers and sisters in an extended family setting. Few high school or college friendships continue through marriage and the childrearing years into retirement. Because of social and geographic mobility, people are less likely to be present at the deaths of relatives or friends. The result is a loss of shared death rituals.

Of course, some families maintain close relations, even when they don't share the same dwelling or live in the same town. Patterns of mobility also vary among individuals and groups. Some ethnic and cultural groups

> I often wonder what it would be like to be born and raised and live one's whole life in the same zip code. I wonder what it would be like to be able to dial all of one's family and friends without an area code. What it would be like not to always be missing one person or the other, one place or the other. What it would be like to return to a family home in which one grew up and still had things stored in the attic.
>
> My family is in area code 405 and my best friend's in 415 and I'm living in 212. The in-laws are in 203. And there are other friends in 213 and 202, in 412 and 214.
>
> Beverly Stephen, "A Mobile Generation in Search of Roots"

continue to place a high value on maintaining strong family ties despite general trends in society. Reduced contact with kin may be partly compensated for by increased contact with friends and neighbors.

Generally speaking, in modern societies there is less intermingling of the generations, a normal part of daily life in earlier times. Consider the experience of two small children on a Halloween trek, going door to door. After knocking on several well-lighted doors in a seniors-only mobile-home park and receiving no response, their cries of "Trick or treat!" were answered by a woman who said, "You'll not get any Halloween treats in this place. Only old people live here, and they leave their lights on for security and safety, not to welcome children on Halloween!"

Life-Extending Technologies

Seriously ill or injured individuals are likely to find themselves surrounded by an astonishing array of machinery. Sophisticated machines monitor such biological functions as brain wave activity, heart rate, body temperature, respiration, blood pressure, pulse, and blood chemistry. Signaling changes in body function by light, sound, and computer printout, such devices can make a crucial difference in situations of life or death. In place of a sense of the inevitability of death, we are now prone to "an exaggerated faith in the ability of scientific medicine to prolong life."[154] This faith has been called "exaggerated optimism" and "irrational exuberance."[155]

Advanced medical technology that seems to one person a godsend, extending life, may seem to another a curse that only prolongs dying. Dignity can be devalued amid technology focused solely on the biological organism. What are the trade-offs in applying medical technologies to the end stage of life? The conventional definition of death as "the cessation of life, the total and permanent cessation of all vital functions" may be superseded by a medicolegal definition, which acknowledges the fact that life can be sustained artificially. In short, the definition of death is not always as straightforward as the simple statement "When you're dead, you're dead."

Thus, medical technology is yet another factor lessening our familiarity with dying and death. Modern medicine tends to distance family and friends from the patient who is dying. The attitude that "what can be done, should be done" increases the odds that technological fixes will be tried, even when success or cure is unlikely. When death does come, it may seem unexpected. Technological medicine promotes a view of death as an event that can be deferred indefinitely rather than as a normal, natural part of life. In short, death has become "a radically unnatural occurrence."[156]

The "medicalization of death" is a significant manifestation of the disappearance of death from the public domain. Although discussion of death occurs to some extent in the public space, death is hidden from public gaze. At the same time, as Chris Shilling notes, "there is a growing demand for representations of death: from war documentaries and news, to violent movies and television series based around hospital casualty departments."[157] All of these demographic and social variables can be understood as sociocultural forces that influence the way we learn about death through childhood and beyond.

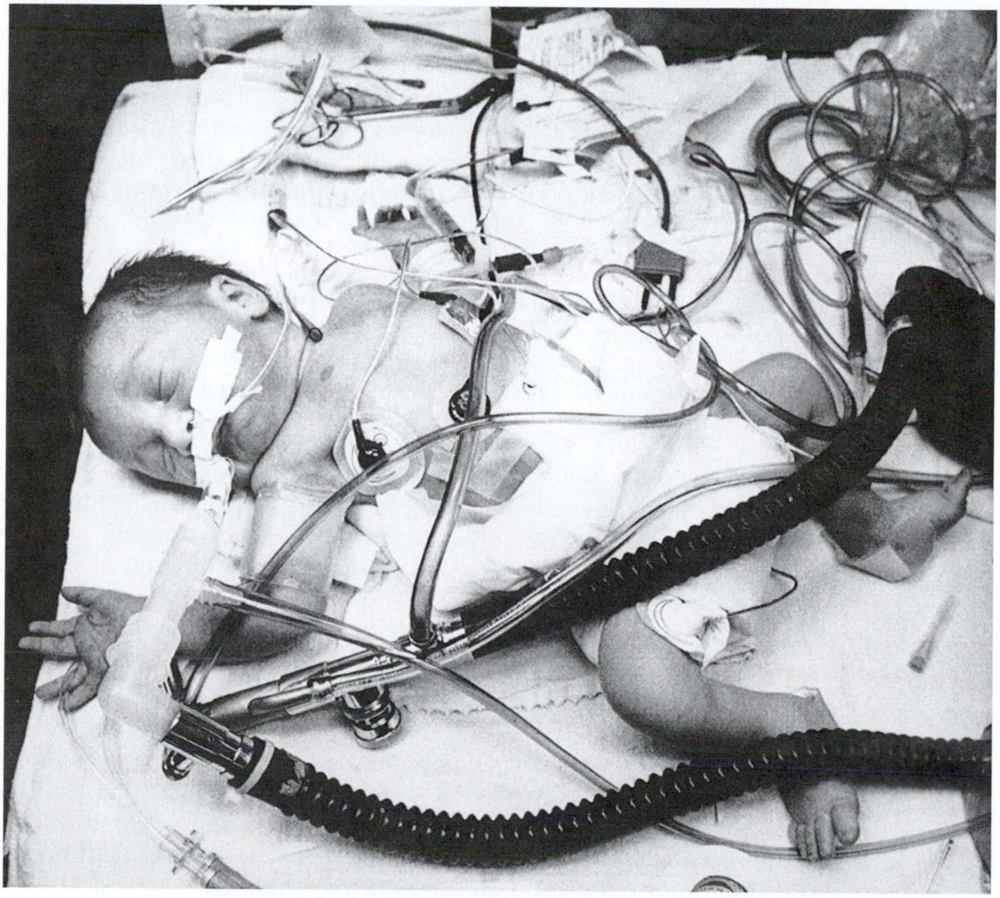

© Clem Murray, AP Photo

Lifelines—tubes and wires monitoring heartbeat, breathing, and blood pressure—increase this premature baby's chances of survival in the intensive care unit of Philadelphia's Children's Hospital. The special-care nursery often becomes an arena for many of the most difficult ethical decisions in medicine.

The Internet and the Digital Age

Another force currently shaping our attitudes and understanding toward death is information and communication technology (ICT). This refers to the integration of telecommunications (telephone lines and wireless signals) and computers, as well as necessary software, middleware, storage, and audio-visual systems, which enable users to access, store, transmit, and manipulate information. These technologies, which have spread rapidly worldwide, are affecting global consciousness regarding death, dying, and bereavement. Scholars note that "the use of the Internet for death-related information and education has expanded to include loss-specific multifaceted websites, social networking for support, interactive counseling, artistic expression, blogging, cyber memorials, and postmortem continuing bonds."[158] Gadgets like smart phones and tablets expand opportunities for connection to the Internet. Tony Walter and colleagues say the evidence indicates that "the internet has significant implications for many current concepts in death studies."[159] It is accurate to say that the Internet and World Wide Web have become part of the modern death system (discussed in Chapter 4). Indeed, ICT influences thanatology in many ways, not only in terms of access to information but also in terms of support for people with life-threatening illness and for those who are bereaved.

The editors of a book about death in the "online universe" report the following story:

> A young man was able to participate in his grandmother's funeral despite being unable to book a flight in time to attend the actual event. Instead, as a musician, he composed a piece in honor of his grandmother, digitally recorded it, and attached it to an email sent to his aunt, who burned it onto a CD and played it less than twelve hours later at the memorial service.[160]

Social networking sites allow for connection to family, friends, and community and are important sources of support for the bereaved.[161] The bereaved may maintain relational continuity with the deceased by posting messages on sites such as Facebook. Indeed, grieving individuals often post messages to the deceased as if the deceased could read the messages.[162] Although it is usual to think of teens and young adults as the "wired" generation, social networking sites like Facebook also receive heavy use by the elderly and the disabled, who are empowered to manage social contacts without leaving home. As Robert Neimeyer says, "We are wired for attachment in a world of impermanence."[163]

Crisis text lines are becoming a new form of hotline to which teens and other individuals who are in crisis can "text" their concerns rather than calling a telephone hotline or using other forms of computer-based chat. One teen, who used a hotline to seek assistance in averting suicidal thoughts, said, "I think teens would definitely use a hotline if they could text to it; most teens keep their feelings to themselves."[164]

Social media are also being integrated into emergency-preparedness efforts. Web-based platforms use information gathered from online communities ("crowd-sourced") to support crisis management, link health care providers, get supplies to those needing them, and aid trapped victims.[165] The Internet can be an avenue providing immediate response to crisis and loss.

Internet activities can reduce social isolation and disenfranchisement by allowing individuals to form online communities devoted to particular losses, such as pet loss. The virtual world offers opportunities to mourn that are not available in the "real" world. However, there can also be negative aspects to social media as grievers experience a lack of privacy. Exposure online may leave some users feeling distressed and violated.

Finally, what about the "digital afterlife"? Observers remark, "In the virtual world, if you have an online presence, you have the issue of your 'digital legacy' to consider as you prepare for your eventual death."[166] What happens to online accounts after a person's death? Families and online companies may find themselves on opposite sides in a battle for access to digital assets: social media accounts, online photos and other records, e-mails, posts, and blogs. Consider a death by suicide. In earlier times, diaries and letters could be examined for clues to the individual's state of mind or the circumstances leading to his or her death. Now, such paper-based artifacts are being replaced by digital files. Whereas a safe deposit box at the bank becomes part of the deceased's estate and whoever controls the estate can open the box, the situation with online assets is less clear. Privacy tends to be a big issue in the online world, and the deceased may not have wanted his or her family or other persons granted access to Internet files. Survivors may have no idea about what their loved one would want to have happen to their online accounts.

With some social media providers, a dead user's account can be memorialized, which leaves it active so friends and family can leave posts in remembrance. Other providers say that accounts are not transferable and simply deactivate an account upon receipt of a death certificate. Companies such as Legacy Locker and Entrustet provide avenues for determining the disposition of Internet accounts after death.

Examining Assumptions

Death is unavoidably part of our lives. Not thinking or not talking about death doesn't remove us from its power. Such ostrichlike behavior only limits our choices for coping with dying and death. As death educator Robert Kavanaugh said, "The unexamined death is not worth dying."[167] Historian David Stannard tells us that in societies in which each person is unique, important, and irreplaceable, death is not ignored but is marked by a "community-wide outpouring of grief for what is a genuine social loss."[168] Conversely, in societies where people feel that "little damage is done to the social fabric by the loss of an individual," death tends not to be acknowledged outside of that person's immediate circle.

Among communities where traditional beliefs, values, and practices are maintained, death is part of the natural rhythm of life. The act of dying, the most private act any person can experience, is a community event. A death initiates an outpouring of social support for the bereaved family and for the wider community. Our values and preferences play an unavoidable part in the quest to examine assumptions and think clearly about death.

Death in a Cosmopolitan Society

At the California Science Center in Los Angeles, a public exhibition of more than 200 cadavers attracted more than 650,000 visitors (doubling the previous record set by an exhibit of *Titanic* artifacts).[169] Titled "Body Worlds: The Anatomical Exhibition of Real Human Bodies," previous exhibitions in Europe and Asia had spawned protests over displaying bodies that had been *plastinated* (a process that involves replacing body fluids with clear, pliable plastic, making it possible to position in dynamic poses not only a whole cadaver but also skeletal bones and internal systems such as blood vessels), thereby offering viewers an "insider's view of the effects of disease and ailments, such as lung disease, hardened arteries, tumors, and ulcers." German physician Gunther von Hagens, inventor of the plastination process, calls the result "anatomic artwork."

Some said the exhibit's popularity was due to the fact that "morbidity has always been a spectator sport," alluding to the exhibit's macabre aspects. Others praised it as an educational opportunity for both children and adults to appreciate firsthand the wonder of the human body, as well as its deterioration from the ravages of disease. What do these contrasting reactions tell us about attitudes toward death? Is the specter of death, positive or negative, in the eyes of the beholder? What do you imagine your own response might be?

The quest for meaningful answers to questions involving human mortality requires us to contemplate what it means to live in a society that scholars describe as "postmodern" and "cosmopolitan."[170] This perspective encourages us to value diversity and pluralism by examining "taken-for-granted" beliefs and considering ideas and practices from other historical periods and cultures. In the contemporary era, individuals are exposed to diverse cultures and a "plurality of life worlds."[171]

Postmodern thought is concerned with the contingency, fragility, and arbitrariness of human life.[172] As one scholar remarked, "Postmodernism can be regarded as a rejection of many, if not most, of the cultural certainties on which life in the West has been structured."[173] It reflects a skepticism about culture and its aims, including a belief in progress in all areas of human endeavor.

In a cosmopolitan world, people are being forced to deal with three related social processes: globalization, accelerated individualization, and consumer societies. As one writer said, "Accelerated individualization has largely emancipated individuals from many ascribed social bonds," resulting in "an unprecedented degree of freedom, but at the same time [creating] an unprecedented task of coping with its consequences."[174]

According to Ulrich Beck, a German scholar and keen observer of the "cosmopolitan society," the human condition in the present century cannot be understood nationally or locally but only globally.[175] British sociologist Anthony Giddens says,

> In a globalizing world, where information and images are routinely transmitted across the globe, we are all regularly in contact with others who think differently, and live differently, from ourselves.[176]

Global concerns are becoming part of local experiences for an increasing number of people.[177]

Your classmates may arrive at different conclusions as they seek appropriate responses to death. Some may prefer an option for swift and low-cost body disposal instead of the traditional funeral. Others might choose a conventional funeral because they feel it provides a necessary framework for meeting the social and psychological needs of survivors (see Figure 1-5). Or consider the likelihood of differing values and attitudes concerning such issues as medical care at the end of life and decisions about whether to withhold or withdraw life-sustaining treatment. Is it feasible to allow space for only one point of view? Or do we need room for diversity of opinion and practice?

Medical technology, demographic changes, shifting disease patterns, urbanization, and professionalization, among other factors, all influence how we die, grieve, and care for our dead. Marina Sozzi, an Italian thanatologist, observes that the wish to die a "natural" death, seen as an event that concludes

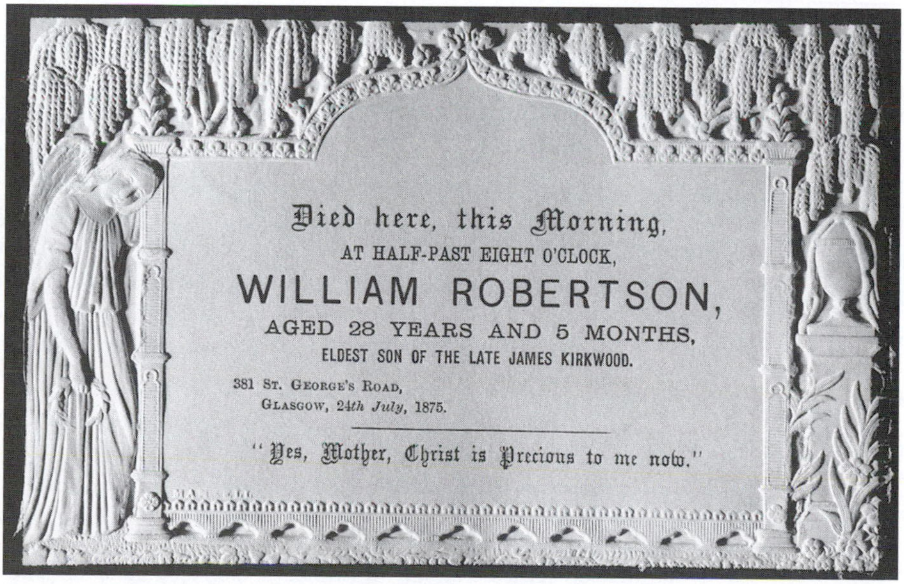

Figure 1-5 *Embossed Linen Death Notification, 1875*
This card exemplifies the formality of nineteenth-century mourning customs. The etiquette books of the period often devoted considerable space to the procedural details associated with the wearing of mourning clothes, the issuance of funeral invitations, and other behaviors appropriate to the survivors of a death.

a genetically determined life cycle, has become a modern myth. By delegating our relationship with death to professionals—doctors, nurses, undertakers, and so on—we try to avoid thinking about mortality and "dream about someone who, equipped with the necessary skills," will guarantee us a "sweet" death with no real loss of self. "Our culture," she says, "has lost the capacity of making the experience of death fecund; thus, death becomes an impersonal deadline of the body, a fatality inscribed inside it, pure biology."[178]

The latest chapter of the modern story of dying is perhaps best termed *managed death.* Even when a prognosis of death has been accepted by medical staff and families, and when further treatments intended to cure have been put aside, there may nevertheless be a strong desire to manage the situation so that it comes out "right." However, as Robert Kastenbaum says, "guidelines for an existentially correct management of death have yet to forthcome."[179] One expression of movement toward managed death involves the aim of ending treatment just at the proper moment so that the person is enabled to die a quiet or peaceful death. Another involves the attempt to control the timing of death even more completely through physician-assisted suicide or euthanasia. In light of such efforts, Daniel Callahan says it seems that death is becoming "just one more choice-and-efficiency issue, to be domesticated along with traffic jams and other excesses of modern life."[180]

Exploring Your Own Losses and Attitudes

Social scientists use the term *cultural lag* to describe the phenomenon of societies' "falling behind" in dealing with new challenges resulting from rapid technological and social change. It may be that we are in a period of cultural lag with respect to dying and death. Recently, a novel forum for discussing death and end-of-life matters has proliferated in venues worldwide, primarily in Europe and the United States: the *death café.* This is an event at which coffee and cake are served in a relaxed setting while people gather to initiate conversation about death-related topics. Organizers aim to create an environment where talking about death is natural and comfortable. The goal is "to increase awareness of death with a view to helping people make the most of their (finite) lives."[181] Glennys Howarth observes, "We appear to be living in a period where the study of death and the recognition of mortality have gained in popularity."[182]

Andrew Ziner says,

> Like nearly every other aspect of our lives, our understandings and feelings about dying and death are derived from our involvement in the myriad of groups, organizations, and institutions that represent our communities and, ultimately, constitute our society. As these religious, economic, legal, and familial structures change over time, we also change. This is because, as social beings, all of the meanings we attach to personal and cultural concerns—including dying and death—are inexorably tied to our social worlds. For example, how do you feel when you hear the word *death?* If you were born a century earlier, would you feel the same way? Is the difference due to individual or social factors?[183]

A perspective informed by values of connectedness and community, which acknowledges and celebrates difference and diversity, can help us discover personally meaningful and socially appropriate choices for the times in which we live and die, giving us a "pluralistic way of understanding and being in the world."[184] After reviewing dozens of studies, researchers found that contemplating mortality brings positive results, such as better health decisions, increased altruism and helpfulness, and decreased militaristic attitudes.[185]

Our attitudes toward death develop out of a lifetime of experiences with significant losses, beginning in childhood and continuing into old age. Exploring the meaning of these losses and their influence on our attitudes and practices is part of a comprehensive study of death and dying. It can be helpful to construct a "lossography," an account of the losses we have experienced, allowing time for investigation and reflection about the circumstances in which they occurred and the ways in which we and significant others in our environment responded to those losses.

It's been said, "The most precious thing in life is its uncertainty."[186]

Further Readings

Christopher A. Dustin and Joanna E. Ziegler. *Practicing Mortality: Art, Philosophy, and Contemplative Seeing.* New York: Palgrave Macmillan, 2005.

Marilyn Johnson. *The Dead Beat: Lost Souls, Lucky Stiffs, and the Perverse Pleasures of Obituaries.* New York: HarperCollins, 2006.

Allan Kellehear, ed. *The Study of Dying: From Autonomy to Transformation.* New York: Cambridge University Press, 2009.

Daniel Liechty, ed. *Death and Denial: Interdisciplinary Perspectives on the Legacy of Ernest Becker.* Westport, Conn.: Praeger, 2002.

Carla J. Sofka, Illene Noppe Cupit, and Kathleen R. Gilbert, eds. *Dying, Death, and Grief in an Online Universe.* New York: Springer, 2012.

Graeme Thomson. *I Shot a Man in Reno: A History of Death by Murder, Suicide, Fire, Flood, Drugs, Disease and Misadventure as Related in Popular Song.* New York: Continuum, 2008.

Adrian Tomer, Grafton T. Eliason, and Paul T. P. Wong, eds. *Existential and Spiritual Issues in Death Attitudes.* New York: Lawrence Erlbaum, 2007.

Irvin D. Yalom. *Staring at the Sun: Overcoming the Terror of Death.* San Francisco: Jossey-Bass, 2008.

Additional resources for this chapter can be found at www.mhhe.com/despelder10e

© Robin Van Doren, Open Doors

A father and son make an offering at the grave of their Chinese ancestors during village cremation ceremonies held in Peliatan, Bali. In this way, religious and cultural traditions are passed along to successive generations through socializing processes that are important to the ongoing life of the community.

CHAPTER 2

Learning About Death: Socialization

Imagine yourself as a child. Someone says, "Everybody's going to ziss one of these days. It happens to all of us. You, too, will ziss." Or, one day as you're playing, you are told, "Don't touch that, it's zissed!" Being an observant child, you notice that, when a person zisses, other people cry and appear to be sad. Over time, as you put together all your experiences of "zissing," you begin to develop some personal feelings and thoughts about what it means to ziss.

The understanding of death evolves like this. As a child grows older, incorporating various experiences of death, his or her concepts and responses to death begin to resemble those of the adults in the culture. Just as a child's understanding of "money" changes over time—at first, it is a matter of little or no concern; later, it seems to come into the child's experience almost magically; and finally, it engages the child's attention and participation in many different ways—so, too, does the child develop new understandings about the meaning of death. As with other aspects of human development, the understanding of death evolves as experiences stimulate reevaluation of previously held knowledge, beliefs, and attitudes.

A Child's Reasoning

A twenty-seven-month-old child had been waking several times each night and screaming hysterically for a bottle of sugar water.[1] This had been going on for two months. His father describes getting up one night for the second or third time and deciding with his wife to use firmness in refusing to meet the child's demand. He went into his son's room and told him that he was too old to have a bottle and would have to go back to sleep without it. The father, his mind made up that enough was enough, started to leave the room.

But then he heard a frightened cry, one of desperation that sounded like the fear of death. Wondering what could be causing the child such alarm, the father turned back into the room, took his son out of the crib, and asked, "What will happen if you don't get your bottle?" The child, no longer hysterical, but very tearful and sniffling, said, "I can't make contact!" The father asked, "What does that mean, 'you can't make contact'?" His son replied, "If I run out of gas, I can't make contact—my engine won't go. You know!"

The father then remembered several family excursions during the previous summer, when vehicles had run out of gas. "What are you afraid will happen if you run out of gas?" Still crying, the child replied, "My motor won't run, and then I'll die." At that point, the father recalled another incident his son had witnessed. Some time earlier, when they were selling an old car, the prospective buyer had tried to start the engine, but the battery was dead, and the engine wouldn't turn over. The child had heard remarks like "It's probably *not making contact,*" "the *motor died,*" and "I guess *the battery's dead.*"

With this in mind, the father asked, "Are you afraid that your bottle is like gasoline and, just like when the car runs out of gas, the car dies; so, if you run out of food, you'll die?" The child nodded his head yes. The father explained, "Well, that's not the same thing at all. You see, when you eat food, your body stores up energy so that you have enough to last you all night. You eat three times a day; we only fill up the car with gas once a week. When the car runs out of gas, it doesn't have any saved up for an emergency. But with people, it isn't anything like that at all. You can go maybe two or three days without eating. And, even if you got hungry, you still wouldn't die. People aren't anything like cars."

This explanation seemed to do little to alleviate the child's anxiety, so the father tried a different tack. "You're worried that you have a motor, just like a car, right?" The child nodded yes. "So," continued the father, "you're worried that, if you run out of gas or run out of food you'll die, just like the motor of a car, right?" Again, the child nodded yes. "Ah, but the car has a key, right? We can turn it on and off anytime we want, right?"

Now the child's body began to relax. "But where is your key?" The father poked around the boy's belly button: "Is this your key?" The child laughed. "Can I turn your motor off and on? See, you're really nothing like a car at all. Nobody can turn you on and off. Once your motor is on, you don't have to worry about it dying. You can sleep through the whole night, and your motor will keep running without you ever having to fill it up with gas. Do you know what I mean?" The child said, "Yes."

"Okay. Now you can sleep without worrying. When you wake in the morning, your motor will still be running. Okay?" Never again did the child wake up in the middle of the night asking for a bottle of warm sugar water.

The father later speculated that two experiences had contributed to his child's concerns: First, the child had decided that sugar water would give him gas because he had overheard his parents saying that a younger sibling had "gas" from drinking sugar water; second, when the child's parakeet died, his question, "What happened to it?" was answered by his father: "Every animal has a motor inside that keeps it going. When a thing dies, it is like when a motor stops running. Its motor just won't run anymore."

In this dialogue between a child and his father, notice how the father's skills in listening and his sensitivity to his child's behavior helped him engage in this kind of conversation. Consider, too, the impressive reasoning that goes on in a child's mind—the way of stringing together concepts, the complex associations of language and death.

A Mature Concept of Death

Some people believe that children do not think about death through infancy, toddlerhood, and the preschool years. As this story illustrates, however, it is more realistic to expect that children will have experiences with death from very early ages. A study conducted by Mark Speece to investigate the impact of death experiences on children ages one to three helps confirm this.[2] Speece says, "It seems safe to conclude that death experiences occur in the lives of a sizable proportion of children of this age and that those children who do have such experiences attempt to deal with and integrate their specific death experiences into their understanding of the world in general."

Slightly over half of the children Speece studied had some experience with death: in some cases, a human death (for example, a grandparent, a cousin, a neighbor); in others, a nonhuman death, such as that of a pet. Speece found that these young children responded to death in observable ways. Some children actively looked for the deceased pet or person. One child became angry when a pet bird that had died would not come back to life. Children questioned the immobility of the deceased and what happens after death, and expressed concern about the welfare of the living.

Through observing and interacting with children at different ages, psychologists have described how children gain a mature understanding of death. In reviewing more than 100 such studies, Mark Speece and Sandor Brent conclude, "It is now generally accepted that the concept of death is not a single, unidimensional concept but is, rather, made up of several relatively distinct subconcepts."[3] A formal statement of the empirical, or observable, facts about death includes four primary components:[4]

1. *Universality.* All living things must eventually die. Death is all-inclusive, inevitable, and unavoidable (although unpredictable in its exact timing; that is, death may occur at any moment to any living thing).
2. *Irreversibility.* Death is irrevocable and final. Organisms that die cannot be made alive again. (This is separate from a belief in a spiritual afterlife.)

3. *Nonfunctionality.* Death involves the cessation of all physiological functioning. All life-defining bodily functions and capabilities cease at death.
4. *Causality.* There are biological reasons for the occurrence of death. This component includes a recognition of both internal (e.g., disease) and external (e.g., physical trauma) causes of death.

A fifth component, *personal mortality,* may be added to this list. A subcomponent of universality, it makes explicit the understanding not only that all living things die but also that each living thing will die ("I will die").

In addition, individuals with a mature understanding of death typically hold *nonempirical* ideas about it as well.[5] Such nonempirical ideas—that is, ideas not subject to scientific proof—deal mainly with the notion that human beings survive in some form beyond the death of the physical body. What happens to an individual's "personality" after he or she dies? Does the self or soul continue to exist after the death of the physical body? If so, what is the nature of this "afterlife"? Developing personally meaningful answers to such questions, which involve what Speece and Brent term "noncorporeal

"ISN'T THAT CUTE? THEY'RE PLAYING 'CORONER'."

continuity," is, for many individuals, part of the process of acquiring a mature understanding of death.

Most children understand by about three or four years of age that death is a changed state. The major aspects of a mature concept of death are mastered in a relatively fixed sequential order between the ages of five and ten.[6] Studies investigating this sequence have generally found that understanding the irreversibility of death occurs first, by age five or six, with the recognition that the dead cannot come back to life. Between the ages of five and eight, a major shift occurs in how children think about biological phenomena and, specifically, how the human body functions to maintain life.[7] In early school years, children come to understand that death affects all living things and that it is characterized by bodily processes ceasing to function. By ages seven to ten, all basic components of a mature concept of death have been acquired. "Death is conceptualized as a fundamentally biological event that inevitably happens to all living things and is ultimately caused by an irreversible breakdown in the functioning of the body."[8] Of course, some children take longer than others to come to this understanding, and some may even resist or defend against acknowledging information related to a mature understanding of death.[9]

The ever-expanding understanding of death during childhood is further refined during adolescence and early adulthood, as individuals consider the social and emotional impact of death on close relationships and contemplate the value of religious or philosophical answers to the meaning of death. Thus, a mature understanding of death goes beyond a biological focus to an appreciation for the life lost, the characteristics that make the loss of life a tragedy.[10]

What a person "knows" about death may change from time to time. We may hold conflicting or contradictory notions about death, especially our own. When facing a distressing situation, an understanding of the facts may give way to a more childlike attitude, such as the notion that we can bargain where death is concerned. A patient told that he or she has only six months to live may imagine that by some magical act, some bargain with God or the universe, the death sentence can be postponed. Thus, although the main evolution toward a mature understanding of death occurs during childhood, how a person understands death fluctuates among different ways of knowing throughout life. Later in this chapter, we discuss the distinctive developmental transitions that pertain to adulthood.

Understanding Death Through the Life Course

The evolving understanding of death is a process of continuous adjustment and refinement. It is part of human development, which refers to the changes in physical, psychological, and social behavior experienced across the life span.[11] By observing children's behavior, developmental psychologists devise theories, or models, to describe the characteristic concerns and interests of children at various ages. These models are like maps that describe the main features of the territory of childhood at different stages of development. The models are useful for describing the characteristics of a typical child at, say, age two or age seven.

Children vary in their individual rates of development—not only physically, but also emotionally, socially, and cognitively. Thus, with respect to a child's understanding of death, paying attention to the *sequence* of development is more pertinent than trying to correlate understanding to a specific *age*. Experience plays an important role. A child who has had firsthand encounters with death may arrive at a more mature understanding of death than is typical of other children of the same age.

Children are active thinkers and learners. Very young children appear to make theory-like assumptions about the world, and they use basic reasoning to make causal explanations about physical, biological, and psychological events.[12] In recent decades, studies have shown infants and young children behaving in ways that imply an understanding of physical and perceptual phenomena at ages younger than previously thought possible.[13]

In tracking the development of the understanding of death in children, it is useful to have a framework within which to place the distinctive attitudes and behaviors that pertain to various phases of childhood. The formal study of children's understanding of death can be traced to the pioneering work of Paul Schilder and David Wechsler (1934).[14] However, studies conducted in the early 1940s by Sylvia Anthony in England and Maria Nagy in Hungary have received greater attention.

To summarize, according to Anthony, children under the age of two have no understanding of "dead," by five they have a limited concept, and by nine they can give general explanations for death; in addition, young children engage in magical thinking (that is, the notion that, for example, angry thoughts or feelings can cause someone's death).[15]

Nagy found three developmental stages in children's understanding of death between the ages of three and ten. Her research showed that, in the first stage (ages three to five), children understood death as somehow being less alive; the dead "live on" under changed circumstances and can return to normal life. In the second stage (ages five to nine), children understood

> We are reading the newspaper on the terrace in our suite in a New York hotel. It is a faultless fall day. Out two-year-old daughter is sitting contentedly beside us, drinking a bottle. She climbs off her chair and squats down, inspecting something on the ground. She pulls the bottle out of her mouth, calls to me and points to a large, motionless bumble bee. She is alarmed, shaking her head back and forth, as if to say "No, no, no!" "The bee stopped," she says. Then she makes a command: "Make it start."
>
> Carol Blue, *Mortality*

death as final but as avoidable and lacking inevitability and personal reference ("I will die"). In the third stage (ages nine and older), children recognized death as the result of a biological process that is final, inevitable, universal, and personal.[16]

Although research generally has indicated that most children have acquired a mature concept of death around the age of nine, recent studies show that children begin to conceptualize death as a biological event at the same time they construct a "biological model" of how the human body functions.[17] By preschool age, an animate/inanimate distinction serves "as the center of a vast cluster of conceptual distinctions," including a naïve theory of biology.[18] Only after children begin to think purposefully about the biological functions of life-sustaining body parts (e.g., the heart is for pumping blood) do they become "life theorizers," able to reason that, without these parts, one would die.[19] Older children are more apt than younger children to state that bodily functions cease at death.[20] In the discussion that follows, children's development is placed within the framework of two major theories or models of human development—namely, those devised by Erik Erikson and Jean Piaget.

The model of human development devised by Erikson focuses on the *stages of psychosocial development,* or the psychosocial milestones, that occur successively throughout a person's life (see Figure 2-1).[21] Each stage involves a crisis, or turning point, that requires a response so that the individual can gain mastery over various issues and further develop a sense of identity. For

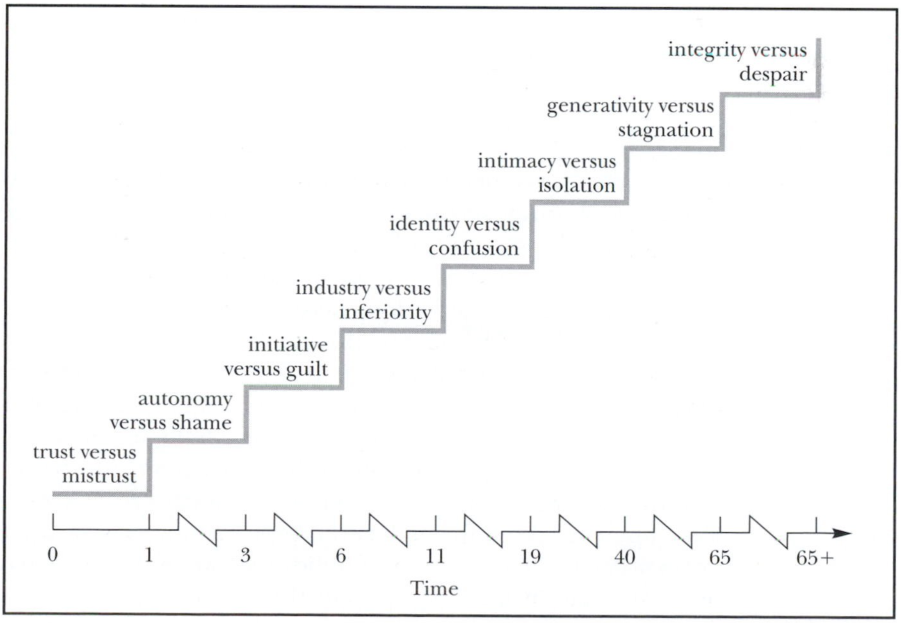

Figure 2-1 *Stages of Psychosocial Development Proposed by Erikson*

TABLE 2-1 *Piaget's Model of Cognitive Development*

Age (approximate)	Developmental Period	Characteristics
Birth–2 years	Sensorimotor	Focused on senses and motor abilities; learns object exists even when not observable (object permanence) and begins to remember and imagine ideas and experiences (mental representation).
2–7 years	Preoperational	Development of symbolic thinking and language to understand the world. (2–4 years) *Preconceptual subperiod:* sense of magical omnipotence; self as center of world; egocentric thought; all natural objects have feelings and intention (will). (4–6 years) *Prelogical subperiod:* beginning problem solving; seeing is believing; trial and error; understanding of other points of view; more socialized speech; gradual decentering of self and discovery of correct relationships.
7–12 years	Concrete operational	Applies logical abilities to understanding concrete ideas; organizes and classifies information; manipulates ideas and experiences symbolically; able to think backward and forward; notion of reversibility; can think logically about things experienced.
12+ years	Formal operational	Reasons logically about abstract ideas and experiences; can think hypothetically about things never experienced; deductive and inductive reasoning; complexity of knowledge; many answers to questions; interest in ethics, politics, social sciences.

Erikson, the basic needs of *connectedness* and *independence* complement and support each other in the successful resolution of each stage. As you think about various stages and the crises associated with them, keep in mind that Erikson believed that all the issues surrounding the development of identity and the mastery of various tasks and skills are present at every period of a person's life. This means that adults deal with issues or crises initially described as having occurred during childhood. Each of the major issues in development is "recycled" whenever events in one's life elicit it.

Jean Piaget's focus was on the *cognitive transformations* that occur during childhood (see Table 2-1).[22] According to Piaget, the basic unit of understanding is a *schema* or scheme, defined as "a pattern of knowing something." Development occurs through two complementary processes: *assimilation* and *accommodation*. The first term implies that we apply our current schemes to new information and incorporate this information into existing schemes. The second term refers to the process of adjusting or modifying our current schemes to handle new information.

Although we are constantly reaching new levels of understanding, Piaget said that at times so many new levels of understanding converge that there occurs a major reorganization in the structure of our thinking. Accordingly, Piaget distinguished four different periods of cognitive development based on the characteristic ways in which individuals organize their experience of the world: *sensorimotor, preoperational, concrete operational,* and *formal operational.* Although children move through these stages in the same sequence, each child's rate of development is unique.

In the following discussion of the years of childhood and adolescence, we make use of both Erikson and Piaget in describing developmental patterns.

Infancy and Toddlerhood

As shown in Figure 2-1, Erikson characterizes the period from birth to roughly one year as predominantly a time of developing a sense of basic *trust* toward the environment. The positive outcome of this developmental "crisis" is *hope.* If the infant's needs are not met, the result may be distrust. Other people in the environment—typically parents—play an important part in development as the infant acquires a sense of trust in others as reliable and nurturant. Moreover, he or she learns not only to trust others, but also that the world is predictable. The death of a caregiver can disrupt building this foundation of trusting others and trusting the environment. Similarly, a death that affects other family members and puts them under stress can adversely affect the infant's developing sense of predictability about the world. When a death occurs in the child's environment, adults need to watch for nonverbal cues that the child might understand more than the adults assume or than is readily apparent.[23]

During the next stage according to Erikson, toddlerhood (roughly one to three years of age), the child grapples with issues of *autonomy* versus shame and doubt. The positive outcome is characterized as *will.* This is a period of "letting go" and "holding on" in both psychosocial and physical development. Toilet training typically occurs during this time. Toddlers make giant gains in object recognition and thinking between the ages of 18 and 24 months. There is a developmental leap in their pretend play (for instance, pretending a laundry basket is a car), a basic form of symbolic thinking.[24] As the toddler explores the environment and develops greater independence, there are inevitably clashes of wills between what the child wants to do and what others want the child to do. Exercising independence is a hallmark of this stage. The death of a significant other, especially a primary caregiver, affects the child's task of pursuing independence and may cause a regression to earlier behaviors, such as clinging, crying, and being more demanding.

Turning to Piaget's model, the first two years of life are characterized as the *sensorimotor period,* as a child develops and strengthens his or her sensory and motor, or physical, abilities. This period starts with the reflex schemes babies are born with and ends with elementary symbol use. At roughly 12 to 18 months, we see "infant scientists" at work with the environment as their laboratory. "They perform miniature experiments in which they deliberately

> Driving my three-year-old daughter to day care before work, I noticed a family of dead raccoons on the road. I quickly sped past, hoping she wouldn't spot them. No such luck.
>
> "Mommy, what was that?"
>
> "Some wood must have fallen from a truck," I fibbed.
>
> "Oh," she said. "Is that what killed all those raccoons?"
>
> Tammy Maas

vary an action in order to see how this variation affects the outcome."[25] As the child accumulates experiences of the flow of events in the environment, he or she gradually begins to perceive patterns that become generalized into schemes, which tie together the common features of actions occurring at different times. Meg Jay says,

> In the first eighteen months of life, the brain experiences its first growth spurt, producing far more neurons than it can use. The infant brain overprepares, readying itself for whatever life brings, such as to speak any language within earshot. This is how we go from being one-year-olds who understand fewer than one hundred words to being six-year-olds who know more than ten thousand.[26]

Between about 14 and 24 months, most children make a transition into the next period. They begin to show insight learning, budding symbol use, and simple pretend play. With symbol use, children are no longer tied to the here and now, nor do they need to act overtly on the environment to think about causality and how things work.

In the beginning, a parent who leaves the room has simply vanished; there is no thought, "My parent is in the other room." Eventually, the child acquires the concept of *object permanence;* an object continues to exist even when one cannot see, hear, or feel it. Piaget says, "a Copernican revolution takes place," with the result that "at the end of this sensory-motor evolution, there are permanent objects, constituting a universe within which the child's own body exists also."[27]

Early Childhood

In Erikson's model, the preschool and kindergarten years (roughly three to six years of age) involve issues of *initiative* versus guilt. The positive outcome is *purpose.* The child is convinced that she *is* a person; now she must find out *what kind* of person she is going to be.[28] The child seeks his or her own direction and purpose yet is concerned about how parents (and other significant adults) perceive these tentative efforts to express individuality. The egocentric orientation of the infant gives way to the socially integrated self of the older child.

Children tend to first acknowledge death in the preschool years. Children may become fascinated with the idea of "gone" or "all gone." For the young child, being dead is an altered state of living or a diminished form of life. A four-year-old girl told Robert Kastenbaum, "They have only dead people to talk to, and dead people don't listen, and they don't play, and they miss all the TV shows they liked."[29] Children in this period typically consider that death is something that happens only to the very sick or aged, and it can be avoided with healthy living and by avoiding situations that are fatal (e.g., car crashes).[30]

This period marks the beginning of the child's moral sense, the ability to function within socially sanctioned modes of behavior. During this period, situations arise that induce feelings of guilt. For instance, a child who has fantasies of doing away with a parent—expressed perhaps by the frustrated scream, "I wish you were dead!"—may feel guilty or shameful about having such thoughts. Reflecting emerging communication skills, the child's concept of death expands quite rapidly during the preschool and kindergarten years.

The body becomes important to children's self-image as they race around on tricycles, learn to cut small pieces of paper precisely, and generally gain greater control over their bodies. During this period, bodily mutilation is one of the death-related fears that may manifest. This preoccupation with the body can be illustrated: A five-year-old witnessed the death of his younger brother, who was killed when the wheel of a truck rolled over his head. The parents, who were considering having a wake in their home, asked the surviving son how he might feel if his younger brother's body were brought into the house for a wake. His question was "Does he look hurt?" Concern about bodily disfigurement is characteristic of this stage of psychosocial development (see Figure 2-2). Children in this age group need to be given accurate information about a death and what caused it so they will not draw erroneous conclusions. Common expressions of grief at this period include sadness, regression, play reenactment, and magical thinking.

In Piaget's model, early childhood is characterized as the *preoperational* period. Cognitive development centers on learning to use language and symbols to represent objects, a huge shift in human development. Because so many changes in thinking emerge during the transition from the preschool to the school years, this period has come to be called the *five-to-seven-year shift.*

How does Piaget's model apply to children's concepts of death? A study conducted by Gerald Koocher supplies a partial answer. Children were asked four questions about death.[31] (You might want to answer these questions for yourself.) The first question was, What makes things die? Children in the preoperational stage used fantasy reasoning, magical thinking, and realistic causes of death (sometimes expressed in egocentric terms). Here are sample responses:

- Gia: "When they eat bad things, like if you went with a stranger and they gave you a candy bar with poison on it. [*The researcher asks, "Anything else?"*] Yes, you can die if you swallow a dirty bug."
- Emilio: "They eat poison and stuff, pills. You'd better wait until your Mom gives them to you. [*Anything else?*] Drinking poison water and stuff like going swimming alone."
- Louis: "A bird might get real sick and die if you catch it. [*Anything else?*] They could eat the wrong foods like aluminum foil. That's all I can think of."

Figure 2-2 *Accident Drawing by a Five-Year-Old*
In this drawing by a five-year-old who witnessed his younger brother's accidental death, the surviving child is depicted as riding a Big Wheel on the left side of the truck that ran over his brother. The four wheels of the truck are shown, and the younger brother's head is drawn next to the wheel farthest to the right. This drawing is similar to one drawn by the child on the night of the fatal accident, when he told his parents, "I can't sleep because I can't get the pictures out of my head." The act of externalizing these disturbing images by making a drawing had therapeutic value for this child in coming to terms with the traumatic experience of his sibling's death.

The understanding of death during the early childhood years is also illustrated in a study done by Helen Swain.[32] Most children in this study expressed the notion that death is reversible, attributing the return of life to the good effects of ambulances, hospitals, or doctors, whose help is often summoned magically, as if a dead person could ring up the hospital and say, "Will you send me an ambulance over here? I'm dead and I need you to fix me up." About two-thirds of the children said that death is unlikely or avoidable or is brought about only by unusual events such as an accident or a catastrophe. About one-third expressed disbelief that death could happen to them or to their families. Nearly half were uncertain about whether they would ever die or else thought they would die only in the remote future.

Middle Childhood or School-Age Period

In Erikson's model, the years from about six to the beginning of puberty correspond to the stage of *industry* versus inferiority. The positive outcome of this stage is *competence*. This is the "industrial age," a period when the child is busy in school, interacting with peers in a variety of ways. The theme is "I am what I learn." As a child's efforts begin to gain recognition and bring satisfaction, he or she may be anxious about those areas in which there is a lack of control or sense of inadequacy. An example is seen in reactions of children to the terrorist attacks of 2001. According to Grace Crist, children in the eight-to-eleven age range had a difficult time navigating what had happened because they weren't old enough to fully grasp the big picture the way adolescents can. At that age, she says, children need details and concrete information to feel a sense of control, but the details of 9/11 were gruesome, making the event frightening and almost impossible to comprehend.[33]

Common grief reactions in the middle childhood period include school and learning problems, phobias, anger, and hypochondriasis. The death of a parent during the school-age years is likely to deprive a child of an important source of recognition. During these years of development, as children learn new tasks, they are also comparing themselves with their peers. When one nine-year-old moved to a different school shortly after her mother's death, she didn't want her new acquaintances to know about the death. When questioned about this, she replied, "Having a dead mother makes me too different from other kids."

In Piaget's framework, this period is denoted by the term *concrete operations.* The child begins to use logic to solve problems and to think logically about things without having to have their relationships demonstrated directly. The ability to do arithmetic, for instance, requires the recognition that numbers are symbols for quantities. Children at this stage are able to

Childhood activities such as "playing dead" can be a means of experimenting with various concepts, trying them on for size, and thus arriving at a more comprehensive and manageable sense of reality.

manipulate concepts in a logical fashion, although typically they do not engage in abstract thinking. In other words, the ability to think logically is applied to objects but not yet to hypotheses, which require the ability to carry out "operations on operations." The characteristic mode of thought in this developmental period emphasizes real-life situations or concrete instances of a problem, not hypothetical or theoretical problems.

During this period, children name both intentional and unintentional means by which a person may die, and they are familiar with a wide range of causes of death. When a death occurs, children are likely to be concerned about their own safety and the safety of other family members. Here are some responses from the children in Koocher's study when asked about causes of death:

- Beatrice: "Knife, arrow, guns, and lots of stuff. You want me to tell you all of them? [*As many as you want.*] Hatchets and animals, and fires and explosions, too."
- José: "Cancer, heart attacks, poison, guns, bullets, or if someone drops a boulder on you."
- Catherine: "Accidents, cars, guns, or a knife. Old age, sickness, taking dope, or drowning."

Adolescence

The period of life called adolescence is conceptualized in terms of three stages: *early adolescence,* from about eleven to fourteen years, which begins with puberty and involves a shift in attachment from parents to peers; *middle adolescence,* about ages fifteen to seventeen, marked by the development of individual self-image, experimentation, and striving for competency, mastery, and control; and *late adolescence,* the years from about eighteen to the early twenties, distinguished by increased self-acceptance, concern for others, and an increasingly future-oriented view of the world.[34] Ken Doka says the key developmental issues of adolescence are often called the three *I*'s: identity, independence, and intimacy.[35] One writer says,

> Childhood is important, but more and more I am curious about what went on in high school. High school and our twenties are not only the time when we have our most self-defining experiences, study after study shows they are also the time when we have our most self-defining *memories.*[36]

It has been pointed out that adolescence is "a period when young people draw on 'repertoires' characteristic of both adulthood and childhood."[37]

In Erikson's model, adolescence is marked by the crisis of *identity* versus confusion (sometimes characterized as role confusion or identity diffusion). The positive outcome of this crisis is *fidelity.* Identity has been defined as "the way in which we adopt certain strategies of action to maintain a connection with others, with our past, and with our own aspirations."[38]

Adolescence is associated with physical and hormonal changes brought about by puberty. It is also a time when, as with the period associated with the first eighteen months of life, "thousands of new connections sprout" in the wiring of the brain, "exponentially increasing our capacity of new learning." Again, the brain overprepares, this time for the "uncertainty of adult life."[39]

This is usually a time for switching schools, with adolescents going from elementary to middle and high schools, where they encounter different policies and focuses. "Adolescents are confronted with a host of unique transitional issues," says Robin Paletti; besides physical changes, "teenagers must also negotiate pressing psychosocial concerns surrounding the attainment of independence, peer acceptance, and self-esteem."[40] Another writer says, "The psychosocial modality of this stage is to be oneself or not to be oneself."[41] As they change into adults and approach the end of their school years, adolescents recognize that they will soon have to leave home and make major decisions about college education and career paths. "With independence looming, the adolescent must negotiate some degree of detachment from the family, provoking feelings of loss."[42]

A bridge is established between the past—the years of childhood and dependency—and the future—the years of adulthood and independence. The central question is, Who am I as an emotional, thinking, physical, and sexual being?

Remember what it was like being a teenager? Becoming more your own person? Striving to express your own ideas and beliefs? Sorting out the tangle of all that's happening to you? Deciding what you want for your life? Adolescence can be confusing and challenging. The achievement of goals and dreams seems nearly within one's grasp; death threatens that achievement. When a close death occurs, common grief reactions during adolescence include denial, depression, anger, somatization (conversion of a mental state into physical symptoms), mood swings, and philosophical questioning. Surviving a close death may also result in a more rapid "growing up."

In Piaget's model, adolescence is characterized by the use of *formal operations*. The fourth and final phase in Piaget's theory, this period begins at about the age of eleven or twelve and extends into adulthood, although a person's fundamental way of seeing the world is thought to be fairly well established by about age fifteen. With the arrival of formal operational thinking, the individual is able to "think about thinking"—that is, to formulate concepts that are abstract or symbolic. Relations of correspondence or implication between complex sets of statements can be perceived, analogies recognized, and assumptions or deductions made. It becomes possible to predict outcomes without having to try them in the real world. In a chess game, for example, formal operations of thought allow players to consider a number of complicated strategies and to predict the likely result of each move, without having to touch a single piece on the board.

In Koocher's study, most of the children who used formal operations of thought were twelve or older, although a few were as young as nine or ten.

The children interviewed by Koocher reflected a mature understanding of death in their responses to the question, What makes things die?

- António: "You mean death in a physical sense? [*Yes.*] Destruction of a vital organ or life force within us."
- George: "They get old and their body gets all worn out, and their organs don't work as well as they used to."
- Paula: "When the heart stops, blood stops circulating. You stop breathing, and that's it. [*Anything else?*] Well, there's lots of ways it can get started, but that's what really happens."

Although adolescents typically demonstrate a mature understanding of death, this does not necessarily mean that there are no differences in the ways adolescents and adults understand and cope with death. For example, an adolescent's understanding of the universality of death may be influenced by a sense of invulnerability ("It can't happen to me"). The concept of personal death may not be easily accepted. In forging a sense of identity, the adolescent is confronted by the need to "reconcile that identity with ultimate disintegration and not being."[43]

Emerging Adulthood

Although adolescence historically has been defined as occupying ages eleven or twelve through eighteen or twenty, some developmentalists have proposed a category, *emerging adulthood,* for the period from the late teens through the twenties, especially ages eighteen to twenty-five. For most young people today, adulthood no longer begins when adolescence ends. Social scientists point out, "Societies have not yet become fully aware of, or begun fully to address, the ramifications of the longer and more varied transition into adult life."[44]

Many individuals in this age range enter a moratorium, postponing commitments and identity decisions. This delay is often associated with the time needed to gain an education or to make choices about a career. This is a time when many possibilities and directions in work, love, and worldview can be imagined. People of this age group no longer view themselves as adolescents, but they may not see themselves entirely as adults either. "Emerging adults can pursue novel and intense experiences more freely than adolescents because they are less likely to be monitored by parents and can pursue them more freely than adults because they are less constrained by roles."[45] The prevalence of certain types of risk behavior—including unprotected sex, substance abuse, risky driving, and binge drinking—appears to peak during the years of emerging adulthood. Like adolescents in this regard, emerging adults may think they are "beyond death."

Early Adulthood

Human development does not stop with childhood's end. The patterns of coping with loss continue to evolve throughout a person's life span. Just as we associate certain developmental tasks and abilities with children of different ages, so, too, we distinguish distinctive phases and transitions during adult life. All too often, we are sensitive to the developmental stages of childhood but tend to ignore the changes that occur in the last sixty or more years of life.[46]

Earlier in this chapter, we discussed the first five stages of psychosocial development proposed by Erik Erikson—namely, those pertaining to the years of childhood and adolescence. The last three stages of psychosocial development, according to Erikson's model, occur during adulthood. As in childhood, each stage of adult life requires a particular developmental response, and each stage builds on previous ones.

Early adulthood (nineteen to forty years) is represented by tension between *intimacy* and isolation. The positive outcome is *love.* This stage involves various forms of commitment and interaction, including sex, friendship, cooperation, partnership, and affiliation. Ken Doka describes this as "a time of looking outward, of beginning families and a career."[47] Because mature love takes the risk of commitment, the death of a loved one may be most devastating during this stage and the next.[48]

Middle Adulthood

The next psychosocial stage according to Erikson is *middle adulthood* (forty to sixty or sixty-five years), and it is characterized by the crisis of *generativity* versus stagnation and self-absorption. The positive outcome is *care.* "Faith in the future, a belief in the species, and the ability to care about others seem to be prerequisites for development in this stage," whereas self-indulgence, boredom, and lack of psychological growth signal a lack of generativity.[49] This stage is characterized by a widening commitment to take care of the people, things, and ideas one has learned to care for. Ken Doka characterizes this period as having "a more settled quality" in that "jobs, careers, family, and friendship networks have probably stabilized."[50] Michele Paludi says, "Middle adulthood appears to be a prime period for experiencing fear of death since it is during this stage of the life cycle that the death of one's parents typically occurs."[51]

"Bloom County," drawing by Berke Breathed, © 1984 by Washington Post Writers Group

Later Adulthood

In reaching *late adulthood,* the eighth and final stage of the life cycle, the crisis to be resolved is that of *integrity* versus despair. The positive outcome of this stage of life is *wisdom.* "People must live with what they have built over their lifetime."[52] If the middle-aged adult is aware of mortality in a general sense, the older person can be described as aware of his or her *own* finitude.[53] Patricia Miller says that integrity involves "acceptance of the limitations of life, a sense of being part of a larger history that includes previous generations, a sense of owning the wisdom of the ages, and a final integration of all the previous stages." She adds that the antithesis of integrity is despair, which has been described as "regret for what one has done or not done with one's life, fear of approaching death, and disgust with oneself."[54] With respect to this, the psychologist M. Brewster Smith stated, "Fear of death seems to me partly a reflection of feeling cheated by life."[55]

Viewing the developmental phases as connected, each building on the ones before, the crisis of this period is especially powerful because of physical decline, outward signs of aging, vulnerability to chronic diseases, and the approaching certainty of death. It is marked by the thought, "This is the life I've had; there is no other; this is it. I don't have options to go back and change things in any significant way." Successfully completing the challenges of this developmental period gives us the strength of wisdom, which Erikson describes as "informed and detached concern with life itself in the face of death itself."[56]

The Evolution of a Mature Concept of Death

Through successive periods of development, individuals progress toward a mature understanding of death and exhibit characteristic responses to loss. Earlier, we looked at children's responses to the question, What makes things die? Their answers to other questions posed by Koocher also correspond to developmental stages. Asked, "How do you make dead things come back to life?" children who thought of death as reversible gave answers like "You can help them; give them hot food and keep them healthy so it won't happen again." Another child said, "No one ever taught me about that, but maybe you could give them some kind of medicine and take them to the hospital to get better." Children in later developmental stages recognized death as permanent: "If it was a tree, you could water it. If it's a person, you could rush them to the emergency room, but it would do no good if they were dead already." Another child said, "Maybe some day we'll be able to do it, but not now. Scientists are working on that problem."

Asked, "When will you die?" younger children gave answers ranging from "When I'm seven" (from a six-year-old) to "Three hundred years." In contrast,

> My granddaughter was helping me cut onions and it stung her eyes. I said, "You'll live." Skylar answered, "Of course I'll live. I'm six. . . ."

older children expected to live a statistically correct life span or a bit more; the usual age at which death was expected was about eighty.

In answer to the researchers' question, "What will happen when you die?" one nine-and-a-half-year-old said, "They'll help me come back alive." The researcher asked, "Who?" "My father, my mother, and my grandfather," the child responded. "They'll keep me in bed and feed me and keep me away from rat poison and stuff." According to some models, a child of nine would understand that none of those measures would work. Thus, this example illustrates the point that age-and-stage correlations provide, at best, a rule of thumb concerning how children develop.

In answer to the same question, an eight-and-a-half-year-old replied, "You go to heaven and all that will be left of you will be a skeleton. My friend has some fossils. A fossil is just a skeleton." Notice how this child used comparison to help interpret what happens when death occurs. An eleven-year-old said, "I'll feel dizzy and tired and pass out, and then they'll bury me and I'll rot away. You just disintegrate and only your bones will be left."

A twelve-year-old said, "I'll have a nice funeral and be buried and leave all my money to my son." One ten-year-old said, "If I tell you, you'll laugh." The researcher assured the child, "No, I won't. I want to know what you really think." Thus encouraged, the child continued, "I think I'm going to be reincarnated as a plant or animal, whatever they need at that particular time." The ability to imagine what things might be like in the future is seen in this child's response.

Agents of Socialization

Acquiring a mature understanding of death is part of the developmental process known as *socialization*—that is, the process by which an individual becomes identified as a member of a particular culture, learning and internalizing the norms, values, rules, and behaviors of society.[57] Classically, primary socialization refers to the preparation of a child for participation in adult society. However, socialization is best seen not as "a process of acquiring a unitary culture" but as involving the development of capacities for diverse cultural practices across the entire life course.[58] For people living in modern, industrialized countries, this life course now spans, with reasonable certainty, 50 to 70 years, and even beyond.[59] How we are socialized seems significantly tied to the fact that we will one day die. "Because death is universal and inevitable, it plays a role in shaping the organization and experience of life."[60]

Although the main phases of socialization occur during the years of childhood, it does not end with the age of majority. On the contrary, it continues throughout life as individuals develop new attitudes, values, and beliefs, as well as new social roles. Nor is it a one-way process whereby individuals simply learn to fit into society. Society's norms and values are modified as its members redefine their social roles and obligations. These are "bi-directional socializing processes that lead to individualized arrangements with changing social contexts."[61]

Socialization has a variety of influences, beginning with the family and extending to peer groups, school and work situations, social clubs, on to vicarious socialization through the popular media and the global "transcultural" environment. As Hannelore Wass says, "Children adopt many values and beliefs from significant adults in their world [including] parents, teachers, public figures, sports heroes, and famous entertainers."[62] Today, children and adults are exposed to a broader range of influences on their socialization than at any other time in history.

Resocialization, a term that refers to the "uprooting and restructuring of basic attitudes, values, or identities," occurs when adults take on new roles that require replacing their existing values and modes of behavior.[63] This occurs, for example, with religious conversion, starting a new job, getting married, having children, or surviving the death of a mate. Widowhood, for example, involves changes in many areas of life, as new roles and activities are taken on. Richard Settersten says, "Resocialization seems increasingly necessary for everyone in a fast-paced and ever-changing world in which life spans seven or more decades."[64]

Secondary socialization is a term used to describe the learning of new rules and behaviors when one becomes a member of a smaller group within the larger society, such as the military, a profession, an urban gang, or a new neighborhood. It occurs, too, when a child enters school with its new rules and expectations. Secondary socialization is generally understood as involving smaller changes than those occurring in primary socialization.

People tend to acquire their learning about dying and death on an ad hoc basis—that is, in a disorganized and impromptu fashion. Formal education about death is offered through courses, seminars, and the like, but these avenues of socialization are not part of most people's experience. The term *tactical socialization* refers to strategies that, for example, hospice caregivers use to informally teach people about death and dying.[65] Tactical socialization involves actively attempting to change people's perceptions and behaviors about some aspect of their social world.

Family

The family is the foundational social institution in all societies, although the definition of "family" varies from place to place and time to time. In the routines of daily life, the beliefs and values of parents are transmitted to their children. The family is the first source of death education in our lives, and its influence continues throughout our lives.[66] It's important to recognize that the dead, especially deceased family members, can also serve as agents of socialization, influencing the living in many ways. Richard Settersten observes, "The influence of the dead may be just as great—or even greater—than that of the living."[67]

Think back to your own childhood. What messages did you receive about death that remain to this day in the back of your mind? Possibly some messages were conveyed directly: "This is what death is" or "This is how we behave in relation to death." Perhaps some messages were indirect: "Let's not talk about it . . . . " How would the rest of that sentence go? Let's not talk about it . . . because it's

> "Mom, if there was a dead rabbit in our house, I would ask you if I could poke it. Then when you said no, I would do it anyway because I want to see if it is alive."
>
> A four-year-old

not something that people talk about? When, as a child, one woman encountered a dead animal on the highway, she was told, "You shouldn't look at it." Her mother admonished, "Put your head down; children shouldn't see that." This is a parental message about appropriate behavior toward death.

Other parental messages about death are communicated unconsciously. Consider the notion of replaceability. A child's pet dies, and the parent says, "It's okay, dear, we'll get another one." Children differ in their emotional response to the death of a family pet; some grieve intensely when a beloved pet dies. Quickly replacing it may not allow time for acknowledging the loss. What lesson about death is taught? Imagine a situation in which a mother's grief over her mate's death is interrupted by her child's remark, "Don't worry, Mommy, we'll get you another one."

The way we learn about death tends to be a result of happenstance rather than of systematic instruction. It is not always possible to pinpoint the genesis of ideas that an individual acquires about death. Consider the following incident, involving two siblings ages eight and ten. When asked to draw a picture of a funeral (see Figure 2-3), they got out their colored pencils and immersed themselves in the task. After a while, Heather (ten) said to Matt (eight), "Hey, you've got smiles on those faces! This is supposed to be a funeral. What are they doing with smiles on their faces?" In her model of appropriate death-related behavior, people don't smile at funerals; to her younger brother, smiles were perfectly acceptable. One can only guess the influences that provoke such strong statements about what kind of behavior is appropriate at funerals.

The lessons about death that are learned in the family are conveyed by actions as well as words. A woman now in her thirties tells the following story: "I remember a time when my mother ran over a cat. I wasn't with her in the car, but I recall my mother coming home and just totally falling apart. She ran into the bedroom and cried for hours. Since that time, I've been extremely conscientious about not killing anything. If there's an insect on me or in my house, I'll pick it up and carry it outside." Parental attitudes, and the attitudes of other family members, shape the values and behaviors not only of the child but also of the adult that the child will become, and they influence how that adult conveys attitudes toward death to his or her own children.

School and Peers

Schools teach more than "reading, 'riting, and 'rithmetic." The social world of a child is dramatically broadened during the school years. Hobbies and sports also connect children to a community and a set of social norms. "The scraps of lore which children learn from each other are at once more real, more immediately serviceable, and more vastly entertaining to them

FUNERAL
no!

Figure 2-3 *Children's Drawings of a Funeral*
Instructed to draw a picture of a funeral, a sister (age ten) and brother (eight) did so. The ten-year-old, whose drawing is at the left, emphasizes the emotional responses of the survivors. We see the picture as if we are looking in (and down) upon their grief. The figures in the first two pews have tears streaming down their faces, and one woman shouts, "No!" At ten, this child reflects on the sorrowful and unwelcome nature of death. When questioned about the empty pews, she said they were for anyone who came late.

The eight-year-old's drawing (above) is viewed from a similar perspective (looking in and down at the scene). Here, we see the survivors grouped around a flag-draped and flower-bedecked coffin. The figures are portrayed with smiles on their faces. The focus in this drawing is on the symbols of death (for example, the casket) and the ceremony rather than on the emotions. During the drawing session, the older sister commented that her brother's picture was "too happy" for a funeral scene.

Disregarding my warning about the toxin I had added to a little reflecting pond behind our home because it was full of mosquito larvae, our son Mark carefully poured a jar of tadpoles into the little pond and watched all of them die in an instant. I heard his screams and ran outdoors to see what had happened. Huge tears were streaming down his face. I picked him up to check his body to see if he had any damage other than from watching all his little tadpoles floating with their white bellies in the air.

He gasped deeply with his arms around my neck and sobbed, "Daddy . . . does this mean that I'll die? Will you die, too, Daddy?" I did my best to assure him that I was not going to die then, nor would he, but that death was a part of our lives and he would certainly be cared for.

And all of a sudden I was aware of what Gerard Manley Hopkins was saying so beautifully in his poem I had read years before. In "Spring and Fall: To a Young Child," he was letting us know that children at an early age (Mark was about four years old) could firmly grasp the concept that everything that lives will ultimately die. During my training in child psychiatry I had been taught that children under the age of eight or nine could not grasp the concept of death. Mark was half that age and knew innately what my professors could not grasp, namely, that it is obvious even to children that everything that lives will die.

William M. Lamers, Jr.

than anything which they learn from grown-ups."[68] Even before the school years, children enter the social world of their peer group as they play with other children of the same age and general social status. Recall how, in chasing games, a touch with the tip of a finger can have a noxious effect, as if the chaser were evil, magic, or diseased, and the touch was contagious.[69] Similarly, in songs and rhymes, children share death imagery, as in the classic "As the Hearse Goes By," which includes the lines

Did you ever think as the hearse goes by
That you may be the next to die?
The worms crawl in, the worms crawl out,
The worms play pinochle on your snout.

With the broadening of a child's social network, there is an increase in learning about death.

Later in life, educational and work settings, clubs and organizations, leisure pursuits, friends and neighbors, and so forth provide further opportunities for peer groups and other social networks to exert a powerful influence on socialization through the life course.

Mass Media and Children's Literature

Television, movies, radio, newspapers, magazines, books, CDs, DVDs, and the Internet—these media have a powerful socializing influence. Although the manner in which death-related content is presented in media intended for children can be evaluated as having both good and bad qualities, these

Little Red Riding Hood

. . . "Dear me, Grandmamma, what great arms you have!"

The wolf replied: "They are so much better to hug you with, my child."

"Why, Grandmamma, what great legs you have got!"

"That is to run the better, my child!"

"But, Grandmamma, what great ears you've got!"

"That is to hear the better, my child."

"But, Grandmamma, what great eyes you've got!"

"They are so much better to see you with, my child."

Then the little girl, who was now very much frightened, said: "Oh, Grandmamma, what great teeth you have got!"

"THEY ARE THE BETTER TO EAT YOU UP!"

With these words the wicked wolf fell upon Little Red Riding Hood and ate her up in a moment.

Journeys Through Bookland, Volume One

media still serve as avenues for learning about death.[70] Media messages communicate cultural attitudes toward death to children, even when the message is not purposely directed to them, as with news reports of disasters. When President John F. Kennedy was assassinated, a classic study found that children tended to select from the details presented by the media those aspects that were consistent with their developmental concerns.[71] Younger children worried about the appearance of the president's body and the effects of the death on his family; older children expressed concerns about the impact of Kennedy's death on the political system.

Many classic children's stories and fairy tales depict death, near deaths, or the threat of death.[72] There are "tales of children abandoned in woods; of daughters poisoned by their mothers' hands; of sons forced to betray their siblings; of men and women struck down by wolves, or imprisoned in windowless towers."[73] Death has often had a place in children's literature, and this is especially true of the earliest versions of familiar stories that parents and other adults share with children. Elizabeth Lamers says, "American children taught to read with textbooks such as *McGuffey's Eclectic Readers* found that death was presented as tragic, but inevitable, and many of the death-related stories conveyed a moral lesson."[74] In the nineteenth century, the violence in children's stories was usually graphic and gory so that it would make the desired moral impression.[75]

Cultural values related to death are also presented in children's stories. Consider, for example, the contrasts between different versions of the tale of Little Red Riding Hood. One version, "Petite Rouge," situates Riding Hood in the swamps and bayous of Louisiana, and another, "Pretty Salma," locates her in an African marketplace.[76] In the traditional version of the story, the wolf eats Little Red Riding Hood, but she is saved by a woodsman who kills the wolf and slits its stomach, allowing Little Red Riding Hood to emerge unharmed. In more recent versions, Little Red Riding Hood's screams alert the woodsman, who chases the wolf and then returns to announce that she will be bothered no more (the killing of the wolf occurs offstage and is not mentioned).[77]

The Chinese tale of "Lon Po Po" ("Granny Wolf") comes from an oral tradition thought to be over a thousand years old. In this version of the story, three young children are left by themselves while their mother goes away to visit their grandmother. The wolf, disguised as Po Po (Grandmother), persuades the children to open the locked door of their house. When they do, he quickly blows out the light. By making perceptive inquiries, however, the oldest child cleverly discovers the wolf's true identity and, with her younger siblings, escapes to the top of a ginkgo tree. Through trickery, the children convince the wolf to step into a basket so that they can haul him up to enjoy the ginkgo nuts. Joining together, the children start hauling up the basket. But, just as it nearly reaches the top of the tree, they let the basket drop to the ground. The story says, "Not only did the wolf bump his head, but he broke his heart to pieces."[78] Climbing down

© Christine DeVault

This grandmother and granddaughter read a story about loss as they share a special moment. Occasions for discussing death arise naturally out of our interactions with children. Often, the most important contribution an adult can make to a child's learning is simply to be a good listener.

to the branches just above the wolf, the children discover that he is "truly dead." Unlike the Western version, which has a solitary child facing the threat of the wolf by herself and ultimately being saved by someone else, the Chinese folk tale emphasizes the value of being part of a group effort to do away with the wolf.

Some children's stories are written with the specific aim of answering their questions about dying and death. In many such books, especially those for young children, death is presented as part of the natural cycle. These stories express the idea that, like the transition from one season to the next, each ending in life is followed by renewal. In choosing a book to read with a younger child or suggesting one for an older reader, it is important to first review the book yourself to evaluate how it presents information about death. Books should be appropriate for a particular situation. For example, *When Dinosaurs Die: A Guide to Understanding Death* was selected when one young boy's kindergarten teacher died unexpectedly. Each time he read and reread this book with his parents, he raised different questions about his teacher's death. Books are published on such topics as learning about and understanding death, the death of a parent, grandparent, sibling, and other relatives and friends, as well as pets (see Figure 2-4 at the end of this chapter for a selection of books about death for children and teens).

It is also important to pay attention to the language the author uses to describe dying, death, and bereavement. Euphemisms such as "closure," "moving on," or "getting over the loss" may signal that an author is unfamiliar with the theories and insights that apply to understanding loss. A story that refers to death as sleep should raise a red flag about the ideas it is communicating to children. Straightforward words such as died, dead, sorrow, and funeral suggest the use of honest and accurate terminology. A book can give an adult and a child an opportunity to begin talking about each other's experiences.

Lullabies also contain themes of death and violence.[79] In every human culture and in every historical period, adults have sung to children. It is said that, with the first lullaby a mother sings to her child, death education begins.[80] Consider the message in this well-known lullaby:

> Rockabye baby, in the treetops.
> When the wind blows, the cradle will rock.
> When the bough breaks, the cradle will fall.
> Down will come baby, cradle and all.

Some lullabies are mourning songs, which describe the death or funeral of a child; others are threat songs that warn of violence if a child does not go to sleep or perform some other action in the expected manner.

Of two hundred nursery rhymes examined in one study, about half described the wonder and beauty of life, whereas the other half dealt with the ways in which humans and animals die or are mistreated.[81] Death-related themes in these rhymes include accounts of murder, choking to death, torment and cruelty, maiming, misery and sorrow, as well as stories of lost or abandoned children and depictions of poverty and want.

Religion

Contemplating one's place in the universe is a crucial aspect of human development, and religions the world over have traditionally been a fertile avenue for such contemplation. Religion is not only a basis for morality and human relationships; it can also give meaning to life.[82] As a fundamental element of culture, religion and, more broadly, spirituality have the potential to shape individual lives and personalities.[83] Many concepts central to religious traditions "are not as opaque to young children as often thought."[84] It has been noted that "while more young people than ever claim to have no religion, there seems to be a growing interest in 'spirituality' among them."[85]

In the United States, more than 90 percent of the population is affiliated with a religious tradition.[86] These traditions are naturally part of a child's socialization. (The role of religion and religious belief is discussed in more detail in Chapter 14.)

Teachable Moments

In the course of their daily lives, opportunities abound for children to learn about dying and death.[87] Consider, for example, a mother who discovers her eleven-year-old son sitting at her new computer writing his will. Taken aback, she pauses for a moment as thoughts race through her head: Why is he writing a will? How did an eleven-year-old become interested in giving away his favorite treasures? Does he believe he is going to die soon? What should I do? What can I say? Gathering her courage, she cautiously adjusts her tone to suggest a neutral stance and asks, "What has made you think about writing a will?"

Turning to her, the joy of accomplishment lighting up his face, the boy says, "I was looking at the menu on your computer and found *Willmaker*. The program came up, and all I have to do is fill in the blanks. It's easy, see? Then I can print out my very own will."

Thus we encounter the concept of the *teachable moment,* a phrase used by educators to describe opportunities for learning that arise out of ordinary experiences. Because of their immediacy, such naturally occurring events are ideal for learning. The learner's questions, enthusiasm, and motivation guide the educational process. If we assume that learning always flows in a single direction, from adult to child, we miss the quintessential quality of education as an interactive process. In the example of the young boy filling in the blanks of a computerized will-making program, the mother appears to occupy most clearly the role of the learner. She learns something about her son's exploration of the new computer and, more important, she learns the crucial lesson of gathering information before reacting.

Suppose this mother, acting out of initial shock at her son's apparent interest in death, had hastily responded, "Stop that! Children shouldn't be thinking about wills or about dying!" A lesson about death would surely be taught, but it wouldn't promote a healthy understanding. It is useful to ask, *What* is being taught? Does the "teaching" result from a conscious design? Or is it unintentionally conveying unhealthy messages about death?

Let's return to our story of the mother and son. Having elicited information without acting on her initial anxiety, the mother can use this conversation as an opportunity to discuss death with her son. She might call attention to the entry for "Designated Guardian for Minor Children," informing her son about the steps she has taken to ensure his well-being ("Did I tell you that Aunt Martha and Uncle John are listed in my will as your guardians?") as well as responding to his concerns ("No, I do not intend to die for a long time"). They might spend a few minutes talking about other aspects of death and how people prepare for it. An atmosphere of openness is promoted as information is exchanged between adult and child. Much learning can take place in a brief conversation.

Teachable moments are often defined in the context of unplanned or unexpected occurrences, but it is useful to recognize that parents, educators, and other adults can intentionally create situations that encourage such opportunities for learning about death.[88] There is no rule that we must wait until such events happen spontaneously. Indeed, in the example given earlier, the mother used her son's experience with the computer program as a way of introducing their subsequent discussion about death. Similarly, in films produced for children, death is frequently part of the plot, and this can lead to a natural discussion about how grief, for example, is portrayed among the various characters.[89] The key to making the most of such opportunities is adequate preparation by trusted adults in the child's environment.

Teachable moments take place not only between adults and children but also between adults. While on an airplane trip, an executive for a large corporation engaged one of this book's authors in conversation. Upon learning the subject of this textbook, his tone changed a bit as he said, "Could I ask your opinion on a personal matter?" The question involved a family dispute about whether the man's five-year-old son should attend his grandfather's burial ceremony at Arlington National Cemetery. He was concerned that the military ceremony—with uniforms, soldiers, and a twenty-one-gun salute—would frighten his son. After he shared additional information about his family and child, suggestions were offered about ways that parental support could be provided to the child during the funeral rites. Hearing these suggestions made it possible for the man to reconsider his earlier decision to

> Recently my seven-year-old son hopped in my lap and we watched the evening news together. The concluding line of a report on environmental pollution was a quote from U.N. scientists predicting that in twenty years the world would be uninhabitable. As the TV switched to a Madison Avenue jingle designed to encourage us to purchase a non-greasy hair tonic, my son turned to me with a terribly small voice and asked: "Dad, how old will I be when we all die?"
>
> Robert D. Barr, *The Social Studies Professional*

exclude the child. With specific recommendations in hand, he decided that his son should be present at his grandfather's funeral. You do not have to be the author of a textbook to offer information that is helpful to people who are coping with death-related issues. In reading this book, you will gain information that can be appropriately shared.

The Death of a Companion Animal

One mother described the responses of her daughters to the deaths of a new litter of baby rabbits.[90] Upon learning the news, the seven-year-old burst into tears and howled, "I don't want them dead." The five-year-old at first stood silently and then asked to call her father at work. She told him, "If you had been here, Daddy, you could have been the rabbits' doctor," reflecting a belief, appropriate for her age, that it should have been possible somehow to save the baby rabbits or restore them to life. Later, when the children began to dig a grave to bury the dead rabbits, the seven-year-old stopped crying for the first time since learning the news, while the five-year-old kept repeating, "The baby rabbits are dead, the baby rabbits are dead," in a monotone.

In the days following the rabbits' deaths, the girls asked many questions. The seven-year-old was particularly interested in questioning a family friend, who was a widow, about her dead husband. How often did she think about him, and why did people have to be taken away from those who loved them, she wanted to know. The five-year-old, meanwhile, continued to mourn silently until her mother encouraged her to express her feelings. Then she began to sob. Finally, she said, "I'm glad I'm only five; you only die when you're old."

The younger child's first concern was for herself, the fear that she herself could die. The older child worried about the durability of relationships. Although each child had a distinctive response to the loss, both children showed a need to be close to their parents during the days following the deaths of the rabbits, and they told the story of the rabbits' deaths again and again as they dealt with their experience.

Adults may wonder how best to help a child cope with the death of a beloved pet. Should one minimize the loss? Obtain a replacement animal? Or should the death be seen as a natural opportunity to help the child consider what death means and explore his or her feelings about the loss? "Pets, whose lives are shorter than [those of] humans, can teach children about the life cycle, including loss."[91]

Of course, it is not only children who are affected by the death of a pet. Kelly McCutcheon and Stephen Fleming point out that "the loss of a pet often involves responsibility for life and death which can make grieving especially difficult. When a pet is seriously ill, the owner is faced with the major decision of whether the pet's life is worth continuing or if the pet should be euthanized."[92]

Pets can mean many different things to their "pet parents."[93] For some people, a pet is viewed as a best friend. A pet may be a bridge to the past, a reminder of happier times or of poignant events. A pet can be a source of support during a loss or other times of stress. For people who are coping with serious illness, a pet may be both a source of comfort and a reason for living. As has been wisely said, "The unique bond with a particular pet can never be duplicated."[94] We may bond again with another pet, but we can never replace the one lost.

Barbara Ambros writes about the changing view of animal spirits in Japan, where pets who had died were regarded as recently as the mid-1990s as becoming vengeful, threatening spirits and now a decade or so later are viewed as loving, faithful spiritual companions. Ambros says, "Pets are often buried and memorialized with rites due to a family member," noting that many pet owners "seem to have a strong urge to perpetuate the bond that they felt with their pet even after the pet's death."[95] A similar transition, albeit without the occult overtones, is found in an account by Michelle Linn-Gust, describing how the role of dogs in families has shifted from hunting and protection to "membership" in the family.[96]

© Albert Lee Strickland

The strong attachment felt toward an animal companion is shown in this homemade tombstone and burial plot. Experiencing grief and memorializing a beloved pet are natural accompaniments to such a loss.

A woman described the reaction of her husband to the death of Iggy, a desert iguana.[97] When the iguana died, her husband "cried throughout the shoebox burial in the backyard." He later said that he was crying "for every pet he had ever loved and lost." The death of a pet can evoke numbness and disbelief, preoccupation with the loss, being drawn toward reminders of the pet, anger, depression, and the whole range of mental and emotional qualities associated with grief following a significant loss. Rather than viewing a pet as a possession, many people feel that a pet is not only a companion but "part of the family."[98]

Those who counsel individuals who are grieving over the loss of a pet emphasize that feelings should be expressed by adults as well as children. The circumstances of an animal's death can influence the grief reaction; for instance, the loss of a pet whose death occurred because of an accident may result in grief of longer duration than that of a pet who died a natural or even a euthanized death.[99] "Pet parents" may experience feelings of guilt and direct responsibility for a companion animal's death by euthanasia; after all, the animal cannot communicate a wish to die explicitly through language in the way humans can in a living will or other advance directive.

When a decision is made to euthanize an animal, some experts advise informing children about the process.[100] They can be told that the animal is in the process of dying and that the veterinarian will assist in this process by giving an injection that helps the pet die without suffering. Children should also be told that this injection is a powerful medicine that is given only to animals, so the child will not fear getting a vaccination or other injection.

Although attachments between humans and pets can be very strong, mourning the loss of a pet sometimes elicits ridicule, or worse. After Hurricane Katrina, some people in authority were unconcerned about stranded companion animals and did not consider them important. Reportedly, rather than argue with survivors about saving a family dog, some local authorities simply shot pets, disregarding the fact that many people who live with an animal consider it important enough to risk their own personal safety to keep a pet from harm.[101] It has been observed that "victims of disaster are often accidentally or forcibly separated from their pets, sometimes permanently, just at the time they need one another most."[102]

People sometimes say that the bereaved pet owner's grief is excessive or that it's an overreaction. After all, "It was only an animal, a mere pet." However, as Allan Kellehear and Jan Fook point out, "Despite the popular tendency in some quarters to trivialize such loss, the general literature on pet–human relations portrays bereaved owners as every bit as beset with the same power and range of emotions as for other kinds of human loss."[103]

In many parts of the country, pet cemeteries exist, and they provide options for the final disposition of a companion animal's remains. The Gateway Pet Cemetery located in Southern California, for example, offers both burial and cremation. Veterinary schools can be good sources of information about disposition options as well as about end-of-life care of companion animals, including "hospice care for pets."[104]

When the bond between an animal and its carer is broken by death, the significance of that loss should be recognized as a natural occasion for mourning.[105] This is true for adults as well as children. Cheri Barton Ross explains,

> A child might decide to wear the cat's collar to feel close to a cat that has died. Some children choose to cuddle or sleep with the pet's bedding. One woman shared that she saved her dog's collar and wore it as a garter—for something blue—under her wedding gown in honor of the dog with whom she had grown up.[106]

Sufficient time for mourning the loss should be allowed before a new animal is acquired. "For some owners, grieving may be facilitated by the presence of another pet, but for others, replacement may never be appropriate."[107] The right time for another pet is likely to be when grief has been integrated sufficiently to enable one to reinvest emotionally in a new pet. As Avery Weisman observes, "The depth of a human–animal bond often exceeds that between a person and close kith and kin."[108]

The Mature Concept of Death Revisited

The process of socialization is complex and ongoing. With new experiences of loss and death, we modify previously held beliefs, exchanging them for new ones that provide a better fit with our current understanding of death and its meaning in our lives. A "mature" concept of death, acquired during childhood, becomes a foundation for further development in adulthood.[109] Sandor Brent and Mark Speece note that a basic understanding of death is "the stable nucleus, or core, of a connotational sphere that the child continues to enrich and elaborate throughout the remainder of life by the addition of all kinds of exceptions, conditions, questions, doubts, and so forth." Instead of the "neat, clean, sharply delineated concepts of formal

> I like especially the small town cemeteries of America where the children come for picnics and games, as we did when I was growing up—wandering among the stones on our own, with no adults about, to regard the mystery and inevitability of death, on its terms and ours. I remember we would watch the funerals from afar in a hushed awe, and I believe that was when I became obsessed not with death itself but with the singular community of death and life together—and life's secrets, life's fears, life's surprises.
>
> Willie Morris, *Shifting Interludes*

scientific theories of reality," the end result of this process may be a kind of "fuzzy" concept that acknowledges the reality of death while leaving room for elaborations about its meaning. Thus, the binary, either-or logic that young children use to grasp the core components of a mature concept of death is a precursor to the greater sophistication in understanding death that comes later in life.[110]

David Plath says,

> We are born alone and we die alone, each an organism genetically unique. But we mature or decline together: In the company of others we mutually domesticate the wild genetic pulse as we go about shaping ourselves into persons after the vision of our group's heritage. Perhaps the growth and aging of an organism can be described well enough in terms of stages and transitions within the individual as a monad entity. But in a social animal the life courses have to be described in terms of a collective fabricating of selves, a mutual building of biographies.[111]

It is said that the single most important thing one can do to influence the development of an infant is to "decide where on earth—in what human community—that infant is going to grow up."[112] Understanding ourselves as cultural beings, we are better able to understand others as cultural beings. Even though we identify (or are identified by others) with a particular group, we are also individuals who sometimes do things our own way. Psychologists tell us that every person is composed of "multiple identities" and that the ability to manage different identities is an important aspect of the self.[113] Culture does not determine behavior but, rather, gives us a "repertoire of ideas and possible actions" through which we understand ourselves, our environment, and our experiences.[114]

Albert Bandura says, "Theorists who approach human development from a life-span perspective treat the environment not as a situational entity, but as a varied succession of life events that differ in their power to affect the direction lives take."[115] The social circles in which one moves, the kinds of people who populate those settings make some types of "intersects" more probable than others. Bandura cites the example of a child living in a crime-ridden neighborhood as being likely to experience chance encounters quite different from those experienced by a child residing at a prep school.

Take a moment to consider your own circumstances. Do you live in a rural, urban, or small-town environment? What region of the country do you live in, the North, East, South, or West? Was your school environment ethnically and religiously diverse, or was it not? Your response to death is likely to be influenced by such factors. Life experiences are powerful in shaping a person's attitudes and beliefs about death. A person may not become fully aware of the impact of childhood experiences with death until adulthood. A ten-year-old's agonized phrase, "It's sickening, don't talk about it!" can survive into adulthood.

Books for Younger Children

Cathy Blanford. *Something Happened.* Illustrated by Phyllis Childers. Western Springs, Ill.: Cathy Blanford, 2008. A clearly illustrated book that discusses pregnancy loss in language easy for young children to understand. Also has information for grieving parents to help their children. Ages 3–7.

Marc Brown. *When Dinosaurs Die: A Guide to Understanding Death.* Illustrated by Laurie Krasny Brown. Boston: Little, Brown, 1996. This cartoon-like book offers comfort and reassurance to children by addressing their fears about death, explaining in simple language the feelings people may have when a loved one dies and ways of remembering someone who has died. Ages 3–8.

Margaret Wise Brown. *The Dead Bird.* Illustrated by Remy Charlip. New York: Morrow, 2004. A simple story in which children find a dead bird and conduct a funeral and burial. Ages 4–8.

Bill Cochran. *The Forever Dog.* Illustrated by Dan Andreasen. New York: HarperCollins, 2007. Mike makes a Forever Plan with his dog Corky to be best friends forever; it works beautifully until Corky dies unexpectedly. In his grief, Mike is angry at Corky for breaking his promise. With his mother's help, Mike realizes the Forever Plan is going to work differently. Corky will be in his heart forever. Ages 4–8.

Bill Cosby. *The Day I Saw My Father Cry.* Illustrated by Varnette P. Honeywood. New York: Scholastic, 2000. The sudden death of a family friend brings lessons in experiencing and expressing grief. Ages 4–10.

Mary Newell DePalma. *A Grand Old Tree.* New York: A. A. Levine, 2005. Clearly illustrated easy-reader picture book about the life cycle. The grand old tree slowly crumbles and becomes part of the earth. The roots of her "grandchildren" sink deep into the earth and are home to many creatures. Ages 4–8.

DyAnne DiSalvo-Ryan. *A Dog Like Jack.* New York: Holiday House, 2001. Story of loving and losing an aged pet. An epilogue contains suggestions for parents about pet loss. Ages 4–8.

Joan Drescher. *The Moon Balloon: A Journey of Hope and Discovery for Children and Families.* Waltham, Mass.: Arvest Press, 2005. A colorful book about hot-air balloons, each of which contains a feeling that a child might have when coping with change. Examples of the balloons include the angry balloon, the tear balloon, the stress balloon, the love balloon, and the giggle balloon. Gives children an opportunity to draw or write about their feelings and offers helpful tips for adults. Ages 6–11.

Wolf Erlbruch. *Duck, Death and the Tulip.* Wellington, New Zealand: Gecko Press, 2008. With a gorgeously drawn colored-pencil style, this book explores a relationship between a duck and Death. The duck becomes friends with Death; they go to the pond where Death (drawn as a clothed skull) becomes chilled. Duck offers to warm Death, spreading her body and feathers over Death. When Duck wakes in the morning, she is still alive and the story continues until the seasons change and she becomes chilled, dying in the night. Death carries her to the great river, places a tulip on her breast. "For a long time he watched her. When she was lost to sight, he was almost a little moved. But that's life, thought Death." A good book to demystify death and begin a discussion. Ages 4–up.

Anne Fontaine. *Ocho Loved Flowers.* Illustrated by Obadinah. Seattle: Stoneleigh Press, 2007. A story about Annie and her cat Ocho. Ocho becomes ill and the veterinarian tells Annie and her mom that Ocho has only one month to live. During Ocho's last month, Annie learns how to help her mom care for him. After Ocho dies, Annie buys flowers in memory of Ocho. Ages 4–8.

(continued)

Figure 2-4 *Books About Death for Children and Teens*
Prepared with the assistance of Dr. Carol F. Berns, cofounder of the Children's Bereavement Center, Miami, Florida. Additional resources can be found on *The Last Dance* website.

Books for Younger Children (continued)

Eiko Kadono. *Grandpa's Soup.* Illustrated by Satomi Ichikawa. Grand Rapids, Mich.: Eerdmans, 1999. After Grandma's death, Grandpa fixes her soup recipe for his friends, including his mice friends. Ages 4–8.

Laurie A. Kanyer. *25 Things to Do When Grandpa Passes Away, Mom and Dad Get Divorced, or the Dog Dies.* Seattle: Parenting Press, 2004. Offers education to parents or other adults who are working with grieving children. The second half of the book describes twenty-five activities to help children experiencing loss, including art and craft activities as well as high-energy outdoor activities. Ages 6–11.

Essie Laflamme. *Caring for Mama Bear: A Story of Love.* Illustrated by Marie Crane-Yvon. Naples, Fla.: Quality of Life Publishing. 2010. Despite her declining health, Mama Bear's days are sprinkled with laughter, family, and love thanks to her sons the Brother Bears. Mama Bear's last weeks are spent at a Hospice House and she is comfortable and feels loved. This story is good for families served by hospice and includes tips and resources for parents. Ages 7–10.

Marisol Munoz-Kiehne. *Since My Brother Died: Desde que Murio Mi Hermano.* Illustrated by Susanna Pitzer. Omaha, Neb.: Centering Corporation. 2008. A young boy talks about how his life has changed since his brother's death, yet he is comforted knowing that he will always love and remember him. The boy's journey is told in English and Spanish and the book includes a resource for parents and professionals. Ages 5–12.

Ellen Sabin. *The Healing Book.* New York: Watering Can Press, 2006. A memory book filled with page after page of opportunities for children to work through grief-related feelings as well as remember the person who died. Excellent tool for adults working with grieving children. Ages 6–13.

Harold Ivan Smith and Joy Johnson. *What Does That Mean?* Omaha, Neb.: Centering Corporation, 2006. A dictionary of death, dying, and grief terms for children. Offers age-appropriate definitions of words that grieving children hear but may not understand. Ages 6–12.

Patricia Smith. *Janna and the Kings.* Illustrated by Aaron Boyd. New York: Lee and Low Books, Inc., 2003. A tender story of Janna, an African American girl, who spends Saturdays with her grandfather and his buddies, the Kings. When Granddaddy dies, Janna is devastated. But when his old friends welcome her, they talk and share memories and she feels his love once again. Ages 5 and up.

Pat Thomas. *I Miss You: A First Look at Death.* Illustrated by Lesley Harker. Hauppauge, N.Y.: Barron's, 2001. "Every day someone is born and every day someone dies" begins this frank and sensitive look at death, including how people die, funerals, a survivor's feelings, and how people of different cultures engage in death rituals. Ages 4–8.

E. B. White. *Charlotte's Web.* Illustrated by Garth Williams. New York: Harper & Row, 1952. Classic story describes grief experienced at the death of a close friend—Charlotte, a spider—and the continuing of life through her offspring. Ages 3–up.

Jeanette Winter. *September Roses.* New York: Farrar, Straus & Giroux, 2004. South African sisters who raise roses come to New York on September 11, 2001. Addresses the sorrow of the terrorist attack and the response of those living through the disaster. A picture book, although not one a child can read because the text is in cursive. Ages 4–8.

Harriet Ziefert. *Ode to Humpty Dumpty.* Illustrated by Seymour Chwast. New York: Houghton Mifflin, 2001. The ultimate book for understanding rituals. A town comes together to memorialize Humpty's death. Ages 5–13.

Books for Older Children and Teens

The Dougy Center (Portland, Ore.). *After a Death: An Activity Book for Children/Después de un fallecimiento,* 2007; *After a Murder: A Workbook for Grieving Kids,* 2002; *After a Suicide: A Workbook for Grieving Kids,* 2001. Interactive workbooks in which children learn from other children who have experienced a death. These workbooks encourage children to express their thoughts and feelings through a variety of activities, including drawings, puzzles, word games, helpful stories, and advice from other kids and adults. Ages 9–up.

Dina Friedman. *Playing Dad's Song.* New York: Farrar, Straus & Giroux, 2006. When Gus was nine, his father died in the attack on the World Trade Center. Gus struggles with missing his father and, at the same time, does not want anyone to ask him about his father. He feels isolated because he is the only person he knows who had a parent die on 9/11. He uses music for comfort and to honor the memory of his father. Ages 9–12.

Carole Geitner. *If Only.* New York: Scholastic Press, 2012. Corinna, a typical eighth grader, whose mother has just died of cancer, gives voice to her experiences of loss, grief, relationships with friends, and other teen concerns in this sensitive and honest book. Ages 12 and up.

Marc Gellman and Thomas Hartman. *Bad Stuff in the News: A Guide to Handling the Headlines.* New York: SeaStar Books, 2002. After seeing a big office building crash to the ground or seeing kids shooting other kids at school, you might think the world is so scary that the only safe place is hiding under your bed. Written to help kids understand and cope with dangers in the world. Includes terrorism, kids killing kids, disasters (both natural and human caused), death through abuse, dangerous sports, diseases that kill, and more. Simple and easy to read. Ages 10–13.

Earl Grollman and Joy Johnson. *A Complete Book About Death for Kids.* Omaha, Neb.: Centering Corporation, 2006. Comprehensive information to help explain death to older children. Complex concepts are clearly defined. Written in easy-to-understand language. Ages 9–12.

Amy Hest. *Remembering Mrs. Rossi.* Illustrated by Heather Maione. Somerville, Mass.: Candlewick Press, 2007. Annie Rossi is eight years old when her mother, a sixth-grade teacher, dies. Her father does his best to do all of the things that Annie's mom did, but no one can replace Annie's mom. Annie is helped when her mother's class creates a special memory book about her (included at the end of this novel). With few books addressing the death of a mother, this one is a standout. Ages 9–12.

Gloria Horsley and Heidi Horsley. *Teen Grief Relief.* Highland City, Fla.: Rainbow Books, 2007. Information for teens and their parents about ways grieving teens can be helped. Easy to read. Includes vignettes from teens who have "been there," as well as activities teens can do to cope with feelings of sadness, anger, and guilt. Ages 12–up.

Carrie Stark Hugus. *Crossing 13: A Memoir of a Father's Suicide.* Denver: Affirm Publications, 2008. A teenage girl discovers her father dead from suicide. Young survivors will identify with and benefit from understanding that their confusing, and often frightening, grief responses are normal. Ages 12–up.

Davida Wills Hurwin. *A Time for Dancing.* New York: Puffin, 1997; reissued 2009. In this powerful novel about how terminal illness affects the lives of friends and others around them, two teenage girls who have been best friends since childhood face mortality when one is diagnosed with histiocytic lymphoma, a deadly cancer. Ages 12 and up.

Amy Goldman Koss. *Side Effects.* New Milford, Conn.: Roaring Brook Press, 2006. The story of teenage Izzy's bout with cancer. Excellently detailed view of Izzy's and her family's coping mechanisms. Teens will identify with her, whether they or someone they know has cancer or they are just curious about life-threatening illness. Ages 9–12.

(continued)

Books for Older Children and Teens (continued)

Erika Leeuwenburgh and Ellen Goldring. *Why Did You Die: Activities to Help Children Cope with Grief and Loss.* Oakland, Calif.: Instant Help Books, 2008. Offers detailed, helpful activities for children who have experienced a death. The first part of the book offers practical information for parents and other adults to help a grieving child. The second half of the book has activities to help grieving children. Ages 9 and up.

Wendy Mass. *Jeremy Fink and the Meaning of Life.* New York: Little, Brown, 2006. When Jeremy was eight, his father died in a car accident. A few months before he turns thirteen, he receives a mysterious wooden box in the mail that his father had created for him before his death. According to Jeremy's father, this box contained the Meaning of Life. There is only one problem: There are no keys! Jeremy spends the summer finding the keys to unlock this precious gift from his beloved father. Ages 9–12.

Sheryl McFarlane. *The Smell of Paint.* Brighton, Mass.: Fitzhenry & Whiteside, 2006. Story of Jess, a high school freshman, whose mother is diagnosed with incurable bone cancer. Jess tries to deal with her mother's illness by herself, not wanting even her closest friends to know. Explores Jess's complicated relationship with her dying mother. Ages 12 and up.

Katherine Paterson. *Bridge to Terabithia.* Illustrations by Donna Diamond. New York: HarperTrophy, 1987; reissued HarperTeen, 2009. In this Newberry award winner, fifth grader Jess's rural world expands when he meets his new neighbor, a tomboy named Leslie. They become best friends and create a secret kingdom in the woods named Terabithia. When Leslie drowns, Jess's life is changed forever. Ages 11 and up.

Lila Perl. *Dying To Know: About Death, Funeral Customs, and Final Resting Places.* Brookfield, Conn.: Twenty-First Century Books, 2001. This small book uses photographs and text to acquaint the reader with death customs and practices in the United States and other parts of the world. Organized into sections that address attitudes and practices from different religions and countries, as well as historical information. Ages 12–18.

Margo Rabb. *Cures for Heartbreak.* New York: Random House, 2008. This book deals with grief and typical teen issues in a straightforward manner with wit and wisdom and a dabbling of sarcasm. Fifteen-year-old Mia Perlman struggles to make sense of her mother's death, her father's illness, and her relationship with her sister. Mia's voice and those of the other characters are genuine, powerful, and raw. Ages 14 and up.

Jordan Sonnenblick. *Drums, Girls, and Dangerous Pie.* New York: Scholastic, 2006. Jeffery is diagnosed with leukemia. Big brother protector Steven says, "So how come when I wasn't looking Jeffy got cancer." Written in the voice of the older sibling, the story touches on many aspects of living with life-threatening illness, including the strain put on his entire family. Ages 11–14.

Staff of the New York Times. *A Nation Challenged: A Visual History of 9/11 and Its Aftermath (Young Reader's Edition).* New York: Scholastic, 2002. Combines stories published in the newspaper and Pulitzer Prize-winning photographs to present an account of terrifying events in an age-appropriate fashion. Ages 9–14.

Peter Lane Taylor and Nicola Christos. *The Secret of Priest's Grotto: A Holocaust Survival Story.* Minneapolis: Kar-Ben, 2007. Remarkable story of the survival of Jewish families who lived in a gypsum cave called Popwa Yama in the Ukraine for 344 days to escape the Gestapo. Includes excerpts from the privately published memoir of Esther Stermer, *We Fight to Survive,* that recount the dark epoch—the darkness being both literal and figurative. Ages 9–12.

Terry Trueman. *Hurricane: A Novel.* New York: HarperCollins, 2008. José, from La Rupa, Honduras, tells the story of surviving a disastrous hurricane. José narrates the story of his life before and after the hurricane. Ages 9–12.

Jamie Lee Wheeler. *Weird Is Normal When Teenagers Grieve.* Naples, Fla.: Quality of Life Publishing. 2010. Jenny is compelling and forthright as she speaks of her father's illness and death when she was fourteen years old. Her sage words and style are rich beyond her years, making this book an excellent resource for teens and adults. At the end of each chapter are bullet points for easy reading and suggestions. Ages 12 and up.

Kazumi Yumoto. *The Friends.* Translated by Cathy Hirano. New York: Farrar, Straus & Giroux, 1996; reissued, 2005. In a story that is both universal and rooted in the country and culture from which it comes, three young boys' fascination with death leads them to form an unexpected friendship with an old man through which they confront their fears and learn to accept the inevitable with a sense of joy in life. Ages 9 and up.

Nan Zastrow. *Ask Me . . . 30 Things I Want You to Know: How to be a Friend to a Survivor of Suicide.* Omaha, Neb.: Centering Corporation, 2008. Straightforward book about helping survivors of suicide. These tips will assist family members and friends of survivors when they are at a loss as to how to help. Ages 16 and up.

Further Readings

David Clark, ed. *The Sociology of Death: Theory, Culture, Practice.* Cambridge, Mass.: Blackwell, 1993.

Lynn Schofield Clark. *From Angels to Aliens: Teenagers, the Media, and the Supernatural.* New York: Oxford University Press, 2003.

Lynne Ann DeSpelder and Albert Lee Strickland. "Culture, Socialization, and Death Education." In *Handbook of Thanatology,* 2nd ed., ed. David K. Meagher and David E. Balk, 323–331. New York: Routledge, 2013.

Patricia H. Miller. *Theories of Developmental Psychology,* 4th ed. New York: Worth, 2002.

Clive F. Seale. *Constructing Death: The Sociology of Dying and Bereavement.* Cambridge: Cambridge University Press, 1998.

Additional resources for this chapter can be found at www.mhhe.com/despelder10e.

In this celebration of Día de los Muertos, *or Day of the Dead, held in a California community, a child enters into the festivities by drawing a skull, an activity that reinforces her identity as a participant in age-old traditions that mark her culture's particular attitudes and behaviors relative to death. In pluralistic societies, such celebrations both perpetuate cultural traditions and allow them to be shared with people from the wider community, who may choose to adopt elements of those traditions in their own lives, thereby creating a distinctive sense of local identity with respect to death-related customs and practices.*

CHAPTER 3

Perspectives on Death: Historical and Cultural

Although death is fundamentally a biological fact, socially shaped ideas and assumptions create its meaning. Consider, for instance, Hindus who live in England and their encounter with cultural imperatives related to death rituals.[1] In India, where there are few undertakers or funeral directors, funeral arrangements are usually made by the deceased's family. Cremation is a public event, and the principal mourner lights the sacred flame of the funeral pyre; in Britain, the body is placed inside a coffin and concealed from view inside the cremator, which is operated by employees of the crematorium. "For the mourners there is neither the smoke to sting their eyes, nor the fire to singe their hair, nor the smell of burning flesh to bring the poignant immediacy and reality of the experience to their consciousness."

This example illustrates how the multicultural nature of today's societies brings challenges to traditional cultural identities. Such challenges apply not only to members of immigrant populations but to people generally. Most people worldwide now develop a bicultural or "hybrid" identity that "combines their local cultural identity with an identity linked to elements of the global culture."[2]

Culture can be defined as "all that in human society which is socially rather than biologically transmitted."[3] Broadening our perspective to include cultures other than our own increases the range of choices available in our encounters with death. In becoming *culturally competent,* we gain the capacity to respond appropriately and skillfully to the diversity encountered in culturally pluralistic societies.

People tend to view the world from a single perspective—their own—and to apply their own cultural criteria as benchmarks for judging the values of other communities. Stereotypes are sometimes used as a learning strategy to organize and interpret information, but in fact there may be more differences within cultural groups than between cultural groups. Engaging the ideas and customs of other cultures is an antidote to *ethnocentrism*—that is, the fallacy of making judgments about others in terms of one's own cultural assumptions and biases.

Society is defined as "a group of people who share a common culture, a common territory, and a common identity; and who feel themselves to constitute a unified and distinct entity which involves interacting in socially structured relationships."[4] Much as in studying the human body, where we look at the structure and function of various organs and their interrelationships, we can view society as an organic whole in which constituent parts work together to maintain each other and the whole society. The *structural view of society* refers to the "enduring and patterned aspects which provide the context and background against which people live out their daily lives."[5]

Social institutions are related in such a way that a change in one leads to changes in others (see Figure 3-1). For example, in northeastern Brazil,

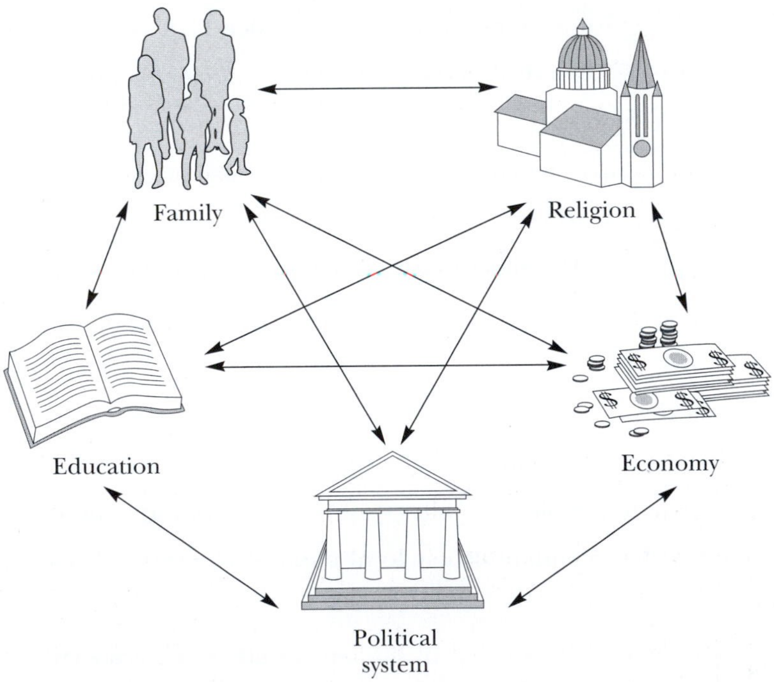

Figure 3-1 *Social Structure*

a region where many people live in extreme poverty, political authorities do not bother to keep accurate statistics about infant mortality among the poor.[6] Looked at from the perspective of social structure, this example illustrates how the economy has an impact on the political system, with consequences that, in turn, affect the social reality of poor Brazilian families.

This view of society helps us appreciate the institutionalized bases of attitudes and behaviors toward death. In North America, cultural expectations about death reflect a social reality consistent with a technology-oriented and bureaucratic society. An appropriate death is one that occurs naturally and is correctly timed—that is, occurs in old age.[7] The bureaucratic aspect of death in modern societies is designed to prevent disruptions and preserve the equilibrium of social life.[8] In this structural framework, death tends to be moved to the periphery of social life.[9]

Symbolic interactionism refers to the idea that people are actively responsive to, and indeed the creators of, the social structures and processes in their lives. In a study of dying Canadian "First Nation" patients and their grieving families in urban hospital settings, researchers found that European Canadian caregivers and Native Canadian patients bring to their encounters differing interpretations of appropriate care.[10] Engaging one another in interactions to resolve conflict between these differing views resulted in changes in attitudes and behaviors of both caregivers and patients. As new "meanings" emerged, the hospital "culture" changed.

When we conform to social norms, our behavior is reinforced or rewarded; when we fail to conform, our behavior is punished or goes unrewarded. *Social learning* also occurs through *vicarious reinforcement,* which takes place when a person observes others reinforced for a behavior but has not been directly reinforced himself or herself. We may not even be aware that we are conforming to some social norms, because they are embedded in our way of life. We accept them as natural, "the way things work."

For instance, in societies today, people are unlikely to consider disposing of a relative's corpse by placing it on a scaffold outdoors where it will gradually decompose; yet, to Native Americans living on the Great Plains in the nineteenth century, platform burial was natural as part of their social norms.

In culturally diverse societies, we have ample opportunities to apply these insights in expanding our understanding of customs and behaviors associated with dying, death, and bereavement. A young Latina who had recently attended her first Anglo funeral said that she was "genuinely puzzled" at the absence of storytelling and gentle humor about the deceased's life. "Everyone was respectful of the family," she said, "but I was surprised that it was all so serious. I'm used to people talking and laughing at funerals." By recognizing that social norms function much like the rules of a game or the script of a drama, we can observe their influence in the ways people grieve and the ceremonies they enact to commemorate death.

Cultures can be thought of as occupying a continuum from "death-welcoming" to "death-denying."[11] Paul Koudounaris reminds us,

> While we tend to think of death as representing an unequivocal, non-negotiable, and irreducible status, its definition and interpretation are matters of context. In the modern Western world, we have come to consider death as a boundary. In many other cultures, it is not—it is conceived simply as a transition, and a dialogue between the living and the dead forms a meaningful part of social discourse.[12]

As you read about various cultures, consider where you might place each of them on the welcoming–denying continuum. Consider, too, where your own cultures—the national, ethnic or subcultural, and family groups of which you are a member—might fit on such a continuum.

Traditional Cultures

Human concern for the dead predates written history. It is not known whether the earliest burials were intended to maintain continuity or communication with the dead or to protect against the harmful power of unburied dead or wandering spirits.[13] Burial of the dead may have begun as a way to avoid unpleasant odors, disease, or dangerous scavengers. In any event, human remains recovered in Europe from the Upper Paleolithic period, about forty thousand to ten thousand years ago, are recognized as intentional burials, accompanied by manufactured objects, personal effects, and other grave goods.[14]

In some burials, the corpse is stained with red ochre and placed in a fetal posture, suggesting revitalization of the body and rebirth (see Figure 3-2).[15] Ornamental shells, stone implements, and food were sometimes buried with the dead, implying belief that such items would be useful in the journey from the land of the living to the land of the dead. Such evidence reminds us that "the dead do not bury themselves, but are treated and disposed of by the living."[16] The Italian philosopher Giambattista Vico classified burial of the dead as a basic social institution and pointed out that humanity received its Latin name *humanitas* from the Latin root word *humare,* which means "to bury."[17]

Origin of Death

The precursors of human attitudes, values, and practices are found in myths—that is, stories that explain ideas or beliefs common to the worldview of a people. What do such stories tell us about how death became part of human experience? In some myths, death becomes part of human experience because ancestral parents or an archetypal figure transgressed divine or natural law, through either poor judgment or disobedience (see Figure 3-3). These stories sometimes involve a test of some person or group. When the test is failed, death becomes a reality. A story told by the Luba of Africa describes how God created a paradise for the first human beings and endowed it with everything needed for their sustenance; however, they were forbidden to eat

Figure 3-2 *Neanderthal Burial*

When the first man, the father of the human race, was being buried, a god passed by the grave and inquired what it meant, for he had never seen a grave before. Upon receiving the information from those about the place of interment that they had just buried their father, he said: "Do not bury him, dig up the body again." "No," they replied, "we cannot do that. He has been dead for four days and smells." "Not so," entreated the god, "dig him up and I promise you that he will live again." But they refused to carry out the divine injunction. Then the god declared, "By disobeying me, you have sealed your own fate. Had you dug up your ancestor, you would have found him alive, and you yourselves when you passed from this world should have been buried as bananas are for four days, after which you shall have been dug up, not rotten, but ripe. But now, as a punishment for your disobedience, you shall die and rot." And whenever they hear this sad tale the Fijians say: "Oh, that those children had dug up that body!"

Figure 3-3 *Fijian Story (Traditional): The Origin of Death*

When Hare heard of Death, he started for his lodge & arrived there crying, shrieking, *My uncles & my aunts must not die!* And then the thought assailed him: *To all things death will come!* He cast his thoughts upon the precipices & they began to fall & crumble. Upon the rocks he cast his thoughts & they became shattered. Under the earth he cast his thoughts & all the things living there stopped moving & their limbs stiffened in death. Up above, toward the skies, he cast his thoughts & the birds flying there suddenly fell to the earth & were dead.

After he entered his lodge he took his blanket and, wrapping it around him, lay down crying. *Not the whole earth will suffice for all those who will die. Oh, there will not be enough earth for them in many places!* There he lay in his corner wrapped up in his blanket, silent.

Figure 3-4 *Winnebago Myth: When Hare Heard of Death*

the bananas in the middle of the field. When humans ate the bananas, it was decreed that humankind would die after a lifetime of toil. This motif is akin to the biblical story of Adam and Eve's transgression in the Garden of Eden, an account of death's origin that persists in the religious traditions of Judaism, Christianity, and Islam.

In some myths, a crucial act that would have ensured immortality was not properly carried out; an *omission* rather than an *action* introduces death to humankind. Some stories tell of a messenger who was supposed to deliver the message of eternal life, but the message was garbled due to malice or forgetfulness, or it did not arrive on time. Among the Winnebago of North America, the trickster figure, Hare, is an example of this motif (see Figure 3-4). Momentarily forgetting his purpose, Hare failed to deliver the life-saving message. In a variant of this motif, two messengers were sent—one bringing immortality, the other bringing death—and the messenger bringing death arrived first.

In the "death in a bundle" motif, death is introduced into human experience when a bundle containing the mortal fate of all humankind is opened, either inadvertently or because of poor choice. A story from Greek mythology told by Aesop is an expression of this motif (see Figure 3-5).

These myths echo a theme that is surprisingly familiar: Death comes from outside; it cuts short an existence that otherwise would be immortal. We understand the biological processes of disease and aging yet still feel that if only this defect could be repaired, we could remain alive. We find ourselves believing that death is foreign, not really part of us.

Names of the Dead

A common practice related to the dead is *name avoidance:* For instance, the deceased might be referred to as "that one," or allusions may be made to particular traits or special qualities a person was known for during his or her lifetime. Thus, "Uncle Joe," who gained renown as an expert fisherman, might be referred to after his death as "that relative who caught many

It was a hot, sultry summer afternoon, and Eros, tired with play and faint from the heat, took shelter in a cool, dark cave. It happened to be the cave of Death himself.

Eros, wanting only to rest, threw himself down carelessly—so carelessly that all his arrows fell out of his quiver.

When he woke he found they had mingled with the arrows of Death, which lay scattered about the floor of the cave. They were so alike Eros could not tell the difference. He knew, however, how many had been in his quiver, and eventually he gathered up the right number.

Of course, Eros took some that belonged to Death and left some of his own behind. And so it is today that we often see the hearts of the old and the dying struck by bolts of Love; and sometimes we see the hearts of the young captured by Death.

Figure 3-5 *Aesop: Eros and Death*

fish." A woman who had displayed extraordinary bravery might be referred to as "that one who showed courage." In some cultures, the deceased is not referred to by name but only by his or her relationship to the speaker.

Name avoidance can be so complete that living people with the same name as the deceased must adopt new names. Among the Penan Geng of central Borneo, naming practices involving death are incorporated into all forms of social discourse.[18] When a person dies, "death names" are given to closest kin. Thus, as a person goes through life, he or she may have a series of names and titles referring to different categories of relationship to the deceased.

Some cultures, instead of avoiding the deceased's name, give it special emphasis. For example, the name may be conferred on a newborn child. Such naming takes place out of a desire to honor the memory of a loved one or to ensure that the soul of the dead person is reincarnated. Among traditional Hawaiians, for example, a child may be named for an ancestor or even named by the gods. Such names are especially important because they are bestowed by gods and communicated through dreams. It is said that naming a child for a relative who has died allows the name to live again.[19]

Causes of Death

Allan Kellehear's description and analysis of the social history of dying—from the Stone Age, to the Pastoral Age with the rise of settled populations, to the Age of the City and the "tame death," and finally the present Cosmopolitan Age—sheds light on how the meaning of death has changed over time (see Table 3-1).

Even with a meaningful explanation about how death came into the world, there remains the question, What causes *individual* human beings to die? The immediate cause of a death from accidental injuries or wounds sustained in battle is clear, but the ultimate cause is open to question: Why did

TABLE 3-1 *A Social History of Dying*

THE STONE AGE "Dawn of Mortal Awareness"	THE PASTORAL AGE "Rise of Settled Populations"
Cause of Death Sudden from trauma, human and animal predators, childbearing, accidents. A short awareness of dying. Dying seen as good or bad if the dead were adequately prepared by survivors for the otherworld journey. *Otherworld Journey* Survivors provided grave goods for other world journey that is fraught with tests and trials; thus, others in the community arranged the social responsibilities on behalf of the "dying." Biological death is not the end point of dying, rather, the end point is extinction of one's identity in the otherworld. *The Challenge* *Anticipating death:* Results in behaviors that are characterized as: Defensive—looking for omens to ward off death, predict the coming of death, identify risks that bring death and avoid them. Acceptance—planning, learning, preparing. Death is either lucky (merciful) or unlucky (bad) for communities, not the individual.	*Cause of Death* Living in close proximity with animals resulted in ecopathogenic infections, bacteria from cows, lice, chickens, fleas. Transmission of crowd-type diseases, infections, parasitic diseases, tuberculosis, and smallpox. A longer awareness of dying. Epidemics led to search for social or spiritual causes, thus imprisonment or death by burning, drowning, torturing of those deemed responsible. *The Good Death* Good death a natural component of the good life where dying had its privileges and obligations. Dying people provided goods for survivors (inheritance). Dying was "tame," that is, its physical rigors and ultimate destination were known and understood as a collective fate. *The Challenge* *Preparing for death:* Distributing inheritance, religious preparations; redistribution of goods as well as emotional impact of loss as part of the community. Death is good or bad for both individuals and community.

this fatal event happen to this person at this particular time? Might it be due to some evil influence, possibly shaped by magic? An explanation may be sought in supernatural causes. Although not subject to proof or disproof, such explanations comfort the bereaved by helping make sense of what otherwise seems inexplicable. The search for answers takes place within an environment that encompasses both the living and the dead. Did the person offend the ancestors or neglect to carry out the prescribed rites for the dead?

When a child dies among the Senufo people of Africa's Ivory Coast, for example, it disturbs the whole community. Illness and death signal the fact that something is "out of balance." To restore a sense of security and proper order, animal sacrifices are offered to purify and protect the community from further calamity.[20] The health of the whole community depends on maintaining a proper relationship with the environment, including its unseen aspects.

TABLE 3-1 *A Social History of Dying (continued)*

THE AGE OF THE CITY "The Tame Death"	**THE COSMOPOLITAN AGE** "Dying as a Trial"
Cause of Death Major degenerative diseases: cancer, heart disease, neurological disease.	*Cause of Death* Dying from AIDS, frailty; organ failure and dementia.
A long dying. Urban social complexity moved dying from the community to a contract of social relationships based on private services and fees paid. Increasing need to tame the uncomfortable physical and social aspects of dying. Professionals involved in efforts to tame the chaos and uncertainty of impending death.	Dying occurs over so long a period that it is confused with chronic illness. Time for dying unclear. Actual "dying persons" difficult to identify. Soaring life expectancy in rich countries. Globalization bringing "new" or revived infections: TB, HIV, SARS.
The Well-Managed Death Power sharing with contractual service providers extended over a longer period of dying and heavily invested in medical management in the final hours or days of dying.	*The Shameful Death* Marked by "dying out of time," either too early or too late in terms of value to society. Global social and economic arrangements blur social divisions, such as location, gender, religion, ethnicity, and social class.
The Challenge *Taming death:* Death is good or bad depending on how well the dying is managed by professionals. How that "wild thing" is tamed depends on a level of prosperity and available health services. The outcome of good/bad dying is transferred solely to the individual. The community is replaced by contracts with professionals.	*The Challenge* *Timing death:* Preparing for or timing death is elusive. Stigmatized deaths both because people live too long (affluence) or die too soon (poverty). Death is good or bad based on trials and tests of this world (residential care or poverty experiences); fear of losing control over timing of death grows globally.

Power of the Dead

In cultures that maintain bonds between the living and the dead, "the land echoes with the voices of the ancestors."[21] The community is a partnership of living and dead. Together, the living and the dead constitute the clan, the tribe, the people. In Balinese society, for example, the village territory belongs to the ancestors, and the living members of the community maintain contact with them to ensure their livelihood and well-being.[22] This understanding is implicit when people refer to the "founding fathers" of a nation or college, who are spoken of metaphorically as "being with us in spirit" as living members of the group celebrate their common purpose with those who preceded them.

In traditional societies, grief may be expressed with loud wails or with silent tears, but almost always there is deep respect for the still-powerful soul of the deceased. If the soul or spirit of the deceased is not treated properly, harm may result. Of special concern are evil-intentioned spirits that wander about aimlessly, seeking to disrupt the well-being of the living. Such spirits are often associated with catastrophic deaths, such as those occurring during childbirth. Conducting prescribed funeral rites ensures the successful journey of the soul into the realm of the dead, a journey that benefits the living.

As unseen members of an ongoing social order, the dead are often allies who can perform services for the living—as interpreters, intermediaries, and ambassadors in the realm beyond the reach of our physical senses. Such communication with the dead can be facilitated by a *shaman*, a visionary in the community who, entering into a trance, projects his or her consciousness to the realm beyond this world and becomes an intermediary between the worlds of living and dead.[23] The shaman contacts the dead and reports back messages that will benefit the living. Because the dead are not bound by human time, *necromancy* (from the Greek, meaning "corpse-prophecy") offers access to past and future events.[24] In the rhythm and flow of communal life, the deceased—in death as in life—is part of the whole.

Western Culture

Beginning in the early Middle Ages, about the year 400, and continuing for a thousand years, people in Western European culture shared a view of the universe as bound together by natural and divine law.[25] The Church influenced the manner in which people died, and offered hope for the afterlife. This outlook generally prevailed until the European Renaissance, or cultural rebirth, which began in Italy in the fourteenth century and lasted into the seventeenth century.

During the early medieval period, people viewed death as a natural component of life and with the understanding that "we shall all die." This reflected a sense of death as the collective destiny of humankind. The dead were "asleep"—in the Church's keeping—with assurance of resurrection at the apocalyptic return of Christ. With this faith, people tended not to fear what awaited them after death. Although this period has been called the Age of Faith, some writers argue that, because of the pervasive influence of the Church, it should be called the Age of Religious Culture.[26]

This sense of a common, collective destiny began to change during the period of the High Middle Ages, about 1000–1450, transforming into an emphasis on the destiny of the individual. The collective idea that "everyone dies" was replaced by an individual acknowledgment, "I will die my own death." This change occurred over the course of several centuries and coincided with a general enrichment of life and culture.

The scientific revolution of the 1500s and 1600s ushered in the Enlightenment, with its emphasis on reason and intellect, in the 1700s. Conventional wisdom was challenged by competing ideas in the religious marketplace and by the revolutionary discoveries of scientists and explorers. This era marked the birth of a modern worldview. People began to feel more ambivalent about death and the afterlife. Death was no longer something to be contemplated only in the realm of the sacred. It became an event that could be manipulated and shaped by human beings.

These modernizing trends accelerated with an industrial revolution from about 1750 to 1900. This 150-year period was a time of rapid technological innovation, mechanization, and urbanization, accompanied by progress in public health and medicine. The attitude toward death during this period emphasized the death of the other, "thy death."

Along with an emphasis on "thy death," the meaning of death focused on separation from the beloved, giving rise to impassioned expressions of grief and desires to memorialize the dead. Hence was born the ideal of the "beautiful death," in which the sad beauty of a loved one's death elicits feelings of melancholy tinged with optimism for eventual reunion with the beloved in a heavenly home. With the death of her prince consort, Albert, in 1861, Queen Victoria of Great Britain set the trend for elaborate funeral etiquette and mourning customs as well as a cult of widowhood.[27] She wore a black mourning bonnet for the rest of her life and often communed with Prince Albert at his grave in the Royal Mausoleum, where she herself was laid to rest after her death in 1901. One custom of the time was "mourning jewelry," rings and brooches, sometimes containing locks of hair, in remembrance of departed loved ones.[28]

Through more than a thousand years in Western culture, attitudes toward death reflected a progression from an emphasis on collective destiny in which "we all shall die," to the more personal awareness of "one's own death," and then to a preoccupation with the deaths of loved ones, "thy death." Despite these changes in emphasis, French historian Philippe Ariès characterizes virtually the whole of this period as one of "tamed death." Death was an ordinary human experience, not something to be hidden away from view or excluded from social life.

According to Ariès, the long era of "tamed death" came to an end early in the twentieth century. World War I (1914–1918) was a major turning point in modern history. It marked the advent of "total war," which affected civilians as well as combatants. It also demonstrated the increasing importance of technology in virtually every aspect of life. In health care, technology would bring about the "medicalization" of dying. The deathbed scene moved from home to hospital. Whereas dying had been a public and communal event, now it became private.[29] Events that had been part of people's ordinary lives were now under the control of professionals. Customary signs of mourning all but disappeared. The prevailing attitude toward death could be described by such terms as "forbidden death," "invisible death," and "death denied."

Death Knells

During many centuries one item of expense for survivors was the fee that must be paid for the ringing of the soul bell. Every cathedral and church of medieval Christendom had such a bell, almost always the largest one in the bell tower.

By the time John Donne wrote the immortal line "for whom the bell tolls," ringing of the soul bell—in a distinctive pattern, or knell—was popularly taken to be merely a public notice that a death had occurred. This use of the soul bell came into importance relatively late, however.

Not simply in Christian Europe but also among primitive tribes and highly developed non-Christian cultures of the Orient, bells have been linked with death. Notes from bells (rung in special fashion) served to help convince a spirit that there was no need to remain close to a useless dead body. At the same time, noise made by bells was considered to be especially effective in driving away the evil spirits who prowled about hoping to seize a newly released soul or to put obstacles in its path.

Ringing of the soul (or passing) bell was long considered so vital that bell ringers demanded, and got, big fees for using it. Still in general use by the British as late as the era of King Charles II in the seventeenth century, bell ringers then regulated the number of strokes of the passing bell so that the general public could determine the age, sex, and social status of the deceased.

Webb Garrison, *Strange Facts About Death*

The Deathbed Scene

"I see and know that my death is near": Thus did the dying person during the Middle Ages acknowledge impending death. Anticipated by natural signs or by inner certainty, dying was understood as manageable. On pious deathbeds, the dying offered their suffering to God with the expectation that everything would take place in a customary manner. Sudden death was rare; even wounds in battle seldom brought instantaneous death. (The possibility of unexpected death was fearful because it caught victims unaware and unable to properly close earthly accounts and turn toward the divine.) Those who kept vigil around the deathbed could confidently say that the dying person "feels her time has come" or "knows he will soon be dead."

Marked by simple and solemn ceremony, dying occurred within the context of familiar practices. Ariès describes a typical Christian death during the early Middle Ages: Lying down, with the head facing east toward Jerusalem and arms crossed over the chest, the dying person expressed sadness at his or her impending end and began "a discreet recollection of beloved beings and things." Family and friends gathered around the deathbed to receive the dying person's pardon for any wrongs they might have done, and all were commended to God. Next, the dying person turned his or her attention away from the earthly realm and toward the divine. With the customary rites completed, nothing more need be said: The dying person was prepared for death.

This deathbed vigil in a Spanish village is characteristic of the way in which human beings have responded to death for thousands of years. Only recently have such scenes been superseded in modern societies by the specter of dying alone, perhaps unconscious, amid the impersonal technological gadgetry of an unfamiliar institutional environment.

Dying was more or less a public ceremony, with the dying person in charge. The recumbent figure in the deathbed, surrounded by family, friends, children, and even passersby, remained the customary deathbed scene until the late nineteenth century, although subtle changes did occur over time. For example, as the destiny of the individual gained more emphasis around the twelfth century, there were corresponding changes in the deathbed scene. Besides the entourage of public participants, there now hovered an invisible army of celestial figures, angels and demons, battling for possession of the dying person's soul. *How* a person died became profoundly important. Death became the *speculum mortis,* the mirror in which the dying person could discover his or her destiny by tallying the moral balance sheet of his or her life. This emphasis on individual responsibility for the destiny of one's soul was communicated in the *memento mori* of the time, "Remember, you must die!" This precept was inscribed on all sorts of objects and trinkets as reminders that death comes to everyone, and there are no exceptions.

During the following centuries, there was little change in the outward aspects of the deathbed scene; family and friends still gathered as participants in the public ritual of a person's dying. But religion was less prominent in the thoughts of the dying person or the grief of survivors. People now compared the act of dying to the emergence of a butterfly from its cocoon. A secular hope for immortality and eventual reunion with loved ones became more important than churchly images of heaven and hell. Gradually, the focus changed from the dying person to his or her survivors.

By the mid-twentieth century, however, the rituals of dying had been overtaken by a technological process in which death occurs by "a series of little steps." Ariès says, "All these little silent deaths have replaced and erased the great dramatic act of death."

Burial Customs

With the rise of Christianity in the early Middle Ages, believers adopted the idea that the saintliness of Christian martyrs was powerful, even in death, and that these saints of the Church could help others avoid the pitfalls of sin and the horrors of hell.[30] It became advantageous to be buried near the grave of a martyr to gain merit by proximity. (A modern analogy might be that of a movie fan being buried near a film star at Forest Lawn or a veteran requesting burial near a Medal of Honor winner, although medieval folk were generally more concerned with the welfare of their souls than with earthly prestige.)

As Christian pilgrims began journeying to venerate martyrs, altars, chapels, and eventually churches were built on or near the martyrs' graves. Initially, only notables and saints of the Church received such honored burial, but eventually ordinary folk came to be buried in common graves located in the churchyards and surrounds of churches and cathedrals.

Charnel Houses

Burial within churchyards led to the development of *charnel houses,* arcades and galleries where the bones of the dead were entrusted to the Church. "The charnels were built on consecrated ground and the bones themselves were considered blessed, as it was believed that they would be resurrected and clothed in divine glory at the Parousia, or Second Coming of Christ."[31] Limbs and skulls were arranged along various parts of the churchyard, as well as within and near the church. (In Paris, it is possible to visit catacombs where, as one visitor exclaimed, "piles of femurs and skulls" are "stacked eight feet high and ten yards deep, as neatly as lumber in an Oregon mill yard.")[32] The bones in these charnels came from common graves, which were periodically opened so that the bones could be safely kept by the Church until the Resurrection.

A similar instance of the desiccation and preservation of corpses is found in Sicily, "where the relationship between the living and the dead is especially strong."[33]

Why would anyone exhibit decaying bodies? One suggestion is that the practice may be a "residual echo" of a much older, pre-Christian belief in the shamanistic power of corpses. Another is that the practice was done to illustrate the inevitability of death and the foolishness of vain human pride.

Library of Congress

This ossuary located at a European monastery is a survival of the medieval charnel house, a gallery of skeletons and skulls and bones.

The public nature of charnel houses and other such exhibits reflects a familiarity with death and with the dead. As Romans had congregated in the Forum, their counterparts in the Middle Ages met in charnel houses, which functioned as public squares. There, they would find shops and merchants, conduct business, dance, gamble, or simply enjoy being together. "As yet unborn," Ariès says, "was the modern idea that the dead person should be installed in a sort of house unto himself, a house of which he was the perpetual owner or at least the long-term tenant, a house in which he would be at home and from which he could not be evicted."

Memorializing the Dead

About the twelfth century, as part of an increasing emphasis on individualism, a desire arose to preserve the identity of the person buried in a particular place. Simple grave markers of the "Here lies John Doe" variety began to appear, as did elaborate effigies—that is, images or representations of the dead—at the burials of notables. The thirteenth-century sepulchral effigy of Jean d'Alluye depicts a recumbent knight in chain mail, sword girded and shield at his side, feet resting on the image of a lion, a vivid expression of the intellectual and social milieu of the age of chivalry, with its tension between faith and heroism. Although effigies were created only for people at the highest social rank, they give us clues about how people of the time viewed death.

Effigies reflect the emerging belief that the bereaved could maintain bonds with the deceased by perpetuating their *memory*. Over time, such memorialization became increasingly important. By the time of the Renaissance, as secular ideas competed with religious beliefs, burials began to take place in cemeteries that were not associated with churches. The opening of the Cemetery of Père Lachaise outside Paris in 1804 signaled the culmination of a dramatic change in Western attitudes toward life and death.[34]

In the United States, the rural cemetery movement began in the 1830s with the aim of replacing the simple, untended graveyards of the Puritans with lush, well-kept cemeteries like Mount Auburn in Cambridge, Massachusetts, and Woodlawn in New York City. Places like Spring Grove in Cincinnati, Ohio, established in 1844 and occupying 733 acres, including a large, undeveloped area of woodland at its center, promoted a new concept of cemetery design in which landscape took precedence over monuments.[35] In parklike settings, the bereaved visited private graves and communed in memory with the deceased.[36] The deceased were imagined to be in a heaven where survivors hoped to be eventually reunited with their loved ones. An interest in occult practices, such as séances and communication with spirits, grew popular.[37] There was a sense of sentimentality that made death seem less final or severe.

Today, except for occasional memorials to the war dead, cemeteries generally do not encourage monuments that interrupt the flat expanses of embedded "grave markers." In the opinion of architectural historian James Curl,

> The neglected cemeteries, poorly designed crematoria, and abysmal tombstone designs of the present insult life itself, for death is an inevitable consequence of birth. By treating the disposal of the dead as though the problem were one of refuse-collection, society devalues life.[38]

The Dance of Death

With origins in the ecstatic dances of pre-Christian times, artistic themes involving the *danse macabre,* or Dance of Death, came to fullest expression in the late thirteenth and early fourteenth centuries.[39] (These themes are termed *macabre* because they tend to produce horror in a beholder.) Partly a reaction to war, famine, and poverty, the Dance of Death was influenced primarily by the mass deaths caused by the plague, or Black Death, which came to Europe via a Black Sea port in 1347.[40] When the first wave of pestilence ended in 1351, a quarter of the European population had died. The plague disrupted the customary ways of death. "Death was no longer the kind caretaker of souls awaiting resurrection."[41] As the plague reminded individuals of their own "fragile grasp on life," it prompted some of them to spend their hours in revelry and orgies—the celebration of a victory, however temporary, over death. As a cultural and artistic phenomenon, the Dance of Death reflects ideas about the *inevitability* and *impartiality* of death.

The danse macabre was expressed through drama, poetry, music, and the visual arts. It was sometimes performed as a masque, a short entertainment in which actors costumed as skeletons danced gaily with figures representing people at all levels of society. Paintings of the Dance of Death depict individuals being escorted to graveyards by skeletons and corpses, a grim reminder of the universality of death. The Dance of Death conveys the notion that, regardless of rank or status, death comes to *all* people and to *each* person. In the oldest

Hans Holbein the Younger, authors' collection

José Guadalupe Posada, Swann Collection, Library of Congress

The somber mood of Hans Holbein's depiction of Die Totentanz, or Dance of Death, contrasts with the treatment of the same theme by Mexican artist José Guadalupe Posada. In Holbein's medieval woodblock print, The Child, we see the anxiety of family members as the skeletal figure of Death ominously takes a child; in Posada's print, there is a sense of gaiety and festivity. Although expressed differently, the two works convey a common message: Death comes to people in all walks of life; no one is exempt.

versions of the Dance of Death, the figure of death seems scarcely to touch the living as it singles them out. Death has a personal meaning but is part of the natural order. In later versions, people are depicted as forcibly taken by death.

By about the fifteenth century, death was portrayed as causing a radical, violent, and complete break between the living and the dead. This is reflected in ghastly themes that involve cadavers and the deterioration of the corpse.

The dance of death seems to have been part of a general obsession with death in the late Middle Ages. In the fifteenth and sixteenth centuries, sculptures of the burial of Christ were popular throughout Western Europe. In contrast to depictions of the dance of death, they were usually not macabre. However, they were likely a response to the same phenomenon: widespread death and suffering. Johan Mackenbach says,

> By providing an example of dignified behavior, entombments may have played a part in development of self-restraint by mourners, just as the *artes moriendi* [art of dying] of the same period provided guidance on the behavior of the dying. It is only after about 1540 that a more vivid, baroque style developed and that expression of emotion became less restrained. In later entombments, Mary faints, and mouths open to cry.[42]

This was also the era of public anatomy dissections, which were attended by ordinary townspeople as well as surgeons and medical students. At the University of Leiden, the "Anatomical Theater" was held in the apse of a church, where human remains were artistically displayed and posed in dramatic gestures. Frank Gonzalez-Crussi cites the example of a child's arm "clad in an infant's lace sleeve" and, held in the child's hand, "between thumb and index finger—as gracefully as an artist's model might hold a flower by the stem—a human eye by the optical nerve."[43]

By the eighteenth and nineteenth centuries, the relationship between love and death, which had been confined mostly to religious martyrdom, was extended to include romantic love. Romances like those of Tristan and Isolde or Romeo and Juliet promoted the idea that where there is love, death can be beautiful, even desirable.

Originally a reaction to fear of sudden death caused by an epidemic of plague, the danse macabre emphasizes the uncertainties of human existence, the knowledge that death can come when least expected and disrupt the most loving relationships. These themes of death's universality and inevitability are also portrayed in the Mexican celebration of Día de los Muertos, the Day of the Dead, and artists draw upon these themes to convey the epidemic nature of AIDS as well as threatening aspects of other potential catastrophes. More subtly, images associated with the Dance of Death persist as skeletons on children's Halloween costumes.

Death Masks

The making of a death mask is an ancient practice, going back to early Egyptian and Roman cultures.[44] In ancient Egypt, where mummification of the body was an important part of the funeral process, a special element of death rites was the creation of a sculpted mask that would be placed on the face of the dead person. The best known example of this is the mask prepared for Tutankhamen, the youthful Egyptian king who died around 1352 BCE.

In European culture, by the Middle Ages, a shift occurred from the use of sculpted masks to the creation of actual death masks. These were typically of royalty and nobility, as well as of other eminent persons, such as poets and philosophers. Examples of this latter category include Dante, Pascal, and Voltaire. A death mask is a wax, plaster, or clay cast taken of a person's face soon after death. This cast is used to make a reproduction of the face to provide a memento for bereaved survivors or to create a portrait of the dead person. Death masks also function as *memento mori,* a reminder to the living that death awaits us all, that we are mortal, similar to the message of the death's-head, or human skull, found on early gravestones.

With the death of Isaac Newton (1643–1727), the creation of a death mask, formerly an honor reserved for members of royalty and the nobility, was extended to an ordinary citizen, a testimony to his human genius as well as the changing social values of the Enlightenment.

A fascinating story about death masks concerns Resusci Anne, also known as CPR Annie, a model used since the beginning of CPR (cardiopulmonary resuscitation) training in the 1960s and still the most popular CPR manikin face.

The designer of Resusci Anne was a Norwegian toy maker, Asmund Laerdal, who had also devised artificial wounds for use in military training. When his friend, Dr. Peter Safer, the father of CPR, asked him to design a device for the new CPR training, Laerdal agreed to participate.

Laerdal decided that the best way to learn resuscitation would be to practice on a manikin; all that was needed was the perfect face. While visiting his parents, Laerdal noticed a mask of a woman's face on their wall. This image was actually a death mask known as "L'Inconnu de la Seine," which means "the unknown woman of the Seine."

This mask is of a beautiful young woman who apparently died by suicide in the river Seine in Paris around the late 1880s. After she was pulled out of the river, workers at the Paris Morgue were struck by her beauty and decided to memorialize it by creating a death mask. Over time, as reproductions of the death mask became available, people, captivated by her beauty and her unknown identity, began to display the mask as art in homes across Europe. Her beguiling smile has been compared to the enigmatic smile of Mona Lisa, whose portrait was painted by Italian Renaissance artist and polymath, Leonardo da Vinci. Now, because of her death mask, the unknown beautiful young woman who drowned is symbolically resuscitated, again and again, in CPR classes around the world.

Invisible Death?

In tracing the manner in which attitudes and behaviors relative to dying and death have changed, a common theme emerges: Human beings always seek to manage death in ways appropriate for their cultural and historical circumstances. Comparing current practices with those of earlier generations, dying and death have become less visible, less part of common experience. For many people today, death is seen as one more disease to conquer. Death is "managed" and "prolonged" as care providers seek mastery. Yet, many others of us seek more meaningful ways of encountering death. We are not satisfied with "one size fits all."

Present attitudes and practices are increasingly starting to reflect a diversity of choices and options as people become dissatisfied with the tendency to compartmentalize, professionalize, and medicalize dying and death. Exploring other cultures can allow us to better appreciate our own attitudes and practices, as well as perhaps introduce us to new possibilities and ways of encountering death.[45] Even when other cultures appear exotic in comparison with what is familiar to us, closer examination usually reveals significant correspondences between the "foreign" and the "familiar."

Cultural Viewpoints

In reading about cultural practices in the following sections, keep in mind the diversity that exists among individuals within a particular cultural heritage. The descriptor "Asian," for example, encompasses individuals of Chinese, Japanese, Korean, Hmong, Vietnamese, Cambodian, and other ancestries—individuals who share certain commonalities while having unique traditions. Within each of these traditions, there is further diversity among individuals.

People of Native American Heritage

Across the United States, there are more than five hundred federally recognized Native American nations, each endowed with unique traditions.[46] Death customs have varied widely, not only geographically, but also through time.[47] It is important to recognize that historical practices were affected by the dramatic social upheavals that accompanied the "westward expansionism" of white society.[48] Within two generations of white contact, it is estimated that 80 percent of the Native people of the Pacific Northwest died from newly introduced diseases to which they had no immunity. Natives throughout the Americas experienced a similar pattern. Scholars note:

> The changes were so comprehensive, the readjustments so massive, the level of human suffering so catastrophic, we can only guess what the experiences of the people might have been. . . . the terrifying sweep of unaccountable and unstoppable death must be understood as a constant backdrop to the history of American Indians.[49]

Maria Yellow Horse Brave Heart describes the "historical trauma" and "historical unresolved grief" that accompanies this intergenerational trauma.[50] The Takini (a Lakota word meaning "to come back to life") Network seeks to address these issues and promote healing among Native people.

In general, Native Americans view death as a normal part of an ongoing life cycle; it is something that does not terminate one's existence but transforms it.[51] Native Americans believe the souls of the dead pass into a spirit world and become part of the spiritual forces that influence every aspect of their lives. However, fear of the dead is very real among some tribes, and some are reluctant to deal with a dead body. Some tribes rely on a mortuary to prepare the deceased for last rites; others maintain their traditional practices to the extent possible.

Of special importance is reverence toward the dead, who are often believed to serve as guardian spirits or special envoys to the spirit world. Chief Seattle (leader of the Suquamish people) said, "To us the ashes of our

L. A. Huffman, Coffrin's Old West Gallery, Bozeman, Montana

In January 1879, frontier photographer L. A. Huffman recorded this scene showing the platform burial of a Sioux warrior who had died only a few days before. In the Great Plains, it was customary to expose the corpse on a scaffold or platform above ground or to place it in the limbs of a tree. This hastened decomposition of the body and aided the soul's journey to the spirit world. Later, the sun-bleached skeleton would be retrieved for burial in sacred grounds.

ancestors are sacred and their resting place is hallowed ground. . . . Be just and deal kindly with my people, for the dead are not powerless. Dead, did I say? There is no death, only a change of worlds."[52]

The land, the whole of the physical environment, is the basic source of American Indian identity and ultimate source of spiritual power.[53] As Old Chief Joseph of the Nez Percé lay dying, he told his son, "Never forget my dying words. This country holds your father's body. Never sell the bones of your father and mother."[54] These words were remembered by Younger Chief Joseph as he led warriors into battle to preserve the sanctity of the lands that held the bones of the ancestral dead. (Disputes about the disposition of artifacts and bones retrieved from sacred burial places by archaeologists and others led the U.S. Congress to enact the Native American Graves Protection and Repatriation Act in 1990 with the purpose of reuniting Native American skeletal remains, funerary items, and ceremonial objects with living members of the cultures that produced them.)[55]

Within Native American societies, there is an emphasis on "living one day at a time, with purpose, grateful for life's blessings, in the knowledge that it could all end abruptly."[56] This relationship to death is typified in the Lakota battle cry: "It's a good day to die!" Stephen Levine says,

> This embodies the possibilities of a life reviewed and completed. A life in which even death is not excluded. I am speaking here of a whole death that succeeds a whole life. . . . When everything is brought up to date, and the heart is turned toward itself, it is a good day to die.[57]

Death may come at any time, and we are wise to be prepared. This outlook is evident in the emphasis Cree people place on being careful to say farewells before leaving on a lengthy or difficult journey; unforeseen death may intervene.[58]

For Native Americans, *death songs* summarize a person's life and acknowledge death as the completion of being, the final act in the drama of earthly existence. In some cases, a death song was "composed spontaneously at the very moment of death" and "chanted with the last breath of the dying person."[59] These death songs express a resolve to meet death fully, to accept it with one's whole being, not in defeat and desperation, but with equanimity and composure.

Time is generally viewed not as linear and progress oriented but rather as cyclic. Åke Hultkrantz says that Native Americans are "mainly interested

Two Death Songs

In the great night my heart will go out
Toward me the darkness comes rattling
In the great night my heart will go out

Papago song by Juana Manwell
(Owl Woman)

The odor of death,
I smell the odor of death
In front of my body.

A song of the Dakota tribe

in how this cycle affects people in this life"; they have "only a vague notion of another existence after death."[60] Rigid beliefs about the state of the dead or the afterlife tend to be of little or no importance. Instead, Hultkrantz says, "One individual might hold several ideas about the dead at the same time [because] different situations call for different interpretations of the fate of humans after death." The Wind River Shoshoni, for example, have a variety of beliefs about death: The dead may travel to another world or may remain on earth as ghosts; they may be born again as people or may transmigrate into "insects, birds, or even inanimate objects like wood and rocks." Hultkrantz says that "most Shoshoni express only a slight interest in the next life and often declare that they know nothing about it."

Historical accounts tell us that the Ohlone of the California coast adorned the corpse with feathers, flowers, and beads, and then wrapped it in blankets and skins. Dance regalia, weapons, a medicine bundle, and other items owned by the deceased were gathered together and, with the corpse, placed on a funeral pyre. Destroying the deceased's possessions helped to facilitate the soul's journey to the "Island of the Dead." This action also removed reminders that might cause the ghost to remain near the living. During the dangerous period, which lasted from six months to a year, the Ohlone considered it disrespectful to utter the deceased's name. In *The Ohlone Way,* Malcolm Margolin writes, "While the mere thought of a dead person brought sorrow, the mention of a dead person's name brought absolute dread."[61] Destroying the deceased's belongings and avoiding his or her name helped confirm the separation of the dead from the living. A similar belief is echoed in a Yokut funeral chant that says, "You are going where you are going; don't look back for your family."

It has been suggested that sedentary tribes, such as the Pueblo and Navajo, express more fear of the dead than nomadic hunters and gatherers, such as the Sioux and Apache.[62] This contrast was found in a study among

Burial Oration

You are dead.
You will go above there to the trail.
That is the spirit trail.
Go there to the beautiful trail.
May it please you not to walk about where I am.
You are dead.
Go there to the beautiful trail above.
That is your way.
Look at the place where you used to wander.
The north trail, the mountains where you used to wander,
    you are leaving.
Listen to me: go there!

Wintu tribe

the Cocopa and Hopi.[63] When a Cocopa dies, surviving family members wail in an "ecstasy of violent grief behavior" that lasts twenty-four hours or more, continuing until the body is cremated. Clothes, food, and other items are burned with the body. Although the deceased needs these goods in the afterlife, the Cocopa also hope this will help persuade the spirit of the dead person to pass on from the earth. Later, a ceremony is held commemorating the deceased. Although the deceased's name cannot be spoken at other times, at this special mourning ceremony, those who have passed into the spirit world are publicly summoned, and their presence may be impersonated by living members of the tribe. The ceremony is intended to both honor the dead and persuade lurking spirits to come out into the open and leave the earthly realm. Whereas the initial cremation ritual is focused on the grief of the bereaved family, the subsequent mourning ceremony is focused on affirming the integrity of the family and the community.

Unlike the Cocopa, the Hopi strive to keep death at a distance. It threatens the "middle way" of order, control, and measured deliberation. This attitude is reflected in Hopi funeral rituals, which are attended by few people and held privately. Mourners are reticent about expressing grief. The Hopi want the whole matter to be "quickly over and best forgotten." They have no desire to invite dead ancestors to a communal gathering. Once a person's spirit leaves the body, it is a different class of being, no longer Hopi. Thus, it is important to make sure that the "dichotomy of quick and dead is sharp and clear."

As these descriptions of the Cocopa and the Hopi show, different social groups may create distinctive responses to death even when they occupy a similar cultural situation. Both Hopi and Cocopa fear the dead, but they cope with this fear differently: The Hopi want to completely avoid the dead, whereas the Cocopa invite the spirits of the dead to join them in ritual celebration, even if only temporarily and under controlled circumstances.

Reflecting on the different emphases within Hopi and Cocopa societies can help us evaluate our own attitudes and values relative to death. What do you find valuable about each of these ways of coping with death?

People of African Heritage

It is said that, for Africans, life is afterlife.[64] Many African peoples believe a person's soul remains "alive" and active as long as at least one individual remains who has known the deceased and remembers his or her name. Death does not extinguish a person's participation in the life and activities of his family and community but rather opens a way to a connection and participation that is different from the mundane mode of the living.[65] The term *ancestor worship* has been used to describe customs such as prayer, sacrifice, or libation, and other acts of respect or reverence shown to the deceased members of a community. However, the respect and rites accorded ancestors are not rites of worship but methods of communication.[66]

As generations come and go and memory fades, the long-dead ancestral members of the community are replaced by the more recently deceased.[67]

Thus, the ongoing community of the "living dead" consists of ancestors who are recalled in the minds of the living. Dominique Zahan says,

> The ancestral community is in a constant state of renewal which is affected in two ways. First, the "newly dead" invariably keep the earthward side of their universe updated and on its feet. Second, there is the continual disappearance of a part of them, the heavenly side, which has become useless because of the weaknesses in the collective memory of those in this world.[68]

This is illustrated by the system of age grouping: Among the Nandi in Kenya, for example, once past childhood, a male member of the tribe moves through the junior and senior warrior levels and eventually enters the age group of senior elders; he next becomes an old man and ultimately, at death, an ancestor, one of the living dead, whose personality is remembered by survivors. When he is no longer remembered, he merges with the anonymous dead. The Nandi believe that, by this time, the dead person's "soul stuff" may have reappeared in a newborn child of the tribe, thus continuing the recurrent pattern of a person's passage through the levels of the age-group system.[69]

Kofi Asare Opoku says that the traditional African attitude toward death is essentially positive because "it is comprehensively integrated into the totality of life."[70] Death is merely the passage from the human world to the spirit world.[71] This attitude can be found in the festive sounds of trumpets and drums played at African funerals. "Music," says Francis Bebey, "is a challenge to human destiny; a refusal to accept the transience of this life; and an attempt to transform the finality of death into another kind of living."[72]

In Africa today, reverence toward the dead retains its importance. When the body of a Nigerian villager of the Ibo people was shipped by air from the United States to her home village, the coffin arrived in damaged condition. Somewhere in transit, her body had been wrapped in burlap and turned upside down—violating strict tribal taboos concerning abuse of a corpse. Despite the family's offerings of yams, money, and wine to appease the insult, tribal members reported seeing the woman's spirit roaming about, and relatives began to experience reversals of fortune, which they characterized as a "curse" due to mistreatment of their dead relative. The woman's son said, "My mother was treated as if she were nothing." Thus, her spirit was angry and not at peace. In bringing suit against the airline to which the body had been entrusted, the son said, "If this had been done to us by an individual, my whole tribe would have gone to war. If I win the case, it would be like bringing back someone's head. It would prove I'm a warrior . . . it will show the gods I have done something against someone who shamed my mother."[73]

> If we knew the home of Death, we would set it on fire.
>
> Acholi funeral song

Delmar Lipp, Eliot Elisofon Archives, National Museum of African Art

A woman and child in mourning are depicted in this Yombe memorial figure from Zaire. Installed in a shed constructed on the grave, such adornments are thought to provide the deceased with companionship or protection in the afterlife.

The LoDagaa of Northern Ghana

The richness of traditional African funeral customs is illustrated by the practices carried out among the LoDagaa, whose funeral ceremonies span at least a six-month period and sometimes continue over several years.[74] They occur in four distinct, successive phases, each focusing on specific aspects of death and bereavement.

The first stage begins at a person's death and lasts six or seven days. During the first several days, the body is prepared for burial, the deceased is mourned by the community, rites are performed to acknowledge the separation of the deceased from the living, kinship ties are affirmed, and some of the social and family roles occupied by the deceased are redistributed. The public ceremonies, which last about three days, conclude with the burial of the corpse. The remaining three or four days of this first stage are devoted to private ceremonies in which preparations are made for redistributing the dead person's property.

About three weeks later, in a second ceremony, the cause of death is established. Rather than considering a snakebite, for example, to be the cause of a person's death, the LoDagaa view the bite as an intermediate agent but not the sole cause of death. The real cause of death lies in a network of spiritual and human relationships. Inquiries are made to uncover any tension that may have existed between the deceased and others.

At the beginning of the rainy season, a third stage of the funeral is held. These rites mark a transitional period in the deceased's passing from the role of the living to that of an ancestor. At this stage, a provisional ancestral shrine is placed on the grave.

The fourth and final stage of LoDagaa ceremonies occurs after the harvest. A final ancestral shrine is constructed and placed on the grave, and close relatives of the deceased are formally released from mourning. The care of offspring is formally transferred to the deceased's tribal "brothers," and final rites conclude redistribution of the deceased's property.

These extended mourning ceremonies serve two main purposes: First, they *separate* the dead person from the bereaved family and from the wider community of the living; social roles formerly held by the deceased are assigned to living persons. Second, they gather together, or *aggregate;* that is, the dead person joins with the ancestors, and the bereaved are reincorporated into the community in a way that reflects their new status. This rhythm of separation and gathering together is common to funeral rites of all cultures. LoDagaa funerals are noteworthy because of the formality with which these functions are accomplished. They provide a model of explicitness in mourning that can be compared and contrasted with our own.

This explicitness is evident in the LoDagaa's use of "mourning restraints" made of leather, fabric, and string. These restraints, which are usually tied around a person's wrist, indicate the degree of relationship of the bereaved to the deceased. At a man's funeral, for example, his father, mother, and widow wear restraints made of hide; his brothers and sisters wear fiber restraints; and his children wear restraints made of string tied around the ankle. The strongest restraints are worn by mourners who had the closest relationship with the deceased, usually through kinship and marriage but sometimes through friendship bonds. Persons with less intimate relationships to the deceased wear weaker mourning restraints. In all cases, one end of the mourning restraint is attached to the bereaved, while the other end is held by a "mourning companion," who assumes responsibility for the bereaved's behavior during the period of intense grief.

The LoDagaa mourning restraints serve two related purposes. First, as objects that can be seen and felt, they validate that the intensity of the bereaved person's grief is appropriate for his or her relationship with the deceased. Second, they discourage expressions of grief that exceed the norms of the community.

In Africa, as elsewhere, social and economic forces of modern times threaten traditions. Even so, customs are carried forward in innovative ways. Among the Yoruba of southwestern Nigeria, for example, obituary publication provides a modern forum for an ancient custom. In newspaper obituaries paid for by family and friends, the deceased's status and prestige are denoted by, among other things, the size of the obituary, which can occupy a full page. Olatunde Bayo Lawuyi says it is common to "mark the return of the dead [through obituary publications] every ten years," although this practice lessens over time.[75] The publication of obituaries, Lawuyi says, "demonstrates the possibility of continuity in ancestral beliefs" and "is a symbolic manifestation of a tradition that has taken a new cultural form."

Traditions Among African Americans

As Ronald Barrett points out, elements of traditional West African practices retain their importance for many African Americans.[76] One of the strongest ties between Africans and their descendants in the United States is evident in the significance given to funeral traditions.[77] In the black church, funerals are called "homegoing" services; sermons and songs refer to themes of "going home." Family members often desire to give the deceased a "big send-off" in the form of an elaborate funeral. Respectful display of the body is important. Barrett says, "The success and survival of most African American funeral homes has historically depended on the physical appearance of loved ones during viewing, which is an important part of African American homegoing celebrations."[78] LaVone Hazell says,

> At times economics underlie cultural decisions regarding the funeral rite. One widow who was making arrangements summed up a pervasive feeling within the African American community, saying, "After working so hard all his life, my husband didn't have much to show for his efforts. The last thing I can do for him is to give him a fine and proper burial." With these words, she used his entire insurance policy on the funeral.[79]

Dying is referred to as a "transition," and belief in the possibility of an ongoing relationship with the person who has passed and of one day being reunited with the deceased loved one is commonly expressed. Family members and extended family are likely to place great importance on gathering at the bedside of a dying patient. Trusting God for health and desiring to hold on to a loved one as long as possible may result in insisting on life-sustaining treatments and avoiding preparations for death. African Americans are less likely than some other groups to complete advance directives or agree to DNR (do not resuscitate) orders. This may be partly out of a concern, due to historical factors, that the health care system would give up on them or provide less than optimal care. Comparatively low use of hospice and other end-of-life services is due in part to similar factors. "Some African Americans may view illness and death as yet another struggle to overcome."[80] Further, accepting a prognosis of terminality may be seen as a lack of faith. People commonly feel that "God is in charge," in control of fate and the timing of death. As a result, they are content to "leave it in God's hands."

African Americans are a diverse group united by a common legacy and a history of oppression and discrimination that has shaped their cultural identity.[81] This legacy "grew from deep African roots, gained a paradoxical strength and resilience from the horrors of mid-passage, and flowered in the slave funeral—a value laden and unifying social event which the slave community in the United States was able to preserve from both physical and ideological onslaughts of the master class."[82] This heritage influences the attitudes and beliefs of African Americans, a group that encompasses individuals of various African, Caribbean, and South American descent.[83] Barrett points out that, in general, "blacks may be characterized as having a holistic view of death and dying, in that birth and death are understood to be part of a cycle or continuum."[84]

People of Hispanic Heritage

People of Hispanic, or Latino, heritage comprise one of the fastest-growing population groups in the United States. Some are fairly recent arrivals; others were living in the Southwest before it became part of the United States. Interconnectedness and interdependence, especially within the family (*familismo*), are highly valued.[85] In decisions about medical care, family is an important voice.

Among people of Cuban heritage, bereavement is generally expressed openly, with loud crying and other physical manifestations. After death, family and friends gather for a wake, or *valorio,* lasting several days. These wakes may take the form of *novenas,* or devotions, consisting of periods of prayer for nine consecutive days, with the final day having the atmosphere of a fiesta. People of Puerto Rican and other Latino heritage have similar practices regarding wakes and novenas.

It is rare to see a hearse or mortuary in rural areas of Brazil. The deceased is likely to be kept in the home until the body is buried, and burial may be in the plot with other family members to "keep the family together."[86]

In Guatemala, it is customary to place the deceased in a simple wooden coffin or casket, which is carried by key family members through town from the church to the cemetery while onlookers show their respect, mourn, and offer flowers. "At Indian funerals, the Mayan priest may spin the coffin at the grave to fool the devil and point the spirit of the deceased toward heaven."[87]

In the United States, Mexicans are the largest segment of the Hispanic population, with over 60 percent of Hispanics being of Mexican descent. The second-largest group, with 9 percent of the Hispanic population, are Puerto Ricans.[88] Although Latinos share many cultural traits, the various groups within the Hispanic population—Cuban, Mexican, Puerto Rican, South American, Central American, and so on—are culturally and socially diverse.[89]

Attitudes Toward Death in Mexico

Mexicans tend to view death as a natural part of life. Mexican poetry is filled with similes comparing life's fragility to a dream, a flower, a river, or a passing breeze.[90] "Because the overall outlook for many Mexicans is one of fatalism, pride may be taken in stoic acceptance of life's adversities."[91] People often confront death with humorous sarcasm. Death elicits an emotional response of impatience, disdain, or irony. It is cast as an equalizer that not even the wealthiest or most privileged can escape.

The skeleton has been called "Mexico's national totem."[92] People from all walks of life, the professor as well as the pilot, are portrayed as *calavera* (skulls or bones), the central icon of *Día de los Muertos,* the Day of the Dead. The intimate association of life and death is seen in one of the most common Day of the Dead motifs: a skeletal bride and groom, donned in white wedding dress and tuxedo. The calavera sculpted in sugar, clay, or papier-mâché or created from elaborate paper cuttings are a reminder that all of us will one day become "dead ones." Under each person's skin are those bones, and the calavera send the message that we need to recognize that fact and become accustomed to the idea that we will die.

The popular engravings of Mexican artist José Guadalupe Posada resemble the medieval danse macabre. Posada created what has become the most universally depicted of all calaveras—La Catrina—a female skeleton foppishly attired to satirize the pretensions of Mexico's upper classes. Posada also illustrated verses, like this one by poet Constancio S. Suárez:

> It is a most sincere truth
> that this adage makes us see:
> only one who was never born
> can never a death's-head be.[93]

A striking awareness of death is displayed in graffiti and ornaments that decorate cars and buses. In churches, the suffering Savior is portrayed with bloody vividness. Obituaries are framed with conspicuous black borders. Surrounded by references to death, the Mexican, says Octavio Paz, "jokes about it, caresses it, sleeps with it, celebrates it [and makes it] one of his favorite toys and his most steadfast love." More soberly, Paz adds, "Death defines life. . . . Each of us dies the death he has made for himself. . . . Death, like life, is not transferable."[94] Folk sayings speak to this connection between death and identity: "Tell me how you die and I will tell you who you are."

Día de los Muertos

When Spanish priests arrived in Mexico, they attempted in vain to suppress Aztec rituals. But they also brought elements from the medieval tradition of the Feast of Fools (associated with carnival, *carne vale,* "farewell to the flesh"), where everything is open to criticism, ridicule, and mockery. This humorous tradition is part of Día de los Muertos, which is now celebrated during the Catholic feasts of All Saints' and All Souls' Days, the Christian feast of commemoration for the dead.[95] The first of these is often devoted to *los angelitos,* young children who have died and who are remembered on November 1. The fiesta of Día de los Muertos combines ancient indigenous customs with introduced Catholic traditions. Besides its celebration in parts of Mexico, the fiesta is also celebrated in other countries of Latin America, including Argentina, Bolivia, Ecuador, Guatemala, Honduras, Nicaragua, Panama, and Peru.

Observances of Day of the Dead are part of folk culture throughout Latin America, testifying to the belief that one's own well-being depends in part on respectfully remembering the dead. "These rituals are rooted in a common feeling of moral obligation to the deceased."[96] Death is satirized while memories of deceased loved ones are cherished by the living.

During late October, the markets of the villages and towns are filled with special handmade items for the fiesta. In the marketplace, there are tall candles for lighting the gravesite and *cempazuchitl* (yellow marigolds used in

Smithsonian Institution

The sugar skull, or calavera, is widely available in the marketplace. Made of sugar and water and decorated with reflective eyes and facial markings made of icing, sugar skulls often have a place at the top for your own name. (In eating your skull, you symbolically become a compadre or companion of death rather than its adversary). Sugar is also used to construct animals who accompany the dead on their journey to and from Mictlan, the place of the dead. The names of deceased relatives are often placed on ornaments such as this skull and these coffins to assure the spirits of the dead that they are not forgotten. This practice also provides solace to the living in the form of tangible symbols of the presence of deceased loved ones.

Mesoamerica since pre-Columbian times to honor the dead), whose petals traditionally are strewn to guide the dead on the path to the family home. Some of the most interesting *cosas de muertos* (things of the dead) are designed to be eaten by the living. *Pan de muerto* (bread of the dead) is an essential food for the fiesta. It is generally made from a light, sweet yeast batter and baked into a characteristic shape depending upon the region of the country. For example, the pan de muerto typical of Mexico City is a round loaf topped by stylized skull and crossbones. Sugar-candy skulls, tissue-paper skeletons, and cardboard coffins poke fun at death. Pulling on a string at the end of a cardboard coffin might open the top and pull up a skull-shaped *muerto* (dead one) to a sitting position.

Stanley Brandes has highlighted some of the characteristics of an artistic representation of the Day of the Dead:[97]

1. It is *ephemeral.* It exists to celebrate the moment and is made for momentary consumption.
2. It is *humorous;* it evokes laughter rather than sadness, enjoyment rather than pain.
3. It is *comical.* The toys and candies are often designed for play; they often have moving parts.
4. It is *small, light, and transportable.* It generally fits in your hand.
5. It is *designed for living people,* not for the deceased.

As a part of the festival, families go to the *panteón* (cemetery) to prepare for the return of their dead. The rituals of cleaning graves, repainting crosses, pulling weeds, redecorating stones, and decorating with flowers is both a rejuvenation of the gravesite and a display of welcome for the dead. Even in the "perpetual care" cemeteries of the United States where Día de los Muertos is celebrated, families will gather at graves to clean and decorate them in anticipation of their dead ones' return. A party-like atmosphere occurs in the graveyards, with families, including children, visiting with one another and their dead loved ones. At night during the fiesta in Xoxo, Oaxaca, the small cemetery is ablaze with lights from tall candles placed around the graves. A *mariache* band circulates, playing tunes for the living and the dead while vendors sell food and drink.

During the festival, families build an *altar de muertos,* or *ofrenda* (altar where offerings are placed) in the home. The placement, size, and materials used to construct the altar for the dead vary. Pictures of the deceased, sacred images such as pictures of Mary, Jesus, or other religious notables such as the Virgin de Guadalupe, are placed on the altar. Food for the ofrenda might include a dish of chicken *mole*—a spicy sauce of some fifty ingredients, including chili peppers, peanuts, and chocolate—or other dishes that were favorites of the deceased. Items familiar to deceased loved ones, such as a package of a particular brand of cigarettes or a bottle of mescal, are set out to entice their spirits to return to the family during the fiesta.

The tall candles, or *ceras,* used in the festival are placed both on the ofrenda and on the grave. It is believed that the spirits of the dead need light to find their way back to the living on their journey to join us. In some communities, the quantity of candles signifies the number of dead ones who are being welcomed home.

Families set off large firecrackers to announce to the dead that it is time to come. In some communities, the dead will join the living in a meal. The sweets, bread, and other delicious items on the ofrenda are first given to the dead. The living will eventually eat them but only after much of their essence and flavor has been consumed by the dead. Among the most traditional observances of the fiesta are those on the Island of Janitzio in Michoacán and in the Zapotec villages in the Valley of Oaxaca.

Día de los Muertos is a time for revolting against ordinary modes of thought and action; the celebration reunites "contradictory elements and principles in order to bring about a renascence of life."[98] Jorge Valadez says,

> The rituals honoring and remembering the dead not only bring members of the community together; they also reinforce the belief that death is a transitional phase in which individuals continue to exist in a different plane while maintaining an important relationship with the living.[99]

Celebrants challenge the boundaries that ordinarily separate the dead from the living. Davíd Carrasco says, "The souls of the dead reassure the living of their continued protection, and the living reassure the dead that they will remember and nurture them in their daily lives."[100] It is important that families pay their respects to the dead, but mourners are cautioned against shedding too many tears; excessive grief may make the pathway traveled by

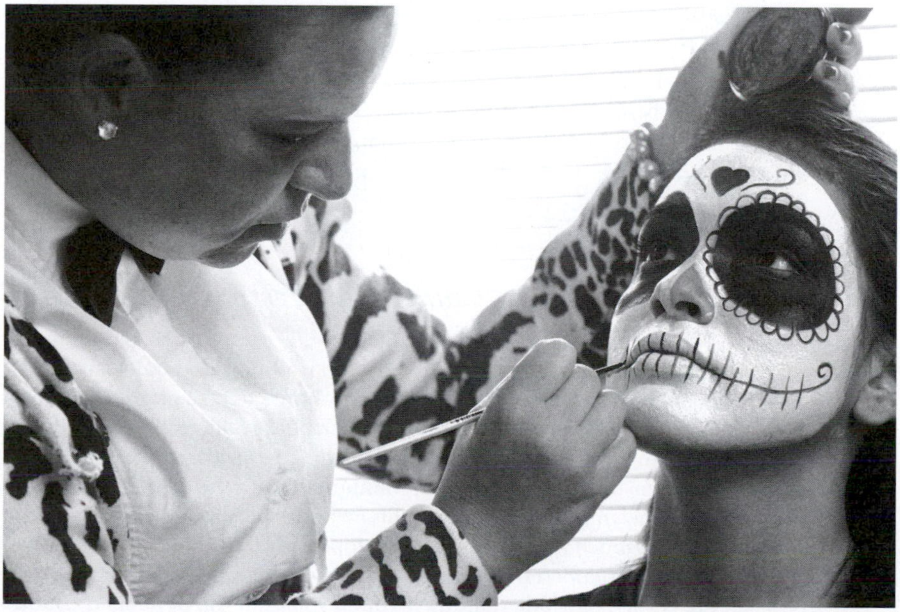

© Shmuel Thaler

At a Day of the Dead festival in the United States, a young woman receives elaborate makeup resembling a sugar skull, or calavera. The artist, who has won awards for her skillful masks, says, "It's refreshing to know that more people are looking at Día de los Muertos; and not just the look, but the tradition."

the dead slippery, burdening them with a tortuous journey as they return to the world of the living at this special time of celebration.

The mainstreaming of this celebration is an example of the "Latinization" of U.S. culture, an occurrence over the past thirty years as a result of the biggest migration flow in the history of the continent. One important reason for the "Mexicanness" of the Day of the Dead in the United States is that Chicano activists in California were engaged in struggles for civil rights during the 1960s and 1970s. They began to organize indigenous-inspired Day of the Dead processions and ofrenda exhibits as a way to honor Mexican American heritage.[101] One participant in Day of the Dead festivities in the United States explains,

> There is no venue in American tradition which lets us honor and celebrate our dead. Once people have died, their memory becomes a private matter for the family. . . . There is no public remembrance past the funeral. It's as if they were swept under the carpet and we move on to the next thing. With Día de los Muertos, the entire community is involved [in a] public acknowledgment of the dead.[102]

People of Asian Heritage

Generally speaking, Asian cultures value interdependence and affiliation over independence and individualism. *Harmony,* a quality manifested in proper conduct, is especially important in interpersonal relationships. In China, for example, this emphasis stems from the fact that descendants of a common ancestor share a lineage that may go back centuries. Important in this regard is the Chinese ideal of *hsiao,* which translates as "filiality" or "filial piety."

Asian heritage encompasses the cultures of India, China, Taiwan, Japan, and Korea. The many diverse cultures of Southeast Asia—Cambodian, Laotian, Hmong, Thai, Burmese, Vietnamese, Indonesian, Singaporean, Malaysian, and Filipino—can be added under the geographical rubric

Pchum Ben, the Cambodian Festival of the Dead

The International Financial Fund and the Global Bank are distressed . . . by Cambodia's failure to adapt its cultural traditions to modern conditions . . . With the country's labor force rising in the early hours to take offerings to departed ancestors, there must be an enormous decline in labor productivity . . . Cambodia cannot afford such an annual blow to its ability to compete in this era of globalization . . . In most Western, developed countries, communion with the dead is restricted to one night per year, known as Halloween . . . This means that Cambodia is spending at least fourteen times as much time as necessary in appeasing its ghosts . . . Cambodian ghosts . . . may well feel offended by a shift to a one-day observance. However . . . Cambodian ghosts are no less patriotic than their counterparts in the developed countries, and can be counted on to make this sacrifice in the national interest.

Phnom Penh Post

"Asian," while acknowledging highly variable distinctions and differences. For example, some of these cultures are predominantly Hindu, others are mainly Buddhist, yet others are Islamic, while still others follow animist-influenced practices or are a mixture of religions.

Filipinos are generally classed within Asian culture; however, diversity in the Philippine Islands and colonization by the Spanish make it problematic to classify Filipinos within a single category.[103] This points up the importance of recognizing that significant differences exist among the various "Asian" cultures.

The Hmong, an Asian ethnic group from the mountainous regions of China, Vietnam, Laos, and Thailand, view life as a journey; death is a phase one goes through when passing from this plane of existence to the next. "Hmong funerals are distinctive with many rituals and may last many days to honor the deceased and their ancestors. The older or more revered the person, the longer the funeral."[104] The primary religious leader is the shaman, or *tu txiv neeb,* who attends to both health and spiritual problems. Animal sacrifice may be made to honor the deceased. In the mountains of their homelands, Hmong funeral customs include firing mortars to alert the village that a death has occurred and slaughtering oxen and buffalo for the funeral ceremony. In the significantly different social environment of mostly urban settings in North America, the traditional elements of Hmong funeral ritual cannot be readily accommodated and have been dramatically changed.[105]

Like other Buddhists, Thais believe that a person is reborn after death, the place of rebirth depending on that person's *karma.* During the funeral, family members may pray for themselves to be reborn in the same family with the same relationship to the deceased in their next life.

In traditional Hindu households, death is a communal affair. Family members perform all the rites and rituals, with males dealing with the male body and females with the female body, from washing, anointing, and dressing, to the construction of the bier on which the corpse is laid and secured with ropes. Last rites are called *antyesti,* and their purpose is to purify the deceased and comfort the bereaved. The deceased is cremated within twenty-four hours following death for both hygienic and spiritual reasons, as Hindus believe a swifter cremation results in more complete release of the soul. Hindus living in the United States may keep their family members' ashes to scatter later in holy rivers upon return to their homeland.[106]

For Sikhs, widely recognized for their turban headdress and whose religion originated in northern India in the fifteenth century, an interdependent approach to decision making is preferred. Thus, many Sikh families choose not to inform the patient of his or her diagnosis or prognosis, believing that such information may hasten the course of death.[107]

Somewhat similarly, traditional Filipinos may not want to plan for death or discuss advance directives because doing so may be "tempting fate." When a person is seriously ill or dying, family members may provide personal care themselves. Following death, some Filipino families celebrate nine days of novenas (discussed in connection with Hispanic heritage).

Filipinos generally believe that life continues beyond death, and caring for the spiritual needs of the dying or dead is a way to ensure the peaceful rest of the soul or spirit.

Ancestors typically occupy a central place in Asian families as deceased members continue to have reciprocal relationships with the living members of the household.[108] When speaking of ancestors, Vietnamese mention the word *thiêng,* meaning "awe-inspiring" and "able to comply with prayers."[109] The living and the dead are dependent on each other; the living perform the necessary ancestral rites, while the dead dispense blessings to their descendants. There is eternal reciprocity between dead ancestors and their heirs.[110] The Chinese philosopher Mencius said that the most unfilial act was to leave no heirs, because there would be no one to perform the necessary ancestral rites. In fact, a recent study notes that in Japan's modern society, some older persons are facing being without "appropriate grave successors" (descendants) and, because of that, find it difficult to imagine their postmortem transformation into ancestors, a situation that causes them to be anxious about death.[111]

In Chinese funerals, specific mourning garments show degrees of kinship between bereaved and deceased (similar to the LoDagaa use of mourning restraints). Following Taoist traditions, Chinese death rituals use ancient principles of *fêng-shui* (literally, "wind-water"), an art of divination concerned with the proper positioning of elements in harmonious relation to one another. It is said that "fêng-shui connects life and death."[112] Fêng-shui aids in determining an auspicious, or favorable, site for dwellings,

Chuang Tzu's wife died. When Hui Tzu went to convey his condolences, he found Chuang Tzu sitting with his legs sprawled out, pounding on a tub and singing.

"You lived with her, she brought up your children, and grew old," said Hui Tzu. "It should be enough simply not to weep at her death. But pounding on a tub and singing—this is going too far, isn't it?"

Chuang Tzu said, "You're wrong. When she first died, do you think I didn't grieve like anyone else? But I looked back to her beginning and the time before she was born. Not only the time before she was born, but the time before she had a body. Not only the time before she had a body, but the time before she had a spirit. In the midst of the jumble of wonder and mystery, a change took place and she had a spirit. Another change and she had a body. Another change and she was born. Now there's been another change and she's dead. It's just like the progression of the four seasons, spring, summer, fall, winter.

"Now she's going to lie down peacefully in a vast room. If I were to follow after her bawling and sobbing, it would show that I don't understand anything about fate. So I stopped."

Chuang Tzu

a matter important for both living and dead, as failure to do so can cause sorrow. Thus, Chinese cemeteries are usually situated on elevated, sloping ground—preferably involving mountains behind and sea in front—with a view of fertile fields, which the ancestors are leaving for their descendants. During funeral ceremonies, the foot of the casket is positioned facing the door so that the spirit or soul of the deceased will have an unobstructed pathway into the next world. Attention to such details assures the bereaved family that everything is done properly to facilitate the ancestor's afterlife journey.

For tradition-minded Japanese, respect for the ancestors provides ways to maintain psychological and emotional links between the living and the dead.[113] However, these links can also give rise to fear of death and concerns about "death pollution," where death and the bad luck it brings can be contaminating. Indeed, "One of the major purposes of the ancestral rites is to move the soul of the newly dead from its ritually polluting, still-earthbound state, into a purified collectivity of the long-dead ancestors of the house and community."[114] The dead gradually lose their individuality and, after a time, merge with the spirits of the ancestors. Historically, in Japan,

> it was the task of the court poets to write laments for the deceased members of the imperial family, usually when they were lying in state at a temporary shrine (*arikinomiya*) prior to interment. It was believed that such poems of mourning would comfort the dead and keep them from returning to this world, dissatisfied by the neglect of the living, to torment people.[115]

Similar fears about death and its pollution are common in Chinese communities. Andy Ho and Cecelia Chan report:

> Common taboos include not talking about death; having no contact with the sick and the dying; avoiding proximity to coffins and dead bodies including their clothing and belongings; and not mentioning the names of dead people for fear of calling back their spirits. Contacts with family members of the deceased are avoided, as they are believed to be bearers of ill fortune and ritually polluted by death. Avoiding the use or invocation of the Chinese word for death (*sǐ*), also meaning four, is commonplace.[116]

During the typical Japanese funeral service, incense is offered and priests read Buddhist scriptures. At this time, the deceased is given a special posthumous or "Buddhist name," which indicates that the material aspect of the person is extinguished. This name (*kaimyo*) is eventually inscribed on an *ihai,* or memorial tablet, that is placed in the family's *butsudan,* or household altar. After the body is cremated, the ashes and some pieces of bone are placed in an urn, which will be interred at the family's grave.

Besides the butsudan in the home, the other main focus of Japanese ancestral rites is the *haka,* the family grave, where ashes of family members are interred. These family memorials may have space for a dozen or more urns. The grave must be maintained properly, which includes cleaning it

© Patrick Dean

This butsudan, prominently situated in the home of a Japanese American family in California, is representative of altars found in Japanese homes, where deceased relatives and ancestors are honored through prayers, gifts of food, and other ways of showing respect. As a focal point for ongoing relationships between the living and dead members of a household, the butsudan is a place where such relationships are demonstrated through concrete actions.

and making offerings to the dead. As with the butsudan, the haka is a place of ritual. Incense and flowers are offered to ancestors, and water is poured over the gravestone, a gesture of purification that dates back to antiquity and that people may now perform without fully recognizing its ancient meaning and symbolism. This tradition of ancestor veneration, or *sosen sūhai,* frames

Death-Song

If they ask for me
  Say: He had some
  Business
In another world.

Sokan

responses to death and loss; the transition to ancestorhood depends not on moral worth but on family loyalty.[117]

In a study of Japanese practices, Christine Valentine reports that "proper treatment of the dead" and the reinforcement of familiar and social ties continue to frame Japanese understandings of bereavement, compared to the Western emphasis on the "therapeutic needs of the bereaved and recovering personal autonomy."[118] Allan Kellehear and Daisuke Tanaka note that Western culture has been shaped by Judeo-Christian assumptions: When people die, they either go to another "realm" or perhaps simply disintegrate. Either way, the dead leave us; they are not here. But the cosmology of Shinto and Buddhism in Japan stresses the view that, although the dead do exist in another world, that world is not sharply divided from the world of the living. The dead and the living have access to each other.[119]

For the Japanese, it is quite ordinary to talk to their ancestors, either at the gravesite or at the family altar in the home, often in conversational ways, telling the deceased about things that are going on in life or asking for advice. Through such activities, the connection between the dead and the living is maintained.

The Chinese behave similarly in honoring ancestors. Traditionally, an ancestor's soul is embodied in a *spirit tablet*—a rectangular piece of wood upon which is engraved the deceased's name, title, and birth and death dates—that is kept on the family's home altar. Many Chinese families maintain memorial walls in their homes, sometimes substituting photographs for spirit tablets, as a way to maintain the presence of the dead within the family.

Paper Offerings

Paper offerings are objects made of paper, many of them handmade and one of a kind, which, by being burnt up, are offered to the beings residing beyond the world of the living: the gods, the ghosts, and the ancestors.[120] Burning accomplishes the vital transformation that sends the items beyond the confines of the living world. The residents of the next world are provided with symbolic money (called Hell Money or Hell Notes) and gold and silver, the latter in the form of ingots and coins made of paper. This "money," which the dead person will spend in the other world, is contributed by mourners and burned in a container during the funeral and on other occasions. Offerings to departed kinsmen are a significant part of both funeral rituals and

© Andy Hau Yan Ho

In the entry to this Hong Kong funeral hall are paper offerings, costing five to six thousand U.S. dollars, that will be burnt for the deceased to send him or her successfully into the afterlife. The Chinese characters, "Jiao Fu," worn by the two figures identify them as sedan chair carriers (porters for a palanquin). Beside the sedan chair carriers, there is a large mansion for the deceased and a Mercedes with driver (a combination of modern and traditional artifacts). A mahjong table is situated behind the car, and the mansion is decorated with protectors and servants to ease the transition of the deceased into the afterlife. The numbers 1628 on the Mercedes convey the meaning: "always a straight road to easy wealth."

rituals of commemoration. The dead are dependents after death, needing the family to supply what they require.

Ancient categories of offerings such as transportation, clothing, housing, and daily necessities are retained, but their specific contents are kept up to date. "Replicas of standard desk telephones have given way to mobile phones; as the mobile phones themselves become more compact and intricate, so do their counterparts in paper."[121]

Traditional belief demands that deceased members of families be remembered, and the ties between the dead and the living maintained. One way to do this is to give gifts to the dead at regular intervals. The busiest times of year are the Lunar New Year and the *ch'ing ming* festival honoring the dead, when shops are packed with customers buying gifts for the ancestors.[122]

Ch'ing ming and O-bon Festivals

The Chinese celebrate the return of deceased ancestors in a spring festival known as *ch'ing ming*, which has been called a kind of Chinese Memorial

Day. Families visit graves and burn paper offerings as a way of showing regard and care for their ancestors.

The Japanese festival of *bon* or *o-bon* is similar to the Chinese ch'ing ming. Usually observed each year in August, o-bon marks the return of ancestral spirits to their families. Known in English as the Festival of the Dead, the Feast of Lanterns (because lamps are lit to guide the spirits on their journeys home), the Feast of All Souls, or simply the midsummer festival, o-bon is an expression of ancient customs relating to the souls of the dead and the reverence due them by the living. In traditional belief, the ancestral spirits and gods descend from their mountain abodes to confer their blessings upon the living.[123]

People of Jewish Heritage

Generally, Jews do not speculate much about life after death. Rather, their focus is on conduct in one's present life. Janice Selekman says, "Death is an expected part of the life cycle; yet, each day is to be appreciated and lived as fully as possible. . . . The goal is to appreciate things and people while one still has them."[124]

As for death rites, a deathbed confessional prayer called the *Viddui* may be said by the dying person or recited by somebody for him or her. Jewish funerals and burials usually take place within twenty-four to forty-eight hours after death. *Shivah* is the term designating the seven-day period that begins with burial. During this period, mourners are "sitting Shivah." This is a time for condolences. *Kaddish,* the Jewish "mourner's prayer," is said in the company of others. Rather than speaking of death, however, it praises God and reaffirms faith.

Although there are differences in timing, it is customary for a tombstone to be placed after the Kaddish period is complete and within one year of the death. At this time, a graveside service, called an unveiling, is held. The anniversary of the death is called a *yahrzeit.* Upon visiting the gravesite, it is customary to place a small stone on the grave to indicate that someone has visited.

Jews have experienced pogroms and exiles throughout their history. The Nazi Holocaust, during World War II, has been a shaping event on Jewish identity, and it continues to affect the lives of American Jews and, specifically, the children of survivors.

People of Celtic Heritage

In ancient times, Celtic people occupied much of central and western Europe, ranging from the British Isles in the west to Turkey and the Black Sea coasts in the east, from Belgium in the north, south to Spain and Italy. It is commonly agreed that all of the European cultures can trace their roots to Celtic origins.[125] The societies of the Celts were led by warriors who justified their authority by skill, courage, and good fortune in battle. Fame after death was the hallmark of human achievement. As someone larger than life but less than divine, the hero was viewed as being in contact with supernatural powers and the *Otherworld,* the world beyond present reality.

Both burial and cremation were practiced at various times in Celtic history. The Celts were often buried with personal effects, clothes, jewelry, and other items that apparently reflected belief in immortality. Articles held dear by the deceased were burned or buried so that they could continue to serve in another life. The status of the deceased and his or her place in the community were indicated by the extent and type of grave goods. Based on archaeological evidence, scholars believe that the Celts enacted elaborate funeral ceremonies involving clan gatherings and feasting at funeral banquets. In one especially lavish burial, probably of a chieftain, tomb furnishings included a large bronze couch on which the body was placed, as well as a four-wheeled vehicle that may have been a hearse or have represented a chariot for traveling to the Otherworld. The tomb contained bronze dishes and drinking horns, enough to accommodate nine people, the number considered ideal for a drinking party, suggesting a ritual feast.

There was a strong sense of communication between the world of the living and the world of the dead. Memory toasts were drunk in honor of the dead. Generally, the dead were helpful to their descendants, especially when reverence was paid to them. Death was viewed as simply a changing of place. Life went on in all its forms in another world, a world of the dead, the Otherworld. When people died in that world, they could be reborn in this world. Thus, a constant exchange of souls took place between the two worlds: Death in the Otherworld brought a soul to this world, and death in this world took a soul to the Otherworld.

Contact between the living and the dead was especially possible during the breach in time known as *Samhain* (November 1), which marked the end of one year and the dawn of the next, according to the Celtic calendar. As the most important festival of the year, the harvest feast of Samhain lasted several days, a time when supernatural communications with the gods as well as the dead could take place. At that time, the walls between this world and the "other" were most transparent, the souls of the dead driven toward the living "like swirling leaves."[126]

The Celtic priesthood, known as *Druids,* presided over the sacrificial rites and interpreted omens.[127] They acted as intermediaries between the world of humankind and the domain of the supernatural. Their main teaching appears to have been immortality of the soul as a future bodily life, not merely as spirit or shadow of life after death. Indeed, the Celts seem to have been among the first peoples to develop a belief in personal immortality. Such beliefs helped the Celts face the fear of death and made them brave in battle.

The part played by battle-goddesses, battle-maids, or *valkyries* is important in both Nordic and Celtic traditions and can be traced back before the Viking Age. Valkyries were thought to haunt the battlefield, where they rejoiced in the bloodshed and deaths of warriors. Described as wearing swords, carrying spears, and riding over air and sea, they were viewed as apportioning victory or defeat in battle and welcoming fallen heroes into *Valhalla,* a place of heavenly honor and glory. The phrase "being a guest in Valhalla" was synonymous with death. Valhalla literally means "hall of the slain." Of great height, it is roofed with golden shields, and its rafters are spears. Valhalla was viewed not as the dwelling place of all the dead but as a place for outstanding heroes. The Celtic attitude toward death in battle can be summarized as follows: "To be a warrior among warriors was the ideal life for the Celt, but to die in a fight surrounded by friends, poets and a hundred dead enemies was the supreme consummation."[128] One writer observes that present attitudes may be similar: "If you watch the commercials that accompany all televised sporting events, you'll note this is still our collective idea of heaven, with scantily clad bimbettes bearing bounteous beer to Victorious Men as their envious admirers leap about shouting Woo."[129]

The Celts, who valued skill in words nearly as much as skill in battle, delighting in word-games and intricate poetic language, also made notable contributions to world literature, perhaps most famously in the legend of King Arthur. Traces of Celtic myth are also found in Chaucer and in Shakespeare's *The Tempest* and *As You Like It,* as well as more recently in Tolkien's *Lord of the Rings,* which contains strong echoes of the Otherworld and includes Druid-like characters in the forms of the magicians Gandalf and Saruman. In Tolkien's *The Hobbit,* the ring lord is called the *Necromancer,* a name from Nordic mythology that means "enchanter" or "wizard" and refers to the sorcerer's skill of speaking with the dead to gain knowledge. There is an elegiac note in Old English poetry, like *Beowulf,* in which there is a sense of grief at the awareness that all things are passing away and life is on loan.[130]

Long after Ireland was converted to Christianity, beliefs and customs associated with Samhain continued. In the mid-twentieth century, for example, arrangements of bread and produce were prepared in rural Irish homes on November 1, "a bowl of water placed on the table," and the doors left unlatched "to let in the souls."[131] A traditional practice in Ireland was for the deceased to be "laid out" at home for a final farewell. In ancient times, at wakes, Gaelic women engaged in "keening," or loud wailing, while men socialized with drinking and conversation. The wake is still an important tradition in contemporary Irish and Irish American families. "A wake is a time of melancholy, rejoicing, pain, and hopefulness as well as a time to share food and drink in honor of the deceased."[132]

Today, more people claim some sort of Celtic identity than at any other time in history. Celtic religious beliefs are being rediscovered as part of the modern resurgence of pagan, nature-venerating, polytheistic religions. (The literal meaning of the word *pagan* is "rural" or "country dweller.") The keening sounds of dirges and laments played on bagpipes and uilleann pipes are part of many funeral processions, especially of police officers and firefighters killed in the line of duty. In short, the Celtic heritage is an important component of European and European American culture.

People of Arab Heritage

Arabs trace their ancestry and traditions to the nomadic desert tribes of the Arabian Peninsula. This cultural heritage is associated with a wide geographic area of North Africa and Southwest Asia, including the countries of Jordan, Iraq, Kuwait, Bahrain, Qatar, the United Arab Emirates, Oman, Yemen, and Saudi Arabia, as well as Algeria, Lebanon, Libya, Morocco, Palestine, Somalia, Sudan, Syria, and Tunisia. *Bedouin* is the term applied to all Arabic-speaking, nomadic tribes in the Middle East.

Different groups of Arabs have distinctive traditions and religious beliefs, as well as differences based on ethnic, linguistic, tribal, regional, religious, socioeconomic, and national identities. Although many Arabs are Muslim, the terms *Arab* and *Muslim* are not synonymous. Nevertheless, this section will focus on Muslim beliefs and practices regarding death.

For most Muslims, death and the afterlife are central tenets of faith.[133] Allah determines how long a person will live. Earthly life is a preparation for eternal life, and death is accepted as God's will. Because of this, discussion of advance directives or end-of-life care may be unwelcome.

Extended periods of mourning may be perceived by some Muslims as contrary to the will of God. Even so, individuals may react dramatically to the death of a family member and engage in strong and expressive grieving. Family, friendship, and social support are sources of strength and comfort, especially in times of illness or crisis.

Among Muslims, as the time of death nears, the deathbed, or at least the person's face, is turned toward Mecca. Islam calls for burial of the deceased as soon as possible. The burial ritual includes cleaning the body and wrapping it in a white cotton shroud. Verses from the Qur'an are read and prayer is recited before the body is buried in a simple tomb. For devout Muslims, life or death is the *will of God*.

People of Oceanian Heritage

The indigenous peoples of the Pacific Islands, or Oceanians, are people who are descended from the original peoples of Hawaii and other Pacific islands, including people of Polynesian, Melanesian, and Micronesian background. They differ in language and culture across many subgroups.[134] The largest Polynesian groups are Hawaiian, Samoan, and Tongan; the largest Micronesian group is Chamorros/Guamanian; and the largest Melanesian group is Fijian.[135]

Key areas of culture for Pacific Islanders are family networks, spirituality, balance, harmony, and values such as are expressed in the Hawaiian terms *lokahi* (unity and harmony), *pono* (goodness, uprightness, proper procedure), *'ohana* (kingroup and social supports), *kokua* (mutual help and cooperation), and *kuleana* (responsibility). These values are evident in the following discussion of culture in Hawaii.

Mixed Plate: Cultural Diversity in Hawaii

The population of Hawaii represents a rich ethnic and cultural blend. The boundaries between different population groups in Hawaii are loosened through social interaction, becoming "soft instead of hard, often overlapping rather than sharply defined," resulting in a situation wherein "no group has totally surrendered the core of its traditional cultural identity."[136] (This may foreshadow what the mainland United States and much of the larger global environment will look like in a few more decades.)

Hawaii is "the only region [in the United States] where all racial groups are minorities and where most of the population has its roots in the Pacific Islands or Asia instead of Europe or Africa."[137] Hawaii was settled by Polynesians who sailed to the Hawaiian archipelago and whose first contact with Europeans came in 1778 with exploration of the Pacific by Captain James Cook.[138] Later, successive waves of immigrants came—including Chinese, Japanese, Portuguese, Okinawans, Koreans, and Filipinos. Today's residents include Caucasians from Europe and North America, Samoans, Vietnamese, Laotians, and Cambodians, as well as African Americans, Latin Americans, Pakistanis, Tongans, Fijians, Micronesians, immigrants from other parts of Oceania, and others. The *pan-ethnic* identity of being a "local" represents "the common identity of people of Hawaii and their shared appreciation of the land, peoples, and cultures of the islands."[139]

Each group has its own story, unique history, and corresponding traditions. Most have their own cultural networks, with their own ways of keeping tradition alive, as well as providing mutual support in times of need. The diversity in Hawaii illustrates the possibility of preserving the cultural richness of distinctive traditions by accommodating and assimilating their expression.

Characteristics of Hawaii's Peoples

The extended family group, or *'ohana,* is at the center of traditional Hawaiian values.[140] Children have an important place in family gatherings, including funerals. The intimate relationships of the 'ohana involve close bonds between living family members and their ancestors.[141] Ancestral remains are sacred, especially those of the *ali'i,* members of the royal family. Indeed, as George Kanahele says, the Hawaiians' love of family is the basis of their love of the land:

> In a religious society in which ancestors were deified as *'aumakua* [gods] and genealogy elevated to prominent status, a place, a home, was much more valued because of its ties with the ancestors. A Hawaiian's birthplace was celebrated not simply because he happened to be born there, but because it was also the place where so many generations of his ancestors were born before him. It was a constant reminder of the vitality of the bloodline and of the preciousness of life past, present, and future.[142]

To be spiritual means to recognize interdependence and strive for harmony among human beings, the land, and higher powers (including both God, called *ke akua,* and personal ancestral guides, called *'aumakua*).[143] Hawaiian identity is spoken of in terms of connectedness to lands, language, and family.[144]

Among the earliest immigrants to Hawaii were the Chinese. Like the Hawaiians, Chinese cultural values emphasize the importance of family and relationships.[145] They also retain elements of traditional funerals and mourning.[146] For example, Chinese funerals in Hawaii typically include paper offerings (such as those discussed earlier in this chapter). Papier-mâché "servant dolls" are placed in front of the casket, and a Taoist priest chants instructions about how to take care of the deceased in Heaven. The boy servant might be told, "Take care of your master; fetch him water and firewood." To the girl servant, the priest might say, "Keep the house clean, and when you go shopping, don't waste your master's money." In the Taoist funeral, which lasts nearly all day, the priest chants and musicians play instruments while family members perform rituals at the priest's direction.

Most cultural groups living in Hawaii share a valuing of family ties and respect for ancestors. John F. McDermott says,

> In all groups, except perhaps the Caucasian, the extended family plays a central role. There is an emphasis on the family as a key social unit, and on family cohesion, family interdependence, and loyalty to the family as central guiding values. The individual is seen as part of a larger network, and duties and obligations, as well as much of the sense of personal security, derive from that context. . . . Caucasians, too, value the family, but they face the world as individuals.[147]

It is appropriate to think of Caucasians as one of many groups that constitute the "cultural mosaic" of the islands. Newcomers often find that this social reality requires some adjustment. Caucasians who move to Hawaii from the United States mainland do not think of themselves as migrants; they view themselves as representing mainstream culture and usually expect others, not themselves, to adapt.[148] Those who remain in Hawaii, however, adapt to the unique culture of Hawaii and assume a "local" identity, which is shared by all the groups living in Hawaii.

Death and Local Identity

The various ethnic groups in Hawaii tend to maintain a distinctive identity and culture while sharing elements of their identity and culture with the overall community. As different ethnic groups became part of the cultural mix in Hawaii, a common language, called *pidgin,* developed and became a symbol of local identity. Borrowing words and grammar from the native tongues of its speakers, pidgin is not only an expressive means of communication among people of disparate backgrounds but also a way for people to identify with their adopted homeland. Today, speaking pidgin allows people to transcend cultural boundaries and establish rapport with each other on the basis of "local" identity.

A Caucasian nurse describes how pidgin was useful in talking with a Filipino man who was dying. As the man's body wasted away, he was frightened. Offering comfort, the nurse told him, "Spirit good, body *pau* [finished]." In using a pidgin word, borrowed from the Hawaiian language, she was able to affirm, in a culturally appropriate and comforting way, the strength of his spirit while acknowledging that the life in his body was being consumed by disease.

Local identity is fostered by familiarity with customs practiced by the different ethnic groups and by flexibility in adopting elements of those customs into one's own life. For instance, the native Hawaiian tradition of feasting at important ceremonial events is widespread among Hawaii's residents. At funerals, mourners often gather after the ritual to share food and conversation. Mortuaries in Hawaii accommodate this by having kitchen and dining facilities where food can be prepared, brought by mourners (potluck), or catered and served to gathered family and friends.

Similarly, funeral announcements in Hawaii usually include the notice "Aloha attire requested," to which mourners respond by wearing colorful shirts or *mu'u* (long "missionary" dresses), along with beautiful and fragrant flower leis. The lei is very special in Hawaiian culture, and different flowers and leis carry symbolic meanings. For example, a *hala* lei is associated with the breath (*ha*) and connotes passing away or dying. The ginger, or *'awapuhi,* lei is a symbol of things that pass too soon, as indicated in the Hawaiian folk saying, "*'Awapuhi lau pala wale,*" or "Ginger leaves yellow too quickly."[149] In the customs of feasting after a funeral and wearing flower leis, traditions associated with the indigenous Hawaiians have been adopted as expressions of local identity and community feeling.

Given the religions practiced in Hawaii—Christianity, Buddhism, and Taoism, among others—mortuaries are generally set up to offer appropriate accoutrements and symbols for each of these traditions. The central portion of the altar at one mortuary is designed as a revolving display so that images and symbols of the appropriate religious tradition can be easily moved into view.

Hawaii's diverse inhabitants have not minimized differences between different ethnic groups so much as learned to appreciate and make room for their expression. The fastest-growing ethnic group in Hawaii is "mixed race," or *hapa.*[150] When people marry outside their heritage group, thereby joining in kinship with families from different cultural traditions, their customs, beliefs, and practices blend together in a new family. As spouses from different traditions adopt elements of each other's culture, their children naturally become acquainted with both cultures.

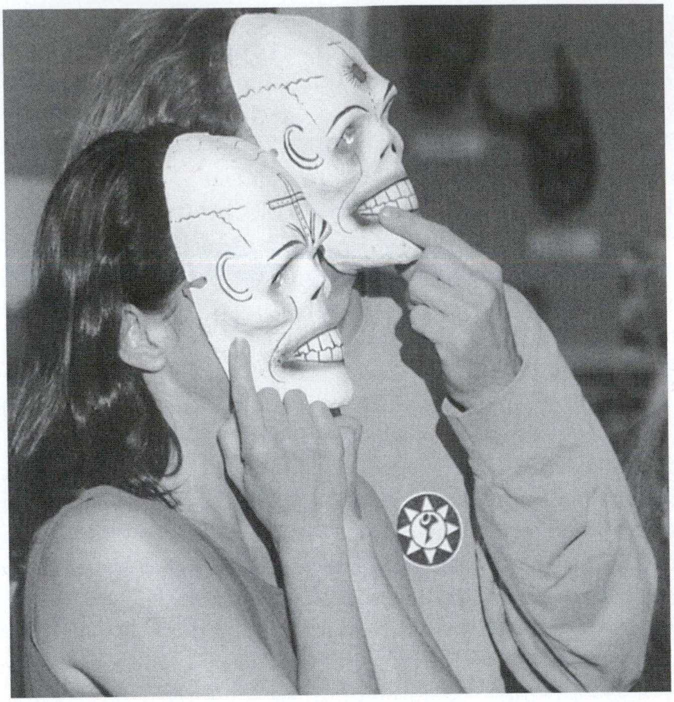

© Patrick Dean

In contemporary societies, where a variety of cultural traditions are practiced by different ethnic and subcultural groups, people may find themselves "trying on" customs and practices that differ from those of their own heritage group. The opportunity to participate in the rites and ceremonies of other cultures, to assume a "local identity," even if only temporarily, can broaden our understanding and expand our range of choices for revitalizing even those customs with which we are most familiar.

Death in Contemporary Multicultural Societies

Modern societies are composed of a number of social groups, each with distinctive customs and lifestyles. The presence of a cultural mosaic created by different ethnic and cultural groups can enrich a society.[151] People sometimes talk or write about "the American way of death," but this phrase conceals what, in fact, are many different "ways of death," reflecting attitudes, beliefs, and customs of culturally diverse groups. David Olson and John DeFrain remind us that "tremendous diversity exists among people who are commonly grouped together."[152]

The ways we cope with death are not created out of thin air. The root meaning of *tradition* is "to hand down." Each generation receives culture from the preceding generation, alters it, and passes it on. This is seen in the film *Bend It Like Beckam,* which tells of a young girl's search for identity in twenty-first-century London. She seeks to renegotiate an identity that combines her ancestral cultural and the culture of a new homeland, occupying what has been termed *third space*.[153] The ancestral culture in this case is that of immigrant and first-generation Punjabi Sikh Indians, and the film shows the struggles tradition-bound cultures must go through as they enter a more freedom-loving modern world.

Ethnicity and other cultural factors have an impact on such matters as coping with life-threatening illness, the perception of pain, social support for the dying, manifestations of grief, mourning styles, and funeral customs.[154] Spanish-speaking people in northern New Mexico continue to practice traditional forms of *recuerdo,* or remembrance, which memorialize the dead and comfort the bereaved.[155] Presented as a written narrative or ballad, the recuerdo tells the story of a person's life in an epic, lyrical, and heroic manner. This is a kind of farewell, a leave-taking, or *la despedida,* on behalf of a deceased person. Such memorials frequently contain reminders of the transitory nature of life and express the notion that life is on loan from God for only a short time.

As Robert Harrison reminds us, mourning rituals are missing something important if they do not "provide the means, or language, to cope with one's own mortality even as they help one cope with the death of others."[156]

Further Readings

Fredrik Fahlander and Terje Oestigaard. *The Materiality of Death: Bodies, Burials, Beliefs.* Oxford: British Archaeologial Reports, 2008.

Ronald L. Grimes. *Deeply into the Bone: Re-Inventing Rites of Passage.* Berkeley: University of California Press, 2000.

Robert Pogue Harrison. *The Dominion of the Dead.* Chicago: University of Chicago Press, 2003.

Allan Kellehear. *A Social History of Dying.* New York: Cambridge University Press, 2007.

Paul Koudounaris. *The Empire of Death: A Cultural History of Ossuaries and Charnel Houses.* London: Thames & Hudson, 2011.

Claudio Lomnitz. *Death and the Idea of Mexico.* Cambridge, Mass.: MIT Press, 2005.

Regina M. Marchi. *Day of the Dead in the USA: The Migration and Transformation of a Cultural Phenomenon.* New Brunswick, N.J.: Rutgers University Press, 2009.

Elaine Nichols, ed. *The Last Miles of the Way: African-American Homegoing Traditions, 1890-Present.* Columbia: South Carolina State Museum, 1989.

Mike Parker Pearson. *The Archaeology of Death and Burial.* College Station: Texas A&M University Press, 2000.

Charles Wilkinson. *Blood Struggle: The Rise of Modern Indian Nations.* New York: Norton, 2005.

Additional resources for this chapter can be found at www.mhhe.com/despelder10e

A death that occurs under suspicious or uncertain circumstances prompts an investigation to determine cause of death. Thus, law enforcement agencies are part of a society's death system—the networks of people, places, times, objects, and symbols that shape an individual's relationship to mortality.

CHAPTER 4

Death Systems: Mortality and Society

Society has an interest in such matters as devising the rules governing organ donation and transplantation, defining and making determinations of death, classifying modes of death into useful categories, regulating the manner in which investigative duties are carried out by coroners and medical examiners, and assessing the degree of criminal intent or negligence when a violent death has occurred. Kaleidoscopic in their diversity, all of these are part of the "death system," a term coined by Robert Kastenbaum to describe "the interpersonal, sociophysical, and symbolic network through which an individual's relationship to mortality is mediated by his or her society."[1]

The components of a death system include *people* (funeral directors, life insurance agents, weapons designers, people who care for the dying), *places* (cemeteries, funeral homes, battlefields, war memorials, disaster sites), *times* (memorial days and religious commemorations such as Good Friday, anniversaries of important battles, Halloween), *objects* (obituaries, tombstones, hearses, the electric chair), and *symbols* (black armbands, funeral music, skull and crossbones, language used to talk about death). In today's societies, the Internet has also become a significant part of the death system (a *thanatechnological* death system).[2]

Although the functions of a death system vary among different societies and at different times in the same society, a death system includes these elements:

1. Warnings and predictions about potentially life-threatening events (storms, tornadoes, and other disasters, as well as advice to specific individuals, such as doctors' reports of laboratory results or mechanics' warnings about faulty brakes)
2. Preventing death (emergency and acute medical care, public health initiatives, antismoking campaigns)
3. Caring for the dying (nurses, trauma workers, family caregivers, hospice staff)
4. Disposing of the dead (mortuaries, cemetery plots, memorialization processes, identification of bodies in disasters)
5. Social consolidation after death (coping with grief, maintaining community bonds, settling estates)
6. Making sense of death (religious or scientific explanations, consolation literature, last words)
7. Killing (capital punishment, war, hunting, raising and marketing of animals)

There are interconnections and mutual influences among these functions. It should be obvious, however, that the elements composing a death system touch on virtually every aspect of social and individual life, ranging from the use of euphemisms on sympathy cards to the medicalization of death. The death system is concerned with managing the phenomenon of death in all its varied manifestations. These include preventing death, disposing of the dead, making sense of death, endorsing socially sanctioned death, and sometimes camouflaging the impact of death on our lives.[3] The death system also defines rules of grieving that "determine who, when, where, how, how long, and for whom people should be sanctioned to grieve;" that is, the "shoulds" and "should nots" that govern individual responses to loss.[4] This is called the "policing" of grief. Similarly, the circumstances surrounding an individual's dying typically occur as a result of decisions made through "a social process of negotiation of meanings."[5] Throughout this text, we highlight different aspects of the death system. In the following pages, we focus particularly on the death system's impact as it relates to defining and certifying death, assessing homicidal acts, regulating organ donation and transplantation, and administering capital punishment. As Kastenbaum says, "the death system regards mortality as intrinsic to all facets of societal functioning."[6]

Certification of Death

Death certificates reflect both a private and a public function in the death system. At first glance, the document used to certify the facts of death appears straightforward, a concise summary of the pertinent data regarding the deceased and the mode and place of death. However, this seemingly simple document has broader implications than one might imagine. Besides its value and purpose as a legal document that affects disposition of property rights, life insurance benefits, pension payments, and so on, the utility of the death certificate extends to such diverse matters as aiding in crime detection, tracing genealogy, and gaining knowledge about the incidence of disease and other aspects of physical and psychological health.

In fact, the official registration of death is considered the most important legal procedure following a death. A death certificate constitutes legal proof of death, and death certificates are required by all jurisdictions in the United States. Although death certificates vary somewhat from state to state, most follow the format outlined by the United States Standard Certificate of Death.

Funeral directors are generally responsible for completing and filing death certificates. "The funeral director obtains personal data from the best source available (usually next of kin) and cause-of-death information from the attending physician, medical examiner, or coroner."[7] When complete, the certificate is filed with the registration authority in the state where the death occurred.

The typical death certificate (see Figure 4-1) provides for four different *modes* of death: accidental, suicidal, homicidal, and natural. However, as Edwin Shneidman points out, the *cause* of death isn't necessarily the same as the *mode* of death.[8] For example, if a death is caused by asphyxiation due to drowning, should it be classified as an accident, a suicide, or a homicide? Any of these modes might apply.

Underlying the distinction between mode and cause is a more complex issue of intentions and subconscious factors, the states of mind and actions, that may have contributed directly or indirectly to the death. For instance, if an intoxicated person jumps into a swimming pool with no one else present and drowns, is the death accidental or suicidal? Does it make a difference whether the alcohol abuse was related to emotional distress and despondency? What is the mode of death if the cocktails were served by a too-generous host? What if the person serving the excessive alcohol were also an heir of the person who died?

Obviously, intentions and subconscious factors can be more complex than the relatively elementary distinctions concerning mode and cause of death now listed on most death certificates. A study done in Marin County, California, to assess the conventional classifications of mode of death as well as the lethality of the deceased's intention revealed that some deaths classified as natural, accidental, and homicidal were precipitated by the deceased's own actions; that is, the deceased had lethal intentions against himself or herself. (The use of a *psychological autopsy* as an investigative tool for reconstructing the intentions and factors leading up to a death is discussed in Chapter 12.) Because death certificates force physicians to simplify what might be a complex medical situation, lack of training is said to be the greatest contributor to the poor quality of mortality data.[9]

The Coroner and the Medical Examiner

Most deaths in the United States result from disease, and the physician attending the patient certifies the cause of death. However, when death occurs in suspicious circumstances or suddenly, and there is no physician to certify

CERTIFICATE OF DEATH
STATE OF CALIFORNIA
USE BLACK INK ONLY / NO ERASURES, WHITEOUTS OR ALTERATIONS
VS-11 (REV 1/03)

STATE FILE NUMBER | LOCAL REGISTRATION NUMBER

DECEDENT'S PERSONAL DATA

1. NAME OF DECEDENT --- FIRST (Given) | 2. MIDDLE | 3. LAST (Family)

AKA. ALSO KNOWN AS --- Include full AKA (FIRST, MIDDLE, LAST) | 4. DATE OF BIRTH mm/dd/ccyy | 5. AGE Yrs. | IF UNDER ONE YEAR: Months, Days | IF UNDER 24 HOURS: Hours, Minutes | 6. SEX

9. BIRTH STATE/FOREIGN COUNTRY | 10. SOCIAL SECURITY NUMBER | 11. EVER IN U.S. ARMED FORCES? ☐ YES ☐ NO ☐ UNK | 12. MARITAL STATUS (at Time of Death) | 7. DATE OF DEATH mm/dd/ccyy | 8. HOUR (24 Hours)

13. EDUCATION --- Highest Level/Degree (see worksheet on back) | 14/15. WAS DECEDENT SPANISH/HISPANIC/LATINO? (If yes, see worksheet on back.) ☐ YES ☐ NO | 16. DECEDENT'S RACE --- Up to 3 races may be listed (see worksheet on back)

17. USUAL OCCUPATION --- Type of work for most of life. DO NOT USE RETIRED | 18. KIND OF BUSINESS OR INDUSTRY (e.g., grocery store, road construction, employment agency, etc.) | 19. YEARS IN OCCUPATION

USUAL RESIDENCE

20. DECEDENT'S RESIDENCE (Street and number or location)

21. CITY | 22. COUNTY/PROVINCE | 23. ZIP CODE | 24. YEARS IN COUNTY | 25. STATE/FOREIGN COUNTRY

INFOR-MANT

26. INFORMANT'S NAME, RELATIONSHIP | 27. INFORMANT'S MAILING ADDRESS (Street and number or rural route number, city or town, state, ZIP)

SPOUSE AND PARENT INFORMATION

28. NAME OF SURVIVING SPOUSE --- FIRST | 29. MIDDLE | 30. LAST (Maiden Name)

31. NAME OF FATHER --- FIRST | 32. MIDDLE | 33. LAST | 34. BIRTH STATE

35. NAME OF MOTHER --- FIRST | 36. MIDDLE | 37. LAST (Maiden) | 38. BIRTH STATE

FUNERAL DIRECTOR/ LOCAL REGISTRAR

39. DISPOSITION DATE mm/dd/ccyy | 40. PLACE OF FINAL DISPOSITION

41. TYPE OF DISPOSITION(S) | 42. SIGNATURE OF EMBALMER ▶ | 43. LICENSE NUMBER

44. NAME OF FUNERAL ESTABLISHMENT | 45. LICENSE NUMBER | 46. SIGNATURE OF LOCAL REGISTRAR ▶ | 47. DATE mm/dd/ccyy

PLACE OF DEATH

101. PLACE OF DEATH | 102. IF HOSPITAL, SPECIFY ONE ☐ IP ☐ ER/OP ☐ DOA | 103. IF OTHER THAN HOSPITAL, SPECIFY ONE ☐ Hospice ☐ Nursing Home/LTC ☐ Decedent's Home ☐ Other

104. COUNTY | 105. FACILITY ADDRESS OR LOCATION WHERE FOUND (Street and number or location) | 106. CITY

CAUSE OF DEATH

107. CAUSE OF DEATH — Enter the chain of events --- diseases, injuries, or complications --- that directly caused death. DO NOT enter terminal events such as cardiac arrest, respiratory arrest, or ventricular fibrillation without showing the etiology. DO NOT ABBREVIATE. | Time Interval Between Onset and Death | 108. DEATH REPORTED TO CORONER? ☐ YES ☐ NO REFERRAL NUMBER

IMMEDIATE CAUSE (Final disease or condition resulting in death) → (A) | (AT)

(B) | (BT) | 109. BIOPSY PERFORMED? ☐ YES ☐ NO

Sequentially, list conditions, if any, leading to cause on Line A. Enter UNDERLYING CAUSE (disease or injury that initiated the events resulting in death) LAST

(C) | (CT) | 110. AUTOPSY PERFORMED? ☐ YES ☐ NO

(D) | (DT) | 111. USED IN DETERMINING CAUSE? ☐ YES ☐ NO

112. OTHER SIGNIFICANT CONDITIONS CONTRIBUTING TO DEATH BUT NOT RESULTING IN THE UNDERLYING CAUSE GIVEN IN 107

113. WAS OPERATION PERFORMED FOR ANY CONDITION IN ITEM 107 OR 112? (If yes, list type of operation and date.) | 113A. IF FEMALE, PREGNANT IN LAST YEAR? ☐ YES ☐ NO ☐ UNK

PHYSICIAN'S CERTIFICATION

114. I CERTIFY THAT TO THE BEST OF MY KNOWLEDGE DEATH OCCURRED AT THE HOUR, DATE, AND PLACE STATED FROM THE CAUSES STATED. Decedent Attended Since (A) mm/dd/ccyy | Decedent Last Seen Alive (B) mm/dd/ccyy | 115. SIGNATURE AND TITLE OF CERTIFIER ▶ | 116. LICENSE NUMBER | 117. DATE mm/dd/ccyy

118. TYPE ATTENDING PHYSICIAN'S NAME, MAILING ADDRESS, ZIP CODE

CORONER'S USE ONLY

119. I CERTIFY THAT IN MY OPINION DEATH OCCURRED AT THE HOUR, DATE, AND PLACE STATED FROM THE CAUSES STATED. MANNER OF DEATH ☐ Natural ☐ Accident ☐ Homicide ☐ Suicide ☐ Pending Investigation ☐ Could not be determined | 120. INJURED AT WORK? ☐ YES ☐ NO ☐ UNK | 121. INJURY DATE mm/dd/ccyy | 122. HOUR (24 Hours)

123. PLACE OF INJURY (e.g., home, construction site, wooded area, etc.)

124. DESCRIBE HOW INJURY OCCURRED (Events which resulted in injury)

125. LOCATION OF INJURY (Street and number, or location, and city, and ZIP)

126. SIGNATURE OF CORONER / DEPUTY CORONER ▶ | 127. DATE mm/dd/ccyy | 128. TYPE NAME, TITLE OF CORONER / DEPUTY CORONER

STATE REGISTRAR | A | B | C | D | E | FAX AUTH. # | CENSUS TRACT

Figure 4-1 *Certificate of Death in Use in California*

A member of the coroner's staff notifies a family about the sudden, unexpected death of a husband and father. Details about the accident and efforts at life-saving intervention are provided in a gentle, open manner, using the family's questions to guide the discussion. A police officer who was on the scene stands by to provide more information if it is requested.

cause of death, the cause must be determined by a coroner or medical examiner, also known as a *death investigator*.[10] Coroners are usually elected officials; medical examiners are usually appointed. The main difference between the two positions, however, has to do with training. Whereas coroners may not possess any special background or training, medical examiners are physicians, generally with advanced training and certification in anatomical and *forensic pathology* (the application of medical knowledge to questions of law).

A Chinese book written in the thirteenth century describes how investigators of the time could distinguish a natural death from an unnatural death by, for example, noting damaged cartilage on the neck and pressure marks on the throat, suggesting death by strangulation.[11]

Observation and analysis are still at the core of forensic examination. Stefan Timmermans says,

> Death investigators are called when something goes seriously wrong. The deceased should have lived. Their death was either unexpected or premature, or the circumstances suggest violence, accident, destructive behavior, abuse, or simple ambiguity. These deaths are *suspicious* because they occurred out of the ordinary.[12]

Cause of death is determined by an investigation that makes use of scientific procedures, possibly including an autopsy (described later in this chapter), toxicology and bacteriology tests, chemical analyses, and any other studies that are needed to arrive at adequate findings. The investigator's queries eventually result in a *thanatography,* a written account of a person's death.[13]

The results of such postmortem examination can play a crucial role in court cases and insurance settlements. Such proceedings may be important not only to law enforcement agencies but also to the families involved: The mode of death—whether due to foul play, negligence, suicide, accident, or natural causes—can have a significant emotional effect on survivors. It may also have an economic effect; for example, some life insurance policies cover only accidental death, whereas others pay twice the face value of the contract in the case of accidental death (double indemnity).

Besides their responsibilities for investigating the cause of death in questionable circumstances, coroners and medical examiners often play a key role in community health programs, such as suicide prevention and drug abuse education.

One death investigator said, "I can't give people back their loved ones. I can't restore their happiness or innocence, can't give back their lives the way they were before. But I can give them the truth. Then they will be free to grieve for the dead, and then free to start living again."[14]

Autopsies

An autopsy (from the Greek *autopsia,* meaning "seeing with one's own eyes") is a detailed medical examination of a body after death to determine cause of death or investigate the nature of changes caused by disease. Once the abdominal cavity is exposed, organs are removed for examination of their internal structure, and small samples may be taken for later analysis. After the autopsy is completed, organs not needed for further study are replaced in the body cavity, and all incisions are closed.

The situations which call for autopsies and the manner in which they are carried out are matters for the death system. The deceased's family may request an autopsy to determine whether any genetic or infectious conditions led to death, or to help resolve questions about possible malpractice. An autopsy may be performed for legal or official reasons (as mentioned in connection with the role of the coroner or medical examiner) or as part of a hospital's teaching or research program. Unlike autopsies performed as part of medical training or at a family's request, those done as part of an investigation conducted by a coroner or medical examiner are required by law.

Except when required by law, an autopsy can be performed only after the next of kin's consent is obtained or when the deceased has donated his or her body for autopsy under the provisions of the Uniform Anatomical Gift Act. Students in medical school practice human dissection in the anatomy lab as one of their early tasks. For many, this is their first encounter with a human cadaver, and it is part of the "white coat" initiation that marks entry into the medical profession. Traditionally, such labs gave students little or no information about the cadavers they were assigned for dissection. The cadavers were given numbers, not names. Recently, some medical schools have been

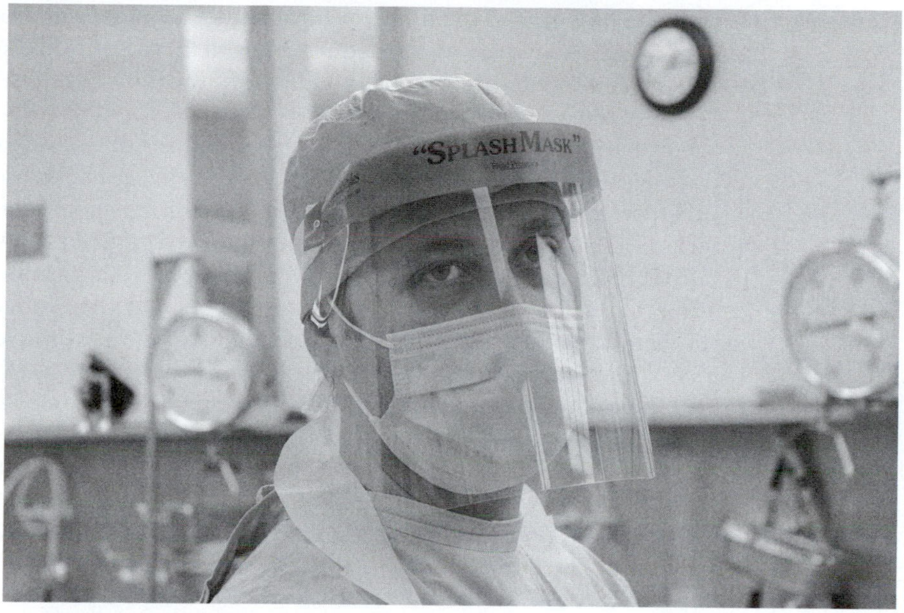

© David Rodriguez

When a coroner's preliminary investigation reveals the need to scientifically determine the cause of death, the corpse is brought to the morgue, where it is held until an autopsy can be performed.

The autopsy, or medical examination to determine the cause of death, is conducted under the coroner's direction when the circumstances of a death are violent, suspicious, or unexplained, or when a death is medically unattended and a doctor is unable to certify the cause of death. All homicides, accidents, and suicides come under the coroner's or medical examiner's jurisdiction.

© David Rodriguez

returning identity to the donors whose bodies are dissected. Videos of donors explaining their reasons for bequeathing their remains are shown, and students learn to view the human cadavers under their care not as anonymous cadavers but as their "first patients."[15]

Forensic techniques for identifying remains are used by the Army Central Identification Laboratory in Hawaii (CILHI) at Hickam Air Force Base, which is responsible for searching for, recovering, and identifying armed service members killed or listed as missing.[16] Organized into three sections, CILHI includes teams devoted to search and recovery, casualty data analysis, and scientific examination of physical evidence in the lab itself. In the lab, recovered remains and other evidence are examined by physical anthropologists and other experts.

Techniques for identifying human remains have become increasingly sophisticated, allowing positive identification to be made not only from fragments of hair or bone but also from DNA analysis based on relatively few cells. In 2003, when the space shuttle *Columbia* broke apart as it reentered Earth's atmosphere, search teams recovered remains from all seven astronauts and forwarded them to the Charles C. Carson Center for Mortuary Affairs at Dover Air Force Base in Delaware. Forensic analysis provided at the Carson Center also had been used to identify the remains of the *Challenger* astronauts in 1986 and the Pentagon victims of the September 2001 terrorist attack. Experts say that disasters such as the attack on the World Trade Center pushed the science of identification technologies to use new methods of chemical analysis and analytical software, enhancing their ability to identify burned or pulverized remains and to work with smaller biological samples of the genetic code that every human cell contains.[17]

In conclusively establishing cause of death, autopsies serve a number of important purposes in law and medicine (see Table 4-1). Physician John Lantos says, "Postmortem examinations have long been recognized as one of the best teaching tools in medicine. They are the final check on whether what we did and what we thought we ought to be doing were correct or whether we missed something."[18] Because autopsies are required in just a few circumstances,

TABLE 4-1 *Reasons for Autopsies*

1. Establish the cause of death
2. Assist in determining the mode of death (i.e., homicide, suicide, etc.)
3. Compare the premortem and postmortem findings
4. Produce accurate vital statistics
5. Monitor public health
6. Assess the quality of medical practice
7. Instruct medical students and physicians
8. Identify new and changing diseases
9. Evaluate the effectiveness of therapies such as drugs, surgical techniques, and prostheses
10. Reassure family members
11. Protect against false liability claims and settle valid claims quickly and fairly

however, many hospitals have discontinued autopsies or no longer have full autopsy facilities. This situation is despite the fact that studies show autopsy results contradicting presumed cause of death in about one-third to nearly half of cases.[19] Consider this figure in light of the fact that the autopsy rate at nonteaching hospitals averages less than 10 percent, and many hospitals have autopsy rates at or near 0 percent despite many deaths. The autopsy rate for deaths in nursing homes is apparently not known. The autopsy, says George Lundberg, editor of the *Journal of the American Medical Association,* is "apparently the victim of a vast cultural delusion of denial." For various reasons, it's as if the result voiced is "do not bother me with the truth." Lundberg says, "The autopsy remains the essence of modern clinical science. It is the one place where truth can be sought, found, and told without conflict of interest."[20]

Recently, private autopsy services have become available to conduct autopsies for a fee on behalf of hospitals and individual clients, many of whom are family members seeking information about hereditary diseases or who suspect malpractice and want evidence that may be obtained through an autopsy. With genetics being found to play a bigger role in a wider range of conditions, some experts believe that accurately knowing a family member's cause of death provides information that can potentially save lives.

Assessing Homicide

Community standards play a role in determining how an act of killing is assessed by a society and its legal-political-judicial system. *Homicide*—the killing of one human being by another—is separated into two categories, criminal and noncriminal, and each of these categories has further distinctions. For example, an act of homicide is considered excusable or justifiable when a person who kills another is found to have acted within certain legal rights, such as that of self-defense, or when the killing is judged an accident involving no gross negligence.

Justifiable homicide nearly doubled in the decade from 2000 to 2010. More individuals are killing other individuals and claiming self-defense, a trend most pronounced in states with "stand your ground" laws that grant more leeway for people to attack and even kill someone who is threatening them. A 2012 article in *The Wall Street Journal* pointed out that in about 60 percent of justifiable homicide cases where the relationship between killer and victim was known, the pair were strangers, a statistic that differs sharply from nonjustifiable homicide cases, where more than three-quarters of victims knew their killers.[21]

Thus, although a murder is necessarily a homicide, a homicide is not always a murder. The law has traditionally recognized two main distinctions within the category of *criminal* homicide: murder and manslaughter. Murder is associated with acts carried out with deliberate intention ("malice aforethought"), and the category of first-degree murder, or "capital murder" in some states, is used to designate killings that are carefully planned (e.g., murder for hire), involve multiple victims or police officers as victims, or take place in conjunction with other serious crimes. Manslaughter is defined as wrongful, unplanned killing done without express or implied malice.

State laws differ in how they distinguish various categories of manslaughter. The basic divide is between voluntary and involuntary manslaughter, although some states do not make this distinction. An example of *voluntary* manslaughter is that of a person who, after being provoked, kills another person in a fight. Such a person is said to have acted in the heat of passion without considering the consequences. When homicide results from criminal carelessness but is unintentional, it is termed an act of *involuntary* manslaughter, as in the case of a fatal automobile accident caused by reckless driving or a death caused by gross negligence. When alcohol is involved, the penalties can be stiff.

Some states that do not make the distinction between voluntary and involuntary combine them as "manslaughter" and add the category *criminally negligent* homicide—an act in which a person ought to have been aware of a substantial and unjustifiable risk of such nature and degree that it is a gross deviation from the standard of care that an ordinary person would have exercised.

In a study of more than three hundred killings that occurred in a major American city, it was found that more than half of the suspects were released before reaching trial.[22] To understand why some homicide cases are not brought to trial, it is necessary to look at how the circumstances of a homicidal act influence its investigation and how the judicial processes determine whether an accused killer is brought to trial.

The medical-legal investigation of an act of homicide generally includes three components: (1) an autopsy to determine the official cause of death; (2) a police investigation to ascertain the facts and gather evidence pertinent to the killing; and (3) various judicial and quasi-judicial procedures carried out by the district attorney's office and the court system to determine whether there is sufficient cause to bring a case to trial.

Fundamental to this investigation is the acknowledgment that homicide is an interpersonal act. That is, it involves a relationship between the killer and the victim: They may have had close domestic ties, have been members of the same family or otherwise related; they may have been friends or associates; or they may have been strangers. In the study referred to above, it was found that "the closer, or more intimate, the relationship is between a killer and his victim, the less likely it is that the killer will be severely punished for his act." In other words, killing a stranger was more likely to result in a stiff penalty than was killing a friend or family member.

The circumstances surrounding a killing, the relationship between the killer and the victim, and the killer's motivation and intention are all weighed to determine how an act of homicide is assessed within the judicial system. Basing its standards on cultural attitudes, the criminal justice system, including the police investigation, sets about the task of determining whether an act of homicide is lawful or unlawful. If it is lawful, the killer is released, and the case is closed. If it is unlawful, a further determination is made as to whether the killing in question was an act of murder, manslaughter, or negligent homicide—and there are various degrees of criminal intent within each of these categories as well. The following set of figures for the United States is instructive:[23]

- 22,000—Number of *criminal homicides* reported (murder and non-negligent manslaughter)
- 15,000—Number of *arrests* reported of persons charged with criminal homicide
- 13,500—Number of homicide cases *prosecuted* (about 90 percent of persons arrested)
- 10,000—Estimated number of homicide *convictions* (about two-thirds of those arrested and nearly three-fourths of those prosecuted)
- 2,000–4,000—Estimated number of *death-eligible defendants* convicted of first-degree murder because of "aggravating circumstances" on which a jury can impose a death sentence
- 300—Average number of *death sentences* imposed annually (about one-tenth of death-eligible defendants)
- 55—Average number of *executions* per year

What are the cultural assumptions by which an act of homicide is judged? Research shows that the legal outcome for a person who kills his wife's lover is quite different from the outcome for a person who combines killing with theft, robbery, or similar criminal acts. An extensive investigation conducted by the *Los Angeles Times* found that people who killed strangers were more

"First of all, you mislabelled this evidence. Second, it looks like you brought the victim in for questioning."

likely to get tough treatment from the criminal justice system than those who killed lovers, relatives, or other people they knew. One police investigator said that when "innocent victims, God-fearing people, end up murdered," other cases "take a back seat" because such killing causes neighborhood terror and therefore must be resolved quickly. However, he added, referring to gang shootings, "When 'Snoopy' kills 'Chilly Willie,' nobody cares."[24]

Society is usually reluctant to become involved in matters that fall within the domain of the family. This appears to be true even with family homicide involving a child victim. Situational elements within a family may result in penalties being imposed on the basis of statutes defining manslaughter or child abuse rather than murder.[25] There are exceptions, however, as in cases of mothers who intentionally kill their children.[26] Nevertheless, a close relationship is believed to involve its own set of mutual responsibilities and obligations—its own "code of justice"—that provides social sanctions for acts that occur within the relationship.

Killings that occur within the family unit or between persons who know one another tend to be viewed as less of a threat to society at large. In contrast, the killer who chooses a stranger as his victim overtly threatens the preservation of the social order. Thus, society devotes its attention to acts of homicide that threaten the preservation of law and order within the larger society.

Capital Punishment

In 2010, forty-six individuals were executed in the United States and, at year's end, about 3,200 were under sentence of death.[27] Most murderers who receive the death penalty are involved in intraracial offenses—that is, cases of whites killing whites or blacks killing blacks. In theory, capital punishment serves a twofold purpose: (1) It punishes the offender and (2) deters other potential offenders. "The theory of deterrence is based on the idea that criminal behavior can be deterred if punishment is swift, certain, and severe enough to counter the benefits or pleasure gained from committing crime."[28]

Although the death penalty has been applied to various offenses since ancient times, the argument is made that it is needlessly cruel and overrated as a deterrent to murder. According to Glenn Vernon,

> Investigations into the ineffectiveness of the death penalty as a deterrent to murder revealed that some murderers were so busy with other things during the events preceding the murder that they simply did not think of the death penalty, and that others were interacting with their victims in such an extremely emotional manner that the consequences of their murderous acts were not even taken into account.[29]

In the United States, most statutes require that a sentence of death be imposed only after evidence is submitted to establish that "aggravating," as opposed to "mitigating," factors were present in the crime. If aggravating factors are found, and the sentence is death, then the case is reviewed by an appellate court. Apart from certain crimes on which the Supreme Court has not ruled (the most notable being treason), the only capital crime (crime punishable with death) in the United States is murder.[30]

Is it inconsistent for society to try to prevent murder by itself engaging in killing? Does capital punishment reinforce the idea that violence solves problems? Citing evidence from psychology and behavioral therapy, which emphasizes the effects of positive reinforcement, Robert Kastenbaum and Ruth Aisenberg say that "there is little evidence to suggest that imposing massive punishment on one individual will 'improve' the behavior of others; on the contrary, it may reinforce hostile fantasies and murderous tendencies."[31] The greatest risk for a potential murderer, they contend, is not the risk of execution "but the risk of being killed by the police, the intended victim, or some bystander."

Yet another argument against capital punishment is the concern for the number of death-row inmates who have been released after evidence of their innocence has been discovered, some of them just days before their scheduled executions. Between 1973 and 2002, more than one hundred death-row inmates were released due to evidence of their innocence that came to light during their imprisonment.[32]

If capital punishment is not an effective deterrent to murder, are there other options? Comparing our present-day system with early Anglo-Saxon and English law and with many non-Western legal systems as well, Henry Lundsgaarde says, "Modern criminal law has completely transformed the ancient view of homicide as a wrong against a victim and his family to its modern version that views homicide as an offense against the state."[33] In short, the modern tendency is to view crime as a social problem. The separation of civil and criminal law—or, more specifically, the separation of personal obligation and criminal liability—eliminates the killer's liability to the *victim as person*. Instead, the violent act is viewed as having been committed against the public at large.

Defining Death

How death is defined and how a determination of death is made are significant matters for a death system to resolve. At first, the definition of death might seem obvious: A person dies, is dead, and the corpse is disposed of. But as soon as someone asks, "What do you mean by 'a person dies'?" this simple definition begins to unravel. Finding a reliable way to define death and to determine when it has occurred can become quite complex. Furthermore, as Allan Kellehear points out, "these problems are not simply biomedical in nature, but fundamentally shaped and driven by a series of important sociological influences."[34]

Think about how you would define *death*. When would you consider yourself to be dead? How would you know that death had occurred in someone else? The answers to these questions range from the definite ("when decay and putrefaction have set in") to the subtler ("when I can no longer take care of myself"). A person using the first method for making a determination of death would hardly be pleased to be judged dead by the standards of the second.

There are historical accounts of people being considered dead who, in fact, were in a condition that only mimicked biological death. As a safeguard

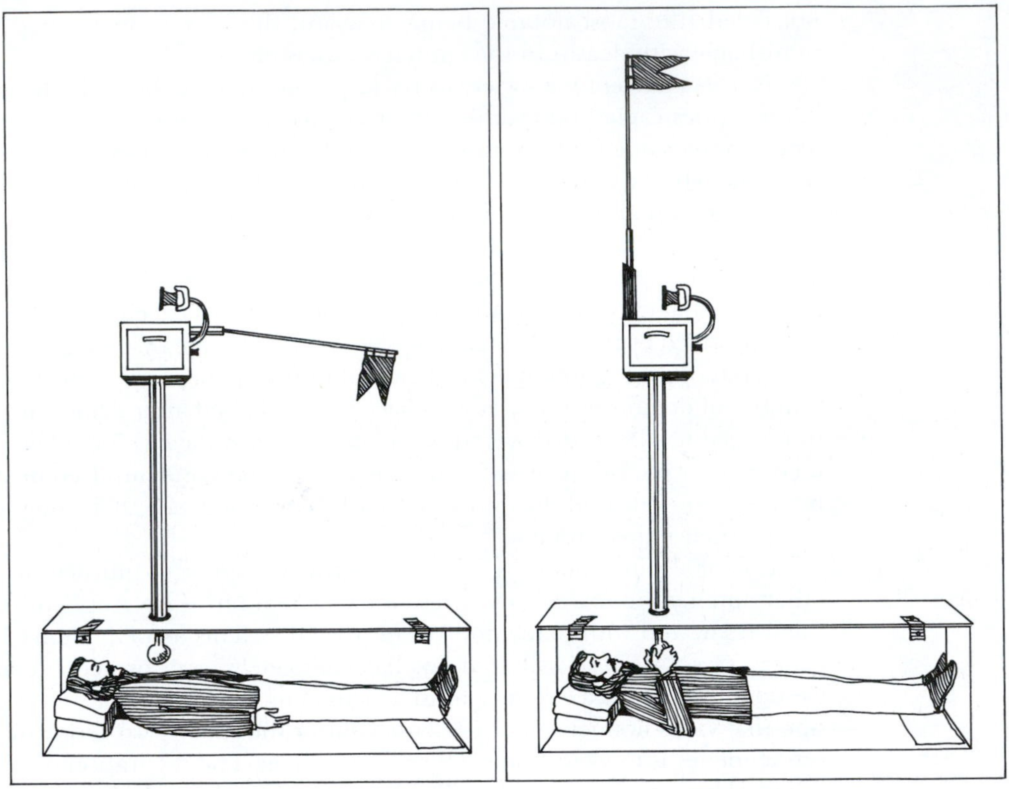

Figure 4-2 *Coffin Bell-Pull Device*
To prevent premature burial in cases of doubtful death, devices such as this French "life-preserving" coffin were invented and patented. If activated, the box above the ground opened to let in air and light, the flag rose, a bell rang, and a light came on to signal that the buried person was still alive. The person who had been mistaken for dead could also call out, and his or her voice would be amplified by the device. The fear of being buried alive stemmed from the period of great plagues and epidemics when, in the hasty disposition of the dead, a mistaken determination of death might result from a state of illness that only mimicked death.

against the threat of being buried alive, in earlier times some people arranged for their bodies to be placed in coffins with bells or some other attention-getting device that the "corpse" could activate after burial should consciousness return after a mistaken determination of death (see Figure 4-2).

The present concern with defining death is, of course, more sophisticated and draws upon scientific data. Yet, even though it is possible to determine when death has occurred by observing certain signs that life has ceased, these signs may be interpreted differently depending on how death is defined. In other words, the way we define death establishes the criteria that are used to determine that a person has died. Five steps can be distinguished in the process of making decisions about the death of a human being:[35]

1. Establish a conceptual understanding of what constitutes death—that is, a definition of death.
2. Decide upon the criteria and procedures that will be used in making a determination that death has occurred.
3. Apply these criteria and procedures *in a particular case* to determine if a person's condition meets the criteria.
4. If the criteria are met, the person is *pronounced dead.*
5. Attest the person's death on *a certificate of record.*

Conventional Signs of Death and New Technology

Historically, the death of the human organism has been determined by the absence of heartbeat and breathing. Most deaths are still determined by the absence of these vital signs. However, when respirators, ventilators, and other life-support systems are used to artificially sustain vital physiological processes, conventional means of determining death by absence of heartbeat and breathing are inadequate. Someone using the conventional vital signs of heartbeat and breathing could declare a patient with permanent loss of brain function "alive" on the basis of *artificially* maintained cardiopulmonary functions.

A number of years ago, before all the discussion about defining brain death and maintaining life on a respirator and so on, a patient of mine, a young pregnant woman at term, suddenly developed extremely high blood pressure. Then she had a stroke and the baby's heartbeat stopped, so we supported her by artificially maintaining blood pressure and other vital functions, including breathing. But she had a complete brain death immediately. And she had lost the baby. We got an EEG [electroencephalogram], and it was completely flat. We repeated it twenty-four hours later, and again it was completely flat.

It was the worst tragedy I've ever seen, because in just a few minutes she was gone and the baby was gone—just within moments. I talked with her husband, her mother, and her father. (Now, this was long before the issues surrounding definition of death had become so contentious that the lawyers got involved.) I told them that the thing to do was turn off the machine. Just as I had not read about all this, they as a family had not read about it. It seemed quite logical to me.

So we picked a time when we were going to do it, and they all came and waited outside the door. I told them again what I was going to do, and they said to go ahead and do it. I went in and turned off the machine. The nurse and I watched her, and in five minutes her pulse rate had stopped. I think this is the proper way to handle this sort of situation when brain death is involved. I think it has a negative effect to continue life support systems for weeks and months. It was a tragedy, and given the tragedy, what options do you have? Continue the life support system or don't continue it. To me, there's no argument whatsoever to continue the life support system.

Quoted from *Death and Dying: The Physician's Perspective,*
a videotape by Elizabeth Bradbury

Therefore, the concept of *brain death* was created as a means of determining whether a person is alive or dead when conventional vital signs are ambiguous because of supportive medical technology. (When brain death occurs, brain stem functions—including spontaneous breathing—are lost, but heartbeat and other vegetative functions related to internal homeostasis can continue because these functions are not completely dependent on the integrity of the brain stem.)[36] Rather than replacing the conventional clinical criteria for determining death—pulse, heartbeat, and respiration—the criteria for brain death supplement them.

However, brain death has been called "an imprecise term." In 2007 testimony before the President's Council on Bioethics, Alan Shewman said, "Contrary to popular belief, brain death is not a settled issue." He pointed to a number of issues indicating "conceptual confusion underlying the superficial consensus."[37] We discuss some of these issues later in this chapter.

In contrast to *clinical death,* a determination of death made according to accepted medical criteria (either the cessation of heartbeat and breathing or the criteria for establishing brain death), *cellular death* refers to a process that results when heartbeat, respiration, and brain activity cease. In this sense, "the process of death is a gradual event where organs and cells die at different rates depending on their resistance to the lack of oxygen."[38]

When a person's breathing and heartbeat are stopped temporarily, as occurs during certain surgical procedures, people sometimes say that the person was "clinically dead" for a period of time. However, such language is imprecise when the cessation of vital functions is reversible.

Cellular death encompasses the breakdown of metabolic processes and results in complete nonfunctionality. Thus, in this sense, the definition of death is "we die because our cells die."[39] Living cells require a continuous input of energy; without it, they degrade into a nonliving collection of molecules. Cellular death is an irreversible process of deterioration in the body's systems and organs. Without oxygen, cells vary in their survival potential. The cells of skin and connective tissues may survive for several hours; the neurons of the brain last only five to eight minutes. When there is a loss of neurons in the midbrain and medulla, the brain center that controls breathing is destroyed; the death of neurons in the cerebral cortex destroys intellectual capacity. The breakdown of metabolic processes, the sum of which is life, causes a loss of organic functions—that is, death. As the cells and tissues of the body die, advanced signs of death become evident: the lack of certain reflexes in the eyes, the fall of body temperature (*algor mortis*), the purple-red discoloration of parts of the body as blood settles (*livor mortis*), and the rigidity of muscles (*rigor mortis*). In a biological sense, death can be defined as the cessation of life due to irreversible changes in cell metabolism. Following these signs, putrefaction and decomposition continue as the corpse is reduced to simpler forms of matter, accompanied by a strong, unpleasant odor. Rarely, a *cadaveric spasm* occurs in which muscular stiffening takes place that crystallizes the last action one did prior to death (e.g., holding a knife tightly); this can be significant in forensic investigations.

> Life is fundamentally based on the maintenance of individual and collective cell function, dependent on the provision of nutrients and oxygen. Cell biology has demonstrated that a layer of human cells, separated from the human organism, may be grown in laboratory culture as long as they are bathed in a sterile supply of nutrients and oxygen. The human being, a complex arrangement of trillions of cells organized into organ systems, requires a cardiopulmonary delivery system (lung, heart, and circulatory system) for oxygen and nutrients to reach the cells. The development and evolution of modern cardiopulmonary resuscitation evolving into cardiopulmonary support technologies have been important advances informing our concepts of life and death.
>
> Sam D. Shemie

Medical technologies make it possible to manipulate the dying process in such a way that some parts of the body stop functioning while other parts can be artificially maintained. Thus, cell death may affect some organs of the body, causing irreversible breakdown, while other organs of the body are still functioning. The capacity of modern medicine to alter the natural sequence and process of cellular death has created a need to rethink how death is defined and institute new procedures for determining when death has occurred.

Conceptual and Empirical Criteria

What is death? How can we determine that a person has died? These questions, though closely related, involve separate issues that must be distinguished. Medical ethicist Robert Veatch outlines four levels that must be addressed in our inquiry concerning the definition and determination of death.[40] The first level involves formally defining *death*. Essentially, this is a conceptual or philosophical endeavor. According to Veatch, "Death means a complete change in the status of a living entity characterized by the irreversible loss of those characteristics that are essentially significant to it." Although this definition may sound rather abstract on first reading, it is really quite precise. It encompasses the deaths not only of human beings but also of nonhuman animals, plants, and cells and indeed can even be understood metaphorically as applying to social phenomena, such as the organization of societies or cultures.

To flesh out this definition, we must turn to Veatch's second level of inquiry, again a conceptual or philosophical question: What is so essentially *significant* about life that its loss is termed *death?* Some possible answers include the flow of vital bodily fluids (breath and blood, for example), the soul, and, in more recent definitions, consciousness. Each of these possible answers is examined more closely in the next section.

The third level that Veatch distinguishes has to do with the *locus* of death: Where in the organism should one look to determine whether death has occurred? This question moves us from the conceptual realm to an empirical

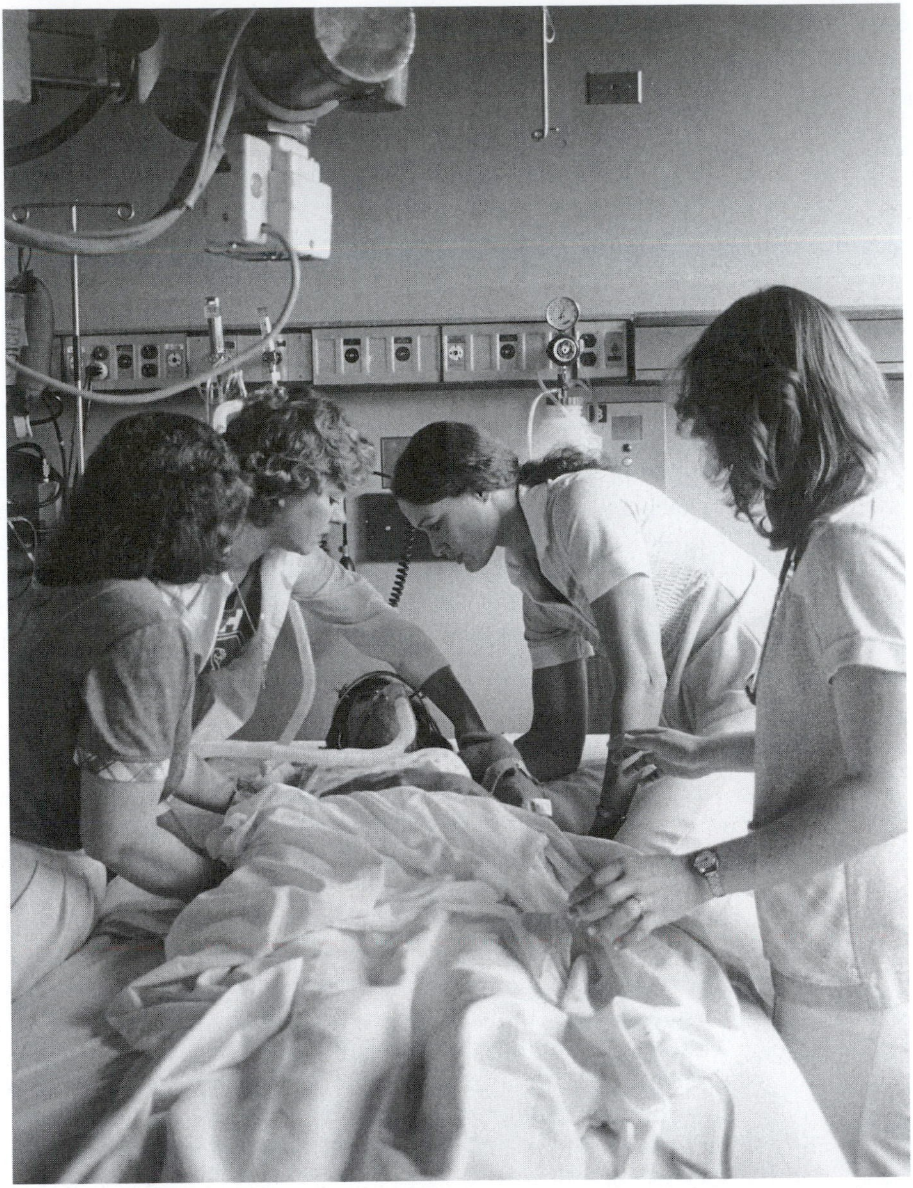

© Mark Tuschman

How death is determined—that is, the criteria used to establish the difference between life and death—depends on how death is defined. What is it about life that makes its absence signify death? What signs should be used to make this determination? Questions about the meaning of life and death are important to caregivers as well as patients who occupy hospital intensive-care units.

inquiry—that is, one based on observation or experience. Notice, however, that the answer to this question depends on the conceptual understanding used to define death.

Veatch's fourth level deals with the following question: What technical tests must be applied at the locus of death to determine if an individual is living or dead?

So, to recap these levels of inquiry: Step one involves formally defining death. Step two adds further content to the definition by pinpointing the significant difference between life and death. Step three locates where one should look for signs of this significant change. And step four gives us some tests, or a set of criteria, that can be used to determine whether an organism is alive or dead. With this process in mind, we now have the tools to examine four different approaches to the definition and determination of death.

Four Approaches to the Definition and Determination of Death

All four of the following approaches to defining and determining death begin with the formal definition of death given earlier by Veatch. From that shared beginning, each approach finds its particular way through subsequent levels of inquiry. As you'll see, each of these approaches relates death to a loss: the first, of the flow of vital fluids; the second, of the soul by the body; the third, of the capacity for bodily integration; the fourth, of the capacity for social interaction. In considering the merits of the various approaches, notice how death is determined according to the way it is defined.

Irreversible Loss of Flow of Vital Fluids

The first approach focuses on the cessation of the flow of vital bodily fluids. With this conceptual understanding of death, one looks to the heart, blood vessels, lungs, and respiratory tract as the locus of death. To determine whether an individual is alive or dead, one would observe the breathing, feel the pulse, and listen to the heartbeat. In addition to these conventional tests, we can include the modern methods of electrocardiogram and direct measurement of oxygen and carbon dioxide levels in the blood because they focus on the same loci and criteria for determining death.

This approach to defining death is adequate for making a determination of death in most cases, even today. When vital functions are artificially sustained by machines, however, no clear determination of death can be made by this definition. Consider, for example, a patient connected to a heart-lung machine that keeps the vital fluids of blood and breath flowing through the body. According to this definition, the patient is alive. If the patient is disconnected from the machine, these vital functions cease, and by this definition the patient is dead.

Thus, the ambiguity of this first approach results from defining death on the basis of physiological criteria that, although intimately related to life processes, do not appear to constitute the most significant criteria for identifying human life.

Irreversible Loss of the Soul from the Body

In the second approach to defining death—one used in many cultures worldwide and from time immemorial—the criterion is the presence or

Knowing What a Human Being Is

Rolling Thunder often repeated, "We do so many unnatural things, we don't know what's natural anymore." One day he and I were sitting on the ground out in the desert. He was describing a young Indian apprentice from another tribe and making designs in the sand with a stick. Suddenly he said, "You people don't even know what a human being is!" I did not see the connection between the subject at hand and that sudden exclamation, but I had learned to understand what he meant by "you people." It was not a judgmental finger-pointing to be taken personally, but a sort of generalized identification to be applied wherever it fit. "You can look right at someone's empty body and think that you're lookin' at the person when they're not even there. Time and time again, you people speed to the scene of an accident, pick up an empty body and take it down the highway at eighty miles an hour, leaving the person miles behind, not knowing what the heck is going on!"

As an example, he then described to me an episode in which he went into the hospital to assist a young lady—a friend of friends—who had been in a head-on collision and was a long time in a coma.

"But the moment I took a good look at the body, I could see she wasn't even there. I had to find her—go get her—and she was way out in the field where the car'd flipped over the cliff, and she was sittin' on a rock. Her friend who was driving was killed. And this one sittin' on the rock, she didn't even know where she was. But, boy, she was determined to stay there. She was totally disoriented. I had to pull her, nearly force her back. Only time we can do that is when we know their own will isn't working—otherwise we always leave it up to their own choice.

"Well, in the early days, most everyone could tell when a person wasn't in their body. That was just natural to see that. That's been lost now, mostly. Only thing I can say is, until you learn to understand these things, you should never, never move an unconscious body. Unconscious means the person is not in there. So treat the body on the scene and never, never move it. Not until you learn how. People can't find their own way back to the body—not when they've been pulled loose that way by some accident or something. Time and time again, traumatized people get abandoned that way. Time and time again, people die in a coma because of that."

Quoted in Doug Boyd, *Mystics, Magicians, and Medicine People: Tales of a Wanderer*

absence of the soul in the body. Within this framework, as long as the soul is present, the person is alive; when the soul leaves, the body dies. Some religious traditions define death in precisely this way.

The locus of the soul has not been scientifically established (nor has its existence), although some believe the soul is related to the breath or the heart or, perhaps, as seventeenth-century philosopher René Descartes believed, to the pineal body, a small protrusion from the center of the brain. For those who hold this concept, the criteria for determining death would presumably involve some means of ascertaining death at the particular locus where the soul is thought to reside. In a study done in 1907, dying people were placed on a sensitive scale to determine whether any weight loss occurred at the moment of death. Researchers noted a loss averaging from one to two ounces, which led to speculations about whether the loss indicated the departure of the soul from the body at death.[41]

To people living in modern societies, this approach to defining death seems irrelevant. Our first difficulty would be to adequately define the soul. Even if this difficulty could be overcome, we would need some way to ascertain whether the soul was present or absent at a given time. Moreover, this definition of death forces an examination of whether death occurs because the soul departs from the body or, conversely, whether the soul departs from the body because death has occurred. In other words, does the soul "animate" the body, giving it life, or do the physiological processes of vitality in the body provide a vessel wherein the soul resides? Such questions may lead to fascinating speculations, but they do little to solve the dilemmas posed by medical practice in a scientific age.

Irreversible Loss of the Capacity for Bodily Integration

In the third approach, death is defined as the irreversible loss of the capacity for bodily integration. That is, "an organism dies when it loses the power to preserve and sustain its self-organizing organization permanently and irreversibly"; in other words, "death is the loss of syntropic capacity or ability."[42] This approach is more sophisticated than the first because it refers not just to the conventional physiological signs of vitality in the body (the flow of breath and blood) but also to the more generalized capability of the body to regulate its own functioning. The approach recognizes the fact that a human being is an integrated organism with capacities for internal regulation through complex homeostatic feedback mechanisms.

This definition at least partly resolves the ambiguity of the first definition because a determination of death would not be made merely because a person's physiological functioning was being maintained by a machine. Rather, a determination of death would be made when the organism no longer had the capacity for bodily integration. The locus for such a determination is currently considered to be the central nervous system—more specifically, the brain. The determination of death that results from this definition is often characterized as brain death (although this term is potentially misleading because it focuses attention on the death of part of the organism, not the whole organism).

According to standards published in 1968 by the Harvard Medical School Ad Hoc Committee to Examine the Definition of Brain Death, brain death involves four essential criteria:[43]

1. Lack of receptivity and response to external stimuli
2. Absence of spontaneous muscular movement and spontaneous breathing
3. Absence of observable reflexes, including brain and spinal reflexes
4. Absence of brain activity, as signified by a flat electroencephalogram (EEG)

The Harvard criteria require a second set of tests to be performed after twenty-four hours have elapsed, and they exclude cases of hypothermia (body temperature below 90 degrees Fahrenheit) as well as situations involving central nervous system depressants, such as barbiturates. After the Harvard definition of brain death, heart-beating brain-dead donors (HBDD) became the major source of transplantable organs, and such donors remain the major source of transplantable organs worldwide.[44]

In 2010, the American Academy of Neurology published an updated guideline on determining brain death to provide more clarity.[45] According to the guideline, there are three signs that a person's brain has permanently stopped functioning. First, the person is comatose and the cause of the coma is known. Second, all brain stem reflexes have permanently stopped working. Third, breathing has permanently stopped. A ventilator, or breathing machine, is needed to keep the body functioning. Further, the guideline concludes that tests such as EEG or cerebral flow studies are not needed for a diagnosis of brain death.

Allan Kellehear observes, "The Harvard deliberations were historically significant because the formulations of brain death developed by their ad hoc committee established the basic criteria from which all subsequent revisions and debates have derived."[46] Procedures for applying these criteria, which have become known as the "whole-brain" definition of death, have been widely adopted when conventional means of determining death are not conclusive. However, over the years, not all experts believe these criteria are unassailable.[47] Some ethicists argue that the clinical tests currently used to determine brain death do not actually satisfy all of the criteria; specifically, varying degrees and kinds of brain function have been found in some individuals pronounced brain dead according to the standard tests. This finding suggests that the tests may not always suffice to show "permanent cessation of functioning of the entire brain." Furthermore, "the tests for brain death are about as good as the operators in charge of the tests and the people interpreting them."[48]

In light of these objections to "brain death" standards, some experts advocate returning to cardiorespiratory criteria as the definition of death. "In medical practice and law, the separation between being alive and being dead should not be ambiguous."[49] However, simply abandoning current methods of determining brain death could create problems because organ transplantation would likely be characterized as a kind of legally sanctioned killing.

Irreversible Loss of the Capacity for Consciousness or Social Interaction

Although the Harvard criteria are widely accepted in clinical settings, some people believe that they fail to specify what is *significant* about human life. Veatch, for example, says that it is the higher functions of the brain—not merely reflex networks that regulate such physiological processes as blood pressure and respiration—that define the essential characteristics of a human being. Thus, the fourth approach to defining death emphasizes the capacity for consciousness and social interaction. The premise of this approach is that,

> Failure to accept clinical definitions of brain death in all its different versions, by the general public or families, is often attributed to their "confusion" about what death actually "looks" like.
>
> Brain dead patients look alive—they are pink and breathing; they sometimes respond to surgical incision with elevated blood pressure and respiration; they are capable of reproduction; they develop bedsores and pneumonia, something that cadavers don't do; and they move in their beds, mimicking restlessness, and grasping at deliberate or accidental stimuli. This is not "confusion," "misapprehension," or "misconceptions" by the general public about those who are brain dead. By most *social* criteria, the brain dead do appear alive.
>
> Allan Kellehear

for a person to be truly human, not only must certain biological processes function, but the social dimension of life—consciousness or personhood—must also be present. Being alive implies a capacity for conscious interaction with one's environment and with other human beings. Therefore, according to this definition, death is determined by the irreversible loss of the capacity for social interaction. The death of a *person* is synonymous with the death of a human being.

Using this approach, where should we look to determine whether an individual is alive or dead? Current scientific evidence points to the neocortex, the outer surface of the brain, where processes essential to consciousness and social interaction are located. In this case, the EEG alone would provide an adequate measure for determining death.

In the debate about how death should be defined, this fourth approach is known as a "higher-brain" theory, which contrasts with the "whole-brain" theory discussed earlier. Karen Gervais represents the higher-brain approach when she writes, "It is loss of consciousness and not loss of biological functioning that should determine when human life is over."[50] Furthermore, she says, "By emphasizing the brain's integrating role in the human organism, the whole-brain theory of death reduces to a lower-brain theory of death." In commenting on the search for a more precise definition of human death, Gervais concludes that we are confronted with a basic choice about the definition of human life—namely, whether we consider a human being as an *organism* or as a *person*.

The current whole-brain definition of death, says Robert Veatch, establishes a view of what is *essential* to being alive that is not shared by all ethnic or religious groups.[51] He argues that, rather than imposing one approach on everyone, the right to "opt out" could be made available to individuals whose beliefs about how to define the death of a human being are in conflict with the whole-brain approach of the Harvard criteria. Although these criteria have been an accepted part of medical practice for more than four decades, questions about defining death are not yet fully resolved.

The Uniform Determination of Death Act

The definition of death touches upon many aspects of our lives. Criminal prosecution, inheritance, taxation, treatment of the corpse, and mourning are all affected by the way society "draws the dividing line between life and death."[52] After publication of the criteria for establishing brain death in 1968, public and legislative discussion began to take place about the need to revise the legal definition of death so as to reflect medical realities.

Finally, in the early 1980s, a presidential commission drafted a model statute that met with broad acceptance and eventually led to uniform laws throughout the United States: the Uniform Determination of Death Act (see Figure 4-3). The President's Commission for the Study of Ethical Problems in Medicine said that the Uniform Determination of Death Act "addresses the matter of 'defining' death at the level of general physiological standards rather than at the level of more abstract concepts or the level of more precise criteria and tests" because such standards and criteria change over time as knowledge and techniques are refined.[53]

To avoid obsolescence as technology advances, the Act does not specify an exact means of diagnosing death. The Act acknowledges that, in most cases, irreversible circulatory and respiratory cessation provides an obvious and sufficient basis for making a determination of death. In other words, these cases permit death to be diagnosed on the basis that breathing and blood flow have stopped and cannot be restored. Thus, if a patient is not being supported on a respirator, there is no need to evaluate brain function before making a determination of death.

The commission said that a statutory definition of death should be separate and distinct from any provisions concerning organ donation. In contrast to earlier proposals, which stated that a person would be "considered dead" when their stated criteria were met, the language of the Uniform Determination of Death Act is clearer and more direct. It states that a person who meets the standards set forth in the law "is dead."

Confusion about the definition of death had arisen, the commission said, "because the same technology not only keeps heart and lungs functioning in some who have irretrievably lost all brain functions, but also sustains other,

---

Uniform Determination of Death Act

1. [*Determination of Death.*] An individual who has sustained either (1) irreversible cessation of circulatory and respiratory functions, or (2) irreversible cessation of all functions of the entire brain, including the brain stem, is dead. A determination of death must be made in accordance with accepted medical standards.
2. [*Uniformity of Construction and Application.*] This Act shall be applied and construed to effectuate its general purpose to make uniform the law with respect to the subject of this Act among states enacting it.

Figure 4-3 *Uniform Determination of Death Act*

less severely injured patients." The result is a "blurring of the important distinction between patients who are *dead* and those who are or may be *dying*." The commission concluded that "proof of an irreversible absence of functions in the entire brain, including the brain stem, provides a highly reliable means of declaring death for respirator-maintained bodies." The commission noted that the Harvard Committee's definition of brain death had been reliable and that "no case has yet been found that met these criteria and regained any brain functions despite continuation of respirator support."

Death is an absolute and single phenomenon, the commission said, arguing that it would radically change the meaning of death to expand the definition of death to include persons who have lost all cognitive functions but are still able to breathe spontaneously. When brain-stem functions remain—for example, when respiration occurs naturally but there is no cognitive awareness—the patient's condition is described as a "persistent vegetative state" (discussed in Chapter 6). Sustained by medical and nursing care, including artificial feeding and antibiotics to fight recurrent infections, such patients may survive for years without a respirator. (The longest such survival, according to the commission's report, was over thirty-seven years.)

The commission cited the nearly universal acceptance of the "whole-brain" concept by both the medical community and the general public. A higher-brain formulation, which would require agreement about the meaning of personhood, does not enjoy such consensus. At the present level of understanding and technique, the commission said, "The 'higher brain' may well exist only as a metaphorical concept, not in reality." In summing up the work of the President's Commission for the Study of Ethical Problems in Medicine, Albert Jonsen says that it "brought conceptual clarity to a confused issue and helped to make good law."[54]

Because guidelines for diagnosing brain death are implemented at the level of the hospital, however, there is wide variability in practice. This can result in differences that are important for determination of death and initiation of transplant procedures. With an increasing number of non-heart-beating donors (NHBD), some doctors believe

> we should move away from an unattainable certification of biological death as the *sine qua non* for organ donation; we should openly admit that NHBD death cannot be defined at a time when organ retrieval is possible and that all we are able to define are socially, morally, and scientifically acceptable criteria for organ donation.[55]

Others suggest more radical alternatives, "deeming it reasonable and feasible to remove organs for transplantation . . . when the patient is either permanently unconscious or when death is imminent."[56] Kellehear says,

> The problem of death is not only a simple technical problem of the brain and its workings but also about how experiences of mortality are mediated by social understandings of death and dying. . . . This means understanding death and dying at the place where biology and biography meet at their intersections with society and history.[57]

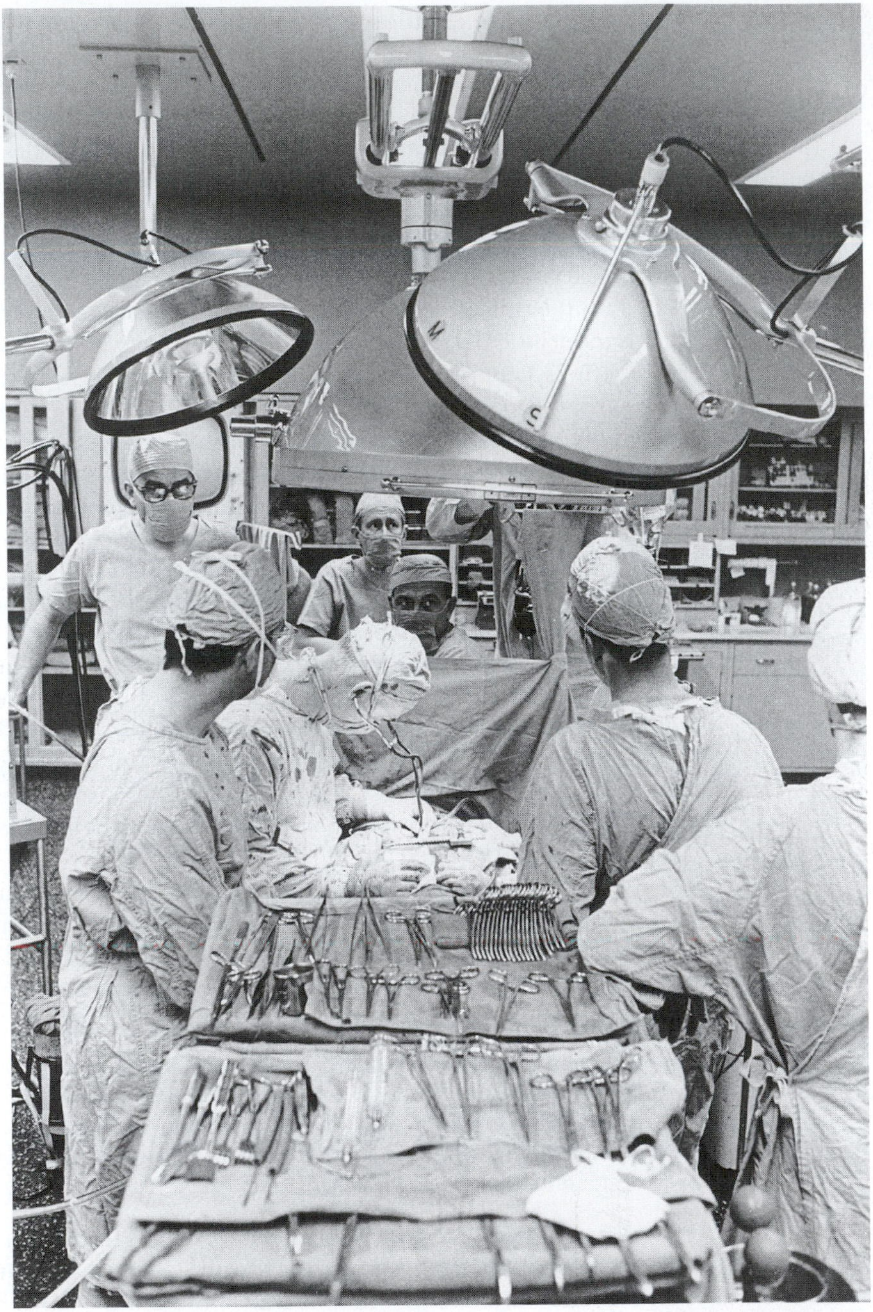

In 1968, at Stanford University Medical Center, Dr. Norman Shumway performed the first successful human heart transplant in the United States. "The father of heart transplantation," Shumway was known as a reticent man who did not like to tout his many accomplishments. Advances in transplantation procedures and related medical therapies make such operations more feasible, yet they also raise questions that are difficult, at times painful, to resolve.

Organ Transplantation and Organ Donation

Of all the innovative medical techniques for saving the lives of patients who were once considered hopelessly ill, perhaps the most dramatic is *organ transplantation,* which is defined as "the transfer of living tissues or cells from a donor to a recipient, with the intention of maintaining the functional integrity of the transplanted tissue in the recipient."[58] Since the day in 1954 when the first kidney transplant, from one identical twin to another, was performed at Peter Bent Brigham Hospital in Boston, organ transplantation has evolved to become part of standard medical practice. In 1967, public interest was heightened as Christiaan Barnard accomplished the first successful adult heart transplant. Other noteworthy events in the history of transplantation include widespread agreement on the definition of brain death in 1968 and discovery of the immunosuppressive drug cyclosporine in 1976.[59] In 2012, the first "breathing lung" transplant was performed in the United States, with the help of an experimental organ-preserving device known as the Organ Care System, which keeps donor lungs "breathing" in a near-physiologic state outside the body during transport.[60] The success of organ transplantation is due largely to such factors as newer immunosuppressants, better patient selection, and earlier intervention, as well as better understanding of the issues related to histocompatibility, the ability of tissues to accept a transplant from a different individual without rejecting it. The growing number of patients on waiting lists for transplants involving the heart, kidney, liver, pancreas, and lung is indicative of the widespread public acceptance of transplantation.

The ideal candidate for a transplant is a patient whose condition is deteriorating despite the best conventional medical treatment available and for whom a transplant offers a reasonable likelihood of recovery. For some transplants, most often a kidney, the donor is a living person; sometimes donor and recipient are members of the same family. When a living donor is unavailable, or when the needed organ (a heart, for example) cannot be taken from a living human being, the organ can be removed from the body of a person who has been declared dead and whose organs are kept viable for transplantation by artificially sustaining physiological functions. About three of every four organs that are transplanted are recovered from deceased donors.[61]

These donors are declared dead by the criteria of either (1) *cardiac death*—that is, death declared on the basis of cardiopulmonary criteria (irreversible cessation of circulatory and respiratory function) or (2) *brain death* (irreversible loss of all functions of the entire brain, including the brain stem). According to the "dead donor rule," organ donation should not hasten or cause death. "As currently practiced, donation after cardiac death raises more concerns than donation after brain death" because the process is more complex and "the potential donor is not dead when life-sustaining measures cease."[62] The intervals between withdrawing care, pronouncing death, and recovering organs are very brief. One professor of medicine said, "The end-of-life experience is changed because organ procurement begins immediately after death has occurred."[63]

Although organ donation is viewed by advocates as offering families "a way to find meaning in the death," David Meagher reports bereaved family members saying that they cannot recall the moment when consent for donation was obtained; in only a small percentage of cases were organ donations discussed before the death. In short, "Family members or others responsible for making donation decisions have reported confusion and uncertainty around the moment of the request," with the result that "family members felt superfluous and ignored afterward."[64]

The Uniform Anatomical Gift Act (UAGA), approved in 1968 by the National Conference of Commissions on Uniform State Laws and enacted in some form in all fifty states, provides for the donation of the body or specific body parts upon the death of the donor. Because of the shortage of donated organs, the Act was revised in 1987 and again in 2006 to simplify organ donation. The Uniform Anatomical Gift Act covers such matters as how anatomical gifts can be made and provides a list of individuals who can authorize organ donation in the absence of donation arrangements made before death. The 2006 revision strengthens prior language barring others from attempting to override an individual's decision to make or refuse to make an anatomical gift. Hospitals are required to have procedures in place that encourage donations. The 2006 revision modified the Act "to permit the use of life support systems at or near death for the purpose of maximizing procurement of organs medically suitable for transplantation."[65]

Some observers note that the primary intent of the 2006 revision was to solve the organ shortage problem. They point out that this creates a potential for conflict with care at the end of life in that it prioritizes care of donor organs over care and comfort of the dying person. Similarly, other physicians and ethicists are emphatic that "care of dying patients takes precedence over organs."[66] It is also argued that "the traditional concepts of life and death are simply inadequate in the settings in which we have to make decisions, in the face of the continuing progress of resuscitation techniques, and the social needs represented by modern transplant medicine."[67]

Margaret Lock calls attention to several reasons for the "growing shortage" of organs: First, there are fewer deaths from car accidents than was the case just a few decades ago, because of better automobile safety devices. Second, trauma units are more effective than they once were in keeping patients with severe head injuries from becoming brain dead. Third, with a rapidly aging population the potential donor pool has decreased. Another factor that contributes to the impression of shortage is the increasing number of patients deemed eligible for transplants, ranging from infants to the elderly and including patients with comorbidities (that is, other medical conditions). Finally, second or third transplants are now routinely done when earlier ones fail. "In other words," Lock says, "the transplant world has broadened its sights and has itself created an increased 'need' for organs at a time when there are many fewer potential donors."[68]

Because not enough organs are donated to meet demand, physicians and organ procurement agencies must function as gatekeepers in choosing

© Don Wright, *The Miami News*

among prospective recipients. For example, many transplant centers will not accept people without insurance or those over age 75. What criteria should be used to allocate organs? Should it be the urgency of the patient's need? Or should it be efficacy, the likelihood of a beneficial result? Every day, with over 100,000 people on the waiting list, about a dozen people die because not enough organs are available.[69] In 1984, the U.S. Congress enacted the National Organ Transplant Act, which instituted a central office to help match donated organs with potential recipients.

The United Network for Organ Sharing (UNOS) operates the Organ Procurement and Transplantation Network (OPTN) under contract with the federal government. The networks are collectively known as OPTN/UNOS, and they maintain lists of people waiting for transplants and track the status of donated organs, with the goal of ensuring both the fairness of distribution and the competence of medical centers where organ transplants are performed.

Advocates of organ transplantation conduct public information campaigns to educate people about the benefits of organ donation and to encourage more individuals to donate.[70] Some potential recipients of organs advertise their need on billboards, in newspapers, or on personal Web sites, hoping a sympathetic person will make a *directed donation* naming them as the specific recipient.[71] Web sites (such as MatchingDonors.com) help donors and recipients find each other so that a directed donation can be made. Patients also increase their chances of obtaining a transplant by enrolling at more than one transplant center—a practice known as multiple listing. Each of these evaluations and enrollments can cost tens of thousands of dollars.[72] The current system favors patients with the means to rush to geographic areas where there is less competition for organs. For example, computer executive Steve Jobs flew in his personal jet from California, with one of the longest transplant lists, to Memphis, where the wait list was shorter, to receive a liver transplant in 2009.[73]

Because so many patients are on waiting lists for organs, and because waiting lists are growing faster than the supply of organs, questions have been raised about the effectiveness of the voluntary approach to organ donation. Some people suggest that donating one's organs after death is a moral duty, and therefore organ donation should be *required* except when a person intentionally "opts out" by signing a refusal to donate. This approach is known as *presumed consent.* Although it has not been tried in the United States, a number of European countries have enacted laws creating presumed consent, or what some call "default to donation." The main ethical objection is a perceived loss of personal autonomy—the belief that it is wrong to take someone's organs without that person's explicit consent.

Many people who have donor cards do not understand why anyone would be reluctant to donate: "To me, it's obvious. If you're not using your organs, let somebody else have them." What prevents people from donating their organs? Research has found that knowledge and attitudes, both of which are cognitive variables, are weak predictors of donor card status. More influential are noncognitive variables, which include a variety of "ick factors" related to posthumous mutilation, respect for the dead, and disgust or squeamishness about having one's organs inside another person; "jinx factors" related to anxieties or superstitions about misfortune that could result from signing a donor card; medical mistrust and skepticism about premature declaration of death; and concerns about body integrity, or the need to maintain the integrity of the body after death lest one face serious afterlife consequences.[74] Native Americans, among others, may hold a belief that one must have all body parts upon death, as a "whole body is needed in the afterlife."[75]

Questions about organ donation ultimately come down to personal values and particular views about the nature of the human body and the way it is perceived. Among the main views are these:[76]

1. *The body as machine.* A mechanistic view of the body, in which organs are "extracted," "salvaged," and "replaced."
2. *The body as an ecological resource.* A form of recycling within the global biomass, in which organs are "harvested," "retrieved," or "recovered."
3. *The body as a potential gift.* A view that emphasizes ownership, in which organs are "donated," "gifted," and "received."
4. *The body as a commodity.* The body as a profitable resource from which organs are "procured" and possibly bought and sold.

Because a human body is a valuable resource, the suggestion has been put forward to make commerce in human organs legal.[77] Under the provisions of the National Organ Transplant Act, it is currently illegal to buy or sell human organs and tissues (except blood). If this were changed, a person's heirs might earn money through selling the deceased's vital organs. Some

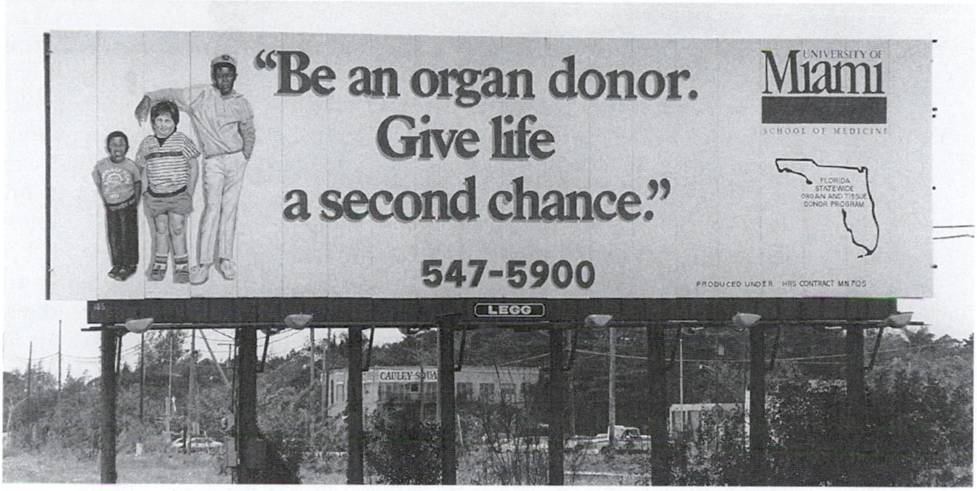

© Albert Lee Strickland

Designed to increase public awareness of organ donation, this billboard on a Florida highway calls particular attention to donations that can save the lives of children.

people envision the possibility of a "futures market" in human organs, with prices fluctuating according to supply and demand. Those who favor making human organs a commodity argue that, as a result of market forces, shortages or surpluses of organs for transplantation would be eliminated. In some areas of the world, there already exists an active "black market" in transplantable organs (notably kidneys). There appears to be growing support to indirectly compensate people who donate organs, possibly through tax credits or grants to help pay for funeral expenses. Generally, the consensus at present is that commercialization is not preferable to the gift model of organ donation.

Most bodies that enter the "cadaver trade" are acquired legally; however, donors may have only a vague notion of how a donated body will be used, not realizing that not all are used for organ transplantation. Besides being used to teach anatomy to medical students, cadavers are used for research experiments and for seminars to demonstrate the latest medical or surgical gadgetry.[78] The federal government regulates organ procurement organizations, but it doesn't regulate the use of bodies and body parts for research and education.

Conflict sometimes occurs between organ procurement agencies and medical examiners (whose role in the death system is discussed later in this chapter). Because coroners and medical examiners have jurisdiction over "suspicious" deaths, organ recovery in such cases depends not only on the permission of next of kin but also on the coroner's or medical examiner's approval. That is to say, organ and tissue procurement sometimes "pits the living against the dead and transplant surgery against criminal justice."[79] Some procurement organizations have succeeded in changing some medical examiner statutes to make the legal requirement of death investigation secondary to organ removal. Some believe that "the determination to procure

> This old lady was in the hospital and her family wanted to put her in a nursing home. She didn't want to go, and she hung herself with her hospital bathrobe. The hospital nurses put her in bed and when the family came, they told them, "Grandma has died. Her heart stopped." They did not mention anything about the suicide. But when the hospital called the medical examiner, they explained how they had found her. The medical examiner conducts a thorough investigation and calls it a suicide and mentions hanging as [one of the] circumstances. The family goes ballistic. For the next two years they call him every week. He has several meetings with them to explain his findings. Nothing helps. Then after two years, he has another meeting with them and asks them, "What would make you happy?" They say that they don't like suicide. That's when he makes his mistake. He says, "Okay, I can't make it a natural death, but I can leave the death undetermined." So he changes the death certificate. About two weeks later, he is contacted by the sheriff. The family has gone to the sheriff and says that he was incompetent because he missed a homicide. The medical examiner explains to the sheriff what has happened, and the sheriff tells the family that he will not investigate. The family accuses the medical examiner of manipulating the sheriff and goes to the attorney general. He in turn checks with the medical examiner and decides not to pursue the case. The family now accuses the attorney general of covering up the examiner's mistakes. They take their case to the board of medical licensure, and the medical examiner almost lost his license.
>
> Stefan Timmermans, *Postmortem: How Medical Examiners Explain Suspicious Deaths*

organs has become so powerful there is almost a predatory obliviousness to where the organs come from and how the donors died."[80] Nancy Scheper-Hughes remarks, "Wherever transplant surgery moves, it challenges customary laws and traditional local practices bearing on the body, death, and social relations."[81]

Medical Ethics: A Cross-Cultural Example

In Japan, ethical, moral, and legal questions involving the definition of death and organ transplantation have been matters of controversy for decades.[82] Debate began in 1968, when Japanese surgeon Dr. Jurō Wada performed the world's second heart transplant, using an organ from a brain-dead donor. Initially admired for his scientific achievement, Wada was soon subjected to intense questioning about alleged disregard for the rights of both donor and recipient. He was accused of illegal human experimentation and of poor judgment in the manner in which he determined the donor's death. At the time, the criteria for establishing brain death were new, and no public consensus existed in Japan concerning this novel definition of death. The Wada case left a legacy of mistrust about brain death and transplantation in Japan.

Among technologically advanced countries, Japan is unique in its reliance on living donors. Although most scientific and technological advances are eagerly adopted in Japan, questions about brain death resulted in a reluctance to actively pursue organ transplantation. Only in 1997 did Japan pass its Organ Transplant Law, which legalized organ procurement from brain-dead donors, although children were still prohibited from donating due to their "inability to make a mature decision." In 2009, this ban was lifted by a law allowing donations by children under fifteen.[83]

The 1997 law also allowed organs to be taken only from brain-dead patients who had given prior written permission for donation of their organs. The 2009 law gave relatives authority to consent to donation when the patient's intentions were unclear.

Japan's debate illustrates how culture influences attitudes and practices related to dying and death. Although the circumstances surrounding the Wada case have had a lingering effect, a sense of mistrust between physicians and patients has long been prevalent in Japan. Until quite recently, most physicians practiced a kind of "closed door" medicine in which patients were neither given information about their health nor permitted to criticize their physicians. The practice of *uso mo hoben,* or expedient lies, was justified by the belief that patients "want to be told warm lies rather than confronting the cold truth."[84] In the Japanese medical system, the consensus has been that patients should leave decision making to their physicians and family members. Many people feel this kind of paternalism is especially worrisome in the context of transplantation procedures. It is feared that, in determining brain death, doctors might give no information to family members and perhaps even lie to them. People also worry that the criteria for brain death may be applied too readily. There is widespread feeling that the definition of brain death is such a critical issue that it should not be decided solely by physicians. In addition, long-term mistrust raises concerns that a market for organs could provoke abuses by physicians.

Traditional beliefs about death may have an even more important influence on attitudes. In Japan, death traditionally has been viewed as a social process, not a medically determined phenomenon. The respect shown to ancestors through various practices attests to an extended process of social death. Physicians may alter the conventional definition of death, but the persistence of traditional views reveals diverse opinions about the meaning of death.

Many Japanese are concerned about keeping the body intact, not only during life but also after death. The body is viewed as a gift from one's parents, one's ancestors. Removal of organs from brain-dead bodies violates the integrity of the body. An aversion to tampering with the corpse of a loved one is related to beliefs that body and soul must be intact as the person goes to the next world. The body must be perfect; if it is not, the soul may become unhappy. Organ transplantation is viewed as mutilation of the body. Whereas people in some societies tend to think of body organs as replaceable parts, the Japanese tend to find in every part of a deceased person's body a fragment of his or her mind and spirit. Related to this issue is Japan's historical concern about impurity. From this viewpoint, procedures involved in organ donation and transplantation defile the body. A person considering organ donation may be dissuaded by the notion that, if organs are taken, "My body is no longer mine."

Another important issue has to do with differing cultural ideas about the "seat of the soul" or "center of the self." In Western biomedicine, the brain—the locus of rational thought—tends to occupy the most important place among the various body parts. As the "seat of the mind," it represents the essence of humanness. In other traditions, the heart, not the brain, is considered the seat of life. Equating life with the functioning of the brain is alien to many Japanese, who place equal if not greater symbolic importance on the heart. A person's true center of spirit and consciousness, the "heart-mind," is traditionally located in the *hara,* or belly.

As this example illustrates, the notion of brain death is culturally constructed. The notion of death as absence of brain function, separate from other bodily functions, is inconsistent with the Japanese perspective on death of the whole person. Making a determination of brain death creates confusion because there remains a beating heart and a warm body. For many Japanese, the procedures involved in organ donation and transplantation result in a "death that cannot be seen," an invisible death.

In addition to the cultural factors already mentioned, Japanese concerns about organ donation and transplantation relate to traditional practices involving the exchange of gifts. In Japan, there are fine-tuned rules governing the flow of gifts. Receiving a gift incurs an obligation to return the favor. With organ donation, giving is viewed as one-way. The recipient of an organ donation cannot offer a countergift. There is no way of repaying such a valuable gift. Moreover, the absence of a social relationship between donor and receiver clouds organ donation with a shadow of commercialization.

The maintenance of cultural identity is important to most Japanese. To unquestioningly adopt Western practices of organ donation and transplantation would involve abandoning history and thereby diminish cultural distinctiveness. A culturally appropriate bioethics would therefore incorporate the influences of Shinto, Buddhist, and Confucian thought as well as modern Western traditions. In reflecting on the Japanese example presented here, we see that cultural differences need not be viewed as barriers that must be overcome but can be seen as opportunities for learning about different ways in which people deal with the complex issues surrounding dying and death.

The Impact of the Death System

The concept of the death system is a helpful model for contemplating how death shapes the social order and, in turn, our individual lives. As a network of people, places, and times as well as objects and symbols, the death system affects our collective and personal relationships to mortality in many ways. In this chapter, we have seen how society develops public policies concerning the definition of death, organ donation and transplantation, certification of death, the roles of coroners and medical examiners, and when and under what circumstances autopsies are performed. As you study topics related to dying and death, you may find it interesting to keep in mind how they fit into the death system. As Kastenbaum says, "Everything that makes a collection of individuals into a society and keeps that society going has implications for our relationship with death."[85]

Further Readings

Stuart Banner. *The Death Penalty: An American History.* Cambridge, Mass.: Harvard University Press, 2003.

Kai Erikson. *A New Species of Trouble: Explorations in Disaster, Trauma, and Community.* New York: W. W. Norton, 1994.

Michele Goodwin. *Black Markets: The Supply and Demand of Body Parts.* New York: Cambridge University Press, 2006.

Sue Holtkamp. *Wrapped in Mourning: The Gift of Life and Organ Donor Family Trauma.* New York: Brunner-Routledge, 2002.

Glennys Howarth. *Death and Dying: A Sociological Introduction.* Malden, Mass.: Polity, 2007.

Susan Orpett Long. *Final Days: Japanese Culture and Choice at the End of Life.* Honolulu: University of Hawaii Press, 2005.

Stuart J. Youngner, Robert M. Arnold, and Renie Schapiro, eds. *The Definition of Death: Contemporary Controversies.* Baltimore: Johns Hopkins University Press, 1999.

Additional resources for this chapter can be found at *www.mhhe.com/despelder10e*

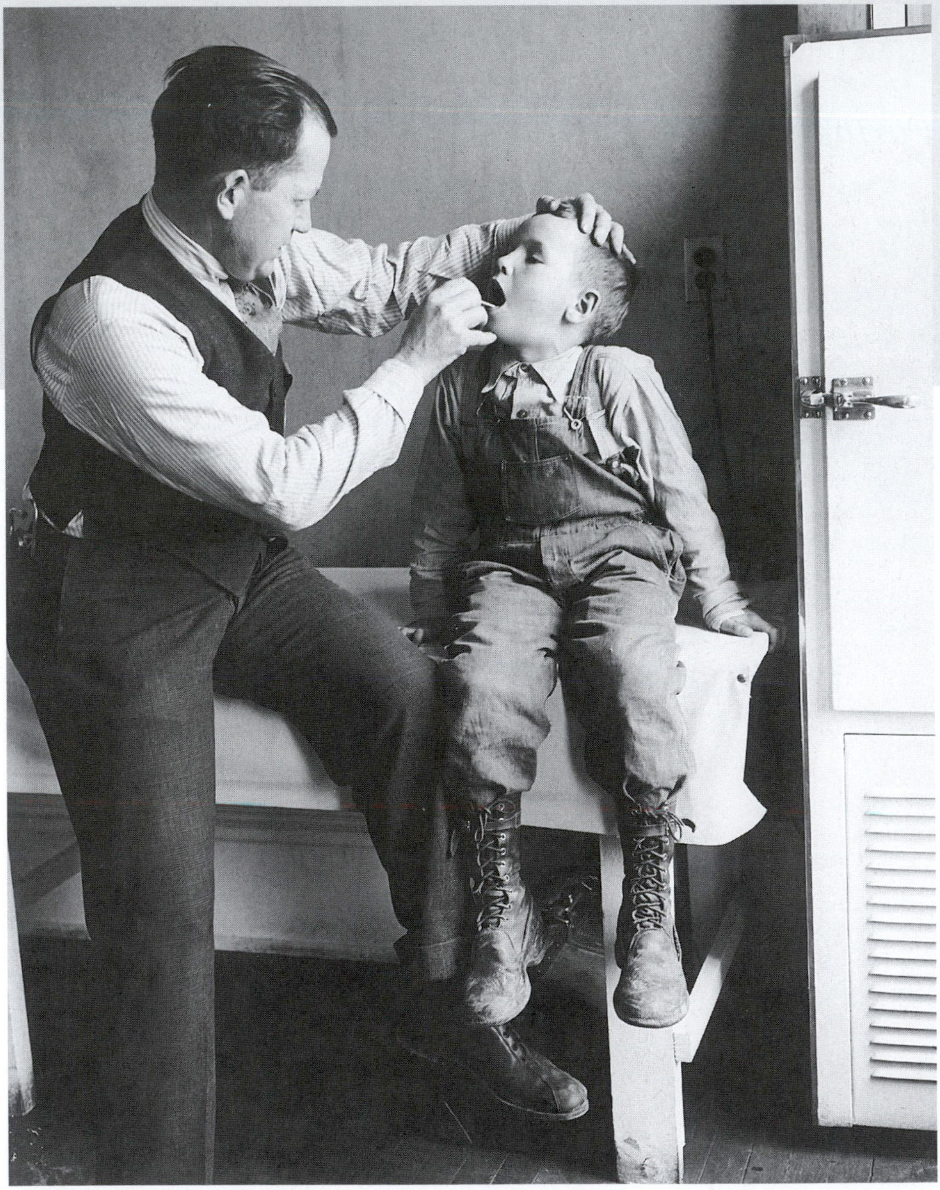

FSA Collection, Library of Congress

In 1935, medical care in Reedsville, West Virginia, seems less formal than that received in the urban clinics and hospitals of today. Although the practice of medicine has been enhanced by new methods of diagnosis and treatment, most people still believe that the relationship between physician and patient is central to the outcome of an illness.

CHAPTER 5

Health Care: Patients, Staff, and Institutions

Think about the end of your life. Most people say they want to live their last days amid the familiar surroundings of home, surrounded by loved ones. But the nature of an illness or lack of necessary support can oblige the dying person to be cared for in an institutional health care setting. Often, an "interventional cascade" surrounds the patient with technology, resulting in unwanted aggressive care at the end of life. "The potential gain in survival even from perfect therapy may be small."[1]

Oriented toward the goal of sustaining life, the health care system sometimes falls short in meeting the needs of dying patients and their families. In 1900, about 80 percent of deaths in the United States occurred in the home. Now, most deaths take place in institutional settings, mainly hospitals and nursing homes. Ira Byock points out that, at present, just over one-fifth of Americans are at home when they die; over 30 percent die in nursing homes; and hospitals remain the site of over 50 percent of deaths in most parts of the country. Moreover, nearly 40 percent of those who die in a hospital spend their last days in an ICU (intensive care unit).[2]

In the past, physicians did as much to console as to cure patients; consolation and comfort were often all that medicine could offer. Now, if treatment is not a cure, we may feel cheated. Physicians become scapegoats if their therapies do not lead to the desired outcome.

Each of the three major categories of institutional medical care—hospitals, nursing homes, and hospices—is intended optimally to serve a specific purpose within the overall health care delivery system. Patients with life-threatening illness usually receive a combination of acute and supportive care. As conditions change, institutional care may alternate with home care.

Hospitals are devoted mainly to acute intensive care of a limited duration. Aggressive medical techniques are used to diagnose symptoms, provide treatment, and sustain life. The typical patient expects to regain well-being after a short period of treatment and then return to normal life. Patients with chronic or life-threatening illness may alternate between receiving acute care in hospitals and obtaining supportive care in nursing homes, from hospices, or at home. Some hospitals are evolving toward an integrated approach by offering a "portfolio" of health care services, which can include outpatient and extended care, as well as palliative care. ("Palliate" originates from the Greek and translates as "to cloak," meaning care that is meant to cloak or prevent the experience of pain or other distressing symptoms. In the context of modern medicine, "palliative" was originally used by Dr. Balfour Mount at Royal Victoria Hospital in Canada.)[3]

Nursing homes (a category that includes convalescent and extended-care facilities) provide long-term residential care for people who are chronically ill and those whose illness does not require acute, intensive care. Most patients in nursing homes eventually return to the community. A smaller percentage of patients includes those who require ongoing supportive care, as well as those who die while being cared for in a nursing home. "Increasingly, the nursing home is the place of care and death for older Americans."[4]

Hospice care is distinguished by its orientation toward the needs of dying patients and their families. The mission of hospice care is to comfort the patient rather than to cure a disease. Hospice is not necessarily a place but, rather, a *program* of caring. Care that matches the aims of hospice can be provided in various settings, including a palliative medicine department within a hospital, a nursing home or residential-care facility, a community hospice, or the home. These options for hospice and palliative care are examined in more detail later in this chapter. (Palliative care services for children are discussed in Chapter 10.)

Modern Health Care

A person admitted to a health care facility expects to receive medical and nursing care appropriate to his or her particular malady. Each element of the health care system—patient, staff, and institution—contributes to the overall quality and nature of health care (see Figure 5-1). To efficiently use staff and facilities, procedures are standardized and routine. When an elderly aunt was dying at home, she could be spoon-fed her favorite homemade soup by a family member. In a hospital or nursing home, she is likely to receive a standard diet, perhaps served impersonally by a harried and overworked aide. Charles Rosenberg observed that "we expect a great deal of our hospitals: alleviation of pain,

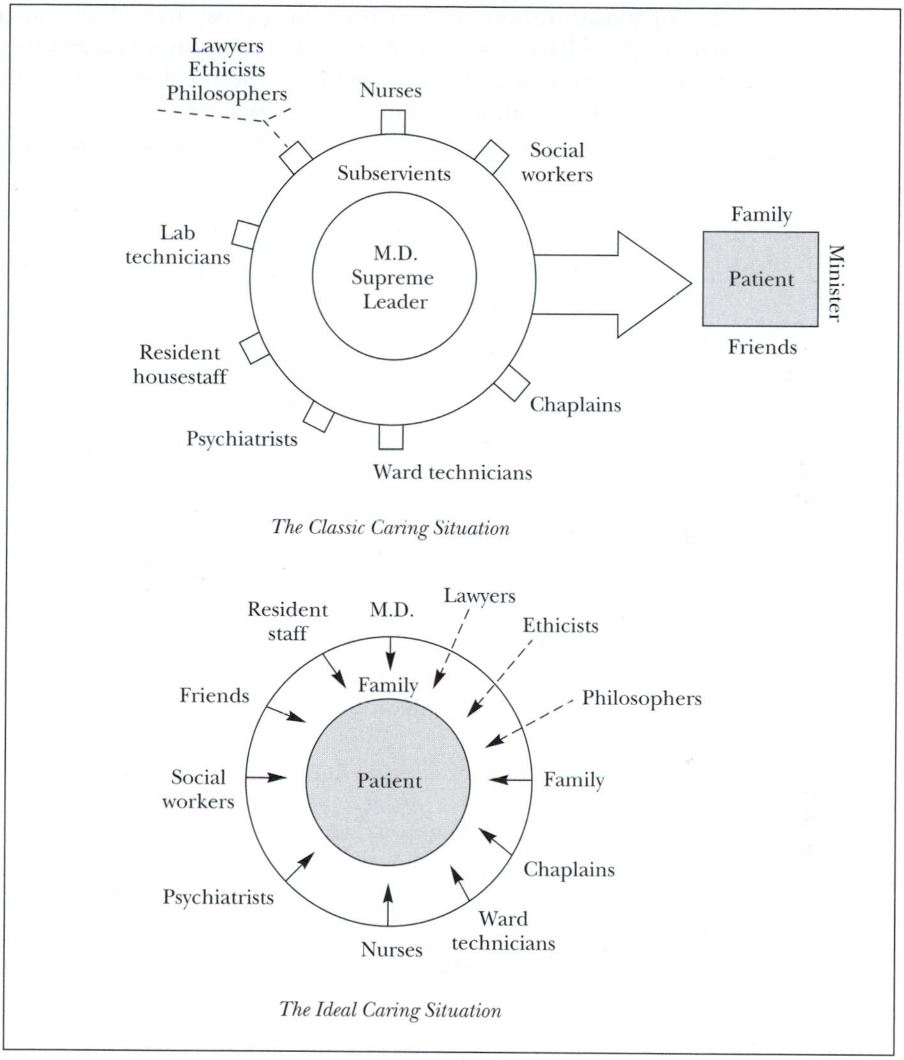

Figure 5-1 *Classic and Ideal Caring Situations*

extension of life, [and] management of death and the awkward and painful circumstances surrounding its approach."[5]

A patient's experience is shaped by rules, regulations, and conventions—written and unwritten. The family of a dying patient may be relegated to a deathwatch in the corridor or the waiting room down the hall, with one person at a time squeezing into the patient's room to keep a bedside vigil. There may be no private space where relatives can meet to discuss concerns with doctors or nurses. Grieving relatives may feel obliged to contain or repress their emotions. In situations that involve dying patients, "the goal must not be simply to provide expert medical care to an individual patient, but to help give voice and connection and meaning to a family."[6]

Abstraction and standardization are aspects of the scientific method, which is the basis for many of the life-saving medical advances we applaud. Less welcome is what happens when these mechanisms make medicine less humane. For instance, reductionism occurs when complex phenomena, such as those present in medicine and patient care, are reduced to overly simple terms that distort the phenomena. It also occurs when only a piece of a given system is acknowledged or considered, instead of the whole system. Another error or aberration is depersonalization, which occurs when dying patients are given less attention because physicians and nurses avoid contact due to their own death anxiety or because of the belief that "nothing more can be done."

Health Care Financing

Our individual and social choices about financing health care influence the options available for care of the seriously ill and dying. As Paul Insel and Walton Roth observe, "Health care is financed by a combination of private and public insurance plans, patient out-of-pocket payments, and government assistance."[7] Spending for health care appears to be unlimited because "the richer a country becomes, the more it will tend to spend."[8]

The United States spends more on health than any other industrialized country. Daniel Callahan says, "There must be limits. American health care is radically American: individualistic, scientifically ambitious, market intoxicated, suspicious of government, and profit-driven."[9] Further, "The improvement of health, the relief of suffering, and the forestalling of death are as open-ended as the exploration of outer space."[10]

The rising costs of health care are due partly to a "technological imperative" that promises an unprecedented range of tools for combating disease. Callahan says there are "many carrots and few sticks" with regard to the rapid rise in technology (see Table 5-1).[11] The constant advances in medical technology effectively extend life longer and longer, which often makes it hard to know when to stop treatment. Some technologists appear

TABLE 5-1 *Some Factors Spurring Medical Technology*

- A long-standing love of technology in all areas of life
- The belief that technology saves lives and relieves suffering
- The notion that it is wrong to decide which treatments are not cost-worthy
- Consumer demand and expectations
- Aggressive promotion and marketing of medical technologies
- Direct-to-consumer advertising of medical technologies
- Competition in the hospital marketplace
- "Defensive medicine" as a prophylactic against malpractice charges
- Health care as a growth industry (new jobs and construction)
- Better fees and reimbursements for technology use than for talking to patients or sitting by the bedside of the dying person
- Belief in endless technological progress

to believe that "death is nothing but a series of preventable diseases to be picked off one by one."[12]

> The most important aim of a health care system should be to help a person go from being a young person to becoming an old person. However, once a person has achieved that goal, there ought to be a reduced obligation on the part of a health system to help someone become indefinitely older, much less as old as that person might like.[13]

Medical advances can be a mixed blessing. Earlier detection of disease, for example, may result in a cure that otherwise would not have been possible, or it may result only in the patient's being aware of his or her disease for a longer period of time.[14] The ability of medicine to predict death at an early stage in some diseases has led to the emergence of a category of experience called "terminal illness."[15] With earlier diagnosis and sophisticated medical care, the "terminal" stage of an illness may now last more than a decade. Callahan says,

> We can readily agree that medical progress and technological innovation have been an enormous human benefit. . . . They have helped to lower death rates from lethal diseases, extended average life expectancies, relieved us of many forms of physical and mental suffering, and have given us a confidence about living into old age, and a good old age at that, in ways impossible for past generations to imagine. Yet if the cost of all those benefits begins to exceed what we can now afford, how do we decide when enough is enough, and just what might count as "enough"?[16]

Reportedly, a quarter of the Medicare budget is spent on the last year of patients' lives and 40 percent of that amount is spent in the last 30 days.[17] George Lundberg, a physician and professor of health policy at Stanford Medical School, says, "We should stop paying physicians and institutions to prolong dying with false hope, bravado, and intensive therapy that only adds to their profit margin."[18]

Of course, it is not just doctors who rush to take advantage of newer and newer technologies. Callahan says, "An astonishing 40 percent of Americans believe that medical technology can always save their lives. The old joke that Americans believe death is just one more disease to be cured is no longer a joke."[19] He asks these questions:[20]

- Should death be seen as the greatest evil that medicine should seek to combat, or would a better quality of life within a finite life span be a better goal?
- Do the elderly need better access to intensive care units and more high-tech medicine to extend their lives, or better long-term and home care and improved economic and social support?
- Does it make any sense that the healthier we get in this country, the *more* we spend on health care, not less?
- Should we be spending three times more of our gross domestic product on health care than on education, when forty years ago these amounts were about the same?

> When my father went back to the hospital a year ago, he was clearly close to the end: His lungs and liver were barely functioning, his abdomen was filling with fluid, and he could no longer lift himself out of bed. The hospital's doctors nonetheless treated him aggressively, punching a hole in his chest to insert a drainage tube, which quickly led to uncontrolled bleeding, an infection, and a plunge in blood pressure. Within 12 hours, my father was in a coma, with no chance of recovery, sustained only by a ventilator and a tangle of multiple IV drips. He spent four days in the ICU, until I overcame the resistance of two doctors and had the machines turned off, as per my dad's living will. Medicare paid upward of $20,000 for these last days of my father's life, during which he received little comfort, moments of agonizing pain and fear, and all the medical care in the world, and then some.
>
> William Falk, *The Week*

Do investments in medical technology result in a better quality of care? The answer seems to be yes. The impact of rising costs, however, raises the question, Is society obligated to provide every medical intervention that a patient believes might be beneficial?

Rationing Scarce Resources

To alleviate pressures on the health care system, experts suggest that resources must be rationed. *Rationing* refers to the allocation of scarce resources among competing individuals. In health care, it is defined as any system that limits the amount of health care a person can receive. Rationing occurs when not all care expected to be beneficial is provided to all patients and, particularly, when a medical benefit valued by a patient must be withheld because of cost. Although physicians have always functioned as gatekeepers in decisions concerning access to therapies deemed best for a patient's welfare, the new era of *managed care* means that they now face the prospect of being forced to engage in "restrictive" gatekeeping and "bedside" rationing, roles that many people view as morally illegitimate in medicine. (Managed care refers to an arrangement for health care in which an organization—such as a health maintenance organization [HMO], a doctor-hospital network, or an insurance company—attempts to control costs by acting as an intermediary between the person seeking care and the physician.) Indeed, some physicians express concern that trends toward closer management are leading to "industrialization" of medicine in which medical care begins to resemble a factory operation.

Daniel Callahan suggests that a "principle of symmetry" is useful in acknowledging the limits of medical care.[21] He says, "A technology should be judged by its likelihood of enhancing a good balance between the extension and saving of life and the quality of life." Conversely, "a health care system that develops and institutionalizes a life-saving technology which has the common result of leaving people chronically ill or with poor quality of life ignores the principle of symmetry."

Decisions about allocating scarce medical resources are not just the purview of experts and legislators. The choices each of us makes in pursuit of well-being influence the health care system and contribute to shaping its character. Madeline Jacobs says, "Modern technology blurs the definitions of good care—what does it mean to heal, especially at the end of life?"[22] Instead of facing costly and likely futile treatments at the end of life, for instance, we may choose to sign an advance directive that makes known our wishes about receiving life-sustaining medical therapies (advance directives are discussed in Chapter 6). "Medicine overreaches itself," Callahan says, "when it sets as its implicit goal that of curing all diseases and infinitely forestalling death."

The Caregiver-Patient Relationship

Aesculapius—according to Greek legend, the first physician—was elevated to the pantheon of gods and, along with Hygeia and Panacea, ruled over health and illness. Medicine—given its association with the elemental experiences of birth, life, and death—carries high symbolic importance. Arthur Frank says, "Medicine is a *play* of boundaries," explaining that "medicine requires both the aura of distance and the approachability that requires renouncing some measure of aura."[23] *Paternalism,* the assumption of parentlike authority by medical practitioners, is seen as infringing on a patient's autonomy or freedom to make medical decisions.[24] Thus, in the present era, the "Aesculapian authority" of physicians is being challenged.

The physician-patient relationship can be viewed as an alliance wherein the physician is an educator, counselor, and expert but not the sole decision maker.[25] (In primary care medicine, the term "doctor" can include individuals who have earned the clinical-oriented degree "DNP," which signifies Doctors of Nursing Practice, or, as some physicians call them, "Noctors.")

Patients' experiences in coping with illness help shape the missions of health care.[26] The social contract between physicians and patients includes qualities of a *covenantal* relationship, which implies a mutuality of interests between providers and patients.[27] This kind of relationship is fostered when providers get to know the patient, empower him or her to share in decision making, and work within the constraints of the situation to respect and accommodate patient choices.

Shared decision making is crucial in medicine generally and perhaps especially in end-of-life care. Preferences or questions about end-of-life care should be part of the discussion when choosing a doctor. Does the doctor have experience caring for people at the end of life? Is he or she willing and able to provide care in a variety of settings—hospital, nursing facility, hospice or palliative care, or the home? Is the doctor familiar with community resources? Any wishes about limiting treatment at the end of life should be discussed. The bottom line is, Will the system accommodate the patient's and his or her family's preferences and plans?

> I clearly made Dr. Mueh nervous. He was clearly up to his ears in patients and spread very thin.
>
> He took 90 minutes to talk to me and my wife about my disease. He started out with terminal care and told me I'd get all the narcotics I would need to eliminate pain and that tubes could be used to provide nourishment.
>
> I was amazed that he talked that way, as if I were dying.
>
> Pierre Bowman, Honolulu *Star-Bulletin*

Disclosing a Life-Threatening Diagnosis

If you were diagnosed as having a life-threatening illness, would you want to know? Some people say, "Of course, I want to know everything that's going on with me!" Others answer, "Spare the truth, I'd rather not know that I could die; ignorance is bliss." The person who has spent a lifetime as a fighter against the odds is likely to have a different response from the person whose typical pattern of coping involves efforts to shun stress. Consider your own attitudes and preferences. Keeping information from a patient may leave him or her in what Avery Weisman called "a state of lonely apprehension."[28]

Surveys indicate that most people do want to be told if diagnosed with a life-threatening illness, but the questions of *when* and *how* such information should be communicated are more difficult to answer. Physicians need to present news of a life-threatening diagnosis in a manner that will serve the best interests of the patient. In deciding how to do this, the doctor must consider the patient's personality, emotional constitution, and capacity for continued function under stress. The patient's familial and sociocultural environment may also be important.

Doctors may worry that knowing all the details about a life-threatening illness could adversely affect a patient's ability to cope. Is minimizing the threat of an illness sometimes in a patient's best interest? Physicians generally subscribe to the belief that hope must be encouraged. Thus, although physicians may disclose the general facts of a life-threatening illness, details may be withheld until the patient takes the initiative by asking specific questions. Members of some cultural and ethnic groups prefer "concealment" rather than full disclosure.[29] That is, families may be aware of a diagnosis or prognosis and attempt to hide the truth from the patient. Furthermore, a patient may not be accustomed to making decisions about his or her medical care; family members may have an important voice. Communication training for physicians generally emphasizes dyadic skills between the physician and separate family members; however, insights available from family systems studies and family therapy can be usefully adapted to goals-of-care family conferences.[30]

Communicating the diagnosis is a crucial event in patient care. How this is done can influence a patient's attitude toward the illness, response to treatment, and ability to cope. The content of such a conversation depends on a number of factors, including the doctor's preferences for breaking bad news, the patient's receptivity to the facts, and the expected prognosis. In conversations that involve a terminal diagnosis, both physicians and patients may be cautious about mentioning dying or death. Patients may be shocked when first given a diagnosis of serious or life-threatening illness, unable to ask questions that will occur to them later. Thus, details can be given in segments. Breaking bad news is not so much a single event as a process.

In his book *Counseling Individuals with Life-Threatening Illness,* Ken Doka offers eight principles that are important when delivering bad news:[31]

1. Keep it simple.
2. Ask yourself, "What does this diagnosis mean to the patient?"
3. Meet on "cool ground" first. Get to know a patient prior to presenting the news.
4. Wait for questions.
5. Do not argue with denial.
6. Ask questions yourself.
7. Do not destroy all hope.
8. Do not say anything that is untrue.

Besides providing a truthful report of the diagnosis, doctors generally should offer advice about the proposed course of treatment and side effects, providing as much detail as the patient desires. A good question to ask is, How much do you want to know about your illness?[32] Ample time should be available to explore the patient's questions and concerns.[33]

Achieving Clear Communication

Clear communication does not happen automatically. Candace West, a sociologist who conducted a study of how doctors and patients relate to each other, found what she calls a "communications chasm" that hinders the healing process.[34] She observed a lack of "social cement"—the introductions, greetings, laughter, and use of patients' names—that is naturally part of ordinary social interactions. West also found that physicians tend to "advance questions which restrict patients' options for answers," and patients tend to be hesitant about questioning their doctors.

Physicians should "listen" with their eyes as well as their ears, paying attention to the nonverbal communication of gestures and body language that reveal a patient's unease or anxiety about what is being discussed. The technology of medical interventions can be an obstacle to effective communication.[35] Richard Sandor, a physician, says, "We detect subtle disturbances of heart rhythm, manipulate faltering blood pressure to within a few millimeters of mercury, and regulate minute changes in blood chemistry, but what about the *person* who is dying?"[36] In the art of medicine, accurate communication has been called "the single most valuable asset of the skilled doctor."[37]

Communication is an interactive and transactional process: One cannot *not* communicate. For instance, think about nonverbal communication, which includes not only facial expressions, gestures, and body postures, but

Maxine was silent. "Is it even worth being treated?" she finally asked.

"You are the only one who can answer that question," I said. "If we don't treat it, it will quickly spread to other cranial nerves and parts of the brain and spinal cord. The quality of your life would be markedly impaired. I want to help sustain as much quality of life for as long as possible."

Maxine opened her eyes.

"I don't want to die," she said, beginning to sob. "I didn't think it would happen so fast, so soon. I'm not really ready to die."

Jerome Groopman, "Dying Words"

also *iconics*—objects that convey meaningful information (such as clothing and jewelry)—and *proxemics* (space and time). For example, consider the time it takes a caregiver to respond to a patient's request for help, or the physical distance established when a physician stands behind a desk while talking to a seated patient. Such labels as M.D. and R.N., as well as such titles as doctor, nurse, and patient, are symbolic identifiers that influence communication.[38] In most medical communications, patients are addressed by their first names, whereas doctors are addressed by their titles.[39]

When patients express a desire to talk about death, caregivers may respond with various strategies that either curtail or encourage such conversations, including (1) reassurance ("You're doing so well"), (2) denial ("Oh, you'll live to be a hundred"), (3) changing the subject ("Let's talk about something more cheerful"), (4) fatalism ("Well, we all have to die sometime"), and (5) discussion ("What happened to make you feel that way?"). Trained to save lives, caregivers may feel helpless when they are not able to offer a cure. Jeanne Quint Benoliel says that "open communication does not necessarily mean open talk about death, but it does mean openness to the patient's verbalized concerns."[40]

Responding to the emotional and spiritual needs of patients and their families can be as important as caring for physical needs. A nurse who steps into the room, sits down by the patient's bed, and displays a willingness to listen is likely to be more effective in providing comfort than one who breezes in, remains standing, and quips, "How're we today? Did we sleep well?" Skillful communication helps in attaining the goals of health care for the whole person.

Doctors and patients sometimes collude to maintain false optimism about recovery by communicating in ways that allow the focus to be on current treatment activities, with disregard for long-term prognosis.[41] The doctor does not want to pronounce a "death sentence," and the patient does not want to hear it.

Writing about his own experiences with serious illness, Norman Cousins pointed out that it is possible to communicate a life-threatening diagnosis as a "challenge rather than a verdict."[42] Communication can promote either a positive attitude, with faith in the ultimate outcome, or a negative attitude, with corresponding feelings of despondence and despair. Clear communication can play an important role in motivating the patient's own "healing system," creating the potential for a positive outcome regardless of the ultimate prognosis.

Providing Total Care

Caring for seriously ill and dying patients involves attending not just to a patient's physical needs but also to his or her mental, emotional, and spiritual needs. This is "whole person" care.[43] Such care usually means continuity of contact between at least one caregiver and the patient, opportunity for the patient to keep informed of his or her condition and prognosis, patient participation in decisions that affect him or her, and behavior by staff members that elicits the patient's trust and confidence.[44] When these guidelines are in place, care can be both *personal* and *comprehensive.*

As death approaches, the patient's family is likely to experience a transition that has been characterized as the patient's "fading away."[45] A period of chaos, confusion, fear, and uncertainty may ensue: "Nothing feels solid anymore." This transition involves a task of redefinition as family members cope with the burden of letting go of the old before picking up the new. Families often find themselves caring for a dying loved one while simultaneously trying to carry on with the normal business of life. Total care means also attending to needs of the patient's family.

Care of the Dying

When Elisabeth Kübler-Ross set out to educate interns in an urban hospital about the dying, she wanted to let terminally ill patients make their own case. Informing staff members of her plan, she was told that no one was dying on their wards; there were only some patients who were "very critically ill."[46] Kübler-Ross's efforts to focus attention on terminally ill patients became an impetus toward compassionate care of the dying.

Dying, like birthing, is a natural event, sometimes better witnessed than managed. Caregivers are called upon to put aside their own beliefs to discover what's appropriate for a particular person in a particular situation. Care of the dying, as Balfour Mount observes, involves both heart and mind: "The dying need the friendship of the heart with its caring, acceptance, vulnerability and reciprocity. They also need the skills of the mind embodied in competent medical care. Neither alone is sufficient."[47]

The timeline for dying has changed over the last several generations. Not only do we, on average, tend to live longer, but we are also more likely to live with chronic disease and disability for months or even years before we die. Most of us will need some level of care during our last days, weeks, months, or even years of life. As life draws to a close, end-of-life care may involve some combination of home care, hospital stays, nursing home care, and hospice or palliative care. (*Palliative care* refers to treatment intended to relieve the symptoms or reduce the severity of an illness without curing the underlying disease.)

Dr. Elisabeth Kübler-Ross, seen here with a patient who has been diagnosed with a life-threatening illness, is widely recognized for her pioneering efforts toward increased awareness on the part of the patient, family, and medical staff relative to the issues that arise in caring for the dying.

Would you prefer to spend your last days or weeks at home, cared for by relatives and friends? Or would you rather have access to sophisticated medical technologies available in a hospital? The course of a disease may be unpredictable, preventing a person from choosing the place where he or she will die or the exact nature of medical care received. Even so, it is prudent to consider possible options. When death is expected, perhaps foreseen as the final chapter of a long illness, there is usually some choice about where death will occur.

Hospice and Palliative Care

The goal of medicine is to restore or sustain a sense of equanimity and personal integrity despite disturbances caused by illness. Often, however, the message heard by dying patients and their families is that nothing more can be done.[48] The response of hospice and palliative care is that, on the contrary, much can be done to help the dying person continue *living* until death, even though recovery or cure is not possible. These models of care go beyond physical needs and seek to relieve suffering by providing total care: physical, psychological, spiritual, and existential.[49] At the end of life, a patient's personal story is not adequately told by what's written on the medical chart.

A useful mnemonic is the 3Cs: high-quality care is competent, compassionate, and coordinated.[50] Such care is provided by a team that may include physicians, nurses, social workers, pharmacists, physical and occupational therapists, chaplains, home health aides, and trained volunteers, as well as family members and friends. This team-oriented approach is intended to provide state-of-the-art care to treat pain and other distressing symptoms, as well as to provide emotional and spiritual support tailored to the needs of the patient and his or her family.

The World Health Organization defines *palliative care* as

> an approach that improves the quality of life of patients and their families facing the problems associated with life-threatening illness, through the prevention and relief of suffering by means of early identification and impeccable assessment and treatment of pain and other problems, physical, psychosocial, and spiritual.[51]

Stephen Connor describes palliative care as a "human right."[52] Yet, a study revealed that palliative care was not being provided at all in half the countries of the world.[53]

The Patient's Story

In learning to think like a medical scientist, I was forgetting the whole patient. To help the patient in times of suffering, the physician must know the patient: not only as a case but as a person. Each patient has a history, a unique story to tell, which goes beyond the information in the medical history. Different patients have different senses of what makes life important to them, what they want out of life, and how far they are willing to go to preserve it. The patient's full story, like any person's story, includes his or her cultural background, childhood circumstances, career, family, religious life, and so on. It includes the patient's self-understanding, appearance, manner of expression, temperament, and character. In short, it includes those attributes that make the patient a person—and not only a person, but this particular person.

Richard B. Gunderman,
"Medicine and the Question of Suffering"

As Joan Teno and Stephen Connor point out, "The central difference between *hospice* and hospital-based palliative care programs is that the latter can admit and serve patients who are still receiving curative therapies. Most hospice programs are Medicare certified, and the Medicare Hospice Benefit generally requires that a patient be given a prognosis of six months or less if the illness runs its normal course. Thus, hospice is a health care system under which the patient decides to forgo curative treatments for the terminal illness. Making a decision about hospice care can be a challenge in which the patient faces a seemingly all-or-nothing decision. The Medicare Hospice Benefit has, in effect, "put hospice in a box with regard to treatment choice," in that patients who want to keep some option of survival open have been excluded.[54] Patients referred to a palliative care service are not required to meet a similar prognostic requirement (see Table 5-2).[55] This distinction will become clearer as we discuss the challenges of care for patients with life-limiting illnesses. For now, consider Teno and Connor's apt summary: "In short, all care provided by hospices is palliative; however, not all palliative care is provided by hospices."

Although the terms *hospice care* and *palliative care* are sometimes used interchangeably, as mentioned above, they also can be differentiated. For example, the *Merck Manual of Diagnosis and Therapy,* a standard medical textbook, defines *hospice* as a type of care specifically designed to minimize suffering for dying patients and their family members; it forgoes most diagnostic testing and life-prolonging treatments in favor of symptom relief, education of patients and family members about appropriate care, and comfort care.[56] Such programs, which are available in virtually all regions of the United States except for a small number of rural areas, can be considered as conforming to the "standard definition" of hospice.

Stephen Connor lists the following among the essential components of hospice programs:[57]

1. The patient and his/her family are the unit of care.
2. Care is provided in the home or in an inpatient facility.
3. Symptom management is the focus of treatment.
4. Treatment is directed toward the "whole person."
5. Care is interdisciplinary.
6. Services are available twenty-four hours a day, seven days a week.

Hospice doesn't prescribe a particular "way of dying."[58] Rather, it seeks to create an environment in which the "seemingly disordered process of dying" can be lived out in a manner that fits the needs and beliefs of the person who is dying.[59] The growth of hospice reflects changing expectations about end-of-life care, "from cure to care, extension of life to quality of life."[60]

According to the National Hospice and Palliative Care Organization (NHPCO), about 5,300 hospice programs in the United States provided care to an estimated 1.65 million patients in 2011; and about 1,059,000 patients died under hospice care, nearly 45 percent of all deaths in the United States that year.[61] In the 1970s, cancer patients made up the largest percentage of

TABLE 5-2 *Comparison of Hospice and Hospital-Based Palliative Care*

	Hospice Programs	Hospital-Based Palliative Care
Patient population	Life-limiting illness; expected prognosis 6 months or less if illness runs its normal course.	Any stage of advanced or life-limiting illness.
Sites of care	Home, nursing home, assisted living facility, hospital, free-standing hospice unit.	Hospital. Provision of services elsewhere (e.g., nursing homes) varies.
Services provided	Pain and symptom management, psychosocial and spiritual support; interdisciplinary team; medical equipment, medications, supplies; family bereavement support for 1 year after death.	Services vary, from single health care provider to interdisciplinary team.
Length of stay	Average length of stay is 2 months; median, 20 days.	Varies, may be episodic care based on needs.
Reimbursement	Set payment per day enrolled, at 1 of 4 levels of care: routine home care, continuous home care, general inpatient care, inpatient respite care.	Reimbursement through existing channels, including CPT (current procedure terminology) and DRGs (diagnosis-related groups). Payment for professional or facility services.
Role of primary care provider (PCP)	Usually continues to provide overall management of care. Hospice medical director consults with PCP.	PCP often requests formal consult with palliative care team. Palliative care service or hospitalist may manage care during inpatient stays.
Key differences	Focus on caring for patient and family or caregivers at the end of life after efforts at curative treatment are no longer effective or patient decides to stop treatment with curative intent.	Focus on palliative care throughout the continuum of a life-limiting illness. Can be delivered concurrently with curative or life-prolonging therapies.

hospice admissions; today, they account for less than half of hospice admissions (37.7 percent), with the majority being patients with chronic illnesses, including unspecified debility, dementia, heart disease, and lung disease. More than 98 percent of families indicate they would recommend hospice services to others.[62]

Besides providing a relatively consistent package of services and benefits designed to meet the needs of patients and families facing life-limiting illness, hospice programs are mandated to provide bereavement follow-up to every family they serve. Patient care is provided in the place the patient calls home, which includes nursing homes and residential facilities as well as private residences. Most of the time hospice care takes place in patients' homes with family members as primary caregivers. "Entering hospice care" usually means affiliating with a *hospice program*—that is, arranging to receive the services of a local hospice.

Hospitals are increasingly incorporating principles of hospice and palliative care into their mission.[63] When nurses are given time to get to know patients and their families, when caregivers are assigned responsibility for individual patients rather than tasks, when supportive relationships exist among staff members, and when there is a policy of open disclosure of diagnosis and prognosis, care of the dying in both hospitals and hospice programs embodies comparable ideals and philosophy regarding end-of-life care. Palliative care is strictly defined as care that affords relief, not necessarily cure; however, it can be combined with curative treatments, allowing patients to battle the effects of disease while benefiting from efforts to improve quality of life.

Hospice and palliative care physician Ira Byock points out that "intensivists and palliative care professionals both care for the sickest patients in the healthcare system. As with patients in an ICU, those referred for palliative care consultation or admitted to hospice programs have life-threatening conditions, often involving multiple organ system failure or insufficiency."[64] In assessing the quality of palliative care or hospice, it is useful to ask, Is the

This exceptionally beautiful and functional facility at Hospice MariaTeresa Chiantore Seràgnoli in Bentivoglio (Bologna), Italy, shelters and cares for cancer and palliative care patients, with the aim of improving quality and dignity of life. Each unit opens onto a private garden where families and friends may visit with patients. It is also a training hospice for the University of Bologna's Accademia della Scienze di Medicina Palliativa.

interdisciplinary team competent? Is there continuity and coordination of care in the services provided? Is care focused on the patient and family? How easy is it to access care? Is the program committed to quality?[65] The goal is to help people live as fully as possible until the end of their lives. Byock says, "Even when it is not possible to add many days to life, the opportunity exists to add life to one's days."[66]

The Origins of Hospice and Palliative Care

The roots of hospice and palliative care are found in age-old customs of hospitality and in "places of welcome" maintained by early Christians to care for pilgrims and travelers.[67] (The words *hotel, hospice,* and *hospital* derive from the Latin *hospitium,* meaning "a place that receives guests.") Whereas Roman hospitals were built on a "military model of efficiency" to provide quick repair of gladiators and slaves, Christian hospices aided injured travelers, the hopelessly ill, and victims of disasters. The dying received special honor, for they were seen as spiritual pilgrims close to God. Among the earliest hospices were those founded in the fourth century by a disciple of Saint Jerome named Fabiola, a wealthy Roman widow who became patron and nurse in caring for the sick and dying. Within the Judeo-Christian religious tradition, the basis for hospice care is found in the concepts of *diakonia* (serving and caring for others), *metanoia* (turning within to a deeper self or divine power), and *kairos* (a unique moment of fulfillment).[68]

The most influential model of modern hospice care is St. Christopher's Hospice in Sydenham, England, founded in 1967 by Dr. Cicely Saunders.[69] (Saunders first trained as a nurse, then as a medical social worker, and finally as a physician.)[70] During the 1940s, while training as a medical social worker, Saunders met David Tasma, a Jewish refugee from Poland who was dying of inoperable cancer. They formulated the vision of a haven where people could find relief from pain and die with dignity. When Tasma died in 1948, he left a small bequest to Saunders, saying, "I'll be a window in your home." Nineteen years later, with the opening of St. Christopher's Hospice, the vision became a reality as a window was dedicated to Tasma's memory.[71]

Named for the patron saint of travelers, St. Christopher's promotes acceptance of dying within an atmosphere of tranquility. St. Christopher's reflects what Saunders called a "high person, low technology and hardware" system of health care.[72] The wards and rooms at St. Christopher's are filled with flowers, photographs, and personal items. Patients are encouraged to pursue their familiar interests and pleasures. Extensive visiting hours allow for interaction between patients and their families, including children and even family pets. When a patient is dying, family, friends, and staff members gather around the bed for farewells. After death, family and friends may spend time with the body if they wish.

Home care is an important adjunct to residential care at St. Christopher's, allowing the benefits of hospice care to be extended to nonresidential patients and families. The hospice staff plans medication schedules, and hospice nurses visit patients to monitor their conditions. Over the years,

St. Christopher's has exemplified many features associated with hospice care, such as providing adequate pain control, treating the patient and his or her family as the unit of care, and achieving the best possible quality of life for dying patients.

In 1963, a visit by Cicely Saunders to the school of nursing at Yale University stimulated interest in hospice care in the United States. When Saunders again visited Yale in 1966, Florence Wald, as dean of Yale's graduate school of nursing, organized a meeting attended by Saunders, Elisabeth Kübler-Ross, Colin Murray Parkes, and others interested in improving care of the dying. Wald, who had worked with terminally ill patients and their families for more than a decade, was instrumental in establishing the first American hospice, which opened in New Haven, Connecticut, in 1974. Its first medical director was Dr. Sylvia Lack, who had previously served at St. Christopher's.

In its early years, hospice was a counterculture among the conventional clinical disciplines in its approach to care. A sign of the positive change that has occurred since that time is the approval (in 2006) of hospice and palliative medicine as a new subspecialty by the American Board of Medical Specialties.[73] Advances in palliative care have been a response to the perception that all too often care for dying patients had become ill considered and inhumane.[74]

Other key events in the modern history of hospice and palliative care include establishment of a hospital-based palliative care team at St. Luke's Hospital in New York City in 1974 and publication of assumptions and principles for terminal care by the International Work Group on Death, Dying, and Bereavement in 1979.[75] Also, in the early 1970s, at Hospice of Marin in California, Dr. William Lamers developed innovative approaches to home care for terminally ill patients. This "home care" model of hospice quickly spread, sponsored by a range of groups from churches and interfaith groups to junior leagues.[76] Hospice programs, Lamers says, were created out of a desire to improve the quality of life for patients with incurable illness, patients who were being slighted in "a health care system that stressed aggressive therapies aimed at cure or rehabilitation, but that seemed to offer disincentives for care aimed at relief of illness."[77]

Challenges for Hospice and Palliative Care

There are challenges in making hospice and palliative care more widely available at life's end.[78] First, because most care is provided in patients' homes, the presence of a primary caregiver available twenty-four hours a day is a near-requirement for receiving hospice services. A primary caregiver may be the patient's spouse, partner, or parent, although other relatives—as well as someone paid by the family or funded by public agencies—can fill this role. Caregivers must be able to accomplish a variety of health-related tasks, such as monitoring vital signs, assessing pain, and administering proper dosages of medications.

Another challenge is funding. Hospice services are covered by Medicare/Medicaid programs as well as by most private health plans, but there are limits on who qualifies. Under the Medicare Hospice Benefit, a patient must provide a doctor's certification that his or her life expectancy is six months or less if the illness trajectory follows its normal course. A review of the accuracy of physicians' clinical predictions of survival in terminally ill patients found that they "consistently overestimate survival."[79] Nicholas Christakis, a hospice physician, says that most doctors decline to prognosticate at all; when they do, they overestimate the patient's remaining days by a factor of two to five. He says, "Most doctors stick to an unspoken code: Don't foresee. If you do, don't foretell. And, if you do that, keep it upbeat and vague."[80]

"HOW DO YOU TELL A MAN HE'S GOT THREE WEEKS TO SETTLE HIS BILL?"

Because of difficulties in stating with certainty that a patient's expected prognosis is less than six months, the "six-months" rule may exclude patients who have conditions difficult to predict. It also results in both physicians and patients deferring hospice until a later stage of illness than is preferable. Because of potential confusion about the six-months rule, the head of the Health Care Financing Administration, which administers the hospice benefit, pointed out that it is a misperception that patients who outlive the six-months rule automatically lose their coverage.[81] The pertinent section of the law states, "six months or less if the illness runs its normal course."[82] Also, patients already enrolled in hospice who outlive this limit can be recertified by a hospice physician, allowing continued care.

Despite this assurance, the challenge faced by hospices is illustrated by the story of San Diego Hospice, one of the largest community-owned, nonprofit hospices in the country, which in its heyday reportedly cared for nearly one thousand patients a day, terminally ill children as well as adults. Its demise and eventual bankruptcy occurred when it faced a Medicare audit that appeared to question its admission practices and the qualifications of patients to receive federal reimbursement for hospice care. At issue was whether San Diego Hospice "allowed patients to stay on service when it could not be proved that they were dying."[83]

Another challenge faced by hospice is broadening access for underserved patient populations. According to NHPCO, in 2011, nearly 83 percent of patients were white/Caucasian, about 9 percent were black or African American, and the remaining patients were identified as Asian, Hawaiian, Pacific Islander, American Indian, multiracial, or other race. Of the total patient population, about 6 percent were identified as of Hispanic or Latino origin, a small percentage considering that this group constitutes approximately 17 percent of the U.S. population.[84]

African American participation is not much greater. For historical reasons, people of color tend to distrust social institutions.[85] A study found that requiring cancer patients to give up curative treatment is detrimental to the neediest patients and contributes to racial disparities in hospice use.[86] Moreover, ethnic groups may have traditions of family and community support when coping with illness and death, whereas most hospice programs reflect mainstream, middle-class values.[87] Richard Payne says,

> African Americans are significantly less likely to prepare a living will, to talk to their doctors about end-of-life care, or to participate in a hospice program. When death is inevitable and imminent, blacks are twice as likely as whites to request life-sustaining treatments that can make dying a miserable experience for both patients and their families. . . . In my experience, many patients, especially African Americans and members of other medically underserved minority groups, tend to think of "palliative care" as "giving up hope." I suspect this is so because many African Americans fear their cultural and personal values will not be respected when they are dying.[88]

When end-of-life decisions are being made, there is potential conflict between European American values of individualism and self-determination and the Afrocentric emphasis on collectivity and family. "Cookie-cutter services that fail to consider the contextual domain in which death and dying occur are likely to be rejected by those who most need assistance at the end of life."[89]

In its early years, hospice was distinguished by the enthusiasm of pioneer-activists who sought to offer services not available from mainstream social service agencies or in conventional medical settings and to provide services on a not-for-profit basis. Now, however, the greatest growth in the number of hospice programs has been establishment of for-profit hospices, which account for about half the total number of programs.[90] According to experts, "Outcome measurement and evaluation is no longer just an option if a hospice or palliative care program is to succeed and establish credibility in the current environment."[91] Bureaucracy and routinization have become additional challenges to hospice care. This prompts the question, Has the philosophy of hospice changed?

Inge Corless, an expert in palliative/hospice care, asks: In our zeal to provide hospice care, are we becoming as paternalistic as the medical practices we often criticize? Do patients need to comply with hospice ideology to receive services? Must all hospice clients engage in a dialogue about death? What gives us the hubris to think we know best?[92]

Critics familiar with the evolution of hospice see a subtle shift from the concept of striving for a "good" death to a more prescriptive "peaceful" death.[93] In the early days, hospices experimented with various approaches to the delivery of services. Now, says Corless, the "politicization of reimbursement for hospice care" brings regulations requiring that all programs seeking certification comply with a set of standards based on one model of care."[94]

The Future of Hospice and Palliative Care

William Lamers suggests that new forms of hospice and palliative care may be needed to meet the challenges of caring for the dying.[95] He outlines three levels of care:

1. *Traditional* hospice care for persons with fairly definable short-term prognoses (for example, advanced, incurable cancers)
2. *Long-term* hospice care for persons with an indeterminate diagnosis who do not require costly therapies to improve quality of life during a prolonged period of dying (for example, chronic, incurable neurologic disorders, such as Alzheimer's disease and amyotrophic lateral sclerosis, or ALS)
3. *High-tech* hospice care for persons who require expensive therapies to maintain reasonable relief of symptoms in the face of a limited, although uncertain, prognosis (for example, advanced AIDS)

An innovative development intended to help individuals avoid having to make a decision between palliative care and hospice is the *open access model of hospice*. "An open access hospice provides treatments that palliate symptoms and enhance the quality of life, even if the treatments are considered to be disease directed."[96] This can be a risky decision for a hospice, however, because the cost of care is increased without a corresponding increase in reimbursement. There is also risk that Medicare may consider treatment too aggressive or inappropriate for hospice and disallow coverage. Thus, whether the open access model of hospice can be sustained is unclear.

A step toward easing this challenge of hospice has been made by some private health insurers, who allow patients to receive curative therapy and hospice care concurrently. Kaiser Permanente, for example, has established an interdisciplinary home-based program, the Palliative Care Project, which helps patients transition gradually from curative therapy to palliative care.

Another potential solution to this challenge is to create a *bridge* that offers patients hospice services earlier than they can be provided under the Medicare Hospice Benefit. "Bridge programs are based on the concept that palliative care experts have long advocated that end-of-life care can be enhanced by better integration of palliative care throughout the continuum of care."[97] Such programs are offered by a hospice in collaboration with a home health agency or other care provider that provides pain and symptom management, consultation, and other supportive services when a patient with a life-limiting condition is not yet ready to elect the hospice benefit. According to the program of care offered by Partners HealthCare, a nonprofit health system founded by Brigham and Women's Hospital and Massachusetts General Hospice,

> Bridge to Hospice is for people who are coping with a life limiting condition and whose prognosis is uncertain. This program provides home care support that they need now, with preparation for future support from hospice. Together, we focus on improving the quality of life for our patients by anticipating and managing possible changes that may occur in their care. This allows for early identification and a seamless transition from home health to hospice care.[98]

The key points to remember about bridge programs is that they apply to a patient who (1) has a life-limiting condition and is receiving curative treatment, (2) requires pain and symptom management and meets the insurer's criteria for home health care, and (3) is hospice appropriate but declines hospice care.

Home Care

Medically supervised end-of-life care that is provided in a patient's home is often referred to as "hospice home care." Such care is directed by physicians, coordinated by nurses, and usually supported by an interdisciplinary team that may include volunteers, family members, and friends. Home care offers a number of potential advantages as a setting for terminal care,

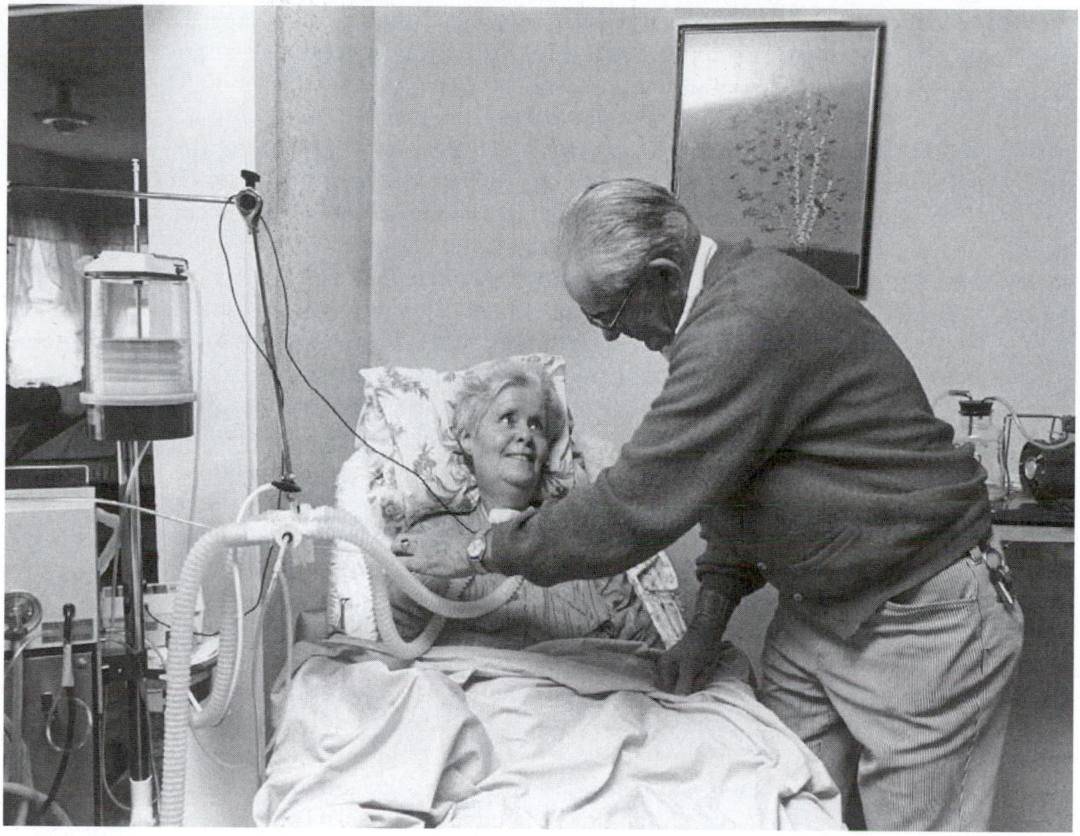
© Carol A. Foote

Home care may not come immediately to mind when one thinks of health care systems, yet this centuries-old tradition of care for the ill and the dying is once again emerging as an option for many. Innovations in sophisticated medical life-support equipment often make it possible for the seriously ill to be cared for using a high level of medical technology within the home.

including the obvious fact that the patient is *at home,* which, for most people, is a "center of meaningful activity and connectedness to family, friends, and community."[99]

At home, instead of having to comply with a schedule of visiting hours and other rules determined by institutional routine, the patient and his or her family enjoy greater flexibility. Home care lessens the need to "live to a timetable" and provides a sense of normalcy that enhances opportunities for the patient to maintain relationships and exercise self-determination. It also allows for a mutuality of care and concern, which families often find gratifying in caring for an ailing family member.

However, to realize these attractive features, home care requires adequate support, preparation, and commitment. Home care can be a twenty-four-hour-a-day job. Whether family member, friend, paid home health aide, or outside volunteer, someone must be available to manage the various tasks that constitute appropriate care of the patient. Although about 40 percent of adult caregivers are men, day-to-day personal and household care is typically shouldered by women, who have traditionally filled the role of "family nurse" and continue to do so, despite social progress in breaking down gender stereotypes in other areas. Even so, family caregivers may be marginalized by health care professionals and denied access to information they may need to do a good job.[100]

The strain of caring for a dying relative may cause the caregiver to be inattentive to his or her own health care needs, with the result that the caregiver becomes sick or run down. Thus, another phenomenon associated with home care is *secondary morbidity,* which refers to "difficulties in the physical, cognitive, emotional, or social spheres of functioning that may be experienced by those closely involved with the terminally ill person."[101] Secondary morbidity can affect professional or volunteer caregivers as well as family members and friends of the dying person. The patient care workload can be lightened by outside support services provided, for example, by visiting nurses. There are likely to be times when it is appropriate to arrange *respite care*—temporary care that gives family members or other caregivers a welcome break.

Social Support

Social support is a key component of care for patients with a life-threatening illness. It can help patients gain better understanding of their illness and provide a forum for sharing ways to cope with fears and enhance physical and emotional well-being. Caregivers are encouraged to cultivate a "listening mind" that allows them to be present to the needs and concerns of both the patient and his or her family. Frank Ostaseski, founding director of Zen Hospice Project, says, "One of our central tasks is to be available when stories are ready to be told."[102]

Organizations dedicated to helping people with specific illnesses—for example, cancer, heart disease, or Alzheimer's—can be found through hospitals and other community agencies. The Internet is another alternative resource. It offers health and medical information, and some sites provide social support. For example, online patient groups demonstrate shared concern for a particular illness or malady and provide a forum for giving and receiving both information and support. Allan Kellehear proposes a type of "health-promoting palliative care" that enlists support "not merely in terms of support groups but also as a wider community issue."[103]

At Stanford Hospital in California, volunteers are enlisted to make sure that no one dies alone.[104] For a patient who outlives his or her close relatives, is estranged from his or her children, or becomes ill far away from family, volunteers come to the hospital and sit with a stranger in his or her final moments. Stanford's "No One Dies Alone" program attempts to humanize the often sterile, clinical setting of the hospital. The volunteers describe sitting with the dying as deeply profound, an honor, and a privilege. Unlike the nursing team, there's no to-do list; it's simply being present.

I Know (I'm Losing You)

Have you ever touched your father's back? No, my fingers tell me, as they try to pull up a similar memory.

There are none. This is a place we have never traveled to, as I try to lift his weary body onto the bedpan.

I recall a photo of him standing in front of our house. He is large, healthy, a stocky body in a dark blue suit.

And now his bowels panic, feed his mind phony information, and as I try to position him, my hands shift and the news shocks me more than the sight of his balls.

O, bag of bones, this is all I'll know of his body, the sharp ridge of spine, the bedsores, the ribs rising up in place like new islands.

I feel him strain as he pushes, for nothing, feel his fingers grip my shoulders. *He is slipping to dust,* my hands inform me, *you'd better remember this.*

Cornelius Eady

Elder Care

Round-the-clock care is sometimes needed to manage the illnesses and debilities that may accompany old age. Listen to conversations about care of a chronically ill older adult, and you may notice language like this: "She couldn't live by herself, so her son took her in," or "He was failing and had to be put in a nursing home." A question like "What will we do with Dad when he is too old and can't manage by himself?" can reflect both loving concern and inadvertent disregard for the aged person. It is not surprising that old people report feelings of being put away, taken in, done to, and otherwise manipulated, their integrity ignored.

Institutional care is likely to be depersonalizing. Residents may feel deprived of self-esteem and integrity. Rules and regulations dictate a style of life that may be far from what the resident would choose for himself or herself. Even a cherished picture of a loved one may find no place in the resident's room: not the bedstand (that's for bedpans), not the wall (patients are frequently moved)—so, where? The answer may be, nowhere.

Gerontologists—people who study the process and the problems of aging—describe how the "psychological railroading" of routinized, bureaucratic environments can result in an *institutional neurosis,* the symptoms of which include "a gradual erosion of the uniqueness of one's personality traits so that residents become increasingly dependent on staff direction for even the most mundane needs."[105] Such favoring of institutional expediency over the needs of living persons cannot be justified.

In the United States, social service programs for older people can be traced to the Depression of the 1930s and the passage of the Social Security

Act of 1935. The Old Age Assistance Act, enacted in 1950, became the first federal program to deal specifically with problems of the aged. Following adoption of the Medicare and Medicaid programs in the mid-1960s, federal assistance became a customary means of providing care for America's elderly.

Nevertheless, questions about how to provide adequate, as well as cost-effective, care of the aged continue to be of public concern, and they become more important as life expectancy increases: Aged people are not only growing in numbers but also making up a larger proportion of the total population. (*Senescence,* the state or process of becoming old, is discussed in Chapter 11.)

Historically, the family has been a haven for ill and aged relatives, and families continue to provide the major portion of care for aged relatives. Indeed, most elders live in their own homes or with their families, who often highly value the care they provide to an older relative. But aged people may require more assistance than relatives or friends can realistically provide.

Home health care may be available to assist the older person in a variety of ways, ranging from medical and nursing visits to helping with preparation of meals, exercise, and other maintenance needs, along with simple (but important) visitation. The decision for institutional care is usually made when a person is no longer able to live independently and his or her family is unable to provide the level of care needed.

There are several alternatives to consider. *Home sharing* is one possibility. This is an option with various configurations: (1) an older homeowner who prefers not to live alone or needs the income rents spare rooms to other older persons, (2) several older adults rent a house or apartment, sharing kitchen and other living spaces as well as household chores, (3) a faith-based or community group sponsors a large home shared by several individuals. *Personal care homes,* also called board-and-care homes, provide care for residents who need minimal assistance and are otherwise able to care for themselves.

Midway between independent living and institutionalization is a form of care called *congregate housing.* This is usually a large facility with individual apartments or a group of small condominiums within a planned neighborhood. This is an option for residents who are mobile and able to care for themselves, although they share meals in a central dining room and enjoy housekeeping services. *Assisted living facilities* provide for residents who cannot live independently, but do not require skilled nursing care. Assistance may include help with bathing, meals, and housekeeping.

Continuing care retirement communities are designed to provide the level of care required by the changing needs of older people. Such communities offer a variety of housing options and services on the same campus. This option is distinguished by its organizational structure, which, like a series of concentric circles or graduated steps, provides the level of care needed by each resident. Within such a community, some individuals essentially live independently, preparing meals in their own apartments or eating in a common dining room when they wish. This type of facility may include various floor plans, from studio apartments to suites of three bedrooms plus den. Such

TABLE 5-3 *Steps in Choosing a Nursing Care Facility*

1. Make a list of local facilities offering the type of services needed.
2. Find out whether the facilities are licensed and certified.
3. Visit the facilities.
4. Prepare a checklist of desirable features and evaluate each facility in light of the needs of the person who would be moving in.
5. Determine the costs.
6. Make your decision.

communities typically offer a variety of recreational services, such as game rooms, libraries, walking paths, and other social and cultural activities, as well as transportation to shopping, art exhibits, and theater events. A person moves to an assisted living unit when help is needed with activities of daily living. A skilled nursing facility is also available on campus when needed, and hospice care may be available on site. These various levels of care within the same campus allow older people to enjoy a sense of security without losing their independence, knowing that help is available when required.

Finally, *skilled nursing facilities* provide comprehensive care, furnishing medical and nursing services as well as dietary supervision.

Despite the image of old people being "dumped" in nursing homes by uncaring relatives, this is rarely the reality. On the contrary, families often delay obtaining care for elders because of reluctance to accept the fact that more help is needed. Entering into institutional care is usually viewed as a personal failure for both the aged person and his or her family. It is pictured as the least desirable option, "a sort of confession to final surrender, a half-way stop on the route to death."[106] However, it may be the only reasonable course open to an aged person. The best outcome follows when adequate information is gathered before making a decision about a particular facility (see Table 5-3). In coming decades, novel types of elder care undoubtedly will be created to accommodate "baby boomers."[107] Perhaps most important for individuals and as a society is the imperative to address the task of envisioning and creating a worthy place for the old who live among us.

Trauma and Emergency Care

It was only little more than half a century ago that hearses stopped doing double-duty as ambulances and emergency medical technicians (EMTs) replaced "ambulance drivers." This led to dramatic change as ERs began to receive patients who previously would not have reached the hospital alive.[108]

In the United States, modern hospital-based trauma care was initiated in 1966 by Robert Freeark at Cook County Hospital in Chicago and William Blaisdell at San Francisco General Hospital. Then, in 1969, R. Adams Cowley formed a comprehensive system of trauma and emergency care by bringing together the Maryland State Police and the Maryland Institute for Emergency

Medical Services to create the first civilian helicopter medevac program. The first *hospital-based* helicopter program was established in 1972 at St. Anthony's Hospital in Denver. These innovations reflect the standard approach to emergency treatment in the United States, which is termed "scoop and run," meaning that accident victims receive minimal on-site treatment from paramedics and are rushed to emergency rooms or trauma centers. "Stay and play" is used to describe an approach in which extensive on-site treatment and stabilization are performed by doctors who arrive at the scene of the accident in mobile hospital units. (This was the approach used to treat Diana, Princess of Wales, when the Mercedes in which she was a passenger crashed in the Alma tunnel in France.)[109]

Many of the procedures now commonplace in trauma care have been adapted from techniques used by the military in combat situations. These include the use of helicopter air ambulances, advances in team surgery and orthopedics, and treatment for burns and shock. In fact, the roots of modern emergency and trauma care can be traced back to the Civil War, when Army Major John Letterman developed a *triage* system for evacuating casualties.

Emergency personnel, including search-and-rescue workers and police officers, engage in the grim task of recovering and identifying the bodies of two people who died in the crash of a helicopter about a thousand yards offshore. Such work is stressful and involves an extensive network of helping professionals who typically receive little or no formal training in methods of coping with the impact of multiple encounters with death, an inevitable consequence of the performance of their duties.

Aimed at reducing time between injury and care, triage involves assigning priorities to patients based on the seriousness of their injuries. Highest priority is given to patients whose injuries are serious but survivable. Lower priorities are assigned to patients with only a remote chance of survival and to those with comparatively minor injuries.

In a recent year, more than 121,000 Americans died from injuries sustained in accidents.[110] About 40 percent of these deaths involved motor vehicle accidents, with falls, drownings, fires, and poisoning and exposure to noxious substances accounting for most of the rest. Experts in emergency care and *trauma* (defined as physical injury) refer to the "golden hour" following accidental injury, of which the first fifteen minutes are especially critical.[111]

Think about the compelling images associated with the drama of life-or-death situations in the emergency room.[112] As one ER staffer said, "You can be sitting there almost lulled to sleep during a quiet period, then suddenly everything is happening at once because there's just been a five-car crackup." Interventions must be rapidly and efficiently mobilized if life is to be sustained. Trauma patients are frequently comatose or incoherent due to shock. The emergency room staff must take action that makes the difference between life and death while receiving little or no feedback from the patient.

Caregivers disagree about whether family members should be present in the ER (or at home when EMTs are called) during cardiac resuscitation.[113] Incorporating family members into such events can be quite challenging, yet

> The worst thing I ever saw was either two babies and their grandmother burnt to death, to nothing, to just charred black lumps that had to be picked up out of smoking rubble, or a guy who wasn't dead yet who was mashed half in two by a truck. I saw a lot of death, and I worked at a small department in a little Mississippi town. It may sound cold, but the dead who were already gone never bothered me as much as the living ones, who were in great amounts of pain and shock, who had to be assured that yes in fact they were not going to die but were going to live if they would just take it easy and relax. You cannot think about a person's pain and do your most efficient job; if your feelings about his feelings are weighing on your mind more than how best to remove his crumpled car door from around his body, you're not doing him any good and should probably step aside and let somebody else operate the tool.
>
> Remove the car from the victim, not the other way around. You can be faced with anything. A car upside down on top of two people, one dead, one alive. A head-on collision, two dead, two alive, one each in each car. A car flipped up on its side against a tree, the driver between the roof and the tree. A burning car with live occupants trapped inside.
>
> Rolling on a call has been likened to soldiers going into combat.
>
> Larry Brown, *On Fire*

some argue that the family deserves the opportunity to be present in what may be the last minutes of the patient's life. As Jerome Groopman points out, "Resuscitations are generally gruesome—physicians occasionally have to split ribs or cut into a windpipe in an effort to keep someone who is bleeding or unconscious alive—and just fifteen percent, at most, are successful."[114] Still, some studies have shown that relatives who *did not* witness resuscitation efforts were more likely to experience anxiety, depression, and post-traumatic symptoms afterwards. Nonetheless, there is a subgroup of the population who appear to be at risk for a severe adverse reaction, including attempted suicide, after witnessing resuscitation.

When a patient dies, members of the staff face the task of delivering bad news to relatives. A doctor usually provides news of a patient's death, perhaps with other staff members on hand. The manner in which such news is communicated often will remain with survivors for a lifetime.

Death Notification

A notification of death "announces a void in the social fabric."[115] Medical personnel are not the only group with the task of delivering "bad news." Emergency personnel, police officers, and firefighters also seek appropriate resources to do effective notification.[116] R. Moroni Leash says, "Death notification is always traumatic. Difficult family dynamics and death scenarios can make it much more complex."[117] For military deaths, the policy of sending a Western Union telegram has been replaced by a personal visit to the next of kin: "We are here to inform you that your son. . . ." Those devastating, dreaded words delivered by a stranger who seems to be the grim reaper launches survivors into the role of the bereaved, and grief is unpredictable. After being told that his son had been killed in Iraq, a Florida man used gasoline and a blowtorch to set fire to the Marines' van, severely burning himself.[118] One writer said that notifiers have the task of uttering "the first lines of a final chapter in a family's life."[119]

In a recent year in the United States, about 45,300 people were killed in motor vehicle crashes, many involving drunk driving, and more than 18,000 died by homicide.[120] Often, deaths occur away from the next of kin, who must be told the news. Selection of the notifier is important, although this task is frequently thrust unexpectedly on emergency personnel. More important than *who* are *how* and *when* and even *where.*

In a hospital, the notifier is usually a physician who was involved in the life-saving efforts. If a physician is not available and family are already present, a nurse may give the notification. As the person ultimately responsible for treatment, however, the physician is thought best able to provide a detailed explanation, and families tend to accept the reality more readily if a physician notifies. However, good arguments can be made for bringing in a social worker, chaplain, or counselor, perhaps even to deliver the initial news if the physician is unavailable or has just finished "running the code" and needs time to decompress.

"I already know he's gone—it's been on the Internet."

When a death occurs "in the field," notification may be done by police officers, firefighters, EMTs, or coroner's staff. The primary notifier is preferably someone who has ample time to discuss the death and who was present with the victim or knows the details that led to the death, because families often ask for more information. This may be someone who provided on-scene medical assistance if family members happen on the scene or survive the accident and have questions about the condition of others.

Often, notification does not occur at the scene of death, meaning that next of kin must be identified and contacted. This can present challenges when the deceased is, for example, an undocumented migrant, a transient, or a teenage runaway. The notifier must be certain of the identity of the deceased to prevent an erroneous notification intended for someone else. Key elements in notification include timely announcement, control of the physical environment, details of the efforts to save the life, explanation of the cause(s) of death, appropriate emotional support, and other resources that could be helpful to

> Generally, the doctor's announcement of the death was made within the first or first two sentences, usually in the course of one long sentence. An interesting feature of his presentation, more common in the DOA situation than in announcements of the deaths of hospital patients, was that in announcing the death he provided, in some way, that the death be presented as having followed a course of "dying." In nearly every scene I witnessed, the doctor's opening remarks contained an historical reference. . . . This was true in accidental as well as "natural" deaths, and true whether or not the physician had any basis for assuming a likely cause of death. . . . Physicians seem to feel in such situations that historicizing their delivery of news, no matter how much their limited knowledge of the case may restrict the range of possibilities, helps not only reduce some of the shock values of "sudden deaths" but aids in the very grasp of the news. The correctness of the physician's supposed cause of death is of secondary significance relative to the sheer fact that he provides some sequential formulation of its generation, some means whereby the occurrence can be placed in a sequence of natural or accidental events. This is felt particularly to be necessary in the DOA circumstance, where many deaths occur with no apparent "reason," particularly the so-called "sudden unexpected death," not uncommon among young adults.
>
> David Sudnow, *Passing On: The Social Organization of Dying*

the bereaved. If it is necessary to make telephone contact, the notifier should plan to direct the conversation and avoid telling more than is appropriate for the circumstance, especially if family dynamics and emotional stability are not known.[121] Plans can be made to meet in person with the family.

Peter Rober and Paul Rosenblatt remind us that the death of a loved one is always painful for a family, and "unexpected deaths are particularly tragic and shattering."[122] The process of making meaning of the loss begins with notification. As family members deal with the available information about the circumstances of the death, they start to create a story about their loss. The manner in which notification is carried out can be significant in shaping the family's experience of grief.

Leash suggests a "sequential notification technique" to prepare the family for the ultimate statement of death. He says, "Coordinate your statements with their emotional responses. By so doing, you allow them to control the flow of the conversation, preparing themselves as you proceed together."[123] In meeting with the family (in this scenario, at the hospital), follow these steps:

1. Ask the family members what they already know about the situation.
2. Bridging from what they know, give a brief description of events that led up to the patient's arrival at the hospital.
3. Give information regarding the resuscitative efforts made on behalf of the patient.
4. Conclude with the victim's response to treatment, the statement of death, and a brief explanation of the cause of death.

In terms of the death system, notification relates to functions in such areas as making sense of death, disposing of the dead, and consolidation after death.

Caregiver Stress and Compassion Fatigue

Health care professionals not only must possess necessary technical skills but also must learn how to deal with their own anxieties about dying and death.[124] The goal of saving every patient may be worthy, but it is not realistic or practical in the context of trauma care, or, indeed, in that of medical care generally. When the circumstances of a death provoke the caregiver's own anxieties or when a death is exceptionally tragic—the death of a child, for example, or the death of several members of a family in an automobile accident on Christmas Eve—it is likely to profoundly affect caregivers.[125] This observation also applies to firefighters, police officers, and other *first-responders* (personnel who are first to arrive at the scene of accidents, disasters, and other life-threatening medical situations), as well as to search-and-rescue personnel.[126] Examples of events likely to have a negative impact on emergency service personnel include

- Disasters
- Incidents involving children
- Events in which victims are known to personnel
- Line-of-duty deaths

The impact of working in a death-saturated environment is evident on the faces of rescue and recovery personnel when disaster occurs. Although it is frequently suggested that such individuals receive *critical incident stress management* (CISM) intervention following traumatic events, the particulars of how best to provide psychosocial aid are neither obvious nor generally agreed upon.[127] Such interventions have received criticism for having little positive effect; some argue that they actually worsen trauma. Others express the view that CISM is ineffective with some groups and beneficial for others.

The essential idea is to allow the person who has experienced trauma a chance to talk about it without receiving judgment or criticism. One scenario involves a three-step approach that addresses the trauma at various stages: First, a *defusing* is done the day of the incident. The purpose of the defusing is to assure the people involved that their feelings are normal, alert them to symptoms to watch for over the short term, and offer them a lifeline (in the form of a telephone number to reach someone they can talk to). Defusings are often informal, sometimes done at the scene. The defusing is followed within two or three days by a *debriefing,* which gives affected individuals a chance to talk about their experiences, discuss coping strategies, identify individuals who may be at risk, and inform them about resources in the community. A debriefing is typically the second level of intervention for people directly affected by the incident, and it may be the first for those not directly involved. The final step is to *follow up* to ensure that the individuals are safe and coping well or to refer them for professional counseling.

© Susan Ragan, AP Photo

Members of the Newburgh, New York, Volunteer Ambulance Corps are overcome with tears at the end of a memorial held for seven children killed at a local elementary school by a tornado. Emergency personnel who work in closely knit communities often have personal relationships with those they serve and thus may experience with special intensity the tragedies that befall their neighbors.

Professionals who provide care for seriously ill and dying people may be more familiar with death than the average person; however, experiences with death can still be stressful, and the frequency of such experiences can lead to *compassion fatigue.* The main sources of stress include feelings of inadequacy, nonreciprocal giving, and too many demands. The biggest threat tends to occur when caregivers feel helpless, seemingly unable to improve the situation. They may ask, Was there something else that could have been done? Caregivers may experience a litany of what-ifs when deaths occur. When caring is defined as curing, caregivers are vulnerable to feelings of failure when a patient dies.[128]

> A person's in the room with me and they're very close to dying and afraid. I can feel the fear of death in myself. I'm working through my fear. I give them an opportunity, silent though it may be, to work through theirs. If I come into a room saying, "Oh, there's nothing to be afraid of. We go through death and then into another rebirth," that's not very useful. That's a way of not dealing with the power of the moment—the suffering in that room in the fellow on the bed, and the suffering in the mind of the fellow next to the bed.
>
> Stephen Levine, *A Gradual Awakening*

When the health care system or other people or phenomena interfere with a carer's ability to provide relief to a dying person's suffering, the result may be *moral distress.* "Moral distress occurs when the clinician knows the appropriate action to take, but is unable to carry it out and feels forced to give care contrary to her values."[129]

In working day in and day out with individuals who are seriously ill and dying, caregivers who become fatigued by grief may be tempted to take refuge in hospital routine and standardized policies as a way of alleviating stress. This can lead to emotional exhaustion, or *burnout,* defined as a reaction to stress in which a carer goes beyond a state of exhaustion and depression to being "past caring."

Danai Papadatou proposes what she terms a "relationship-centered" approach, the basic idea of which is that "care cannot be perceived or understood independently of the relationships in which it occurs."[130] She says,

> No matter how "expert" we become—or strive to appear—dying and bereaved people remind us that we are human and equal in the face of death. We all die—some sooner, others later. In this field of work, we are all affected by the transience of life, the irreversibility of death, the suffering that loss engenders, and an existential quest for meaning.

The death of a patient whom caregivers have come to know well is likely to evoke grief. Papadatou says, "We hold onto memories of patients who, through their experience, provided us with opportunities to review our work, our practices, and our lives."[131]

It is important for carers to maintain balance in all the professional and personal dimensions of life: occupational, physical, intellectual, social, emotional, and spiritual. When care for the caregiver is recognized as crucial to being fit to provide empathetic care, caregiver stress and compassion fatigue can be minimized.

A Changing Health Care System

Care of dying persons takes place within a health care system that is undergoing rapid change. Some of these changes are due to financial issues that simultaneously result in moves to ration scarce health care resources while other initiatives seek to broaden access to health care for poor and underserved segments of the population. There are various ways of measuring the outcome of health care choices in relation to available resources. For example, the concept of "quality-adjusted life years" (or QALYs) is concerned with a balance between *length* of life and *quality* of life.[132] The idea behind QALYs is that individuals may be willing to accept a trade-off: A person might equate the prospect of living *fewer* years in *perfect* health with the prospect of living *more* years in *less-than-perfect* health. Decisions about this trade-off and other matters inherent in the health care system must be made by society as well as individuals.

The boundary where patient and staff meet—that is, the caregiver-patient relationship—is crucial to the assessment of quality health care. Clear communication is essential, especially in the context of serious or life-threatening illness. Equally important in this context is the provision of total care to patients with life-limiting diagnoses.

In response to this need, recent decades have seen dramatic growth in hospices and palliative care. Although this type of care has become an important part of the overall health care system, there are still challenges that must be addressed to carry adequate care of the dying into the future. Some of the main challenges have been discussed in this chapter.

Similarly, dramatic advances in trauma and emergency care have resulted in life-saving innovations that bring benefits to a large number of patients and their families. Notification of death to families often contains information regarding the resuscitative efforts made on behalf of the patient. As the following chapter shows, however, CPR (cardiopulmonary resuscitation) has brought many questions of its own when applied in the context of a life-limited or dying patient. This is one of the most pressing questions concerning end-of-life issues and ethics—and how such issues and ethics play out in the health care system.

Options for elder care have expanded in recent years as well. Daniel Callahan points out that "the retirement of the baby boomers will be the great demographic event of the first half of the twenty-first century, just as the birth of that generation was the great demographic event of the last half of the twentieth century."[133] In consequence, society will confront issues related to aging and the aged—and their interaction with the health care system—in new and possibly unforeseen ways.

Allan Kellehear says, "The question of seamless social support for end-of-life care finds its answer, however ambitious and daunting the task, in community care."[134] We explore the model of *compassionate cities* and how it applies to end-of-life care in Chapter 15.

Further Readings

Ira Byock. *The Best Care Possible: A Physician's Quest to Transform Care Through the End of Life.* New York: Avery Penguin, 2012.

Daniel Callahan. *Taming the Beloved Beast: How Medical Technology Costs Are Destroying Our Health Care System.* Princeton, N.J.: Princeton University Press, 2009.

Helen Chapple. *No Place for Dying: Hospitals and the Ideology of Dying.* Walnut Creek, Calif.: Left Coast Press, 2010.

Stephen R. Connor. *Hospice and Palliative Care: The Essential Guide,* 2nd ed. New York: Routledge, 2009.

Marilyn J. Field and Christine K. Cassel, eds. *Approaching Death: Improving Care at the End of Life.* Washington, D.C.: National Academy Press, 1997.

Sharon R. Kaufman. . . . *And a Time to Die: How American Hospitals Shape the End of Life.* New York: Scribner, 2005.

Stanley Joel Reiser. *Technological Medicine: The Changing World of Doctors and Patients.* New York: Cambridge University Press, 2009.

Irene Renzenbrink, ed. *Caregiver Stress and Staff Support in Illness, Dying, and Bereavement.* New York: Oxford University Press, 2011.

Additional resources for this chapter can be found at www.mhhe.com/despelder10e

Adequate planning helps ensure that we do not unnecessarily add to the burdens carried by our survivors when we die. Such planning includes consideration not only of the disposition of our estate but also of the content of our advance directives. Although some end-of-life issues are easily decided, others may require us to intensely consider alternatives. Our thoughtful choices will likely reflect our own personal and family values as well as social and cultural preferences.

CHAPTER 6

End-of-Life Issues and Decisions

A sudden stroke severely incapacitated a divorced woman in her late fifties who had been living independently. Nothing had been discussed or written about her wishes in the event such an incapacitating event occurred. As her condition worsened, her four brothers and sisters, five children, their partners, and nieces and nephews began to discuss what "Mom would have wanted." Not surprisingly, many conflicting notions were expressed. There were arguments by phone and in person. After the woman died, family members who had been most vocal never spoke to one another again.

Choices concerning end-of-life care are best made by individuals, families, and caregivers, who, acting together, form a community of interest with firsthand knowledge about a particular case and the will to make moral decisions.[1] Some decisions involve matters that can be dealt with long before an individual is faced with the crisis of an illness or debility. These include activities like making a will, establishing a living trust, obtaining life insurance, and completing an advance directive to express wishes about medical treatment in the event one becomes incapacitated. Other decisions are likely to arise when a person is near death. These include such matters as choosing to withhold or withdraw treatments and considering physician-assisted death or aid-in-dying. Finally, some issues are initiated earlier in life but are not completed until after a person's death. These include the settling of a person's estate through probate and the disbursement of proceeds from insurance and other death benefits to survivors.

Decision making in the end-of-life (EOL) context has been defined as "the aspects of life-threatening illness/terminal illness that involve choices and decisions about actions to be taken, for individuals, families, and professional caregivers."[2] We expand this definition to include issues and decisions that pertain more generally to the end of a person's life, not just those that pertain to the specific period when end-of-life care is provided.

The reason for thinking about ethics and developing skills to deal creatively with ethical issues is not so that we can adopt some particular set of principles, but, rather, so we can exercise powers of reflection and consider possibilities and options that enable us to think for ourselves. It seems there is never a good time for EOL planning. We tend to say, "I'm an active person, I've got things to do, I'll get to it when there's time." The result, for most of us, is that end-of-life planning is placed low on our list of priorities.

The end-of-life issues and decisions discussed in this chapter deserve consideration at an early stage of life. When we acknowledge the inevitability of death, we can prepare for it. Planning helps ensure that we do not add to the burdens carried by our survivors. Many issues can be anticipated, considered, and discussed with close relatives and trusted friends. Thus, it is wise to begin considering EOL issues and decisions as soon as possible and then periodically review and revise choices throughout life.

Principles of Medical Ethics

To provide a framework for discussing informed consent, withdrawing or withholding medical treatment, euthanasia, physician-assisted death, and other issues relevant to end-of-life care, it is worthwhile to review some guiding principles of medical ethics.[3] To begin, *ethics* is concerned with the investigation of what is good and bad, especially as these concepts relate to moral duties and obligations. Such an investigation results in a set of moral principles or values that guide behavior. When we think of *morals,* or moral principles, we are dealing essentially with notions of right and wrong. Although the two terms—*morals* and *ethics*—are closely related, we can distinguish them in one way by noting that morals involve conforming to established codes or accepted notions of right and wrong, whereas ethics involve more subtle or challenging questions. The pursuit of ethics is characterized by efforts to answer the question, What is the good? and its corollary, What is to be done?

In applying ethical principles to the realm of medicine, several concepts have importance. The first of these, *autonomy,* refers to an individual's right to be self-governing—that is, to exercise self-direction, freedom, and moral independence. Our personal autonomy is limited by the rights of others to exercise their autonomy, and it also may be limited by society, which exercises rights in the name of the community. One example is the requirement that a traveler must obtain inoculations before being granted a visa to enter certain countries; the traveler's autonomy is restricted by concerns about public health imposed by the larger community.

Thus, limits may be placed on a person's autonomy and autonomy may be challenged. Such challenges can include, among other things, the impact of decisions on the welfare of the individual, the interests of others, including caregivers, and society's interest in the allocation of scarce resources.[4] Culture and religious beliefs influence how individuals exercise their autonomy. For some cultural groups, family members have a primary, or at least equal, voice in decisions about a patient's care.[5] Individual autonomy is offset by respect for the values of others with whom one has a significant relationship. If decisions are made without considering their effect on the "family commons," those choices may be overridden. Thus, within limits, the principle of autonomy promotes "respect for persons" as people negotiate the medical system.

Another fundamental principle in medical care is *beneficence,* which involves doing good or conferring benefits that enhance personal or social well-being. This principle is sometimes expressed by its counterpart, *nonmaleficence,* or the injunction to "do no harm." In the context of caregiver-patient relationships, this principle requires that physicians not abandon a patient even when a patient makes decisions or takes actions that the physician believes are ill advised.[6]

Finally, medical ethics is concerned with the principle of *justice.* Like "the good," justice is not easy to define, although it includes qualities of impartiality and fairness as well as right and proper action. Justice implies going beyond one's own feelings, prejudices, and desires to find an appropriate balance among conflicting interests. As you consider the issues discussed in this chapter, keep in mind the fundamental ethical principles of autonomy, beneficence, and justice. Physician John Lantos says, "The goal of medical ethics, it seems, should not be to develop rules that will minimize the need for individual virtues but to develop virtues that will minimize the need for rules."[7]

Informed Consent to Treatment

Patients have a right to be informed about their medical condition and about the proposed plan of treatment. We see our doctor to obtain medication to cure the flu or mend a broken arm, and we may give little thought to alternative treatments. We tend to rely on the physician's judgment by accepting the diagnosis and going along with the proposed treatment. By following the doctor's advice, we expect to achieve a speedy recovery. The *etiology,* or cause, of the disease or injury generally concerns us less than obtaining relief from its symptoms. However, when an illness is serious or life threatening, a patient's informed consent is more significant. Several treatment plans may be presented, each with its own set of potential risks and benefits. Which treatment promises the best results? The fewest undesirable side effects?

Principles of Informed Consent

Informed consent is based on three legal principles: First, the patient must be *competent* to give consent. Second, consent must be given *freely.* Third, consent must be based on an *adequate understanding* of the proposed

Nurse: Did they mention anything about a tube through your nose?
Patient: Yes, I'm gonna have a tube in my nose.
Nurse: You're going to have the tube down for a couple of days or longer. It depends. So you're going to be NPO, nothing by mouth, and also you're going to have IV fluid.
Patient: I know. For three or four days, they told me that already. I don't like it, though.
Nurse: You don't have any choice.
Patient: Yes, I don't have any choice, I know.
Nurse: Like it or not, you don't have any choice. (laughter) After you come back, we'll ask you to do a lot of coughing and deep breathing to exercise your lungs.
Patient: Oh, we'll see how I feel.
Nurse: (emphasis) No matter how you feel, you have to do that!

President's Commission for the Study of Ethical Problems in Medicine and Biomedical and Behavioral Research, *Making Health Care Decisions: A Report on the Ethical and Legal Implications of the Patient–Practitioner Relationship*

treatment, including any potential risks. Although the phrase *informed consent* did not achieve legal definition until 1957, its antecedents go back hundreds of years to English common law. The President's Commission for the Study of Ethical Problems in Medicine remarked that "the legal doctrine of informed consent imposes on physicians two general duties: to disclose information about treatment to patients and to obtain their consent before proceeding with treatment."[8] Although informed consent involves inquiring about patients' desires to receive medical procedures to cure their conditions, in terminal cases, the issue becomes less "informed consent" of how to cure than "truth telling" about the end of life.[9]

Informed consent ideally occurs within a context of shared decision making based on mutual respect. Because people differ in their attitudes toward autonomy and information gathering in medical care, the process of obtaining informed consent must be flexible. Some patients are more interested in being *informed* than in being fully involved in *decision making*.

Most physicians believe they have a duty to truthfully inform patients about a life-threatening condition, but this has not always been the case. A study in 1961 found that most doctors had a strong and general tendency to *withhold* information.[10] None of the doctors surveyed at that time reported a policy of telling every patient about a life-threatening diagnosis. Only about 12 percent said they would usually inform patients about a diagnosis of incurable cancer. Even when patients were informed, the disease was often described euphemistically. Doctors might tell the patient that he or she had a "lesion" or a "mass." Some doctors were more precise, using a description such as "growth," "tumor," or "hyperplastic tissue." In many instances, the description was phrased to suggest that the cancer was benign, or adjectives were used to temper the impact of the diagnosis. Thus, a tumor was said to be "suspicious" or "degenerated." Such descriptions allowed physicians to give a general explanation of the medical situation while eliciting the patient's cooperation in the proposed course of treatment.

By the late 1970s, the climate of truth telling had seemingly changed significantly. A study done in 1977 found an almost complete reversal of attitudes; about 97 percent of the doctors surveyed indicated that they would usually tell patients the truth about a diagnosis.[11] A review of this study, however, revealed methodological and theoretical shortcomings that undermined the claim of a shift in physicians' behaviors.[12] The picture became a bit clearer in a follow-up study (by the authors of the 1977 paper), which found that doctors reported that they were willing to engage in some deception when situations involved complicated or sensitive ethical issues.[13] Researchers said that physicians "appear to justify their decisions in terms of the consequences and to place a higher value on their patients' welfare and keeping patients' confidences than truth telling for its own sake."

Offering information about *prognosis*—that is, the expected course of the disease—can be a problem for physicians. It can be difficult to predict life expectancy or predict how a disease will run its course in a particular patient. Statistics about the usual course of a disease provide a rough idea of the odds of survival, and a doctor's clinical experience may also be a guide. Still, because of uncertainty, some doctors prefer to offer hope by describing recoveries without also mentioning the likelihood that most people who have such a condition will die.[14] Daniel Callahan says, "Medicine finds it harder and harder to locate the line between living and dying, and thus to know when to stop treatment."[15]

Informed consent can be especially important when medical care is provided by a team of specialists whose responsibilities are defined less by patients' needs than by particular diseases or organ systems. In some cases, it may seem as if no doctor has responsibility for the overall care of the patient. The patient may be unsure who to ask for information and advice.

To the extent that a course of treatment is elective, the outcome uncertain, and the procedure experimental, informed consent becomes correspondingly more important. For example, drawing a blood sample is a common procedure that entails little risk to the patient. Consequently, we do not expect to receive a detailed explanation of risks when we roll up our sleeve for the needle. However, a complicated surgical procedure, one with a nearly equal proportion of risks and benefits, makes a patient's informed consent crucial.

Preferences Regarding Informed Consent

What constitutes sufficient information on which the patient can base a decision? Some patients take an active role in their treatment, even proposing alternatives to their physician. Others prefer to follow the plan suggested by their doctor, not wanting to know about potential risks or the percentage of failures. Full disclosure is a help to some patients, a hindrance to others. Such variation among patient attitudes presents a dilemma for the medical practitioner.

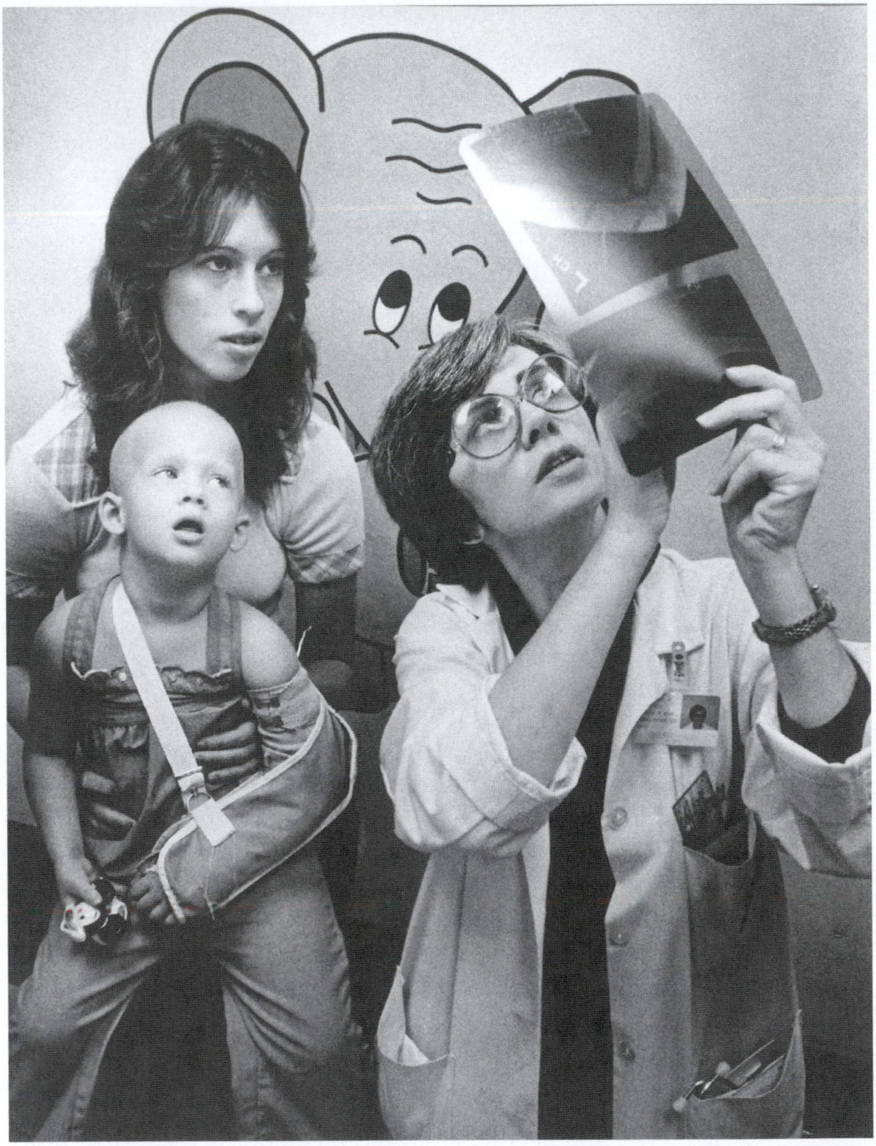

Informed consent is a fundamental ethical principle in medicine. Even fairly routine procedures, such as mending a small fracture, may become complicated when the patient is leukemic, as is this child: Alternatives must be weighed more carefully before a course of treatment is chosen.

Additionally, members of a patient's family may have their own agendas that complicate informed consent and medical decision making. Margot White and John Fletcher describe a case in which the spouse of a dying patient told doctors, "You can't tell my husband he's dying; it will kill him."[16] She insisted that the truth of her husband's illness be withheld from him, refusing the doctors' requests to speak with him about his condition and his preferences for treatment. From the wife's point of view, she knew her husband better than anyone—certainly better than the doctors—and she knew what was best for him. For the staff, however, her "interference" caused concern about thwarting or compromising the patient's autonomy and right to know.

Informed consent is closely tied to the quality of communication between physician and patient. A study designed to assess communication between physicians and seriously ill patients at the end of life found disturbing shortcomings.[17] (The study, known by its acronym, SUPPORT, was a multicenter "Study to Understand Prognoses and Preferences for Outcomes and Risks of Treatment.") Researchers found that fewer than half (41 percent) of the patients reported talking to their doctors about prognosis or CPR (cardiopulmonary resuscitation); that is, efforts to restart a patient's heart and breathing, which range from relatively simple actions, such as external chest compression, to advanced interventions that involve electric shock, insertion of a tube to open airways, injection of medication into the heart, and open chest heart massage. "Physicians misunderstood patient preferences regarding CPR in 80% of cases. When patients wanted CPR withheld, a do-not-resuscitate order was never written in 50% of cases."[18] In short, physicians were oblivious to the reality that some patients near the end of their lives would not want CPR administered. Furthermore the study revealed that half of the patients who died had moderate or severe pain during their final three days of life. Madeline Jacobs says, "The SUPPORT study revealed that people were suffering terrible deaths in hospitals, in pain, and with no power to control the last stage of their lives."[19]

Findings from Phase 2 of the study were even more troubling in terms of informed consent and patient preferences. The SUPPORT investigators assigned specially trained nurse advocates to help make patients' wishes known. Despite this intervention, there was no improvement in physician-patient communication. One expert stated, "The SUPPORT investigators underestimated the tenacity of physicians in continuing to care for patients the way they always have."[20] A little bit of education for patients and physicians was not enough to overcome the difficulty of appropriately caring for the dying.

The fact is, patients may not want disruptive medical technologies at the end of life, preferring to be allowed to die as peacefully as possible. This preference can be recognized in the medical setting by designating the patient as "DNR (meaning, Do Not Resuscitate)," "No Code," or "CMO" (Comfort Measures Only)—all of which are intended to inform medical and nursing staff not to perform CPR. Sharon Kaufman says,

> In 1965, CPR was reclassified from an exclusively medical procedure, used only in certain kinds of cases, to a universal emergency procedure that anyone could perform. By implication, anyone, anywhere, could benefit from CPR. The formal DNR order came into being in 1974. Yet consent for emergency resuscitation was, and, still is, presumed.[21]

Lack of communication may cause DNR orders to be ignored even when they exist. Families facing end-of-life decisions frequently want more guidance than they receive. Yet, doctors may be uncertain about the best course with respect to risks and benefits for a patient. There are three categories to consider in CPR decisions:

1. *CPR is a plausible option.* For example, a patient who has chronic illness that has not reached end stage.
2. *Recommend against CPR.* For example, a patient with end-stage advanced illness.
3. *Do not offer CPR.* For example, a patient who is imminently dying.

Should a decision not to offer CPR be disclosed to patients or their surrogates (persons who serve as substitute decision makers)? Whereas a decision not to offer treatment for other illnesses—for example, a patient dying of renal failure from complications of metastatic cancer—is not questioned, resuscitation is viewed differently from other medical procedures.[22]

Patients may not realize that they must speak up if they do not want emergency attempts at resuscitation. Indeed, most patients and families do not know what to want when faced with specific directives about options that are generated by institutional routines.[23] Without a DNR order, hospital policies generally require that CPR be initiated immediately if a patient is in cardiac arrest or a similar medical emergency. Even when a physician has entered a DNR order on the patient's chart, it may not contain specific guidance about which treatments should be initiated and which withheld. Does the order not to initiate CPR mean that *other* life-saving medical interventions should be done? Or should *all* such interventions be withheld? If medical heroics are to be avoided, who decides whether a particular intervention is "heroic" or "ordinary" in a given set of circumstances? When a

> When I was a junior physician in a hospital, we were once called urgently to the bedside of a lady of ninety. The nurse had used the term "cardiac arrest"—the old lady's heart had stopped (as hearts are apt to do, around ninety!). But because the cardiac arrest alarm was raised, I and the other houseman launched into a full-scale resuscitation. With violent drugs injected directly into the heart, blasts of electric current through her chest, noise and chaos, she had anything but a peaceful death. On reflection we realized that all this had been inappropriate, but nothing in our medical student training gave us any guide. Indeed once the emergency is in the air, there is not time to weigh up the pros and cons. The decision is rarely a doctor's anyway, because usually the only person on the scene when an emergency occurs is a nurse—probably a relatively junior one if it is nighttime—and she decides whether or not to resuscitate. Needless to say, it is a very courageous nurse who decides not to. Once things have started, it is very difficult for the doctor when he arrives to stop everything, particularly if the patient is showing signs of reviving.
>
> Richard Lamerton, *Care of the Dying*

patient's attending physician is not present on the scene to determine the appropriate level of treatment, it can put other medical and nursing staff in a quandary about what to do. It is not always straightforward to simply "follow doctor's orders."

Many physicians have not been trained to move from aggressive to palliative care, nor are they familiar with the principles of care associated with palliative medicine. The momentum in medicine naturally moves toward providing life-sustaining treatment. Thus, a patient's wish to refuse CPR or other life-sustaining interventions simply may not be on a doctor's "radar screen."

Although forced, coercive treatment is rare, caregivers can—unwittingly or not—exert undue influence on patients by means of subtle or overt manipulation. Once the patient is admitted to a health care institution, cooperation with caregivers is expected. The tacit communication may be that the patient has no choice. Informed consent requires cooperation between patient and physician in seeking the common goal of optimal and appropriate health care.

Choosing Death

Techniques for cardiopulmonary resuscitation (CPR) and artificial respiration allow physicians to intervene in the "normal" dying process. The human organism can be kept functioning despite the cessation of normal heart, brain, respiratory, or kidney function. (Note, however, that the portrayal of CPR on television medical shows generally presents a misleading picture of the frequency with which such resuscitation results in "miracles.")[24] When medical technologies spare patients' lives and enable them to resume more or less normal functioning, the results are gratifying. But the same technologies that prolong life can also prolong dying.

The conventional understanding of the Hippocratic oath, named for the ancient Greek physician Hippocrates, acknowledges that medical treatment is sometimes futile; that is, it is ineffective and has no possibility to "cure, ameliorate, improve, or restore a quality of life that would be satisfactory to the patient."[25] Should futile treatment be withheld or withdrawn when doing so is virtually certain to result in the patient's death? Alternatively, should treatment be continued with no reasonable hope of improvement? What is the proper balance between sustaining life and preventing suffering?

Surrounded by an array of machinery and tubes, the patient may seem less a human person than an extension of medical technology. Reviewing the range of modern medical technologies, the President's Commission for the Study of Ethical Problems in Medicine concluded, "For almost any life-threatening condition, some intervention is capable of delaying the moment of death. Matters that were once the province of fate have now become a matter of human choice."[26]

Often, the medical slogan seems to be "Keep the patient alive at all costs." Patients and their families usually find it difficult to make a decision to limit treatment, to stop "doing everything that can be done." Yet, striving to keep patients alive by all means and at any cost is also questioned. At times, in the medical arena, "the available choices are between dying sooner and comfortably and living slightly longer by receiving aggressive therapy, which may prolong the dying process, increase discomfort and dependence, and decrease the quality of life."[27] Does a person have a "right to die" when suffering outweighs the benefits of continued existence?[28]

Ethical debates about this question have become prominent since the landmark case of Karen Ann Quinlan in 1975. At age twenty-one, after a party at a local bar, she was found in her bed not breathing. Karen was admitted to the intensive care unit of a New Jersey hospital. She was in a coma. (See Table 6-1 for a description of disorders of consciousness, including coma and vegetative state.)

Soon Karen's breathing was sustained by a mechanical MA-1 respirator and she received artificial nutrition. When she remained unresponsive over the next several months, her parents asked that the respirator be disconnected so that nature could take its course. But hospital officials denied their request. Eventually, the petition reached the New Jersey Supreme Court, which ruled that artificial respiration could be discontinued.[29] Karen was taken off the respirator. To the surprise of many people, she continued to breathe unaided. She was transferred to a nursing care facility and lived in a vegetative state until her death in June 1985 at age thirty-one, having become a focal point for issues pertaining to "death with dignity."

After Quinlan, both state and federal courts issued rulings concerned with removal of life-sustaining treatment, including feeding tubes that supply nutrition and hydration to patients. Noteworthy was the case of Nancy Beth Cruzan, heard before the United States Supreme Court in 1990.[30] As a result of injuries sustained in a car crash in 1983, at age twenty-five Nancy was left in a vegetative state. Although she was resuscitated by paramedics, her brain had been deprived of oxygen for so long that she never regained consciousness. For nourishment, Nancy's physicians implanted a feeding tube in her stomach, the only form of life support she was receiving, a treatment that physicians said could prolong her life for as long as thirty years.

After waiting four years for a recovery, Nancy's parents, granted guardianship by the court, asked that the feeding tube be taken out, basing their request on Nancy's right to be free from "unwarranted bodily intrusions." The hospital refused, and the Missouri Supreme Court denied the Cruzans' petition, ruling that, without "clear and convincing evidence" of Nancy's consent, her parents could not exercise her right to refuse treatment. The state's "unqualified" interest in preserving life should prevail.

(*Clear and convincing* is a legal term, indicating a standard of proof between the heaviest burden of proof, *beyond a reasonable doubt,* which is used in criminal cases, and *a preponderance of the evidence,* a "more likely than not" standard, which is used in most civil cases.)[31]

The Missouri court's decision was appealed to the United States Supreme Court, which ruled that the right to refuse treatment, even if life sustaining, is constitutionally protected. However, the Court said states are justified in

TABLE 6-1 *Disorders of Consciousness*

Coma—A state of profound unconsciousness and unresponsiveness. Usually, after a few days or weeks, patients either regain consciousness, progress to a vegetative state, or die (if the entire brain or brain stem is permanently nonfunctional, then the diagnosis is brain death rather than coma).

Vegetative state—In this state, coma has progressed to a state of wakefulness; eyes may be open and the patient may respond reflexively to painful stimuli, but there is no detectable awareness. There is some functioning of the upper brain stem. A deep coma without detectable awareness, the vegetative state is characterized as "awake but unaware." Some investigators propose the description "unresponsive wakefulness syndrome." It has also been called "hopelessly conscious."

Persistent vegetative state—This is a wakeful unconscious state that lasts longer than a few weeks. Recovery depends largely on the extent of injury to the brain. Because *persistent* suggests irreversibility, the terms *post-coma unresponsiveness* and *vegetative coma* have been suggested as substitutes.

Permanent vegetative state—A vegetative state is considered *permanent* after three or twelve months, depending on the nature of the injury. If from oxygen deprivation, as with cardiac arrest or drowning, it is considered permanent after three months. If from traumatic brain injury, such as a motor vehicle accident or a fall, it is designated permanent after twelve months. (A word of caution when reading articles or books that use the abbreviation *PVS:* Although originally used to designate a "persistent" state, because of inherent ambiguity, it is also used to refer to a "permanent" state.)

Minimally conscious state (MCS)—Unlike the vegetative state, with which the MCS may be confused, this is a state of *consciousness.* It includes varying degrees of cortical injury. Patients exhibit fluctuating or intermittent periods of awareness of self and environment. A relatively new category of disorders of consciousness, MCS is a condition of severely altered consciousness in which minimal but definite behavioral evidence of self or environmental awareness is demonstrated. For example, MCS patients smile or cry appropriately in response to the content of emotional topics or stimuli, give gestural or verbal yes/no responses (regardless of accuracy) that are directly responsive to linguistic content of questions, and reach for objects in ways that demonstrate a clear relationship between object location and direction of reach. Such responses are not merely reflexive.

Locked-in syndrome—Not strictly a disorder of consciousness, this state involves paralysis of most muscles, except ocular muscles of the eyes; the patient is conscious, has awareness, sleep-wake cycles, and meaningful behavior (e.g., eye movement). The patient is aware and awake, but cannot move or communicate verbally. Total locked-in syndrome is similar, except the eyes are also paralyzed.

requiring that only the patient herself or himself can make such a decision. Because Nancy apparently had not made a clear expression of her wishes prior to her injury and ensuing unconscious state, Missouri was not bound to honor her parents' request.

A few months later, however, in light of testimony from several of Nancy's friends that she had expressed her wish "not to live like a vegetable," a Missouri state court ruled that the standard of "clear and convincing" evidence of Nancy's wishes had been met, and the court granted permission to remove the feeding tube. Thirteen days later and seven years after her car accident, Nancy Cruzan died. Her family said, "She showed no sign of discomfort or distress in any way. . . . There remains no question that we made the choice she would want."

Following Quinlan and Cruzan, the next name to capture widespread public attention was Terri Schiavo, who collapsed in her home in February 1990, experiencing a cardiac arrest that led to coma and subsequently a vegetative state.[32] Eight years later, Michael Schiavo, her husband and guardian, petitioned a Florida court to remove her feeding tube, an action opposed by Terri's parents, who argued that she was conscious. Over the next five years, there was a struggle in the courts to determine whether life support should be withdrawn, a struggle compounded by the fact that Terri had not completed an advance directive, although the court found evidence that she would not have wanted to be kept alive on a machine.

Terri's parents, however, argued that Terri was not in a vegetative state and, instead, was in a "minimally conscious state," saying that her actions showed response to external stimuli, not merely reflex behavior. This assertion led to more court hearings to determine whether new therapies could help restore Terri's cognitive function. By this time, the case was being played out in the media.

Terri's feeding tube was removed and, within a week, the Florida legislature passed "Terri's Law," which gave Governor Jeb Bush authority to intervene on behalf of the parents and order reinsertion of the tube. A flurry of court hearings ensued and Terri's Law was overturned by the Florida Supreme Court.

A time and date for removal of the feeding tube were again set by the court, a ruling that sparked an upsurge of federal involvement in the case. The U.S. Congress subpoenaed Terri Schiavo to testify at a "field hearing," and President Bush signed a bill that transferred jurisdiction to the federal courts. (Critics pointed out that never before had Congress used its subpoena power to obtain testimony from someone in a persistent vegetative state.)[33] Within a matter of days, further appeals were denied and the U.S. Supreme Court declined to grant judicial review, thus ending the legal options of Terri's parents.

As Madeline Jacobs observed, "The involvement of the press and ultimately the political system . . . turned this private tragedy into a public circus."[34] "Experts" kept providing Schiavo's parents with "proof" that therapies might work or with testimonies that kept their hopes alive, resulting in a "tragic misperception about Schiavo's likelihood of recovery."

Ultimately, the feeding tube was removed and, on March 31, 2005, Terri died. The subsequent autopsy revealed extensive brain damage, with Terri's brain only half the weight expected for a woman of her age, height, and weight. The report said the damage was "irreversible."[35] Perhaps because of the "culture wars" the Schiavo case generated, discussion of the terms *vegetative state, coma,* and *minimally conscious state* became part of widespread public discourse.[36]

> Ms. Schiavo died after a long odyssey that polarized her family and sparked international debate. The collision of faith, medicine, law, and politics jolted many of us into a discussion of such complex social concerns as to when life-sustaining treatment may or may not be removed from a patient with a catastrophic illness.
>
> Of the thousands of people who die each day, two-thirds will involve some element of a decision that a family will have to make.
>
> Rabbi Earl A. Grollman, "Can We Talk?"

Schiavo exposed three modern myths about life and death:[37] First, that death with dignity is easily attainable so long as people make living wills (a type of advance directive, discussed later in this chapter). Second, that only patients themselves are permitted to take quality of life into account when making life-sustaining decisions. Third, that medical innovations and miracle cures bring a promise of extending life indefinitely. Kathy Cerminara said, "The waves kicked up by the Schiavo storm will ebb and flow long after the gavel has struck for the final time in the courtroom."[38]

Withholding or Withdrawing Treatment

The right of a competent patient to refuse unwanted treatment is generally established in both law and medical practice. This can mean either withholding (not starting) a treatment or withdrawing (stopping) a treatment once it has been started. The consensus is that there is no medical or ethical distinction between withholding and withdrawing treatment. The choice to forgo life-sustaining treatment involves refusing treatments that would be expected to extend life. Such treatments include cardiopulmonary resuscitation, advanced cardiac life support, renal dialysis, nutritional support and hydration, mechanical ventilation, organ transplantation and other surgery, pacemakers, chemotherapy, and antibiotics. Even when a patient decides not to receive life-sustaining treatments, he or she ordinarily continues to receive supportive medical care. The right to refuse treatment remains constitutionally protected even when a patient is unable to communicate. Although specific requirements vary, all of the states authorize some type of written advance directive to honor decisions of individuals who have previously recorded their wishes and have become unable to speak for themselves.

When a treatment that could sustain life is withheld or withdrawn, some people have called this practice *passive euthanasia,* although this term is considered a misnomer because it tends to confuse the widely accepted practice of withholding or withdrawing treatment with the generally unacceptable and unlawful practice of taking active steps to cause death. It can be argued that "passive euthanasia" is not euthanasia at all but, rather, letting nature take its course.

The distinction between "allowing to die" (withholding or withdrawing treatment) and "helping to die" (taking steps to cause a patient's death) is important in discussions about a right to die; many ethicists and physicians (as well as the general public) are willing to permit the former but not the latter (see Figure 6-1). As you look at this figure, consider your own attitudes about choices that hasten death.

Physician-Assisted Death

Assisted death (also called assisted suicide) refers to providing someone with the means to kill himself or herself, knowing that the recipient intends to use them to end his or her life. In *physician-assisted death,* a physician helps a patient hasten his or her death by providing lethal drugs, offering advice on methods of suicide, or assisting with other interventions—at the patient's explicit request—with the understanding that the patient plans to use them to end his or her life.[39] The patient, not the doctor, administers the fatal dose.[40]

In 1997, the U.S. Supreme Court reviewed two cases relating to physician-assisted death.[41] The decisions in these cases (*Washington v. Glucksberg* and *Vacco v. Quill*) are important for several reasons. First, the Court upheld the distinction between, on the one hand, withholding or withdrawing treatment and, on the other hand, physician-assisted death. In doing so, the Court clarified its ruling in the Cruzan case, noting that the right to *refuse treatment* is based on the right to maintain one's bodily integrity, not on a right to *hasten death.* When treatment is withheld or withdrawn, the Court said, the intent is to honor the patient's wishes, not to cause death. Second, the Court affirmed the rights of states to craft policy concerning physician-assisted

Most Acceptable

Withdraw artificial life support from a patient who cannot live without such intervention

Withdraw artificial feeding or hydration from a patient who does not require any other artificial life support

Provide pain relief to a patient, knowing that it may hasten death (the so-called *double effect;* that is, treating pain *and* hastening death)

Provide a terminally ill patient with the means to kill himself or herself (e.g., write a prescription for pain medication or sleeping pills that, if taken as an overdose, will result in death)

Administer a lethal injection to a patient who is severely or terminally ill

Least Acceptable

Figure 6-1 *Public Acceptance of Hastening Death*
Note: Involuntary euthanasia occurs when someone acts arbitrarily, without the patient's consent, to end the patient's life.

death, prohibiting it, as most states now do, or permitting it under some regulatory system. A third finding of importance in the Supreme Court's 1997 rulings about physician-assisted death relates to the concept of *double effect* (discussed later in this chapter).

Currently, physician-assisted death is permitted by legislation enacted in the states of Oregon and Washington and by court ruling in the state of Montana. In May 2013, the Vermont senate passed and the governor signed the "Patient Choice and Control at End of Life Act," adding Vermont to the list. Voters in Washington state passed an initiative in 2008 that is substantially similar to the Death with Dignity Act passed by Oregon voters in 1994 and, after surviving judicial challenges, reaffirmed in 1997. So far, right-to-die groups working to change laws in other states have been unsuccessful.

The Oregon Death with Dignity Act (DWDA) allows physicians to prescribe lethal medication to terminally ill patients. Doctors who are opposed to aid-in-dying can refuse to participate, and the provisions of the law are available only to individuals who are legal residents of Oregon. In March 1998, an elderly woman with breast cancer became the first known person to die under the law, taking a lethal dose of barbiturates prescribed by her doctor.

During 2008, 88 prescriptions for lethal medications under the provisions of the DWDA were written; of these, 54 patients took the medications and died, 22 died of their underlying disease, and 12 were alive at the end of the year.[42] In addition, 6 patients with earlier prescriptions died from taking the medications, resulting in a total of 60 deaths during 2008. Since the law was passed in 1997, a total of 401 patients have died with the assistance of their physicians. Most patients died at home (97 percent). The decision to request a prescription for lethal medication was associated mainly with patients' concerns about loss of autonomy, decreasing ability to participate in activities that make life enjoyable, and loss of dignity.

In a summary of the Oregon experiment, palliative care physician Timothy Quill and Jane Greenlaw note that the practice of physician-assisted death is stable and relatively rare:

> Although there were few physician-assisted deaths, there was much conversation on the topic—one in 50 patients talked with the doctors and one in six talked with their families about the possibility. We also know that pain management has improved in Oregon, hospice utilization is among the highest in the nation, and there is a statewide program to record patients' wishes about cardiopulmonary resuscitation.[43]

Ira Byock, a hospice and palliative care physician, emphasizes the need for physicians and other caregivers to become more competent in pain management and other aspects of palliative medicine.[44] Others—including John Pridonoff, a former executive director of the Hemlock Society (which advocates assisted suicide and the "right to die")—argue that hospice and aid-in-dying can be complementary aspects of a comprehensive approach to end-of-life decisions.[45]

Daymond J. Hartley, *Detroit Free Press*

Seen here testifying in a Michigan courtroom, Dr. Jack Kevorkian became a symbol of the public debate about ethical and legal issues surrounding physician-assisted suicide. After reportedly assisting in the deaths of at least 130 people over a period of ten years, Kevorkian was found guilty of giving a man a lethal injection and sentenced to prison.

Although the trend has been toward greater freedom for individuals to choose when and how they will die, physician-assisted death continues to spark debate. In 2001, U.S. Attorney General John Ashcroft issued a directive stating that "prescribing, dispensing, or administering federally controlled substances to assist suicide violates the Controlled Substances Act." This interpretation authorized the Drug Enforcement Administration (DEA) to pursue criminal prosecution of Oregon physicians who write prescriptions under that state's Death with Dignity Act. Court cases ensued and, in January 2006, the U.S. Supreme Court ruled in *Gonzales v. Oregon* that the attorney general (then Alberto Gonzales) was not empowered to prohibit doctors from prescribing drugs under Oregon's laws.

The Rule of Double Effect

In the medical management of pain, the *rule of double effect* states that a harmful effect of treatment, even if it results in death, is permissible if the harm is not intended and occurs as a side effect of a beneficial action. Sometimes, the dosages of medication needed to relieve a patient's pain (especially at the end stage of some diseases) must be increased to levels that can cause respiratory depression, resulting in the patient's death, a practice sometimes referred to as "terminal sedation."[46] Thus, the relief of suffering (the intended good effect) may have a bad effect that is foreseen but not the primary intention. The Court said that such medication for pain, even if it hastens death, is not physician-assisted death if the intent is to relieve pain.

A study of patients with advanced disease in the Emilia-Romagna region of Italy found that overall survival was not statistically different between palliatively sedated and unsedated patients, leading researchers to conclude that palliative sedation therapy does not hasten the death of patients with advanced disease even when death occurs fairly rapidly after sedation.[47] Commenting on this study, physician Drew Rosielle notes that these were patients with a median survival of about ten days and only a quarter of the sedated patients received what is termed "deep" or "terminal" sedation. Says Rosielle, the important point is, first, that "imminently dying patients are imminently dying patients" and, second, that questions of life-prolongation are really secondary to relieving pain and other symptoms in such patients. "A peaceful, comfortable death should be the preeminent treatment goal when someone is dying, and we don't need to twist ourselves into ethical knots about it."[48] This maxim is echoed in a statement by the American Medical Association:

> It is the ethical obligation of a physician to offer palliative sedation to unconsciousness as an option for the relief of intractable symptoms [at the end of life] when symptoms cannot be diminished through all other means of palliation.[49]

Euthanasia

Illegal in the United States and distinguished from withdrawing or withholding treatment, *euthanasia* (from the Greek, "easy death") involves a deliberate act to end another person's life.[50] It is generally understood as the intentional act of killing someone who would otherwise suffer from an incurable and painful disease. An example is the case of "Debbie," a twenty-year-old woman with terminal ovarian cancer whose death was hastened by a physician called to her bedside in the middle of the night, not having previously known the patient. Seeing her distressful condition and hearing her say, "Let's get this over with," he decided without further discussion to "give her rest" by preparing a fatal injection.[51] Were Debbie's words meant as a request for the physician's help in her dying? The circumstances in this case are ambiguous.

At present, euthanasia has found greatest acceptance in the Netherlands, where physicians are legally permitted to give lethal injections to patients who request death.[52] (Euthanasia has also been legal in Belgium since 2002 and in Luxembourg since 2008; physician-assisted death has been legal in Switzerland since 1942.) The guidelines for euthanasia include the presence of a terminal diagnosis, the patient's voluntary consent and unwavering desire to die, suffering that the patient finds unbearable, a second medical opinion (recommended but not required), and documentation and reporting of the death. In the Benelux countries, there is the view that a physician's responsibility to respond to a patient's suffering is a *force majeure* (superior or irresistible force) that has precedence over normal laws.

Palliative Care and the Right to Die

In thinking about options at the end of life, we need to recognize that a "one size fits all" approach to medical treatment and decision making is likely to fit relatively few. Our preferences are influenced by both our individual beliefs and the cultural or ethnic traditions that help define who we are as human beings. Decisions about hastening death are usually arrived at because of the pain and suffering experienced by the patient or perceived by caregivers and family members. The challenge, ethicists say, is not to legalize euthanasia but to transform care of the dying.

Objections to euthanasia sometimes take the form of "wedge" or "slippery slope" arguments. This reflects the view that one should not permit acts that, even if moral in themselves, would pave the way for subsequent acts that would be immoral. If euthanasia is permitted for people with incurable illness, it could become a wedge or slippery slope toward expansion of euthanasia to the aged, the mentally incompetent, the severely handicapped, or other "burdens on society."

Charles Dougherty argues that questions about taking steps to intentionally hasten death should be considered within the context of society's "common good."[53] Emphasizing individual choice can make us lose sight of the fact that no aspect of human experience is wholly personal and private. In fact, says Dougherty, "The way we die—when, under what circumstances, and from what cause or reason—is shaped in profound ways by relationships with others and by large social and institutional forces." If dying in the medical setting involves pain and suffering and costs too much, the common good of society could be served by taking measures that "add simplicity and dignity to the process of dying and contain unnecessary spending." Dougherty suggests practical steps toward realizing this common good, such as the following:

1. Increasing the use of home hospice care
2. Developing strategies for more aggressive pain management
3. Refining protocols for timely diagnosis of terminal illness
4. Making the right to refuse extraordinary care universally available to patients
5. Expanding the use of DNR orders to avoid prolonged, expensive, and unnecessary care at the end of life

6. Providing universal access to an appropriate combination of care options (home, hospice, and so on)
7. Instituting a health insurance system that ensures adequate and appropriate care for everyone

Nutrition and Hydration

Because of the symbolic significance of nourishment, removing artificial nutrition and hydration tends to evoke deep-rooted human feelings about food and drink, as well as the image of "starving" a person to death. This causes some people to characterize removal of artificial nutrition and hydration as "intentional killing."

Should an exception to a patient's right to refuse treatment be made for artificial feeding? Answering this question requires exploring the distinction between ordinary and extraordinary care. *Ordinary care* is generally defined as the use of conventional, proven therapies. In contrast, *extraordinary measures* usually involve some kind of life-sustaining intervention. Such measures are usually temporary until the patient is able to resume normal biological functioning.

Of course, therapies that are usually considered ordinary may be extraordinary or even intrusive, depending on the circumstances. Using antibiotics to treat pneumonia, a practice that generally fits into the category of ordinary care, may be viewed as extraordinary when such drugs are administered to a person who is actively dying. The distinction between ordinary and extraordinary therapies also becomes blurred in situations where a series of medical interventions, each one in itself "ordinary," combine in such a way that the net result is an "extraordinary" effort to sustain life. Although some medical ethicists argue that a clear dividing line is needed between ordinary and extraordinary treatment, Thomas Attig says it is likely that "a definitive rule dividing ordinary and extraordinary treatment will forever elude us."[54]

Because we tend to think of nourishment as ordinary care, withholding it brings up images of causing the patient's death by starvation. But such images may be inaccurate for several reasons. First, the invasive nature of delivering such nourishment, and the skills required to administer it, argue against the perception that it is merely providing simple care. Second, artificial nourishment causes discomfort to many patients, especially those who are close to dying. Feeding tubes and intravenous lines may add to a patient's suffering at the end of life.

Accordingly, normal, everyday sentiments about the symbolic meaning of food and water "cannot be transferred without distortion to the hospital world" and, indeed, "authentic sentiment may demand discontinuance of artificial feeding."[55] Acknowledging that issues around nourishment are highly charged emotionally, Dena Davis says, "We need to be very careful to sort out the physiological aspects of providing nutrition from the social phenomenon of 'feeding.'"[56] When a person is actively dying, the removal of artificial nutrition and hydration can be good palliative care.

Seriously Ill Newborns

In hospitals with specialized neonatal intensive care units (NICUs), newborns who are born prematurely or with serious medical problems are routinely treated. Some of these babies, however, will never be capable of living what most people consider a normal life. Such infants suffer from cardiopulmonary ailments, brain damage, or other serious congenital defects or dysfunction. Whereas in the past such conditions would have quickly resulted in death, now, because of specialized neonatal care, babies born with life-threatening conditions often survive. Alan Fleishman says, "Predicting outcomes in the first days of life is difficult in most circumstances and creates the fundamental dilemma of deciding treatment options in the face of not knowing the future of the infant's life."[57]

Is medical intervention the course of action to take in every case? Should the infant's projected quality of life be considered? For example, should a newborn with an intestinal blockage be spared by surgical intervention? Is the answer always yes, that life should be saved, or does the answer change according to circumstances? Is the answer the same if the infant with intestinal blockage is also severely brain damaged?

In the past, it was often thought to be part of the job of health care providers to answer such questions and make life-or-death choices. Today, the family—indeed, the larger community—has a role in such decisions. However, "parental refusal of a life-sustaining therapy does not relieve the physician from an ethical duty to the child."[58] The principle known as the "best interest of the child" must be taken into account.

Consider an infant born with his entire left side malformed, with no left eye and very little of a left ear; some of his vertebrae were not fused. Also afflicted with a tracheoesophageal fistula (an abnormality of the windpipe and the canal that leads to the stomach), he could not be fed by mouth. Air leaked into his stomach instead of going to the lungs, and fluid from the stomach pushed up into the lungs. One doctor commented, "It takes little imagination to think there were further internal difficulties as well." In the ensuing days, the infant's condition steadily worsened. Pneumonia set in; his reflexes became impaired; and, because of poor circulation, severe brain damage was suspected. Despite the seriousness of all these factors, the immediate threat to his survival, the tracheoesophageal fistula, could be corrected by a fairly easy surgical procedure. The debate began when the parents refused to give their consent to surgery. Some doctors treating the child believed surgery was warranted and took the case to court. The judge ruled against the parents and ordered the surgery, declaring that "at the moment of live birth, there exists a human being entitled to the fullest protection of the law."[59]

In another case, which contrasts with the one just described, the mother of a premature baby overheard a doctor describing her infant as having Down syndrome with the added complication that the intestines were blocked. This kind of blockage can be corrected by ordinary surgery; without correction, the child could not be fed and would die. One physician argued that the degree of mental retardation in children with Down syndrome cannot be predicted; and, in the physician's words, "They're almost always trainable. They can hold simple jobs, and they're famous for being happy children. When further complications do not appear, a long life can be anticipated." However, the mother felt that "it would be unfair" to her other children if a retarded child were brought into the home. Her husband supported this decision, and they refused consent for surgery. Unlike the case of the first infant described above, this time the hospital staff did not seek a court order to override the parents' decision against surgical intervention. The child was placed in a side room and, eleven days later, died.

Think about the differences between these two cases. In the first, the severely malformed infant seemed to have less chance of survival or of living a normal life than the infant in the second example. Yet, the hospital staff in the first case chose to seek a court order granting surgery, whereas the staff at the second hospital chose to abide by the parents' wishes. In the second case, did the physicians and the parents adequately explore the child's right to life? It could be argued that the withholding of ordinary means of treatment (that is, surgery) was in fact an *extraordinary* nonintervention.

Whatever our feelings about the decisions described, notice a distinction between ethical issues involving infants and those involving adults. Generally, with adults, all procedures that might prolong life have been tried or at least presented to the patient. In cases involving newborns, the question of whether to treat or withhold treatment cannot be discussed with the patient; thus, decisions are made by others, who will, it is hoped, act in the child's best interest. The tough part, of course, is determining "the child's best interest."[60]

Generally speaking, federal regulations state that physicians should use reasonable medical judgment in making treatment recommendations. Regulations also state that physicians should involve parents in the decision-making process. Exceptions to the requirement to provide treatment may be made only when one of the following conditions applies:

- The infant is irreversibly comatose.
- The provision of such treatment would merely prolong dying or not be effective in ameliorating or correcting all of the infant's life-threatening conditions or otherwise would be futile in terms of the survival of the infant.
- The provision of such treatment would be virtually futile in terms of the survival of the infant and the treatment itself under such circumstances would be inhumane.

As Alan Fleishman says, "Continued treatment should not be forced when hope for benefit is uncertain."[61]

Advance Directives

Advance directives have generated considerable controversy; opponents argue that they are a step toward euthanasia, and proponents counter that they safeguard patients' rights to determine the manner of care at the end of life (see the letters in Figure 6-2). In a general sense, an *advance directive* is any statement made by a competent person about choices for medical treatment should he or she become unable to make such decisions or communicate them at some time in the future.[62] A recent study in California found that, although an overwhelming majority of the state's residents said they would prefer to die at home, fewer than one in four have written instructions about how and where they would like to die.[63] One type of advance directive is the *living will,* which Louis Kutner proposed in 1967.[64] Essentially, a living will allows an individual to refuse life-sustaining treatment in the event he or she is terminally ill and the administration of life-sustaining procedures would only prolong the dying process. In 1976, California adopted the Natural Death Act, thereby becoming the first state to give legal recognition to the living will.[65] The Act was described as "a piece of legislation that encourages

---

Editor: If the governor signs the bill currently before him, this will become the first state to legalize suicide.

I believe this measure is immoral, bizarre, and tainted with Mephistophelian connotations.

Legislators, at all levels, should legislate laws pertaining only to life, as we know it. Death, in any manner, is nature's absolute domain, and no one should attempt to trespass on that domain.

I trust the governor is wise enough and sane enough to veto the bill presently lying heavily and cadaverously on his desk.

Editor: We have explored this bill and its implications in death and fully support the right of an individual, who wishes to do so, to be allowed to make a legally recognized written directive requesting withdrawal of life-support systems when these procedures would serve no purpose except to artificially delay the moment of death.

We reiterate our belief in the basic human right of an individual to control his destiny. We have communicated our support of this bill to the legislature and to the governor.

Editor: This bill, and all other natural-death or death-with-dignity bills, is based on a faulty premise. For when we react to tubes, oxygen and other paraphernalia, our concern is with daintiness, not dignity.

Dignity is the quality of mind having to do with worth, nobility, and forbearance. The dying, with the help of the living, can have dignity—no matter what functions of control are lost.

Instead of unplugging and abandoning our dying patients, we should work to achieve truly compassionate care for them in hospices like those in London, England, and New Haven, Connecticut.

Editor: No physician is required by law to use extraordinary means of preserving life, and none has ever been convicted for failing to do so.

So the real purpose of death-with-dignity or natural-death bills must be to set the stage for letting doctors take positive action: giving lethal injections or denying ordinary means of care to patients who may be handicapped or burdensome to society.

We must be suspicious of any trend which offers death as a solution to problems, no matter how heart-rending those problems may be.

Editor: The bill allowing an adult of sound mind to refuse extraordinary life-preservation measures reaffirms for me the value of life. Life is active choosing toward greater fulfillment and reduced suffering, not the beating of a heart in a pain-wracked and hopeless body. This bill is a public and legal recognition of that principle.

Figure 6-2 *Letters to the Editor*

a patient to participate in his or her own terminal care" and as legislation that "underscores the role of technology as another clinical option, not a necessity."[66] By the end of the twentieth century, all states had passed some form of living will legislation.

Questions have been raised, however, about whether living wills are the best choice to accomplish their stated goals. Some observers suggest that "living wills fail not for want of effort, or education, or intelligence, or good will, but because of stubborn traits of human psychology and persistent features of social organization."[67] Among the concerns are these:[68]

1. *For living wills to be effective, people must have them.* Most Americans do not.
2. *Individuals must decide what treatment they would want if incompetent.* People often do not know enough about illnesses and treatments to make future life-or-death decisions about them. Further, their preferences about life-sustaining treatment change over time and across contexts.
3. *Individuals must accurately and lucidly state that preference.* People often have trouble reaching well-considered EOL decisions and may issue inconsistent instructions.
4. *A living will must be available to people making decisions for the patient.* "It can be a long road from the draftee's chair to the ICU bed." The living will may be signed years before it needs to be used, and its existence and location may have vanished in the mists of time. One study found that 62 percent of patients with a living will do not give their living will to their physician.
5. *People must understand and heed the living will's instructions.* Living wills are not self-executing. Someone must decide whether a medical situation described in the living will has arisen and what action the living will directs.

Another concern is that, because living wills are not physician orders, their directives cannot be followed by emergency medical technicians (EMTs). Finally, a presidential council on bioethics commented that "living wills make autonomy and self-determination the primary values at a time of life when one is no longer autonomous or self-determining, and when what one needs is loyal and loving care."[69]

An alternative to the living will is the standardized document known as Physician Orders for Life-Sustaining Treatment (POLST), which can be used together with other advance directives. POLST transfers a patient's wishes into a set of medical orders that must be followed. Developed in Oregon and fully or partially implemented in an increasing number of states, POLST is a two-sided form that "spells out directions for resuscitation, medical interventions, antibiotics, and artificial feeding."[70] It provides both a summary of an individual's advance-directive decisions and the physician's order. It can inform emergency medical services personnel about a patient's wishes for life-sustaining procedures, such as CPR. It is also intended to solve the problem of respecting DNR orders when a patient is transferred from nursing home to hospital. POLST is designed for individuals with serious or life-threatening illness. It governs medical issues considered likely to arise in the near term, usually within the year. One of the primary purposes of POLST—which in

People may be uncertain about their preferences regarding future life-or-death decisions. Engaging in open discussion with a knowledgeable and trusted physician can help individuals think about the alternatives. Having a document such as the Physician Orders for Life-Sustaining Treatment (POLST) can help ensure compliance with one's choices.

some states is called by other names, such as MOLST, meaning "Medical Orders for Life-Sustaining Treatment"—is to initiate "rich conversations" between patients and their medical providers.[71]

The second important type of advance directive is the *health care proxy* (also known as a *durable power of attorney for health care*). Some commentators believe that health care proxies have advantages over living wills, in part because they are simpler and more straightforward. The health care proxy makes it possible to appoint another person, called a *proxy* (also known as a *surrogate*) to represent you in making decisions about medical treatment if you become unable to do so. He or she may be a relative, friend, or attorney, someone with whom you have discussed your treatment preferences. As your representative, the proxy you appoint is expected to act in accordance with your wishes as stated in an advance directive or as otherwise made known. When a surrogate makes decisions for an incapacitated or incompetent patient, it is known as *substituted judgment.*

Ideally, the surrogate will use all available evidence to determine as accurately as possible how the patient would have decided if he or she were capable. A court may take away the proxy's power to make decisions if he or she (1) authorizes any illegal act, (2) acts contrary to the patient's known desires, or (3) where those desires are not known, does anything clearly contrary to the patient's best interests. Completing a health care proxy can provide an additional safeguard that preferences about life-sustaining treatment will be followed. Whether used as an adjunct to a living will or on its own to name a proxy for health care decisions, it is crucial that one's preferences and choices are known and available when the need arises.

The document known as Five Wishes, created by the organization Aging with Dignity, combines a living will and a health care power of attorney. It also addresses matters of comfort care and spirituality. Here is a summary of the five wishes:

- Wish 1: *The person I want to make care decisions for me when I can't.* This section is an assignment of a health care agent, proxy, or surrogate to act on your behalf.
- Wish 2: *The kind of medical treatment I want or don't want.* This section is a living will; it lets you specify what life support treatment means to you and when you would and would not want it.
- Wish 3: *How comfortable I want to be.* This section address matters of comfort care, including pain management, personal grooming, and whether you want to know about options for hospice care, for example.
- Wish 4: *How I want people to treat me.* This section is concerned with personal matters, such as whether you want to be at home during the illness, to have your hand held, to have others praying for you, and to die at home, among other concerns.
- Wish 5: *What I want my loved ones to know.* This section deals with how you want to be remembered, your wishes regarding funeral or memorial plans, as well as body disposition, and other matters that may be important to you, such as forgiveness.

Notice that wishes one and two, once signed, are both legal documents in states where Five Wishes meets regulatory requirements.[72]

In 1990, the United States Congress enacted the Patient Self-Determination Act (PSDA).[73] It requires providers of services under the Medicare and Medicaid programs to inform patients of their rights to appoint a health care proxy and draw up written instructions concerning limits to medical care to be activated if they become incapacitated. Specifically, patients have rights to[74]

1. participate in and direct their own health care decisions
2. accept or refuse medical or surgical treatment
3. prepare an advance directive

The PSDA has been described as a "medical Miranda warning" (referring to the requirement that police officers advise arrested suspects of their legal rights) due to its requirement that patients be advised of their rights regarding advance directives and life-sustaining treatment. Recalling the earlier discussion of the SUPPORT study (see the section on "Informed Consent"), which was done just five years after passage of the PSDA, it seems that, despite its aims of improving planning around goals of care, the Act has been none too successful in terms of improving communication between patients and providers.

Using Advance Directives

Completing an advance directive is one step toward improving the chances that your treatment preferences will be honored if you become incapacitated. But physicians and other medical staff cannot follow advance directives if they don't know about them or if the instructions are too vague to give direction about what should be done. In addition, laws governing advance directives vary for different states, making it important to be sure you have the forms that apply where you live.[75]

After you complete an advance directive, review it occasionally to be sure the preferences expressed in the directive continue to match your wishes. Without periodic review and clear conversations with trusted persons who can see that its provisions are carried out, an advance directive may not accomplish its intended purpose.

In some cases, an advance directive may be less a directive than a request. Uncertainty about the course of a disease may cause doctors to be wary of deciding that a patient is in a terminal condition. Individuals should discuss issues of end-of-life care with their primary doctor and other physicians from whom they receive treatment, as well as with family members, *before* a situation occurs in which the advance directive becomes necessary.

If you are called upon to help someone create his or her advance directive, it is wise to recall the old saying, "We have two ears and one mouth." The message is that we should listen twice as much as we talk. It has been pointed out, "If you wait at least seven seconds after someone stops speaking, chances are good that they'll continue talking, perhaps revealing something they've been hesitant to say."[76] The drafting of an advance directive should not be hurried or ill considered. It warrants a generous intent to listen and accept what is heard.

Because advance directives become effective when medical intervention is needed and a patient is unable to communicate his or her wishes, the directive could be implemented in a situation the patient had not foreseen. Consider the case of a woman in her seventies who entered a hospital for hip replacement surgery and, along with other admission forms, was given an advance directive to sign. While recovering from surgery, she had an unexpected cardiac arrest. Rather than starting a resuscitation attempt, however, the medical staff assumed that—because she had signed the directive—she wanted no resuscitation. The woman died. Although this woman was not terminally ill, by signing a document providing evidence that she did not want to be kept alive if in a grave medical condition, the power to interpret her wishes was put into the hands of medical staff. Was the outcome what she intended?

Nor should one be complacent in thinking that all will necessarily go smoothly so long as an advance directive has been completed and signed. Zelda Foster, a social worker and educator, describes the struggle to ensure that her ninety-three-year-old father's wishes were respected by medical

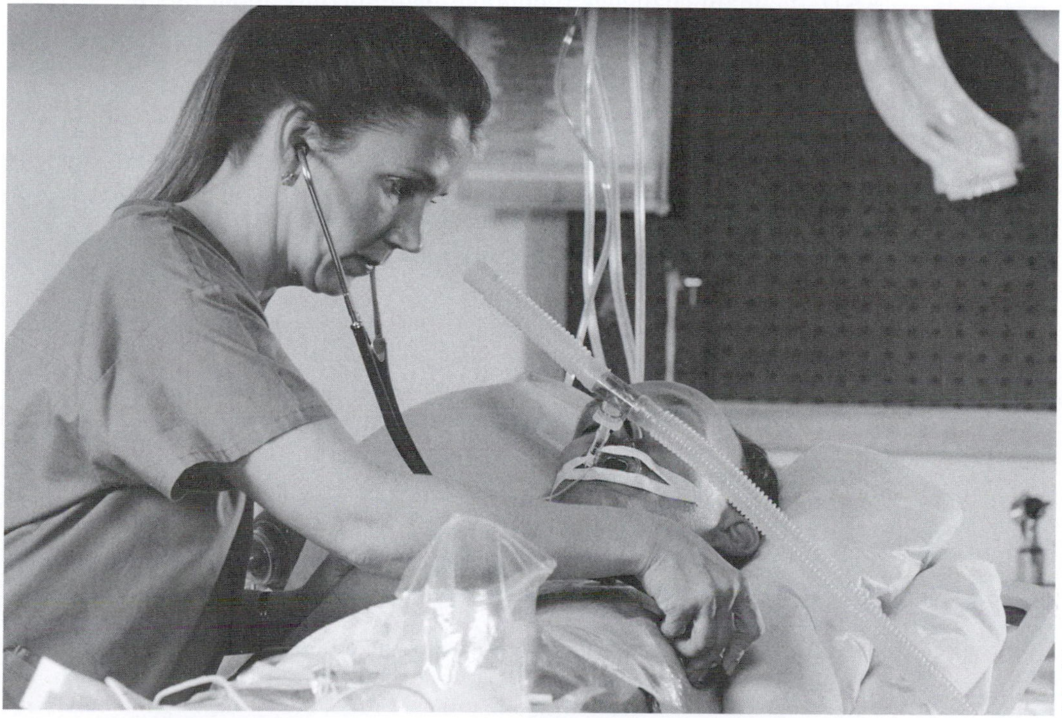

A physician works with a patient in the Intensive Care Unit, where time for decision making may be short. The goal of knowing and following an individual's wishes for life-sustaining treatment is challenging in situations where minutes count.

personnel after he was brought to an emergency room and attached to life-support machines.[77] Despite having her father's health care proxy in hand, the staff seemed to be unfamiliar with its purpose. The hospital administrators insisted that Foster's family obtain a court order to enforce the proxy's provisions. Ms. Foster noted that "the hospital has created one obstacle after another to challenge our rightful request that our father be allowed to die with dignity." As the Supreme Court made clear in the case of Nancy Beth Cruzan, advance directives offer a means for providing clear and convincing evidence of one's wishes for life-sustaining treatment in critical situations; however, they do not resolve all the difficulties that may accompany end-of-life care.

Advance Directives and Emergency Care

Do-not-resuscitate (DNR) orders are another type of advance directive. Unless given other instructions, hospital staff and emergency personnel will start CPR to help patients whose hearts have stopped or who have stopped breathing. As mentioned earlier in the chapter, a DNR is a directive stating that you don't want to be resuscitated. (There are proposals to replace DNR orders with Allow Natural Death orders, which are said to be more compassionate and readily accepted by patients and their families. Whether DNR or AND, the main challenge is eliminating ambiguity about the intended plan of treatment and clearly communicating this to caregivers.[78]) In the hospital, a DNR order is put in your medical chart by your doctor. But what about outside the hospital?

I was in the ready room listening to Netcom calls being transmitted to the local fire agencies and EMT first-responders. Mostly routine calls were the order of the day when one scenario caught my ear.

***

Netcom: Medic 4, respond to 119 Wasatch Blvd. for a woman with faint pulse, not alert, and no responses.

Medic 4: Responding.

A couple of minutes passed before the next transmission:

Netcom: Medic 4, additional information, the subject is a 70-year-old woman, unconscious, no pulse.

Medic 4: Copy that.

Once again, there was a brief pause between messages. Then:

Netcom: Medic 4, on the Wasatch Blvd. call, subject unconscious, no vital signs. She has a DNR order, but they want transport to hospital.

***

I had heard such calls many times before, but on this day I thought to myself, "Wow, guess the nursing home didn't want the patient to die on their watch, so even though she was already dead, they wanted to get her to the hospital where her death would be pronounced."

James Scott, EMT Supervisor

Emergency care provided by paramedics, EMTs, and other personnel is considered a boon when it helps save lives, but it may be less welcome when it results in interventions that save the lives of those who would rather die naturally. Once 911 is dialed, it sets in motion a response intended to save life. First-responders are generally not in a position to make decisions about who wants to be saved and who doesn't. In fact, they are legally *required* to initiate CPR unless there is clear evidence that the person has a valid DNR order provided by his or her physician.

Imagine a dying person, at home surrounded by family and close friends, prepared to let nature take its course. When the person begins to experience difficulty breathing, however, someone watching this passage toward death may have an impulse to *do* something to relieve the apparent suffering. A spontaneous call to 911 can result in the dying person's being resuscitated and being placed on life-support equipment, with the result that the last hours or days of life are played out as a crisis.

Individuals who do not want CPR or other life-saving interventions must ensure that their instructions are readily available to emergency personnel who may be called to the scene. Medic-Alert bracelets or wallet cards may be helpful in signaling the fact that a person should not receive CPR. In some states, instructions can be made known in a Physician Orders for Life-Sustaining Treatment (POLST), discussed earlier.

Inheritance: Wills, Probate, and Living Trusts

Individuals with life-limiting illnesses and their families often turn to counselors and other mental health professionals to help explore their fears, uncertainties, and conflicts, as well as to devise a plan to meet the prospects that lie ahead; an attorney can be an important part of that team. Estate planning not only optimizes survivors' financial security but also helps ensure peace of mind, both for the bereaved and for the person who has taken steps to put his or her affairs in order. In addition, by preparing the legal documents, an attorney can help ensure that a person's wishes about organ donation or advance directives for medical care are carried out.

Barton Bernstein outlines three basic legal stages that apply in cases of terminal illness when death follows expected medical probabilities.[79] The

> The clock wound by Elizabeth still ticked, storing in its spring the pressure of her hand. Life cannot be cut off quickly. One cannot be dead until the things he changed are dead. His effect is the only evidence of his life. While there remains even a plaintive memory a person cannot be cut off, dead. A man's life dies as a commotion in a still pool dies, in little waves, spreading and growing back towards stillness.
>
> John Steinbeck, *To a God Unknown*

first stage involves long-range planning, in which the terminally ill person arranges his or her legal and financial affairs for the eventuality of death. During the *second* stage, which occurs shortly before death, the survivors gather pertinent legal papers, obtain sufficient funds to cover immediate expenses, and notify the attorney and insurance representative so they will be ready to make a smooth transition of the deceased's legal and financial affairs. Also at this time, if the dying person intends to make an organ donation or other anatomical gift (discussed in Chapter 4), the appropriate medical personnel are alerted.

In the *third* stage of legal activity, which follows the death, the will is delivered to an attorney for probate (the process of settling an estate). The effort that went into planning is now rewarded in the survivors' certainty that affairs have not been left to chance. The survivors can confront their loss without the distraction and worry of complex legal and financial entanglements. About the process of estate planning and will drafting, Kaja Whitehouse says, "Every seemingly irritating or daunting concept or procedure offers a way for you to take away a small bit of the sting and the pain that those you love will have to go through."[80]

Wills

A *will* is a legal document expressing a person's intentions and wishes for the disposition of his or her property after death. It is a declaration of how a person's *estate*—that is, money, property, and other possessions—will be distributed to one's heirs and beneficiaries upon that person's death. The term *devise* applies to real property, *legacy* applies to money, and *bequest* applies to nonmonetary personal property, although you will often hear the terms *legacy* and *bequest* used more generally, even by attorneys. Jackson Rainer says,

> A will is the best way to determine the distribution of personal belongings and assets, to provide for family needs regarding underage children, to plan wisely for taxes, and to make charitable contributions. Only by having a will can the individual be assured that personal wishes will be carried out after death.[81]

Conferring a kind of immortality on the *testator* (the person making the will), a will can be thought of as the deceased's last words. During the life of the testator, a will can be changed, replaced, or revoked. Upon the testator's death, it becomes a legal instrument that governs the distribution of his or her estate. (A glossary of additional terms related to inheritance is provided in Table 6-2).

A will can evoke powerful emotions, embodying as it does the testator's feelings and intentions toward his or her survivors, possibly affecting the intensity or course of grief.[82] People usually think of the will as simply a tool for estate planning, perhaps overlooking its comforting and possibly therapeutic effects for both the testator and his or her survivors.

TABLE 6-2 Terms Related to Wills and Inheritance

Administrator: A person appointed by the court (in the absence of a will, or if no executor is named in one) to carry out the steps necessary to settling an estate. When an administrator is to be appointed, state law requires the drawing up of a preferential list of candidates. Assuming that the necessary qualifications are met, the order of preference typically begins with the spouse of the deceased and continues successively through the deceased's children, grandchildren, parents, siblings, more distant next of kin, and a public administrator.

Attestation clause: A statement signed by the persons who witness the testator's making of the will.

Codicil: An amendment to a will.

Conditional will: A type of formally executed will that states that certain actions will take place provided that a specified future event occurs. For example, suppose a testator wishes to bequeath money or property to a potential beneficiary who is incapable of self-care but who has a reasonable chance of recovery. With a conditional will, the money or property could be held in trust for that person until the conditions specified in the will (e.g., recovery) have been satisfied. A problem of conditional wills lies in the difficulty of stipulating with exactitude the nature of events and circumstances that might occur in the future.

Executor: A person named by the testator in his or her will to see that the provisions in the will are carried out properly.

Holographic will: A will written entirely by the hand of the person signing it. Some states do not recognize holographic wills as valid, and those that do generally have stringent conditions for such a document to be deemed valid. Not considered a substitute for a formally executed will.

Intestate: The condition of having made no valid will.

Mutual will: A type of formally executed will that contains reciprocal provisions. May be used by husbands and wives who wish to leave everything to the other spouse with no restrictions, although it limits the range of choices that are available when a will is executed individually.

Nuncupative will: A will made orally. Many states do not recognize a nuncupative will or do so only under extremely limited circumstances. A few states admit an oral will if the person makes it in fear of imminent death or in the expectation of receiving mortal injuries, and the peril does result in death. A nuncupative will may also be valid when made by a soldier or sailor engaged in military service or by a mariner at sea; in these instances, the individual need not be in immediate peril. Generally, an oral will must be witnessed by at least two persons who attest that the will is indeed a statement of the testator's wishes.

Probate: The process by which an estate is settled and the property distributed. This process generally occupies an average of nine to twelve months, though it may be longer or shorter, depending on circumstances and the complexity of the estate.

The person who makes a will must have the mental capacity to understand the nature of the document and the consequences of signing it. He or she must understand the nature and extent of the property being distributed by the will and be able to identify the persons who, by convention, ought to be considered when making a will, whether or not they actually become beneficiaries. Given these conditions and in the absence of any significant delusions, the testator is said to be of sound mind, capable of executing a legal will. State laws generally specify a minimum age at which a person can make a legal will—usually eighteen, though in several states as young as fourteen—and various other requirements, such as the presence of witnesses and execution of the document in a proper form.

Besides standard clauses, such as a declaration that the document constitutes the person's last will and testament (along with a statement revoking previous wills, if applicable), a will may include information about the property to be distributed, the names of children and other heirs, and specific bequests and allocations of property, as well as information concerning the establishment of trusts, the granting of powers to a trustee and/or guardian, other provisions for disposition of property, and payment of taxes, debts, and expenses of administration. Not all these items are necessarily part of every will, nor is a will limited to the items listed here.

The privilege of determining how one's property will be distributed after death is not available in all societies, nor is it without limitations. In some countries, the government assumes control over the settlement of a person's affairs; in other countries, including the United States, a person has considerable liberty in determining how property will be distributed. Still, depending on the laws of a particular state, enforcing and carrying out the provisions of a will may be constrained by circumstances affecting one's heirs. For example, someone may try to avoid willing anything to his or her spouse, but if the will is contested, a court may overturn it. State statutes usually stipulate that a surviving spouse cannot be disinherited. Some statutes require that dependent children be provided for in the will. As a rule of thumb, anything that conflicts with ordinary standards of social conduct may be invalid if the will is contested.

In making a will, it is generally advisable to involve close family members, or at least one's spouse, to prevent problems that can arise when actions are taken without the knowledge of those who will be affected. When survivors discover that things are not as expected or customary, it may add to the burden of grief. In loving families, usually everyone has some idea of what is going to happen when the will becomes effective. There may be valid reasons for not disclosing the details of a will. But the testator can tell his or her survivors something like, "Call Rick, my attorney; he knows where my will is and can help you in handling my estate." Some legal experts suggest that there ought to be a governmental or administrative program whereby wills, as well as other important documents such as advance directives, could be registered ahead of time and be readily available when they are needed (in fact, some states—for example, Maryland and Virginia—allow a testator to record his or her will in the courthouse with the county or city register of wills).

In addition to drafting a will, some advisors recommend completing what has been termed a "family love letter."[83] Besides providing basic information to family members about assets and liabilities, this document also

Inheritance

When I was ten years old, my father died. And at that time, of course, I thought my father was the best and finest man there ever was. And some years later when I was eighteen and I began to mingle in the adult community, I introduced myself to strangers and they would ask me if John Estrada was my father. When I said yes, they would say, "Well, let me shake your hand. He was a fine man and a good friend of mine." And then they would tell me wonderful stories about him. Since that time, I have hoped that when I am gone, some people might meet my children and say to them that I was a good man and a good friend. To me that is a finer inheritance than any material possession.

Fred Estrada

communicates personal desires after death, from choice of pallbearers to tombstone engravings. One financial services firm gives clients a nineteen-page document that begins, "Dear Loved Ones" and includes a number of topics that could provide clarity during a time of confusion. Financial advisors say the letter is helpful because it compiles data in one place and facilitates working with clients on various EOL issues and strategies. It can also help prevent family conflicts or disagreements that might arise after death.

Of course, bequeathing nonfinancial legacies, such as personal values or family stories, is not new. So-called *ethical wills* were described three thousand years ago in the Hebrew Bible as a means to pass on wisdom and love to future generations. Ethical wills can include family history, values, blessings, expressions of love, summary of life's lessons, hopes and dreams for children and grandchildren, pride, and desires for forgiveness.[84] Usually written when facing challenging life situations, they can be among the most cherished and meaningful gifts left to family members and community of friends.

The Formally Executed Will

The *formally executed will* is the conventional document used for specifying a person's wishes for the distribution of his or her estate after death (see Figure 6-3). If carefully prepared, it not only has sufficient clarity of purpose and expression to withstand a court's scrutiny but also can help ease the burden and stress on survivors.

In making a formally executed will, most people find it beneficial to consult an attorney. A comprehensive review of an estate requires that legal records and other information be gathered. Several meetings may be required to carefully determine the nature of the property and the testator's wishes for its distribution. Once the will's content is determined and its provisions set, the attorney has it prepared and an appointment is made for its formal execution. On that occasion, the will is reviewed, two (or, in some

Will of Tomás Antonio Yorba

In the name of the Holy Trinity, Father, Son, and the Holy Ghost, three distinct persons and one true God, Amen.

1st Clause. Know all [men] who may read this my last will and testament: that I—Tomás Antonio Yorba, native born resident of this department of California, legitimate son of Antonio Yorba and Josefa Grijalva—being sick, but, by divine mercy, in the full enjoyment of my reason, memory and understanding, believing, as I firmly do, in all the mysteries of our holy Catholic faith, which faith is natural to me, since I have lived in it from my infancy and I declare that I want to live in it as a faithful Christian and true Catholic, trusting that, for this reason, his divine Majesty will have mercy on me and will pardon all my sins, through the mysteries of our Lord Jesus Christ and the intercession of his most holy mother, who is my protector and benefactress in these my last moments, so that together with my guardian angel, with St. Joseph, my own name's saint, and all the other saints of my devotion and all the other hosts of heaven, they will assist me before the grand tribunal of God, before which all mortals must render account of their actions—make and decree this my last will and testament as follows, in ordinary paper because of lack of stamped paper.

2nd Clause. Firstly, I commend my soul to God who created it, and my body to the earth, from whence it was fashioned, and it is my wish that I be buried in the church of the Mission of San Gabriel in the shroud of our father St. Francis, the funeral to be according to what my executors and heirs consider that I deserve and is befitting.

3rd Clause. Item: In regard to the expense of the funeral and masses, these should be drawn from the fifth of my estate, according to the disposition of my executors, and I leave the residue of this fifth to my son Juan.

4th Clause. I declare that with respect to my debts, my heirs and executors should collect and pay any legal claims that may turn up or be due according to law. Item: I declare to have been married to Doña Vicenta Sepúlveda, legitimate daughter of Don Francisco Sepúlveda and Doña Ramona Sepúlveda, of this neighborhood, by which marriage I had five children named: (1) Juan; (2) Guadalupe, deceased; (3) José Antonio; (4) Josefa; (5) Ramona. The first being 10 years old, the second died

Figure 6-3 *Historical Will*
Social custom plays a significant part in the making of a will. The will of Don Tomás Antonio Yorba, dating from the period of Mexican rule in California, presents an illuminating contrast to the modern will with its emphasis on the distribution of the testator's property. Although Yorba's estate was among the largest of the time—consisting of a Spanish land grant of 62,000 acres known as the Rancho Santiago de Santa Ana in Southern California—only a small fraction of his will relates to matters affecting the distribution of the estate to his heirs.

states, three) disinterested persons are brought in to serve as witnesses, and the testator acknowledges that the document accurately reflects his or her wishes and signs it. Although preparation of the will may involve weeks or even months of thoughtful consideration and planning, the actual signing can take less than five minutes.

Amending or Revoking a Will

A will is not cast in stone; it can be changed as the testator's situation changes. A will can be revoked and replaced by an entirely new will, or only certain parts of it can be amended. Amending a will is a means of adding at the age of three, the third six years old, the fourth four years old, and the fifth two years old. Item: I declare to have given my wife jewels of some value as a wedding present, but I do not remember how many nor their value; but they must be in her possession, since I gave them to her. Item: According to my reckoning I have about 2,000 head of cattle, 900 ewes and their respective males, three herds of about 100 mares and their stallions, and three donkeys; about 21 tame horses, 7 tame and 12 unbroken mules; and lastly, whatever cattle, horses or mules may turn up with my brand which may not have been legally sold. Item: I declare to have the right—through inheritance from my father—to part of Middle Santa Ana and Lower Santana, known to be of the Yorbas. I have in Middle Santa Ana an adobe house, its roof being part timber and part thatched, consisting of 18 rooms, including the soap-house. Item: I declare that I have two vineyards with wooden fences which are now planted with bearing vines and some fruit trees; also a section of enclosed land.

5th Clause. I declare that it is my wish to name as executors and guardians of my estate, first, my brother, Don Bernardo Yorba, and second, Don Raimundo Yorba, by joint approval, to whom I give all my vested power, as much as may be necessary, to go in and examine my property for the benefit of my heirs in carrying out this will, and I grant them the power to procure another associate [executor] to expedite its due execution, whom I consider appointed as a matter of course, granting him the same authority as those previously named.

6th Clause. I name as my heirs my children and my wife, in the form and manner indicated by the law, following the necessary inventory.

7th Clause. In this my last will, I annul and void whatever will or wills, codicil or codicils, I may have previously made, so that they may stand nullified with or without judicial process, now and forever, since I definitely desire that the present testamentary disposition be my last will, codicil, and final wish, in the manner and form most legally valid. To this effect I beg Don Vicente Sanchez, Judge of 1st *instancia,* to exercise his authority in probating this will.

To which I, the citizen Vicente Sanchez, 1st constitutional Alcalde and Judge of the 1st *instancia* of the city of Los Angeles, certify; and I affirm that the present testamentary disposition was made in my presence, and that the testator, Don Tomás Antonio Yorba, although ill, finds himself in the full command of his faculties and natural understanding, and, to attest it, I do this before the assistant witnesses—the citizens Ramon Aguilar and Ignacio Coronel—the other instrumental witnesses being the citizens Bautista Mutriel and Mariano Martinez; on the 28th day of the month of January, 1845. The testator did not sign because of physical inability, but Don Juan Bandini signed for him.

Figure 6-3 *(continued)*

new provisions without having to rewrite it entirely. A testator who, after the will has been executed, acquires valuable property, such as an art collection, might want to make a specific provision for the new property without disturbing other parts of his or her estate plan. A *codicil,* which is executed in much the same manner as a will, accomplishes that objective. All wills should be reviewed periodically to determine whether changed circumstances call for revision.

When the addition of codicils makes a will unwieldy or potentially confusing, it is time to review the entire will and make a new one. States vary in their requirements for legally revoking a will. Generally, the testator's intent to revoke the will must be demonstrated; the accidental burning of a will, for instance, does not imply revocation. If someone turns up with an earlier will, it may be difficult to prove that it was revoked if a subsequent will does not explicitly say so. When in doubt, seek legal advice.

Probate

The period of *probate* allows time for the deceased's affairs to be resolved, debts and taxes paid, and arrangements made to receive funds that were owed to the deceased. During the course of probate, the validity of the will is proved; an executor or administrator of the estate is appointed; the necessary matters for settling the estate are carried out; and with the probate court's approval, the decedent's property is distributed to beneficiaries. If the deceased left a valid will, property is distributed in accordance with its terms. When a person dies *intestate*—that is, without having left a valid will—property is distributed according to rules set up by the state.

The Duties of the Executor or Administrator

Someone has to be responsible for carrying out all the steps necessary to settling an estate through probate. This is the role of the executor or administrator. As the decedent's personal representative, this person may be an *executor* named in the will or an *administrator* appointed by the court. Whereas an executor named by the testator is permitted to act more or less independently in the management of the estate provided that he or she acts prudently, a court-appointed administrator may be required to obtain the court's approval before proceeding with necessary decisions. In either case, executor or administrator, the personal representative generally must meet certain requirements stipulated by the law of the state in which probate occurs.

Although being named as executor of someone's will is often seen as an honor, it can be a time-consuming, complex, emotionally frustrating, and exhausting experience, even for a modestly sized estate.[85] The initial tasks are to thoroughly read the will and any other instructions from the deceased, register the will with the court, determine the estate's heirs, and inventory all property and assets to determine what is distributed via the will versus what goes directly to an heir outside of the will, such as life insurance or a retirement account.

Interested parties must be notified of the death. This is generally accomplished in two ways. First, parties who are likely to be interested in the settlement of the estate are notified of the death by mail and, if they request it, are sent a copy of the will. Second, a legal notification of the death is published in appropriate newspapers (see Figure 6-4). This notice serves three purposes in the probate process: (1) It announces that someone is ready to prove the legal validity of the will of the decedent; (2) it acknowledges that someone is petitioning to be appointed by the court to begin probate; and (3) it gives notice of the death to creditors so that outstanding claims against the decedent can be submitted for settlement.

When a surviving spouse is the estate's primary or sole heir, the inventory of personal and household goods can be less meticulous, though items that

NOTICE OF DEATH OF
LEE D. WILLIAMS
AND OF PETITION TO
ADMINISTER ESTATE
Case Number: 11111

To all heirs, beneficiaries, creditors, contingent creditors, and persons who may be otherwise interested in the will or estate of LEE D. WILLIAMS.

A petition has been filed by JANE DOE, in the Superior Court of Santa Cruz County requesting that JANE DOE be appointed as personal representative to administer the estate of the decedent.

A hearing on the petition will be held on March 22, 1982, at 8:30 a.m. in Dept III, located at 701 Ocean Street, Santa Cruz, California 95060.

IF YOU OBJECT to the granting of the petition, you should either appear at the hearing and state your objections or file written objections with the court before the hearing. Your appearance may be in person or by your attorney.

IF YOU ARE A CREDITOR or a contingent creditor of the deceased, you must file your claim with the court or present it to the personal representative appointed by the court within four months from the date of first issuance of letters as provided in section 700 of the California Probate Code. The time for filing claims will not expire prior to four months from the date of the hearing noticed above.

YOU MAY EXAMINE the file kept by the court. If you are a person interested in the estate, you may file a request with the court to receive special notice of the filing of the inventory of estate assets and of the petitions, accounts and reports described in section 1200 of the California Probate Code.

s/ JOHN P. SMITH
Attorney for the Petitioner

JOHN P. SMITH
9999 Pacific Avenue
Santa Cruz, CA 95060
March 7, 9, 14

Figure 6-4 *Newspaper Notice to Creditors*

have significant worth, such as paintings, jewelry, and antiques, are specified. Important papers are gathered, including insurance policies, Social Security and pension information, military service records, and other documents that require review and possibly action.

The executor or administrator is responsible for managing the estate pending its final disbursement to heirs. This includes determining valid creditor claims and making sure the estate pays off any debts. Tax returns may need to be filed on behalf of the decedent and the estate. An allowance may need to be paid to the deceased's spouse or to minor children for their support during probate. If the decedent was in business or was a stockholder in a corporation, the personal representative must manage a smooth transition that benefits the estate. When a personal representative is not knowledgeable about the law, he or she usually enlists the aid of an attorney to make certain that legal requirements are satisfied.

Finally, an accounting of the estate's property and a schedule for distributing it to the beneficiaries are prepared and submitted for approval by the probate court. Once the court's approval is obtained, the property is distributed, and receipts are obtained to certify that the distribution has been made correctly. Assuming that everything has been carried out properly, the court then discharges the personal representative. The estate is settled.

Laws of Intestate Succession

Statistics show that most people die without leaving a will. A recent study showed that only 44 percent of adults have a will.[86] Perhaps the failure to plan ahead by making a will is attributable to the discomfort many people feel about their own mortality. Or perhaps, overwhelmed by busyness, we neglect to plan, with the questionable excuse that we are not yet at an age when death is statistically probable. Whatever the reason, dying without having made a will can lead to unnecessary hardships for our survivors, even when an estate is modest in size.

Failure to prepare a will may result in a distribution of property that is not compatible with a person's wishes nor best suited to the interests and needs of heirs. In the absence of a will, property is distributed according to

End-of-life decisions touch on many aspects of dying and death, ranging from legal matters relating to wills, living trusts, and the settling of estates to issues such as advance directives. This young couple review the documents they have prepared—including those that cover provisions for care of their minor children—with the help of their attorney.

guidelines established in state law. The state generally tries to accomplish what it believes the deceased would have done had he or she actually made a will. Nevertheless, the laws that dictate the disbursement of property, the care of minor children, and all the matters that pertain to settling the estate reflect society's ideas of fair play and justice. Thus, the values of society, rather than the deceased's personal values, determine the outcome.

Although the laws of intestate succession differ among states, some general patterns prevail. In community-property states, for example, all community property goes to the surviving spouse. In separate property or non-community-property states, when there is only one child, an estate is generally divided equally between child and surviving spouse. If there is more than one child, usually one-third of the estate goes to the surviving spouse, and the remaining two-thirds is divided equally among the children.

If there is no surviving spouse, property is divided among the lineal descendants (children and grandchildren who are in the decedent's "lineage"); if there are no lineal descendants, disbursement is made to the deceased's parents; if they are not living, property is likely to be divided among the deceased's surviving siblings; if there are none, the estate may be divided among the deceased's siblings' children. In attempting to settle an estate, the court will make a determined effort to locate surviving heirs. If none can be found, the proceeds go to the state. These are some typical disbursements; however, when a person dies intestate, everything depends on the exact wording and interpretation of the statutes in a particular state.

Living Trusts

Living trusts can minimize the costs of passing one's estate to heirs, and they can avoid the publicity about an estate that accompanies public proceedings. In fact, they can be a substitute for engaging in the complicated process of going through probate. In addition, living trusts may be used to avoid or minimize inheritance taxes that would otherwise have to be paid on the value of an estate.

There are four main categories of trusts, based on when the trusts become effective and who owns the assets in the trust. Depending on when a trust goes into effect, it is either a living or a testamentary trust. A *living trust* becomes effective immediately, whereas a *testamentary trust* becomes effective only at the death of the grantor. Sometimes, testamentary trusts are created within wills. The second distinction about a trust is whether it is revocable or

> When it comes to divide an estate, the politest men quarrel.
>
> Ralph Waldo Emerson, *Journals* (1863)

"We cannot write a life policy for your husband, Mrs. Blaine, because he is already dead. In insurance terms, that is considered a preëxisting condition."

irrevocable. With a *revocable trust,* the grantor retains ownership and control of the property in the trust and can change the terms of the trust, including changing the individuals designated trustees and beneficiaries. With an *irrevocable trust,* ownership and control of property is given to others (trustees) and the grantor no longer owns or controls the property; thus, it is not possible for the grantor to enact changes to the trust.

The trustees of a trust can be the grantor who is making the trust, family members, friends, professionals (accountants or attorneys, for example), a bank or trust company, or a combination of these. A person who establishes a revocable, living trust will likely name himself or herself as sole trustee. The beneficiaries of a trust can be anyone the grantor designates, although beneficiary distributions are generally to family members or charities.

All decisions about wills, probate, and living trusts should be carefully considered and, in most cases, it is prudent to have the advice of an attorney who is well versed in such matters.

Insurance and Death Benefits

In the United States, the first life insurance company was established in 1759 by the Presbyterian Synod of Philadelphia for its ministers. Although life insurance did not become common until the middle of the nineteenth century, it is now a huge industry. Most American households include at least one member who owns some form of life insurance.[87]

Depending on a person's age and health, life insurance can be a convenient way of leaving a basic estate for our beneficiaries after we die. It may represent a small portion of a large estate or the major portion of a smaller estate. Insurance plans can be designed in a number of ways and to suit many purposes. Some policies are part of a total investment portfolio that can be drawn upon during the insured's lifetime. Other policies provide benefit payments only after the death of the insured.

Life insurance offers some advantages not available with other investments. For example, life insurance benefits payable to a named beneficiary (not the decedent's estate) are not subject to attachment by creditors. Also, unlike assets that must be processed through probate, insurance benefits usually become available immediately following death. These benefits can have important psychological and emotional value, possibly providing relief and a sense of security to a surviving spouse or other dependents in the period soon after death. Knowing that money is available to cover anticipated expenses may help to reduce stress.

In estate planning, people sometimes focus solely on the breadwinner of the family and fail to consider the economic value that would be lost with the death of a nonworking spouse. Following the death of his wife, one man described the financial burdens he incurred with the added expenses of child care. The nonworking spouse, as well as the working spouse, should be considered as part of a comprehensive estate plan.

A recent development allows terminally ill patients to sell their life insurance policies to "viatical settlement companies" so that they can pay medical bills, travel, or purchase things they want to enjoy before dying. A *viatical settlement* allows a person with terminal illness to sell his or her life insurance policy before death and receive payment for a percentage of its face value. Viatical settlement companies typically pay about 70 percent of the face value of the policy, and the policy is cashed in for its full value after the policyholder's death. For example, on a policy with a face value of $100,000, the settlement company might pay $70,000 to the policyholder. Patients with less than a year to live usually receive a higher percentage of face value than those expected to live longer. When the patient dies and the policy is cashed in, the settlement company pockets the difference between what was paid to the policyholder and the face amount of the policy, less its operating expenses. Some mainstream insurers offer similar options. As with any area of financial planning, it is wise to compare choices.

Many survivors qualify for benefits from programs like Social Security and the Veterans Administration. To obtain current information about such death-benefit programs, call or write the appropriate government agency. A person entitled to benefits under one or more of these programs may not receive them unless a claim is filed. Moreover, delays in filing may result in a loss of benefits. A comprehensive estate plan includes consideration of benefits that accrue from government programs, as well as those related to employee or union pension programs.

Burial in a national cemetery, such as the Black Hills National Cemetery in South Dakota, is a benefit made available to veterans who have served in American military forces during wartime. Such cemeteries have been established across the United States. Other death benefits for veterans include a lump-sum payment to help defray burial expenses and, under certain circumstances, direct payments to survivors.

© Albert Lee Strickland

Death of a Son

"I'm not happy because I no more my son already. . . . I miss him. Even if I get my money, I no more my loved one, my son. I'm not interested in money. Every day, after work, even if I feel tired, I no miss to go visit my boy. Sometimes I cry. Sometimes I give food [for his grave]. Soda. His favorite—Kentucky Fried Chicken. Sometimes fried saimin. Then I give an orange. Ice cream. . . . One day after the crash, my boy, he come my house in spirit. He tell me, 'Daddy, I miss you. I no more hands. I no more eyes.' Ho, I cry."

Figure 6-5 *Death of a Son*

When a death results from negligence, other death benefits may be payable to survivors. Such benefits sometimes result from court cases that attempt to place a value on the deceased's life and what the loss represents to his or her survivors. Although settlements of this kind may indeed be helpful to survivors, the monetary amount of a settlement, no matter how large, is poor compensation for the loss of a loved one (see Figure 6-5).

Dealing with legal and financial matters surrounding dying and death can be a burden when a person is grieving the death of a loved one or coping with the impending death of a family member. Yet, crucial and even irrevocable decisions often must be made at times like these. Preparation can help ease the burden. Although one cannot plan for every contingency, it is possible to become aware of the range of legalities that may impinge on our experiences of death and dying and, acting out of that recognition, to take appropriate steps to prepare ourselves for the inevitable eventualities.

Considering End-of-Life Issues and Decisions

Studies of the factors that patients, family members, physicians, and care providers consider important at the end of life include pain and symptom management, communication with one's physician, preparation for death, and the opportunity to achieve a sense of completion. "Whereas physicians tend to focus on physical aspects, patients and families tend to view the end of life with broader psychosocial and spiritual meaning, shaped by a lifetime of experiences."[88] The challenge to medicine, then, say researchers, is to "design flexible care systems that permit a variety of expressions of a good death." In her study, *And a Time to Die: How American Hospitals Shape the End of Life,* Sharon Kaufman observes,

> Waiting for death—without an institutionally imposed concern for how long it takes—was necessary and time-consuming in the 1960s. Death today is mostly *decided,* not waited for.
>
> "The deathwatch has given way," said one thoughtful ICU nurse, "to saving a life or offering the best palliative care possible, to heading full bore into strategies and techniques for mastering death by staving it off or by choosing the time for it."[89]

In reviewing the rapidity with which issues and decisions involving the end of life have come to public interest during the past few decades, bioethicist Leon Kass observes that "today the ethics business is booming"; medical schools now offer courses in medical ethics, hospitals establish ethics committees, courts adjudicate ethical conflicts, and blue-ribbon commissions analyze and pronounce on ethical issues.[90] Yet, Kass argues, much of this "action" is really just talk—philosophical theorizing and rational analysis—with comparatively little time devoted to "what genuinely moves people to act—their motives and passions." This is not to say that analysis and theorizing are irrelevant, but the "morality of ordinary practice" is where the rubber meets the road. Kass points out that every human encounter is an ethical encounter, an occasion for the practice and cultivation of virtue and respect. Jitaro Mizuno says, "The place where ethical problems occur is not in an isolated individual consciousness, but rather in the relationship of person to person."[91]

Writing about care of individuals at the end of life, one scholar asks: "Are we not getting better at managing death? Or is it that death itself cannot be controlled, cannot be managed?"[92]

Our choices about end-of-life issues result not only from our personal values but also from values present within our particular ethnic or cultural group. Different value systems produce different attitudes about the end of life. Richard Gilbert says,

> End-of-life care requires us to at least be available to the dying and their loved ones around the issues of meaning, beliefs, rituals, and their longing for peace as they face whatever may be ahead for them. . . . It requires us to stand firmly in their presence as guest, nonjudgmentally, while also tracking our own spiritual/religious issues, challenges, and shortcomings.[93]

Concerns about issues pertaining to the end of life do not affect merely the realm of public policy but also bear directly, often poignantly, on the lives of individuals and families.

Further Readings

Jeffrey Paul Bishop. *The Anticipatory Corpse: Medicine, Power, and the Care of the Dying.* Notre Dame, Ind.: University of Notre Dame Press, 2011.

Michael C. Brannigan and Judith A. Boss. *Healthcare Ethics in a Diverse Society.* Boston: McGraw-Hill, 2001.

Denis Clifford and Cora Jordan. *Plan Your Estate,* 8th ed. Berkeley, Calif.: Nolo Press, 2006.

Susan Dolan and Audrey Vizzard. *The End of Life Advisor: Personal, Legal, and Medical Considerations for a Peaceful, Dignified Death.* New York: Kaplan, 2009.

Donald E. Gelfand and others. *End-of-Life Stories: Crossing Disciplinary Boundaries.* New York: Springer, 2005.

John Griffiths, Heleen Weyers, and Maurice Adams. *Euthanasia and Law in Europe.* Portland, Ore: Hart, 2008.

Matt Weinberg, ed. *Medical Ethics: Applying Theories and Principles to the Patient Encounter.* Buffalo, N.Y.: Prometheus, 2001.

James L. Werth, Jr., and Dean Blevins, eds. *Decision Making Near the End of Life: Issues, Developments, and Future Directions.* New York: Routledge, 2008.

Additional resources for this chapter can be found at www.mhhe.com/despelder10e

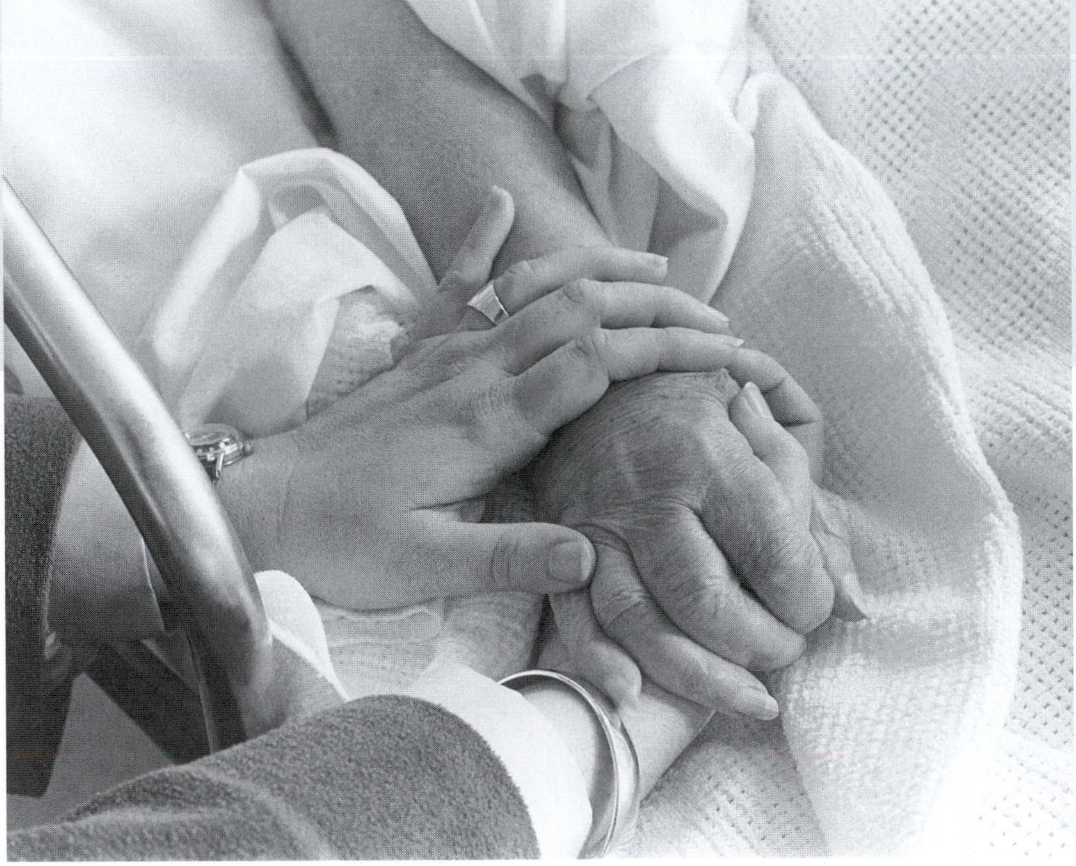

© Carol A. Foote

Total care for the patient with a life-threatening illness includes warm, intimate contact with caring persons who are able to listen and share the patient's concerns.

CHAPTER 7

Facing Death: Living with Life-Threatening Illness

One day, you wake up and notice symptoms in your body that you associate with a serious illness. What goes through your mind? Perhaps you just barely admit to yourself the possibility that you're "really sick," then quickly push away such thoughts and go on with your day's activities. "After all," you say, "there's no reason to suspect it's anything serious; it's probably nothing." You don't want to tempt fate by looking too closely.

You forget about it for a while. But, more and more persistently, the symptoms demand your attention. "This better not be anything serious," you tell yourself, "I've got too much to do." Yet, in some part of your mind, you recognize that it could be serious. You begin to admit your concern, feeling a bit anxious about what the symptoms might mean, how they might affect your life.

You make an appointment with your doctor, describe your symptoms, submit to an examination, and wait for the results. Perhaps right away, or maybe only after additional tests are completed, you learn the diagnosis. Your doctor informs you that you have a tumor, a malignancy. Cancer.

Now your thoughts and emotions really become agitated: "What can be done? How are the doctors going to treat this illness? What kind of changes will I have to make in my life? Should I postpone the trip I've been planning? What course of treatment should be followed? Are there side effects? Can this kind of cancer be cured? Will it be painful? Will

I die?" As the drama unfolds, you find ways to cope with the crisis. Earlier fears about symptoms are transformed into concerns about diagnosis, treatment, and outcome.

As time passes, you experience a remission: The tumor appears to have stopped growing. The doctors are optimistic. Still, you wonder whether the cancer is really gone for good. Cancer used to mean a terminal prognosis; now, because of early detection and treatment advances, it is not always a fatal disease. Despite good reports from your doctors, you wonder whether you will be a "cancer victim" or a "cancer survivor." Your health status is up in the air. You are in limbo. You're happy that things seem to be going well, but optimism is mixed with uncertainty and fear. Perhaps after a while you begin to relax and feel less anxious about the cancer returning. It seems your cancer was curable.

However, sooner or later you may notice the recurrence of symptoms, signaling the cancer's return. You fear the spreading of the cancer to other areas of your body. Cancer symbolizes the worst fears of our age: pain, wasting away, suffering, and death.

Thoughts of dying may become more predominant. Attention is focused on enacting the role of patient with a life-threatening illness. When nothing more can be done to stop the progression of the disease, fear or anxiety about the prospect of dying is difficult to avoid. Still, fear is balanced by hope. We hope for a remission, a change for the better that doctors haven't foreseen. We may fight to the end with the attitude, "I've always outwitted the percentages. Why not now?" Or we may take a different approach, coping with the end of life by making the most of the time we have left, surrounding ourselves with those closest to us, and accepting our fate. As a physician who had been diagnosed with a life-threatening illness said, "The attitude, 'I'm going to beat this thing' makes everyone who dies a loser. Death is a fight that no one can win."[1]

Life-threatening diseases confront us with our mortality, exposing our anxiety about being separated from all that we love, our fear of pain, and the imagined horror of dying.

Of course, cancer—the focus of the preceding scenario—is only one category of life-threatening illness. For example, heart disease and stroke are also killers.[2] The main forms of heart and circulatory disease are atherosclerosis (thickening and hardening of the arteries), coronary and peripheral artery disease, congestive heart failure, congenital heart disease, rheumatic heart disease, and heart valve problems. Stroke—also called a cerebrovascular accident (CVA)—refers to an impeded blood supply to some part of the brain, resulting in destruction of brain cells. Although people think of heart disease as a malady of modern life, CT scans of mummies from three continents show hardened arteries, evidence suggesting that humans may have a predisposition to cardiovascular disease as they age.[3]

Sometimes serious heart or cerebrovascular disorders have no symptoms until they reach a late stage. Sudden cardiac death refers to unexpected death from cardiac arrest, usually due to arrhythmia (disruption of the

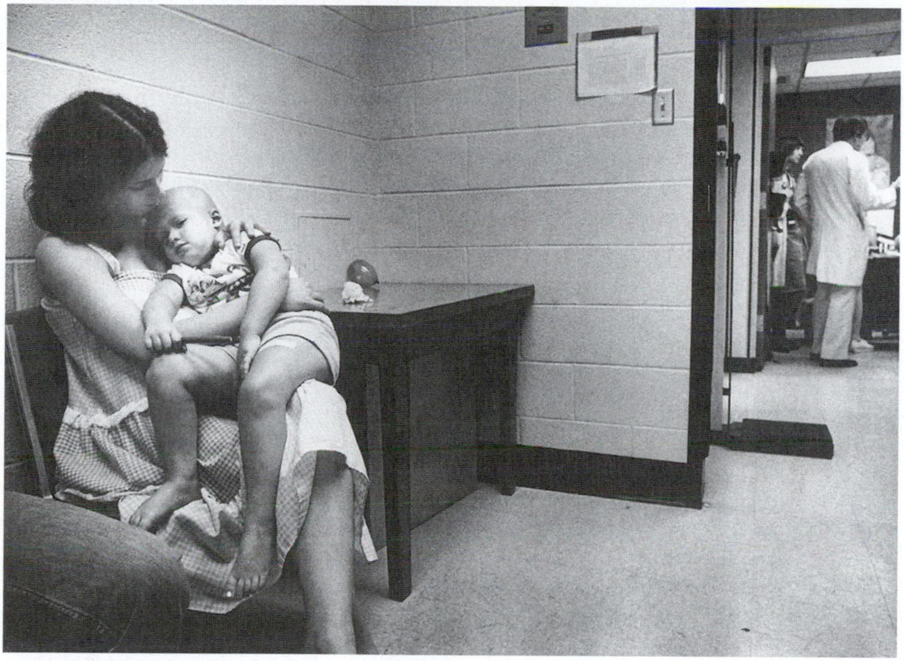

© Burton Steele, *Times-Picayune*

With her seriously ill daughter, this mother waits for the test results that will help determine the next step in care and treatment.

heart's electrical conduction system in which it beats too quickly, too slowly, or irregularly). This category of disease does not always cause sudden, unexpected death. For example, damage to heart muscle can result in a heart attack, or myocardial infarction, that becomes a threat that must be dealt with over time.

In addition to cancer, heart disease, and stroke, other leading causes of death in the United States include accidents, Alzheimer's disease, and suicide. These ways of "facing death" are discussed in later chapters. However, except for some parts of the discussion of treatment options, which focus particularly on cancer, the material in this chapter is pertinent to life-threatening illnesses generally. In our discussion of treatment options, we focus particularly on cancer for two reasons: First, it symbolizes for many people the nature of life-threatening or terminal illness; second, many of the medical and palliative care options now available to patients with life-threatening diseases were initially developed as a result of efforts to improve cancer care.

Personal and Social Meanings of Life-Threatening Illness

Life-threatening diseases are sometimes treated as taboo (from the Polynesian word *tapu*, meaning "marked off"), as if fraught with mystical danger.[4]

This can lead to avoidance of people, places, and objects associated with the forbidden condition. Kay Toombs says,

> Diagnoses are permeated with personal and cultural meanings. The dread diseases—cancer, heart disease, AIDS—carry with them a particularly powerful symbolic significance. In living an illness, one is forced not only to deal with the physical symptoms of disease but also to confront the meanings associated with the diagnosis—particularly with respect to the response of others.[5]

A pattern of taboo and avoidance can cause friends and relatives as well as caregivers to abandon the patient, creating a kind of "social death"; the patient feels walled off from the rest of society as somehow "in-valid." (Researchers note that, although cancer still carries a stigma, it is nothing like it was before celebrities started "coming out" about the disease.)[6]

A person who fails to achieve or retain good health may feel guilty: "Am I responsible for bringing this illness on myself?" Magical thinking—assuming oneself responsible though it's not clear just how—can place an additional burden on a patient with life-threatening illness: "If I had done this or not done that, maybe I wouldn't be in this predicament." The pursuit of wellness becomes a kind of moral virtue.

In addition, serious and life-threatening diseases are expensive, incurring costs related to hospitalization, outpatient therapy, office visits, and medications. Besides medical care, there are incidental costs associated with transportation, support services, child care, and temporary housing for patients who travel long distances to receive specialized care. Time off from work results in lost earnings. Looking at the family as a system, as the illness affects the patient, it also affects family life; and this pattern is reciprocal. When all these things are considered, in addition to the stress and problems inherent in the care of a life-limiting illness, we begin to agree with the summary expressed by Ira Byock, "We make dying a lot harder than it has to be."[7]

Education, counseling, and support groups can help individuals cope with life-threatening illness. Acquiring information about the disease and its treatment, sharing experiences with others in an environment of mutual support, using counseling services to clarify issues, and finding ways of communicating more effectively with caregivers as well as family and friends—all of these are examples of positive approaches to dealing with life-threatening

> I sat in our yard, a peaceful wooded place in the hills filled with the sound of birds, and just breathed in the scent of bay trees and pine. I knew that my life would never be the same—my work life, my family life, and the way I felt physically every day would all be different. I also knew that I couldn't imagine what this would feel like: chemotherapy, radiation, pain, daily nausea, and eventual fading away into death. I had watched many patients experience this but never asked them what it felt like. I was about to find out. I was embarking on a very challenging journey, to say the least. I sat there enjoying the last thirty minutes of my existence before cancer would become the life focus for both my family and me.
>
> Lee Lipsenthal, *Enjoy Every Sandwich*

illness, restoring some sense of personal control over one's life. Nevertheless, there may be overwhelming feelings of loss on all levels. Byock says, "The fundamental nature of illness is not medical; it is personal. . . . Illness is the interaction of a person with a disease."[8]

Coping with Life-Threatening Illness

Every disease has its own set of problems and challenges, and each person copes in his or her own way.[9] How people respond to illness is shaped by personality, psychological makeup, family patterns, and social environment. Arthur Frank says, "Critical illness teaches us that to be alive is to be constantly at risk, but the risk greater than dying is living less than well."[10]

Religious faith and spiritual beliefs can be important allies in coping with life-threatening illness. Patients and their families may be comforted by faith that helps them face the abyss of death and somehow make sense of existence.[11] Faith can promote a sense of self-confidence, peacefulness, and purpose.

Charles Corr identifies four primary dimensions in coping with dying: physical, psychological, social, and spiritual (see Table 7-1).[12] This highlights the fact that coping involves more than just body or mind. The spiritual dimension, it should be noted, is not exclusively religious; rather, it encompasses a person's basic values and sources of meaning about life and death. This model shifts our perspective from a narrow or limited view of coping with the threat of dying to one that is holistic.

Awareness of Dying

Observing family interactions in response to life-threatening illness, sociologists Barney Glaser and Anselm Strauss noted four distinctive ways in which a context of awareness about dying shapes communication styles.[13] In the *closed awareness* context, the dying person is not aware of his or her impending death, although others may know. This context is characterized by a lack of communication about the person's illness or the prospect of his or her death.

In the *suspected awareness* context, a person suspects his or her prognosis, but this suspicion is not verified by those who know. The dying person may try to confirm or deny his or her suspicions by testing family members, friends, and medical staff in an effort to elicit information known by others but not openly shared. Despite this secrecy, the patient observes the disruptions in family communication patterns caused by the illness and senses

TABLE 7-1 *Four Primary Dimensions in Coping with Dying*

1. *Physical.* Involves satisfying bodily needs and minimizing physical distress in ways consistent with other values.
2. *Psychological.* Involves maximizing psychological security, autonomy, and richness in living.
3. *Social.* Involves sustaining and enhancing significant interpersonal relationships and addressing the social implications of dying.
4. *Spiritual.* Involves identifying, developing, or reaffirming sources of spiritual energy or meaning and, in so doing, fostering hope.

others' anxiety about the illness, thus tending to confirm suspicions. Kenneth Doka tells a story that illustrates this: One patient said his first inkling of impending dying occurred when he told his wife that he wanted to plant an herb garden next spring. Grasping his hand tightly, his wife said, with tears in her eyes, "Of course you will, dear." The man said wryly, "She never before showed so much emotion about my gardening."[14]

The *mutual pretense* context is like a dance in which participants sidestep direct communication about the patient's condition. This can lead to complicated though usually unspoken rules of behavior intended to sustain the illusion that the patient is getting well. Participants exchange subtle signals that the style of communication used to cope with the crisis is to pretend that things are normal. Everyone, the patient included, recognizes that death will be the outcome, but all act as if the patient will recover. In the short term, mutual pretense can be a useful strategy for coping with a difficult and painful situation.

Underlying mutual pretense is the notion that everyone should avoid "dangerous" or "threatening" topics, such as facts about the disease, its prognosis, medical procedures, the deaths of other patients with the same disease, and future plans and events that will likely occur after the patient dies. When something happens that threatens to break the fiction and disclose the reality, the parties to mutual pretense act as if the threatening event had not occurred. People may respond to the risk of disclosure by becoming angry or withdrawn, or they may avoid further communication by saying they need to go out for a walk or make a phone call. Mutual pretense may be carried on right to the end, even when unspoken rules are occasionally violated in ways that could have revealed the patient's condition.

Glaser and Strauss's fourth designation, the context of *open awareness,* is one in which death is acknowledged and discussed. Open awareness does not necessarily make death easier to accept, but it does allow for the possibility of sharing support in ways that are not readily available with the other awareness contexts.

As new information about the disease comes to light or the course of the disease changes, the context of awareness may change. For example, mutual pretense may dominate through a succession of medical procedures; then, with receipt of new test results, participants may begin to openly acknowledge the illness as life threatening. As circumstances change, the awareness context may shift.

Adapting to "Living-Dying"

Living with a life-threatening illness can be described as a "living-dying" experience, during which patients and families fluctuate between denial and acceptance.[15] Avery Weisman described this coping process as involving *middle knowledge;* that is, individuals seek a balance between sustaining hope and acknowledging the reality.[16]

Based on her work with dying patients, more than forty years ago, Elisabeth Kübler-Ross developed a description of common emotional and psychological responses to life-threatening illness.[17] "At the heart of Kübler-Ross's work was her concern for the patient and her wish that every physician be able to

But You Look So Good

It's with me each day.
I wake, thinking
Today it will go away.
But the pain seems to stay . . .
Persistent, resistant, consistent.
People say,
But you look so good.
If only I could
Feel like I look.
Or, should
I look bad?
So they'll know
How I feel
is real.
Do they doubt?
I wish the pain
Was on the outside—
something you see.
Not only the pain
Do I need to survive,
But also my
Paranoid imaginings
Of others' disbelief.

Judy Ellsworth

fully imagine the patient's suffering and act accordingly."[18] She reminded her students and readers of how important it is to pay attention to dying people, who have much to teach us about our shared humanity and the final stages of life with all its anxieties, fears, and hopes.[19]

Perhaps you have heard or read about the five stages associated with Kübler-Ross's model: denial, anger, bargaining, depression, and acceptance. Receiving the diagnosis of a life-threatening illness, a person may respond with avoidance or denial. Bargaining, or attempting to strike a deal with fate or with God, occurs as a patient tries to find a way to avoid the inevitable. Expressions of anger can mask anxiety about the encounter with serious illness and its meaning. It may be manifest as displaced hostility, perhaps directed toward a caregiver, as displayed in complaints about food or other aspects of care: "Why can't you fix me a good cup of tea? You know I can't do it for myself!"

As the illness progresses, weakening the body, an individual's attempts to be stoic may be replaced by depression, a profound sense of loss. Kübler-Ross distinguished two kinds of depression: *reactive* depression, which is a response to disruptions caused by the disease, and *preparatory* depression, which is related to the awareness that one is dying and must prepare for death.

In coping with a life-threatening illness and its accompanying losses, an individual may ultimately find some acceptance or resolution. Rather than giving up or losing hope, "acceptance" implies facing one's mortality in a manner that is essentially positive. Consider the words of writer Harold Brodkey as he faced the prospect of dying from AIDS:

> I have liked my life. I like my life at present, being ill. I like the people I deal with. I don't feel I am being whisked off the stage or murdered and stuffed in a laundry hamper while my life is incomplete. It's my turn to die—I can see that is interesting to some people but not that it is tragic. Yes, I was left out of some things and was cheated over a lifetime in a bad way but who isn't and so what? I had a lot of privileges as well. Sometimes I'm sad about its being over but I'm that way about books and sunsets and conversations.[20]

The "Kübler-Ross" model has been portrayed in cartoons and on television shows, such as *The Simpsons.* The acronym DABDA is used by medical students preparing for their exams. The idea that these five stages occur in a linear progression—and that a person is supposed to move through them sequentially and eventually wind up at acceptance—became a prescription for how people *should* cope with the process of living-dying. In reality, each person's pathway is unique, determined by such factors as the specific nature of the illness, his or her personality, and the helping resources available in his or her environment.

Kübler-Ross stimulated a better understanding of how people experience the prospect of dying. However, this model became, for a time, *the* way to cope, despite the fact that Kübler-Ross herself said that patients tend to go back and forth among the various "stages" during the course of an illness and may experience different stages at the same time. People sometimes interpret denial as a bad thing, something the dying person should "get over" or move beyond. But this interpretation ignores the fact that denial can be healthy and an effective way of coping. Whether denial is adaptive or maladaptive depends on its timing and duration, as well as the nature of the perceived threat. Facing reality is not always the healthiest choice; there are times when game-playing or acting as if circumstances were otherwise is appropriate.

Moving beyond Kübler-Ross, in focusing on the tasks that individuals manage at different phases of a life-threatening illness, Kenneth Doka provides a useful model of the chronology of living-dying (see Table 7-2).[21] This model describes an *acute* phase, initiated by the diagnosis; a *chronic* phase, living with the disease; and a *terminal* phase, coping with impending death. Doka points out that, in some cases, two additional phases may occur: first, a *prediagnostic* phase, during which a person suspects the illness and may seek medical attention; and, second, a *recovery* phase, which follows the cure or remission of a previously life-threatening disease. As you think about the tasks that pertain to each of these phases, keep in mind that serious illness doesn't automatically liberate a person from the ordinary challenges of life. Doka says, "Life-threatening illness is only part of life."[22] All the previous issues and problems of life remain part of the larger struggle of life and living.

Patterns of Coping

Herman Feifel points out that patterns of coping with a life-threatening illness vary in significant fashion.[23] Thus, we need to keep in mind both the

TABLE 7-2 *Tasks in Coping with Life-Threatening Illness*

Acute Phase	Chronic Phase	Terminal Phase
Understand the disease.	Manage symptoms and side effects.	Manage discomfort, pain, incapacitation, other symptoms.
Maximize health and lifestyle.	Carry out health regimens.	Cope with health procedures and institutional stress.
Optimize coping strengths.	Manage stress and examine coping behaviors.	Manage stress and examine coping behaviors.
Develop strategies to deal with issues created by disease.	Normalize life to extent possible in face of disease.	Prepare for death and say goodbye.
Explore effect of diagnosis on self and others.	Maximize social support and preserve self-concept.	Sustain self-concept and appropriate relationships with others.
Express feelings and fears.	Express feelings and fears.	Express feelings and fears.
Integrate present reality into sense of past and future.	Find meaning in uncertainty and suffering.	Find meaning in life and death.

highly individual nature of coping styles and the fact that a person can have various ways of coping with life-threatening illness. It is not feasible to rely solely on some "standard" model of the dying process to tell us how a given individual is likely to behave or what he or she is likely to feel or think. We must pay attention to the dying person's own *life story* (see Figure 7-1).

Avery Weisman observed that coping effectively with life-threatening illness involves three interrelated tasks: first, confronting the problem and revising one's plans as necessary; second, keeping communication open and wisely using the help offered by others; and third, maintaining a sense of optimism and hope.[24] Weisman suggested that the process of coping with terminal illness consists of three phases: (1) from the time symptoms are noticed until the diagnosis is confirmed, (2) the time between diagnosis and the final decline, and (3) from decline to death.[25] Among the "landmarks" that characterize the journey through terminal illness are the following:

1. *Existential plight.* A crisis of self-identity begins with the initial shock of diagnosis as the person attempts to come to terms with the life-altering news.
2. *Mitigation and accommodation.* When treatment begins, the reality of the illness becomes part of the person's life as adjustments and accommodations are made.

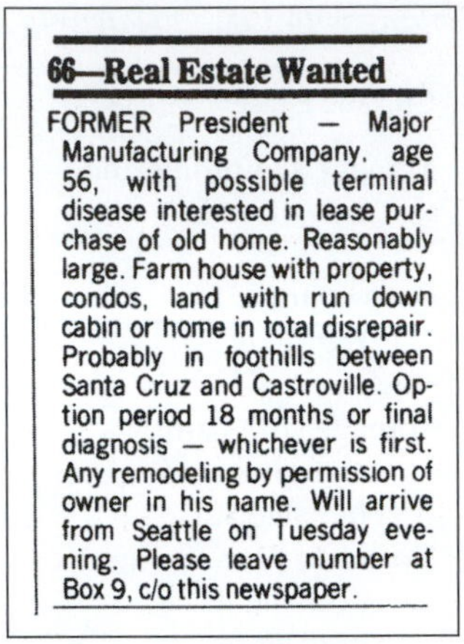

66—Real Estate Wanted

FORMER President — Major Manufacturing Company, age 56, with possible terminal disease interested in lease purchase of old home. Reasonably large. Farm house with property, condos, land with run down cabin or home in total disrepair. Probably in foothills between Santa Cruz and Castroville. Option period 18 months or final diagnosis — whichever is first. Any remodeling by permission of owner in his name. Will arrive from Seattle on Tuesday evening. Please leave number at Box 9, c/o this newspaper.

Figure 7-1 *Life Change with Life-Threatening Illness: Real Estate Want Ad*
The confrontation with a life-threatening illness may activate desires to accomplish in the present plans that previously had been visualized as occurring in the future.

3. *Preterminality and terminality.* When no cure or extension of life is in the offing, the individual confronts progressive decline and deterioration as the limits of life become increasingly clear. As the end draws near, palliative care replaces curative therapy as the dying person prepares for death.

Although life-threatening illness disrupts virtually all aspects of a person's life, it has been known for a long time that there is a vital link between finding meaning and achieving a sense of mastery.[26] The threat of a potentially fatal illness evokes a variety of responses to make the threat manageable. Psychologically, these responses can be divided into two categories: defense mechanisms and coping strategies.[27] *Defense mechanisms* occur unintentionally and without conscious effort or awareness; they function to change a person's internal psychological states, not the external reality. *Coping strategies* involve conscious, purposeful effort; they are employed with the intention of solving a problem situation. Although coping strategies are generally viewed more positively than defense mechanisms, both involve psychological processes that can help ease a distressful situation. Denial, for example, is a defense mechanism that is sometimes adaptive and sometimes not, depending on the person and the situation. In the short term, denial can give a person "breathing room" in living with a distressing situation; over the longer term, however, defenses may hinder a positive outcome if they prevent a person from mobilizing needed resources and taking appropriate action. Consider the example of a person who uses denial to delay seeking medical attention because of his or her fear about illness.[28] Edwin Shneidman says, "Intermittent denial is the ubiquitous psychological feature of the dying process."[29]

Therese Rando identifies three major psychological and behavioral patterns that individuals use in coping with the threat of death: (1) retreat and conservation of energy, (2) exclusion from the threat of death, and (3) attempting to master or control the threat of death.[30] The main aim of the mental processes and behaviors involved in coping is to establish control over a stressful situation. This generally requires different coping strategies working in concert. As with an orchestra, wherein particular instruments come to the fore at a given time while other instruments await their turn, the various coping strategies may be employed at different times to achieve different purposes. One way of distinguishing different strategies is to examine their purpose and focus. *Emotion-focused coping,* for example, helps regulate the level of distress. It allows a person to escape the impact of the stressful situation by reframing it or distancing himself or herself from it. Reframing a situation to put it in a positive light can reduce the sense of threat. Another strategy, *problem-focused coping,* deals with managing the problem that is causing distress. An individual who seeks out information about a diagnosis and takes an active role in determining options is engaging in problem-focused coping. A hallmark of this style of coping is the pursuit of personally meaningful goals. Recalling that the main aim of coping is to establish a sense of control, it is noteworthy that a greater sense of control is associated with problem-focused coping. A third strategy, *meaning-based coping,* helps maintain a person's sense of positive well-being. Examples include giving up goals that are no longer achievable and formulating new ones, making some sense of what is happening, and, where possible, finding benefit in the distressing situation. In searching for meaning, people often turn to spiritual beliefs for insight in making the best of a bad situation. Finding some redeeming value in loss can make the burden easier to bear (see Figure 7-2).

People vary their styles of coping depending on opportunities for problem solving, the intensity of their emotional responses and their ability to regulate them, and the changes in their environment as the distressing situation unfolds. Thus, coping strategies are dynamic rather than static. They are also interdependent, each supplementing the others.[31] Thus, the overall pattern of coping resembles a more or less continual flow or oscillation among various styles.

How individuals respond to stressful circumstances is largely determined by who they are—by their enduring dispositions and personalities.[32] People who apparently cope best with life-threatening illness often exhibit a "fighting spirit" that views the illness not only as a threat but also as a challenge.[33] Such people strive to inform themselves about their illness and take an active part in treatment decisions. They are optimistic and try to discover positive meaning in ordinary events. Holding to a positive outlook despite distressing circumstances involves creating a sense of meaning bigger than the threat. In the context of life-threatening illness, this encompasses a person's ability to comprehend the implications an illness has for the future as well as for his or her ability to accomplish goals, maintain relationships, and sustain a sense of personal vitality, competence, and power.

Maintaining Coping Potency

From the moment one notices unusual symptoms, through the ups and downs of treatment, and on to the final moments of life, hope and honesty are often delicately balanced—honesty to face reality as it is, hope that the outcome is positive. The capacity to maintain a sense of self-worth, to set

Dear Friends,

In company with our dear Mother Earth, I have arrived at the time of autumn in my worldly life, that time of transition between life and death. Before long, just as the leaves drop from the trees to continue Life's cycle of generation and regeneration, so will my body be shed and become part of the muttering earth. Like the tree gathering in energy to prepare itself for winter, I feel a need to gather energy for the process of dying. Also, I want to share a last celebration with you dear friends. To do this, I have planned a ritual of transition to take place on Sunday, November 3, at 2:30 p.m. here at my home.

I would love it if you can participate with your presence; and if you cannot, I would appreciate your joining us in spirit with loving energy via the ethers that afternoon.

If you can come, please bring a pillow to sit on and a symbolic gift of your energy and blessing for me in this process I am going through—something from nature (rock, shell, feather, etc.); a poem, picture or song; something written or drawn; or whatever you are inspired to bring. Please also bring a casserole, salad or dessert or beverage to contribute to our potluck supper following the ritual.

There is a new joy that is beginning to be realized in me as I acknowledge the prospect of having a spirit float free of my tired body. I look forward to sharing this with you too.

Love and blessings,

Joan Conn

Figure 7-2 *Invitation to a Going-Away Party*
Ritual and companionship can assist in dealing with impending death. This celebration was attended by close friends and family, who said the occasion was an extremely moving experience. Knowing that she would soon die from cancer, Joan created a ritual that involved drawing a line on the floor and, in her weakened condition, she was helped across it by her ex-husband and her children while members of the gathering played music and sang. Although such an event would not be appropriate for everyone, Joan's farewell party aptly reflected her lifestyle and values. She died seven months later.

goals and strive to meet them, to exercise choice out of an awareness of one's power to meet challenges, to engage in active interactions with one's environment—all of these reflect a "coping potency" that sustains the will to live in the face of death. It has long been a truism in medicine that hope plays a key role in a patient's ability to live with illness.

Reportedly, both John Adams and Thomas Jefferson, although gravely ill, managed to live until July 4, 1826, the fiftieth anniversary of the signing of the Declaration of Independence. According to his physician, Jefferson's last words were, "Is it the Fourth?" This story raises the question, Do individuals have the ability to delay or defer death so they can observe an anniversary or other important event?[34]

The object of hope changes over time. Hope that the symptoms mean nothing gives way to hope that there will be a cure. When hope for a cure is no longer possible, one may hope for more time. When time runs out, one hopes for a pain-free death. Hope is sustained by focusing on meaningful aspects of life.[35]

Doctors often attempt to instill hope in patients by the manner in which they discuss a disease and its treatment. They talk about taking things one step at a time, first controlling pain or other symptoms. Or they may use analogies, likening the process of coping with a serious illness to climbing a mountain, which can be hard but potentially successful as long as one keeps advancing to the top. This metaphor suggests that the doctor can help "pull the patient to safer, higher ground." One oncologist explains, "You have to give people something to wake up for in the morning, otherwise they might as well take some cyanide."[36] In putting the best face on bad news, doctors see themselves in the role of "the patient's cheerleader." Yet it is also the case that "sometimes the only real hope you can offer a dying person is that you will accompany them to their death and respect their wishes to the best of your ability."[37]

I got the news that I was sick on the afternoon of my thirty-ninth birthday. It took a bit of time, travel, and a series of wretched tests to get the specific diagnosis, but by then the main blow had been delivered, and that main blow is what matters. I have an incurable cancer in my blood. The disease is as rare as it is mysterious, killing some people quickly and sparing others for decades, afflicting some with all manner of miseries and disabilities and leaving others relatively healthy until the end. Of all the doctors I have seen, not one has been willing to venture even a vague prognosis.

Conventional wisdom says that tragedy will cause either extreme closeness or estrangement in a couple. We'd been married less than a year when we got the news of the cancer.

In those early days after the diagnosis, when we mostly just sat on the couch and cried, I alone was dying, but we were mourning very much together. And what we were mourning was not my death, exactly, but the death of the life we had imagined with each other.

Christian Wiman, "Love Bade Me Welcome"

Treatment Options and Issues

The options for treating life-threatening illness vary with the nature of the disease and the patient's particular situation. Some diseases that are life-threatening can be cured by relatively simple treatment. Others diminish or become stabilized with treatment. With yet others, there is little hope of survival. People who are seriously ill have reasonable expectations of the following:[38]

- To have one's pain and other symptoms regularly assessed and competently treated.
- To have adequate information about one's condition and treatments, in clear and simple terms.
- To have care coordinated between visits and among physicians and health programs involved in one's care.
- To have crises prevented when possible and have clear plans in place for managing emergencies.
- To have enough nurses and aides on staff to provide safe and high-quality care.
- To have one's family supported in giving care and, eventually, in their grief.

The range of available choices for treating disease depends to an extent on circumstances in society at large. Disparities in access to health care are obvious. Individuals who fit the category of the urban poor tell "indignity stories" that occur in treatment experiences, causing them to ask, "Can you give me respect?"[39] Conversely, patients at the high end of the socioeconomic scale may encounter problems as a result of a greater access to care. A *New York Times* article observed, "You end up with the phenomenon of specialists referring to other specialists, with nobody coordinating, which results in confused messages, more referrals, more hospitalizations, deterioration in health care and a more anxious patient."[40]

Dignity is important for all human beings, perhaps especially so in the dramas and circumstances that accompany the end of life. Harvey Max Chochinov points out that dignity is defined as "the quality or state of being worthy, honored, or esteemed."[41] He adds: "Dignity provides an overarching framework that may guide the physician, patient, and family in defining the objectives and therapeutic considerations fundamental at the end of life." In studies conducted in Hong Kong, Andy Ho and his colleagues concluded:

> As dignity is a value- and cultural-laden concept that encompasses a wide spectrum of physical, psychosocial, spiritual, familial, and cultural issues, greater awareness of ethnic diversity is required for all palliative care workers. Yet, most end-of-life interventions still focus prominently on pain and symptoms control, while holistic care and familial support are limited.[42]

Another example of how social choices affect treatment options is demonstrated in the medical emergency of heart attack, which typically occurs when a blockage in a coronary artery cuts off the blood supply to a region of the heart. Half of the deaths from heart attack occur in the first three to four hours after the onset of symptoms. The sooner treatment begins, the better the chances of survival. Victims who receive early treatment have a survival rate of about 90 percent. The key to life-saving help is a rapid emergency response. Some communities, recognizing that sudden cardiac death is a pressing public health problem, have funded sophisticated mobile cardiac care units; other communities consider these units too costly.

As mentioned earlier, our focus in this section is primarily treatment options for cancer. Nevertheless, much of what is presented—especially concerning alternative therapies and pain management—applies generally to life-threatening illness.

As a general term, *cancer* encompasses many types of malignant, or potentially lethal, growths that occur in the body. Essentially, cancer is the abnormal, uncontrolled multiplication of cells.[43] The most common types of cancer in the United States are prostate, breast, lung, colorectal, urinary and bladder, kidney, oral cavity and pharynx, and pancreas cancers; melanoma; non-Hodgkin's lymphoma; leukemia; and cancers of the female reproductive tract (cervical, uterine, and ovarian cancer). Cancer cells can develop in any tissue within any organ.

Because there are many categories and types of cancer, some experts propose that cancer is best understood as a process, of which *time* is a critical dimension.[44] Cancer growth may be fast or slow; it may take weeks or years. Cancer is classified according to how it has spread in the body. This process is called *staging*. It denotes the extent of disease and helps determine treatment decisions as well as prognosis (see Table 7-3). Tumors are typically assessed in three ways: (1) extent of the primary tumor, (2) absence or presence of lymph node involvement, and (3) absence or presence of distant metastases. First affecting tissues in one part of the body, cancer may spread, either by invading adjacent tissues or by *metastasis*, a process whereby diseased cells travel in the blood or lymphatic system or through body tracts to more distant parts of the body. The speed at which cancer progresses affects how the patient and his or her family cope with the illness.

TABLE 7-3 *Cancer Staging*

Stage	Description
0	"Carcinoma in situ": An early cancer that is present only in cells where it originated; that is, it has not spread into surrounding tissue.
I–IV	More extensive cancer, with higher numbers indicating greater tumor size or degree to which cancer has spread to nearby lymph nodes or organs adjacent to primary tumor. For descriptive and statistical analysis, invasive cancers are categorized as *local*, *regional*, or *distant* based on the extent of spread.

TABLE 7-4 *Medical Treatment Word List*

Alkylating agents: A family of chemotherapeutic drugs that combine with DNA (genetic substance) to prevent normal cell division.

Analgesic: A drug used for reducing pain.

Antimetabolites: A family of chemotherapeutic drugs that interfere with the processes of DNA production and thus prevent normal cell division.

Benign: Not malignant. [See *malignant.*]

Biopsy: The surgical removal of a small portion of tissue for diagnosis.

Blood count: A laboratory study to evaluate the number of white cells, red cells, and platelets.

Bone marrow: A soft substance found within bone cavities, ordinarily composed of fat and developing red cells, white cells, and platelets.

Cancer: A condition involving the proliferation of malignant cells that are capable of invading normal tissues.

Chemotherapy: The treatment of disease by chemicals (drugs) introduced into the bloodstream by injection or taken by mouth as tablets.

Cobalt treatment: A form of radiotherapy that uses gamma rays generated from the breakdown of radioactive cobalt-60.

Colostomy: The surgical formation of an artificial anus in the abdominal wall so the colon can drain feces into a bag.

Coma: A condition of decreased mental function in which the individual is incapable of responding to any stimulus, including painful stimuli.

Cyanotic: A blue appearance of the skin, lips, or fingernails as the result of low oxygen content of the circulating blood.

Diagnosis: The process by which a disease is identified.

DNA: The abbreviation for deoxyribonucleic acid, the building block of the genes, responsible for the passing of hereditary characteristics from cell to cell.

Hodgkin's disease: A form of tumor that arises in a single lymph node and may spread, first to local lymph nodes, then to distant ones, and finally to other tissues, commonly the spleen, liver, and bone marrow.

Immunotherapy: A method of cancer therapy that stimulates the body defenses (the immune system) to attack cancer cells or modify a specific disease state.

Intravenous (IV): Pertaining to the administration of a drug or of fluid directly into a vein.

Leukemia: A malignant proliferation of white blood cells in the bone marrow; cancer of the blood cells.

Lymph nodes: Organized clusters of lymphocytes through which the tissue fluids drain upon returning to the blood circulation; they act as the first line of defense, filtering out and destroying infective organisms or cancer cells and initiating the generalized immune response.

Successful treatment of cancer requires that all cancerous tissue be destroyed or removed; otherwise, the disease recurs. In treating cancer, attention is focused on the primary tumor and its metastases. No single therapy is effective for all types of cancer. A therapy that has a high success rate with one type of cancer may be ineffective with another. Some cancers require a combination of therapies. There also may be a need for an *adjuvant therapy* (an auxiliary remedy which aids or assists another; other key terms used in cancer care are defined in Table 7-4). When a cure is not possible, palliation

TABLE 7-4 *(continued)*

Malignant: Having the potential to be lethal if not successfully treated. All cancers are malignant by definition.
Melanoma: A cancer of the pigment cells of the skin, usually arising in a preexisting pigmented area (mole).
Metastasis: The establishment of a secondary site or multiple sites of cancer separate from the primary or original site.
Multimodality therapy: The use of more than one modality for cure or palliation (abatement) of cancer.
Myelogram: The introduction of radiopaque dye into the sac surrounding the spinal cord, a process that makes it possible to see tumor involvement of the spinal cord or nerve roots on X-ray.
Oncologist: An internist (specialist in internal medicine dealing with nonsurgical treatment of disease) who has further specialized in cancer therapy and has expertise in both chemotherapy and the handling of problems that arise during the course of the disease.
Parkinson's disease: A degenerative disease of the brain resulting in tremor and rigid muscles.
Prognosis: An estimate of the outcome of a disease based on the status of the patient and accumulated information about the disease and its treatment.
Prosthesis: An artificial structure designed to replace or approximate a normal one.
Regression: The diminution of cancerous involvement, usually as the result of therapy; it is manifested by decreased size of the tumor (or tumors) or its clinical evidence in fewer locations.
Relapse: The reappearance of cancer following a period of remission.
Remission: The temporary disappearance of evident active cancer, occurring either spontaneously or as the result of therapy.
Sarcoma: A cancer of connective tissue, bone, cartilage, fat, muscle, nerve sheath, blood vessels, or lymphoid system.
Subcutaneous cyst: A cyst located beneath the skin; usually benign.
Symptom: A manifestation or complaint of disease as described by the patient, as opposed to one found by the doctor's examination; the latter is referred to as a *sign*.
Terminal: Pertaining to the condition of decline toward death, from which not even a brief reversal can be expected.
Therapeutic procedure: A procedure intended to offer palliation (abatement) or cure of a condition or disease.
Toxicity: The state of being poisonous; that is, injurious to health or dangerous to life.
Tumor: A mass or swelling. A tumor can be either benign or malignant.

of symptoms using some or all of the following therapies may improve the quality and duration of life. Patients need enough information to clearly understand the risks and benefits of each therapy, as well as to assess the consequences of pursuing a different course of action.

Surgery

Surgery is the oldest and most common form of cancer therapy, and some cancers are curable in early stages with surgery alone.[45] Surgery is commonly used in treating many other diseases as well. Although surgery is a

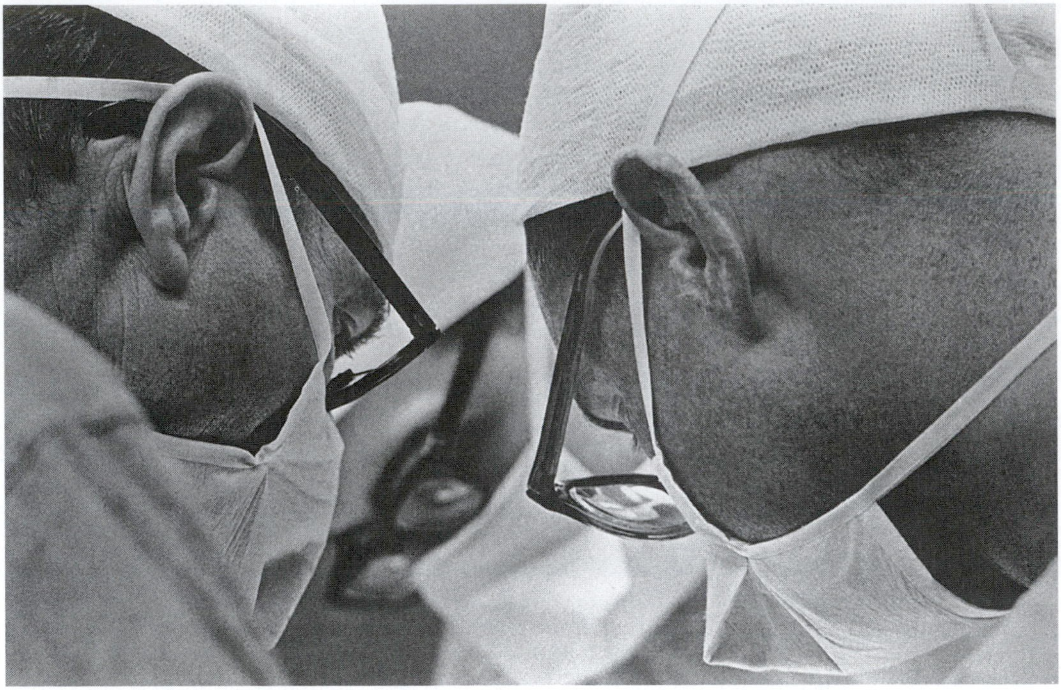

Surgery is a commonly used therapy in treating cancers. Advances in surgical technology and in surgeons' skills have resulted in notable successes in treatment. Palliative surgery may be done to relieve symptoms and restore quality of life when a cure is unlikely or an attempt at cure produces adverse effects that are unacceptable to the patient.

routine medical practice, it can also be seen as a "violation of the body" the side effects of which may include disfigurement, disability, or loss of bodily function.

The diagnosis of cancer is usually established by a biopsy, a tissue sample surgically removed and examined for the presence of cancerous cells. To stop the growth of cancer and prevent it from spreading, surgery usually involves removing not only the malignant organ or tissue but also adjacent healthy tissue. In addition to its role as a primary treatment for many types of cancer, surgery is used as a therapeutic option in treating pain.[46]

Radiation Therapy

Soon after the discovery of radium in 1898, it was recognized that radiation could be used to treat cancer. Radiation therapy uses ionizing radiation to preferentially destroy cells that divide rapidly.[47] Although radiation affects both normal and cancerous tissues, cancer cells are damaged more seriously because they usually grow more rapidly than normal cells. Radiation plays a key role in the treatment of some cancers, and it is used as an adjunct to chemotherapy in others. Even when radiation does not provide a cure, it may be used as a palliative therapy to relieve symptoms and thus improve quality of life.

Patients who receive radiation therapy are usually scheduled for frequent treatments over a period of several months. The radiation dose is prescribed on the basis of the stage of the disease and the patient's ability to withstand side effects, which can include nausea, vomiting, tiredness, and general weakness.

Chemotherapy

Chemotherapy has been called the leading weapon for increasing the number of patients who can be cured of cancer. It involves the use of toxic drugs to kill cancer cells.[48] Some cancers are cured by chemotherapy; others respond but aren't cured; and still others are resistant.

This form of therapy developed from the observation that toxic effects of mustard gases during World War I included damage to bone marrow. Clinical trials began after World War II. The ideal chemotherapeutic agent would attack cancerous cells in the body without affecting healthy tissue. The dose must be strong enough to kill the cancer or slow its growth but not so potent that it seriously harms the patient. Although chemotherapy may provide some palliation, it is also associated with substantial toxic effects.[49]

All chemotherapeutic agents basically work by blocking metabolic processes involved in cellular division. As a result, they damage healthy as well as diseased tissue. However, because cancer cells divide more rapidly than most normal cells, chemotherapy preferentially affects cancerous cells. Whether a particular drug prevents cells from making genetic material (DNA), blocks nucleic acid synthesis, or stops cell division and induces other cellular changes, chemotherapeutic agents owe their effectiveness to the fact that they are poisonous.

Chemotherapy is an important treatment in many types of cancers despite the fact that it usually causes distressing side effects, including hair loss, nausea, sleeplessness, problems with eating and digestion, mouth sores, ulceration and bleeding in the gastrointestinal tract, and other toxic effects.

Alternative Therapies

Paul Insel and Walton Roth observe, "One of the important characteristics of Western medicine is the belief that disease is caused by identifiable physical factors." They add: "Another feature that distinguishes Western biomedicine from other medical systems is the concept that almost every disease

> The oncology bargain is that, in return for at least the chance of a few more useful years, you agree to submit to chemotherapy and then, if you are lucky with that, to radiation or even surgery. So here's the wager: You stick around for a bit, but in return we are going to need some things from you. These things may include your taste buds, your ability to concentrate, your ability to digest, and the hair on your head.
>
> Christopher Hitchens, *Mortality*

is defined by a certain set of signs (physical manifestations) and symptoms (the effects on an individual), and that they are similar in most patients suffering from the disease."[50]

The conventional medical system is based, therefore, on describing health-related phenomena by using scientific explanations, which is to say explanations that are[51]

- Empirical (based on evidence of the senses and objective observation)
- Rational (follow rules of logic and are consistent with known facts)
- Parsimonious (explain phenomena by use of fewest causes)
- Rigorously evaluated (capable of verification)
- Tentative (open to new or better evidence)

Patients are often willing to try unproven treatments when standard therapies fail. For instance, they try to gain entrance into clinical trials of therapies that are being investigated for possible efficacy. Doctors point out, however, that experimental drugs are not therapies; they are research compounds that may end up causing more harm than good.[52] Physicians warn that patients, "often grasping at straws, need to be informed and wary of those who falsely promise cure."[53]

However, people sometimes find mainstream medicine lacking in its ability to address the patient as a whole person, not just the recipient of a "doctor-centered" treatment regimen. The result is growing interest in so-called *complementary and alternative medicine (CAM)*—sometimes referred to as "integrative medicine"—which comprises a diverse set of healing philosophies, therapies, and products (see Table 7-5).[54] While some of these are

TABLE 7-5 *Complementary and Alternative Therapies*

Mind-Body Interventions	Systems-Oriented Approaches	Manual Healing Methods
Psychotherapy and support groups	Traditional Chinese medicine	Osteopathic medicine
Meditation	Acupuncture and acupressure	Chiropractic treatment
Imagery	Herbal medicine and diet/nutritional approaches	Massage therapy
Hypnosis and biofeedback	Community-based practices (for example, Native American sweat lodges and Latin American *curanderismo*)	Biofield therapeutics (that is, laying on of hands)
Yoga, dance therapy, other movement therapies	Ayurveda (India)	Reflexology
Music therapy and art therapy	Homeopathic medicine	"Body work" (for example, Rolfing, Trager, Feldenkrais method, Alexander technique, shiatsu)
Prayer and mental healing	Naturopathic medicine	Bioenergetics

Figure 7-3 *Good Cells and Bad Cells: A Child's Drawing*
In this drawing by a child with cancer, the health-giving good cells are depicted as being victorious over the diseased bad cells. Such imaginative techniques can be ways of enlisting the patient's internal resources as an adjunct to conventional therapies.

unorthodox techniques considered harmful by the medical establishment, others are compatible with conventional medicine.[55]

In managing pain, for example, adjuvant methods may include psychotherapy and other mind-body interventions (meditation, imagery, biofeedback, and so on), as well as physical therapy and other forms of manual healing. In conjunction with chemotherapy, patients may use *visualization* to imagine the therapeutic agent inside the body as it helps to restore well-being. Such techniques help patients mobilize their inner healing resources by imagining the diseased parts of the body becoming well again (see Figure 7-3).

At Shibata Hospital in Japan, conventional treatment is accompanied by a psychotherapeutic technique called *ikigai ryoho,* or meaningful-life therapy.[56] The idea behind this therapy is that, even when we are terminally ill, we can "take responsibility for what to do in the time remaining to us." Thus, patients begin by acknowledging their own suffering and gradually proceed to the recognition that others also suffer, then to an acceptance of the reality of the illness, and finally to "an ability to live fully and deeply within the realistic limits posed by the illness."

Cross-cultural issues are becoming more important in conventional medicine as well.[57] Instead of viewing such beliefs as irrational or wrong, physicians are increasingly recognizing that optimal care is often achieved by judiciously combining conventional biomedicine and folk beliefs, or *ethnomedicine*. This means physicians must entertain the possibility that practices other than the "culture of biomedicine" may be effective. Arthur Kleinman says, "If you can't see that your own culture has its own set of interests, emotions, and biases, how can you expect to deal successfully with someone else's culture?"[58]

Traditional tribal beliefs are integrated into conventional medicine to present a holistic approach that Lori Arviso Alvord offers to her Navajo patients.[59] In this way, Alvord "bridges two worlds of medicine—traditional Navajo healing and conventional Western medicine—to treat the whole patient."[60] When Alvord, a graduate of Stanford University School of Medicine, returned to her Navajo community, she discovered that, although she was a good doctor, she "was not always a good healer."

> I went back to the healers of my tribe to learn what a surgical residency could not teach me. From them I have heard a resounding message: Everything in life is connected. Learn to understand the bonds between humans, spirit, and nature. Realize that our illness and our healing alike come from maintaining strong and healthy relationships in every aspect of our lives.[61]

Gerry Cox points out that "the basis of care of the dying in Indian culture lies in nature and healing rituals."[62]

Among some Mexican Americans, traditional practices of *curanderismo* (from the Spanish verb *curar*, "to heal") are an important part of total health care.[63] A study comparing folk healing and biomedicine concluded, "In the search for the alleviation of pain, pragmatism prevails; people judge the treatments they are given by their effects."[64]

A standard medical text states, "If the goal is the maintenance of or a return to health, all available mechanisms should be used."[65] Many physicians caution, however, that "respect for multiculturalism should not be used as a sentimental excuse to abandon one's professional obligation to serve the patient's best interest."[66]

The Placebo Effect

As the definition of medical treatment is changing, so too are attitudes about placebos. In 2008, Harvard created an institute dedicated to their study, the Program in Placebo Studies and the Therapeutic Encounter.[67] What is a placebo? Steven Perlmutter, a doctor and attorney, defines it as "a substance with no known specific pharmacologic activity for the condition being treated."[68] Placebos may be not only sugar tablets, an isotonic saline solution, and other non-drug interventions, but also so-called impure placebos—substances that have known therapeutic actions but not for the disease in question. A common example is an antibiotic for a non-bacterial infection. In the case of procedures such as surgery, a *sham* procedure is used.[69]

An interesting historical note: The word *placebo* comes from the Latin for "I will please." In medieval times, hired mourners participated in Vespers for the Dead. Because they were hired, the mourners' emotions were considered insincere. People called them 'placebos.'"[70]

The "placebo effect" is the positive response to a treatment that a person believes to be an effective therapy. Researchers have found that "simply believing in a treatment can be as effective as the treatment itself."[71] In other words, our expectations have a profound impact on healing, even if "it's all in your head." Perlmutter says, "In general, injections are more potent than oral medication, capsules work better than tablets, brightly colored remedies are more efficacious than muted colors, and two pills work better than one."[72] A placebo may be justified when physicians think a patient may go "doctor-shopping" and receive inappropriate or overly aggressive treatment from a less skilled or more self-serving provider, or when there is a risk of dangerous "Google self-treatment." Studies show that common indications for placebo use include pain and the desire to avoid informing patients that treatment possibilities are exhausted. Perlmutter points out, "When the disease is incurable and the situation is hopeless, the placebo offers a 'treatment' option."[73]

Unorthodox Treatment

What comes to mind when you hear the word *unorthodox?* Ineffective? Outside the establishment? Unorthodox therapies are methods of treatment that the medical establishment considers unproved or potentially harmful. The advocates of such remedies may be branded as quacks, charlatans, or frauds and their methods characterized as updated editions of Dr. Feelgood's Medicine Show, a form of snake oil medicine that, even if intrinsically harmless, diverts individuals from conventional medicine, which could help them.

Even in the best circumstances, alternative approaches typically make use of unproved therapies—that is, therapies that have not been subjected to rigorous scientific testing. Such unproved therapies may be launched in the mass media or via the Internet, a primary source of information on health issues for many people. A study in Italy found that patients are willing to try therapies of unknown efficacy in the hope of being cured: "Ignorance about the benefits of a treatment is what keeps hope alive, whereas knowledge requires coming to terms with uncertainty especially when the benefit of a treatment (such as palliative chemotherapy) is limited."[74]

That a cure could be found in the pits of apricots or shark cartilage stretches credibility; indeed, such "cures" may be not only controversial but also dangerous. Yet, many common medications derive from seemingly unlikely sources. Digitalis, in continuous use for more than two hundred years and prescribed for heart ailments, comes from the plant foxglove. Penicillin is naturally produced from molds. The active ingredient of aspirin is close kin to a substance found in the bark and leaves of the white willow. Perhaps the source of a proposed medicinal substance should concern us less than the question, Does it work? In China, about 1700 plants are commonly used as medicines, and in India that number is about 2500. As scientists seek out "undiscovered" drugs used by healers around the world, the study of medicinal plants is increasingly important to pharmacology.[75] Indeed, "Much of the pharmacopoeia of present-day scientific medicine originated in the folk medicine of native people, and many drugs used today are derived from plants."[76]

The debate over the medical use of marijuana has involved conflicts between law and medicine because the substance in question is not only an unproved therapy but also a generally illegal one.[77] A review by the Institute of Medicine concluded that marijuana appears to have a natural role in modulating and easing pain as well as in treating wasting syndrome, nausea, appetite loss, and anxiety. It noted that studies show that marijuana and other cannabinoids "may provide useful adjuncts to existing medications."[78] However, a statement from the federal Food and Drug Administration (FDA) said there were no sound scientific studies to support the medical use of marijuana.[79] Many physicians, as well as patients, believe further clinical trials could resolve the question. However, the federal Drug Enforcement Administration (DEA) routinely refuses to grant universities and pharmaceutical companies permission to research marijuana use.[80] The outcome of this ongoing debate remains to be seen.

Anson Shupe and Jeffrey Hadden use the term *symbolic healing* to identify the varied therapies known under such names as "faith healing," "supernatural healing," and "folk healing."[81] What we take to be meaningful—what we believe—potentially affects the functioning of our bodies. As human beings, we live within a series of overlapping environments: biological, social, and cultural. Cross-culturally, most healing systems describe illness as "an imbalance among different realms of a patient's life." When alternative therapies help restore this balance, they are an adjunct to conventional medical treatment. Adjunctive therapies of this kind are characterized as "complementary therapies."

Shortly before his death, Norman Cousins said, "The great tragedy of life is not death but what dies inside us while we live."[82] The reality of living with serious or terminal illness can wreak damage on the human spirit, damage that conventional medical therapies alone may not repair. It may be a mistake to confront patients with an either-or situation, forcing them to choose between conventional and alternative treatments. There are times when rigidly defending standard practices can do more harm than good.

Pain Management

Pain is the most common symptom in terminally ill patients. "Physical, often unbearable, suffering is part of everyday life in the world of palliative care."[83] A recent review of studies conducted between 1987 and 2007 found that nearly one of two patients with cancer pain is undertreated, a condition usually attributed to the inappropriate use of opioids.[84] Pain is now viewed as a "fifth vital sign," one that should be added to the four vital signs (temperature, pulse, respiration, and blood pressure) recorded and assessed as a standard part of patient care.[85]

Pain is a complex, multidimensional phenomenon; the type and severity of pain can be important diagnostic tools.[86] *Acute pain* is "an essential biological signal of the potential for or the extent of injury."[87] It is a protective mechanism that prompts the sufferer to remove or withdraw from the source of the pain.[88] *Chronic pain,* in contrast, is usually defined as pain that persists longer than three to six months. When pain lasts this long, it loses its adaptive role. Chronic pain may be accompanied by sleep disturbances, loss of appetite, weight loss, and depression. It may also result in diminished sexual interest and corresponding changes in closeness and intimacy.[89] It can result from physical mechanisms (somatogenic pain), psychological mechanisms (psychogenic pain), the activation of pain-sensitive nerve fibers (nociceptive pain), or nerve-tissue damage (neuropathic pain).

The Language of Pain

People often speak of pain as if it were a well-defined entity, but, in fact, as Linda Garro points out, pain is "subjective in nature and ultimately unshareable."[90] Garro says, "Pain cannot be directly measured or observed; it is a perceptual experience that can only be communicated through verbal means and/or by behavior interpreted as indicating pain." Culturally related belief systems have a dramatic impact on how patients "represent" their illness, as well as on their coping responses.

Languages differ in their lexicon for talking about pain. When describing pain, English speakers use such terms as *pain, hurt, sore,* and *ache.* Qualifiers are added to make the description match the experience. We talk about having a "burning" or "stabbing" pain or about "unbearable ache" or "soreness in the shoulder." Notice the tendency to treat pain as an object: "I have a pain." For Thai speakers, the basic terms for describing pain are verbs, referring to the active perception of sensations and often conveying the location of the pain as well; for example, "suffering focused abdominal pain" or "feeling irritated by an abrasion." Pain is described not as an object but as a perceptual process. Our response to pain, at least in part, is culturally shaped.

Treating Pain

Yvette Colón of the American Pain Foundation points out that "the belief that pain is real is a critical first step in assessing and managing that pain."[91] Effective treatment of pain requires attention to, among other factors, its

> The family of an elderly terminal cancer patient sued a nursing home that unilaterally reduced his pain medication without seeking approval from his doctor, a decision that caused the 75-year-old patient increased suffering. Deciding that the patient was "addicted to morphine," the nursing home staff substituted a "mild tranquilizer," which failed to control his pain. In response to the lawsuit, the nursing director at the facility said: "I have never heard of giving such high doses, at such frequent intervals. . . . The staff and I did not think he needed that much morphine."
>
> Maureen Cushing, "Pain Management on Trial"

severity, location, quality, duration, and course, as well as the "meaning" of pain to the patient. Patients may experience different mechanisms of pain operating simultaneously.[92] It is important to distinguish between pain and *suffering*, especially with patients, "whose suffering may be due as much to loss of function and fear of impending death as to pain."[93]

Pain is generally managed in a stepwise approach, beginning with basic non-opioid pain relievers such as aspirin, acetaminophen, and nonsteroidal anti-inflammatories (NSAIDs); then, if necessary, moving to opioid derivatives like codeine or tramadol; and, if pain is not relieved, using strong opioids such as morphine and fentanyl.[94] A combination of treatments is usually most effective. Numerous studies have shown that when these guidelines are followed, 90 percent of patients are pain free.[95] Colón says, "Something can always be done to manage pain."

The most useful agents for the treatment of pain associated with advanced disease are opioid analgesics. Yet, 80 percent of the world's population lacks adequate access to opiod medications for pain control.[96] Morphine is the gold standard of analgesics and a cornerstone for management of serious pain, although the development of new drugs and formulations of different opioids has enlarged the therapeutic arsenal.[97] Morphine works effectively to manage pain because it taps into the body's own pain relief system, the neurotransmitters, one class of which is chemically similar to morphine.

The good news is that (1) it is not difficult to assess and treat pain and that (2) physicians and other medical personnel are paying more attention to pain.[98] The not-so-good news is that there are doctors, nurses, and pharmacists whose misunderstandings about opioid analgesics, such as morphine, prevent patients from receiving adequate pain control.[99]

Pain specialists say that medicine has the means to alleviate the pain and suffering of almost all dying patients; it is the will to treat pain effectively that is lacking (see Table 7-6). There is a distinction between addiction (in which drug-seeking behavior occurs in an effort to reproduce the high) and physical dependence (which simply results in an abstinence syndrome after the

TABLE 7-6 *Factors That Inhibit Adequate Pain Control*

- Medical personnel have concerns that patients may become addicted, so they either don't prescribe appropriate drugs or prescribe only low, insufficient doses of medications that would be helpful in adequate dosages.
- Physicians are afraid to prescribe powerful narcotics due to concern about prosecution by overzealous law enforcers.
- Patients feel they should silently live with pain as a sign of moral strength or stoicism.
- Patients worry that, if they use strong painkillers now, nothing will be available later when pain may become worse; in fact, however, for most people there is no upper limit to the ability of narcotics like morphine to control pain.
- Many doctors really don't know much about how to control pain. There is a severe lack of training and information about the principles of pain management and palliative medicine.

"If it's any consolation, toward the end he was high as a kite."

patient stops taking the drug). A common misconception is that patients with severe pain obtain pleasant, euphoric sensations from drugs.

Governmental regulation can adversely affect pain management as an unintended side effect of fighting abuse. A Medscape poll of physicians found that 86 percent said there was little or no cooperation between clinicians and the DEA. Thus, the "politics of pain management" is a factor in determining whether pain is treated adequately.

Advances in pain management are occurring as the pathways of pain and its mechanisms become better understood. Pain can be treated with a variety of medical techniques, including nerve blocks, electrical stimulation of nerves, and neurosurgery. Patient-controlled analgesia (PCA), a mechanism that allows patients to determine for themselves the best timing of pain relief, is often more effective than relying on caregivers for an injection or a tablet after pain has worsened. Epidural and intraspinal drug delivery—placement of a slow, steady stream of morphine directly into the spinal column—is used effectively with some dying patients. In addition, antidepressants and other drugs are prescribed to relieve anxiety, confusion, and depression. Finally, drugs can be given to minimize the distressing effects of constipation, nausea, respiratory depression, and other physical symptoms.

Controlling pain in patients near the end of life presents a formidable challenge requiring specialized attention by skilled professionals. However, effective techniques for pain control are known and accessible. Hospice and palliative care practitioners have been at the forefront in calling attention to adequate pain management, especially in terms of responding to a patient's "total pain," which includes physical, psychological, social, and spiritual components.[100]

The Dying Trajectory

Our expectations about dying may be quite different from what most people actually experience. Young adults tend to imagine themselves living into old age and then quickly dying at home, alert and lucid until the end.[101] Pain and discomforts of dying tend to be absent from these imagined deathbed scenes. Our pictures of dying may be influenced more by images from movies and other media than by what is likely to actually occur.

The concept of a *trajectory of dying* is useful for understanding patients' experiences as they near death. Although sudden death from an unexpected cause—a massive heart attack or an accident, for example—is one type of dying trajectory, our focus here is on deaths that occur when there is forewarning. Among these, some trajectories involve a steady and fairly predictable decline. This is the case with many cancers, which tend to follow the course of a progressive disease with a terminal phase. Other kinds of advanced chronic illness involve a long period of slow decline marked by episodes of crisis, the last of which proves to be "suddenly" fatal.

We can also distinguish between different stages in a dying trajectory: namely, a period in which a person is known to be terminally ill but is living with a life expectancy of perhaps weeks or months, possibly years; and a later period in which death is imminent and the person is described as "actively dying." The way such trajectories are estimated—their duration and expected course—can affect both patients and caregivers and can influence their actions. Deaths that occur "out of time" (too quickly or too slowly) may pose special difficulties.

In addition to the *expected quick* trajectory, in which an individual makes a sudden exit, as in accidents or other emergency situations when life or death hangs in the balance, researchers have described the *lingering* trajectory, in which a patient's life fades away slowly and inevitably.[102] This second trajectory, which applies to people with progressive chronic illnesses who are receiving palliative care, can be further subdivided into three distinct trajectories for different diseases (see Figure 7-4).[103]

- *Trajectory 1:* Short period of evident decline. There is a reasonably predictable decline over a period of weeks, months, or, in some cases, years. This is a trajectory with steady progression and usually a clear terminal phase. There is usually time to anticipate palliative needs and plan for end-of-life care. This is typically the case with cancer.

- *Trajectory 2:* Long-term limitations with intermittent serious episodes. This is a trajectory with gradual decline, punctuated by periods of acute deterioration and some recovery, with seemingly unexpected "sudden" death. Heart failure and respiratory illnesses are examples.
- *Trajectory 3:* Prolonged gradual decline or "dwindling." This is a trajectory of progressive disability from an already low level of cognitive or physical functioning, with patients dying from minor physical events that may seem trivial, but, occurring in combination with declining reserves, prove fatal. Examples include death in old age from such illnesses as Alzheimer's or other dementia, or from generalized frailty of multiple body systems.

An acute stroke, for instance, could result in a swift decline, as in trajectory 1; a series of smaller strokes and recovery could mimic trajectory 2; and gradual decline due to stroke sequelae could parallel trajectory 3. A central point is that different models of care will be appropriate for people with different illness trajectories. "The key to caring well for people who will die in the (relatively) near future is to understand how they may die, and then plan appropriately."[104]

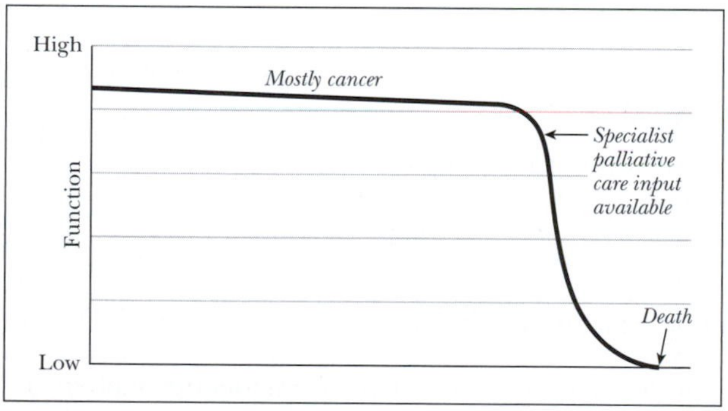

Figure 7-4 *(a)* *Trajectory 1*

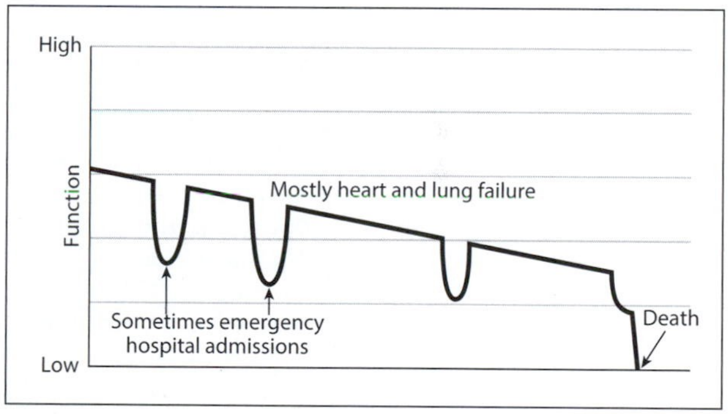

Figure 7-4 *(b)* *Trajectory 2*

The three trajectories of decline shown here are typical of chronic illness, especially in the elderly. Trajectory 1, typical of cancer, depicts a steady progression of disease followed by a relatively rapid period of decline preceding death. Trajectory 2, typical of organ failure, shows long-term limitations with occasional serious episodes requiring emergency hospital admissions, followed by a final episode leading to a "sudden" death. Trajectory 3, typical of frailty, dementia, and disabling stroke, presents prolonged decline with gradual disability and generalized failure of multiple systems.

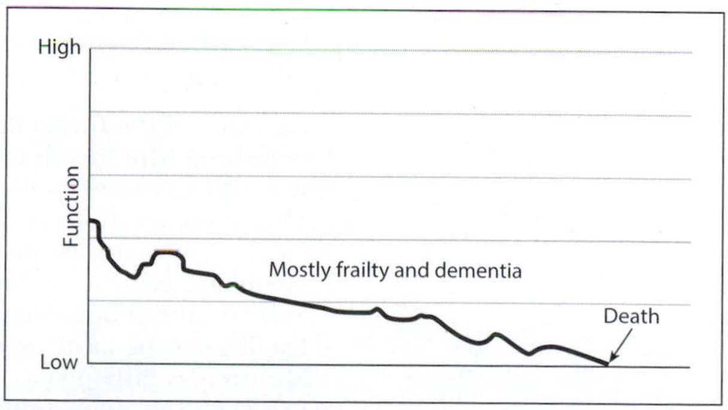

Figure 7-4 *(c)* *Trajectory 3*

The end of life is characterized by what is termed *active dying* (see Table 7-7). Among the signs that death is near are loss of appetite, excessive fatigue and sleep, increased physical weakness, and social withdrawal. The end stage is expected to last only hours or at most a few days. Pain should be treated aggressively as part of a comprehensive approach to comfort care. Some patients, even near death, still have concerns about addiction or want to delay pain medication "until it is really needed" or want to maintain control by "using the pain as a reminder that they are still living."[105]

During this phase, a dying person may exhibit irregular breathing or shortness of breath, nausea and vomiting, incontinence, and decreased appetite and thirst. People near the end of life are often more comfortable without food or liquids.

Dying patients may also experience confusion, delirium, disorientation, and diminished consciousness, as well as anxiety, agitation, and restlessness. A distinction is made between restlessness as a general symptom and the medical emergency referred to as *terminal restlessness* (also referred to as *terminal delirium* and *agitation delirium*).[106] Symptoms can include inability to maintain

TABLE 7-7 *Signs of "Active Dying"*

Common Symptoms During Last Days or Hours . . .

- Body systems slow down.
- Breathing pattern changes and becomes irregular (for example, shallow breaths followed by deep breath; periods of panting).
- Difficulty breathing (dyspnea).
- Congestion (noisy and moist breathing; gurgling sounds).
- Decrease in appetite and thirst.
- Nausea and vomiting.
- Incontinence.
- Sweating.
- Restlessness and agitation (for example, jerking, twitching, pulling at bed linen or clothing).
- Disorientation and confusion (for example, about time, place, identity of people).
- Decreased socialization; progressive detachment.
- Changes in skin color as circulation decreases (limbs may become cool and perhaps bluish or mottled).
- Increased sleeping.
- Decrease in consciousness.

At Time of Death . . .

- Relaxing of the throat muscles or secretions in the throat may cause noisy breathing (the "death rattle").
- Breathing ceases.
- Muscle contractions may occur, and the chest may heave as if to breathe.
- Heart may beat a few minutes after breathing stops, and a brief seizure may occur.
- Heartbeat ceases.
- Person cannot be aroused.
- Eyelids may be partly open with the eyes in a fixed stare.
- Mouth may fall open as the jaw relaxes.
- Bowel and bladder contents may be released.

attention or relax, disturbances in sleep or rest patterns, mumbling speech, twitching, trying to climb out of bed, picking at clothes, and other agitated motor activity. Such symptoms can be disturbing and even overwhelming for families who are unfamiliar with behaviors near the end of life.

As death becomes imminent, relaxation of the throat muscles or secretions in the throat may cause the person's breathing to become noisy, resulting in a sound called the "death rattle." Dying persons usually are not aware of this noisy breathing. If the sound unnerves family or caregivers, medication or repositioning the person can help. Just before death, the dying person may take a breath and sigh or shudder. After death, unless the person had a rare infectious disease, family and friends may stay with the body for a time as they make their farewells.

The Social Role of the Dying Patient

Eric Cassell writes, "There are two distinct things happening to the terminally ill: the death of the body and the passing of the person."[107] The death of the body is a physical phenomenon, whereas the passing of the person is nonphysical (social, emotional, psychological, spiritual). When we focus on the former and neglect the latter, biological death may be preceded by *social death.*

"Being healthy" is a vital characteristic of our social world. Sociologist Talcott Parsons tells us that illness is accompanied by a particular social role.[108] A sick person is obligated to engage in a supervised attempt to get well. Like all social roles—parent, child, student, employee, spouse—the role of the "person who is sick" includes rights and responsibilities. Illness tends to excuse a person from his or her usual tasks. Other people make allowances for our behavior. We are granted the right to be sick. Whereas taking off from work just to enjoy a day in the sun is frowned upon, absence due to illness elicits sympathy rather than reprimands. The sick person not only enjoys exemptions from usual social obligations but also is given special care. Such care is part of the role of being sick, of being a patient. But these "rights" are balanced by responsibilities. The sick person must cooperate with his or her caregivers. You've got to take your medicine.

In coping with life-threatening illness, individuals often find ways to redefine their situation so that they still feel "healthy." A woman with metastatic cancer said, "I am really very healthy. I just have this problem, but I am still me." Her statement shows a sense of self-integrity that demonstrates an ability to go on with life despite the disease.[109]

When life-threatening illness becomes terminal illness, the parameters of the "sick role" described by Parsons do not apply. Now, illness is no longer a temporary condition expected to be followed by a return to wellness. However, society has not clearly defined a social role for the dying person.[110] Even when circumstances are contrary, the dying person may be urged to deny the reality of his or her experience, to hope for recovery. This can result in actions that are incongruous. Consider, for example, the image of an end-stage, terminally ill person being rushed to the ICU (intensive care unit) and subjected

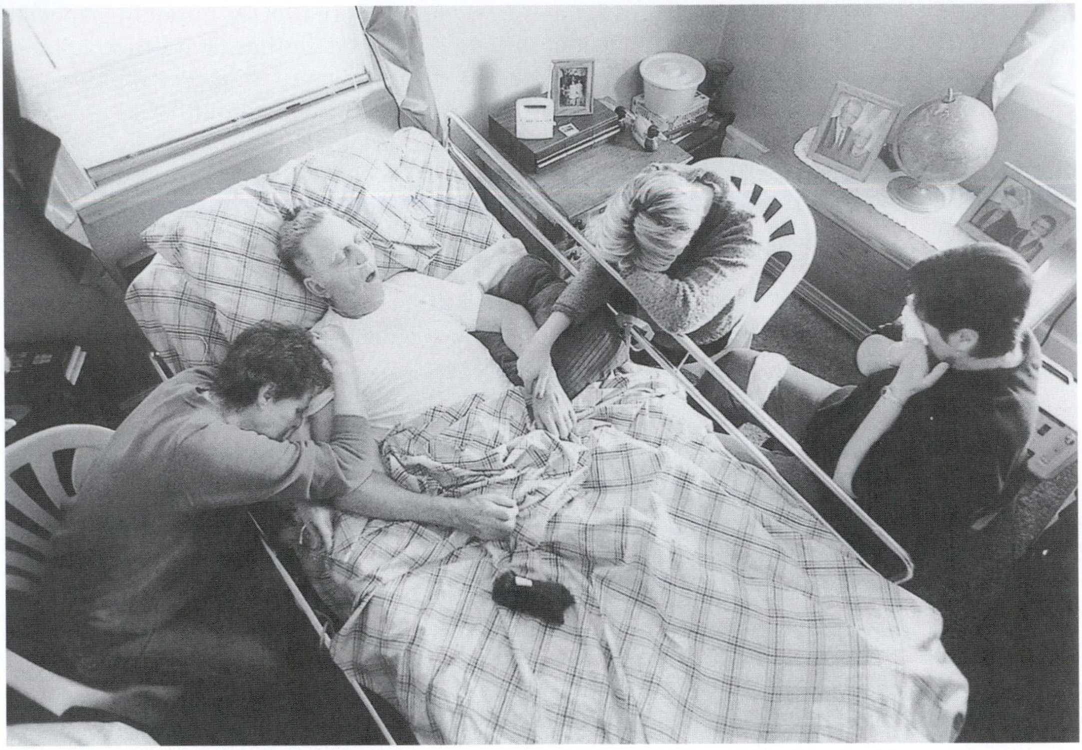

© Jeff Siner, *Charlotte Observer*

After being diagnosed with a recurrence of cancer, Vernon Nantz chose to be cared for at home by family and friends, with the support of hospice. In his last days, Vernon's family united in tears and prayers, sharing a vigil around his bedside, as he drifted away to the peaceful end he sought.

to heroic attempts to sustain his or her life. This image is real more often than we wish to admit.

What would an appropriate social role for the dying look like? First, the dying person would not be expected to maintain the appearance of expecting to live forever, of getting well again, of sustaining false hope. Instead, he or she would be encouraged to mobilize the resources necessary for attending to the prospect of death. Relatives and friends, accepting this changed perspective as natural, would allow the patient to set his or her own agenda about activities and relationships as the end of life draws closer.[111] In a study of "farewells by the dying," most people wanted to express their farewells through giving gifts, writing letters, and informal conversations with those closest to them.[112] Valued relationships are important for most people right to the end of life. Ira Byock suggests that persons who are dying—and, indeed, this suggestion is for everyone—make a point of expressing the "four things that matter": Please forgive me. I forgive you. Thank you. I love you.[113]

As a person begins to recognize his or her impending death, this acknowledgment may stimulate a period of *life review,* an assessment of one's accomplishments in life: What have I achieved or failed to achieve? How have I contributed to others' well-being or to the betterment of humankind? Have I met my expectations for a life well lived? How will my reputation fare after I'm gone? Has life been "fair"? Has "good luck" outweighed the bad? In short, what is the "balance sheet" of my life?

Reviewing the course of a life can empower that person to make the choices he or she values in completing the last chapter of life. Reviewing relationships and events, the person gains an opportunity to complete unfinished business. However, as Stephen Connor says:

> Hospice and palliative care workers cannot impose their ideas of how one should react or respond. They may have the idea that dying people should always say goodbye to their families. This is laudable, but in each life there are many different relationships, and not all of them can be resolved. All people die with some unfinished business.[114]

As a person realizes that he or she is nearing the end of life, the most important thing may be "to believe that life has, if not a purpose, at least a singularity that makes it memorable."[115]

In his work as a volunteer with Capital Hospice (now Capital Caring) in Arlington, Virginia, Thomas Lyons describes how a patient's review of his or her life can result in a precious legacy for family and friends:

> These patients tell me their personal story while I film them. I edit the result and add text, titles, and music to produce a personalized DVD, which contains the image of the person, their voice, their expressions and gestures, and the stories they cherish enough to tell at the end of their life. They, of course, do this to be remembered, and I do my best to provide this service for them.[116]

Lyons says his experience is that hospice patients who want to make a Legacy Movie fall into three categories: (1) They want to leave their life story for their family, (2) They want to leave a personal message for a spouse, young children, or grandchildren, or (3) They want to recollect and review the worthwhile memories of a lifetime, which distracts them from their present circumstances and helps them validate themselves. "It is my honor to help them fulfill any of these goals," says Lyons.

Allan Kellehear reminds us that experiences of courage, love, and positive transformation are an under-described phenomenon in the literature of dying.[117] These are qualities that make facing death bearable. Living with life-threatening illness is not all suffering, sadness, anger, and fear. Ira Byock says, "In assisting people with the difficult tasks of life completion, palliative care extends beyond management of symptoms to focus on the priorities of the individual and family."[118] We see, then, that a social role of the dying encompasses spiritual needs as well as physical and emotional ones. Spiritual needs include:[119]

1. *The need for meaning and purpose.* This involves reviewing one's life (including relationships, work, other achievements, and religious concerns) and attempting to make sense of it, to place it within a larger perspective that has meaning.

> "How are you doing?" Every day millions of people ask that question to millions of other people who respond "Fine," even though both may be suffering greatly. The ending of a life can offer precious opportunities for authentic connections between people who care deeply for each other but may withhold their feelings to maintain a façade of strength and protect a loved one from overwhelming emotions. The admission of fears and anxieties does not indicate weakness. Listening to one another exchange honest expressions of sadness and loss as well as words of love can be both gratifying and consoling.
>
> Susan Dolan and Audrey Vizzard, *The End of Life Advisor*

2. *The need for hope and creativity.* Whereas the first item involves looking back over one's life to discover meaning and purpose, this one is oriented toward the future. It may involve the aspiration for improved well-being, for being free of pain; the desire to accomplish a personal goal or to achieve reconciliation with others; or the hope of an afterlife. This need may also center on the hope "that that which has been of meaning and purpose to the individual may be affirmed by those who are important to him or her."
3. *The need to give and receive love.* "We all need to be reassured that we are loved and that others need our love."[120] Reconciliation is a key element in satisfying this human spiritual need.

Being with Someone Who is Dying

People often feel uncomfortable in the presence of someone diagnosed with a life-threatening illness. What can we say? How should we act? Perhaps it seems that anything we might think of to express our thoughts or feelings would come out as nothing more than a stale platitude. Discomfort may be exhibited through either excessive sympathy or obsessive avoidance while we shy away from real communication. As an antidote to such responses, it is helpful to keep in mind that the essence of caregiving is to leave your own agenda at the door and to be present to whatever the person needs. Keep in mind, too, the crucial difference between dying (still alive) and death.

Often, the only task that matters in being with someone who is dying is to sit still and listen to the stories. In a talk to volunteers at San Francisco's Zen Hospice Project, Tenshin Reb Anderson expressed it this way: "Stay close and do nothing."[121] Near the end of life, an individual may attend to a variety of interrelated concerns and activities, such as these:[122]

- Re-examining beliefs
- Reconciling life choices
- Exploring lifetime contributions
- Examining loving relationships
- Exploring ideas and beliefs about an afterlife
- Discovering meaning

By staying close and doing nothing special, we can accompany the person we love along the passage to death's door.

In an essay titled "The Eyes of a Dying Man," Japanese author Yasunari Kawabata suggests that the human longing for beauty is realized in a special way by people who are dying. This theme is echoed in his stories as well. For example, in "The Moon in the Water," a dying man finds an enhanced appreciation of the beauty of nature. In *The Sound of the Mountain,* an aged man, approaching death, enjoys an intensified awareness of the beauty of the heroine Kikuko. Finally, in "House of the Sleeping Beauties," the "beauties" are all the more beautiful because they are seen through the eyes of old Eguchi, who knows his days are numbered.[123]

Being with someone who is seriously ill or dying, we confront our own mortality. We come to appreciate how precious life is and how uncertain. Few occasions in life present us with the chance to be so vulnerable to aspects of ourselves that are usually kept hidden. Jitaro Mizuno says, "It is through the act of caring for another person that the existence of what we call 'the self' becomes clear."[124] Being with someone who is dying can surprise us with moments of grace and beauty. In describing the end of her mother's life and her death, Janmarie Silvera describes how the blossoming of a "huge, luminous full moon" through a hospital window became an occasion of "wonderment," a moment of intimacy acknowledging both life and death.[125]

Further Readings

Joan Berzoff and Phyllis R. Silverman. *Living with Dying: A Handbook for End-of-Life Healthcare Practitioners.* New York: Columbia University Press, 2004.

Pauline W. Chen. *Final Exam: A Surgeon's Reflections on Mortality.* New York: Knopf, 2007.

Kenneth J. Doka and Amy S. Tucci, eds. *Beyond Kübler-Ross: New Perspectives on Death, Dying, and Grief.* Washington, D.C.: Hospice Foundation of America, 2011.

Christopher Hitchens. *Mortality.* New York: Twelve, 2012.

Allan Kellehear. *The Inner Life of the Dying Person.* New York: Columbia University Press, 2014.

Joanne Lynn, Joan Harrold, and Janice Lynch Schuster. *Handbook for Mortals: Guidance for People Facing Serious Illness,* 2nd ed. New York: Oxford University Press, 2011.

Ernest H. Rosenbaum and Isadora Rosenbaum. *Supportive Cancer Care: The Complete Guide for Patients and Their Families.* Naperville, Ill.: Sourcebooks, 2001.

L. Eugene Thomas. "Personal Reflections on Terminal Illness After Twenty Years of Teaching a Death and Dying Course," *Omega: Journal of Death and Dying* 43, no. 2 (2001): 119–127.

Jonathan S. Watts and Tomatsu Yoshiharu, eds. *Buddhist Care for the Dying and Bereaved.* Boston: Wisdom, 2012.

Additional resources for this chapter can be found at www.mhhe.com/despelder10e

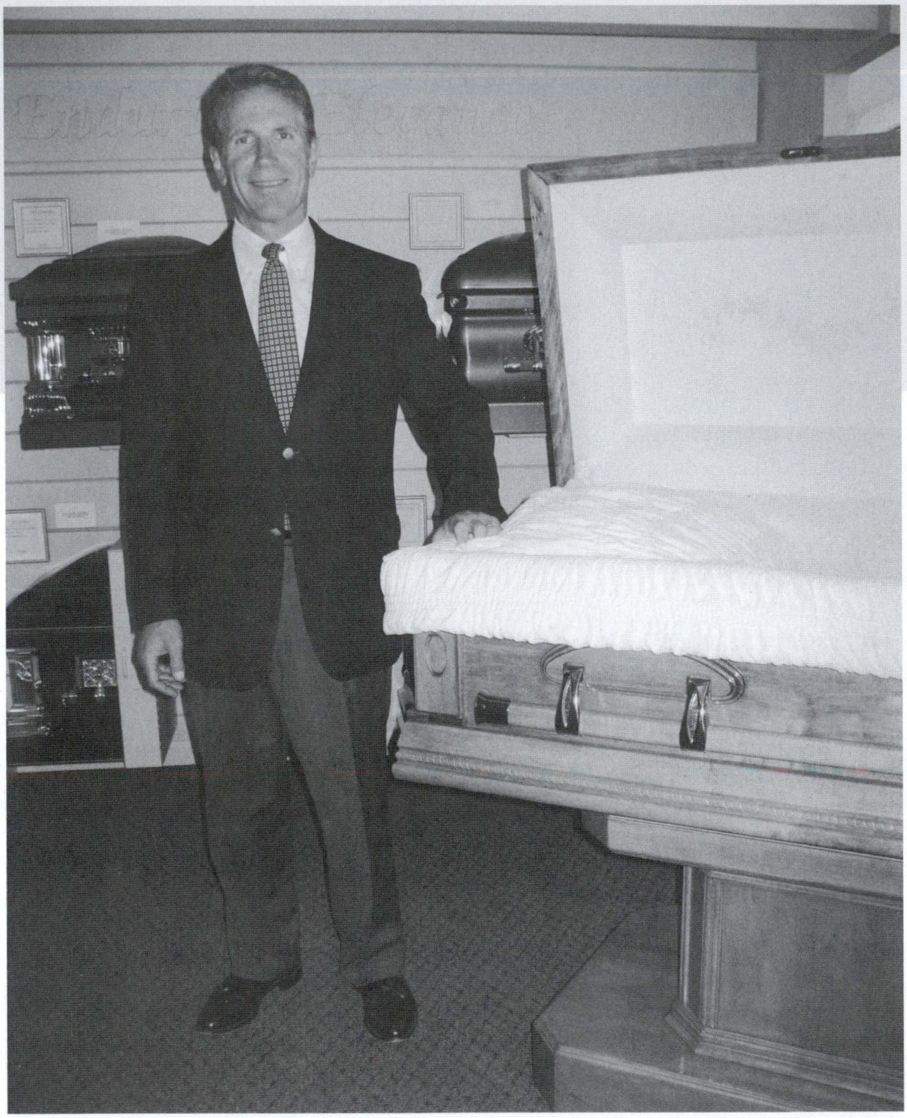

Familiarity with the choices available in funeral services can help us appreciate our many options, perhaps alleviating some of the stress of making such choices in the midst of crisis. The roles of the funeral director and others who can provide assistance in coping with the practical matters of death may also be better understood.

CHAPTER 8

Last Rites: Funerals and Body Disposition

Funeral rites have been characterized as "the most significant of the rites of passage in our progress from womb to tomb."[1] As you begin to think about the significance of funerals, consider these questions: Who does the funeral serve, the living or the dead? What is the purpose, socially and psychologically, of last rites? How do the ceremonies that a community enacts to mark the passing of one of its members express, through symbol and metaphor, how death is perceived within a particular social group?[2] Consider the following description of the royal funeral for Alexander the Great.

> The hearse itself took two years to build and took the form of an Ionic temple, roofed with gold, inside which Alexander's mummy was enclosed in a golden sarcophagus over which was draped his purple cloak. Golden nets prevented the profane gaze from falling on it and no fewer than 64 mules were needed to drag the hearse on its lengthy processional route.[3]

What messages did this funeral communicate to the onlookers? In what ways was this a fitting ceremony within Alexander's social group? Did these actions fulfill the purposes of last rites?

Funeral ritual "permits meaningful action at a chaotic time" and "offers cues as to what we are supposed to feel and models how we are to mourn."[4] Thus, funerals can have an effect on how we grieve. Learning the technique of ritual is likened to learning to play a musical instrument: "Once we master the scales and chords and gain sufficient dexterity in the use of our fingers, we can play the piano in such a manner as to release our aesthetic feelings. This inner ecstasy of performance is open to those who practice ritual as well."[5]

In contrast to cultures that view the funeral as a means to prepare the dead for a successful migration to the afterworld, funerals in the United States are focused mainly on the welfare of survivors. Funerals provide a setting wherein the bereaved family makes a public statement that one of its members has died. The wider community uses the occasion to respond with sympathy and support for the bereaved. Vanderlyn Pine points out that the funeral historically has addressed four major social functions:[6]

1. It serves to acknowledge and commemorate a person's death.
2. It provides a setting for the disposition of the dead body.
3. It assists in reorienting the bereaved to their lives, which have been ruptured by the death.
4. It demonstrates reciprocal economic and social obligations between the bereaved and their social world.

Traditionally, funeral rites begin with the gathering of family and friends for a "deathwatch" to accompany the dying person in his or her last hours, and they formally end with the disposition of the corpse (see Table 8-1). Historically, in African American culture, it was customary, immediately after a death, to have a "settin' up," at which friends and family would stay with the body as the soul or spirit began its journey to the next world.[7]

In other contexts, "settin' up" is referred to as a *wake*. A wake is a vigil (usually) held prior to burial at which those close to the deceased keep watch over the body. Wakes are said to "have a transforming effect on friends and family, not only helping them adjust to life without the departed, but also re-creating their bonds."[8] Another funeral tradition is the "funeral meal."[9] It sometimes takes place during the wake; in other instances, it takes place after the ceremony and disposition. In the South, for example, people gather and bring foods that were favored by the deceased as well as other regional favorites—fried chicken, greens, baked beans, ham, molasses pie, macaroni and cheese, iced tea—and share a meal as well as memories. There can be a sense of "sacred space and time" as the bereaved enjoy food and fellowship. Depending on individual and cultural preferences, funerals today do not always include all of the traditional elements shown in Table 8-1, and some of them may be abbreviated.

Music may be employed to evoke the emotions of the bereaved or memories of the deceased.[10] Selection of music is often very important. Considerations include the role of music in shaping and managing the ceremony, providing comfort to survivors, and creating meaning relative to the life of the deceased and his or her relationships with the bereaved. Sue Adamson and Margaret Holloway say, "Music is not just an important *feature* of contemporary funerals, it offers an interpretive lens through which we may understand the complex interweaving of personalized, customized meanings with social and cultural purposes and traditional frames of reference."[11]

Samuel Barber's *Adagio for Strings* was played at the funerals of Franklin Delano Roosevelt and John F. Kennedy. This piece of music is often used

TABLE 8-1 *Elements of Funeral Ritual*

1. *Deathwatch* (also known as the "death vigil" or "sitting up"). As death nears, relatives and friends gather to say farewells and show respect for the dying person, as well as to give support and care to his or her family. Historically, a deathwatch might continue for hours, days, or even weeks or months.
2. *Preparation of the deceased.* Involves various tasks associated with preparing the corpse for ultimate disposition, usually burial or cremation.
3. *Wake* (also known as "visitation" or "calling hours"). Traditionally held on the night after death occurs, this practice involves laying out the corpse and keeping a watch or "wake" over it. Historically, wakes were observed as a safeguard against premature burial, as an opportunity to pay respects to the deceased, and, in some cultures, as an occasion for lively festivities focused on allaying fears by "rousing the ghost."

   With changes in the social patterns of mourning, the traditional wake has been transformed into the practice of setting aside time for viewing of the body prior to the funeral service. As with traditional wakes, the modern visitation offers opportunities for social interactions that can be healing in the aftermath of loss.
4. *Funeral.* As the centerpiece of the ritual surrounding death, the funeral is a rite of passage for both the deceased and his or her survivors. Services are usually held in a mortuary chapel or church, although they may be held in the home or at the gravesite. The body may or may not be present; if it is present, the casket may be open or closed. Funeral services typically include music, prayers, readings from scripture or other poetry or prose, a eulogy honoring the life of the deceased, and, less frequently, a funeral sermon focusing on the role of death in human life in general. In modern times, funerals are usually held within a few days after death, and they are increasingly scheduled in the evening or on weekends so mourners who work during the week can attend the service.
5. *Procession.* Traditionally, funerals include a procession conveying the corpse from the site of the funeral to the place of burial. It is considered an honor to be among the friends and relatives chosen to carry the deceased's body to its final resting place. Funerals for national leaders and other notables may include a lengthy procession, or cortege, in which the corpse is attended by honorary pallbearers.
6. *Committal.* A ceremony held at the grave or crematorium, the committal service is held after, or sometimes in lieu of, the funeral service. When it follows a funeral service, it usually consists of a brief ceremony focusing on disposition of the deceased's remains.
7. *Disposal of the corpse.* In modern societies, disposition usually means burial or cremation.

as background for solemn reflections. Chopin's *Funeral March* and George Frederick Handel's *Dead March* are also favored by many funeral planners.[12]

The "second line" march (or jazz funeral) of New Orleans brass bands are processions that typically occur alongside a conventional funeral at a church or mortuary.

> The tradition of funerals with brass bands is rooted in the many benevolent associations that sprang up among African Americans in New Orleans and offered, among other things, burial insurance to members. Another benefit was the option of having a brass band (or bands) play for your funeral, both as a celebration of life and as a throwback to the ancient Christian and African traditions of rejoicing when you die.[13]

On the walk to the cemetery, the music is slow, dirgelike, and solemn. Returning, it is fast, joyful, and uplifting. This New Orleans tradition, which has elements of both African and Afro-Caribbean traditions, has been called "a celebration of the soul's entrance into heaven."[14]

On the value of learning about death rituals in other cultures, William Hoy says, "Through the exploration of rituals, new insights develop about the way the world's people face death in their families and communities."[15] Review the descriptions given in Table 8-1 and consider which of the elements you believe would have value in planning a funeral for a loved one or which you would want to have included as part of your own last rites.

Psychosocial Aspects of Last Rites

Just as people gather to commemorate other major transitions in a person's life, such as birth and marriage, funerals and memorial services are rites of passage that honor a person's life in a community and acknowledge his or her passing from that community. Funerals and memorial services provide a framework that allows survivors to support one another as they cope with their loss and express their grief. The presence of death rites in every human culture suggests that they serve innate human needs. Thomas Lynch, author of *The Undertaking: Life Studies from the Dismal Trade,* makes the observation that "funerals are the way we close the gap between the death that happens and the death that matters."[16]

Announcement of Death

When a person dies, first to learn of it, besides those present at the time of death, are usually members of the person's immediate family. Then, in a widening circle of relatives, friends, and acquaintances, others affected by the death are notified. In his classic study *Passing On: The Social Organization of Dying,* David Sudnow observed that announcements of death usually occur in a consistent pattern from the immediate family to the wider community (see Figure 8-1).[17] Those with closest relationships to the deceased are told first, followed by those with less intimate relationships. Futhermore, announcements generally take place between people in a peer relationship. For example, a bereaved mother might first call the child who had been closest to the deceased, and that person then calls other brothers and sisters. They in turn notify more distant kin. A similar pattern occurs among people not directly related to the deceased. For instance, a coworker or neighbor who learns of the death tells others who had a similar relationship with the deceased. Ideally, this process—taking in a gradually widening circle of relatives, friends, and acquaintances—continues until everyone affected by the death is notified.

Human beings have an inherent need to respond to the death of someone who has been significant to them. Thus, it is important for this notification process to occur in a timely fashion so that those affected by the death are able to come together in a spirit of mutual support to grieve their loss.

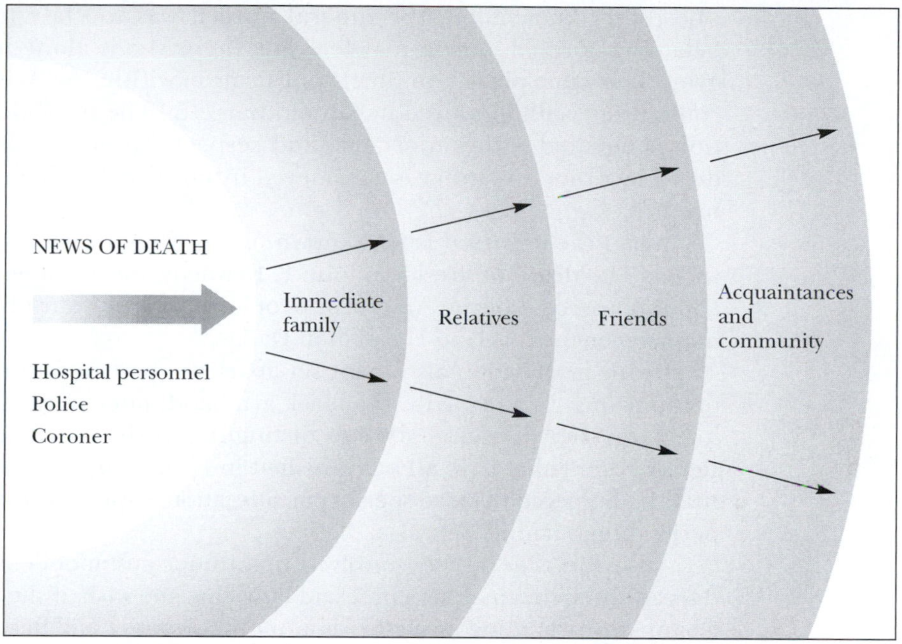

Figure 8-1 *Widening Circles of Death Announcement*

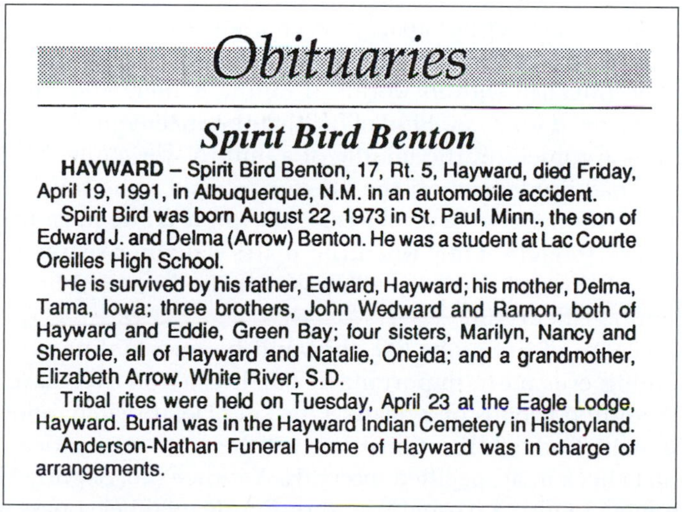

Obituaries

Spirit Bird Benton

HAYWARD – Spirit Bird Benton, 17, Rt. 5, Hayward, died Friday, April 19, 1991, in Albuquerque, N.M. in an automobile accident.

Spirit Bird was born August 22, 1973 in St. Paul, Minn., the son of Edward J. and Delma (Arrow) Benton. He was a student at Lac Courte Oreilles High School.

He is survived by his father, Edward, Hayward; his mother, Delma, Tama, Iowa; three brothers, John Wedward and Ramon, both of Hayward and Eddie, Green Bay; four sisters, Marilyn, Nancy and Sherrole, all of Hayward and Natalie, Oneida; and a grandmother, Elizabeth Arrow, White River, S.D.

Tribal rites were held on Tuesday, April 23 at the Eagle Lodge, Hayward. Burial was in the Hayward Indian Cemetery in Historyland.

Anderson-Nathan Funeral Home of Hayward was in charge of arrangements.

Figure 8-2 *Newspaper Obituary*

Announcements of death also take place by means of notices and obituaries that appear in newspapers (see Figure 8-2). When an announcement does not appear in a timely fashion, it can be upsetting. The following complaint is typical: "The obituary did not appear in the newspaper until the morning of the funeral. We had a number of calls and letters from people who didn't know about the funeral until it was too late to attend." The belatedly notified person may feel that he or she is alone in dealing with grief. The value placed on timely notification within the African American community is underscored by Ronald Barrett: "The immediacy of notification is equated with importance and respect. To not be informed of the death in a timely manner is considered insensitive, lacking respect, and an insult."[18]

When the deceased is well known, news of the death is broadcast more widely. The death of President John F. Kennedy, for example, was known by about 90 percent of the American people within an hour of its official pronouncement at Parkland Hospital in Dallas.[19]

Death notification also helps set apart the bereaved during the period of mourning. Traditionally, the black armband, mourning colors and clothing, and other signs and symbols distinguished the bereaved person. Such signs of mourning have all but vanished in North America. Still, people feel that the bereaved deserve special consideration, especially during the initial period of mourning.

A woman who became involved in a minor automobile accident several days after the death of her child said later that she wished she could have had a banner proclaiming her status as a "mother whose child has just died." With no outward symbol of her bereavement, she was subjected, as any of us would be, to the strain of waiting around and filling in seemingly endless accident report forms. Had she lived in a small town, the process of death notification itself might have set her apart in such a way that the task of completing the paperwork would have been made easier.

The Internet, with its worlds of online gamers and social networks, has created a need for a new kind of death announcement.[20] When one man died after an argument in the middle of a multiplayer game, his friends thought that he had just logged off the site and needed some time to cool off. When he didn't return after several weeks, they figured he must have been angrier than they thought. Only when the man's daughter searched online for the guild he belonged to did his fellow gamers find out that he had died from an abdominal aneurysm.

Because of situations like this, and because online social networks are becoming ever more important in our lives, Web sites have been set up to notify online friends of a death. One site, Deathswitch, allows people to set up e-mail death notifications that will be sent automatically if the person doesn't check in at specified intervals. Another site, Slightly Morbid, requires customers to give a trusted friend or family member a password to start the announcement process. One gamer commented, "People die all the time, but you never really think about how people online are real people and could die and you'd never know about it."[21]

The Internet sometimes brings announcement of death that outruns the coroner's notification. A mother whose son died in an automobile accident learned of his death through a Facebook posting while the coroner was on her way to notify the family.

Library of Congress

The funeral has traditionally been a time when family and friends come together to pay respects and to say farewells. It is a time of mutual support for the bereaved and of tribute to the deceased. The display of flowers surrounding this coffin bespeaks the affection felt for the deceased while she was alive and the sense of loss at her absence from the community.

Mutual Support

When people learn about the death of a person who is significant to them, they tend to gather together, closing ranks to provide support and comfort in their mutual bereavement. This emotional and social support is directed primarily toward the bereaved family. When a small child asked her mother why they were going to visit a bereaved family, the mother replied, "It's important for people to know that you care." What we think we can or cannot do for the bereaved family matters little; what counts is that we show our care and concern. J. Z. Young says, "Probably the very act of coming together symbolizes communication."[22] Assembling as a community reassures us that we are part of a larger whole, thereby strengthening our individual lives.

Gathering at the home of the bereaved is a unique social occasion. Some people stay only a short time, express condolences, and leave. Others, usually relatives or close friends, stay for a longer time, perhaps assisting with the preparation of food, caring for children, helping with funeral arrangements, greeting visitors, and doing whatever else needs doing.

Funeral rituals embody the rhythms of separation and integration. Death is a change of status both for the person who dies and for his or her survivors. This change of status is reflected in language when we refer to someone as a "widow" or "widower." This special designation for a bereaved spouse affirms the social and psychological impact associated with the death of a mate. Based on a cross-cultural investigation of funeral rites, Vernon Reynolds and Ralph Tanner conclude,

> The importance of the rituals of death is that they are socioreligious requirements which have to be carried out by the bereaved within the social context of friends, relatives, and neighbors who are less bereaved. The bereaved are not left alone to generate and multiply the psychosomatic symptoms of their grief, but are required to be active, and in many cultures there is a special role for bereaved persons over quite a long period . . . at the end of which their recovery from bereavement is well advanced.[23]

Impetus for Coping with Loss

Announcements, visiting the bereaved, and other after-death rituals are forms of social interaction that provide a potent psychological impetus for realizing a loss. While these social interactions are crucial, it is important to remember that the death of a person is experienced not only within a social setting but also within the psyche of the bereaved individual. When death occurs, an immediate concern of survivors is the disposition of the corpse. This process involves both a mental activity (deciding what is to be done) and a physical activity (carrying out the action decided upon). Making arrangements for the disposition of the body engages survivors in a process that reinforces the recognition that the deceased person is really dead. This acknowledgment occurs whether the survivor actively constructs the coffin and digs the grave or simply talks with someone about funeral arrangements.

The funeral itself offers a range of opportunities for the bereaved to engage in activities that promote expression of grief. Survivors may place items that are significant to the deceased in the casket. The practice of burying *grave goods,* or funerary artifacts, with the dead is found in many cultures.[24] Jewelry, photographs, rosaries, Bibles or other special books, favorite hats, military medals, stuffed animals, and organizational emblems are among the items commonly placed in caskets. Tobacco, alcohol, and articles related to a favorite activity such as golf or fishing are other examples of grave goods. The placing of such grave goods is a mourning practice that is meaningful to survivors. When a widely known and beloved German funeral director died, family and friends placed various items in his casket, arranging cookies his grandchildren had baked on his stomach to commemorate the fact that he enjoyed eating well. The final disposition of a dead body is surrounded by a web of social, cultural, religious, psychological, and personal considerations that determine how this task is accomplished.

> If you have an uncomfortable feeling about funerals, which are the accepted social pattern for confronting death in our culture, if you try to avoid or eliminate them, that might be a sign that you're dealing with major residual death anxiety. That's one of the things that shows up in our culture: the way people delude themselves and retreat from the major therapeutic resources that are provided culturally. There's a notion that if we have a mini-funeral, we'll have mini-grief. But we know that the exact opposite is true.
>
> The more you reduce your emotional acting out at the time of the event, the more you prolong the pain of grief and postpone the therapeutic work of mourning.
>
> That's why in a culture such as ours, where you have an unwise management of grief, you have a very large proportion of illness responses after the death experience. People act it out physically rather than doing it psychologically or socially. That's a very heavy weight.
>
> But in primitive cultures, such as the aboriginals in Australia, where you have almost a two-week funeral process, where there are all kinds of acting out of deep feelings, you come to the end of that two weeks, and a major portion of the grief work has been done, and the survivor is ready to move into the period of resolution through the mourning process, which takes quite a bit longer, usually.
>
> Edgar N. Jackson, from an interview with the authors

Funerals in the United States

Few people personally care for their own dead in modern societies. Most hire professionals—funeral directors or morticians—to provide services and merchandise for conducting a funeral service and handling various tasks involved in caring for the dead. Because we are unfamiliar with these tasks and choices, the funeral business tends to be viewed as a "mystery business." Critics claim that mortuaries, by their very nature, are in a position to take advantage of their customers. This claim is made despite the fact that most people give funeral directors high marks for the services they provide at a distressing time. Beyond this, it has been noted that, in African American communities, black funeral directors not only are seen as important members of their communities, but often have had key roles in civil rights struggles as well.

To counteract the potential for abuses, the U.S. Federal Trade Commission (FTC) implemented the Trade Regulation Rule on Funeral Industry Practices in 1984.[25] The Funeral Rule, as it is called, stipulates that funeral service providers must give detailed information about prices and legal requirements to people who are arranging funerals. It requires the disclosure of itemized prices both over the telephone and in writing. Misrepresentations about the disposition of human remains are prohibited, as are certain practices, such as embalming for a fee without prior permission, requiring customers to purchase caskets for a direct cremation, or making the purchase of any funeral good or service conditional on the purchase of any other funeral good or service. The FTC Funeral Rule is the outcome of a historical process that has removed death from the purview of family and friends and placed it in the hands of professionals.

The Rise of Professional Funeral Services

When families themselves took care of the disposition of their dead, criticisms would have been irrelevant. And, of course, there was no profit motive. Disposition of the dead was simply a human task to be carried out by the family and community. At a time when the family's ceremonial occasions involving death were held within the home, the "undertaker," when he came upon the scene during the Colonial era, mainly functioned as a merchant who supplied materials and funeral paraphernalia—such items as the casket and carriage, door badges and scarves, special clothing, memorial cards and announcements, robes, pillows, gauze, candles, ornaments, and so on—for mourning rituals (see Figure 8-3).

During the later decades of the nineteenth century, the undertaker assumed a larger role in caring for the dead.[26] No longer merely a tradesman who furnished goods to bereaved families, the undertaker became a provider of services. He began to actually take part in the disposition of the dead: laying out the body for the wake, transporting it to the church for the funeral, and, finally, taking it to the cemetery for burial. With the coming of smaller houses and urbanization, the place for viewing the body moved from the parlor of the family home to a room reserved for such use by the tradesman-undertaker. The funeral "parlor" in town became a substitute for the ceremonial room that people no longer had in their own homes. This one-room funeral parlor was the forerunner of the present-day funeral home or mortuary.

Also around this time, undertakers were becoming "morticians" and were starting to view themselves as "funeral *directors*."[27] For instance, the Funeral Directors National Association, established in the 1880s—now the National Funeral Directors Association (NFDA)—was among the first

Figure 8-3 *City Directory Listing for a Cabinet Maker and Supplier of Funeral Furnishings, circa 1850*

of the new trade organizations designed to promote funeral service businesses as well as establish standards. Early trade publications, such as *The Casket* and *Sunnyside,* helped to facilitate communication among funeral directors.

What is the job of a funeral director like? Gary Benito says, "Our entire client load is comprised of people on the worst day of their life. We're confronted every day with our mortality." His partner, Vince Azzaro, says, "A lot of the job is simply guiding people through the red tape and bureacracy that have grown up around the disposition of a body."[28]

> The stress of getting every detail right, from the choice of flowers to how a pastor pronounces the deceased's name is intense, leaving undertakers emotionally exhausted by the end of the day. They're charged with cramming into two days the same amount of organizing wedding planners take a year to pull off. At the same time, they have to treat each family as if they're the only people walking through the door.[29]

Although some funeral homes handle fewer than fifty calls per year and are often run by husband and wife, others handle hundreds of calls and may be owned by small companies or large corporations. The average funeral home handles 112 calls per year.[30]

Many mortuaries have expanded their services to include "aftercare" programs, which can range from simply telephoning a bereaved spouse to see how he or she is doing to offering counseling or support groups for bereaved customers. Mortuary staff may attend training programs to prepare themselves for this kind of aftercare or, in some cases, the funeral home hires a psychologist or grief counselor to manage such services. Many funeral directors view this offering of aftercare service—this extension of their professional services—as a contemporary expression of "old-fashioned neighborly concern."[31]

The clergy has traditionally played a major role in assisting bereaved families in making funeral arrangements. Whereas funerals were once commonly held in churches, they are now likely to be held in funeral chapels. The move from church to mortuary (along with the more dominant role of mortuary personnel) has sometimes put a strain on relationships between clergy and funeral directors. Some clergy are bringing funeral services back into church and taking a greater role in funeral arrangements. Some churches have even started operating their own "funeral businesses" or have contracted with firms that agree to provide funerals for parishioners.

During the past several decades, conglomeration in the funeral industry has become a major trend and a much-debated topic. Large multinational corporations that own hundreds of funeral homes are purchasing neighborhood "mom-and-pop" funeral homes, many of which have been family owned and operated for generations. Many observers wonder whether the personal touch provided by locally owned funeral homes will be lost with corporate ownership. In some communities, customers of funeral homes that were once family owned but now are owned by corporations "vote with their feet" as they switch to mortuary establishments that are devoted to local ownership and personal service.

Even though we are accustomed to turning over care of our dead to professionals, the fact that someone is profiting from such services may seem somehow macabre. When a corpse belongs to someone we loved, the common aversion to touching a dead body may be mixed with guilt. Unconscious resentment may be felt toward the funeral director or mortician who prepares the body of our loved one for final disposition. Pulled in opposing directions, we experience a confusing range of emotions regarding our dead: aversion, guilt, resentment, anxiety, and affection. Lack of familiarity with the dead can result in funeral directors and funeral establishments becoming a lightning rod for criticisms.

Criticisms of Funeral Practices

Funerals have attracted criticism of various kinds since ancient times. The Greek philosopher Herodotus, in the fourth century BCE, spoke critically about what he called "lavish displays for the dead." Funeral practices in the United States have received their share of criticism as well. One of the earliest criticisms was directed not just at funeral practices but at the funeral itself. Published in 1926, Bertram Puckle's *Funeral Customs: Their Origin and Development* argued that the modern funeral was merely the vestige of a "pagan" superstitious fear of the dead. Like Herodotus, Puckle was especially critical of elaborate ceremonies for the dead.

In 1959, the commercialism and conspicuous display connected with funerals were documented by LeRoy Bowman in *The American Funeral: A Study in Guilt, Extravagance, and Sublimity.*[32] Bowman was especially interested in the social and psychological value of funerals. He was concerned that modern funerals were overlaid with such ostentation that the essential meaning and dignity of funeral rites had all but disappeared. The funeral, Bowman said,

> Visiting with a family in a funeral home one night, we witnessed a woman enter the visiting room. She approached the casket and burst into convulsive tears. Two men stood up and supported her on either side as she sobbed loudly. The mother of the deceased man leaned over to me and said, "Brother Wayne, do you know that woman?" I had never seen her before. Everyone in the room was whispering and looking. "Who is that?" they were asking.
>
> After this loud display, the men escorted the woman to a folding chair, where she gradually calmed herself. Finally, one of the men asked her how she was acquainted with his brother, Bill.
>
> She raised her head and asked, "Bill?"
>
> "Yes, that's my brother Bill."
>
> The mystery lady stood, looked in the casket, and said, "Oh, I'm sorry . . . I'm in the wrong room," and quickly exited.
>
> As we all doubled over with laughter, Bill's widow said, "I was fixin' to get up there and find out WHO she was and WHY she was so upset that Bill was dead!"
>
> Wayne Delk, *U.S. Gospel News*

"appears to be an anachronism, an elaboration of early customs rather than the adaptation to modern needs that it should be." To Bowman, the funeral director was a tradesman, selling wares that were unnecessary and unwanted. Bowman believed that consumers could avoid the potential for exploitation associated with the materialistic features of contemporary practices by becoming aware of the essential social, psychological, and spiritual functions of funeral rituals. The function of the funeral director, said Bowman, should be to help the family fulfill its own wishes. He also argued for greater flexibility in funeral service: "The uniformity of present usage," he said, "should give way to individually adapted procedures, whatever they may be."

In 1963, two books appeared that brought widespread public attention to funeral practices in the United States: Jessica Mitford's *The American Way of Death* and Ruth M. Harmer's *The High Cost of Dying*. Both Mitford and Harmer were critical of what they viewed as excessive materialism in funeral practices. These books, especially Mitford's *The American Way of Death*, stimulated lobbying by advocates for greater governmental regulation of funeral businesses.

Mitford employed a heavy dose of satire in making the case that conventional funeral practices were bizarre and morbid; efforts to disguise and prettify death made it more grotesque. The language used by funeral industry personnel became a special target of Mitford's wit. She took issue with the euphemisms employed to soften the reality of death: the metamorphosis of coffins into "caskets," hearses into "coaches," flowers into "floral tributes," and cremated ashes into "cremains." The corpse, she said, now lies in state in the "slumber room." The undertaker, now a "funeral director," displays a solid-copper "Colonial Classic Beauty" casket, replete with "Perfect-Posture" adjustable mattress, in a choice of "60 color-matched shades." The deceased wears "handmade original fashions" from a "gravewear couturiere" and "Nature-Glo, the ultimate in cosmetic grooming."[33] Mitford's use of wry humor in her critical examination of funeral practices was reminiscent of Evelyn Waugh's earlier novel, *The Loved One* (1948), in which Waugh employed satire to poke fun at what he believed were hypocritical and death-avoiding attitudes about funerals.

Despite these criticisms of funeral practices, most people appear to be satisfied with the quality of service provided by their local mortuaries. Funeral directors often receive expressions of gratitude from the people they serve for their help in sorting out the events that immediately follow the death of a loved one. A willingness to "go the extra mile" is typical of funeral directors. Most funeral directors are committed to meeting the needs and wishes of bereaved families, even when they vary from standard practices, as the following story illustrates.

When a Dutch couple died unexpectedly while traveling in South America, their relatives felt that the couple's intimacy and sharing in life should be carried through to their death rites. They wanted the couple buried together in one coffin and in one grave. Although this request had never been made before, the funeral establishment checked applicable laws and found that they did not prohibit the family's wishes being carried out. There

William E. Rosemund, U.S. Army Photo

Thousands of American citizens joined in the funeral observance honoring the Unknown Serviceman of the Vietnam Era. Here the procession is crossing Memorial Bridge between a Marine honor cordon, on its way to Arlington National Cemetery. Replete with full military honors, the funeral was an occasion for expressing national gratitude and grief in response to the ultimate sacrifice of those who died in the wartime service of their country.

were practical problems, however. No company made a double casket. Acting quickly, the funeral home found a craftsman who was able to make a special casket by working overtime, and with a few adjustments all went smoothly. The funeral director said, "We are proud that we have been able to arrange this committal for the couple in which, for the children, the love between their parents was confirmed."[34]

New and Rediscovered Memorial Choices

The Internet has ushered in a variety of innovative services related to funerals and memorials. Individuals can make online purchases of funeral goods, including caskets. The Internet has become the site of cyber tributes and even webcasts of funeral services, or *cyberfunerals.* Carla Sofka says, "A cyberfuneral, also known as funeral-casting or memorial webcasting, is the broadcasting via the World Wide Web of a ritual to commemorate an individual's life and death."[35] Cameras placed in the mortuary or chapel can transmit video of the funeral to "cybermourners" via the Internet.[36] Such funeral-casts may be viewed live or "on demand," on an individual monitor or projected onto a large screen for an audience. According to Sofka, the barriers overcome by funeral-casting include limitations created by geographic distance, work obligations, or the requirements of a religious or spiritual ritual (for example, burial within twenty-four hours according to some religious practices), as well as by an inability to travel due to physical or health matters, the cost of airfare, or the need to remain at home to care for young children.

Memorial pages on the Internet allow mourners to post condolences and share grief online. For example, Legacy.com is a media company that collaborates with more than 800 newspapers to provide ways for the bereaved to express condolences and shape remembrances through online obituaries and memorials. It draws more than 18 million visitors each month.[37] Web sites known as "virtual cemeteries" or "memorial gardens" provide space for photographs and biographical information about the dead, and visitors have opportunities to sign guest books and leave "digital flowers."[38] According to Pamela Roberts,

> Analysis suggests that rather than serving as a poor substitute for traditional bereavement activities, Web memorialization is a valued addition, allowing the bereaved to enhance their relationship with the dead and to increase and deepen their connections with others who have suffered a loss.[39]

High-tech innovations are also resulting in new styles of electronic gravesite memorials. One such offering allows survivors to compile a "visual eulogy" of a deceased loved one, whereby photographs, the deceased's life story and family history, and other such gleanings of a life well lived are electronically stored and can be displayed on a small video monitor that is installed into a traditional grave marker. Containing up to 250 pages of information, this personalized memorial "allows a person's life story to be remembered for generations to come."[40]

Memorialization opportunities abound in the world of the twenty-first century. For example, with the growing popularity of cremation, entrepreneurs have developed, or rediscovered, innovative ways of memorializing a deceased loved one. Several firms offer "cremation jewelry," locket-style pendants, which can be worn around the neck or displayed in special holders, that hold a small bit of cremated remains.

In some parts of the United States, T-shirts are worn as a way of memorializing victims of violence as well as persons who died in accidents or from illnesses. The custom apparently began in New Orleans and has since been adopted elsewhere. As "wearable tombstones," these shirts are characterized as "a uniquely modern twist on the ancient ritual of honoring the dead." One woman in her early twenties has memorial T-shirts for eight family members and friends murdered in and around her neighborhood. A man in his early thirties says, "Now I got more T-shirts than friends." The shirts are worn to wakes and funerals, on the anniversaries of the deaths, on the victim's birthday, when visiting the gravesite, or just when someone is missed.[41] Memorials are also found in the form of "memorial wall art" painted on buildings.[42]

Roadside memorials, also called *descansos* (literally, "resting places"), have spread from a regional southwestern Hispanic usage to appear throughout

© David Goldman, AP Photo

Epitaphs and messages written by friends and relatives are displayed on a photograph of a hip-hop musician at his funeral. Such spontaneous sentiments are characteristic of the innovative personalized or "life-centered" rituals that are increasingly becoming the norm for rituals today.

the United States.[43] They range from a simple cross to a more elaborate memorial. Typically, great pains are taken to place the memorial with precision at the site where death occurred. They are not farewells as much as efforts to maintain a sense of continuity with the deceased who "knows what is taking place at the scene of his or her death." As such memorials have become more mainstream, they are sometimes erected by state road crews to memorialize coworkers killed while working on highways.

Although roadside memorials seem to be a new phenomenon, such "marking of travel-related deaths" has a long history. Prehistoric traders buried their dead beside the trails of Europe. Roadside memorials, as it happens, are "far older than roadways and nearly as old as travel itself."[44]

Memorial wall art, roadside crosses, sidewalk memorials, floral offerings, and cyber memorials are all examples of what are called "spontaneous shrines." Such shrines were seen following deaths from the Newtown school shootings, the Boston marathon bombings, and the death of Princess Diana, when resources of cut flowers throughout Europe were almost totally depleted by the demand, and they were seen in the aftermath of 9/11 in the photocopied snapshots and portraits that, Sylvia Grider says, "reinforced the function of spontaneous shrines as sites for communication between the living and the dead."[45] Grider points out that some mourners spend a great deal of time preparing their tributes and make special pilgrimages to place their offerings at the shrines. She says, "Part of our shared humanity is feeling a sense of loss from the deaths of our fellow humans."[46]

Selecting Funeral Services

In commemorating a person's life and death, the choice of last rites may involve a traditional funeral ceremony or a simple memorial service. Whereas the casketed body is typically present at a funeral, it is not at a memorial service. In some cases, both a funeral and a memorial service are held, the former within a few days after death and the latter sometime later (perhaps in a different town, where the deceased had a large social network). Although individuals and families sometimes express a preference that no funeral services be held, bereaved relatives and friends usually want to honor and pay respect to the deceased and express their grief through ceremony.

After a death occurs, survivors are confronted by a number of tasks that demand attention in preparing for last rites (see Table 8-2). Some tasks can be dealt with before a person's death, and preparations can be made for completing others. It can be helpful to have done some of this homework before death occurs. In making choices, it can be worthwhile to remember that a meaningful funeral or memorial service can be designed in many different ways. Decisions about one's own last rites are ideally made with a view to the needs and wishes of one's survivors. In making plans or arrangements, you may want to review the various elements that are traditionally part of after-death rituals (discussed earlier in this chapter).

TABLE 8-2 *Funeral Tasks for Survivors*

- Make a list of relatives, friends, and colleagues who should be made aware that the death has occurred, and inform them as soon as possible.
- Find out if the deceased left instructions regarding a funeral or memorial service, or for disposition of his or her body, whether burial, cremation, or some form of "green" disposition.
- If no prior plan is in place, consider what type of funeral arrangement and body disposition would be appropriate.
- If professional help is needed, contact a funeral home, mortuary, or memorial society.
- Consider relevant cultural or religious factors
- Gather information and write the obituary. Consider including such items as the deceased's age, birthplace, cause of death, occupation or life's work, academic degrees, memberships, military service, and religious affiliation; the names and relationships of the nearest survivors; and the time and place of the funeral or memorial service you are planning.
- Ask friends to help coordinate meals for the first days following the death and to assist with other tasks and child care, if necessary.
- If relatives or friends will be coming from out of the area, ask a friend or family member to help with travel arrangements, such as transportation and lodging.
- If a funeral service is planned, choose and notify the individuals who will be pallbearers and who will assume other roles in the ceremony, such as officiator or clergy, ushers, and persons who will present the eulogy/eulogies.
- Gather photographs and other mementos for a memory book, memory board, or memorial Web site.
- If you want to have a memorial brochure with photos and information about the deceased, enlist the aid of friends and family to create it and have it printed.
- Don't let too many cooks into the kitchen; that is, rely on your close-knit support system when it's time to make decisions.
- Did I do what my loved one wanted? Did I do the right thing? If you feel assured in answering these questions, be confident that you have served the memory of your loved one honorably.

The purchase of funeral services is a transaction unique in commerce. Most people give it little thought until they find themselves in the midst of an emotional crisis. As with other purchases, the customer who winds up with the fewest regrets is likely to be the one who has taken time beforehand to investigate his or her options. When arrangements for funeral services are made during a crisis, the customer must make an on-the-spot decision. Caskets do not bear a notice saying, "Return in thirty days if not completely satisfied." Once made, the decision is final.

Selecting funeral services differs from the way we make most other purchases. When purchasing a new car, for example, you can shop around and test-drive various makes and models. If you encounter a salesperson who uses high-pressure tactics, you can either submit or walk away; you have a clear choice. Yet, the circumstances surrounding the purchase of funeral services rarely allow for objectivity or coolheadedness. The bereaved is usually not in a position to simply walk away and compare prices elsewhere. Once a death has occurred, it may be too late to investigate options. (However, there is no law that prohibits moving a body from one funeral home to another.)

It is unfortunate when an expensive casket or lavish display becomes the focal point of a funeral merely because survivors are attempting to assuage guilt or compensate for unresolved conflict with the deceased. Spending a huge sum of money on a funeral may, in some circumstances, thwart the real purpose of last rites—namely, to effect a kind of closure on the deceased's life and comfort the bereaved. As Thomas Lynch, a funeral director and poet-essayist, says, "In even the best of caskets, it never all fits—all that we'd like to bury in them: the hurt and forgiveness, the anger and pain, the praise and thanksgiving, the emptiness and exaltations, the untidy feelings when someone dies."[47]

The funeral is a setting for private sorrow and public loss whereby the burden of grief is reduced by sharing with others. Last rites effect the disposition of the corpse while acknowledging that a life has been lived. Funeral rituals are a statement from survivors to the community: "We have lost someone, and we are grieving." The purpose of the funeral can be realized whether it is garnished with diamonds and rubies or with poetry and a song.

Funeral Service Charges

The National Funeral Directors Association distinguishes four categories of costs in a conventional funeral. The first category includes services provided by the funeral director and mortuary staff, the use of mortuary facilities and equipment, and the casket and any other funeral merchandise selected by the customer.

The second category pertains to the disposition of the body. This can include the purchase of a gravesite and costs for opening and closing the grave; or, if aboveground entombment is chosen, the cost of a mausoleum crypt; or, if the body is cremated, the cost of cremation and subsequent interment, entombment, or scattering of the cremated remains, as well as the cost of an urn to hold the ashes, if desired.

The third category involves costs related to memorialization. For burials, this can include a monument or marker for the grave; for cremated remains, it can include an inscription or plaque for the niche (recessed compartment) in a *columbarium,* an aboveground structure with a series of niches for urns.

The fourth category involves miscellaneous expenses. These may include a clergy member's honorarium, the use of limousines and additional vehicles (if not included in the funeral services category), flowers, death notices in newspapers, and transportation of the body outside the local area, if necessary.

It has become an FTC requirement for all funeral businesses to provide itemized price information on a general price list so that customers can compare prices or choose only those elements of a funeral they want. It is important to note that FTC requirements do not prohibit funeral directors from also offering "package" funerals for a single price.

Funeral costs vary among regions of the country as well as between rural and metropolitan areas. As with other goods and services, costs have risen over recent decades. According to surveys conducted periodically by the NFDA, average cost of an adult funeral, including casket but excluding burial vault and cemetery costs, was about $1,800 in 1980, $3,700 in 1990, $5,200 in 2000, and $6,600 in 2009.[48] With about 2.5 million people in the United States dying each year, expenditures for funeral, cemetery, and other such "death care" services total about $15.2 billion.[49] As of 2012, there were about 19,700 funeral homes in the United States. Eighty-six percent of these funeral homes were owned by individuals, families, or closely held companies and 14 percent were owned by publicly traded stock corporations.[50] Although most funeral service firms are small businesses, considered in the aggregate, disposition of the dead is big business.

Comparing the Costs

Even when itemized, costs quoted by different funeral homes may be difficult to compare. Funeral providers do not always offer exactly the same goods and services, and they may have different ways of presenting prices. Nevertheless, it is useful to distinguish the usual charges (see Table 8-3). You may find it interesting to compare prices in your own area with these national ranges by obtaining information from local funeral homes.

Professional Services

Funeral costs include a basic charge for services provided by mortuary staff, such as arranging the funeral, consulting with family members and clergy, directing the visitation and funeral ceremony, and preparing and

TABLE 8-3 *Funeral Costs*

Services	
Professional service fee	$1,817
Transfer of remains to funeral home	$250
Embalming	$628
Other body preparation	$200
Use of staff/facilities for viewing	$395
Use of staff/facilities for funeral ceremony	$450
Use of hearse	$275
Use of service car/van	$125
Merchandise	
Casket (metal)	$2,295
Memorial cards	$125
Burial vault	$1,195

filing necessary notices and authorizations related to body disposition. The latter may include filing the death certificate and certain claims for death benefits.

The fee for professional services also covers a share of the overhead and business expenses required to maintain facilities and staff. Mortuary facilities usually require a large capital investment because of their specialized design. The typical funeral business is located in a large, possibly colonial style, building. The floor plan may be designed especially to function as a funeral home. Funerals have been compared to theatrical presentations, with certain activities taking place "off stage."[51] The backstage area, hidden from the public's gaze, is where the body is embalmed and cosmetized for its eventual role in the funeral.

Besides the fee for professional services, mortuaries usually charge an "intake fee" for transferring remains from the place of death to the mortuary, and there may be a surcharge for after-hours (night or weekend) pickup. Cemetery or crematory services, flowers, placement of newspaper notices, and other incidental costs are usually billed separately.

(As an alternative pricing method, the FTC rule allows funeral providers to include the professional service fee as part of the cost of caskets. When this is done, however, a description of such services must appear on the casket price list.)

The FTC Funeral Rule also specifies that, with direct cremation or immediate burial, the fee for professional services must be included in the price quoted for those methods of disposition. Similarly, the fee for professional services must be included in prices quoted for forwarding remains to another funeral home or receiving remains from another funeral home.

Embalming

Embalming methods have differed among cultures, and preservation of the corpse has varied correspondingly. The mummification of royalty and members of the upper class practiced in classical antiquity by the Egyptians is a notable example of embalming. Other noteworthy examples from more modern times include the body of the Soviet Union's founder, Vladimir Lenin, displayed in a mausoleum in Red Square. Lenin's embalmment became a model for other leaders whose bodies have been put on display, Ho Chi Minh in Hanoi and Mao Zedong in Tiananmen Square, for example.

A body destined for burial or cremation may or may not be embalmed. If the body will be viewed during a wake or will be present at the funeral, however, embalming is generally done (although facilities with "cold rooms" may substitute for embalming).

In *Death to Dust,* Kenneth Iserson says, "Originally, embalming meant placing balm, essentially natural sap and aromatic substances, on a corpse."[52] In modern usage, embalming involves removing the blood and other fluids in the body and replacing them with chemicals to disinfect and temporarily retard deterioration of the corpse.

In the United States, embalming was adopted around the time of the Civil War, as funeral homes like Brown & Alexander in Washington, D.C., began to make embalming available to their clientele. Brown was a medical doctor whose interest in embalming grew out of his training in anatomy and his marriage to the daughter of the man who founded Kirk & Nice in Philadelphia, the oldest funeral home in the United States, which began operation in 1761. After witnessing embalming demonstrations by a French doctor in New York City, Brown decided to offer this service at no charge for "soldiers who may be so unfortunate as to die or be killed while at the seat of war and away from their families and friends."[53] The funeral procession for President Abraham Lincoln, which traveled by train from Washington, D.C., to Springfield, Illinois, was a public event that significantly increased awareness of embalming.[54] During this period, however, other means of temporarily retarding decomposition of the corpse remained in use (see Figure 8-4).

In the United States, embalming is usually considered a practical necessity by most mortuary establishments when a body will be viewed. With few exceptions, however, the FTC Funeral Rule requires that mortuaries obtain

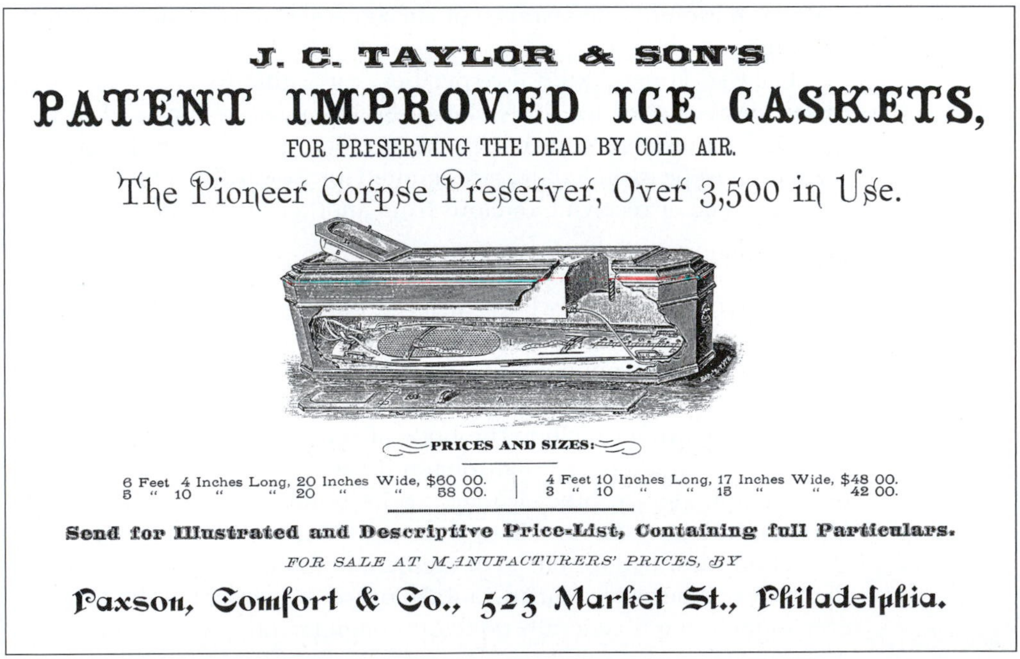

Figure 8-4 *Refrigerated Casket Advertisement, 1881*
Undertakers of the 1880s could keep a body for viewing over a longer period of time by using an ice casket, such as the one shown in this advertisement. When embalming became widespread, these cold-air preservation devices became obsolete.

express permission to embalm from the family in order to charge a fee for the procedure.[55] Furthermore, the mortuary's price list must include the following disclosure next to the price for embalming:

> Except in certain special cases, embalming is not required by law. Embalming may be necessary, however, if you select certain funeral arrangements, such as a funeral with viewing. If you do not want embalming, you usually have the right to choose an arrangement which does not require you to pay for it, such as direct cremation or immediate burial.

Some mortuaries have a combined fee for both embalming and body preparation; others itemize the procedures separately. In addition to basic antiseptic hygiene procedures, body preparation may include cosmetology, hair styling, and manicuring, as well as dressing the body, placing it in the casket, and composing it for viewing.

If refrigeration or a "cold room" is available, a mortuary may offer the alternative of storing a body for a short time without embalming. Refrigeration usually costs a little less than embalming. A refrigerated, unembalmed body will remain relatively preserved for about three days, although some mortuaries may have a policy of not holding an unembalmed body longer than forty-eight hours.

Caskets

Most people feel that the casket is the centerpiece of a traditional funeral because of its symbolic and emotional value in honoring the deceased. The average amount spent on a casket is about $2,300. When it comes to buying a casket, however, customers have a wide range of choices, and prices are highly variable. Choices range from inexpensive cardboard containers all the way to solid mahogany, copper, or bronze caskets that cost thousands of dollars. Most funeral homes offer caskets in a range of prices.

Caskets at the lower end of the price range are typically made of cloth-covered plywood or pressboard and contain a mattress that is likely to be made of straw covered with an acetate sheet. At the next pricing level, refinements appear. The casket may be covered with copper or bronze sheathing and the mattress constructed with springs and topped by a layer of foam rubber with a covering of acetate material. In this middle range, gasketed steel caskets are available with devices intended to ensure an airtight environment within the casket. (Although this may provide solace for some people, any added protection is debatable.) The gasketed steel casket is the most popular choice in the United States.

The price of a top-of-the-line casket ranges from about $7,000 upward to $50,000 or more. For this sum, there are caskets constructed of mahogany, copper, or bronze and fitted out with all the embellishments of the casket manufacturer's art.

The FTC rule requires funeral providers to supply customers with a list of the prices and descriptions of available caskets. This may be done either on the general price list or on a separate casket price list. In addition, the FTC rule stipulates that customers have the right to buy a casket from a supplier different from the funeral home contracted to handle all the other aspects of the funeral service and burial. In addition, mortuaries may not charge handling fees on caskets purchased elsewhere.

The FTC rule led to an increase in the number of casket discounters, some of which are operated as small chains. Although many discounters are storefront businesses or are even located in shopping malls, some are set up so that customers can order caskets via a toll-free number or on the Internet. In 2009, Walmart announced that it had added caskets and urns to its retail Web site. The warehouse club Costco had been selling these items online even earlier. Traditional, handmade wooden caskets are also available from some monastic communities, such as those made by Trappist monks at New Melleray Abbey in Iowa. Mortuaries are joining this trend by opening their own "funeral shops," where caskets and funeral accessories are sold at discounted prices.

Despite the opportunity to avoid part of the markup on caskets, individuals may not feel comfortable buying funeral merchandise at discount. Not only do funeral homes provide "one-stop shopping" for merchandise and services, but the notion of "skimping" on a loved one's funeral may be troubling. Nevertheless, for some people, casket retailers appear to be an idea whose time has come. The Regale Funeral Store in London, England, a "funeral supermarket," offers flowers, memorials, caskets, urns, and other funeral paraphernalia in a supermarket-style shopping hall, with the prices of all products and services clearly itemized and priced.[56]

People are usually surprised to learn that there is no law requiring that a body destined for cremation must be placed in a casket. Most crematoria require only that the body be delivered in a rigid container. Mortuaries sell a body-sized cardboard box that suffices for this purpose. The FTC rule prohibits funeral providers from telling consumers that state or local law requires them to purchase a casket when they want to arrange a direct cremation (that is, a cremation that occurs without formal viewing of the remains or any visitation or ceremony with the body present). The FTC rule stipulates that firms offering direct cremation provide the following disclosure:

> If you want to arrange a direct cremation, you can use an unfinished wood box or an alternative container. Alternative containers can be made of materials like heavy cardboard or composition materials (with or without an outside covering), or pouches of canvas.

Outer Burial Containers

If outer burial containers (vaults or grave liners) are offered for sale by a funeral home, prices must be listed, either separately or on the general price list, and the following disclosure must be made:

> In most areas of the country, no state or local law makes you buy a container to surround the casket in the grave. However, many cemeteries require that you have such a container so that the grave will not sink in. Either a burial vault or a grave liner will satisfy these requirements.

Because many funeral businesses do not sell burial vaults or grave liners, this item may not appear on the price lists of mortuaries in your area.

Facilities and Vehicles

The use of a visitation or viewing room is a common component of most funerals. In the itemized listing of prices, the funeral establishment may use whatever method of pricing it prefers or follow common practice in its area. For example, various settings in the funeral home might be listed, along with the charges for each by day, half day, or hour. Similarly, if funeral ceremonies can be held in a chapel at the funeral home, a charge for the chapel's use will be specified. When other facilities are made available to customers (for example, tent and chairs for graveside services), the charges must be stated on the price list.

According to the FTC rule, charges for the use of a hearse, limousine, or other automotive equipment provided by the mortuary must be itemized separately on the general price list. Family members, pallbearers, or other participants (such as clergy) often use vehicles provided by a funeral home. A "flower car" (or van) may be engaged to transport floral arrangements from the place where the funeral is held to the cemetery or crematorium. A fee will also be assessed when a motorcycle escort is hired to be part of the procession.

Miscellaneous Charges

In the miscellaneous category are charges for goods or services provided directly by the funeral home, as well as charges incurred on behalf of the customer from outside sources. The latter include cash-advance items, such as floral arrangements and newspaper notices. The customer may be billed for the actual amounts of the items, or the funeral provider may add a surcharge for arranging these cash-advance items. If an additional charge is made, a notice to that effect must be shown on the general price list.

The FTC rule specifically mentions that memorial cards must be itemized if the funeral provider sells those items or performs the service of filling out and sending them for customers.

The miscellaneous charges category may also include the cost of burial garments purchased from the mortuary, any fees or honoraria for pallbearers, or an honorarium for the clergyperson who conducts the funeral service.

Direct Cremations and Immediate Burials

Most mortuaries offer direct cremations and immediate burials to customers. These methods of body disposition generally do not involve any formal viewing of the remains or any visitation or ceremony with the body present. (Some mortuaries respond to requests for viewing or informal ceremonies by placing the body on a cloth-covered gurney.)

If direct cremation or immediate burial is offered by a funeral home, the cost—which includes the fee for professional services—is shown on the general price list. When direct cremation is selected, the customer must be

© Robin Van Doren, Open Doors

A papier-mâché bull symbolizing the deceased's caste is a focal point of this cremation ceremony in a Balinese village. According to local custom, corpses are buried until families accumulate the necessary funds to pay for the cremation ritual; at that time, the body is disinterred, wrapped in cloth, and placed, along with various offerings, in ritual objects such as the bull shown here at the cremation site.

given the option of providing the container or of purchasing an unfinished pine box or alternative container (such as a box made of cardboard, plywood, or composition material). Similarly, for immediate burials, the customer can provide a container or purchase a simple casket, such as one made of wood

> Assume that we are confronted with the dead body of a man. What disposition shall we make of it? Shall we lay it in a boat that is set adrift? Shall we take the heart from it and bury it in one place and the rest of the body in another? Shall we expose it to wild animals? Burn it on a pyre? Push it into a pit to rot with other bodies? Boil it until the flesh falls off the bones, and throw the flesh away and treasure the bones? Such questions provoke others which may not be consciously articulated, such as: "What do men generally think this body is?" And, "What do they think is a proper way of dealing with it?"
>
> Robert W. Habenstein and William M. Lamers, *The History of American Funeral Directing*

and covered with cloth. (If a funeral home offers immediate burials but does not offer direct cremations, the FTC rule does not require the firm to make available an alternative container or unfinished wood box, although a funeral director might choose to do so.)

Funeral and Memorial Societies

Funeral and memorial societies are nonprofit, cooperative organizations that offer body disposition to members at a reduced cost by providing simplicity and economy in after-death arrangements. They are generally minimalist with respect to disposition of the corpse—either immediate cremation or immediate burial—although some offer other options at a higher cost. Such societies represent a response to consumers' wishes for low-cost, simple methods of body disposition.

Body Disposition

Speaking of the need for appropriate disposal of the dead, Stephen Prothero says, "Death rites remind us that corpses are feared as well as feted. Though the dead arrive at funerals as honored guests, at the party's climax they are summarily shown the door."[57]

Think for a moment about what you would choose to be done with your body after you die. When people in the United States are asked their preferences, responses usually fall into one of the following categories: earth burial, entombment in a mausoleum crypt, cremation, or donation to science. In ancient Greece, from the sixth century BCE, it was considered criminal not to give the dead body a tomb, condemning it to roam the banks of the Styx, the dreaded river of the underworld.

Some recent innovations in body disposition—green or woodland burials, space burials, and cryonics, for example—are mentioned in a later section titled "New Directions in Funerals and Body Disposition." Here, we focus on conventional choices available to individuals and families.

Corpses must be disposed of for sanitary reasons, though it is unlikely that a person's choice of *how* to accomplish disposition is influenced by that fact. The method chosen is more likely to involve social, cultural, religious, psychological, and personal considerations. Reynolds and Tanner point out that "dead bodies have to be disposed of and religions often provide the rules and personnel for this, even when the dead and their survivors are not specifically religious."[58] For example, Judaism, Christianity, and Islam typically practice ground burial, whereas Hindus and Buddhists prefer cremation. Each method of disposing of the corpse has symbolic meanings that are important to followers of the respective religions. For example, among Hindus, cremation is seen as a gesture of purification and symbol of the transitory nature of human life. Orthodox Judaism, in contrast, views cremation as a form of idolatry; burial returns the body to the "dust" from whence it was created by God. Other branches of Judaism have less strict views about the ban on cremation. In Christianity, prohibition against cremation is no longer universal, having been replaced by a diversity of viewpoints; some churches support or tolerate cremation, whereas others require or strongly prefer ground burial.

In *Death to Dust,* Kenneth Iserson reports that "an unembalmed adult body buried six feet deep in ordinary soil without a coffin normally takes ten to twelve years to decompose down to the bony skeleton; a child's body takes about half that time."[59] Environmental conditions can delay or hasten decomposition; for example, corpses buried in coffins or caskets take longer to decompose than those buried without such containers, and bodies directly exposed to the environment will generally be reduced to skeletons rather quickly.

The decomposition of the body is hastened in some societies by washing the flesh from the bones when the corpse is partially decomposed; parts of the body are then retained as a memorial. In other societies, open-air disposal is practiced; the body is left to the elements, where it generally decomposes quite rapidly (except in very dry, desert climates, where heat removes the moisture from the body, acting thereby to preserve it). Some Indian tribes of the plains constructed platforms on which the corpse was exposed to the effects of the sun, wind, and rain. In some societies, vultures or other animals consume the remains of the dead. In India, for example, one can see scaffolds known as high *dakhmas* (towers of silence) on Bombay's fashionable Marabar Hill, where the Parsi community disposes of its dead by leaving corpses to be devoured by birds of prey. As followers of Zoroaster, they regard earth, fire, and water as sacred and therefore not to be defiled by the dead.

A method of body disposal practiced by mariners since ancient times is water burial, or burial at sea. Depending on circumstances and cultural practices, this form of body disposition might involve either ceremonially sliding the corpse off the side of a ship or placing the corpse inside a boat that is set aflame and then set adrift. The Norwegian ship burials of the Viking Age present an interesting twist on this method of body disposal by combining the

Burial at sea is a naval tradition the world over, particularly during times of war. Here the body of a seaman is committed to the deep during burial services aboard the USS Ranger.

"burial at sea" theme with ground burial.[60] The dead were laid in a wooden grave chamber and placed in a ship along with grave goods, and the whole was covered by an earthen mound.

Donation to medical science is another method of body disposition. The person who chooses this may gain satisfaction from the notion that he or she is making a contribution to the advancement of knowledge: "My body will serve a useful function even after I'm gone." This is a somewhat limited option, however, because medical schools and other such institutions require relatively few cadavers. When a body has been donated to science, the final disposition of the remains may be left to the discretion of the institution that received the donation. Usually, however, the next of kin is usually given a say in determining the final disposition once the medical or scientific purposes of the donation have been achieved. Most medical schools and research institutions have policies to ensure that cadavers are treated ethically and disposed of properly. In some cases, a memorial service is held to acknowledge the gift represented by the donation of the body to science.[61]

From the burials of prehistory to space-age cryonics, human beings have chosen from a variety of alternatives for disposing of the dead. Although few people give much thought to the subject of body disposition, it is nonetheless fraught with emotional and psychological importance, as the following story illustrates: When Major Edward Strombeck was killed in a plane crash while on duty in Vietnam, the military cremated his body and forwarded the ashes by mail to his home in Hawaii.[62] Shocked at the lack of proper ceremony, his mother and other family members expressed their dismay and gained the attention of U.S. Senator Daniel Inouye. The result was a change in policy, which ordered that the ashes of military personnel must be escorted home with dignity and honor. Proper disposition of human remains is a matter of considerable significance not only to the immediate survivors but also to the larger community. What do your own preferences regarding body disposition tell you about your attitudes toward and beliefs about death?

Burial

It's been said that no land in the United States is more sacred than the square mile of Arlington National Cemetery. It is a place "where the living meet the dead and where national history is intertwined with personal loss."[63] This poignant sentiment bespeaks the value that historically has been conferred on a "place" for the dead. *Cemetery* comes from the Greek, meaning "sleeping chamber." Related words include *necropolis,* or city of the dead, referring especially to the large cemeteries with elaborate monuments that were outside ancient cities, and *graveyard,* which, in Western European history, was usually located near a church. Sir Raymond Firth says, "Cemeteries offer a rich field for anthropological study because they illustrate the emotional and symbolic meaning attached to material objects in human culture, including even the bodies of the dead."[64] Other writers point out that the cemetery is not only a place, but also a process. "In it the thoughts and feelings of the bereaved are evoked and constrained in their culturally appropriate behavioural expression."[65] Commenting on passage of the Native American Grave Protection and Repatriation Act by Congress in 1990, Michael Kammen says, "Returning bodies to their rightful places becomes a symbolic way of reordering a disruptive and confusing world."[66]

The term *burial* encompasses a wide range of practices. It may involve digging a single grave in the soil, or it may refer to entombment in a mausoleum (of which the Taj Mahal and the pyramids in Egypt are examples). The whole body can be buried, just the bones, or even cremated remains. In parts of the world, cemetery plots are purchased outright; elsewhere, a burial plot is merely rented for a number of years.[67] In some cemeteries, everyone is equal in death; in others, the social distinctions that held sway in life are perpetuated by dividing burial space into classes, with better placement of graves for those who occupy first-class ranks.[68]

In addition to the cost of a cemetery plot, cemeteries usually require a grave liner or vault to support the earth around and above the casket. This adds about $1,000 to the cost of ground burial, although vaults that are designed (but not guaranteed) to seal out moisture cost considerably more.

The cost of entombment in a mausoleum or crypt averages about $2,000, although, as always, prices vary. At the mausoleum recently completed beneath the Cathedral of Our Lady of the Angels in Los Angeles, the 1300 invitation-only crypts start at about $50,000 each and are available to individuals who made substantial contributions to the building of the cathedral (space in one of the six semiprivate chapels or a crypt near one of the stained-glass windows will cost much more).[69] Historically, the term *crypt* denotes a subterranean burial vault or chamber often situated beneath the floor of a church. In modern usage, the term also refers to space in a *mausoleum,* an aboveground structure of concrete, marble, or other stone in which one or more bodies are entombed. The most expensive crypt spaces are usually those at eye level, with less expensive spaces at the top and bottom. (The Queen of Heaven mausoleum complex in Chicago, the world's largest Catholic mausoleum, has space for 33,000 bodies.)[70] The opening and closing of a grave or crypt normally involves additional charges.

Simple bronze or stone grave markers generally cost several hundred dollars; nameplates for mausoleum crypts cost a bit less. More elaborate memorials, if they are permitted by a cemetery (some permit only flat-on-the-ground markers), cost from several hundred to many thousands of dollars.

Mausoleum crypts, such as those seen here in Oaxaca, Mexico, are an alternative to underground burial that is found in many parts of the world. When space is at a premium, bodies may be removed from the chambers after a period of time and given underground burial or other disposition.

Finally, some cemeteries assess an endowment or "perpetual care" cost that subsidizes upkeep of the cemetery, although this fee is sometimes included in the basic cost for burial or entombment.

With a growing number of cremations, traditional cemetery burial is becoming more of a lifestyle choice.[71]

Cremation

Using intense heat, approximately 2000 to 2500 degrees Fahrenheit, *cremation* reduces the organic components of a body to a mineralized skeleton through a process of dehydration and oxidation. In the United States, the practice of cremation as a method of body disposal dates from the nineteenth century (although it had been customary for some Native American cultural groups for centuries). In Europe, the practice is considerably older, going back at least to the Bronze Age. Cremation is the most common method of body disposal in many countries, including India and Japan, and it has found growing acceptance in the United States in recent decades. Currently, cremation is the method of body disposition chosen in slightly over 40 percent of final dispositions in the United States.[72]

Cremation has been accomplished by various methods, from a simple wood fire to sophisticated electric or gas retorts. In the United States, natural gas is the most commonly used fuel. An average-size body takes about one and one-half hours to be reduced to a mineralized skeleton, which is put through a "cremulator" that reduces the bone fragments to a granular state, often referred to as "ashes." (The term *ashes* leads some people to believe that the cremated remains will look and feel like wood or paper ashes. Actually, they are very small pieces of bone, which look and feel like coarse coral sands whose shell-like components are worn by the wind and waves.)

Environmental concerns have led to "green" techniques that can substitute for the conventional cremation process. *Resomation* (alkaline hydrolysis), for example, is a chemical process that reduces a human cadaver to a few pounds of bone fragments in a timeframe approximately equal to fire cremation. Bones are then dried and ground into ash. The process of *cryomation* is the virtual opposite of fire cremation and alkaline hydrolysis. Akin to the freeze-drying used to dehydrate food for space travel and long-term preservation, cryomation involves immersing the body into a liquid nitrogen bath, freezing the cadaver into brittle particles that can be pulverized into fine powder. William Hoy says, "Like cremation, their older 'cousin,' technologies such as resomation and cryomation neither interfere with funeral rituals nor take their place."[73]

Cremated remains can be buried, placed in a columbarium niche, put into an urn kept by the family or interred in an urn garden, or scattered at sea or on land. State and local laws may restrict how some of these options are carried out. Although scattering cremated remains is a popular method of final disposition and usually the least costly, some people who have decided to scatter "ashes" later regret it because, as one woman said about her husband,

"I have no place to take him a flower." When remains are scattered at sea, over a forest, or in some similar locale, people may find that they miss the emotional power of a *specific place* where one can visit the deceased loved one. (The provision of GPS coordinates of longitude and latitude might relieve this concern for some.) In Japanese cemeteries, *haka*—small, private family mausolea that fit on a standard cemetery plot—hold a dozen crematory urns. This setting has been called "the Asian equivalent of a European family plot with a hedge growing around it."[74] As land for burials becomes more expensive, mainstream cemeteries may respond to the increasing popularity of cremation by offering landscaped "garden" plots that have space for several urns, thereby allowing several generations to be buried and memorialized in a family plot.

Survivors may choose to memorialize the deceased in conjunction with cremation, just as with traditional burials. Urns to hold cremated remains can be purchased at prices from about $50 to $400, though more expensive urns are available. If cremated remains are to be entombed, columbarium niches (small vaults in which the urns are placed) are available; the cost depends on the size and location of the niche. Among some families and ethnic groups, a family tomb is the resting place for the ashes of several generations of the dead. For cremated remains, memorialization may include an inscription or plaque on a columbarium niche or a special urn to hold the ashes.

Memorialization

Grave markers and monuments are examples of how people have traditionally chosen to honor and remember their dead. Memorials can be structures as large as the Taj Mahal or as tall as the obelisk in Washington, D.C., honoring the first president of the United States. Or they can be as small as a postal stamp. The faces of presidents and prime ministers, kings and queens, writers and painters, and all manner of personalities are printed on postage stamps as a way to honor and remember those whom a nation finds worthy. When wartime British prime minister Winston Churchill died in 1965, some 287 stamps were issued by 73 countries within a year of his death. The runner-up was John F. Kennedy, for whom 183 stamps were issued by 44 countries.[75]

The U.S. Department of Veterans Affairs offers at least thirty-nine different emblems to designate a veteran's belief, from the expected Christian (the cross), Buddhist (the wheel of dharma), Muslim (the crescent and star), and Jewish (the Star of David), to more recently adopted symbols representing Wicca (the pentacle), humanist, and atheist.

In some African American communities, obituaries have been turned into memorials celebrating and honoring the life of the deceased. Colorful funeral booklets with testimonial prose and photos describe the highlights of a person's life in magazine format. Printing technologies make it possible to quickly produce as many copies as needed of the memorial magazines, which are seen as simply another step in the progression of African American style. One writer comments, "Some people rate an obituary. And then some people rate an entire magazine."[76]

Marion Pinsdorf notes that widows have been "image makers" for dead husbands both in history and in modern times.[77] She cites Mrs. George Armstrong Custer's example of stage-managing the general's funeral to gain the greatest impact visually and historically. Yoko Ono is a modern example who "organized and sanitized" John Lennon's life. Other widows who acted to enhance the memorialization of their husbands include Jacqueline Kennedy, Coretta Scott King, and Susan Eakins (widow of painter Thomas Eakins). In some cases, image triumphs over deeds as widows strive to make "dead heroes" of their husbands.

Conventional forms of memorialization are not the only options for achieving the purpose of a memorial: namely, to commemorate (remind) and to celebrate (honor and give public notice). A memorial may be a keepsake, memento, or memoir, as well as a sculpture or structure made of concrete or bricks. A memorial functions to "keep interest alive" and "preserve remembrance."

Laws Regulating Body Disposition

As a general rule, the deceased's next of kin is responsible for arranging for the final disposition of the body. State laws and local ordinances, however, may govern the manner in which disposition can be effected. For example, some communities have ordinances prohibiting burial within city limits.

When the deceased has left no money to cover the cost of body disposition, and his or her relatives are unwilling or unable to pay, the state may be forced to step in and handle the details. Counties generally have an "indigent burial fund" for such cases. The public administrator's office may distinguish between "inconvenient to pay" and "unable to pay." When funds are not available from private sources, the county picks up the cost. The county may have a contract with a local mortuary that provides direct cremation and burial of the cremated remains. If the next of kin opposes cremation, the corpse may be placed in a casket and buried in a plot donated by a cemetery (or, again, paid for out of community funds).

Located in a setting of great natural beauty on the Hawaiian island of Oahu, this Chinese cemetery is situated on a hillside that gently slopes down toward the city of Honolulu and the ocean beyond. Following Chinese custom and in accord with the principles of fêng-shui, care is taken to ensure proper siting of the grave to facilitate the journey of the deceased's spirit to the afterlife. As with this cemetery located above a bustling, metropolitan city, certain aspects of traditional practices retain importance even in modern social settings.

New Directions in Funerals and Body Disposition

Whereas grieving families used to be faced with two basic choices—how much to spend on a casket and where to bury their deceased loved one—now they encounter dozens of options for care and disposal of the deceased, ranging from presenting video biographies of the deceased at the funeral to wearing jewelry made from cremated remains.

Even the selection of a casket is changing. In place of the conventional "selection" room, typically a fairly large space filled with caskets of various styles and costs, mortuaries are installing high-tech, touchscreen monitors and software that allow families to choose from a larger range of caskets than could be housed in a selection room, and that also serve as an information center about products and services available for both burials and cremations. One funeral director says, "Many families tell us they dread the thought of walking into a showroom surrounded by caskets and having to choose." The new technology, which goes by names like "Family Advisor," eases some of that mental anguish while allowing the mortuary to provide a wider selection of merchandise, even allowing families to design their own casket through the touchscreen interface.

Kathleen Garces-Foley says, "The choices available to the modern family may feel like a burden, but they also present an opportunity to create a funeral experience that is personally meaningful."[78] Funeral directors have had to stay abreast of these changes as people seek new options and choices in funerals and memorials. A new generation of funeral directors is emerging and beginning to see themselves less as morticians and more as event planners.[79] (Some people are calling them "hipster undertakers.") Garces-Foley says, "Inventive energy is being put into the creation of death rites that are personally meaningful."[80]

The San Francisco Columbarium recently held a gala party for its "future residents." While music played and food and beverages were served, the mortuary helped people share ideas for decorating their vaults. Marilyn Yalom says that, although such an event "may appear bizarre to many Americans who generally think of death in less entertaining terms," this was not just a San Francisco phenomenon but "part of a larger trend to make resting places more user friendly."[81]

Personalized funerals, which adapt many elements of conventional funerals, are increasingly preferred as more "authentic" rituals.[82] For example, eulogies in honor of the deceased usually remain part of the ritual, but they are likely to be spoken not just by clergy but also by family and friends. Such "shared eulogies" may even expand into open, spontaneous sharing by those present, causing some clergy to complain that such eulogies neglect "the comfort religion offers the grieving" and "can become a space for telling stories about the good 'ole times."[83]

Personalized funerals are also called "life-centered" funerals, because the focus is placed on the life and the relationships of the deceased, not on

> As a testament to changing times, funeral-cremation providers must be reminded that valuables on bodies might no longer only include ordinary items such as rings, watches, earrings, necklaces, bracelets, anklets, and toe rings nor be confined to ears, toes, fingers, necks or wrists. Body piercing is common. Diligence now requires thoroughly inspecting other parts of the body that may contain valuables. The tongue, chest, navel, pubic areas and nasal cavity must be inspected.
>
> Michael Kubasak and William M. Lamers, Jr., *Traversing the Minefield—Best Practice: Reducing Risk in Funeral-Cremation Service*

religious teachings about death or the afterlife. Favorite music is played, and favorite poems may be read. Douglas Davies says that such ceremonies "reflect life rather than confront the bereaved with beliefs they may not hold."[84]

Movement toward personalization is also seen in the growing popularity of a "do-it-yourself" orientation toward last rites. This development has been described variously as a "natural funeral," "home funeral," and "family-directed funeral" (as distinguished from a funeral directed by a licensed mortician). A guidebook for such funerals states:

> A home funeral is a noncommercial, family-centered response to death that involves the family and social community in the care and preparation of the body for burial or cremation and/or in planning and carrying out related rituals or ceremonies and/or in the burial or cremation itself. It is differentiated from the institutional funeral by its emphasis on minimal, noninvasive care and preparation of the body, on its reliance on the family's own social networks for assistance and support, and on the relative or total absence of commercial funeral providers in its proceedings.[85]

Survivors may be guided through their choices by a "death midwife," a person who is familiar with the options and knows how to negotiate the sometimes complex bureacracy of conventional funeral rules.[86]

For body disposition, conventional choices in burial and cremation have been joined by new-age options. "Natural," "woodland," or "green" burials increasingly have come to public attention and are becoming an option for some people, although one that is not yet widely available.[87] Green burials first became institutionalized in England in the 1990s before being introduced in the United States.[88] A green burial connotes body disposal in a natural setting, with no embalming. The body is wrapped in a shroud or placed in a biodegradable coffin (see Figure 8-5).[89] The emphasis is on materials that naturally return to the earth. Toxic materials are forbidden (see Table 8-4). In Sweden, an organization named Promessa, led by an ecologist, is pioneering a method of burial that does not involve embalming fluid; rather it uses liquid nitrogen to remove water from the body, transforming it to dust. The recycled body is then used as fertilizer.

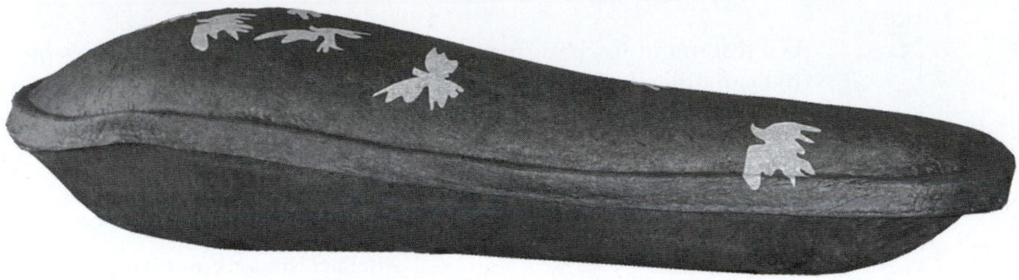

Courtesy of www.ecopod.co.uk

Figure 8-5 *The Ecopod*
The Ecopod, made in England, is a recyclable casket made from post-consumer newspapers churned with water and a natural plant hardener to make paper clay, which is then laid by hand into molds for the lids and base. The outer surface is covered with a design printed on a sheet of paper made from mulberry pulp. Cotton webbing and removable bamboo handles complete the Ecopod.

In green cemeteries, a natural marker, such as a tree or special rock, may be permitted, but the setting is free of tombstones or mausoleums. The goal is a "sustainable" cemetery.

Individuals are also choosing a form of ocean burial called an "eternal reef," in which cremated remains are integrated into a small, constructed "reef" that is lowered into the ocean and that soon becomes a habitat for sea animals.[90] Green burials, whether on land or in the ocean, appeal especially to those who live by the "reduce, reuse, recycle" lifestyle.

The "gonzo" journalist Hunter S. Thompson chose a unique send-off as a method of disposition when his ashes were blasted into the sky carried by red, white, and blue fireworks. Six months to the day after he shot himself to death at his home, guests watched "as his ashes exploded with fireworks, lingered in great puffs of milky smoke, then vanished."[91]

Another option is a "space burial." In this form of disposition, cremated remains are loaded onto a rocket and launched into space, where they orbit Earth and after a few weeks descend into the atmosphere and are totally incinerated. A more costly variation provides rocket transport of the cremated remains to the Moon or beyond.

TABLE 8-4 *Environmental Impact of Burial*

Burial inters more than a body. What else goes under the ground each year in the United States?

- 30 million board feet of casket wood, including tropical hardwoods
- 90,000 tons of steel, more than enough to build the Golden Gate Bridge
- 1.6 million tons of concrete in burial vaults
- Over 800,000 gallons of embalming fluid, more than enough to fill an Olympic-size pool

Strictly speaking, *cryonics,* or cryogenic suspension, is not a method of body disposal but rather an experimental technology. It has nevertheless attracted attention as a unique way to deal with a body after death. Cryogenic suspension involves preserving a corpse (or only the head) by freezing it in liquid nitrogen and keeping it frozen until some future time when medical science is sophisticated enough to allow for resuscitation and continued life.

Remembrance Rituals and Linking Objects

Bereaved people may find solace through remembrance or leave-taking rituals that differ from, or become an adjunct to, conventional funeral rites and services. Such rituals of remembrance or continuity typically use *linking objects;* that is, any physical object or image that serves to connect a mourner in a comforting or constructive way with a deceased loved one. Lou LaGrand, a longtime grief counselor, says,

> Linking objects are in effect transitional objects that assist the mourner in maintaining a healthy bond of remembrance and thanksgiving as one begins the journey to find new ways to reinvest emotional energy into life. . . . These objects are one type of learning tool to bring empathy, understanding, and awareness that love never dies into the experience of massive change.[92]

Some writers express the view that linking objects are a "chain" that should be broken. Although it is true that holding onto possessions of the deceased may be done in a manner that is not helpful in adjusting to a loss and moving forward, it is also true that discarding every reminder of the deceased can be equally unhelpful. Indeed, the use of linking objects in remembrance ritual can help individuals move from a maladaptive to an adaptive style of grieving.[93] In effect, it is a form of "directive mourning therapy" that allows grieving survivors to take symbolic leave of the deceased.[94]

Memorial garden

This is her first garden. It's a memorial garden. It is a place to visit her still and have a chat. The garden is another way of keeping in touch. I come every week on Thursday since she died. To tidy up, trim, cut the grass, put fresh water in, change the flowers that others bring. I feel she's still with me. I used to see her every day when she was living. I worked where she lived and I would see her and have a cup of tea and a chat. Although Mum's no longer alive, I still have a chat—for five minutes after I tidy up; I tell her what's going on.

East End resident whose mother was buried
at the City of London Cemetery

Examples of using linking objects to create a ritual of remembrance or continuity include writing a farewell letter to the deceased and subsequently burying or burning it. An activity like this can be followed by a "reunion" ritual, perhaps in the form of a ceremonial dinner with family and friends. In this way, the rhythms of separation and joining found in traditional rituals can be adapted to the circumstances of a particular person. It is usually appropriate to strike a balance between the *linking* activities that maintain the survivor's ties to the past and the *bridging* activities that lead the survivor to a future without the deceased. The following story is illustrative.

> Sometimes you get what you need.
>
> A woman whose older brother died in a plane crash over the ocean (where his body was never found) decided she needed to honor his memory some thirty-three years after his death. Until then, she had lived in a seaside town, in a house facing the ocean with her drapes closed so that she didn't have to look at her brother's "killer."
>
> With encouragement from her counselor, the woman chose long-stemmed red roses, one for each year her brother had been dead. She took the flowers, some music, and a few poems to a cliff overlooking the ocean. Her plan was to have a simple ceremony by herself. She would cast the roses, one by one, into the ocean—something peaceful as well as forgiving of the ocean for keeping her brother's body.
>
> Being unfamiliar with the waves in the chosen spot, she began her ceremony. She threw a rose off the cliff. The ocean current and waves hurled and smashed it back to the cliff. With each rose, the ocean seemingly refused to take her offering. By the time the last rose was gone, she was down on her hands and knees, at the cliff's edge, crying and swearing.
>
> Her peaceful ritual had become a catharsis for years of pain and grief at the sudden loss of an adored sibling. When she again became aware of her surroundings, she checked to see if anyone had observed her loud temper tantrum, remarking later that the ritual turned out to be exactly what she needed but hadn't planned.

Making Meaningful Choices

Willliam Lamers, Sr., defined the funeral as "an organized, purposeful, time-limited, flexible, group-centered response to death."[95] In light of the varied and diverse styles of funeral service now available, does this definition apply to our current approaches to caring for the dead? What values guide our actions in memorializing the dead and meeting the emotional needs of survivors? The choices we make concerning funerals and body disposition increasingly reflect personal rather than community judgments.

If the monolithic and perhaps stereotypical "American funeral" is disappearing, it is being replaced by a broader range of options. Reflecting cultural diversity, funeral directors generally have at least some familiarity not only with the rituals practiced in Judaism and Christianity but also with Buddhist, Hindu, and Muslim services as well as nonreligious humanistic and fraternal rites. Rather than being locked into a "conventional funeral," people can now choose from a wide range of resources that allow them to create or adapt funeral customs from both religious and secular traditions. There are many ways to deal meaningfully and appropriately with death. Becoming aware of the alternatives enables us to make meaningful choices.

Some people prefer a minimal role in caring for their dead; others seek to participate actively. The experience of a family following the death of a young son is illustrative. There were no plans for a formal funeral ceremony. The body would be cremated and the ashes scattered. Before the body was to be cremated, the family found themselves experiencing the acute grief that comes with a sudden and intimate loss. As they tried to come to terms with their emotions and the loss of their son, someone in their circle of friends suggested that they put their energy into building a coffin. Soon, friends and members of the family, including the five-year-old older brother of the child who was killed, were busily engaged in the task of constructing a coffin. Later, they said they were relieved to have had the opportunity to "do something." Building the coffin became a meaningful way to honor the dead child as well as a means of working through their feelings (see Figure 8-6).

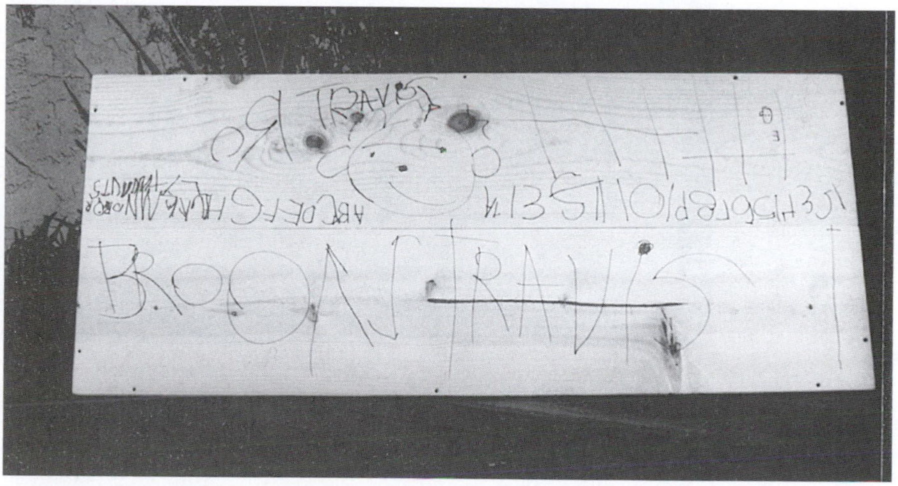

Figure 8-6 *Three Views of a Child's Coffin*
Top View: When the wooden coffin constructed by the family and friends had been completed, the surviving child ran his hand over the surface and voiced his approval but said that it "needs something more." He gathered his marking pens and began to ornament the coffin with drawings. The inscriptions on the outer surface of the lid show the child's interest in identifying by name and by picture the fact that this coffin was built for his brother. His own participation in the making of the coffin is also connoted by the inclusion of his name and by the demonstration of his newly developed skills with the use of numerals and letters.

Figure 8-6 *(continued)*
Detail of Lid Interior: In this close-up of a portion of the interior lid, viewed from left to right, one can see a chrysalis—indicating a transition from caterpillar to butterfly—along with some of the younger brother's favorite television characters: Big Bird, Oscar the Grouch, and Cookie Monster. *Interior of Lid:* In contrast to the matter-of-fact inscriptions placed on the outer surface, the inside of the coffin lid is filled with representations of experiences, events, and objects that brought joy into the life of the child's younger brother. Many of the dead child's favorite activities, such as listening to the stereo with headphones and sitting on a horse at grandma's house, are depicted. The surviving child depicts himself as sad because of his brother's death, yet also as happy because of the shared experiences he enjoyed with his brother. It is interesting to notice the degree of detail and the variety of images placed on the interior of the coffin lid.

Traditional practices are being altered by the fast pace of modern life. Attendance at funerals is down; fewer people "have the time" to take off from work or other activities for a mourning ceremony that seems somehow optional. Yet the desire to participate in such ceremonies persists, as evidenced by the advent of technologies—cyberfunerals and memorial webcasting, for instance—that allow distant mourners to feel they are included in funerals and memorials when they can't be physically present. These new options attest to the strength of the bonds between the living and the dead and the desire to connect with others in bereavement.

Whether these are adequate substitutes for intimate, face-to-face social support provided by conventional services is questioned. What does it say about how we manage our lives when we are too busy to join together with other mourners to acknowledge the passing of a person who was loved and respected as part of our community of friends and family?

There are those who believe that substituting a memorial service for a traditional funeral is lacking in several respects: First, it usually does not take place when feelings about a loss are most intense. Second, members of the family are not as exposed to the fact that death has occurred, nor do they participate as fully as they would in making funeral arrangements and going through the funeralization process. Third, the body is not present at a memorial service, thus removing the therapeutic benefit that comes with fixing the fact of death in the minds of mourners.[96] Alan Wolfelt, director of the Center for Loss and Life Transition, says, "Opponents of viewing [the body] often describe it as unseemly, expensive, undignified, and unnecessary. Yet, seeing and spending time with the body allows for last good-byes and visual confirmation that someone loved is indeed dead."[97]

At Pütz-Roth, an innovative funeral establishment in Bergisch Gladbach, Germany, mourners are encouraged to give themselves sufficient time to grieve after a loved one's death. In a homelike environment, the bereaved family and friends are offered opportunities to spend time with the body over a period of several days before final disposition of the remains (see Figure 8-7). The bodies of the dead are not embalmed but instead are kept in a "cool room." When family and friends come, the body is moved to a sitting room, where the bereaved have access to a kitchen facility for keeping beverages or making snacks. In addition to comfortable seating and soothing artworks, each room has windows that look out on natural surroundings and that also let in the sounds of running water and birdsong. Amid this natural setting, as the body begins to show signs of deterioration, the mourners are subtly encouraged to recognize that all things have a beginning and an ending and that grief involves letting go of the physical aspects of the deceased while finding a "place in the heart for grief."[98]

The social support that accompanies meaningful ritual need not be limited to the period immediately following a death. In traditional Hawaiian culture, for example, the bereaved community holds a memorial feast on the first-year anniversary of the day of death for any person—man, woman, child,

Figure 8-7 Mourners at Pütz-Roth in Bergisch Gladbach, Germany, are given opportunities to sit with their deceased loved ones in a serene, homelike environment that aids their coming to terms with the death. This innovative funeral establishment is a model for helping the bereaved find a place in the heart for grief.

even a newborn baby.[99] For the extended family, this is considered "one of the three greatest occasions, the others being the feasts of rejoicing for the first-born and the marriage festival." Although this memorial occasion is called the *'aha'aina waimaka,* or "feast of tears," because it embraces everyone who had shed tears out of respect and love for the deceased, it is in fact "a happy occasion, a joyful reunion of all who had previously shed tears together." One participant said: "There was drinking, eating, singing and dancing. We had a *lu'au* when all the grief was done."

Further Readings

Lisa Takeuchi Cullen. *Remember Me: A Lively Tour of the New American Way of Death.* New York: HarperCollins, 2006.

Douglas J. Davies. *Death, Ritual, and Belief: The Rhetoric of Funeral Rites,* 2nd ed. London: Continuum, 2002.

Keith Eggener. *Cemeteries: Library of Congress Visual Sourcebooks in Architecture, Design & Engineering.* New York: Norton, 2010.

Mark Harris. *Grave Matters: A Journey Through the Modern Funeral Industry to a Natural Way of Burial.* New York: Scribner, 2007.

William G. Hoy. *Do Funerals Matter? The Purposes and Practices of Death Rituals in Global Perspective.* New York: Routledge, 2013.

Kenneth V. Iserson. *Death to Dust: What Happens to Dead Bodies?* 2nd ed. Tucson: Galen Press, 2001.

Thomas Lynch. *The Undertaking: Life Studies from the Dismal Trade.* New York: Norton, 1997.

Marilyn Yalom. *The American Resting Place: Four Hundred Years of History Through Our Cemeteries and Burial Grounds.* Boston: Houghton Mifflin, 2008.

Additional resources for this chapter can be found at www.mhhe.com/despelder10e

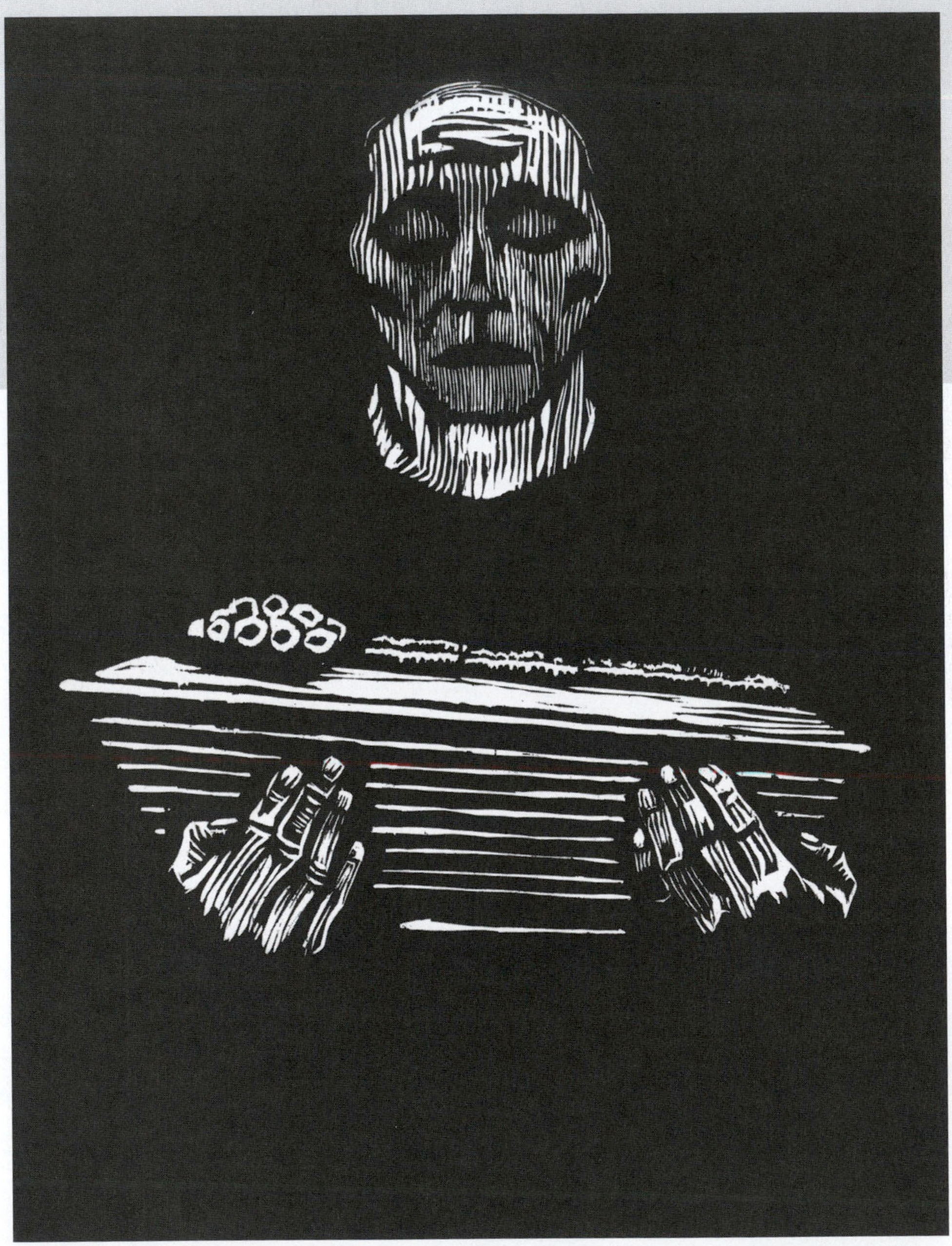

Käthe Kollwitz, Library of Congress

The profound effect of loss on survivors is starkly depicted in this woodcut by German artist Käthe Kollwitz.

CHAPTER 9

Survivors: Understanding the Experience of Loss

We are all survivors. Even if we have not experienced the death of someone close, we are survivors of losses that occur in our lives because of changes and endings. The loss of a job, the ending of a relationship, transitions from one school or neighborhood to another—such losses are sometimes called "little deaths," and, in varying degrees, all can involve grief. Recall some of the little deaths in your own life. Remember the responses they evoked in you? Georges Bataille writes,

> It is a naive opinion that links death closely to sorrow. The tears of the living, which respond to its coming, are themselves far from having a meaning opposite to joy. Far from being sorrowful, the tears are the expression of a keen awareness of shared life grasped in its intimacy.[1]

Grief can be a unifying rather than an alienating human experience. Bereaved individuals often describe themselves as stronger, more competent, more mature, more independent, better able to face other crises of life. "Bereavement challenges people to find a way to continue their lives following loss while dealing with the thoughts, feelings, and imagery that accompany adjustment to the reality that a loved one has died."[2] One bereaved father said, "Living without my son has meant adding another room onto the house in my mind; not so I can shut the door on his death, but so I can move in and out of the experience of my loss."[3]

> Working through our endings allows us to redefine
> our relationships, to surrender what is dead
> and to accept what is alive,
> and to be in the world more fully to face the
> new situation.
>
> Stanley Keleman, *Living Your Dying*

When the Chicago White Sox played their last game at Old Comiskey Park, many fans experienced grief that was a response to losses associated with their memories of attending games at "the world's greatest baseball palace."[4] One fan recalled attending a game at the park with six of his friends before leaving for combat. He said, "Three of those guys eventually were killed in the war, and I guess I'm sayin' goodbye to them. This park was my bond with them and now I'm gonna lose that tie." Another fan said that his fondest memories of his father were associated with ball games they attended together at the stadium. He said, "As a son, I went back to recapture the warmth and contentment I always had felt sitting in those 'special' seats—I went back to visit my father. . . . When Old Comiskey closed that autumn day . . . I lost something. I lost a very real connection to the feelings a six-year-old boy has for his father."

While you are reading about the experiences of loss due to death, it is important to remember that there are many other occasions for loss in life. These losses occur in the "death" of a relationship, a job, a family bond, a home, as well as many other endings. Throughout our life we amass collections of friends and treasured possessions. When we lose something precious to us, we are left with feelings. Whether it is a friend or a treasured object, the loss can be difficult. Some say that it's as if a part of you has gone missing. Having close relationships helps us feel less alone in the world. When we lose someone or something that is valuable to us, we are survivors.[5]

Loss occurs when something is left behind—something we no longer have, whether by choice or circumstances. For example, even the initiator of the end of a relationship is not immune to experiences of grief. One student who had survived both the loss of a marriage because of death and another relationship to a welcomed divorce said, "The death was easier in that it was the end of the relationship and I had great support for my loss. The divorce was much worse as the relationship, changed as it was, the kids, custody arrangements, and running into my ex-partner around town with a new mate remained 'alive.'" As you read about being a survivor, think about the losses you've experienced. You will find that many of the issues discussed apply to other losses in your life as well as to losses from death.

Bereavement, Grief, and Mourning

Knowing the definitions of *bereavement, grief,* and *mourning* can broaden our understanding of what it means to be a survivor. Each of these terms refers to a distinct aspect of the encounter with loss.[6]

Bereavement is defined as the objective event of loss. It comes from a root word meaning "shorn off or torn up"—as if something precious had been suddenly yanked away by a disruptive force. Thus, *bereavement* conveys a sense of deprivation, that some part of ourselves has been stripped away against our will, that we have been robbed. Although bereavement can disrupt our lives, it is appropriate to understand it as an event that is normal in human experience.

Grief is the reaction to loss. There is no one right or universal way to experience and respond to loss.[7] Grief is highly variable. It encompasses thoughts and feelings as well as physical, behavioral, and spiritual responses. These reactions may appear immediately after the bereaved learns of the death, or they may be delayed; they may even be absent. No particular survivor will necessarily experience all of them, nor must all be present.

Mental or cognitive distress in grief may manifest as disbelief, confusion, anxiety, tension, pain, a pervasive sense of disorganization, and depression. Things and events may seem unreal, sensory responses undependable and erratic. Or the bereaved may have heightened perceptual and emotional

© Albert Lee Strickland

The passionate nature of grief is vividly portrayed by the "stone screams" in this detail from the Lamentation *by the fifteenth-century artist Niccolò dell'Arca. The artist, who took his name from* arca, *the Italian word for "tomb," created this powerful work for the church of Santa Maria della Vita in Bologna, Italy. Mary Magdalene, on the right, is shown in horrified disbelief as she looks down at the dead Christ. On the left, Mary of Cleofe (St. Mary Cleophas) gestures, "I cannot look," as she backs away, shrieking.*

sensitivity to people and events. Especially in the early period after a loss, survivors may appear depressed. They may also experience periods of euphoria. The bereaved person may be preoccupied with images of the deceased, experienced in dreams, or may feel a sense of the deceased's presence. Paranormal or psychic experiences in which the dead appear or communicate with the living are not unusual.

Emotions in grief may include sadness, longing, loneliness, sorrow, self-pity, anguish, guilt, and anger, as well as relief. The bereaved may express outrage at the apparent injustice of the loss. Inability to control events may leave the bereaved person feeling frustrated and impotent. If the world could be arranged more to his or her liking, it would not have included this loss. By recognizing that grief can involve a very wide range of feelings, even conflicting ones, we become better able to cope.

Physically, grief may be exhibited in frequent sighing, shortness of breath, tightness of the throat, a feeling of emptiness in the abdomen, muscle weakness, chills, tremors, nervous system hyperactivity, insomnia or other sleep disruptions, and changes in appetite. It may also be manifested physically as "wandering about" or aimless wandering, a condition psychologists refer to as *psychomotor agitation.*

Behaviors associated with grief include crying and "searching" for the deceased. Bereaved people may talk incessantly about the deceased and the circumstances of the death. Or they may talk about everything *but* the loss. At times, survivors may be highly irritable or even hostile. They may withdraw from social interactions, or they may exhibit a kind of frenetic overactivity and general restlessness, as if they didn't know what to do with themselves.

Religious or spiritual beliefs may be reexamined as a person tries to find meaning in a loss. Bereaved people may also turn to such beliefs as a source of consolation and comfort in coping with loss. A significant loss can cause us to question our fundamental assumptions about the world and our place in it, undermining beliefs we had taken for granted. When loss shatters our "assumptive world," a world we expect to be stable and reliable, healing the rifts may require us to relearn how to live in all the dimensions affected by the loss.[8]

Thus, grief involves the whole person and is manifest in a variety of ways: mentally, emotionally, physically, behaviorally, and spiritually. When we limit

Grief Is Its Own Size

The interesting thing about grief, I think, is that it is its own size. It is not the size of you. It is its own size. And grief comes to you. You know what I mean? I've always liked that phrase "He was visited by grief," because that's really what it is. Grief is its own thing. It's not like it's in me and I'm going to deal with it. It's a thing, and you have to be okay with its presence. If you try to ignore it, it will be like a wolf at your door.

Stephen Colbert, talking about deaths
of family members 40 years later

the definition of grief, it reduces our chances of accepting all of the reactions to loss we may experience. Many kinds of thoughts, feelings, behaviors, and so on are a normal part of grief.

Mourning is closely related to grief and is often used as a synonym for it. However, the term *mourning* refers not so much to the *reaction* to loss but rather to the *process* by which a bereaved person integrates the loss into his or her ongoing life. This process is determined at least partly by social and cultural norms for expressing grief. Grief and mourning are the natural pathways toward coping with loss.

Typical mourning behaviors include wearing black armbands or clothes of subdued colors and, if the deceased was a public figure, flying the national flag at half-mast. In earlier times, the *mater dolorosa,* a veiled woman in black clothing, represented the socially prescribed way of mourning. In some cultures widows wear black for years following the death of a spouse as a public way of acknowledging their loss, their changed status, and their grief. Altering one's appearance as a sign of mourning occurs in many societies. Among some Native Americans, a person's hair is shorn as a way of signifying that he or she is mourning. "To cut the hair short is a symbolic and actual sacrifice in memory and respect of the one lost. It is also an immediate sign to visitors that such a loss has taken place. It is a strong visual symbol of grief."[9]

A theme common to mourning behaviors cross-culturally is that the bereaved are different and that this difference diminishes with time. This is seen in customs that involve seclusion of the bereaved. Seclusion forces the survivor to abstain from social relationships. You may have heard someone say, "That family experienced a death and is in mourning; they aren't going out socially." Seclusion serves two purposes during the period of mourning: First, it allows survivors to shelter their grief from the world; second, it prevents survivors from forgetting the deceased too quickly.[10]

In the United States, mourning customs are not as formal or as socially regulated as they once were. Lacking well-defined rules, bereaved people sometimes experience conflict about what constitutes appropriate mourning behavior, as illustrated by the following story: A young girl wrote to an advice columnist about a "sweet sixteen" party that her dying father asked the family to celebrate for her, even if the party should occur on the day of his funeral. The girl said that, although she did not feel like having a party, family members decided to honor the promise to her father. So the party was held two days after her father's death, and it turned out to be a good experience for all who attended. The problem, she wrote, arose when several relatives became horrified because, in their view, enjoying a party was not appropriate during a time of mourning. What advice would you have given to this girl?

"Appropriate" mourning behavior is difficult to define in culturally diverse societies. It is wise to suspend judgments or preconceptions about what is "correct," recognizing instead that many different kinds of mourning behaviors can be appropriate for different people and circumstances.

Tasks of Mourning

This description of the tasks of grief, or tasks of mourning, is associated with J. William Worden. Before going on to discuss several different perspectives on the process of grieving, Worden's description provides a useful overview.

The first task is to *accept the reality* of the loss.[11] "Denying the facts of the loss," says Worden, "can vary in degree from a slight distortion to a full-blown delusion." One signpost in the journey is the survivor's choice of words when talking about the deceased person. Most significant is the transition from present to past tense, from *is* to *was,* as, for example, from "Randy is a wonderful carpenter" to "Randy was a wonderful carpenter."

The second task is to *process the pain* of grief. This includes physical as well as emotional and behavioral pain. As Worden says, "Not everyone experiences the same intensity of pain or feels it in the same way, but it is impossible to lose someone you have been deeply attached to without experiencing some level of pain." In accomplishing this task, humor can lighten the weight of grief, providing respite as survivors cope with loss.

The third task is to *adjust to a world without the deceased.* It takes time to make this adjustment, especially when a relationship was of long duration and exceptional closeness. The many roles fulfilled by the deceased in the bereaved's life may not be fully recognized until after the loss. The changed environment of a "world without the deceased" encompasses physical, emotional, mental, behavioral, and spiritual dimensions of life. This change is symbolized by actions such as rearranging the furniture or changing the place settings at the dining table.

The fourth task is to *find an enduring connection with the deceased in the midst of embarking on a new life.* Accomplishing this task involves the recognition that, although one does not forget or stop loving the deceased person, there are other people one can love.

Therese Rando offers yet another perspective on the tasks of grief, or mourning.[12] She calls these tasks the "Six R's":

1. Recognize the loss (acknowledge and understand the death).
2. React to the separation (experience the pain; feel, identify, accept, and express the reaction to loss; and identify and mourn secondary losses).
3. Recollect and reexperience the deceased and the relationship (review and remember realistically; revive and reexperience the feelings).
4. Relinquish the old attachments to the deceased and the old assumptive world.
5. Readjust to move adaptively into the new world without forgetting the old (develop a new relationship with the deceased, adopt new ways of being in the world, form a new identity).
6. Reinvest (the emotional energy that was invested in the relationship with the deceased needs to be reinvested where it can return some of the emotional gratification that was lost with the death).

Notice that healthy grief involves recognizing the reality of the loss, adjusting to a world without the deceased without forgetting the old, and

> All that day I walked alone. In the afternoon I looked for a church, went into a café, and finally left on the bus, carrying with me more grief and sorrow than I had ever borne before, my body in tatters and my whole life a moan.
>
> Oscar Lewis, *A Death in the Sanchez Family*

finding a connection with the deceased that allows one to discover new ways of being in the world and a new life.

Models of Grief

The notion that there is a consistent pattern to grief and mourning may bring us solace when we are bereaved. Human beings appear to have an affinity for patterns and models that help them make sense of complex phenomena.[13] However, although models may provide a "snapshot" of a dynamic process, they tend to oversimplify and distort reality. With this caveat in mind, it is still worthwhile to examine some of the major efforts to create models for understanding how individuals grieve and mourn. We begin with the perspective of "grief work," associated with Sigmund Freud, and then discuss several models that have been proposed to more accurately or thoroughly capture the nature of grief and how it is experienced, and complete the discussion of models with a review of efforts to arrive at an integrated model of grief.

Working Through Grief

The concept of "working through grief" received major emphasis in Freud's 1917 paper, "Mourning and Melancholia."[14] The central message of the *grief work* perspective is usually understood as the idea that it is necessary for the bereaved to "let go"of the affectional bonds of attachment to the deceased by gradually "working through" these attachments and relinquishing them. John Bowlby's publication of a three-part work in 1969, 1973, and 1982 contributed significantly to the understanding of the nature of our attachments and the process by which they are relinquished.[15]

According to *attachment theory*, when a person recognizes that an object (someone loved) to which he or she is attached no longer exists, grief arises, along with a defensive psychological demand to withdraw libido (energy) from the object. This demand to withdraw energy is likely to meet with resistance, causing the survivor to temporarily turn away from reality in an attempt to cling to the lost object. As the grief work continues, the energy previously invested eventually becomes detached from the object, and the ego (personality) is freed of its attachment so that new relationships can be formed. As Therese Rando points out, according to this model,

> Mourning is initiated by the need to detach from the lost object, and the reason mourning is such a struggle is that the human being never willingly abandons an emotional attachment, and only does so when he or she learns that it is better to relinquish the object than to try to hold on to it now that it is lost.[16]

In "The Symptomatology and Management of Acute Grief" (1944), a landmark article based on the author's involvement as a psychiatrist treating the survivors of a nightclub fire in which 492 people died, Erich Lindemann observed,

> The duration of a grief reaction seems to depend upon the success with which a person does the *grief work,* namely, emancipation from the bondage to the deceased, readjustment to the environment in which the deceased is missing, and the formation of new relationships.[17]

Lindemann added that the main obstacle to successful grief work was the fact that many people "try to avoid the intense distress connected with the grief experience and to avoid the expression of emotion necessary for it."

The grief-work model has been widely accepted as the standard formulation for understanding and helping people accommodate to loss. However, its apparent emphasis on the need for bereaved individuals to break their relational bonds with the deceased has been questioned. Colin Murray Parkes points out, "Each love relationship is unique, and theoretical models which assume that libido can be withdrawn from one object in order to become invested in another similar object, fail to recognize this uniqueness."[18] Parkes says, "The emotion that is the *sine qua non* [essential quality] of grief is *pining or yearning for the lost person* who is intensely missed."[19]

The conventional formulation of the grief-work model seems to imply that everyone must work through grief in a similar fashion to recover from a loss. In reality, however, there may be no universal way of coping with grief. Cross-cultural studies reveal diversity in grief and mourning.[20] Grief is highly individualistic. Furthermore, it is influenced by a variety of situational factors, such as type of death, circumstances of the loss, and so on.

Margaret Stroebe asks a number of pertinent questions about this model: Is it really necessary to work through grief in order to adapt to a loss? Are there occasions when, or persons for whom, grief work is *not* adaptive? Where does one draw the line between healthy and unhealthy grief work? Stroebe points out that, within the range of normal grief reactions, suppression or avoidance of confrontation with memories related to the deceased can be as effective a strategy as "working through" grief.[21]

Nonetheless, the model of "working through grief" advances several worthwhile points to consider in thinking about grief and mourning: First, it describes grief as an *adaptive response* to loss. Second, it states that the reality of the loss must be *confronted and accepted.* Third, it acknowledges that grieving is an *active process that occurs over time.* Let's look at how these points are dealt with in other models of grief.

Continuing Bonds with the Deceased

The idea that healthy grief means relinquishing affectional ties with the deceased is giving way to a perspective that more accurately describes the range of behaviors and emotions that human beings experience when experiencing loss. In this view, rather than severing ties, the bereaved person acknowledges

Edward V. Gillon, Jr.

© Albert Lee Strickland

Contemporary memorial stories often reflect a similar emphasis on the unending love felt by survivors for the deceased and on the faith that bonds forged during a person's lifetime can remain strong despite death.

The nineteenth-century Romantic view of death is reflected in the Lawson memorial, which characterizes both the devotion of the bereaved to the deceased and the belief that loving relationships continue beyond the mortal framework of the human life span.

the loss and yet maintains an enduring connection with the deceased. In other words, the deceased loved one is integrated into the bereaved person's ongoing life so the relationship is sustained beyond death. This is called "continuing bonds," and it occurs in various ways. Some cultures create continuing bonds in the context of rituals that locate the deceased in the realm of beloved ancestors. Recall, for example, African traditions that celebrate relationships with the "living-dead" or the Japanese custom of maintaining a household shrine for ancestors. Other cultures and individuals define such bonds as keeping a special place for the deceased in one's heart and mind.[22] Whatever the cultural context, "an adaptive response to loss will generally balance attention to the challenges of life with a flexible but ongoing connection to the deceased."[23]

Dennis Klass observes that bereaved parents often find solace by maintaining bonds with their children who died.[24] "Memory," Klass says, "binds family and communities together." Through religious beliefs and objects that link the parents with memories of the child, a kind of immortality is granted to the child in the lives of surviving family members. Klass points out that the death of a child challenges parents' worldviews—that is, their basic assumptions about how the universe functions and their place in the world. Making sense of such a loss is facilitated by maintaining an "inner representation" of the dead child that allows for continuing interactions so that the significance of the child's life is not forgotten or diminished.[25] Work done by Phyllis Silverman, Steven Nickman, and J. William Worden supports the notion that children likewise maintain connections with deceased parents through memories and linking objects (discussed in Chapter 8).[26]

Therese Rando says, "The development of a healthy new relationship with the deceased is a crucial part of the mourning process when the person lost has been integral to the mourner's life."[27] Whether maintaining continuing bonds with the deceased reflects a healthy adjustment to loss depends on two criteria: First, does the mourner truly recognize that the person is dead and understand the implications of the death? Second, is the mourner moving adaptively into his or her new life?[28]

Klass states that continuing bonds are collectively held. We see this when people visit cemeteries. "The bonds with the individual dead person are thus interwoven with the bonds to the other dead buried there, as well as to the other living people."[29] In comments about the social bond between human beings, Lyn Lofland suggests the following are among the "threads of connectedness" or "ties that bind" us to one another:

> We are linked to others by the *roles* we play, by the *help* we receive, by the wider *network* of others made available to us, by the *selves* others create and sustain, by the comforting *myths* they allow us, by the *reality* they validate for us, and by the *futures* they make possible.[30]

Telling the "Story": Narrative Reconstruction

When someone we love dies, we face the prospect of revising and re-forming our life story. John Kelly suggests that by contemplating grieving in terms of a narrative, or story, we cope with loss by re-forming our story so that we integrate the deceased into our lives in a new way and adjust our relationships in ways that restore wholeness.[31] In the context of grief, narrative reconstruction has to do with how an individual weaves a story about transitions and life events into an interpretation of meaning and possibility. Jerome Bruner says stories, or narratives, are "a version of reality" that reflect how we organize our experience and our memory of human happenings.[32]

Through narrative, the story of grief can be told without the constraint of having to conform to a particular model of how it should be or what it should feel like or what should be thought. In a sense, it is the "real" story. In telling and retelling it, the story gradually reveals the dimensions of grief in ways that allow survivors to carry on despite loss. Carolyn Ellis describes how telling the story of her brother's death in an airplane crash not only gives meaning to the loss but also helps in "reconstructing" her life:

> Each writing and reading of my text has permitted me to relive my brother's death from an aesthetic distance, a place that allows me to experience the experience but with an awareness that I am not actually again *in* this situation, and thus I muster the courage to continue grieving.[33]

In telling the story of loss, Ellis says, "We can make true a plot in which we play the part of, and become in the playing, actual 'survivors.'"

Mary Anne Sedney and her colleagues note that "every death creates a story, or a set of stories, to tell."[34] Coping with grief involves telling the story. Conversing with others, we not only gain appreciation of the deceased's life but also come to a revised assessment of our own life. "Through storytelling, the diverse meanings of life experience and existence are woven into a whole."[35]

One way we "keep" those we have lost to death is to talk about them with family, friends, and neighbors who knew them. Describing how this process occurred with the death of a former girlfriend, Tony Walter says, "This was not social support for an intrinsically personal grief process, but an intrinsically social *process* in which we negotiated and re-negotiated who Corina was, how she had died, and what she had meant to us."[36] Sharing the story of a loss provides emotional relief, promotes the search for meaning, and brings people together in support of one another. Kathleen Gilbert says, "We need to create stories to make order of disorder and to find meaning in the meaningless."[37] This is all part of the "reworking of the life narrative."[38] "Giving grief voice" by telling our stories about the dead and listening to the stories others tell helps us move on with our lives without leaving our loved ones behind.[39]

The Dual Process Model of Coping

One of the most important recent contributions to understanding grief is the dual process model of coping with bereavement proposed by Margaret Stroebe and Henk Schut.[40] According to the dual process model, the bereaved person experiences and expresses both *loss-oriented* and *restoration-oriented* coping behaviors. Depending on individual as well as cultural characteristics, each of these behaviors occurs in varying proportions. There is "oscillation," movement back and forth, between these aspects of coping.

Examples of loss-oriented coping include yearning for the deceased, looking at old photographs, crying about the death, and so on. Restoration-oriented coping includes mastering tasks that had been taken care of by the deceased (such as cooking or handling the finances), dealing with arrangements for reorganizing one's life (such as selling the house or moving to another area), developing a new identity (such as changing status from spouse to widower or from parent to parent of deceased child), and so on.

Thus, on the one hand, loss-oriented coping involves "concentrating on, dealing with, [or] processing some aspect of the loss experience." Restoration-oriented coping, on the other hand, involves making the changes that are required to cope with the "secondary consequences" of loss—all those aspects of the bereaved's life that require rearrangement in the wake of the loss.

Central to this model is the understanding that grief is a dynamic process. It involves movement—oscillation or alternation—between loss-oriented and restoration-oriented coping. It avoids getting stuck in an either-or framework whereby the bereaved must either "let go" of the deceased or "hold on" to memories. In coping with loss, the bereaved at times will be actively confronting the loss; at other times, he or she will avoid troubling memories, be distracted, or seek relief by turning attention to other things. Over time, movement between these ways of coping leads to adjustment to the loss.

The Two-Track Model of Bereavement

In this model, developed by Simon Shimshon Rubin, the loss process is conceptualized along two distinct but interactive tracks that attend to aspects of the loss (see Table 9-1).[41] Track I is concerned with biopsychosocial functioning in the wake of the loss. Track II focuses on the bereaved's ongoing or continuing relationship to the deceased.

From this perspective, in the first track loss is examined along a range of dimensions of *functioning,* where the terms *recovery, growth, continuing difficulties,* or *inadequate adaptation* may apply. The second track, the *continuing relationship to the deceased,* considers the nature of transforming that relationship, which typically involves both an acceptance of the death and a transformed connection with the deceased. As time passes, bereaved individuals are likely to experience changes in their perspective on themselves and on the nature of their relational bond to the deceased. For example, a widow's relationship to her young husband who died at twenty-five will probably have different meanings across her life trajectory of possibly an additional sixty years.

Rubin and his colleagues point out that, while relationship to another person is what initiates grief and the loss response, professionals as well as lay people tend to respond as if the relationship with the deceased is neither central or of particular significance.[42] However, an unbalanced emphasis on Track I, the biopsychosocial elements of bereavement, can miss an important aspect of adaptation to loss. The two-track model calls for a coordinated, balanced view of bereavement.

TABLE 9-1 *The Two-Track Model of Bereavement: A Multidimensional View*

Track I: General Biopsychosocial Functioning	Track II: Ongoing Relationship to the Deceased
• Anxiety • Depressive affect and cognitions • Somatic (physical) and health concerns • Behaviors and symptoms associated with psychiatric problems • Posttraumatic stress and other emotional difficulties • Quality of family relationships • Quality of other interpersonal relationships • Self-esteem and self-worth • Meaning structure in life • Investment in work • Investment in life tasks	• Narrative construction of the relationship • Imagery and memory • Emotional distance • Positive affect vis-à-vis deceased • Negative affect vis-à-vis deceased • Preoccupation with the loss and the lost • Idealization • Conflict and problems with the deceased • Presence of various elements of loss process (shock, searching, disorganization and reorganization) • Impact of memories on self-perception • Memorialization and transformation of the loss experience and the relationship with the deceased

Rubin explains that four main points serve to orient the observer to the process of grief: First, the loss of a close relationship usually has a major impact on the bereaved. Fixed patterns of functioning undergo change in intrapersonal, behavioral, biological, and interpersonal areas. When the initial response to loss has subsided, we would expect a return to adaptive functioning, although not necessarily identical to the states prior to the loss. Second, the initial challenge of response to loss requires the bereaved to accept the reality that death has occurred. Rubin says, "As the loss process unfolds, the narrowing of the lived relationship to the deceased is characterized by its opposite, an intensive psychological focus on the relationship and the deceased." Third, as time passes, the acuteness of the response to loss subsides. "Some of the changes that buffeted the bereaved will have disappeared and others will recede with time." Fourth, after a lapse of a significant amount of time (for some persons and for some losses, measured in weeks; for others, measured in years), the bereaved will achieve a new level of organization in his or her life. With this new organization, "It is now possible to look for a balance along the dimension of functioning as well as along that of relationship to the deceased." Rubin and colleagues say, "The management of one's life following the loss of a loved one is intimately associated with how the ongoing relationship with the complex of memories, thoughts, emotions, and needs [is] associated with the person who has died."[43]

Toward an Integrated Model of Grief

Colin Murray Parkes points to three main influences on a person's course of grieving:[44]

1. The urge to look back, cry, and search for what is lost
2. The urge to look forward, explore the world that emerges out of the loss, and discover what can be carried forward from the past into the future
3. The social and cultural pressures that influence how the first two urges are inhibited or expressed

It has been suggested that the major theorists should compare their theories to identify commonalities and differences with the aim of reaching some agreement on a professional vocabulary of grief. Hannelore Wass points out, "An integrated theory of grief is a pipe dream," but adds, "We all have to dream, don't we?"[45]

We know that an integrated understanding of grief must look beyond the individual and encompass the family system as well as the wider culture. Janice Nadeau says, "Individual grief is profoundly shaped by the family context in which it occurs, and the grief of an individual has profound effects on the family."[46] Nancy Moos says, "Families and family grief processes are inextricably linked to individual grief and recovery."[47] The family and its patterns of interaction are often crucial determinants of whether grief is dealt with in a healthy or a dysfunctional manner.

Although there is no standard way of coping with loss, all of the models discussed here represent contributions to a more complex and refined understanding of grief and mourning.[48] In thinking about the *personal meaning* of a loss, Stephen Fleming and Paul Robinson observe,

> You do not find meaning in *death,* you find meaning in the *life* that was lived. Central to the struggle to find meaning in the life that was lived is the notion of the deceased's legacy. The legacy is the appreciation of how knowing and loving the deceased has irrevocably changed the survivor, thus realizing the transition from losing what one has to having what one has lost.[49]

The Experience of Grief

People often ask, What is normal grief? How long should a person actively be grieving? If the bereaved is not "over" the loss by a certain time, does it mean he or she is grieving or mourning inappropriately? Such questions require us to consider the circumstances of a death as well as other factors that influence a person's experience. Individuals who are newly bereaved may be alarmed by the flood of reactions they experience. "Grief, at times, may be experienced as frightening, overwhelming, even 'crazy-making.'"[50] It can be helpful to have an understanding about how grief is likely to be expressed over time.

Mental Versus Emotional Responses

When there is a substantial difference between a survivor's emotional and mental responses to death, and the survivor believes only one response can be right, the result is conflict. To expect the head and the heart to react exactly the same to loss is unrealistic; disparity between thoughts and feelings is likely. In grief, many different emotions will be felt, and many different thoughts will arise. By allowing them all and not judging the rightness and wrongness of particular emotions or thoughts, a bereaved person is more likely to experience grief as healing.

Survivors may have rigid rules about emotions that can be expressed in grief—such as where and when it is acceptable to be angry or to be open to the pain and release an intense outburst of sadness. Permission to experience and express feelings is of key importance. "How can I be mad at someone for dying?" Yet, anger may indeed be present in grief. Consider the example of someone who died by suicide or as a result of driving while intoxicated. Of course, survivors may be angry even if the death was seemingly unavoidable and beyond the victim's control. One young mother told of walking past a photograph of her recently deceased child and noticing, amid her grief and pain, a small voice within blurting out, "Brat! How could you die and leave me as you did!" How could she be angry at her child for dying? We might be tempted to think this mother's behavior inappropriate. Yet, survivors need to give themselves permission to experience their feelings, perhaps to feel anger at the person for having died and anger at themselves for not having been able to prevent the death. As Ira Byock observes, "Anger is a way of holding sadness at bay."[51]

The Course of Grief

To describe the course of grief as a series of phases seems to suggest a linear progression from the first stage through the second and so on, until the process has been completed. Such a scenario might be comforting to someone who would like to have a ready-made outline for evaluating the journey after loss. We need to be cautious about applying such schemata to the experience of a particular survivor. The different phases of grief "may overlap, may be of varying and unpredictable duration, occur in any order, may be present simultaneously, and may disappear or reappear at random."[52]

In the first hours or days following a death, grief usually manifests in shock and numbness, feelings of being stunned as well as of feelings of disbelief. There may be an expression of denial—"No! This can't be true!"—especially if the death was sudden and unexpected. Even when a death is anticipated, grief is not necessarily diminished when the loss becomes real.

During the initial period of grief, the sense of confusion and disorganization can be overwhelming, as if the bereaved person, motionless and helpless, is stranded in the middle of a fast-flowing stream while water and debris rush about him or her. Bewildered by the shock of the loss, a bereaved individual may be vulnerable and seek protection by withdrawing. Another survivor might process the death differently, wading into the water. The early period of grief is set against the requirement for survivors to attend to decisions and activities related to disposition of the deceased's body. This is normally a time when the bereaved are occupied with arranging for funeral services, as well as starting to sort out the deceased's personal and family affairs. Engaging in

Edward C. Clark, Life Magazine, © Time Inc.

Tears stream down the face of accordion player Graham Jackson as the body of President Franklin Delano Roosevelt is carried to the train at Warm Springs, Georgia, the day after his death—a poignant example of how bereaved persons express their loss in public as well as private.

such activities within the context of community can help promote acceptance of the reality of the death and allow survivors to begin moving beyond the acute period of grief. As relatives and friends gather to support one another, the funeral can be a focal point that helps reintegrate distraught and disoriented grievers after the disruption caused by death.[53]

In its middle period, grief is characterized by anxiety, apathy, and pining for the deceased. Despair is likely to be felt, as "feelings of disbelief give way to the realization that there will be no reprieve and that the reality is neither a horrible hoax nor a bad dream."[54] Bereaved individuals may repeatedly go over the events surrounding the loss, wishing to undo the calamity and make everything as it was before. Pangs of grief are felt as the bereaved person deeply experiences the pain of separation and the intense yearning for the one who died.

During this phase, which can last some time, survivors often experience volatile emotions, which suggests the image of a volcano that at times gives off steam and at other times appears relatively dormant. Rage and resentment may be felt and expressed toward persons or institutions that might have somehow prevented the death "if only things had been different." Anger may be directed toward the deceased loved one whose "abandonment" causes such pain, as well as toward God ("How could you let this happen?") or about the situation itself ("How could this happen to me?"). Hostile or negative feelings may in turn give rise to guilt.

The predominant emotion during the middle period of grief is likely to be sadness accompanied by longing and loneliness as various needs and dependencies that had been satisfied by the deceased become painfully apparent. Time is filled with if-onlys and what-ifs as the bereaved comes to terms with the reality: The loved one is dead. Starting to accept the unwelcome fact that the loss is real and cannot be changed, the bereaved person is likely to review and sort through all the bits of interaction that created his or her relationship with the deceased. This can involve an intense reexperiencing of the history of the relationship. Over a period of weeks or months, the process goes on, as the bonds of the relationship that *was* are gradually undone and a new relationship with the deceased is created as part of the survivor's ongoing life.

This is usually a painful time. Yet, it is a time when the bereaved may not have much social support from relatives and friends, who were more present during the earlier period. After the funeral, the bereaved may be left alone with his or her grief. When acting to comfort a grieving person, it's helpful to remember that social support after the acute phase can facilitate opportunities for the bereaved to talk about the loss and express grief. A counselor offers the advice that a supportive person should not ask, "How are you doing?" unless there is at least forty-five minutes to listen to the answer. Be prepared to hear, "I'm okay," as a preface to a lengthy description of painful issues.

There is no predetermined timetable in grief. In restoring one's well-being, however, the last phase of "active" grief is marked by a sense of resolution, recovery, reintegration, and transformation as the bereaved person moves forward with a life that is irrevocably changed but worth living. Physical and mental balance is reestablished. The turmoil of grief subsides; it no longer dominates every waking hour. This is not to say that sadness goes away completely; rather, it gradually recedes into the background. Grief is no longer "heavy"; a weight has been lifted. At times, adapting to loss may feel like a betrayal of the deceased loved one, but it is healthy to once again engage life and become oriented toward the future.

The impact of change on recently bereaved people may affect virtually every detail of life: The family unit is different; social realities are no longer the same; legal and financial matters require attention. Bereaved people face the question, How can I make the necessary adjustment in each of these areas? Survivors are sometimes urged to take a hand in the practical management of their everyday affairs soon after bereavement, but it can be useful to limit, insofar as possible, the number of changes made, especially in the first few months after loss.

Anniversaries, birthdays, and other reminders are likely to stimulate active grieving from time to time. New losses may reactivate grief for an earlier loss. Adjusting to loss doesn't mean forgetting or minimizing the significance of the lost relationship. It is not "getting over the grief" in some absolute or final sense but rather a process of "living with the loss."

When you recall a loss in your life, you may remember the emotions, thoughts, physical reactions, and behaviors associated with grief. Perhaps all these reactions were happening at once. Part of you may have been in shock while another part was calm. Distinguishing the waypoints of grief can help us better comprehend "how grief works." Even so, the experience itself resembles a series of dance steps more than it does a cross-country walk.

The Duration of Grief

How long does grief last? Six months? A year? People sometimes assume that normal grief lasts only a short time. This assumption can place unrealistic expectations on a bereaved person. What happens when grief appears to continue beyond some arbitrarily defined limit? Counselors, psychotherapists, and other professionals who work with people who are grieving usually endorse the axiom that grief has no absolute end point or timetable.

When signs of painful and deeply felt grief persist, along with other disturbances, this could be an indication of unhealthy and dysfunctional grief. This may be the case, for example, when an individual exhibits symptoms of depression, especially if compounded by other emotional problems, substance abuse, or suicidal thoughts. Help is warranted when unhealthy grieving puts bereaved individuals at risk. In general, however, a cautious approach is preferred before labeling certain manifestations of grief "prolonged" or "abnormal."[55]

The onset of intense grief years after a loss may be mistaken as abnormal when it is actually a normal response to a new loss and, therefore, a time-appropriate response rather than a delayed one.[56] This is illustrated in the experience of a young woman who reported intense grief over the death of her husband, though he had died nearly four years earlier. Bewildered, she said, "I don't understand myself; it feels almost like the day he died." In conversation with a counselor, she discovered the event that triggered her pain: Within a few days, the couple's seven-year-old daughter would be celebrating her first communion. Although happily remarried, successfully back to work, and obviously adjusting to her loss, this devoutly religious woman grieved the absence of her child's father from a celebration that had been discussed and anticipated since the child's birth.

Individuals may also experience a resurfacing of grief stimulated by a public death. Researchers call this a "ripple effect." For example, in the week following the highly publicized death of Diana, Princess of Wales, South Australia's largest cemetery reported having more visitors than on Mother's Day, traditionally the busiest visitation day of the year.[57] Individual grief was called forth by the death of a public figure.

Survivors may experience a recurrence of grief for a significant loss at various times throughout their lives when something brings freshly to mind the recognition that what once was is no more. For example, a person who was bereaved as a child by a parent's death may grieve that death anew many years later when his or her own child is born. A study of bereaved spouses found that the effects of loss are often sustained over an extended period of time that is more appropriately termed a "life transition" than a "life crisis," with survivors grieving in some fashion for the rest of their lives.[58]

Perhaps in your own life you recognize a recurrence of grief for earlier losses. For example, people often grieve the loss of childhood and its special experiences. A woman mentioned visiting her parents after some years of living on her own; one day, while poking around in the attic, her mother opened a trunk and pulled out a collection of dolls that had belonged to the daughter when she was a child. Seeing the dolls evoked grief for the childhood that had ended years earlier. She said, "I looked at those dolls and their tiny clothes, and I got in touch with the loss of that time in my life when my mother had made clothes for my dolls and taken care of me. There I was, sitting in the attic, just bawling." Perhaps you have experienced a similar situation? Some event, picture, place, song, or other stimulus provokes grief related to something or someone no longer present. Stephen Fleming and Paul Robinson point out that the meaning of loss is negotiated and renegotiated over time; in effect, moving from a "going on" to an "ongoing" perspective of the loss.[59]

Complications of Grief

Therese Rando lists the following as examples of situations that heighten the risk of what she termed *complicated mourning*:[60]

1. Sudden and unanticipated death, especially when it is traumatic, violent, mutilating, or random
2. Death from an overly lengthy illness
3. Death of a child

4. The bereaved's perception that the death was somehow preventable
5. A relationship between the bereaved and the deceased that was markedly angry or ambivalent, or markedly dependent
6. The bereaved's prior or concurrent mental health problems or unaccommodated losses and stresses
7. The bereaved's perceived lack of social support

These are examples of situations that might hamper the bereaved's ability to adapt to life without the deceased. They affect the journey through grief.

Robert Hansson and Margaret Stroebe write, "It is important to remember that bereavement is a normal, emotional reaction to the loss of a loved person, not a psychiatric disorder, even though in some cases it is associated with higher risks of intense symptomatology."[61] Determining whether grief is complicated is not as simple as picking up a checklist and marking off the appropriate items. Rando says, "What may be an appropriate response in one circumstance for an individual mourner may be a highly pathological response for a different mourner in other circumstances." In reviewing the circumstances that may complicate grief, notice that complicating circumstances alone do not justify labeling a person's grief "abnormal" or "pathological." For example, a parent who experiences the death of his or her child due to random violence may be confronted by a mode of bereavement that is inherently *complicated,* but this fact alone does not lead us to conclude that the parent's grief will be *dysfunctional.*

Rando says that all forms of complicated grief involve attempts to do two things: (1) to deny, repress, or avoid aspects of the loss, its pain, and the full realization of its implications for the mourner; and (2) to hold onto, and avoid relinquishing, the lost loved one. When grief is suppressed, and emotional engagement with the loss is absent or diminished, or when grief is so boundless that it becomes totally overwhelming, it sets the stage for a poor adjustment. According to Rando, the prevalence of complicated grief is increasing due to a variety of social processes, including urbanization, secularization, and deritualization, as well as violence, availability of guns, social alienation, substance abuse, and a general sense of hopelessness.[62]

Attachment has a role in complicated grief. According to John Bowlby and Mary Ainsworth, during the early years of life, children develop what is called an *internal working model* of primary attachment relationships. This model, or attachment style, can be of various types, such as avoidant attachment, secure attachment, and anxious-ambivalent attachment. The working model developed by the child functions as a basic pattern for viewing the world and guides future relationships. The quality of a person's attachment style has significant implications for how he or she grieves. Having a history of insecure or anxious attachment styles, especially when replicated in the mourner-decedent relationship, puts grievers at risk for complicated bereavement reactions.[63]

In their article "Mourning and Meaning," Robert Neimeyer, Holly Prigerson, and Betty Davies say that complicated grief can be viewed as "the inability to reconstruct a meaningful personal reality" and is "an outcome to which

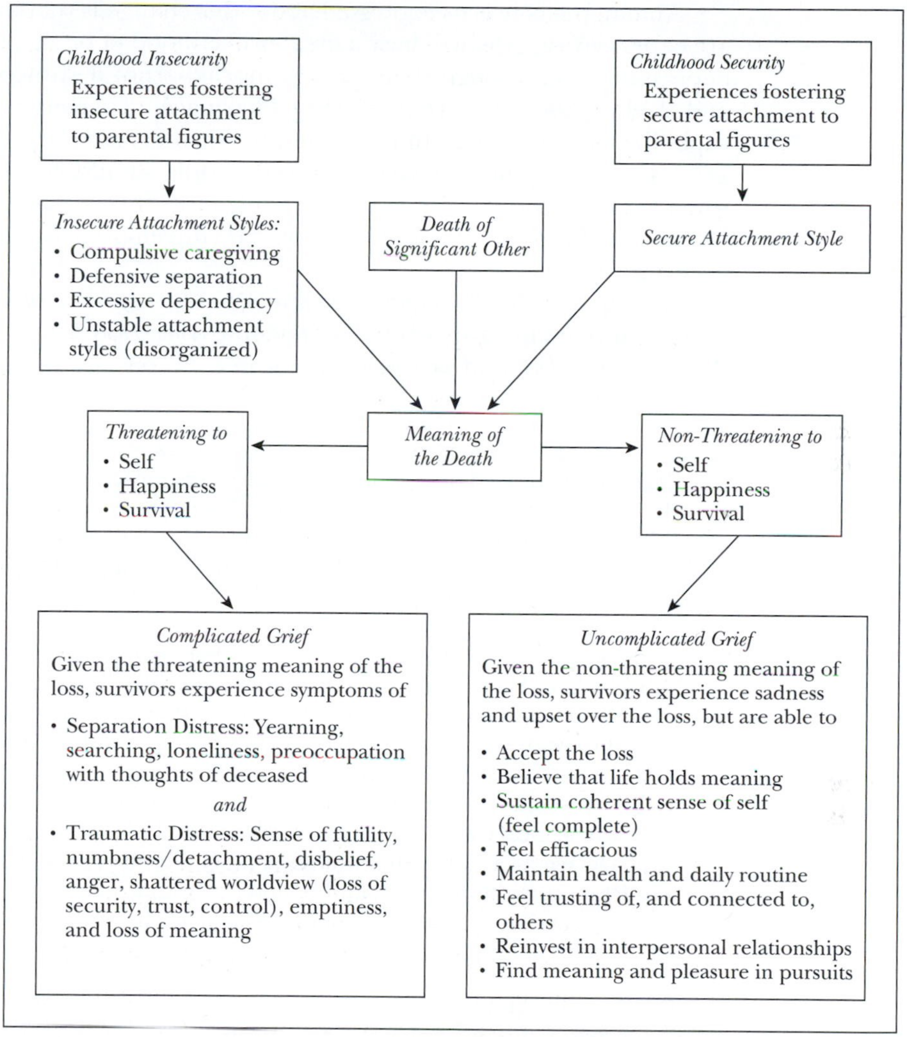

Figure 9-1 *Pathways to Complicated Grief and Uncomplicated Grief*

individuals with insecure working models of self and relationships are especially vulnerable" (see Figure 9-1).[64]

Recently, a new edition of the *Diagnostic and Statistical Manual of Mental Disorders (DSM-5),* a reference used by mental health professionals, was published in the United States. In it, a change was made from the previous edition (*DSM-4*). That edition included a so-called bereavement exclusion, which instructed that a diagnosis of depression or adjustment disorder should *not* be made in the immediate aftermath of a significant death. This "exclusion" was deleted from the new *DSM-5*. The argument for removal was "that it does not make sense to exclude bereavement *if the symptoms fit the criteria* for depression while other stressors, such as divorce or job loss, are not excluded."[65]

Among the concerns expressed about this change is that individuals who are experiencing grief will have a greater likelihood of being prescribed anti-depressants even though their grief is "normal," not dysfunctional. Sadness and "feeling down" is part of grieving. Pharmaceutical companies may try to capitalize on this change in the *DSM-5* by "medicalizing" or "pathologizing" grief, promoting the idea that bereaved people should consult a physician when they are coping with a loss. The lesson in this is that people need to be careful of treating loss and its accompanying emotions as if medication is necessary.

In response to the change in the DSM-5, a group of internationally renowned thanatologists wrote a statement, *When Does A Broken Heart Become A Mental Disorder?*, and provided the answer, "Rarely, if ever." The statement pointed out:

> Grief is not the same experience as major depressive disorder. It is not an illness to be treated or cured. It is a healthy response to a painful reality that one's world is forever altered and will never be the same. Absorbing this loss, and adapting to all the changes it unleashes, has its own unique course for every person and will not be stilled or stopped by quick fixes or simple solutions. Death is a life-altering event, but grief is not a pathological condition.
>
> There is a strong likelihood that newly bereaved people will qualify for a diagnosis of Major Depressive Disorder just two weeks after a death even though their reactions are normal. Antidepressants have not been shown to be helpful with grief-related depressive symptoms, and there is accumulating evidence of long-term negative effects of being on antidepressants. We need to ask why psychiatry is pathologizing grief and therefore making inappropriate pharmacological treatment easier. And we should not overlook the self-interest of pharmaceutical companies who see a new and substantial market for antidepressants, currently a multi-billion dollar industry.
>
> The caution here? Be wary of physicians or other medical professionals who rush to prescribe anti depressants to address your grief.[66]

Phyllis Silverman points out that there can be tension "between those who focus on grieving behavior as symptoms of psychiatric problems and those who see mourning as an expected life-cycle transition, the pain that is to be expected under the circumstances."[67] It appears to be the case that normal and complicated (or prolonged) grief fall along different ends of the same continuum.[68] As Margaret Stroebe and Henk Schut comment, "bereavement is a normal life event with—sometimes—complicated reactions."[69]

The Mortality of Bereavement

During the fifteenth century, grief was a legal cause of death that could be listed on death certificates. The death of a loved one involves many concurrent changes, or *secondary losses,* that add to the bereaved's vulnerability. Can a grieving person really die of a "broken heart"?[70] What determines the outcome is not so much stress itself as the person's ability to cope with it. Stephen Oppenheimer, a neurologist, says, "It's an old wives' tale that a person can die of a broken heart. . . . But, many old wives' tales are true."[71] Stress can throw the heart into an irregular and fatal heartbeat. Oppenheimer studies the brain's insular cortex, an area of the nervous system that controls breathing and heartbeat and that links up with the limbic system, which deals with anger, fear, sadness, and other emotions. He says that damage to the insular cortex may render a person susceptible to a chaotic heartbeat called ventricular fibrillation, leading to cardiac arrest and, thus, a "broken heart."

In reviewing the "broken heart" phenomenon, Margaret Stroebe concludes that "both the direct consequences of loss of a loved one, or a broken heart, and secondary effects, or the stress of bereavement, are responsible for the bereavement-mortality relationship."[72] She adds, "When extreme grief coincides with severe life stresses during bereavement, the risk to life is likely to be greatest of all."

The stress of bereavement appears to aggravate physical conditions that may have been inactive, causing symptoms to appear or develop more rapidly. An early study of a small community in Wales found that the death rate among bereaved individuals during the first year of bereavement was nearly seven times that of the general population.[73] Another study found a diminished immune response among widowers during the first months following bereavement.[74] Other studies have shown significant depression of lymphocyte (T-cell) function following bereavement.[75]

George Engel investigated the possible relationship between stress and sudden death.[76] After compiling a number of case reports, Engel classified stressful situations into eight categories, four of which can be considered as either a direct or an indirect component of grief and mourning: (1) the impact of the death of a close person, (2) the stress of acute grief, (3) the stress that occurs with mourning, and (4) the loss of status or self-esteem following bereavement.

At first glance, loss of self-esteem may not seem especially relevant. However, guilt tends to lower self-esteem, and guilt is a common experience in grief. Consider the bereaved person who says, "If only I had tried harder or done something differently, my loved one might not have died." The changed circumstances of daily life may also tend to diminish a survivor's self-esteem. A widower who used to attend social functions with his spouse may now be left off the guest list; a widow may decline social events that she believes are for "couples only." Tighter finances may lower self-esteem. Loss of status that had been enjoyed due to a deceased mate's professional or community standing can have a similar effect.

There is intriguing evidence that hints of the possibility that the reaction to loss can contribute to illness and even death. But no direct cause-and-effect link has been established between bereavement and onset of disease. Colin Murray Parkes says, "The fact that bereavement may be followed by death from heart disease does not prove that grief itself is a cause of death."[77]

Variables Influencing Grief

Just as no two individuals are exactly alike, no two experiences of grief are exactly alike. There may be similarities, but the circumstances of death, the personality and social roles of the bereaved, the relationship with the deceased—these are among the factors that influence grief and mourning and make each experience of grief unique. These factors offer clues about why some deaths are especially devastating to survivors. In thinking about some of the variables that influence a survivor's grief, the following are some fundamental questions: Who died? How did the death occur? What was the quality of the survivor's relationship to the deceased? Is there any "unfinished business"? What prior losses has the survivor experienced? Were there complicating factors about the death? Was the loss socially sanctioned? (See "Social Support and Disenfranchised Grief" later in this chapter.) Are there financial and legal matters that remain to be dealt with in the wake of the death? Each of these questions provokes further investigation.

Survivor's Model of the World

A survivor's response to loss is conditioned by his or her model of the world—that is, by his or her perception of reality and assumptions about how the world works. How a person copes with loss—the death of a mate, another family member, or a close friend—tends to be consistent with how that individual copes with everyday stresses and small losses of daily living. In considering how a person's model of the world applies to bereavement, Edgar Jackson identified four factors that are especially important: personality, social roles, perception of the deceased's importance, and values.[78]

Personality

Self-concept is an important determinant of how a person responds to death. The person with an immature or dependent personality is vulnerable to the loss of someone in whom much emotional capital has been invested.

> The upper middles would probably drink themselves silly at the funeral. Although a few years ago this would have been frowned on. When my husband in the sixties announced that he intended to leave £200 in his will for a booze-up for his friends, his lawyer talked him out of it, saying it was in bad taste and would upset people. The same year his grandmother died, and after the funeral, recovering from the innate vulgarity of the cremation service when the gramophone record stuck on 'Abi-abi-abi-abi-de with me', the whole family trooped home and discovered some crates of Australian burgundy under the stairs. A rip-roaring party ensued and soon a lower middle busybody who lived next door came bustling over to see if anything was wrong. Whereupon my father-in-law, holding a glass and seeing her coming up the path, uttered the immortal line: 'Who is this intruding on our grief?'
>
> Jilly Cooper, *Class*

Perhaps in an attempt to compensate for feelings of inadequacy, the dependent personality has projected part of his or her identity onto another person. With the death of that person, more of the survivor's projected self is involved in the loss. In contrast, the person with greater self-esteem and stronger self-concept is not as prone to such overcompensation. Thus, grief is quite likely to be less devastating. Similarly, people who report a high degree of purpose in life tend to cope more effectively with bereavement than do people who report a low purpose in life.[79]

Cultural Context and Social Roles

Grief is shaped by social context.[80] It is influenced by norms prescribing the emotions appropriate within a culture for a given situation. To some extent, the human response to loss is culturally learned. This is apparent in differences sometimes observed between bereaved males and females in various cultural settings. Wolfgang and Margaret Stroebe point out:

> Grief is channeled in all cultures along specified lines [and] there are substantial differences in the rules laid down by cultures as to how long the deceased should be grieved over and how long mourning should last. . . . What is sanctioned or prohibited in one culture may differ dramatically from what is or is not permitted in another.[81]

Daniel Callahan says, "Every great culture has had a characteristic view of death, ordinarily accompanied by public rituals, customary practices, and time-honored patterns of communal grief."[82]

In examining bereavement and loss in two Muslim communities—one in Egypt, the other in Bali—Unni Wikan describes how culture is a potent shaper and organizer of the way people respond to loss.[83] Although both societies share a common religious heritage, one encourages mourners to express their sorrow in wails and lamentations, whereas the other encourages mourners to contain their sorrow and maintain a quiet and essentially cheerful countenance. Grief is embedded in a web of complex relationships.[84]

The question is sometimes asked, Are there "universals" in grief—that is, do people in all cultures have essentially the same response to loss in terms of their grief? Although this question is not completely resolved, it is clear that the cultural environment is an important factor in shaping a person's grief and mourning. It may be that people do not "naturally" grieve any more than they "naturally" laugh or cry.[85] Stephen Connor says, "Grief is not a universal process with typical symptoms. There are a wide range of individual and cultural differences in the way people grieve. What is normal in one culture may be quite aberrant in another."[86]

Perceived Relationship with the Deceased

The survivor's perception of the relative importance of the deceased also shapes the experience of grief. Was the deceased an important person in the bereaved's life? Is the bereaved's life likely to be significantly changed by the death? Think for a moment about the various relationships in your life—parents, children, neighbors, coworkers, teachers, friends, lovers, and so on. Generally speaking, the death of a family member or other close relative is perceived as more important than the death of a coworker or neighbor. But the outward form of the relationship is not the only determinant of the deceased's importance to a survivor. The death of a close friend may parallel the mourning patterns associated with surviving a death within the family.[87] Reports of death in the media may even prompt "vicarious grief" experiences, especially if they involve events or circumstances that have special poignancy to the griever.[88]

Whatever the outward form—kin, friend, neighbor, or mate—relationships vary according to degree of intimacy, perception of each other's roles, expectations of the other person, and the quality of the relationship itself. In some instances, a person's relationship with his or her parents may reflect socially defined roles of "parent" and "child" more than feelings of friendship or personal intimacy. For others, a parent may occupy additional roles of business associate, neighbor, and friend. These differing roles and expectations result in different perceptions that are likely to shape the experience of grief when a parent dies.

David Des Granges, Tate Gallery, London

This portrait of the Saltonstall family, painted in 1611 by David Des Granges, provides a record of living family members and their relational links with the deceased, whose influence is still felt. The husband and father, Sir Richard, is portrayed as if standing at the bedside of his dead wife, whose arm reaches toward their two children. Seated in the chair and holding her baby, the newest member of the family, is Sir Richard's second wife, whom he married three years after the death of his first wife.

In his paper "Human Grief: A Model for Prediction and Intervention," Larry Bugen observed that a death involving someone central to the survivor's life generally will be more affecting than the death of someone who is perceived to be on the periphery.[89] Bugen added that grief can also be predicted to some extent by a survivor's belief about the circumstances of the death—that is, whether the death was preventable or not. For instance, given a *central* relationship between the survivor and the deceased and the belief that the death was *preventable,* mourning would be expected to be both intense and prolonged. However, if a survivor had a *peripheral* relationship with the deceased and believed that the death was *not preventable,* mourning could be expected to be less intense as well as of shorter duration.

It is also important to mention the effect of *ambivalence* on the course of grief. Ambivalence involves a push-pull struggle between love and hate, and it may be subtle or dramatic. Perhaps no relationship is entirely free of ambivalence, but when it is intense and ongoing, ambivalence complicates grieving.

Relationship with the deceased may also be considered in terms of a survivor's *perceived similarity* to the deceased. This hypothesis suggests that the more similar to the deceased a survivor believes he or she is, the greater the grief reaction is likely to be.[90] (Perceived similarity is also a factor in the formation of support groups that are composed of people who have experienced similar losses.)

Values and Beliefs

We sometimes hear people say things like, "Of course, his wife misses him terribly, but she is relieved that he is no longer enduring such pain and suffering." Knowing the husband's suffering is over lessens the wife's grief at his death. More generally, a person's value structure—that is, the relative worth he or she assigns to different experiences and outcomes—is yet another influence on grief. Values that include a place for death in a person's philosophy of life can be a factor in how that person experiences loss and grief.

Religious and spiritual beliefs influence how individuals relate to values and the meaning of death; thus, they play a role in shaping the experience of loss and grief. Even with hope of an eventual reunion with the deceased loved one, the immediate reality must be recognized. Although religious faith may be consoling and comforting, the path of grief still must be trod. Richard Leliaert says, "To suggest that faith itself can drive out the pain of bereavement is to counsel badly."[91]

Coping Patterns and Gender

People sometimes believe that "men don't cry, women do," thus associating with only one gender a behavior that applies to human beings generally. Gender stereotypes portray women as more emotional than men, a notion that is sometimes interpreted as a sign that women are better able to cope with grief. It is important to understand that, although gender influences patterns of grief and mourning, it does *not* determine them.

Terry Martin and Kenneth Doka point out that there are many effective ways of expressing and adapting to loss and that women as well as men

A Letter from the Canadian Prairie

Heather Brae, Alberta
January 12, 1906

Miss Jennie Magee
Dear Sister:

You will be surprised to hear from me after so many years. Well I have bad news for you. My Dear little wife is Dead and I am the lonelyist Man in all the world. She gave Birth to little Daughter on the 27th of December three Days after she went out of her mind and on the 7th of January she took Pnumonia and Died about half past three in the afternoon. We buried her tuesday afternoon in a little cemetary on the Prarry about 15 miles from here. I am writing to you to see if you will come and keep house for me and raise my little Baby. I would not like to influence you in any way as I am afraid you would be lonely when I have to go from home as I will now and again. You are used to so much stir in the city. I have 400 acres of Land and I have 9 or ten cows and some hens. If you come you can make all you can out of the Butter and eggs and I might be able to Pay you a small wage . . . . Write and let me know as soon as Possible what you think about the Proposition. I am writing to the rest tonight to let them know the bad news. I think this is all at Present from your affectionate Brother.

William Magee

Linda Rasmussen, Lorna Rasmussen,
Candace Savage, and Anne Wheeler,
A Harvest Yet to Reap: A History of Prairie Women

make use of various coping strategies.[92] They identify two patterns of grieving: *intuitive* and *instrumental.* In the first, individuals experience and express grief in an affective way (feelings or emotions as distinguished from thought or action); in the second, grief is experienced physically, such as in restlessness or mental activity. Although the first pattern tends to be associated with women and the second with men, Martin and Doka reject the notion that one pattern is inherently better than the other, along with the bias that correlates these patterns with gender. In fact, both patterns can be effective ways of coping, and both men and women make use of them.

Another model that goes beyond gender stereotypes and allows an understanding of individual patterns involves a distinction between two styles, linear and systemic.[93]

In the *linear* style of thinking and communicating, processes continue one after another: step one, step two, step three, and so on. Thus, people who use a linear style have thought processes that move from one point to the next and involve "doing" something. Advice is for problem solving, and intimacy is usually doing something together. Language is for giving information, protection, or gaining advantage. A symbol of the linear style could be a straight line.

In contrast, the *systemic* mode could easily be symbolized by a spider's web. In this style of thinking and communicating, processes move from one point on the web to another, leading linear thinkers to ask, "How did you get there?" Systemic thinkers have thought processes that move quickly through connections and involve "being." The emphasis is on feelings. Listening, not problem solving, is expected. Intimacy is shared feelings. Language is for bonding and building connections. If you compare these two polarities, you can easily see the differences between these two styles.

An example of the linear coping approach is starting an organization devoted to assisting survivors, such as Mothers Against Drunk Drivers (MADD), which was begun by a woman whose child was killed by a drunk driver. A person using a linear mode seeks to provide solutions to problems expressed by another, rather than merely listening and extending sympathy. For example, in the linear style someone might offer Internet resources that explain treatment options, provide books to read, and the like. Writing about loss experiences intended to help inform others in similar circumstances is characteristic of a linear style. Other examples of this style include preparing for death by planning a funeral, updating a will, and organizing important papers that will be needed after death.

Systemic patterns revolve around "being." Operating in a systemic coping mode, an individual might attend a survivor's support group in order to make connections with people whose losses are similar. Providing a listening ear for problems expressed by another without offering solutions is a hallmark of the systemic mode. When writing, someone operating in a systemic mode will likely write about his or her loss experiences as a means to sort out feelings and understand reactions. Offering suggestions for funeral options whereby the survivors can choose what is best for them is an indication of someone acting systemically.

With respect to grief, someone operating systemically will likely experience and express grief emotionally, whereas a linear expression involves physical or mental activity. As with instrumental versus intuitional differences, notice that the linear mode tends to be associated with men and the systemic mode with women. However, keep in mind that the phrase "Men don't cry, women do" is a gender stereotype, and stereotypes do not explain the vast richness of diversity within a given population. Both patterns are effective ways of coping with loss, and both men and women use them.

Mode of Death

How a person dies affects a survivor's grief. Consider the ways in which people die: the grandmother who dies quietly in her sleep, the child who is pronounced DOA after a bicycle crash, the bystander caught in the crossfire of violence, a despondent person who dies by suicide, the chronically ill patient who dies a lingering death. The mode of death—accidental, homicidal, suicidal, or natural—has an impact on the nature of grief, as does the survivor's previous experience with that type of death.[94]

The circumstances of a death influence whether it is likely to involve *high grief* or *low grief*.[95] A high-grief death is characterized by intense reactions; a

Many people believe the death of a young child to be the most heartrending of all bereavement experiences—what researchers term a high-grief death *because it tends to elicit a tremendous sense of loss.*

low-grief death is perceived as less devastating, and thus grief is likely to be less intense. The death of a child is often cited as the classic example of a high-grief death.

Some losses are characterized as "ambiguous" because they are in some way incomplete or uncertain. Examples include losses where the body is present but the mind is absent (such as Alzheimer's, chronic mental illness, head trauma, addictions), as well as those where the body is absent but the person is psychologically present in the lives of family members and friends (such as military personnel missing in action, missing children, hostages).[96] Such ambiguity can make adjusting to loss more difficult.

Anticipated Death

The phenomenon of *anticipatory grief,* or anticipatory mourning, can be understood as a reaction to the awareness of an impending loss. This awareness may be accompanied by a recognition of associated losses.[97] Some people believe that an expected or anticipated death, as is often the case with chronic or long-term illnesses, is easier to cope with than a death that occurs suddenly, without warning.[98] Others believe that grief experienced before a death occurs does not diminish the grief experienced when the anticipated loss becomes an objective fact.

Sudden Death

Yvonne Ameche described her experience on the night two policemen came to her door with news of her son's unexpected death. Despite having experienced the deaths of her grandparents during her childhood and, later, the deaths of both her parents, Ameche said, "I don't know if anything prepared me for the knock on the door the night Paul died. . . . I remember reeling back [and feeling] like I had been physically assaulted."[99] The sense of overwhelming shock caused by the unexpected nature of her son's death was accompanied by feelings that her own familiar sense of self had been "lost" as well. The journey of survivorship from head to heart, as Ameche describes it, "where I started to internalize what I had so carefully intellectualized," took a long time and, she adds, "it was a long time before I felt like myself."

Survivors who are bereft because of a sudden death usually want information, often in considerable detail, to help them begin to make sense of the loss. Hospital staff, emergency personnel, and others who deal with traumatic deaths need to offer this information in a sensitive, compassionate manner. (See "Death Notification" in Chapter 5.) The abrupt breaking of ties between the deceased and his or her survivors makes sudden death a category of bereavement that many people consider especially difficult.

Suicide

People who survive a loved one's death by suicide are often left feeling bewildered: "Oh, my God, he did it to himself!" The impact of suicide can intensify survivors' feelings of blame and guilt. If someone close to us was in such pain that he or she died by suicide, we may be burdened by guilty questions: "Why didn't I see the predicament and do more to help? What could have been done to respond to the cry for help?" In a series of interviews with individuals bereaved by suicide, Carol Van Dongen concluded,

> A consistent theme throughout survivors' experiences was an intense need to understand why the suicide had occurred and what were the implications of the death for themselves and their family. Survivors agonized over possible reasons for the suicide, as well as how the death was affecting them now and what it might mean in the future.[100]

Besides guilt and self-questioning, survivors may direct feelings of anger and blame toward the person who died by suicide. Suicide is seen as the ultimate affront, the final insult—one that, because it cannot be answered, compounds survivors' frustration and anger. When a suicide is actually witnessed by family or friends, it is likely to add to the trauma of the loss.[101]

Feelings of guilt and blame may be made more difficult to cope with because of societal attitudes. Survivors may be "held responsible" for a death by suicide, as if somehow complicit. This kind of negativity may be even directed toward the parents of a child who died by suicide.[102] Such attitudes can result in a lack of social support. Because suicide is usually unexpected, the shock of suddenness magnifies the bereaved's sense that the death occurred "out of time" or was inappropriate.

Homicide

When a loved one dies as a victim of homicide, the survivor may experience the world as dangerous and cruel, unsafe and unfair. Furthermore, as Lula Redmond points out, "The raw wound of the grieving homicide survivor is overtly and covertly affected by the performance of law enforcement officials, criminal justice practitioners, media personnel, and others after a murder."[103] Dealing with the criminal justice system extends the active grieving period as the case drags on, with no assurance that the result will give the survivor a sense of justice being done. Among the "trigger events" that Redmond cites as restimulating grief are these:

1. Identification of the assailant
2. Sensing (hearing, smelling, and so on) something that elicits recollection of an experience acutely associated with the traumatic event
3. Anniversaries of the event
4. Holidays and other significant events in the life of the family (such as birthdays)
5. Hearings, trials, appeals, and other criminal justice proceedings
6. Media reports about the event or about similar events

Survivors of murder victims face a number of obstacles in adjusting to the loss. The survivor may have to give depositions to attorneys and possibly testify in court. He or she may be surprised to learn that the charge of murder is a crime against the *state,* not against the *loved one* for whom the survivor grieves. Prosecutors may decide to plea-bargain or reduce the charge to a lesser offense, and they may do so without consulting the bereaved family. As the case proceeds through the judicial system, survivors can find themselves facing the defendant in the courtroom or in the courthouse corridor. Character witnesses may describe the defendant as a good and honorable person. Survivors may have to contend with the defendant's receiving a light sentence or even being released. In other cases, the crime may never be solved, or it may not be prosecuted because of insufficient evidence to bring the case to trial. These are special circumstances that make grieving a homicide death especially difficult.

Disaster

People who survive a disaster in which others died become survivors twice over—survivors of a catastrophic event that could have ended their own lives and survivors of the deaths of others, often friends or relatives. Because such survivors may feel that they did not deserve to live when others did not survive, a sense of profound guilt can accompany the anguish and sorrow of grief. Relief at having survived catastrophic and threatening circumstances—a natural human response—may be accompanied by intense questioning: Why did I survive while others very much like me perished? Such feelings are often intensified by catastrophic events involving untimely or unwarranted deaths of others. *Survivor guilt* at being alive while others died can be hard to cope with.[104] Survivors of the Nazi Holocaust typically express a deep sense of guilt about having survived the camps and torture while others did not survive.[105] Veterans whose comrades were killed in combat often feel much the same way. (Other aspects of coping with the aftermath of disaster are discussed in Chapter 13.)

Multiple Losses and Bereavement Burnout

Experiencing multiple losses can intensify grief. Catastrophe, whether natural or human caused, can cause survivors to become overwhelmed by loss, so devastated that they become emotionally numb and disoriented, preventing the expression of normal grief.

In the wake of multiple losses, survivors may feel that they have "run out of tears," that they are bereft of emotional resources to express further feelings of grief.[106] The experience of multiple losses can result in what has been termed *bereavement burnout*. It's as if the normal expression of grief is short-circuited by an unending experience of loss.

Social Support and Disenfranchised Grief

The experience of grief and mourning also varies according to the kind of social support available to the bereaved. In some communities and religious traditions, social support is provided within an organized framework that ensures caring concern for the bereaved. Among religious Jewish families, for example, there are specific customs associated with *aninut,* the period between death and interment; *keriah,* the rending of the garment by the bereaved, which allows expression of deep anger in response to grief in a controlled, religiously sanctioned manner; the *hesped,* or eulogy, in which the virtues of the deceased are recounted in a way that elicits the natural expression of grief; *seudat havraah,* the meal of condolence, which recognizes that the first meal after the interment should be provided by the mourner's friends or neighbors as a way of offering consolation; the *kaddish* prayer, which subliminally transfers the focus from the deceased to the living; and *shivah,* the seven days of mourning that give structure to the early period of grief.[107] Social support of this kind can be immensely helpful to mourners.

Conversely, when social support is lacking, mourners may experience an added burden in dealing with a loss. For example, after the death of an unborn child, whether through miscarriage or abortion, bereaved persons may receive little or no social support of the kind that comforts survivors of other types of bereavement. In most cases, there is no funeral or other formal observance of the death; the loss may not be acknowledged at all by the larger

Pam Price, UPI/Corbis-Bettmann Newsphotos

Family members leave the church after attending the funeral of a son and brother. Providing community support for the bereaved, such social rituals exhibit a blending of private grief and public mourning that offers solace during the early days of grief.

community. Occurrences of this kind can involve what Ken Doka has termed *disenfranchised grief*—that is, grief experienced in connection with a loss that is not socially supported or acknowledged through the usual rituals.[108]

When grief is disenfranchised, either because the significance of the loss is not recognized or because the relationship between the deceased and the bereaved is not socially sanctioned, the bereaved person has little or no opportunity to mourn publicly. Bereaved same-sex mates of persons who die may face this situation. Survivors may receive comparatively little support from the broader community as they cope with their loss. How many community resources, such as spousal support groups, are welcoming of persons with a different sexual orientation? Obviously, the answer to this question varies depending on the community and the mind-set of a particular support group. For example, in one community, a support group for parents who experience neonatal loss integrated lesbian couples whose babies had died, thus providing a measure of community support. When a death is treated by society as if it were not a significant loss, the process of adjustment is unnecessarily made difficult for survivors.

Grief may also be disenfranchised not because of the circumstances of the loss but because of certain qualities that others may wittingly or unwittingly associate with the bereaved. Darlene Kloeppel and Sheila Hollins point out that complications may occur when a death in the family is combined with a grieving family member's having a mental handicap.[109] These complications may affect both the family's functioning and the handicapped person's mourning. Kloeppel and Hollins add that "death and mental retardation are both taboo subjects in our society" and that "taboos elicit fear and avoidance."

Family support can be central to determining whether the survivor is encouraged to cope not only with grief but also with the many practical issues that accompany bereavement. An illustration of this is the situation in western Nigeria, where a widow has no rights of inheritance to her deceased husband's estate; all possessions revert to the husband's family. Kemi Adamolekun points out that the social support provided by in-laws, or the lack of it, is an important factor in how these widows mourn their loss.[110] Complicated grieving was especially noted when in-laws held the widow somehow responsible for her husband's death and when in-laws took steps to dispossess the widow and her children of property. One observer at an African funeral said, "When a widow cries uncontrollably at her husband's burial, she is not crying only for the loss, but for herself, because of the ordeal ahead of her." Indeed, a common saying is that widowhood should not be wished even for an enemy.

Language can also disenfranchise. What expectations do we communicate when we talk about "working through" or "getting over" a loss? When it turns out that grief is not so readily "resolved" and "closure" is not realized, the bereaved may feel somehow deficient, as if something must be wrong with them. Phyllis Silverman observes that our way of talking about grief influences both how we understand it and how we cope with it.[111]

Unfinished Business

Unfinished business can be aptly termed "business that goes on after death." Something is incomplete. The content of unfinished business, how it is handled, and how the survivor is affected by it all have an impact on mourning. Unfinished business can be thought of in one or both of two ways relative to its effect on survivors: first is the fact of death itself; second is the relationship between deceased and survivor. As to the first, perhaps an earlier death of a parent, child, sibling, or someone else close continues to be a vivid reminder of the survivor's uncertainty and fears about death. Regardless of an individual's particular beliefs or values, the more "finished" the business of death is—that is, the more a survivor feels resolved within himself or herself—the easier it will be to accept death and to cope with it. If a person rails against death, refusing to make a place for it, grief is likely to be more difficult to accept. Accepting death, giving it a place in our lives, allows us to be finished with otherwise unresolved issues about death itself.

Second, and perhaps more crucial, is the unfinished business between the deceased and the survivor. Something in the relationship was left incomplete—perhaps some long-standing conflict was never resolved while the deceased was alive, and now it's too late. Unfinished business can include things that were and were not said, things done or not done. Bereaved people often say that the things left unsaid or undone seem to come back to haunt them and make mourning more painful. The sense of never being able to resolve conflicts left by unfinished business amplifies the suffering. Consider the image of a son standing over his father's grave saying, "If only we had been closer, Dad. We ought to have taken more time to visit each other." It may be possible to resolve unfinished business by dealing with issues through the help of creative or therapeutic interventions, but it is generally better to resolve unfinished business daily, in all our relationships and especially our intimate ones.

Unfinished business can also relate to the plans and dreams that the bereaved person had shared with the deceased. Perhaps there were places they had talked about going together at some time in the future; now, these travel plans will never be fulfilled. Perhaps the survivor and the deceased shared dreams related to family matters—plans about their children or retirement years, for example. Such plans and dreams can touch on a number of areas in a survivor's life. Death brings an end to all that had involved the presence of the deceased.

Deathbed promises constitute a particular kind of unfinished business. Picture the classic scene in which the person who is dying elicits some promise from the survivor to perform a particular action after the person dies. Most survivors agree to enact the promise, whether or not they really want to comply with the deathbed request. Thus, a deathbed promise can later create conflict for the survivor, who may be torn between fulfilling the promise and taking another course of action. Whereas some people carry through a deathbed promise and find it to be a gratifying choice, others find that deathbed promises need to be reevaluated in the light of their own wishes and circumstances.

Grief Counseling and Grief Therapy

Because society is increasingly diverse, we cannot always easily determine what may or may not be "healthy grieving." Howard Winokuer and Darcy Harris state, "One of the most important aspects of grief that differentiates it from other issues that clients bring into the counseling relationship is that the grieving process itself is an adaptive response and not a form of pathology."[112] The task is to develop new concepts and approaches that can aid in understanding the *differentiated* experiences of bereaved people.[113] In some circumstances, survivors may seek professional help to cope with their grief. J. William Worden differentiates grief *counseling,* which involves helping people facilitate normal or uncomplicated grief, from grief *therapy,* which involves specialized techniques to help people with abnormal or complicated grief reactions.[114] Worden also says that counselors and therapists are challenged to work with issues of trauma and to know how to perform triage among those needing traumatic intervention and those who need bereavement intervention.[115] It seems that the more complicated the grief appears to be or to become, the better the chances of interventions leading to positive results.[116]

In recent years, articles have been published both in scholarly journals and in the popular press suggesting that grief counseling may be more harmful than helpful. One article states, "Grief counseling may sometimes make matters worse."[117] Another states, "Grief counseling does not appear to be very effective, most probably because many of the people who receive it would do just as well (and perhaps in some cases better) without it."[118]

In a recent study, Dale Larson and William Hoyt conclude that this pessimistic view of grief counseling was initiated by an unpublished dissertation that did not have the benefit of peer review. They say, "There is no empirical or statistical foundation for these claims."[119] According to Larson and Hoyt, there is no reason to believe that grief counseling is less effective than other forms of counseling or psychotherapy, which have positive outcomes for various forms of psychological distress. A study of treatments for traumatized children found that, whereas cognitive-behavioral therapy shows benefits, the results are not as clear for psychodynamic therapy, art therapy, drug therapy, play therapy, or psychological debriefing.[120] With limited data available at present, additional research is needed to clarify whether or not grief counseling—with its various techniques—is an effective treatment for normally bereaved people.

Grief counseling on the Internet raises additional questions. Cybertherapy, e-therapy, teletherapy, Web-based counseling—a variety of names are used to describe mental health services delivered via the Internet. Perhaps this should not be surprising when it is considered that the history of indirect treatment can be traced back to Freud's practice of providing psychoanalysis by letter when necessary because of geographic distance.[121] Are such cyber services appropriate or effective?

In discussing the efficacy of grief counseling, several questions present themselves, the first of which is, Do grievers need counseling? Phyllis Silverman reminds us that the bereaved "need comfort, support, and help as they deal with their grief and find a new direction for their lives. Who should that helping person be in our postmodern society—grief counselor, family, and/or friend?"[122] David Crenshaw says, "Throughout the life span

Grief Counseling on the Internet

Picture the following scene: a client enters a coffee shop on the entry level of a large office building in a major U.S. city on the eastern seaboard and selects a comfortable, overstuffed chair in a secluded corner. With the technological assistance of a very smart phone and local wireless access to the Internet, the client participates in a real-time, video-conference grief-counseling session with an expert provider located on the West Coast, who was recommended as the best counselor available for the client's particular loss. The client wears a wireless headset to hear the counselor's comments and responds into a sensitive microphone that transmits clearly what the client says when speaking no louder than a library voice. On the telephone screen, the client can see the grief counselor, who is seated at a desktop computer with Webcam in an office at the counselor's home 3,000 miles away. When the client's cup of coffee is finished, and the 50-minute therapy "hour" is over, both parties sign off, and the bill is paid over the Internet by credit card. Does this sound futuristic?

Louis A. Gamino and R. Hal Ritter, Jr.,
Ethical Practice in Grief Counseling

the primary intervention for most bereaved children, adults, and families is some form of bereavement support. The majority will receive this support from their families, church, synagogue, or mosque, their school, or the larger community."[123]

When additional intervention or professional help is needed, the bereaved may turn to counseling or therapy. Here the question becomes, Is the counselor death competent? What is *death competence?* In their book titled *Ethical Practice in Grief Counseling,* Louis Gamino and Hal Ritter define the term to mean the counselor's specialized skill in tolerating and managing clients' problems related to dying, death, and bereavement.[124] They liken it to a three-layer cake in which death competence rests on a solid stratum of emotional competence that itself rests on a bedrock of cognitive competence. Dennis Klass offers an additional caveat when he advises, "If we want to hold ourselves out as experts in helping the bereaved, we need to have a rather good grasp of the symbols by which people find meaning or lose meaning, and the religious traditions (even the secular religion that believes in "spirituality") that supply those symbols."[125]

In contrast to the death-competent counselor or therapist, Gamino and Ritter remark that "individuals who deliberately try to solve their own problems in grieving through the professional role of grief counselor are really clients masquerading as counselors."[126]

Bereaved people who experience traumatic death, who have dysfunctional attachment styles, or who, because of other factors (such as those mentioned earlier in this chapter), are susceptible to complications may benefit from help in coping with grief. More research is needed to answer the question whether grief counseling is efficacious for normally bereaved people.

Margaret Stroebe and her colleagues suggest that we "search for an appreciative understanding of grief in all its varieties." In part, "this would mean curtailing the search for ideal therapeutic practices and focusing instead on tailor-made treatments."[127]

Support for the Bereaved

When a person experiences a significant loss, he or she may initially feel and behave much like a frightened child. A hug may be more comforting than words. Having someone who can simply listen is helpful. The key to being a good listener is to refrain from making judgments about whether the feelings expressed by a bereaved person are "right" or "wrong," "good" or "bad." Talking and crying, even yelling in rage, are ways of coping with intense emotions. In offering support to the bereaved, a basic guideline is not to expect them to be "strong" and "brave" or to hold back their feelings. The emotions and thoughts evoked by loss may not be expected, but they can be valid within a survivor's experience.

The role of the wake in Hawaiian culture illustrates how social support can provide opportunities for the bereaved to engage in a controlled expression of anger and hostility that leads to a lessening of guilt and anxiety. Everyone in the *'ohana,* or extended family, attends the wake, including children. With each new arrival, a relative might say—as if telling the dead person—"Here comes Keone, your old fishing companion," or "Tutu is coming in now; remember how she used to massage you when you were sick?" The assembled mourners address the dead, recalling their memories and sometimes describing their feelings of abandonment or even scolding the deceased. A fishing companion might exclaim, "Why you mean, go off when we gon' go fishing! Now who I go fish with?" Or a wife might say, "You had no business to go. You should be ashamed. We need you."[128] Scolding the corpse gives survivors an opportunity to vent hostility toward the dead who had abandoned them. What a contrast to the idea that one should "not speak ill of the dead," which encourages suppressing feelings of anger at the deceased.

As a culturally condoned vehicle for expressing grief, funerals and other death-related community gatherings facilitate mourning by providing a social framework for coping with the fact of death. Funerals and other rituals can help survivors begin to integrate a loss into their lives. Donna Schuurman offers insight in this regard: "I look at rituals not as closure; I don't think the word closure goes with death. I look at them as punctuation. Ritual gives the mourner the opportunity to mark that something special has happened."[129] (Or, as Robert Neimeyer has said, "Closure is for bank accounts, not for love accounts.")[130]

For some, funerals are occasions of weeping and wailing; for others, stoic and subdued emotions are the rule. Different styles of mourning behavior can be equally valid and appropriate. Whereas dense social networks—small or medium-sized Israeli kibbutzim, for example—have social structures that allow mourning to take place within an intimate circle of family, friends, neighbors, and coworkers, looser social networks may need funerals and other rituals to provide a structure wherein support can be offered to the bereaved.[131]

Social support is critical during the later course of grief, just as it is during the first days and weeks after a loss. Bereaved people should be able to rely on receiving support from those they trust. They need to be reassured that it is appropriate to express grief. They may also need permission to occasionally give themselves a break from grieving. As they move forward with life, bereaved individuals may be helped by encouragement from others to face the world confidently. The anniversary following a significant loss is usually a time of renewed grieving, when the support of others is important and appreciated. Knowing that others remember and acknowledge the loss, and that they take time to "touch base," is usually perceived as very supportive.

Besides receiving social support from individuals who form their network of friends and relations, bereaved people may want to share their stories and concerns through organized support groups. Most such groups are based on perceived similarity. Having experienced similar losses, members of support groups come together to talk with each other as they integrate those losses into their lives. Widow-to-widow groups, for example, provide opportunities for women to share experiences of being a woman alone and encourage one another in the task of coping with the death of a spouse. Military families receive bereavement support through the Tragedy Assistance Program for Survivors (T.A.P.S.), which offers peer-to-peer support, counseling referrals, survivor seminars, and other types of help.[132] Other organizations, such as The Compassionate Friends (TCF) and Bereaved Families of Ontario (BFO), assist families who are coping with the death of a child. In describing the aims of BFO, Stephen Fleming and Leslie Balmer note that it is "designed to facilitate the grieving process, emancipate the bereaved from crippling attachments to the deceased, assuage fears that one is 'going crazy,' educate the survivors about the nature and dynamics of grief to normalize their experience, and promote the usual curative qualities found in groups (the installation of hope, altruism, group cohesiveness, catharsis, and insight)."[133] Some support groups are composed entirely of peers; others are led by a trained professional or lay counselor. Hospice and palliative care programs usually have trained volunteers to help families cope with grief.

Bereavement as an Opportunity for Growth

When life's events bring loss into our lives, we might wish there was some potion we could access that would induce forgetfulness of pain and sorrow, what the Greeks called *nepenthe,* something capable of causing the end of suffering and grief. Viewing bereavement as an opportunity for growth can be difficult at first, but this perspective can promote gradual movement toward accommodating the loss. As the bereaved person begins to reformulate the loss, it frees up energy that had been bound to the past. As John Schneider says, "There is a change in perceptual set from focusing on limits to focusing on potential; from coping to growth; and from problems to challenges."[134] The tragic event of a death is reformulated in a way that doesn't shut out new possibilities. Loss can be transformed in ways that place it within a context of growth. This reframing can carry over into other areas of the person's life so that beliefs and assumptions that were once limiting are reassessed with greater self-confidence and self-awareness, making possible significant and rewarding life changes.

Turning to inner sources of creativity can give form to the experience of grief. Creatively responding to loss can bring forth remarkable results. Those who work with the bereaved can spark a grieving person's creative response, as in the case of a young woman who had experienced the sudden, unexpected death of her son at birth. Overwhelmed by feelings of sadness, depression, and an inability to do anything other than grieve, she was despairing of words to communicate her feelings. In a counseling session six months after her son's death, she remarked, "I haven't touched a lump of clay since Justin died." The obvious question was, What had she done with clay before his death? She said that her sculptures of whales and seals had sold at a local seaside crafts shop. The counselor pointed out that the reason for her inability to return to her art might lie in the products of her creative energies. Although whales and seals might one day reemerge from the lumps of clay, her creativity at present might take a different form. The client agreed to find a quiet moment when she would put her hands to the lump of clay as an experiment to see what might emerge.

Both the bereaved mother and the counselor were amazed at the results (see Figures 9-2 a, b, c). Over the course of twelve months, a series of some twenty-two figures emerged. The earliest were naked; later works were draped with a blanket; and, with the final pieces, the fabric of the blanket had been turned into clothing. The mother's creativity not only gave form to her loss but also manifested an unconscious understanding of the process of recovery and the integration of her loss. Subsequently, the sculptures were photographed and published along with her prose, giving comfort to other survivors.[135]

People maintain connections with deceased loved ones through memories, as well as through personal and social rituals that provide a "space" in their ongoing lives for acknowledging affection and love for the deceased. The journey of grief has benefited from theory, research, and clinical experience, which have deepened our appreciation of the lifelong impact of bereavement on survivors.[136] Bereavement, grief, and mourning are complementary threads in the fabric of life, part of the warp and weft of human experience.

Figure 9-2*(a) Anguish of Loss*

Figure 9-2*(b) Sharing the Grief*

Figure 9-2*(c) Collapsing*

"The anguish of loss is overpowering and vast," begins the prose accompanying the sculpture by Julie Fritsch pictured here, part of the series created following the death of her son. "Sharing the grief" states the theme of the second sculpture, acknowledging that "together we must comfort and be comforted." The third sculpture portrays the bereaved artist "collapsing from the weight of emotions I cannot control." The prose accompanying this sculpture continues: "Drained of any ability to cope or carry on, I must collapse now. And feel myself overcome by absolute grief."

Further Readings

Thomas Attig. *How We Grieve: Relearning the World,* 2nd ed. New York: Oxford University Press, 2010.

Sandra M. Gilbert. *Death's Door: Modern Dying and the Ways We Grieve.* New York: Norton, 2006.

Robert E. Goss and Dennis Klass. *Dead but Not Lost: Grief Narratives in Religious Traditions.* Walnut Creek, Calif.: AltaMira Press, 2005.

Nancy R. Hooyman and Betty J. Kramer. *Living Through Loss: Interventions Across the Life Span*. New York: Columbia University Press, 2006.

Robert A. Neimeyer, Darcy L. Harris, Howard R. Winokuer, and Gordon F. Thornton, eds. *Grief and Bereavement in Contemporary Society: Bridging Research and Practice*. New York: Routledge, 2011.

Colin Murray Parkes and Holly G. Prigerson. *Bereavement: Studies of Grief in Adult Life*, 4th ed. New York: Routledge, 2010.

Margaret S. Stroebe, Robert O. Hansson, Henk Schut, and Wolfgang Stroebe, eds. *Handbook of Bereavement Research and Practice: Advances in Theory and Intervention*. Washington, D.C.: American Psychological Association, 2008.

Christine Valentine. *Bereavement Narratives: Continuing Bonds in the Twenty-First Century*. New York: Routledge, 2008.

Additional resources for this chapter can be found at www.mhhe.com/despelder10e

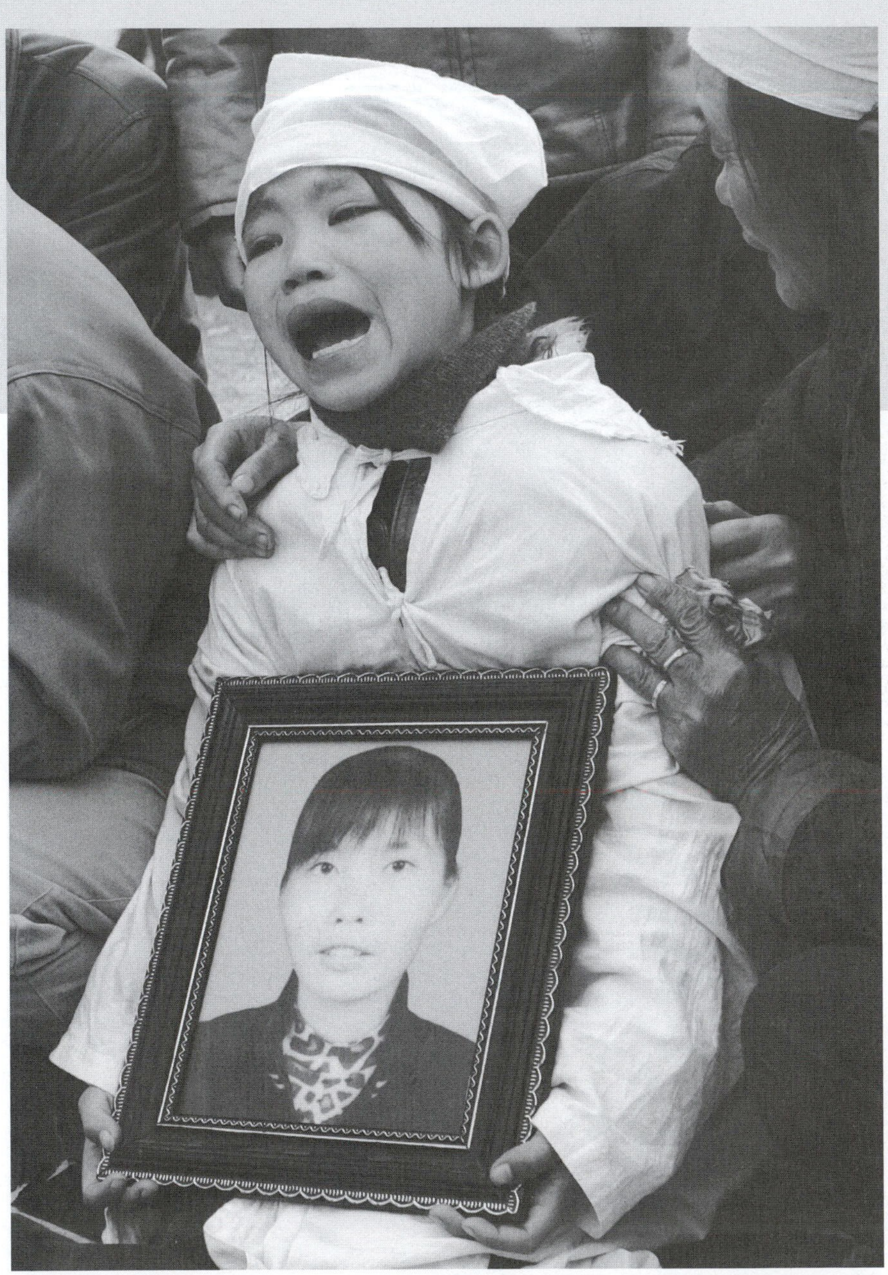

© Mark Ralson/AFP/Getty Images

A child feels the death of a parent or other close family member or friend as deeply as do adult survivors. This young Chinese girl holds a picture of her mother, who died in an earthquake. The girl's hat and white clothes, known as Pi Ma Dai Xiao, make up the traditional garments worn in Chinese funerals to signify mourning the death of a parent.

CHAPTER 10

Death in the Lives of Children and Adolescents

Parents and other adults have natural concerns about what to tell children about death. How can we help a child cope with death? How should we start the discussion? What is the child able to understand? Deaths that are sudden and unexpected or that result from suicide or homicide complicate issues the child faces in coping with loss.[1] Although children tend to be resilient in coping with tragedies in their lives, adults can play a crucial role in guiding a child through grief by listening to the child's concerns and communicating support for the child's well-being. Family patterns and styles of communication influence a child's or adolescent's ability to understand and cope with loss.

According to the International Work Group on Death, Dying, and Bereavement, "All too often, the needs of children and adolescents who encounter issues related to death are not properly acknowledged or appreciated by adults."[2] Loss due to death is part of life for children as well as adults. Yet, it is a topic that society as a whole tries to shield from children.[3] When a loss occurs in a child's life, attempts are often made to minimize its effects. The death of a pet, for example, may be swiftly followed by its replacement with another animal. However, this strategy for comfort may be of limited benefit. Severing an attachment to someone special is a significant loss. A more constructive approach is to help children explore their feelings about death. Despite our wish to spare children the pain of bereavement, death is a fact of life that eventually cannot be ignored.

Cpl. Edward Belfer, U.S. Army Photo

Children experience the impact of war on their lives in a variety of ways. For the German child seen here, war brought a stark encounter with death. This child was one of many German citizens who, at the end of World War II, were ordered by the provisional military government of the U.S. Third Army to view the exhumed bodies of Russians, Poles, and Czechs killed while imprisoned in the concentration camp at Flossenberg. For Amanda Wille (facing page), the impact of war was felt in terms of the anticipated loss of her father, a Navy computer technician, as he prepared to board the USS John F. Kennedy for service during the Persian Gulf War. Understanding only that her father was going away, the three-year-old seemed anxious and bewildered until she found a piece of string on the Norfolk, Virginia, dock. After her father broke the string and tied one piece around his wrist and the other around hers, Amanda cried and hugged him goodbye.

Whether or not they receive instruction, children develop their own concepts about death, even when the topic is considered taboo. How a child experiences and copes with death is likely to correspond to his or her developmental phase.[4] (The process of learning about death is discussed in Chapter 2.) Children who have had death experience appear to have a more complete understanding of death than their inexperienced age-mates.[5]

One six-year-old who witnessed the accidental death of her sibling expressed a clear understanding that death is final, that people die, and that

© Robin Layton Kinsley

she herself could die. She was concerned about how she could protect herself and her friends from the dangerous circumstances that had led to her brother's death. Her attitude was displayed in admonitions to schoolmates that they should try to prevent accidents.

Besides being survivors of tragedy or a close death, children and adolescents sometimes encounter death in the context of being challenged to cope with serious and possibly life-limiting illness. An Institute of Medicine report states: "We can and should do more than we are currently doing to prevent the physical and emotional suffering of dying children and . . . to respect the personal dignity of the dying child."[6] This is discussed later in this chapter.

Children want to know about death, just as they want to learn about all the things they encounter in their lives. One child wrote, "Dear God, what's it like when you die? Nobody will tell me. I just want to know. I don't want to do it."

Experiences with Death

Children who experience firsthand the reality of death through war or violence, or in connection with other forms of catastrophic death, often exhibit a fatalistic attitude that contrasts with the attitude of children whose experiences of death occur in more benign circumstances. A diary written by a young girl in war-torn Sarajevo highlights the effects of violence on children. Zlata Filipovic's diary displays an evolution from the ordinary concerns of teenage life to a shattering preoccupation with destruction and death as warfare disrupts normal life. In one entry, Zlata writes, "War has crossed out the day and replaced it with horror, and now horrors are unfolding instead of days."[7]

A study of the psychosocial effects of war among displaced children in Southern Darfur found that increased exposure to war experiences led to higher levels of traumatic reactions, depression, and grief symptoms.[8] War experiences included abduction, hiding to protect oneself, being raped, being forced to fight and to kill or hurt family members, and death of a parent. A separate study in Uganda found children who said they had to keep quiet about such deaths, not only because it was too painful to talk about but also because they were afraid of retaliation by those who had a hand in the killings.[9] James Garbarino says, "Few issues challenge our moral, intellectual, and political resources as does the topic of children and community violence—war, violent crime on the streets, and other forms of armed conflict."[10]

Many children and teenagers growing up in America's cities experience warlike disruptions due to drug-related violence and gang warfare, a situation that writer, actor, and musician Ice-T characterizes as "the killing fields" of America (see Figures 10-1 and 10-2).[11] When children in an urban school in Germany were asked about the ways people die, violent deaths were described as being caused by "weapons" and "sharp knives." Conspicuously absent was any use of the word *gun*.[12] In Germany, firearms are strictly regulated and not readily available to the populace.

Children who have witnessed violence or experienced it indirectly, such as losing a parent to murder, may develop posttraumatic stress disorder (PTSD) or other harmful disorders. A task force on traumatic events among children and adolescents found that individual and group cognitive-behavioral therapy is helpful in relieving symptoms of PTSD, depression, anxiety, and related problems by addressing distortions of perception regarding self-blame, safety, and the trustworthiness of others.[13]

Figure 10-1 *Ways People Die: Children's Images*
Above: A seven-year-old African American boy in a large midwestern city draws a picture of murder by decapitation. (In separate incidents, two young girls in his city had recently been killed in this manner.)
Below: In contrast, the drawing created by a seven-year-old Caucasian boy attending Catholic school in a small California town portrays the child's concept that people die when "God calls you home." Notice the child's depiction of the voice of God and heavenly "pearly gates."

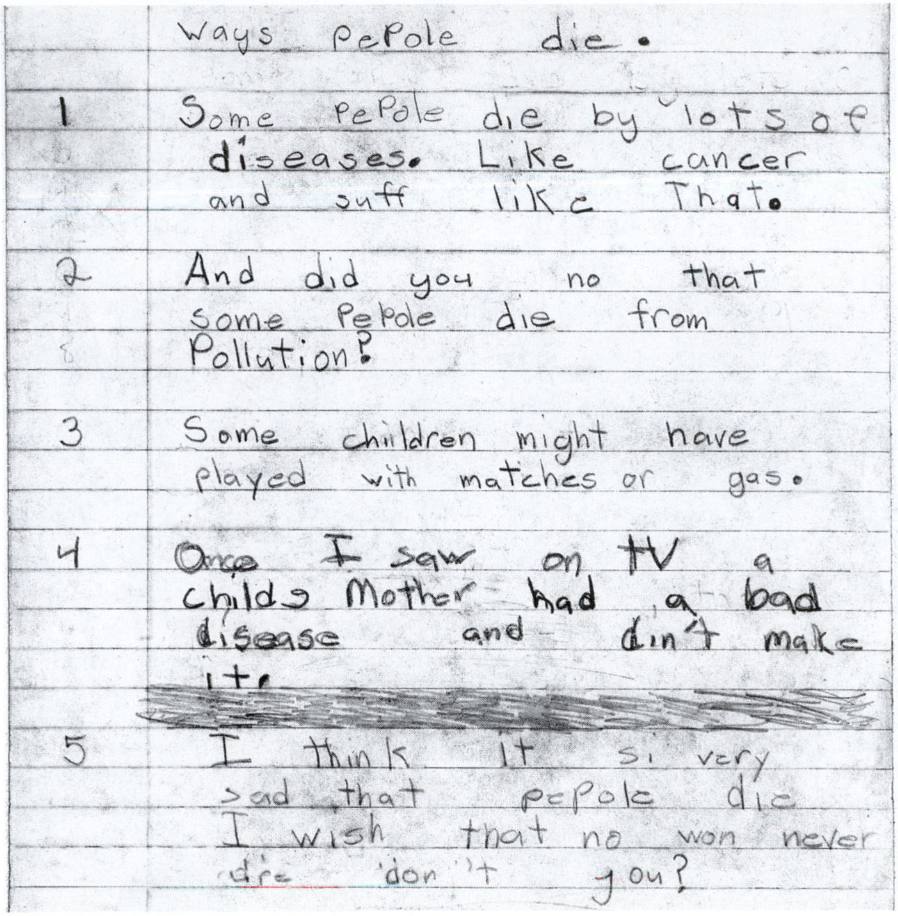

Ways Pepole die.

1 Some pePole die by lots of diseases. Like cancer and suff like That.

2 And did you no that some PePole die from Pollution?

3 Some children might have played with matches or gas.

4 Once I saw on TV a childs Mother had a bad disease and din't make it.

5 I think it si very sad that pepole die I wish that no won never die don't you?

Figure 10-2 *Ways People Die: Children's Explanations*
Environment, including both time and place, influences a child's understanding of death. The impact of environment on children's views of death can be evoked by asking them to make a list or draw a picture in response to the question, What are the ways people die? The list shown above was written by a seven-year-old Caucasian girl living in a small coastal California town. It stands in sharp contrast to the thirteen-item response (facing page) written by a seven-year-old African American boy living in a major midwestern city. Although both lists were created by children of the same age, the second list reflects the circumstances of life in an inner-city metropolitan environment. Whereas the first child's list focuses on diseases and accidents, the second child's explanation shows familiarity with a broad range of causes of death, few of which relate to "natural" events. His illustration of item number 11, "cut your head off," is shown in Figure 10-1.

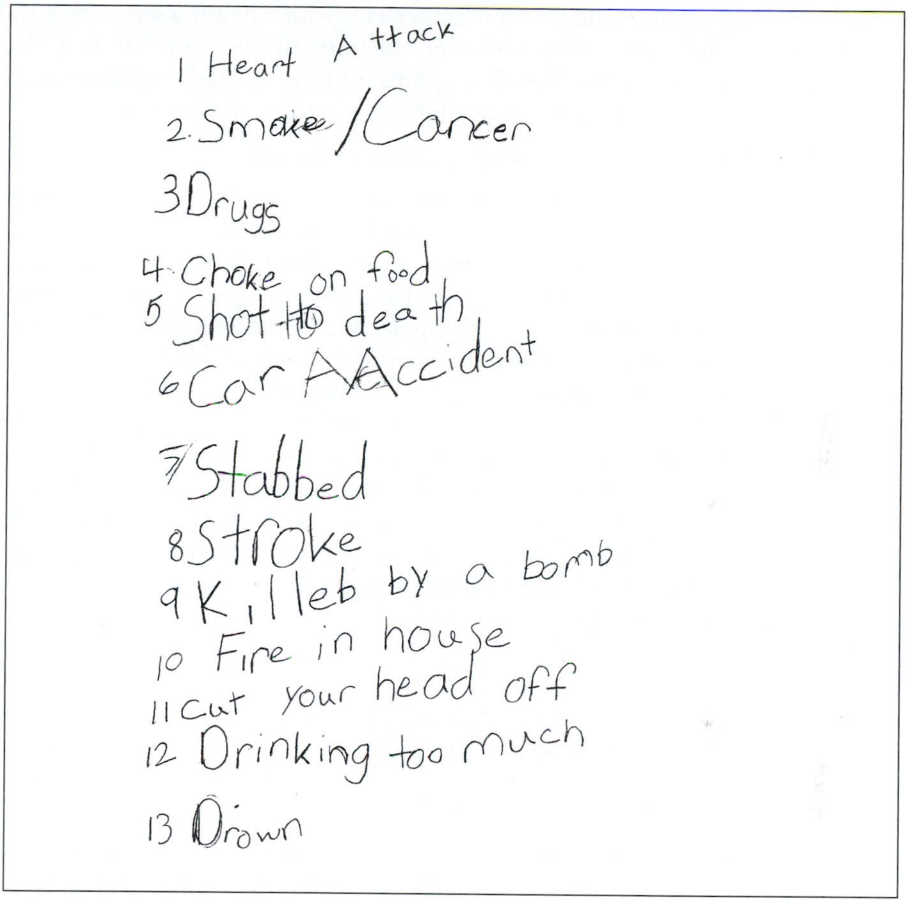

1 Heart Attack
2. Smoke/Cancer
3 Drugs
4. Choke on food
5 Shot to death
6 Car Accident
7 Stabbed
8 Stroke
9 Killeb by a bomb
10 Fire in house
11 Cut your head off
12 Orinking too much
13 Orown

Chance encounters or fortuitous happenings may be beneficial or detrimental, depending on the nature and interplay of personal and social forces. Some detrimental confrontations occur in which the affected person simply happened to be in the wrong place at the wrong time.

> They may get injured, maimed, or deeply enmeshed in nightmarish events that leave debilitating effects. In tragic cases, as when an innocent victim is unexpectedly caught in a cross fire and killed by a drive-by shooting, the unfortunate victim is no longer around to provide narratives.[14]

When questioned about the ways people die, children in violent or death-saturated environments tend to answer quite differently from children whose lives are comparatively sheltered from such experiences.

Children as Survivors of a Close Death

A particular child's response to loss reflects the influence of such factors as age, stage of mental and emotional development, patterns of interaction and communication within his or her family, relationship with the person who has died, and previous experiences with death. Generally speaking, bereaved children experience grief reactions similar to those experienced by adults. However, children differ from adults in cognitive abilities, need for identification figures, and dependence on adults for support.

The Bereaved Child's Experience of Grief

A story about Monica, a three-year-old who nearly drowned when her house collapsed into the raging water of Hurricane Katrina, can add to our understanding of children's grief.[15] After the disaster waned, each time she got into the tub, Monica reacted as if she were going to drown. At first whimpering, then sobbing softly, and finally wailing as the tub began to fill. She learned in the storm that those she loves and who love her can't always protect her. Faith in her parents' ability to protect her was shattered. As a result of the hurricane, school-age children struggled with intrusive thoughts and their anxiety manifested in physical symptoms like stomachaches. For adolescents, depression set in as they realized it could be years before they could be back in their homes.

Certain expressions of grief are prevalent during early childhood.[16] These include regression, magical thinking, guilt over "causing" a death, helplessness, and wishful thoughts about the return of the deceased. Older children typically exhibit anger, concerns about health, or school problems.

> Coping strategies change as one matures. For example, children often try to derive comfort by seeking comfort from others, denying at times the impact of the loss, adhering to familiar activities and routines, using fantasy to ameliorate aspects of the loss. As they enter adolescence, young persons begin to engage in more effective behavioral coping strategies (for example, help seeking, problem solving, expressing feelings).[17]

Adolescents begin to engage in cognitive coping strategies, such as search for meaning, positive reappraisal, and acceptance of the loss. In doing so, they are likely to make use of the Internet and social networking sites.

Adolescents' developmental tasks of feeling in control, attaining a sense of mastery, and being able to predict events are compromised by death.[18] In a study of adolescents' responses to the terror attacks of September 11, 2001, researchers found that adolescents (especially girls) were frightened and reported concerns about dying from other disasters, such as tornadoes or earthquakes. These anxiety reactions are consistent with adolescents' developmental issues related to vulnerability to death. Resilience, too, was seen in their efforts to make a coherent narrative of the events and to refocus on their daily living.[19] Indeed, some researchers and clinicians suggest that resilience can be a key protective factor.[20] In a study of African American teen girls who had experienced the homicidal death of a friend, Celeste Johnson found that they demonstrated resilience in their ability to "move on" with their lives by calling upon reserves of motivation and meaning-making in their lives.[21]

If a child believes he or she may have played a role in the events that led to a death, guilt may predominate among emotions experienced. It is important to openly discuss the circumstances surrounding the death and give the child opportunities to explore the troubling aspects of his or her grief. When children are left on their own to figure out how to cope with confused feelings of guilt and blame, traumatic effects may persist into adulthood. To illustrate, in one situation, which involved three brothers playing with a loaded gun, the youngest pushed the oldest, who held the gun as a bullet was discharged, killing the third sibling. "I have always struggled with myself about whether my brother would have died if I hadn't tried to push my other brother away," said a thirty-year-old man, recalling events that had taken place more than a quarter of a century earlier. "I always thought I did the right thing in *trying* to prevent the accident, but no one ever talked with me about my feelings. For years, I cried myself to sleep alone in my bed at night." Even when it is obvious to others in the environment that a child bears no responsibility for a death, he or she should be encouraged to share his or her perceptions and beliefs about how the death occurred. The child's experience can be different from that of the adults.

In coping with loss, children sometimes selectively forget or try to reconstruct reality in a more desirable and comfortable way. A child may not recall how frightened she was by the sight of a sibling lying ill in a hospital bed surrounded by awesome medical paraphernalia; or the child may remember a protracted illness with long stays in the hospital as if the sibling had been away from home only briefly for a few tests. The forgotten details or reconstructed images provide a way to cope without being overwhelmed by painful memories.

Despite significant advances in the understanding of grief, some pediatric medical journals continue to rely on the Kübler-Ross model as a description of the "stages of grief" children experience with loss.[22] The wise parent or counselor will expand this framework by making use of other strategies for understanding grief (such as those discussed in Chapter 9).

The Death of a Parent

Of all the deaths that may be experienced in childhood, the most affecting is likely to be the death of a parent.[23] A parent's death is perceived as a loss of security, nurture, and affection—a loss of the emotional and psychological support upon which the child could formerly rely. Coping may be complicated when the death results from suicide or homicide.[24] In the United States, it is reported that more than 2 million children and adolescents younger than eighteen (roughly 3.5 percent) have experienced the death of a parent.[25]

> Death leaves a gap not only from the lack of the physical presence, but also from the part the parent played in defining and directing the family life. Parents are role models, teachers, nurturers, and framers of family traditions. Each child loses someone different, depending on their parent's role in the family and also on the child's relationship to that parent.[26]

Based on data obtained from the Child Bereavement Study, Phyllis Silverman and her colleagues conclude that children who have lost a parent typically establish a set of memories, feelings, and actions that the child draws on

> Even young children sense that they are different from other kids after a parent dies. During one of The Dougy Center's "Littles" groups for three to five year olds, Luke got a splinter in his finger while climbing on the playhouse outside. He went inside with an adult facilitator for a Band-Aid, trailed by his buddy, Mario. Both of these preschoolers' fathers had died in car accidents. As Luke's finger was washed and the Band-Aid applied, Mario said that he too had a "boo-boo" and needed a Band-Aid. When the facilitator asked him where his boo-boo was, he replied, "It's invis'ble. All of us kids at The Dougy Center have invis'ble boo-boos, 'cause we all had someone die." He knew, even at four, that he was different from other kids.
>
> Donna Schuurman, *Never the Same: Coming to Terms with the Death of a Parent*

in "reconstructing" an image of the dead parent.[27] This involves building an "inner representation" that allows the child to sustain his or her relationship with the deceased parent, and "this relationship changes as the child matures and as the intensity of grief lessens." The child negotiates and renegotiates the meaning of the loss over time. The loss is permanent; the process of coping with it changes.

When the death of a parent occurs when a child is very young, grief may involve mourning the years of relationship that were lost due to the parent's premature death. There can be a lingering sense of "never having known" the deceased parent. Consider, for example, the situation of a parent who dies as a result of war. Powerful emotions may lie buried for years until some stimulus—perhaps the discovery of the parent's military papers or a visit to a war memorial—brings the loss to the surface. Sharing the loss with others can aid healing. Ways of forming an understanding of the loss may include talking to other veterans, allowing the child to fill in the picture of a deceased parent whom he or she had not been able to fully know.

Children sometimes take responsibility as they struggle to understand a close death. For example, a child whose parent died of cancer might remember times when she was noisy and her parent needed to rest. "Maybe if I had been quiet," the child thinks, "Mom would have gotten well." The very fact that the parent is dead while the child is alive may cause children to experience "survivor's guilt." A drawing made by a four-year-old whose father had died of leukemia illustrates this (see Figure 10-3). Some time after his father's death, as the child was playing with pencils and drawing paper, he asked his mother how to spell various words. Attracted by the child's activity, his mother noticed that he had drawn a picture of his father. In the drawing, the father was saying to the child, "I am mad at you!" Surprised at this depiction of her husband's anger toward her son, the mother asked, "Why would your father have been mad at you?" The child explained, "Because you and I can still play together and Dad can't." Amid the confusing feelings resulting from his father's death, the child was attempting to come to terms with the fact of his survivorship.

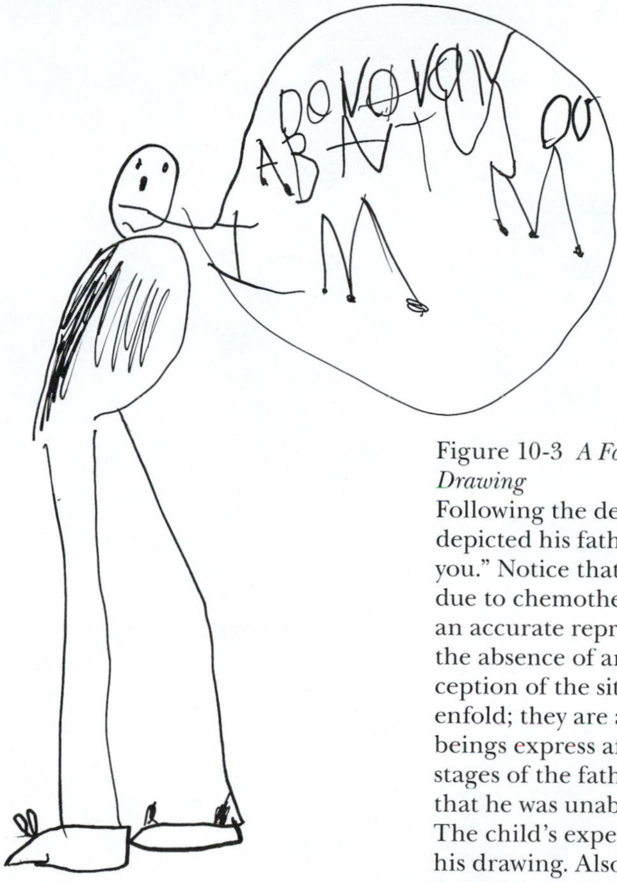

Figure 10-3 *A Four-Year-Old's "I Am Mad at You" Drawing*
Following the death of his father, a four-year-old has depicted his father saying, "Donovan, I am mad at you." Notice that the father is portrayed as being bald due to chemotherapy treatments. Whereas baldness is an accurate representation of the father's appearance, the absence of arms reflects the child's emotional perception of the situation. Arms reach out; they hug and enfold; they are a common means by which human beings express affection for one another. In the later stages of the father's illness, the pain was so great that he was unable to gather the child into his arms. The child's experience of this has been depicted in his drawing. Also notice that the drawing shows the father's body facing the viewer, yet his feet are drawn at an angle as if they are walking off the page. Again, the drawing reflects the child's experience, this time showing the father's movement out of his life. Importantly, the child's mother used the occasion of this drawing as an opportunity to talk with the child about his present feelings regarding his father's death.

Now, in working with this child as a survivor, his mother did a very wise thing. She said, "Tell me about this picture." She asked open-ended questions, which allowed her to elicit information about the child's feelings and respond directly to the child's concerns. Using art with bereaved children helps them work through grief by providing a safe, focused environment for expressing their concerns and feelings.

The Death of a Sibling

One effect of a sibling's death may be to increase the surviving child's sense of vulnerability to death, especially when siblings are close in age. When

© Karen Saltzman

Siblings enjoy a special relationship, one conjoining both rivalries and mutual affection and love. The death of a brother or sister thus severs a unique human relationship. The surviving child may feel the loss more intensely because of identification with the deceased brother or sister. The surviving child recognizes that he or she is also not immune to dying at an early age.

a child dies, most of the attention is focused on the parents rather than on the dead child's surviving siblings. As Betty Davies points out, relatively little attention has been devoted to sibling bereavement.[28] Yet, in countries like the United States, where families tend to be small, the death of a sibling can make the surviving child an *only* child. Losing a brother or sister can be a lonely experience. As one child said, "It was like my mom and dad had each other, and I had no one." With the parents grieving their own loss, the surviving child may also experience losing his or her parents as they were once known.

The brother or sister may have been a protector or caregiver as well as a playmate. The surviving child may grieve the loss of this unique relationship, worried that the protection and care given by the sibling are no longer available and yet relieved or even pleased that, with the sibling's absence, he or she can now be closer to the center of attention in the family. Such a mixture of emotions can produce guilt and confusion as a child comes to terms with the sibling's death.

Children typically look to their parents for help in understanding and coping with a sibling's death and its effects on the family. In studies of adolescent sibling bereavement, the support considered most helpful by the bereaved teenagers was perceived as "people being there for me."[29] Dysfunctional family patterns impair the surviving child's ability to cope. Such responses range from overt resentment of the surviving child to attempts to re-create in that child the qualities of the deceased child. As parents come to terms with a child's death, they may unintentionally minimize contact with the surviving child. The living child can be a painful reminder of the child now lost. Conversely, parents may become overprotective of the surviving child. Parental responses like these may be present to a lesser extent even in families that appear to be coping successfully.

The bereaved child must be given opportunities to acknowledge and express his or her grief. If a child talks about feeling guilty, one can ask, "What would it take to forgive yourself?" Feelings of guilt are often related to normal sibling rivalry. The sister at whom one angrily yells, "I hate you!" in the morning may be lying dead at the morgue in the afternoon, the victim of a bicycle accident. To a young child, anger directed toward a person and that person's subsequent death might be viewed as a cause-and-effect relationship.

This assumption of responsibility is sometimes displayed as a preoccupation with the "should haves." One five-year-old whose younger brother was run over by a truck while they were outside playing told his mother later, "I should have . . . I should have." He saw himself as his younger brother's protector, responsible for his safety. His mother asked him, "You should have what?" He replied, "I just should have!"

His mother then asked, "What do you mean, you 'should have'?" The boy answered, "I should have looked, I should have known, I should have . . . "—a flood of "should haves" about being his brother's guardian and protector. Taking the child into her arms, his mother said, "I understand, honey. Daddy's got the 'should haves.' Mommy's got the 'should haves.' We all have them. It's okay to have them. And it's okay to know that everybody could have done something differently, and that they *would* have if they'd had a choice."

Allowing a child to be a participant in the family's experience helps the child cope with crisis, as we see exemplified in a drawing by the five-year-old who saw his younger brother killed (see Figure 10-4). The drawing represents "the day my brother was killed"; the point of greatest stress is shown to be the period of time when he was left at a neighbor's house while his parents were at the hospital. Even more frightening than seeing the wheel of the truck roll over his brother's head was the feeling of being left alone, separated from the rest of his family, not knowing what was happening with his parents and his younger brother.

This child's parents not only encouraged the child to express his feelings but also sought out resources as additional support for coping with the tragedy. Just as the child's work with spontaneous drawings helped bring to light his anger at being left out, the parents received support by sharing their experience with others who had survived similar experiences and by calling on therapeutic resources in their community.

Figure 10-4 *A Five-Year-Old's "Crooked Day" Drawing*
In this drawing of "The Crooked Day," a five-year-old boy depicts his experience of the events that transpired on the day his brother received fatal injuries in an accident. Contrary to what might be assumed about this drawing, the places on the line where the greatest stress is indicated occurred after the accident itself. The sharp dip in the line at the left-hand side of the drawing represents the accident; the point at which the line crosses back on itself denotes the time when the surviving child was left with a neighbor while his parents were at the hospital with his brother. This was a period of uncertainty and confusion, and the child was angry about not being with the other members of his family. The point at which his parents returned and informed him of his brother's death is indicated by the vertical slash marks, which were literally stabbed onto the paper. The jagged line connoting the remainder of the day represents the emotional upheaval that occurred as the child and his parents together focused their attention on coping with the initial shock of their loss. Importantly, the drawing ends with an upward slanting line that is indicative of an essentially positive attitude—the child's ability to deal constructively with his experience of loss. This drawing demonstrates that even a simple artistic expression, such as a line depicting the chronology of events, can reveal a wealth of detail about a child's experience of a traumatic event such as death.

For adolescents bereaved by a sibling's death, efforts to cope with the loss may be intertwined with the developmental task of formulating a personal sense of the meaning of life, a task that usually includes intense questioning about the value of religious beliefs and the existence of God. David Balk points out that the death of a sibling shatters "trust in a benign, innocent universe" and various "questions about the nature of life and death, about good and evil, and about the meaning of life become personal."[30] Coping with a sibling's death can bring about a greater maturity in cognitive development, social reasoning, moral judgment, identity formation, and religious understanding. Indeed, bereaved young people often cite religion as an important resource for coping with loss, reporting that it offers a source of meaning that provides solace as they search for significance in the aftermath of tragedy. A sense of the "ongoing presence" of the sibling bond is also reported by bereaved adolescents, as they continue the "conversation" with a deceased brother or sister and take time to "catch up" on things that have been going on in their lives.[31]

Children with Life-Threatening Illnesses

"Mental first aid" may be needed by children with life-threatening illness to help them cope with disturbing thoughts and feelings. Such assistance may mean simply comforting the child and being supportive through a difficult or painful procedure, or it may require more substantive intervention to deal with anxiety, guilt, anger, or other conflicting or unresolved emotions. Caring for children requires a flexible approach. A child who feels unsure about what is happening may have fantasies that are more frightening than the truth. A supportive atmosphere in which the child feels free to express his or her fears diminishes feelings of separation and loneliness. Care of children who are seriously ill goes beyond physical care. As an Institute of Medicine panel stated, "We can and must reduce the number of those who fail to receive consistent, competent care that meets not only their physical needs, but their emotional, spiritual, and cultural ones as well."[32]

Some suggestions for communication with seriously ill children are given in Table 10-1. In early childhood, the experience of serious illness is likely to be characterized by possibly frightening periods of hospitalization, painful and incomprehensible procedures, periods of separation from familiar adults, limitations caused by the disease and treatment, and communication issues (especially when parents are reluctant to inform the child). For a school-age child, major issues may include a sense of stigma and impaired self-concept, interactions with peers, managing the illness within the school environment (such as intermittent absences and poor academic performance), side effects of treatment, and issues with parents concerning autonomy. For an adolescent, concerns may focus on being forced into a dependent role when trying to achieve independence, impaired body image and impaired self-concept, limited ability to establish ties with peers, questioning of beliefs, and ambivalence or open conflict with parents.

TABLE 10-1 *Suggestions for Communication with Seriously Ill Children*

Age	Approach
0–2	Provide maximum physical relief and comfort.
2–7	Minimize child's separation from parents. Evaluate for feelings of guilt.
7–11	Foster child's sense of control and mastery. Evaluate for feelings of abandonment or body mutilation. Provide details about treatment. Maintain access to peers.
12+	Be clear, honest, direct. Support reasonable measures for independence. Provide privacy. Reinforce self-esteem and body image. Allow ventilation of anger. Maintain access to peers. Consider mutual support groups.

Parents and other adults often find it difficult to respond to a seriously ill child's or teen's questions. Such questions can evoke uncertainty and may be met with silence or other forms of avoidance. Is it ethical, or even possible, to withhold information about a serious or life-threatening illness from a child or adolescent? This poses a dilemma for those who might wish to keep troubling news from them. William Bartholome observes that "the most daunting problem facing parents and caregivers who are caring for a terminally ill child is that the person they are caring for lives in a different reality."[33]

The Child's Perception of Serious Illness

Younger children's perception of their illnesses can be remarkable. Marie-Bénédicte Dembour writes movingly about the "conscious death" of a two-year-old, describing how the child behaved with obvious awareness and curiosity as her parents and doctors discussed her prognosis and her treatment was carried out.[34]

Studying children in a leukemia ward, Myra Bluebond-Langner observed that seriously ill children were usually able to guess their condition by interpreting how people behave toward them.[35] Crying or avoidance behaviors were interpreted as indicating the serious nature of the disease. The children in the leukemia ward, most of whom were between the ages of three and nine, were able to accurately assess the seriousness of their illness even though adults had not shared this information with them. Although they sometimes discussed their illnesses with their peers, these children refrained from doing so with adults. Recognizing that such conversations made adults uncomfortable, the children talked about the taboo topics among themselves, much as children discuss other forbidden topics, out of range of adult hearing.

Over time, the children's interpretations of their conditions changed. At first, the illness was seen as acute, then chronic, and finally fatal. Medications were first "healing agents," then "something that prolongs life." As their perception of the drugs changed from being "always effective" to "effective sometimes" to "not really effective at all," their attitudes and behaviors toward taking medication likewise changed.

The children tended to know a great deal about the world of the hospital, its staff and procedures, and the experiences of other leukemic children, making comments like "Jeffrey's in his first relapse" and noticing when other children died. Although the children did not always know the exact name of the disease afflicting them, they typically displayed considerable knowledge about its treatment and prognosis.

In the "cancer narratives" of adolescents and young adults, researchers said that "we hear their sense of pain and anger at losing control over making their own decisions; we also hear about ways of coping, the support of friends, and ways that they view their physical and psychological selves as they progress through treatment."[36]

Spontaneous drawings and other forms of art therapy are excellent methods for working with young children, helping them explore and express feelings that otherwise might remain hidden yet be disturbing.[37] This was shown in a study conducted at G. Gaslini Children's Hospital in Genova, Italy.[38] The children, affected by leukemia and other cancers, ranged in age from four to fourteen years (median eight years). The children used drawings "as a stage to dramatize their needs, wishes, anxieties, and joys." The drawings depicted their relationship to the disease, the hospital, and the environment in general. The researchers concluded that art therapy is a "vitally important means of narrative communication for severely sick children" that allows them to express their need for truth and for communication. They said that the study confirmed their theory that art therapy is warranted as part of the total care of severely ill hospitalized children.

The Child's Coping Mechanisms

How a child perceives an illness and the manner in which he or she responds to it depend on age, the nature of the illness and its treatment, family relationships, and the child's own personal history. The main concerns experienced by seriously ill children tend to match their understanding of death. For example, children under five years old tend to be most distressed by separation from the mother. Children from roughly ages five to nine tend to be most concerned about the discomforting and possibly disfiguring effects of the disease and related medical procedures. Older children tend to be anxious in response to other children's deaths. The way a child copes with such concerns is influenced by his or her perception of the meaning and likely consequences of an illness.

A child's illness can result in absences from school, changes in family patterns, increased dependency on others, and financial or emotional strain on the child's family. Other sources of stress and grief include medical concerns, such as the presence of pain and possibly the visible effects of the disease or treatment, which may have symbolic significance depending on the child's age and the part of the body affected.

To cope with the anxiety and confusion that accompany serious or life-threatening illness, children use various coping mechanisms. Although a child's stage of development influences his or her capacity for drawing on both internal and external resources, even very young children exhibit a wide range of coping mechanisms. Children use distancing strategies to limit the number of people with whom they have close relationships, thus reducing the number of opportunities for a distressing interaction. In this way, a child selects from the whole situation only those aspects or those people that seem least threatening. This coping mechanism allows the child to construct as safe and secure an environment as possible given the circumstances.

Children may cope with a painful medical procedure by making a deal that allows some desire to be fulfilled once the pain has been endured: "After I get my shot, can I play with my toys?" In dealing with an overwhelming situation, sick children may regress to behavior patterns that recall a less demanding, more comfortable time in their lives. Children may revert to baby talk or "forget" their toilet training during stressful times. A child whose illness prevents him or her from engaging in a competitive sport may cope by finding a substitute for the desired activity by playing board games in a highly competitive way. One might envision scenes of sick children racing through the hospital corridors, IV bottles swinging from their wheelchairs, in a spontaneous competition. Children undergoing chemotherapy may become fatigued and exhibit depressed mood and other affective changes, as well as such physical consequences as nausea/vomiting and sleepiness (frequent napping).[39] As do adults, children use varied coping mechanisms as they confront uncomfortable and frightening aspects of a potentially life-limiting illness. Even very small children know when they are very sick, and they are often far more aware of death than adults realize.[40]

Providing and Organizing Care

"Was there someone in charge of your child's medical care?"

"Yes, me. Coordinating the various doctors, nurses, and treatments was the most frustrating part of the process."

The Institute of Medicine panel mentioned earlier reported the above dialogue with a parent of a seriously ill child. The panel said: "The diagnosis of a child's life-threatening medical condition often launches child and family into a complex and confusing world of technologically sophisticated treatments, arcane terminology, and highly specialized personnel and organizations."[41]

Caring for a child who is dying involves more than just medical treatment. The child and his or her whole family should receive appropriate social, psychological, and spiritual care. Researchers note that "children's spiritual growth appears to parallel physical and psychosocial growth."[42] Providing optimal care involves implementing the principle of whole-person care for children as well as adults. The Institute of Medicine panel found that "too often, children with fatal or potentially fatal conditions and their families fail to receive competent, compassionate, and consistent care that meets their physical, emotional, and spiritual needs."[43]

Pediatric Hospice and Palliative Care

Children with life-limiting conditions can receive care in children's hospitals, hospices with established pediatric programs, and other institutions that care for children with such conditions, as well as at home. One goal of residential hospice care is to offer an alternative to hospitalization when a child requires more intensive assessment, symptom management, and care planning than can be successfully provided at home. Stephen Connor says, "In general, dedicated pediatric palliative care services are like islands of excellence in the sea of children's health care in the United States."[44]

There are relatively few hospice programs intended to specifically serve dying children and their families. The first was Helen House, founded in England in 1982. In 1995, pediatric palliative care was initiated in British Columbia, Canada: Canuck Place, which was the first freestanding children's hospice in North America. George Mark Children's House, founded in 2004 in the San Francisco Bay area, was the first freestanding pediatric palliative care center in the United States. Other notable children's hospice programs include Edmarc Hospice for Children in Virginia and Suncoast Hospice in Florida. Typically, such programs provide services through all stages of a child's illness, including physician and nursing support, pain and symptom management, respite care, music and play therapy, and end-of-life care, with counseling services available to all members of the child's family.

As mentioned in an earlier chapter, the Medicare Hospice Benefit specifies that hospice care is reimbursed only when (1) a physician determines that the patient has a prognosis of six months or less, and (2) the patient forgoes curative treatment. To remedy this limitation, the state of California recently passed the Nick Snow Children's Hospice and Palliative Care Act, which requires the state Department of Health Services to submit a waiver that allows children with life-limiting conditions to receive both palliative and curative care.[45] The goal is to promote the development of a comprehensive pediatric palliative care demonstration program that improves quality of life for children and their family members.

Home-based palliative care is an important option in the care of terminally ill children. Hospice Hawaii is among the "adult" hospices that have recently expanded services to terminally ill children. "With children," one social worker at Hospice Hawaii explains, "you have to think outside of the box."[46] Ida Martinson, a nurse-educator who helped pioneer such care, observes,

> The greatest barrier [to providing effective care to dying children and their families] is the difficulty in accepting the reality of the dying child by the parents and physicians as well as the nurses. No one wants a child to die, so continued treatment goes beyond what is desirable and useful for the child.[47]

Martinson says, "Parents may have difficulty in realizing that the care they are providing their child in the home is as good—and most likely better than—what we health care professionals could provide in the hospital."

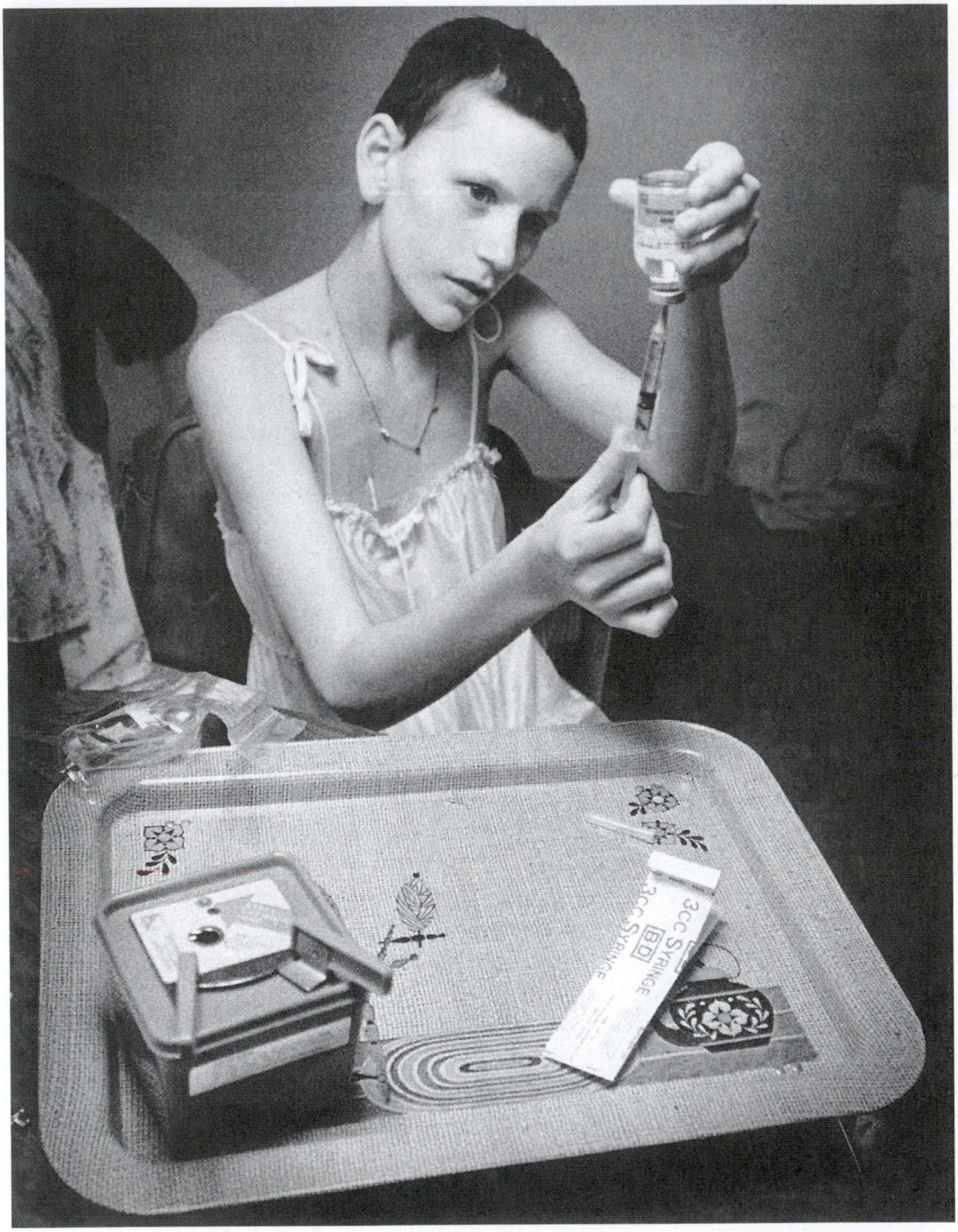

Theresa Aubin, *Bremerton Sun*

Adolescents and older children with life-threatening illnesses may take on increasing responsibilities for their daily treatment regimes. Here, a young cancer patient flushes her venous access catheter, the route used to administer chemotherapy, which must be cleaned nightly.

Decisions About Medical Treatment

Seriously ill children and adolescents are not merely passive participants in the medical and social events that occur because of their illness. Depending on the child and his or her stage of developmental sophistication, he or she may have opinions about the course of illness and treatment and may wish to exercise some degree of autonomy and choice in making medical decisions. Studies confirm adolescents' willingness and ability to participate in end-of-life decisions.[48] Nevertheless, parents, the medical staff, and other adults may be uncertain about, or even resistant to, the idea of a child or an adolescent making decisions about such possible life-or-death matters.

According to Louis Gamino and Hal Ritter, the Rule of Sevens, based on English common law, gives parents and health care providers a guideline for assessing a minor child's capacity to participate in medical decision making.[49] Until the age of seven, a child is understood to be an immature minor with no capacity for medical decision making. For a child ages seven to fourteen, it is thought possible that the child may object to a medical procedure. Children in this age group are moving toward a status as "mature minors," and their increasing cognitive capacities need to be honored. If the significant adults disagree with the child, there may be reasons for contradicting their claim of the child's incapacity to make a decision. Finally, during ages fourteen to twenty-one, the adolescent's or young adult's views are considered more carefully, as if he or she has capacity for medical decision making. These individuals are considered mature minors who have capacity for decision, though there may be reasons for overriding their wishes. The greater the harm that could occur as a result of following the child's or adolescent's wishes, the stronger the argument for overriding them.

Gamino and Ritter argue that, although the legal right of *consent* for treating children remains with the parent, health care providers should work to secure a child's *assent,* or agreement to the proposed treatment or procedure. Disagreements sometimes end up in the courts. As Gamino and Ritter point out,

> In situations where mature minors want a different decision about their medical treatment than that being chosen by the parents, courts often invoke the 50% Risk Rule in addition to the Rule of Sevens. If the mature minor is refusing treatment, and the various risks of not receiving the treatment are less than 50%, then the court will generally rule in favor of the mature minor. On the other hand, if the risks to the child of no treatment are greater than 50%, then the courts will generally rule in favor of the parents to proceed with a decision for treatment.[50]

Because of the recognition that, at least on some levels, adolescents are maturing more quickly than in the past, some legal analysts suggest that teenage decision making should be simplified by instituting laws that "recognize legal age of consent by an adolescent to routine and standard medical and surgical procedures as 16 years of age."[51] Of course, this proposal is not as simple when medical procedures pertain to life-threatening and serious illness.

William Bartholome, a physician and professor of pediatrics, states, "Many of the problems involved in responding to the needs of dying children belong to the 'big people' involved."[52] Adults sometimes question whether it is better to tell or not to tell; that is, they wonder about the appropriate action to take in terms of being truthful with children about a serious or life-limiting illness. Such questions are legitimate and must be considered with the aim of achieving a responsible balance between presenting the facts or truth to a child and refraining from unnecessarily adding to his or her anxieties, concerns, and fears. The goal of respecting the child is much more than just being truthful (see Table 10-1). Bartholome says, "Children have a right to be treated as developing persons, as persons with a developing capacity for rationality, autonomy, and participation in health care decision making."[53]

Caring for a Seriously Ill Child

A study of fathers who cared for a child with life-limiting illness characterized their experience as "living in the dragon's shadow" and "battling the dragon."[54] It was a continuous process that required strength, willpower, and work. In the fathers' perceptions, they (and their ill children) "struggled valiantly to overcome the dragon's power."

The ill child is thrust into a more or less alien world of hospitals and medical paraphernalia. Illness separates children from their familiar surroundings and the people they love. Even as a child becomes accustomed to the rhythms of life in and out of hospital, new therapies or unfamiliar medical settings or personnel can make everything again seem out of whack. Changes in expected routine can be upsetting, adding to the child's anxieties and fears. Each time a child returns to the hospital, he or she is a different person, at a new stage of development, with different fears and expectations. Some children are resilient in response to the stressors of treatment, debilitating side effects, and the day-to-day experience of living with serious illness; others have difficulty coping with all the varied acute and chronic stressors that accompany a life-threatening illness.

The participation of family members in some aspects of care can be comforting to a child. Although professionals are usually better equipped to care for a child's medical needs, parents have special expertise in the nontechnical aspects of care. Parents can be involved in activities like bathing the child, assisting at mealtimes, tucking the child in at night, and emotionally supporting the child. Parents should carefully consider whether it is in the child's best interest for them to be involved in performing medical procedures that might cause the child pain. Generally speaking, parents should focus on their parenting role rather than trying to perform the role of a nurse.

The crisis of a child's illness can lead to a breakdown in communication. A young girl told a hospital staffer, "I know I'm going to die. I want to talk to Mother, but she won't let me. I know she's hurting, but I'm the one who's dying." When told of this conversation by the staff member, the girl's mother replied angrily, "She wouldn't be thinking of dying if you hadn't made her talk about it."

The communication between mother and daughter went from bad to worse. Still refusing to discuss her daughter's feelings, the mother's style of communication degenerated into baby talk: "Her doesn't feel goody today. . . . her doesn't want to talk." A lack of openness was hampering satisfaction of the child's (as well as the parent's) needs for affection and reassurance.

Support Groups for Children

Community support is an important supplement to a family's internal support system. Many organizations that offer support during the crises of life-threatening illness and bereavement have programs for all members of a family, including children. For example, The Compassionate Friends and the Bereaved Families of Ontario not only serve bereaved parents but also serve children and adolescents. The Dougy Center for Grieving Children in Portland, Oregon, has been so successful in providing bereavement support programs to its community that it conducts facilitator trainings worldwide.

The Hospice of Frederick County in Maryland has an innovative outreach program, Camp Jamie, in which bereaved children are paired with a group of caring adults, called "Big Buddies," some of whom are also recovering from losses.[55] Named after a hospice patient who died before his third birthday, Camp Jamie provides children with "a haven to learn about coping with grief." In a mountain setting, participants enjoy recreational activities and have opportunities to explore their losses in a safe environment among peers and "big buddies." In addition to grief education and support, campers also enjoy activities, such as fishing, team games, arts/crafts, hiking, sing-alongs, campfires with storytellers, and the Camp Jamie Olympics. There are opportunities for the children to express themselves and develop bonds with others. Through interactions with other children and adults, campers learn that they are not alone in their grief.

Similar programs have developed across the United States over the past decades. Camp Erin, for example, is "the largest nationwide network of free bereavement camps for children and teens ages 6–17 who have experienced the death of someone close to them."[56] These camps provide a weekend-long experience of traditional camp activities combined with grief education and emotional support. Each Camp Erin is facilitated through a partnership with a local bereavement agency. In Southern California, one such agency is Morning Star. As a nationally acclaimed support center for grieving children, teens, and their families, Morning Star offers Camp Erin to bereaved children during summers. It is staffed by professional grief counselors and there is no charge to attendees.

Besides organizations offering bereavement support to children and teens, other organizations provide support for the crises that accompany life-threatening illness. HUGS—an acronym that stands for Help, Understanding, and Group Support for Hawaii's Seriously Ill Children and Their Families—was founded in 1982 by a small group of volunteers who recognized the many challenges and stressors that families with seriously ill children face. HUGS offers a wide range of services, including crisis support, hospital and home visits, transportation to medical appointments, recreational activities, and respite care. The mission of HUGS is "to help families stay together in the face of overwhelming adversity."[57]

The Starlight Children's Foundation, founded in 1983, is an organization dedicated to improving the quality of life for children with chronic and life-threatening medical conditions.[58] The foundation has chapters and offices located throughout the United States and facilities in Canada, the United Kingdom, Australia, and Japan. The foundation's "high-tech" and "high-touch" programs are designed to help children better understand and manage their illnesses and connect families with others facing similar challenges to create a community so that no one feels alone. The foundation does this by providing education, entertainment, and family events that help sick children cope with the pain, fear, and isolation of prolonged illness. Among its programs are "Starlight Sites," hospital environments where pediatric patients can relax, play, and interact with other children during their hospital stay, and "Starbright World," an online social network for teens with chronic and life-threatening medical conditions, and their siblings. Sick teens are able to connect with other teens that are at home or in the hospital. Users post pictures, chat, post blogs and bulletins, and find new friends in similar situations.[59]

Organizations that exist to grant the wishes of children who have been given a limited or uncertain prognosis are another support. Examples include the Sunshine Foundation, founded in 1976, and the Make-A-Wish Foundation, founded in 1980.[60] After the founding of Make-A-Wish, interest in granting wishes spread across the country and to other nations. The organization now grants wishes through its 62 chapters located throughout the United States, and it also operates in 47 other countries on five continents through affiliates. Through the efforts of such groups, seriously ill children and their families are able to take a vacation together or fulfill some other wish that seems impossible without outside help.

Telephone support groups are a type of organized social support that has been effectively used with varied populations, including children. The telephone was first used as a method of outreach for suicide prevention by the Samaritans in London in 1953. Later, the Pediatric Branch of the National Cancer Institute created a telephone network to offer social support to

"Peanuts," drawing by Charles Schulz, © 1995 United Features Syndicate, Inc.

HIV-infected children. Organizers said the telephone offered "a sense of confidentiality not afforded in face-to-face groups," thus providing "a creative and therapeutic way to help HIV-infected children and their family members cope with the impact this disease had on their lives."[61]

Helping Children Cope with Change and Loss

Never overlook a child's concerns or take them lightly when the child wants to talk about a close friend or loved one who has died. Encourage the child or adolescent to express his or her feelings about the loss. Heather Servaty-Seib observes that, although "friends are central to the daily life" of teens, the grief of young people for deceased friends "generally goes unnoticed, is minimized, or is misunderstood."[62] Tailor any intervention or strategy to the individual's needs and situation. Children usually cope more easily with their feelings in a crisis when they feel included as participants in the unfolding experience. If they are excluded, or if their questions go unanswered, uncertainty creates more anxiety and confusion. When an adult is also struggling to cope with a traumatic experience, it may be difficult to provide an explanation of the painful circumstances to a child. The child's feelings and concerns may be dismissed or ignored. Even when adults agree that children have a right to know the truth, they may feel uncomfortable about giving them painful and disturbing news. They may ask themselves, Would knowing the truth cause the child more harm than good? In most instances, the child's natural curiosity effectively eliminates the option of withholding such information.

Responding to a child's natural inquisitiveness and concern does not mean that one needs to overwhelm the child with excessive detail, nor does it mean "talking down" to the child, as if he or she were incapable of comprehension. Nevertheless, a child's manner of perceiving, experiencing, and coping with change needs to be considered by parents and others who wish to be helpful. This implies responding to the child's questions and concerns on the basis of his or her ability to understand. As a general guideline for discussing death with a child, it is important to keep the explanation simple, stick to basic facts, and verify what the child has understood.

Bibliotherapy—that is, using books as an aid to coping—can facilitate discussion between adults and children and create opportunities for sharing thoughts and feelings (a selection of books about death for children and teens can be found in Chapter 2).[63]

Discussing Death Before a Crisis Occurs

In explaining death to children, honesty is in first place. Be aware, however, that a parent who sets a ground rule that it's okay to be open and honest in talking about death may find that there are times when the child wants to initiate a discussion, and the parent is tired or would rather avoid the subject. If talking about death is part of normal life and not a reaction to crisis, choosing a good time is more of a possibility.

The Lesson

'Your father's gone,' my bald headmaster said.
His shiny dome and brown tobacco jar
Splintered at once in tears. It wasn't grief.
I cried for knowledge which was bitterer
Than any grief. For there and then I knew
That grief has uses—that a father dead
Could bind the bully's fist a week or two;
And then I cried for shame, then for relief.

I was a month past ten when I learnt this:
I still remember how the noise was stilled
In school-assembly when my grief came in.
Some goldfish in a bowl quietly sculled
Around their shining prison on its shelf.
They were indifferent. All the other eyes
Were turned towards me. Somewhere in myself
Pride, like a goldfish, flashed a sudden fin.

Edward Lucie-Smith

Second, don't put off introducing the topic of death. When a close death precedes the discussion, the parent is faced with the need to provide an explanation in the midst of crisis. This unfortunate situation arises when a parent puts off discussing death "because it's not really going to happen," only to find that "it's happening right now, and my child has to be told something." In these circumstances, the explanation to the child is likely to be charged with all the emotions the parent is dealing with, making clear communication more difficult. Thus, it is a good idea to make use of teachable moments—occasions that come up in everyday activities—for talking with children about death (see discussion of teachable moments in Chapter 2).

Third, set the explanation to the child's level of understanding. By using as a guide the child's interest and ability to understand, the parent can provide an explanation that is appropriate to the child's particular circumstances.

When talking with children about death, it is important to verify what they think you've told them. Have them tell you what they learned or heard you saying about death. Children generalize from known concepts to make new experiences fit. This may lead to a very literal interpretation of new information, especially among young children, who tend to emphasize the concreteness of things. Recognizing this, strive to keep your communication free of associations that could be confusing. Metaphorical explanations about death may help you draw a child-sized picture as an aid to understanding, but unless fact and fancy are clearly distinguished, the child may grasp the fanciful details instead of the underlying facts the analogy was meant to convey. This is illustrated in the following story: A five-year-old girl was told that her grandfather's cancer was like a seed that grew in his body; it grew and grew

A Cemetery Conversation with Sofia at Five Years Old

Sofia: "What are the dead people doing in the earth?"
Francesco: "They rest."
Sofia: "Are they bored?"
Francesco (smiling): "To death!"
Sofia (sad): "Do they rest always?"
Francesco: "Maybe they come out at night to talk to each other or perhaps to dance."
Sofia: "Impossible! They are dead!"

until he couldn't live in his body anymore, and he died. Her parents didn't notice that, ever afterward, all through childhood, she never ate another seed. Not one. Not a cucumber seed, watermelon seed, no seeds. Finally, at age twenty-one, she was asked, "Why are you avoiding the seeds? Isn't that a little bizarre? What's wrong with the seeds?" Her automatic response was, "You swallow them, and you die." After all those years, she saw the fallacy of her compulsion to avoid eating seeds. It would have been useful if someone had asked her when she was five, "What will happen if you swallow that seed?"

Discussions When a Family Member Is Seriously Ill

When a member of a child's family is seriously ill, family routine is disrupted. If the truth about the illness is kept from the child, he or she may become confused about the reasons for changes in the family's usual pattern of interactions. The child may feel rejected, left out of family activities, or ignored for no apparent reason: "Why are my parents so nice to my sister, but they ignore me all the time?" or "Geez, I get into trouble about every little thing, while my brother gets off scot-free no matter what he does!" Siblings of a seriously ill child may be alarmed by changes in the sick child's appearance due to disease or side effects of treatment.[64] In some cases, there may be multiple losses, unpredictable living arrangements, and changes of school, as well as the possibility of issues involving stigma, secrecy, and shame.

Although open communication is important in helping a child cope with the crisis, explanations must be suited to the child's cognitive capacity. A very young child whose parent is seriously ill might be told simply, "Mommy has an ouch in her tummy which the doctors are trying to fix." A school-age child could be given a more complex explanation, such as that the parent needs medical treatment because something is growing in her stomach that doesn't belong there.

Anxiety about a parent's or sibling's illness may be displayed in varied ways. Children may feel neglected and resent adjustments they must make in their own lives. A child may be angry because "Mommy isn't here," yet feel guilty because he or she imagines somehow "causing Mommy's illness." To counteract these feelings, help the child feel that he or she is a fully participating member of the family. Encourage the child to be part of the process of dealing with the illness.

The child can participate in caring for the sick family member in appropriate ways. For example, a child might pick a bouquet or make a drawing as a gift. Such activities allow the child to express his or her feelings in a creative way. Although children cannot be protected from the reality of death, their experiences of it can be made less difficult if they have sensitive, caring support from those closest to them.

Discussions in the Aftermath of Loss

Understanding another person's experience requires the art of listening. This is true when talking with a child or an adolescent as well as when talking with adults. The aim is to discover what the other person thinks, feels, and believes: What does he or she find important? What are his or her concerns, fears, hopes? If a need for support or assistance is being expressed, what kind of help is he or she asking for? Questions of this kind are important in helping children cope with loss. Rob Zucker says, "Grieving adults can become so overwhelmed that they lose sight of their obligations to their grieving children."[65] We need to be willing *to listen and to accept the reality of the child's experience.*

When death disrupts familiar patterns of living, the result can be confusion and conflict, creating a tangle of emotions and thoughts that are hard to sort out. In the midst of this, children may be asked to remain "unseen and unheard," thus thwarting their natural tendencies to explore and grapple with the emotions and thoughts generated by change. Paying attention to a child's behavior is useful for gathering information about his or her experience of crisis. Crying, for instance, is a natural response to the loss of someone significant. Admonishing a child to "Be brave!" or "Be a little man and buck up!" denies the validity of the child's spontaneous emotion. Be aware, however, that an absence of tears should not be interpreted as an absence of grief.

In helping children cope with loss, adults must strive to *answer the child's questions honestly and directly.* Explanations should be truthful to the facts and should be as concrete as possible. Telling a child that her goldfish "went to heaven" may cause her to make an elaborate picture of the pearly gates and different sections of heaven: Here is goldfish heaven, cat heaven, and over here is people heaven—a very logical concept that makes sense to a child. A study of images of heaven in children's storybooks found that heaven was typically portrayed in a simplistic fashion. The stories presented "a generic image of heaven" combined with cultural beliefs suggesting that "death is not the end of life, but a continuation."[66] Regardless of the therapeutic value of assuring children that they are able to maintain bonds with a deceased loved one, we need to be careful that the concepts we convey to a child don't turn out to be dysfunctional.

One woman recalled that, when she was three or four, a favorite dog suddenly "went to live on a farm." Not until she was about seven did she realize that the dog really wasn't living at the puppy farm. When she realized that in fact her beloved dog was dead, she felt angry and upset that she hadn't had the opportunity to properly say good-bye.

Similarly, religious beliefs are an important part of how death is understood in many families. Parents want to share these beliefs with their children

Hasse Persson/Expressen Stockholm/Sweden

The classmates of a murdered child carry his coffin to the grave. The rituals and ceremonies surrounding death can provide an avenue for children and adolescents to express their grief and to begin the process of coming to terms with loss.

when coping with the death of a family member or friend. Children may indeed be comforted by such beliefs, but they deserve to be told that these are *beliefs*. Talk about them in a way that avoids confusing the child. For example, a parent's concept of an afterlife may be different from what a child is

> *Small boy.* "Where do animals go when they die?"
> *Small girl.* "All good animals go to heaven, but the bad ones go to the Natural History Museum."
>
> Caption to drawing by E. H. Shepard, *Punch*, 1929

able to understand. A child who is told that "God took Daddy to be with him in heaven" may not feel very kindly toward a being who could be so capricious and inconsiderate of the child's feelings.

For the same reason, fairy tales, metaphors, and the like should be avoided or used with care because children may take such explanations of death literally. Consider the case of a four-year-old whose brother (nine) told him that daddy had gone to heaven. The four-year-old promptly went and told his mother, "My daddy's on the roof!" She said, "What? Who told you that?" He said, "Andrew did." The older brother then explained, "We were looking out the window and I told him that daddy was in heaven up there." To the four-year-old, the highest "up there" was up on the roof. If you tell a four-year-old that someone who has died is "up there," and you also say that Santa Claus lands on the roof on Christmas Eve, he may decide that Santa Claus and the person who has died are great buddies. He might make up stories about how they work together, making toys, feeding the reindeer, and so on.

The concreteness of a young child's concepts about death is also illustrated in the experience of a woman whose first encounter with death occurred when she was three and a half years old, and her mother died. It seemed that her mother had just disappeared; she didn't know what had happened to her. Some time later, she began to realize that her mother had died, and she started asking questions. Some people told her that her mother had been buried, and her thought was, "Why don't they dig her up?" Others said that her mother had gone to heaven, so she kept looking at the sky, watching for her. With both of these concepts running through her young mind, she did her best to figure out, "How can my mother be buried in heaven?"

When asked about their experiences involving a close death, children often say that the most difficult times were when they did not know what was happening. A child whose diagnosis of serious illness was withheld from her by her family said later, "We'd always done everything with each other knowing what was going on. Suddenly, it was different. That scared me more than what was happening to my body. It felt like my family was becoming strangers."[67] Sudden change in family communication patterns can be alarming to a child, heightening anxiety about the crisis. A child who is kept from the funeral of a close friend or relative may feel anxious about not being included in an activity that had obvious importance to the significant adults in his or her life. Some children may not want to attend a funeral. Those who do, however, tend to report that it helped them acknowledge the death, provided an occasion for honoring the deceased person, and made it possible for them to receive social support and comfort.[68]

The best gauge of a child's readiness to be informed about a potentially painful situation is the child's own interest, usually expressed through questions. Using these questions as a guide, caregivers can give straightforward answers without burdening the child with facts irrelevant to his or her understanding of the situation. Most important, children in crisis situations need to be reassured that they are loved.

Children are apt to point out any inconsistencies in what we tell them about death. When one three-year-old's playmate was killed, his mother explained to him that Jesus had come and taken his friend to heaven. His response was, "Well, that's an awful thing to do; I want to play with him. Jesus isn't very nice if he comes down here and takes my friend from me." In discussing death with a child, it is crucial to consider the child's belief system, the kind of thought processes he or she uses to understand the world. Then, from your very first statement, ask yourself, "If I explain death in this way, how will it be understood by the child?"

Adults tend to worry about children's encounters with death. Are they doing all right? Will they be okay? Is death going to be too hard for them to handle? Can they survive this particular loss? Erik Erikson said, "Healthy children will not fear life if their parents have the integrity not to fear death."[69]

Further Readings

David E. Balk and Charles A. Corr, eds., *Adolescent Encounters with Death, Bereavement, and Coping*. New York: Springer, 2009.

Mary Dixon-Woods, Bridget Young, and David Heney. *Rethinking Experiences of Childhood Cancer: A Multidisciplinary Approach to Chronic Childhood Illness.* Maidenhead, Berkshire: Open University Press, 2005.

Kenneth J. Doka and Amy S. Tucci, eds. *Living with Grief: Children and Adolescents.* Washington, D.C.: Hospice Foundation of America, 2008.

Marilyn J. Field and Richard E. Behrman, eds. *When Children Die: Improving Palliative and End-of-Life Care for Children and Their Families.* Washington, D.C.: National Academies Press, 2003.

Phyllis Silverman and Madelyn Kelly. *A Parent's Guide to Raising Grieving Children: Rebuilding Your Family After the Death of a Loved One.* New York: Oxford University Press, 2009.

Carolyn Ambler Walter and Judith L. M. McCoyd. *Grief and Loss Across the Lifespan: A Biopsychosocial Perspective.* New York: Springer, 2009.

Leigh A. Woznick and Carol D. Goodheart. *Living with Childhood Cancer: A Practical Guide to Help Families Cope.* Washington, D.C.: American Psychological Association, 2002.

Additional resources for this chapter can be found at www.mhhe.com/despelder10e

Holding their dead baby, this Harlem couple finds comfort in the sharing of their memories and their grief as they acknowledge the death of their firstborn child. Of all the losses that can be experienced during adult life, most people feel that the death of a child is the most painful.

CHAPTER 11

Death in the Lives of Adults

Take a moment to reflect on the losses that have occurred in your own life, both during childhood and more recently. How have these experiences differed? In what ways are they similar? How has your orientation to loss changed as you've gotten older? What kinds of coping mechanisms have been beneficial in moving through the experience of loss?

Some of the losses discussed in connection with childhood and adolescence occur in adulthood also.[1] The death of a brother or sister, or other close relative. The death of a parent. The deaths of friends. Peter Marris says, "Grieving for loss is the most profoundly innovative learning we undertake in our adult lives."[2]

In this chapter we look at the death of a friend and death of a parent occurring in adult life, as well as parental bereavement, including childbearing losses, and death of a life partner. The chapter concludes with an examination of the losses that typically accompany the end of the life course. You will probably find it useful to briefly review the discussion of developmental challenges associated with the phases of adulthood in Chapter 2.

Death and the College Student

College students are generally situated within the age groups of *emerging adulthood* (roughly ages eighteen to twenty-five) and the early years of *early adulthood* (ages twenty to forty). They are typically involved in expanding the scope of various forms of commitment and interaction in their lives—sex, friendship, cooperation, partnership, and affiliation. These years involve a tension between intimacy and isolation. In *Death and the College Student,* Edwin Shneidman collected brief essays on death and related topics written by students in a death education course taught at Harvard.[3] Class was scheduled in a room with twenty chairs; two hundred students appeared for the first class meeting, and 155 completed the course. Essays were wide-ranging and included topics such as combat death, philosophy, the death cult of James Dean, motives for self-destruction, and suicide. Many essays reflect what Shneidman called "metacrises"—crises related to incidents that occurred out of phase with the students' chronological age. Paging through these essays, it is evident that death was significant in the lives of these students.

Surveys reveal that a considerable number of college students are within twelve months of a family or friend death, and about a third to nearly half are within twenty-four months of bereavement. "In terms of adverse life events, death loss was the most common" such event among undergraduates.[4] A study by Heather Servaty-Seib found that bereaved college students are at risk for decreased academic performance and dropout. Students earned significantly lower GPAs during the semester of their death loss.[5]

Young adults, somewhat like adolescents, may think they are "beyond death." This can result in risky behaviors, such as unprotected sex, substance abuse, binge drinking, and careless or incautious driving. Car accidents are the leading cause of death for college students. In some instances, these accidents are alcohol-related; at other times, they are caused by dangerous activities like texting while driving. On some occasions, they are the result of youthful exuberance, "having fun," without necessary attention to the tasks of driving. Whatever the reason, automobile-related accidents can be a significant source of death and bereavement experiences among college students.

> I remember her as she lay in her hospital bed in July. Unable finally to deny the pain. And for the first time in our relationship of 21 years forced to allow someone else to take care of her. My father could not stand the sight and so he stayed outside, pacing up and down in the hallways. I could not help staring at her. Disbelief that this person with tubes running in and out like entrances and exits on a freeway was the same woman who just six months before had laughed gaily and danced at my wedding.
>
> Ruth Kramer Ziony, "Scream of Consciousness"

Suicide is the second-leading cause of death among college students. Suicides of individuals in this age group, whose lives were mostly ahead of them, leave the lingering question, What beautiful things might have existed in the void now left behind? Despite efforts by college officials to create a safety net, the suicide rate on campus has remained relatively static. Psychologist Thomas Joiner compares suicide on campus to a hurricane: "It's a catastrophe."[6]

One theory is that young people are becoming more concerned about rewards, status, and success—all of which tend to create stress. Although counseling is usually available through college health programs, the amount of time that can be devoted to talking with an individual student about emotional or other problems is limited. The result may be, as with health care generally, a prescription for an antidepressant or other mood-altering drug, when talking about a problem may have been more effective than receiving medication. (Suicide of young adults and possible interventions are discussed in Chapter 12.)

College students are also at risk of infectious diseases, such as bacterial meningitis. Because college students usually come to campus from widely dispersed locales and live in close quarters, bacteria can readily multiply. Although immunizations are available, and students may receive them prior to arriving on campus, vaccines are not always 100 percent effective.

Violence—both random acts and acts occurring within known victim-perpetrator relationships—is another threat, one that can come without

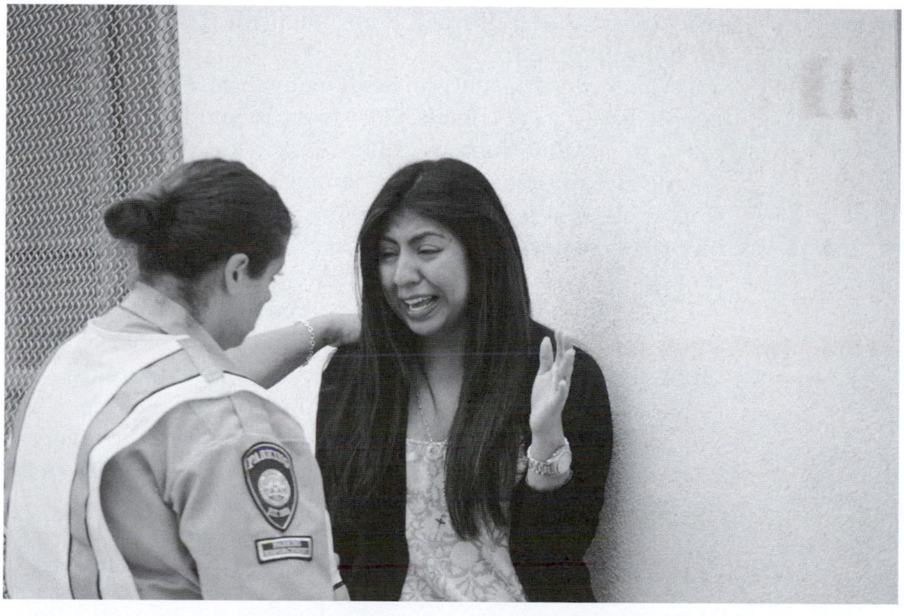

At Santa Monica College, Priscilla Morales cries as she is consoled by a parking enforcement officer after a series of killings by a gunman with an assault-style rifle in June 2013. Morales was in the college library when the gunman, who had previously been a student at the college, opened fire on students. He was shot to death by police when he exchanged gunfire with them.

warning. Young people are disproportionately represented among victims of violence. (Violence and steps to reduce it are discussed in Chapter 13.)

Finally, individuals attending college usually question traditional religious practices and their own spiritual development. Typical questions include these: What am I going to do with my life? What kind of person do I want to be? How am I going to leave my mark before I eventually die? For most students, these kinds of questions are important, and they often involve, at least tangentially, dying and death. As a diverse group—ethnically, socioeconomically, religiously, and politically—students on campuses today are generally active in dealing with core existential questions.[7]

The Death of a Friend

The death of a close friend is a loss that evokes grief similar to reactions following the death of a relative.[8] Yet there are fewer opportunities to openly mourn. In this sense, a friend's death can result in disenfranchised grief (discussed in Chapter 9). Whereas most employers provide at least some type of bereavement leave when death occurs in an employee's family, such leave is unlikely to be provided when a close friend dies, even when the mourner and the deceased have been friends for years. There is a tendency to believe that the most important human relationships are found *within,* not *outside,* families. But friendship involves similar bonds. Because of changes in family structure, social and geographical mobility, and other psychological or cultural factors, friendship ties are increasingly important for many people.

The term *friend* encompasses many different kinds of relationships. Most people have casual friends, close friends, and best friends, as well as "special-purpose" friends such as colleagues, associates, and acquaintances. Many people identify a mate as their best friend; when death ends a paired relationship, it packs a double whammy because it also means the loss of the surviving partner's best friend. Some friends do not see each other often, but, when they do get together, their friendship "picks up where we left off."

For older adults, friendships can be more important than family relationships. For example, despite the fact that many older women live alone, they often say that they are not lonely because of the mutually supportive relationships they have developed and maintained with a circle of friends.[9]

Friendships are important. When a friend dies, grief needs to be acknowledged. Even when society tends to disenfranchise such grief, it is nonetheless important to do what is needed to mourn the loss.

The Death of a Parent

Many people say that a parent's death is the hardest thing they have dealt with in their lives. Even when the parent has been ill beforehand, the ensuing grief can include a variety of emotions: sadness over the loss; relief at the ending of the parent's suffering; anxiety because a kind of "protection against death" symbolized by a parent's presence is gone; and memories, painful as well as comforting. In most cases, the death of a parent represents the loss of a long-term relationship characterized by nurture and unconditional support. Parents are often described as "always being there when the chips are really down, no matter what." In other instances, a parent's death may bring an ending to a relationship that was troubling or dysfunctional. The reaction may be either relief or regret that there is no longer a chance for reconciliation.

Individual siblings may experience a parent's death in very different ways. A study by Miriam and Sidney Moss revealed several themes that emerged from the narratives of two sisters regarding the death of their father:[10]

1. Each sister described very different perceptions of the family and of the father while disconfirming many aspects of the other sister's view.
2. Each sister had a close bond and a caring relationship with her sister, although they were different in personality, attitudes toward caregiving for parents, and their views of life.
3. Each sister saw different meanings and realities related to the father's death, based partly on their non-shared experiences in the past.

For midlife adults, a parent's death is an important symbolic event.[11] It may initiate a period of upheaval and transition. Most people report that the death of a parent changes their outlook on life, often spurring them on to examine their lives more closely, to begin changing what they don't like, and to appreciate more fully their ongoing relationships. A study of middle-aged African American women who were coping with the deaths of their elderly mothers found that religious beliefs provided important ways of thinking about and coping with their mothers' deaths.[12] Besides facilitating a sense of readiness for the anticipated loss, religious themes also helped in the "development of a new tie that permits restructuring life with mom's emotional, if not physical, presence."[13]

Any death reminds us of our own mortality, but a parent's death can cause a person to realize, perhaps for the first time, that he or she has become an adult. Thus, the death of a parent can result in a "developmental push," which may lead to a "more mature stance in parentally bereaved adults who no longer think of themselves as children."[14]

When both parents have died, there may be a consequent role change for the adult child, who no longer has his or her parents to fall back on, even if only in imagination. There is often a sense that, if real trouble comes, a child can call on his or her parents. With the deaths of one's parents, that sense of security is gone. The bereaved adult child may feel that there is no longer anyone who would be willing to answer his or her call for help unconditionally. After the deaths of both her parents, one woman said that although she knew friends and other relatives loved and cared about her, she felt that her parents' love had been unique and irreplaceable. Adjusting to the death of one's parents can involve both holding on and letting go, as the bereaved

You Don't Miss Your Water

At home, my mother wakes up and spends some of her day
talking back to my father's empty chair.
In Florida, my sister experiences the occasional dream in
which my father returns; they chat.
He's been dead and gone for a little over a year. How it would
please me to hear his unrecorded voice again, now alive
only in the minds of those who remember him.
If I could, if as in the old spiritual, I could actually get a direct
phone link to the other side, I could call him up, tell him
about this small prize of a week I've had teaching poetry
at a ski resort a few miles from Lake Tahoe, imagination
jackpot, brief paradise of letters.
How could I make him believe that I have gotten all of this,
this modern apartment, this pond in front of my window,
all from the writing of a few good lines of verse, my father,
who distrusted anything he couldn't get his hands on?
Most likely, he would listen, then ask me, as he always did, just
for safety's sake, if my wife still had her good paying job.
And I can't tell you why, but this afternoon, I wouldn't become
hot and stuffy from his concern, think "old fool" and gripe
back *Of course I'm still teaching college. It's summer, you know?*
This afternoon, I miss his difficult waters, and when he'd ask, as
he always would, *How're they treating you?* I'd love to answer
back, *Fine, daddy. They're paying me to write about your life.*

Cornelius Eady

person simultaneously recognizes the reality of death and treasures comforting memories of the deceased.[15]

Perhaps because of a mother's traditional role as the primary nurturing caregiver, many people believe that the death of a mother is harder to cope with than the death of a father.[16] Another factor may be the fact that, statistically, fathers tend to die before mothers. Thus, a mother's death often represents the loss of having parents, as the bereaved adult child experiences reactive grief over the death of the other parent as well.

Generally, for adult children, a parent's death is less likely to evoke intense grief than, for instance, the death of a child. The reason for this is probably related to the fact that an adult child is involved in his or her own life; feelings of attachment to parents have been redirected to some extent toward others, such as a partner and children. Nevertheless, it puts a strain on a relationship when the person whose parent has died feels that his or her partner is not offering as much emotional support as needed or expected or does not understand the impact of the loss.[17] The parent-child bond has unique symbolic importance and, with the death of a parent, the bereaved child mourns the loss of that special relationship.

Parental Bereavement

The death of a child represents the untimely loss of a potential future, the "ultimate deprivation."[18] A child's death upsets the expectation that the old die first and are replaced by the young. Death may be viewed as appropriate in old age, but in technologically advanced countries we expect that a child will outlive his or her parents. In parts of the world today, as in earlier times, a newborn or infant is not really viewed as a "person" until he or she has lived long enough to exhibit the likelihood of ongoing life. In most societies, however, the death of a child is considered the least natural of deaths.[19] Bereaved parents often maintain an inner representation of the dead child, an "image" sustained through memories and spiritual beliefs.[20]

A child's existence grants a kind of immortality to the parent; this is ripped away when the child dies. Parents envision their children graduating from school, getting married, raising their own children—all the various milestones and occasions that constitute a sense of continuity into the future. Death brings an end to the plans and hopes for a child's life.

Käthe Kollwitz, Library of Congress

The overwhelming grief of parental bereavement is expressed in the soft-ground etching Überfahren (Passing Over), by Käthe Kollwitz, whose art became a means of working through her own sorrow following the death of a child. The dead child is carried by adults bent with the burden of grief; other children look on.

Symbolically and actually, a child's death is contrary to the caring task of adulthood. When the basic function of parenting is understood as protecting one's child and nurturing his or her well-being, this responsibility is thwarted by a child's death. *Parenting* is generally defined as protecting and caring for a child until he or she can act independently in the world. Thus, the death of a child may be experienced as the ultimate lack of protection, the ultimate breakdown and failure in being a "good parent." A study by Paul Rosenblatt showed that after a child's death parents tended to become more protective of their other children, exhibiting greater vigilance, more rapid response to signs of trouble, and greater awareness of child vulnerability.[21] Among the Cree of North America, infants were given "ghost-protective" moccasins to wear. Holes were cut in the bottom of the moccasins to safeguard the baby from death. If the spirit of an ancestor appeared and beckoned, the infant could refuse to go, pointing out that his or her moccasins "needed mending."[22]

Many issues of parental bereavement span the adult life cycle. They are present for twenty-year-old parents and eighty-year-old parents. They are experienced by parents of grown children as well as by parents of infants. A sixty-five-year-old widowed mother may feel considerable loss of security when her thirty-five-year-old child dies suddenly. One such woman said, "He was going to take care of me when I got old; now I have no one." Whether or not her son would have indeed taken on the responsibility she envisioned, his death represented the loss of *her* imagined future. The interdependency between parent and child makes the death of a child a profound loss.[23]

Childbearing Losses

Pregnancy is a major life transition for adults, the expected result of which is the birth of a viable, healthy baby. Miscarriage, stillbirth, or neonatal death is not the anticipated outcome. These are all forms of *perinatal loss* (loss pertaining to the periods before, during, or after the time of birth).

Miscarriage occurs prior to the twentieth week of pregnancy. Also known as *spontaneous abortion,* it is defined as "loss of the products of conception before the fetus is viable."[24] Most miscarriages are due to chromosomal abnormalities in the fetus. *Stillbirth,* also referred to as *sudden intrauterine death,* is defined as occurring between the twentieth week of gestation (pregnancy) and the time of birth, resulting in delivery of a dead child. The distinction between miscarriage and stillbirth is based on the fact that most fetuses are viable—that is, able to survive outside the mother's body—after the twentieth week of pregnancy. In contrast to miscarriage, which occurs naturally, *induced abortion* (also called *artificial* or *therapeutic abortion*) is brought about intentionally, with the aim of ending a pregnancy by mechanical means or drugs.

Infant death, a term referring to death that occurs before a child's first birthday, is often subdivided into the period of *neonatal* death, defined as occurring during the first twenty-eight days following birth, and *postneonatal* death, occurring after the first twenty-eight days and up to eleven months

> When we bury the old, we bury the known past, the past we imagine sometimes better than it was, but the past all the same, a portion of which we inhabited. Memory is the overwhelming theme, the eventual comfort.
>
> But burying infants, we bury the future, unwieldy and unknown, full of promise and possibilities, outcomes punctuated by our rosy hopes. The grief has no borders, no limits, no known ends, and the little infant graves that edge the corners and fencerows of every cemetery are never quite big enough to contain that grief. Some sadnesses are permanent. Dead babies do not give us memories. They give us dreams.
>
> Thomas Lynch, *The Undertaking: Life Studies from the Dismal Trade*

following birth (some definitions extend the postneonatal period to encompass the period from age twenty-eight days to under one year). We discuss these childbearing losses in greater detail later in this chapter.

> Pregnancy, induced and spontaneous abortion (miscarriage), stillbirth, and infant death all take their meanings from the lives of those who experience them and the social worlds in which they occur. . . . The physical reality (at what point a death occurs), the social reality (the definition *as* death as well as the significance of that death), and the psychological reality (the grief associated with that death) are all constructed within particular, and various, social contexts.[25]

Reproductive loss also includes losses resulting from infertility and sterility. Whereas *infertility* refers to "diminished or absent capacity to produce offspring," *sterility* denotes "complete inability to produce offspring" due to inability either to conceive (female) or to induce conception (male).[26] Despite advances in medical treatment for infertility, many couples remain childless, their urges to reproduce frustrated by forces beyond their control.

Another example of reproductive loss involves giving up a child for *adoption*. Although this might not initially be thought of as a childbearing loss because it generally results from choice, grief may accompany such decisions nonetheless. Adoption can be envisioned as a triangle, with its three sides being the relinquishing parents (generally the birth mother), the adoptee, and the adoptive parents.[27] Each of these parties faces different issues. Psychologists point out,

> In a society that defines women as mothers, mothers-to-be, or childless, the woman who has given birth and then relinquished her child for adoption is an enigma. Having signed away her legal claim to the child, she is often perceived as the most unnatural of women, a rejecting mother. [But] the maternal experience does not end with the signing of surrender papers.[28]

A comprehensive view of childbearing loss also includes the birth of a child with a severe impairment, such as a congenital deformity or a mental disability. Parents may have difficulty accepting the reality that their child is not as they had dreamed; they may grieve the loss of the "perfect" or "wished-for" child.[29]

Bereavement in connection with childbearing or reproductive loss covers a broad range of related losses. People may assume that the loss of a baby during the early stages of pregnancy evokes feelings of disappointment, not grief. To the parents, who have dreamed about the baby even before its conception, the loss is likely to be very real, prompting grief infused with confusion and pain. In the following sections, we examine in more detail losses resulting from miscarriage, induced abortion, stillbirth, neonatal death, and sudden infant death syndrome.

Miscarriage

Parents may be told that miscarriage is simply "nature's way" of weeding out genetic anomalies. Such a remark offers little or no consolation to grieving parents; it was *their* baby that nature decided to eliminate. Platitudes that minimize or deny the loss are unhelpful. When parents experience a series of miscarriages, loss is compounded upon loss.

Parents may have difficulty identifying their loss precisely or making sense of what has happened. After a miscarriage, one young mother's grief was complicated because she had no remains to be buried. "I didn't know where my baby was," she said. Even though a miscarriage may have occurred many years ago, grief for an unborn baby can recur with other significant life events—for example, at the birth of a subsequent child or the onset of menopause. A particular marker, such as reaching age forty or age sixty-five, can reawaken feelings of grief.

Induced Abortion

Although induced abortion is also termed *elective abortion,* in many cases it is less a choice than a medical necessity. Some people assume that women who elect to terminate a pregnancy do not experience grief, but this is not always true. Although women may experience relief after an abortion, some experience a period of deep sadness that may be characterized by feelings of guilt, anger, or regret. If a woman feels that she was pressured into sexual intercourse or into the abortion, along with grief for the loss, she may feel bitter.[30] Grief after elective abortion can be just as real as grief after involuntary fetal or infant loss.[31] "For a woman who experiences a pregnancy loss as a tragedy, it is a tragedy; and for a woman who experiences a loss as relief, it is a relief."[32] The emotional reaction to induced abortion varies. Similar questions apply to men who participate in decisions about elective abortion.

In some cases, the repercussions are not felt until much later. One woman, who had chosen to abort a pregnancy as a young adult because she and her partner felt their relationship couldn't withstand the pressures of raising a child at that time, experienced great remorse when they later found themselves unable to have other children. "That may have been our only chance," she lamented. Subsequent pregnancy loss may be experienced as "retribution" for an earlier abortion.

Conflicting views about abortion may place the bereaved in a dilemma: Those who believe a loss occurred may not sanction the act, whereas those who sanction the act may not recognize that grief for a perceived loss needs to be expressed and legitimized. Complications in grieving may be exacerbated when customary sources of solace and social support are not readily available.[33]

When the decision for an abortion is made because of adverse information about the health of the fetus, the inherent conflict about the choice may add to parents' grief. Many genetic diseases are identified by tests during the early stages of pregnancy; when the results are unfavorable, terminating the pregnancy may seem the best or only choice. Some tests, however, can be done only well into the pregnancy, after the mother has already felt the fetus moving. Parents who decide in favor of a therapeutic abortion may worry that no one will understand their "choice" and that they will be judged harshly. Furthermore, in this situation, couples may face not only the loss of a particular baby but also the possibility of a childless future; biological considerations or genetic risk may preclude the choice to conceive again.

In Japan, at places like Hase Temple near Kamakura and Shiun Jizo Temple north of Tokyo, tiny stone statues called *mizuko* represent children conceived but never born.[34] Some wear bibs and stocking caps. Placed alongside them are toy milk bottles, dolls, and twirling pinwheels, along with memorials written by their sponsors—women who chose to have an abortion rather

Seen here are a few of the more than fifty thousand mizuko, *or "water children," at Hase Temple near Kamakura, Japan. For the parents who sponsor a statue, they represent a ritual resolution of grief for the souls of unborn babies.*

than give birth. The statues, each one costing several hundred dollars, are erected as repositories for the souls of unborn babies. At Hase Temple, the mizuko are watched over by a thirty-foot-tall wooden statue of the Japanese Goddess of Mercy, who is also the patroness of safe birth. Even though abortion is common in Japan, "mizuko worship" bears witness to an intense desire to acknowledge the unborn fetus.

Stillbirth

"Instead of giving birth, I gave death," said a mother whose daughter was born dead. Instead of a cradle, there is a grave; instead of a receiving blanket, there are burial clothes; instead of a birth certificate, there is a death certificate. Many stillbirths occur at or near full term to otherwise apparently healthy infants.[35] After a stillbirth, "a family's wishes and hopes and dreams—the individuals' illusions about what life *ought* to be—are quickly shattered by the reality of what life really *is*."[36]

Researchers point out that data on the prevalence of stillbirth may be inaccurate because of poor documentation and underreporting.[37] In the past, it was standard practice for hospitals to take over management of stillbirth and remove the dead infant as quickly as possible with the aim of avoiding or minimizing the psychological trauma. "Women trusted those in authority as to whether or not they should see their stillborn babies."[38] As Irving Leon points out,

> The death of a baby was an unspeakable event in a hospital. Hushed silence greeted the delivery of a stillborn. The baby was whisked away before parents could see and hold their child. They were told to forget what happened and have another baby as soon as possible. The mother was given tranquilizers if she became too upset, if she "lost it" (meaning that she was grieving over what she *had* lost).[39]

Today, in most hospitals the situation is different, and grief for childbearing loss is respected. Hospital staff are now likely to encourage parents to see and hold their baby. A recent large study of mothers who had experienced stillbirth found that the great majority saw (95 percent) and held (90 percent) their stillborn babies. Very few expressed regret. Researchers noted that "rituals, such as holding, caressing, and caring for the dead body of a loved one, have been used universally by humans throughout history and across cultures as a way of realizing and coping with loss, and they have been described as the *antidote to powerlessness*."[40]

A postmortem photograph of the child may assist in the process of grieving.[41] Parents may hold a memorial service for the stillborn baby, a choice that not only acknowledges the reality of what has happened but also provides an opportunity to find meaning and solace by sharing grief with others. Family support is especially important. In one study, family support was the only form of support associated with reduced maternal anxiety and depression after a stillbirth. Researchers noted that "stillbirth is often an isolating, marginalizing experience for women," and "the social support of many bereaved mothers falters."[42]

Some hospitals give bereaved parents an information packet that includes a certificate of stillbirth, which acknowledges the birth as well as the death of the child. Linking objects (discussed in Chapter 8), such as a lock of hair, a photograph, and the receiving blanket, can be comforting to parents. Nearly 90 percent of the parents included in a study by John DeFrain named their stillborn baby, thereby recognizing that it was indeed part of the family, no matter how briefly: "Naming seemed to help show others that the baby really existed and was important, not just something to be thrown away and forgotten."[43] The hurt may fade as time passes; the memories do not.

Neonatal Death

When a baby is born alive but with life-threatening disabilities due to prematurity or congenital defects, the ensuing period of uncertainty about the baby's survival can be a nightmare for parents. Parents may experience an overwhelming sense of frustration and futility as medical interventions

© Albert Lee Strickland

The items placed around the grave of this infant in Hawaii—balloons, flowers, and jars of baby food—bespeak the parents' loss and acknowledge the enduring bonds of even a short-lived relationship.

are discussed, are attempted, and perhaps fail. Sometimes a baby born with one or more life-threatening conditions embarks on a life-or-death struggle that lasts weeks. During this time, parents may have to make difficult ethical choices that determine whether the baby lives or dies. Meanwhile, costs incurred in keeping the baby alive continue to mount. If the baby does die, parents might resent the medical institution and its personnel, feeling as if they survived a painful and futile ordeal only to be billed later for the experience.

In circumstances involving a critically ill newborn, *any* decision may haunt parents as they repeatedly ask themselves if they made the right choice. Caregivers who appreciate the heart-wrenching ethical dilemmas that occur in the context of neonatal intensive care are in a position to provide sensitive care and support to parents facing the prospect of making and living with these difficult decisions. When the life of a critically ill infant is being sustained by extraordinary medical means, the decision to terminate artificial support ought to be handled with as much grace as circumstances allow. One young neonatologist remarked, "One of the most difficult and important things for me to learn was to hand over the baby to the parents so it could die in their arms."

Sudden Infant Death Syndrome

Sudden infant death syndrome (SIDS) is defined as a death of an apparently healthy infant usually before one year of age and of unknown or no definitive cause.[44] Risk factors include low birth weight, prematurity, mother's age less than twenty years, maternal drug use or smoking during pregnancy, overly cold or overly hot environment, and soft bedding.

The unexpected nature of the death, the age of the child and of the parents (who are generally young and may be experiencing an intimate death for the first time), and uncertainty about the cause of death combine to make SIDS deaths a difficult loss for all concerned.

Because the cause of death is not certain and because of generalized concerns about the possibility of child abuse, law enforcement personnel may question whether the parents are responsible. Tragically, parents do sometimes murder their own infants and try to pass off the deaths as natural or accidental. The search for a cause of death in SIDS cases is characterized by lack of clarity. Because of this and because SIDS support groups have circulated information about the adverse effects of misdirected accusations toward grieving parents, police and other investigators are usually sensitive in handling cases that might involve SIDS. Even so, parents may question themselves just as sternly: Was the death somehow due to something they did or left undone? Could it have been prevented?

Continuing research into the causes of SIDS may help avoid some parental guilt. Researchers at Children's Hospital in Boston found that babies who died of SIDS had defects in the brain stem. These defects undermined the action of the chemical serotonin, which is critical to breathing and arousal. Other researchers cautioned that, although infants who die with SIDS have

> After her daughter's death, there was no one to blame but herself. Nothing anyone said would convince her otherwise. One doctor who had only just met her told her she was a very good mother and should stop feeling guilty. A friend insisted that she needed to stop blaming herself or she would lose her mind. All of their efforts failed to eliminate Julia's persistent magical belief that she was to blame for her child's death. At last, when the autopsy results arrived, her child's doctor explained how a very rare illness killed her daughter, and that due to the rapid onset of symptoms, it would even have gone undetected if her baby had been admitted to the pediatric ICU before showing any symptoms whatsoever. In effect, not even the best medical minds could have saved her child. Julia was finally satisfied that she was not responsible, but this only caused her more distress. If random tragedies like her daughter's death could happen, she thought, then no parent can completely ensure the safety of his or her child. Unable now to blame even herself, she was filled with anxiety about the countless ways her children could be at risk.
>
> Robert Zucker, *The Journey Through Grief and Loss*

anomalies with serotonin function, there are other brain-chemical systems that have not been thoroughly studied and may play equally strong roles.[45] Studies continue. In the meantime, the unexplained nature of SIDS deaths can lead survivors to embark on a quest for answers that may not be available.

Grief for "Unlived" Lives

The kinds of losses discussed here involve grief for "unlived" lives. Judith Savage says, "Childbearing losses are mourned not only for what was, but also for what might have been."[46] Grief is felt not only for the physical loss but also for symbolic losses. Parents mourn "the child of the imagination, that part of themselves which seems now to have no possibility of embodiment in the world." Writing from the perspective of a Jungian psychologist who by age thirty-three had experienced multiple losses (her adoptive and biological parents, her two brothers, and her infant son), Savage says,

> By unraveling the mystery of the imaginative relationship, that is, the projections of the self onto the unborn child, it becomes clear that primary relationships are not composed merely of interchangeable functional attributes and roles but are uniquely personal bonds that are generated from deep within and are as much a reflection of the individual soul as they are an accurate reflection of the other.[47]

It is important to be aware of two distinct yet related realities: the *actual* relationship and the *symbolic* nature of the parent-child bond. Grieving parents often talk about lost companionship, lost dreams—all the ways in which the child would have enriched their lives. Such discussion is concerned with the actual loss. The symbolic loss relates to the meaning attached to the relationship, as when an individual, by parenting a child, becomes a nurturing, supportive guide. A bereaved father said, "Not only have I lost a son who might follow in my footsteps, but, without him, I have no feet." It was important for this father to acknowledge and mourn both the loss of his son and the loss of meaning and purpose in his own life. The image of the lost child activates powerful associations, which become part of a natural process guiding the bereaved parent's journey toward wholeness.

Anger may be focused on the dead child, resulting in confusing and tangled emotions. We may think, What kind of parent could be angry at an innocent infant? Yet, anger is a natural response to loss. As one woman said of her stillborn daughter, "Why did she just drop in and out of my life? Why did she bother coming at all?" Emotional responses may be accompanied by auditory or kinesthetic deceptions: A baby cries in the night, waking parents from sleep; the baby kicks inside the womb, yet there is no pregnancy, no live child.

Grief following a childbearing loss also may be influenced by the parents' perceptions that the loss is neither understood nor acknowledged by others. Bereaved parents report hearing insensitive comments, such as "It must be easier, since you didn't get too attached." Well-intentioned family members and friends may attempt to minimize the death in an effort to console the bereaved parent. They may say, "You're young; you can have another baby," unaware that such a comment, although possibly true, is inappropriate: No other child will replace the one who died. This kind of advice and comment is especially difficult for couples who postponed having children—they may feel an added constraint of time that compounds the experience of loss.

The Death of an Older Child

Many of the issues discussed in the preceding section pertain as well to parents' grief following the death of an older child, adolescent, or young adult. The meaning of such a death is usually more complex, however, because the relationship between parent and child has been of longer duration, with a larger store of memories. A child represents many things to a parent. As Beverly Raphael reminds us, a child is "a part of the self, and of the loved partner; a representation of generations past; the genes of the forebears; the hope of the future; a source of love, pleasure, even narcissistic delight; a tie or a burden; and sometimes a symbol of the worst parts of the self and others."[48] Over time, the bond between parent and child takes on increasing complexity.

Among the major causes of death among individuals between the ages of five and twenty-four, accidents top the list.[49] As the most prominent cause of death during the first half of the human life span, injury is characterized as "the last major plague of the young."[50] Although more children and adolescents die from injuries received in accidents than from the effects of disease, the circumstances and challenges of a child with life-threatening illness are usually viewed as especially poignant. Perhaps we feel, justifiably or not, that an accident is something that just "happens" and therefore is not preventable, whereas we expect medicine to provide a cure for disease.

When a child's life is threatened by serious illness, it affects the whole fabric of family life. Parents and siblings, along with other relatives, are all involved in coping with the illness. (See "Caring for a Seriously Ill Child" in

Chapter 10.) Few families are able to sustain total openness to the reality of a child's terminal illness throughout what may be a long process from diagnosis of the disease to the child's death. At times, a seriously ill child may function quite normally, and the routine of medical care becomes just another aspect of family life. At other times, the illness requires parents and other family members to deal intensely and decisively with changes in the child's condition. Those around the child may feel challenged as they try to adjust to shifts between hope for recovery and acceptance of terminality, all while trying to support the child in the best way possible.

Parents seem to have a somewhat easier time coping when they do not base their personal identities solely on their role as parents. In other words, although parenting is an important part of their lives, it does not comprise the whole of their self-image, which encompasses other accomplishments and values as well. Some parents manage not only to cope with and survive the devastating loss of a child but to grow from the experience. Such parents are able to "respond to a [child's] severe illness by making a more mature reevaluation of their lives and achieving a truer vision of what counts," says Jerome Schulman. "They learn to make each new day more enriching."[51]

The Death of an Adult Child

For a young or middle-aged adult to die while his or her parents live on seems unnatural. It is a death "out of sequence." The consequent loss of parenthood may become a kind of "perpetual bereavement," in which the struggle to understand the meaning of the death continues all through life.[52]

The older parent who survives the death of an adult child may also have lost a caregiver. The child, a source of comfort and security, is gone. There may also be a sense of "competing" with the dead child's spouse or children for the role of "most bereaved." Who has priority in receiving care and comfort? The death of an adult child sometimes requires parents to assume care of grandchildren, a result that can be emotionally as well as economically disruptive.

Parents who suffer the death of a child already grown to adulthood may find themselves alone in coping with their grief. In contrast to the situation of parents who lose younger children or individuals who survive the death of

> We had waited, agonizing through the nights and days without sleep, startled by nearly any sound, unable to eat, simply staring at our meals. Suddenly in a few seconds of radio time it was over. My first son, whose birth had brought me so much joy that I jumped up in a hall outside the room where he was born and touched the ceiling—the child, the scholar, the preacher, the boy singing and smiling, the son—all of it was gone. And Ebenezer was so quiet. All through the church as the staff learned what had happened, the tears flowed, but almost completely in silence.
>
> Martin Luther King, Sr.

a spouse, few support resources are available to help parents cope with the death of an adult child. Yet, the death of a child—at whatever age—is always a significant loss.

Coping with Bereavement as a Couple

One concern following the death of a child is the impact it has on the bond between partners. Some people believe that the stress of coping with a child's death will make or break a relationship. Clinicians sometimes note the presence of a kind of "general chaos," a pervasive sense that the parents have been robbed of past and future. With such a traumatic event, parents expect, and are expected, to support each other. But the energy expended by each partner in coping with his or her own grief can deplete the emotional resources needed for mutual support. Some bereaved parents report that in addition to losing a child, they felt they had lost their partner for a time. The death of a child has the potential to either improve or worsen a marital relationship.[53] It may have the paradoxical effect of creating a feeling of estrangement and a strong bond between parents at the same time.[54]

Even though they share the same loss, parents might have different grieving styles, which can leave each of them feeling isolated and unsupported by the only person who shares the magnitude of the loss. Although in some cases the mother's loss may be more physical and less abstract, fathers often struggle with feeling powerless to support and protect their loved ones.[55] Also, individual differences in values, beliefs, and expectations may cause conflicts in coping styles, thereby reducing the sense of commonality in a couple's grief experience.[56] Parents do not necessarily grieve in an asynchronous or "roller-coaster" pattern, but they may find themselves grieving "out of synch" with one another at times.

The sense of commonality in a couple's grief is also affected by their view of themselves as a *couple*. They may have difficulty reaching agreement about the best way to regain a sense of stability and meaning in life after their child's death. Despite each partner's desire and expectation to "go through grief" together, differences in grieving styles may create conflict about whether one's partner is behaving appropriately.

Conflict can arise out of each partner's *interpretation* of the other's behavior. A husband who contains his grief so that he can "be there" for his wife may be perceived by his spouse as cold and unfeeling. The desire to be caring and protective can be misinterpreted, resulting in conflict rather than comfort. Disagreement can also relate to issues about what constitutes "proper" mourning behavior, the couple's "public face" of grief.

Reducing conflict and promoting positive interactions between grieving partners requires the willingness of each to engage in open and honest communication. In this way, each partner's emotional expression of loss helps validate the reality of the other's perceptions. Crying together can be helpful in resolving conflict and working through the loss. Accepting differences and being flexible about roles helps. One characteristic of couples who report little conflict is a positive view of each other and their relationship.

The "bridges" between partners have various qualities. Bonds may be as strong as a suspension bridge embedded in concrete or as weak as one made of wooden planks and bark. Using the analogy of the weight of a large truck being driven over a flimsy bridge reveals that some relationships are fragile and likely will not support the burden of loss. Yet, who is to say that a poorly constructed partnership might not have been broken regardless of the death of a child? Some couples recognize that their bridges need upgrades and seek resources and support to stabilize and strengthen their relationship. Other couples move into a circle of blame and destruction. It is not predetermined that a child's death will cause the loss of the pair bond as well. In fact, a study conducted for The Compassionate Friends, a self-help group of bereaved parents, found that the divorce rate of couples who had lost a child was far below the national divorce rate (16 percent versus about 50 percent) and that, of the couples who divorced after the death of a child, only about 40 percent felt that the death had contributed to the divorce.[57]

Coming to terms with a partner's behavior is enhanced by the ability to *reframe* each other's behavior in a positive way. For example, a husband who views sobbing as "breaking down" can alter his perception so that crying is seen as emotionally cleansing and valuable, making it possible to explain the behavior in positive terms rather than judging it as inappropriate or dysfunctional. When unsettling behavior is seen as providing emotional release, it allows a mate to support the expression instead of trying to curtail it.

Social Support in Parental Bereavement

Relatives and friends of bereaved parents have many ways to offer support, including simply listening, sending cards or letters of condolence, bringing food, doing housework or other chores, caring for other children in the family, sharing their own grief over the loss, giving the parents time to be alone, and so on. Individuals who are willing to talk openly with a parent about his or her grief in the wake of a child's death are important sources of support in parental bereavement.

In additional, social support organizations are available to provide various types of parental bereavement services. The Compassionate Friends, which has chapters across the nation, offers support to bereaved parents across a broad spectrum of losses. Another group, the Candlelighters Childhood Cancer Foundation, focuses on support for children with cancer, their parents, and other family members. Two groups, Mothers Against Drunk Driving (MADD) and Parents of Murdered Children (POMC), combine social support with political advocacy. Such groups of bereaved parents who have experienced similar losses constitute what some people have called "communities of feeling" within which grief is shared.[58]

It is important to keep in mind that people are different, as are their attachments to their children. Bereaved parents should not be expected to "follow a script" or enact some "right way" to grieve. Social support should be offered in ways that recognize individual differences and promote genuine empathy.

Spousal Bereavement

The ties between two people in a paired relationship are usually so closely interwoven that, as Beverly Raphael says, the death of one partner may "cut across the very meaning of the other's existence."[59] Even though we recognize the possibility, the likelihood, that one spouse will die before the other, such thoughts are usually kept safely in the background. The pressing activities of daily life occupy our attention until one day the possibility becomes a reality that can't be ignored.

The aftermath of spousal bereavement has been described as follows: "Everyday occurrences underscore the absence of your mate. Sitting down to breakfast, or dinner, opening mail, hearing a special song, going to bed, all become sources of pain when they were formerly sources of pleasure. Each day is full of challenges and heartbreaks."[60]

A spouse's death requires an adjustment from being a couple to being single, a transition that is likely to be especially hard for the survivor who is also a parent. With children to care for and nurture, there is the added burden of single parenthood. The way a particular person adjusts to the role of newly widowed person depends on a host of sociocultural, personal, and circumstantial factors.

Factors Influencing Spousal Bereavement

Although the death of a mate is the most intensively studied of all losses during adulthood, research has generally focused on a brief time span immediately after bereavement; there are few studies of the enduring effects of a partner's death.[61] It is also noteworthy that studies of spousal, or conjugal, bereavement have generally focused on heterosexually paired relationships while mostly ignoring homosexual couples who make lifelong commitments to each other. In same-sex relationships, grief following the death of a partner may be exacerbated by conflict with a mate's parents who have never made peace with their son's or daughter's sexual orientation or lifestyle. "If I was effectively nonexistent to them before," one surviving mate said, "I really vanished after my partner died. For years, they denied our commitment to each other; now they acted as if they could completely erase me! They claimed everything: the body, our home, and, seemingly, my right to grieve." It is important to recognize that grief over the loss of a mate is independent of legal or social sanctions about the nature of a relationship.

The patterns of intimacy and interaction between spouses are an important determinant of how the loss of a partner will be experienced by a survivor. Whereas one couple may derive their primary satisfaction from shared activities, another couple enjoys greater independence. In some relationships, the focus is on children; in others, the adult partners take precedence. Furthermore, the patterns of a given relationship tend to be in flux as circumstances change over time.

Consider the differences in outlook between an older couple, who have shared their lives over many years, and a young couple, who have been

Jack Delano, FSA Collection, Library of Congress

Mr. and Mrs. Andrew Lyman, Polish farmers living near Windsor Lakes, Connecticut, exemplify some of the qualities that contribute to a close relationship. When such a bond is severed by death, the effect is felt in every area of the survivor's life.

together only a short time. The death of a mate in old age typically follows a lifetime of mutual commitment and shared experiences. Spousal death may not be a "surprise" to older adults, but often it "sets off an intertwined set of circumstances endemic to being old."[62]

In contrast, a young couple is just setting out to build a world together and, when a partner dies, the survivor must remake previously shared goals. During the years from youth to old age, a person's standard of living and overall quality of life are also likely to change, thus affecting the meaning and reality of loss.

Spousal bereavement also elicits distinct behaviors related to culturally sanctioned gender roles. In one culture, a widower might avoid crying publicly because to do so would be viewed as weak and shameful. A widower in another culture, conversely, might express his grief through many tears and loud crying because not to do so would suggest a weakness in ability to love. As Robert Stettersten says, "Culture structures the ways lives are lived."[63]

Individuals who have lived out traditional gender roles may find the transition to widowhood especially hard. Learning to manage unfamiliar role responsibilities in the midst of grief can be a formidable task, intensifying feelings of helplessness. The widow who has never written a check or the widower who has never prepared dinner is confronted not only with grief at losing a loved one but also with major role readjustments. New skills must be learned to manage the needs of daily life. Widowed persons whose lifestyles include multiple roles—such as parent; employee; friend; student; hobbyist; or participant in community, political, and religious organizations—appear to make an easier adjustment than do those with fewer role involvements.

In the first year after the death of a mate, there are higher rates of illness and death among widows and widowers; aged people are particularly at risk. This is partly explained by the observation that individuals tend to neglect their own health problems while caring for an ailing spouse. In addition, a survivor's ties to the outside world may have diminished while caring for his or her spouse, thus increasing feelings of loneliness following bereavement. A study of more than fifty-five thousand widows found that women widowed less than a year reported "substantially higher rates of depression and poorer social functioning, overall mental health, and general health than longer term widows."[64] After a three-year period of time, however, these widows showed marked improvements in their functioning, which researchers attributed to the "resilience of older women" and their capacity for reestablishing social connections.

Adverse effects of spousal death appear to be more common among widowers, perhaps because men with conventional gender roles find it difficult to manage domestic matters that were once left to the now-deceased spouse. Widowers also may be less likely than widows to seek help from others, a trait of "self-reliance" that may be associated with gender roles. As Judith Stillion points out, men who care for an ailing partner over an extended period of time may be at a disadvantage in coping with the onset of normal physical and psychological problems of bereavement if "their socialization prohibits them from asking for help, showing strain, or even, in some instances, recognizing and discussing their feelings with helping professionals."[65]

Relief following the death of a spouse, although little discussed, is an emotion that may be experienced by people who have cared for an ailing spouse over a long period of time. In such cases, death may be viewed as ending an ailing loved one's suffering. Less socially accepted or acknowledged is relief experienced when a mate's death is the welcome end to an unsatisfactory relationship.

Because women statistically live longer than men, it is estimated that three out of four married women will be widowed at one time or another. Widows who want to remarry face not only social pressures but also a lack of eligible men. However, it has been suggested that widowhood is less difficult for women than retirement is for men. This is because there are many other widows with whom to share leisure time and activities; thus, a woman's status may increase with widowhood, whereas a man's status usually decreases at retirement.

Social Support for Bereaved Spouses

The death of a mate results in the loss of a primary source of social interactions and alters a person's social role in the community. The availability of a stable social support network can be crucial in determining how bereaved spouses adjust to their changed status. A study by Rebecca Utz and colleagues found that widowed persons used social participation "as an active coping strategy to deal with the negative effects of widowhood."[66] Informal activities, such as getting together with friends and telephone contact, were particularly important as aspects of daily life that are affected by late-life bereavement. Formal social participation, researchers concluded, may not provide the emotional and instrumental support that informal social participation does. Because friendships are based on common interests and lifestyles, maintaining relationships with nonrelatives appears to be important. Participation in leisure activities with friends may help widowed people cope with role transitions and maintain a sense of resiliency and positive morale despite difficult life changes.

Family relationships, in contrast, may pose a potential psychological threat to the widowed elderly because they contain elements of role reversal between the adult child and the aging parent that suggest or demand dependency from the aged widow or widower. Furthermore, an adult child's experience of the loss differs from that of the bereaved spouse, who is likely to value the loss as more significant than does the child and to feel the effects of the loss more intensely with respect to physical and emotional health.[67]

One of the most valuable resources for the recently widowed is contact with peers—that is, other bereaved people who have lost a mate and who can serve as role models during the subsequent period of adjustment. Exposed to the role model's accepting attitude, the newly widowed person learns to live with the painful or difficult feelings of grief and gain perspective on them.

Following the pioneering work of Phyllis Silverman at Harvard University Medical School, the Widowed Persons Service (WPS) began in 1973 to implement a concept of mutual help to widowed individuals.[68] The Widowed Persons Service, whose parent organization is the American Association

> "What would you like for breakfast, Jack?" I asked my son-in-law on Sunday, the day after the funeral.
>
> "A fried egg, over," he replied.
>
> Such a simple thing. Yet, I'd never fried an egg.
>
> Oh, we often had them on weekends; but my husband was the breakfast cook, while I dashed up and down the steps putting clothes in the washer, running the vacuum, and all the other tasks always awaiting a working wife.
>
> I stood there, the frying pan in one hand, the egg in the other.
>
> How many times in the future would I find myself standing the same way? How many things had I never done? How many things had I taken for granted?
>
> Maxine Dowd Jensen, *The Warming of Winter*

of Retired Persons (AARP), offers newly widowed people help provided by trained volunteers who themselves have been widowed, the key to the effectiveness of such programs.

Aging and the Aged

The stereotyped image of an aged person is marked by such outward signs as dry and wrinkled skin, graying hair, baldness, failing eyesight, hearing loss, stiff joints, and general physical debility. Indeed, the physical signs of *senescence,* or the process of becoming old, are rightly associated with the aging of the human organism. (Senescence can be thought of in terms of vulnerability; the risk that an illness or an injury will prove fatal increases with age.) Most elderly individuals experience some *chronic* conditions. These can be divided into three categories: (1) nonfatal chronic illness, (2) serious and eventually fatal chronic illness, and (3) frailty.[69]

> Common nonfatal chronic conditions include arthritis and hearing or vision problems. The common fatal chronic conditions are cancers, organ system failures, dementia, and strokes. Frailty is the fragility of multiple body systems as the customary reserves diminish with age and disease. Frailty is a fatal chronic condition; small upsets cause cascading health problems.[70]

Many illnesses and disabilities—with accompanying losses in many areas of life—occur most commonly among people aged fifty or older.[71] However, age alone is a poor predictor of outcome for a particular individual.[72]

Older people who practice life-enhancing activities—challenging their minds, maintaining physical fitness, eating wisely, reducing stress, and so on—increase the chances of "age-proofing" their lives.[73] Old age can be a season of life satisfaction and ego integrity or one of dissatisfaction, despair, and disgust. One writer said, "Growing old is like being increasingly punished for a crime we did not commit."[74] This accounts for some of the reasons given by aged people for accepting death as an alternative to continued existence (see Table 11-1). Suicide may be seen by some older people as a

TABLE 11-1 *Some Reasons Given by Aged People for Accepting Death*

Death is preferable to inactivity.
Death is preferable to the loss of the ability to be useful.
Death is preferable to becoming a burden.
Death is preferable to loss of mental faculties.
Death is preferable to living with progressively deteriorating physical health and concomitant physical discomfort.

rational choice that offers release from severe illness or other hardships of old age. Some of the factors influencing suicide among older adults are discussed in Chapter 12.

Bereavement is one of many stressors that characterize the challenges faced by the older adult.[75] As we age, we not only experience with increasing frequency the deaths of others, we also come closer to our own death. A philosopher writes, "Death is always close for the elderly, internalized. Many may not face it, but most are well aware of it. As with the young, the time of death is uncertain, but the elderly are more likely to realize that we may die in the very next instant."[76]

Dementia—the loss, usually progressive, of cognitive and intellectual functions—affects about 5 to 10 percent of people over age 65 and as many as 30 to 50 percent of people older than 85 years.[77] This loss of brain function affects memory, language, judgment, and behavior. It may be accompanied by emotional problems and personality changes. Alzheimer's disease—named after a German neurologist—is the most common form of dementia. It is a progressive mental deterioration marked by loss of memory and ability to calculate, confusion, and disorientation. It usually begins in late middle or later adulthood and results in death in five to ten years. "The disease is twice as common among women as among men, partly because women have a longer life expectancy."[78] Mortality from Alzheimer's disease has steadily increased during the past three decades.[79] With the aging of the post–World War II "baby boom" generation, the number of Alzheimer's patients is expected to swell, "making the need for adequate diagnostic techniques and therapies more pressing."[80]

The President's Council on Bioethics reports, "We are on the threshold of the first-ever 'mass geriatric society.'"[81] (*Geriatrics* is the branch of medicine that deals with old age and the treatment of physical and mental disorders in older adults.)[82] Although the chairman of the council stated, "It is the best of times to be old," the sobering fact is that "the most common trajectory toward death is a lengthy period of debility, frailty, and dementia lasting not months, but years." The twenty-first century is being characterized as a century of aging.[83] Others call the aging of societies a "silver tsunami."

When are you "old"? From the time in early childhood when a person of twenty-one appeared quite old and a person of forty seemed ancient, our perception of "old" gradually recedes as we celebrate more birthdays. At class reunions, *each* person can hardly believe how much older *other* classmates appear![84] A person festively celebrating his or her thirtieth or fortieth birthday may find these milestones of life bringing thoughts about the meaning of growing older and the lost opportunities that occur in taking one particular path in life rather than another.[85]

Aging doesn't begin at fifty or sixty-five or eighty-five. At this moment, we are all aging. Interestingly, the expectations most people have about aging or being old differ from the actual experience. Young adults typically expect problems among older people to be more serious than they actually are for those who experience them.

Bernice Neugarten reports that when she first developed a course on Adult Development and Aging, "It was generally assumed that you reached a plateau simply called adulthood and you lived on that plateau until you went over the cliff at age sixty-five."[86] The changing health status of older adults is acknowledged in the National Council on Aging's use of the terms *young-old* for people ages sixty to seventy-five, *middle-old* for those seventy-five to eighty-five, and *old-old* for those over the age of eighty-five. This last group is the fastest-growing segment of the aged population. As a "highly selected" group of survivors, they tend not to match stereotypes of advanced age as a time of fragility and dependency.

(Even these age categories may be outdated. One writer says that in 2004 he was placing ages 55–64 into the "nearly old" and 95+ into the "oldest old" categories. Within the next few years, he suspects he will be splitting the 95+ group into 95–104 as "oldest old" and 105+ as "hyper old.")

Most people would subscribe to the goal of improving the quality of life while "compressing" morbidity, or illness, and extending "active" life expectancy.[87] How long can we expect to live in the best of circumstances? Whereas *life span* is defined as "a theoretically projected length of life based on the maximum potential of the human body in the best environment," a more practical concept might be that of the *health span*, which refers to "the period of life when one is generally healthy and free from chronic or serious disease."[88] Making the period of debilitating illness briefer enables people to enjoy good health and stay active until quite near the end of their lives. Perhaps, in place of a "natural life span," we should think in terms of a "full life."

In contrast to their stereotypical image, old people tend to be more individually distinct than any other segment of the population: They have had more years to create unique life histories. (It is important to keep in mind that older people are different from one another, even within the same age category.)[89] Neugarten says, "People are 'open systems,' interacting with the people around them. All their experiences leave traces."[90] Mutual respect, faith, communion with others, and concern with existential issues of life are essential to the well-being of the aged.[91] Beyond that, "there is considerable evidence that spiritual concerns, experience, and development become increasingly important for many people in middle and later life."[92]

© Albert Lee Strickland

After a lifetime together, spouses engage in the activities of daily living out of a history of habit and familiarity. Preserving independence becomes a crucial goal of people in the years of maturity.

In a memoir written at the age of eighty-nine, Diana Athill says,

> From up here I can look back and see that, although a human life is less than the blink of an eyelid in terms of the universe, within its own framework it is amazingly capacious, so that it can contain many opposites. One life can contain serenity and tumult, heartbreak and happiness, coldness and warmth, grabbing and giving—and also more particular opposites such as a neurotic conviction that one is a flop and a consciousness of success amounting to smugness.[93]

In a summing up, she adds, "Minuscule though every individual, every 'self' is, he/she/it is an object through which life is being expressed and leaves some sort of contribution to the world."[94]

Daniel Callahan points out that, while we are right to acknowledge individual *differences* among the aged, it is important to appreciate the "*shared* features of old age, the features that make it meaningful to talk about the aged as a group and about old age as an inherent part of individual life."[95] In seeking what Callahan terms a "public meaning" of aging, we need to reflect on "what kind of elderly person we want ourselves to be and what ideal character traits we would like to promote and support." In considering one's own future status as an elder, it is worth noting that attempts to meet *all* the needs of the elderly must inevitably fail, especially if those needs are defined as the avoidance of disease and frailty.

While There Is Time

I carry the folding chair
for my mother
I carry the shawl
the large straw hat
to shield her from the glare
She leans her small weight
on my arm   Frail legs unsteady
feet now cramped with pain

Each day we sit for hours
at the ocean   The sun is hot
but she is wrapped and swathed
her hands are icy cold
they hide their ache
beneath the blanket

Her eyes follow the
movement that surrounds us
the romp of children
flight of gulls
the strong young surfers
challenging the sea

When the visit is ended
when my mother leaves
I will burst from the house
run empty-handed to the beach
hold out my arms
and swoop like a bird
my hands will tag children
as I pass

I will run and run
until I fall
and weep
for the crushed feet
the gnarled fingers
for her longing
I will run for both of us

Maude Meehan

Old age is a time for bringing plans to completion or relinquishing the responsibility for uncompleted projects to others younger than oneself, for reflection and summing up, and for preparing for one's own death. Jay Rosenberg says, "The fact that each of us will someday die shapes and colors our consciousness."[96] One sign of a rational person

> is that he lives a life appropriate to a dying being—that he acknowledges without denial and without complaint the unavoidable transitoriness of his own existence, accepts with dignity and with grace the inevitable passage from youth to old age, which is the outward sign of that transitoriness, and prudently plans and provides for his own death and, to the extent that he can, for the well-being and betterment of those whose lives will continue after his life, and thus his very being, has come to an end.[97]

Occasionally, we read or hear stories about old people being "left" to die alone, as if they have been abandoned. Some people, however, choose to die this way. Dying alone is different from dying lonely. The image of a person dying alone is often portrayed as a negative outcome, perhaps due to the person's antisocial behavior or neglect by family, neighbors, or social services. A typical story line pictures individuals who die alone as "fearful, lonely, even pathetic figures who need help despite themselves or their lifestyles."[98] The idea that older people may be exercising independence or autonomy at the end of life and do not want attention from the community usually receives little consideration. Rarely is it thought that these "service refusers" represent a desire to simply be left alone. The fact is, some people would rather die at home alone, rather than having to put up with "interfering" medical or health care workers, or members of their own community, who might expose them to the risk of being placed into an institution. For these people, dying alone is dignified and dying surrounded by machines is not dignified.

The positive images and meanings of growing old are eroded when we regard old age as a pathological state or as an avoidable affliction. In some societies, the aged hold special status as the "elders" of a community. Elderly women in the African American community, for example, occupy a special place as they continue the oral traditions of passing on cultural meanings to succeeding generations.[99] Respect for elders is similarly found among Native American peoples.[100] In the broader society, the wish seems to be that the old "age gracefully."

Although many older people living with serious illness are said to be "living on thin ice"—with prognoses that might be some years or less than a week—growing old is not essentially a "medical problem." Robert Butler says, "None of us knows whether we have already had the best years of our lives or whether the best are yet to come. But the greatest of human possibilities remain to the very end of life—the possibilities for love and feeling, reconciliation and resolution."[101] As the culminating phase of human life, the period of old age or maturity is an appropriate time to focus on the tasks specific to that part of the human journey. Butler says,

> After one has lived a life of meaning, death may lose much of its terror. For what we fear most is not really death but a meaningless and absurd life. I believe most human beings can accept the basic fairness of each generation's taking its turn on the face of the planet if they are not cheated out of the full measure of their turn.[102]

Further Readings

Robert C. Atchley. *Spirituality and Aging.* Baltimore: Johns Hopkins University Press, 2009.

Donna S. Davenport. *Singing Mother Home: A Psychologist's Journey Through Anticipatory Grief.* Denton: University of North Texas Press, 2002.

Norman M. Hadler. *Rethinking Aging: Growing Old and Living Well in an Overtreated Society.* Chapel Hill: University of North Carolina Press, 2011.

Robert O. Hansson and Margaret S. Stroebe. *Bereavement in Late Life: Coping, Adaptation, and Developmental Influences.* Washington, D.C.: American Psychological Association, 2006.

Therese A. Rando, ed. *Parental Loss of a Child.* Champaign, Ill.: Research Press, 1986.

Paul C. Rosenblatt. *Parent Grief: Narratives of Loss and Relationship.* Philadelphia: Brunner/Mazel, 2000.

Phyllis R. Silverman. *Widow to Widow: How the Bereaved Help One Another,* 2nd ed. New York: Brunner-Routledge, 2004.

Debra Umberson. *Death of a Parent: Transition to a New Adult Identity.* New York: Cambridge University Press, 2003.

Additional resources for this chapter can be found at www.mhhe.com/despelder10e

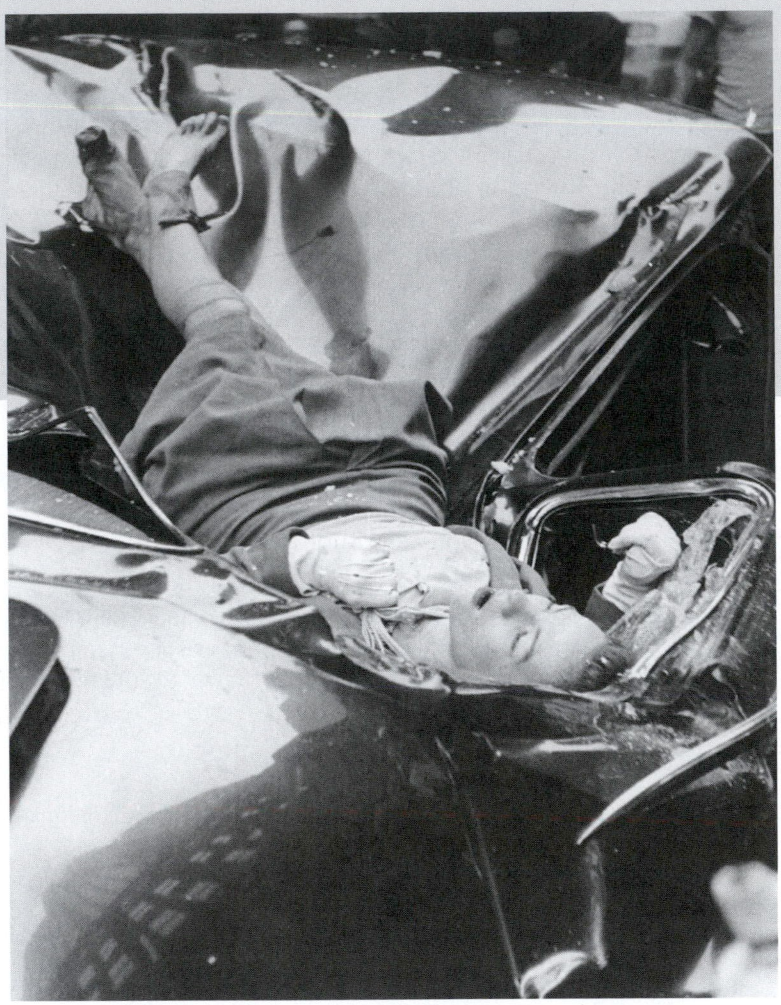

After plummeting eighty-six floors from the observation deck of the Empire State Building—visible in the metallic reflection at lower left—this young woman lies dead, the victim of suicide.

CHAPTER 12

Suicide

Altruistic suicide—that is, the giving of one's life for others or for a greater good—has occurred since human beings first banded together in clans. Imagine, for example, a situation in which an individual volunteered to draw the attention of a herd of animals and thereby allow other members of a hunting party to more easily trap the animals. The likelihood of surviving the onrushing herd was low. The reward for the clan was survival.

Among nomadic peoples, altruistic suicide among the elderly or infirm was accepted as a way to maintain the mobility needed for the survival of the group. Honor was given to the person who, recognizing that the end of life was near, willingly left the community for certain death. Historically and across cultures, suicide also has been recognized as a way to express ultimate commitment to a moral or philosophical principle.

These examples of altruistic suicide may not conform to the ideas most people have when they hear the word *suicide*. Although it has been documented throughout recorded history, Judith Stillion says that "suicide is arguably the most complex and the least understood of all human behaviors."[1]

Why would someone end his or her own life? People question the awesome fact that each of us has the power to decide whether or not we live. Questions about *intention* and *choice* are central in understanding suicide and other self-destructive behaviors. Usually, no single answer explains *why* a person dies by suicide. Kay Redfield Jamison says,

> Suicide is a death like no other, and those who are left behind to struggle with it must confront a pain like no other. They are left with the shock and the unending "what if's." They are left with anger and guilt and, now and again, a terrible sense of relief. They are left to a bank of questions from others, both asked and unasked, about Why; they are left to the silence of others, who are horrified, embarrassed, or unable to cobble together a note of condolence, an embrace, or a comment; and they are left with the assumption by others—and themselves—that more could have been done.[2]

As a complex human behavior, suicide involves diverse motives and intentions.

Comprehending Suicide

As you consider what might influence a person to die by suicide, you may think, "There's nothing that could cause me to end my own life intentionally." For individuals who are confident about their resources to deal with the demands of life, suicide seems a radical solution indeed. In the search for answers about suicide, our first step must be to find a framework for organizing this complexity into manageable form. The four definitions of suicide given in Table 12-1 help establish a framework useful for all of these approaches.

Notice that each definition emphasizes certain aspects of suicidal intention and behavior. The standard dictionary definition is a good starting point for understanding suicide, although it is vague. As you review the different definitions, pay attention to how each explains the dynamics of suicide. Notice, too, that suicidal behavior may be immediate or long term. Thus, alcohol abuse can be suicidal behavior because, in attempting to solve existential problems, it makes use of something that can be fatal over time. Ask yourself, What kinds of human behavior does the definition include? Is suicide a specific act, or is it a behavioral process? What is the context of suicide? What are the circumstances in which it occurs?

TABLE 12-1 *Four Definitions of Suicide*

Suicide is . . .
The act or an instance of taking one's own life voluntarily and intentionally, especially by a person of years of discretion and of sound mind. (*Webster's New Collegiate Dictionary*)
Self-killing deriving from one's inability or refusal to accept the terms of the human condition. (Ronald W. Maris)
All behavior that seeks and finds the solution to an existential problem by making an attempt on the life of the subject. (Jean Baechler)
The human act of self-inflicted, self-intentioned cessation. (Edwin Shneidman)

> You may notice that I have not used the common terminology "committed suicide." It's because I believe this phrase incorrectly and unfairly accuses the suicide victim of an act over which they had no control. (If they had control, they would not have suicided. If they had, in other words, been in their right mind, they would not have taken their life.) The topic of "rational suicide" or physician-assisted suicide/death with dignity, as in the case of debilitating terminal illness, is a whole other topic of its own and outside the scope of these comments. The word "commit" is frequently paired with negatively judged acts: commit adultery, commit murder, commit a crime, commit a felony. I strongly believe that, because the suicidal person's mind is not working properly, there is a moment where suicide is no longer a choice. . . . If at that moment the person has access to the means to die, the suicide will happen. If at that moment the person is prevented from suiciding because he or she does not have the means, the suicide can be prevented. People refer to suicide as an "easy way out," but if you think about it, would it be easy for someone who is thinking clearly to slit their wrist, jump off a bridge, or pull the trigger of a gun?
>
> Donna Schuurman, *Never the Same: Coming to Terms with the Death of a Parent*

Suicidal behavior includes three types of self-destruction: (1) *completed suicide,* (2) *attempted suicide,* and (3) *suicidal gestures.* (Thoughts and plans about suicide are referred to as *suicidal ideation.*) The first of these results in death, whereas the second is intended to be self-lethal but does not result in death. The third category represents attempts with low lethal potential, such as inflicting superficial scratches on the wrist or overdosing on vitamins. Although suicidal gestures are often "pleas for help" from individuals who still wish to live, they should not be dismissed lightly.[3]

Statistical Issues

In the most recent year for which statistics are available, over 38,000 people died by suicide in the United States.[4] For the nation as a whole, suicide ranked tenth among all causes of death. It ranked third among persons fifteen to twenty-four years of age and second among those twenty-five to thirty-four years old.[5] Among those who die by suicide, males outnumber females by about four to one. In contrast to the male-female ratio for *deaths* by suicide, about three females *attempt* suicide for every male who does so.[6] According to a recent study, more than eight million Americans seriously consider suicide each year.[7]

Besides the cost in terms of lives lost, suicide has a powerful impact on those who are left to grieve a death by suicide. Pioneering suicidologist Edwin Shneidman says that the person who dies by suicide "puts his psychological skeleton in the survivor's emotional closet."[8] It is estimated that each suicide affects at least six other people. These survivors of suicide include family members, friends, significant others, and loved ones. Based on an average of one suicide every eighteen minutes in the United States, this means that there are at least six new survivors every eighteen minutes as well. "Those who are left behind in the wake of suicide are left to deal with the guilt and the anger, to sift the good memories from the bad, and to try to understand an inexplicable act."[9]

The actual number of suicide deaths each year is likely to be much higher than statistics indicate. There is general agreement that official counts understate the number of suicides, perhaps by as much as half. A death is unlikely to be classified as a suicide unless the coroner or medical examiner suspects suicide because of the deceased's history of suicidal tendencies or acts of self-injury, or because the deceased left a note, or because the circumstances of death clearly point to suicide. "A suicide classification is therefore neither a matter of elimination nor a default option. Rather, it is a manner of death that must be positively demonstrated. This has been called 'the fifty-one percent rule of suicide.'"[10]

In some cases, an examination of circumstances surrounding an automobile accident, for example, leads to the conclusion that what seemed an accident was really a suicide in disguise. In fact, some authorities believe that if such "autocides" were added to known statistics, suicide would be ranked as the number-one killer of young people.

When the circumstances of a death are equivocal (meaning that the causes are uncertain or unclear), and there are questions about whether the manner of death was suicide or accident, it is likely to be classified as accidental unless a careful investigation proves otherwise. One investigator says, "When it's not a simple black or white case but one full of gray values, we never end up in the suicide range. You owe that to the family and the decedent."[11]

Victim-precipitated homicide also may mask a person's suicidal intent. Someone who deliberately provokes others by flashing a knife, wielding a gun, or goading others with threats of violence may be attempting to enlist the unwitting help of others in causing his or her own death. Individuals can create violent situations in which they are likely to be killed, thereby possibly "dying as heroes."[12] A subcategory of victim-precipitated homicide, "suicide by cop," occurs when individuals engage in life-threatening and criminal actions that force police to shoot and kill them.[13] Researchers say there are two categories of suicide by cop: (1) the "fleeing felon," who tries to escape and, once cornered, decides he is going out in a "blaze of glory," and (2) the emotionally disturbed person who is seeking a way out of mental pain or some life failure. This distinction is recognized in the advice: It's one thing to kill a "bad guy," and quite another to kill a "sad guy."[14] Similarly, research indicates that some individuals murder others and then seek the death penalty as a form of suicide, a situation that has been termed the "murder-suicide syndrome."[15] All these types of victim-precipitated deaths are variously classified as homicide, suicide, or undetermined.[16]

In summarizing the difficulties in compiling accurate suicide statistics, Shneidman says,

> Because of religious and bureaucratic prejudices, family sensitivity, differences in the proceedings of coroner's hearings and postmortem examinations, and the shadowy distinctions between suicides and accidents—in short, the unwillingness to recognize the act for what it is—knowledge of the extent to which suicide pervades modern society is diminished and distorted.[17]

The Psychological Autopsy

Developed in 1961—primarily by Norman Farberow, Edwin Shneidman, and Robert Litman—the *psychological autopsy* is an impartial investigation by behavioral scientists to look for the motivational or intentional aspects of cases of ambiguous death.[18] The findings of a psychological autopsy improve the accuracy of death classification. Such an autopsy attempts to re-create the personality and lifestyle of the deceased and the known circumstances of his or her death. Information gathered from interviews, documents, and other materials is used to determine the mode of death: natural, accident, suicide, or homicide.[19] With this information in hand, "The historical gestalt [pattern] that emerges from the data can clarify the most probable mode of death."[20]

Of particular importance is the information pieced together from interviews with the deceased's friends and relatives, as well as other members of the community. This involves learning about current and previous stressors, psychiatric and medical histories, and the general lifestyle of the deceased, as well as any communication about suicidal intent. The person's routine in the days and hours before death is considered carefully as investigators try to create a picture of the person's character, personality, and state of mind. Based on an assessment of all the data gathered, a judgment is made about the mode of death (see Table 12-2).

An explosion aboard the USS *Iowa* that killed forty-seven sailors brought increased public attention to the use of psychological autopsies.[21] Based on an "equivocal death analysis" conducted by the FBI, the U.S. Navy attributed the tragedy to alleged suicidal acts by Gunner's Mate Clayton Hartwig. Because of questions about the investigation, the House Armed Services Committee convened a panel of distinguished psychologists to conduct a peer review of the FBI's report and the Navy's subsequent conclusion. After weighing the evidence, the committee rejected the Navy's allegation that Hartwig intentionally caused the explosion; they characterized the inquiry as an "investigative failure," particularly with respect to

TABLE 12-2 *Four Purposes of the Psychological Autopsy*

1. To help clarify the mode of death: natural, accident, suicide, or homicide (a classification system known by the acronym NASH). Note that *mode* of death differs from *cause* of death. The mode of death may be uncertain, although the cause may be clear.
2. To determine why a death occurred at a particular time; in other words, to examine the possible connection between the individual's psychology or state of mind and the timing of his or her death.
3. To gain data that may prove useful in predicting suicide and assessing the lethality of the suicidal person, thus helping clinicians and others identify trends in suicidal behavior and high-risk groups.
4. To obtain information that can be of therapeutic value to survivors in resolving emotional turmoil and questions that follow upon a loved one's death by suicide.

the FBI's analysis. Later tests indicated that the blast may have been due to mechanical error. The Navy ultimately recanted its allegations of Hartwig's responsibility, and the Chief of Naval Operations issued a formal apology to Hartwig's family.

In commenting about the case, the committee's psychologists cited several limitations of reconstructive psychological procedures, including the FBI's equivocal death analysis and psychological autopsies (see Table 12-3). They concluded that such psychological reconstruction should not result in an assertion of "categorical conclusions about the precise mental state or actions suspected of the actor at the time of his or her demise."[22] At present, the judiciary appears undecided about the admissibility of psychological autopsies as evidence; some courts admit them into evidence, whereas others exclude them.

The Hartwig case demonstrates that a lack of scientific precision may result in erroneous conclusions about the data collected through the use of psychological autopsies. Proponents of such investigative techniques point out that even *medical* autopsies are not perfect—yet they are viewed as having the potential to clarify circumstances surrounding death.

Despite its limitations, the psychological autopsy has proved to be a useful tool in assessing risk factors for suicide, especially factors that place young people at risk.[23] However, recently it has been pointed out that using a psychological autopsy to establish a diagnosis of a mental disorder does not produce valid results, and researchers say such efforts should be abandoned.[24] Nonetheless, they endorse uses of psychological autopsies that focus on adding to the understanding of suicide, a goal more in line with the original intent of such tools. As both an investigative approach and a research tool, it seems clear the psychological autopsy deepens our understanding of suicide and suicidal behavior.

TABLE 12-3 *Limitations of the Psychological Autopsy*

1. *Lack of standardized procedures.* Several guidelines for conducting a psychological autopsy have been proposed, but a set of standardized procedures does not exist. Thus, critics question the reliability and validity of psychological autopsies. Proponents, on the other hand, argue that wide latitude is needed to accommodate unique situations.
2. *Retrospective nature.* Examiners are required to offer observations or opinions about a person's past mental state.
3. *Distorted information.* Third-party informants may distort representations of the decedent for a variety of reasons. Everyone who participates in a psychological autopsy has some stake in its outcome. Information from friends or relatives may be biased; public agencies may shape the story to fit certain preconceived parameters.
4. *Lack of availability.* The individual of interest may not be available for examination, a fact that makes this the greatest limitation of the psychological autopsy.
5. *Too few studies.* There are few studies examining the reliability and validity of data obtained by psychological autopsies.

Explanatory Theories of Suicide

The study of suicide has followed mainly two lines of theoretical investigation: (1) the sociological model, which has its foundation in the work of nineteenth-century French sociologist Emile Durkheim, and (2) the psychological model, which is based on the work of Viennese psychoanalyst Sigmund Freud. Most scholars pursue an integrated approach to understanding suicide, one that combines sociological and psychological insights. Moreover, David Lester points out, "There is some evidence that theories of suicide proposed by Western scholars may not be applicable to other nations and cultures."[25] Thus, he asks, "Which culturally specific ethnic variables have been overlooked that might be important?" Lester says, "More work needs to be done on taking the ideas about suicide held in nonWestern societies and exploring whether new and different hypotheses, and even comprehensive theories of suicide, can be developed from them."[26] Although the following discussion can provide a good foundation, there is more to be done toward fully understanding suicide.

The Social Context of Suicide

The sociological model, as its name implies, focuses on the relationship between the individual and society. People live within networks of social relationships ranging from the family to society as a whole, and social forces influence the circumstances surrounding suicide. Durkheim theorized that these social forces are manifested in the degree of integration and regulation present in a given society.[27]

Degree of Social Integration

The degree to which a person is part of (integrated into) his or her society is important. At one extreme, we find situations in which the individual feels alienated from the institutions and traditions of his or her society. This is known as *low integration* or *low belongingness.*[28] The person has too few ties with his or her community. Without an adequate sense of social connectedness, a person becomes overly dependent upon his or her own resources. In this type of social environment, the suicides that occur are termed *egoistic.* An individual's mental energies are concentrated on the self to such an extent that social sanctions against suicide are ineffective. People who are disenfranchised or who live at the fringes of society may have no reason to hold to life-affirming values, because they do not experience themselves as meaningfully related to the community. In Durkheim's view, when a person is detached from society, individual personality takes precedence over collective personality. Egoistic suicide is a type of suicide that springs from excessive individualism.

Conversely, when a person has a strong degree of social connectedness and integration, he or she may identify with its values or causes to such an extent that the sense of his or her own personal identity is diminished. Under certain circumstances, the values or customs of the group may demand suicide. This is the case in what Durkheim called *altruistic* or *institutional suicide,* which has been defined as "the self-destruction demanded by a society . . . as a price for being a member of that society."[29]

In feudal Japan, for example, when samurai warriors sacrificed their lives to maintain the honor or reputation of their lords, their society viewed such suicide as heroic. In certain circumstances, ritual disembowelment, called *seppuku* or *hara-kiri,* was culturally accepted and expected, and it was accomplished by a prescribed etiquette.[30] When a warrior experienced disgrace in battle, seppuku was a way to regain honor. It demonstrated devotion to a superior, and the samurai might be expected to exhibit his devotion in this manner upon the death of his lord. At other times, seppuku could be an honorable way for a samurai to make a public statement of disagreement with a corrupt superior. Such acts were widely revered by Japanese people when they were based on authentic moral intentions. Suicide as protest also occurred during the Vietnam War, when Buddhist monks died by self-immolation to protest their country's governmental policies. According to Durkheim, highly integrated societies naturally encourage altruistic and fatalistic suicide.[31]

Flames engulf the body of Buddhist monk Thich Quang Duc, whose self-immolation in downtown Saigon on June 11, 1963, was intended as a protest against persecution of Buddhists by the government of South Vietnam.

Similarly, historically, certain castes in India were expected to practice *satī* (also called *suttee*), which called for a "faithful wife" to die on the fire as her husband's body was burned on the cremation pyre. Such self-immolation, or "following into death," was condoned by religious and cultural beliefs.[32] Reluctance to enact such ritual suicide could meet with social disapproval. Indeed, a reluctant widow might be "helped" onto the burning pyre. To these examples of seppuku and satī could be added the deaths of kamikaze pilots in Japan's air attack corps during World War II and the example of the dedicated captain who goes down with the ship. In discussing altruistic suicide, Durkheim introduced the concept of *heroic suicide* in referring to deaths in combat, as in the case of Medal of Honor recipients who voluntarily sacrificed their own lives to save the lives of others.[33]

Mass suicide, defined as the simultaneous suicide of the members of a social group, also occurs within a highly integrated social context. Researchers have denoted two types of mass suicide: (1) *hetero-induced,* which typically occurs in defeated and colonized populations, and (2) *self-induced,* in which the motivation is related to a distorted evaluation of reality. An example of the first type occurred in 219 BCE, when the Carthaginian commander Hannibal sacked the commune of Sagunto. Its leading citizens, preferring death to capture, died together by suicide. This is a type of suicide enacted by soldiers who realize they are losing the battle. The second type has become familiar in recent decades, when the "mystic delirium" within a sect has led to the self-destruction of the group as an act of self-assertiveness.[34]

For example, on November 20, 1978, at a previously little-noticed jungle clearing in Jonestown, Guyana, more than nine hundred people died in what is considered the largest mass suicide in history.[35] Family members died in one another's arms as the Reverend Jim Jones, in hypnotic tones from his throne above the crowd, instructed the followers of his Peoples Temple community to drink cyanide-laced fruit punch. In 1993, in Waco, Texas, seventy-five followers of David Koresh's Branch Davidians died among the flames after setting fire to their camp. More recently, the desire to leave this planet for a better existence in a "parallel dimension" led to the mass suicide in 1997 of thirty-nine members of the Heaven's Gate cult in a San Diego suburb.[36]

Degree of Social Regulation

In Durkheim's model, insufficient social regulation creates the conditions for *anomic suicides.* In the typical example, the relationship between an individual and society is suddenly shattered or disrupted. Such social estrangement is characterized by the term *anomie* (from the Greek *anomia,* meaning "lawlessness"). The classic example of this situation occurs when societies undergo rapid social change, and people lose their moorings to traditional values and lifeways. Suicide among youth worldwide is partly attributed to cultural changes whereby individualism and autonomy tend to loosen bonds between individuals and society. Anomie (lack of regulation) and egoism (lack of integration) reinforce each other.

Sudden trauma or catastrophe can also weaken the ties between an individual and society. The loss of a job, the amputation of a limb, the death of a close friend or family member—any of these losses can be an anomic event. Any disruptive change—whether positive or negative—can precipitate a state of anomie.

At the other extreme of regulation, we find societies characterized by excessive social constraints. Lack of freedom and absence of choice can generate a sense of fatalism, a feeling that there is nowhere to turn and that nothing good can be achieved. This produces what Durkheim termed *fatalistic suicide.* Suicide in jail is due partly to the rigid regulation found in such environments. (When three Guantanamo Bay detainees died by hanging themselves with fabricated nooses made from clothes and bedsheets, another detainee explained what led to their deaths by saying, "I would rather die than live here forever without rights.")[37]

Viewed from a social perspective, suicide is caused by a disturbance in the ties between an individual and society. An imbalance in the degree of social regulation or social integration, or both, heightens the potential for suicide. Thus, according to the sociological explanation, each form of suicide—egoistic, altruistic, anomic, fatalistic—is related to a particular kind of interplay between society and the individual.

Psychological Insights About Suicide

Drawing on theories proposed by Sigmund Freud, the psychological model of suicide focuses attention on the mental and emotional processes, both conscious and unconscious, that occur within the mind of an individual. It assumes that a person's behavior is determined by both past experience and current reality. Among the key insights from psychological studies of suicide are the following:

1. The *acute* suicidal crisis is of relatively brief duration; that is, it lasts hours or days rather than weeks or months—though it may recur. A person is at the peak of self-destructiveness for a short time and gets help, cools off, or dies.
2. The suicidal person is likely to be *ambivalent* about ending his or her life. A person on the brink of suicide both wants to die and doesn't want to die. While plans for self-destruction are being made, the person also entertains fantasies of rescue or intervention.
3. Most suicidal events are *dyadic* events—that is, two-person events. In some way, they involve both a suicidal person and a significant other.

Suicide Note Written by a Married Man, Age 45

My darling,
May her guts rot in hell—I loved her so much.

Henry

In the psychological view, suicide involves strong unconscious hostility. Under conditions of enormous stress, the intrapsychic pressures impelling a person toward self-destruction increase to the point that they overwhelm the defense mechanisms of the ego, or self. This, in turn, causes a regression to primitive ego states, which involve powerful forces of *aggression*. Whereas murder is aggression turned upon another, suicide is aggression turned upon oneself. In this sense, suicide may be viewed as murder in the 180th degree. In the German language, suicide is murder of the self, *Selbstmord*.

Even with aggressive forces mobilized, however, the urge toward self-preservation works against the self's acquiescence in its own death. Thus, another psychological process comes into play: *ambivalence*. Analysis of suicidal behavior usually reveals the presence of conflicting forces that compete for the greater share of the person's mental energies. Suicidal persons tend to be indecisive. They may even count on being rescued. Shneidman says the prototypical suicidal person wants "to cut his throat and to cry for help at the same time."[38]

Even when a person appears to be intent on suicide, the natural urge toward self-preservation works against the self's acceptance of its own death. At issue is the will to live versus the will to die. "Most people who commit acts of self-damage with more or less conscious self-destructive intent do not want either to live or to die, but to do both at the same time."[39]

The balance between these opposing polarities may be delicate, with an otherwise minor incident tipping the scales one way or the other. Although one of these forces is eventually stronger than the other, the weaker one nevertheless affects the person's behavior. Suicidal acts are often examples of risk-taking behavior or gambles. The outcome of the conflict between the self-destructive and life-preserving impulses depends on a variety of factors, some of which are outside the individual's control.

Toward an Integrated Understanding of Suicide

In an illuminating study of the death of Socrates, Sam Silverman reviewed the factors that may have entered into his decision to drink the hemlock (a poisonous herb) given to him. Among these factors were his awareness of aging, his declining relationships with others, his marriage and family life, and the political context of the times and his place in it. "He must have been tired, disillusioned, and generally depressed by how things had gone and by his age," Silverman says.[40] Furthermore, his support systems were crumbling. Because he believed that suicide was not permitted, however, it wasn't an option. Silverman suggests that Socrates chose, in essence, "suicide by cop," letting a jury of his Athenian peers decide his fate.

Because suicidal behavior is multidimensional and multifaceted, the social and psychological explanations of suicide interact in an integrated fashion. After devoting a lifetime to studying suicide, Edwin Shneidman distilled his learning into five words: *Suicide is caused by psychache*.[41] Shneidman says: "Psychache is at the dark heart of suicide; no psychache, no suicide."[42] However, Shneidman points out that over 99 percent of individuals who

Richard Cory

Whenever Richard Cory went down town,
We people on the pavement looked at him:
He was a gentleman from sole to crown,
Clean favored, and imperially slim.

And he was always quietly arrayed,
And he was always human when he talked;
But still he fluttered pulses when he said,
"Good-morning," and he glittered when he walked.

And he was rich—yes, richer than a king—
And admirably schooled in every grace:
In fine, we thought that he was everything
To make us wish that we were in his place.

So on we worked, and waited for the light,
And went without the meat, and cursed the bread;
And Richard Cory, one calm summer night,
Went home and put a bullet through his head.

Edwin Arlington Robinson

suffer from even severe psychache do not kill themselves. He observes, "Much psychache without suicide; no suicide without psychache."[43]

The term "psychache" refers to the unbearable mental pain that is caused by the frustration of a person's most important needs, which are unique to each individual. Shneidman believes that most suicide cases tend to exhibit themselves in one of four clusters of frustrated psychological needs:[44]

1. Thwarted love, acceptance, or belonging
2. Fractured control, helplessness, and frustration
3. Assaulted self-image and avoidance of shame, defeat, humiliation, and disgrace
4. Ruptured key relationships and attendant grief and bereftness

Suicide has been called "a very bad decision on a very bad day." It is the outcome of a person's desire to reduce intolerable pain. An individual who is suicidal is likely to be in a state of isolated desperation, a dark corner where it seems there is no hope of relief. A common theme among the various paths to suicide is that it is seen as the ultimate form of gaining control over insurmountable difficulties in life.

The sequence leading to suicide often begins with interactions between biochemical imbalances in the brain, personality factors, and life stress. Most suicides are the outcome of a disease in the brain, an illness such as depression, anxiety, schizophrenia, bipolar (manic-depressive) disorder, or some other mood disorder. Clinical depression, a state of intense sadness and self-reproach, is a major risk factor. A key aspect of depression is the person's sense of *hopelessness.* Suicide risk is also higher with some personality disorders, such as borderline and antisocial personality, especially when combined with substance abuse. (Alcohol or substance abuse is a contributing cause in many suicides.) Whereas mental illness is an *ongoing* risk factor for suicide, the specific *timing* of suicidal acts tends to be related to stressful life events. Nonetheless, virtually everyone who dies by suicide experiences one or more mental disorders at the time of death.[45]

In studies of attempted and completed suicides, there appears to be a neurobiological determinant related to the brain's reduced ability to make and use serotonin, a key neurotransmitter. Serotonin is lower in suicide attempters, and postmortem studies of suicide victims reveal decreased serotonin activity in the prefrontal cortex.[46] Low levels of serotonin (5-HT) or its neurotransmitter metabolite (5-HIAA) may be correlated with suicidal behavior. Serotonin levels appear to be related to a calming influence on the mind and, when levels are low, to an increased risk of suicide. As scientists learn more about the role of biological markers like serotonin, it may be possible to reduce vulnerability to suicide by identifying individuals at risk and offering appropriate therapy.

Many people are not aware of the role of brain disease in suicide. As a result, they tend to treat suicide as a failure of personal responsibility and as a matter of shame. This mistaken attitude can severely limit an understanding of suicide. In fact, our recognition of the strong connection between diseases of the brain and suicide challenges the conventional notion that suicide is chosen by a person out of his or her free and rational choice.

Some Types of Suicide

Various classification schemes have been applied to suicide to comprehend its cultural and personal meanings (see Table 12-4). To provide a more complete picture of suicide and other self-destructive behaviors, it is worthwhile to look more closely at a few typical categories of suicide. Notice that an instance of suicide may include elements from more than one category.

Suicide as Escape

Suicide may be a means to put an end to intense physical pain or mental anguish. In such cases, it is called *surcease* suicide, an escape "forced by life's becoming literally unbearable."[47] A person with a severely debilitating or terminal illness may view suicide as a way to gain release from burdensome suffering. Ending one's life in such a situation is sometimes termed *rational suicide* because the reasoning used—that death will bring release from pain—conforms to normal logic. Physician-assisted death (discussed in Chapter 6) can be considered an example of this type of suicide.

In other instances, a desire to escape through suicide results from destructive logic. When an individual's self-concept or sense of identity is confused, and when this confusion is coupled with problems in relating to

TABLE 12-4 *Meanings of Suicide*

Some Cultural Meanings of Suicide

Suicide is sinful: A crime against nature, a revolt against the preordained order of the universe.

Suicide is criminal: It violates the ties that exist, the social contract between persons in a society.

Suicide is weakness or madness: It reflects limitations or deviancy ("He must have been crazy" or "He couldn't take it").

Suicide is the Great Death, as in *seppuku, suttee,* and other culturally approved forms of ritual suicide.

Suicide is the rational alternative: The outcome of a "balance-sheet" approach that sizes up the situation and determines the best option.

Some Individual Meanings of Suicide

Suicide is reunion with a lost loved one: A way to " join the deceased."

Suicide is rest and refuge: A way out of a burdensome and depressing situation.

Suicide is getting back: A way of expressing resentment and revenge at being rejected or hurt.

Suicide is the penalty for failure: A response to disappointment and frustration at not meeting one's own expectations or those of others.

Suicide is a mistake: The attempt was made as a cry for help and was not intended to be fatal, but there was no rescue or intervention, and the outcome was death.

others, it can result in the person's self-perception as a failure. In this case, suicide may be termed *referred,* bringing to mind the analogy of a physical pain that is experienced at some distance from its source. An inflammation of the liver may be experienced as pain in the shoulder. Just as this physical phenomenon is characterized as referred pain, so the root causes of referred suicide are likewise only indirectly related to the end result—namely, suicide. The intention to end one's life is not based on a dispassionate or rational assessment of the situation but, instead, results from an overwhelming sense of anguish and confusion about one's options.

In China, suicide has become the leading cause of death among young adults, a quarter million of whom die by suicide each year, while another three million make suicide attempts.[48] Many are college students who leave notes expressing regret at failing to live up to their parents' expectations. These expectations may be related to something outside the person ("If I can't be a good enough daughter to please my parents, I give up!") or to feelings of frustration ("Everybody thinks I'm doing okay, but I feel rotten"). Not performing up to expectations or role definitions can provoke a crisis of self-concept that leads to a desire to escape the unsatisfactory situation.

Desire to escape may arise from loss of meaning in one's life. Despite significant accomplishments, a person may feel, "Okay, now what?" Accumulating successes one after another may seem a Sisyphean effort, a continual struggle for achievement without a corresponding sense of accomplishment. Conversely, success may be accompanied by feelings of dissatisfaction—"If

Käthe Kollwitz, Library of Congress

Depression, hopelessness, despair, and psychache are depicted in this lithograph, Nachdenkende Frau, by Käthe Kollwitz. Such intense sadness is caused by frustration of a person's most important needs and is a major risk factor for suicide.

this is success, it's not worth the effort." The causal chain begins with events that fall short of standards and expectations.[49] The individual seeks to escape from a negative sense of self. Drastic measures seem acceptable, and suicide becomes the ultimate step in the effort to find release.

Cry for Help

Considered as a *cry for help,* suicide aims to force a change. The person no longer wishes to continue living life as it is. The goal is not to die but to solve some problem. Suicide, or the threat of suicide, is perceived, at least temporarily, as a means of eliminating the problem. Suicidal behavior is, in effect,

The Suicide

When the suicide moved in across the street,
People knew her as the woman with blonde hair.
She hadn't decided on her method yet.

A gun? Some pills? The blood released from its knot
of life? At first, there was nothing to fear
When the suicide moved in across the street.

She couldn't sleep at all, she said. At night
She wove her drunken mind around a star.
She hadn't decided on her method yet.

Later, they read the signs: the way each thought
Stumbled on the grass, the telling whisper.
When the suicide moved in across the street,

She tried to tell them how immediate
Death was, how soft, its under-wings like Mother.
She hadn't decided on her method yet.

They didn't hear. She asked for tea, the gate
Closing in her eyes. She asked for sugar.
When the suicide moved in across the street,
She hadn't decided on her method yet.

Kim Bridgeford

a message that "something has to change in my life; I can't go on living this way." In distinguishing between a suicide threat and a suicide attempt, some definitions may be appropriate:

> A suicide *threat* is "any interpersonal action, verbal or non-verbal, without a direct self-injurious component, that a reasonable person would interpret as communicating or suggesting that suicidal behavior might occur in the near future." A suicide *attempt* is "a self-inflicted, potentially injurious behavior with a non-fatal outcome for which there is evidence (either explicit or implicit) of intent to die."[50]

Some experts express the view that self-harm, such as cutting one's wrist or taking a drug overdose, can be considered an act of "self-preservation" or even "self-assertion."[51] From this perspective, self-injury among young people could be viewed as a coping mechanism to deal with emotional distress and validated as representing a young person coping the best way he or she can. Looked at in this way, efforts can be taken to help the young person move away from self-harm toward safer and healthier methods of coping. The intent may be to express frustration or gain attention, but the danger of a fatal outcome is not acknowledged. Many suicide attempts represent a kind of communication that says, in effect, "I am deadly serious; you'd better pay attention!" This message may be directed inwardly to oneself or meant for others.

There may be two distinct populations of individuals who engage in suicidal behavior: (1) *attempters* (who tend to make repeated but not lethal attempts) and (2) *completers* (whose first attempt typically results in death). Attempters and completers may have quite different aims with regard to their suicidal acts.[52] "Intention in the behavior may or may not be to die, or may or may not be to inflict injury or pain on oneself."[53] Some suicidologists believe that attempted suicide should be viewed as the norm, whereas completed suicide should be seen as a failed behavior in which a person inappropriately died.

A cry for help is associated with individuals who threaten or attempt suicide, as distinct from those who actually kill themselves. Often, in the first group the *lethality* of the attempt is low. (Lethality refers to capability of causing death). It appears the aim of the behavior is to communicate to others how desperate or unhappy the person feels. When low-lethality suicidal behavior is met with defensive hostility or attempts to minimize its seriousness, however, the risk of suicide may increase, along with the possibility that a future attempt will be lethal. In responding to the cry for help, it is crucial to recognize that a problem exists and take steps toward expanding communication and proposing remedies. Whatever the intention, suicidal behavior can be deadly. Psychological autopsies indicate that some people who have died by suicide didn't intend their actions to result in death, but help didn't arrive in time.

Attempted suicides outnumber completed suicides by a significant margin. A standard estimate is that there are twenty-five attempts for every death by suicide. There are more suicide attempts among females than among males, whereas males die by suicide more often than do females. These gender differences may be explained partly by the methods chosen; males tend to use more lethal methods, such as guns, whereas females tend to take pills or slash wrists. (Unfortunately, this gap may be narrowing, as females appear to be adopting increasingly lethal methods, such as firearms.) Alcohol abuse, a risk factor for suicide, is also more common among males. Furthermore, it may be that males consider a "failed" suicide attempt to be cowardly or unmasculine and therefore make a special effort to be "successful." Besides this "suicidal success syndrome," males are less likely than females to report suicidal thoughts or seek help. By trying to hide their feelings of depression or hopelessness, males are less likely to seek out suicide prevention or crisis intervention programs.

People who survive a suicide attempt may view their continued existence as a second chance or "bonus life." If this opportunity is used well, the person may arrive at a more positive self-identity and find ways to get beyond the pain that led to the attempted suicide. By altering the distressing situation or one's attitude toward it, a cry for help may lead to constructive change and healing.

Suicide Note Written by a Divorced Woman, Age 61

You cops will want to know why I did it, well just let us say that I lived 61 years too many.

People have always put obstacles in my way. One of the great ones is leaving this world when you want to and have nothing to live for.

I am not insane. My mind was never more clear. It has been a long day. The motor got so hot it would not run so I just had to sit here and wait. The breaks were against me to the very last.

The sun is leaving the hill now so hope nothing else happens.

Subintentioned and Chronic Suicide

As defined by Edwin Shneidman, a *subintentioned* death is "one in which the person plays some partial, covert, subliminal, or unconscious role in hastening his own demise."[54] Some fatalities reported as accidents result from the victim's taking unnecessary and unwise risks. Such behavior might be called careless or imprudent. Probing deeper into causes, however, reveals that accidents are sometimes the end result of a self-destructive pattern of behavior. Similarly, homicide investigations sometimes turn up evidence of subintentional factors that led a victim to behave in ways that provoked his or her death at another's hands.

Besides subintentioned death, Shneidman delineates two other patterns of death-related behaviors: *intentioned* and *unintentioned.* Table 12-5 presents an outline of these three patterns. Notice that, within each of these categories, a person might exhibit a variety of attitudes and behaviors regarding death. As you review this table, ask yourself: Where do I stand on this list? What does that tell me about my own regard for life and death?

Chronic suicide, a term coined by Karl Menninger, refers to individuals who destroy themselves by means of drugs, alcohol, smoking, reckless living, and the like. Although individuals who shorten their lives by chronic suicide may consciously find the idea of suicide repugnant or unacceptable, an analysis of their lifestyles typically reveals the presence of a "death wish."

Risk Factors Influencing Suicide

Another way to increase our understanding of suicide is to examine risk factors that influence suicide and suicidal behaviors. Besides the neurobiological and genetic factors discussed earlier in this chapter, here we focus on risk factors related to culture, personality, and the individual situation. Typically, various risk factors overlap and are mutually influential in a particular instance of suicidal behavior.

TABLE 12-5 *Patterns of Death-Related Behavior and Attitudes*

Intentioned Death: Death resulting from the suicide's direct, conscious behavior to bring it about. A variety of attitudes or motives may be operative:

The *death seeker* wishes to end consciousness and commits the suicidal act in such a way that rescue is unlikely.

The *death initiator* expects to die in the near future and wants to choose the time and circumstances of death.

The *death ignorer* believes that death ends only physical existence and that the person continues to exist in another manner.

The *death darer* gambles with death or, as Shneidman says, "bets his life on a relatively low objective probability that he will survive" (such as by playing Russian roulette).

Subintentioned Death: Death resulting from a person's patterns of management or style of living, although death was not the conscious, direct aim of the person's actions:

The *death chancer,* although in many ways like the death darer, may want higher odds of survival.

The *death hastener* may expedite his or her death by substance abuse (drugs, alcohol, and the like) or by failing to safeguard well-being (for example, by inadequate nutrition or precautions against disease or by disregard of available treatments).

The *death facilitator* offers little resistance to death, making it easy for death to occur, as in the deaths of patients whose energies, or "will to live," are low because of their illness.

The *death capitulator* is one who, usually out of a great fear of death, plays a subintentional role in his or her own death, as may a person upon whom a so-called voodoo death has been put, or as may a person who believes that someone admitted to a hospital is bound to die.

The *death experimenter* does not consciously wish to die but lives on the brink, usually in a "befogged state of consciousness" that may be related to taking drugs in such ways that he or she may become comatose or even die with little concern.

Unintentioned Death: Death in which the decedent plays no significant causative role. However, various attitudes toward death may shape the experience of dying:

The *death welcomer,* though not hastening death, looks forward to it (as might an aged person who feels unable to manage adequately or satisfactorily).

The *death accepter* is resigned to his or her fate; the style of acceptance may be passive, philosophical, resigned, heroic, realistic, or mature.

The *death postponer* hopes to put death off for as long as possible.

The *death disdainer* feels, in Shneidman's words, "above any involvement in the stopping of the vital processes."

The *death fearer* is fearful of and possibly phobic about anything related to death; death is something to be fought and hated.

The *death feigner* pretends to be in mortal danger or pretends to perform a suicidal act without being in actual danger, possibly in an attempt to gain attention or to manipulate others.

Culture

Cultural messages about suicide acceptability can influence the kinds of behavior engaged in by members of a social group. For example, a society or group may believe that suicide to end physical suffering from terminal disease is more acceptable than suicide to escape mental pain or other life problems. It has been pointed out that suicide has different meanings for different cultures.

Cultural disruption and stress appear to play a part in suicide among Native Americans. Forced onto reservations, their cultures undermined, native peoples of North America have undergone severe dislocations. Conflicts between their traditional ways and the ways of contemporary white society can lead to feelings of powerlessness and anxiety. An added burden is experienced by Native Americans who live in large cities, where support systems, family ties, and traditional customs are lacking. These stresses, sometimes combined with such dysfunctional behaviors as alcohol and drug abuse, can heighten suicide risk.

Kathleen Erwin has examined how social factors may influence gay and lesbian suicide.[55] Explanations for the elevated rate of suicide among homosexual populations have been sought mostly in theories centering on individual psychology. More recently, however, the antecedents of gay and lesbian suicide have been located in a sociocultural model that highlights the role of social forces that have been intolerant and oppressive toward homosexuals. The earlier focus on individual psychology is being balanced by a recognition that social factors are important, perhaps decisive, in suicide among homosexuals.

Within African American communities, many young people consider suicide a weak, cowardly way out of their problems, a view that is also held by many of their elders. The rate of suicide among African Americans is lower than the rate among white Americans, a phenomenon due at least partly to a common perception among African Americans that suicide is a "white thing." Kevin Early and Ronald Akers report that religion and family play important roles in "buffering" social forces that might otherwise promote suicide among African Americans. Early and Akers found that suicide is typically viewed as "inherently contradictory to the black experience and a complete denial of black identity and culture."[56]

The acceptability of violence as a solution to problems is another cultural factor that affects suicide risk. The availability of lethal weapons as well as the prevalence of violence in the media contribute to a sense that violence is an acceptable alternative when the going gets rough. Easy access to guns is an important factor in suicide among children and young adults, who are increasingly using guns to end their lives instead of methods that are more likely to fail. The apparent acceptance of violence in our lives can change posturing into deadly deeds.

In considering cultural messages, the idea that suicide is contagious has a long history. Following publication of Johann Wolfgang von Goethe's *The*

TABLE 12-6 *Pro-Life Versus Pro-Death Forces*

Belief that problems can promote growth	Belief that problems are intolerable
Perceived ability to solve life problems	Perception that life problems are intractable or unyielding
Willingness to struggle and suffer if necessary	Sense of entitlement to a rewarding life
A healthy fear of death and its aftermath	A philosophical stance that sees suicide as a means of obtaining relief

Sorrows of Young Werther in 1774, an epidemic of suicide among young people was thought to be stimulated by the book. The influence of suggestion on suicidal behavior has been termed the "Werther effect." The question of whether such a "contagious" or imitative effect actually exists remains controversial. (Suicide "clusters" are discussed later in this chapter.) What is clear is the fact that the social environment is a significant influence on suicide and suicidal behaviors.

Cultural factors in suicide are highlighted in what Brian Barry calls "the balance between pro-life and pro-death forces operating at any given time" (see Table 12-6).[57] In Barry's view, people in modern societies have accepted two fundamental assumptions about life that no previous generation has embraced so thoroughly: first, the belief that we deserve significant fulfillment in our jobs, marriages, and overall lives; and second, the belief that, rather than accepting unalterable circumstances, we must live and die on our own terms. In other words, not only do we aspire to a good life, but we have convinced ourselves that we are entitled to it. If this sense of entitlement is not realized, we may feel it's appropriate to protest by removing ourselves from an intolerable situation, even when the outcome is death.

Suicide bombings, too, reflect an understanding that the cultural collective—religion, sect, nation—is more important than the individual, leading to the terrorist's belief that he or she is engaged in a worthy struggle that makes suicidal sacrifice not only desirable but imperative (this topic is discussed in Chapter 13).

Personality

Some people seem to live with a basic optimism; others, with a basic pessimism. This personality difference can have an impact on the onset of suicidal thoughts. Fear or anxiety about death may also influence suicidal behavior. A higher degree of anxiety may inhibit suicidal behavior, whereas perceiving death as an attractive prospect may encourage it. Thus, the meanings attributed to death may influence the way individuals evaluate the possibility of suicide. Personality factors that contribute to suicidal thoughts and behaviors include low self-esteem, difficulties with intimate relationships, hopelessness, lack of coping skills, feelings of stagnation, and despair.

Suicide Note Written by a Married Man, Age 74

What is a few short years to live in hell. That is all I get around here.

No more I will pay the bills.

No more I will drive the car.

No more I will wash, iron & mend any clothes.

No more I will have to eat the leftover articles that was cooked the day before.

This is no way to live.

Either is it any way to die.

Her grub I can not eat.

At night I can not sleep.

I married the wrong nag-nag-nag and I lost my life.

W.S.

To the undertaker

We have got plenty money to give me a decent burial. Don't let my wife kid you by saying she has not got any money.

Give this note to the cops.

Give me liberty or give me death.

W.S.

An individual's fascination with the "mystique" of death, especially self-willed death, can increase suicide risk. Some suicides appear to be related to a "poetic" or "romantic" attraction to death. Following the example of Thomas Chatterton, who killed himself in 1770 at the age of seventeen, the Romantics thought of death as "the great inspirer" and "the great consoler." In other words, death is a lover to be courted. The poet Sylvia Plath wrote, "I will marry dark death, the thief of the daytime."[58] Do the suicides of such writers as Ernest Hemingway, Anne Sexton, and Plath herself, and, more recently, the suicide of musician Kurt Cobain, reflect a desire to embrace the mystery of death? Or do they result from commonplace human experiences? Investigated deeply, failure to find meaning in life and relationship problems are common threads. As someone said, "The death of love evokes the love of death."

The Individual Situation

The intersection of culture and personality creates the unique life situation experienced by a particular person. Every person is subject to a constellation of environmental factors that involve varying degrees of suicide risk. These include the social forces existing within society as a whole, as well as the particular characteristics associated with an individual's family, economic situation, and so on.

Stressful life events are associated with suicidal behaviors. For example, individuals who have been bereaved as a result of suicide may be vulnerable to increased risk of suicide themselves. In *crisis suicide,* the usual example is that of an adolescent who experiences traumatic change in his or her life, such as loss of a loved one or threatened loss of status in school.

With the wars in Iraq and Afghanistan, suicide rates in the military have risen rapidly, surpassing rates for society at large. In 2012, there were more deaths in the military from suicide than from combat.[59] More troubling, the military may be undercounting the problem because of the way it calculates the suicide rate. There is an increase in the number of military family members killing themselves as well. Senior officers have convened teleconferences to discuss causes and what needs to be done to help reduce these suicides.[60] Besides military personnel simply "falling through the cracks," other factors noted are working long, solitary hours; errors in mental health screening; health workers failing to recognize signs of distress; outdated assessment questionnaires; and even high-energy drinks taken in combination with drugs soldiers take for combat stress (one such drink has 100 milligrams of caffeine per can, 25 percent more than Red Bull and about three times as much as a can of Diet Coke). Numerous reports have been commissioned and many dollars spent on research and prevention programs, yet experts concede they are not much closer to understanding the root causes of why military suicide is rising so fast.

An emerging consensus among researchers is that, just as among civilians, a dauntingly complex web of factors usually underlies military suicide: mental illness, sexual or physical abuse, addictions, failed relationships, financial struggles. A recent report found that half of the troops who killed themselves had experienced the failure of an intimate relationship and about a quarter had received diagnoses of substance abuse.

An Institute of Medicine study reported that being deployed to a war zone can result in numerous adverse outcomes, and suicidal ideation, suicide attempts, and suicide are increasingly associated with modern military service.[61] The report noted that the relative risk of suicide is higher in individuals deployed to combat zones than in those never deployed. It said, "Some risk factors might be mitigated or prevented, but others, such as deployment and combat exposure, are difficult to prevent in a military population."[62]

Deployment and exposure to combat can act as catalysts that worsen existing problems in a service member's life, like drug abuse, or cause new ones, like posttraumatic stress disorder or traumatic brain injuries, which may contribute to suicidal behavior. Yet, some researchers contend, deployment and combat by themselves cannot explain the spiking suicide rates. Some reports indicate that, in recent years, about half of service members who killed themselves had never deployed to Iraq or Afghanistan, and more than 80 percent had never been in combat.

This has caused some commentators to point out that the United States has been engaged in wars for more than a decade; and, it is argued, some of them are waged only to increase global dominance. The traditional ideals of *duty, honor, country* may not be as applicable to current military conflicts as they once were. In his farewell address to cadets at West Point in 1962, General Douglas MacArthur said:

> Those three hallowed words reverently dictate what you ought to be, what you can be, what you will be. . . . The code which those words perpetuate embraces the highest moral laws and will stand the test of any ethics or philosophies ever promulgated for the uplift of mankind. Its requirements are for the things that are right, and its restraints are from the things that are wrong.[63]

Do these words, which speak of "morals" and "ethics," and the "uplift" of humankind, still provide a basis for the motives and consequence of contemporary wars? Could it be that one or more of Durkheim's explanations of suicide—anomie or fatalism perhaps—suggest that a lessening of traditional values of honor and a feeling that there is nowhere to turn and that nothing good can be achieved are at least partly responsible for suicides among the military and veterans, and their families?

Recently, in another example of perhaps diminished expectations and purpose, the suicide rate among the middle-aged in the United States has shown a dramatic spike. The highest increases have been among men in their fifties and women in their early sixties. Although there are so far no large-scale studies to explain the reasons for this increase in "boomer" suicides (referring to the baby boomer generation now passing through those ages), some observers point out that a reluctance to accept the realities of aging may be among the causes. "To those growing up in the 50s and 60s, America seemed to promise a limitless array of possibilities," as well as the freedom to "embrace new ways of living."[64] Now, this illusion of virtually unlimited choice is being shattered by the recognition that the expectation of "leading glorious lives didn't come to fruition." This uptick in suicide rates among boomers, who are at ages when rates have historically been stable (for men) or beginning to decline (for women), may be due to social or historical events, the so-called *period effect*.[65] With individuals ending their lives at their supposed peak, the question is being asked: What's gotten so rotten in the modern world? Moreover, in mainstream society, we don't venerate or honor our elders as some cultures do. All these factors may be part of the explanation for a rising suicide rate among the late middle-aged.

Physicians are another group in which suicidal risk is a matter of concern. On average, the United States loses the equivalent of an entire medical school class to suicide each year (as many as four hundred physicians).[66] Depression is a leading risk factor, coupled with knowledge of and access to lethal means of suicide. The report noted that, although female physicians attempt suicide far less often than their counterparts in the general population, their completion rates equal those of male physicians and, thus, far exceed those of the general population.

The influence of peers also affects an individual's suicide risk, especially among adolescents and young adults. A study of suicide among young Micronesian males found an "epidemic-like" increase during a twenty-year period.[67] This period was marked by rapid sociocultural transformation, as traditional styles of living gave way to a capitalist economy and modern forms of education, employment, health services, and technology. Investigators found links among the suicides, with several occurring among a small circle of friends over several months. There were also cases of self-destructive behavior in reaction to the suicide of a friend or relative, as well as suicide pacts between two or more people. Taken together, these phenomena pointed to the existence of a "suicide subculture" wherein suicide leads to another suicide. In an environment characterized by a general familiarity with and acceptance of the *idea* of suicide, suicide had become a culturally patterned and partly collective response to personal dilemmas and problems.

Finally, an individual's experience of loneliness, of being alone, can be a significant factor in suicide. It is not so much a matter of how many supportive people an individual has in his or her life that counts. Rather, it is that individual's *perception* of support that matters. According to Thomas Joiner, people (men especially) can become so focused on status, money, and success that they become oblivious to the fact that they are lonely. Indeed, they may push away friends and family members who sense something unhealthy and try to intervene. Yet, when questioned, such people (again it seems, men especially) do not acknowledge the fact of their loneliness. Joiner concludes: "Loneliness is a vicious killer. It preferentially stalks men. Like the victims of many killers, the victims of loneliness don't realize the danger until it's too late."[68]

Life-Span Perspectives on Suicide

The risk factors for suicide change through life as human beings encounter changing circumstances related to different periods of human development. The causes of suicide among adolescents, for example, tend to be distinct from those of people in old age. In studying various risks that pertain to different segments of the life span, notice which factors affect people of all ages and which factors tend to exert a particular influence on people in specific age groups.

Childhood

Suicide is rarely reported in young children, but many researchers and clinicians believe that suicidal behavior is found among even very young children. Because suicide risk is higher among those who have made an earlier attempt, children with a history of suicidal ideation or suicide attempt are at risk for multiple recurrence of suicidal ideas or acts.[69]

Researchers believe that the rate of suicide among children would be higher if childhood accidents were examined more carefully for intent. Some of the childhood deaths resulting from running in front of cars or plastic bag suffocation are probably intentional rather than accidental. Although young children usually do not have access to sophisticated means of self-destruction as do people at older ages, they nevertheless engage in acts of self-harm, and some kill themselves. In the case of young children, however, labeling a death as suicide may be problematic because of questions about whether a child possesses a mature concept of death and thus is fully aware of the consequences of his or her actions.[70] (Recall the discussion of childhood development in Chapter 2.) There is evidence that children who attempt suicide, especially those on the cusp between childhood and adolescence, tend to be in a transitional stage between concrete operational thought and formal operational thought, which may involve heightened vulnerability to suicidal ideation and behaviors.[71]

Adolescence and Early Adulthood

Adolescent suicide begins to appear in the age group of ten- to fourteen-year-olds and increases significantly among older adolescents and young adults, which suggests that developmental changes play a role, possibly one related to cognitive development and conceptualization of death.

Social disruption is an important factor in self-destructive behaviors among the young. Psychiatric diagnosis, dysfunctional personality traits, and psychosocial problems also increase the risk of suicide. Suicide in adolescents is linked with interpersonal conflict (with parents as well as boyfriends or girlfriends), interpersonal losses (including disruption of a romantic attachment, as well as other separations), and external stressors (most notably legal or disciplinary problems, which are often related to tendencies to engage in impulsive violence).[72] Being a victim of bullying or cyberbullying, or engaging in risky sexual behavior, especially at younger ages, also appears to increase suicidal risk.[73]

Family problems are significant. Suicidal young people tend to be exposed to family violence, disengaged families and deficient family support, physical abuse, parental suicidal behavior, instability in their living situations, and other acute and chronic stressors related to family life. The young person's response to such turmoil may give rise to a variety of affective and cognitive states, such as rage, hopelessness, despair, guilt, revenge, self-punishment, and retaliatory abandonment.[74] Substance abuse is a common

Suicide Note Written by a Single Woman, Age 21

My dearest Andrew,

It seems as if I have been spending all my life apologizing to you for things that happened whether they were my fault or not.

I am enclosing your pin because I want you to think of what you took from me every time you see it.

I don't want you to think I would kill myself over you because you're not worth any emotion at all. It is what you cost me that hurts and nothing can replace it.

theme, both in families and among young suicide-prone individuals. Active substance abuse, combined with depression and the availability of a handgun, is potentially lethal.

Upheavals in family life and in lifestyles generally add to the pressures experienced by young people. Suicide may be seen as a way to impose some control over confusing and upsetting events or to escape them. As Paulina Kernberg points out,

> An important meaning of suicide is that it can serve as an act of mastery, of ultimate control, of competency in individuals who are suffering loss of a sense of control over themselves and their lives. It is, as it were, the ultimate "locus of control."[75]

Substance abuse, delinquency, and suicide are linked on a continuum of "escape behaviors" in which young people engage to avoid feelings of depression and hopelessness. Risk-taking behavior may represent a way out for the individual who no longer cares whether he or she lives or dies. Flirting with death, as in "playing chicken," may be engaged in with little concern for the outcome. When substance abuse and risky behaviors no longer provide

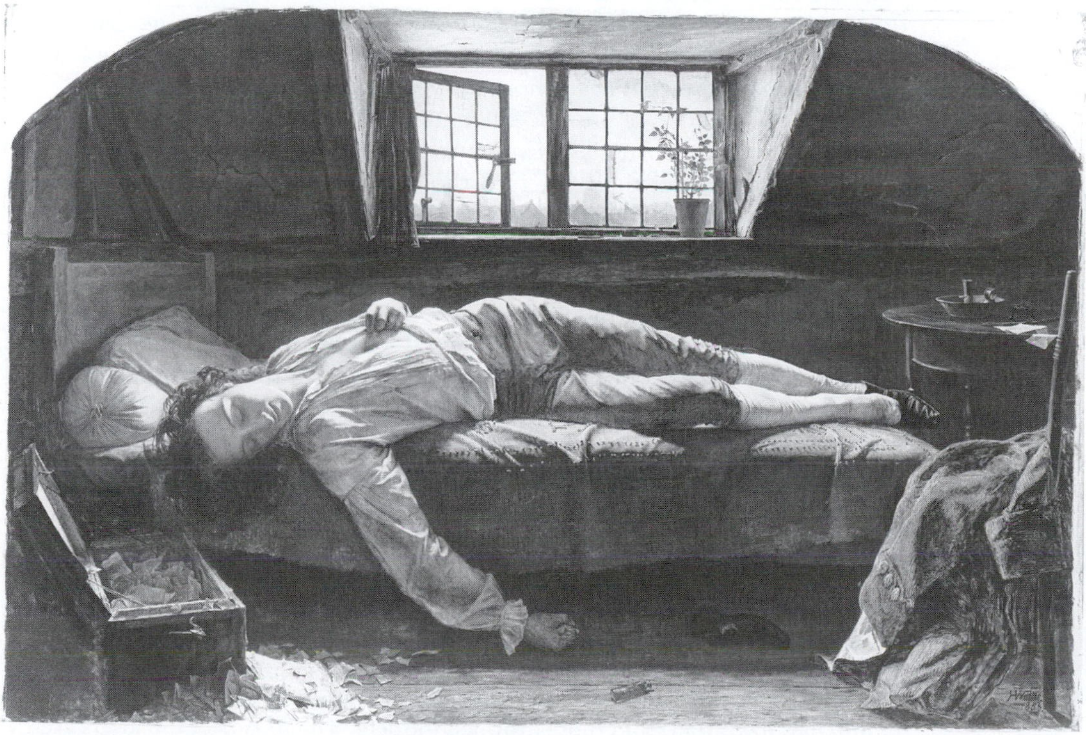

Henry Wallis, Tate Gallery, London

Unable to earn a living by writing and too proud to accept food offered to him by his landlady, this seventeen-year-old killed himself by taking poison. Painted in 1856 by Henry Wallis, The Death of Chatterton *depicts an adolescent suicide that was precipitated by crisis arising out of the developmental transition from child to adult.*

sufficient distraction from painful lives, young people may opt for suicide to provide the ultimate numbness.[76]

Adolescents and young adults may be susceptible to a kind of "contagion," whereby one person's suicide triggers another. So-called *cluster suicides* typically take place within the same locale, are closely related in time, and involve the same method.[77] (Mass suicide can be considered as a special form of clustering.) The term *copycat suicide* is also used to describe cluster suicides, especially when imitation occurs in connection with the depiction of a suicide in the media. In a study of two Texas clusters, researchers concluded that exposure to reports of suicides may affect individuals who are already at risk. Sensational or romanticized media coverage may foster an affinity with those who die by suicide and confer an aura of celebrity on them. In suicide-susceptible individuals, this could evoke the impression that suicide will claim special—albeit posthumous—attention from their family and peers.

Suicide pacts are a similar phenomenon in that they relate to an arrangement between two or more people who determine to kill themselves at the same time and usually in the same place.[78] Four teenagers in New Jersey, two boys and two girls, decided to die together by sitting in a car with the motor running inside a locked garage. Reportedly, they were distraught over the death of a friend. They were discovered dead the next morning. Two days later, another suicide pact took the lives of two teenage girls in Illinois who killed themselves in similar fashion.

Another instance of adolescents entering into a suicide pact involved a boy and girl who reportedly became obsessed with the possibility of reincarnation. They crashed their car into their old junior high school building, causing the boy to be killed instantly. The girl, who apparently had last-second doubts about reincarnation, barely survived by diving under the car's dashboard.

An unusual and one-sided version of the suicide pact occurs in the phenomenon of graveside suicides, in which a pathological grief reaction leads a bereaved person to kill himself or herself at the grave of a deceased loved one. Cemeteries are symbolic of the reunion of the living and the dead, and graveside suicides are analogous to a death pact between two persons in which the second person's death occurs as a reaction to the death of the first person, without the knowledge of the first person.[79]

> Romeo and Juliet also embody another popular misconception: that of the great suicidal passion. It seems that those who die for love usually do so by mistake and ill-luck. It is said that the London police can always distinguish, among the corpses fished out of the Thames, between those who have drowned themselves because of unhappy love affairs and those drowned for debt. The fingers of the lovers are almost invariably lacerated by their attempts to save themselves by clinging to the piers of the bridges. In contrast, the debtors apparently go down like slabs of concrete, apparently without struggle and without afterthought.
>
> A. Alvarez, *The Savage God*

In Japan, mental health authorities are concerned about the phenomenon of "net suicide," or suicide pacts arranged between strangers who meet on the Internet.[80] Although similarly arranged suicides have occurred to a limited degree elsewhere, in Japan the incidence of such suicides has averaged about sixty people (twenty cases of net suicide) a year. With mass media publicity, more people are accessing "suicide Web sites," which has led to the secondary effect of "chain suicide," whereby one suicide facilitates the occurrence of a subsequent suicide (discussed earlier in reference to copycat suicides).

Whereas the motives for suicide among adolescents often involve issues relating to family and peer relationships, for young adults the major issues tend to involve academic achievement, courtship, family formation, and career. A desire for perfection, whether socially or self-imposed, can lead to suicidal ideation when accomplishments fall short of ideals. One study found an exceptionally high rate of suicide among men ages twenty to thirty-four years who had been recently widowed.[81]

At present, the most promising approaches for reducing suicide among young people appear to be in two major areas: first, providing treatment for disorders that increase the risk of suicide, such as depression, substance abuse, and family conflict; and, second, targeting prevention efforts at high-risk groups, such as affectively disordered young men who exhibit substance abuse and other antisocial behavior. The treatment options include hospitalization for psychological evaluation, subsequent close outpatient follow-up, removal of firearms and securing of lethal medications from the home, and therapy for any associated psychiatric disorder.[82]

Middle Adulthood

Middle age, roughly between ages thirty-five or forty and sixty-five, has been called the "terra incognita" of the human life span. This is a period of generativity, of giving back to society some of the gifts of nurture and sustenance received during earlier periods of life. It is a time of shifting from valuing physical capabilities to valuing wisdom, of building new relationships as old ones are lost or altered, and of gaining greater flexibility in life. This part of the life span has also been characterized as "middlescence," suggesting that, for many adults, middle age may be as turbulent as adolescence.

This is also a time of coping with the loss of dreams and ambitions, coming to terms with the realization that one may not reach the goal of being a great artist, writer, or company president, or whatever vision one had for oneself earlier in life. It may not be possible to achieve a perfect marriage or raise perfect children.

The motive for suicidal behavior may be related to difficulties in an individual's career or marriage. In some cases, the nature of the career itself has an impact on suicidal behavior, as may be the case with the relatively high rate of suicide among police officers. The major factors influencing suicide among the middle-aged often include an accumulation of negative life events, affective disorders—especially major depression—and alcoholism.

Late Adulthood

Although teenage suicide attracts more media attention, elderly people are at higher risk for suicide than any other age group. This is especially true of elderly white males, particularly widowers. Major risk factors include being divorced or widowed, living alone, and psychiatric or physical illness.[83] Older people are not as likely as people in younger age groups to have expressed suicidal ideation or to have made a previous suicide attempt.[84] Researchers seem to agree that elderly people who attempt suicide genuinely want to die, unlike younger people, whose attempts are often a cry for help (see Figure 12-1).[85]

Double suicides (a type of suicide pact) occur with greatest frequency among the elderly. The typical double suicide involves an older couple with one or both partners physically ill. Heavy alcohol use by one or both partners is also common. Such couples tend to be dependent on each other and isolated from external sources of support. There seems to be a "special chemistry" between couples who die by suicide together, with the more suicidal partner dominant and the more ambivalent partner passive in the relationship.[86]

Contemplating Suicide

Imagine for a moment the progression of thoughts of someone considering suicide. Assume that, in some situation, suicide appears to be the only recourse or at least an option to be considered further. The next step might involve formulating some means of killing oneself. At this point, the means have not been acquired, but the possibilities are considered.

Many people have reached this stage—perhaps through mere fantasizing or perhaps with serious intentions. For some, the shock of recognizing that one is harboring such thoughts is enough to force a more life-affirming decision. For others, the next step toward suicide is taken, a step that greatly raises the level of lethality with regard to suicidal intention.

This stage involves acquiring the means to kill oneself, setting into motion the logistics that make suicide a real possibility. This stage is reflected in the remark, People die by suicide when they have both the desire to die and the ability to die. A change of mind away from suicide is still possible. Otherwise, the final step in the suicidal progression comes into play: actually using the means that have been acquired to proceed with the suicidal act.

These steps toward lethality have been described as occurring in a definite sequence, but they are likely to be experienced as anything but logical and orderly. Still, recognizing the steps that must be taken to carry out the suicidal act is helpful for understanding both the amount of sustained effort involved and the many decision points at which a change of mind or outside intervention is possible.

Sometimes a particular method is chosen because of the image it represents to the suicidal individual. One might imagine drowning as a dreamy kind of death, a merging back into the universe. Or one might associate an overdose of sleeping pills with the death of a movie star. Despite the image

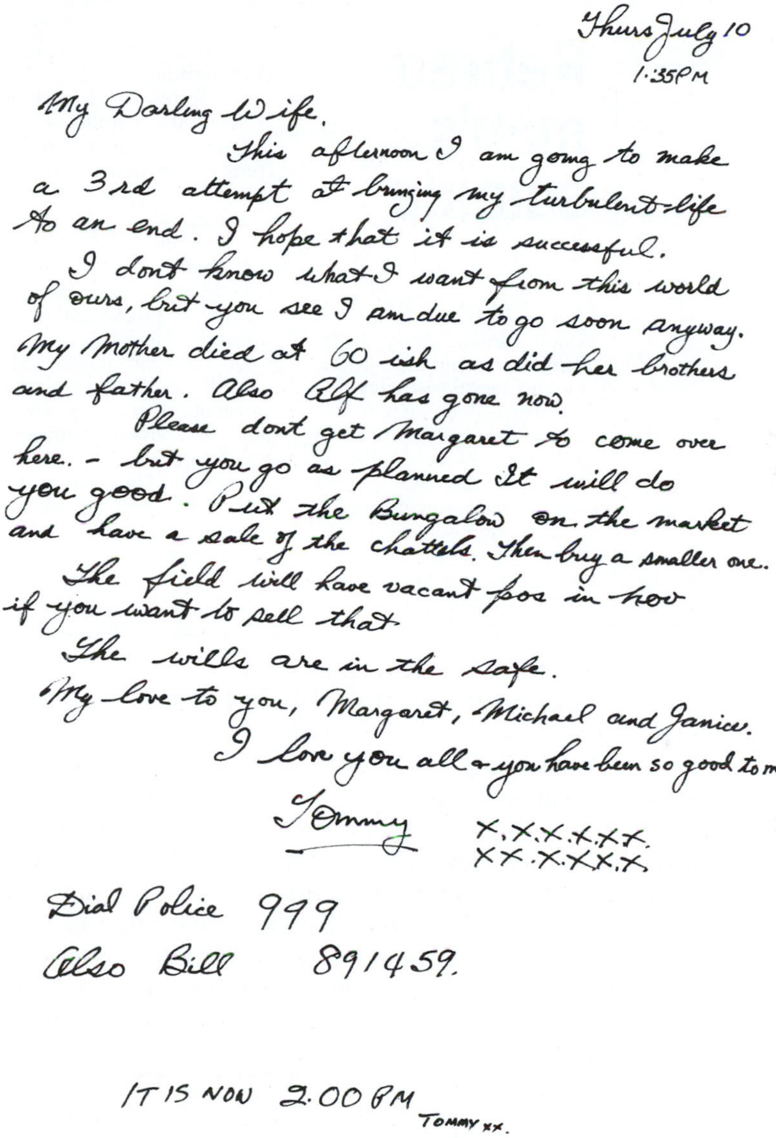

Thurs July 10
1:35PM

My Darling Wife,

This afternoon I am going to make a 3rd attempt at bringing my turbulent life to an end. I hope that it is successful.

I dont know what I want from this world of ours, but you see I am due to go soon anyway. My Mother died at 60 ish as did her brothers and father. Also Alf has gone now.

Please dont get Margaret to come over here. – but you go as planned It will do you good. Put the Bungalow on the market and have a sale of the chattels. Then buy a smaller one.

The field will have vacant pos in Nov if you want to sell that

The wills are in the safe.

My love to you, Margaret, Michael and Janice.

I love you all & you have been so good to me

Tommy X.X.X.X.X.X. XX.X.XX.X

Dial Police 999

Also Bill 891459.

IT IS NOW 2.00PM
TOMMY xx.

Figure 12-1 *Suicide Note and Report of Death*
The facts of suicide as reported in a newspaper may reveal little of the intense human factors—the personal and social dynamics—that precipitated the suicidal act. Compare this handwritten note with the corresponding report on the following page.

Retired man's suicide

A HYTHE man aged 64 killed himself because he could not stand old age, an inquest heard yesterday.

Retired maintenance engineer Aubrey Heathfield Aylmore, who lived at Forest Front, Hythe, was found dead in his car by his wife.

The inquest heard that Mrs. Heathfield Aylmore had been to a WI meeting and returned home an hour later than planned.

She found her husband's body in the garage with a length of hose pipe running from the exhaust into the car.

A note was found in which Mr. Heathfield Aylmore said that this was his third suicide attempt and that he wanted to "put an end to my turbulent life."

Dr. Richard Goodbody, consultant pathologist, said cause of death was asphyxia due to carbon monoxide poisoning.

Coroner Mr. Harry Roe said that Mr. Heathfield Aylmore had been depressed at the thought of growing old.

associated with a particular method, the reality is likely to be quite different. Some people who overdose on drugs do so expecting a quiet or peaceful death. But the actual effects of a suicidal drug overdose are usually far from peaceful or serene.

Sometimes a particular method of suicide is chosen for its anticipated impact on survivors. A study of suicide notes found that people using horrific methods of suicide often communicated that rejection was a critical factor in the decision for self-injury.[87] An individual who wants survivors to "really pay for all the grief they caused me" might select a method that graphically communicates this rage. Someone who did not want to "make a scene" might select a method imagined as being less disturbing to survivors.

Resume

Razors pain you;
Rivers are damp;
Acids stain you;
And drugs cause cramp.
Guns aren't lawful;
Nooses give;
Gas smells awful;
You might as well live.

Dorothy Parker

> Once you've pulled the trigger, it's done. You can't change your mind.
>
> Not like swimming out from the shore, or taking pills, or wrapping your head in a dry-cleaning bag, or sitting in the car with an exhaust hose threaded through the window, or using a knife or a razor—all those methods that allow for second thoughts: what am I doing? In the midst of killing yourself, you might begin to consider emergency rescue plans. Swimming back. Throwing up. Unwrapping the bag. Opening the car door and getting out. A tourniquet, a call to 911.
>
> Even jumping allows for vacillation (no rescue possible there, but all that awful time to regret it on the way down).
>
> With the gun lying on your tongue, the deed and the result are pretty much simultaneous.
>
> There's no separation between action and oblivion.
>
> Joan Wickersham, *The Suicide Index*

Experience and familiarity also influence the choice of suicidal method. An experienced hunter, knowledgeable about rifles, might be inclined to turn to a firearm for suicide because of its accessibility and familiarity. Someone who understands the effects of various drugs might use them to concoct a fatal overdose. In short, the method of suicide tends to reflect a person's experience and state of mind. It may be a spontaneous choice, in which the person uses whatever lethal devices are readily at hand, or it may be the outcome of deliberate thought and even research.

Choosing a method of killing oneself can be likened to making travel arrangements for a cross-country trip. A person wanting to travel from the West Coast to the East Coast must consider the kinds of transportation available—automobile, train, airplane, and so on. Some of these are quite rapid; others are relatively slow and deliberate. For example, once you board an airplane and it lifts off the runway, there is no opportunity to change your mind and disembark before reaching the destination. However, if you were bicycling from coast to coast, you would have innumerable opportunities to decide on a different destination.

Similarly, some methods of suicide offer little hope of changing one's mind after the lethal act is initiated. Once the trigger is pulled on a revolver placed next to one's skull, there's virtually no possibility of altering the likelihood of a fatal outcome. However, the would-be suicide who cuts his or her wrists or takes an overdose of drugs *might* have time to alter an otherwise fatal outcome by seeking medical help. If help is not forthcoming, the likelihood of dying may be as great as with a gunshot wound to the head—but there is a chance of intervention. Among methods used for the suicidal act, then, there is an order of lethality.

Suicide Notes

Suicide notes have been called "cryptic maps of ill-advised journeys."[88] Such notes are usually written in the minutes or hours preceding suicide. Although it is often assumed that nearly all suicides leave notes for their survivors, in fact only about one in six people who complete suicide write a final message.[89] As a partial record of the mental state of suicides, such notes are of immense interest to scholars and helping professionals, not to mention bereaved families. Imagine yourself in circumstances that would lead to writing a suicide note. What kinds of things would you want to say in your last words to your survivors?

Actual suicide notes display a variety of messages and intentions. Some notes explain to survivors the decision to die by suicide. Others express anger or blame. Conversely, some notes emphasize that the suicide is "no one's fault." The messages in suicide notes range from sweeping statements of the writer's philosophy or credo regarding suicide to detailed listings of practical chores that will require attention after the writer's death. For example, one note instructs survivors, "The cat needs to go to the vet next Tuesday; don't miss the appointment or you'll be charged for it. The car is due for servicing a week from Friday." Suicide notes represent the writer's "last chance to take care of business, decide who gets what, or to make funeral wishes known."[90]

Suicide notes may include expressions of love, hate, shame, disgrace, fear of insanity, self-abnegation; feelings of rejection; explanations for the suicidal act or defense of the right to take one's life; disavowal of a survivor's responsibility

Suicide Note Written by a Married Man, Age 45

Dear Claudia,

You win, I can't take it any longer. I know you have been waiting for this to happen. I hope it makes you very happy, this is not an easy thing to do, but I've got to the point where there is nothing to live for, a little bit of kindness from you would of made everything so different, but all that ever interested you was the *dollar.*

It is pretty hard for me to do anything when you are so greedy even with this house you couldn't even be fair with that, well it's all yours now and you won't have to see the Lawyer anymore.

I wish you would give my personal things to Danny, you couldn't get much from selling them anyway, you still have my insurance, it isn't much but it will be enough to take care of my debts and still have a few bucks left.

You always told me that I was the one that made Sharon take her life, in fact you said I killed her, but you know down deep in your heart it was you that made her do what she did, and now you have two deaths to your credit, it should make you feel very proud.

Good By Kid

P.S. Disregard all the mean things I've said in this letter, I have said a lot of things to you I didn't really mean and I hope you get well and wish you the best of everything.

Cathy—don't come in.

Call your mother, she will know what to do.

Love,
Daddy

Cathy don't go in the bedroom.

for the suicide; instructions for distributing property and possessions. They typically display dichotomies of logic, hostility toward others mixed with self-blame, the use of particular names and specific instructions to survivors, and a sense of decisiveness about suicide. Suicide notes often convey an intense love-hate ambivalence toward survivors, as expressed succinctly in the following note:

> Dear Betty:
> I hate you.
> Love,
> George

This example of ambivalence also points up the dyadic nature of suicide—here, involving husband and wife. Suicide notes provide clues about the intentions that lead a person to suicide but rarely tell the whole story—and they often raise more questions than they answer. The message in a suicide note may come as a surprise to survivors who had no hint of the feelings described by the writer. Suicide notes can have a significant effect on survivors. Whether the final message is one of affection or blame, survivors have no opportunity to respond. Death by suicide represents the ultimate last word.

Suicide Prevention, Intervention, and Postvention

Starting in 1953, Chad Varah, an Anglican clergyman, developed a telephone service in London staffed mainly with volunteers whose goal was to "befriend the suicidal and despairing." This service, called The Samaritans, has become an international movement, and Varah has been hailed as "suicidology's most powerful practitioner" and "the patron saint of the suicide prevention volunteer."[91]

In the United States, a comparable milestone was the founding of the Los Angeles Suicide Prevention Center in 1958 by Norman Farberow and Edwin Shneidman.[92]

> The importance of the Los Angeles Suicide Prevention Center cannot be overstated in any history of suicide. The work begun in that center by Shneidman and his associates, and expanded upon later when Shneidman became director of the Suicide Center in the National Institute of Mental Health, changed the nation's view of suicide and suicidal behavior. The most important change was a shift away from seeing suicide as an act committed by an insane person to seeing it as an act committed by a person who felt overwhelming ambivalence toward life.[93]

The activities of the Los Angeles Suicide Prevention Center exemplify the understanding of suicide as a subset of a larger class of self-destructive behaviors, all of which require attention.

The typical suicide prevention center operates as a telephone-answering center with round-the-clock availability to people in crisis. Hotline services are mainly intended to serve as a short-term resource for people contemplating suicide. The caller's anonymity is respected, and his or her expressed need for help is accepted unquestioningly. Staff members—some of them professionals, many of them volunteers who receive training—use crisis intervention strategies to reduce the caller's distress. Like other public health services, suicide crisis centers vary in their standards of professionalism; overall, however, they have a positive impact on countless people.

One hotline volunteer described the reaction of a caller when asked, "Who will find your body?" The answer, "My kids when they get home from elementary school," was enough to cause the caller to rethink the suicidal impulse and prompt a reaching out for resources.

Prevention

There is little reason to be optimistic about preventing suicide, if by "prevention" we mean eliminating it from human behavior. The causes of human unhappiness and dissatisfaction would have to be eliminated. But efforts to create a social utopia must inevitably fall short of perfection. This is not to say that efforts to relieve human suffering are not worth pursuing, only that they are inherently limited.

In any program of suicide prevention, an essential element is education. The lessons to be learned, which can be applied across the life span, include the following key points: First, it is crucial to acknowledge the truth that life is complex and that everyone will inevitably have experiences of disappointment, failure, and loss in life. Second, we can learn to deal with such experiences by developing appropriate coping techniques, including skills of critical thinking. Individuals "who form a habit of analyzing situations from a variety of perspectives, asking appropriate questions, and testing the reality of their own thinking are far less likely to settle easily into the cognitive inflexibility that focuses on suicide as *the* solution."[94] A corollary of such coping skills involves the cultivation of a sense of humor, especially the ability to laugh at oneself and at life's problems, to see the humor in situations. It is also important to learn to set appropriate and attainable goals. Positive self-esteem is a preventative against suicide. Studies have also shown that religiosity (that is, how religious a person is) potentially serves as a protective factor against suicidal behavior.[95] Yet, the influence of religion is often overlooked or minimized.

Another strategy for prevention involves setting up physical barriers in places where suicides are likely to occur. In Washington, D.C., the number-one jump site historically has been the Duke Ellington Bridge, a three-arch concrete structure with pedestrian lookouts. After three suicides from the bridge within a ten-day period, authorities ordered the construction of an eight-foot-high fence. However, the construction was opposed by neighborhood groups and by the National Trust for Historic Preservation because the fence would block scenic views and diminish the architectural aesthetics of the structure. Further, it was argued, such protective fences do not prevent suicides. The barrier was installed, however, and only one suicide occurred from the Ellington Bridge during the next four years. This is in comparison with ten suicides from the nearby Taft Bridge, which had no fence.[96] Although it appears the fence did prevent some suicides, there are too many variables and unknowns to reach a confident conclusion. It is possible that individuals who would have jumped from the Ellington Bridge simply found other ways to kill themselves. To a suicide-prone person, what is the meaning of a bridge barrier? Could it at least alleviate the sense of crisis that drove an individual to consider suicide? These questions are difficult to answer, but intervention during a suicidal crisis can reduce its lethality and give the would-be suicide an opportunity to reassess a painful situation and perhaps find a more constructive, healthier solution.

Intervention

Suicide intervention emphasizes short-term care and treatment of persons who are actively experiencing a suicidal crisis. The aim is to reduce the lethality of the crisis. Although many suicide intervention programs are called "suicide prevention centers," such programs generally use theories and techniques common to crisis intervention. Antoon Leenaars notes,

> Suicide intervention is optimally practiced in cooperation with a number of colleagues, representing various disciplines, and even individuals outside the helping professions. . . . The treatment of a suicidal person should reflect the learning and response of individuals with different points of view.[97]

Unfortunately, researchers have found that a surprisingly high percentage of the interventionists studied were apt to respond, "Come on now, things can't be all that bad." Or a client calls in and says, "I'm thinking about suicide," and the counselor responds, "You say you're suicidal, but what's really bothering you?" In both of these examples, there is an implicit negation of the suicide threat.[98]

When individuals express suicidal thoughts or exhibit suicidal ideation, several avenues of exploration can be helpful:[99]

1. *Imminence.* How soon does the person expect to suicide? Is it a future thought or a present plan?
2. *Provocation.* What has happened to make the suicide feasible now? Is the person experiencing a new crisis or problem?
3. *Plan.* Does the person have a plan? How well defined is that plan?
4. *Means.* Are the means to complete the plan available to the person? Are circumstances such that the person can carry it off?

The cardinal rule in suicide intervention is to *do something.* The basic questions are "Where do you hurt?" and "How can I help you?"[100] Thus, suicide intervention involves (1) taking threats seriously; (2) watching for clues to suicidal intentions and behaviors; (3) answering cries for help by offering support, understanding, and compassion; (4) confronting the problem by asking questions ("Are you considering killing yourself?") and being unafraid to discuss death by suicide with the person in crisis; (5) obtaining professional help to manage the crisis; and (6) offering constructive alternatives to suicide. A key theme of suicide intervention is that talking is a positive step toward resolving the crisis.

Graffiti

I find a snapshot
buried in my father's drawer.
A picture of the grandfather I never knew.
Small, stooped yet dignified he stands
beside my brother's wicker pram
surrounded by his family.
My mother tells the story, hidden in the past
of the last time she saw him.
She was big with child, and so allowed to sit
while his two daughters served the sons
who gathered at the table.
Grandma who reigned as always at the head
arranged the seating of those sons
not in the order of their age
but of the weekly wage they earned
and without question brought to her.

I learn that you, mild gentle man
never at home in the new language, the new land,
subdued by failure, each passing year withdrew
further into old world memories, and silence.
Rising that evening from the table, as usual
scarcely noticed as you went to lie down
on your narrow bed, there was no sign, no signal.
Only that as you passed, you bent
with a shy unaccustomed show of tenderness
to murmur "*Liebchen*" and to kiss my mother's head.
She tells me that I leaped and struggled in her womb
when from your room you shattered silence
with a shot. Your life exploding
sudden messages across blank walls in bursts of red.

Maude Meehan

Postvention

Suicide *postvention,* a term coined by Edwin Shneidman, refers to the assistance given to *all* survivors of suicide: those who attempt suicide, as well as the families, friends, and associates of those who die by suicide. The bereaved survivors of suicide often experience feelings of guilt and self-blame.[101] Those left behind face such questions as "Did she have a choice?" If yes, then the suicide did something unforgivable. If no, then the question becomes "How can we blame the victim?" Joan Wickersham, whose father died by suicide, says it's as if the victim leaves the message, "I'm gone, and you can't even be sure who it is that's gone, because you never knew me."[102] Survivors who witness someone die by suicide may face special challenges.[103] (Grief issues for people bereaved by suicide are discussed in Chapter 9.) Postvention efforts often play an important role in suicide prevention.

Helping a Person Who Is in Suicidal Crisis

Warnings that an individual is considering suicide may be communicated in a variety of ways. Evans and Farberow point out that suicidal intent may be expressed in four main ways: (1) *verbal direct* ("I will shoot myself if you leave me"), (2) *verbal indirect* ("A life without love is a life without meaning"), (3) *behavioral direct* (for example, a chronically ill person hoarding pills), and (4) *behavioral indirect.*[104] Among the warning signs that fall under this last category, Evans and Farberow mention these:

1. Giving away prized possessions, making a will, or attending to other "final" arrangements
2. Sudden and extreme changes in eating habits or sleep patterns
3. Withdrawal from friends or family, or other major behavioral changes accompanied by depression
4. Changes in school or job performance
5. Personality changes, such as nervousness, outbursts of anger, or apathy about health or appearance
6. Use of drugs or alcohol

The recent suicide of a friend or relative, or a history of previous suicide attempts, should also be taken as a warning sign of suicide risk.

A number of commonly held beliefs or myths have grown up about suicide and about the kind of person who is likely to die by suicide. Unfortunately, many of these beliefs—because false—are harmful, for they have the effect of depriving the suicidal person of needed help. For example, the notion that people who talk about suicide don't kill themselves has been called the "grand old myth of suicide," one that may be used to excuse the failure to respond to another person's cry for help, or even to justify words or actions that actually encourage a suicidal act. When a teen chatted about his intentions and then broadcast his suicide from a lethal mixture of drugs on a webcam, other bloggers urged and even taunted the young man to go ahead with the suicide.[105]

In fact, most people who engage in suicidal acts do communicate their intentions to others as hints, direct threats, preparations for suicide, or other self-destructive behaviors. When such cries for help go unheeded by friends, family members, coworkers, or health care personnel, the end result can be tragic.

If a person says, "I feel like killing myself," that statement should not be taken lightly or brushed aside with the quick response, "Oh, well, you'll probably feel better tomorrow." To the person in crisis, there may seem little hope of a tomorrow at all. Pay attention to the message being communicated.

Similarly, responding to a suicidal statement with a provocation—"You wouldn't be capable of suicide!"—or with a tone of moral superiority—"I don't want to hear such unhealthy talk!"—can worsen rather than ease the crisis. A litany of the "good reasons" why the person should not die by suicide also offers little practical assistance to a person in crisis.

Stanley Forman, *Boston Herald American*

Once a person is this close to the suicidal act, the chance of a successful intervention is usually slight. Fortunately, in this dramatic instance intervention was successful.

More helpful is listening carefully to exactly what the person is communicating; the tone and context of statements should reveal to the sensitive listener something about the communicator's intent. Often, remarks about suicide are made in an offhand manner: "If I don't get that job, I'll kill myself!" Perhaps the remark is intended as a figure of speech, much as in the joking threat, "I'll kill you for that!" There is a tendency to discount such statements in a culture where "talk is cheap" and "actions speak louder than words."[106] Suicidal threats need to be taken seriously. To do otherwise is to fall prey to the myth that talking about suicide means the person will not really go through with it. Knowing the patterns of suicidal behavior can help distinguish facts from fallacies. It is also helpful to become acquainted with the crisis intervention resources available in your community.

Lastly, it is important to recognize that no one can take *ultimate* responsibility for another human being's decision to end his or her life. This recognition may go against the wish to preserve life, yet there are limits to what can be done to assist another person in crisis. In the short term, it may be feasible to keep someone from taking his or her life. Constant vigilance or custodial care can prevent suicide during an acute suicidal crisis. Over the longer term, however, taking responsibility for preventing someone else's suicide is likely to be unsuccessful. A terminally ill man dying in great pain said to his wife, "You'd better keep my medication out of reach, because I don't want to keep up this struggle any longer." The wife had to decide whether she could take responsibility for whether he would continue to live with pain or end his life by an overdose. After much soul searching, she concluded that, although she had compassion for his predicament, she could not take responsibility for safeguarding his medication, doling out one pill at a time, constantly fearful that he might locate the drugs and attempt suicide anyway.

Not taking responsibility does not mean that one must go to the opposite extreme: "Well, if you're going to kill yourself, then get it over with!" Although there are limits to how much one person can *protect* another, it is always possible to offer life-affirming support and compassion. A person who seems intent on suicide may be hoping for some intervention. The person who is cast in the role of helper in such a drama can affirm the fact that there are choices other than suicide. It is important to sustain or stimulate that person's desire to live.

One way to help people in crisis is to help them discover what about themselves *can* matter, however small or insignificant it may seem. It is important to find something that matters *to the person.* What are the possibilities of sustaining that value into the present? Asking the person what he or she needs in order to feel worthwhile may be a matter of survival. In the short term, external support can help to ensure survival during the height of crisis.

Suicidal thoughts and behaviors indicate a critical loss of a person's belief that he or she is someone who matters. The feeling that nothing matters, in the sense that one's life is in complete disarray, is not by itself the stimulus for suicide. More important is the person's belief that "*I* don't matter." Those two streams of thought in combination—the sense that the external situation is unsatisfactory and that one does not matter enough to improve it—can be lethal. It is important to remember, "Suicide is a permanent solution to what is most likely a temporary problem."[107]

Further Readings

George Howe Colt. *November of the Soul: The Enigma of Suicide.* New York: Scribner, 2006.

Fred Cutter. *Art and the Wish to Die.* Chicago: Nelson-Hall, 1983.

Norman L. Farberow, ed. *Suicide in Different Cultures.* Baltimore: University Park Press, 1975.

Keith Hawton and Kees van Heeringen, eds. *The International Handbook of Suicide and Attempted Suicide.* New York: Wiley, 2000.

Thomas Joiner. *Why People Die by Suicide.* Cambridge, Mass.: Harvard University Press, 2005.

Updesh Kumar and Manas K. Mandal, eds. *Suicidal Behavior: Assessment of People-at-Risk.* Los Angeles: Sage, 2010.

Edwin S. Shneidman. *Comprehending Suicide: Landmarks in 20th-Century Suicidology.* Washington, D.C.: American Psychological Association, 2001.

Joan Wickersham. *The Suicide Index: Putting My Father's Death in Order.* New York: Harcourt, 2008.

Additional resources for this chapter can be found at www.mhhe.com/despelder10e

"Death's Intrusion," © Clint Brown, from the series "The Plague Drawings"

Calling attention to the perils posed by threatening encounters with death—accidents, disasters, violence, war, terrorism, and epidemic diseases—this drawing depicts victims embraced by Azrael, the angel of death.

CHAPTER 13

Risks, Perils, and Traumatic Death

In 1721, the novelist Daniel Defoe wrote *A Journal of the Plague Year,* a fictional account of the Great Plague that had devastated London in 1665. Victims exhibited symptoms similar to the pestilence caused by the Black Death, a deadly pandemic that swept Europe in the fourteenth century. Drawing on published accounts and his recollection of tales heard during childhood, he vividly depicted a plague-stricken city and the terror of its helpless citizens, confronted by a horror they could not comprehend. What prompted Defoe to write about a plague that had taken place two generations earlier? He knew that a plague again threatened to sweep across Europe, a plague that potentially could cause death and destruction on the scale of the Great Plague of 1665. He wrote to alert a largely indifferent populace to the threat so that precautions could be taken to avert catastrophe.

Why this history lesson? Today, we no longer fear the Black Death. Yet, as individuals and as societies we are subject to risks and perils that are no less threatening than the more easily identified plague of Defoe's time. The essayist E. B. White wrote, "To confront death, in any guise, is to identify with the victim and face what is unsettling and sobering."[1]

As we engage in life's pursuits—on our jobs, in our recreational activities, and in other pursuits—we encounter subtle and sometimes dramatic perils that expose us to the possibility of imminent injury or destruction. The word *peril,* which dates from the thirteenth century, refers to the risk of being injured, destroyed, or lost. Perils are evident in accidents,

The Fast Lane Takes Its Toll

I was ripped off the bike and slammed face first into the van, carving a very nice *Pirates of the Caribbean* scar from my hairline down my forehead, across my left eye, and down over the bridge of my nose—all deep into my skull. Very cool looking.

I remember once standing in line at Spago's, barking at Wolfgang's people because they sat other customers before me. There were 10 people waiting when I showed (unannounced), and I expected to be immediately moved to the front of the line, not *second* to the front. Those were my values. That's what I thought was important. That's what I thought was fun. And that's what I thought was power.

Now I spend 15 minutes 50 times every day trying to bend one finger two degrees as part of my physical therapy. As you can imagine, I am no longer quite as concerned with my position in line at Spago's.

Stephen St. Croix, *Life in the Fast Lane*

disasters, violence, war, terrorism, emerging epidemic diseases, and other instances of traumatic death. Anthony Giddens says, "We live in a world where hazards created by ourselves are as, or more, threatening than those that come from outside."[2] Some of these encounters with death are termed "megadeaths" because of the massive loss of life that typically occurs.[3] No one is immune to risks.

After a classroom discussion about various activities, one student said, "It seems we're coming around to the point that everything we do involves risks. You could even stab yourself with a knitting needle!" Perhaps, but falling backward from a rocking chair while knitting would strike most people as less risky than, say, driving a formula race car or heading out on an expedition to the Himalayas.

Accidents and Injuries

In contrast to intentional injuries, which are inflicted purposefully by oneself or another person, an injury that occurs when no harm is intended is considered an *unintentional* injury.[4] Is this category of injury due to accidents that happen because of "fate" or simple "bad luck"? The definition of an accident as an event that occurs "by chance or from unknown causes" can be expanded with the recognition that accidents also occur because of carelessness, lack of awareness, or ignorance. Suppose a gun is brought into a household. The very presence of the gun increases from zero the chance that there may be an accidental firing of the weapon. Of course, such an event may never happen. But if a gun were *not* in the home, there would be *no* chance of an accidental firing.

Paul Insel and Walton Roth tell us that "most injuries are caused by a combination of human and environmental factors," adding that "a common human factor that leads to injuries is risk-taking behavior."[5] We discuss violence and intentional injuries later in this chapter. Here we focus on unintentional injuries: motor vehicle injuries, home injuries (falls, fires, suffocation and choking, firearms), leisure injuries (sport, recreation), weather-related injuries (heat, cold, wind, lightning, flooding), and work injuries, to list the main categories.

The choices people make affect the probabilities of accidents. Drivers who have been drinking tend to take greater risks than do sober drivers. A driver's judgment and performance are inversely related to the amount of alcohol consumed, whereas a driver's tendency to overrate his or her driving abilities is directly related to the amount imbibed. About half of the drivers involved in accidents are under the influence of alcohol. One-third of all traffic *fatalities* involve drivers with a blood alcohol content (BAC) of 0.8 percent (the legal limit in all states) or higher.[6]

Young drivers tend to be disproportionately at fault for the crashes in which they are involved.[7] Lack of experience compounded by unsafe use of cell phones, iPods, CD players, and the like can be deadly. To increase teen driver safety, some states have instituted "graduated driver license" laws that help teens gain experience incrementally. In California, for example, the law requires drivers under age eighteen to have their license for a year before being allowed to drive between 11 p.m. and 5 a.m. or before being allowed to transport passengers under the age of twenty without an adult in the car.

Unsafe conditions in the environment are sometimes called "accidents waiting to happen." Such conditions may be due to negligence or simply ignorance of the threat. Consider the situation of a swimming pool left unattended and easily accessible to young children; if a toddler happens by, falls into the pool, and drowns, the owner of the pool and the child's guardians may be judged negligent.

A *wrongful death* occurs when a person is killed due to the negligence or misconduct of another individual, company, or entity. A lawsuit for wrongful death may be brought by the decedent's immediate family members, usually surviving spouses and children, sometimes parents. Wrongful death claims arise out of a number of circumstances, such as automobile or airplane accidents or exposure to hazardous conditions. *Wrongful* implies that a death could have been avoided by different actions or choices on the part of the person(s) involved. Thus, in cases of wrongful death, there is someone to blame or hold accountable.[8]

Unsafe conditions are often related to the attitudes and value systems of the person or group responsible or of society as a whole. It is naive to believe that the risks we encounter in our lives can be totally eliminated; nonetheless, usually they can be minimized. Lack of resolve to take necessary actions in correcting unsafe conditions prompts the question, How negligent must a society be before "accidental" deaths are tantamount to homicide?[9]

Risk Taking

The degree of risk we assume is subject to our own choices about how to live our lives. In this sense, "*Risk* refers to hazards that are actively assessed in relation to future possibilities."[10] Our willingness to take risks is influenced

To keep from tumbling through space at 125 miles per hour, this mile-high skydiver spreads arms and legs to control freefall before opening the parachute. Although risks are ever present in our lives, we expose ourselves to many of them by personal choice.

UPI/Corbis-Bettmann Newsphotos

by the images communicated in the media and popular culture. Devotees of a strain of hip-hop music called *hyphy* engage in stunts in which a driver gets out of his car and dances around to a hip-hop beat on top of the slowly moving vehicle.[11] Called "ghost-riding the whip," this stunt has led to numerous minor injuries and has killed at least two people.

In some cases, we can exercise considerable choice about the nature and degree of risk to which we are exposed. Think about your own life. What risks do you face in connection with your job, leisure activities, and overall lifestyle? Are any of these risks potentially life threatening? Do you take "calculated" risks? Are some risks avoidable?

Some occupations involve dangers that most people, if given a choice, would avoid. Such jobs include high-rise window washer, movie stuntperson, test pilot, and explosives expert, as well as police officer and firefighter. We could add scientists who handle hazardous materials, mine workers, electricians, heavy-equipment operators, and farmworkers who use toxic pesticides. As you add your own examples to this list, notice whether they involve the risk of sudden death (as from an explosion or a fall from a high-rise building) or long-term exposure to hazardous materials or conditions. Sometimes, risks that could harm or kill are identified only after years of exposure to a hazardous condition. Other times, people accept risks as something that "comes with the territory," like the hazards encountered in such professional sports as football.

In Japan, job-related stress is legally recognized as a cause of death.[12] Mostly affecting men in their prime working years, victims of *karoshi*—sudden death from overwork—are found in virtually every occupational category. Karoshi is characterized as a buildup of fatigue caused by "long hours of work that clearly exceed all normal physiological limitations," disruptions in an individual's normal daily rhythms (often related to travel or lengthy commutes), and other job-related strains placed on workers. The rise of global markets (with corresponding time differences) has forced workers to conduct business far into the night after the normal day's work has been completed. Karoshi is accompanied by a growing recognition that exhaustion induced by chronic overwork can harm or kill even the healthiest person.

The possibility of death is also found in recreational activities: mountain climbing, parachuting, scuba diving, motorcycle racing, and the like. Such activities are sometimes characterized as thrill seeking, although this phrase suggests motives that participants in these activities might not ascribe to themselves. However, one climber said, "Without the possibility of death, adventure is not possible."[13]

Although mountain climbing involves obvious risks, two climbers can relate to these risks differently. One climber displays an attitude of abandon that could only be called foolhardy or death defying. The other devotes many hours to obtaining instruction, preparing equipment, conditioning for the climb, and asking advice from experienced climbers before deciding to set foot on a mountain. In short, risk can be minimized. An activity may be attractive to some individuals *because* of its inherent risk; other people accept risk as inseparable from other attractive features of the activity. When behavior involves doing dangerous things just for the thrill of it, or as a way to

> I stared in a horrified trance as a figure appeared, frozen in the air for the briefest moment, its arms outstretched above its head as if in utterly hopeless supplication. Then it continued its relaxed, cart-wheeling descent, with only the thundering crashes attesting to its frightening impacts on the rock. It disappeared into a gully.
>
> "Don't look!" I screamed to my wife, who was, of course, as helplessly transfixed as I was. And the sounds continued. After a time, the figure came into view at the base of the gully and continued down the pile of rubble below. My last view of it is frozen in time. The figure's arm was curled easily over its head, and its posture was one of relaxation, of napping. It drifted down that last boulder field like an autumn leaf down a rippling brook. Then it disappeared under the trees, and only the pebbles continued to clatter down the rock. Suddenly it was very, very still.
>
> I looked down to Debby and had to articulate the obvious: "That was a man," I said quietly, numbly.
>
> William G. Higgins, "Groundfall"

"laugh in the face of death," it may represent an attempt to deny fear or anxiety about death.[14] Baruch Fischhoff and John Kadvany observe,

> Popular wisdom holds that teens have a unique sense of invulnerability. That belief can seemingly explain many dubious teen risk decisions. "They think that nothing can happen to them." Evidence suggests more complex explanations.
>
> Contrary to the myth of perceived invulnerability, many teens exaggerate their chances of dying young, so much so that they might take risks because they do not expect to live, rather than because they do not expect to die.[15]

When death results from a high-risk sport or similar activity, it can have a strong impact on others who engage in the same activity. In addition to its effect on those most immediately involved (for example, people who rented equipment or provided instruction to the deceased), the death may affect the larger community of participants in the sport. Such a death challenges the assumption that cautious practice of the sport ensures safety.[16] Rumors may circulate that the deceased failed to take necessary precautions or followed an unwise course of action. Such rumors may serve to mitigate feelings of guilt about having been unable to prevent the death. "Blaming the victim" can be a means of coping that allows individuals to feel comfortable continuing the activity despite the risks.

Disasters

At a magnitude of 9.0, the Great East Japan Earthquake of March 11, 2011, triggered a massive tsunami and dealt unprecedented damage to a wide area spanning from the regions of Tōhoku to Kanto. It is considered the most powerful earthquake ever to hit Japan. Although Japan had hazard maps indicating areas that would be flooded in a tsunami, the resulting tsunami caused by the Tōhoku earthquake "inundated a far wider range of areas than those anticipated in the maps."[17] The tsunami waves reached heights of more than 130 feet and traveled six miles inland. Entire towns were devastated. The death toll was about 16,000 people, with more than 6,000 injured, and nearly 2,700 missing.[18]

Particularly important was damage caused by the tsunami to Japan's nuclear reactors, especially the meltdowns, explosions, and radioactive leakage at the Fukushima Daiichi Complex; associated evacuation zones affected over 200,000 residents, many of whom were still "nuclear refugees" months later.[19] Tests showed that winds carried radioactive particles much farther than initially thought, leading to the realization that there was an "enormous spread of radiation."[20] Experts said it was the second-worst nuclear accident in history (following Chernobyl in the Ukraine).

Devastating, too, was the 2008 earthquake in Sichuan, China, at the edge of the Qinghai-Tibet Plateau:

> Nothing prepares you for the desolation of a city recovering from an earthquake. It's not the physical destruction that is so difficult to confront, although that is bad enough. Rather, it's the people. Traumatized people.

© JIJI PRESS/AFP/Getty Images

Caused by the 2011 Tōhoku earthquake, a tsunami with waves, in some places, reaching more than 120 feet above sea level overflows a floodwall, tossing cars, as it surges into the city of Miyako in northern Japan. Only a small number of boats survived from the town's 960-ship fishing fleet. The city was devastated.

> The roof of the world suddenly collapsed and shifted east, crushing all those people in isolated farmhouses, in whole villages such as Fei Shui, provincial towns such as An, and large cities such as Mianyang.
>
> In Beichuan, the epicenter of the earthquake, most of the buildings were still standing after the initial shock. People were standing around thanking their lucky stars when a mountain collapsed into the valley and buried everyone. Just like that. Ten thousand residents dead and buried in seconds. The community of Beichuan has been wiped off the face of the earth.[21]

The magnitude 8.0 Great Sichuan Earthquake affected 46 million people. It killed more than 69,000 people. Over 18,000 were listed as missing. Nearly 375,000 were injured. It was the deadliest earthquake in China since the 1976 Tangshan earthquake, which reportedly killed at least 240,000 people. Persistent heavy rains and landslides affected rescue efforts. Strong aftershocks continued for months after the main quake. Due to China's "one-child" policy, many parents lost their only child when thousands of schools collapsed in the quake. The scale of the disaster prompted the Chinese government to dispose of dead bodies with little ceremony, closing the door on any opportunity family members had of identifying their kin by sight and celebrating traditional Chinese death rituals.

Although the term is sometimes applied loosely to any event with negative consequences, a *disaster* is generally defined as a life-threatening event that affects many people, usually within a brief period of time, bringing sudden or great misfortune. Earthquakes and hurricanes are commonly associated with major disasters, but floods and fires can also be among the causes. Consider the following account of the 2009 bushfires in Australia:

> They were the most dangerous weather conditions, and they colluded to propel 190 separate fires on winds up to 95 kilometers per hours to raze 2,000 houses, schools, shops, community centers, even entire towns. We could have sat shocked and numbed as the horror toll of Australia's worst natural disaster climbed to an incomprehensible tally of more than 200 dead and an incalculable loss of pets, stock, and wildlife.
>
> In the wake of this, the instantaneous response of people of compassion across the world was to ask themselves: What can I do? How can I help people who have lost everything?[22]

A similar compassionate response to disasters, both among victims themselves and by those outside the affected area, leads to a narrative of help that is sometimes ignored in media reports. For example, in the wake of Hurricane Katrina, in contrast to media accounts of criminal activity and other negative portrayals of New Orleanians, especially those most vulnerable, "insider accounts" revealed that survivors showed a depth of compassion and introspection rarely seen or heard in news stories. Disaster survivors' stories are among their most important remaining possessions (see Figure 13-1). Many emerge from the ruins with little more than memories and their accounts of heroism and endurance.[23]

Disasters result from natural phenomena—such as those just described—as well as from human activities. This latter category includes chemical spills, building collapses, nuclear contamination, fires, and airplane crashes. It includes devastating industrial accidents, as with the fire at the Triangle Shirtwaist Company, a garment factory, that killed 146 young women in New York City in 1911, which still rates as the worst industrial factory fire in the United States. The worst factory fire ever occurred in 1993, when a toy factory in Thailand killed 188 workers and severely injured 469 more. The actual death toll may have been higher because the four-story building collapsed and many bodies were incinerated, some never to be found. In both of these disasters, it was reported that failures on the part of factory owners, elected officials, and bureaucracies responsible for enforcing public safety and health standards had resulted in unsafe working conditions that led to disaster.[24]

On April 24, 2013, an eight-story building in the capital city of Bangladesh collapsed. When the search for the dead concluded, the toll was more than 1100, mainly garment workers who had been ordered to return to work despite warnings about cracks that had been discovered in the building the previous day. Moreover, the upper four floors had been constructed without a permit, and architects warned that the structure was not strong enough to support the weight and vibration of heavy machinery. All these warnings were ignored by the building's owner.

© Haruna Sato

Figure 13-1 *Japanese Child's Tsunami Drawing*
A first-grade child's portrayal of the tsunami caused by the Tōhoku earthquake shows a torrent of water as 33-foot waves triggered by the earthquake sweeps into her city of Kesennuma, a port on the coast near the quake's epicenter. She draws the swirling wall of water carrying people, cars, and fish as it begins to engulf houses in the town of more than 73,000 people. The sun, drawn in red with large black eyes and an open mouth, looks down upon the devastation. Haruna and her older sister, Natsumi, expressed the hope that, through their drawings, "as many people as possible in the world can learn what happened to them."

What is your reaction to reading about these recent events in Australia, Bangladesh, China, and Japan? What can we learn about disasters and our responses to them?

Risk theorists point out that modern technological systems are complex and fail in ways that cannot always be anticipated, with minor events unexpectedly interacting to produce a major problem, a phenomenon that Charles Perrow calls a "normal accident."[25] As one writer concludes, "We have constructed a world in which the potential for high-tech catastrophe is embedded in the fabric of day-to-day life."[26] Experts say that disasters are becoming more frequent worldwide, now happening at a rate of about 1000 a year. Climate change may be a factor. They are also "becoming more catastrophic, as population growth makes increasing numbers of people vulnerable to the impact of disasters."[27]

Reducing the Impact of Disasters

Communities can decrease the risk of injury and death by taking precautionary measures to lessen the impact of a potential disaster. Adequate warnings of an impending disaster may be withheld due to greed, political expediency, uncertainty about the nature and extent of the threat, or concerns about causing panic. The tragedy that followed the eruption in 1902 of the Mount Pelée volcano, on the island of Martinique in the West Indies, shows how information that could warn potential disaster victims may be mismanaged, with disastrous consequences. The officials of the nearby community of Saint-Pierre were alerted to the likelihood that the volcano would erupt. But, concerned that the population would panic if notified and thus thwart their plans for an upcoming local election, officials withheld warning of the danger from the populace. As a result, almost the entire population of the small community was incinerated. The May 1980 eruption of Mount St. Helens, in Washington state, provides comparison. Even though this eruption was larger, only sixty lives were lost, compared with the 30,000 casualties resulting from the eruption of Mount Pelée. In part, this difference was due to adequate warnings of the hazard and timely establishment of a restricted zone of access.[28]

Individuals who live in areas where disasters are a common occurrence—for instance, earthquake or hurricane—may rationalize the danger as "playing the percentages." Similarly, predictions of potential disasters are often met with the response, "I've never been affected before. Why should I worry now?" This is the apparent attitude of people who, hearing about an incoming tsunami, head for the ocean. It seems that people deliberately underestimate the risks to themselves.[29]

Warnings are not always timely or adequate, as with the 2004 Indian Ocean tsunami triggered by a magnitude 9.0 earthquake off the Indonesian island of Sumatra. Traveling at a speed of 500 miles an hour, the tsunami brought huge waves to coastal areas across the Indian Ocean, killing over 230,000 people in more than a dozen countries. Especially hard hit were Indonesia, Sri Lanka, India, and Thailand. Relief workers had to get food, water, and medical supplies into remote areas where roads had been destroyed, as well as identify dead and missing, a job made difficult by the large number of tourists vacationing in the region. As plans were put into practice for a better warning system, experts concluded that equally needed were more effective systems of evacuation and disaster relief.

Similar conclusions accompanied events when Hurricane Katrina came ashore in southern Louisiana in August 2005. It killed more than 1500, left hundreds of thousands homeless, laid waste to 90,000 square miles of land, and ravaged one of America's most storied cities.[30] The storm surge obliterated coastal communities. The suffering of survivors continued for days and weeks after the storm passed. A Senate investigation reported a "failure of government at all levels to plan, prepare for, and respond aggressively to the storm."[31]

> On the day before a hurricane hits, the phone rings. A man's voice speaks; he sounds like a computer, like he has an iron throat. I cannot remember exactly what he says, but I remember it in general. *Mandatory evacuation. Hurricane making landfall tomorrow. If you choose to stay in your home and have not evacuated by this time, we are not responsible. You have been warned.* And *these could be the consequences of your actions.* There is a list. And I do not know if he says this, but this is what it feels like: *You can die.*
>
> This is when the hurricane becomes real.
>
> Jesmyn Ward, *Salvage the Bones*

Coping with the Aftermath of Disaster

What can be done when disaster strikes? What kind of help is needed in its aftermath? Imagine the situation: People are injured, some are missing, others are dead. In the wake of a disaster, the survivors may experience an "existential crisis" marked by a profound sense of emptiness and despair.[32] They are likely to be in a state of shock, uncertain of the whereabouts of loved ones and about the future. Community grief can be a complex process that takes months or years to fully resolve.[33] One writer says, "Where counseling is provided, the focus should be on providing information and support, helping the community towards its own recovery."[34]

Among the first steps to be taken in responding to a disaster are a set of core actions collectively defined as *psychological first aid.* Following the onset of disaster, the actions of local, regional, or national authorities lie in three areas: (1) the rescue and treatment of survivors; (2) the repair and maintenance of basic services; and (3) the recovery and management of bodies.[35] Meeting the immediate needs of survivors—providing food and shelter, caring for medical needs, and restoring vital community services—is essential. Even as attention is focused on physical needs, however, the emotional needs of survivors must be addressed.[36] Ministering to these needs might include forming a missing persons group to help alleviate the anxieties of survivors worried about the safety of relatives.

Locating and caring for the dead is an important aspect of helping survivors cope with the trauma of disaster. The humanitarian care and treatment of the dead have an important effect on the recovery of a community after any disaster.[37] The comment of one relief agency worker, "It doesn't really make too much sense to dig up the dead and then go and bury them again," reveals an unfortunate ignorance of the human emotions that surround disposition of the dead. Although most efforts directed toward coping with disaster are focused on the emergency or crisis period, regaining emotional stability can take years. The disaster response team that comes to assist survivors recovering from disaster is usually present for only a brief time; it rapidly dissolves with the end of the emergency period.

© Thomas Dworzak, Magnum Photos

With federal support lacking, local and state death systems in Louisiana were overwhelmed. Bodies of the dead lay in the streets of New Orleans for days following Hurricane Katrina's devastation, a scene that most of the U.S. population thought could never occur in their country.

Responding to disasters usually requires priority setting, rationing, and triage, all of which can involve coercive measures that override individual liberty and property rights.[38] When disasters involve traumatic death, the minimal goals that must be kept in mind for strategies of intervention include the following:[39]

1. Normalizing the situation
2. Minimizing recovery time
3. Reducing distress
4. Restoring function
5. Mobilizing resources

Also to be considered are the helpers who come to the aid of the survivors of a disaster. They may also become "survivors" because of their intense encounter with human suffering and tragedy. Consider the experience of a Kansas City doctor who arrived at the scene of a hotel disaster to find, among the debris left when a balcony collapsed onto the lobby below, bodies chopped in half, decapitated, and maimed. He watched as a critically injured man's leg, trapped under a fallen beam, was amputated with a chain saw. When things returned more or less to normal, he said that he felt the need to spend some time away from reminders of the disaster to cope with his own experience as a survivor.

> The recent discovery that humans have only twice as many genes as fruitflies has tipped the balance in the nature-nurture debate back to nurture. On this evidence it is our culture, history and belief-systems which make us what we are. We look at the rest of nature and see carnivores killing to eat, but we do not see zebras forming armies to wage war on gnus. It is only humans, with their congenital vice of inventing differences of politics and faith, who murder one another because they disagree, and what makes the tragedy more poignant is that the less secure their grounds for belief, the more anxious and violent their adherence to it—and the greater their readiness to kill and die in its defence.
>
> A. C. Grayling, *Life, Sex, and Ideas*

When a storm dumped twenty inches of rain in one night on a coastal community in California, residents awoke the next morning to the news that twenty-two people had been killed, more than a hundred families had lost their homes, and another 3000 homes had been severely damaged. Within a few days, an impromptu organization was set up to help survivors deal with the psychological trauma of their losses. Known as Project COPE (Counseling Ordinary People in Emergencies), it provided counseling to disaster victims and coordinated the services of more than a hundred mental health professionals.[40] Counselors found that the grief reactions of people who had lost loved ones or property were heightened by the sudden, capricious nature of their losses. Some who had lost only material possessions felt guilty for mourning the loss of property when others had had family members die. Some felt guilty for surviving the disaster. Those made homeless by the storm felt isolated and alone. Bureaucratic delay and uncooperative insurance companies and government agencies caused people to feel angry and frustrated. Many victims felt anxious, vulnerable, and depressed. For some, old problems related to personal or relationship issues reemerged in the aftermath of the disaster.

COPE set up programs to respond to each of these problems. Survivors were reassured that their reactions were normal and their grief legitimate. Counselors helped them sort out their priorities so they could begin to solve problems created by the disaster. Emergency crews and relief workers were included in these helping efforts. Although we cannot eliminate the encounter with death that accompanies disaster, steps can be taken to reduce its impact, preserve life, and demonstrate compassion for survivors.

Violence

Violence is one of the most potent of our encounters with death. It can affect our thoughts and actions even when we have not been victimized ourselves. Potentially, anyone may become its victim. In the most recent year for which statistics are available, nearly 14,000 murders occurred in the United States.[41] In two-thirds of these, firearms were used as the murder weapon. While almost 15 percent of these murders were related to the commission of a felony, about 85 percent were related to gang killings, alcohol-influenced brawls, "romantic triangles," arguments over money or property, and other, unspecified causes.

Emergency room physicians report being besieged by patients whose injuries are identical to wounds incurred by soldiers in combat. These wounds result from semi-automatic assault weapons that fire dozens of bullets per minute at several times the velocity of an ordinary pistol: "Organs that would have been merely grazed or even cleanly pierced by a handgun bullet are exploded by assault weapon fire, requiring massive transfusions of blood."[42]

Young people are disproportionately represented among victims of violence.[43] One of the most troubling aspects of handgun violence "is the fact that children very often are the victims of fatal gunshot wounds, self-inflicted either intentionally or accidentally, or received as innocent bystanders in scenes of domestic or street violence."[44] Rap musician Ice-T has drawn attention to the condition of his hometown, South Central Los Angeles. Gang warfare, he says, is comparable to other wars: Members of gangs are like "veterans from war," and "thousands of people have died on each side of this bloody battlefield."[45]

In Detroit, a mother whose sixteen-year-old son had been shot while walking to a neighborhood store with friends told a reporter that similar shootings occurred every night. "They shoot like it's their job or something," she said. "All I want to do is move to someplace safe," she added. "Someplace where there's no shooting on your block or the next block over. That's all. That's good enough. Just two safe blocks."[46]

Violence resulting from gang warfare has even intruded upon the serene setting of the cemetery. In Anaheim, California, two men died of multiple gunshot wounds they received while visiting the graves of two fellow gang members who had been murdered the previous year.[47]

For some, guns are more than just weapons; they are potent symbols of power and energy. One young man said,

> When you are carrying a gun, I think other people can tell. Some kind of way a gun makes you light up. If you don't have a gun on you, a dude might mug you down. People don't mug you if you've got your gun on. They can detect something about you that wasn't there before.[48]

Children who witness violence have been called "silent victims." They may be physically unharmed but are nevertheless emotionally affected as they hear gunshots outside their homes, witness shootings on the playground, or have a family member (often an older sibling) involved with violence.[49] In describing a community-based approach to violence prevention in Richmond, California, Larry Cohen and Susan Swift remark,

> Interpersonal violence, although most concentrated among youth in densely populated, low-income communities, affects everyone in the United States. An awareness of violence permeates the environment, determining where people prefer to live, where they shop, how they respond to strangers on the streets, where they walk and drive, and how late at night they stay outside of their homes. Unlike any other environmental threat, violence has turned into a public health epidemic.[50]

Random Violence

The most threatening of violent acts are those that occur without apparent cause. Victims are selected seemingly at random, thus heightening anxiety that violence could unexpectedly confront anyone. In July 2012, a mass shooting inside a movie theater in Aurora, Colorado, killed twelve people and injured seventy others. In December of the same year, a gunman fatally shot twenty children and six adult staff members in a mass murder at Sandy Hook Elementary School in Newtown, Connecticut. People expressed feelings of being personally threatened because these violent acts had taken place "so close to home."

One woman described a potential encounter with death that began innocently enough when she answered a knock on her door. Recognizing a former schoolmate whom she hadn't seen in a long time, she invited him in, and they began to chat. She began to feel uneasy, although she couldn't say why. About two months later, she heard on the news that her visitor had been arrested (he was subsequently convicted) for the brutal murders of several young women. The murders had occurred around the time of his unexpected visit. Recalling the experience, this woman commented, "I sometimes wonder how close we are to death at times and just not realize it. It seems we really never know."

Serial Killers and Mass Murderers

Serial killers, the category of murderer encountered by the woman just described, take the lives of several victims over a span of time. *Mass murderers,* in contrast, kill many victims at once, in one place, such as a school or place of employment. Reviewing the motivations of serial killers, Dana DeHart and John Mahoney conclude that "one of the more disturbing aspects of serial murder is that virtually everyone is at some risk. Even cautious and circumspect persons are not safe from a serial killer; the victims need not provoke or even be acquainted with the killer."[51]

In 2007, in two separate attacks about two hours apart, a twenty-three-year-old senior at Virginia Tech in Blacksburg killed twenty-seven students and five teachers and wounded many others before killing himself. The massacre was reportedly the deadliest shooting incident by a single gunman in U.S. history. The shooter, Seung-Huo Cho, mentioned "martyrs like Eric and Dylan," apparently referring to the perpetrators of shootings at Columbine High School. Cho had previously received therapy for a severe anxiety disorder, although the university had not been informed of this diagnosis because of federal privacy laws. This event, like those that preceded it and those that followed it, sparked debate about U.S. laws and culture, particularly gun violence, firearms laws, privacy issues, and the mental health system.

Mass murders and serial killings are not limited to the United States, however. In 2002, a gunman shot sixteen people before killing himself at a school in eastern Germany. And, in 2009, a seventeen-year-old former student at a technical school near Stuttgart, Germany, killed nine students and three teachers before continuing his murderous spree, killing several passers-by before being killed by police in a shoot-out. Nor is mass murder

(c) Kevin Higley, AP Photo

Distraught students grieve the violent deaths of friends in the aftermath of a shooting rampage carried out by schoolmates on their campus.

an affliction only of our current times. In 1927, in Michigan, a school board official killed his wife, then blew up the town's school, killing a total of forty-four people, including thirty-nine students and teachers.

Familicide

Familicide is the murder of family members by another family member.[52] In other words, familicide is a multiple-victim homicide in which the killer's spouse or partner and one or more children are killed. Although familicide is relatively rare, it is nevertheless the most common form of mass killing. It is distinguished from other types of mass murder in that victims are family members rather than being anonymous or unknown to the murderer. Most familicides are perpetrated by men, who, after the murders, kill themselves as well. Regardless of gender, familicide is often followed by the suicide of the murderer.

Among the reasons cited for familicide are custody disputes following marital separation; a parent's wish to stop children's suffering, perhaps due to domestic violence or sexual abuse; feelings of shame resulting from a job loss or perceived inability to provide for family members; other financial reversals; and a history of mental illness, including severe depression or psychosis, such as schizophrenia or a manic-depressive disorder.

Some experts find that women are more likely to kill their children than men are, whereas men are more likely to kill both their children and their spouse. Women may have different motives or reasons for familicide than do men. Women tend to kill their children because of a delusional sense of altruism, or selflessness. Mothers are more likely than fathers to be diagnosed as mentally ill at the time of their offenses.

For someone who is psychotically depressed, the whole world is dull gray, and one's children are seen through a lens of suffering and emotional pain, causing the killer to believe that the children, too, are suffering. Thus, the killer may believe that they would be better off in heaven or some other paradise. Killing is perceived as a selfless decision, one carried out with the hope of relieving suffering but with horrific results.

Psychosis can lead a perpetrator to believe that the killing of a child is done with the goal of ending the child's suffering or because the child is demonically possessed. In the second case, the killer may see the child not as suffering but as unredeemably evil. For the protection of others, he or she must be killed.

Familicide also encompasses murders in which a parent or parents and other relatives such as siblings, in-laws, or grandparents are killed. The killing of a close relative is referred to as parricide. Parricide is commonly associated with delusional or faulty mental processes. Patricide is the act of killing one's father, and it is most often committed by a son against the father. Other terms related to familicide include filicide (the killing of one's child or children), mariticide (the killing of one's spouse), and fratricide or sororicide (the killing of one's brother or sister).

Steps Toward Reducing Violence

The term *psychic maneuvers* has been used to describe the factors that facilitate murder and other homicidal acts (see Table 13-1). You may find it interesting to review this list three times. First, consider how each of these psychic maneuvers might function in your own life. Notice that they do violence to ourselves and others, even when they function far more subtly than the overt act of homicide. Second, note how these psychic maneuvers function within society, how they contribute to violence between individuals and between groups. The third time, consider how each of these psychic maneuvers may be a dysfunctional strategy found in conflicts between nations.

Victims sometimes play a role in encouraging violent acts against themselves. Homicide investigators have found that victims are not always as innocent as might initially be assumed. Consider the example of a husband who has been repeatedly threatened by his angry wife, who wields a loaded revolver. His response to this threat is, "Go ahead, you might just as well kill me." What can be said about his role as a victim in such circumstances? Or consider another such incident: A daughter, overhearing her parents arguing, tries to intercede but is told by her mother, "Never mind, honey, let him kill me." After the daughter leaves the house to seek assistance, her father obtains a revolver from another room and shoots and kills the girl's mother.

Investigators note that, during domestic strife, wives have made statements like "What are you going to do, big man, kill me?" coupled with dares like "You haven't got the guts." Such statements combine "elements of

TABLE 13-1 *Factors Favoring Violence*

Anything that physically or psychologically separates the potential killer from the victim. For example, the use of a gun leads to a concentration on the means (pulling the trigger) rather than the end result (the death of a person). Psychological separation occurs when the victim is perceived as fundamentally different from oneself.

Anything that permits the killer to define murder as something else, such as "making an example of the victim," "making the world safe for democracy," "implementing the final solution," or "exterminating the terrorists."

Anything that fosters perceiving people as objects or as less than human. This happens when victims become "cases," "subjects," or "numbers," as well as when the killing occurs from a distance, as with high-altitude bombing or submarine warfare.

Anything that permits one to escape responsibility by blaming someone else: "I was just carrying out orders."

Anything that encourages seeing oneself as debased or worthless: "If I'm treated like a rat, I might as well act like one. What have I got to lose?"

Anything that reduces self-control or that is believed to have this effect: alcohol, mind-altering drugs, hypnotism, mass frenzy, and the like.

Anything that forces a hasty decision or that does not permit time for "cooling off." That is, a situation may force one to decide to shoot or not to shoot with no opportunity for deliberation.

Anything that encourages a person to feel above or outside the law: The notion that rank, prestige, wealth, or the like makes it possible for one to "get away with murder."

seduction and lethality."[53] In some instances, there are indications that the victim not only seemed to be "asking for it" but also was the one responsible for escalating the conflict to the level of physical violence.

While recognizing that victims sometimes do contribute to bringing violence on themselves, we should be cautious about blaming victims. Lula Redmond underscores the fact that labeling victims as bad, careless, seductive, or "with the wrong crowd," or as somehow "asking for it," denies the reality that everyone is vulnerable to victimization.[54] Blaming the victim is a convenient, albeit erroneous, way to overcome one's own sense of vulnerability and thereby regain a sense of personal security. If suitable "explanations" can be found for a victim's death, they provide convincing, though perhaps unwarranted, proof that a similar encounter *could never* happen in one's own life.

More effective than blaming the victim is understanding the factors that favor violence and taking action to reduce their presence in our own lives and in society as a whole. Discovering ways to break the cycle of violence is important, whether in the home, the community, or the world at large.[55]

The sense of social isolation that helps breed violence is counteracted when families take care to communicate positive community values. When residents work together to create a safe and orderly environment and when neighbors themselves take a measure of responsibility for maintaining social order, studies show that violence is reduced.[56] Cohen and Swift argue that "stopping the momentum of violence requires a 'critical mass' of people who are willing to speak out and to work together to change the structures and policies that frame the way we live."[57]

War

Within the context of ordinary human interaction, our moral and legal codes stand in strict opposition to killing. In war, however, killing is not only accepted but may be heroic. War abrogates conventional sanctions against killing by substituting a different set of conventions and rules about moral conduct. The expectation that one will kill and, if necessary, die for one's country is a concomitant of war. As Arnold Toynbee says, "The fundamental postulate of war is that, in war, killing is not murder."[58]

At the beginning, World War I seemed to many people little more than a game, almost idyllic, even ennobling and beautiful. Of course, such sentiments did not last. The war's devastatingly huge impact, especially on Europe, simply states the obvious. It has been called "the turning point in the history of the earth."[59]

In Dalton Trumbo's classic antiwar novel, *Johnny Got His Gun,* we find a veteran "without arms legs ears eyes nose mouth" who devises a means of communicating with the outside world by "tapping out" messages on his pillow with his head.[60] He asks to be taken outside, where he can become an "educational exhibit" to teach people "all there was to know about war." He thinks to himself, "That would be a great thing to concentrate war in one stump of a body and to show it to people so they could see the difference between a war that's in newspaper headlines and liberty loan drives and a war that is fought out lonesomely in the mud somewhere, a war between a man and a high explosive shell."

In more than twenty countries around the world, children are direct participants in war. An estimated 200,000 to 300,000 children serve as soldiers for both rebel groups and government forces in armed conflicts. According to a United Nations report, these child soldiers, girls as well as boys, are forcibly recruited as combatants, denied a childhood, and often subjected to horrific violence.[61]

Chivalrous notions of combat, in which mounted men-at-arms meet gallantly to do battle on an uninhabited hill or plain, have been replaced in modern times by the reality of mass technological warfare.

Technological Alienation

In recalling the epic battles of Achilles and Agamemnon, of the legendary King Arthur and the Knights of the Round Table, or of the samurai in medieval Japan, we encounter a view of warfare as heroic. The enemy is seen as a worthy opponent with whom one is engaged in a "metaphysic of struggle."[62] This sense of chivalry is now largely absent from warfare. Instead of individual initiative and courage, modern warfare emphasizes bureaucratic cooperation and calculation. *Technological alienation* has been called the most characteristic feature of the modern war machine.[63]

Not until World War I did warfare involve civilians on a large scale. In April of 1937, during the Spanish Civil War, the world was horrified by the aerial bombing of the Basque town of Guernica that killed civilians of both sexes and all ages. By the end of World War II, civilian victims of warfare outnumbered military casualties. The estimated number of civilians killed during the Second World War is shown here: Britain (70,000), France (391,000), Japan (953,000), Germany (2,000,000), Soviet Union (7,700,000), and China (20,000,000).[64] In the recent war in Iraq, it is estimated that civilian deaths may have accounted for 90 percent of total deaths.[65]

Early warfare had limits: the bow and arrow, the bullet from a gun, the artillery shell. These conventional limits of warfare were radically altered with the advent of the atomic bomb, unleashed on Hiroshima and Nagasaki in August 1945.

> The ease of access to target and the instant nature of macro-impact [large-scale destruction] mean that both the choice of city and the identity of the victim have become completely randomized, and human technology has reached a final platform of self-destructiveness. . . . At Hiroshima and Nagasaki, the "city of the dead" is finally transformed from a metaphor into a literal reality.[66]

At Hiroshima, the bomb fell near the center of the city, and its explosive force, heat, and radiation engulfed all of the city. A soldier who saw the city the next day left this description:

> I could find nothing but a wide stretch of burned ruins with a lot of debris. Where had the former city of Hiroshima gone? . . . The seven rivers that ran through the city were full of corpses, soot, smoke, and charred driftwood, stretching like black lines through Hiroshima, which was reduced to ashes.[67]

The characteristic human response to such carnage is one of *psychic numbing*. Exposed to mass death, the self-protective psychological response is to become insensitive and unfeeling. "Jet pilots who coolly drop bombs on people they never see tend not to feel what goes on at the receiving end," and "those of us who watch such bombing on TV undergo a different though not unrelated desensitization."[68]

Because of the sheer horror of it, we tend to think the bombing of Hiroshima was the worst attack on a city in history. But, as Ward Wilson points out, "the first of the conventional raids, a night attack on Tokyo on March 9–10, 1945, remains the single most destructive attack on a city in the history of war."[69]

Confronted by the death-dealing potential of modern weaponry, it is worth remembering the story of Dalton Trumbo's veteran, who wanted to be a living exhibit of the ravaging, destructive effects of war. His request was denied, the story explains, because "he was a perfect picture of the future and they were afraid to let anyone see what the future was like." Images of the dead and dying, of the emaciated, of terrified children, and of ravaged cities seem not to fit the earlier codes of noble sacrifice.[70]

The dropping of the atomic bombs on Japan seems to have marked the removal of all moral restraints. Distinctions between combatants and noncombatants had been blurred, if not erased. According to a widely cited study by the International Red Cross, nine out of ten casualties in modern warfare are civilians—men, women, and children who simply "got in the way of somebody's war."[71]

Glenn Vernon observes that "confrontation with wartime killing may be one of the most difficult experiences of those who have been taught to avoid killing."[72]

The Conversion of the Warrior

War activates a special set of conventions that make it psychologically possible for individuals to go against the grain of what they have learned about right and wrong—to put aside ordinary rules of moral conduct. As long as the combatant "keeps more or less faithfully to the recognized rules," Toynbee says, "most of humankind have been willing to alter their moral sense in such

> Perhaps the whole root of our trouble, the human trouble, is that we will sacrifice all the beauty of our lives, will imprison ourselves in totems, taboos, crosses, blood sacrifices, steeples, mosques, races, armies, flags, nations, in order to deny the fact of death, which is the only fact we have. It seems to me that one ought to rejoice in the *fact* of death—ought to decide, indeed, to *earn* one's death by confronting with passion the conundrum of life. One is responsible to life: It is the small beacon in that terrifying darkness from which we come and to which we shall return. One must negotiate this passage as nobly as possible, for the sake of those who are coming after us.
>
> James Baldwin

a way as to regard the killer in war as 'being righteous.'"[73] One convention of warfare, Toynbee points out, is to dress the part. The psychological effect of the uniform is that it "symbolizes the abrogation of the normal taboo on killing fellow human beings: it replaces this taboo by a duty to kill them."

The tension and hyperalertness of combat can produce an addictive "high." A Marine who fought in the Gulf War describes the moments before combat:

> We are all afraid, but show this in various ways—violent indifference, fake ease, standard-issue bravura. We are afraid, but that doesn't mean we don't want to fight. It occurs to me that we will never be young again. . . . The supposedly anti-war films have failed. Now is my time to step into the newest combat zone.[74]

Joel Baruch, another combat veteran, says, "Changes in personality and mood are rooted in the special climate of the combat zone. These mutations evolve in such a wily fashion that the person who undergoes them is not aware of the alterations himself."[75] The conventions of war are mind- and personality-altering. Here is Baruch's account of his first encounter with death on the battlefield:

> Stone dead, he was. Eyes wide open, staring at nothing. A thin veneer of blood curling at the corner of his lips. Two gaping holes in his chest. Right leg half gone. My first combat fatality. A lifeless body where only moments before a heart beat its customary seventy pumps in one orbit of the minute hand. It is one thing to hear about death; to watch it happen is quite another. I went over to the nearest tree and vomited my guts out.

By his next experience of combat death, however, Baruch began to question whether he was becoming callous and unfeeling: "I was becoming impervious to the death of my fellow soldiers, and, in addition, I was negating the possibility of my own . . . demise." Another veteran explains,

> Social context is much more important than most people realize. We pretty much live within the boundaries of one social context. If you lived in a different society, you would consider a different set of behaviors as normal. What's bewildering and frightening in the combat situation is how quickly "normal" can change.[76]

Each of us experiences differences in our behavior according to social context. How we behave among our relatives is likely to be different from how we behave among strangers or business associates. Usually, such differences are subtle and rarely met head on. The contradictory values that exist for the soldier in combat, however, require what the veteran just quoted calls "a much more total 'schizophrenia'":

> When you're there you don't really remember what it's like to come back into the social context of a society where killing is abhorrent. And, when you come back home, you don't really remember the context of the combat situation, except perhaps in your nightmares.

A soldier who fought in the Iraq War with the 1st Infantry Division said, "I don't think we should be fighting a war there for any reason whatsoever, but . . . there's no politics involved when it actually happens, when it comes down to you having to exchange rounds with someone."[77] Heroic intentions and patriotic feelings may be reasons for donning the uniform, but in combat the emphasis is likely to be on survival.[78]

When societies reflect on their participation in war, they often speak in terms of patriotism, the heroism of fighting for one's country, the need to defend the things that are held dear. When we listen to the words of those who have experienced combat, however, we hear a different value system at work. We hear about individuals fighting for their lives.

Coping with the Aftermath of War

Combatants do not necessarily resolve their losses merely by leaving the war zone or by being discharged from military service. They may experience nightmares and flashbacks to traumatic scenes. Many experience such symptoms as numbness, irritability, depression, relationship problems, and survivor's guilt at having survived when others did not.

The term *posttraumatic stress disorder* (PTSD) has been used to describe such symptoms, although such reactions have also been termed *delayed grief syndrome* or *posttraumatic grief disorder.*[79] Known as "shell shock" during World War I and "battle fatigue" during World War II, PTSD first became prominent in the aftermath of the Vietnam War.

Psychiatrist Jonathan Shay finds parallels between the grief and rage experienced by modern combat veterans and the description in Homer's

© Steve Ruark, AP Photo

An Army casualty team moves a transfer case containing the remains of Spc. Javier Sanchez, Jr., who died in Afghanistan, in the hills south of Kabul, when his unit was attacked with an improvised explosive device (IED) while on patrol.

Iliad of similar symptoms experienced by warriors who fought in the Trojan Wars three thousand years ago.[80] In the *Iliad,* we read about chilling atrocities committed by Achilles in a berserk rage following the battlefield death of his friend Patroclus. Shay says, "There have been technological changes, but there have been no changes to the human mind and heart and soul." One of the lessons to be learned from the *Iliad,* says Shay, is that soldiers should be allowed to grieve: "Snatching bodies off the battlefield in black bags and spiriting them back to stateside mortuaries without permitting comrades to mourn the fallen is profoundly damaging to survivors."

Combat leaves haunting memories. After the shooting stops, the mind must sort out the almost incomprehensible facts of war. One helicopter door gunner told his friends to stop boasting about achieving high casualties after he saw dead enemy troops for the first time. "It's different when you see their faces, with blood coming out of their wounds," he said.[81] A Marine captain who served in Afghanistan said:

> My squad saw a motorcycle racing toward us. The two riders did not respond to our shouts to stop, and we began firing and killed them. The riders turned out to be unarmed civilians, and one looked no older than 16. Every day I think about those people and others whose deaths I ordered. I am haunted by the feeling that "I'm no longer the 'good' person I once thought I was."[82]

The Veterans Administration has a phrase for this feeling: *moral injury.* Even if killing is necessary in war, taking the lives of other human beings violates a deep prohibition that often cannot be rationalized away.

Of the more than 2.3 million soldiers who have served in Afghanistan and Iraq, the Veterans Administration has treated more than 210,000 for posttraumatic stress disorder while acknowledging a much bigger epidemic that is hidden because the stigma of mental health problems prevents many veterans from seeking help. Veterans are returning to "a county largely oblivious to the wars in which they served, heightening their feelings of loneliness and alienation."[83] Reports indicate that the military has been remiss in treating PTSD. Confusing paperwork and inconsistent guidelines are among the factors that have hindered the services in dealing with behavioral care issues. The recent past has also seen an epidemic increase in the number of military suicides and suicides of veterans (discussed in Chapter 12).[84] Meditation, hundred-mile "Last Patrol" walks, sweat-lodge rituals, honoring dances, and other traditional as well as novel activities have helped some veterans come to terms with their experiences and heal from wounds received in war. Some Iraq veterans have attended a unique fly-fishing camp in Idaho geared to help veterans with severe traumatic brain injury rebuild physical skills, rediscover confidence and independence, and reintegrate into their communities. Before camp, therapists consult with each veteran and help them identify goals and map out a plan to achieve them. Afterwards, they follow up with the veterans for three years. The veterans learn to recognize what triggers their stress and how to manage it through recreation. One veteran said, "Everything I lost, they gave it back to me tenfold."[85]

One more month, I thought. He would have been home in one more month.

Figure 13-2 *A Widow's Lament*

Besides PTSD and other mental health issues, thousands of veterans are returning with catastrophic injuries, such as double and triple amputations and debilitating spinal cord damage. Improvised explosive devices are causing an increase in traumatic brain injuries, considered the "signature injury" of these wars.[86]

The families of men and women in the military make sacrifices that often go unnoticed (see Figure 13-2). In recalling her odyssey as the wife of a Marine Corps officer, Marian Novak says, "I watched my husband train for war; I waited thirteen months for him to return from it; and then I waited another fifteen years for him to truly come home."[87] War creates a "phantom army" composed of the spouses, children, parents, and friends who serve invisibly at home. Lee Woodruff, whose husband was seriously injured during the Iraq War, said,

> I bristled when, in an effort to make me feel better, people would say to me, "Things happen for a reason" or "God doesn't give you more than you can handle." It felt like greeting-card philosophy to try to package something so complex into bite-sized chunks.[88]

The euphemistic term "collateral damage" encompasses not only the civilian deaths that occur in a war zone but also the grief experienced by families whose lives are disrupted by the injury or death of loved ones serving in war zones.

The Vietnam Veterans Memorial in Washington, D.C., has become a "wailing wall" for the families and friends of the more than fifty-eight thousand whose names are engraved there, as well as for those who served and survived. Many visitors have left mementos, ranging from a pair of old cowboy boots found at the base of the memorial shortly after its dedication, to teddy bears, baseball caps, newspaper clippings, diaries, and tear-stained letters. One of the first letters was left by the mother of an army sergeant whose death had occurred nearly fifteen years before her visit. In the letter, she described finding her son's name for the first time:

> We had been looking for about a half-hour when your father quietly said, "Honey, here it is." As I looked to where his hand was touching the black wall, I saw your name, William R. Stock.
>
> My heart seemed to stop. I felt as though I couldn't breathe. It was like a bad dream. I felt as though I was freezing. My teeth chattered. God, how it hurt.[89]

Making War, Making Peace

About war and terrorist threats, Wilton S. Dillon wrote: "Understanding is not to forgive and forget, alone, but a way to inform us in developing our

Mickey Sanborn, U.S. Air Force Photo

Among the most poignant losses experienced in life are those related to war. The Vietnam Veterans Memorial in Washington, D.C., is a focal point for the grief of individuals and a nation. For many who served in wartime, as well as for other survivors, the effects are pervasive. Here, visitors ponder the names of individuals engraved on the face of the memorial's black wall, which reflects back the viewers' images, accentuating the personal impact of loss.

strategies by genuinely knowing ourselves as well as others while preparing to make war and, ultimately, peace."[90]

War is defined as a condition of hostile conflict between opposing forces, each of which believes its vital interests are at stake and seeks to impose control on the opposing side through the use of force. In the classic nineteenth-century study *On War,* Karl von Clausewitz described war as the continuation of political policy by other means. John Horgan says, "War, once invented, becomes a tradition, a custom, a habit, and its own cause."[91]

Human beings may have an innate tendency to divide the world into "us" and "them."

> In the beginning we create the enemy. Before the weapon comes the image. We *think* others to death and then invent the battle-axe or the ballistic missiles with which to actually kill them. Propaganda precedes technology. . . . It seems unlikely that we will have any considerable success in controlling warfare unless we come to understand the logic of political paranoia, and the process of creating propaganda that justifies our hostility.[92]

Dennis Klass, an expert on the subject of grief and on the phenomenon of continuing bonds of the bereaved with the dead (discussed in Chapter 9), points out that such bonds do not always lead to peace and harmony. "We only need to watch the nightly news to see that bonds with the dead play an integral role in long and bitter wars."[93]

Joining with others against a common enemy creates a sense of community and connectedness. Through an analysis of news stories, Debra Umberson and Kristin Henderson distinguished four major themes in how media reports generate public support for war while facilitating denial of death: (1) rhetorical devices that distance the reader from death and encourage denial of death in the war, (2) official denial of responsibility for war-related deaths and reassurance to the public that death will be "minimal," (3) rhetoric that prepares the public for death in war and to view the deaths as just, and (4) ambiguity and uncertainty about the actual death toll from the war.[94]

If we come to view other human beings as hostile, even ambiguous actions may be perceived as threatening. When we act to defend ourselves against this perceived threat, their reaction confirms our initial assumption (see Table 13-2). It is important to recognize, however, that sometimes our images of the enemy are accurate. Sam Keen says, "Short of utopia there are real enemies. It is a luxury of the naive and sheltered to think that right thinking, good intentions, and better communication techniques will turn all enemies into friends."[95] However, it is still good advice to "do no harm" insofar as possible; in other words, "whatever we do, we shouldn't make a bad situation worse."[96]

Viewed symbolically, war allows us to ritually affirm our own deathlessness by killing the enemy, who *is* Death. This idea is reflected in the promise made by some religions that warriors who fall in battle go directly to Valhalla or Paradise. "War as the bringer of death," says Keen, "wears the face of horror, but also of ecstasy."[97]

TABLE 13-2 *Images of the Enemy*

- The enemy as stranger. "Us" versus "Them."
- The enemy as aggressor. "Good" versus "Evil."
- The faceless enemy. "Human beings" versus "Dehumanized barbarians."
- The enemy as enemy of God; war as applied theology. "Holy" versus "Unholy."
- The enemy as barbarian (threat to culture, heathen, pagan).
- The greedy enemy (appetite for empire).
- The enemy as criminal, as committer of atrocities, as torturer (anarchists, terrorists, outlaws).
- The enemy as torturer or sadist.
- The enemy as rapist, desecrator of women and children. ("Woman as bait and trophy.")
- The enemy as beast, reptile, insect, germ. (Gives sanctions for extermination.)
- The enemy as death. ("The ultimate threat.")
- The enemy as worthy opponent. ("Heroic warfare or chivalry.") Examples: The epic battles of Achilles and Agamemnon, King Arthur and the Knights of the Round Table, the samurai in medieval Japan.

Genocide

Genocide, defined as the deliberate and systematic effort to destroy an entire national, racial, political, or cultural group, occurred with horrendous results during the twentieth century.[98] The term *genocide* (from the Greek word *genos,* "family, tribe, race," and the Latin *-cide,* "killing") was coined in 1944 by a Polish jurist named Raphael Limkin who had studied the Armenian genocide, which occurred early in the twentieth century. There is no consensus about how many lives were lost in the Armenian genocide, but estimates range from 300,000 to 1.5 million.

Between 1941 and 1945, Nazi Germany exterminated six million Jews in the Holocaust and killed another five million people deemed to be political opponents, mentally ill, retarded, or somehow "genetically inferior." The Holocaust Museum in Washington, D.C., memorializes this period of genocide.

When the Khmer Rouge came to power in Cambodia, two million Cambodians died from execution and starvation, an example of *autogenocide,* a group's killing of its own people. After the assassination of the president of Rwanda in 1994, as many as a million people, mainly members of the Tutsi tribe, were massacred in an attempt to exterminate them. The genocide in Darfur (Sudan), as Robert Kastenbaum points out, demonstrates that "large-scale violence did not end with the 20th century and its staggering toll of death and destruction."[99]

In the wake of traumatic bereavement from such losses, there may be few opportunities to grieve. For example, in Rwanda, many of the dead did not receive proper funeral rituals. According to Rwandan beliefs, says Paul Rosenblatt, "when proper funeral and mourning practices are not followed, misfortunes arise."[100] The neglect or repression of grief may contribute to further genocide by perpetuating a cycle of violence focused on revenge.

At Buchenwald, near Weimar, Germany, a few of the dead are piled in a yard awaiting burial following the invasion by the Allies. Starvation and disease due to unsanitary living conditions, as well as the incessant torture of prisoners, caused an average of two hundred deaths each day at this infamous Nazi concentration camp.

Colin Murray Parkes says, "It is not unreasonable to hope that any action to encourage people to grieve and express their discontent in controlled and safe ways might reduce the risk of uncontrolled violence."[101]

Terrorism

Speaking to the often random nature of terrorist acts, someone said, "It is not the bullet with my name on it that worries me; it is the one that says, To whom it may concern."[102] In a sense, terrorism is like other homicidal acts that occur between strangers. Yet, many terrorist acts have more in common with warfare, which is aimed at specific targets and goals. The complex nature of terrorism is apparent in the fact that, although there are more than one hundred definitions of *terrorism,* no single definition is universally accepted.

Among the common elements of terrorism is the use or threat of violence to create fear among both its direct victims and a wider audience. Even when attacks are apparently random, their victims and locations are often chosen for their shock value. The aim is to destroy the sense of security people normally feel in familiar places. Thus, terrorists frequently target schools, shopping centers, bus stops, restaurants, night clubs, and other locations where people gather. The definition developed by the U.S. State Department emphasizes the indiscriminate nature of terrorism, describing it as "premeditated, politically motivated violence perpetrated against noncombatant targets by sub-national groups or clandestine agents, usually intended to influence an audience."[103]

Although this definition captures key points, it is incomplete for several reasons. First, many terrorist acts do not target "noncombatants," or civilians, but rather are aimed against military or police forces. Second, terrorist acts may be perpetrated by states as well as "sub-national groups." Third, the phrase "politically motivated" is insufficient, because much terrorism has religious or quasi-religious sources. Another criticism is that many such definitions tend to treat terrorism as a type of *crime* rather than defining it as *war*.[104] The proposal to treat terrorism as war is not universally accepted, however, because war generally has been defined as "a state of usually open and declared armed hostile conflict between states or nations."[105] Terrorist acts do not fit this definition. Furthermore, war is generally viewed as an activity conducted according to socially recognized rules. In other words, war is a social construct that is recognized in custom and law. The rules of war are spelled out in international agreements like the Geneva Convention, which describes such matters as the appropriate treatment of prisoners of war and of the sick, wounded, and dead in battle. In contrast, terrorism occurs outside the boundaries of social sanctions that regulate conduct between individuals and between groups.[106]

The debate about how to define terrorism, and whether it should be classified and prosecuted as a criminal act or an act of war, is being shaped by the methods and manner of terrorist activities. On one hand, the use of household items like pressure cookers, as were used by the Boston Marathon terrorists, shows that even familiar items can maim and kill indiscriminately. On the other hand, in their desire to attract publicity designed to generate widespread fear, terrorists engage in dramatic and high-profile attacks, including hijackings, hostage takings, kidnappings, car bombings, and frequently suicide bombings. Terrorism has been called the "weapon of the weakest," but, increasingly, terrorists make use of sophisticated weapons and strategies.

In the *Encyclopedia of Terrorism,* Cindy Combs and Martin Slann highlight some of the key features of present-day terrorism by observing that it is "a synthesis of war and theater, a dramatization of the most proscribed kinds of violence—that which is perpetrated on innocent victims—played before an audience in the hope of creating a mood of fear."[107] As one scholar notes, "The meaning of terrorism is socially constructed."[108] In achieving their goals, terrorists often rely on the *amplification effect,* whereby their actions are broadcast through the media to a much larger audience than merely the one in the location where the action occurs, thus giving their acts greater significance. From this standpoint, the media's interest in sensational news and the terrorists' desire for publicity are linked.

Terrorist attacks often seem to be directed at random targets, but they are also directed at politically or culturally important targets. Terrorists' goals are aided by the element of surprise and the pervasive sense of fear generated among the threatened population. Acts of terrorism threaten our assumptive world, heightening our awareness of mortality and increasing our feelings of vulnerability.[109]

September 11, 2001

The events that culminated in the bloodiest day on U.S. soil since the Civil War began shortly before 9:00 a.m. on Tuesday, September 11, 2001, when terrorists piloted a hijacked jetliner into the North Tower of the World Trade Center (WTC) in New York City.[110] Roughly fifteen minutes later, a second airplane crashed into the South Tower of the WTC, erasing any doubt about whether the first crash was a horrible accident or an intentional act. As the nation went on alert and emergency personnel responded to the disaster in New York, a third jet was flown into the Pentagon, a symbol of U.S. military power, just outside Washington, D.C., and a fourth jet crashed into a field near Shanksville, Pennsylvania, a result of passengers on the flight thwarting the terrorists' apparent intentions to strike the U.S. Capitol or the White House. It was determined that the hijackings and suicide attacks were perpetrated by nineteen militants associated with an Islamic extremist group known as al-Qaeda.

Harold Dow, a correspondent for CBS News, said, "The media were very much a part of the terrorists' plan. From the time the first plane went in, they gave the media time to get down there to record the second plane. These pictures were shown all over the world; that's their trophy."[111]

Thousands of people witnessed the attacks firsthand, and millions, perhaps more than two billion worldwide, watched the tragedy unfold on television. Because of the time of day, the event "could be seen anywhere, in both hemispheres, any latitude, any culture, throughout the world, live—something that we've never had happen before."[112] The events were witnessed in real time, as the "terrorist moment" took place in a "global public space" created by extensive media coverage.[113] The most disturbing images were those of people falling or jumping to their deaths, most from the North Tower, the first tower to be hit (see Figure 13-3). Later analysis of videotapes showed that at least sixty people died this way.[114] In comparing coverage by print and television media, David Friend remarks that, whereas "the video would show mass murder, the still image would hint at split seconds when a man or woman had been taken from this earth."[115]

The most dramatic and devastating result of the attacks was the collapse of the 110-story Twin Towers of the WTC, killing more than 2,400 workers

Figure 13-3 *Child's 9/11 Drawing*
A young child's portrayal of the terrorist attack on the Twin Towers in New York City shows the towers in flames as individuals who were trapped in the devastation on the upper floors jump to their deaths. At the far left, an airplane is depicted at what appears to be the moment of impact, while a fire truck and rescue personnel approach the site from the opposite side. At the top of the drawing, the child includes a written affirmation, "You are the best," and she signs the drawing with an affectionate "Love, Briana."

and hundreds of firefighters. Having no way to escape, people trapped in the buildings or on hijacked airplanes made telephone calls to loved ones or left poignant messages on answering machines in their last moments.

Besides conventional news media, the Internet was a major medium for disseminating news of the attacks. People used the Internet to seek information about what happened, who died, who survived, and the extent of the damage. Despite the massive death toll caused by the attack on the Twin Towers, more than fifteen thousand people managed to escape.[116] An online "survivor registry," where people could post their names to let friends and loved ones know they had survived, received more than one million "hits" on September 11 and the next day, as people turned to the Internet to exchange information.[117] The Internet also functioned as a virtual space where individuals who died were identified and commemorated. People from eighty countries around the world, engaged in ordinary life activities, became victims of a desire to make a point, weaken a government, express a grievance.[118]

Rescue, Recovery, and Mourning

Rescue and recovery operations began immediately, but the initial hope of finding a large number of survivors in the rubble was soon replaced by the grim realization that efforts would mainly involve retrieving and identifying the dead. Hundreds of photographs of the missing posted by friends and family members throughout New York City in the days after the attack became memorials to loved ones.[119] In the end, only eighteen people were recovered alive from the collapsed Twin Towers.[120]

Even though the principle that human remains ought to be treated with dignity is almost universally accepted, the application of this rule in extraordinary situations can generate volatile emotions. In Israel, where the commandment to bury the dead is a basic rule in Jewish law, a volunteer organization known as ZAKA (an acronym for Zihui Korbanot Ason, Hebrew for "Identification of Disaster Victims") responds to terrorist incidents to collect remains and identify as many parts as they can, including blood, so that as much of a victim's body as possible can be buried. Doing this kind of rescue and "cleanup" work, seeing firsthand the gruesome violence done to human beings, is stressful and can trigger intense grief. To help volunteers cope with such traumatic experiences, ZAKA regularly schedules counseling workshops, family days, and other programs where members can discuss their feelings in an atmosphere of mutual support.[121]

Whereas Israelis may be familiar with the stresses of life under terrorism, many of the people engaged in recovery at the WTC were much less accustomed to its grisly effects. Frustrated because of the awesome death toll, and grieving the deaths of so many individuals both known and unknown, those who toiled at Ground Zero shared with the wider community a sense of uncertainty and confusion about how to cope. Problems in recovering and identifying victims' remains, as well as the scope and extent of devastation, were among factors that added to the impact of the terrorism of 9/11.

Just days after the attacks, the *New York Times* began publishing a special feature, "Portraits of Grief," which evolved into a kind of shrine that offered vignettes about people who had died. Unlike formal obituaries, these were quick sketches that suggested some spark of life that made each person special. They served to highlight a person's unique humanity and interests, not his or her status or achievements. This new form of reportage represented what one writer called a "kind of haiku obit"—journalism as tribute, as homage, as witness, and as solace.[122]

The Mind of the Terrorist

From the moment the second airplane hit the South Tower of the WTC, confirming the fact that the events were intentional, people asked what could motivate human beings to perpetrate such acts of violence against innocent citizens. Is it even possible to understand the mind of a terrorist? Despite the unparalleled military arsenal of the United States, a successful attack on the symbols of power and wealth in the Western world was carried out by men wielding box cutters, creating the most spectacular terrorist event in history.[123] Yet, such violence was not unprecedented, nor was it merely a chance occurrence devised by nineteen amateurs acting on their own. On the contrary, the attacks were the deliberate result of careful planning by al-Qaeda, an organization with operations in as many as sixty countries worldwide.[124] In its use of sophisticated information technology and small cells of terrorists who operate for long periods independently, al-Qaeda is representative of a new kind of combat organization, one that operates on a global scale as a "fighting network."[125]

Why do organizations like al-Qaeda exist, and why do individuals become allied with them to the extent that they are willing to sacrifice their lives in suicide attacks? Much of the terrorism in recent decades has had a religious or quasi-religious component whereby terrorists combine fanatical hatred of the secular state with a vision of themselves as defenders of an ancient faith. The secular world, having betrayed the true faith, is seen as "evil"; therefore, it is the duty of the "righteous" to engage in a moral and spiritual struggle between good and evil (see Table 13-3).

The idea of martyrdom (from Greek, *martys*, "witness") took shape in the early years of the second century CE, when Christians who refused to sacrifice to the Roman emperor were subjected to the extreme penalty, death by torture or other horrific means.[126] Their enthusiasm for a martyr's death, arranged by an external agent with the complicity of the victim, was seen in reports of radiant joy, smiles, and even laughter.

Mark Juergensmeyer says, "Concepts of cosmic war are accompanied by strong claims of moral justification and an enduring absolutism that transforms worldly struggles into sacred battles."[127] Such views are adopted by individuals who seek to impose their own concepts of right and wrong on those who fail to share their views. Terrorism has tended to develop as part of revivalist movements that promote a return to fundamentalism in religious matters. In the mind of the terrorist, it is permissible, even necessary, to kill, because he or she is doing it for a higher purpose.

Suicide bombings exemplify the terrorist's belief that he or she is engaged in a worthy and just struggle, one that makes sacrifice not only desirable but also imperative. The collective—religion, sect, nation—is more important than the individual. Suicide missions are usually easy to plan because no escape route is needed and, once a suicide terrorist heads for the target, even if he or she does not succeed in reaching it, some damage likely can be inflicted on the enemy while the terrorist is being apprehended.[128]

TABLE 13-3 *Justifications for Terrorist Violence*

- Those who practice revolutionary violence and state repression always claim to champion noble causes and values.
- Policies that advocate extreme violence always cite religious goals to justify behavior, such as to defend faith or human rights.
- The perpetrators of violent acts maintain that they are freedom fighters (in the case of revolutionaries) or the champions of law and social order (in the case of governments).

Psychologist Aaron Beck describes terrorists as "prisoners of hate."[129] Harboring a profound sense of being wronged, they call for revenge against those whom they view as their oppressors. Beck says, "Terrorists who execute well-planned acts of destruction are not deranged"; rather, they are "possessed by a cool hatred toward the designated enemy," which allows them to be "cold and calculating in carrying out their grand design." Terrorists of the "lone wolf" variety may perpetrate their violent acts in support of some group, movement, or ideology, but they do so alone, outside of any command or organizational structure. Timothy McVeigh, convicted of the Oklahoma City bombing that killed 168 people, is often cited as a classic example of "lone wolf" terrorism. Shashi Tharoor says,

> Terrorism emerges from blind hatred of an Other, and that in turn is the product of three factors: fear, rage, and incomprehension. Fear of what the Other might do to you, rage at what you believe the Other has done to you, and incomprehension about who or what the Other really is. . . . If terrorism is to be tackled and ended, we will have to deal with each of these three factors by attacking the ignorance that sustains them. We will have to learn to see ourselves as others see us, learn to recognize hatred and deal with its causes, learn to dispel fear, and, above all, simply learn about each other.[130]

Describing the twenty-first century as "the global century," Tharoor argues that, as never before, "the tragedies of our time are global in origin and reach," and "tackling them is a global responsibility that must be assumed by us all."

Horrendous Death

Daniel Leviton and William Wendt use the term *horrendous death* to describe "a form of premature death which is ugly, fashioned by man, without any trace of grace, totally unnecessary, and, as they say of pornography, lacking any redeeming social value. It is a category of death that typically affects large numbers of people."[131] It is death caused by war, homicide, holocaust, terrorism, starvation, and poisoning of the environment.[132] Horrendous death typically involves the motivation to kill, maim, injure, torture, or otherwise destroy another human being. Such acts are often the work of humiliated individuals who seek to reverse their status from victim to perpetrator. Leviton says, "The horrendous death concept is about preventable death and the process of prevention. It is about addressing causes as well as symptoms."[133] The first step in eliminating or at least reducing horrendous deaths involves confronting the wish to deny their reality. Leviton further says,

> It is hypothesized that the more horrible the type or style of dying and/or death is perceived, the greater the fear; the greater the fear, the greater the denial; and the greater the denial, the less chance of action to eliminate the very causes of such torturous deaths.[134]

The threat of nuclear destruction would seem to fit within this category. Fallout shelters and classroom "duck and cover" trainings are now viewed as relics of an earlier age. Many people believe the threat of nuclear destruction

"Disarmament Talks," © 1987 Ralph Steadman, Swann Collection, Library of Congress

disappeared with the end of the Cold War. Stephen Younger points to a reason for such belief:

> A significant portion of the U.S. population, including many members of Congress, came of age after the end of the Cold War. To them, nuclear weapons are anachronisms, holdovers of a conflict read about in history books or seen in movies.[135]

Sometimes, as with the nuclear threat, horrendous deaths are treated as aberrant or anomalous. Yet, they involve enormous costs for present as well as future generations.

Emerging Infectious Diseases

Pestilence derives from the Latin word for plague. It began to be used in the fourteenth century when bubonic and pneumonic plagues ravaged Europe, and themes of grim terror became common in literature, such as Geoffrey Chaucer's "The Pardoner's Tale." Today, a similar threat is represented by emerging infectious diseases. (Whereas *epidemic* is defined as a rapidly spreading disease or condition, *pandemic* refers to a widespread epidemic.)

The worst infectious disease episode in modern times was the 1918 pandemic caused by an influenza virus that killed as many as forty million people worldwide.[136] In the United States, a quarter of the population had the flu, and more than half a million people died. Many of the thousands of young men crammed onto World War I troop ships were just developing the flu as they left the United States. After a week's crossing of the Atlantic, the ships arrived in France with hundreds of sick servicemen, many of whom died.

In the early twentieth century, infectious diseases predominated among the main causes of death, and epidemic infections caused global havoc. Subsequent advances in public health and medicine so dramatically altered patterns of morbidity and mortality that many people have become complacent about the threat of infectious diseases. Yet, virologists fear that some of the currently emerging viruses are a bigger threat than the 1918 virus.[137]

The World Health Organization defines an emerging disease as one that has appeared in a population for the first time or that may have existed previously but is rapidly increasing in incidence or geographic range. These emerging and re-emerging epidemic diseases pose an ongoing threat to global health security.[138] Among diseases of concern are avian and other forms of influenza, Rift Valley fever, SARS (severe acute respiratory syndrome), coronavirus infections, smallpox, and viral hemorrhagic fevers (Ebola, Marburg, Lassa, Crimean-Congo hemorrhagic fever, etc.).

AIDS (acquired immune deficiency disease) may be a harbinger of other emerging diseases that will threaten the health of human beings worldwide in coming decades. According to a United Nations report, HIV/AIDS is one of the most destructive epidemics in recorded history. At the end of 2011, an estimated 34 million people were living with HIV worldwide.[139] Data from that year shows 1.7 million AIDS-related adult and child deaths, and 2.5 million people newly infected. Sub-Saharan Africa remains the most affected region.

The Response to AIDS

For many people, AIDS is synonymous with death: a dread disease, contagious and epidemic, a modern plague.[140] Looking at AIDS in historical perspective, Charles Rosenberg says,

> Mortality is built into our bodies, into our modes of behavior, and into our place in the planet's ecology. Like other epidemics, AIDS has served well to remind us, finally, of these ultimate realities.[141]

Robert Kastenbaum says that the symbolism of AIDS embodies the stigma of earlier forms of catastrophic dying: disfiguration, dementia, and skeletonization. It conveys multiple meanings about human vanity and pride, divine punishment, attack by an enemy from within, the terror of life in death and the despair of death in life, and the romantic exit of brilliant and beautiful doomed youth.[142] Many survivors—the friends, neighbors, business associates, and relatives of people who died from AIDS—have experienced multiple losses.

It is important to distinguish between AIDS and human immunodeficiency virus (HIV), which causes AIDS. Although a blood test can be used to screen people for HIV infection, people infected with the virus are usually not aware of it until symptoms become evident years later. The pattern of progression from HIV infection to AIDS is not entirely clear. However, the consensus has been that almost all HIV-infected persons eventually develop AIDS. In recent years, the greatest impact of AIDS in the United States has been among African Americans and Hispanics.

For some marginalized people, the view of AIDS is quite different from the view held in society's mainstream: AIDS appears to be a form of race or class warfare, "a virus created in a government or CIA laboratory in an attempt

© Carolyn Jones, from *Living Proof, Courage in the Face of AIDS*

Zoë Lorenz and her daughter Candice are among the many people affected by AIDS. Zoë saw her father die from AIDS, plagued not only by the disease but by the humiliation and shame so often associated with it. Now afflicted with the virus herself, Zoë says, "I have a beautiful four-year-old daughter who has beat the odds and remains HIV negative. So many people have the attitude that I should go off and die somewhere alone. They don't see the tragedy of this child losing her mommy. I don't need to be proud that I have AIDS, but I won't be ashamed that I do. I don't want to feel that I have to tell people I've got cancer or some other acceptable disease."

to 'clean up' a seemingly dirty population."[143] The fact that such a view exists is itself evidence of the gap between the haves and have-nots of society.

AIDS is concentrated in the developing world, where it is wiping out gains in life expectancy made in recent decades. In the United States, AIDS mainly affects intravenous (IV) drug users, hemophiliacs, and recipients of blood transfusions, as well as the sexual partners of individuals infected with the virus. In other parts of the world, it is transmitted mainly through heterosexual contact.

AIDS reminds us that infectious diseases remain a threat and that human beings remain uncertain about how to respond to epidemic disease. When confronted by a new disease with an unknown mode of transmission, people become anxious and fearful. As the initial panic recedes, more thoughtful and helpful measures are implemented.

Living with AIDS

The prognosis for AIDS patients has much improved, as newer drugs have become available. Besides new drugs, there are advances in understanding the biology of HIV infectivity and the role of natural chemicals called chemokines in suppressing HIV's ability to infect cells. With new treatment options, the focus is changing from "dying of AIDS" to "living with HIV and AIDS." Patients who had depleted their financial resources for care or other expenses at what had seemed the end of their lives are now confronted by the need to reappraise their planning for "last days" and to reconstruct their lives so as to include a future that didn't seem likely until quite recently (see Figure 13-4). For AIDS patients who lack financial resources to pay for expensive drugs or lack access to sophisticated health care, the future is bleaker.

The Threat of Emerging Diseases

If AIDS is a harbinger of things to come, what lessons do we need to learn? Three of the most important involve (1) early identification of people who are at risk for disease, (2) a shift to community and public health perspectives, and (3) the need to address health problems on a global scale.[144] In recent decades, localized epidemics of a number of emerging diseases have occurred, many of them related to hemorrhagic fever viruses, such as the Marburg, Ebola, Lassa, and hantaviruses, as well as yellow fever, swine flu (the pandemic H1N1 virus is an example), Legionnaires' disease (*Legionella*), and cholera.[145] Bernard Le Guenno of the Pasteur Institute in Paris says,

> Hemorrhagic fever viruses are among the most threatening examples of what are commonly termed emerging pathogens. They are not really new. Mutations or genetic recombinations between existing viruses can increase virulence, but what appear to be novel viruses are generally viruses that have existed for millions of years and merely come to light when environmental conditions change. The changes allow the virus to multiply and spread in host organisms. New illnesses may then sometimes become apparent.[146]

Patrick Olson, an epidemiologist at the Naval Medical Center in San Diego, theorizes that the plague that struck the Greek city of Athens in 430 BCE, reported by the Athenian general and historian Thucydides, was caused by the deadly Ebola virus (named after a river in the Congo).[147] Olson finds parallels between the ancient and modern accounts. Fever, diarrhea, and severe weakness are prominent symptoms. As with the Athenian plague, Ebola claims almost all of its victims, and quickly; most infected people die within two weeks. Ebola outbreaks usually last only a few weeks because its victims die faster than they are able to spread the virus, which disappears for a time only to reemerge later.

One year ago today, I told my colleagues that I was dying of AIDS. I had been fighting it for years—the illness and the telling. . . . But now I was gaunt, tired, and rather sure I was losing the battle.

I was happily dying—and about to go on a Mexican vacation. I felt I had made my peace with death and, in a way, was looking forward to it. I had blown my mother's estate, about $180,000, on living for the moment, eating in the best restaurants and taking three or four foreign vacations a year. There was no time to lose, and I was determined to go out in style.

What has happened in the past year, at least for me, is a miracle that couldn't have taken place at any other moment. Thanks to the arrival of the new drugs called protease inhibitors, I am probably more likely to be hit by a truck than to die of AIDS.

I stopped the presses on my obituary. Oddly enough, the return from my near-death experience was at first very annoying. I had a few adjustments to make. I had to start thinking again about my bills. . . . We had to start living within our means. . . . I have had to re-energize myself for the daily grind. I'm even thinking about cleaning the basement.

But I'm not out of the woods.

Some HIV-negative men are guilt-ridden when they see so many of their friends dying. I feel guilty that I am getting the best possible medical care, because it is unavailable to most of the world's AIDS sufferers, and to the poor and uninsured in this country.

Figure 13-4 *Back to a Future*

To better understand the interactions of people and plagues, epidemiologists are gathering data from studying outbreaks caused by "bugs" in the virtual world of online gaming. When a viruslike epidemic started causing the deaths of characters in the online game *World of Warcraft,* epidemiologists studied the risk reactions of players to the inadvertent plague, gaining information about human behaviors in the face of threat.[148]

In studying how emerging diseases are disseminated in urban societies, Rodrick and Deborah Wallace conclude that physical and social disruption intensifies the pathological behaviors and conditions that promote the rapid spread of infectious diseases.[149] Abandonment of inner-city areas results in what the Wallaces term "urban desertification" or "social thanatology."[150] The devastation and disintegration in some urban areas is characterized as "unprecedented in a modern industrialized state short of the aftermath of total war."[151] Among disadvantaged populations, a lack of crucial municipal services leads to what Richard Rothenberg of the U.S. Centers for Disease Control and Prevention calls "the metastasis of dangerous behavior."[152]

Experts believe that many viruses reside harmlessly in birds and occasionally infect pigs, where they are changed into a new form of the virus that can affect humans.[153] Deprived of their natural hosts, some of these microorganisms have begun to jump to humans, where there is no such equilibrium. "As we have seen with the Ebola and AIDS viruses," says William Clark, the results "can be disastrous."[154] Since the advent of penicillin, people have become complacent about infectious diseases, believing that epidemics are no longer a threat. But the pandemic of AIDS shows that complacency is ill advised.

Traumatic Death

In its root meaning, *trauma* is defined as a wound, a piercing. In psychological terms, it refers to a disordered psychic or behavioral state resulting from severe mental or emotional stress. The human response to trauma, says Jeffrey Kauffman, is one "in which the cohesion of the self is shattered, producing a diversity of symptoms and other life-redefining consequences."[155] Traumatic deaths occur in the context of many topics covered in this chapter, including disasters, homicide, genocide, combat, terrorism, and epidemics, as well as in the context of topics discussed in earlier chapters, such as suicide (Chapter 12).

Traumatic deaths are often characterized by suddenness and lack of anticipation; preventability and/or randomness; the level of violence, mutilation, and destruction; and the fact of multiple deaths.[156] Such deaths, says Lillian Range, are "out of the ordinary, directly experienced, and perceived as threatening survival and self-preservation." In short, they shatter our assumptive world. The result, Range says, is that "individuals confront their own mortality and recognize their fragility as physical creatures."[157]

Risks and perils—accidents, disasters, violence, homicide, war, terrorism, epidemic diseases—affect us as we go about our daily lives. Sometimes, the encounter is subtle; at others, it is overt, calling into action our ability to cope. The failure to find adequate means of coping with these encounters with death represents a threat to the survival of society as well as the individual.

Further Readings

Jonathan Barker. *The No-Nonsense Guide to Global Terrorism,* 2nd ed. Oxford: New Internationalist, 2008.

Mia Bloom. *Dying to Kill: The Allure of Suicide Terror.* New York: Columbia University Press, 2005.

Feargal Cochrane. *Ending Wars.* Malden, Mass.: Polity, 2008.

Walter Laqueur. *No End to War: Terrorism in the Twenty-First Century.* New York: Continuum, 2003.

Gus Martin. *Understanding Terrorism: Challenges, Perspectives, and Issues,* 3rd ed. Los Angeles: Sage, 2010.

Randolph Roth. *American Homicide.* Cambridge, Mass.: Harvard University Press, 2009.

Jake Tapper. *The Outpost: An Untold Story of American Valor.* New York: Little, Brown, 2012.

Trish Wood. *What Was Asked of Us: An Oral History of the Iraq War by the Soldiers Who Fought It.* New York: Little, Brown, 2006.

Additional resources for this chapter can be found at www.mhhe.com/despelder10e

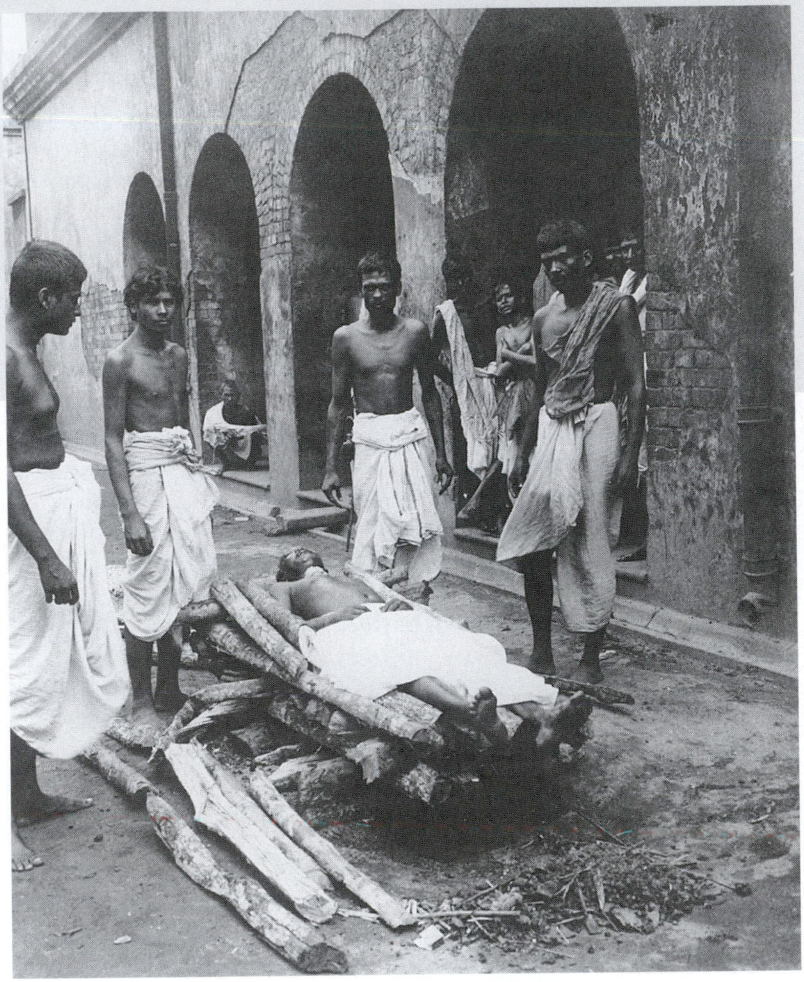

Library of Congress

The corpse placed on the funeral pyre, these men prepare to light the cremation fire. Cremation has been a traditional practice in India, where Hindus believe that "even as the person casts off worn-out clothes and puts on others that are new, so the embodied Self casts off worn-out bodies and enters into others that are new."

CHAPTER 14

Beyond Death / After Life

Death—and then what?

Some people have a ready answer to this question: "When you're dead, you're dead—that's it!" or "You go through a transition and take birth in another body," or "After you die, you go to heaven." Each of these responses reflects a particular understanding of the meaning of human existence. Beliefs about life after death occupy a broad spectrum, from the notion that death spells the end to the notion that the "soul" or "self" lives on after death in some fashion. Answering the question, What happens after I die? has occupied the attention of human beings since the dawn of consciousness.

Examining the death customs of the ancient Egyptians, we find a culture focused on preparing for the afterlife.[1] The body was mortal. Yet, within it were immortal elements: the *Ba,* a soul or psychic force, and the *Ka,* a spiritual double representing the creative and sustaining power of life. At death, the Ka flew to the afterlife, while the Ba lived on in the body. As the permanent dwelling place of the Ba, the body was preserved by mummification and protected by a wooden coffin, sometimes placed within a stone sarcophagus, or limestone coffin. Providing a home for the Ba (often depicted in the form of a bird hovering above the deceased) ensured that the deceased would enjoy the afterlife. However, if the Ba were destroyed, the deceased would suffer "the second death, the death that really did come as the end." Thus, preserving the physical form, as mummy or statue, was necessary for survival.

Concern with immortality—that is, survival after physical death—is cut from the same cloth as questions about the meaning of life and its corollary question, How, then, should one live? Responses to these questions reflect a person's values and beliefs about human experience and the nature of reality. Andrew Greeley says, "We are born with two incurable diseases: *life,* from which we die, and *hope,* which says maybe death isn't the end."[2]

Death can be a tricky question for people. Bob Dylan describes how reviewers of his album *Time Out of Mind* understood that it dealt with "mortality," but not a single critic applied this recognition to himself; it was, Dylan said, as if "whoever's writing about the record has got eternal life and the singer doesn't."[3] Our philosophy of life influences our philosophy of death. Conversely, our understanding of death and its meaning affects the way we live.

According to Socrates, "The unexamined life is not worth living." Such self-investigation includes discovery of what one believes about the consequences of death. Ambivalence about belief in survival after death is aptly described in an anecdote related by Bertrand Russell: A woman whose daughter had recently died was asked what she thought had become of her daughter's soul. She replied, "Oh, well, I suppose she is enjoying eternal bliss, but I wish you wouldn't talk about such unpleasant subjects."[4]

Exploring your beliefs about immortality may not result in an easier acceptance of death—nor should it necessarily. After all, the prospect of immortality is not always looked upon favorably.[5] Nevertheless, such an exploration can lead to a more coherent philosophy of life and death, making possible a congruence between hopes and perceptions. Even when we are settled upon a belief system, exposure to other views can both broaden our understanding of different responses to death and enhance appreciation of our own beliefs. In this chapter, we explore the meaning of mortality by investigating some of the ways that cultures, Eastern and Western, answer the question, What happens after death? These answers provide grist for the mill of our own contemplation about this ultimate human concern.

Traditional Concepts About Life After Death

The notion that life continues in some form after death is one of the oldest concepts held by human beings. In some of the earliest graves, archaeologists have uncovered skeletons that were bound by hands and feet into a fetal position, perhaps indicating beliefs about "rebirth" into other forms of existence following death. (Rebirth, in one form or another, has been characterized

> It is wonderful that five thousand years have now elapsed since the creation of the world, and still it is undecided whether or not there has ever been an instance of the spirit of any person appearing after death. All argument is against it; but all belief is for it.
>
> James Boswell, *Life of Johnson*

as the "most persistent image of afterlife in the history of religion.")[6] In traditional societies, death represents a change of status, a transition from the land of the living to the land of the dead.

Judgment is a key feature of many beliefs about what follows death. Among the various concepts of afterlife among traditional Hawaiians, for

William Hodges, Bishop Museum

The platform burial of a Tahitian chief is depicted in this drawing by William Hodges, made during Captain Cook's second voyage to the South Pacific in the 1770s.

In a world populated by unseen spirits who could exert their influence for good or evil upon the living, the death of a chief or other important person occasioned a spectacular display of grief, which was presided over by a chief mourner (right). *Usually a priest or close relative of the deceased, the chief mourner wore an elaborate costume of pearl shells and the feathers of tropic birds. Rattling a pearl shell clapper and brandishing a long wooden weapon inset with sharks' teeth, the chief mourner was accompanied by other weapon-carrying men who could strike anyone in their way, thus helping ensure that funeral rites were carried out in a manner that would offend neither the living nor the dead.*

Bishop Museum

example, was the belief that a person who had offended a god or who had harmed others would suffer eternal punishment.[7] Such an unworthy soul became a wandering spirit, "forever homeless, forever hungry." The ancestor-gods had the power to punish or reward the released spirit or even to send it back to the body. Misfortune could result when a person had neither loving relatives to care for the corpse nor the guardianship of family ancestor-gods, who help souls find their way to the world of spirits. Those who had lived worthily were welcomed into eternity, whereas those who had done misdeeds, without repenting of or correcting them, were punished. The reward for a good life was reunion with those closest to the family-loving Hawaiians: one's own ancestors.

To understand the consciousness from which such a view of immortality arises, the notion of selfhood in Western cultures must be put aside momentarily. Against an emphasis on individual identity and the self, imagine a mentality in which group identity is all-encompassing. The family, the clan, the people—these social groups represent the loci of communal consciousness within which the thoughts and actions of the individual are subsumed. Thus, traditional beliefs are less concerned with individual survival than with continuation of the community and its common heritage. Having shared in the life of the group, the individual is part of its ultimate destiny, a destiny that transcends death.

Jewish Beliefs About Death and Resurrection

Although the Bible takes death seriously, it does not present a systematic "theology of death" or the afterlife.[8] The biblical story describes a people focused on their communal destiny. Individuals are actors in an unfolding drama, its final outcome foretold in the promises made by Yahweh (the biblical proper name for God). The emphasis is on faith—faith in the people of Israel as a community with a common destiny and faith in Yahweh, whose promises will be realized in the unfolding of the divine plan. For example, as the patriarch Abraham lay dying, his last thoughts were hope for the survival of his progeny so that these promises could be realized. Abraham's vision is reenacted by biblical heroes in one circumstance after another as they affirm Israel's communal destiny. By contributing to this destiny, the righteous person is part of the continuing story of the people as a whole. "According to Jewish tradition, our lives are measured by our deeds and by whether we have lived up to our full potential."[9]

In the story of Job's encounter with adversity, the possibility of life beyond death appears bleak: "As a cloud fades away and disappears, so a person who goes down to the grave will not come up from it."[10] Resignation toward death is echoed in the other wisdom books—including Proverbs, Ecclesiastes, and some of the Psalms—which present the thought of the ancient Hebrew sages on the question of human destiny. Righteous conduct is advised because it leads to harmony in the present life, not because it guarantees future rewards for the individual.

> There is always hope for a tree:
> when felled, it can start its life again;
> its shoots continue to sprout.
>
> Its roots may be decayed in the earth,
> its stump withering in the soil,
>
> but let it scent the water, and it buds,
> and puts out branches like a plant new set.
>
> But man? He dies, and lifeless he remains;
> man breathes his last, and then where is he?
>
> The waters of the sea may disappear,
> all the rivers may run dry or drain away;
>
> but man, once in his resting place, will never rise again.
> The heavens will wear away before he wakes,
> before he rises from his sleep.
>
> Job 14:7–12, *The Jerusalem Bible*

Between the time of Job and the later prophets, however, there was a gradual change from resignation to hopefulness in the face of death. In the apocalyptic, or visionary, writings of such prophets as Daniel and Ezekiel, we find the strands of thought that are eventually woven together in ideas about the resurrection of the body. Daniel envisions a future in which the "sleeping" dead will awaken, "some to everlasting life, some to everlasting disgrace."[11] This development in Hebrew thought would greatly influence Christian theology. Stated succinctly, it "consists in the belief that, at the end of time, the bodies of the dead will be resurrected from the grave and reconstituted."[12]

Hints of this change are also evident in the meanings ascribed over time to the Hebrew word *She'ol,* which in early usage is generally defined as the underworld of all the dead, a shadowy realm of ghostly, disembodied souls (much like the Hades of Greek mythology). A story gives an account of necromancy in which King Saul requests the witch of Endor to summon the spirit of the dead prophet Samuel. Asked by Saul to describe what she sees, the witch replies, "I see a ghost [*elohim* = superhuman being] rising up from the earth [She'ol]." With further refinement of these concepts, the shadowy underworld of She'ol is divided into two distinct realms: Gehinom (hell) and Pardes (heaven or paradise).[13]

In the main, ideas about resurrection of the body found in the writings of the prophets did not alter the essential understanding of the human person as an undivided psychophysical entity. Wheeler Robinson says, "The Hebrew idea of personality is an animated body, and not an incarnated soul."[14] In other words, it is not as if the soul *takes* a body; rather, the body *has* life. Concepts like body or soul cannot be abstracted from the integrity of the human person.

> I knew my former father-in-law from the time I was thirteen. Although I had divorced many years ago, he remained a second father to me. Kurt was born in Germany. He left for Holland on the day of Kristallnacht. He arrived here penniless and went on to become an extremely successful business man. In coming to this country, he left his entire family. With the exception of an uncle, they all died in the Holocaust. He remained an observant Jew and did not talk much about the Holocaust until the last two years of his life. Since he never knew when his parents, sisters, and other loved ones died, he observed the *yahrzeit* (anniversary of their deaths) on Yom Kippur (the day of atonement).
>
> Just before Rosh Hashanah two years ago, he became very ill and was hospitalized. Following an old European tradition, in the synagogue on Rosh Hashanah he was given a new Hebrew name (so that when the angel of death came looking for him, he wouldn't find him). I went to visit him in the hospital that day. He was in and out of consciousness. I doubt that he consciously knew who I was, and I'm sure was not aware of the day. When he did speak, he was speaking only in German. I said my good-bye to him and left. He remained alive for the entire ten-day period (often referred to as the Days of Awe) and (I believe) went to be with his loved ones on Yom Kippur.
>
> Barbara J. Paul

The consensus expressed by the biblical writers seems to be, "Our present existence is of God; if there is life hereafter, it will also be God's gift. Why be anxious about death? What matters is to live righteously." The faith of Israel is sustained through customs like the *minyan* (a quorum or minimum number of individuals required for communal worship) and the reciting of *kaddish* (a liturgical expression of praise to God, which functions as a kind of "memorial prayer"), as well as in the practice of *shivah* (period of formal mourning, traditionally seven days). An Aramaic doxology, kaddish is essentially a pledge from the living to dedicate one's life to the God of Life.[15] It is recited by mourners during the first eleven months after death and then on the anniversary, or *yahrzeit,* of the death of a loved one. In Judaism, the customary mourning rituals help the bereaved face the reality of death, give honor to the deceased, and engage in a reaffirmation of *life.*[16]

Classical Greek Concepts of Immortality

The ancient Greeks held a variety of views about what might follow the death of the body.[17] Generally, however, the afterworld was not an attractive prospect. Hades, the realm of the dead, was typically pictured as a shadowy place inhabited by bloodless phantoms, an image that evoked despair. The heroes in Greek drama are often portrayed as raging against death.[18]

In the Athenian democracy, what mattered was the survival of the *polis,* the corporate existence of the city-state. Personal immortality was important only to the extent that it affected the survival of the community. A person could achieve social immortality by being a good citizen—that is, by

> For the whole world is the sepulchre of famous men, and it is not the epitaph upon monuments set up in their own land that alone commemorates them, but also in lands not their own there abides in each breast an unwritten memorial of them, planted in the heart rather than graven on stone.
>
> Thucydides, *The Peloponnesian War*

performing actions directed toward the common good. Because the community remembers heroic acts, the hero achieves a renown that extends beyond his or her lifetime.

For those who sought more than symbolic immortality, assurances of happiness beyond death could be obtained by participating as an initiate in one of the mystery religions (any of various secret cults that offered religious experiences not provided by the official public religions). By dedicating themselves to rites prescribed by the priests of the mystery cult, initiates exchanged the grim picture of bloodless phantoms in the afterworld for the more promising one of an idyllic future in paradise.

Among the early Greek philosophers, most thought of life and death as aspects of an ever-changing, eternal flux. They typically believed that the soul was a vital principle that continued in some fashion after death but did not imagine it surviving as a distinct entity. If something of the "soul" continued beyond death, it merged with the stuff of the universe.

Later, Pythagoras taught that conduct during life determined the destiny of the soul after death. Through practicing discipline and purification, one could influence transmigration—that is, migration of the soul from one body or state to another in successive rounds of births and deaths—resulting in eventual union with the Divine or Universal Absolute. These beliefs drew upon the Orphic mystery religions of ancient Greece (dedicated to the hero Orpheus and emphasizing ideas about purification and the afterlife), which went back to the cult of Dionysus.

The idea that a person's conduct in this life somehow could influence existence in the afterlife contrasted with the predominant view of an indistinct immortality in which all human beings participated, regardless of their actions. Eventually, the beliefs of Pythagoras and his followers would be adopted in somewhat altered form during the pre-Christian era, and the relationship between righteous conduct and immortality would be further refined during the early centuries of Christianity.

> Speak not smoothly of death, I beseech you, O famous Odysseus. Better by far to remain on earth the thrall of another . . . rather than reign sole king in the realm of bodyless phantoms.
>
> Homer, *The Odyssey*

> He who has lived as a true philosopher has reason to be of good cheer when he is about to die, and that after death he may hope to receive the greatest good in the other world. . . . For I deem that the true disciple of philosophy . . . is ever pursuing death and dying; and if this is true, why, having had the desire of death all his life long, should he repine at the arrival of that which he has been always pursuing and desiring?
>
> Plato, *Phaedo*

With Socrates, there are further signs of the shift from a social immortality predicated on the life of the community to the possibility of personal survival after death. Precisely what Socrates believed is unclear, although he apparently favored the notion that the soul survives the death of the body. On his deathbed, he describes a sense of anticipation at the prospect of communion with the spirits of the great in the afterworld. In the *Apology,* however, he describes death as *either* eternal bliss *or* dreamless sleep. In the *Phaedo,* Plato advanced a number of "proofs" that the soul is eternal and is released from the body at death. The dualism of body and soul is emphasized, and their respective fates are distinguished: Because it is mortal, the body is subject to corruption; the soul is immortal and therefore not subject to death.

Christian Beliefs About the Afterlife

The principal insight of both Jewish and Christian thought has two main premises: first, "that human beings are creatures, composites of dust and God's animating breath," and second, "that they are created in the image and likeness of God, with a destiny—a royal dignity—that overtakes their finite status."[19] In the New Testament, writings about dying and death derive from Jewish traditions as interpreted in the light of Jesus' death and resurrection. The life, death, and resurrection of Jesus is the model of ultimate reality for Christians, a model realized through faith. Oscar Cullman wrote that only a person who takes death seriously *as death* is able to "comprehend the Easter exultation of the primitive Christian community and understand that the whole thinking of the New Testament is governed by belief in the Resurrection."[20] In using the phrase, "death as death," Cullman contrasts the Christian view of Resurrection with belief in immortality, which is "only a *negative* assertion: the soul does *not* die." Resurrection, however is "a *positive* assertion," in which the whole person, "who has really died, is recalled to life by a new act of creation by God."[21]

Boniface Ramsey expresses a similar view: "No matter how much the early Christians may have mourned their dead, and no matter how much they may have experienced some fear of death, nonetheless the basic attitude toward death was radically different from that of the pagans," whose views he describes as fatalistic, joyless, filled with despair and an irreparable sense of loss.[22]

> Behold, I show you a mystery: We shall not all sleep, but we shall all be changed. In a moment, in the twinkling of an eye, at the last trump: for the trumpet shall sound, and the dead shall be raised incorruptible, and we shall be changed. For this corruptible must put on incorruption, and this mortal must put on immortality. So when this corruptible shall have put on incorruption, and this mortal shall have put on immortality, then shall be brought to pass the saying that is written, Death is swallowed up in victory. O death, where is thy sting? O grave, where is thy victory?
>
> I Corinthians, 15

For early Christians like the Apostle Paul, death was vanquished by Christ's resurrection. "As Paul sees it, the Christian certainty of the life to come comes from the fact that the Christian's Savior is one who was dead and is alive again."[23] Resurrection is presented in Paul's writings as a special kind of bodily existence, but it also has a symbolic or spiritual meaning. The promise of immortality, which was implicit in the Hebrew scriptures, is defined in the Christian view as "personal and bodily resurrection from the dead."[24] Ignatius, an early father of the Church, called the Eucharist "medicine of immortality, an antidote against death."[25]

At the same time, the Greek understanding of body and soul was a persistent influence on early Christian thought. In this view, the soul is immortal; it is part of the human person that exists in a disembodied state after death. This understanding interacted richly with Hebrew thought during the formative years of Christianity. Milton Gatch says about this period,

> The notion of resurrection and of the restoration of an elect people continued to be prominent. But the idea of a disembodied afterlife for the soul was also current and led to the conception of some sort of afterlife between the separation and the reunion of soul and body. From a picture of death as the inauguration of a sleep which would last until the divinely instituted resurrection, there emerged a picture of death as the beginning of quiescence for the body and of a continued life for the soul, the nature of which remained more or less undefined.[26]

Gradually, Church doctrine began to accommodate the idea that an intermediate period of purification between death and resurrection provided for the removal of obstacles to "the full enjoyment of eternal union with God."[27]

This intermediate state came to be known as *purgatory*.[28] In the writings of Dante and Thomas Aquinas, earlier concepts of death, which focused on eventual resurrection of the body, are subordinated to a more pronounced emphasis on the soul's immortality after death. Jerry Walls says, "It is hard to exaggerate the long-term significance of [Dante's poem, *Purgatorio*] for the fortunes of the doctrine of purgatory."[29] Jacques Le Goff wrote that Dante not only "rescued Purgatory from the infernalization to which the Church subjected it in the thirteenth century," but also that he "more than anyone else made Purgatory the intermediate region of the other world."[30]

Anthony Thiselton expresses a prominent view: "The main focus in the New Testament lies not chiefly in the experience of the individual, but on the last great cosmos acts of God, namely, the Return of Christ (often called after

Foto Biblioteca Apostolica Vaticana

This scene from Dante's Divine Comedy shows the guide Charon ferrying worthy souls up the River Styx toward Paradise. Unable to reach the heavenly kingdom, the unworthy, immersed in the river, struggle in despair.

the Greek term the *Parousia*), the Last Judgment, and the resurrection of the dead, as well as what follows these "Last Things."[31] Carol Zaleski says,

> The classical Christian view, expressed in countless catechisms and confessions, is that upon death the souls of the blessed enter immediately into the divine presence, where they enjoy the unmediated vision of God, join in the angelic liturgy, and attend to the needs of the living who turn to them for intercession. . . . They await the return of Christ, the resurrection of the dead, and the renewal of all creation. Their bliss is perfect after its kind; but until the soul regains its body, and the whole body of Christ is complete in all its members, this perfection is, paradoxically, an unfinished work.[32]

The interplay between the concepts of resurrection and immortality is illustrated by two tombstone inscriptions from the colonial period found in a cemetery in New Haven, Connecticut.[33] On the first tombstone, the inscription reads, "Sleeping, but will someday meet her maker." The second is inscribed, "Gone to his eternal reward." Whereas the first inscription suggests an intermediate state of "soul-sleep" followed by resurrection of the body at some time in the future, the second inscription proposes the immortality of the soul, which continues to exist even though the body dies. The apparent contrast between these inscriptions is incongruous when you consider that these two individuals were married to each other and are buried side by side. Yet, one is "sleeping," while the other is "gone." In these tombstone inscriptions, we see a curious example of how contrasting ideas about the afterlife can coexist.

Indeed, both of these ideas about the afterlife can be found today, although comparatively few Christians believe in the literal "soul-sleep" of the dead or waiting until the end of the world before experiencing their heavenly reward. The predominant view is this:

> After death and the separation of the soul from the body through death, the bodiless and intermediate state of the soul follows; after the intermediate state of the soul, the resurrection and judgment; after the resurrection and judgment, two-fold eternity: *Paradise* or *Hell*.[34]

As for the nature of Paradise or Hell, figurative phraseology like "the heavenly Jerusalem" or "the great tribulation" is used to convey ideas about

Go Down, Death—A Funeral Sermon

Weep not, weep not,
She is not dead;
She's resting in the bosom of Jesus.
Heart-broken husband—weep no more;
Grief-stricken son—weep no more;
Left-lonesome daughter—weep no more;
She's only just gone home.

James Weldon Johnson

the *conditions* of souls after death rather than exact descriptions. As a "pilgrim people" poised between the ascension of Christ and the realization of the kingdom of God, Christians see themselves as part of a "narrative of hope" that dawned at the beginning of human history, a journey of faith in which death can be understood as "coming home."[35]

The Afterlife in Islamic Tradition

The third of the great religious traditions stemming from the patriarch Abraham is Islam. Like Judaism and Christianity, Islam shares the Semitic religious heritage of monotheism, God's revelation through the prophets, and accountability for one's actions at the Day of Judgment. *Islam* means "peace" or "submission" (peace comes from submission to transcendent reality, the Divine). A *Muslim* is an adherent of Islam—that is, a person who has submitted to and is at peace with God. The five main duties of Islam are declaration of faith, prayer five times a day, almsgiving, fasting from dawn to sunset during the sacred month of Ramadan, and a pilgrimage to Mecca.

The Islamic message came through Muhammad, who received his call to be a prophet in 610 CE, when he was about forty. It is recorded in the Qur'an (meaning "readings," and more familiarly spelled phonetically as *Koran* in the West). According to Muslims, the Qur'an "does not abrogate or nullify, but rather corrects the scriptures preserved by the Jewish and Christian communities."[36] Frithjof Schuon notes that the doctrine of Islam hangs on two statements: First, "There is no divinity (or reality) outside the only Divinity (or Absolute)" and, second, "Muhammad is the Envoy (the mouthpiece, intermediary, or manifestation)."[37]

A basic premise of Qur'anic teaching about death is that God determines the span of a person's life: "He creates man and also causes him to die."[38] After death, Allah (God) judges a person's conduct. The Book of Deeds, wherein are recorded good and bad actions, will be opened, and each person will be consigned to either everlasting bliss or everlasting torment. "For the Muslim, life on earth is the seedbed of an eternal future."[39]

The Islamic vision of the afterlife is both spiritual and physical.[40] "Since the Last Day will be accompanied by bodily resurrection," says John Esposito, "the pleasures of heaven and the pain of hell will be fully experienced."[41] Heaven is a paradise of "perpetual peace and bliss with flowing rivers, beautiful gardens, and the enjoyment of one's spouses (multiple marriage partners are permitted in Islam) and beautiful, dark-eyed female companions (*houris*)." The terrors of hell are described in equally physical terms.

> The happiness of the drop is to
> die in the river.
>
> Ghazal of Ghalib

Some Muslims believe that, after a person dies, "two black-faced, blue-eyed angels named Munkar and Nakir visit the grave and interrogate the deceased about his beliefs and deeds in life." Depending on the answers, the deceased is comforted or punished. Thus, "At a Muslim funeral a mourner may approach a corpse as it is about to be laid in the tomb and whisper instructions for answering these questions."[42] It is also believed by some Muslims that "no one should precede the corpse in the funeral procession because the angels of death go before it."[43]

When death nears, the dying person may be read passages from the Qur'an to help ensure a righteous state of mind and facilitate an easy release. After death, a ritual washing, or ablution, is done—except in the case of a martyr, in which case washing is not done "in order not to remove traces of blood which are the hallmark of his martyrdom."[44] The funeral should be conducted without elaborate ceremony, with the body wrapped in white cloth and laid in a simple, unmarked grave. No coffin comes between the body and the earth to which it returns. Some Muslims believe the grave should be deep enough for the dead person to sit up without his or her head appearing above ground when the time comes to answer questions at the Last Judgment. The grave is laid out on a north-south axis, with the deceased's face turned toward the East—that is, toward Mecca—so that it is symbolically in a state of prayer. Burial follows as soon as possible after death. On hearing of someone's death, it is customary to say, "Allah Karim": From God we came and to him we shall return.[45]

The goal of Muslims is to die in the knowledge that one has submitted to the transcendent reality and has passed the test of this life. The moment of death is considered a call to prayer. "The underlying belief is that one should and can take comfort knowing that life and death are in accord with God's will, that the soul returns to God, and that the community is supportive of the bereaved."[46]

Death and Immortality in Asian Religions

Western thought typically makes distinctions, points up contrasts, establishes differences. Experiences are analyzed as being *either* this *or* that. Life is the opposite of death, death is the enemy of life; life is "good"; death, "evil." In Asian cultures, by comparison, the characteristic mode of thought emphasizes the integrity of the whole rather than distinctions between constituent parts. Whereas Western thought distinguishes between "either/or," Eastern thought subsumes such distinctions within a holistic "both/and" approach.

This view of reality is reflected in sacred texts of the East. In Chinese tradition, for example, the *Book of Changes,* or *I Ching* (Yijing), one of the greatest literary works of Asia, postulates the basic circumstance of change in the universe; life and death are different manifestations of a constantly changing reality. As depicted in the symbol of the *Tao* (literally, "the way"; the process of nature by which all things change), the contrasting aspects of reality interpenetrate one another. Thus, death and life are not mutually exclusive opposites but, rather, complementary facets of an underlying process revealed in cycles of birth, decay, and death. Like a pendulum swinging through its arc, the completion of one cycle heralds the beginning of another. Chuang Tzu expressed the traditional Chinese attitude toward death as follows:

> Life and death are fated—constant as the succession of dark and dawn, a matter of Heaven. I received life because the time had come; I will lose it because the order of things passes on.[47]

Observing this process, the sages of the East developed the concept of reincarnation, or transmigration (the passing at death from one state of existence to another, or of the soul from one body to another). Some people understand this process in a physical way: "I will take birth in another body following the death of my present body." In other words, reincarnation implies a continuity of personal identity from incarnation to incarnation. Other people shun a materialistic understanding, adopting the view that there is, in fact, no "I" to be reborn. Something may indeed be carried over from one state to the next, but this "something" is impersonal, formless, and ineffable.

In China, Confucianism dealt with the external world of politics and social interactions, while Daoism addressed the inner world of spiritual exploration and transformation. By practicing various spiritual techniques, advanced practitioners were supposedly able to gradually purify and transmute their bodies, a transformative process that eliminated impurities and culminated in an immortal body.[48]

Hindu Teachings About Death and Rebirth

The terms *Hindu* and *Hinduism* refer to the beliefs, practices, and socioreligious institutions that developed from the civilization of the Indo-European-speaking peoples who settled in India in the last centuries of the second millennium BCE. In Hinduism, death has been called "the personification of time (*mahakala*) and the foundation of the cosmo-moral order (*dharma*)."[49] Among the distinguishing features of Hinduism is belief in transmigration of the soul. This is termed *samsara,* which refers to "wandering," "journeying" or "passing through" a series of incarnational experiences. What links these experiences is *karma,* which can be roughly defined as the moral law of cause and effect. The thoughts and actions of the past determine the present state of being; and, in turn, present choices influence future states. This karmic process pertains to the ever-changing flow of moment-to-moment experience as well as to successive rounds of deaths and rebirths. As each moment conditions the next, karma governs the reincarnational flow of being. In the *Bhagavad-Gita,* Krishna tells Arjuna,

> For death is a certainty for him who has been born,
> and birth is a certainty for him who has died.
> Therefore, for what is unavoidable thou shouldst not grieve.

In a commentary on this passage, Nikhilananda adds, "It is not proper to grieve for beings which are mere combinations of cause and effect."[50]

Los Angeles County Museum of Art

The cosmic dance of the Hindu deity Shiva, an ever-changing flow of creation and dissolution, embodies the fundamental equilibrium between life and death, the underlying reality behind appearances. As the Lord of the Dance, Shiva is portrayed with one foot on the demon of ignorance and poised for the next step.

Behind the apparent separateness of individual beings is a unitary reality. Just as the ocean is composed of innumerable drops of water, undifferentiated being manifests itself in human experience as apparently separate selves. "Underlying man's personality and animating it is a reservoir of being that never dies, is never exhausted, and is without limit in awareness and bliss. This infinite center of life, this hidden self or *Atman,* is no less than *Brahman,* the Godhead."[51]

Hinduism teaches that it is possible to free ourselves from the illusion of separate selfhood, with its attendant pain. Attachment to, or identification with, the concept of "self" as separate and distinct causes suffering in the present life and perpetuates the endless wheel of births and deaths, the wheel of karma. Liberation (*moksha*) from fate and the cycles of history involves the recognition that life and death are beyond such mistaken notions of self-identity. "The one who has attained *moksha* can see the eternal in the temporal and the temporal in the eternal."[52] The *Bhagavad-Gita* says,

> Worn-out garments are shed by the body:
> Worn-out bodies are shed by the dweller.

Nikhilananda says, "In the act of giving up the old body or entering into the new body, the real Self does not undergo any change whatsoever. . . . Brahman, through Its inscrutable *maya* (illusion), creates a body, identifies Itself with it, and regards Itself as an individual, or embodied, soul."[53]

Death is inescapable. What is born passes away (see Figure 14-1). Yet, for the person "whose consciousness has become stabilized by the insight that it is the very nature of things to come-to-be and pass-away," there is no "occasion either for rejoicing over birth or grieving over death."[54]

Hinduism offers various rites and practices that help in awakening to truth. For example, one practice involves imagining one's own death and the fate of the body, its return to elemental matter in the grave or on the funeral pyre. Another practice involves paying close attention to the transitory and ever-changing nature of one's own being, moment to moment. Other practices involve meditation in the presence of a dead body or at burial or cremation grounds. By consciously confronting mortality, one becomes reoriented toward the transcendent dimensions of reality. The aim is to let go of conditioned existence. This is "the death that conquers death."[55]

Day after day
some of those
who live on the earth
go to the house of death
and those who remain
hope to stay the same forever
what could be stranger.

Figure 14-1 *Mahābhārata*

The Buddhist Understanding of Death

Buddhism is named after the historical Buddha ("the awakened one"), Siddhartha Gautama, who taught in India around the sixth to fourth centuries BCE. Like Hinduism, Buddhist doctrine explains that the universe is the product of karma, and the goal is escape from the suffering of *samsara,* the cycle of births and deaths. The aim is *nirvana,* which means "extinction," as when a flame goes out when deprived of fuel. *Nirvana* is defined as an "unconditioned state beyond birth and death that is reached after all ignorance and craving have been extinguished and all karma, which is the cause of rebirth, has been dissolved."[56]

In this view, there is no "self" to survive after death or to be reborn. Everything is transitory and impermanent (*anicca*), in continual unease and unrest (*dukkha*), and substanceless (*anatta*). In the Buddhist view, karma is seen as the universal principle of causality that underlies the stream of "psychophysical" events. Dōgen, founder of the Soto Zen sect of Buddhism, says, "Life constantly changes, moment by moment, in each of its stages, whether we want it to or not. Without even a moment's pause our karma causes us to transmigrate continuously."[57]

This transmigration can be likened to impressing a seal onto wax, or to transferring energy in a game of billiards when the cue ball strikes the cluster of balls, creating new energy events. "Rebirth does not involve the transfer of a substance, but the continuation of a process."[58] Carl Becker says Buddha spoke of "rebirth, as opposed to the notion of reincarnation that might imply that a single soul was reincarnated in several consecutive bodies. Rebirth, on the other hand, suggests a causal continuity between one birth and the next without requiring that the two be identified as the same person."[59]

From the Buddhist perspective, it could be said that there are two kinds of death: continuous and regular. Continuous death is the "passing show" of phenomenal experience, constantly arising and passing away, moment by moment. Regular, or corporeal, death is the physical cessation of vital body functions at the end of a lifetime. "For the enlightened person, death happens; that is all. And one is in perfect accord with the event."[60]

Buddhist meditation is described as "in one sense a death rite, although it is seldom called that. Meditation practice is about sitting attentively on the abyss between life and death without clinging to life as if it were good or fleeing death as if it were bad."[61] Dōgen said, "The thorough clarification of the meaning of birth and death—this is the most important problem of all for Buddhists."[62]

> Thus shall you think of all this fleeting world:
> A star at dawn, a bubble in a stream;
> A flash of lightning in a summer cloud.
> A phantom, an illusion, a dream.
>
> Buddha, *The Diamond Sutra*

Skulls and skeletons are a common theme in Zen painting. Often humorous—sometimes shocking—these images lead both artist and viewer to contemplate the impermanent nature of material existence. In the Buddhist view, only when impermanence is directly confronted and deeply understood can freedom, bliss, and enlightenment become possible.

Bodhidharma Ink

Like Hinduism, Buddhism teaches that it is necessary to renounce the desires and cravings that maintain the delusion of a separate self. When all attachments are dropped, the incessant round of birth-decay-death is given no further fuel. How does one awaken to this reality, to nirvana? "Zen sects emphasize the need to prepare for death. Preparation means spiritual readiness, including the recognition that all things are impermanent."[63] Dōgen says, "Simply understand that birth and death are in themselves *nirvana*, there being no birth-death to be hated or *nirvana* to be desired. Then, for the first time you will be freed from birth and death."[64]

The paradox of Dōgen's statement about birth-death and the importance of using death as a means of awakening to truth is echoed in the words of Hakuin, who is known as the reviver of the Rinzai sect, the other great Zen Buddhist lineage in Japan.[65] For those who wish to investigate their true nature, Hakuin advised meditation on the word *shi*, the character for death. To do this, he suggested a *koan* (a teaching question): "After you are dead and cremated, where has the main character [the chief actor or one's "original face"] gone?" Hakuin wrote,

> Among all the teaching and instructions, the word *death* has the most unpleasant and disgusting connotations. Yet if you once suddenly penetrate this "death" koan, you will find that there is no more felicitous teaching than this instruction that serves as the key to the realm in which birth and death are transcended, where the place in which you stand is the Diamond indestructible, and where you have become a divine immortal, unaging and undying. The word *death* is the vital essential that the warrior must first determine for himself.

Dying well includes values of composure, living in the moment, and cultivating strength to die alone.[66] There is an emphasis on the importance of a calm and meditative mental state at the time of death, which is significant

Though it will die soon
The voice of the cicada
Shows no sign of this.

Bashō

not only because of transmigration of the consciousness but also more simply in terms of a "good death": one that is filled with peace rather than struggle and angst.[67]

The period immediately after death is considered an especially opportune time for gaining insight. The priest at a Buddhist funeral, for example, speaks directly to the deceased, expounding on the teachings that can awaken the intermediate being to the true nature of existence. Philip Kapleau says, "The funeral and subsequent services thus represent literally a 'once in a lifetime' opportunity to awaken the deceased and thereby liberate him from the binding chain of birth-and-death."[68]

It is important to recognize that, like most religions, Buddhism contains diverse practices and sects. In Japan alone, these include Shingon, founded by Kūkai (774–835); Jodo, founded by Hônen (1133–1212); Zen (Rinzai and Sōtō); Jôdo Shinshū (aka Shin Buddhism), founded by Shinran (1173–1262); and Nichiren (aka Nichirenshū), founded by Nichiren (1222–1282). Jôdo Shinshū ("True Pure Land School"), for example, is a form of Pure Land Buddhism, known as the "easy path," in which faith in the power of Amida Buddha and chanting of the *nembutsu* (the name of Amida) brings liberation.[69]

Despite differences between the various sects, virtually all perform funeral rites that assume a personal existence that continues after death. In

© Albert Lee Strickland

In the Japanese section of this cemetery on the island of Oahu, graves holding the ashes of deceased members of the community are ornamented with Buddhist symbols of the Wheel of Dharma and the Lotus.

doing so, they diverge from the teachings of Buddha. George Tanabe points out, "Śākyamuni [one of the titles of Buddha] taught the nonexistence of souls (*anātman*), and the absence of souls leaves nothing to commemorate after death."[70] He adds: "Human sentiments make the core elements of Japanese funerals resilient to the persuasions of orthodoxies. In the end, love and affection hold sway over both theory and practice."[71]

After-Death States in Tibetan Buddhism

According to W. Y. Evans-Wentz, "Buddhists and Hindus alike believe that the last thought at the moment of death determines the character of the next incarnation."[72] On this point, the Buddha said, "Rebirth arises from two causes: the last thought of the previous life as its governing principle and the actions of the previous life as its basis. The stopping of the last thought is known as decease; the appearance of the first thought as rebirth."[73] Scriptures like the *Bardo Thödol,* or *The Tibetan Book of the Dead,* as it is better known in the West, are meant to influence the thoughts of the dying person during the transitional period of life-death-rebirth. Indeed, the *Bardo Thödol* is also known as "The Book of Natural Liberation." Here is an excerpt:

> Listen carefully; be attentive and alert. Death has come to you. It is time for you to depart this world. While you must face this reality alone, know that you are not the only one, for death comes to all. Do not cling to life because of sentiment, and do not fear to go on. You do not have the power to stay.[74]

Although *bardo* is often interpreted as an intermediate or transitional state between death and rebirth, it can be translated as "gap" or "interval of suspension." In this sense, it refers to a number of "in between" or transitional conditions.[75] Chögyam Trungpa suggests that the term refers not only to the interval between death and rebirth but also to "suspension within the living situation."[76] The *Bardo Thödol* and similar texts are commonly read as a person is dying. (A similar practice occurs in the Hindu tradition, in which the *Bhagavad-Gita* is read.) Such texts can serve as a guide for the living as well as the dying. Chögyam Trungpa says that the *Bardo Thödol* deals with "the principle of birth and death recurring constantly in this life." Indeed, in this view, "The bardo experience is part of our basic psychological make-up."

The *Bardo Thödol* offers counsel about how to use these experiences—some terrifying, some benign—to awaken to a more enlightened incarnation. Although acknowledging that these experiences likely appear quite real to the bardo traveler, the text emphasizes that the deities or demons encountered are simply apparitions, the experiencer's own projections. They do not represent ultimate or transcendent perfection but, rather, steps on the way. (Some scholars believe, as Christopher Carr argues, that modern near-death experiences, or NDEs, "describe, at most, the beginning of death processes, whereas the Tibetan books of the dead describe entire death processes.")[77]

The Consolations of Religion

From the foregoing survey of beliefs about death and the afterlife in various traditions, it is clear that, for many people, if not most, religion offers pathways toward understanding and coping with dying and death. In this sense, the "religious culture of death" provides an interpretative framework within which to find a positive meaning in an otherwise negative or tragic event.[78] In stressful situations, religion enhances coping resources by fostering self-esteem and a sense of control through, for example, trust and faith in God.[79] Even in so-called secular societies, religion plays a significant role in attitudes and behaviors toward death (see Table 14-1).

According to Lucy Bregman, the death awareness movement has gained much from its connection with religion and spirituality. Bregman says,

> Spiritual beliefs and practices provide an interpretation of the dying process, aid in the developmental task of transcendence, and afford comfort to dying individuals and their family members.[80]

For dying patients and their families, religion may offer solace, suggest some meaning in dying, and provide rituals that help ease the pangs of grief. Vernon Reynolds and Ralph Tanner note that religion is concerned with "ministering to the dying person, preparing him or her for the world to come, generally being involved with his physical needs and psychological feelings at this time, and likewise helping those who are especially close."[81]

A significant theme in the work of W. E. B. Du Bois, a pioneering American sociologist of religion, is the insight that religious institutions do more than connect people with God; they connect people to one another.[82]

It is useful to distinguish between two related concepts: *religiosity* and *spirituality*. Although a partial definition of spirituality is "to be concerned with religious values," it is understood more broadly as a search for ultimate meaning and purpose in life, which may or may not be directly related to

TABLE 14-1 *Four Functions of Religion in Societies*

1. Religion provides a shared set of beliefs, values, and norms around which people can form a common identity. Thus, religion is a unifier, "the social glue that binds a group together by giving it a common set of values."
2. Religion provides answers to the "big questions" about human existence and purpose. It addresses issues of life and death, outlines the kind of life people are expected to lead, and explains what happens to them after they die.
3. Religion often provides a foundation for the norms and laws of a society. Laws acquire a moral as well as a legal force when they are embedded in religious values.
4. Religion is a source of emotional and psychological support to people, especially at times of crisis.

a particular religious tradition. "It entails connection to self-chosen and/or religious beliefs, values, and practices that give meaning to life, thereby inspiring and motivating individuals to achieve their optimal being."[83] It emphasizes "a personal search for connection with a larger sacredness" and "a bonding with others that cannot be severed, not even by death."[84]

The consolations of a religious or spiritual orientation are likely to depend on the manner in which that person makes such an orientation part of his or her life. For instance, the experience of someone who attends religious services mainly because they create opportunities for social interaction is likely to be very different from that of someone who participates because he or she finds deep personal meaning in religious creeds and beliefs. In this sense, religiosity embraces several dimensions, including these:[85]

1. Experiential religiosity (emotional ties to a religion)
2. Ritualistic religiosity (participation in religious ceremonies)
3. Ideological religiosity (religious commitment)
4. Consequential religiosity (degree to which religion is integrated into the person's daily life)
5. Intellectual religiosity (knowledge about the religion's traditions, beliefs, and practices)

Any or all of these dimensions can have an impact on how a person faces death and copes with loss. For example, a young Filipino American man whose father had died talked about the comfort he felt in connection with a funeral mass held in the church where his family worshipped. Commenting on the language and other symbols present in the service, he said, "You know, I've never thought much about what those prayers are about, but the soothing rhythms of the chants and the pungent smell of the incense caused me to feel that my dad is somehow still being cared for, that he's really okay." This young man's experience includes aspects of experiential, ritualistic, and consequential religiosity.

Secular Concepts of Immortality

"Mortality teaches us a lot about life, if we let it," says palliative care physician Ira Byock. "One thing it teaches is that human life is inherently spiritual, whether or not a person has a religion."[86]

In technology-oriented and economics-driven societies—both East and West—traditional religious and philosophical beliefs about the purpose of life or the nature of death no longer enjoy universal acceptance as they did when societies and communities were more cohesive. For many people, death has been divorced from religious and mythic connotations. *Secularization* is "the process in modern societies whereby religious ideas, practice, and organizations lose their influence in the face of scientific and other knowledge."[87] Traditional beliefs no longer carry the same weight in a social milieu that emphasizes rationalism and scientific method. Colin Murray Parkes says, "Secularism is essentially rational; it is the faith that we must rely on our reason in all matters, and that reason must take precedence over other ways of perceiving reality."[88] Theological or philosophical discussions about the afterlife may seem to resemble the famous debate about the number of dancing angels that will fit on the head of a pin. Yet, vestiges of traditional concepts about death and the afterlife remain part of our modern consciousness.

The Abrahamic religious traditions—Judaism, Christianity, and Islam—present a linear picture of human history, describing a progression of events that begins with creation and eventuates in the resolution of the cosmic story at the end of time. Such an orientation leads to an interest in *eschatologies*—that is, pictures of the ultimate state, doctrines of last things. From the wellsprings of the Judeo-Christian tradition and Greek thought, people in Western culture have predominantly framed their beliefs about the afterlife in a historical context oriented toward the future. The predominant viewpoint in Western culture is that human beings live a single life; that the soul survives death, perhaps in a disembodied state; that at some future time each soul will be judged; and that, depending on one's conduct during earthly existence, the aftermath will be either hellish torment or heavenly bliss. This view is challenged by modern ways of thinking about human existence and death.

Among the most influential secular alternatives to religious orientations are humanism, positivism, and existentialism. *Humanism* (a doctrine, attitude, or way of life centered on human interests or values) emphasizes human intellectual and cultural achievements rather than divine intervention and the supernaturalism of religion.[89] It tends to reflect an antireligious, even atheistic, stance in which human beings are the measure of all things. *Positivism,* a school of thought associated with science, reflects the belief that religious or metaphysical modes of knowing are imperfect and that "positive knowledge" is based on what can be directly observed in nature and in human activities. *Existentialism* is an intellectual and artistic movement that also influences secular attitudes about life and death. In its inquiry into the meaning of human experience, existentialism disavows the comforting answers offered by religion or social convention. Instead, it focuses squarely on our individual responsibility for making choices that define who we are and what we will become. The "human predicament" is such that we cannot shirk our responsibility for making difficult but crucial choices that shape our existence. According to Kenneth McLeish,

> We are self-creating creatures: we can choose what we want to be, and choose to be it. The moment of choice, the leap into existence, comes between two fixed points: the nothingness from which we come and the nothingness to which we return after we die. Our glory is the self-defining choice; our agony is that we need to make it.[90]

It is not unusual for a person to hold several competing worldviews at the same time, perhaps combining elements of religious faith carried over from childhood with elements of the viewpoints and attitudes represented by one or more of the secular alternatives just discussed.

Secular, or nonreligious, responses to questions about survival after death often reflect ideas about some kind of *symbolic immortality*.[91] These ideas include the biological continuity that results from having children who sustain a person's genetic legacy through succeeding generations, thus conferring a kind of personal immortality. Other "children" that symbolically convey personal immortality include those produced through creative works of art, contributions to a field of knowledge, and even heroic or helpful deeds. A person who has arranged for his or her body to be donated after death for the purpose of medical research gains a kind of "medical immortality" through training new physicians or advancing medical science. The fact that we are all members of one human race means that the good things we do and our contributions to the welfare of others extend beyond our deaths, thereby conferring a kind of "communal immortality" as our good deeds continue to resonate with a positive influence on humankind.

Today, despite the option of unbelief, most people in the United States affirm belief in God. Nearly 80 percent say they believe in life after death.[92] Researchers note that images of what the afterlife might be like generally involve union with God, peace and tranquility, and reunion with relatives.[93] One study of college undergraduates found that more than 90 percent believe that "one is reunited with family and friends, that the afterlife is comforting, that there is Heaven, and that the transition is peaceful."[94] It is apparent that religious ideas continue to play a role in both personal and social thought.

Although the assurances of religion can be comforting, Simone Weil presents a complementary approach:

> Not to believe in the immortality of the soul, but to look upon the whole of life as destined to prepare for the moment of death; not to believe in God, but to love the universe, always, even in the throes of anguish, as a home—there lies the road toward faith by way of atheism. This is the same faith as that which shines resplendent in religious symbols.[95]

The Roman Stoic, Marcus Aurelius, who lived in the second century of the present era, expressed similar thoughts. "The constant recollection of death," he said, "is the test of human conduct."[96]

Questions about immortality and "life after death" engage our thoughts. When religious answers do not suffice, a search for scientific proof of "something beyond" ensues. The search for satisfying answers about what lies beyond death is illustrated by widespread interest in near-death experiences.

Near-Death Experiences: At the Threshold of Death

Stories of travel to other worlds can be found in virtually all cultures. The traveler may be a hero, a shaman, a prophet, a king, or even an ordinary mortal who passes through the gates of death and returns with a message for the living. Examples of such journeys include the heavenly ascent of the prophet Muhammad and the heavenly visions of Enoch and the Apostle Paul, as well as Odysseus's and Gilgamesh's epic adventures to the underworld, and the descent of the goddess Inanna.

Carol Zaleski identifies three forms of the *otherworld* journey: (1) the journey to the underworld, (2) the ascent to higher worlds, and (3) the fantastic voyage.[97] The common thread of all such journeys, says Zaleski, is the "story," which is shaped not only by what appear to be universal laws of symbolic experience but also by the experiences of a given culture. Belief in a future life was historically based on religious experience; today, near-death experiences are often cited by people as a reason for such belief.[98] *Near-death experiences (NDEs)* are "profound psychological events with transcendental and mystical elements, typically occurring to individuals close to death or in situations of intense physical or emotional danger."[99]

The publication in 1975 of Raymond Moody's *Life After Life* sparked the current interest in otherworld journeys and, more specifically, in near-death experiences. These accounts by individuals who have come back from the edge of death provide fascinating glimpses into a paranormal, or scientifically unexplainable, order of existence that seemingly transcends the limits of biological life. Some people view NDEs as proof that the human personality survives death. Others assign psychological or neurophysiological causes to NDEs, describing them as naturalistic responses to the stress of facing a life-threatening danger. What are the components of a typical near-death experience?

NDEs: A Composite Picture

Suppose, in a horrific accident or acute medical crisis, you find yourself suddenly faced by an overwhelming encounter with death. Perhaps, almost beyond awareness, you begin to realize you're not going to make it; you're going to die.

It's like a dream, yet the experience seems more real than ordinary waking consciousness. Your vision and hearing are extremely acute. Sensory perceptions are heightened, and your thought processes are vividly clear, rational. Somehow, you are no longer bound to your body. Becoming aware of this feeling of disconnectedness, you realize that you are, in fact, separate from the body, floating free, as you look down at the mangled or suffering body and recognize it as your own.

You may feel a bit lonely, drifting in space, although there is a pervasive sense of calm, a serenity that was rarely if ever experienced in the body. The constraints of time and space seem irrelevant, unreal. As you move away from the once-familiar world of the now-dead body, you enter a darkness, a tunnel, a transitional stage in your journey.

Now you notice a light, more brilliant than could have been imagined during your earthly existence. It beckons, drawing you onward, its golden hues heralding your approach to the other side. The whole of your life is experienced in a nearly instantaneous matrix of flashbacks, impressions of your prior life, events, places, people: your life reviewed and projected on the transparent screen of consciousness.

As you begin to enter the light, you glimpse a world of unimaginable and unspeakable brilliance and beauty. Someone is greeting you, perhaps a loved one, or perhaps you become aware of Jesus or Moses or Muhammad or another being of ineffable grace. But now you realize that you cannot enter fully into the light, not yet, not this time.

Dimensions of Near-Death Experiences

Many people emerge from a near-death experience with a greater appreciation of life, a determination to make better use of the opportunities presented to them. Often, they are more self-confident, more able to cope with the difficulties of life. Relationships become more important and material comforts less important. NDE researcher Kenneth Ring says the typical near-death experiencer "has achieved a sense of what is important in life and strives to live in accordance with his understanding of what matters."[100] Near-death experiencers report dramatic reductions in death anxiety and fear of death, which leads to altered life goals and values and to enhanced health, well-being, tranquility, and zest for life.[101] People who experience NDEs exhibit many features associated with the "conversion" stories of life-changing religious experiences.

In outline, our imaginary NDE is typical of reports by those who have actually had such experiences. Four core elements have been identified as characteristic of NDEs: The person (1) hears the news of his or her death, (2) departs from the body, (3) encounters significant others, and (4) returns to the body. However, this "typical" NDE is experienced variously by different individuals. In one sample, only about 33 percent of respondents experienced themselves as separate from their bodies, 23 percent experienced the entry into a dark tunnel or transitional stage, 16 percent experienced seeing a bright light, and 10 percent experienced themselves as actually entering the light (though only for a "peek" into the unearthly surroundings). Ring found that NDEs resulting from illness were more likely to be complete—to have all of these characteristic core elements—than were NDEs resulting from accidents. Over half of the NDEs related to accidents, however, included an experience of *panoramic memory,* or life review, compared to only 16 percent of those whose NDE was related to illness or attempted suicide.

Life review, in itself a fascinating feature of NDEs, usually consists of vivid and almost instantaneous visions of the person's whole life or "selected highlights" of it.[102] The life review may appear in an orderly sequence, or it may happen "all at once." Either way, it apparently occurs without any conscious control or effort on the part of the experiencer. Life "review" may include visions of the future, with experiencers visualizing their death, the reactions of friends and relatives, and events at the funeral.

The encounter with a presence—a feature of NDEs typically related to the "tunnel" experience—usually involves seeing deceased relatives or friends or sensing a religious figure. This presence has often been understood as a

Palace of the Doges, Venice

In Hieronymus Bosch's portrayal of the Ascent into the Empyrean—the highest heaven in medieval cosmology—the soul, purged of its impurities, approaches the end of its long journey and union with the Divine.

representation of the "higher self," but this is not always the case.[103] William Serdahely describes an eight-year-old boy who was "comforted by two of his family's pets who had died prior to the incident."[104] These encounters with a presence are sometimes linked to the decision to return, to terminate the NDE. Some experiencers believe that the decision to return to earthly life is made for them; others report that they arrived at this decision themselves. Usually, the decision to return relates in some way to unfinished business or to responsibilities that the person must attend to before his or her death.

The majority of NDEs are characterized by feelings of joy, peace, and cosmic unity, but some are distressing and frightening.[105] These "hellish" NDEs may include imagery and sounds of torment, as well as demonic beings. An initial period of terror is, in some instances, followed by peaceful resolution. In other cases, the aftermath of the NDE brings a sense of emptiness and despair. In yet other instances, a benevolent guide accompanies the experiencer through the disconcerting experience. Some scholars think that hellish NDEs may be a truncated version of the typically radiant NDE; that is, hellish NDEs are *incomplete* NDEs. Another explanation highlights the fact that many saintly persons and mystics—St. Teresa of Avila and St. John of the Cross, to name two examples—reported frightening visions while engaged in deep prayer or meditation. A hellish NDE could therefore be a "purification experience," a kind of "dark night of the soul," as St. John of the Cross described his distressing religious experiences. What are we to make of near-death experiences? How should they be interpreted?

Interpreting Near-Death Experiences

Near-death experiences are fascinating. To some they suggest (or confirm) hoped-for possibilities of an afterlife or immortality. Others view near-death experiences as some sort of psychological phenomenon that may tell us something about the nature of human consciousness. To those who hold this view, NDEs are not "glimpses into a world beyond, but insights into the world within the human mind."[106] To still others, NDEs are related to psychodynamic processes that occur when the self is threatened by annihilation. NDEs are initiated in the presence of a belief that one is dying—whether or not one is in fact close to death.[107] Some of the theories devised to explain near-death experiences are listed in Table 14-2.[108]

For early Hawaiians, observations of *apparent* death, or persons who had "left the body prematurely," were interpreted in accordance with their beliefs about the ancestor-gods.[109] On each island, there was a special promontory overlooking the sea; this was the *leina,* or leaping place, of the soul or spirit on its journey to the realm of the ancestors. If, on its way to the leina, a soul was met by an ancestor-god and sent back, the body would revive. Otherwise, the ancestor-god would lead it safely to and over the leina; once beyond that hurdle, the soul was safe with the ancestors.

For various reasons (often, though not always, having to do with a person's behavior), an ancestor-god might delay a soul's acceptance into eternity. For instance, if a person died before his or her earthly work was done, the

TABLE 14-2 *Theories of the Near-Death Experience*

1. Neuropsychological theories:
   - A. *Temporal lobe paroxysm,* or limbic lobe syndrome: Seizurelike neural discharges in the temporal lobe or, more generally, in the limbic system.
   - B. *Cerebral anoxia,* or oxygen deprivation: Shortage of oxygen in the brain.
   - C. *Endorphin release:* Release of certain neurotransmitters associated with analgesic (pain-killing) effects and a sense of psychological well-being.
   - D. *Massive cortical disinhibition:* Loss of control over the random activity of the central nervous system.
   - E. *False sight:* Hallucinatory imagery arising from structures in the brain and nervous system.
   - F. *Drugs:* Side effects.
   - G. *Sensory deprivation.*
2. Psychological theories:
   - A. *Depersonalization:* Psychological detachment from one's body; in this case, a defensive reaction to the perceived threat of death. May be accompanied by hyperalertness.
   - B. *Motivated fantasy:* A type of "defensive" fantasy that basically proposes that experiencers have an impression of surviving death because they desire to survive death.
   - C. *Archetypes:* Images associated with various elements of the near-death experience are "wired" into the brain as mythological archetypes of our common humanity.
3. Metaphysical theories:
   - A. *Soul travel:* Transitional journey of the soul or spirit to another mode of existence or realm of reality (e.g., "heaven"); proof of life after death.
   - B. *Psychic vision:* Glimpses into another mode of reality, though not necessarily providing proof of soul-survival after death.

ancestor-god conducted the soul back to the body. "Sometimes when it is not yet time to die," reports Mary Pukui, "the relatives [ancestors] stand in the road and make you go back. Then the breath returns to the body with a crowing sound, *o'o-a-moa.*"[110]

Albert Heim, a Swiss geologist and mountain climber, is thought to have been the first to systematically gather data on NDEs.[111] During the early part of the twentieth century, Heim interviewed some thirty skiers and climbers who had been involved in accidents resulting in paranormal experiences. Heim's subjects experienced such phenomena as detachment from their bodies and panoramic memory, or life review.

The data compiled by Heim were subsequently reviewed by psychoanalytic pioneer Oskar Pfister, who explained NDEs as being caused by shock and depersonalization in the face of impending death. In other words, when a person's life is threatened, psychological defense mechanisms may come into play, giving rise to the phenomena associated with NDEs. Pfister's interpretation continues to be elaborated by present-day researchers who believe NDEs can be explained without resorting to the hypothesis that they prove life after death.

According to Russell Noyes and Roy Kletti, when the self is confronted by mortal danger, defensive reactions may result in a sense of depersonalization.[112]

Their model, which may be the most comprehensive psychological explanation of NDEs offered thus far, distinguishes three stages in the typical near-death experience: (1) resistance, (2) life review, and (3) transcendence. The first stage, *resistance,* includes the processes of recognizing the danger, struggling against it, and finally accepting death as imminent. Such acceptance, or surrender, marks the beginning of the second stage, which is characterized by *life review.* As the self detaches from its bodily representation, panoramic memories occur and appear to encompass a person's whole life. Life review is often accompanied by affirmation of the meaning of one's existence and its integration into the universal order of things. The third stage, *transcendence,* occurs as there is further detachment from one's individual existence. It is characterized by an increasingly transcendental, or cosmic, consciousness that replaces limited ego- or self-identity.

Calm detachment, heightened sensory awareness, life review or panoramic memory, and mystical consciousness are all phenomena associated with the ego's protective response to the possibility of its own demise. In other words, the threat of death stimulates various psychological processes that allow the ego, or experiencing self, to "escape" the threat. Because these processes dissociate the experiencing self from the body, death is perceived as a threat only to the *body,* not to the perceiving "self." It is important to notice that a psychological interpretation of NDEs does not necessarily invalidate any possible spiritual meaning that may be associated with NDEs.

In seeking the meaning of NDEs, some researchers follow the lines of inquiry founded in the late nineteenth century by parapsychologists. To adequately understand NDEs, these researchers say, one must go beyond the usual boundaries of scientific inquiry. In short, we must be prepared to accept the possibility, which is not scientifically verifiable, that NDEs are in fact what they seem to be—that is, valid experiences of states of consciousness that transcend the death of the body. In this view, NDEs teach us that the *appearance* of death is not the same as the *experience* of death. In conducting cross-cultural studies of near-death experiences, Karlis Osis and Erlendur Haraldsson concluded that the evidence strongly suggests life after death.[113] They reported that "neither medical, nor psychological, nor cultural conditioning can explain away deathbed visions." Supporting this conclusion is the observation that some deathbed visions include apparitions contrary to the experiencer's expectations, such as "apparitions of persons the person thought were still living, but who in fact were dead," as well as apparitions that do not conform to cultural stereotypes, as with dying children who are "surprised to see 'angels' without wings." The idea that NDEs strongly suggest, or even prove, that there is life after death seems to resonate with many people. In national surveys, most adult Americans answer yes to the question, Do you believe in life after death?[114]

In summary, then, two distinct explanations have been offered to explain near-death experiences. In the first, NDEs offer proof of survival after death. NDEs are what they appear to be: experiences of life after death. In the second explanation, NDEs are a response to the threat of death and destruction of the self. This response focuses on the brain or nervous system and results from an ego-defensive reaction to a life-threatening situation.

Each explanation offers a model, or representation, of "how the world works." Louis Appleby, writing in the *British Medical Journal,* says that the explanations put forward to explain NDEs share one attribute: Each requires a form of faith.[115] The explanation that best suits your own perception of how things work is likely to be accepted most readily. There remains, however, another approach to interpreting the significance of near-death experiences. Perhaps both of the explanations are valid: There is life after death, and there is also a psychological phenomenon involving various defense mechanisms whereby the personality is radically altered as the transition from one state to the next is negotiated. In Carol Zaleski's view, "We need to find a middle path between the extremes of dismissing near-death experience as 'nothing but' and embracing it as 'proof.'"[116]

Raymond Moody, who coined the term *near-death experiences,* now prefers to characterize NDEs as part of a "paranormal death syndrome," which includes apparitions of "death-bed escorts" frequently reported by individuals who are near death.[117] Concerning the way his findings about NDEs have been interpreted over the years, Moody is disturbed when people discuss NDEs as if they provide scientific evidence or proof of life after death. The prospect of finding scientific proof of life after death is, he says, "unthinkable." To Moody, NDEs represent a "wading out collectively into a domain of experience that has been closed for the most part to us until the past few decades and which is now opening up due to the developments and techniques of cardiopulmonary resuscitation." People who have experienced NDEs and shared their stories are enabling us all "to move across a frontier of consciousness."

On the subject of how best to interpret NDEs, Herman Feifel's remarks are pertinent:

> What is somewhat disquieting is the claim by some that near-death experiences are evidence for and proof of the existence of an after-life. There may well be life after death, but jumping to that conclusion from reported near-death experiences reflects more a leap of faith than judicious scientific assessment. This in no way minimizes the reality of these occurrences for the people who declare them. I just think that in weighing the evidence in this area we have less far-fetched and more parsimonious interpretations within the canons of science that can explain these phenomena. What strikes me about many of these out-of-body reports is the hunger for meaning and purpose they suggest in this age of faltering faith.[118]

Robert Kastenbaum cautions us to be careful about readily accepting the "fantastic voyage" implied by most life-after-death accounts.[119] He says,

> The happily-ever-after theme threatens to draw attention away from the actual situations of the dying persons, their loved ones, and their care givers over the days, weeks, and months preceding death. What happens up to the point of the fabulous transition from life to death recedes into the background. This could not be more unfortunate. The background, after all, is where these people are actually living until death comes.

Finally, we should consider three points expressed by Charles Garfield, who has worked extensively with dying patients:[120]

1. Not everyone dies a blissful, accepting death.
2. Context is a powerful variable in altered-state experiences. A supportive environment for the dying person may be an important factor in determining whether the outcome is a positive altered-state experience for the dying.
3. The "happily ever after" stance toward death may represent a form of denial when what is really needed by the dying person is a demonstration of real concern and real caring in his or her present experience.

Whatever beliefs one may hold about life after death, Garfield says, "Let us have the courage to realize that death often will be a bitter pill to swallow."

Death Themes in Dreams and Psychedelic Experiences

Fascinating "hints" about afterlife possibilities have also been conveyed through "death dreams" and experiences with psychedelic or mind-altering drugs. "Dreams offer a vivid illustration of our lifelong awareness of death, giving voice to the unconscious fears, wishes, and desires that surround the brute fact of human finitude."[121]

Marie-Louise von Franz says that, compared to near-death experiences, which tend to be schematic and more culture bound, the death imagery in dreams is richer in graphic detail and more subtle.[122] Among older people, dreams often appear to be psychically preparing them for impending death by symbolically indicating "the end of bodily life and the explicit continuation of psychic life after death." Using the medium of dreams, the unconscious communicates a comforting message—namely, that there *is* an afterlife.

> All of the dreams of people who are facing death indicate that the unconscious . . . prepares consciousness not for a definite end but for a profound transformation and for a kind of continuation of the life process which, however, is unimaginable to everyday consciousness.[123]

Death dreams incorporate a great variety of alchemical and mythological motifs, including themes associated with the growth of vegetation or flowering plants; the divine marriage of the soul with the cosmos; travel through a dark, narrow passageway, or through fire or water, to new birth; sacrifice or transformation of the old body; shifting ego- or soul-identity; and resurrection.

The journey through a dark passageway toward "a light at the end of the tunnel" is a common motif not only in dreams and NDEs but in numerous mythological traditions. Indeed, many mythologies embody a comparison of the sun's path with the mystery of life and death. Among Egyptians, for example, the sun was viewed as the goal of the soul's journey along the pathway of the dead. The sun symbolizes the source of *awareness,* of becoming conscious. Franz says, "This also lies behind the widespread custom of lighting candles

British Museum

The Egyptian papyrus of Hunefer depicts the Hall of Judgment and the Great Balance, where the deceased's soul is weighed against the feather of truth. Beneath the scales, the Devourer of Souls awaits the unjust while Horus is ready to lead the just to Osiris, the lord of the underworld, and to a pleasurable afterlife.

and letting them burn in mortuary rooms and on tombs and graves," which is a form of "analogy magic through which new life and an awakening to new consciousness is granted to the deceased."[124]

Turning to death imagery in connection with the use of psychedelic drugs, it is interesting to note that, although LSD (lysergic acid diethylamide) was first synthesized in 1938 by the Swiss chemist Albert Hoffman, its biochemical action on the brain is still not completely understood.[125] Nevertheless, its amplifying and catalyzing effects on the mind are well documented. From the earliest studies of LSD, researchers noticed that it activates "unconscious material from deep levels of the personality."[126] It apparently opens up areas of religious and spiritual experience that are intrinsic to the human personality but independent of a person's cultural or religious background. Most notably, it often leads to a "shattering encounter" with critical aspects of human existence: birth, decay, and death.

In the early 1960s, Eric Kast of the Chicago Medical School began studies of the pain-relieving effects of LSD and other psychedelic substances on patients who were suffering intense pain from a life-threatening illness.[127] Besides relieving the symptoms of physical pain and discomfort, LSD therapy diminished emotional symptoms, such as depression, anxiety, tension, insomnia, and psychological withdrawal. LSD seemed to accomplish these results by altering the patient's learned response to pain—that is, the patient's anticipation of pain based on past experiences. By becoming free of this conditioning, the patient was more oriented to the present and thus able to respond to sensations as they were actually experienced rather than to an image of pain that had grown more and more distressing over time. Noting that pain is a composite phenomenon that has both a neurophysiological component (the pain sensation) and a psychological component (the pain affect), Stanislav Grof and Joan Halifax conclude that the primary influence of psychedelic therapy seems to be in modifying the psychological component.

Perhaps more significant than diminution of pain was a change of attitude toward death and dying among patients. After the psychedelic session, patients typically displayed a diminished fear of death and less anxiety about the life-threatening implications of the illness. According to Grof and Halifax, "Dying persons who had transcendental experiences developed a deep belief in the ultimate unity of all creation; they often experienced themselves as integral parts of it, including their disease and the often painful situations they were facing."[128]

Many patients exhibited a greater responsiveness to their families and their environment. Self-respect and morale were enhanced, and they showed greater appreciation of the subtleties of everyday life. The fact that such transcendental experiences were induced in randomly selected subjects was considered to be strong evidence that "matrices for such experiences exist in the unconscious as a normal constituent of the human personality."[129] (Although the consensus among researchers was that there was enough positive evidence

Now Let the Weeping Cease (Hymn)

Now let the weeping cease
Let no one mourn again
The love of God will bring you
 peace
There is no end

The Gospel at Colonus

to justify continued research with LSD for therapeutic purposes such as pain relief, the "religious fervor of casual users and their calls for social revolution evoked a backlash that transformed LSD into a pariah substance and triggered laws that made its use in any context illegal.")[130]

As with the phenomena discussed in connection with NDEs, the psychedelic experience typically includes phenomena that are not scientifically explainable. Grof and Halifax point out that persons "unsophisticated in anthropology and mythology experience images, episodes, and even entire thematic sequences that bear a striking resemblance to the descriptions of the posthumous journey of the soul and the death-rebirth mysteries of various cultures."[131] As with NDEs, the result is usually a significantly altered outlook with respect to the meaning of life and death. The evidence accumulated through reports of near-death experiences, as well as psychedelic experiences, has led some researchers to the view that modern science should broaden its perspective on the nature of human consciousness. Stanislav Grof says, "Reality is always larger and more complex than the most elaborate and encompassing theory."[132]

Beliefs About Death: A Wall or a Door?

One writer comments, "Despite myths of an afterlife, the promises of sacred texts, and the hopes of the faithful, none of us really knows *what* continues, and if it does, *where* it goes or *how* it gets there."[133] In the last analysis, then, what shall we believe about personal immortality or the afterlife? Can we anticipate an ultimately fulfilling experience after death, as seems to be true from reports of near-death experiences? Or are such experiences merely psychological projections, wish-fulfilling fantasies that mask the terror of confronting one's own demise? Furthermore, what shall we say about various religious understandings? Do their concepts of the afterlife have some basis in reality? Or should we adopt a strictly scientific approach to such questions? Two basic philosophical views about death and the afterlife can be summarized as follows: Death is either a *wall* or a *door.*[134]

We can imagine many variations on these two positions regarding what happens at death. Indeed, the doctrines of the various religions and the explanations offered for paranormal experiences are just such variations. For example, stating a Christian perspective, we could say that death appears to be a wall, but at some time in the future—at the Resurrection—it will turn out to have been a door. The Hindu concept of reincarnation would suggest that death is a door, not a wall. Buddhists might respond that death is both a door and a wall, and it is neither. A standard psychological explanation of NDEs might support the view that death is a wall that is experienced as a door. Or perhaps the door and the wall are simply alternative ways of experiencing the same reality.

In the end, a statement made by the International Work Group on Death, Dying and Bereavement may be our best guide: "Dying is more than a biological occurrence. It is a human, social, and spiritual event, [but] too often the spiritual dimension of patients is neglected."[135] A close relationship between religion and health has existed since ancient times. Caregivers need to recognize and acknowledge the spiritual component of patient care. Appropriate resources should be offered to those who wish them. Each person's spiritual beliefs and preferences are to be respected.[136]

What we believe about death and the afterlife can influence the actions taken when we or others near death. If we have a materialist view, seeing death as a wall, we may insist that life-sustaining efforts be carried out to the end. Conversely, if we believe in continued existence after death, we may prefer to spend our final hours on earth in preparation for a transition into another mode of existence. Similarly, a bereaved person may find solace in his or her belief about what lies beyond death. The person who views death as the end may be reassured that the suffering of a loved one truly ends at death. Another person finds comfort in believing that the personality survives physical death. By understanding our own beliefs about death, we are able to "care more adequately for each other when death—wall or door—comes to those we love."[137]

Further Readings

John Bowker. *The Meanings of Death.* New York: Cambridge University Press, 1991.

Ben Bradley, Fred Feldman, and Jens Johansson, eds. *The Oxford Handbook of Philosophy of Death.* New York: Oxford University Press, 2012.

David Chidester. *Patterns of Transcendence: Religion, Death, and Dying.* 2nd ed. Belmont, Calif.: Wadsworth, 2002.

Kathleen Garces-Foley, ed. *Death and Religion in a Changing World.* Armonk, N.Y.: M. E. Sharpe, 2006.

Alister E. McGrath. *A Brief History of Heaven.* Malden, Mass.: Blackwell, 2003.

Samuel Scheffler. *Death and the Afterlife.* New York: Oxford University Press, 2013.

Alan F. Segal. *Life After Death: A History of the Afterlife in the Religions of the West.* New York: Doubleday, 2004.

Gregory Shushan. *Conceptions of the Afterlife in Early Civilizations: Universalism, Constructivism, and Near-Death Experience.* New York: Continuum, 2009.

Jane Idelman Smith and Yvonne Yazbeck Haddad. *The Islamic Understanding of Death and Resurrection*. New York: Oxford University Press, 2002.

Jacqueline I. Stone and Mariko Namba Walter, eds. *Death and the Afterlife in Japanese Buddhism*. Honolulu: University of Hawaii Press, 2008.

Richard P. Taylor. *Death and the Afterlife: A Cultural Encyclopedia*. Santa Barbara, Calif.: ABC-CLIO, 2000.

Jerry L. Walls. *Purgatory: The Logic of Total Transformation*. Oxford: Oxford University Press, 2012.

Additional resources for this chapter can be found at www.mhhe.com/despelder10e

© Albert Lee Strickland

The path ahead at times may appear to be clearly marked. Looking ahead, however, the final destination is not so evident. What lies in the distance, around the next bend? The personal and social choices about dying and death are like walking a pathway on which our steps into the immediate future may seem obvious, but it is not always clear what choices lie ahead.

CHAPTER 15

The Path Ahead: Personal and Social Choices

A Chinese folk tale, "The Mortal King," draws attention to the fact that the desire for immortality has its own pitfalls.[1] Surveying his realm one day, a king is struck by the awesome thought that someday he will die and lose it all. "I wish we could live forever!" he says. "That would be wonderful!" Encouraged by his friends, the king fantasizes how great it would be if they were never to grow old and die. Of all his companions, only one refrains from delighting in this prospect. Instead, he bows to the king and explains, "If we all lived forever as you suggest, why, then, all the great heroes of history would still live among us; compared to them, we would be fit only to plow the fields or be clerks in the provinces."

Does this Chinese folk tale have meaning for us? Acknowledging a place for death in our lives can awaken us to the preciousness of life. In the Japanese classic, *The Tale of Genji*, the phrase *mono no aware* is generally translated as "the sorrow of human existence," but Donald Keene points out that it might be better translated as "a sensitivity to things"; that is, as a recognition of the perishability of beauty and human happiness.[2]

In previous chapters, we have seen many different attitudes toward death and dying. In our relationship with death, we are both survivors and experiencers. One student said, "Confronting death has put me in touch with life."

Think about your own relationship to death. What place does death have in your life? What kinds of meanings does death hold for you? Are death and dying compartmentalized in a category all their own, or are they woven into the fabric of your experience?

Reflecting on the study of death and dying, a student remarked, "The thought of death had always created a lot of fear; now I find something fascinating about exploring my own feelings about death and the way that society relates to death." Another student said, "I see now what a big part denial and mutual pretense played in my family's experience of death; the subject of death has *really* been taboo."

As you think about the various topics covered in this book, what do you notice concerning your understanding of death? Has learning about death and dying changed your attitudes toward death? Has it expanded your perspectives? Do the terms *death* and *dying* elicit the same thoughts and emotions as when you first began your study?

Death is the ultimate challenge to human vanity or pretension. "In the last analysis," says sociologist David Clark, "human societies are merely men and women banded together in the face of death."[3] Death may be devalued, even denied for a time, but it cannot be eluded.

Exploring Death and Dying

"When I thought about my own death," a student remarked, "I slammed the door, thinking of all the things I still want to do in my lifetime. Now, I've become a bit more calm, a bit more balanced about it." Another said, "Before I got involved in studying death, I wasn't really down with it, especially my own death, even though I haven't had many personal encounters with death. Now I feel that facing my own death is not as difficult, really, as being a survivor of other people's deaths."

For some, investigation of death and dying allows a more accurate perception of what one can do to protect or to be responsible for another. A parent said, "I've learned about letting go where my children are concerned. No matter how much you might wish it were otherwise, you can never shield your loved ones from everything."

Responding to this awareness, another student said, "I learned how important it is to appreciate people while you've got them." An awareness of death can focus attention on the importance of taking care of unfinished business, saying the things that need to be said, and not being anxious about those things that do not. As one student expressed it, her study of death and dying had impressed upon her a sense of "the precariousness of life."

As Thomas Attig points out, coming to terms with our own finiteness and mortality can be understood as a grieving process.[4] Such self-mourning is really a lifelong process of coming to terms with impermanence, uncertainty, and vulnerability—qualities inherent in being mortal.

Jerry Soloway, UPI/Corbis-Bettmann Newsphotos

Death can be viewed as a burden or as a blessing. Its meaning changes as circumstances change and as our understanding evolves toward new recognitions of its place in our lives.

The close examination of death can bring insights that help dissipate long-held feelings of guilt or blame about a loved one's death. The study of death and dying can help to put previously unsettling experiences into perspective. It can open up new and creative possibilities that result in an easier, more comfortable relationship with others and with life itself.

For one man who had felt frustrated, resentful, and guilty about his brother's death twenty-five years earlier, the study of death allowed opportunities to explore unexpressed and unresolved grief. As the "stored tears" began to be expressed, he summed up the benefit of his exploration of death: "It feels so good to get rid of that ache."

The study of death and dying can bring benefits related to professional concerns. One nurse said, "When death occurs on the ward, people often think, 'Oh, well, you're a nurse; it shouldn't bother you.' But it does. . . . I really

I took your Death and Dying class while trying to cope with the transition from working full-time to taking care of my dad, a stroke and cancer patient. After being convinced for ages that he could die any day, he left us at last, more than 2 years later than anyone (including him!) ever expected.

The lessons I learned in your class are helping me immensely. For example, when I learned that the word bereavement comes from a root word meaning "shorn off," I made a resolution at the time to cut off all my hair when he died. Sure enough, I was then a newly shorn sheep.

Now, my hair is back down below my ears, though not yet to my shoulders. Hair growth, and grief—both take a while.

A student in a Death and Dying class

miss the patient; it's a real loss." A clerk in an emergency room described the new and more helpful choices she could use in relating to survivors:

> My desk is in the same area with the survivors of an ER [emergency room] death. I used to feel a pain right in the pit of my stomach, wondering what to say to them. I thought I should be able to comfort them in some way, that I should somehow offer them words of wisdom. But now I don't feel that way. I've learned how important it is to simply listen, to be supportive just by being there, instead of trying to find some words that will magically make it all go away.

The study of death and dying can be academically intriguing. Learning about the meaning of death in feudal Japan, for example, provides an appreciation that goes beyond the aesthetic or historical approach to cross-cultural understanding. The willingness of a society to engage in activities that pose risks for the well-being of its citizens reveals something of the social consensus with regard to the value of human life. The attitudes in a culture are reflected in programs for care of the dying. Funeral customs reflect a society's attitudes toward intimate relationships. For the person with an inquiring mind, investigating a society's relationship with death opens up larger patterns of belief and behavior.

Cultural Competence

Some of the "lessons taught" in death studies are still based on middle-class, white populations. Darrell Crase asks the rhetorical question, "Black people do die, don't they?"[5] In a culturally diverse environment, this question applies to people from other ethnic backgrounds as well. Among the most insightful research findings and theories in recent decades have been those that resulted from scholars taking a broad, cross-cultural view of dying, death, and bereavement.

Stereotypes will trip you up every time. There is no formula or recipe for understanding a particular cultural group. While generalizations about beliefs and practices can be helpful guides, it is nonetheless true that the map is not the territory. Norms can be used only as a guide. You cannot assume that all individuals of a particular religion, race, or cultural or national group share the same beliefs. Each person is unique.

Rather than making an assumption about an individual's attitudes and beliefs, it is important to be *curious* and to *listen.* Even if the person sitting next to you looks like he or she comes from the same background that you do, there is no way to learn the similarities and differences without being curious. Understanding culture requires knowledge of how an individual defines his or her heritage. Skin color, for example, is probably not going to be the determining factor in matters of death, dying, and bereavement.[6] You must also consider other factors, including geographic location, rural or urban setting, family influences, and the number of generations from immigration to a particular country. Heritage is best understood by exploring cultural associations, spirituality, and social class.[7] When it comes to cultural issues, the most important thing is to approach each individual with openness and curiosity.

Another essential is the ability to *gather information* about practices, rituals, and patterns of belief. Rather than "knowing" the answers, it is best to suspend assumptions and ask questions about attitudes, beliefs, and rituals. Ask an open-ended question, such as "How does that help you cope?" (If it doesn't, then listen to how or why it doesn't.) This is where good listening comes into play.

Various terms have been used to identify the skills that are needed: *cultural accommodation, cultural diversity, cultural sensitivity,* and *cultural competence.* The last term has been defined as "the process by which individuals and systems respond respectfully and effectively to people of all cultures, languages, classes, races, ethnic backgrounds, religions, and other diversity factors in a manner that recognizes, affirms, and values the worth of individuals, families, and communities and protects and preserves the dignity of each."[8]

It can also be helpful to consider the "Iceberg Theory of Culture." According to this model, the vast majority of culture is below the surface. What we see initially are such things as art, clothing, music, literature, food, and celebrations. Dig a bit deeper and we find "deep culture." Near sea level, this arena teaches us about such things as child rearing and socialization, patterns of decision making, and rules of descent. Dig even deeper, or should we say, dive deeper, and you'll find patterns of handling emotions, conversational patterns in various contexts, concepts of status, and the nature of friendship. There is much else to discover at this deep sea level.

And now a little story:[9]

As the television camera was turned off, the interviewer turned and asked quietly, "Why are Anglo funerals so serious?" Answering this question appropriately requires the ability to explore, consider, and respond to cultural differences. Take our television reporter. Notice that she used the word *Anglo.* Considering her word choice, her name, and her appearance, you might guess that her background is Hispanic. Her use of the word *serious* also deserves attention.

It is best to gather information before responding. Recall the reporter's question. What kind of response might help gain a better understanding of her heritage? A useful question might be, "What has been your experience with Anglo funerals?" She probably isn't asking about a British Anglo-Saxon funeral. More likely, she is asking about Caucasian funerals in the United States as contrasted to rituals of her own family or ethnic group. By matching her language and using the term *Anglo* in response, she is likely to provide more specific information.

She describes two recent deaths, one of a Caucasian colleague and the other of a family member. The contrasts between the two funeral ceremonies were quite perplexing to this young woman. The Caucasian funeral was a Protestant service held at a mortuary. The young reporter described her experience at the visitation and funeral for her colleague. She arrived at the mortuary to find the deceased's body in a small, empty room. Walking through the door, she noticed a condolence book set out for her to sign. She did so, briefly viewed the body, and left. During the funeral, the family sat behind closed curtains, cut off from the view of the casket and the mourners sitting in the public portion of the funeral chapel.

The funeral for her uncle was held in his parish church (Catholic) in an area of Miami, Florida, populated mostly by Cuban immigrants. The funeral itself was preceded by several days and nights of viewing at a funeral home, where family members, including small children, visited. Cuban music played in the background, and central to the gathering were jokes, laughter, and stories about the deceased. Laughing and crying together, the family visited with other members of the community who came to pay their respects.

As she talks about the differences in the funeral rituals, her use of the word *serious* is placed in context. Now, we have more information about the cultural differences that spark her curiosity. As you imagine the contrast between these two gatherings, it makes sense that, to the reporter, one seemed to be more "serious" (solemn and staid) than the other. Attitudes that we bring from our cultural experiences reflect the practices that are a familiar part of our heritage. Paying attention to how people use language can reveal a great deal about personal as well as cultural attitudes toward death.[10]

A comparison of bereavement customs among ethnic and other cultural groups in the United States shows that, "while adapting partly to Western patterns, these groups also adhere to the bereavement procedures of their own cultures."[11] Although death is fundamentally a biological fact, socially shaped ideas and assumptions create its meaning.

New Directions in Thanatology

One job of a thanatologist is to provide clients and students with materials that deepen their understandings about death. A second job is to stimulate thinking about attitudes concerning issues in the field. These two tasks are designed to bring about a balance between the affective and the cognitive, or emotional and intellectual, aspects of thanatology. A further task in thanatology is to engage in actions that build toward a better quality of civilized life, especially with regard to such events and experiences as war and environmental catastrophe.

© Robin Van Doren, Open Doors

During a cremation ceremony in Bali, young men carry a papier-mâché tiger containing the remains of a villager through the center of town to a temple outside the village, where the actual cremation will take place. On the way, they run, halt abruptly, shout and make noise, and turn the palanquin around and around to confuse the spirit so that it leaves the earthly realm and journeys to the afterworld.

Thanatology is a diverse, expanding, and maturing field of study and practice. In this section, we take a brief tour of some tasks and topics that constitute new directions in thanatology. We focus particularly on efforts (1) to gain a global perspective and (2) to narrow the gap between theorists and practitioners so that research findings are better integrated into practice.

Gaining a Global Perspective

If you lived in Germany in recent years, you might have received an invitation to participate in an exhibit designed to make people more attentive and aware of their mortality. As Fritz Roth was packing his bags for another trip to speak about death, dying, and bereavement—as well as about the philosophy of his unique funeral establishment, Pütz-Roth—he wondered what different people might pack in a suitcase for their last journey. He invited more than a hundred individuals from across Germany— some prominent individuals, some artists, some young people, and some elderly—to participate by preparing a suitcase sent to them by Pütz-Roth.

What would the suitcases contain? Would the items be similar or vastly different? Sentimental or practical? Memories of life or equipment for the final journey? The instructions required the suitcases to be arranged so that when they were opened they would show, without being unpacked, the individual's thoughts on the finiteness of life. It was hoped that the "suitcases for the last journey" would be as varied as the worldviews of the individuals participating. And, as the suitcases were returned to Pütz-Roth, so it was. Some people returned empty cases, explaining that the task was overwhelming. Others intentionally left the case empty, indicating their rationale on attached placards. But most of the cases were filled, and each person described not only the contents but also the accompanying philosophy (see Figure 15-1).

What began with one man's curiosity grew into an art exhibit about personal mortality. From the exhibit came a film by Phillip Engels, titled *To The Afterlife and Back,* that was shown on German television. A book with images and descriptions of the individuals' varied choices for the suitcase project was also published, *Einmal Jenseits und Zurück: Ein Koffer für die Letzte Reise* (Beyond and Back: A Case for the Last Journey).[12]

International programs in thanatology typically have pioneers who worked to make a difference in attitudes and practices toward death in a variety of ways: forming organizations, spearheading government programs, and preparing educational offerings, for example. Some of these efforts mirror those found in North America; others are unique, such as the German suitcase project.

From New Zealand, Margaret Agee, a professor at the University of Auckland, says that funeral practices are being influenced by traditional customs of the indigenous Maori. For example, *pakeha* (ethnically European or white) families are choosing to have the body at home prior to the funeral, as the Maori people do, either at home or in the *marae* (meeting house) during the *tangi* (a memorializing process held over several days). Also, celebrants are often facilitators, not ordained clergy. New choices come from exposure to and adaptation of different customs.

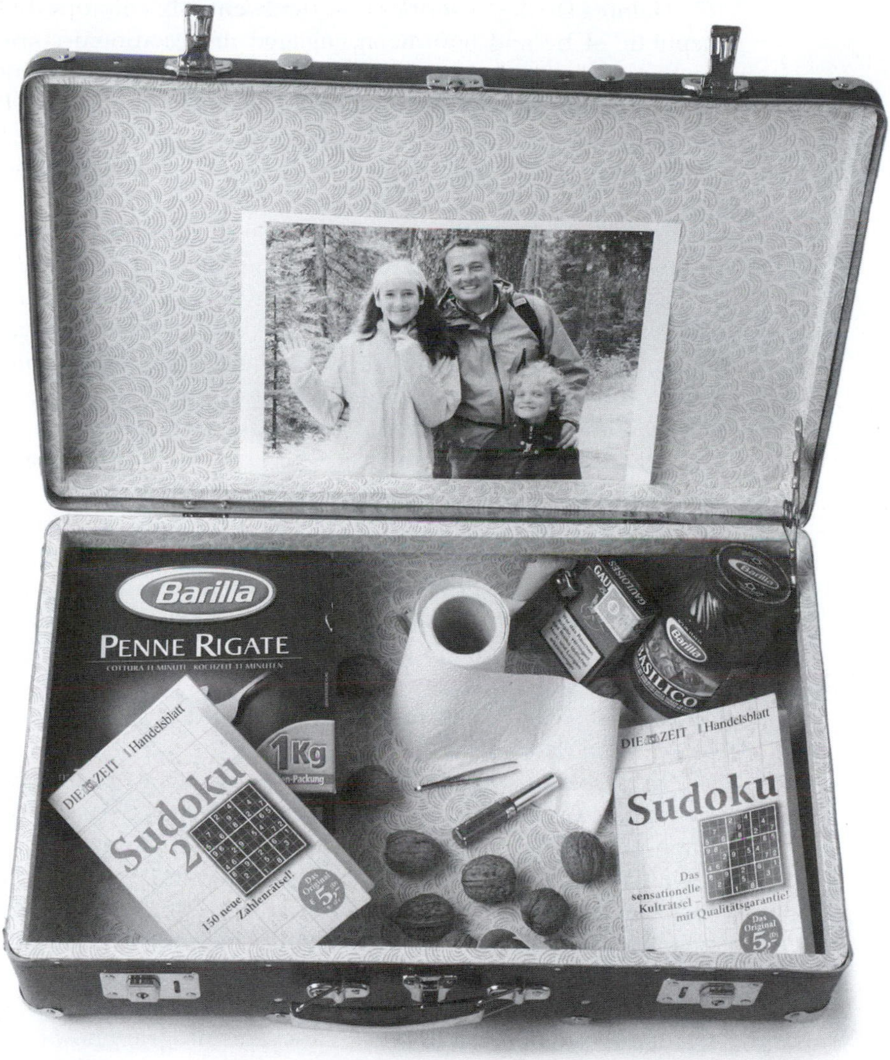

Figure 15-1 *Suitcase for the Last Journey*
I am taking . . . Family photo—for the heart. Noodles—for the mood. Nuts—for the brain. Tweezers—what every woman needs. Sudoku books—against boredom. Lighter—for more light. Lip gloss—for more glamour. Cigarettes—for something a bit sinful. *Susanne Fröhlich, author and TV show host.*

In Limerick, Ireland, language and customs from history are used to describe end-of-life care. Sinéad Donnelly tells how palliative care services use the term *meitheal* to describe a multidisciplinary approach.[13] *Meitheal* is an Irish word that traditionally denotes a group of neighbors in a rural community who come together to help in a particular task, such as harvesting or cutting turf. Through this word choice, a sense of the past, and how it informs the present in relation to community support, is emphasized.

Dolores Dooley describes how the twenty-six counties that constitute the Republic of Ireland have been engaged in a "national conversation" about death and the process of dying.[14] Topics being discussed include how a "good death" is understood, how hospitals can deliver better end-of-life care, preferences about being informed of a terminal condition, advance directives, pain management, life-prolonging technologies, physician-assisted death, and other aspects of the thanatology enterprise.

In Hong Kong, Amy Chow, a professor at the University of Hong Kong, says that courses on death and dying, at all levels, are oversubscribed, and most Chinese are willing to share their bereavement experiences with others, including family, friends, and colleagues.[15] Traditions and rituals, such as ancestor worship, ghost festivals, and elaborate Taoist funeral rites, lend a sense of mystery to the experience of bereavement.

In Italy, Francesco Campione conducts a master's program in dying, death, and bereavement at the University of Bologna, and he edits two book series. He plans to publish Italian contributions to thanatology as well as translations of the best of the international literature. Campione also began an organization, Progetto Rivivere, that uses the Internet to help children with death and bereavement. Counselors who work online are psychologists trained to work with families and children. Francesco says the biggest problem in Italy is overcoming cultural resistance to talking about death. However, he believes that people are ready to ask for advice about how to discuss death with children, which is why he began his program at that level.

In Barbados, Deiann Sobers, Acting Director of the National Assistance Board and Coordinator of Bereavement Support Services, says that the program she directs is a component of a holistic approach to psychological, social, physical, and spiritual care. Facilitators are social workers, nurses, doctors, clergy, fire officers, police officers, educators, and funeral directors who provide counseling for persons dealing with loss by death, divorce, fire, and natural disasters. There are also support groups for parents whose babies are stillborn or die immediately after birth. Nearly 2300 volunteers have been trained to provide bereavement care. This program now extends to the hospital, the Ministry of Education Student Services, the Barbados Cancer Society, the Cancer Support Services, governmental as well as nongovernmental employee assistance programs, and the clergy.

Early Australians were portrayed as hardy, resourceful people too busy colonizing a harsh and unfamiliar landscape to waste time shedding a tear or grieving. This attitude, still held by some, is slowly changing to more open acceptance and willingness to acknowledge losses. Rose Cooper reports that, in recent decades, Australia has been developing education in the fields of loss, grief, and thanatology generally. Despite Australia's familiarity with natural disaster, it took a train wreck to kick-start the formalizing of education and coordinated services. In January 1977, a commuter train derailed and tore away the piers of a bridge in suburban Sydney, resulting in the deaths of eighty-three people. The Granville train disaster was the catalyst for forming the National Association for Loss and Grief (NALAG) later that year. NALAG now operates in all the mainland states of Australia and offers community education and an accreditation program for counselors.

In Sydney, Australia, Mal and Di McKissock's Bereavement Care Centre is engaged in enrolling the first students in a master's honors program specializing in bereavement counseling. The Bereavement Care Centre, established in 1981, offers bereavement care that includes counseling, educational courses, books and DVDs, and other information and resources for bereaved adults and children.

Victoria University of Technology in Melbourne offered its first thanatology program in 1995, the Graduate Diploma in Loss and Grief Counseling. From beginnings in 1996, the Australian Centre for Grief and Bereavement in Melbourne is the largest provider of grief and bereavement education in the country, offering a range of counseling training programs, specialist short courses, and consultation to industry.

Juan Camilo Algarra Pryor, a Bogotá psychologist, describes the contributions of Isa de Jaramillo in his country, calling her the "mother of thanatology" in Colombia. In addition to initiating Fundación Omega, Jaramillo has published extensively, most recently *Morir Bien.*[16] Professionals and laypersons from around the country have participated in seminars sponsored by Fundación Omega. Juan says, "It's a pity, but in such a violent, war-stricken country as ours, professionals in the field of psychology turn their backs to death-related work. In a group of one hundred students in psychology at my school, I was the only one interested. I had to turn to Fundación Omega and Isa Jaramillo's books for instruction."

Another organization, Fundación Vida por Amor a Ellos, provides individual therapy as well as support groups for children, parents, and family of the terminally ill; suicide survivors; siblings; widows and widowers; and people who are separated. They have also devised a program to offer grief counseling and support through mortuaries in Colombia.

Palliative care is being provided at a hospice in Bogotá, and the University del Rosario in Bogotá may soon begin a residency program in palliative care for medical doctors. As far as is known, the only course offering for university students is at Universidad de los Andes, Bogotá.

In Japan, an Association for Death Education and Grief Counseling was founded in 1982 by Alfons Deeken, a Jesuit priest and philosopher. Before that, prolonging the life of a patient usually had been the main concern of doctors, whereas quality of life of the dying was neglected. Today, the changes in interest and understanding of death and dying, hospice care, bereavement, and grief in Japanese society are profound. There are currently chapters of the association in fifty Japanese cities.[17]

It is interesting to consider terms used to describe thanatology in Japanese. Thanatology is usually translated as *shiseigaku. Shi* means "death," *sei* means "life," and *gaku* means "learning" or "study." Thus, *shiseigaku* literally means "the study of death and life." The primary death education organization in Japan is called *Seitoshi wo Kangaeru Kai.* That means "the association for thinking about life and death." Thus, in this case, life comes first. Deeken uses the words *shi eno jyunbi kyouiku,* meaning "preparatory education" for death. Some

My Death

"Death is our eternal companion,"
Don Juan said with a most serious
air. "It is always to our left, at
an arm's length. . . . It has always been
watching you. It always will until
the day it taps you."

Carlos Castaneda

My death
looks exactly like me,
She lives to my left,
at exactly an arm's length.
She has my face, hair, hands;
she ages
as I grow older.

Sometimes, at night,
my death awakens me
or else appears in dreams
I did not write.
Sometimes a sudden wind
blows from nowhere,
& I look left
& see my death.
Alive, I write
with my right hand only.
When I am dead,
I shall write with my left.

But later I will have to write
through others.
I may appear
to future poets
as their deaths.

Erica Jong

school teachers recently seem to prefer *inochi no kyoiku,* which is translated "the education of life." *Inochi* means "life." Inochi no kyoiku includes not only topics about death and bereavement but also topics about the preciousness of life, life stages, and so on. With this phrase, the word death, *shi,* is omitted from death studies at the elementary and secondary school levels.[18]

From this whirlwind global tour, it's clear that our international colleagues are busy initiating unique art explorations, historical and cultural adaptations, academic and publishing projects, and governmental and nongovernmental programs, as well as bereavement and end-of-life services to meet the needs of individuals and families in their respective communities.[19]

Bridging Research and Practice

Do counselors, therapists, other health professionals, and caregivers in general use the knowledge and insights derived from thanatological research? Or is there a cultural split between researchers and clinicians? Examining issues in thanatology more than two decades ago, Robert Kastenbaum remarked that there were few signs of practitioners making much use of either research or theory in their work with patients or with the bereaved. He said it appears "that many practitioners in the area of terminal care and bereavement have neither an up-to-date mastery of thanatological research nor a secure grasp of the historical and theoretical dimensions." Kastenbaum concluded that

> at the worst, perhaps, we have sketched a picture of practitioners who fail to read a literature that wouldn't help them very much anyway. The academicians continue to tread their mills . . . with only each other to amuse, while the practitioners base their services on individual experiences and a grab-bag of unexamined assumptions and "facts" whose veridicality has seldom been tested, let alone established.[20]

Echoing such thoughts, Myra Bluebond-Langner observed, "While the quantity of research has increased, what more do we actually know? Has progress in thanatology kept pace with publication? What differences have our efforts made in the care of dying patients and their families, and in our own responses to death and impending disasters?"[21]

In concluding a book that aimed for a collaboration between researchers and practitioners, the editors summed up the challenge:

> The pairing of coauthors was something of a "blind date," in the sense that we suggested collaborations between prominent theorists or scientists on the one hand and practicing professionals on the other, many of whom had never met prior to being invited to write together. Not all of these arranged marriages worked out amicably! Suspicions arose on both sides of the dialogical divide. [This highlights] the challenge of fostering dialogue across communities that differ in style, focus, institutional context, and "closeness" to the reality of human suffering and resilience.[22]

Efforts are being made to span the gap between research and practice.[23] John Jordan says, "Theory is the bridge over which empirical findings can cross into the world of the practitioner." In building this bridge, he encouraged researchers to "explain with more clarity and depth what their findings could mean for clinical practice."[24] David Balk refers to a "scholarship of application," a dynamic exchange between theory and practice, that can make research "a useful form of gaining knowledge."[25]

Creating Compassionate Cities

Communities give individuals roots, a sense of place, and a location within the broader scheme of human affairs. Allan Kellehear says, "The question of seamless social support for end-of-life care finds its answer, however ambitious and daunting the task, in community care."[26] In the twenty-first century, our "identities will be layered along a continuum from local to global."[27] National boundaries will mean less as people begin to have enough in common to share a transnational identity. This identity "involves the ability to live ethnically and culturally in both the global and local spheres at the same time."[28]

This has important implications with respect to death and dying and to the goal of creating *compassionate cities,* a term coined by Kellehear to denote "a model of public health that encourages community participation in all types of end-of-life care."[29] Ira Byock, a palliative care and hospice physician, echoes Kellehear's vision in imagining a "Care-Full Society."[30] This kind of care is not limited to hospice or palliative care.

> Every day people die in road traumas, suicides, and homicides, and disasters take people in hundreds and thousands at a time. Aside from death from old age, there are also tolls of death from the political and social plight of indigenous peoples all over the world. From civil wars to the negative health effects of dispossession, our current understandings about caring for those dying and experiencing loss have yet to be inclusive of these people and contexts.[31]

Culture and individual personality shape our attitudes toward death. What we understand of death and what meanings we ascribe to it become significant to the extent that we construct a meaningful relationship with the experience of death and dying in our lives. This grave marker expresses a memorialization that is consonant with the lifestyles of both the deceased and her survivors.

Kellehear says, "These widespread experiences of endings, and the losses that inevitably emerge in their wake, are the most important potential basis of our interpersonal and international connection with one another."[32]

Moreover, they could be a promising basis for an innovative public health program that recognizes the need for community involvement and consideration of death as a fact of life.[33] What, then, are some of the defining characteristics of a "compassionate city"?[34]

- It meets the special needs of its aged, those living with life-threatening illness, and those living with loss.
- It recognizes and plans to accommodate the economically disadvantaged, including rural and remote populations, indigenous people, and the homeless.
- It preserves and promotes a community's spiritual traditions and storytellers.
- It has a strong commitment to social and cultural differences.

What do we need to start creating compassionate cities? First, death education for everyone.[35] Early in the twenty-first century, a newspaper series of fifteen articles, *Finding Our Way: Living with Dying in America,* appeared in more than 160 papers and reached millions of people in the United States.[36] It included articles on palliative care, advance directives, grief, funerals, elder care, and other topics in thanatology. Perhaps we are already under way.

Robert Goss and Dennis Klass note that human bonds based in shared pain "do not fit easily into the cultural narrative of consumer capitalism in which happiness is regarded as the normal human condition."[37]

Thus, the ideal of creating compassionate cities remains a challenge for thanatology and public health. However, two lessons from our past experience provide encouragement: First, care of the dying has been *normal and routine* for families and communities; second, past patterns of community care have illustrated the importance of *community relationships* in that care. With the increase in our dependence on others to care for our dying and dead, we have lost sight of these lessons. As a result, death knowledge has become professional knowledge, not personal knowledge.[38]

Herman Feifel calls attention to the need to "integrate existing knowledge concerning death and grief into our communal and public institutions."[39] People who are involved in death education, counseling, and care must participate in the work of formulating public policies that impinge on those areas of concern. Acknowledging that the still-young field of thanatology (and the so-called death awareness movement) has many tasks facing it,

> What will you say right before they put you six feet under?
> Will you say?
> "I wish I would have. . . ."
> "I wish I could have. . . ."
> "I wish I should have. . . ."
> Or will you say, "I did it all. Thank you and good night."
>
> Gene Simmons

Feifel says that it can already be credited with a number of significant contributions to our collective well-being:

> The [death] movement has been a major force in broadening our grasp of the phenomenology of illness, in helping humanize medical relationships and health care, and in advancing the rights of the dying. It is highpointing values that undergird the vitality of human response to catastrophe and loss. Furthermore, it is contributing to reconstituting the integrity of our splintered wholeness. More important, perhaps, it is sensitizing us to our common humanity, which is all too eroded in the present world. It may be somewhat hyperbolic, but I believe that how we regard death and how we treat the dying and survivors are prime indications of a civilization's intention and target.[40]

In commenting on the message put forward by Elisabeth Kübler-Ross, Dame Cicely Saunders, and Mother Teresa of Calcutta, Robert Fulton and Greg Owen note that it was also about "essential religious and spiritual values that extend beyond the immediate goal of care for the dying."[41] Death awareness fosters "compassionate acts of service" that are founded on recognition of the identity and worth of each human being.

Living with Death and Dying

As you review the varied perspectives covered in your study of death and dying, take a moment to assess the areas that seem particularly valuable to you. What insights did you gain by examining how death is seen in other cultures? How does your study of children's responses to death relate to your own experiences as a child or as an adult? What have you learned about your risk-taking behaviors? What choices would you now make regarding funeral ritual, terminal care, life-sustaining medical technologies? In sum, ask yourself, "What have I learned that can be helpful to me as a survivor of others' deaths—and in confronting my own death?" Have you become more comfortable in thinking about death and discussing it with others?

The media are sometimes playful with images of death (see Figure 15-2). Recently, an advertisement in several high-fashion magazines used death imagery to showcase the desirable qualities of the product being promoted (see Figure 15-3). However, in "pushing the envelope" of advertising design, the manufacturer, ad agency, and others involved in the project received letters from disgruntled readers who found the use of such imagery offensive and tasteless. Do you suppose this reaction might have been different if the letter writers had been more comfortable with thinking about dying and death?

In considering the personal value derived from thinking about and exploring the meanings of death, notice how the study of death and dying engages both your mental faculties and your emotions. You may also notice that your exploration of death has a rippling effect, extending outward to your social circles and relationships with others. Has a greater awareness of death had an impact on the quality of your relationships with family members and friends or with the person down the street or at the neighborhood shop?

Figure 15-2 *Death Imagery in the Media*
"Lifetime Guarantee! Get *Rolling Stone* forever, or 'til death do us part. Disclaimer: Non-transferable (without proof of reincarnation)."

Alfred Killilea says, "Rather than threatening to deprive life of all meaning, death deepens an appreciation of life and the capacity of every person to give life to others."[42]

Humanizing Death and Dying

Many people are encouraged by what appears to be increasing openness about death in society. There are signs that the circumstances surrounding death are being brought back into the personal control of the individuals and

Figure 15-3 *Death Imagery in Advertising Design*

families who are closest to a particular death. Traditional customs and practices are being revived in new ways.

The curricula of death education and thanatology are also being refined and new directions explored. There is ongoing discussion about the goals of death education. Should death education aim to *alleviate* discomfort and anxiety about dying and death? If acceptance of death is thought to be "superior" to denial, that notion needs to be investigated and validated.[43]

It is appropriate to question whether apparent openness toward death is sometimes only illusory. When death becomes just another topic of casual (or sensational) discussion on television talk shows, does it reflect a kind of minimizing or devaluing of death? Is "openness" about death always to be applauded? Or does it sometimes reflect a nervous effort to achieve "death without regrets"? Death is not fully known when its description is limited to rosy projections and fantasies about the good death.

Death is an intensely human experience. We can balance our fears with openness. We can understand the dynamics of grief. We can make room for loss and change in our lives and in the lives of others. Death need not always be seen as something foreign to our nature, a foe to be fought to the bitter end. In *A Pattern Language: Towns, Building, Construction,* Christopher Alexander and his coauthors suggest, "No people who turn their backs on death can be alive. The presence of the dead among the living will be a daily fact in any society which encourages its people to live."[44]

We should beware, however, of becoming merely casual. Otherwise, we may find we have confronted only our *image* of death, not death itself. An increased casualness toward death is very evident in modern society. Consider, for example, the growing number of death notices that bear the announcement "No services are planned." Yet, few individuals die without leaving survivors who are affected by the loss. Is death a solitary or a communal event? Can I truly say that my death is "my own"? Or is death an event whose significance ripples outward to touch not only the lives of friends and loved ones but also the lives of casual acquaintances and even strangers in ways little understood?

Defining the Good Death

There is no single definition of what constitutes a *good* death. Caregivers and other individuals who promote palliative care and hospice often define a good death as a "peaceful death."[45] In ancient Greece, to die young, in the fullness of one's creative energies, was considered exceptional luck. In our society, death at a young age is considered a misfortune. The death of a young person just embarking on an independent life or of someone in the prime of life seems a great tragedy. "There is a widespread fantasy that one might reach 80 or 90 years in good health and die in one's sleep. But the epidemiological reality is rather different."[46]

The good death can be defined in many different ways. To an anthropologist interested in how our lives are celebrated in rites of passage, it might be something like the following: "Dying a good death is a ceremonially stylized way of exiting gracefully. By ritualized means, a grim necessity is transformed into a dignified and exemplary demise."[47] A religious concept of a good death, by contrast, might be defined as "one in which the person dies in a properly sanctified state."[48] How might you define a good death? Consider all of the factors—age, mode of death, surroundings, and so on—that would enter into your concept of a good death. Is your definition of a good death the same for yourself and for others? Some may question whether there can be any such thing as a good death. "Death is never good," they might say. "It can only cause pain and sadness."

Robert Kastenbaum has enumerated some thoughts about what constitutes the good death, and we list them briefly here:[49]

1. People should be spared extreme physical, mental, and spiritual suffering at the end of their lives.
2. A good death should enact the highest values held by society. "Communal values are affirmed when people end their lives in a congruent manner."
3. The good death affirms our most significant personal relationships.
4. The good death is transfiguring. "One experiences an epiphany—a profound sense of beauty, love, or understanding. . . . The moment of death becomes the peak experience of life."
5. The good death is simply the final phase of the good life. "People should die as they have lived. . . . Why try to reshape a person's life at the last moment?"
6. The good death is coherent. "It is a story, a drama that makes sense, that satisfies our need for closure."

Another effort to define the components of a good death is shown in Table 15-1. Notice that this definition, which was published in a medical

TABLE 15-1 *Components of a Good Death*

Pain and symptom management. Minimizing the likelihood of dying in pain or suffering "breakthrough pain" by providing adequate analgesia and other forms of pain relief.

Clear decision making. Empowering the dying person by striving for clear communication between the patient, his or her family, and the medical team. Discussing vital end-of-life decisions before crisis occurs and emotional reserves are low.

Preparation for death. Knowing what to expect during the end-stage of illness relative to the physical and psychosocial changes likely to occur as death approaches. Planning for actions to be taken following death. Exploring one's own feelings about death.

Completion. Acknowledging the importance of spirituality and other avenues of meaning making, including life review, resolving conflicts, spending time with family and friends, enacting significant cultural rituals, and saying goodbye.

Contributing to others. Sharing meaningful aspects of oneself through tangible or intangible gifts, such as gifts of time, concern for others, and understanding gained through personal reflection.

Affirmation of the whole person. Seeing the dying person not as a "disease" but in the context of his or her life, values, and preferences.

journal, focuses as much on the *caregiver's* tasks in making a good death possible as it does on the tasks of the dying person. Compare this list with Kastenbaum's description. Would combining these lists create a more complete or more comprehensive definition?

An alternative way of defining a good death has been offered by Stu Farber and his colleagues. They propose the term *respectful death,* defined as "a nonjudgmental relationship between parties." It is "a process of respectful exploration of the goals and values of patients and families at the end of life rather than a prescription for successfully achieving 'a good death.'"[50] Like the components given in Table 15-1, the concept of a respectful death emphasizes the mutuality of caregivers and patients.

Another way to think about the definition of a good death is to construct it in terms of an *appropriate* death. What makes some deaths seem more appropriate than others? Our answers are influenced by cultural values and by social context. Avery Weisman describes some of the elements that constitute the definition of appropriate death in contemporary societies.[51]

First, an appropriate death is relatively pain free; suffering is kept to a minimum. The social and emotional needs of the dying person are met to the fullest extent possible. There is no impoverishment of crucial human resources. Within the limits imposed by disabilities, the dying person is free to operate effectively as an individual and to enjoy mobility and independence. In addition, the dying person is able to recognize and resolve, as far as possible, any residual personal and social conflicts. The person is allowed to satisfy his or her wishes in ways that are consistent with the situation and with his or her self-identity and self-esteem.

As death approaches, the dying person is allowed to freely choose to relinquish control over various aspects of his or her life, turning over control to people in whom confidence and trust have been placed. The dying person also may choose to seek out or to relinquish relationships with significant others. In other words, the person chooses a comfortable level of social interaction.

Weisman said that to achieve an appropriate death, we must first rid ourselves of the notion that death is *never* appropriate. Such a belief acts as a self-fulfilling prophecy. It stops us from creating the possibility of a more appropriate death.

For an appropriate death to become possible, the dying person must be protected from needless, dehumanizing, and demeaning procedures. The person's preferences about pain control and consciousness, and about the extent of solitude or gregarious interaction desired, should be respected. "An appropriate death," Weisman says, "is a death that someone might choose for himself—had he a choice."

Finally, we turn to the criteria for a good death suggested by Edwin Shneidman, a respected thanatologist and suicidologist. (See Table 15-2.) At the age of eighty-nine, Shneidman's ideas about the good death represent the fruits of thoughtful contemplation, reflecting back on a life well lived. It is clearly focused on the dying person, though it acknowledges a continuity

TABLE 15-2 *Ten Criteria for a Good Death*

Natural. Rather than accident, suicide, or homicide.

Mature. Elderly, near the pinnacle of mental functioning but old enough to have experienced and savored life.

Expected. Neither sudden nor unexpected; some warning of impending death.

Honorable. A positive obituary filled with honorifics (conveying honor).

Prepared. Plans made for the legalities surrounding death, such as funeral arrangements, wills, and trusts.

Accepted. "Willing the obligatory"; gracefully accepting the inevitable.

Civilized. Loved ones present; the dying scene enlivened by fresh flowers, beautiful pictures, and cherished music.

Generative. To have passed down the "wisdom of the tribe" to younger generations; to have shared memories and histories.

Rueful. To experience the contemplative emotions of sadness and regret without collapse; to die with some projects left undone; to "teach the paradigm that no life is completely complete."

Peaceable. The dying scene be filled with amicability and love and with relief from physical pain.

that includes family and younger generations. The good death, in this sense, involves more than just a civilized deathbed scene; it encompasses the dying person's "post-self," the self left behind in memory and the community. Shneidman says, "Have your dying be a courtly death, among the best things that you ever did."[52]

The death of Charles Lindbergh exemplifies many of the features of a good or appropriate death.[53] Lindbergh was diagnosed with lymphoma. Until he died two years later, he continued living an active life, traveling and promoting the cause of conservation. When chemotherapy became ineffective, Lindbergh made arrangements for eventual burial on his beloved island of Maui. As his condition grew worse, he was hospitalized for several months, but the best efforts of his physicians could not alter the consequences or course of the disease. Lindbergh then asked that a cabin on Maui be obtained, and he was flown "home to Maui," where, with two nurses, his physician, and his family, he spent the last eight days of his life in the environment he loved.

During these last days, Lindbergh gave instructions for the construction of his grave and conduct of his funeral, requesting that people attend in their work clothes. As Dr. Milton Howell, one of Lindbergh's physicians, describes this period, "There was time for reminiscing, time for discussion, and time for laughter."

Finally, Lindbergh lapsed into a coma and died twelve hours later. In accordance with his wishes, there had been no medical heroics. Dr. Howell says, "Death was another event in his life, as natural as his birth had been in Minnesota more than seventy-two years before."

Perhaps a good death presupposes, in some respects, a good life. Throughout history, philosophers have proposed both religious and secular

© Carol A. Foote

The contemplation of death and its meaning will determine how we and our children think about and behave toward death in the decades ahead.

models that describe the qualities of a good life. In his essays on the transience of life, the medieval Buddhist monk Kenkō wrote,

> When I see the things people do in their struggle to get ahead, it reminds me of someone building a snowman on a spring day, making ornaments of precious metals and stones to decorate it, and then erecting a hall to house it.[54]

If, as Kastenbaum says, the good death is simply the final phase of the good life, we ought to contemplate in this very moment our preparations for a good death.

Death in the Future

During the past century, better living conditions and treatments for infectious diseases enabled people to live long enough to be old enough to suffer from cardiovascular disease, cancers, and other degenerative conditions. The discoveries, inventions, and applications of twenty-first-century medicine will continue to push death farther into the future for those able to access the newest treatments.[55] Individuals who live beyond 100 years, *centenarians,* are healthier because of genetics, common sense, or maybe just luck. In people who live the average life span, diseases of old age strike earlier and last longer.[56] A publication of the National Center for Health Statistics recently

The Angel of Death

The Angel of Death is always with me—
the hard wild flowers of his teeth,
his body like cigar smoke
swaying through a small town jail.

He is the wind that scrapes through our months,
the train wheels grinding over our syllables.
He is the footstep continually pacing through our chests,
the small wound in the soul,
the meteor puncturing the atmosphere.
And sometimes he is merely a quiet between the start of an act
and its completion,
a silence so loud
it shakes you like a tree.

It is only then you look up from the wars,
from the kisses,
from the signing of the business agreements;
It is only then you observe the dimensions
housed in the air of each day,
each moment;

only then you hear the old caressing the cold rims of their sleep,
hear the middle-aged women in love with their pillows
weeping into the gray expanse of each dawn,
where young men, dozing in alleys,
envision their loneliness to be a beautiful girl
and do not know they are part of a young girl's dream,
as she does not know that she is the dream in the sleep
of middle-aged women and old men,
and that all are contained in a gray wind
that scrapes through our months.

noted that the elimination of heart disease as a cause of death would add almost four years to life expectancy at birth, and elimination of cancer would add more than three years.[57] What life expectancy might people look forward to in the future? "Our understandings of what is *natural* about human life, including the ways we respond to illness, grow older, and die, are forever being remade."[58]

Imagine the social patterns of death and dying fifty years from now. Think about the issues discussed in previous chapters, and consider present realities and possibilities. What speculations can you make about how our relationship with death and dying will change by the middle years of the twenty-first century? Looking into the future, what do you expect will be the questions about death and dying that will demand attention from individuals and societies? Consider the effects of an older population. In the United

But soon we forget that the dead sleep in buried cities,
that our hearts contain them in ripe vaults,
We forget that beautiful women dry into parchment
and ball players collapse into ash;
that geography wrinkles and smoothes like the expressions on a face,
and that not even children
can pick the white fruit from the night sky.

And how *could* we laugh while looking at the face
that falls apart like wet tobacco?
How could we wake each morning
to hear the muffled gong beating inside us,
our mouths full of shadows, our rooms filled with a black dust?

Still,
it is humiliating to be born a bottle:
to be filled with air, emptied, filled again;
to be filled with water, emptied, filled again;
and, finally, to be filled with earth.

And yet I am glad that The Angel of Death is always with me:
his footsteps quicken my own,
his silence makes me speak,
his wind freshens the weather of my day.
And it is because of him
I no longer think
that with each beat
my heart
is a planet drowning from within
but an ocean filling for the first time.

Morton Marcus

States, it is estimated that the number of people age sixty-five and over will grow to nearly 64 million by the year 2025 and to more than 88 million by 2050.[59] Stewart Brand says, "The countries that got rich before they got old are in increasing trouble."[60] The average birthrate in long-urbanized, developed countries is down to 1.56 children per female; in some places, it's below 1.2. Brand calls these "extinction numbers." Majority populations will be old, with few or no children to care for them, with a national economy that is expiring for lack of young workers. Can we imagine that care of the dying will become "big business," as corporations expand their role as surrogate caregivers for the aged and dying?

Think about the kinds of rituals or ceremonies that, decades from now, will surround the dead. Writing about the rapid pace of social change among societies in the South Pacific, Ron Crocombe comments on the trend of reducing the time devoted to funerals, marriages, births, and other such occasions of community celebration.[61] Increasingly, they are being moved from day to night and weekday to weekend. "Most traditional social rituals took more time than can be spared today," he says, "both because there are many more things to do, and because each person is doing different things."[62] Although our values and judgments play a role in determining how we spend our time, such decisions are rarely made independently of social norms and practices. If our work schedule conflicts with a midweek funeral, we may be reluctant to insist on time off unless the deceased is a close relative. As notions about community rituals and the use of time change, what kinds of funeral practices and services might evolve in response to such changes?

How might changing circumstances affect traditional patterns for disposition of the dead? Will there be enough land to continue the practice of burials? Or might we see a substitution of high-rise cemeteries, cities of the dead towering above the landscape of the living? This is already happening in Japan, where burial space in large cities like Tokyo is at a premium. Changes in methods of carrying out last rites will occur as people create new choices.

What types of social services for help in coping with the death of a loved one will be available in the years to come? Who could have foreseen the advent of specialized support and advocacy groups like Parents of Murdered Children and Mothers Against Drunk Driving? In recent years, innovative forms of social support—as well as resources for learning about death, dying, and bereavement—have become available on the Internet and the World Wide Web.[63] What other developments in bereavement, grief, and mourning may take place in the coming years?

Recent decades have also seen increased emphasis on counseling or therapy following bereavement. In the future, might there be "grief clinics" available for emergencies? Would these clinics—much like present health institutions—send out reminders for individuals to come in for a bereavement checkup before the anniversary date of a significant death? Perhaps the time is not far off when some kind of professional assistance in coping with grief is the norm. Would this be a good thing or not?

If such life-threatening illnesses as cancer and heart disease become matters of routine prevention or cure in the future, what other diseases will endanger our survival? Given the rapid pace of medical innovation, what change do you imagine will occur within even as short a time as the next decade? The prognosis for a given illness may change from very poor to exceptionally good within the span of a few years. At the same time, diseases previously unknown present new threats. As a case in point: Who could have foreseen the implications of AIDS? Yet, it quickly assumed proportions comparable to the great plagues of the Middle Ages in terms of public fear and uncertainty. Will new diseases and threats cause similar distress in the future?

It is difficult to imagine a time when *no* disease or illness will be life threatening. Yet we have lived through many technological advances that now make it possible to sustain life beyond measures conceivable by earlier generations. Perhaps "off-the-shelf" replaceable body parts will sustain life when conventional methods prove futile. If there is a "bionic" human in our future, what values should guide the use of such technologies, and who will decide?

In Damon Knight's science fiction story, "Masks," a man who has suffered physically devastating injuries is repaired with functional artificial body parts.[64] But his mechanically sustained life causes him to question what constitutes a living human being. Robin Cook's novel, *Coma,* describes "surgery patients" who "undergo suspicious anesthesiology mishaps, become brain dead, and are stockpiled as waiting donors at the mysterious 'Jefferson Institute.'"[65]

Will medical scientists develop techniques to more accurately predict the time of a person's death? This theme is explored in Clifford Simak's "Death Scene" and in Robert Heinlein's "Life-Line."[66] These stories suggest that the moment of one's death might be better left unknown. Although such explorations in speculative fiction are typically located in the future, in a setting different from our own, and often incorporate elements of fantasy, the themes investigated bear on present possibilities and on current dilemmas of ethical choice.

What changes are likely to occur in the health care system? What will be the quality of life—and of dying? In the story "Golden Acres," Kit Reed envisions a future in which the administrators of an institution for the aged make life-or-death decisions about the inmates in order to make room for new arrivals.[67] Golden Acres provides everything for its residents except the possibility of living out their lives in the way they wish. Reed's story focuses on a resident who refuses to accept society's neglect of its aged members. As the protagonist describes it, Golden Acres is "a vast boneyard." Will that bleak description apply to the prospects facing the aged members of our own communities?

What about threats of global warming? Or other global disaster? One scientist writes, "Comets are a real problem, and can do nearly as much damage as asteroids. . . . This is serious business, and the extent to which we all live on a knife-edge in relation to the devastation from these objects is very unsettling to those of us who keep track of these things."[68] He continues,

> On August 10, 1972, a famous daytime "fireball" skipped across the Grand Teton Mountains in Wyoming before returning harmlessly back to space over Canada. This object was estimated to be 200 yards across. If it had landed on one of thousands of towns or cities, it would have left a crater a half mile across. Needless to say, the inhabitants would have had absolutely no useful warning, and nowhere to escape.[69]

In learning from our encounters with dying and death that life is precious and precarious, we must also consider how the insights we've gained can be compassionately applied to the life of the planet as a whole. The poet Gary Snyder writes,

> The extinction of a species, each one a pilgrim of four billion years of evolution, is an irreversible loss. The ending of the lines of so many creatures with whom we have traveled this far is an occasion of profound sorrow and grief. Death can be accepted and to some degree transformed. But the loss of lineages and all their future young is not something to accept. It must be rigorously and intelligently resisted.[70]

Postscript and Farewell

Death education sometimes has immediate, practical consequences. At the conclusion of a course on death and dying, a student said, "It has helped me and my family deal with my mother's serious illness." For others, the practical application may be less immediate. Yet, as one student said, "I've gained a lot of useful information which may not be applicable to my life right now, but I know now that information and help is available and I didn't know that before."

Many people who complete a course in death and dying find that their explorations have consequences for their lives that had not been foreseen when they first signed up for the course. One student said, "To me, this study

has focused on more than just death; it has dealt with living, like a class on philosophy." Another student expressed the value of her death explorations as having "expanded my faith in the resilience of the human spirit." After describing how several individuals faced the prospect of dying, Sandra Bertman concluded that a common thread was the sense of "connectedness, affinity with all mankind: past, present, alive, dead."[71]

The study of death and dying includes components of information and data, of course, and it also embraces a wisdom arising out of the human encounter with death. This wisdom involves "a different kind of knowing, an integrative approach that refuses to look aside from the real human situation of uncertainty and ultimate death."[72] To be sure, death education does pertain to practical aspects of the individual and psychosocial encounter with death. But it offers more than that. Awareness of death and dying brings an added dimension to the experience of living. It brings us into the present and serves as a reminder of the precious precariousness of life and the value of compassion through the ordinary as well as extraordinary circumstances of human experience.

Further Readings

Cecilia Lan-wan Chan and others. *In Celebration of Life: A Self-Help Journey on Preparing a Good Death and Living with Loss and Bereavement.* Hong Kong: Centre on Behavioral Health, University of Hong Kong, 2009.

Allan Kellehear. *Compassionate Cities: Public Health and End-of-Life Care.* New York: Routledge, 2005.

David K. Meagher and David E. Balk, eds. *Handbook of Thanatology,* 2nd ed. New York: Routledge, 2013.

Edwin S. Shneidman. *A Commonsense Book of Death: Reflections at Ninety of a Lifelong Thanatologist.* Lanham, Md.: Rowman & Littlefield, 2008.

Mark C. Taylor. *Field Notes from Elsewhere: Reflections on Dying and Living.* New York: Columbia University Press, 2009.

Barry Vincent. *Philosophical Thinking About Death and Dying.* Belmont, Calif.: Thomson Wadsworth, 2007.

Additional resources for this chapter can be found at www.mhhe.com/despelder10e

EPILOGUE

It's late. I wonder what Death will look like. A drooling ogre? Perhaps an unblinking skull, the Grim Reaper? A veiled mistress with beckoning arms? The standard forms. Or maybe Death will be a polished young man in a three-piece suit, all smiles and sincerity and confidence. What a disappointment that would be. No, I prefer the scythe—no ambiguity, no surrender . . . no dickering. What's that? . . . I hear him. He's here.

"May I come in?"

I nod. It's the young man who left me two days ago to knock on the doors of his neighbors' homes. "Well . . . ?" My breath is shorter than I thought.

He smiles, looks down at his hands, then at me. "Well, I did as you said. It didn't take long before I realized that I wasn't going to find a household that hadn't been touched by death."

"How many did you go to?"

He covers his mouth with his hand a moment, trying to hide his pride, I guess. "All of them."

"All?"

"Every house. . . . I'm very stubborn."

We both smile. My wheezing is worse, and he notices. He shows his concern, and I can see that he understands what is happening.

"You're dying, aren't you, old man?"

I close my eyes in answer. When I open them again, he is at my side.

"Is there someone I should get for you? Your family?"

"Gone."

"Some friend?"

"Gone. All gone . . . except for you." The young man nods, then pulls his chair over next to my own. He takes my hand. I rest a moment. "There is something you must do for me," I wheeze. "When I'm dead, burn this house and everything in it, including me."

"Leave nothing behind?"

"This is only a filthy old shack. I'm leaving behind the only thing that anyone really can leave behind . . . the difference I've made in the lives of the people I've met." I squeeze his hand as best I can. He squeezes back. "Oh . . . and this." I try to lift the book in my lap—my book. He sees me struggling and picks it up for me. "You take this. It's yours." His eyes widen.

"But I don't deserve—"

"There isn't time for that now!" He nods and lays the book on his lap. Good, that's done. Moments pass. It gets quieter. . . . I must close my eyes. I witness again the glory of ten thousand mornings, ten thousand afternoons, ten thousand nights . . . then they, too, fade. All that's left is the sound of our breathing and the wind. Time slows. Time changes. Where is the scythe? The young man's hand leaves mine, and I hear his footsteps recede . . . stop . . . return. He sits down, and I feel his hand on mine. He opens my fingers and lays something cool and light in my palm, all lace and limbs . . . the ballerina.

Now I can go.

David Gordon

NOTES

CHAPTER 1

1. See Philip A. Mellor and Chris Shilling, "Modernity, Self-Identity and the Sequestration of Death," *Sociology: The Journal of the British Sociological Association* 27, no. 3 (1993): 411–431; and Tony Walter, "Modern Death: Taboo or Not Taboo?" *Sociology* 25 (May 1991): 293–310.

2. Regis Martin, *The Last Things: Death, Judgment, Heaven, Hell* (San Francisco: Ignatius Press, 1998), p. 64.

3. Sami Pihlström, "Death—Mine or the Other's? On the Possibility of Philosophical Thanatology," *Mortality* 6, no. 3 (2001): 265–286; quote, pp. 266, 280.

4. Steve Jobs, "You've Got to Find What You Love," *Stanford Report,* June 14, 2005.

5. David Friend, *Watching the World Change: The Stories Behind the Images of 9/11* (New York: Farrar, Straus, and Giroux, 2006), p. 32.

6. See Lynne Ann DeSpelder, "September 11, 2001 and the Internet," *Mortality* 8, no. 1 (2003): 88–89.

7. Robert Kastenbaum, *Death, Society, and Human Experience* (St. Louis: Mosby, 1977), p. 93.

8. Marilyn Johnson, *The Dead Beat: Lost Souls, Lucky Stiffs, and the Perverse Pleasures of Obituaries* (New York: HarperCollins, 2006), pp. 91, 106, 117, 223.

9. Jack Lule, "News Strategies and the Death of Huey Newton," in *The Path Ahead: Readings in Death and Dying,* ed. Lynne Ann DeSpelder and Albert Lee Strickland, 33–40 (Mountain View, Calif.: Mayfield, 1995).

10. Robert Fulton and Greg Owen, "Death and Society in Twentieth Century America," *Omega: Journal of Death and Dying* 18, no. 4 (1987–1988): 379–395. See also Dan Nimmo and James E. Combs, *Nightly Horrors: Crisis Coverage by Television Network News* (Knoxville: University of Tennessee Press, 1985).

11. National Safety Council, 2009. Estimates based on data from National Center for Health Statistics and U.S. Census Bureau.

12. J. Sean McCleneghan, "'Reality Violence' on TV News: It Began with Vietnam," *The Social Science Journal* 39 (2002): 593–598.

13. McCleneghan, "'Reality Violence,'" p. 595. The man referred to was Daniel V. Jones.

14. Allan Kellehear, *Compassionate Cities: Public Health and End-of-Life Care* (New York: Routledge, 2005), p. 105.

15. Kellehear, *Compassionate Cities,* p. 106.

16. George Gerbner, "Death in Prime Time: Notes on the Symbolic Functions of Dying in the Mass Media," *Annals of the American Academy of Political and Social Science* 447 (January 1980): 64–70.

17. Transcript, "The Mean World Syndrome: Media Violence & the Cultivation of Fear," featuring George Gerbner and Michael Morgan, Media Education Foundation, 2010; www.mediaed.org.

18. Jacque Lynn Foltyn, "Dead Sexy: Post-Disaster/Terrorism Voyeurism and the Corpse, Pop Culture's New Porn Star" (paper presented at the Centre for Death and Society, Bath, U.K., 2006).

19. Frederic B. Tate, "Impoverishment of Death Symbolism: The Negative Consequences," *Death Studies* 13, no. 3 (1989): 305–317.

20. Dolf Zillmann, "The Psychology of the Appeal of Portrayals of Violence," in *Why We Watch: The Attractions of Violent Entertainment,* ed. J. H. Goldstein, 179–211 (New York: Oxford University Press, 1998).

21. Colin McGinn, *The Power of Movies: How Screen and Mind Interact* (New York: Pantheon, 2005), p. 14. See also Lynn Schofield Clark, *From Angels to Aliens: Teenagers, the Media, and the Supernatural* (New York: Oxford University Press, 2003), p. 13; and Fran McInerny, "Cinematic Visions of Dying," in *The Study of Dying: From Autonomy to Transformation,* ed. Allan Kellehear, 211–232 (New York: Cambridge University Press, 2009).

22. Hannelore Wass, "A Perspective on the Current State of Death Education," *Death Studies* 28, no. 4 (2004): 289–308.

23. Bill Bryson, *The Mother Tongue: English and How It Got That Way* (New York: Perennial, 2001), p. 189.

24. Marsha McGee, "Faith, Fantasy, and Flowers: A Content Analysis of the American Sympathy Card," *Omega: Journal of Death and Dying* 11, no. 1 (1980–1981): 27, 29.

25. Lorraine Hedtke and John Winslade, "The Use of the Subjunctive in Re-Membering Conversations With Those Who Are Grieving," *Omega: Journal of Death and Dying* 50, no. 3 (2004): 197–215.

26. Alynn Day Harvey, "Evidence of a Tense Shift in Personal Experience Narratives," *Empirical Studies of the Arts* 4, no. 2 (1986): 151–162.

27. Lera Boroditsky, "Linguistic Relativity," in *Encyclopedia of Cognitive Science,* ed. Lynn Nadel (London: Macmillan, 2003), pp. 917–921; esp. 920.

28. Joy S. Berger, *Music of the Soul: Composing Life Out of Loss* (New York: Routledge, 2006), p. 3.

29. Ted Gioia, *Healing Songs* (Durham: Duke University Press, 2006), pp. 24, 32.

30. Robert McDowell, *Poetry as Spiritual Practice* (New York: Free Press, 2008), p. 216.

31. G. Chew and T. J. Mathiesen, "Thrēnos," *The New Grove Dictionary of Music Online;* www.grovemusic.com.

32. Donovan J. Ochs, *Consolatory Rhetoric: Grief, Symbol, and Ritual in the Greco-Roman Era* (Columbia, S.C.: University of South Carolina Press, 1993), p. 50.

33. See Michael Herzfeld, "In Defiance of Destiny: The Management of Time and Gender at a Cretan Funeral," *American Ethnologist* 20, no. 2 (1993): 241–255.

34. De Martino is discussed in James S. Amelang, "Mourning Becomes Eclectic: Ritual Lament and the Problem of Continuity," *Past & Present,* no. 187 (2005): 3–31.

35. Gail Holst-Warhaft, *The Cue for Passion: Grief and Its Political Uses* (Cambridge, Mass.: Harvard University Press, 2000), p. 200. About this lament, see also Loring M. Danforth, *The Death Ritual of Rural Greece* (Princeton, N.J.: Princeton University Press, 1982), p. 143.

36. See Amy Clarkson, "Dying in the Opera," *Pallimed,* http://arts.pallimed.org/2009/10/dying-in-opera.html.

37. Bruce L. Plopper and M. Ernest Ness, "Death as Portrayed to Adolescents Through Top 40 Rock and Roll Music," *Adolescence* 28, no. 112 (Winter 1993): 793–807.

38. David Margolick, *Strange Fruit: Billie Holiday, Café Society, and an Early Cry for Civil Rights* (Philadelphia: Running Press, 2000), p. 17.

39. Glenn Watkins, *Proof Through the Night: Music and the Great War* (Berkeley: University of California Press, 2001), pp. 257–259.

40. Graeme Thomson, *I Shot a Man in Reno: A History of Death by Murder, Suicide, Fire, Flood, Drugs, Disaster, Disease, and General Misadventure as Related in Popular Song* (New York: Continuum, 2008), p. 59.

41. Elijah Wald, *Narcocorrido: A Journey into the Music of Drugs, Guns, and Guerrillas* (New York: HarperCollins, 2002).

42. Edward Hirsch, *How to Read a Poem* (San Diego: Harvest, 1999), p. 271.

43. Charles Reagan Wilson, "Digging Up Bones: Death in Country Music," in *You Wrote My Life: Lyrical Themes in Country Music,* ed. Melton A. McLaurin and Richard A. Peterson, 113–129 (Philadelphia: Gordon and Breach, 1992), p. 115.

44. Wilson, "Digging Up Bones," p. 126.

45. George S. Kanahele, ed., *Hawaiian Music and Musicians* (Honolulu: University Press of Hawaii, 1979), pp. 53, 56.

46. Marguerite K. Ashford, Bishop Museum, Honolulu, personal communication.

47. See Albert Lee Strickland, "The Healing Power of Music in Bereavement," *The Forum: Association for Death Education and Counseling* 29, no. 2 (2003): 4–5.

48. See Richard A. Pacholski, "Death Themes in Music: Resources and Research Opportunities for Death Educators," *Death Studies* 10, no. 3 (1986): 239–263.

49. For a survey, see Robert F. Weir, ed., *Death in Literature* (New York: Columbia University Press, 1980).

50. Ted Bowman, "Using Literary Resources in Bereavement Work: Evoking Words for Grief," *The Forum: Association for Death Education and Counseling* 29, no. 2 (2003): 8–9.

51. Jahan Ramazani, *Poetry of Mourning: The Modern Elegy from Hardy to Heaney* (Chicago: University of Chicago Press, 1994), pp. 1, 361.

52. Albert Lee Strickland, "Elegy," in *The A-Z of Death & Dying: Social, Medical, and Cultural Aspects,* ed. Michael John Brennan (Santa Barbara, Calif.: ABC-Clio/Greenwood, 2014).

53. Robert McDowell, *Poetry as Spiritual Practice* (New York: Free Press, 2008), p. 216.

54. William M. Lamers, Jr., "The Little Sounds of Grief: Poetry and Grief" (paper presented at the 21st International Death, Grief, and Bereavement Conference, University of Wisconsin, LaCrosse, May 28, 2003).

55. Hirsch, *How to Read a Poem,* p. 80.

56. See Terrence Des Pres, *The Survivor: An Anatomy of Life in the Death Camps* (New York: Oxford University Press, 1976); Lawrence L. Langer, *Versions of Survival: The Holocaust and the Human Spirit* (Albany: State University of New York Press, 1982) and *Holocaust Testimonies: The Ruins of Memory* (New Haven, Conn.: Yale University Press, 1991); Lawrence L. Langer, ed., *Art from the Ashes: A Holocaust Anthology* (New York: Oxford University Press, 1995); and Alvin H. Rosenfeld, *A Double Dying: Reflections on Holocaust Literature* (Bloomington: Indiana University Press, 1980).

57. Lawrence Langer, *The Age of Atrocity: Death in Modern Literature* (Boston: Beacon Press, 1978).

58. Frederick J. Hoffman, *The Mortal No: Death and the Modern Imagination* (Princeton, N.J.: Princeton University Press, 1964).

59. William Ruehlmann, *Saint with a Gun: The Unlawful American Private Eye* (New York: New York University Press, 1984), p. 9.

60. Elizabeth D. Samet, "Teaching Poetry to Soldiers in a Post-Heroic Age," *Armed Forces & Society* 29, no. 1 (2002): 109–127.

61. See Richard A. Pacholski, "Death Themes in the Visual Arts: Resources and Research Opportunities for Death Educators," *Death Studies* 10, no. 1 (1986): 59–74.

62. Kirk Varnedoe, "Dreams of a Summer Night," *Portfolio* (November–December 1982), p. 93.

63. Suse Lowenstein, quoted in Ann F. de Jong Hodgson, "Interviews and Issues: Dark Elegy," *Illness, Crises and Loss* 4, nos. 3–4 (1995): 18–38; quote, p. 21. The sculpture is located in Livingston, New Jersey.

64. Fritz Eichenberg, *Dance of Death: A Graphic Commentary on the Danse Macabre Through the Centuries* (New York: Abbeville, 1983).

65. See Martha V. Pike and Janice Gray Armstrong, *A Time to Mourn: Expressions of Grief in Nineteenth Century America* (Stony Brook, N.Y.: The Museums at Stony Brook, 1980); and Anita Schorsch, *Mourning Becomes America: Mourning Art in the New Nation* (Philadelphia: Main Street Press, 1976).

66. Cindy Ruskin, *The Quilt: Stories from the Names Project* (New York: Pocket Books, 1988).

67. Robert E. Goss and Dennis Klass, *Dead But Not Lost: Grief Narratives in Religious Traditions* (Walnut Creek, Calif.: AltaMira, 2005), p. 276.

68. Maxine Borowsky Junge, "Mourning, Memory and Life Itself: The AIDS Quilt and the Vietnam Veterans' Memorial Wall," *Arts in Psychotherapy* 26, no. 3 (1999): 195–203. See also Michael Franklin, "AIDS Iconography and Cultural Transformation: Visual and Artistic Responses to the AIDS Crisis," *The Arts in Psychotherapy* 20, no. 4 (1993): 299–316. For a minority view regarding the Quilt, see Daniel Harris, "Making Kitsch from AIDS," *Harper's Magazine* (July 1994), pp. 55–60.

69. See Jose Cardenas, "Sympathy Crafted by Hand," *The Los Angeles Times,* May 4, 2004; and Michael M. Phillips, "Quilters' Busy Hands Can't Quite Keep Up with Deaths in Iraq," *The Wall Street Journal,* August 30, 2005.

70. Quoted in Cardenas, "Sympathy Crafted by Hand."

71. Holst-Warhaft, *The Cue for Passion,* p. 189.

72. Andrew Whitmarsh, "'We Will Remember Them': Memory and Commemoration in War Museums," *Journal of Conservation and Museum Studies,* Issue 7 (November 2001): 1–15; quote pp. 1, 11.

73. See John Breen, "The Dead and the Living in the Land of Peace: Sociology of the Yasukuni Shrine," *Mortality* 9, no. 1 (2004): 77–82; John Breen, "Yasukuni Shrine: Ritual and Memory," *Japan Focus* 293 (2005); John Breen, ed., *Yasukuni, the War Dead, and the Struggle for Japan's Past* (New York: Columbia University Press, 2008); Andrew M. McGreevy, "Arlington National Cemetery and Yasukuni Jinja: History, Memory, and the Sacred," *Japan Focus* 293 (2005); and Daiki Shibuichi, "The Yasukuni Shrine Dispute and the Politics of Identity in Japan: Why All the Fuss?" *Asian Survey* 45, no. 2 (March/April 2005): 197–215.

74. Carla Sofka, "History and Healing: Museums as Healing Spaces," *The International Journal of the Inclusive Museum,* Volume 2 (Champaign, Ill.: Common Ground, 2009).

75. International Work Group on Death, Dying, and Bereavement, "The Arts and Humanities in Health Care and Education," *Death Studies* 24, no. 5 (2000): 365–375; quote p. 366.

76. Sandra L. Bertman, "Volts of Connection: The Arts as Shock Therapy," *Grief Matters: The Australian Journal of Grief and Bereavement* 3, no. 3 (2000): 51–53; see also, by Bertman, *Facing Death: Images, Insights, and Interventions* (Philadelphia: Taylor & Francis, 1991).

77. See James A. Thorson, "Did You Ever See a Hearse Go By? Some Thoughts on Gallows Humor," *Journal of American Culture* 16, no. 2 (1993): 17–24; quote p. 18.

78. David Lester, "Reflections on Jokes and Cartoons About Suicide," *Death Studies* 36 (2012): 664–674, p. 668.

79. Neil J. Elgee, "Laughing at Death," *The Psychoanalytic Review* 90, no. 4 (2003): 475–497; quote p. 495.

80. Mary N. Hall, "Laughing as We Go" (paper presented at the annual meeting of the Forum for Death Education and Counseling, Philadelphia, April 1985); see also Mary N. Hall and Paula T. Rappe, "Humor and Critical Incident Stress," in *The Path Ahead,* ed. DeSpelder and Strickland, 289–294.

81. John C. Meyer, "Humor as a Double-Edged Sword: Four Functions of Humor in Communication," *Communication Theory* 10, no. 3 (2000): 310–331; example from p. 321.

82. Thorson, "Did You Ever See a Hearse Go By," p. 18.

83. Linda D. Henman, "Humor as a Coping Mechanism: Lessons from POWs," *Humor: International Journal of Humor Research* 14, no. 1 (2001): 83–94; quote p. 86.

84. Linda Francis, Kathleen Monahan, and Candyce Berger, "A Laughing Matter? The Uses of Humor in Medical Institutions," *Motivation and Emotion* 23, no. 2 (1999): 155–174. See also Fabio Sala, Edward Krupat, and Debra Roter, "Satisfaction and the Use of Humor by Physicians and Patients," *Psychology and Health* 17, no. 3 (2002): 269–280.

85. Vera M. Robinson, *Humor and the Health Professions: The Therapeutic Use of Humor in Health Care,* 2nd ed. (Thorofare, N.J.: Slack, 1991), pp. 50, 53.

86. Jamie L. Goldenberg, Tom Pyszczynski, Shannon K. McCoy, Jeff Greenberg, and Sheldon Solomon, "Death, Sex, Love, and Neuroticism: Why is Sex Such a Problem?" *Journal of Personality and Social Psychology* 77, no. 6 (1999): 1173–1187; quote p. 1175.

87. Ester R. Shapiro, "Culture and Socialization in Assessment and Intervention," in *Handbook of Thanatology,* 2nd ed., ed. David K. Meagher and David E. Balk, 193–207 (New York: Routledge, 2013), p. 197.

88. Norman Wirzba, *Food and Faith: A Theology of Eating* (New York: Cambridge University Press, 2011), pp. 1, 2.

89. Tom Arcaro and Ted Cox, "Human Existence as a Waltz of Eros and Thanatos," *Humanity & Society* 12, no. 1 (1988): 75–94.

90. Francesco Campione, *Manifesto della Tanatologia* [Manifesto of Thanatology] (Bologna: Cooperativa Libraria Universitaria Editrice Bologna, 2005).

91. International Work Group on Death, Dying, and Bereavement, "Existential Questions and Their Moral Implications," *Omega: Journal of Death and Dying* 43, no. 1: 1–6; quote p. 1.

92. Robert Kastenbaum, "Reconstructing Death in Postmodern Society," in *The Path Ahead,* ed. DeSpelder and Strickland, 7–18; quote p. 8.

93. Robert Kastenbaum, "Death Writ Large," *Death Studies* 28, no. 4 (2004): 375–392; quote p. 390.

94. Herman Feifel, "The Thanatological Movement: Respice, Adspice, Prospice," *Loss, Grief, and Care* 6, no. 1 (1992): 5–16, esp. pp. 11–12.

95. Calvin Conzelus Moore and John B. Williamson, "The Universal Fear of Death and the Cultural Response," in *Handbook of Death and Dying,* ed. Clifton D. Bryant (Thousand Oaks, Calif.: Sage, 2003), pp. 3–13.

96. Bert Hayslip, Jr., "Death Denial: Hiding and Camouflaging Death," in *Handbook of Death and Dying,* ed. Bryant, 34–42; quote p. 35.

97. Hayslip, "Death Denial," p. 35.

98. Lindsay Prior, "Actuarial Visions of Death: Life, Death, Chance in the Modern World," in *The Changing Face of Death: Historical Accounts of Death and Disposal,* ed. Peter C. Jupp and Glennys Howarth, 177–193 (New York: St. Martin's, 1997), p. 189.

99. Thomas McGuane. *The Longest Silence: A Life in Fishing.* New York: Knopf, 1999, p. x.

100. Avery Weisman, *The Realization of Death* (New York: Jason Aronson, 1974), p. 5.

101. Talcott Parsons, "Death in American Society: A Brief Working Paper," *American Behavioral Scientist* 6, no. 9 (1963): 61–65.

102. See Robert A. Neimeyer and David Van Brunt, "Death Anxiety," in *Dying: Facing the Facts,* 3rd ed., ed. Hannelore Wass and Robert A. Neimeyer, 49–88 (Washington, D.C.: Taylor & Francis, 1995).

103. Robert A. Neimeyer, Richard P. Moser, and Joachim Wittkowski, "Assessing Attitudes Toward Dying and Death: Psychometric Considerations," *Omega: Journal of Death and Dying* 47, no. 1 (2003): 45–76; quote pp. 46–47. See also Robert A. Neimeyer, *Death Anxiety Handbook: Research, Instrumentation, and Application* (Washington, D.C.: Taylor & Francis, 1993).

104. J. A. Beshai and Mohamed A. Naboulsi, "Existential Perspectives on Death Anxiety," *Psychological Reports* 95 (2004): 507–513; quote p. 511.

105. Robert A. Neimeyer, "Death Anxiety Research: The State of the Art" (paper presented at the annual meeting of the Association for Death Education and Counseling, Duluth, Minnesota, April 1991). See also Neimeyer, "Death Anxiety," in *Encyclopedia of Death and the Human Experience,* ed. Clifton D. Bryant and Dennis L. Peck, 296–299 (Thousand Oaks, Calif.: Sage, 2009).

106. Robert A. Neimeyer, Joachim Wittkowski, and Richard P. Moser, "Psychological Research on Death Attitudes: An Overview and Evaluation," *Death Studies* 28 (2004): 309–339; quote p. 331.

107. Robert Kastenbaum, "Theory, Research, and Application: Some Critical Issues for Thanatology," *Omega: Journal of Death and Dying* 18, no. 4 (1987–1988): 397–410.

108. Herman Feifel, "Psychology and Death: Meaningful Rediscovery," in *The Path Ahead,* ed. DeSpelder and Strickland, pp. 19–28.

109. Brian L. Burke, Andy Martens, and Erik H. Faucher, "Two Decades of Terror Management Theory: a Meta-Analysis of Mortality Salience Research," *Personality & Social Psychology Review* 14, no. 2 (2010): 155–195. Study shows MS hypothesis of TMT provides moderate to large effects.

110. Maxine Sheets-Johnstone, "Size, Power, Death: Constituents in the Making of Human Morality," *Journal of Consciousness Studies* 9, no. 2 (2002): 49–67.

111. Lillian M. Range, "Historical and Contemporary Perspectives on Traumatic Death," in *Handbook of Thanatology,* 2nd ed., ed. Meagher and Balk, p. 293.

112. Tom Pyszczynski, Jeff Greenberg, and Sheldon Solomon, "Proximal and Distal Defense: A New Perspective on Unconscious Motivation," *Current Directions in Psychological Science* 9, no. 5 (2000): 156–160.

113. Sheldon Solomon, Jeff Greenberg, and Tom Pyszczynski, "Tales from the Crypt: On the Role of Death in Life," *Zygon: Journal of Religion and Science* 33, no. 1 (1998): 9–43; quote, p. 13. See also Sheldon Solomon, Jeff Greenberg, and Tom Pyszczynski, "A Terror Management Theory of Social Behavior: The Psychological Functions of Esteem and Cultural Worldview," in *Advances in Experimental Social Psychology* 24, ed. M. P. Zanna (New York: Academic Press): 93–159.

114. Sheldon Solomon, Jeff Greenberg, and Tom Pyszczynski, "Pride and Prejudice: Fear of Death and Social Behavior," *Current Directions in Psychological Science* 9, no. 6 (2000): 200–204; quote p. 201.

115. Sam Keen, "The Heroics of Everyday Life: A Theorist of Death Confronts His Own End," *Psychology Today,* April 1974. See also Daniel Liechty, "The Denial of Death Revisited," *Death Studies* 23, no. 8 (1999): 757–760; and "Reaction to Mortality: An Interdisciplinary Organizing Principle for the Human Sciences," *Zygon: Journal of Religion and Science* 33, no. 1 (1998): 45–58. See also Jeffrey Kauffmann, *Awareness of Mortality* (Amityville, N.Y.: Baywood, 1995).

116. Tom Pyszczynski, Jeff Greenberg, and Sheldon Solomon, "Why Do We Need What We Need? A Terror Management Perspective on the Roots of Human Social Motivation," *Psychological Inquiry* 8, no. 1 (1997): 1–20.

117. Jeff Greenberg, Sheldon Solomon, and Tom Pyszczynski, "Terror Management Theory of Self-Esteem and Cultural Worldviews: Empirical Assessments and Conceptual Refinements," *Advances in Experimental Social Psychology* 29 (1997): 61–139; quote p. 100.

118. Robert Kastenbaum, "Should We Manage Terror—If We Could?" *Omega: Journal of Death and Dying* 59, no. 4 (2009): 271–304; esp. pp. 287, 288.

119. Robert Kastenbaum, "Sad to Say: Is It Time for Sorrow Management Theory?," *Omega: Journal of Death and Dying* 62, no. 4 (2010–2011): 305–327; quote p. 323.

120. Robert C. Solomon, "Death Fetishism, Morbid Solipsism," in *Death and Philosophy,* ed. Jeff Malpas and Robert C. Solomon, 152–176 (New York: Routledge, 1998); quote pp. 174–175.

121. F. David Martin, "Facing Death at 80: Memory and the Holy," *Soundings: An Interdisciplinary Journal* 83, no. 2 (Summmer 2000): 301–330.

122. Patrick Vernon Dean, "Is Death Education a 'Nasty Little Secret'? A Call to Break the Alleged Silence," in *The Path Ahead,* ed. DeSpelder and Strickland, pp. 323–326.

123. Vanderlyn R. Pine, "A Socio-Historical Portrait of Death Education," *Death Education* 1, no. 1 (1977): 57–84; see also Pine, "The Age of Maturity for Death Education: A Socio-Historical Portrait of the Era 1976–1985," *Death Studies* 10, no. 3 (1986): 209–231; and Dan Leviton, "The Scope of Death Education," *Death Education* 1, no. 1 (1977): 41–56.

124. Darrell Crase, "Death Education: Its Diversity and Multidisciplinary Focus," *Death Studies* 13, no. 1 (1989): 25–29.

125. Thomas Attig, "Person-Centered Death Education," *Death Studies* 16, no. 4 (1992): 357–370.

126. Gorer's essay was originally published in the journal *Encounter* in 1955; it was later reprinted in his 1965 book, *Death, Grief, and Mourning in Contemporary Britain.* For an account of the essay's influence, see Ian Andrews, "Pornography of Death," in *Encyclopedia of Death and Dying,* ed. Glennys Howarth and Oliver Leaman, 361–362 (New York: Routledge, 2001).

127. Lindsay Prior, *The Social Organization of Death* (London: Macmillan, 1989), esp. pp. 4–12. See also Neil Small, "Theories of Grief: A Critical Review," in *Grief, Mourning, and Death Ritual,* ed. Jenny Hockey, Jeanne Katz, and Neil Small, 19–48 (Buckingham: Open University Press, 2001); esp. pp. 21–24.

128. The symposium was titled "The Concept of Death and Its Relation to Behavior."

129. Herman Feifel, "Psychology and Death: Meaningful Rediscovery," in *The Path Ahead,* ed. DeSpelder and Strickland, pp. 19–28.

130. Kenneth J. Doka, E. Neil Heflin-Wells, Terry L. Martin, Lula M. Redmon, and Sherry R. Schacter, "The Organization of Thanatology," *Omega: Journal of Death and Dying* 63, no. 2 (2011): 113–124; esp. p. 115.

131. Robert Kastenbaum, "Omega: Pre-History of a Journal," *Omega: Journal of Death and Dying* 48, no. 1 (2003): 69–84.

132. The Foundation of Thanatology, through its symposia and publication, served an important role early in the development of the field. See also Darrell Crase and Dan Leviton, "Forum for Death Education and Counseling: Its History, Impact, and Future," *Death Studies* 11, no. 5 (1987): 345–359; Kenneth J. Doka, et. al., "The Organization of Thanatology," *Omega: Journal of Death and Dying* 63, no. 2 (2011): 113–124; John E. Fryer, "The Goose," *Illness, Crisis, and Loss* (January 2003): 65–69; and Judith M. Stillion, "Association for Death Education and Counseling: An Organization for Our Times and for Our Future," *Death Studies* 13, no. 2 (1989): 191–201.

133. See Lynne Ann DeSpelder and Albert Lee Strickland, "The Life of a Death Textbook and Its Authors," *The Forum: Newsletter of the Association for Death Education and Counseling* 30 (First Quarter, 2004): 8–9.

134. Sarah Brabant, DeAnn Kalich, and Brooke O. Breaux, "The *Psychology Today* 'You and Death' Questionnaire Revisited," *Omega: Journal of Death and Dying* 58, no. 3 (2008–2009): 193–211; quote from pp. 210–211.

135. The first of these was *Encyclopedia of Death,* ed. Robert Kastenbaum and Beatrice Kastenbaum (Phoenix: Oryx Press, 1989); see also *Encyclopedia of Death and Dying,* ed. Glennys Howarth and Oliver Leaman (London and New York: Routledge, 2001); *Macmillan Encyclopedia of Death and Dying,* ed. Robert Kastenbaum (New York: Macmillan, 2003); *Handbook of Death and Dying,* ed. Clifton D. Bryant (Thousand Oaks, Calif.: Sage, 2003); Dana K. Cassell, Robert C. Salinas, and Peter A. S. Winn, *The Encyclopedia of Death and Dying* (New York: Facts on File, 2005); and *Encyclopedia of Death and the Human Experience,* ed. Clifton D. Bryant and Dennis L. Peck (Thousand Oaks, Calif.: Sage, 2009).

136. See entry "United States," by Lynne Ann DeSpelder and Albert Lee Strickland, in *Encyclopedia of Death and Dying,* ed. Howarth and Leaman, pp. 460–463.

137. Luciana Mascarenhas Fonseca and Ines Testoni, "The Emergence of Thanatology and Current Practice in Death Education," *Omega: Journal of Death and Dying* 64, no. 2 (2011–2012): 157–169; quote p. 163. Italics added.

138. Hannelore Wass, "Visions in Death Education," in *The Path Ahead,* ed. DeSpelder and Strickland, pp. 327–334.

139. See, for example, James K. Crissman, *Death and Dying in Central Appalachia: Changing Attitudes and Practices* (Urbana: University of Illinois Press, 1994); and James J. Farrell, *Inventing the American Way of Death, 1830–1920* (Philadelphia: Temple University Press, 1980).

140. U.S. Census Bureau, "Expectation of Life at Birth," *Historical Statistics of the United States, Colonial Times to 1970* (Washington, D.C.: Government Printing Office), p. 55; and Arialdi M. Miniño, "Death in the United States, 2011," *NCHS Data Brief,* no. 115 (Hyattsville, Md.: National Center for Health Statistics, 2013), p. 1.

141. "Nation Digest," *The Washington Post,* August 20, 2009.

142. Miniño, "Death in the United States, 2011," pp. 1–2.

143. Rachel Ehrenberg, "Modern Living Vastly Extends Life," *Science News* (November 17, 2012), p. 10.

144. Miniño, "Death in the United States, 2011," p. 4.

145. "Deaths and Death Rates," *Historical Statistics of the United States,* p. 59; and Miniño, "Death in the United States, 2011," p. 1.

146. Vincent DiGirolamo, "Newsboy Funerals: Tales of Sorrow and Solidarity in Urban America," *Journal of Social History* 36, no. 1 (2002): 5–20; esp. p. 7.

147. Jennie Benford, "Victorian Mourning at the Frick," *The Forum: Newsletter of the Association for Death Education and Counseling* 22, no. 1 (January–February 1996): 7–8.

148. U.S. Census Bureau, "Deaths and Death Rates by Leading Causes of Death," *Statistical Abstract of the United States, 2009,* 128th ed. (Washington, D.C.: Government Printing Office, 2008), p. 86. See also Donna L. Hoyert, "75 Years of Mortality in the United States, 1935–2010," *NCHS Data Brief,* no. 88 (March 2012).

149. John Allen Paulos, *A Mathematician Reads the Newspaper* (New York: Basic, 1995), p. 139.

150. S. Jay Olshansky and A. Brian Ault, "The Fourth Stage of the Epidemiologic Transition: The Age of Delayed Degenerative Diseases," *Milbank Quarterly* 64, no. 3 (1986): 355–391.

151. "Annual Estimates of the Population by Age," *Historical Statistics of the United States,* p. 10; and U.S. Census Bureau, "Resident Population by Age," *Statistical Abstract of the United States: 2012,* 131st ed. (Washington, D.C., 2011); http://www.census.gov/compendia/statab/.

152. Charlotte A. Schoenborn and Kathleen M. Heyman, "Health Characteristics of Adults Aged 55 Years and Over: United States: 2004–2007," *National Health Statistics Reports,* no. 16 (July 8, 2009): 1–32; esp. p. 1.

153. "Resident Population by Age: 1900 to 1997," *Statistical Abstract of the United States: 1999,* p. 869; and Donna L. Hoyert and Jiaquan Xu, "Deaths: Preliminary Data for 2011," *National Vital Statistics Reports* 61, no. 6 (Hyattsville, Md.: National Center for Health Statistics, 2012), p. 8.

154. Burden S. Lundgren and Clare A. Houseman, "Banishing Death: The Disappearance of the Appreciation of Mortality," *Omega: Journal of Death and Dying* 61, no. 3 (2010): 223–249; esp. p. 241.

155. Lundgren and Houseman, "Banishing Death," pp. 241, 245.

156. Chris Shilling, *The Body and Social Theory,* 2nd ed. (Thousand Oaks, Calif.: Sage, 2003), p. 167.

157. Shilling, *Body and Social Theory,* p. 165.

158. Anne M. Smith and Corinne Cavuoti, "Thanatology in the Digital Age," in *Handbook of Thanatology,* 2nd ed., ed. Meagher and Balk, p. 429.

159. Tony Walter et al., "Does the Internet Change How We Die and Mourn? Overview and Analysis," *Omega: Journal of Death and Dying* 64, no. 4 (2011–2012): 275–302; quote p. 276.

160. Paraphrased from Carla J. Sofka, Illene Noppe Cupit, and Kathleen R. Gilbert, eds., *Dying, Death, and Grief in an Online Universe* (New York: Springer, 2012), p. 262.

161. Anne M. Smith and Corinne Cavuoti, "Thanatology in the Digital Age," in *Handbook of Thanatology,* 2nd ed., ed. Meagher and Balk, p. 431. See also Margaret S. Stroebe, Karolijne Van Der Houwen, and Henk Schut, "Bereavement Support, Intervention, and Research on the Internet: A Critical Review," in *Handbook of Bereavement Research and Practice: Advances in Theory and Intervention,* ed. Margaret S. Stroebe, Robert O. Hansson, Henk Schut, and Wolfgang Stroebe (Washington, D.C.: American Psychological Association, 2008), pp. 551–574.

162. Jocelyn M. DeGroot, "Maintaining Relational Continuity with the Deceased on Facebook," *Omega: Journal of Death and Dying* 65, no. 3 (2012): 195–212.

163. Robert A. Neimeyer, quoted in "Attachment at a Distance: Grief Therapy in the Virtual World," in *Dying, Death, and Grief in an Online Universe,* 103–118; quote p. 115.

164. Leanne Italie, "Crisis Hotlines Turning to Text to Reach Teens," *AP Online* (March 29, 2013).

165. Raina M. Merchant, Stacy Elmer, and Nicole Lurie, "Integrating Social Media into Emergency-Preparedness Efforts," *New England Journal of Medicine* 365, no. 4 (July 28, 2011): 289–291.

166. Sofka, Cupit, and Gilbert, *Dying, Death, and Grief in an Online Universe,* p. 4.

167. Robert E. Kavanaugh, *Facing Death* (Los Angeles: Nash, 1972).

168. David E. Stannard, *The Puritan Way of Death: A Study in Religion, Culture, and Social Change* (New York: Oxford University Press, 1977).

169. Information from exhibit brochure and stories in *The Los Angeles Times* by Diane Haithman, January 22, 2005, and Tonya Alanez, January 24, 2005.

170. Paul Duro and others, "Postmodernism," in *Key Ideas in Human Thought,* ed. Kenneth McLeish, 584–585 (New York: Facts on File, 1993). See also William Simon, C. Allen Haney, and Russell Buenteo, "The Postmodernization of Death and Dying," *Symbolic Interaction* 16, no. 4 (1993): 411–426.

171. Chris Schilling and Philip A. Mellor, *The Sociological Imagination: Elementary Forms of Social and Moral Life* (Thousand Oaks, Calif.: Sage, 2001), p. 195.

172. Schilling and Mellor, *The Sociological Imagination,* p. 191.

173. Stuart Sim, ed., *The Routledge Companion to Postmodernism,* 2nd ed. (New York: Routledge, 2005), p. vii.

174. Masa Higo, "Surviving Death Anxieties in Liquid Modern Times: Examining Zygmunt Bauman's Cultural Theory of Death and Dying," *Omega: Journal of Death and Dying* 65, no. 3 (2012): 221–238; esp. 228, 232.

175. Ulrich Beck, "The Cosmopolitan Society and Its Enemies," *Theory, Culture & Society* 19, nos. 1–2 (2002): 17–44; quote from p. 17.

176. Anthony Giddens, *Runaway World: How Globalization Is Reshaping Our Lives* (New York: Routledge, 2000), p. 23.

177. Daniel Levy and Natan Sznaider, "Memory Unbound: The Holocaust and the Formation of Cosmopolitan Memory," *European Journal of Social Theory* 51, no. 1 (2002): 87–106.

178. Marina Sozzi, "The Myth of Natural Death" (paper presented at the meeting of the International Association of Thanatology and Suicidology, Bologna, Italy, June 2005).

179. Robert Kastenbaum, "Should We Manage Terror," p. 295.

180. Daniel Callahan, "Frustrated Mastery: The Cultural Context of Death in America—Caring for Patients at the End of Life," *Western Journal of Medicine* 163, no. 3 (1995): 226–230.

181. "What is Death Café"? http://www.deathcafe.com/p/what-is-death-cafe.html.

182. Glennys Howarth, *Death and Dying: A Sociological Introduction* (Malden, Mass.: Polity, 2006), p. 1.

183. Andrew S. Ziner, Department of Sociology, University of North Dakota, personal communication, May 1994.

184. See Nancy J. Moules, "Postmodernism and the Sacred: Reclaiming Connection in Our Greater-than-Human Worlds," *Journal of Marital and Family Therapy* 26, no. 2 (2000): 229–240.

185. "The Bright Side of Death: Awareness of Mortality Can Result in Positive Behaviors," http://www.sciencedaily.com/releases/2012/04/120430164359.htm.

186. Yoshida Kenkō, quoted by Donald Keene, "Kenkō: Essays in Idleness (*Tsurezureguswa*)," in *Approaches to the Asian Classics*, edited by Wm. Theodore de Bary and Irene Bloom (New York: Columbia University Press, 1990), p. 314.

CHAPTER 2

1. Sandor B. Brent, "Puns, Metaphors, and Misunderstandings in a Two-Year-Old's Conception of Death," *Omega: Journal of Death and Dying* 8, no. 4 (1977–1978): 285–293. The son, now an adult, has no recollection of this experience. Dr. Brent, a psychologist, believes that this indicates a successfully managed event. (Personal communication.)

2. Mark W. Speece, "Very Young Children's Experiences with and Reactions to Death" (master's thesis, Wayne State University, 1983).

3. Mark W. Speece and Sandor B. Brent, "The Development of Children's Understanding of Death," in *Handbook of Childhood Death and Bereavement,* ed. Charles A. Corr and Donna M. Corr, 29–50 (New York: Springer, 1996).

4. Brenda L. Kenyon, "Current Research in Children's Conceptions of Death: A Critical Review," *Omega: Journal of Death and Dying* 43, no. 1 (2001): 63–91; Mark W. Speece and Sandor B. Brent, "Children's Understanding of Death: A Review of Three Components of a Death Concept," *Child Development* 55, no. 5 (October 1984): 1671–1686; and Speece and Brent, "The Acquisition of a Mature Understanding of Three Components of the Concept of Death," *Death Studies* 16, no. 3 (1992): 211–229.

5. See Sandor B. Brent and Mark W. Speece, "'Adult' Conceptualization of Irreversibility: Implications for the Development of the Concept of Death," *Death Studies* 17, no. 3 (1993): 203–224.

6. Virginia Slaughter and Maya Griffiths, "Death Understanding and Fear of Death in Young Children," *Clinical Child Psychology and Psychiatry* 12, no. 4 (2007): 525–535; esp. p. 526.

7. Virginia Slaughter, "Young Children's Understanding of Death," *Australian Psychologist* 40, no. 3 (2005): 179–186; and Virginia Slaughter and Michelle Lyons, "Learning about Life and Death in Early Childhood," *Cognitive Psychology* 46, no. 1 (2003): 1–30. See also Susan Carey, *Conceptual Change in Childhood* (Cambridge, Mass.: MIT Press, 1985); and, also by Carey, "On the Origin of Causal Understanding," in *Causal Cognition: A Multidisciplinary Debate,* ed. D. Sperber, D. Premack, and A. Premack (New York: Oxford University Press, 1995).

8. Slaughter and Griffiths, "Death Understanding and Fear of Death in Young Children," pp. 526–527.

9. Slaughter and Griffiths, "Death Understanding and Fear of Death in Young Children," p. 533.

10. Kenyon, "Current Research in Children's Conceptions of Death," p. 87.

11. Eric B. Shiraev and David A. Levy, *Cross-Cultural Psychology: Critical Thinking and Contemporary Applications,* 5th ed. (Boston: Pearson, 2013), p. 19.

12. Kang Lee, "Scientific Reasoning: Introduction," in *Childhood Cognitive Development: The Essential Readings,* ed. Lee, 265–266 (Oxford: Blackwell, 2000).

13. Ross D. Parke, Peter A. Ornstein, John J. Rieser, and Carolyn Zahn-Waxler, "The Past as Prologue: An

Overview of a Century of Developmental Psychology," in *A Century of Developmental Psychology*, ed. Parke et al. (Washington, D.C.: American Psychological Association, 1994), p. 12.

14. Paul Schilder and David Wechsler, "The Attitudes of Children Toward Death," *Journal of Genetic Psychology* 45 (1934): 406–451.

15. Sylvia Anthony, *The Discovery of Death in Childhood and After* (New York: Basic Books, 1972), revised edition of *The Child's Discovery of Death: A Study in Child Psychology* (London: Kegan Paul, 1940).

16. Maria H. Nagy, "The Child's Theories Concerning Death," *Journal of Genetic Psychology* 73 (1948): 3–27.

17. Slaughter, "Young Children's Understanding of Death."

18. Susan A. Gelman and John E. Opfer, "Development of the Animate-Inanimate Distinction," in *Blackwell Handbook of Childhood Cognitive Development,* ed. Usha Goswami, 151–166 (Oxford: Blackwell, 2004).

19. Jesse M. Bering, Carlos Hernández Blasi, and David F. Bjorklund, "The Development of 'Afterlife' Beliefs in Religiously and Secularly Schooled Children," *British Journal of Developmental Psychology* 23 (2005): 587–607; quote p. 589.

20. Jesse M. Bering and David F. Bjorklund, "The Natural Emergence of Reasoning about the Afterlife as a Development Regularity," *Developmental Psychology* 40, no. 2 (2004): 217–233.

21. Erik Erikson, *Childhood and Society* (New York: Norton, 1950).

22. Jean Piaget, *The Child and Reality: Problems of Genetic Psychology,* trans. Arnold Rosin (New York: Grossman, 1973), and *The Child's Conception of the World* (London: Routledge & Kegan Paul, 1929).

23. Robert Zucker, *The Journey Through Grief and Loss: Helping Yourself and Your Child When Grief Is Shared* (New York: St. Martin's, 2009), p. 37.

24. Bruce Bower, "Toddler Worldview Shifts at Age 2," *Science News* (August 16, 2008), p. 12.

25. Patricia Miller, *Theories of Developmental Psychology,* 4th ed. (New York: Worth, 2002), p. 42.

26. Meg Jay, *The Defining Decade: Why Your Twenties Matter—And How to Make the Most of Them Now* (New York: Twelve, 2012), p. 139.

27. From a conversation with Jean Piaget in Richard I. Evans, *The Making of Psychology: Discussions with Creative Contributors* (New York: Knopf, 1976), p. 46.

28. Miller, *Theories of Developmental Psychology,* p. 153.

29. Robert Kastenbaum, *On Our Way: The Final Passage Through Life and Death* (Berkeley: University of California Press, 2004), p. 367.

30. Slaughter and Griffiths, "Death Understanding and Fear of Death in Young Children," p. 526.

31. Gerald P. Koocher, "Childhood, Death, and Cognitive Development," *Developmental Psychology* 9, no. 3 (1973): 369–375; "Talking with Children About Death," *American Journal of Orthopsychiatry* 44, no. 3 (April 1974): 404–411; and "Conversations with Children About Death," *Journal of Clinical Child Psychology* (Summer 1974): 19–21.

32. Helen L. Swain, "Childhood Views of Death," *Death Education* 2, no. 4 (1979): 341–358.

33. Quoted in Claudia Kalb and Aku Ammah-Tagoe, "Generation 9/11: Children Who Watched the Tragedy Unfold Are Now On the Brink of Adulthood," *Newsweek,* September 8, 2009.

34. See Mary Alice Varga and Robin Paletti, "Life Span Issues and Dying," in *Handbook of Thanatology,* 2nd ed., ed. David K. Meagher and David E. Balk, 25–31 (New York: Routledge, 2013), p. 28; and David E. Balk, "Adolescent Development: The Backstory to Adolescent Encounters with Death and Bereavement," in *Adolescent Encounters with Death, Bereavement, and Coping,* ed. David E. Balk and Charles A. Corr, 3–20 (New York: Springer, 2009), esp. pp. 4–5.

35. Ken Doka, *Counseling Individuals with Life-Threatening Illness* (New York: Springer, 2009), p. 118.

36. Jay, *Defining Decade,* pp. 107–108.

37. Mary Dixon-Woods, Bridget Young, and David Heney, *Rethinking Experiences of Childhood Cancer: A Multidisciplinary Approach to Chronic Childhood Illness* (Berksnire: Open University Press, 2005), p. 17.

38. Lynn Schofield Clark, *From Angels to Aliens: Teenagers, the Media, and the Supernatural* (New York: Oxford University Press, 2003), p. 11.

39. Jay, *Defining Decade,* p. 1407.

40. Mary Alice Varga and Robin Paletti, "Life Span Issues and Dying," in *Handbook of Thanatology,* 2nd ed., ed. David K. Meagher and David E. Balk, 25–31 (New York: Routledge, 2013); quote p. 28.

41. Miller, *Theories of Developmental Psychology,* p. 155.

42. Illene Cupit Noppe and Lloyd D. Noppe, "Adolescent Experiences with Death: Letting Go of Immortality," *Journal of Mental Health Counseling* 26, no. 2 (2004): 146–167; quote p. 154.

43. Lloyd D. Noppe and Illene C. Noppe, "Dialectical Themes in Adolescent Conceptions of Death," *Journal of Adolescent Research* 6, no. 1 (1991): 28–42.

44. Richard A. Settersten, Jr., and Barbara Ray, "What's Going On With Young People Today? The Long and Twisting Path to Adulthood," *Future of Children* 20, no. 1 (2010): 19–36; quote p. 36.

45. Jeffrey Jensen Arnett, "Emerging Adulthood: A Theory of Development from the Late Teens Through the Twenties," *American Psychologist* 55, no. 5 (2000): 469–480; quote p. 475. See also Jeffrey Jensen Arnett et al., *Debating Emerging Adulthood: Stage or Process?* (New York: Oxford University Press, 2011).

46. Yoko Yamada, "Models of Life-Span Development Psychology: A Construction of the Generative Life Model Including the Concept of Death," *Kyoto University Research Studies in Education* 47 (2002): 39–62; esp. p. 46.

47. Kenneth J. Doka, *Counseling Individuals with Life-Threatening Illness* (New York: Springer, 2009), p. 120.

48. Charles W. Brice, "Mourning Throughout the Life Cycle," *American Journal of Psychoanalysis* 42, no. 4 (1982): 320–321.

49. Patricia H. Miller, *Theories of Developmental Psychology,* 4th ed. (New York: Worth, 2002), p. 156.

50. Doka, *Counseling Individuals with Life-Threatening Illness,* p. 120.

51. Michele A. Paludi, ed., *Human Development in Multicultural Contexts* (Upper Saddle River, N.J.: Prentice-Hall, 2002), p. 190.

52. Miller, *Theories of Developmental Psychology,* p. 156.

53. Doka, *Counseling Individuals with Life-Threatening Illness,* p. 121.

54. Miller, *Theories of Developmental Psychology,* p. 156.

55. M. Brewster Smith, "The Case of Brew," *Journal of Personality* 73, no. 5 (2005): 1111–1140; quote p. 1136.

56. Erik H. Erikson, *The Life Cycle Completed: A Review* (New York: Norton, 1982), p. 67. See also Paul B. Baltes and Ursula M. Staudinger, "Wisdom: A Metaheuristic (Pragmatic) to Orchestrate Mind and Virtue Toward Excellence," *American Psychologist* 55, no. 1 (2000): 122–136; and Christina Rōcke and Katie E. Cherry, "Death at the End of the 20th Century: Individual Processes and Developmental Tasks in Old Age," *International Journal of Aging and Human Development* 54, no. 4 (2002): 315–333.

57. Hilary N. Weaver, *Explorations in Cultural Competence: Journeys to the Four Directions* (Belmont, Calif.: Brooks/Cole, 2005), p. 25.

58. Frederick Erickson, "Culture and Human Development," *Human Development* 45 (2002): 299–306; quote p. 303.

59. Richard A. Settersten, Jr., "Socialization and the Life Course: New Frontiers in Theory and Research," in *New Frontiers in Socialization,* ed. Richard A. Settersten, Jr., and Timothy J. Owens, 13–40 (Amsterdam: JAI, 2002), p. 15.

60. Settersten, "Socialization and the Life Course," p. 20.

61. Walter R. Heinz, "Self-Socialization and Post-Traditional Society," in *New Frontiers in Socialization,* ed. Settersten and Owens, 41–64; p. 44.

62. Hannelore Wass, "Death Education for Children," in *Dying, Death, and Bereavement: A Challenge for Living,* 2nd ed., ed. Inge Corless, Barbara B. Germino, and Mary A. Pittman, 25–41 (New York: Springer, 2003); quote p. 27.

63. Norman Goodman, *Introduction to Sociology* (New York: HarperCollins, 1992), pp. 84–85.

64. Settersten, "Socialization and the Life Course," p. 34.

65. Mark A. Mesler, "Negotiating Life for the Dying: Hospice and the Strategy of Tactical Socialization," *Death Studies* 19, no. 3 (1995): 235–255.

66. Kathleen R. Gilbert and Colleen I. Murray, "The Family, Larger Systems, and Death Education," in *Handbook of Thanatology,* 2nd ed., ed. David K. Meagher and David E. Balk, 367–377 (New York: Routledge, 2013), p. 367.

67. Settersten, "Socialization and the Life Course," p. 30.

68. Iona Opie and Peter Opie, *The Lore and Language of Schoolchildren* (Oxford: Clarendon, 1959), p. 1.

69. Iona Opie and Peter Opie, *Children's Games in Street and Playground* (Oxford: Clarendon, 1969), pp. 62, 75.

70. Meredith Cox, Erin Garrett, and James A. Graham, "Death in Disney Films: Implications for Children's Understanding of Death," *Omega: Journal of Death and Dying* 50, no. 4 (2004–2005): 267–280.

71. Martha Wolfenstein and Gilbert Kliman, eds., *Children and the Death of a President: Multi-Disciplinary Studies* (Garden City, N.Y.: Anchor Press/Doubleday, 1965), esp. pp. 217–239.

72. See Maria Tatar, ed., *The Annotated Classic Fairy Tales* (New York: Norton, 2002).

73. Terri Windling, "On Tolkien and Fairy-Tales," in *Meditations on Middle-Earth,* ed. Karen Haber (New York: St. Martin's, 2001), pp. 215–229; quote p. 227.

74. Elizabeth P. Lamers, "Children, Death, and Fairy Tales," *Omega: Journal of Death and Dying* 31, no. 2 (1995): 151–167. See also Joan Acocella, "Once Upon a Time: The Lure of the Fairy Tale," *The New Yorker* (July 23, 2012): 73–78.

75. Carolyn Marvin, "On Violence in Media," *Journal of Communication* 50, no. 1 (2000): 142–149.

76. Sheila Hébert-Collins, *Petite Rouge: A Cajun Twist to an Old Tale* (Gretna, La.: Pelican, 1997); Niki Daly, *Pretty Salma: A Little Red Riding Story from Africa* (New York: Clarion, 2007).

77. See Eve Morel, ed., *Fairy Tales and Fables* (New York: Grosset & Dunlap, 1970), pp. 11–13; and Catherine Orenstein, *Little Red Riding Hood Uncloaked: Sex, Morality, and the Evolution of a Fairy Tale* (New York: Basic Books, 2002).

78. Ed Young, trans., *Lon Po Po: A Red-Riding Hood Story from China* (New York: Philomel Books, 1989).

79. Kalle Achte and others, "Themes of Death and Violence in Lullabies of Different Countries," *Omega: Journal of Death and Dying* 20, no. 3 (1989–1990): 193–204.

80. Sandra L. Bertman, "Death Education in the Face of a Taboo," in *Concerning Death: A Practical Guide for the Living,* ed. Earl A. Grollman (Boston: Beacon Press, 1974), p. 334.

81. Reported by Richard Lonetto, *Children's Conceptions of Death* (New York: Springer, 1980), p. 9.

82. Davina A. Allen and others, "Religion," in *Key Ideas in Human Thought,* ed. Kenneth McLeish (New York: Facts on File, 1993), pp. 626–627.

83. Robert A. Emmons, "Religion in the Psychology of Personality: An Introduction," *Journal of Personality* 67, no. 6 (1999): 873–888. See also Alfred Kracher, "The Study of Religion: Conversation Point for Theology and Science," *Zygon: Journal of Religion and Science* 35, no. 4 (2000): 827–848. See also Kenneth J. Doka, "Religion, Spirituality, and Assessment and Intervention," in *Handbook of Thanatology,* 2nd ed., ed. David K. Meagher and David E. Balk, 209–217 (New York: Routledge, 2013).

84. Justin L. Barrett, "Exploring the Natural Foundations of Religion," *Trends in Cognitive Sciences* 4, no. 1 (2000): 29–34.

85. Clark, *From Angels to Aliens,* p. 9.

86. Michael E. McCullough and others, "Religious Involvement and Mortality: A Meta-Analytic Review," *Health Psychology* 19, no. 3 (2000): 211–222.

87. Lynne Ann DeSpelder and Albert Lee Strickland, "Using Life Experiences as a Way of Helping Children Understand Death," in *Beyond the Innocence of Childhood: Factors Influencing Children and Adolescents' Perceptions and Attitudes Toward Death,* ed. David W. Adams and Eleanor J. Deveau, 45–54 (Amityville, N.Y.: Baywood, 1995).

88. Lynne Ann DeSpelder and Nathalie Prettyman, *A Guidebook for Teaching Family Living* (Boston: Allyn & Bacon, 1980), pp. 130–134.

89. See Mary Anne Sedney, "Children's Grief Narratives in Popular Films," *Omega: Journal of Death and Dying* 39, no. 4 (1999): 315–324.

90. Ute Carson, "A Child Loses a Pet," *Death Education* 3 (1980): 399–404.

91. Kenneth R. Kaufman and Nathaniel D. Kaufman, "And Then the Dog Died," *Death Studies* 30 (2006): 61–76; quote p. 63.

92. Kelly A. McCutcheon and Stephen J. Fleming, "Grief Resulting from Euthanasia and Natural Death of Companion Animals," *Omega: Journal of Death and Dying* 44, no. 2 (2001–2002): 169–188.

93. Cheri Barton Ross and Jane Baron-Sorensen, *Pet Loss and Human Emotion: A Guide to Recovery,* 2nd ed. (New York: Routledge, 2007), p. 6.

94. Ross and Baron-Sorensen, *Pet Loss and Human Emotion,* 2nd ed., p. 122.

95. Barbara Ambros, "Vengeful Spirits or Loving Spiritual Companions? Changing Views of Animal Spirits in Contemporary Japan," *Asian Ethnology* 69, no. 1 (2010): 35–67; quotes pp. 36, 60.

96. Michelle Linn-Gust, "From the Backyard to the Pet Bed: The Changing Role of Animals in Society," *The Forum* 33, no. 11 (April 2007): 1, 3–4.

97. Jane Brody, "When Your Pet Dies," *Honolulu Star-Bulletin & Advertiser,* December 8, 1985.

98. See Morris A. Wessel, "Loss of a Pet," in *A Challenge for Living: Dying, Death, and Bereavement,* 2nd ed., ed. Inge B. Corless, Barbara B. Germino, and Mary A. Pittman (New York: Springer, 2003), pp. 303, 305.

99. See Lynn A. Planchon and others, "Death of a Companion Cat or Dog and Human Bereavement: Psychosocial Variables," *Society & Animals* 10, no. 1 (2002): 93–105.

100. Cheri Barton Ross, *Pet Loss and Children: Establishing a Healthy Foundation* (New York: Routledge, 2005), p. 40.

101. Stanley Coren, *The Modern Dog: A Joyful Explanation of How We Live With Dogs Today* (New York: Free Press, 2008), p. 164.

102. Ross and Baron-Sorensen, *Pet Loss and Human Emotion,* pp. 174–175.

103. Allan Kellehear and Jan Fook, "Lassie Come Home: A Study of 'Lost Pet' Notices," *Omega: Journal of Death and Dying* 34, no. 3 (1996–1997): 191–202; quote p. 192.

104. See www.aspca.org for further information.

105. See Lynn A. Planchon, Donald I. Templer, Shelley Stokes, and Jacqueline Keller, "Death of a Companion Cat or Dog and Human Bereavement: Psychosocial Variables," *Society & Animals* 10, no. 1 (2002): 93–105.

106. Ross, *Pet Loss and Children,* p. 98.

107. McCutcheon and Fleming, "Grief Resulting from Euthanasia and Natural Death of Companion Animals."

108. Avery D. Weisman, "Bereavement and Companion Animals," in *The Path Ahead: Readings in Death and Dying,* ed. Lynne Ann DeSpelder and Albert Lee Strickland, 276–280 (Mountain View, Calif.: Mayfield, 1995); quote p. 280.

109. Sandor B. Brent and Mark W. Speece, "'Adult' Conceptualization of Irreversibility: Implications for the Development of the Concept of Death," *Death Studies* 17, no. 3 (1993): 203–224.

110. Sandor B. Brent and others, "The Development of the Concept of Death Among Chinese and U.S. Children 3–17 Years of Age: From Binary to 'Fuzzy' Concepts?" *Omega: Journal of Death and Dying* 33, no. 1 (1996): 67–83. See also Shu Ching Yang and Shih-Fen Chen, "A Phenomenographic Approach to the Meaning of Death: A Chinese Perspective," *Death Studies* 26, no. 2 (2002): 143–175.

111. David W. Plath, "Resistance at Forty-Eight: Old-Age Brinksmanship and Japanese Life Course Pathways," in *Aging and Life Course Transitions: An Interdisciplinary Perspective,* ed. Tamara K. Hareven and Kathleen J. Adams, 109–125 (New York: Guilford Press, 1982).

112. Thomas S. Weisner, "Ecocultural Understanding of Children's Developmental Pathways," *Human Development* 45, no. 4 (2002): 275–281; quote p. 276.

113. Martin Sokefeld, "Debating Self, Identity, and Culture in Anthropology," *Current Anthropology* 40, no. 4 (1999): 417–447.

114. Linda M. Hunt, "Beyond Cultural Competence: Applying Humility to Clinical Settings," *The Park Ridge Center Bulletin* (November–December 2001): 3–4.

115. Albert Bandura, "Exploration of Fortuitous Determinants of Life Paths," *Psychological Inquiry* 9, no. 2 (1998): 95–115; quote p. 97.

CHAPTER *3*

1. Pittu Laungani, "Death and Bereavement in India and England: A Comparative Analysis," *Mortality* 1, no. 2 (1996): 191–212.

2. Jeffrey Jensen Arnett, "The Psychology of Globalization," *American Psychologist* 57, no. 10 (2002): 774–783. See also Mary Buchholtz, "Youth and Cultural Practice," *Annual Review of Anthropology* 31 (2002): 525–552.

3. Gordon Marshall, ed., *The Concise Oxford Dictionary of Sociology* (New York: Oxford University Press, 1994), p. 104. See also Don Brenneis, "Some Cases for Culture," *Human Development* 45, no. 4 (2002): 264–269; and Frederick Erickson, "Culture and Human Development," *Human Development* 45, no. 4 (2002): 299–306.

4. Norman Goodman, *Introduction to Sociology* (New York: HarperCollins, 1992), p. 42.

5. Davina A. Allen, "Structure," in *Key Ideas in Human Thought,* ed. Kenneth McLeish, 508–509 (New York: Facts on File, 1993), p. 716.

6. Nancy Scheper-Hughes, "Death Without Weeping: The Violence of Everyday Life in Brazil," in *The Path Ahead: Readings in Death and Dying,* ed. Lynne Ann DeSpelder and Albert Lee Strickland (Mountain View, Calif.: Mayfield, 1995), pp. 41–58.

7. Kathy Charmaz, "Conceptual Approaches to the Study of Death," *Death and Identity,* 3rd ed., ed. Robert Fulton and Robert Bendiksen (Philadelphia: Charles Press, 1993), pp. 44–45.

8. Robert Blauner, "Death and Social Structure," in *Death and Identity,* rev. ed., ed. Robert Fulton (Bowie, Md.: Charles Press, 1976), pp. 35–59.

9. Robert Bendiksen, "The Sociology of Death," in *Death and Identity,* rev. ed., ed. Fulton, pp. 59–81.

10. Joseph M. Kaufert and John D. O'Neil, "Cultural Mediation of Dying and Grieving Among Native Canadian Patients in Urban Hospitals," in *The Path Ahead,* ed. DeSpelder and Strickland, pp. 59–74.

11. See Ernest Becker, *The Denial of Death* (New York: Free Press, 1973).

12. Paul Koudounaris, *The Empire of Death: A Cultural History of Ossuaries and Charnel Houses* (London: Thames & Hudson, 2011), p. 11.

13. Dana K. Cassell, Robert C. Salinas, and Peter A. S. Winn, *The Encyclopedia of Death and Dying* (New York: Facts on File, 2005), p. xv.

14. See, for example, Ben Harder, "Evolving in Their Graves: Early Burials Hold Clues to Human Origins," *Science News* 160 (December 15, 2001): 380–381. On the origin of "religious feeling" in funeral practices, see Ina Wunn, "Beginning of Religion," *Numen: International Review for the History of Religions* 47, no. 4 (2000): 417–452.

15. The use of blood-red oxide to decorate corpses is possibly the earliest widespread funeral custom. Red ochre was mined in Africa by the earliest *Homo sapiens sapiens;* it appeared in Europe in Neanderthal funeral practices and was used in burials throughout Europe, Africa, Asia, Australia, and the Americas. If we imagine the earth as a living organism, hematite is analogous to the blood of Mother Earth.

16. Mike Parker Pearson, *The Archaeology of Death and Burial* (College Station: Texas A&M University Press, 2000), p. 3.

17. Giambattista Vico, *The First New Science,* ed. and trans. Leon Pompa (Cambridge: Cambridge University Press, 2002), p. 263.

18. J. Peter Brosius, "Father Dead, Mother Dead: Bereavement and Fictive Death in Penan Geng Society," *Omega: Journal of Death and Dying* 32, no. 3 (1995–1996): 197–226.

19. E. S. Craighill Handy and Mary Kawena Pukui, *The Polynesian Family System in Ka-'u, Hawai'i* (Rutland, Vt.: Charles E. Tuttle, 1972), pp. 98–101.

20. Anita J. Glaze, *Art and Death in a Senufo Village* (Bloomington: Indiana University Press, 1981), pp. 150–151.

21. Ninian Smart, *The Long Search* (Boston: Little, Brown, 1977), p. 231.

22. Carol Warren, "Disrupted Death Ceremonies: Popular Culture and the Ethnography of Bali," *Oceania* 64, no. 1 (September 1993): 36–56.

23. See Neville Drury, *The Elements of Shamanism* (Dorset, U.K.: Element Books, 1989); David Riches, "Shamanism: The Key to Religion," *The Journal of the Royal Anthropological Institute* 29, no. 2 (1994): 381–405; and Lyle B. Steadman and Craig T. Palmer, "Visiting Dead Ancestors: Shamans as Interpreters of Religious Traditions," *Zygon: Journal of Religion and Science* 29, no. 2 (1994): 173–189.

24. Kenneth McLeish, "Necromancy," in *Key Ideas in Human Thought,* ed. McLeish, 508–509 (New York: Facts on File, 1993).

25. Important studies include Philippe Ariès, *Western Attitudes Toward Death: From the Middle Ages to the Present* (Baltimore: Johns Hopkins University Press, 1974) and *The Hour of Our Death* (New York: Knopf, 1981); Paul Binsky, *Medieval Death: Ritual and Representation* (London: British Museum Press, 1996); T. S. R. Boase, *Death in the Middle Ages: Mortality, Judgment and Remembrance* (New York: McGraw-Hill, 1972); Jacques Choron, *Death and Western Thought* (New York: Macmillan, 1963); Patrick J. Geary, *Living with the Dead in the Middle Ages* (Ithaca, N.Y.: Cornell University Press, 1994); Ian Gentles, "Funeral Customs in Historical Context," *Journal of Palliative Care* 4, no. 3 (1988): 16–20; and Frederick S. Paxton, *Christianizing Death: The Creation of a Ritual Process in Early Medieval Europe* (New York: Cornell University Press, 1990). Except where otherwise noted, quoted material is from Ariès.

26. C. John Sommerville, "Stark's Age of Faith Argument and the Secularization of Things: A Commentary," *Sociology of Religion* 63, no. 3 (2002): 361–372; esp. p. 362.

27. See Elisabeth Darby and Nicola Smith, *The Cult of the Prince Consort* (New Haven, Conn.: Yale University Press, 1983); Patricia Jalland, *Death in the Victorian Family* (New York: Oxford University Press, 1996); and John Morley, *Death, Heaven, and the Victorians* (Pittsburgh: University of Pittsburgh Press, 1971).

28. Oscar Lenius, *A Well-Dressed Gentleman's Pocket Guide* (London: Prion, 1998), p. 209.

29. See, for example, Philip A. Mellor and Chris Schilling, "Modernity, Self-Identity, and the Sequestration of Death," *Sociology* 27, no. 3 (August 1993): 411–431; and Charles O. Jackson, "Death Shall Have No Dominion: The Passing of the World of the Dead in America," in *Death and Dying: Views from Many Cultures,* ed. Richard A. Kalish, 47–55 (New York: Baywood, 1980).

30. See Peter Brown, *The Cult of the Saints: Its Rise and Function in Latin Christianity* (Chicago: University of Chicago Press, 1981); and Geary, *Living with the Dead in the Middle Ages.*

31. Koudounaris, *The Empire of Death,* p. 16.

32. Rob Kay, *Santa Cruz Sentinel,* March 20, 1983. See also "Empire of the Dead," *Smithsonian* (April 2000).

33. A. A. Gill, "Where the Dead Don't Sleep," *National Geographic* 215, no. 2 (February 2009): 118–133; quote p. 122.

34. Richard A. Etlin, *The Architecture of Death: The Transformation of the Cemetery in Eighteenth-Century Paris* (Cambridge, Mass.: MIT Press, 1984).

35. Kenneth T. Jackson and Camilo José Vergara, *Silent Cities: The Evolution of the American Cemetery* (New York: Princeton Architectural Press, 1989), pp. 22–23.

36. See David E. Stannard, *The Puritan Way of Death: A Study in Religion, Culture, and Social Change* (New York: Oxford University Press, 1977) and "Calm Dwellings: The Brief, Sentimental Age of the Rural Cemetery," *American Heritage* 30, no. 5 (August–September 1979): 42–55, and, edited by Stannard, *Death in America* (Philadelphia: University of Pennsylvania Press, 1975); also Michael Vovelle, "A Century and One-Half of American Epitaphs: Toward the Study of Collective Attitudes About Death," *Comparative Studies in Society and History* 22, no. 4 (October 1980): 534–547.

37. Ray S. Anderson, *Theology, Death and Dying* (New York: Basil Blackwood, 1986), pp. 105–107.

38. James Stevens Curl, *A Celebration of Death: An Introduction to Some of the Buildings, Monuments, and Settings of Funerary Architecture in the Western European Tradition* (New York: Charles Scribner's Sons, 1980), p. 367.

39. See, for example, John Cohen, "Death and the Danse Macabre," *History Today* (August 1982): 35–40; and Fritz Eichenberg, *Dance of Death: A Graphic Commentary on the Danse Macabre Through the Centuries* (New York: Abbeville, 1983).

40. See, for example, Norman F. Cantor, *In the Wake of the Plague: The Black Death and the World It Made* (New York: Free Press, 2001); and Colin Platt, *King Death: The Black Death and Its Aftermath in Late-Medieval England* (London: University College of London Press, 1996).

41. David Herlihy, *The Black Death and the Transformation of the West* (Cambridge, Mass.: Harvard University Press, 1997), pp. 63, 64.

42. Johan P. Mackenbach, "Dead Body with Mourners: Medical Reflections on the Emtombment of Christ," *British Medical Journal* 327 (July 26, 2003): 215–217; quote p. 217.

43. Frank Gonzalez-Crussi, "Anatomy and Old Lace: An Eighteenth-Century Attitude Toward Death," *The Sciences* (January–February 1988): 48–49.

44. Discussion based on Albert Lee Strickland, "Death Masks," in *The A–Z of Death & Dying: Social, Medical, and Cultural Aspects,* ed. Michael John Brennan (Santa Barbara, Calif.: ABC-Clio/Greenwood, 2014). See also Ernst Benkard, *Undying Faces: A Collection of Death Masks,* trans. Margaret M. Green (New York: Norton, 1929).

45. The ensuing discussion of various cultural viewpoints benefits from the following important studies: Miguel A. Pérez and Raffy R. Luquis, eds., *Cultural Competence in Health Education and Health Promotion* (San Francisco: Jossey-Bass, 2008); Larry D. Purnell, *Transcultural Health Care: A Culturally Competent Approach,* 4th ed. (Philadelphia: F. A. Davis, 2013); and Hilary N. Weaver, *Explorations in Cultural Competence: Journeys to the Four Directions* (Belmont, Calif.: Brooks/Cole, 2005).

46. Charles Wilkinson, *Blood Struggle: The Rise of Modern Indian Nations* (New York: Norton, 2005), p. 353.

47. Cassell, Salinas, and Winn, *The Encyclopedia of Death and Dying,* p. xxii.

48. See Donald Bahr, "Bad News: The Predicament of Native American Mythology," *Ethnohistory* 48, no. 4 (2001): 587–612; and Carl Waldman, *Atlas of the North American Indian* (New York: Facts on File, 1985).

49. Theda Perdue and Michael D. Green, *North American Indians: A Very Short Introduction* (New York: Oxford University Press, 2010), pp. 16–17.

50. http://historicaltrauma.com/.

51. Andrea C. Walker, "Building Bridges in American Indian Bereavement Research," *Omega: Journal of Death and Dying* 59, no. 4 (2009): 351–367; esp. p. 355.

52. Quoted in Vine Deloria, Jr., *God Is Red* (New York: Dell, 1973), pp. 176–177. See also Frank Waters, "Two Views of Nature: White and Indian," *The South Dakota Review,* May 1964, pp. 28–29.

53. Clara Sue Kidwell and Alan Velie, *Native American Studies* (Lincoln: University of Nebraska Press, 2005), pp. 11, 21.

54. Chief Joseph, "White Takeover of Indian Land: An Indian's View," in *Christopher Columbus and His Legacy: Opposing Viewpoints,* ed. Mary Ellen Jones, 123–132 (San Diego: Greenhaven, 1992), esp. p. 129.

55. Robson Bonnichsen and Alan L. Schneider, "Battle of the Bones," *The Sciences* 40, no. 4 (2000): 40–46. See also "Human Remains: Contemporary Issues," in *Death Studies* 14, no. 6 (1990), ed. Glen W. Davidson and Larry W. Zimmerman.

56. Louise B. Halfe, "The Circle: Death and Dying from a Native Perspective," *Journal of Palliative Care* 5, no. 1 (1989): 37–41. See also Paul Radin, *The Road of Life and Death: A Ritual Drama of the American Indians* (Princeton, N.J.: Princeton University Press, 1973).

57. Stephen Levine, *A Year to Live: How to Live This Year as If It Were Your Last* (New York: Bell Tower, 1997), p. 154.

58. Richard J. Preston and Sarah C. Preston, "Death and Grieving Among Northern Forest Hunters: An East Cree Example," in *Coping with the Final Tragedy: Cultural Variation in Dying and Grieving,* ed. David R. Counts and Dorothy A. Counts, 135–155 (Amityville, N.Y.: Baywood, 1991).

59. Jamake Highwater, *The Primal Mind: Vision and Reality in Indian America* (New York: Harper & Row, 1981), p. 165.

60. Åke Hultkrantz, *Native Religions of North America: The Power of Visions and Fertility* (New York: Harper & Row, 1987). See also, by Hultkrantz, *The Religions of the American Indians* (Berkeley: University of California Press, 1979), *The Study of American Indian Religions* (New York: Crossroad, 1983), and *Shamanic Healing and Ritual Drama: Health and Medicine in Native North American Religious Tradition* (New York: Crossroad, 1992).

61. Malcolm Margolin, *The Ohlone Way: Indian Life in the San Francisco Monterey Bay Area* (Berkeley, Calif.: Heyday Books, 1978), pp. 145–149.

62. Gerry R. Cox, "Native American Spirituality, Illness, Dying, and Death" (paper presented at the annual meeting of the Midwest Sociological Society, Chicago, 1995).

63. David G. Mandelbaum, "Social Uses of Funeral Rites," in *The Meaning of Death,* ed. Herman Feifel, 189–217 (New York: McGraw-Hill, 1959).

64. John E. Reinhardt, *Life . . . Afterlife: African Funerary Sculpture* (Washington, D.C.: National Museum of African Art, 1982). On African religious thought, see John S. Mbiti, *African Religions and Philosophy* (Garden City, N.Y.: Anchor/Doubleday, 1970); and Dominique Zahan, *The Religion, Spirituality, and Thought of Traditional Africa* (Chicago: University of Chicago Press, 1979).

65. Meyer Fortes, "An Introductory Commentary," in *Ancestors,* ed. William Newell (The Hague: Moulton, 1976), p. 5.

66. Steadman and Palmer, "Visiting Dead Ancestors," p. 177.

67. Noel Q. King, *Religions of Africa: A Pilgrimage into Traditional Religions* (New York: Harper & Row, 1970), pp. 13–14; see also, by King, *Christian and Muslim in Africa* (New York: Harper & Row, 1971), p. 95.

68. Dominique Zahan, "Some Reflections on African Spirituality," in *African Spirituality: Forms, Meanings, and Expressions,* ed. Jacob K. Olupona, 3–25 (New York: Crossroad, 2000), p. 12.

69. King, *Religions of Africa,* p. 68. See also Sjaak Van Der Geest, "'I Want to Go!' How Older People in Ghana Look Forward to Death," *Ageing and Society* 22 (2002): 7–28.

70. Kofi Asare Opoku, "African Perspectives on Death and Dying," in *Perspectives on Death and Dying: Cross-Cultural and Multidisciplinary Views,* ed. Arthur Berger and others, 14–23 (Philadelphia: Charles Press, 1989).

71. Ogbu U. Kalu, "Ancestral Spirituality and Society in Africa," in *African Spirituality: Forms, Meanings, and Expressions,* ed. Jacob K. Olupona, 54–84 (New York: Crossroad, 2000), p. 54.

72. Francis Bebey, *African Music: A People's Art* (Brooklyn, N.Y.: Lawrence Hill, 1975), p. 126.

73. From a story by Robert Dvorchak, *The Los Angeles Times,* July 8, 1990.

74. Jack Goody, *Death, Property, and the Ancestors: A Study of the Mortuary Customs of the LoDagaa of West Africa* (Stanford, Calif.: Stanford University Press, 1962).

75. Olatunde Bayo Lawuyi, "Obituary and Ancestral Worship: Analysis of a Contemporary Cultural Form in Nigeria," *Sociological Analysis* 48, no. 4 (1988): 372–379. See also Kemi Adamolekun, "Survivors' Motives for Extravagant Funerals Among the Yorubas of Western Nigeria," *Death Studies* 25, no. 7 (2001): 609–619; and A. Odasuo Alali, "Management of Death and Grief in Obituary and in Memoriam Pages of Nigerian Newspapers," *Psychological Reports* 73 (1993): 835–842.

76. Ronald Keith Barrett, "Contemporary African-American Funeral Rites and Traditions," in *The Path Ahead,* ed. DeSpelder and Strickland, pp. 80–82; "Psychocultural Influences on African-American Attitudes Toward Death, Dying, and Funeral Rites," in *Personal Care in an Impersonal World: A Multidimensional Look at Bereavement,* ed. John D. Morgan (Amityville, N.Y.: Baywood, 1995), pp. 213–230.

77. Jennifer Hildebrand, "Funerals," in *Greenwood Encyclopedia of African American Folklore,* ed. Anand Prahlad (Westport, Conn.: Greenwood, 2005), p. 482.

78. Ronald K. Barrett, personal communication.

79. LaVone V. Hazell, "Cross-Cultural Funeral Rites," *The Forum: Newsletter of the Association for Death Education and Counseling* 24, no. 3 (1998): 1, 10–11; quote p. 10.

80. Kimberly S. Johnson, Katja I. Elbert-Avila, and James A. Tulsky, "The Influence of Spiritual Beliefs and Practices on the Treatment Preferences of African Americans: A Review of the Literature," *Journal of the American Geriatrics Society* 53 (2005): 711–719.

81. Weaver, *Explorations in Cultural Competence,* p. 112.

82. David R. Roediger, "And Die in Dixie: Funerals, Death & Heaven in the Slave Community, 1700–1865," *The Massachusetts Review* 22, no. 1 (Spring 1981): 163–183.

83. Pérez and Luquis, *Cultural Competence in Health Education and Health Promotion,* p. 13.

84. Ronald K. Barrett, "Death and Dying in the Black Experience: An Interview with Ronald K. Barrett," *Innovations in End-of-Life Care* 3, no. 5 (2001); www.edu .org.;lastacts.

85. Weaver, *Explorations in Cultural Competence,* p. 145.

86. Margo Simon Coler and Maria Adriana Felix Coler, "People of Brazilian Heritage," http:// resources.fadavis.com/purnell4e/bonus_chapters/ Ch27_001-011.pdf.

87. Tina A. Ellis and Larry D. Purnell, "People of Guatemalan Heritage," http://resources.fadavis.com/ purnell4e/bonus_chapters/Ch31_001-014.pdf.

88. Leylha Ahuile, "Ready for Prime Time," *Publishers Weekly* (April 1, 2014), p. 3 (special section, "Spanish Language Publishing").

89. Pérez and Luquis, *Cultural Competence in Health Education and Health Promotion,* p. 13.

90. Miguel León-Portilla, "Those Made Worthy by Divine Sacrifice: The Faith of Ancient Mexico," in *South and Meso-American Native Spirituality: From the Cult of the Feathered Serpent to the Theology of Liberation,* ed. Gary H. Gossen, 41–64 (New York: Crossroad, 1993), p. 56.

91. Rich Zoucha and Cecelia A. Zamarripa, "People of Mexican Heritage," in *Transcultural Health Care,* ed. Purnell, 374–390; p. 384.

92. Luis Cardoza y Arogón, quoted in Claudio Lomnitz, *Death and the Idea of Mexico* (Cambridge, Mass.: MIT Press, 2005), p. 23.

93. Quoted in Rafael Jesús González, *El Corazón de la Muerte: Altars and Offerings for Days of the Dead* (Berkeley, Calif.: Heyday Books, 2005), p. 26.

94. Octavio Paz, *The Labyrinth of Solitude: Life and Thought in Mexico* (New York: Grove Press, 1961); quote p. 54.

95. See, by Mary J. Andrade, *Through the Eyes of the Soul, Día de Muertos en Mexico: Michoacan,* 2nd ed. (San Jose, Calif.: La Oferta, 1999), *Through the Eyes of the Soul, Día de Muertos en Mexico: Oaxaca* (San Jose, Calif.: La Oferta, 1999), and *Through the Eyes of the Soul, Día de Muertos en Mexico: Mexico City, Mixquic, and Morelos* (San Jose, Calif.: La Oferta 2000). See also Barbara Brodman, *The Mexican Cult of Death in Myth and Literature* (Gainesville: University of Florida Press, 1976); Elizabeth Carmichael and Chloë Sayer, *The Skeleton at the Feast: The Day of the Dead in Mexico* (London: British Museum Press, 1991); Robert Childs and Patricia B. Altman, *Vive tu Recuerdo: Living Traditions of the Mexican Days of the Dead* (Los Angeles: Museum of Cultural History, UCLA, 1982); Juanita Garciagodoy, *Digging the Days of the Dead: A Reading of Mexico's Dias de Muertos* (Niwot, Colo.: University Press of Colorado, 1998); Judith Strupp Green, "The Days of the Dead in Oaxaca, Mexico: An Historical Inquiry," in *Death and Dying: Views from Many Cultures,* ed. Kalish, pp. 56–71; John Greenleigh and Rosalind Rosoff Beimler, *The Days of the Dead: Mexico's Festival of Communion with the Departed* (San Francisco: HarperCollins, 1991); Rafael Jesús González, *El Corazón de la Muerte: Altars and Offerings for Days of the Dead* (Berkeley, Calif.: Heyday Books, 2005); Patricia Fernández Kelly, "Death in Mexican Folk Culture," *American Quarterly* 26, no. 5 (December 1974): 516–535; Claudio Lomnitz, *Death and the Idea of Mexico* (Cambridge, Mass.: MIT Press, 2005); Joan Moore, "The Death Culture of Mexico and Mexican Americans," in *Death and Dying: Views from Many Cultures,* ed. Kalish, pp. 72–91; Patricia Osuna and David K. Reynolds, "A Funeral in Mexico: Description and Analysis," *Omega: Journal of Death and Dying* 1, no. 3 (1970): 249–269.

96. Regina M. Marchi, *Day of the Dead in the USA: The Migration and Transformation of a Cultural Phenomenon* (New Brunswick, N.J.: Rutgers University Press, 2009), p. 40.

97. Stanley Brandes, *Skulls to the Living, Bread to the Dead: The Day of the Dead in Mexico and Beyond* (Malden, Mass.: Blackwell, 2006), pp. 48–50.

98. Paz, *Labyrinth of Solitude.*

99. Jorge Valadez, "Pre-Columbian and Modern Philosophical Perspectives in Latin America," in *From Africa to Zen: An Invitation to World Philosophy,* ed. Robert C. Solomon and Kathleen M. Higgins, 81–124 (Lanham, Md.: Rowman and Littlefield, 1993), p. 107.

100. Davíd Carrasco, "Religions of Mesoamerica: Cosmovision and Ceremonial Centers," in *Religious Traditions of the World,* ed. H. Byron Earhart, 107–253 (San Francisco: HarperCollins, 1992); quote pp. 232–233.

101. Marchi, *Day of the Dead in the USA,* p. 37.

102. Quoted in Marchi, *Day of the Dead in the USA,* p. 103.

103. Weaver, *Explorations in Cultural Competence,* p. 167.

104. Larry Purnell, "People of Hmong Heritage," in *Transcultural Health Care,* ed. Purnell, 310–318; p. 316.

105. Christopher L. Hayes and Richard A. Kalish, "Death-Related Experiences and Funerary Practices of the Hmong Refugee in the United States," in *The Path Ahead,* ed. DeSpelder and Strickland, pp. 75–79.

106. Jaya Jambunathan, "People of Hindu Heritage," in *Transcultural Health Care,* ed. Purnell, 288–309; p. 302.

107. Shanil Ebrahim, Sheena Bance, and Kerry W. Bowman, "Sikh Perspectives Towards Death and End-of-Life Care," *Journal of Palliative Care* 27, no. 2 (2011): 170–174.

108. See, for example: H. Byron Earhart, "Religions of Japan: Many Traditions Within One Sacred Way," in *Religious Traditions of the World,* ed. Earhart, 1075–1186 (San Francisco: HarperCollins, 1992); Dennis Klass, "Ancestor Worship in Japan: Dependence and the Resolution of Grief," *Omega: Journal of Death and Dying* 33, no. 4 (1996): 279–302; Hajime Nakamura, *Ways of Thinking of Eastern Peoples: India, China, Tibet, Japan,* trans. and ed. Philip P. Wiener (Honolulu: University of Hawaii Press, 1964); Sokyo Ono, *Shinto: The Kami Way* (Rutland, Vt.: Charles E. Tuttle, 1962); Daniel L. Overmyer, "Religions of China: The World as a Living System," in *Religious Traditions of the World,* ed. Earhart, 973–1073; Ian Reader, *Religion in Contemporary Japan* (Honolulu: University of Hawaii Press, 1991); Robert J. Smith, *Ancestor Worship in Contemporary Japan* (Stanford, Calif.: Stanford University Press, 1974); Yamaori Tetsuo, "The Metamorphosis of Ancestors," *Japan Quarterly* 33,

no. 1 (January–March 1986): 50–53; and James L. Watson and Evelyn S. Rawski, eds., *Death Ritual in Late Imperial and Modern China* (Berkeley: University of California Press, 1988).

109. Kate Jellema, "Everywhere Incense Burning: Remembering Ancestors in Dôi Moí Vietnam," *Journal of Southeast Asian Studies* 38, no. 3 (2007): 457–492; esp. p. 473.

110. Inge Rösch-Rhomberg, "Hierarchical Opposition and the Concept of *um-yang* (*yin-yang*): A Reevaluation of Values in the Light of the Symbolism of Korean Rituals for the Dead," *Anthropos* 89 (1994): 471–491.

111. Satsuki Kawano, "A Sociocultural Analysis of Death Anxiety Among Older Japanese Urbanites in a Citizens' Movement," *Omega: Journal of Death and Dying* 62, no. 4 (2010–2011): 369–386.

112. Wanyan Shaoyuan, *Exploring Fêng-shui* (Singapore: McGraw-Hill, 2010), p. 6. See also Ole Bruun, *An Introduction to Feng Shui* (Cambridge: Cambridge University Press, 2008); Richard Creightmore, *Feng Shui: Secrets of Chinese Geomancy* (New York: Walker, 2012), esp. pp. 2, 4, 14; and Derek Walters, *The Feng Shui Handbook: A Practical Guide to Chinese Geomancy and Harmony* (San Francisco: Aquarian/Thorsons, 1991), esp. p. 165.

113. Yamaori Tetsuo, "The Metamorphosis of Ancestors," *Japan Quarterly* 33, no. 1 (January–March 1986): 50–53.

114. *Keys to the Japanese Heart and Soul* (Tokyo: Kodansha, 1996), p. 169.

115. Donald Keene, *The Pleasures of Japanese Literature* (New York: Columbia University Press, 1988), p. 53.

116. Andy Hau Yan Ho and Cecilia Lai Wan Chan, "Liberating Dying People and Bereaved Families from the Oppression of Death and Loss in Chinese Societies: A Public Health Approach," in *Governing Death and Loss: Empowerment, Involvement and Participation,* ed. Steve Conway, 119–128 (New York: Oxford University Press, 2011), p. 119.

117. Christine Valentine, "Negotiating a Loved One's Dying in Contemporary Japanese Society," *Mortality* 14, no. 1 (2009): 34–52; esp. pp. 36, 37.

118. Christine Valentine, "Bereavement in Japan: Contemporary Responses to Traditional Forms," paper presented at a conference of the Centre for Death and Society, Bath, U.K., March 26, 2009.

119. Allan Kellehear and Daisuke Tanaka, "Supporting Bereavement in Society: Comparisons Between Australia and Japan," *Grief Matters: The Australian Journal of Grief and Bereavement* 7, no. 1 (Autumn 2004): 4–7.

120. Janet Lee Scott, *For Gods, Ghosts and Ancestors: The Chinese Tradition of Paper Offerings* (Hong Kong: Hong Kong University Press, 2007), pp. 2, 20, 104, 114. See also Roderick Cave, *Chinese Paper Offerings* (Hong Kong: Oxford University Press, 1998).

121. Scott, *For Gods, Ghosts and Ancestors,* p. 129.

122. Scott, *For Gods, Ghosts and Ancestors,* pp. 104, 150.

123. Tetsuo, "Metamorphosis of Ancestors," p. 51.

124. Janice Selekman, "People of Jewish Heritage," in *Transcultural Health Care,* ed. Purnell, 339–356; p. 349.

125. See, for example, Barry Cunliffe, *The Ancient Celts* (New York: Oxford University Press, 1997); Hilda Ellis Davidson, *Myths and Symbols in Pagan Europe: Early Scandinavian and Celtic Religions* (Manchester, U.K.: Manchester University Press, 1988), and *The Lost Beliefs of Northern Europe* (London: Routledge, 1993); Peter Berresford Ellis, *The Celtic Empire: The First Millennium of Celtic History 1000 BC–AD 51* (New York: Carroll & Graf, 2001); Ronald Hutton, *The Pagan Religions of the Ancient British Isles: Their Nature and Legacy* (Malden, Mass.: Blackwell, 1991); Prudence Jones and Nigel Pennick, *A History of Pagan Europe* (London: Routledge, 1995); J. A. MacCulloch, *The Celtic and Scandinavian Religions* (London: Hutchinson's University Library, 1948); Sabatino Moscati, ed., *The Celts* (New York: Rizzoli, 1991); Dáithé Ó'Hógáin, *The Celts: A History* (Cork: Boydell, 2020); and Ward Rutherford, *Celtic Mythology* (London: Thorsons, 1995).

126. Sandra M. Gilbert, *Death's Door: Modern Dying and the Ways We Grieve* (New York: Norton, 2006), p. 1.

127. See, for example, Nora K. Chadwick, *The Druids* (Cardiff: University of Wales Press, 1966); Paul R. Lonigan, *The Druids: Priests of the Ancient Celts* (Westport, Conn.: Greenwood, 1996).

128. John Sharkey, *Celtic Mysteries: The Ancient Religion* (New York: Thames & Hudson, 1975), p. 10.

129. James R. Babb, *River Music: A Fly Fisher's Four Seasons* (Guilford, Conn.: Lyons Press, 2001), p. 176.

130. Elizabeth Kantor, *The Politically Incorrect Guide to English and American Literature* (Washington, D.C.: Regnery, 2006), p. 15.

131. Jack Santino, *The Hallowed Eve: Dimensions of Culture in a Calendar Festival in Northern Ireland* (Lexington: University Press of Kentucky, 1998), p. 90.

132. Stephanie Myers Schim, "People of Irish Heritage," http://resources.fadavis.com/purnell4e/bonus_chapters/Ch33_001-013.pdf.

133. Humayun Ansari, "Burying the Dead: Making Muslim Space in Britain," *Historical Research* 80, no. 210 (November 2007): 545–566.

134. Pérez and Luquis, *Cultural Competence in Health Education and Health Promotion,* p. 16.

135. Weaver, *Explorations in Cultural Competence,* p. 191.

136. John F. McDermott, Jr., "Toward an Interethnic Society," in *People and Cultures of Hawaii,* ed. McDermott, Tseng, and Maretzki, p. 231.

137. Eleanor C. Nordyke, *The Peopling of Hawai'i,* 2nd ed. (Honolulu: University of Hawaii Press, 1989), p. 1.

138. Patrick Vinton Kirch, *Feathered Gods and Fishhooks: An Introduction to Hawaiian Archeology and Prehistory* (Honolulu: University of Hawaii Press, 1985), p. 298.

139. Jonathan Y. Okamura, "Why There Are No Asian Americans in Hawai'i: The Continuing Significance of Local Identity," *Social Process in Hawaii* 35 (1994): 161–178.

140. See Benjamin B. C. Young, "The Hawaiians," in *People and Cultures of Hawaii: A Psychocultural Profile,* ed. John F. McDermott, Jr., Wen-Shing Tseng, and Thomas W. Maretzki, 5–24 (Honolulu: John A. Burns School of Medicine and University of Hawaii Press, 1980).

141. Mary Kawena Pukui, E. W. Haertig, and Catherine A. Lee, *Nana I Ke Kumu (Look to the Source),* 2 vols. (Honolulu: Hui Hanai; Queen Lili'uokalani Children's Center, 1972). A study conducted in the 1930s found families still tracing their lineage from ancestors who were viewed as spiritual guardians of their descendants and who often interceded in very practical ways. See E. S. Craighill Handy and Mary Kawena Pukui, *The Polynesian Family System in Ka-'u, Hawai'i* (Rutland, Vt.: Charles E. Tuttle, 1972).

142. George Hu'eu Sanford Kanahele, *Ku Kanaka, Stand Tall: A Search for Hawaiian Values* (Honolulu: University of Hawaii Press, 1986), p. 182. On the soul after death and realms of the spirits of the dead, see also Donald D. Kilolani Mitchell, *Resource Units in Hawaiian Culture* (Honolulu: Kamehameha Schools Press, 1982), pp. 84–86.

143. Kathryn L. Braun, Noreen Mokuau, G. Haunani Hunt, Momi Kaanoi, and Carolyn C. Gotay, "Supports and Obstacles to Cancer Survival for Hawaii's Native People," *Cancer Practice* 10, no. 4 (2002): 192–200; esp. p. 193.

144. Margaret J. Maaka, Kathryn H. Au, Yvonne K. Lefcourt, and L. Pauahi Bogac, "Raccoon? Wass Dat? Hawaiian Preservice Teachers Reconceptualize Culture, Literacy, and Schooling," in *Reconceptualizing Literacy in the New Age of Multiculturalism and Pluralism,* ed. R. Schmidt and P. B. Mosenthal, 341–366 (Greenwich, Conn.: Information Age, 2001), p. 344.

145. Nordyke, *The Peopling of Hawai'i,* p. 52; see also Walter F. Char and others, "The Chinese," in *People and Cultures of Hawaii,* ed. McDermott, Tseng, and Maretzki, pp. 53–72.

146. This discussion of contemporary Chinese funeral customs in Hawaii is based on interviews by the authors with Anna Ordenstein and Ken Ordenstein who, along with their Chinese-Hawaiian-Jewish-Portuguese forebears, have provided funeral services to residents of Hawaii over the course of five generations. We are grateful for their assistance.

147. John F. McDermott, Jr., "Toward an Interethnic Society," in *People and Cultures of Hawaii,* ed. McDermott, Tseng, and Maretzki, p. 231; see also Wayne S. Wooden, *What Price Paradise? Changing Social Patterns in Hawaii* (Washington, D.C.: University Press of America, 1981).

148. McDermott, "Toward an Interethnic Society," pp. 229–230; see also Elvi Whittaker, *The Mainland Haole: The White Experience in Hawaii* (New York: Columbia University Press, 1986).

149. Mary Kawena Pukui and Samuel H. Elbert, *Hawaiian Dictionary,* rev. ed. (Honolulu: University of Hawaii Press, 1986), p. 34.

150. Paul Spickard, quoted in Susan Yim, "Hapa in Hawai'i," *Honolulu* (December 1994), pp. 44–47, 90, 92.

151. Goodman, *Introduction to Sociology,* p. 37.

152. David H. Olson and John DeFrain, *Marriage and Family: Diversity and Strengths* (Mountain View, Calif.: Mayfield, 1994), p. 37.

153. Katie Algeo, "Teaching Cultural Geography with 'Bend It Like Beckham,'" *Journal of Geography* 106, no. 3 (2007): 133–143.

154. See M. Eisenbruch, "Cross-Cultural Aspects of Bereavement: Ethnic and Cultural Variations in the Development of Bereavement Practices," *Culture, Medicine, and Psychiatry* 8 (1984): 315–347; and Jimy M. Sanders, "Ethnic Boundaries and Identity in Plural Societies," *Annual Review of Sociology* 28 (2002): 327–357.

155. Alvin O. Korte, "*Despedidas* as Reflections of Death in Hispanic New Mexico," *Omega: Journal of Death and Dying* 32, no. 4 (1995–1996): 245–267.

156. Robert Pogue Harrison, *The Dominion of the Dead* (Chicago: University of Chicago Press, 2003), p. 70.

CHAPTER 4

1. Robert Kastenbaum, "Death System," in *Encyclopedia of Death,* ed. Robert Kastenbaum and Beatrice Kastenbaum, 90–93 (Phoenix, Ariz.: Oryx Press, 1989); and Kenneth J. Doka, "Death System," in *Macmillan Encyclopedia of Death and Dying,* ed. Robert Kastenbaum, 222–223 (New York: Macmillan, 2003).

2. Carla J. Sofka, Illene Noppe Cupit, and Kathleen R. Gilbert, eds., *Dying, Death, and Grief in an Online Universe* (New York: Springer, 2012), p. 6.

3. Bert Hayslip, Jr., "Death Denial: Hiding and Camouflaging Death," in *Handbook of Death & Dying,* ed. Clifton D. Bryant, 34–42 (Thousand Oaks, Calif.: Sage, 2003); esp. p. 35.

4. Darcy Harris, "Healing the Narcissistic Injury of Death in the Context of Western Society," in *The Shame of Death, Grief, and Trauma,* ed. Jeffrey Kauffman, 75–86 (New York: Routledge, 2010), p. 80. See also Kenneth J. Doka, *Disenfranchised Grief: Recognizing Hidden Sorrow* (Lexington, Mass.: Lexington Books, 1989).

5. Susan Orpett Long, *Final Days: Japanese Culture and Choice at the End of Life* (Honolulu: University of Hawaii Press, 2005), p. 3.

6. Robert Kastenbaum, "Should We Manage Terror—If We Could?" *Omega: Journal of Death and Dying* 59, no. 4 (2009): 271–304; esp. 297.

7. Robert A. Hahn and others, "The Recording of Demographic Information on Death Certificates: A National Survey of Funeral Directors," *Public Health Reports* 117 (January–February 2002): 37–43; quote p. 38.

8. Edwin S. Shneidman, *Deaths of Man* (New York: Quadrangle Books, 1973), pp. 121–130.

9. Chris Kaiser, "Heart Disease Not as Pervasive as Reported," MedPage Today (May 21, 2013); www.medpagetoday.com/PublicHealthPolicy/GeneralProfessionalIssues/39303.

10. Brad Randall, *Death Investigation: The Basics* (Tucson, Ariz.: Galen, 1997), p. 1. On the functioning of a big-city coroner's office, see Tony Blanche and Brad Schreiber, *Death in Paradise: An Illustrated History of the Los Angeles County Department of Coroner* (Los Angeles: General Publishing Group, 1998).

11. Deborah Noyes, "Forensic Science," in *Encyclopedia of the End: Mysterious Death in Fact, Fancy, Folklore, and More,* ed. Deborah Noyes (Boston: Houghton Mifflin, 2008), p. 50.

12. Stefan Timmermans, *Postmortem: How Medical Examiners Explain Suspicious Deaths* (Chicago: University of Chicago Press, 2006), p. viii.

13. Timmermans, *Postmortem,* p. 43.

14. Quoted in Timmermans, *Postmortem,* p. 272.

15. Ernest F. Talarico, Jr., "A Change in Paradigm: Giving Back Identity to Donors in the Anatomy Laboratory," *Clinical Anatomy* 26, no. 2 (2013): 161–172.

16. Jon Yoshishige, "Searching for Answers: Lab Identifies Remains of Soldiers, Civilians," *Honolulu Advertiser,* August 8, 1993.

17. Joseph B. Verrengia, "Remains of Columbia Crew Recovered," *Associated Press Online,* February 2, 2003.

18. John D. Lantos, *Do We Still Need Doctors?* (New York: Routledge, 1997), pp. 129–130.

19. George D. Lundberg, "Low-Tech Autopsies in the Era of High-Tech Medicine: Continued Value for Quality Assurance and Patient Safety," *JAMA* 280, no. 14 (October 14, 1998): 1273–1274.

20. George D. Lundberg, "Who Does Not Like Autopsies and Why," *MedPage Today* (February 20, 2012); http://www.medpagetoday.com/Columns/At-Large/31264.

21. Joe Palazzolo and Rob Barry, "More Killings Called Self-Defense," *The Wall Street Journal Weekend* (March 31–April 1), p. A1.

22. Henry Lundsgaarde, *Murder in Space City: A Cultural Analysis of Houston Homicide Patterns* (New York: Oxford University Press, 1977).

23. Hugo Adam Bedau, "An Abolitionist's Survey of the Death Penalty in America," in *Debating the Death Penalty: Should America Have Capital Punishment?* ed. Hugo Bedau and Paul Cassell (New York: Oxford University Press, 2004), pp. 26–27.

24. Ted Rohrlich and Fredric N. Tulsky, "Not All L.A. Murder Cases Are Equal," *The Los Angeles Times,* December 3, 1995.

25. See N. Prabha Unnithan, "The Processing of Homicide Cases with Child Victims: Systemic and Situational Contingencies," *Journal of Criminal Justice* 22, no. 1 (1994): 41–50, and "Children as Victims of Homicide: Making Claims, Formulating Categories, and Constructing Social Problems," *Deviant Behavior* 15, no. 1 (1994): 63–83.

26. Catharine R. Stimpson, "Do These Deaths Surpass Understanding? The Literary Figure of the Mother Who Murders," *Triquarterly* 124 (2006): 46–61; see also George B. Palermo, "Murderous Parents," *International Journal of Offender Therapy and Comparative Criminology* 46, no. 2 (2002): 123–143.

27. "Prisoners Executed Under Civil Authority" and "Prisoners Under Sentence of Death," *Statistical Abstract of the United States: 2012,* 131st ed. (Washington, D.C., 2011); http://www.census.gov/compendia/statab/.

28. Roman Espejo, ed., *Does Capital Punishment Deter Crime?* (Farmington Hills, Mich.: Greenhaven, 2003), p. 7.

29. Glenn M. Vernon, *Sociology of Death: An Analysis of Death-Related Behavior* (New York: Ronald Press, 1970). See also Dennis J. Stevens, "The Death Sentence and Inmate Attitudes," *Crime & Delinquency* 38, no. 2 (1992): 272–279.

30. Hugo A. Bedau, "Capital Punishment," *Academic American Encyclopedia Online,* March 1991.

31. Kastenbaum and Aisenberg, *The Psychology of Death* (New York: Springer, 1972), pp. 284–285.

32. Linda R. Monk, *The Words We Live By: Your Annotated Constitution* (New York: Stonesong, 2003), p. 187. On the risk of innocent deaths occurring in the operation of the death penalty, see James S. Liebman, "Rates of Reversible Error and the Risk of Wrongful Execution," *Judicature* 86, no. 2 (2002): 78–82.

33. Lundsgaarde, *Murder in Space City,* p. 146.

34. Allan Kellehear, "Dying As a Social Relationship: A Sociological Review of Debates on the Determination of Death," *Social Science & Medicine* 66 (2008): 1533–1544.

35. Douglas N. Walton, *On Defining Death: An Analytic Study of the Concept of Death in Philosophy and Medical Ethics* (Montreal: McGill-Queen's University Press, 1979).

36. Ronald E. Cranford, "The Persistent Vegetative State: The Medical Reality," in *Medical Ethics: Applying Theories and Principles to the Patient Encounter,* ed. Matt Weinberg, 111–120 (Amherst, N.Y.: Prometheus, 2001).

37. D. Alan Shewman, transcript, "Session 5: Responses to the Council's White Paper, 'Controversies in the Determination of Death,'" The President's Council on Bioethics (November 9, 2007).

38. Sam D. Shemie, "Clarifying the Paradigm for the Ethics of Donation and Transplantation: Was 'Dead' Really So Clear Before Organ Donation?" *Philosophy, Ethics, and Humanities in Medicine* 2 (August 24, 2007): 18.

39. William R. Clark, *Sex and the Origins of Death* (New York: Oxford University Press, 1996), p. 171.

40. Robert M. Veatch, *Death, Dying, and the Biological Revolution: Our Last Quest for Responsibility,* rev. ed. (New Haven, Conn.: Yale University Press, 1989).

41. Duncan MacDougall, "Hypothesis Concerning Soul Substance Together with Experimental Evidence of the Existence of Such Substance," *Journal of the American Society for Psychical Research* 1, no. 5 (May 1907): 237–244.

42. Jay F. Rosenberg, *Thinking Clearly About Death* (Englewood Cliffs, N.J.: Prentice-Hall, 1983), p. 106.

43. "A Definition of Irreversible Coma: Report of the Ad Hoc Committee of the Harvard Medical School to Examine the Definition of Brain Death," *Journal of the American Medical Association* 205, no. 6 (August 5, 1968): 337–340.

44. N. Zamperetti, R. Bellomo, and C. Ronco, "Defining Death in Non-Heart Beating Donors," *Journal of Medical Ethics* 29 (2003): 182–185.

45. Press release, "New AAN Guideline for Determining Brain Death Provides More Clarity and Direction," www.aan.com. See also Eelco F. M. Wijdicks et al., "Evidence-Based Guideline Update: Determining Brain Death in Adults," *Neurology* 74 (June 8, 2010): 1911–1918.

46. Kellehear, "Dying as a Social Relationship," p. 1534. Kellehear notes that some researchers conclude that the transplant lobby exerted a powerful influence within the medical community at the time of these deliberations.

47. See James L. Bernat, "The Biophilosophical Basis of Whole-Brain Death," *Social Philosophy & Policy* 19, no. 2 (2002): 324–342; Gary Greenberg, "As Good as Dead: Is There Really Such a Thing as Brain Death?," *The New Yorker,* August 13, 2001, pp. 36–41; K. G. Karakatsanis and J. N. Tsanakas, "A Critique on the Concept of 'Brain Death,'" *Issues in Law and Medicine* 18, no. 2 (2002): 127–141; R. D. Truog, "Is It Time to Abandon Brain Death?" *Hastings Center Report* 27, no. 1 (1997): 29–37; and Robert M. Veatch, "The Impending Collapse of the Whole-Brain Definition of Death," *Hastings Center Report* 23, no. 4 (1993): 18–24. See also John P. Lizza, "Persons and Death: What's Metaphysically Wrong with Our Current Statutory Definition of Death?" *Journal of Medicine and Philosophy* 18 (1993): 351–374.

48. Kellehear, "Dying as a Social Relationship," p. 1536.

49. Shemie, "Clarifying the Paradigm for the Ethics of Donation and Transplantation," p. 18.

50. Karen G. Gervais, "Advancing the Definition of Death: A Philosophical Essay," *Medical Humanities Review* 3 (July 1989): 7–19; and, by Gervais, *Redefining Death* (New Haven, Conn.: Yale University Press, 1986).

51. Robert M. Veatch, "What Counts as Basic Health Care? Private Values and Public Policy," *Hastings Center Report* 24, no. 3 (1994): 20–21.

52. President's Commission for the Study of Ethical Problems in Medicine and Biomedical and Behavioral Research, *Defining Death: A Report on the Medical, Legal and Ethical Issues in the Determination of Death* (Washington, D.C.: Government Printing Office, 1981), p. 45.

53. President's Commission, *Defining Death.*

54. Albert R. Jonsen, *The Birth of Bioethics* (New York: Oxford University Press, 1998), pp. 238–244.

55. Zamperetti, Bellomo, and Ronco, "Defining Death in Non-Heart Beating Donors," p. 184.

56. Zamperetti, Bellomo, and Ronco, "Defining Death," p. 184.

57. Kellehear, "Dying as a Social Relationship," p. 1541.

58. Mark H. Beers and Robert Berkow, eds., *The Merck Manual of Diagnosis and Therapy,* 17th ed. (Whitehouse Station, N.J.: Merck Research Laboratories, 1999), p. 1067.

59. Leonard L. Bailey, "Organ Transplantation: A Paradigm of Medical Progress," *Hastings Center Report* (January–February 1990): 24–28; see also Susan L. Smith, "Progress in Clinical Organ Transplantation," www.medscape.com.

60. "First 'Breathing Lung' Transplant in United States," www.sciencedaily.com/releases/2012/11/121126130928.htm.

61. Robert Steinbrook, "Organ Donation After Cardiac Death," *New England Journal of Medicine* 357, no. 3 (July 19, 2007): 209–213; esp. p. 209.

62. Steinbrook, "Organ Donation After Cardiac Death," p. 211.

63. Steinbrook, "Organ Donation After Cardiac Death," quote p. 211. See also The President's Council on Bioethics, *Controversies in the Determination of Death* (Washington, D.C.: 2008).

64. David K. Meagher, "Ethical and Legal Issues and Loss, Grief and Mourning," in *Handbook of Thanatology,* 2nd ed., ed. David K. Meagher and David E. Balk, 179–190 (New York: Routledge, 2013), p. 183.

65. Joseph L. Verheijde, Mohamed Y. Rady, and Joan L. McGregor, "The United States Revised Uniform Anatomical Gift Act (2006): New Challenges to Balancing Patient Rights and Physician Responsibilities," *Philosophy, Ethics, and Humanities in Medicine* 2, (September 12, 2007): 19–21.

66. Michael A. DeVita and Arthur L. Caplan, "Caring for Organs or for Patients? Ethical Concerns about the Uniform Anatomical Gift Act (2006)," *Annals of Internal Medicine* 147, no. 12 (2007): 876–879.

67. Zamperetti, Bellomo, and Ronco, "Defining Death in Non-Heart Beating Donors," p. 184.

68. Margaret Lock, "Human Body Parts as Therapeutic Tools: Contradictory Discourses and Transformed Subjectivities," *Qualitative Health Research* 12, no. 10 (2002): 1406–1418; quote p. 1407.

69. Arthur Caplan, "Organ Transplantation," in *From Birth to Death and Bench to Clinic: The Hastings Center Bioethics Briefing Book for Journalists, Policymakers, and Campaigns,* ed. Mary Crowley, 129–132 (Garrison, N.Y.: The Hastings Center, 2008); and United Network for Organ Sharing (www.unos.org).

70. See, for example, Cheryl L. Albright et al., "Choosing to be a Designated Organ Donor on Their First Driver's License: Actions, Opinions, Intentions, and Barriers of Asian American and Pacific Islander Adolescents in Hawaii," *Progress in Transplantation* 20, no. 4 (2010): 392–400; Elisa J. Gordon, Jillian Rodde, and Juan Carlos Calcedo, "Quality of Internet Education about Living Kidney Donation for Hispanics," *Progress in Transplantation* 22, no. 3 (2012): 294–302.

71. Louis A. Gamino and R. Hal Ritter, Jr., *Ethical Practice in Grief Counseling* (New York: Springer, 2009), p. 153.

72. Caplan, "Organ Transplantation," p. 130.

73. John Lauerman and Connie Guglielmo, "Jobs Travel to Transplant Mecca Shows System Flaws," Bloomberg.com.

74. Susan E. Morgan, Michael T. Stephenson, Tyler R. Harrison, Walid A. Afifi, and Shawn D. Long, "Facts versus 'Feelings': How Rational Is the Decision to Become an Organ Donor?" *Journal of Health Psychology* 13 (2008): 644–658.

75. Felicia Schanche Hodge, Patricia Bellanger, and Connie Norman, "Organ Donation and Transplantation: A Dialogue with American Indian Healers and Western Health-Care Providers," *American Indian Culture and Research Journal* 35, no. 3 (2011); 79–90; quote p. 87.

76. Margaret Robbins, "The Donation of Organs for Transplantation: The Donor Families," in *Contemporary Issues in the Sociology of Death, Dying, and Disposal,* ed. Glennys Howarth and Peter C. Jupp, 179–192 (New York: St. Martin's, 1996).

77. See Julia D. Mahoney, "The Market for Human Tissue," *Virginia Law Review* 86, no. 2 (2000): 163–223; and Laura A. Siminoff and Mary Beth Mercer, "Public Policy, Public Opinion, and Consent for Organ Donation," *Cambridge Quarterly of Healthcare Ethics* 10, no. 4 (2001): 377–386.

78. Annie Cheney, *Body Brokers: Inside America's Underground Trade in Human Remains* (New York: Broadway, 2006), pp. 8–10.

79. Timmermans, *Postmortem,* pp. 226–227; see also Chapter 6, "The Organ and Tissue Trade," pp. 225–249.

80. Renee C. Fox and Judith P. Swazey, *Spare Parts: Organ Replacement in American Society* (New York: Oxford University Press, 1992), p. 206.

81. Nancy Scheper-Hughes, "The Global Traffic in Human Organs," *Current Anthropology* 41, no. 2 (2000): 191–224; quote p. 194. On the way in which a unique set of social and religious conditions facilitated acceptance of brain death and organ transplantation in the United States during the late 1960s, see William R. LaFleur, "From Agape to Organs: Religious

Differences Between Japan and America in Judging the Ethics of the Transplant," *Zygon: Journal of Religion and Science* 37, no. 3 (2002): 623–642. For different religious views, see Laurence J. O'Connell, "The Religious and Spiritual Perspective Toward Human Organ Donation and Transplantation," in *The Ethics of Organ Transplantation,* ed. Wayne Shelton and John Balint, 277–292 (New York: JAI Press, 2001).

82. This case study draws on the following sources: Albert R. Jonsen, "Ethical Issues in Organ Transplantation," in *Medical Ethics,* 2nd ed., ed. Robert M. Veatch (Boston: Jones & Bartlett, 1997), pp. 239–274; Rihito Kimura, "Organ Transplantation and Brain-Death in Japan: Cultural, Legal, and Bioethical Background," *Annals of Transplantation* 3, no. 3 (1998): 5–58; Darryl Macer, "Bioethics in and from Asia," *Journal of Medical Ethics* 25 (1999): 293–295; Masahiro Morioka, "Bioethics and Japanese Culture: Brain Death, Patients' Rights, and Cultural Factors," *Eubios Journal of Asian and International Bioethics* 5 (1995): 87–90; Emiko Ohnuki-Tierney, "Brain Death and Organ Transplantation: Cultural Bases of Medical Technology," *Current Anthropology* 35, no. 3 (1994): 233–254; and Mona Newsome Wicks, "Brain Death and Transplantation: The Japanese," www.medscape.com.

83. Mari Yamaguchi, "Japan Lifts Ban on Children Donating Organs," AP News Online, July 13, 2009.

84. Michihiro Matsumoto and Lafayette De Mente Boyé, *Japanese Nuance in Plain English* (Tokyo: Kodansha, 2007), p. 35.

85. Robert Kastenbaum, *Death, Society, and Human Experience,* 7th ed. (Needham Heights, Mass.: Allyn & Bacon, 2001), p. 62.

CHAPTER 5

1. Richard A. Deyo, "Cascade Effects of Medical Technology," *Annual Review of Public Health* 23 (2002): 23–44; quote p. 29.

2. Ira Byock, *The Best Care Possible: A Physician's Quest to Transform Care Through the End of Life* (New York: Avery Penguin, 2012), p. 3.

3. Stephen R. Connor, *Hospice and Palliative Care: The Essential Guide,* 2nd ed. (New York: Routledge, 2009), p. 2.

4. Vanessa M. P. Johnson, Joan M. Teno, Meg Bourbonniere, and Vincent Mor, "Palliative Care Needs of Cancer Patients in U.S. Nursing Homes," *Journal of Palliative Medicine* 8, no. 2 (2005): 273–279.

5. Charles E. Rosenberg, "Institutionalized Ambiguity: Conflict and Continuity in the American Hospital," *Second Opinion* 12 (November 1989): 63–73.

6. Joshua Hauser and John Lantos, "Stories of Caring and Connection," *Hastings Center Report* 30, no. 2 (2000): 44–47.

7. Paul M. Insel and Walton T. Roth, *Connect Core Concepts in Health,* 13th ed. (New York: McGraw-Hill, 2013), p. 584.

8. Alastair Gray, "International Patterns of Health Care, 1960 to the 1990s," in *Caring for Health: History and Diversity,* ed. Charles Webster, Health and Disease Series, Book 6 (Buckingham, U.K.: Open University Press, 1994), p. 174. See also Thomas S. Bodenheimer and Kevin Grumbach, *Understanding Health Policy: A Clinical Approach,* 3rd ed. (New York: Lange Medical Books, 2002).

9. Daniel Callahan, *Taming the Beloved Beast: How Medical Technology Costs Are Destroying Our Health Care System* (Princeton, N.J.: Princeton University Press, 2009), p. 7.

10. Callahan, *Taming the Beloved Beast,* p. 9.

11. Callahan, *Taming the Beloved Beast,* pp. 47, 151.

12. Callahan, *Taming the Beloved Beast,* p. 152.

13. Callahan, *Taming the Beloved Beast,* p. 177.

14. Howard M. Spiro, "If It Ain't Broke," *Science & Medicine* 3, no. 6 (November–December 1996): 4–5.

15. Clive F. Seale, "Changing Patterns of Death and Dying," *Social Science and Medicine* 51 (2000): 917–930.

16. Callahan, *Taming the Beloved Beast,* p. 3.

17. Madeline Jacobs, "Ethical and Legal Issues Related to Dying and End-of-Life Care," in *Handbook of Thanatology,* 2nd ed., ed. David K. Meagher and David E. Balk, 43–49 (New York: Routledge, 2013), p. 43.

18. George D. Lundberg, "How to Rein in Medical Costs, RIGHT NOW," http://thehealthcareblog.com/blog/2009/08/11/how-to-rein-in-medical-costs-right-now.

19. Daniel Callahan, "Health Care Costs and Medical Technology," 79–92, *The Hastings Center Bioethics Briefing Book* (Garrison, N.Y.: The Hastings Center, 2009), p. 80.

20. Callahan, "Health Care Costs and Medical Technology," p. 82.

21. Daniel Callahan, "The Limits of Medical Progress: A Principle of Symmetry," in *The Path Ahead: Readings in Death and Dying,* ed. Lynne Ann DeSpelder and Albert Lee Strickland, 103–105 (Mountain View, Calif.: Mayfield, 1995), p. 104. See also, by Callahan, *What Kind of Life: The Limits of Medical Progress* (New York: Simon & Schuster, 1990).

22. Madeline Jacobs, "Ethical and Legal Issues Related to Dying and End-of-Life Care," in *Handbook of Thanatology,* 2nd ed., ed. Meagher and Balk, p. 47.

23. Arthur W. Frank, "The Painter and the Cameraman: Boundaries in Clinical Relationships," *Theoretical Medicine* 23 (2002): 219–232; quote p. 231.

24. Michael D. Fetters and Howard Brody, "The Epidemiology of Bioethics," *Journal of Clinical Ethics* 10, no. 2 (1999): 107–115.

25. See Dan W. Brock, "The Ideal of Shared Decision Making Between Physicians and Patients," *Kennedy Institute of Ethics Journal* (March 1991): 28–47; and Christine K. Cassel, "The Patient-Physician Covenant: An Affirmation of Asklepios," *Annals of Internal Medicine* 124 (1996): 604–606.

26. Stanley Joel Reiser, "The Era of the Patient: Using the Experience of Illness in Shaping the Missions of Health Care," in *The Path Ahead,* ed. DeSpelder and Strickland, pp. 106–115.

27. C. D. Bessinger, "Doctoring: The Philosophic Milieu," *Southern Medical Journal* 81, no. 12 (1988): 1558–1562. See also William Campbell Felch, *The Secret(s) of Good Patient Care: Thoughts on Medicine in the 21st Century* (Westport, Conn.: Praeger, 1996); and Edmund D. Pellegrino and David C. Thomasma, *A Philosophical Basis for Medical Practice: Towards a Philosophy and Ethic of the Healing Professions* (New York: Oxford University Press, 1981).

28. Stephen R. Connor, "The Family, Larger Systems, and Dying," in *Handbook of Thanatology,* 2nd ed., ed. David K. Meagher and David E. Balk, p. 41. This phrase is attributed to Avery Weisman, *On Dying and Denying* (1972).

29. See, for example, Dieter Birnbacher, "Predictive Medicine: The Right to Know and the Right Not to Know," *Acta Analytica: Philosophy and Psychology* 16 (2001): 35–47; Todd S. Elwyn, Michael D. Fetters, Hiroki Sasaki, and Tsukada Tsuda, "Responsibility and Cancer Disclosure in Japan," *Social Science & Medicine* 54, no. 2 (2002): 281–293; and Stan A. Kaplowitz, Shelly Campo, and Wai Tat Chiu, "Cancer Patients' Desires for Communication of Prognosis Information," *Health Communication* 14, no. 2 (2002): 221–241.

30. Blair Sumner Mynatt and Robyn L. Mowery, "The Family, Larger Systems, and End-of-Life Decision Making," in *Handbook of Thanatology,* 2nd ed., ed. Meagher and Balk, p. 99f.

31. Kenneth J. Doka, *Counseling Individuals with Life-Threatening Illness* (New York: Springer, 2009), pp. 35–36.

32. Thomas J. Smith, "Tell It Like It Is," *Journal of Clinical Oncology* 18, no. 19 (2000): 3441–3445.

33. For a model of such discussion, see Ernest Rosenbaum, "Oncology/Hematology and Psychosocial Support of the Cancer Patient," in *Psychosocial Care of the Dying Patient,* ed. Charles A. Garfield, 169–184 (New York: McGraw-Hill, 1978).

34. Candace West, *Routine Complications: Troubles with Talk Between Doctors and Patients* (Bloomington: Indiana University Press, 1984).

35. Sandra L. Bertman, Michael D. Wertheimer, and H. Brownell Wheeler, "Humanities in Surgery, a Life-Threatening Situation: Communicating the Diagnosis," *Death Studies* 10, no. 5 (1986): 431–439.

36. Richard S. Sandor, "On Death and Coding," in *The Path Ahead,* ed. DeSpelder and Strickland, pp. 144–147.

37. Eugene A. Stead, Jr., *A Way of Thinking: A Primer on the Art of Being a Doctor* (Durham, N.C.: Carolina Academic Press, 1995), p. 126. See also Susan E. Hickman, "Improving Communication Near the End of Life," *American Behavioral Scientist* 46, no. 2 (2002): 252–267.

38. Albert Lee Strickland and Lynne Ann DeSpelder, "Communicating About Death and Dying," in *Dying, Death, and Bereavement: A Challenge for Living,* 2nd ed., ed. Inge Corless, Barbara B. Germino, and Mary A. Pittman, 7–24 (New York: Springer, 2003).

39. S. M. Johnson and M. E. Kurtz, "Name Usage in Clinical Practice: Ethnic and Gender Disparities," *Humane Medicine* 11, no. 3 (1995): 106–109. See also Gary L. Brase and Jillian Richmond, "The White-Coat Effect: Physician Attire and Perceived Authority, Friendliness, and Attractiveness," *Journal of Applied Social Psychology* 34, no. 12 (2004): 2469–2481; Felicity Goodyear-Smith and Stephen Buetow, "Power Issues in the Doctor-Patient Relationship," *Health Care Analysis* 9, no. 4 (2001): 449–462; and Robert M. Veatch, "White Coat Ceremonies: A Second Opinion," *Journal of Medical Ethics* 28, no. 1 (2002): 5–9.

40. Jeanne Quint Benoliel, "Health Care Providers and Dying Patients: Critical Issues in Terminal Care," *Omega: Journal of Death and Dying* 18, no. 4 (1987–1988): 341–363; quote p. 345.

41. Anne-Mei The, Tony Hak, Gerard Koëter, and Gerrit van der Wal, "Collusion in Doctor-Patient Communication about Imminent Death: An Ethnographic Study," *British Medical Journal* 321 (December 2, 2000): 1376–1381.

42. "Tapping Human Potential: An Interview with Norman Cousins," *Second Opinion* 14 (July 1990): 57–71.

43. See Balfour Mount, "Whole Person Care: Beyond Psychosocial and Physical Needs," *American Journal of Hospice and Palliative Care* 10, no. 1 (January–February 1993): 28–37.

44. Marilee Ivars Donovan and Sandra Girton Pierce, *Cancer Care Nursing* (New York: Appleton-Century-Crofts, 1976), p. 32.

45. Betty Davies and others, *Fading Away: The Experience of Transition in Families with Terminal Illness* (Amityville, N.Y.: Baywood, 1996).

46. Elisabeth Kübler-Ross, *On Death and Dying* (New York: Macmillan, 1969), p. 249. For a biographical account of Kübler-Ross's experiences, see Elisabeth Kübler-Ross, *The Wheel of Life: A Memoir of Living and Dying* (New York: Scribner, 1997).

47. Balfour M. Mount, "Keeping the Mission," in *The Path Ahead,* ed. DeSpelder and Strickland, pp. 125–132, quote p. 125.

48. Inge B. Corless, "Settings for Terminal Care," *Omega: Journal of Death and Dying* 18, no. 4 (1987–1988): 319–340.

49. See Rien M. J. P. A. Janssens, Zbigniew Zylicz, and Henk A. M. J. Ten Have, "Articulating the Concept of Palliative Care: Philosophical and Theological Perspectives," *Journal of Palliative Care* 15, no. 2 (1999): 38–44; and Allan Kellehear, "Spirituality and Palliative Care: A Model of Needs," *Palliative Medicine* 14 (2000): 149–155.

50. Joan M. Teno and Stephen R. Connor, "Referring a Patient and Family to High-Quality Palliative Care at the Close of Life," *JAMA* 301, no. 6 (February 11, 2009): 651–659; quote p. 655.

51. Reported in Teno and Connor, "Referring a Patient and Family to High-Quality Palliative Care at the Close of Life," p. 652.

52. Stephen R. Connor, "Palliative Care is a Human Right," *ADEC Forum* 37, no. 3 (2011): 1, 3–4, 10.

53. Study commissioned by the Worldwide Palliative Care Alliance. See M. Wright et al., "Mapping Levels of Palliative Care Development," *Journal of Pain and Symptom Management* 35 (2008): 469–485.

54. Stephen R. Connor, *Hospice and Palliative Care: The Essential Guide,* 2nd ed., p. 215.

55. Teno and Connor, "Referring a Patient and Family to High-Quality Palliative Care at the Close of Life," p. 654.

56. Mark H. Beers, ed., *The Merck Manual of Diagnosis and Therapy,* 18th ed. (Whitehouse Station, N.J.: Merck Research Laboratories, 2006), p. 2763. It is noteworthy that there is no entry for "palliative" in the *Manual's* index.

57. Connor, *Hospice and Palliative Care: The Essential Guide,* p. 8.

58. See F. Ackerman, "Goldilocks and Mrs. Ilych: A Critical Look at the 'Philosophy of Hospice,'" *Cambridge Quarterly of Healthcare Ethics* 6, no. 3 (1997): 314–324.

59. See Katherine Froggatt, "Rites of Passage and the Hospice Culture," *Mortality* 2, no. 2 (1997): 123–136.

60. David S. Greer, Vincent Mor, and Robert Kastenbaum, "Concepts, Questions, and Research Priorities," in *The Hospice Experiment,* ed. Vincent Mor, David S. Greer, and Robert Kastenbaum (Baltimore: Johns Hopkins University Press, 1988), p. 249. See also Marcia Lattanzi-Licht, John J. Mahoney, and Galen W. Miller, *The Hospice Choice: In Pursuit of a Peaceful Death* (New York: Fireside, 1998).

61. *NHPCO Facts and Figures: Hospice Care in America 2012,* www.nhpco.org.

62. Stephen R. Connor, Joan Teno, Carol Spench, and Neal Smith, "Family Evaluation of Hospice Care," *Journal of Pain and Symptom Management* 30, no. 1 (2005): 9–17.

63. R. Sean Morrison, Catherine Maroney-Galin, Peter D. Kravolec, and Diane E. Meier, "The Growth of Palliative Care Programs in United States Hospitals," *Journal of Palliative Medicine* 8, no. 6 (2005): 1127–1134.

64. Ira Byock, "Improving Palliative Care in Intensive Care Units: Identifying Strategies and Interventions That Work," *Critical Care Medicine* 34, no. 11 (2006): S302–S305; quote p. S303.

65. Stephen R. Connor, "JAMA Article Provides Valuable Guidance," *NHPCO Newsline* (April 2009): 1–2, 4–5. See also NHPCO, *Hospice Care: A Consumer's Guide to Selecting a Hospice Program,* which can be downloaded free from www.caringinfo.org.

66. Ira Byock, "Palliative Care," in *On Our Own Terms: Moyers on Dying,* ed. Public Affairs Television (New York: WNET, 2000), pp. 10–11. See also, by Byock, "End-of-Life Care: A Public Health Crisis and an Opportunity for Managed Care," *American Journal of Managed Care* 7, no. 12 (2001): 1123–1132.

67. See William E. Phipps, "The Origin of Hospices/Hospitals," *Death Studies* 12, no. 2 (1988): 91–99; Susan Lynn Sloan, "The Hospice Movement: A Study in the Diffusion of Innovative Palliative Care," *American Journal of Hospice and Palliative Care* (May–June 1992): 24–31; and Sandol Stoddard, "Hospice in the United States: An Overview," *Journal of Palliative Care* 5, no. 3 (1989): 10–19.

68. James Luther Adams, "Palliative Care in the Light of Early Christian Concepts," *Journal of Palliative Care* 5, no. 3 (1989): 5–8.

69. See Thelma Ingles, "St. Christopher's Hospice," in *A Hospice Handbook: A New Way to Care for the Dying,* ed.

Michael P. Hamilton and Helen F. Reid, 45–56 (Grand Rapids, Mich.: Eerdmans, 1980). See also Cicely Saunders, "The Evolution of Palliative Care," *Patient Education and Counseling* 41, no. 1 (2000): 7–13.

70. Connor, *Hospice and Palliative Care: The Essential Guide,* p. 4.

71. Cicely Saunders, personal communication.

72. Quoted in Constance Holden, "Hospices for the Dying, Relief from Pain and Fear," in *Hospice Handbook,* ed. Hamilton and Reid, p. 61.

73. Stephen R. Connor, "The Family, Larger Systems, and Dying," in *Handbook of Thanatology,* 2nd ed., ed. Meagher and Balk, 33–41 (New York: Routledge, 2013), p. 37.

74. Ira Byock, "The Ethics of Loving Care," *Health Progress* 85, no. 4 (2004): 12–19, 57.

75. International Work Group on Death, Dying, and Bereavement, *Statements on Death, Dying, and Bereavement* (London, Ont.: IWG, 1994).

76. Kenneth J. Doka, "Historical and Contemporary Perspectives on Dying," in *Handbook of Thanatology,* 2nd ed., ed. Meagher and Balk, 17–23 (New York: Routledge, 2013), p. 19. See also Andrea Fontana and Jennifer Reid Keene, *Death and Dying in America* (Malden, Mass.: Polity, 2009), p. 41.

77. William M. Lamers, Jr., "Hospice: Enhancing the Quality of Life," in *The Path Ahead,* ed. DeSpelder and Strickland, pp. 116–124.

78. For a report compiled by the National Hospice Work Group, see Bruce Jennings, True Ryndes, Carol D'Onofrio, and Mary Ann Baily, *Access to Hospice Care: Expanding Boundaries, Overcoming Barriers: Hastings Center Report Special Supplement* 33, no. 2 (2003): S3–S59.

79. Paul Glare and others, "A Systematic Review of Physicians' Survival Predictions in Terminally Ill Cancer Patients," *British Medical Journal* 327 (July 26, 2003): 195–198.

80. Quoted in article by Jeff Sharlet, "The Truth Can Comfort the Dying," *Chronicle of Higher Education* 46, no. 21 (January 28, 2000): A20–A24.

81. Lucette Lagnado, "Medicare Head Tackles Criticism on Hospice Care," *The Wall Street Journal,* September 15, 2000; and Nancy-Ann Min DeParle, Administrator, Health Care Financing Administration, "Letter to Medicare Hospices," September 12, 2000.

82. Code of Federal Regulations, Title 42, Chapter IV, Part 418, Certification of Terminal Illness (current to March 1, 2010).

83. Paul Sisson, "Scripps Wins Bidding for Hospice Property" (April 30, 2013); www.utsandiego.com/news/2013/Apr/30/sharp-san-diego-hospice-auction/. See also press release, "San Diego Hospice and Scripps Health Joint Statement: San Diego Hospice Announces Intent to Close," February 13, 2013.

84. *NHPCO Facts and Figures,* p. 7; and "Resident Population by Race, Hispanic Origin, and Age: 2009," *Statistical Abstract of the United States: 2012,* 131st ed. (Washington, D.C., 2011); http://www.census.gov/compendia/statab/.

85. Ronald K. Barrett, "Blacks, Death, Dying, and Funerals: Things You've Wondered About but Thought It Politically Incorrect to Ask" (keynote presentation, King's College 15th International Conference on Death and Bereavement, London, Ontario, May 12, 1997). See also Harold P. Freeman and Richard Payne, "Racial Injustice in Health Care," *New England Journal of Medicine* 342, no. 14 (April 6, 2000): 1045–1047; and Harold P. Freeman, Richard Payne, and Louis W. Sullivan, "Racial Injustice in Health Care: How Should It Be Addressed?" *Medical Crossfire* 2, no. 8 (2000): 31–33.

86. David J. Casarett and others, "The Terrible Choice: Re-Evaluating Hospice Eligibility Criteria for Cancer," *Journal of Clinical Oncology* 27, no. 6 (2009): 953–959; and Jessica Fishman and others, "Race, Treatment Preferences, and Hospice Enrollment: Eligibility Criteria May Exclude Patients with Greatest Needs for Care," *Cancer* 115, no. 3 (2009): 689–697. See also Alexander K. Smith, Craig C. Earle, and Ellen P. McCarthy, "Racial and Ethnic Differences in End-of-Life Care in Fee-for-Service Medicare Beneficiaries with Advanced Cancer," *Journal of the American Geriatrics Society* 57 (January 2009): 153–158.

87. Sandol Stoddard, quoted in Sloan, "The Hospice Movement: A Study in the Diffusion of Innovative Palliative Care," 24–31.

88. Richard Payne, "At the End of Life, Color Still Divides," *The Washington Post,* February 15, 2000. See also Leslie J. Blackhall and others, "Ethnicity and Attitudes Towards Life Sustaining Technology," *Social Science & Medicine* 48, no. 12 (1999): 1779–1789; Eric L. Krakauer, Christopher Crenner, and Ken Fox, "Barriers to Optimum End-of-Life Care for Minority Patients," *Journal of the American Geriatrics Society* 50, no. 1 (2002): 182–190; and "Palliative Care in African-American Communities" (whole issue), *Innovations in End-of-Life Care: An International Online Journal* 3, no. 5 (September–October 2001) www.2.edu.org/lastacts/crntisue.asp.

89. Carole A. Winston, Paula Leshner, Jennifer Kramer, and Gillian Allen, "Overcoming Barriers to Access and Utilization of Hospice and Palliative Care Services in African-American Communities," *Omega: Journal of Death and Dying* 50, no. 2 (2004–2005): 151–163; quote p. 161.

90. "The Debate in Hospice Care," *Journal of Oncology Practice* 4, no. 3 (2008): 153–157.

91. Stephen R. Connor, Martha Tecca, Judi Lund-Person, and Joan Teno, "Measuring Hospice Care," *Journal of Pain and Symptom Management* 28, no. 4 (2004): 316–328; quote p. 325.

92. Inge B. Corless, "Hospice and Hope: An Incompatible Duo," *American Journal of Hospice and Palliative Care* (May–June 1992): 10–12.

93. See Nicky James and David Field, "The Routinization of Hospice: Charisma and Bureaucratization," *Social Science & Medicine* 34, no. 12 (1992): 1363–1375.

94. Corless, "Settings for Terminal Care," p. 331.

95. William M. Lamers, Jr., "Hospice Care and Its Effect on the Grieving Process," in *Living with Grief When Illness Is Prolonged,* ed. Kenneth J. Doka and Joyce Davidson, 67–82 (Washington, D.C.: Hospice Foundation of America, 1997). See also, by Lamers, "Defining Hospice and Palliative Care: Some Further Thoughts," *Journal of Pain & Palliative Care Pharmacotherapy* 16, no. 3 (2002): 65–71; and Inge B. Corless, "Palliative Care: One Does Not Need to Be Terminally Ill," in *The Nursing Profession and Beyond,* ed. Norma L. Chasha, 561–573 (Thousand Oaks, Calif.: Sage, 2001).

96. "The Debate in Hospice Care," p. 155.

97. "The Debate in Hospice Care," p. 156.

98. Information from www.partners.org.

99. Pam Brown, Betty Davies, and Nola Martens, "Families in Supportive Care--Part II: Palliative Care at Home: A Viable Care Setting," *Journal of Palliative Care* 6, no. 3 (1990): 21–27. See also Tony Chapman, "There's No Place Like Home," *Theory, Culture & Society* 18, no. 6 (2001): 135–146.

100. Carol Levine, "Family Caregiving," 63–67, *The Hastings Center Bioethics Briefing Book* (Garrison, N.Y.: The Hastings Center, 2009), p. 63.

101. Sylvia Sherwood, Robert Kastenbaum, John N. Morris, and Susan M. Wright, "The First Months of Bereavement," in *The Hospice Experiment,* ed. Vincent Mor, David S. Greer, and Robert Kastenbaum (Baltimore: Johns Hopkins University Press, 1988), p. 150.

102. Frank Ostaseski, "Stories of Lives Lived and Now Ending," *Inquiring Mind: A Journal of the Vipassana Community* 10, no. 2 (Spring 1994): 14–16.

103. Allan Kellehear, "Health-Promoting Palliative Care: Developing a Social Model for Practice," *Mortality* 4, no. 1 (1999): 75–82; quote p. 77.

104. April Dembosky, "Stanford Program Ensures No One Dies Alone," *The Mercury News;* www.mercurynews.com August 21, 2009

105. Jon Hendricks and C. Davis Hendricks, *Aging in Mass Society: Myths and Realities* (Cambridge, Mass.: Winthrop, 1977), pp. 284–285.

106. Hendricks and Hendricks, *Aging in Mass Society,* p. 282.

107. See Muriel R. Gillick, "Do We Need to Create Geriatric Hospitals?" *Journal of the American Geriatrics Society* 50, no. 1 (2002): 174–177.

108. Arthur L. Kellerman and Ricardo Martinez, "The ER, Fifty Years On," *New England Journal of Medicine* 364, no. 24 (June 15, 2011): 2278–2279.

109. Michael Nurok, "The Death of a Princess and the Formulation of Medical Competence," *Social Science & Medicine* 53 (2001): 1427–1438; quote p. 1436. See also Thomas A. Sancton, "Death of a Princess: Did Princess Diana Have to Die? A Study in French Emergency Medicine," *The Internet Journal of Rescue and Disaster Medicine* 1, no. 2 (2000).

110. "Deaths and Death Rates by Selected Causes," *Statistical Abstract of the United States: 2012,* 131st ed. (Washington, D.C., 2011); http://www.census.gov/compendia/statab/.

111. See, for example, Mickey Eisenberg, *Life in the Balance: Emergency Medicine and the Quest to Reverse Sudden Death* (New York: Oxford University Press, 1997).

112. See, for example, Frank Huyler, *The Blood of Strangers: Stories from Emergency Medicine* (Berkeley: University of California Press, 1999).

113. "Family Presence During Cardiac Resuscitation," *New England Journal of Medicine* 368, no. 11 (March 14, 2013): 1060–1062. This article includes opposing commentary by James Downer and Patricia A. Kritek.

114. Jerome Groopman, "Being There: Should Patients' Families See What Happens in the Emergency Room?" *The New Yorker* (April 3, 2006): 34–39; quote p. 34.

115. James K. Crissman and Mary A. Crissman, "Notifications of Death," in *Macmillan Encyclopedia of Death and Dying,* ed. Robert Kastenbaum (New York: Macmillan, 2003), p. 620.

116. Resources include Kenneth V. Iserson, *Grave Words: Notifying Survivors About Sudden, Unexpected Deaths* (Tucson, Ariz.: Galen Press, 1999); R. Moroni Leash, *Death Notification: A Practical Guide to the Process* (Hinesburg, Vt.: Upper Access, 1994); Janice H. Lord, *Breaking the Bad News with Concern for the Professional and Compassion for the Survivor* (Washington, D.C.: U.S. Department of Justice, n.d.); C. A. J. McLauchlan, "Handling Distressed Relatives and Breaking Bad News," *British Medical Journal* 301 (November 17, 1990): 1145–1149; and Alan Stewart and Janice Harris Lord,

"The Death Notification Process," in *Handbook of Death & Dying,* ed. Clifton D. Bryant, 513–522 (Thousand Oaks, Calif.: Sage, 2003).

117. Leash, *Death Notification,* p. 25. See also Alan E. Stewart, "Complicated Bereavement and Posttraumatic Stress Disorder Following Fatal Car Crashes: Recommendations for Death Notification Practice," *Death Studies* 23 (1999): 289–321.

118. Roger Ray, "Death Notification: A Dreaded Duty," *The Orlando Sentinel,* March 21, 2005.

119. Julian Guthrie, "The Saddest Duty: Informing Families of Loss," *San Francisco Chronicle,* April 6, 2003.

120. "Deaths and Death Rates by Selected Causes," *Statistical Abstract of the United States: 2012,* 131st ed. (Washington, D.C., 2011); http://www.census.gov/compendia/statab/.

121. Leash, *Death Notification,* p. 48.

122. Peter Rober and Paul C. Rosenblatt, "Selected Discourse in a First Conversation About a Family Death in James Agee's Novel, *A Death in the Family,*" *Death Studies* 37 (2013): 172–194. This novel describes three days in the life of a family confronted with the husband/father's death in a road accident.

123. Leash, *Death Notification,* p. 52.

124. William M. Lamers, Jr., "How Patient Deaths Affect Health Professionals: A Plea for More Open Communication," *Journal of Pharmaceutical Care in Pain & Symptom Control* 5, no. 3 (1997): 59–71.

125. See Danai Papadatou, "A Proposed Model of Health Professionals' Grieving Process," *Omega: Journal of Death and Dying* 41, no. 1 (2000): 59–77.

126. See, for example, John D. Sugimoto and Kevin Ann Oltjenbruns, "The Environment of Death and Its Influence on Police Officers in the United States," *Omega: Journal of Death and Dying* 43, no. 2 (2001): 145–155; and Laurence Miller, "Tough Guys: Psychotherapeutic Strategies with Law Enforcement and Emergency Services Personnel," in *Stress Management in Law Enforcement,* ed. Leonard Territo and James D. Sewell, 317–332 (Durham, N.C.: Carolina Academic Press, 1999).

127. Morag B. Harris, Mustafa Baloğlu, and James R. Stacks, "Mental Health of Trauma-Exposed Firefighters and Critical Incident Stress Debriefing," *Journal of Loss and Trauma* 7 (2002): 223–238.

128. See Patricia Boston, Anna Towers, and David Barnard, "Embracing Vulnerability: Risk and Empathy in Palliative Care," *Journal of Palliative Care* 17, no. 4 (2001): 248–253; and Judi Webster and Linda J. Kristjanson, "'But Isn't It Depressing?': The Vitality of Palliative Care," *Journal of Palliative Care* 18, no. 1 (2002): 15–24.

129. Pallimed: A Hospice and Palliative Medicine Blog (May 22, 2013). See also David E. Weissman, "Moral Distress in Palliative Care," *Journal of Palliative Medicine* 12, no. 10 (2009): 865–866.

130. Danai Papadatou, *In the Face of Death: Professionals Who Care for the Dying and the Bereaved* (New York: Springer, 2009), p. 13.

131. Papadatou, *In the Face of Death,* p. 172.

132. See Graham Loomes and Lynda McKenzie, "The Use of QALYs in Health Care Decision Making," *Social Science & Medicine* 28 (1989): 299–308; and Erik Nord, "The QALY: A Measure of Social Value Rather Than Individual Utility?" *Health Economics* 3 (1993): 89–93, as well as "The Trade-Off Between Severity of Illness and Treatment Effect in Cost-Value Analysis of Health Care," *Health Policy* 24 (1993): 227–238.

133. Callahan, *Taming the Beloved Beast,* p. 7.

134. Allan Kellehear, *Compassionate Cities: Public Health and End of Life Care* (New York: Routledge, 2005), p. x.

CHAPTER 6

1. Alexander Morgan Capron, "The Burden of Decision," *Hastings Center Report* (May–June 1990): 36–41.

2. "Introduction to Part 2," in *Handbook of Thanatology,* 2nd ed., ed. David K. Meagher and David E. Balk (New York: Routledge, 2013), p. 51.

3. On the history of medical ethics, see Albert R. Jonsen, *The Birth of Bioethics* (New York: Oxford University Press, 1998).

4. Alan Meisel, "End-of-Life Care," 51–54, *The Hastings Center Bioethics Briefing Book* (Garrison, N.Y.: The Hastings Center, 2009).

5. See Karen Bullock, "The Influence of Culture on End-of-Life Decision Making," *Journal of Social Work in End-of-Life & Palliative Care* 7, no. 1 (2011): 83–98.

6. Timothy E. Quill and Christine K. Cassel, "Nonabandonment: A Central Obligation for Physicians," *Annals of Internal Medicine* 122, no. 5 (1995): 368–374.

7. John D. Lantos, *Do We Still Need Doctors?* (New York: Routledge, 1997), pp. 47–48.

8. The President's Commission for the Study of Ethical Problems in Medicine and Biomedical and Behavioral Research, *Making Health Care Decisions: The Ethical and Legal Implications of Informed Consent in the Patient-Practitioner Relationship,* vol. 1, *Report,* and vol. 3, *Studies on the Foundations of Informed Consent* (Washington, D.C.: Government Printing Office, 1982).

9. Carl B. Becker, "Japan: Challenges of Caring for the Aging and Dying," in *Buddhist Care for the Dying and Bereaved,* ed. Jonathan S. Watts and Yosiharu Tomatsu, 19–36 (Boston: Wisdom, 2012), p. 24.

10. Donald Oken, "What to Tell Cancer Patients: A Study of Medical Attitudes," *JAMA* 175 (1961): 1120–1128.

11. D. H. Novack and others, "Changes in Physicians' Attitudes Toward Telling the Cancer Patient," *JAMA* 241 (March 2, 1979): 897–900.

12. See Daniel J. Klenow and George A. Youngs, "Changes in Doctor/Patient Communication of a Terminal Prognosis: A Selective Review and Critique," *Death Studies* 11, no. 4 (1987): 263–277.

13. D. H. Novack and others, "Physicians' Attitudes Toward Using Deception to Resolve Difficult Ethical Problems," *JAMA* 261 (May 26, 1989): 2980–2985.

14. Robert Berkow, ed., *The Merck Manual of Medical Information: Home Edition* (Whitehouse Station, N.J.: Merck Research Laboratories, 1997), p. 16.

15. Daniel Callahan, *The Troubled Dream of Life: Living with Mortality* (New York: Simon & Schuster, 1993), p. 48.

16. Margot L. White and John C. Fletcher, "The Story of Mr. and Mrs. Doe: 'You Can't Tell My Husband He's Dying; It Will Kill Him,'" in *The Path Ahead: Readings in Death and Dying,* ed. Lynne Ann DeSpelder and Albert Lee Strickland (Mountain View, Calif.: Mayfield, 1995), pp. 148–153.

17. The SUPPORT Principal Investigators, "A Controlled Trial to Improve Care for Seriously Ill Hospitalized Patients: The Study to Understand Prognoses and Preferences for Outcomes and Risks of Treatment (SUPPORT)," *Journal of the American Medical Association* 274, no. 20 (1995): 1591–1598. See also in *Journal of the American Geriatrics Society* 48, no. 5 (2000): Russell S. Phillips and others, "Findings from SUPPORT and HELP: An Introduction" (pp. S1–S5); Neil S. Wenger and others, "Physician Understanding of Patient Resuscitation Preferences: Insights and Clinical Implications" (pp. S44–S51); and Carol E. Golin and others, "A Prospective Study of Patient-Physician Communication About Resuscitation" (pp. S52–S60).

18. Stephen R. Connor, *Hospice and Palliative Care: The Essential Guide,* 2nd ed. (New York: Routledge, 2009), p. 39.

19. Madeline Jacobs, "Ethical and Legal Issues Related to Dying and End-of-Life Care," in *Handbook of Thanatology,* 2nd ed., ed. Meagher and Balk, 43–49; quote p. 49.

20. Stephen R. Connor, *Hospice and Palliative Care: The Essential Guide,* 2nd ed. (New York: Routledge, 2009), p. 94.

21. Sharon R. Kaufman, *And a Time to Die: How American Hospitals Shape the End of Life* (New York: Scribner, 2005), pp. 116–117.

22. Josh Lakin, "Discussing CPR: What Makes It So Different?" *GeriPal: Geriatrics and Palliative Care Blog* (May 24, 2013).

23. Kaufman, *And a Time to Die,* pp. 49, 74.

24. S. J. Diem and J. D. Lantos, "Cardiopulmonary Resuscitation on Television: Miracles and Misinformation," *New England Journal of Medicine* 334, no. 24 (1996): 1578–1582.

25. A. Halevy and B. A. Brody, "A Multi-Institutional Collaborative Policy on Medical Futility," *Journal of the American Medical Association* 276, no. 7 (1996): 571–574. See also Donald Joralemon, "Reading Futility: Reflections on a Bioethical Concept," *Cambridge Quarterly of Healthcare Ethics* 11, no. 2 (2002): 127–133.

26. President's Commission for the Study of Ethical Problems in Medicine and Biomedical and Behavioral Research, *Summing Up: Final Report on Studies of the Ethical and Legal Problems in Medicine and Biomedical and Behavioral Research* (Washington, D.C.: Government Printing Office, March 1983), p. 31. See also the companion volume, *Deciding to Forego Life-Sustaining Treatment: A Report on the Ethical, Medical, and Legal Issues in Treatment Decisions* (Washington, D.C.: Government Printing Office, March 1983).

27. Berkow, ed., *Merck Manual of Medical Information: Home Edition,* p. 16.

28. See, by C. G. Prado, *Choosing to Die: Elective Death and Multiculturalism* (New York: Cambridge University Press, 2008), which addresses the question of when and whether it is rational to end one's life to escape devastating terminal illness; *Coping with Choices to Die* (New York: Cambridge University Press, 2011), which deals with the reasoning that needs to be done by family and friends of individuals who choose to die; and *The Last Choice: Preemptive Suicide in Advanced Age,* 2nd ed. (Westport, Conn.: Greenwood, 1998), which puts forth the argument that there are good reasons to end one's life as an unforced anticipation of demeaning and agonizing developments.

29. *In the Matter of Karen Quinlan: The Complete Legal Briefs, Court Proceedings and Decisions in the Superior Court of New Jersey* (1975) and *In the Matter of Karen Quinlan, Volume 2: The Complete Briefs, Oral Arguments, and Opinion in the New Jersey Supreme Court* (1976; Arlington, Va.: University Publications of America).

30. Background to the Cruzan case and arguments on both sides of the issue can be found in *Hastings Center Report* (January–February 1990): 38–50. See also Ron

Hamel, "The Supreme Court's Decision in the *Cruzan* Case: A Synopsis," *Bulletin of the Park Ridge Center* (September 1990): 18, 20; and Thane Josef Messinger, "A Gentle and Easy Death: From Ancient Greece to Beyond Cruzan Toward a Reasoned Legal Response to the Societal Dilemma of Euthanasia," *Denver University Law Review* 71, no. 1 (1993): 175–251.

31. Lois Shepherd, *If That Ever Happens to Me: Making Life and Death Decisions After Terri Schiavo* (Chapel Hill: University of North Carolina Press, 2009), p. 67.

32. See Arthur L. Caplan, James J. McCartney, and Dominic A. Sisti, eds., *The Case of Terri Schiavo: Ethics at the End of Life* (Amherst, N.Y.: Prometheus, 2006); Kenneth Goodman, ed., *The Case of Terri Schiavo: Ethics, Politics, and Death in the 21st Century* (New York: Oxford University Press, 2009); and Shepherd, *If That Ever Happens to Me.*

33. Jon Eisenberg, *Using Terri: The Religious Right's Conspiracy to Take Away Our Rights* (San Francisco: HarperCollins, 2005), p. 160. The term *persistent vegetative state* was coined in 1972 by Scottish neurosurgeon Bryan Jennett and American neurologist Fred Plum in the medical journal *The Lancet.*

34. Madeline Jacobs, "Ethical and Legal Issues in End-of-Life Decision Making," pp. 102, 103.

35. William Colby, *Unplugged: Reclaiming Our Right to Die in America* (New York: Amacom, 2006), p. 95.

36. Kenneth Goodman, "Ethics Schmethics: The Schiavo Case and the Culture Wars," *University of Miami Law Review* 61, no. 3 (2007): 863–870. See also Ronald E. Cranford, "What is a Minimally Conscious State," *Western Journal of Medicine* 176 (2002): 129–130; Joseph J. Fins, "Brain Injury: The Vegetative and Minimally Conscious States," 15–19, *The Hastings Center Bioethics Briefing Book* (Garrison, N.Y.: The Hastings Center, 2009); and J. T. Giacino and others, "The Minimally Conscious State: Definition and Diagnostic Criteria," *Neurology* 58 (2002): 349–353. For a review of the underlying mechanisms and classification of disorders of consciousness, see Andrew M. Goldfine and Nicholas D. Schiff, "Consciousness: Its Neurobiology and the Major Classes of Impairment," *Neurologic Clinics* 29, no. 4 (2011): 723–737.

37. Rebecca Dresser, "Schiavo and Contemporary Myths about Dying," *University of Miami Law Review* 61, no. 3 (2007): 821–846.

38. Kathy L. Cerminara, "Tracking the Storm: The Far-Reaching Power of the Forces Propelling the Schiavo Case," *Stetson Law Review* 35, no. 1 (2005): 147–178, quote p. 176; and "Theresa Marie Schiavo's Long Road to Peace," *Death Studies* 30, no. 2 (2006): 101–112. See also, in the same issue of *Death Studies,* Peter H. Ditto, "What Would Terri Want? On the Psychological Challenges of Surrogate Decision Making," pp. 135–148.

39. See Steve Perlmutter, "Physician-Assisted Suicide: A Medicolegal Inquiry," *Michigan State University Journal of Medicine & Law* 15 (Spring 2011): 203–225. See also Howard Brody, "Assisted Death: A Compassionate Response to a Medical Failure," *New England Journal of Medicine* 327 (November 5, 1992): 1384–1388; Eugenie Anne Gifford, "*Artes Moriendi:* Active Euthanasia and the Art of Dying," *UCLA Law Review* 40 (1993): 1545–1585; and Albert R. Jonsen, "Living with Euthanasia: A Futuristic Scenario," *Journal of Medicine and Philosophy* 18 (1993): 241–251.

40. Physician-assisted suicide (PAS) conducted by Michigan pathologist Jack Kevorkian brought the issue of hastened deaths of patients to widespread media and public attention during the 1990s. At the time of his sentencing in 1999 for the second-degree murder of Thomas Youk, Dr. Kevorkian had provided aid-in-dying to more than 100 individuals since he began his active crusade to legalize physician-assisted suicide in 1990.

41. See Choice in Dying, "Physician-Assisted Suicide: *Vacco v. Quill* and *Washington v. Glucksberg,*" www.choices.org/sctdec.htm; John Dinan, "Rights and the Political Process: Physician Assisted Suicide in the Aftermath of *Washington v. Glucksberg,*" *Publius: The Journal of Federalism* 31, no. 4 (2001): 1–21; and James L. Werth, Jr., and Judith R. Gordon, "Amicus Curiae Brief for the United States Supreme Court on Mental Health Issues Associated with 'Physician-Assisted Suicide,'" *Journal of Counseling & Development* 80, no. 2 (2002): 160–172.

42. Oregon Health Division, "2008 Summary of Oregon's Death with Dignity Act," http://oregon.gov/DHS/ph/pas/ar-index.shtml.

43. Timothy E. Quill and Jane Greenlaw, "Physician-Assisted Death," in *The Hastings Center Bioethics Briefing Book,* pp. 137–141 (Garrison, N.Y.: The Hastings Center, 2009); quote p. 138.

44. Ira Byock, "Dying: After the Court Ruling," *The Wall Street Journal,* June 25, 1997, p. A14.

45. John A. Pridonoff, "Introduction," in *Hospice and Hemlock: Retaining Dignity, Integrity, and Self-Respect in End-of-Life Decisions,* ed. Michele A. Trepkowski (Eugene, Ore.: Hemlock Society, 1993).

46. See P. Rousseau, "Terminal Sedation in the Care of Dying Patients," *Archives of Internal Medicine* 1556, no. 16 (1996): 1785–1786.

47. M. Maltoni and others, "Palliative Sedation Therapy Does Not Hasten Death: Results from a Prospective Multicenter Study," *Annals of Oncology* 20 (2009): 1163–1169.

48. Drew Rosielle, "Palliative Sedation and Shortened Survival," *Pallimed,* www.pallimed.org, July 2, 2009.

49. Quoted in Quill and Greenlaw, "Physician-Assisted Death," p. 141.

50. Euthanasia can be involuntary, nonvoluntary, or voluntary. *Involuntary* euthanasia refers to the death of a patient by a medical practitioner *without* the patient's consent. A notorious example was the medicalized killing done by the Nazi regime. Involuntary euthanasia is usually considered murder. *Nonvoluntary* euthanasia occurs when a surrogate decision maker (not the patient himself or herself) asks a physician for assistance to end another person's life. This could occur, for instance, when a family member assumes life-or-death decisions for an ailing relative. Nonvoluntary euthanasia is the category usually applied to child euthanasia when a seriously ill child is deemed incompetent to make a decision for himself or herself. *Voluntary* euthanasia is the intentional termination of a patient's life at his or her request by someone other than the patient. In practice, this usually means that a competent patient requests direct assistance to die, and he or she receives assistance from a qualified medical practitioner.

51. "It's Over, Debbie," *Journal of the American Medical Association* 259, no. 2 (January 8, 1988): 272.

52. See Raphael Cohen-Almagor, "Why the Netherlands?" *Journal of Law, Medicine & Ethics* 30, no. 1 (2002): 95–104, and "'Culture of Death' in the Netherlands: Dutch Perspectives," *Issues in Law & Medicine* 17, no. 2 (2001): 167–179; Herbert Hendin, "The Dutch Experience," *Issues in Law & Medicine* 17, no. 3 (2002): 223–246; and Herman H. van der Kloot Meijburg, "How Health Care Institutions in the Netherlands Approach Physician-Assisted Death," *Omega: Journal of Death and Dying* 32, no. 3 (1995–1996): 179–196.

53. Charles J. Dougherty, "The Common Good, Terminal Illness, and Euthanasia," in *The Path Ahead,* ed. DeSpelder and Strickland, pp. 154–164.

54. Thomas Attig, "Can We Talk? On the Elusiveness of Dialogue," *Death Studies* 19, no. 1 (1995): 1–19.

55. R. J. Connelly, "The Sentiment Argument for Artificial Feeding of the Dying," *Omega: Journal of Death and Dying* 20, no. 3 (1989–1990): 229–237. See also Germain Grisez and Kevin O'Rourke, "Should Nutrition and Hydration Be Provided to Permanently Unconscious and Other Mentally Disabled Persons," *Issues in Law & Medicine* 5 (1989): 165–196; James J. McCartney and Jane Mary Trau, "Cessation of the Artificial Delivery of Food and Fluids: Defining Terminal Illness and Care," *Death Studies* 14, no. 5 (1990): 435–444; Steven H. Miles, "Nourishment and the Ethics of Lament," *Linacre Quarterly* 56 (August 1989): 64–69; and J. Slomka, "What Do Apple Pie and Motherhood Have to Do with Feeding Tubes and Caring for the Patient?" *Archives of Internal Medicine* 155, no. 12 (1995): 1258–1263.

56. Dena S. Davis, "Old and Thin," *Second Opinion* 15 (November 1990): 26–32; see also, in the same issue, Ronald M. Green, "Old and Thin: A Response," pp. 34–39. On Japanese attitudes toward withdrawing nutrition and hydration, see Emiko Konishi, Anne J. Davis, and Toshiaki Aiba, "The Ethics of Withdrawing Artificial Food and Fluid from Terminally Ill Patients: An End-of-Life Dilemma for Japanese Nurses and Families," *Nursing Ethics* 9, no. 1 (2002): 7–19.

57. Alan R. Fleishman, "Neonatal Care," in *The Hastings Center Bioethics Briefing Book,* pp. 121–124 (Garrison, N.Y.: The Hastings Center, 2009); quote p. 121.

58. Fleishman, "Neonatal Care," p. 122.

59. Quoted in Richard A. McCormick, "To Save or Let Die: The Dilemma of Modern Medicine," in *Ethical Issues in Death and Dying,* ed. Robert F. Weir (New York: Columbia University Press, 1977), pp. 173–184.

60. See, for example, Peter A. Clark, "Medical Futility in Pediatrics: Is It Time for a Public Policy?" *Journal of Public Health Policy* 23, no. 1 (2002): 66–89; and John J. Paris, Jeffrey Ferranti, and Frank Reardon, "From the Johns Hopkins Baby to Baby Miller: What Have We Learned from Four Decades of Reflection on Neonatal Cases?" *Journal of Clinical Ethics* 12, no. 3 (2001): 207–214.

61. Alan R. Fleishman, "Neonatal Care," p. 124.

62. See Peter H. Ditto and others, "Advance Directives as Acts of Communication," *Archives of Internal Medicine* 161 (2001): 421–430; Angela Fagerlin and others, "Projection in Surrogate Decisions About Life-Sustaining Medical Treatments," *Health Psychology* 20, no. 3 (2001): 166–175; and Angela Fagerlin and others, "The Use of Advance Directives in End-of-Life Decision Making: Problems and Possibilities," *American Behavioral Scientist* 46, no. 2 (2002): 268–283.

63. Lisa M. Krieger, "New Survey Sheds Light on Californians' End-of-Life Wishes," *San Jose Mercury News* (February 14, 2012), A10.

64. Judi Lund Person, "Regulatory Issues in the Care of Dying," in *Dying, Death, and Bereavement: A Challenge for Living,* 2nd ed., ed. Inge B. Corless, Barbara B. Germino, and Mary A. Pittman (New York: Springer, 2003), p. 205.

65. California Medical Association, "California Natural Death Act," www.cmanet.org.

66. Quotes by H. Harrison Sadler, M.D., in "California's Natural Death Act—Medical Staff Conference, University of California, San Francisco," *Western Journal of Medicine* 128 (1978): 318–330.

67. Angela Fagerlin and Carl E. Schneider, "Enough: The Failure of the Living Will," *Hastings Center Report* 34, no. 2 (2004): 30–42; quote p. 38.

68. Fagerlin and Schneider, "Enough," pp. 30–42.

69. President's Council on Bioethics, *Ethical Caregiving in Our Aging Society* (Washington, D.C.: Government Printing Office, 2005), p. 55.

70. Current information can be found at www.POLST.org.

71. Marilyn J. Field and Christine K. Cassel, eds., *Approaching Death: Improving Care at the End of Life* (Washington, D.C.: National Academies Press, 1997).

72. Information can be found at www.agingwithdignity.org.

73. The authors thank Senator John C. Danforth, sponsor of this measure, for providing information about its provisions. See also Elizabeth Leibold McCloskey, "The Patient Self-Determination Act," *Kennedy Institute of Ethics Journal* 1, no. 2 (1991): 163–169.

74. Madeline Jacobs, "Ethical and Legal Issues in End-of-Life Decision Making," p. 104.

75. Information and forms for each state can be downloaded from Caring Connections at www.caringinfo.org.

76. Susan Dolan and Audrey Vizzard, *The End of Life Advisor: Personal, Legal, and Medical Considerations for a Peaceful, Dignified Death* (New York: Kaplan, 2009), p. 73.

77. Zelda Foster, "The Struggle to End My Father's Life," in *Dying, Death, and Bereavement,* 2nd ed., ed. Corless, Germino, and Pittman, pp. 79–85. See also Reneé Semonin Holleran, "When Is Dead, Dead? The Ethics of Resuscitation in Emergency Care," *Nursing Clinics of North America* 37, no. 1 (2002): 11–18.

78. Christian Sinclair, "Do Not (Attempt) Resuscitation vs. Allow Natural Death," *Pallimed,* www.pallimed.org, March 5, 2009.

79. Barton E. Bernstein, "Lawyer and Counselor as an Interdisciplinary Team: Interfacing for the Terminally Ill," *Death Education* 1, no. 3 (Fall 1977): 277–291; "Lawyer and Therapist as an Interdisciplinary Team: Serving the Terminally Ill," *Death Education* 3, no. 1 (Spring 1979): 11–19; and "Lawyer and Therapist as an Interdisciplinary Team: Serving the Survivors," *Death Education* 4, no. 2 (Summer 1980): 179–188.

80. Kaja Whitehouse, *What Your Lawyer May Not Tell You About Your Family's Will* (New York: Warner, 2006), p. 219.

81. Jackson P. Rainer, "Ethical and Legal Issues in Assessment and Intervention," in *Handbook of Thanatology,* 2nd ed., ed. Meagher and Balk, pp. 255–261; quote p. 260.

82. See Kenneth J. Doka, "The Monkey's Paw: The Role of Inheritance in the Resolution of Grief," *Death Studies* 16, no. 1 (1992): 45–58. For a cross-cultural comparison of inheritance practices, see Misa Izuhara, "Care and Inheritance: Japanese and English Perspectives on the 'Generational Contract,'" *Ageing and Society* 22 (2002): 61–77.

83. Colleen DeBaise, "'Family Letters' Go Beyond Wills," *The Wall Street Journal* (November 16, 2005), p. D3.

84. See www.ethicalwill.com; and Barry K. Baines, *Ethical Wills: Putting Your Values on Paper* (New York: Perseus, 2002).

85. Richard Costa, "Challenges of Being an Estate Executor," *Capitola Soquel Times* (May 1, 2006), p. 31.

86. Survey by EZLaw Wills and Estate Planning, reported in *The Week* (September 9, 2011), p. 34.

87. See Joseph M. Belth, *Life Insurance: A Consumer's Handbook,* 2nd ed. (Bloomington: Indiana University Press, 1985).

88. Karen E. Steinhauser, Nicholas A. Christakis, and others, "Factors Considered Important at the End of Life by Patients, Family, Physicians, and Other Care Providers," *JAMA* 284, no. 19 (November 15, 2000): 2476–2482.

89. Kaufman, *And a Time to Die,* p. 93.

90. Leon R. Kass, "Practicing Ethics: Where's the Action?" *Hastings Center Report* (January–February 1990): 5–12.

91. Jitaro Mizuno, "A Caring Heart and Integrated Knowledge: An Ethics Which Inquires into the Relationship Between the Self and Others," Reitaku University, Japan.

92. Jeffrey P. Bishop, *The Anticipatory Corpse: Medicine, Power, and the Care of the Dying* (Notre Dame, Ind.: University of Notre Dame Press, 2011), p. 7. See also, by Bishop and others, "Reviving the Conversation Around CPR/DNR," *American Journal of Bioethics* 10, no. 1 (2010): 61–67.

93. Richard B. Gilbert, "End-of-Life Care: Spirituality and Religion," in *Handbook of Thanatology,* 2nd ed., ed. Meagher Balk, pp. 63–71; quote p. 63.

CHAPTER 7

1. Lee Lipsenthal, *Enjoy Every Sandwich: Living Each Day As If It Were Your Last* (New York: Crown Archetype, 2011), p. 110.

2. Paul M. Insel and Walton T. Roth, *Connect Core Concepts in Health,* 13th ed. (New York: McGraw-Hill, 2013), pp. 414, 428–429, 432.

3. Randall C. Thompson et al., "Atherosclerosis Across 4000 Years of Human History: The Horus Study of Four Ancient Populations," *The Lancet Early Online Publication* (March 11, 2013).

4. Cassandra Lorius, "Taboo," in *Key Ideas in Human Thought,* ed. Kenneth McLeish (New York: Facts on File, 1993), p. 731.

5. S. Kay Toombs, "Chronic Illness and the Goals of Medicine," *Second Opinion* 21, no. 1 (July 1995): 11–19. See also Charles E. Rosenberg, "The Tyranny of Diagnosis: Specific Entities and Individual Experience," *Milbank Quarterly* 80, no. 2 (2002): 237–260.

6. S. Lochlann Jain, "Survival Odds: Mortality in Corporate Time," *Current Anthropology* 52, Supplement 3 (April 2011): S45–S55.

7. Ira Byock, *The Best Care Possible: A Physician's Quest to Transform Care Through the End of Life* (New York: Avery, 2012), p. 1.

8. Byock, *The Best Care Possible,* pp. 25, 26.

9. See Maggie Callanan and Patricia Kelley. *Final Gifts: Understanding the Special Awareness, Needs, and Communications of the Dying* (New York: Bantam, 1997).

10. Arthur W. Frank, "The Pedagogy of Suffering: Moral Dimensions of Psychological Therapy and Research with the Ill," *Theory & Psychology* 2, no. 4 (1992): 467–485.

11. See Kevin P. Kaut, "Religion, Spirituality, and Existentialism Near the End of Life: Implications for Assessment and Application," *American Behavioral Scientist* 46, no. 2 (2002): 220–234.

12. Charles A. Corr, "A Task-Based Approach to Coping with Dying," *Omega: Journal of Death and Dying* 24, no. 2 (1991–1992): 81–94. See also Charles A. Corr and Kenneth J. Doka, "Current Models of Death, Dying, and Bereavement," *Critical Care Nursing Clinics of North America* 6, no. 3 (1994): 545–552.

13. Barney G. Glaser and Anselm L. Strauss, *Awareness of Dying* (Chicago: Aldine, 1965). See also Neil Small and Merryn Gott, "The Contemporary Relevance of Glaser and Strauss," *Mortality* 17, no. 4 (2012): 355–377.

14. Kenneth J. Doka, *Counseling Individuals with Life-Threatening Illness* (New York: Springer, 2009), p. 206.

15. E. Mansell Pattison, *The Experience of Dying* (Englewood Cliffs, N.J.: Prentice-Hall, 1977), and "The Living-Dying Process," in *Psychological Care of the Dying,* ed. Charles Garfield (New York: McGraw-Hill, 1978), pp. 163–168. See also Karin L. Olson and others, "Linking Trajectories of Illness and Dying," *Omega: Journal of Death and Dying* 42, no. 4 (2001): 293–308.

16. Avery D. Weisman, *On Dying and Denying: A Psychiatric Study of Terminality* (New York: Behavioral Publications, 1972).

17. Elisabeth Kübler-Ross, *On Death and Dying* (New York: Macmillan, 1969). See also Colin Murray Parkes, "Classics Revisited: Elisabeth Kübler-Ross, *On Death and Dying:* A Reappraisal," *Mortality* 18, no. 1 (2013): 94–97.

18. Abraham Verghese, "On Death and Dying," *The Wall Street Journal,* August 31, 2004.

19. Charles A. Corr and Donna M. Corr, "Culture, Socialization, and Dying," in *Handbook of Thanatology,* 2nd ed., ed. David K. Meagher and David E. Balk, 3–8 (New York: Routledge, 2013), p. 8. See also Charles A. Corr, "Coping with Dying: Lessons That We Should and Should Not Learn from the Work of Elisabeth Kübler-Ross," *Death Studies* 17 (1993): 69–83.

20. Harold Brodkey, "To My Readers," in *The Path Ahead: Readings in Death and Dying,* ed. Lynne Ann DeSpelder and Albert Lee Strickland (Mountain View, Calif.: Mayfield, 1995), pp. 295–300; quote p. 298. See also Robert Connelly, "Living with Death: The Meaning of Acceptance," *Journal of Humanistic Psychology* 43, no. 1 (2003): 45–63.

21. Kenneth J. Doka, "Coping with Life-Threatening Illness: A Task Model," *Omega: Journal of Death and Dying* 32, no. 2 (1995–1996): 111–122. See also Doka, *Counseling Individuals with Life-Threatening Illness,* and *Living with Life-Threatening Illness: A Guide for Patients, Their Families, and Caregivers* (New York: Lexington, 1993).

22. Doka, "Coping with Life-Threatening Illness," p. 120.

23. Herman Feifel, "Psychology and Death: Meaningful Rediscovery," in *The Path Ahead,* ed. DeSpelder and Strickland, pp. 19–28; quote p. 23. See also Susan Folkman and Steven Greer, "Promoting Psychological Well-Being in the Face of Serious Illness: When Theory, Research and Practice Inform Each Other," *Psycho-Oncology* 9, no. 1 (2000): 11–19. See also Susan Folkman, "Positive Psychological States and Coping with Severe Stress," *Social Science & Medicine* 45, no. 8 (1997): 1207–1221; and Susan Folkman and Judith Tedlie Moskowitz, "Positive Affect and the Other Side of Coping," *American Psychologist* 55, no. 6 (2000): 647–654.

24. Avery D. Weisman, *The Coping Capacity: On the Nature of Being Mortal* (New York: Human Sciences Press, 1986).

25. Weisman, *On Dying and Denying.* See also, by Weisman, *Coping with Cancer* (New York: McGraw-Hill, 1979); and "Thanatology," in *Comprehensive Textbook of Psychiatry,* ed. O. Kaplan (Baltimore: Williams & Wilkins, 1980).

26. Betsy L. Fife, "The Measurement of Meaning in Illness," *Social Science & Medicine* 40, no. 8 (1995): 1021–1028. See also, by Fife, "The Conceptualization of Meaning in Illness," *Social Science & Medicine* 38, no. 2 (1994): 309–316.

27. See Phoebe Cramer, "Coping and Defense Mechanisms: What's the Difference?" *Journal of Personality* 66, no. 6 (1998): 919–946; and "Defense Mechanisms in Psychology Today: Further Processes for Adaptation," *American Psychologist* 55, no. 6 (2000): 637–646.

28. Russell Noyes, Jr., and others, "Illness Fears in the General Population," *Psychosomatic Medicine* 62, no. 3 (2000): 318–325.

29. Edwin S. Shneidman, *Lives and Deaths: Selections from the Works of Edwin S. Shneidman,* ed. Antoon A. Leenaars (Philadelphia: Brunner-Mazel, 1999), p. 260.

30. Therese A. Rando, *Grief, Dying, and Death: Clinical Interventions for Caregivers* (Lexington, Mass.: Lexington, 1993).

31. Richard S. Lazarus, "Toward Better Research on Stress and Coping," *American Psychologist* 55, no. 6 (2000): 665–673.

32. Mark R. Somerfield and Robert R. McCrae, "Stress and Coping Research: Methodological Challenges, Theoretical Advances, and Clinical Applications," *American Psychologist* 55, no. 6 (2000): 620–625.

33. Folkman and Greer, "Promoting Psychological Well-Being in the Face of Serious Illness."

34. On deferred demises, see Bruce Bower, "Death Waits for No One," *Science News* 165, no. 23 (2004): 356; and Judith A. Skala and Kenneth E. Freedland, "Death Takes a Raincheck," *Psychosomatic Medicine* 66 (2004): 382–386.

35. Tone Rustøen and Ingela Wiklund, "Hope in Newly Diagnosed Patients with Cancer," *Cancer Nursing* 23, no. 3 (2000): 214–219. See also Jaklin Eliott and Ian Olver, "The Discursive Properties of 'Hope': A Qualitative Analysis of Cancer Patients' Speech," *Qualitative Health Research* 12, no. 2 (2002): 173–193.

36. Mary-Jo Del Vecchio Good and others, "Oncology and Narrative Time," *Social Science & Medicine* 38, no. 6 (1994): 855–862.

37. Robert L. Wrenn, Dan Levinson, and Danai Papadatou, *End of Life Decisions: Guidelines for the Health Care Provider* (Tucson: University of Arizona Health Sciences Center, 1996), p. 20.

38. Byock, *The Best Care Possible,* p. 244.

39. Anne Hughes, Betty Davies, and Maria Gudmundsdottir, "'Can You Give Me Respect?': Experiences of the Urban Poor on a Dedicated AIDS Nursing Home Unit," *Journal of the Association of Nurses in AIDS Care* 19, no. 5 (2008): 342–356; and Anne Hughes, Maria Gudmundsdottir, and Betty Davies, "Everyday Struggling to Survive: Experiences of the Urban Poor Living with Advanced Cancer," *Oncology Nursing Forum* 34, no. 6 (2007): 1113–1118.

40. Anemona Hartocollis and Ford Fessenden, "In New York City, Two Versions of End-of-Life Care," *New York Times,* May 30, 2008, http://www.nytimes.com/2008/05/30/nyregion/30hospitals.html?_r=0#. See also Kevin Fiscella and Kathleen Holt, "Racial Disparity in Hypertension Control: Tallying the Death Toll," *Annals of Family Medicine* 6, no. 6 (2008): 497–502.

41. Harvey Max Chochinov, "Dignity-Conserving Care: A New Model for Palliative Care: Helping the Patient Feel Valued," *JAMA* 287, no. 17 (2002): 2253–2260; quote p. 2254.

42. Andy Hau Yan Ho et al., "Living and Dying with Dignity in Chinese Society: Perspectives of Older Palliative Care Patients in Hong Kong," *Age and Ageing* 42, no. 4 (2013): 455–461. See also Ho and others, "Dignity Amidst Liminality: Healing Within Suffering Among Chinese Terminal Cancer Patients," *Death Studies* (2013), in press, as well as Cecilia L. W. Chan and others, "The Blessings and Curses of Filial Piety on Dignity at the End of Life: Lived Experiences of Hong Kong Chinese Adult Children Caregivers," *Journal of Ethnic and Cultural Diversity in Social Work* 21 (2012): 277–296.

43. Insel and Roth, *Connect Core Concepts in Health,* p. 444.

44. Paolo Venies, "Definition and Classification of Cancer: Monothetic or Polythetic?" *Theoretical Medicine* 14 (1993): 249–256.

45. Robert Berkow, ed., *The Merck Manual of Diagnosis and Therapy,* 16th ed. (Rahway, N.J.: Merck Research Laboratories, 1992), p. 1275.

46. Laurence McCahill and Betty Ferrell, "Palliative Surgery for Cancer Pain," *Western Journal of Medicine* 176, no. 2 (2002): 107–110.

47. See Berkow, ed., *Merck Manual of Diagnosis and Therapy,* 16th ed., pp. 1276–1277; *Merck Manual of Medical Information: Home Edition* (Whitehouse Station, N.J.: Merck Research Laboratories, 1997), p. 801; and R. A. Hope and others, *Oxford Handbook of Clinical Medicine,* 3rd ed. (New York: Oxford University Press, 1994), p. 768.

48. See Berkow, ed., *Merck Manual of Diagnosis and Therapy,* 16th ed., pp. 55, 1277, 1287; and *Merck Manual: Home Edition,* pp. 799, 802; and Hope and others, *Oxford Handbook of Clinical Medicine,* 3rd ed., p. 768.

49. Jane C. Weeks et al., "Patients' Expectations about Effects of Chemotherapy for Advanced Cancer," *New England Journal of Medicine* 367 (October 25, 2012): 1616–1625.

50. Insel and Roth, *Connect Core Concepts in Health,* p. 565.

51. Insel and Roth, *Connect Core Concepts in Health,* p. 566.

52. Roxanne Nelson, "Framework for Experimental Drug Use in Terminally Ill Patients," *Medscape Medical News,* www.medscape.com.

53. Berkow, ed., *Merck Manual of Diagnosis and Therapy,* 16th ed., p. 1263.

54. The National Center for Complementary and Alternative Medicine (NCCAM) is the federal government's lead agency for scientific research on complementary and alternative medicine. It is one of the twenty-seven institutes and centers that make up the National Institutes of Health (NIH) within the U.S. Department of Health and Human Services. See http://nccam.nih.gov/about/ataglance.

55. Terri A. Winnick, "From Quackery to 'Complementary' Medicine: The American Medical Profession Confronts Alternative Therapies," *Social Problems* 52, no. 1 (2005): 38–61. For critical views on CAM, see the website Quackwatch (www.quackwatch.org).

56. David K. Reynolds, *A Thousand Waves: A Sensible Life Style for Sensitive People* (New York: Quill/Morrow, 1990).

57. See Josep M. Comelles, "The Role of Local Knowledge in Medical Practice: A Trans-Historical Perspective," *Culture Medicine and Psychiatry* 24, no. 1 (2000): 41–75.

58. Quoted in Anne Fadiman, *The Spirit Catches You and You Fall Down: A Hmong Child, Her American Doctors, and the Collision of Two Cultures* (New York: Farrar, Straus and Giroux, 1997), p. 261. See also Arthur Kleinman, *Patients and Healers in the Context of Culture* (Berkeley: University of California Press, 1980).

59. Lori Arviso Alvord and Elizabeth Cohen Van Pelt, *The Scalpel and the Silver Bear* (New York: Bantam, 1999).

60. Biography, Dr. Lori Arviso Alvord, National Library of Medicine. www.nlm.nih.gov/changingthefaceofmedicine/physicians/biography_7.html.

61. Biograpy, Dr. Lori Arviso Alvord.

62. Gerry Cox, *Death and the American Indian* (Omaha, Neb.: Grief Illustrated Press, 2010), p. 55. See also Gerry R. Cox, "The Native American Way of Death," in *Handbook of Death and Dying,* ed. Clifton D. Bryant, 631–639 (Thousand Oaks, Calif.: Sage, 2003).

63. Robert T. Trotter II and Juan Antonio Chavira, *Curanderismo: Mexican-American Folk Healing,* 2nd ed. (Athens: University of Georgia Press, 1997).

64. Kaja Finkler, "Sacred Healing and Biomedicine Compared," *Medical Anthropology Quarterly* 8, no. 2 (June 1994): 178–197.

65. Berkow, ed., *Merck Manual of Diagnosis and Therapy,* 16th ed., pp. 2593–2596.

66. Lawrence J. Schneiderman, "Alternative Medicine or Alternatives to Medicine? A Physician's Perspective," *Cambridge Quarterly of Healthcare Ethics* 9, no. 1 (2000): 83–97.

67. Michael Specter, "The Power of Nothing," *The New Yorker* (December 12, 2008), pp. 30–36.

68. Steven B. Perlmutter, "Clinical Use of Placebos: Medicine, Neuroscience, Ethics, and the Law," 8 *Tennessee Journal of Law and Policy* 8 (2012).

69. Insel and Roth, *Connect Core Concepts in Health,* pp. 566–567.

70. Michael Specter, "The Power of Nothing," *The New Yorker* (December 12, 2008), p. 31.

71. Specter, Power of Nothing," p. 31.

72. Perlmutter, "Clinical Use of Placebos."

73. Perlmutter, "Clinical Use of Placebos."

74. Rodolfo Passalacqua, Francesco Campione, and Caterina Caminiti, "Patients' Opinions, Feelings, and Attitudes After a Campaign to Promote the Di Bella Therapy," *The Lancet* 353 (April 17, 1999): 1310–1314; quote p. 1313.

75. Doris M. Schoenhoff, *The Barefoot Expert: The Interface of Computerized Knowledge Systems and Indigenous Knowledge Systems* (Westport, Conn.: Greenwood, 1993), pp. 13–14.

76. Insel and Roth, *Connect Core Concepts in Health,* p. 579.

77. "Medicinal Use of Marijuana," *New England Journal of Medicine* 368 (February 28, 2013): 866–868.

78. Stanley J. Watson, John A. Benson, Jr., and Janet E. Joy, "Marijuana and Medicine: Assessing the Science Base," *Archives of General Psychiatry* 57 (2000): 547–552. See also Inge B. Corless and others, "Marijuana Effectiveness as an HIV Self-Care Strategy," *Clinical Nursing Research* 18, no. 2 (2009): 172–193; Franjo Grotenhermen, "The Medical Use of Cannabis in Germany,"

Journal of Drug Issues 32, no. 2 (2002): 607–633; and Donald I. Templer, Hiroko Arikawa, and Patrick C. Gariety, "Psychotropic Drugs in Terminally Ill Patients: A Review of the Clinical and Research Literature," *Omega: Journal of Death and Dying* 49, no. 3 (2004): 249–274.

79. Gregory T. Carter and Bruce Mirken, "Medical Marijuana: Politics Trumps Science at the FDA," *Medscape General Medicine*, May 24, 2006, www.medscape.com.

80. "Is Marijuana Bad for You? *The Week* (November 30, 2012), p. 11.

81. Anson Shupe and Jeffrey K. Hadden, "Symbolic Healing," *Second Opinion* 12 (November 1989): 74–97.

82. "Tapping Human Potential: An Interview with Norman Cousins," *Second Opinion* 14 (July 1990): 57–71. See also Norman Cousins, *Anatomy of an Illness as Perceived by the Patient: Reflections on Healing and Regeneration* (New York: Norton, 1979).

83. Kjell Kallenberg and Carl-Rheinhold Brakenhielm, "Pain and Suffering as Existential Questions in Palliative Care," *European Journal of Palliative Care* 1, no. 1 (1994): 54–56.

84. S. Deandrea, M. Montanari, L. Moja, and G. Apolone, "Prevalence of Undertreatment in Cancer Pain: A Review of Published Literature," *Annals of Oncology* 19, no. 12 (2008): 1985–1991.

85. Marcia K. Merboth and Susan Barnason, "Managing Pain: The Fifth Vital Sign," *Nursing Clinics of North America* 35, no. 2 (2000): 375–383. See also Marni Jackson, *Pain: The Fifth Vital Sign* (New York: Crown, 2002).

86. Alison Twycross, "Education About Pain: A Neglected Area?" *Nurse Education Today* 20, no. 3 (2000): 244–253. See also, by Twycross, "Educating Nurses About Pain Management: The Way Forward," *Journal of Clinical Nursing* 11, no. 6 (2002): 705–714.

87. Berkow, ed., *Merck Manual of Diagnosis and Therapy*, 16th ed., p. 1409.

88. *Dorland's Illustrated Medical Dictionary*, 26th ed. (Philadelphia: Saunders, 1985), p. 954.

89. Yasmin Hawkins and others, "Changes in Sexuality and Intimacy After the Diagnosis and Treatment of Cancer: The Experience of Partners in a Sexual Relationship with a Person with Cancer," *Cancer Nursing* 32, no. 4 (2009): 271–280.

90. Linda C. Garro, "Culture, Pain and Cancer," *Journal of Palliative Care* 6, no. 3 (1990): 34–44. See also David B. Morris, *The Culture of Pain* (Berkeley: University of California Press, 1991).

91. "Interview with Yvette Colón," *Hospice Foundation of America*, www.hospicefoundation.org.

92. Perry G. Fine and Clarinda Mac Low, "The Last Chance for Comfort: An Update on Pain Management at the End of Life," *Medscape*, December 26, 2005, www.medscape.com.

93. Berkow, ed., *Merck Manual of Diagnosis and Therapy*, 16th ed., pp. 1409, 1412. See also Fredrica A. Preston, Siew Tzuh Tang, and Ruth McCorkle, "Symptom Management for the Terminally Ill," in *Dying, Death, and Bereavement: A Challenge for Living*, 2nd ed., ed. Inge Corless, Barbara B. Germino, and Mary A. Pittman (New York: Springer, 2003), pp. 145–180.

94. See Fine and Low, "The Last Chance for Comfort."

95. Ana Blasco, Miguel Berzosa, Vega Iranzo, and Carlos Camps, "Update in Cancer Pain," *Cancer & Chemotherapy Reviews* 4, no. 2 (2009): 95–109.

96. Stephen R. Connor, "Palliative Care is a Human Right," *ADEC Forum* 37, no. 3 (2011): 1, 3–4, 10.

97. Ana Blasco, Miguel Berzosa, Vega Iranzo, and Carlos Camps, "Update in Cancer Pain," *Medscape Cancer & Chemotherapy Reviews*, August 28, 2009, www.medscape.com.

98. See Betty Rolling Ferrell, ed., "Issues in Cancer Pain Management: Models of Success," *Cancer Practice* 10, Supplement 1 (2002): whole issue.

99. See Karen L. Schumacher and others, "Pain Management Autobiographies and Reluctance to Use Opioids for Cancer Pain Management," *Cancer Nursing* 25, no. 2 (2002): 125–133; and James L. Werth, Jr., "Reinterpreting the Controlled Substances Act: Predictions for the Effect on Pain Relief," *Behavioral Sciences and the Law* 20, no. 3 (2002): 287–305.

100. See David Clark, "'Total Pain': Disciplinary Power and the Body in the Work of Cicely Saunders, 1958–1967," *Social Science & Medicine* 49 (1999): 727–736.

101. Robert Kastenbaum and Claude Normand, "Deathbed Scenes as Imagined by the Young and Experienced by the Old," *Death Studies* 14, no. 3 (1990): 201–217.

102. Barney G. Glaser and Anselm L. Strauss, *Time for Dying* (Chicago: Aldine, 1968). See also Pattison, *The Experience of Dying*.

103. Scott A. Murray, Marilyn Kendall, Kirsty Boyd, and Aziz Sheikh, "Illness Trajectories and Palliative Care," *British Medical Journal* 330 (2005): 1007–1011.

104. Murray and others, "Illness Trajectories and Palliative Care," p. 1011.

105. Inge B. Corless, "Dying Well: Symptom Control Within Hospice Care," in *Annual Review of Nursing Research*, vol. 12, ed. J. J. Fitzpatrick and J. S. Stevenson (New York: Springer, 1994), pp. 125–146.

106. See Diane M. Thomas and Brenda Moretta Guerrero, "Terminal Restlessness in the Dying: Hospice Attitudes and Practices," *Omega: Journal of Death and Dying* 46, no. 1 (2002–2003): 77–90.

107. Eric J. Cassell, "Dying in a Technological Society," in *Death Inside Out: The Hastings Center Report,* ed. Peter Steinfels and Robert M. Veatch (New York: Harper & Row, 1974), pp. 43–48; see also, by Cassell, *The Nature of Suffering and the Goals of Medicine* (New York: Oxford University Press, 1991); Glaser and Strauss, *Awareness of Dying;* and David Sudnow, *Passing On: The Social Organization of Dying* (Englewood Cliffs, N.J.: Prentice-Hall, 1967).

108. Talcott Parsons, *The Social System* (New York: Free Press, 1951).

109. Marjorie Kagawa-Singer, "Redefining Health: Living with Cancer," *Social Science & Medicine* 37, no. 3 (1993): 295–304.

110. See Russell Noyes, Jr., and John Clancy, "The Dying Role: Its Relevance to Improved Patient Care," *Psychiatry* 40 (February 1977): 41–47.

111. Robert J. Baugher and others, "A Comparison of Terminally Ill Persons at Various Time Periods to Death," *Omega: Journal of Death and Dying* 20, no. 2 (1989–1990): 103–155.

112. Allan Kellehear and Terry Lewin, "Farewells by the Dying: A Sociological Study," *Omega: Journal of Death and Dying* 19, no. 4 (1988–1989): 275–292.

113. Byock, *The Best Care Possible,* p. 76.

114. Stephen R. Connor, *Hospice and Palliative Care: The Essential Guide,* 2nd ed. (New York: Routledge, 2009), p. 12.

115. Arthur W. Frank, "The Pedagogy of Suffering: Moral Dimensions of Psychological Therapy and Research with the Ill," *Theory & Psychology* 2, no. 4 (1992): 467–485; see also, by Frank, "What Kind of Phoenix? Illness and Self-Knowledge," *Second Opinion* 18, no. 2 (October 1992): 31–41.

116. Thomas Lyons, e-mail message to authors, May 25, 2013.

117. Allan Kellehear, *The Inner Life of the Dying Person* (New York: Columbia University Press, in press).

118. Ira Byock, "Personal Health and Human Development in Life-Threatening Conditions," in *Handbook of Psychiatry in Palliative Medicine,* 2nd ed., ed. Harvey Max Chochinov and William Breitbart, 281–299 (New York: Oxford University Press, 2009). See also Ira Byock, *Dying Well: The Prospect for Growth at the End of Life* (New York: Riverhead, 1997).

119. Roderick Cosh, "Spiritual Care of the Dying," in *Dying, Death, and Bereavement: A Challenge for Living,* ed. Corless, Germino, and Pittman, pp. 131–143.

120. Cosh, "Spiritual Care of the Dying," p. 136.

121. Tenshin Reb Anderson, quoted by Frank Ostaseski, "Stories of Lives Lived and Now Ending," *Inquiring Mind: A Journal of the Vipassana Community* 10, no. 2 (Spring 1994), p. 29.

122. Marcia Lattanzi-Licht, "Religion, Spirituality, and Dying," in *Handbook of Thanatology,* 2nd ed., ed. Meagher and Balk, 9–16; p. 10.

123. Makoto Ueda, *Modern Japanese Writers and the Nature of Literature* (Stanford, Calif.: Stanford University Press, 1976), p. 193.

124. Jitaro Mizuno, "A Caring Heart and Integrated Knowledge: An Ethics Which Inquires into the Relationship Between the Self and Others" (Reitaku University, Japan, 2005). Unpublished manuscript.

125. Janmarie Silvera, "Crossing the Border," in *The Path Ahead,* ed. DeSpelder and Strickland, pp. 301–302.

CHAPTER 8

1. Mike Parker Pearson, *The Archaeology of Death and Burial* (College Station: Texas A&M University Press, 2000), p. 194. See also Robert W. Habenstein and William M. Lamers, *Funeral Customs the World Over,* rev. ed. (Milwaukee: Bulfin Printers, 1974).

2. See Lynne Ann DeSpelder and Albert Lee Strickland, "Ceremonies," in *Encyclopedia of Death and Dying,* ed. Glennys Howarth and Oliver Leaman (New York: Routledge, 2001), pp. 84–85.

3. Dominic Janes, *Romans and Christians* (Charleston, S.C.: Tempus, 2002), p. 32.

4. Christopher Hall, "For As Long As It Takes," February 22, 2009, www.theage.com.au. See also Amitai Etzioni, "Toward a Theory of Public Ritual," *Sociological Theory* 18, no. 1 (2000): 44–59.

5. David L. Hall and Roger T. Ames, "Understanding Order: The Chinese Perspective," in *From Africa to Zen: An Invitation to World Philosophy,* ed. Robert S. Solomon and Kathleen M. Higgins, 1–23 (Lanham, Md.: Rowman and Littlefield, 1993), p. 8.

6. Vanderlyn R. Pine, "Funerals: Life's Final Ceremony," in *A Challenge for Living: Dying, Death, and Bereavement,* ed. Inge B. Corless, Barbara B. Germino, and Mary A. Pittman (Boston: Jones & Bartlett, 1995), pp. 159–171. See also Jenny Hockey, "Encountering the 'Reality of Death' Through Professional Discourse: The Matter of Materiality," *Mortality* 1, no. 1 (1996): 45–60.

7. Jennifer Hildebrand, "Funerals," in *Greenwood Encyclopedia of African American Folklore,* ed. Anand Prahlad, 478–479 (Westport, Conn.: Greenwood, 2005).

8. Michael A. Goldwasser, "Wakes," in *Greenwood Encyclopedia of African American Folklore,* ed. Anand Prahlad, 1359–1361 (Westport, Conn.: Greenwood, 2005); see also, by Goldwasser, in the same volume, "Nine-Night Rituals," pp. 908–909.

9. See Charles Reagan Wilson, "Funerals," in *Folklife,* ed. Glenn Hinson and William Ferris, Volume 14 of *Encyclopedia of Southern Culture* (Chapel Hill: University of North Carolina Press, 2009), pp. 102–104.

10. Glenys Caswell, "Beyond Words: Some Uses of Music in the Funeral Setting," *Omega: Journal of Death and Dying* 64, no. 4 (2011–2012): 319–334.

11. Sue Adamson and Margaret Holloway, "A Sound Track of Your Life: Music in Contemporary UK Funerals," *Omega: Journal of Death and Dying* 65, no. 1 (2012): 33–54; quote p. 49.

12. Deborah Noye, *Encyclopedia of the End: Mysterious Death in Fact, Fancy, Folklore, and More* (Boston: Houghton Mifflin, 2008), p. 93.

13. Alma Williams Freeman, "A Special Love: Spirit of New Orleans," *The International Review of African American Art* 17, no. 2 (2002): 14–15.

14. Hilary Mac Austin, "Brass Bands," in *Greenwood Encyclopedia of African American Folklore,* ed. Anand Prahlad, 156 (Westport, Conn.: Greenwood, 2005). See also Tashel C. Bordere, "Second-Lining at Death in New Orleans," *The Forum: Newsletter of the Association for Death Education and Counseling* 31, no. 4 (2005): 1, 3.

15. William G. Hoy, *Do Funerals Matter? The Purposes and Practices of Death Rituals in Global Perspective* (New York: Routledge, 2013), p. 22.

16. Thomas Lynch, *The Undertaking: Life Studies from the Dismal Trade* (New York: Norton, 1997), p. 21.

17. David Sudnow, *Passing On: The Social Organization of Dying* (Englewood Cliffs, N.J.: Prentice-Hall, 1967), pp. 153–168.

18. Ronald K. Barrett, "Contemporary African-American Funeral Rites and Traditions," in *The Path Ahead: Readings in Death and Dying,* ed. Lynne Ann DeSpelder and Albert Lee Strickland (Mountain View, Calif.: Mayfield, 1995), pp. 80–92, quote p. 88; and, also by Barrett, "The Legacy of Traditional African-American Funeral Rites," *Thanos* 16 (October 1994): 18–20; "Affirming and Reclaiming African-American Funeral Rites," *The Director* 66, no. 11 (October 1994): 36–40; and "Psychocultural Influences on African American Attitudes Toward Death, Dying, and Funeral Rites," in *Personal Care in an Impersonal World,* ed. John Morgan (Amityville, N.Y.: Baywood, 1993), pp. 213–230. See also Elaine Nichols, ed., *The Last Miles of the Way: African-American Homegoing Traditions, 1890–Present* (Columbia: South Carolina State Museum, 1989).

19. See Ben H. Bagdikian, *The Information Machines: Their Impact on Men and the Media* (New York: Harper & Row, 1971), pp. 39, 59; and Bradley Greenberg, "Diffusion of News of the Kennedy Assassination," *Public Opinion Quarterly* 28, no. 2 (Summer 1964): 225–232.

20. See Peter Svensson, "Deaths of Gamers Leave Their Online Lives in Limbo," *Associated Press* (March 14, 2009).

21. Quoted in Daniel Landis, "WoW Gamer Kicked from Guild, Too Dead To Log In," *Philadelphia Gaming News Examiner* (March 15, 2009).

22. J. Z. Young, *Programs of the Brain* (New York: Oxford University Press, 1978), p. 255.

23. Vernon Reynolds and Ralph Tanner, *The Social Ecology of Religion* (New York: Oxford University Press, 1995), p. 213.

24. John R. Elliott, "Funerary Artifacts in Contemporary America," *Death Studies* 14, no. 6 (1990): 601–612.

25. Federal Trade Commission, *Compliance Guidelines: Trade Regulation Rule on Funeral Industry Practices* (Washington, D.C., 1984).

26. See Robert W. Habenstein and William M. Lamers, *The History of American Funeral Directing* (Milwaukee: Bulfin Printers, 1962). See also Gary Laderman, *Rest in Peace: A Cultural History of Death and the Funeral Home in Twentieth-Century America* (New York: Oxford University Press, 2003).

27. See Glennys Howarth, *Last Rites: The Work of the Modern Funeral Director* (Amityville, N.Y.: Baywood, 1996).

28. Benito and Azzaro quotes from Jeanene Harlick, "Local Undertakers Survive Recession, Stave Off Stereotypes," *Santa Cruz Sentinel,* June 2, 2003.

29. Harlick, "Local Undertakers Survive Recession, Stave Off Stereotypes."

30. NFDA Funeral Service Facts. http://nfda.org/about-funeral-service-/trends-and-statistics.html.

31. O. Duane Weeks and Catherine Johnson, "Developing a Successful Aftercare Program," *The Director* 67, no. 12 (December 1995): 12–18.

32. LeRoy Bowman, *The American Funeral: A Study in Guilt, Extravagance, and Sublimity* (Washington, D.C.: Public Affairs Press, 1959).

33. Jessica Mitford, *The American Way of Death* (New York: Simon & Schuster, 1963), pp. 16–19.

34. D. van Vuure, "The Relatives Asked for a Duo-Committal for Their Parents," *Thanos* 22 (1996): 28–30.

35. Carla Sofka, "Cyberfunerals," in *Encyclopedia of Death and the Human Experience,* ed. Clifton D. Bryant and Dennis L. Peak, 249–251 (Thousand Oaks, Calif.: Sage, 2009), pp. 249–250.

36. See, for example, Andre Van Gemert, "The Digital Death," *Thanos* 21 (1996): 18–21; Lucette Lagnado, "Phone Eulogies, Cybermourners Make Funerals into Virtual Events," *The Wall Street Journal,* August 21, 1996, p. B1.

37. www.Legacy.com/NS/about/. See also Janice Hume and Bonnie Bressers, "Obituaries Online: New Connections with the Living—And the Dead," *Omega: Journal of Death and Dying* 60, no. 3 (2009–2010): 255–271.

38. Examples include Virtual Memorial Gardens, Dearly Departed, Empty Arms, Garden of Remembrance, The Virtual Memorial Company, and World Wide Cemetery. For current Web addresses, an online search is recommended.

39. Pamela Roberts, "The Living and the Dead: Community in the Virtual Cemetery," *Omega: Journal of Death and Dying* 49, no. 1 (2004): 57–76; quote p. 57.

40. Brochure, Leif Technologies, 1997.

41. Dan Morse, "Shirts for the Dead Are the New Rage in Some Inner Cities," *The Wall Street Journal,* February 4, 1999. For a related version of inner-city memorialization, see Martha Cooper and Joseph Sciorra, *R.I.P.: Memorial Wall Art* (New York: Henry Holt, 1994).

42. Cooper and Sciorra, *R.I.P.: Memorial Wall Art.*

43. Charles O. Collins and Charles D. Rhine, "Roadside Memorials," *Omega: Journal of Death and Dying* 47, no. 3 (2003): 221–244. See also Holly Everett, *Roadside Crosses in Contemporary Memorial Culture* (Denton: University of North Texas Press, 2002); and Jon K. Reid and Cynthia L. Reid, "A Cross Marks the Spot: A Study of Roadside Death Memorials in Texas and Oklahoma," *Death Studies* 25 (2001): 341–356.

44. Jennifer Clark and Ashley Cheshire, "RIP by the Roadside: A Comparative Study of Roadside Memorials in New South Wales, Australia, and Texas, United States," *Omega: Journal of Death and Dying* 48, no. 3 (2003–2004): 203–222; quote p. 204.

45. Sylvia Grider, "Spontaneous Shrines and Public Memorialization," in *Death and Religion in a Changing World,* ed. Kathleen Garces-Foley, 246–264 (Armonk, N.Y.: M. E. Sharpe, 2006), p. 255.

46. Grider, "Spontaneous Shrines and Public Memorialization," p. 262.

47. Lynch, *The Undertaking,* p. 191.

48. Data from the NFDA General Price List Survey.

49. "Other Services––Estimated Revenue," *Statistical Abstract of the United States: 2012,* 131st ed. (Washington, D.C., 2011). http://www.census.gov/compendia/statab/.

50. NFDA Funeral Service Facts. http://nfda.org/about-funeral-service-/trends-and-statistics.html.

51. Ronny E. Turner and Charles Edgley, "Death as Theatre: A Dramaturgical Analysis of the American Funeral," *Sociology and Social Research* 60, no. 4 (1976): 377–392. See also Liam Hyland and Janice M. Morse, "Orchestrating Comfort: The Role of Funeral Directors," *Death Studies* 19, no. 5 (1995): 453–474.

52. Kenneth V. Iserson, *Death to Dust: What Happens to Dead Bodies?* 2nd ed. (Tucson, Ariz.: Galen Press, 2001), p. 226; see also pp. 241–257 for a detailed description of embalming and other body-preparation procedures.

53. Edward C. Johnson and Melissa Johnson Williams, "Dr. Charles DeCosta Brown, Civil War Embalming Surgeon and the Masonic Order," *American Funeral Director* 120, no. 9 (September 1997): 74–78.

54. Vanderlyn Pine, "The Care of the Dead: A Historical Portrait," in *Death and Dying: Challenge and Change,* ed. Robert Fulton, Eric Markusen, Greg Owen, and Jane L. Scheiber (San Francisco: Boyd & Fraser, 1978), p. 276; see also, by Pine, *Caretaker of the Dead: The American Funeral Director* (New York: Irvington, 1985).

55. Briefly summarized, exceptions to this requirement occur when (1) state or local law requires embalming or (2) there are "exigent circumstances," such as (a) when a family member or other authorized person cannot be contacted despite diligent efforts, and (b) there is no reason to believe the family does not want embalming, and (c) after the body has been embalmed, the family is notified that no fee will be charged if they choose a funeral that does not require embalming.

56. *Thanos* 24 (1997): 9.

57. Stephen Prothero, *Purified by Fire: A History of Cremation in America* (Berkeley: University of California Press, 2001), p. 2.

58. Reynolds and Tanner, *The Social Ecology of Religion,* p. 221.

59. Iserson, *Death to Dust,* p. 390.

60. See Niels Bonde and Arne Emil Christensen, "Dendrochronological Dating for the Viking Age Ship Burials at Oseberg, Gokstad, and Tune, Norway," *Antiquity* 67 (1993): 575–583.

61. See Bruce A. Iverson, "Bodies for Science," *Death Studies* 14, no. 6 (1990): 577–587; Robert D. Reece

and Jesse H. Ziegler, "How a Medical School (Wright State University) Takes Leave of Human Remains," *Death Studies* 14, no. 6 (1990): 589–600; and Kathleen A. Schotzinger and Elizabeth Kirkley Best, "Closure and the Cadaver Experience: A Memorial Service for Deeded Bodies," *Omega: Journal of Death and Dying* 18, no. 3 (1987–1988): 217–227.

62. *Honolulu Star-Bulletin & Advertiser,* June 3, 1984.

63. Rick Atkinson, "The Nation's Cemetery," *National Geographic* (June 2007), pp. 121–137.

64. Sir Raymond Firth, "Foreword," in *The Secret Cemetery,* by Doris Frances, Leonie Kellaher, and Georgina Neophytou (Oxford: Berg, 2005), p. xv.

65. Doris Frances, Leonie Kellaher, and Georgina Neophytou, *The Secret Cemetery* (Oxford: Berg, 2005), p. 197.

66. Michael Kammen, *Digging Up the Dead: A History of Notable American Reburials* (Chicago: University of Chicago Press, 2010), p. 198.

67. Jack Goody and Cesare Poppi, "Flowers and Bones: Approaches to the Dead in Anglo-American and Italian Cemeteries," *Comparative Studies in Society and History* 36, no. 1 (1994): 146–175.

68. See Diane O. Bennett, "Bury Me in Second Class: Contested Symbols in a Greek Cemetery," *Anthropological Quarterly* 67, no. 3 (1994): 122–134.

69. "L.A.'s Well-to-Do Get Burial Space," *Associated Press,* February 10, 2002. http://www.apnewsarchive.com/2002/L-A-s-Well-to-Do-Get-Burial-Space/id-8b35c5a0d712cd98b74b804bb8c14105.

70. Douglas Keister, "A Brief History of the Community Mausoleum," *American Cemetery* 69, no. 9 (September 1997): 20–21, 50–52.

71. See Hali J. Weiss, "In the Long Run: Staying Relevant Amidst Cultural Change," *Cemetery Management* (January 1995): 14–16; and, also by Weiss, "Dust to Dust: Transforming the American Cemetery," *Tikkun* 10, no. 5 (1996): 21–25.

72. NFDA, Cremation Facts. Accessed June 22, 2013. http://nfda.org/about-funeral-service-/trends-and-statistics.html.

73. Hoy, *Do Funerals Matter?* p. 125.

74. Sally Gribbin, "The Social Crisis Facing the Cremation Industry," *Cemetery Management* (January 1994), reprint.

75. James Mackay, *The Guinness Book of Stamps Facts & Feats* (New York: Canopy, 1992), pp. 157–158; see also Charles A. Fricke, "Death and Funeral Notices on U.S. Postal Cards," *Scott Stamp Monthly* 13, no. 7 (1995): 9, 22.

76. Angelo B. Henderson, "In Detroit, Blacks Turn the Staid Obit Into a Glossy Art," *The Wall Street Journal,* May 1, 2000.

77. Marion K. Pinsdorf, "Greater Dead Heroes than Live Husbands: Widows as Image-Makers," *Public Relations Review* 28 (2002): 283–299.

78. Kathleen Garces-Foley, "Funerals of the Unaffiliated," *Omega: Journal of Death and Dying* 46, no. 4 (2002–2003): 287–302; quote p. 288.

79. Steve Kurutz, "Grave New World," *Details* (March 2003), pp. 147–148.

80. Kathleen Garces-Foley and Justin S. Holcomb, "Contemporary American Funerals: Personalizing Tradition," in *Death and Religion in a Changing World,* ed. Kathleen Garces-Foley, 207–227 (Armonk, N.Y.: M. E. Sharpe, 2006), p. 208.

81. Marilyn Yalom, *The American Resting Place: Four Hundred Years of History Through Our Cemeteries and Burial Grounds* (Boston: Houghton Mifflin, 2008), p. 274.

82. Garces-Foley and Holcomb, "Contemporary American Funerals: Personalizing Tradition," p. 208.

83. Garces-Foley, "Funerals of the Unaffiliated," p. 295.

84. Douglas J. Davies, "Forms of Disposal," in *Death and Religion in a Changing World,* ed. Kathleen Garces-Foley, 228–245 (Armonk, N.Y.: M. E. Sharpe, 2006), p. 240.

85. Excerpted from *Undertaken with Love: A Home Funeral Guide for Congregations and Communities* (Oak Ridge, N.C.: Home Funeral Committee Manual Publishing Group, 2009), p. 5.

86. For information on preplanning a home- or family-directed funeral, contact Final Passages, PO Box 1721, Sebastopol, CA 95473, or www.finalpassages.org.

87. See, for example, Bob Butz, *Going Out Green: One Man's Adventure Planning His Own Burial* (Traverse City, Mich.: Spirituality & Health, 2009).

88. Garces-Foley and Holcomb, "Contemporary American Funerals: Personalizing Tradition," p. 221.

89. The Ecopod coffin, for example, is a recycled paper coffin. See www.ecopod.co.uk or www.naturalburialcompany.com.

90. Eternal Reefs, Inc., www.eternalreefs.com.

91. Katharine Q. Seelye, "Ashes-to-Fireworks Send-Off for an 'Outlaw' Writer," *The New York Times,* August 22, 2005.

92. Lou LaGrand, "How to Use Linking Objects as You Mourn and Continue with Life," http://ezinearticles.com/?How-to-Use-Linking-Objects-as-You-Mourn-and-Continue-with-Life&id=594394.

93. Nancy C. Reeves and Frederic J. Boersma, "The Therapeutic Use of Ritual in Maladaptive Grieving," *Omega: Journal of Death and Dying* 20, no. 4 (1989–1990): 281–291.

94. Onno van der Hart, *Coping with Loss: The Therapeutic Use of Leave-Taking Ritual* (New York: Irvington, 1988); and, also by van der Hart, "An Imaginary Leave-Taking Ritual in Mourning Therapy: A Brief Communication," *The International Journal of Clinical and Experimental Hypnosis* 36, no. 2 (1988): 63–69.

95. William Lamers, Sr., quoted in *Concerning Death: A Practical Guide for the Living,* ed. Earl Grollman (Boston: Beacon Press, 1974), and in *Successful Funeral Service Practice,* ed. Howard C. Raether (Englewood Cliffs, N.J.: Prentice-Hall, 1971).

96. William M. Lamers, Jr., "Funerals Are Good for People: M.D.'s Included," *Medical Economics* (June 23, 1969): 1–4.

97. Alan Wolfelt, "Understanding the Trend Toward Deritualization of the Funeral," *The Forum: Newsletter of the Association for Death Education and Counseling* 20, no. 6 (November–December 1994): 1, 15–17.

98. Sabine Bode and Fritz Roth, *Der Trauer Eine Heimat Geben: Für Einen Lebendigen Umgang mit dem Tod* [Giving Grief a Home] (Bergisch Gladbach, Ger.: Gustav Lübbe Verlag, 1998), and *Trauer hat Viele Farben* [Grief Has Many Colors] (Bergisch Gladbach, Ger.: Ehrenwirth, 2004).

99. E. S. Craighill Handy and Mary Kawena Pukui, *The Polynesian Family System in Ka-'u, Hawai'i* (Rutland, Vt.: Charles E. Tuttle, 1972), p. 157; and Mary Kawena Pukui, E. W. Haertig, and Catherine A. Lee, *Nana I Ke Kumu (Look to the Source),* vol. 1 (Honolulu: Hui Hanai; Queen Lili'uokalani Children's Center, 1972), p. 139.

CHAPTER *9*

1. Georges Bataille, "Sacrifice, the Festival, and the Principles of the Sacred World," *Theory of Religion,* trans. Robert Hurley (New York: Zone Books, 1992), p. 48.

2. Simon Shimson Rubin, Ruth Malkinson, and Eliezer Wiztum, "On Bereavement Interventions: Controversy and Consensus," in *Handbook of Thanatology,* 2nd ed., ed. David K. Meagher and David E. Balk, 263–272 (New York: Routledge, 2013), p. 265.

3. Personal communication.

4. Bob Krizek, "Goodbye Old Friend: A Son's Farewell to Comiskey Park," *Omega: Journal of Death and Dying* 25, no. 2 (1992): 87–93.

5. An adaptation of an anonymous reading used in many funeral and memorial services.

6. See Lynne Ann DeSpelder and Albert Lee Strickland, "Loss," in *Encyclopedia of Death and Dying,* ed. Glennys Howarth and Oliver Leaman (New York: Routledge, 2001), pp. 288–289.

7. Simon Shimson Rubin, Ruth Malkinson, and Eliezer Wiztum, "On Bereavement Interventions, Controversy and Consensus," in *Handbook of Thanatology,* 2nd ed., ed. Meagher and Balk, 263–272; p. 264.

8. See Thomas A. Attig, *How We Grieve: Relearning the World* (New York: Oxford University Press, 1996); and Jeffrey Kauffman, ed., *Loss of the Assumptive World: A Theory of Traumatic Loss* (New York: Brunner-Routledge, 2002).

9. Terry Tafoya, "The Widow as Butterfly: Treatment of Grief/Depression Among the Sahaptin," unpublished paper.

10. Philippe Ariès, "The Reversal of Death: Changes in Attitudes Toward Death in Western Societies," in *Death in America,* ed. David E. Stannard (Philadelphia: University of Pennsylvania Press, 1975), pp. 134–158.

11. J. William Worden, *Grief Counseling and Grief Therapy: A Handbook for the Mental Health Practitioner,* 4th ed. (New York: Springer, 2009), esp. pp. 39–53.

12. Therese A. Rando, *Treatment of Complicated Mourning* (Champaign, Ill.: Research Press, 1993).

13. See Robert M. Sapolsky, "The Solace of Patterns," *The Sciences* 34, no. 6 (November–December 1994): 14–16.

14. Sigmund Freud, "Mourning and Melancholia," *Collected Papers,* vol. 4 (New York: Basic Books, 1959), pp. 152–170. Originally published in 1917. See also Lorraine Siggins, "Mourning: A Critical Survey of the Literature," *International Journal of Psycho-Analysis* 47 (1966): 14–25.

15. See John Bowlby's three-volume work, *Attachment and Loss* (New York: Basic Books): vol. 1, *Attachment* (1969); vol. 2, *Separation: Anxiety and Anger* (1973); and vol. 3, *Loss: Sadness and Depression* (1982); and *The Making and Breaking of Affectional Bonds* (London: Tavistock, 1979). See also Dale Vincent Hardt, "An Investigation of the Stages of Bereavement," *Omega: Journal of Death and Dying* 9, no. 3 (1978–1979): 279–285; and Dennis Klass, "John Bowlby's Model of Grief and the Problem of Identification," *Omega: Journal of Death and Dying* 18, no. 1 (1987–1988): 13–32.

16. Therese A. Rando, "Grief and Mourning: Accommodating to Loss," in *Dying: Facing the Facts,* 3rd ed., ed. Hannelore Wass and Robert A. Neimeyer (Washington, D.C.: Taylor & Francis, 1995), pp. 211–241; quote p. 212.

17. Erich Lindemann, "The Symptomatology and Management of Acute Grief," *American Journal of Psychiatry* 101 (1944): 141–148.

18. Colin Murray Parkes, "Research: Bereavement," *Omega: Journal of Death and Dying* 18, no. 4 (1987–1988): 365–377; quote p. 366.

19. Colin Murray Parkes, "Complicated Grief in the *DSM-5:* Problems and Solutions," in *Beyond Kübler-Ross: New Perspectives on Death, Dying, and Grief,* ed. Kenneth J. Doka and Amy S. Tucci, 93–111 (Washington, D.C.: Hospice Foundation of America, 2011), p. 94.

20. See Dennis Klass, "Developing a Cross-Cultural Model of Grief: The State of the Field," *Omega: Journal of Death and Dying* 39, no. 3 (1999): 153–178.

21. Margaret Stroebe, "Coping with Bereavement: A Review of the Grief Work Hypothesis," *Omega: Journal of Death and Dying* 26, no. 1 (1992–1993): 19–42. See also George A. Bonanno, ed., "New Directions in Bereavement Research and Theory (special issue)," *American Behavioral Scientist* 44, no. 3 (2001); Torill Christine Lindstrøm, "'It Ain't Necessarily So': Challenging Mainstream Thinking About Bereavement," *Family & Community Health* 25, no. 1 (2002): 11–21; R. J. Russac, Nina S. Steighner, and Angela I. Canto, "Grief Work Versus Continuing Bonds: A Call for Paradigm Integration or Replacement?" *Death Studies* 26, no. 6 (2002): 463–478; and Margaret Stroebe and others, "Does Disclosure of Emotions Facilitate Recovery from Bereavement? Evidence from Two Prospective Studies," *Journal of Consulting and Clinical Psychology* 70, no. 1 (2002): 169–178.

22. See Dennis Klass and Robert Goss, "Spiritual Bonds to the Dead in Cross-Cultural and Historical Perspective: Comparative Religion and Modern Grief," *Death Studies* 23, no. 6 (1999): 547–567.

23. Simon Shimson Rubin, Ruth Malkinson, and Eliezer Wiztum, "On Bereavement Interventions: Controversy and Consensus," in *Handbook of Thanatology,* 2nd ed., ed. Meagher and Balk, 263–272; p. 265.

24. Dennis Klass, "Solace and Immortality: Bereaved Parents' Continuing Bond with Their Children," in *The Path Ahead,* ed. DeSpelder and Strickland, pp. 246–259.

25. Dennis Klass, "The Inner Representation of the Dead Child and the Worldviews of Bereaved Parents," *Omega: Journal of Death and Dying* 26, no. 4 (1992–1993): 255–272.

26. Phyllis R. Silverman, Steven Nickman, and J. William Worden, "Detachment Revisited: The Child's Reconstruction of a Dead Parent," in *The Path Ahead,* ed. DeSpelder and Strickland, pp. 260–270.

27. Rando, *Treatment of Complicated Mourning,* p. 53.

28. See Simon Shimshon Rubin, "Psychodynamic Therapy with the Bereaved: Listening for Conflict, Relationship, and Transference," *Omega: Journal of Death and Dying* 39, no. 2 (1999): 83–98; and Paul A. Boelen and others, "Continuing Bonds and Grief: A Prospective Analysis," *Death Studies* 30 (2006): 767–776.

29. Dennis Klass, "Continuing Conversation about Continuing Bonds," *Death Studies* 30 (2006): 843–858; quote p. 851.

30. Lyn H. Lofland, "Loss and Human Connection: An Exploration into the Nature of the Social Bond," in *Personality, Roles, and Social Behavior,* ed. William Ickes and Eric S. Knowles (New York: Springer-Verlag, 1982), pp. 219–242.

31. John D. Kelly, "Grief: Re-forming Life's Story," in *The Path Ahead,* ed. DeSpelder and Strickland, pp. 242–245.

32. Jerome Bruner, "The Narrative Construction of Reality," *Critical Inquiry* 18 (1991): 1–21; quote p. 4.

33. Carolyn Ellis, "'There Are Survivors': Telling a Story of Sudden Death," *Sociological Quarterly* 34, no. 4 (1993): 711–730.

34. Mary Anne Sedney, John E. Baker, and Esther Gross, "'The Story' of a Death: Therapeutic Considerations with Bereaved Families," *Journal of Marital and Family Therapy* 20, no. 3 (1994): 287–296. See also Jack J. Bauer and George A. Bonanno, "Continuity amid Discontinuity: Bridging One's Past and Present in Stories of Conjugal Bereavement," *Narrative Inquiry* 11, no. 1 (2001): 123–158; Kathleen R. Gilbert, "Taking a Narrative Approach to Grief Research: Finding Meaning in Stories," *Death Studies* 26, no. 3 (2002): 223–239; and Brian Schiff, Chaim Noy, and Bertram J. Cohler, "Collected Stories in the Life Narratives of Holocaust Survivors," *Narrative Inquiry* 11, no. 1 (2001): 159–193.

35. Jane Harper Chelf and others, "Storytelling: A Strategy for Living and Coping with Cancer," *Cancer Nursing* 23, no. 1 (2000): 1–5.

36. Tony Walter, "A New Model of Grief: Bereavement and Biography," *Mortality* 1, no. 1 (1996): 7–25, quote p. 13; see also James A. Thorson, "Qualitative Thanatology," *Mortality* 1, no. 2 (1996): 177–190.

37. Quoted in Kathleen Fowler, "So New, So New: Art and Heart in Women's Grief Memoirs," *Women's Studies* 36, no. 7 (2007): 525–549.

38. Simon Shimson Rubin, Ruth Malkinson, and Eliezer Wiztum, "On Bereavement Interventions: Controversy and Consensus," in *Handbook of Thanatology,* 2nd ed., ed. Meagher and Balk, 263–272; p. 271.

39. See George A. Bonanno, Anthony Papa, and Kathleen O'Neill, "Loss and Human Resilience," *Applied & Preventive Psychology* 10, no. 3 (2001): 193–206; Louis A. Gamino, Nancy S. Hogan, and Kenneth W. Sewell, "Feeling the Absence: A Content Analysis from the Scott and White Grief Study," *Death Studies* 26, no. 10 (2002): 793–813; Judith A. Murray, "Loss as a Universal Concept: A Review of the Literature to Identify Common Aspects of Loss in Diverse Situations," *Journal of Loss and Trauma* 6, no. 3 (2001): 219–241; and Robert A. Neimeyer, "Reauthoring Life Narratives: Grief Therapy as Meaning Reconstruction," *Israel Journal of Psychiatry and Related Sciences* 38, nos. 3–4 (2001): 171–183.

40. Margaret Stroebe and Henk Schut, "The Dual Process Model of Coping with Bereavement" (paper presented at the Meeting of the International Work Group on Death, Dying, and Bereavement, Oxford, U.K., June 1995); see also Stroebe and Schut, "The Dual Process Model of Bereavement: Rationale and Description," *Death Studies* 23, no. 3 (1999): 197–224.

41. Simon Shimshon Rubin, "The Two-Track Model of Bereavement: Overview, Retrospect, and Prospect," *Death Studies* 23 (1999): 681–714.

42. Simon Shimson Rubin, Ruth Malkinson, and Eliezer Wiztum, "On Bereavement Interventions: Controversy and Consensus," in *Handbook of Thanatology*, 2nd ed., ed. Meagher and Balk, 263–272; p. 267.

43. Ruth Malkinson, Simon Shimshon Rubin, and Eliezer Witztum, "Therapeutic Issues and the Relationship to the Deceased: Working Clinically with the Two-Track Model of Bereavement," *Death Studies* 30, no. 9 (2006): 797–815; esp. pp. 811–812. See also Ruth Malkinson, *Cognitive Grief Therapy: Constructing a Rational Meaning to Life Following Loss* (New York: Norton, 2007); Ruth Malkinson, Simon Shimshon Rubin, and Eliezer Witztum, eds., *Traumatic and Nontraumatic Loss and Bereavement: Clinical Theory and Practice* (Madison, Conn.: Psychosocial Press, 2000); and Rubin, "Two-Track Model of Bereavement," pp. 709–710.

44. Colin Murray Parkes, "Bereavement in Adult Life," *British Medical Journal* 316 (1998): 856–859, and "Facing Loss," *British Medical Journal* 316 (1998): 1521–1524. See also, by Parkes, "Bereavement Dissected: A Reexamination of the Basic Components Influencing the Reaction to Loss," *Israel Journal of Psychiatry and Related Sciences* 38, nos. 3–4 (2001): 150–156, and "Grief: Lessons from the Past, Visions for the Future," *Death Studies* 26, no. 5 (2002): 367–385.

45. Hannelore Wass, personal communication, September 15, 2009.

46. Janice Winchester Nadeau, "Meaning-Making in Bereaved Families," in *Handbook of Bereavement Research and Practice: Advances in Theory and Intervention*, ed. Margaret S. Stroebe, Robert O. Hansson, Henk Schut, and Wolfgang Stroebe, 511–530 (Washington, D.C.: American Psychological Association, 2008), p. 513. See also Nadeau, *Families Making Sense of Death* (Thousand Oaks, Calif.: Sage, 1997).

47. Nancy L. Moos, "An Integrative Model of Grief," *Death Studies* 19, no. 4 (1995): 337–364, quote p. 337. See also Froma Walsh and Monica McGoldrick, eds., *Living Beyond Loss: Death in the Family*, 2nd ed. (New York: Norton, 2004).

48. See Robert A. Neimeyer and John R. Jordan, "Historical and Contemporary Perspectives on Assessment and Intervention," in *Handbook of Thanatology*, 2nd ed., ed. Meagher and Balk, 219–237; p. 224.

49. Stephen J. Fleming and Paul J. Robinson, "The Application of Cognitive Therapy to the Bereaved," in *The Challenge of Cognitive Therapy: Applications to Nontraditional Populations*, ed. T. M. Vallis, J. L. Howes, and P. C. Miller (New York: Plenum Press, 1991), pp. 135–158.

50. Fleming and Robinson, "Application of Cognitive Therapy to the Bereaved."

51. Ira Byock, *The Best Care Possible: A Physician's Quest to Transform Care Through the End of Life* (New York: Avery, 2012), p. 92.

52. Sandra L. Bertman, Helen K. Sumpter, and Harry L. Green, "Bereavement and Grief," in *Introduction to Clinical Medicine*, ed. Harry L. Green (Philadelphia: B. C. Decker, 1991), p. 682.

53. See Liam Hyland and Janice M. Morse, "Orchestrating Comfort: The Role of Funeral Directors," *Death Studies* 19, no. 5 (1995): 453–474.

54. Bertman, Sumpter, and Green, "Bereavement and Grief," p. 682.

55. See Beverly Raphael and Christine Minkov, "Abnormal Grief," *Current Opinion in Psychiatry* 12, no. 1 (1999): 99–102.

56. Sarah Brabant, "Old Pain or New Pain: A Social Psychological Approach to Recurrent Grief," *Omega: Journal of Death and Dying* 20, no. 4 (1989–1990): 273–279.

57. M. A. Bull, S. Clark, and K. Duszynski, "Lessons from a Community's Response to the Death of Diana, Princess of Wales," *Omega: Journal of Death and Dying* 46, no. 1 (2002): 35–49.

58. Ira O. Glick, Robert S. Weiss, and Colin Murray Parkes, *The First Year of Bereavement* (New York: Wiley, 1974), p. viii; see also Colin Murray Parkes and Robert S. Weiss, *Recovery from Bereavement* (New York: Basic Books, 1983); and Robert S. Weiss, "Loss and Recovery," *Journal of Social Issues* 44, no. 3 (1988): 37–52.

59. Stephen Fleming and Paul Robinson, "Grief and Cognitive-Behavioral Therapy: The Reconstruction of Meaning," in *Handbook of Bereavement Research: Consequences, Coping, and Care,* ed. Margaret S. Stroebe, Robert O. Hansson, Wolfgang Stroebe, and Henk Schut, 647–669 (Washington, D.C.: American Psychological Association, 2001), p. 647.

60. Therese A. Rando, *The Treatment of Complicated Mourning* (Champaign, Ill.: Research Press, 1993).

61. Robert O. Hansson and Margaret S. Stroebe, *Bereavement in Late Life: Coping, Adaptation, and Developmental Influences* (Washington, D.C.: American Psychological Association, 2007), p. 172.

62. Therese A. Rando, "The Increasing Prevalence of Complicated Mourning: The Onslaught Is Just Beginning," *Omega: Journal of Death and Dying* 26, no. 1 (1992–1993): 43–59.

63. See Louis A. Gamino and R. Hal Ritter, Jr., *Ethical Practice in Grief Counseling* (New York: Springer, 2009), pp. 250–252. See also Heather L. Servaty-Seib, "Connections Between Counseling Theories and Current Theories of Grief and Mourning," *Journal of Mental Health Counseling* 26, no. 2 (2004): 125–145; esp. pp. 136–140.

64. Robert A. Neimeyer, Holly G. Prigerson, and Betty Davies, "Mourning and Meaning," *American Behavioral Science* 46, no. 2 (2002): 235–251.

65. Kenneth J. Doka, "Grief and the DSM: A Brief Q & A," *Huffpost Healthy Living* (May 29, 2013); italics added.

66. Excerpted from the statement developed by a work group at the meeting of the International Work Group on Death, Dying and Bereavement (IWG) in Victoria, British Columbia on April 28–May 3, 2013. This statement represents the opinions of the authors, not the opinions of the Board or membership of IWG. The full text of the statement can be found on the European Association of Palliative Care Blog, http://eapcnet.wordpress.com/2013/05/20/when-does-a-broken-heart-become-a-mental-disorder.

67. Phyllis R. Silverman, "Dying and Bereavement in Historical Perspective," in *Living with Dying: A Handbook for End-of-Life Care Practitioners,* ed. Joan Berzoff and Phyllis R. Silverman (New York: Columbia University Press, 2004), pp. 128–149; quote p. 144.

68. Jason M. Holland, Robert A. Neimeyer, Paul A. Boelen, and Holly G. Prigerson, "The Underlying Structure of Grief: A Taxometric Investigation of Prolonged and Normal Reactions to Loss," *Journal of Psychopathology and Behavior Assessment* 31, no. 3 (2009): 190–201.

69. Margaret Stroebe and Henk Schut, "Complicated Grief: A Conceptual Analysis of the Field," *Omega: Journal of Death and Dying* 52, no. 1 (2005–2006): 53–70; quote p. 67.

70. See Jerome F. Fredrick, "Grief as a Disease Process," *Omega: Journal of Death and Dying* 7, no. 4 (1976–1977): 297–305; and Edgar N. Jackson, "The Physiology of Crisis," in his *Coping with the Crises of Your Life* (New York: Hawthorne Books, 1974), pp. 48–55.

71. Quoted in Jerry E. Bishop, "Secrets of the Heart: Can It Be 'Broken'?" *The Wall Street Journal,* February 14, 1994.

72. Margaret S. Stroebe, "The Broken Heart Phenomenon: An Examination of the Mortality of Bereavement," *Journal of Community & Applied Social Psychology* 4 (1994): 47–61.

73. W. D. Rees and S. G. Lutkins, "The Mortality of Bereavement," *British Medical Journal* 4 (1967): 13–16.

74. See Nicholas R. Hall and Allan L. Goldstein, "Thinking Well: The Chemical Links Between Emotions and Health," *The Sciences* 26, no. 2 (March/April 1986): 34–40.

75. For a review of these studies, see Colin Murray Parkes, "Research: Bereavement," *Omega: Journal of Death and Dying* 18, no. 4 (1987–1988): 365–377.

76. George L. Engel, "Sudden and Rapid Death During Psychological Stress," *Annals of Internal Medicine* 74 (1971); see also, by Engel, "Emotional Stress and Sudden Death," *Psychology Today,* November 1977.

77. Colin Murray Parkes, "The Broken Heart," in his *Bereavement: Studies of Grief in Adult Life,* 3rd ed. (Philadelphia: Routledge, 2001), pp. 14–30; quote p. 17.

78. Edgar N. Jackson, *Understanding Grief: Its Roots, Dynamics, and Treatment* (Nashville: Abingdon Press, 1957), p. 27; see also, by Jackson, *The Many Faces of Grief* (Nashville: Abingdon Press, 1977). In an interview with the authors, Dr. Jackson described how the death of his young son became the impetus for his studies of grief, which became a mechanism for coping with, understanding, and coming to terms with the loss.

79. Karen S. Pfost, Michael J. Stevens, and Anne B. Wessels, "Relationship of Purpose in Life to Grief Experiences in Response to the Death of a Significant Other," *Death Studies* 13, no. 4 (1989): 371–378.

80. See Paul C. Rosenblatt, "Grief: The Social Context of Private Feelings," *Journal of Social Issues* 44, no. 3 (1988): 67–78. See also Carolyn Ambler Walter and Judith L. M. McCoyd, *Grief and Loss Across the Lifespan: A Biopsychosocial Perspective* (New York: Springer, 2009).

81. Wolfgang Stroebe and Margaret Stroebe, "Is Grief Universal? Cultural Variations in the Emotional Reaction to Loss," in *Death and Identity,* 3rd ed., ed. Fulton and Bendiksen, p. 197.

82. Daniel Callahan, *The Troubled Dream of Life: Living with Mortality* (New York: Simon & Schuster, 1993), p. 15.

83. Unni Wikan, "Bereavement and Loss in Two Muslim Communities: Egypt and Bali Compared," *Social Science & Medicine* 27, no. 5 (1988): 451–460.

84. Alicia Skinner Cook, "The Family, Larger Systems, and Loss, Grief, and Mourning," in *Handbook of Thanatology,* 2nd ed., ed. Meagher and Balk, 171–178; p. 171.

85. Greg Owen, Robert Fulton, and Eric Marcusen, "Death at a Distance: A Study of Family Bereavement," in *Death and Identity,* 3rd ed., ed. Fulton and Bendiksen, p. 241.

86. Stephen R. Connor, *Hospice and Palliative Care: The Essential Guide,* 2nd ed. (New York: Routledge, 2009), p. 88.

87. Fred Sklar and Shirley F. Hartley, "Close Friends as Survivors: Bereavement Patterns in a 'Hidden' Population," *Omega: Journal of Death and Dying* 21, no. 2 (1990): 103–112.

88. See entry on "Grief, Vicarious," by Lynne Ann DeSpelder and Albert Lee Strickland, in *Encyclopedia of Death and Dying,* ed. Howarth and Leaman, pp. 225–226.

89. Larry A. Bugen, "Human Grief: A Model for Prediction and Intervention," *American Journal of Orthopsychiatry* 47, no. 2 (1977): 196–206.

90. Robert J. Smith, John H. Lingle, and Timothy C. Brock, "Reactions to Death as a Function of Perceived Similarity to the Deceased," *Omega: Journal of Death and Dying* 9, no. 2 (1978–1979): 125–138.

91. Richard M. Leliaert, "Spiritual Side of 'Good Grief': What Happened to Holy Saturday?" *Death Studies* 13, no. 2 (1989): 103–117; quote p. 103.

92. Terry L. Martin and Kenneth J. Doka, *Men Don't Cry . . . Women Do: Transcending Gender Stereotypes of Grief* (Philadelphia: Brunner/Mazel, 2000); see also, by Martin and Doka, "Revisiting Masculine Grief," in *Living with Grief: Who We Are, How We Grieve,* ed. Kenneth J. Doka and Joyce D. Davidson (Washington, D.C.: Hospice Foundation of America, 1998), pp. 133–142; and Judith M. Stillion and Susan B. Noviello, "Living and Dying in Different Worlds: Gender Differences in Violent Death and Grief," *Illness, Crisis & Loss* 9, no. 3 (2001): 247–259.

93. Lynne Ann DeSpelder, "Culture and Gender: Diversity in Dying, Death, and Bereavement" (paper presented at the VI International Congress of the International Association of Thanatology and Suicidology, Bologna, Italy, June 2005).

94. Arlene Sheskin and Samuel E. Wallace, "Differing Bereavements: Suicide, Natural, and Accidental Death," *Omega: Journal of Death and Dying* 7, no. 3 (1976): 229–242.

95. See Robert L. Fulton, "Death, Grief, and Social Recuperation," *Omega: Journal of Death and Dying* 1, no. 1 (1970): 23–28; and Bruce J. Horacek, "A Heuristic Model of Grieving After High-Grief Death," *Death Studies* 19, no. 1 (1995): 21–31.

96. See Pauline Boss, *Ambiguous Loss: Learning to Live with Unresolved Grief* (Cambridge, Mass.: Harvard University Press, 1999).

97. Therese A. Rando, *Loss and Anticipatory Grief* (Lexington, Mass.: Lexington, 1986), p. 24.

98. See Bernard Schoenberg, Arthur C. Carr, Austin H. Kutscher, David Peretz, and Ivan K. Goldberg, eds., *Anticipatory Grief* (New York: Columbia University Press, 1974), p. 4.

99. Yvonne K. Ameche, "A Story of Loss and Survivorship," *Death Studies* 14, no. 2 (1990): 185–198.

100. Carol J. Van Dongen, "Social Context of Postsuicide Bereavement," *Death Studies* 17, no. 2 (1993): 125–141; quote p. 130.

101. See Charles P. McDowell, Joseph M. Rothberg, and Ronald J. Koshes, "Witnessed Suicides," *Suicide and Life-Threatening Behavior* 24, no. 3 (1994): 213–223.

102. Francoise M. Reynolds and Peter Cimbolic, "Attitudes Toward Suicide Survivors as a Function of Survivors' Relationship to the Victim," *Omega: Journal of Death and Dying* 19, no. 2 (1988–1989): 125–133.

103. Lula M. Redmond, *Surviving When Someone You Love Was Murdered: A Professional's Guide to Group Therapy for Families and Friends of Murder Victims* (Clearwater, Fla.: Psychological Consultation and Education Services, 1989), p. 38.

104. See entry on survivors' grief, by Lynne Ann DeSpelder and Albert Lee Strickland, in *Encyclopedia of Death and Dying,* ed. Howarth and Leaman, pp. 221–223.

105. Terrence Des Pres, *The Survivor* (New York: Oxford University Press, 1976; Pocket Books, 1977); and Lawrence L. Langer, *Versions of Survival: The Holocaust and the Human Spirit* (Albany: State University of New York Press, 1982). See also Robert Jay Lifton, *Death in Life: Survivors of Hiroshima* (New York: Simon & Schuster, 1967).

106. See J. William Worden, "Grieving a Loss from AIDS," *Hospice Journal* 7 (1991): 143–150.

107. Ruben Schindler, "Mourning and Bereavement Among Jewish Religious Families: A Time for Reflection and Recovery," *Omega: Journal of Death and Dying* 33, no. 2 (1996): 121–129.

108. See Kenneth J. Doka, "Disenfranchised Grief," in *The Path Ahead,* ed. DeSpelder and Strickland, pp. 271–275; and, edited by Doka, *Disenfranchised Grief: Recognizing Hidden Sorrow* (Lexington, Mass.: Lexington, 1989); and *Disenfranchised Grief: New Directions, Challenges, and Strategies for Practice* (Champaign, Ill.: Research Press, 2002).

109. Darlene A. Kloeppel and Sheila Hollins, "Double Handicap: Mental Retardation and Death in the Family," *Death Studies* 13, no. 1 (1989): 31–38.

110. Kemi Adamolekun, "In-Laws' Behavior as a Social Factor in Subsequent Temporary Upsurges of Grief in Western Nigeria," *Omega: Journal of Death and Dying* 31, no. 1 (1995): 23–34. See also M. A. Sossou, "Widowhood Practices in West Africa: The Silent Victims," *International Journal of Social Welfare* 11, no. 3 (2002): 201–209.

111. Phyllis R. Silverman, "Social Support and Mutual Help for the Bereaved," in *Dying, Death, and Bereavement: A Challenge for Living,* 2nd ed., ed. Inge Corless, Barbara B. Germino, and Mary A. Pittman (New York: Springer, 2003), pp. 247–265.

112. Howard R. Winokuer and Darcy L. Harris, *Principles and Practice of Grief Counseling* (New York: Springer, 2012), p. 15.

113. Glennys Howarth, "Dismantling the Boundaries Between Life and Death," *Mortality* 5, no. 2 (2000): 127–138.

114. Worden, *Grief Counseling and Grief Therapy,* 4th ed., p. 83.

115. David K. Meagher, "Grief Counseling for the New Millennium: An Interview with J. William Worden," *The Thanatology Newsletter* 2, no. 4 (2002): 10–12. See also Lawrence G. Calhoun and Richard G. Tedeshi, eds., *Handbook of Posttraumatic Growth: Research and Practice* (Mahwah, N.J.: Lawrence Erlbaum, 2006).

116. Henk Schut, Margaret S. Stroebe, Jan Van Den Bout, and Maaike Terheggen, "The Efficacy of Bereavement Interventions: Determining Who Benefits," in *Handbook of Bereavement Research: Consequences, Coping, and Care,* ed. Stroebe and others, 705–737; p. 731.

117. Jane E. Brody, "Often, Time Beats Therapy for Treating Grief," *The New York Times,* January 27, 2004.

118. John R. Jordan and Robert A. Neimeyer, "Does Grief Counseling Work?" *Death Studies* 27 (2003): 765–786; quote p. 781.

119. Dale G. Larson and William T. Hoyt, "What Has Become of Grief Counseling? An Evaluation of the Empirical Foundations of the New Pessimism," *Professional Psychology: Research and Practice* 38, no. 4 (2007): 347–355; quote p. 354. See also Connor, *Hospice and Palliative Care: The Essential Guide,* 2nd ed., p. 89.

120. Study by Task Force on Community Preventive Services, published in *American Journal of Preventive Medicine* (September 2008) and reported by Bruce Bower, "Study Evaluates Kids' Therapies," *Science News* (September 27, 2008), p. 11.

121. Louis A. Gamino and R. Hal Ritter, Jr., *Ethical Practice in Grief Counseling* (New York: Springer, 2009), p. 215. See also Margaret S. Stroebe, Karolijne Van Der Houwen, and Henk Schut, "Bereavement Support, Intervention, and Research on the Internet: A Critical Review," in *Handbook of Bereavement Research and Practice: Advances in Theory and Intervention,* ed. Stroebe and others, pp. 551–574.

122. Silverman, "Dying and Bereavement in Historical Perspective," p. 145.

123. David A. Crenshaw, "Life Span Issues and Assessment and Intervention," in *Handbook of Thanatology,* 2nd ed., ed. Meagher and Balk, 239–244; p. 242.

124. Louis A. Gamino and R. Hal Ritter, Jr., *Ethical Practice in Grief Counseling* (New York: Springer, 2009), p. 31.

125. Dennis Klass, "Religion and Spirituality in Loss, Grief, and Mourning," in *Handbook of Thanatology,* 2nd ed., ed. Meagher and Balk, 127–134; pp. 128–129, 133.

126. Louis A. Gamino and R. Hal Ritter, Jr., *Ethical Practice in Grief Counseling* (New York: Springer, 2009), p. 38.

127. Margaret Stroebe, Mary M. Gergen, Kenneth J. Gergen, and Wolfgang Stroebe, "Broken Hearts or Broken Bonds: Love and Death in Historical Perspective," in *The Path Ahead: Readings in Death and Dying,* ed. Lynne Ann DeSpelder and Albert Lee Strickland (Mountain View, Calif.: Mayfield, 1995), pp. 231–241.

128. Mary Kawena Pukui, E. W. Haertig, and Catherine A. Lee, *Nana I Ke Kumu (Look to the Source),* vol. 1 (Honolulu: Hui Hanai; Queen Lili'uokalani Children's Center, 1972), pp. 135–136, 141.

129. Quoted in Ari L. Goldman, "Confronting Grief, Not Burying It," *The New York Times,* September 7, 2003.

130. Quoted in Jane E. Brody, "Often, Time Beats Therapy for Treating Grief," *The New York Times,* January 27, 2004.

131. Nissan Rubin, "Social Networks and Mourning: A Comparative Approach," *Omega: Journal of Death and Dying* 21, no. 2 (1990): 113–127. See also Jason Castle, "Grief Rituals: Aspects That Facilitate Adjustment to Bereavement," *Journal of Loss & Trauma* 8, no. 1 (2003): 41–71.

132. For more information, contact T.A.P.S., 2001 S Street NW, Suite 300, Washington, DC 20009; (800) 959-8277.

133. Stephen J. Fleming and Leslie Balmer, "Bereaved Families of Ontario: A Mutual-Help Model for Families Experiencing Death," in *The Path Ahead,* ed. DeSpelder and Strickland, pp. 281–288; quote p. 288.

134. John Schneider, *Stress, Loss, and Grief: Understanding Their Origins and Growth Potential* (Baltimore: University Park Press, 1984), pp. 66–76.

135. Julie Fritsch with Sherokee Ilse, *The Anguish of Loss* (Maple Plain, Minn.: Wintergreen Press, 1988).

136. Simon Shimson Rubin, Ruth Malkinson, and Eliezer Wiztum, "On Bereavement Interventions: Controversy and Consensus," in *Handbook of Thanatology,* 2nd ed., ed. Meagher and Balk, 263–272; p. 263. See also Margaret S. Stroebe, Robert O. Hansson, and Henk Schut, "Bereavement Research: 21st Century Prospects," in *Handbook of Bereavement Research and Practice: Advances in Theory and Intervention,* ed. Stroebe and others, pp. 577–603.

CHAPTER *10*

1. See Linda Goldman, *Breaking the Silence: A Guide to Helping Children with Complicated Grief—Suicide, Homicide, AIDS, Violence, and Abuse,* 2nd ed. (New York: Brunner-Routledge, 2001).

2. International Work Group on Death, Dying, and Bereavement, "Children, Adolescents, and Death: Myths, Realities, and Challenges," *Death Studies* 23 (1999): 443–463.

3. Mary Louise Branch and Sabrina A. Brinson, "Gone But Not Forgotton: Children's Experience with Attachment, Separation, and Loss," *Reclaiming Children and Youth* 16, no. 3 (Fall 2007): 41–45.

4. See David W. Adams and Eleanor J. Deveau, eds., *Beyond the Innocence of Childhood.* 3 vols. (Amityville, N.Y.: Baywood, 1995); and Phyllis Rolfe Silverman, *Never Too Young to Know: Death in Children's Lives* (New York: Oxford University Press, 2000).

5. See, for example, Fotini Bonoti, Angeliki Leondari, and Adelais Mastora, "Exploring Children's Understanding of Death: Through Drawings and the Death Concept Questionnaire," *Death Studies* 37 (2013): 47–60.

6. Marilyn J. Field and Richard E. Behrman, eds., *When Children Die: Improving Palliative and End-of-Life Care for Children and Their Families* (Washington, D.C.: National Academies Press, 2003), p. xv.

7. Zlata Filipovic, "Zlata's Diary: A Child's Life in Sarajevo," in *The Path Ahead: Readings in Death and Dying,* ed. Lynne Ann DeSpelder and Albert Lee Strickland, (Mountain View, Calif.: Mayfield, 1995); pp. 175–178; quote p. 178.

8. Dorothy Morgos, J. William Worden, and Leila Gupta, "Psychosocial Effects of War Experiences Among Displaced Children in Southern Darfur," *Omega: Journal of Death and Dying* 56, no. 3 (2008): 229–253.

9. Marian Tankink, "'The Moment I Became Born-Again the Pain Disappeared': The Healing of Devastating War Memories in Born-Again Churches in Mbarara District, Southwest Uganda," *Transcultural Psychiatry* 44, no. 2 (2007): 203–231.

10. James Garbarino, "Challenges We Face in Understanding Children and War: A Personal Essay," in *The Path Ahead,* ed. DeSpelder and Strickland, 169–174; quote p. 169.

11. Ice-T, "The Killing Fields," in *The Path Ahead,* ed. DeSpelder and Strickland, pp. 179–181.

12. Ronald Keith Barrett and Lynne Ann DeSpelder, "Ways People Die: The Influence of Environment on a Child's View of Death" (paper presented at the annual meeting of the Association for Death Education and Counseling, Washington, D.C., June 26, 1997).

13. Task Force on Community Preventive Services, "Recommendations to Reduce Psychological Harm from Traumatic Events Among Children and Adolescents," *American Journal of Preventive Medicine* 35, no. 3 (2008): 314–316.

14. Albert Bandura, "Exploration of Fortuitous Determinants of Life Paths," *Psychological Inquiry* 9, no. 2 (1998): 95–115; quote p. 96.

15. Rukmini Callimachi, "Katrina's Children Struggle with Fears," *Santa Cruz Sentinel,* April 23, 2006.

16. Kevin Ann Oltjenbruns, "Developmental Context of Childhood: Grief and Regrief Pheonomena," in *Handbook of Bereavement Research: Consequences, Coping, and Care,* ed. Margaret S. Stroebe, Robert O. Hansson, Wolfgang Stroebe, and Henk Schut, 169–197 (Washington, D.C.: American Psyhological Association, 2001), pp. 176–177.

17. Kevin Ann Oltjenbruns, "Lifespan Issues and Loss, Grief, and Mourning: Childhood and Adolescence," in *Handbook of Thanatology,* 2nd ed., ed. David K. Meagher and David E. Balk, 149–155 (New York: Routledge, 2013), p. 153.

18. Illene C. Noppe and Lloyd D. Noppe, "Adolescent Experiences with Death: Letting Go of Immortality," *Journal of Mental Health Counseling* 26, no. 2 (2004): 146–167.

19. Illene C. Noppe, Lloyd D. Noppe, and Denise Bartell, "Terrorism and Resilience: Adolescents' and Teachers' Responses to September 11, 2001," *Death Studies* 30 (2006): 41–60.

20. Russell C. Hurd, "A Teenager Revisits Her Father's Death During Childhood: A Study in Resilience and Healthy Mourning," *Adolescence* 39, no. 154 (2004): 337–354.

21. Celeste M. Johnson, "African-American Teen Girls Grieve the Loss of Friends to Homicide: Meaning-Making and Resilience," *Omega: Journal of Death and Dying* 61, no. 2 (2010): 121–143.

22. See, for example, Jeffrey Lancaster, "Developmental Stages, Grief, and a Child's Response to Death," *Pediatric Annals* 40, no. 5 (2011): 277–281.

23. See entry on death of parents, by Lynne Ann DeSpelder and Albert Lee Strickland, in *Encyclopedia of Death and Dying,* ed. Glennys Howarth and Oliver Leaman, 346–347 (New York: Routledge, 2001). See also Donna Schuurman, *Never the Same: Coming to Terms with the Death of a Parent* (New York: St. Martin's, 2003); and J. William Worden, *Children and Grief: When a Parent Dies* (New York: Guilford Press, 1996). Classic studies include Erna Furman, *A Child's Parent Dies: Studies in Childhood Bereavement* (New Haven, Conn.: Yale University Press, 1974); and Robert A. Furman, "The Child's Reaction to Death in the Family," in *Loss and Grief: Psychological Management in Medical Practice,* ed. Bernard Schoenberg et al., 70–86 (New York: Columbia University Press, 1970).

24. Margo Requarth, *After a Parent's Suicide: Helping Children Heal* (Sebastopol, Calif.: Healing Hearts, 2006).

25. Grace H. Christ, Karolynn Siegel, and Adolph E. Christ, "It Never Really Hit Me . . . Until It Actually Happened," *JAMA: Journal of the American Medical Association* 288, no. 10 (September 11, 2002): 1269–1278.

26. Phyllis R. Silverman and Madelyn Kelly, *A Parent's Guide to Raising Grieving Children: Rebuilding Your Family After the Death of a Loved One* (New York: Oxford University Press, 2009), p. 89.

27. Phyllis R. Silverman, Steven Nickman, and J. William Worden, "Detachment Revisited: The Child's Reconstruction of a Dead Parent," in *The Path Ahead,* ed. DeSpelder and Strickland, pp. 260–270.

28. Betty Davies, "The Study of Sibling Bereavement: An Historical Perspective," in *Dying, Death, and Bereavement,* 2nd ed., ed. Corless, Germino, and Pittman, pp. 287–302. See also, by Davies, *Shadows in the Sun: The Experience of Sibling Bereavement in Childhood* (Washington, D.C.: Taylor & Francis, 1999).

29. Nancy S. Hogan and Lydia DeSantis, "Things That Help and Hinder Adolescent Sibling Bereavement," *Western Journal of Nursing Research* 16, no. 2 (1994): 132–153.

30. David E. Balk, "Sibling Death, Adolescent Bereavement, and Religion," *Death Studies* 15, no. 1 (1991): 1–20.

31. Nancy Hogan and Lydia DeSantis, "Adolescent Sibling Bereavement: An Ongoing Attachment," *Qualitative Health Research* 2, no. 2 (1992): 159–177.

32. Field and Behrman, eds., *When Children Die,* p. xv.

33. William G. Bartholome, "Care of the Dying Child: The Demands of Ethics," in *The Path Ahead,* ed. DeSpelder and Strickland, 133–143; quote p. 136. See also Judith M. Stillion and Danai Papadatou, "Suffer the Children: An Examination of Psychosocial Issues in Children and Adolescents with Terminal Illness," *American Behavioral Scientist* 46, no. 2 (2002): 299–315.

34. Marie-Bénédicte Dembour, "The Conscious Death of a Two-Year-Old," *Omega: Journal of Death and Dying* 38, no. 3 (1998–1999): 187–200.

35. Myra Bluebond-Langner, *The Private Worlds of Dying Children* (Princeton, N.J.: Princeton University Press, 1978).

36. Rebecca R. Kameny and David J. Bearison, "Cancer Narratives of Adolescents and Young Adults: A Quantitative and Qualitative Analysis," Children's Health Care 31, no. 2 (2002): 143–173; quote from p. 144.

37. See Gregg M. Furth, *The Secret World of Drawings: Healing Through Art* (Boston: Sigo Press, 1988); and Maare E. Tamm and Anna Granqvist, "The Meaning of Death for Children and Adolescents: A Phenomenographic Study of Drawings," *Death Studies* 19, no. 3 (1995): 203–222.

38. Luisa M. Massimo and Daniela A. Zarri, "In Tribute to Luigi Castagnetta—Drawings: A Narrative Approach for Children with Cancer," *Annals of the New York Academy of Sciences* 1089 (2006): xvi–xxiii.

39. Stan F. Whitsett and others, "Chemotherapy-Related Fatigue in Childhood Cancer: Correlates, Consequences, and Coping Strategies," *Journal of Pediatric Oncology Nursing* 25, no. 2 (2008): 86–96.

40. Field and Behrman,eds.,*When Children Die,* p. 323.

41. Field and Behrman, eds., *When Children Die,* p. 180.

42. Betty Davies and others, "Addressing Spirituality in Pediatric Hospice and Palliative Care," *Journal of Palliative Care* 18, no. 1 (2002): 59–67.

43. Field and Behrman, eds., *When Children Die,* p. 3.

44. Stephen R. Connor, *Hospice and Palliative Care: The Essential Guide,* 2nd ed. (New York: Routledge, 2009), p. 217.

45. Program Overview (http://www.dhcs.ca.gov/services/ppc/Pages/ProgramOverview.aspx#top). See also Children's Hospice and Palliative Care Coalition (www.childrenshospice.org).

46. Tiffany Hill, "Kid-Size Care," *Honolulu Magazine* (November 2011), p. 48.

47. "Children's Hospice: An Omega Interview [by Robert Kastenbaum] with Ida M. Martinson," *Omega: Journal of Death and Dying* 31, no. 4 (1995): 253–261.

48. Andrea C. Walker, "Life Span Issues and End-of-Life Decision Making," in *Handbook of Thanatology,* 2nd ed., ed. Meagher and Balk, 81–89; p. 83.

49. Louis A. Gamino and R. Hal Ritter, Jr., *Ethical Practice in Grief Counseling* (New York: Springer, 2009), p. 142.

50. Gamino and Ritter, *Ethical Practice in Grief Counseling,* p. 143.

51. Andrew Newman, "Adolescent Consent to Routine Medical and Surgical Treatment: A Proposal to Simplify the Law of Teenage Medical Decision-Making," *Journal of Legal Medicine* 22 (2001): 501–532; quote p. 528.

52. Bartholome, "Care of the Dying Child," p. 133.

53. Bartholome, "Care of the Dying Child," p. 141.

54. Betty Davies and others, "Living in the Dragon's Shadow: Fathers' Experiences of a Child's Life-Limiting Illness," *Death Studies 28* (2004): 111–135.

55. Dana Cable, Laurel Cucchi, Faye Lopez, and Terry Martin, "Camp Jamie," *American Journal of Hospice and Palliative Care* 9, no. 5 (1992): 18–21.

56. https://www.moyerfoundation.org/programs/camperin.aspx.

57. *HUGS Fact Sheet.* Contact HUGS (Help, Understanding, and Group Support for Hawaii's Seriously Ill Children and Their Families), 3636 Kilauea Avenue, Honolulu, HI 96816; (808) 732–4846; www.hugslove.org.

58. Starlight Children's Foundation International, 5900 Wilshire Blvd., Suite 2530, Los Angeles, CA 90036, (323) 634–0080; www.starlight.org.

59. See the following, published in *Children's Health Care* 31, no. 1 (2002): Haven B. Battles and Lori S. Wiener, "Starbright World: Effects of an Electronic Network on the Social Environment of Children with Life-Threatening Illnesses," pp. 47–68; and Ruth T. Brokstein, Susan O. Cohen, and Gary A. Walco, "Starbright World and Psychological Adjustment in Children with Cancer: A Clinical Series," pp. 29–45.

60. Sunshine Foundation, 1041 Mill Creek Drive, Feasterville, PA 19052, (215) 396–4770 or (800) 767–1976, www.sunshinefoundation.org; Make-A-Wish Foundation, Suite 400, 4742 24th Street, Phoenix, AZ 85106, (602) 279–9474 or (800) 722–9474; www.wish.org.

61. Lori S. Wiener and others, "National Telephone Support Groups: A New Avenue Toward Psychosocial Support for HIV-Infected Children and Their Families," *Social Work with Groups* 16, no. 3 (1993): 55–71.

62. Heather L. Servaty-Seib, "Death of a Friend During Adolescence," in *Adolescent Encounters with Death, Bereavement, and Coping,* ed. David E. Balk and Charles A. Corr, 217–235 (New York: Springer, 2009), p. 218.

63. See the special issue of *Omega: Journal of Death and Dying* 48, no. 4 (2004) on death-related literature for children, esp. Carol F. Berns, "Bibliotherapy: The Use of Literature in Working with Bereaved Children," pp. 321–336, and Donna Schuurman, "Literature for Adults to Assist Them in Helping Bereaved Children," pp. 415–424.

64. See Myra Bluebond-Langner, *In the Shadow of Illness: Parents and Siblings of the Chronically Ill Child* (Princeton, N.J.: Princeton University Press, 1996), and "Worlds of Dying Children and Their Well Siblings," *Death Studies* 13, no. 1 (1989): 1–16.

65. Robert Zucker, *The Journey Through Grief and Loss: Helping Yourself and Your Child When Grief Is Shared* (New York: St. Martin's, 2009), p. 2.

66. Nancy L. Malcom, "Images of Heaven and the Spiritual Afterlife: Qualitative Analysis of Children's Storybooks about Death, Dying, Grief, and Bereavement," *Omega: Journal of Death and Dying* 62, no. 1 (2010–2011): 51–76; quote p. 69.

67. This and the following anecdote from Jo-Eileen Gyulay, *The Dying Child* (New York: McGraw-Hill, 1978), pp. 17–18.

68. See Mary A. Fristad and others, "The Role of Ritual in Children's Bereavement," *Omega: Journal of Death and Dying* 42, no. 4 (2001): 321–339; and Phyllis R. Silverman and J. William Worden, "Children's Understanding of Funeral Ritual," *Omega: Journal of Death and Dying* 25, no. 4 (1992): 319–331.

69. Erik Erikson, *Childhood and Society* (New York: Norton, 1950), p. 233.

CHAPTER *11*

1. See, for example, Catherine M. Sanders, *Grief, the Mourning After: Dealing with Adult Bereavement,* 2nd ed. (New York: Wiley, 1989).

2. Peter Marris, "Holding onto Meaning Through the Life Cycle," in *Challenges of the Third Age: Meaning and Purpose in Later Life,* ed. Robert S. Weiss and Scott A. Bass (New York: Oxford University Press, 2002). Kindle edition.

3. Edwin S. Shneidman, *Death and the College Student* (New York: Behavioral Publications, 1972).

4. Sara J. Tedrick Parikh and Heather L. Servaty-Seib, "College Students' Beliefs about Supporting a Grieving Peer," *Death Studies* 37 (2013): 653–669; quote p. 653.

5. Heather L. Servaty-Seib and Lou Ann Hamilton, "Educational Performance and Persistence of Bereaved College Students," *Journal of College Student Development* 47, no. 2 (2006): 225–234; see also Heather L. Servaty-Seib and Deborah J. Taub, "Bereavement and College Students: The Role of Counseling Psychology," *The Counseling Psychologist* 38, no. 7 (2010): 947–975.

6. Leslie Williams Hale, "College Suicide: Second-Leading Cause of Student Death Hits Home in Southwest Florida," *Naples Daily News* (January 1, 2012).

7. *The Spiritual Life of College Students: A National Study of College Students' Search for Meaning and Purpose* (Higher Education Research Institute, University of California, Los Angeles, n.d.).

8. Harold Ivan Smith, *Friendgrief: An Absence Called Presence* (Amityville, N.Y.: Baywood, 2000).

9. See Rosemary Blieszner, "'She'll Be on My Heart': Intimacy Among Friends," *Generations: Journal of the American Society on Aging* 25, no. 2 (2001): 48–54.

10. Miriam S. Moss and Sidney Z. Moss, "Meaning of the Death of an Elderly Father: Two Sisters' Perspectives," *Omega: Journal of Death and Dying* 66, no. 3 (2012–2013): 195–213; esp. p. 208.

11. See entry on death of parents, by Lynne Ann DeSpelder and Albert Lee Strickland, in *Encyclopedia of Death and Dying,* ed. Glennys Howarth and Oliver Leaman (New York: Routledge, 2001), pp. 346–347.

12. Sharon Hines Smith, "'Fret No More My Child . . . For I'm All Over Heaven All Day': Religious Beliefs in the Bereavement of African American, Middle-Aged Daughters Coping with the Death of an Elderly Mother," *Death Studies* 26 (2002): 309–323.

13. Smith, "'Fret No More My Child' . . . ," p. 320.

14. Marion Osterweis, Fredric Solomon, and Morris Green, eds., *Bereavement: Reactions, Consequences, and Care* (Washington, D.C.: National Academy Press, 1984), p. 85.

15. Miriam S. Moss, Sidney Z. Moss, Robert Rubinstein, and Nancy Resch, "Impact of Elderly Mother's Death on Middle Aged Daughters," *International Journal of Aging and Human Development* 37, no. 1 (1992–1993): 1–22.

16. See Harold Ivan Smith, *Grieving the Death of a Mother* (Minneapolis: Augsburg, 2003).

17. Debra Umberson and Meichu D. Chen, "Effects of a Parent's Death on Adult Children: Relationship Salience and Reaction to Loss," *American Sociological Review* 59, no. 1 (1994): 152–168.

18. Laura R. Umphrey and Joanne Cacciatore, "Coping with the Ultimate Deprivation: Narrative Themes in a Parental Bereavement Support Group," *Omega: Journal of Death and Dying* 63, no. 2 (2011): 141–160.

19. Laura S. Smart, "Parental Bereavement in Anglo American History," *Omega: Journal of Death and Dying* 28, no. 1 (1993–1994): 49–61.

20. Dennis Klass, "Solace and Immortality: Bereaved Parents' Continuing Bond with Their Children," in *The Path Ahead: Readings in Death and Dying,* ed. Lynne Ann DeSpelder and Albert Lee Strickland, 246–259 (Mountain View, Calif.: Mayfield, 1995); and Klass, *The Spiritual Lives of Bereaved Parents* (Philadelphia: Brunner/Mazel, 1999).

21. Paul C. Rosenblatt, "Protective Parenting After the Death of a Child," *Journal of Personal and Interpersonal Loss* 5 (2000): 343–360.

22. Exhibition note, "Native Peoples," Glenbow Museum, Calgary, Alberta, Canada.

23. See, for example, Harriett Sarnoff Schiff, *The Bereaved Parent* (New York: Crown, 1977); and Kay Talbot, *What Forever Means After the Death of a Child: Transcending the Trauma, Living with the Loss* (New York: Brunner-Routledge, 2002).

24. *Dorland's Illustrated Medical Dictionary,* 26th ed. (Philadelphia: Saunders, 1985), p. 828.

25. Wendy Simonds and Barbara Katz Rothman, *Centuries of Solace: Expressions of Maternal Grief in Popular Literature* (Philadelphia: Temple University Press, 1992), p. 252.

26. *Dorland's Illustrated Medical Dictionary,* pp. 664, 1251.

27. Rose Cooper, "Unrecognized Losses in Child Adoption," in *Disenfranchised Grief: New Directions, Challenges, and Strategies for Practice,* ed. Kenneth J. Doka, Chapter 17 (Champaign, Ill.: Research Press, 2002).

28. Leverett Millen and Samuel Roll, "Solomon's Mothers: A Special Case of Pathological Bereavement," *American Journal of Orthopsychiatry* 55, no. 3 (1985): 411–418.

29. Glen W. Davidson, "Death of a Wished-for Child: A Case Study," *Death Education* 1, no. 3 (1977): 265–275. See also Susan Roos, *Chronic Sorrow: A Living Loss* (New York: Brunner-Routledge, 2002).

30. Paul M. Insel and Walton T. Roth, *Connect Core Concepts in Health,* 13th ed. (New York: McGraw-Hill, 2013), p. 185.

31. Larry G. Peppers, "Grief and Elective Abortion: Breaking the Emotional Bond?" *Omega: Journal of Death and Dying* 18, no. 1 (1987–1988): 1–12.

32. Simonds and Rothman, *Centuries of Solace,* p. 259.

33. Kenneth J. Doka, "Disenfranchised Grief" (paper presented at the annual meeting of the Association for Death Education and Counseling, Atlanta, Spring 1986); and, edited by Doka, *Disenfranchised Grief: New Directions, Challenges, and Strategies for Practice* (Champaign, Ill.: Research Press, 2002).

34. See William R. LaFleur, *Liquid Life: Abortion and Buddhism in Japan* (Princeton, N.J.: Princeton University Press, 1992). See also Dennis Klass and Amy Olwen Heath, "Grief and Abortion: *Mizuko Kuyo,* the Japanese Ritual Resolution," *Omega: Journal of Death and Dying* 34, no. 1 (1996–1997): 1–14; and Takada Yoshihito and James M. Vardaman, Jr., *Talking about Buddhism* (Tokyo: Kodansha, 1997), pp. 183–185.

35. Joanne Cacciatore, "The Silent Birth: A Feminist Perspective," *Social Work* 54, no. 1 (January 2009): 91–95.

36. John DeFrain and others, "The Psychological Effects of a Stillbirth on Surviving Family Members," *Omega: Journal of Death and Dying* 22, no. 2 (1990–1991): 81–108.

37. Joanne Cacciatore and Suzanne Bushfield, "Stillbirth: A Sociopolitical Issue," *Affilia* 23, no. 4 (2008): 378–387.

38. Joanne Cacciatore, Ingela Rådestad, and J. Frederik Frøen, "Effects of Contact with Stillborn Babies on Maternal Anxiety and Depression," *Birth* 35, no. 4 (December 2008): 313–320; quote p. 313.

39. Irving G. Leon, "Perinatal Loss: Choreographing Grief on the Obstetric Unit," *American Journal of Orthopsychiatry* 62, no. 1 (1992): 7–8.

40. Cacciatore, Rådestad, and Frøen, "Effects of Contact with Stillborn Babies," p. 319.

41. Jay Ruby, "Portraying the Dead," *Omega: Journal of Death and Dying* 19, no. 1 (1988–1989): 1–20; and Joy Johnson and S. Marvin Johnson, with James H. Cunningham and Irwin J. Weinfeld, *A Most Important Picture: A Very Tender Manual for Taking Pictures of Stillborn Babies and Infants Who Die* (Omaha: Centering Corp., 1985).

42. Joanne Cacciatore, Stephen Schnebly, and J. Frederik Frøen, "The Effects of Social Support on Maternal Anxiety and Depression After Stillbirth," *Health and Social Care in the Community* 17, no. 2 (2009): 167–176; quote p. 167.

43. DeFrain and others, "Psychological Effects of a Stillbirth," p. 87.

44. *Merriam-Webster's Collegiate Dictionary,* 11th ed. (Springfield, Mass., 2003), p. 1248. Cf. Mark H. Beers and others, eds., *The Merck Manual of Diagnosis and Therapy,* 18th ed. (Whitehouse Station, N.J.: Merck Research Laboratories, 2006), pp. 2402–2403.

45. See J. Rehmeyer, "Abated Breath: Serotonin Problems May Contribute to SIDS," *Science News* 170, no. 19 (November 4, 2006): 294, and "Finding the Cause of SIDS," *The Week* (November 17, 2006), p. 22.

46. Judith A. Savage, *Mourning Unlived Lives: A Psychological Study of Childbearing Loss* (Wilmette, Ill.: Chiron, 1989).

47. Savage, *Mourning Unlived Lives,* p. xiii.

48. Beverly Raphael, *The Anatomy of Bereavement* (New York: Basic Books, 1983), p. 229.

49. "Deaths by Age and Selected Causes: 2007," *Statistical Abstract of the United States: 2012,* 131st ed. (Washington, D.C., 2011). http://www.census.gov/compendia/statab/.

50. Committee on Trauma Research, National Research Council, *Injury in America: A Continuing Public Health Problem* (Washington, D.C.: National Academy Press, 1985).

51. Jerome L. Schulman, *Coping with Tragedy: Successfully Facing the Problem of a Seriously Ill Child* (Chicago: Follett, 1976), p. 335. See also Marilyn McCubbin and others, "Family Resiliency in Childhood Cancer," *Family Relations* 51, no. 2 (2002): 103–111.

52. Kay Talbot, "Mothers Now Childless: Survival After the Death of an Only Child," *Omega: Journal of Death and Dying* 34, no. 3 (1996–1997): 177–189. See also, by Talbot, *What Forever Means After the Death of a Child.*

53. Laura S. Smart, "The Marital Helping Relationship Following Pregnancy Loss and Infant Death," *Journal of Family Issues* 13, no. 1 (1992): 81–98.

54. Dennis Klass, *Parental Grief: Solace and Resolution* (New York: Springer, 1988).

55. Joanne Cacciatore, John DeFrain, Kara L. C. Jones, and Hawk Jones, "Stillbirth and the Couple: A Gender-Based Exploration," *Journal of Family Social Work* 11, no. 4 (2008): 351–372; esp. p. 354.

56. Kathleen R. Gilbert, "Interactive Grief and Coping in the Marital Dyad," *Death Studies* 13, no. 6 (1989): 605–626. See also Kathleen R. Gilbert and Laura S. Smart, *Coping with Infant or Fetal Loss: The Couple's Healing Process* (New York: Brunner/Mazel, 1992).

57. *When a Child Dies: A Survey of Bereaved Parents* (Oak Brook, Ill.: The Compassionate Friends, 2006).

58. Gordon Riches and Pam Dawson, "Communities of Feeling: The Culture of Bereaved Parents," *Mortality* 1, no. 2 (1996): 143–161.

59. Raphael, *Anatomy of Bereavement,* p. 177.

60. Savine Gross Weizman and Phyllis Kamm, *About Mourning: Support and Guidance for the Bereaved* (New York: Human Sciences, 1985), p. 130.

61. See Ira O. Glick, Robert S. Weiss, and Colin Murray Parkes, *The First Year of Bereavement* (New York: Wiley, 1974), and its follow-up by Colin Murray Parkes and Robert S. Weiss, *Recovery from Bereavement* (New York: Basic Books, 1983).

62. David E. Balk, "Life Span Issues and Loss, Grief, and Mourning: Adulthood," *Handbook of Thanatology,* 2nd ed., ed. David K. Meagher and David E. Balk, 157–169 (New York: Routledge, 2013), p.168.

63. Richard A. Settersten, Jr., "Social Sources of Meaning in Later Life," in *Challenges of the Third Age,* ed. Weiss and Bass.

64. Sara Wilcox and others, "The Effects of Widowhood on Physical and Mental Health, Health Behaviors, and Health Outcomes: The Women's Health Initiative," *Health Psychology* 22, no. 5 (2003): 1–10.

65. Judith M. Stillion, *Death and the Sexes: An Examination of Differential Longevity, Attitudes, Behaviors, and Coping Skills* (Washington, D.C.: Hemisphere, 1985). See also Scott Campbell and Phyllis R. Silverman, *Widower: When Men Are Left Alone* (Amityville, N.Y.: Baywood, 1996); Luann M. Daggett, "Living with Loss: Middle-Aged Men Face Spousal Bereavement," *Qualitative Health Research* 12, no. 5 (2002): 625–639; Geraldine P. Mineau, Ken R. Smith, and Lee L. Bean, "Historical Trends of Survival Among Widows and Widowers," *Social Science & Medicine* 54, no. 2 (2002): 245–254; and John M. O'Brien, Linda M. Forrest, and Ann E. Austin, "Death of a Partner: Perspectives of Heterosexual and Gay Men," *Journal of Health Psychology* 7, no. 3 (2002): 317–328.

66. Rebecca L. Utz and others, "The Effect of Widowhood on Older Adults' Social Participation: An Evaluation of Activity, Disengagement, and Continuity Theories," *The Gerontologist* 42, no. 4 (2002): 522–533; quote, p. 530.

67. See Karen L. Fingerman, "A Distant Closeness: Intimacy Between Parents and Their Children in Later Life," *Generations: Journal of the American Society on Aging* 25, no. 2 (2001): 26–33.

68. See Phyllis R. Silverman, *Widow to Widow: How the Bereaved Help One Another,* 2nd ed. (New York: Brunner-Routledge, 2004); and also by Silverman, "Widowhood as the Next Stage in the Life Cycle," in *Widows: North America,* ed. Helena Z. Lopata (Durham, N.C.: Duke University Press, 1987), and "The Widow-to-Widow Program: An Experiment in Preventive Intervention," *Mental Hygiene* 53, no. 3 (1969), a landmark report by Silverman on her work at Harvard Medical School's Laboratory of Community Psychiatry. See also Helena Z. Lopata, *Widowhood in an American City* (Cambridge, Mass.: Schenkman, 1973), *Women as Widows: Support Systems* (New York: Elsevier, 1979), and *Current Widowhood: Myths and Realities* (Thousand Oaks, Calif.: Sage, 1996).

69. Joanne Lynn and David M. Anderson, *Living Well at the End of Life: Adapting Health Care to Serious Chronic Illness in Old Age,*" Rand Health White Paper (Santa Monica, Calif.: Rand, 2003), p. 4.

70. Lynn and Anderson, *Living Well at the End of Life,* pp. 4–5.

71. Julia Holmes and others, "Aging Differently: Physical Limitations Among Adults Aged 50 Years and Over: United States, 2001–2007," *National Center for Health Statistics Data Brief,* no. 20 (July 2009).

72. R. A. Hope and others, *Oxford Handbook of Clinical Medicine,* 3rd ed. (Oxford: Oxford University Press, 1994), p. 64.

73. Insel and Roth, *Connect Core Concepts in Health,* pp.623–626.

74. F. David Martin, "Facing Death at 80: Memory and the Holy," *Soundings: An Interdisciplinary Journal* 83, no. 2 (Summer 2000): 301–330; quote p. 304.

75. Balk, "Life Span Issues and Loss, Grief, and Mourning: Adulthood," p. 168.

76. Martin, "Facing Death at 80," p. 304. See also Sharon R. Kaufman, *The Ageless Self: Sources of Meaning in Later Life* (Madison: University of Wisconsin Press, 1995).

77. *Stedman's Medical Dictionary,* 26th ed. (Baltimore: Williams & Wilkins, 1995), p. 492; and Insel and Roth, *Connect Core Concepts in Health,* p. 630.

78. Beers et al., *The Merck Manual of Diagnosis and Therapy,* p. 1815.

79. Betzaida Tejada-Vera, "Mortality from Alzheimer's Disease in the United States: Data for 2000 and 2010," *NCHS Data Brief,* no. 116 (Hyattsville, Md.: National Center for Health Statistics, 2013), p. 1.

80. *Stedman's Medical Dictinoary,* p. 492.

81. Leon Kass, Chairman, President's Council on Bioethics, "Letter of Transmittal," *Taking Care: Ethical Caregiving in Our Aging Society,* September 2005. http://bioethics.georgetown.edu/pcbe/reports/taking_care/taking_care.pdf.

82. Gary R. VanderBos, ed., *APA Dictionary of Psychology* (Washington, D.C.: American Psychological Association, 2007), p. 408.

83. Chris Wilson, "The Century Ahead," *Daedalus* 135, no. 1 (Winter 2006): 5–8.

84. James M. Henslin, *Sociology: A Down-to-Earth Approach,* 9th ed. (Boston: Pearson, 2008), p. 377.

85. See Stanley Brandes, *Forty: The Age and the Symbol* (Nashville: University of Tennessee Press, 1985).

86. Bernice L. Neugarten, "Growing as Long as We Live," *Second Opinion* 15 (November 1990): 42–51.

87. James F. Fries, Lawrence W. Green, and Sol Levine, "Health Promotion and the Compression of Morbidity," *Lancet* (March 4, 1989): 481–483; see also, by Fries, "The Compression of Morbidity," *Milbank Memorial Fund Quarterly* 61 (1983): 397–419.

88. Insel and Roth, *Connect Core Concepts in Health,* p. 632.

89. Bert Hayslip, Jr., Julie Hicks Patrick, and Paul E. Panek, *Adult Development and Aging,* 5th ed. (Malabar, Fla.: Krieger, 2011), p. 15.

90. Neugarten, "Growing as Long as We Live."

91. Sandra L. Bertman, "Aging Grace: Treatment of the Aged in the Arts," *Death Studies* 13, no. 6 (1989): 517–535. See also Pamela T. Amoss and Steven Harrell, eds., *Other Ways of Growing Old: Anthropological Perspectives* (Palo Alto, Calif.: Stanford University Press, 1981).

92. Robert C. Atchley, *Spirituality and Aging* (Baltimore: Johns Hopkins University Press, 2009), p. 4.

93. Diana Athill, *Somewhere Towards the End: A Memoir* (New York: Norton, 2009), p. 177.

94. Athill, *Somewhere Towards the End,* p. 180.

95. Daniel Callahan, "Can Old Age Be Given a Public Meaning?" *Second Opinion* 15 (November 1990): 12–23.

96. Jay F. Rosenberg, *Thinking Clearly About Death* (Englewood Cliffs, N.J.: Prentice-Hall, 1983), p. 208.

97. Rosenberg, *Thinking Clearly About Death,* pp. 211–212.

98. Allan Kellehear, "Dying Alone—and *Preferably* Alone? Agency, Resistance, and Dissent at the End of Life," *International Journal of Ageing and Later Life* 4, no. 1 (2009): 5–21.

99. Jane W. Peterson, "Age of Wisdom: Elderly Black Women in Family and Church," in *The Cultural Context of Aging: Worldwide Perspectives,* ed. Jay Sokolovsky (New York: Bergin & Garvey, 1990), pp. 213–227.

100. See, for example, Cesare Marino, "Honor the Elders: Symbolic Associations with Old Age in Traditional Eastern Cherokee Culture," *Journal of Cherokee Studies* 13 (1988): 3–18.

101. Robert N. Butler, *Why Survive? Being Old in America* (New York: Harper & Row, 1975); quote p. 421. See also Robert N. Butler. *The Longevity Revolution: The Benefits and Challenges of Living a Long Life.* New York: Public Affairs, 2008.

102. Butler, *Why Survive?,* p. 422.

CHAPTER 12

1. Judith M. Stillion, "Premature Exits: Understanding Suicide," in *The Path Ahead: Readings in Death and Dying,* ed. Lynne Ann DeSpelder and Albert Lee Strickland, 182–197 (Mountain View, Calif.: Mayfield, 1995), p. 182.

2. Kay Redfield Jamison, *Night Falls Fast: Understanding Suicide* (New York: Knopf, 1999), p. 292.

3. Mark H. Beers and others, eds., *The Merck Manual of Diagnosis and Therapy,* 18th ed. (Whitehouse Station, N.J.: Merck Research Laboratories, 2006), p. 1741.

4. Donna L. Hoyert and Jiaquan Xu, "Deaths: Preliminary Data for 2011," *National Vital Statistics Reports* 61, no. 6 (Hyattsville, Md.: National Center for Health Statistics, 2012), p. 4.

5. "Deaths and Death Rates by Leading Causes of Death and Age: 2007," *Statistical Abstract of the United States: 2012,* 131st ed. (Washington, D.C., 2011). http://www.census.gov/compendia/statab/.

6. Beers and others, eds., *The Merck Manual of Diagnosis and Therapy,* p. 1741.

7. News Release, Substance Abuse and Mental Health Services Administration, September 17, 2009, www.samha.gov.

8. Edwin S. Shneidman, *Comprehending Suicide: Landmarks in 20th Century Suicidology* (Washington, D.C.: American Psychological Association, 2001), p. 154.

9. Jamison, *Night Falls Fast,* p. 291.

10. Stefan Timmermans, *Postmortem: How Medical Examiners Explain Suspicious Deaths* (Chicago: University of Chicago Press, 2006), p. 92.

11. Quoted in Timmermans, *Postmortem,* p. 96.

12. Glen Evans and Norman L. Farberow, *The Encyclopedia of Suicide* (New York: Facts on File, 1988), p. 268.

13. See Robert J. Homant and Daniel B. Kennedy, "Suicide by Police: A Proposed Typology of Law Enforcement Officer-Assisted Suicide," *Policing: An International Journal of Police Strategies & Management* 23, no. 3 (2000): 339–355; and Vivian B. Lord, "Law Enforcement-Assisted Suicide," *Criminal Justice and Behavior* 27, no. 3 (2000): 401–419.

14. Julia Dahl, "How to Stop Suicide by Cop," *Miller-McCune* (March-April 2011), pp. 66–73.

15. Katherine Van Wormer and Chuk Odiah, "The Psychology of the Suicide-Murder and the Death Penalty," *Journal of Criminal Justice* 27, no. 4 (1999): 361–370.

16. Timmermans, *Postmortem,* p. 185.

17. Edwin S. Shneidman, "Suicide," in *Death: Current Perspectives,* 2nd ed., ed. Shneidman (Mountain View, Calif.: Mayfield, 1980), p. 432.

18. James R. P. Ogloff and Randy K. Otto, "Psychological Autopsy: Clinical and Legal Perspectives," *Saint Louis University Law Journal* 37, no. 3 (Spring 1993): 607–646. See also Edwin S. Shneidman, *Clues to Suicide* (New York: McGraw-Hill, 1957); and, by Avery D. Weisman, *The Psychological Autopsy* (New York: Human Sciences Press, 1968) and *The Realization of Death: A Guide for the Psychological Autopsy* (Northvale, N.J.: Aronson, 1974).

19. For an example of the data-gathering approach used in psychological autopsies, see Tracy L. Cross, Karyn Gust-Brey, and P. Bonny Ball, "A Psychological Autopsy of the Suicide of an Academically Gifted Student: Researchers' and Parents' Perspectives," *Gifted Child Quarterly* 46, no. 4 (2002): 247–264.

20. Thomas J. Young, "Procedures and Problems in Conducting a Psychological Autopsy," *International Journal of Offender Therapy and Comparative Criminology* 36, no. 1 (Spring 1992): 43–52.

21. See Norman Poythress and others, "APA's Expert Panel in the Congressional Review of the USS 'Iowa' Incident," *American Psychologist* 48, no. 1 (January 1993): 8–15; Randy K. Otto and others, "An Empirical Study of the Reports of APA's Peer Review Panel in the Congressional Review of the U.S.S. IOWA Incident," *Journal of Personality Assessment* 61, no. 3 (December 1993): 425–442; Ogloff and Otto, "Psychological Autopsy: Clinical and Legal Perspectives"; and Charles C. Thompson II, *A Glimpse of Hell: The Explosion on the USS* Iowa *and Its Cover-Up* (New York: Norton, 1999).

22. Quoted material from Poythress and others, "APA's Expert Panel."

23. See David A. Brent, "The Psychological Autopsy: Methodological Considerations for the Study of Adolescent Suicide," *Suicide and Life-Threatening Behavior* 19 (Spring 1989): 43–57; and Mohammad Shafi and others, "Psychological Autopsy of Completed Suicide in Children and Adolescents," *American Journal of Psychiatry* 142 (1985): 1061–1064.

24. Heidi Hjelmeland and others, "Psychological Autopsy Studies as Diagnostic Tools: Are They Methodologically Flawed?" *Death Studies* 36, no. 7 (2012): 605–626.

25. David Lester, "Theories of Suicide," in *Suicide Among Racial and Ethnic Minority Groups: Theory, Research, and Practice,* ed. Frederick T. L. Leong and Mark M. Leach, pp. 39–53 (New York: Routledge); quote p. 44.

26. Roy F. Baumeister, "Suicide as Escape from Self," *Psychological Review* 97 (1990): 90–113; and Lester, "Theories of Suicide," p. 51

27. Emile Durkheim, *Suicide: A Study in Sociology* (New York: Free Press, 1951).

28. Thomas Joiner, *Why People Die by Suicide* (Cambridge, Mass.: Harvard University Press, 2005), p. 34.

29. Norman Farberow, "The History of Suicide," in Evans and Farberow, *Encyclopedia of Suicide,* p. viii.

30. Jack Seward, *Hara-Kiri: Japanese Ritual Suicide* (Rutland, Vt.: Charles E. Tuttle, 1968). See also Robert Jay Lifton, Shuichi Kato, and Michael R. Reich, *Six Lives, Six Deaths: Portraits from Modern Japan* (New Haven, Conn.: Yale University Press, 1979).

31. See Jerome Young, "Morals, Suicide, and Psychiatry: A View from Japan," *Bioethics* 16, no. 5 (2002): 412–424.

32. See Catherine Weinberger-Thomas, *Ashes of Immortality: Widow-Burning in India* (Chicago: University of Chicago Press, 1999).

33. Jeffrey W. Riemer, "Durkheim's 'Heroic Suicide' in Military Combat," *Armed Forces & Society* 25, no. 1 (1998): 103–120. See also Albert Axell, "The Kamikaze Mindset," *History Today* 52, no. 9 (2002): 3–4; and Bernard Millot, *Divine Thunder: The Life and Death of the Kamikazes* (New York: McCall, 1971).

34. Iginia Mancinelli and others, "Mass Suicide: Historical and Psychodynamic Considerations," *Suicide and Life-Threatening Behavior* 32, no. 1 (2002): 91–100.

35. See David Chidester, *Salvation and Suicide: An Interpretation of Jim Jones, the Peoples Temple, and Jonestown* (Bloomington: Indiana University Press, 1988); Jose I. Lasaga, "Death in Jonestown: Techniques of Political Control by a Paranoid Leader," *Suicide and Life-Threatening Behavior* 10, no. 4 (1980): 210–213; and Richard H. Seiden, "Reverend Jones on Suicide," *Suicide and Life-Threatening Behavior* 9, no. 2 (1979): 116–119. For an overview of mass suicide, see Iginia Mancinelli, Anna Comparelli, Paolo Girardi, and Roberto Tatarelli, "Mass Suicide: Historical and Psychodynamic Considerations," *Suicide and Life-Threatening Behavior* 32, no. 1 (2002): 91–100.

36. Susan Raine, "Reconceptualizing the Human Body: Heaven's Gate and the Quest for Divine Transformation," *Religion* 35 (2005): 98–117.

37. Andrew Selsky and Jennifer Loven, "3 Gitmo Inmates Hanged Themselves," *Associated Press Online*, June 10, 2006.

38. Edwin S. Shneidman, "Suicide," *Encyclopedia Britannica*, vol. 21 (Chicago: William Benton, 1973), p. 385.

39. Erwin Stengel, "A Matter of Communication," in *On the Nature of Suicide*, ed. Edwin S. Shneidman (San Francisco: Jossey-Bass, 1969), pp. 78–79.

40. Sam Silverman, "The Death of Socrates: A Holistic Re-Examination," *Omega: Journal of Death and Dying* 61, no. 1 (2010): 71–84.

41. Edwin S. Shneidman, "Suicide as Psychache," *Journal of Nervous and Mental Disease* 181, no. 3 (1993): 147–149, and "Some Controversies in Suicidology: Toward a Mentalistic Discipline," *Suicide and Life-Threatening Behavior* 23, no. 4 (1993): 292–298.

42. Shneidman, *Comprehending Suicide*, p. 200.

43. Edwin S. Shneidman, personal communication.

44. Shneidman, *Comprehending Suicide*, pp. 202–203.

45. Thomas Joiner, *Why People Die By Suicide* (Cambridge, Mass.: Harvard University Press, 2005), p. 201.

46. J. John Mann and others, "The Neurobiology of Suicide Risk: A Review for the Clinician," *Journal of Clinical Psychiatry* 60, Supplement 2 (1999): 7–11.

47. C. G. Prado, *The Last Choice: Preemptive Suicide in Advanced Age*, 2nd ed. (Westport, Conn.: Greenwood, 1998), p. 6.

48. "Suicide Epidemic," *The Week*, August 5, 2005.

49. Roy F. Baumeister, "Suicide as Escape from Self," *Psychological Review* 97 (1990): 90–113.

50. Quoted material from Chad E. Morrow, Craig J. Bryan, and Kathryn Kanzler Appolonio, "Empirically Based Assessment of Suicide Risk," in *Suicidal Behavior: Assessment of People-at-Risk*, ed. Updesh Kumar and Manas K. Mandel, 20–41 (Los Angeles: Sage, 2010), p. 25.

51. See, for example, Danny Nugus, "Choosing Life," *Counseling Children and Young People* (March 2009): 32–37.

52. Ronald W. Maris, *Pathways to Suicide: A Survey of Self-Destructive Behaviors* (Baltimore: Johns Hopkins University Press, 1981), and *Understanding and Preventing Suicide* (New York: Guilford Press, 1988). On the ambiguity concerning the degree of self-harm intended in suicide attempts, see Barry M. Wagner, Steven A. Wong, and David A. Jobes, "Mental Health Professionals' Determinations of Adolescent Suicide Attempts," *Suicide and Life-Threatening Behavior* 32, no. 3 (2002): 284–300.

53. Evans and Farberow, *Encyclopedia of Suicide*, p. 21.

54. Edwin S. Shneidman, *Deaths of Man* (New York: Quadrangle Books, 1973), pp. 81–90.

55. Kathleen Erwin, "Interpreting the Evidence: Competing Paradigms and the Emergence of Lesbian and Gay Suicide as a 'Social Fact,'" in *The Path Ahead*, ed. DeSpelder and Strickland, pp. 211–220.

56. Kevin E. Early and Ronald L. Akers, "'It's a White Thing'—An Exploration of Beliefs About Suicide in the African-American Community," in *The Path Ahead*, ed. DeSpelder and Strickland, pp. 198–210. See also Kevin E. Early, *Religion and Suicide in the African-American Community* (Westport, Conn.: Greenwood, 1992).

57. Brian Barry, "Suicide: The Ultimate Escape," *Death Studies* 13, no. 2 (1989): 185–190; quote p. 188.

58. See Alfred Alvarez, *The Savage God: A Study of Suicide* (New York: Random House, 1971).

59. Susan L. Ruth, "Suicide Rates Among Military Family Members Are On the Rise," *Washington Times* (June 17, 2013).

60. Ann Scott Tyson and Greg Jaffe, "Generals Find Suicide a Frustrating Enemy," *The Washington Post* (May 23, 2009).

61. Committee on the Assessment of Readjustment Needs of Military Personnel, Veterans, and Their Families, *Returning Home from Iraq and Afghanistan* (Washington, D.C.: National Academies Press, 2013), pp. 110, 120.

62. Committee, *Returning Home from Iraq and Afghanistan*, p. 111.

63. Douglas MacArthur, "Duty, Honor, Country" (speech upon receipt of the Sylvanus Thayer Award for outstanding service to the nation, United States Military Academy, West Point, May 12, 1962). http://www.nationalcenter.org/MacArthurFarewell.html.

64. Tara Bahrampour, "Baby Boomers Are Killing Themselves at an Alarming Rate, Raising Question: Why?" *Washington Post.* http://www.washingtonpost.com/local/baby-boomers-are-killing-themselves-at-an-alarming-rate-begging-question-why/2013/06/03/d98acc7a-c41f-11e2-8c3b-0b5e9247e8ca_story.html.

65. See Julie A. Phillips and others, "Understanding Recent Changes in Suicide Rates Among the Middle-Aged: Period or Cohort Effects?" *Public Health Reports* 125, no. 5 (2010): 680–688.

66. Louise B. Andrew, "Physician Suicide," *eMedicine,* July 10, 2008, http://emedicine.medscape.com/article/806779-overview.

67. Donald H. Rubinstein, "Epidemic Suicide Among Micronesian Adolescents," *Social Science & Medicine* 17 (1983): 657–665, and "Suicide in Micronesia," in *Culture, Youth and Suicide in the Pacific: Papers from an East-West Center Conference,* ed. Francis X. Hezel, Donald H. Rubinstein, and Geoffrey M. White (Honolulu: Pacific Islands Study Program, University of Hawaii, 1985), pp. 88–111.

68. Thomas Joiner, *Lonely at the Top: The High Cost of Men's Success* (New York: Palgrave Macmillan, 2011), p. 45

69. Cynthia R. Pfeffer and others, "Suicidal Children Grow Up: Suicidal Episodes and Effects of Treatment During Follow-Up," *Journal of the American Academy of Child and Adolescent Psychiatry* 33, no. 2 (1994): 225–230.

70. See Brian L. Mishara, "Conceptions of Death and Suicide in Children Ages 6–12 and Their Implications for Suicide Prevention," *Suicide and Life-Threatening Behavior* 29, no. 2 (1999): 105–118.

71. C. J. Lennings, "A Cognitive Understanding of Adolescent Suicide," *Genetic, Social, and General Psychology Monographs* 120, no. 3 (1994): 289–307.

72. David A. Brent and others, "Stressful Life Events: Psychopathology and Adolescent Suicide: A Case Control Study," *Suicide and Life-Threatening Behavior* 23, no. 3 (1993): 179–187. See also Stephen Briggs, "Working with the Risk of Suicide in Young People," *Journal of Social Work Practice* 16, no. 2 (2002): 135–148.

73. Kristi Kendrick and others, "Bullying, Cyberbullying, and Teen Suicidality: Results from the 2011 Youth Risk Behavior Survey," *APA 2013,* Abstract NR7-13.

74. Herbert Hendin, "Psychodynamics of Suicide, with Particular Reference to the Young," *American Journal of Psychiatry* 148, no. 9 (1991): 1150–1158.

75. Paulina F. Kernberg, "Psychological Interventions for the Suicidal Adolescent," *American Journal of Psychotherapy* 48, no. 1 (1994): 52–63.

76. Lennings, "A Cognitive Understanding of Adolescent Suicide."

77. See M. S. Gould, S. Wallenstein, and L. Davidson, "Suicide Clusters: A Critical Review," *Suicide and Life-Threatening Behavior* 19 (Spring 1989): 17–29; and James A. Mercy and others, "Is Suicide Contagious? A Study of the Relation Between Exposure to the Suicidal Behavior of Others and Nearly Lethal Suicide Attempts," *American Journal of Epidemiology* 154, no. 2 (2001): 120–127.

78. Examples from Evans and Farberow, *Encyclopedia of Suicide,* pp. 26–27, 72, 254.

79. Bruce L. Danto, Mark L. Taff, and Lauren R. Boglioli, "Graveside Deaths," *Omega: Journal of Death and Dying* 33, no. 4 (1996): 265–278.

80. Ayumi Naito, "Internet Suicide in Japan: Implications for Child and Adolescent Mental Health," *Clinical Child Psychology and Psychiatry* 12, no. 4 (2007): 583–597.

81. Jason B. Luoma and Jane L. Pearson, "Suicide and Marital Status in the United States, 1991–1996: Is Widowhood a Risk Factor?" *American Journal of Public Health* 92, no. 9 (2002): 1518–1522.

82. Benjamin N. Shain and the Committee on Adolescence, "Suicide and Suicide Attempts in Adolescents," *Pediatrics* 120 (2007): 669–676.

83. Y. Conwell and J. L. Pearson, "Suicidal Behaviors in Older Adults," *American Journal of Geriatric Psychiatry* 10, no. 4 (2002): 359–361; and, in the same issue, C. L. Turvey and others, "Risk Factors for Late-Life Suicide: A Prospective, Community-Based Study," pp. 398–406.

84. Susanne S. Carney and others, "Suicide over 60: The San Diego Study," *Journal of the American Geriatrics Society* 42 (1994): 174–180.

85. J. Conrad Glass, Jr., and Susan E. Reed, "To Live or Die: A Look at Elderly Suicide," *Educational Gerontology* 19 (1993): 767–778.

86. Judith M. Stillion, Eugene E. McDowell, and Jacque H. May, *Suicide Across the Life Span: Premature Exits* (New York: Hemisphere, 1989), pp. 180–181.

87. Antoon A. Leenaars and David Lester, "The Significance of the Method Chosen for Suicide in Understanding the Psychodynamics of the Suicidal Individual," *Omega: Journal of Death and Dying* 19, no. 4 (1988–1989): 311–314.

88. Edwin S. Shneidman, "Self-Destruction: Suicide Notes and Tragic Lives," in *Death: Current Perspectives,* 2nd ed., ed. Shneidman, p. 467; and, by Shneidman, "A Bibliography of Suicide Notes: 1856–1979," in *Suicide and Life-Threatening Behavior* 9, no. 1 (Spring 1979): 57–59.

89. Beers and others, eds., *The Merck Manual of Diagnosis and Therapy,* p. 1741.

90. Stephen T. Black, "Comparing Genuine and Simulated Suicide Notes: A New Perspective," *Journal of Consulting and Clinical Psychology* 61, no. 4 (1993): 699–702.

91. Shneidman, *Comprehending Suicide,* pp. 167, 170.

92. Evans and Farberow, *Encyclopedia of Suicide,* p. 187.

93. Stillion, McDowell, and May, *Suicide Across the Life Span,* p. 13.

94. Stillion, McDowell, and May, *Suicide Across the Life Span,* p. 194.

95. D. Lizardi and R. E. Golding, "Religion and Suicide: Buddhism, Native American and African Religions, Atheism, and Agnosticism," *Journal of Religion and Health* 49 (2010): 377–384.

96. Patrick W. O'Carroll, Morton M. Silverman, and Alan L. Berman, "Community Suicide Prevention: The Effectiveness of Bridge Barriers," *Suicide and Life-Threatening Behavior* 24, no. 1 (Spring 1994): 89–99.

97. Antoon A. Leenaars, "Crisis Intervention with Highly Lethal Suicidal People," *Death Studies* 18, no. 4 (1994): 341–360.

98. Robert A. Neimeyer and Angela M. Pfeiffer, "The Ten Most Common Errors of Suicide Interventionists," in *Treatment of Suicidal People,* ed. Antoon A. Leenaars, John T. Maltsberger, and Robert A. Neimeyer, 207–224 (Washington, D.C.: Taylor & Francis, 1994), pp. 210, 212.

99. Kenneth J. Doka, *Counseling Individuals with Life-Threatening Illness* (New York: Springer, 2009), p. 206.

100. Shneidman, *Comprehending Suicide,* p. 203.

101. See Alison Wertheimer, *A Special Scar: The Experiences of People Bereaved by Suicide,* 2nd ed. (Philadelphia: Brunner-Routledge, 2001).

102. Joan Wickersham, *The Suicide Index: Putting My Father's Death in Order* (New York: Harcourt, 2008), p. 158.

103. See Charles P. McDowell, Joseph M. Rothberg, and Ronald J. Koshes, "Witnessed Suicides," *Suicide and Life-Threatening Behavior* 24, no. 3 (1994): 213–223.

104. Evans and Farberow, *Encyclopedia of Suicide,* pp. 58–59, 63.

105. Adam H. Beasley, David Smiley, and Evan S. Benn, "Pembroke Pines Teen Broadcasts Suicide on Webcam," *Miami Herald Online* (November 21, 2008); and Fred Tasker, "Teen's Webcam Suicide Raises Red Flags for Copycats, Experts Say," *Miami Herald Online* (November 22, 2008).

106. Jack D. Douglas, *The Social Meanings of Suicide* (Princeton, N.J.: Princeton University Press, 1967), pp. 324ff.

107. Stillion, McDowell, and May, *Suicide Across the Life Span,* p. 24.

CHAPTER *13*

1. From *Letters of E. B. White,* collected and edited by Dorothy Lobrano Guth (New York: Harper & Row, 1976), p. 558.

2. Anthony Giddens, *Runaway World: How Globalization Is Reshaping Our Lives* (New York: Routledge, 2000), p. 52.

3. See Jerome Rosenberg and Dennis L. Peck, "Megadeaths," in *Handbook of Death & Dying,* 223–235, edited by Clifton D. Bryant (Thousand Oaks, Calif.: Sage, 2003).

4. Paul M. Insel and Walton T. Roth, *Connect Core Concepts in Health,* 13th ed. (New York: McGraw-Hill, 2013), p. 592.

5. Insel and Roth, *Connect Core Concepts in Health,* p. 593.

6. Insel and Roth, *Connect Core Concepts in Health,* p. 259.

7. "Auto Club Analysis Shows that California Teens 15–17 at Fault in 68 Percent of Fatal Crashes," *Santa Cruz Sentinel,* January 19, 2006.

8. Louis A. Gamino and R. Hal Ritter, Jr., *Ethical Practice in Grief Counseling* (New York: Springer, 2009), p. 286.

9. Robert Kastenbaum and Ruth Aisenberg, *The Psychology of Death: Concise Edition* (New York: Springer, 1976), p. 319. See also Alan E. Stewart and Janice Harris Lord, "Motor Vehicle Crash Versus Accident: A Change in Terminology Is Necessary," *Journal of Traumatic Stress* 15, no. 4 (2002): 333–335.

10. Giddens, *Runaway World,* p. 40.

11. Garance Burke, "Hip-Hop Car Stunt Leaves Two Dead," *Santa Cruz Sentinel,* December 29, 2006.

12. Kawahito Hiroshi, "Death and the Corporate Warrior," *Japan Quarterly* 38 (April–June 1991): 149–157.

13. Reinhold Messner, quoted in Caroline Alexander, "Greatest Mountaineer," *National Geographic* 210, no. 5 (November 2006): 44.

14. James A. Thorson and F. C. Powell, "To Laugh in the Face of Death: The Games That Lethal People Play," *Omega: Journal of Death and Dying* 21, no. 3 (1990): 225–239.

15. Baruch Fischhoff and John Kadvany, *Risk: A Very Short Introduction* (New York: Oxford University Press, 2011), p. 90.

16. Kenneth J. Doka, Eric C. Schwartz, and Catherine Schwarz, "Risky Business: Observations on the Nature of Death in Hazardous Sports," *Omega: Journal of Death and Dying* 21, no. 3 (1990): 215–223.

17. *Highlighting Japan* (March 2013), p. 6.

18. National Police Agency of Japan. http://www.npa.go.jp/archive/keibi/biki/higaijokyo_e.pdf.

19. Lucille Craft, "Japan's Nuclear Refugees," *National Geographic* (December 2011): 92–111

20. "Hot Spots and Blind Spots," *The Economist* (December 8, 2011), p. 54. See also Evan Osnos, "The Fallout," *The New Yorker* (October 17, 2011), pp. 46–61.

21. Compiled from Edward Wong, "China Begins Burying Its Unknown Quake Victims," *International Herald Tribune*, February 12, 2009; and Brian Hennessy, "Earthquake in Sichuan, China: The Aftermath," *On Line Opinion*, http://www.onlineopinion.com.au/view.asp?article=8437.

22. Compiled from Australian news reports provided by Rose Cooper, who provides grief support services in Ocean Grove, Australia.

23. Carl Lindahl, "Legends of Hurricane Katrina: The Right to Be Wrong, Survivor-to-Survivor Storytelling, and Healing," *Journal of American Folklore* 125 (2012): 139–176; esp. p. 171.

24. William Greider, Introduction: "Who Will Protect the Working Girl," in *The Triangle Fire*, by Leon Stein, v–xvi (Ithaca, N.Y.: Cornell University Press, 2001).

25. Charles Perrow, *Normal Accidents: Living with High-Risk Technology* (New York: Basic Books, 1984).

26. Malcolm Gladwell, "Blowup," *The New Yorker*, January 22, 1996, pp. 32–36.

27. John Maurice, "Mitigating Disasters—A Promising Start," *The Lancet* 381, issue 9878 (May 11, 2913): 1611–1613.

28. Robert I. Tilling, U.S. Geological Survey, *Eruptions of Mount St. Helens: Past, Present, and Future* (Washington, D.C.: Government Printing Office, n.d.).

29. Philip Sarre, "Natural Hazards," in *Key Ideas in Human Thought*, ed. Kenneth McLeish, 502–504 (New York: Facts on File, 1993).

30. U.S. Senate, Committee on Homeland Security and Governmental Affairs, *Hurricane Katrina: A Nation Still Unprepared* (Washington, D.C.: Government Printing Office, 2006), p. 21. See also Christopher Cooper and Robert Block, *Disaster: Hurricane Katrina and the Failure of Homeland Security* (New York: Times Books, 2006).

31. U.S. Senate, *Hurricane Katrina*, p. 2.

32. Neil Thompson, "The Ontology of Disaster," *Death Studies* 19, no. 5 (1995): 501–510. See also International Work Group on Death, Dying, and Bereavement, "Assumptions and Principles about Psychosocial Aspects of Disasters," *Death Studies* 26, no. 6 (2002): 449–462.

33. Jennifer L. Matheson, "Assessment and Intervention in the Family and Larger Systems," in *Handbook of Thanatology*, 2nd ed., ed. David K. Meagher and David E. Balk, 245–254 (New York: Routledge, 2013), p. 251.

34. Mark Creamer, Director of Australian Center for Posttraumatic Mental Health, "An Initial Focus on the Trauma May Damage the Recovery Process," *The Age*, http://www.theage.com.au/federal-politics/counselling-must-hit-the-right-targets-20090209-8287.html.

35. Pan American Health Organization, *Management of Dead Bodies in Disaster Situations* (Washington, D.C.: PAHO, 2004), p. xi.

36. Fran H. Norris, Matthew J. Friedman, and Patricia J. Watson, "60,000 Disaster Victims Speak, Parts I and II," *Psychiatry* 65, no. 3 (2002): 207–260.

37. Pan American Health Organization, *Management of Dead Bodies in Disaster Situations;* see also Oliver Morgan, ed., *Management of Dead Bodies After Disasters: A Field Manual for First Responders* (Washington, D.C.: PAHO, 2006).

38. Bruce Jennings, "Disaster Planning and Public Health," *The Hastings Center Bioethics Briefing Book*, 41–44 (Garrison, N.Y.: The Hastings Center, 2009).

39. David K. Meagher, "Ethical and Legal Issues in Traumatic Death," in *Handbook of Thanatology*, 2nd ed., ed. Meagher and Balk, 311–320; p. 315.

40. Beverly McLeod, "In the Wake of Disaster," *Psychology Today*, October 1984, pp. 54–57.

41. "Murder Victims—Circumstances and Weapons Used or Cause of Death," *Statistical Abstract of the United States: 2012*, 131st ed. (Washington, D.C., 2011). http://www.census.gov/compendia/statab/.

42. "'Vietnam Style' Triage Techniques Used to Treat Urban Assault Weapon Injuries," *Bulletin of the Park Ridge Center* (May 1989): 11–12.

43. See Ronald K. Barrett, "Urban Adolescent Homicidal Violence: An Emerging Public Health Concern," *Urban League Review* 16, no. 2 (1993): 67–75.

44. American Medical Association, Council on Scientific Affairs, "Firearms Injuries and Deaths: A Critical Public Health Issue," *Public Health Reports* 104 (1989): 111–120. See also Leland Ropp and others, "Death in the City: An American Childhood Tragedy," *Journal of the American Medical Association* 267, no. 21 (1992): 2905–2910.

45. Ice-T, "The Killing Fields," in *The Path Ahead: Readings in Death and Dying,* ed. Lynne Ann DeSpelder and Albert Lee Strickland, 178–181 (Mountain View, Calif.: Mayfield, 1995).

46. Mitch Albom, "Random Shooting Paralyzes Football Player," *Detroit Free Press,* December 28, 1994, p. C1.

47. Bruce L. Danto, Mark L. Taff, and Lauren R. Boglioli, "Graveside Deaths," *Omega: Journal of Death and Dying* 33, no. 4 (1996): 265–278.

48. Quoted in Drew Leder, "Guns and Voices," *Second Opinion* 20, no. 2 (1994): 83–89.

49. Betsy McAlister Groves and others, "Silent Victims: Children Who Witness Violence," *Journal of the American Medical Association* 269, no. 2 (1993): 262–264.

50. Larry Cohen and Susan Swift, "A Public Health Approach to the Violence Epidemic in the United States," *Environment and Urbanization* 5, no. 2 (1993): 50–66. See also Mary R. Jackman, "Violence in Social Life," *Annual Review of Sociology* 28 (2002): 387–415; and Stephen J. Morewitz, *Death Threats and Violence: New Research and Clinical Perspectives* (New York: Springer, 2008).

51. Dana D. DeHart and John M. Mahoney, "The Serial Murderer's Motivations: An Interdisciplinary Review," *Omega: Journal of Death and Dying* 29, no. 1 (1994): 29–45. See also T. D. Dogra and others, "A Psychological Profile of a Serial Killer: A Case Report," *Omega: Journal of Death and Dying* 65, no. 4 (2012): 299–316.

52. Discussion based on Albert Lee Strickland, "Familicide," in *The A-Z of Death & Dying: Social, Medical, and Cultural Aspects,* ed. Michael John Brennan (Santa Barbara, Calif.: ABC-Clio/Greenwood, 2014). See also George B. Palermo, "Murderous Parents," *International Journal of Offender Therapy and Comparative Criminology* 46, no. 2 (2002): 123–143.

53. Kastenbaum and Aisenberg, *Psychology of Death,* pp. 281–282.

54. Lula M. Redmond, *Surviving When Someone You Love Was Murdered: A Professional's Guide to Group Grief Therapy for Families and Friends of Murder Victims* (Clearwater, Fla.: Psychological Consultation and Education Services, 1989), p. 37.

55. See International Work Group on Death, Dying, and Bereavement, "Breaking the Cycles of Violence," *Death Studies* 29, no. 7 (2005): 585–600; and "Armed Conflict: A Model for Understanding and Intervention," *Death Studies* 37, no. 1 (2013): 61–88.

56. Robert J. Sampson, Stephen W. Raudenbush, and Felton Earls, "Neighborhoods and Violent Crime: A Multilevel Study of Collective Efficacy," *Science* 277 (August 15, 1997): 918–923.

57. Cohen and Swift, "A Public Health Approach to the Violence Epidemic in the United States."

58. Arnold Toynbee, "Death in War," in *Death and Dying: Challenge and Change,* ed. Robert Fulton and others (Reading, Mass.: Addison-Wesley, 1978), p. 367.

59. James Lachlan Macleod, "'Greater Love Hath No Man Than This': Scotland's Conflicting Religious Reponses to Death in the Great War," *Scottish Historical Review* 81, no. 211 (April 2002): 70–96; quote p. 70.

60. Dalton Trumbo, *Johnny Got His Gun* (New York: Bantam Books, 1970), pp. 214, 224.

61. United Nations Population Fund, "Overview of Adolescent Life," *State of World Population 2003,* http://www.unfpa.org/swp/2003/english/ch1/index.htm.

62. Sam Keen, *Faces of the Enemy: Reflections of the Hostile Imagination* (San Francisco: Harper & Row, 1986), p. 71.

63. Gil Elliot, "Agents of Death," in *Death: Current Perspectives,* 3rd ed., ed. Edwin S. Shneidman (Mountain View, Calif.: Mayfield, 1984), pp. 422–440.

64. Gus Martin, *Understanding Terrorism: Challenges, Perspectives, and Issues,* 3rd ed. (Thousand Oaks, Calif.: Sage, 2010), p. 31.

65. Andrea Fontana and Jennifer Reid Keene, *Death and Dying in America* (Malden, Mass.: Polity, 2009), p. 131.

66. Elliot, "Agents of Death," pp. 422–440.

67. Quoted in Shono Naomi, "Mute Reminders of Hiroshima's Atomic Bombing," *Japan Quarterly* (July–September 1993): 267–272. See also Robert Jay Lifton, "Psychological Effects of the Atomic Bomb in Hiroshima: The Theme of Death," in *The Threat of Impending Disaster: Contributions to the Psychology of Stress,* ed. George H. Grosser, Henry Wechsler, and Milton Greenblatt (Cambridge, Mass.: MIT Press, 1964), pp. 152–193.

68. Robert Jay Lifton and Eric Olson, *Living and Dying* (New York: Praeger, 1974), p. 32.

69. Ward Wilson, *Five Myths about Nuclear Weapons* (Boston: Houghton Mifflin, 2013), p. 32.

70. Gail Holst-Warhaft, *The Cue for Passion: Grief and Its Political Uses* (Cambridge, Mass.: Harvard University Press, 2000), p. 174.

71. World Campaign for the Protection of Victims of War, International Red Cross and Red Crescent Movement. See also James Garbarino, "Challenges We Face in Understanding Children and War: A Personal Essay," in *The Path Ahead,* ed. DeSpelder and Strickland, pp. 169–174.

72. Glenn M. Vernon, *Sociology of Death: An Analysis of Death-Related Behavior* (New York: Ronald Press, 1970), p. 46.

73. Toynbee, "Death in War," p. 367.

74. Anthony Swofford, *Jarhead: A Marine's Chronicle of the Gulf War and Other Battles* (New York: Scribner, 2003), p. 7.

75. Joel Baruch, "Combat Death," in *Death: Current Perspectives,* ed. Shneidman, pp. 92–93. Reprinted from *Suicide and Life-Threatening Behavior* 2, no. 3 (1972): 209–216.

76. Interview with military veteran, n.d.

77. Quoted in Trish Wood, *What Was Asked of Us: An Oral History of the Iraq War by the Soldiers Who Fought It* (New York: Little, Brown, 2006), p. 127.

78. See Robert Jay Lifton, *Home from the War: Vietnam Veterans, Neither Victims Nor Executioners* (New York: Basic Books, 1985); and Harvey J. Schwartz, "Fear of the Dead: The Role of Social Ritual in Neutralizing Fantasies from Combat," in *Psychotherapy of the Combat Veteran,* ed. H. J. Schwartz (New York: SP Medical & Scientific Books, 1984), pp. 253–267.

79. See Harold A. Widdison and Howard G. Salisbury, "The Delayed Stress Syndrome: A Pathological Delayed Grief Reaction?" *Omega: Journal of Death and Dying* 20, no. 4 (1989–1990): 293–306.

80. Quoted in Michael Browning, "Homer's 'Iliad' Has Lessons for Vietnam Nightmare," *Honolulu Advertiser,* February 12, 1995, pp. B1, B4. See also Jonathan Shay, *Achilles in Vietnam: Combat Trauma and the Undoing of Character* (New York: Atheneum, 1994).

81. Paul Recer, "A Different Johnny," Associated Press wire story, March 3, 1991.

82. Timothy Kudo, "What War Does to Soldiers," *The Week* (February 8, 2013); from a story originally published in *The Washington Post.*

83. "A Tough Homecoming," *The Week* (January 27, 2012), p. 11.

84. Gene Johnson, "Report Details Flaws in Army's Handling of PTSD," http://www.armytimes.com/article/20130308/BENEFITS05/303080301/Report-details-flaws-in-Army-s-handling-of-PTSD.

85. Jessie L. Bonner, "Iraq Veterans Use Fly Fishing as Therapy, Finding Comfort on the Water," *AP News,* October 18, 2009.

86. "A Tough Homecoming," p. 11.

87. Marian Faye Novak, *Lonely Girls with Burning Eyes: A Wife Recalls Her Husband's Journey Home from Vietnam* (Boston: Little, Brown, 1991), p. 3.

88. Lee Woodruff and Bob Woodruff, *In an Instant: A Family's Journey of Love and Healing* (New York: Random House, 2007), p. 140.

89. From an account by Barbara Carton, Washington Park Service, in the *Honolulu Star-Bulletin & Advertiser,* August 11, 1985.

90. Wilton S. Dillon, "Reflections on Coping: Then, Now, and Tomorrow," *Cosmos Journal* (Washington, D.C.: The Cosmos Club, 2001).

91. John Horgan, *The End of War* (San Francisco: McSweeney's, 2012), p. 102.

92. Keen, *Faces of the Enemy,* pp. 10–14.

93. Dennis Klass, "Grief, Religion, and Spirituality," in *Death and Religion in a Changing World,* 283–304, edited by Kathleen Garces-Foley (Armonk, N.Y.: M. E. Sharpe, 2006), p. 301, slightly edited.

94. Debra Umberson and Kristin Henderson, "The Social Construction of Death in the Gulf War," *Omega: Journal of Death and Dying* 25, no. 1 (1992): 1–15.

95. Keen, *Faces of the Enemy,* pp. 180–181.

96. Horgan, *The End of War,* p. 165.

97. Keen, *Faces of the Enemy,* p. 137.

98. Ervin Staub, *The Roots of Evil: The Origins of Genocide and Other Group Violence* (New York: Cambridge University Press, 1989). See also, by Staub, "Genocide and Mass Killing: Origins, Prevention, Healing, and Reconciliation," *Political Psychology* 21 (2000): 367–382.

99. Robert Kastenbaum, "Grieving in Contemporary Society," in *Handbook of Bereavement Research and Practice: Advances in Theory and Intervention,* ed. Margaret S. Stroebe, Robert O. Hansson, Henk Schut, and Wolfgang Stroebe, 67–85 (Washington, D.C.: American Psychological Association, 2008), p. 79.

100. Paul Rosenblatt, "Grief Across Cultures: A Review and Research Agenda," in *Handbook of Bereavement Research and Practice,* ed. Stroebe and others, 207–222; quote p. 214. See also, in the same volume, Colin Murray Parkes, "Bereavement Following Disasters," pp. 463–484.

101. Colin Murray Parkes, "Genocide in Rwanda: Personal Reflections," *Mortality* 1, no. 1 (1996): 95–110.

102. Anonymous epigraph in Aref M. Al-Kattar, *Religion and Terrorism: An Interfaith Perspective* (Westport, Conn.: Praeger, 2003), p. 3.

103. See Philip Jenkins, *Images of Terror: What We Can and Can't Know About Terrorism* (New York: Aldine de Gruyter, 2003), p. 28; and Walter Laqueur, *No End to War: Terrorism in the Twenty-First Century* (New York: Continuum, 2003), p. 233.

104. See, for example, Caleb Carr, *The Lessons of Terror: A History of Warfare Against Civilians, Why It Has Always Failed and Why It Will Fail Again* (New York: Random House, 2002), pp. 7, 9, 12–14.

105. *Merriam-Webster's Collegiate Dictionary,* 11th ed. (Springfield, Mass.: Merriam-Webster, 2003), p. 1049.

106. Walter Laqueur, *The Age of Terrorism* (Boston: Little, Brown, 1987), p. 72.

107. Cindy C. Combs and Martin Slann, *Encyclopedia of Terrorism* (New York: Facts on File, 2002), pp. 208–211.

108. Joseph S. Tuman, *Communicating Terror: The Rhetorical Dimensions of Terrorism,* 2nd ed. (Thousand Oaks, Calif.: Sage, 210), p. xiii.

109. Tom Pyszczynski, Sheldon Solomon, and Jeff Greenberg, *In the Wake of 9/11: The Psychology of Terror* (Washington, D.C.: American Psychological Association, 2003), pp. 8, 16, 127.

110. On September 17, 1862, in the Battle of Antietam, 6,000 were killed outright or mortally wounded, and another 16,000 were wounded and survived. At least 620,000 died during the course of the Civil War. See James M. McPherson, "The Lesson of Antietam," *The American Scholar* 71, no. 1 (2002): 64–65.

111. Harold Dow, quoted in Cathy Trost and Alicia C. Shepard, *Running Toward Danger: Stories Behind the Breaking News of 9/11* (Lanham, Md.: Rowman & Littlefield, 2002), p. 247.

112. David Friend, *Watching the World Change: The Stories Behind the Images of 9/11* (New York: Farrar, Straus & Giroux, 2006), p. 32.

113. Nilüfer Göle, "Close Encounters, Islam, Modernity, and Violence," in *Understanding September 11,* ed. Craig Calhoun, Paul Price, and Ashley Timmer (New York: New Press, 2002), pp. 332–344. See also CBS News, *What We Saw: The Events of September 11 in Words, Pictures, and Video* (New York: Simon & Schuster, 2002).

114. Richard Bernstein and Staff of The New York Times, *Out of the Blue: The Story of September 11, 2001, From Jihad to Ground Zero* (New York: Times Books, 2002), p. 3. See also Brian Doyle, "Leap," *The American Scholar* 71, no. 1 (2002): 69–70.

115. Friend, *Watching the World Change,* p. 35.

116. William Langewiesche, *American Ground: Unbuilding the World Trade Center* (New York: North Point, 2002), p. 45.

117. Lynne Ann DeSpelder, "September 11, 2001, and the Internet," *Mortality* 8, no. 1 (2003): 88–89.

118. Craig Calhoun, Paul Price, and Ashley Timmer, "Introduction," in Calhoun, Price, and Timmer, *Understanding September 11,* p. 4. See also Shashi Tharoor, "The Global Century," *The American Scholar* 71, no. 1 (2002): 66–68.

119. See Marita Sturken, "Memorializing Absence," in Calhoun, Price, and Timmer, *Understanding September 11,* pp. 374–384, esp. 378–381.

120. Langewiesche, *American Ground,* p. 99.

121. Loolwa Khazzoom, "For ZAKA Rescue Volunteers, Grisly Deaths Are a Part of Life." loolwa.com/for-zaka-rescue-volunteers-grisly-deaths-are-a-part-of-life/.

122. Michael Schudson, "What's Unusual About Covering Politics as Usual," in *Journalism After September 11,* ed. Barbie Zelizer and Stuart Allan (New York: Routledge, 2002), pp. 38–39; see also introduction by Zelizer and Allan, pp. 8–9.

123. Philip Jenkins, *Images of Terror: What We Can and Can't Know About Terrorism* (New York: Aldine de Gruyter, 2003), pp. 82–83.

124. Combs and Slann, *Encyclopedia of Terrorism,* p. 166.

125. Bruce D. Berkowitz, *The New Face of War: How War Will Be Fought in the 21st Century* (New York: Free Press, 2003), pp. 16–17; see also Philip Bobbitt, *The Shield of Achilles: War, Peace, and the Course of History* (New York: Knopf, 2002), pp. 811, 821.

126. G. W. Bowersock, *Martyrdom and Rome* (Cambridge: Cambridge University Press, 1995), pp. 17–18, 25, 59, 61.

127. Mark Juergensmeyer, "Religious Terror and Global War," in *Understanding September 11,* ed. Calhoun, Price, and Timmer, pp. 27–49; quote p. 29. See also Kelton Cobb, "Violent Faith," in *11 September: Religious Perspectives on the Causes and Consequences,* ed. Ian Markham and Ibrahim M. Abu-Rabi (Oxford: OneWorld, 2002), pp. 136–163; and Bruce Lincoln, *Holy Terrors: Thinking About Religion After September 11* (Chicago: University of Chicago Press, 2003).

128. Laqueur, *No End to War,* pp. 71, 91.

129. Aaron T. Beck, "Prisoners of Hate," *Behaviour Research and Therapy* 40, no. 3 (2002): 209–216, and *Prisoners of Hate: The Cognitive Basis of Anger, Hostility, and Violence* (New York: HarperCollins, 1999).

130. Tharoor, "Global Century," p. 68.

131. Daniel Leviton, "Horrendous Death: Improving the Quality of Global Health," in *The Path Ahead,* ed. DeSpelder and Strickland, pp. 165–168; see also, edited by Leviton, *Horrendous Death, Health, and Well-Being* (New York: Hemisphere, 1991), and *Horrendous Death and Health: Toward Action* (New York: Taylor and Francis, 1991). See also Richard A. Pacholski, "Teaching Nuclear Holocaust, the Basic Thanatological Topic," *Death Studies* 13, no. 2 (1989): 175–183.

132. Daniel Leviton and William Wendt, "Death Education: Toward Individual and Global Well-Being," *Death Education* 7, no. 4 (1983): 369–384; quote p. 301.

133. Daniel Leviton, "Horrendous Death," in *Death and the Quest for Meaning: Essays in Honor of Herman Feifel,* ed. Stephen Strack (Northvale, N.J.: Jason Aronson, 1997), pp. 301–327; quote p. 303.

134. Leviton, "Horrendous Death," p. 309.

135. Stephen M. Younger, *The Bomb: A New History* (New York: HarperCollins, 2009), p. 10.

136. J. Travis, "New Drugs Beat Old Flu," *Science News* 162 (September 28, 2002): 196.

137. Travis, "New Drugs Beat Old Flu." See also Monica Schoch-Spana, "'Hospital's Full-Up': The 1918 Influenza Pandemic," *Public Health Reports* 116 (2001): 32–33.

138. UN World Health Organization, Global Alert and Response (GAR); http://www.who.int/csr/en/.

139. Joint United Nations Programme on HIV/AIDS (UNAIDS); www.unaids.org/en/dataanalysis/datatools/aidsinfo/.

140. See Mary Catherine Bateson and Richard Goldsby, *Thinking AIDS: The Social Response to the Biological Threat* (Reading, Mass.: Addison-Wesley, 1988); Douglas Crimp, ed., *AIDS: Cultural Analysis, Cultural Activism* (Cambridge, Mass.: MIT Press, 1988); Albert R. Jonsen and Jeff Stryker, eds., *The Social Impact of AIDS* (Washington, D.C.: National Academy Press, 1993); Eve K. Nichols, *Mobilizing Against AIDS,* rev. ed. (Cambridge, Mass.: Harvard University Press, 1989); and Randy Shilts, *And the Band Played On: Politics, People, and the AIDS Epidemic* (New York: Viking Penguin, 1988).

141. Charles E. Rosenberg, "What Is an Epidemic? AIDS in Historical Perspective," in *The Path Ahead,* ed. DeSpelder and Strickland, pp. 29–32.

142. Robert Kastenbaum, "Reconstructing Death in Postmodern Society," in *The Path Ahead,* ed. DeSpelder and Strickland, pp. 7–18.

143. Mitchell Duneier, *Slim's Table: Race, Respectability, and Masculinity* (Chicago: University of Chicago Press, 1992), p. 75.

144. Margaret A. Chesney, "Health Psychology in the 21st Century: Acquired Immunodeficiency Syndrome as a Harbinger of Things to Come," *Health Psychology* 12, no. 4 (1993): 259–268.

145. See Laurie Garrett, *The Coming Plague: Newly Emerging Diseases in a World Out of Balance* (New York: Farrar, Straus & Giroux, 1994). See also Robert Berkow, ed., *The Merck Manual of Diagnosis and Therapy,* 16th ed. (Rahway, N.J.: Merck Research Laboratories, 1992), pp. 211–220.

146. Bernard Le Guenno, "Emerging Viruses," *Scientific American* (October 1995): 56–64.

147. See Gunjan Sinha and Burkhard Bilger, "Skeletons in the Attic: Has the Scourge of Athens Returned to Haunt Us?" *The Sciences* 36, no. 5 (September–October 1996): 11; and Matt Crenson, "Researcher: Plague Sparked Ebola," *Associated Press Online* (January 20, 1997).

148. Brian Vastag, "Virtual Worlds, Real Science: Epidemiologists, Social Scientists Flock to the Online World," *Science News* 172, no. 17 (October 27, 2007): 264–265.

149. Rodrick Wallace and Deborah Wallace, "Inner-City Disease and the Public Health of the Suburbs: The Sociogeographical Dispersion of Point-Source Infection," *Environment and Planning Abstracts* 25 (1993): 1707–1723; and "The Coming Crisis of Public Health in the Suburbs," *Milbank Quarterly* 71, no. 4 (1993): 543–564. See also Rodrick Wallace and others, "Will AIDS Be Contained Within U.S. Minority Urban Populations?" *Social Science & Medicine* 39, no. 8 (1994): 1051–1062.

150. Rodrick Wallace and John Pittman, "Recurrence of Contagious Urban Desertification and the Social Thanatology of New York City," *Environment and Planning Abstracts* 24 (June 1992): 1–6.

151. Wallace and Pittmann, "Recurrence of Contagious Urban Desertification," p. 1.

152. Richard Rothenberg, "Chronicle of an Epidemic Foretold: A Response to the Wallaces," *Milbank Quarterly* 71, no. 4 (1993): 565–574.

153. Paul Recer, "Origin of 1918 Flu Pandemic Found," *Associated Press Online* (March 20, 1997).

154. William R. Clark, *Sex and the Origins of Death* (New York: Oxford University Press, 1996), p. 177.

155. Jeffrey Kauffman, "Culture, Socialization, and Traumatic Death," in *Handbook of Thanatology,* 2nd ed., ed. Meagher and Balk, 275–284; quote p. 275. See also Jeffrey Kauffman, *Loss of the Assumptive World: A Theory of Traumatic Loss* (New York: Routledge, 2002).

156. Lillian M. Range, "Historical and Contemporary Perspectives on Traumatic Death," in *Handbook of Thanatology,* 2nd ed., ed. Meagher and Balk, 291–296; p. 291.

157. Range, "Historical and Contemporary Perspectives on Traumatic Death," p. 273.

CHAPTER 14

1. This account is based on "Coffins and Sarcophagi," exhibition note, Metropolitan Museum of Art, New York; Henri Frankfort, *Ancient Egyptian Religion: An Interpretation* (New York: Harper & Row, 1948, 1961); Manfred Lurker, *The Gods and Symbols of Ancient Egypt* (New York: Thames & Hudson, 1980); A. J. Spencer, *Death in Ancient Egypt* (New York: Penguin, 1982); and Barbara Watterson, *The Gods of Ancient Egypt* (New York: Facts on File, 1984).

2. Quoted in Jeffery L. Sheler, "Heaven in the Age of Reason," *U.S. News & World Report* 122, no. 12 (1997): 65–66; italics added.

3. Interview with Mikal Gilmore, *Rolling Stone* (December 22, 2001).

4. Bertrand Russell, *Unpopular Essays* (New York: Simon & Schuster, 1950), p. 141.

5. See "The Problem of Immortality," in Jacques Choron, *Death and Modern Man* (New York: Collier, 1964).

6. Geddes MacGregor, *Images of Afterlife: Beliefs from Antiquity to Modern Times* (New York: Paragon House, 1992), p. 209.

7. Mary Kawena Pukui, E. W. Haertig, and Catherine A. Lee, *Nana I Ke Kumu (Look to the Source),* vols. 1 and 2 (Honolulu: Hui Hanai; Queen Lili'uokalani Children's Center, 1972). See also E. S. Craighill Handy and Mary Kawena Pukui, *The Polynesian Family System in Ka-'u, Hawai'i* (Rutland, Vt.: Charles E. Tuttle, 1972).

8. Ray S. Anderson, *Theology, Death and Dying* (New York: Basil Blackwell, 1986), p. 38.

9. Ellen Levine, "Jewish Views and Customs on Death," in *Death and Bereavement Across Cultures,* ed. Colin Murray Parkes, Pitti Laungani, and Bill Young (New York: Routledge, 1997), pp. 98–130.

10. Job 7:9, *The Jerusalem Bible.* See also Job 14:7–12.

11. Daniel 12:2, *The Jerusalem Bible.*

12. Stephen J. Vicchio, "Against Raising Hope of Raising the Dead: Contra Moody and Kübler-Ross," *Essence: Issues in the Study of Ageing, Dying and Death* 3, no. 2 (1979): 63.

13. See Lou H. Silberman in "Death in the Hebrew Bible and Apocalyptic Literature," in *Perspectives on Death,* ed. L. O. Mills (Nashville: Abingdon Press, 1969), pp. 13–32. The "Samuel" story is told in the first book of Samuel (28:3–25).

14. H. Wheeler Robinson, "Hebrew Psychology," in *The People and the Book,* ed. Arthur S. Peake (London: Oxford University Press, 1925), pp. 353–382.

15. See, for example, Leon Wieseltier, *Kaddish* (New York: Knopf, 1998).

16. Earl A. Grollman, "The Ritualistic and Theological Approach of the Jew," in *Explaining Death to Children,* ed. Grollman (Boston: Beacon Press, 1967), pp. 223–245; and Jonathan Boyarin, "Death and the *Minyan,*" *Cultural Anthropology* 9, no. 1 (1994): 3–22.

17. See Jasper Griffin, *Homer on Life and Death* (Oxford: Clarendon Press, 1980).

18. See C. Fred Alford, "Greek Tragedy and the Place of Death in Life: A Psychoanalytic Perspective," *Psychoanalysis and Contemporary Thought* 15, no. 2 (1992): 129–159.

19. Carol Zaleski, "In Defense of Immortality," *First Things* (August–September 2000): 36–42; quote p. 40.

20. Oscar Cullman, *Immortality of the Soul or Resurrection of the Dead? The Witness of the New Testament* (London: Epworth Press, 1958), pp. 26–27.

21. Cullman, *Immortality of the Soul or Resurrection of the Dead?,* p. 27.

22. Boniface Ramsey, *Beginning to Read the Fathers* (New York: Paulist Press, 1985), p. 218.

23. William Barclay, *Introducing the Bible* (Nashville: Abingdon Press, 1972), p. 123.

24. Anderson, *Theology, Death and Dying,* p. 59. See also Murray J. Harris, *Raised Immortal: Resurrection and Immortality in the New Testament* (Grand Rapids, Mich.: Eerdmans, 1985).

25. John D. Zizioulas, "The Early Christian Community," in *Christian Spirituality: Origins to the Twelfth Century,* ed. Bernard McGinn and John Meyendorff, 23–43 (New York: Crossroad, 1992), p. 31.

26. Milton McC. Gatch, *Death: Meaning and Mortality in Christian Thought and Contemporary Culture* (New York: Seabury Press, 1969), p. 78.

27. Richard P. McBrien, *The HarperCollins Encyclopedia of Catholicism* (San Francisco: HarperCollins, 1995),

p. 1070. See also Alan E. Bernstein, *The Formation of Hell: Death and Retribution in the Ancient and Early Christian Worlds* (Ithaca, N.Y.: Cornell University Press, 1993); Stephen Greenblatt, *Hamlet in Purgatory* (Princeton, N.J.: Princeton University Press, 2001); and Jacques Le Goff, *The Birth of Purgatory* (Chicago: University of Chicago Press, 1984).

28. Purgatory is not to be confused with *limbo,* "a place or state where unbaptized persons enjoy a natural happiness, though they remain excluded from the Beatific Vision." See McBrien, *The HarperCollins Encyclopedia of Catholicism,* p. 771.

29. Jerry L. Walls, *Purgatory: The Logic of Total Transformation* (New York: Oxford University Press, 2012), p. 25.

30. Jacques Le Goff, *The Birth of Purgatory,* trans. Arthur Goldhammer (Chicago: The University of Chicago Press, 1984), p. 58.

31. Anthony C. Thiselton, *The Last Things: A New Approach* (London: SPCK, 2012), p. 1.

32. Zaleski, "In Defense of Immortality," quote p. 41. See also Alister E. McGrath, "Last Things: The Christian Hope" (Chapter 18), in *Christian Theology: An Introduction,* 3rd ed. (Malden, Mass.: Blackwell, 2001), pp. 553–577.

33. Vicchio, "Against Raising Hope," p. 62. See also Gordon E. Geddes, *Welcome Joy: Death in Puritan New England* (Ann Arbor, Mich.: UMI Research Press, 1981); and David E. Stannard, *The Puritan Way of Death: A Study of Religion, Culture, and Social Change* (New York: Oxford University Press, 1977).

34. Constantine Callinicos, *Beyond the Grave: An Orthodox Theology of Eschatology,* trans. George Dimopoulos and Leslie Jerome Newville (Scranton, Penn.: Christian Orthodox Editions, 1969), p. 158. See also Stanley Samuel Harakas, *Health and Medicine in the Eastern Orthodox Tradition: Faith, Liturgy, and Wholeness* (New York: Crossroad, 1990), esp. pp. 151–159.

35. Peter C. Phan, *Responses to 101 Questions on Death and Eternal Life* (New York: Paulist Press, 1997), pp. 18, 129. See also Douglas Connelly, *Bible Prophecy for Blockheads: A User-Friendly Look at the End Times* (Grand Rapids, Mich.: Zondervan, 2002), pp. 164–166; and Regis Martin, *The Last Things: Death, Judgment, Heaven, Hell* (San Francisco: Ignatius, 1998), p. 118.

36. John L. Esposito, *Islam: The Straight Path* (New York: Oxford University Press, 1988), p. 22.

37. Frithjof Schuon, *Understanding Islam* (Baltimore: Penguin, 1972), p. 16.

38. Alfred T. Welch, "Death and Dying in the Qur'an," in *Religious Encounters with Death: Insights from the History and Anthropology of Religions,* ed. Frank E. Reynolds and Earle H. Waugh (University Park: Pennsylvania State University Press, 1977), p. 184. See also Shahzad Bashir, "Deciphering the Cosmos from Creation to Apocalypse: The Hurufiyya Movement and Medieval Islamic Esotericism," in *Imagining the End: Visions of Apocalypse from the Ancient Middle East to Modern America,* ed. Abbas Amanat and Magnus Bernhardsson (London: I. B. Tauris, 2002), pp. 168–184; and "Enshrining Divinity: The Death and Memorialization of Fazlallah Astarabadi in Hurufi Thought," *Muslim World* 90, nos. 3–4 (2000): 289–308.

39. Huston Smith, *The Religions of Man* (New York: New American Library, 1958), p. 215.

40. See J. I. Smith and Y. Haddad, *The Islamic Understanding of Death and Resurrection* (Albany: State University of New York Press, 1981).

41. Esposito, *Islam: The Straight Path,* p. 35.

42. Welch, "Death and Dying in the Qur'an," p. 193.

43. D. S. Roberts, *Islam: A Concise Introduction* (San Francisco: Harper and Row, 1981), p. 128.

44. Roberts, *Islam,* p. 128. See also Suzanne Evans, "The Scent of a Martyr," *Numen: International Review for the History of Religions* 49, no. 2 (2002): 193–211.

45. Abdul Latif Al Hoa, *Islam* (New York: Bookwright Press, 1987), p. 20.

46. Hend Yasien-Esmael and Simon Shimson Rubin, "The Meaning Structures of Muslim Bereavements in Israel: Religious Traditions, Mourning Practices, and Human Experience," *Death Studies* 29 (2005): 495–518.

47. Chuang Tzu, *Basic Writings,* trans. Burton Watson (New York: Columbia University Press, 1964), p. 76.

48. Mario Poceski, *Introducing Chinese Religions* (New York: Routledge, 2009), p. 76.

49. T. N. Madan, "Dying with Dignity," *Social Science & Medicine* 35, no. 4 (1992): 425–432.

50. *Bhagavad-Gita* II.27, trans. Swami Nikhilananda (New York: Ramakrishna-Vivekananda Center, 1952), p. 79.

51. Smith, *Religions of Man,* p. 34.

52. E. M. Jackson, "Moksha," in *Key Ideas in Human Thought,* ed. Kenneth McLeish (New York: Facts on File, 1993), pp. 482–483.

53. *Bhagavad-Gita* II.22, trans. Nikhilananda, p. 77.

54. J. Bruce Long, "Death as a Necessity and a Gift in Hindu Mythology," in *Religious Encounters with Death,* ed. Reynolds and Waugh, p. 92; see also pp. 73–96.

55. David R. Kinsley in "The 'Death That Conquers Death': Dying to the World in Medieval Hinduism," in *Religious Encounters with Death,* ed. Reynolds and Waugh, pp. 97–108. See also Pittu Laungani, "Death in a Hindu Family," in *Death and Bereavement Across Cultures,* pp. 52–72.

56. Philip Kapleau, *Zen: Dawn in the West* (Garden City, N.Y.: Anchor Press/Doubleday, 1979), p. 296. See also, ed. Kapleau, *The Wheel of Death: A Collection of Writings from Zen Buddhist and Other Sources on Death-Rebirth-Dying* (New York: Harper and Row, 1971), and *The Wheel of Life and Death: A Practical and Spiritual Guide* (New York: Doubleday, 1989).

57. "Awakening to the Bodhi-Mind (Hotsu Bodaishin)," from the Shobo-Genzo, in *Zen Master Dogen,* trans. Yuho Yokoi, p. 109.

58. Kapleau, *Zen: Dawn in the West,* pp. 67–68.

59. Carl B. Becker, *Breaking the Circle: Death and the Afterlife in Buddhism* (Carbondale: Southern Illinois University Press, 1993), p. 7.

60. Ronald L. Grimes, *Deeply into the Bone: Re-Inventing Rites of Passage* (Berkeley: University of California Press, 2000), p. 225.

61. Grimes, *Deeply into the Bone,* p. 224.

62. "The Meaning of Practice-Enlightenment (Susho-gi)," in *Zen Master Dōgen: An Introduction with Selected Writings,* trans. Yuho Yokoi (New York/Tokyo: Weatherhill, 1976), p. 58.

63. Susan Orpett Long, *Final Days: Japanese Culture and Choice at the End of Life* (Honolulu: University of Hawaii Press, 2005), p. 69.

64. "The Meaning of Practice-Enlightenment (Shusho-gi)," p. 58.

65. *The Zen Master Hakuin: Selected Writings,* trans. Philip B. Yampolsky (New York: Columbia University Press, 1971), p. 219.

66. Long, *Final Days,* p. 69.

67. Jonathan S. Watts, "Introduction," in *Buddhist Care for the Dying and Bereaved,* 1–17, ed. Jonathan S. Watts and Yosiharu Tomatsu (Boston: Wisdom, 2012), pp. 4–5.

68. Kapleau, *Zen: Dawn in the West,* p. 69.

69. For more on Pure Land Buddhism, see "The Afterlife in Pure Land Buddhism," Chapter 3, pp. 46–62, in Becker, *Breaking the Circle: Death and the Afterlife in Buddhism.*

70. George J. Tanabe, Jr., "The Orthodox Heresy of Buddhist Funerals," in *Death and the Afterlife in Japanese Buddhism,* ed. Jacqueline I. Stone and Mariko Namba Walter, 325–348 (Honolulu: University of Hawaii Press, 2008), p. 328.

71. Tanabe, "The Orthodox Heresy of Buddhist Funerals," p. 345.

72. W. Y. Evans-Wentz, *The Tibetan Book of the Dead: or, the After-Death Experiences on the Bardo Plane, According to Lama Kazi Dawa-Samup's English Rendering* (New York: Oxford University Press, 1960).

73. Quoted in Kapleau, *Zen: Dawn in the West,* p. 68.

74. Quoted in William R. Clark, *Sex and the Origins of Death* (New York: Oxford University Press, 1996), p. 159.

75. See Robert E. Goss and Dennis Klass, "Tibetan Buddhism and the Resolution of Grief: The Bardo-Thodol for the Dying and Grieving," *Death Studies* 21 (1997): 377–395.

76. Francesca Fremantle and Chögyam Trungpa, eds., *The Tibetan Book of the Dead: The Great Liberation Through Hearing in the Bardo, by Guru Rinpoche According to Karma Lingpa* (Boulder, Colo.: Shambhala, 1975).

77. Christopher Carr, "Death and Near-Death: A Comparison of Tibetan and Euro-American Experiences," *Journal of Transpersonal Psychology* 25, no. 1 (1993): 59–110. See also Uwe P. Gielen, "A Death on the Roof of the World," in *Death and Bereavement Across Cultures,* pp. 73–97.

78. See Paul Badham and Linda Badham, eds., *Death and Immortality in the Religions of the World* (New York: Paragon House, 1987).

79. Karolynn Siegel, Stanley J. Anderman, and Eric W. Schrimshaw, "Religion and Coping with Health-Related Stress," *Psychology and Health* 16 (2001): 631–653.

80. Lucy Bregman, "The Roles of Religions in the Death Awareness Movement," *The Forum* 32, no. 2 (2006): 4–5, quote p. 4.

81. Vernon Reynolds and Ralph Tanner, *The Social Ecology of Religion* (New York: Oxford University Press, 1995), p. 211.

82. Phil Zuckerman, "The Sociology of Religion of W. E. B. Du Bois," *Sociology of Religion* 63, no. 2 (2002): 239–253.

83. Ruth A. Tanyi, "Towards Clarification of the Meaning of Spirituality," *Journal of Advanced Nursing* 39, no. 5 (2002): 500–509; quote, p. 506.

84. Ralph L. Piedmont, "Does Spirituality Represent the Sixth Factor of Personality? Spiritual Transcendence and the Five-Factor Model," *Journal of Personality* 67, no. 6 (1999): 987–1013; quoted material 988–989.

85. Norman Goodman, *Introduction to Sociology* (New York: HarperCollins, 1992), p. 215.

86. Ira R. Byock, "To Life! Reflections on Spirituality, Palliative Practice, and Politics," *American Journal of Hospice & Palliative Medicine* 23, no. 6 (2007): 436–438; quote, p. 436.

87. Davina A. Allen, "Secularization," in *Key Ideas in Human Thought,* ed. McLeish, p. 668. See also Charles Taylor, *A Secular Age* (Cambridge, Mass.: Harvard University Press, 2007); and James Turner, *Without God, Without Creed: The Origins of Unbelief in America* (Baltimore: Johns Hopkins University Press, 1985).

88. Colin Murray Parkes, "Conclusions II: Attachments and Losses in Cross-Cultural Perspective," in *Death and Bereavement Across Cultures,* pp. 233–243; quote p. 234.

89. E. M. Jackson and Kenneth McLeish, "Humanism," in *Key Ideas in Human Thought,* ed. McLeish, pp. 355–356.

90. Kenneth McLeish, "Existentialism," in *Key Ideas in Human Thought,* ed. McLeish, pp. 265–266; quote p. 265. See also William Barrett, *Irrational Man: A Study in Existential Philosophy* (New York: Doubleday, 1958), and *Death of the Soul: From Descartes to the Computer* (New York: Anchor/Doubleday, 1986).

91. See Robert J. Lifton, *The Future of Immortality and Other Essays for a Nuclear Age* (New York: Basic Books, 1987), and *The Broken Connection: On Death and the Continuity of Life* (New York: Basic Books, 1983; reprint, Washington, D.C.: American Psychiatric Press, 1996).

92. Sheler, "Heaven in the Age of Reason"; see also Jeffery L. Sheler, "Hell's Sober Comeback," *U.S. News & World Report,* March 25, 1991, pp. 56–57; and Daniel J. Klenow and Robert C. Bolin, "Belief in an Afterlife: A National Survey," *Omega: Journal of Death and Dying* 20, no. 1 (1989–1990): 63–74.

93. Andrew M. Greeley and Michael Hout, "Americans' Increasing Belief in Life After Death: Religious Competition and Acculturation," *American Sociological Review* 64, no. 6 (1999): 813–835.

94. David Lester and others, "What Is the Afterlife Like? Undergraduate Beliefs about the Afterlife," *Omega: Journal of Death and Dying* 44, no. 2 (2001–2002): 113–126.

95. Quoted in David Cockburn, "Simone Weil on Death," *Mortality* 2, no. 1 (1997): 63–72.

96. *The Meditations of Marcus Aurelius,* trans. George Long, *The Harvard Classics,* vol. 2, ed. Charles W. Elliot, pp. 193–301; see especially section II, 5 and 11, pp. 201–202.

97. Carol Zaleski, *Otherworld Journeys: Accounts of Near-Death Experience in Medieval and Modern Times* (New York: Oxford University Press, 1987).

98. Paul Badham, "Religious and Near-Death Experience in Relation to Belief in a Future Life," *Mortality* 2, no. 1 (1997): 7–21.

99. Bruce Greyson, "Near-Death Experiences," in *Varieties of Anomalous Experience: Examining the Scientific Evidence,* ed. Etzel Cardeña, Steven Jay Lynn, and Stanley Krippner (Washington, D.C.: American Psychological Association, 2000), pp. 315–352; definition pp. 315–316.

100. Kenneth Ring, *Life at Death: A Scientific Investigation of the Near-Death Experience* (New York: Coward, McCann & Geoghegan, 1980), and *Heading Toward Omega: In Search of the Meaning of the Near-Death Experience* (New York: Morrow, 1984). See also Bruce Greyson, "Varieties of Near-Death Experience," *Psychiatry* 56 (1993): 390–399; and Raymond A. Moody, Jr., *Life After Life,* and its sequel, *Reflections on Life After Life* (various editions).

101. Bruce Greyson, "Reduced Death Threat in Near-Death Experiencers," in *Death Anxiety Handbook: Research, Instrumentation, and Application,* ed. Robert A. Neimeyer (Washington, D.C.: Taylor & Francis, 1994), pp. 169–179, esp. pp. 169, 177.

102. H. J. Irwin, *An Introduction to Parapsychology* (Jefferson, N.C.: McFarland, 1989), pp. 188–190.

103. William J. Serdahely, "The Near-Death Experience: Is the Presence Always the Higher Self?" *Omega: Journal of Death and Dying* 18, no. 2 (1987–1988): 129–134.

104. William J. Serdahely, "A Pediatric Near-Death Experience: Tunnel Variants," *Omega: Journal of Death and Dying* 20, no. 1 (1989–1990): 55–62. See also William J. Serdahely and Barbara A. Walker, "A Near-Death Experience at Birth," *Death Studies* 14, no. 2 (1990): 177–183.

105. See Bruce Greyson and Nancy Evans Bush, "Distressing Near-Death Experiences," *Psychiatry* 55 (February 1992): 95–110; and P. M. H. Atwater, "Is There a Hell? Surprising Observations About the Near-Death Experience," *Journal of Near-Death Studies* 10, no. 3 (Spring 1992): 149–160.

106. Brendan I. Koerner, "Is There Life After Death?" *U.S. News & World Report* 122, no. 12 (1997): 59–64.

107. Ian Stevenson, Emily W. Cook, and Nicholas McClean-Rice, "Are Persons Reporting 'Near-Death Experiences' Really Near Death? A Study of Medical Records," *Omega: Journal of Death and Dying* 20, no. 1 (1989–1990): 45–54.

108. For an introduction to the main points of view, see Stephen J. Vicchio, "Near-Death Experiences: A Critical Review of the Literature and Some Questions for Further Study," *Essence: Issues in the Study of Ageing, Dying and Death* 5, no. 1 (1981): 77–89. See also James E. Alcock, "Psychology and Near-Death Experiences," *The Skeptical Inquirer* 3, no. 3 (Spring 1979): 25–41; Michael B. Sabom, *Recollections of Death: A Medical Investigation* (New York: Harper and Row, 1981); and Stephen J. Vicchio, "Near-Death Experiences: Some Logical Problems and Questions for Further Study," *Anabiosis: The Journal of the International Association for Near-Death Studies* (1981): 66–87. The history of research into NDEs is traced in Stanislav Grof and Joan Halifax, *The Human Encounter with Death* (New York: E. P. Dutton, 1978), Chapter 7, "Consciousness and the Threshold of Death," pp. 131–157.

109. See Handy and Pukui, *The Polynesian Family System in Ka-'u, Hawai'i;* Donald D. Kilolani Mitchell, *Resource Units in Hawaiian Culture* (Honolulu: Kamehameha Schools Press, 1982); and Pukui, Haertig, and Lee, *Nana I Ke Kumu (Look to the Source),* vols. 1 and 2.

110. Pukui, Haertig, and Lee, *Nana I Ke Kumu (Look to the Source),* vol. 1, p. 40.

111. See Roy Kletti and Russell Noyes, Jr., "Mental States in Mortal Danger," which includes a translation of Oskar Pfister's 1930 paper commenting on Heim's observations, in *Essence: Issues in the Study of Ageing, Dying and Death* 5, no. 1 (1981): 5–20.

112. See Russell Noyes, Jr., "Dying and Mystical Consciousness," *Journal of Thanatology* I (1971): 25–41; Russell Noyes, Jr., and Roy Kletti, "Depersonalization in the Face of Life-Threatening Danger: An Interpretation," *Omega: Journal of Death and Dying* 7, no. 2 (1976): 103–114, and "Panoramic Memory: A Response to the Threat of Death," *Omega: Journal of Death and Dying* 8, no. 3 (1977): 181–194; Russell Noyes, Jr., "Near-Death Experiences: Their Interpretation and Significance," in *Between Life and Death,* ed. Robert Kastenbaum (New York: Springer, 1979), pp. 73–78; and Russell Noyes, Jr., "The Encounter with Life-Threatening Danger: Its Nature and Impact," *Essence: Issues in the Study of Ageing, Dying and Death* 5, no. 1 (1981): 21–32.

113. Karlis Osis and Erlendur Haraldsson, "Deathbed Observations of Physicians and Nurses: A Cross-Cultural Survey," in *The Signet Handbook of Parapsychology,* ed. Martin Ebon (New York: Signet/NAL, 1978); and, by Osis and Haraldsson, *At the Hour of Death* (New York: Avon Books, 1977). See also, by Haraldsson, "Survey of Claimed Encounters with the Dead," *Omega: Journal of Death and Dying* 19, no. 2 (1988–1989): 103–113.

114. George Gallup, Jr., *Adventures in Immortality* (New York: McGraw-Hill, 1982). See also Sheler, "Heaven in the Age of Reason"; Greeley and Hout, "Americans' Increasing Belief in Life After Death"; and Klenow and Bolin, "Belief in an Afterlife: A National Survey."

115. Louis Appleby, *British Medical Journal* 298 (April 15, 1989): 976–977. See also Michael Potts, "Sensory Experiences in Near-Death Experiences and the Thomistic View of the Soul," *International Journal for Philosophy of Religion* 49, no. 2 (2001): 85–100.

116. Zaleski, *Otherworld Journeys,* p. 182.

117. Raymond A. Moody, Jr., "An Omega Interview [by Robert Kastenbaum]," *Omega: Journal of Death and Dying* 31, no. 2 (1995): 87–97.

118. From a conversation between Herman Feifel and John Morgan, "Humanity Has to Be the Model," *Death Studies* 10, no. 1 (1986): 1–9.

119. Robert Kastenbaum, "Happily Ever After," in *Between Life and Death,* ed. Kastenbaum, pp. 17, 19. See also Bruce Greyson, "Near-Death Experiences and Deathbed Visions," in *The Study of Dying: From Autonomy to Transformation,* ed. Allan Kellehear, 253–275 (New York: Cambridge University Press, 2009).

120. Charles A. Garfield, "The Dying Patient's Concern with 'Life After Death,'" in *Between Life and Death,* ed. Kastenbaum, pp. 52–57.

121. Kelly Bulkeley and Patricia Bulkley, *Dreaming Beyond Death: A Guide to Pre-Death Dreams and Visions* (Boston: Beacon Press, 2005), p. 12.

122. Marie-Louise von Franz, *On Death and Dreams: A Jungian Interpretation* (Boston: Shambhala, 1986), pp. viii–ix.

123. Franz, *On Death and Dreams,* p. 156.

124. Franz, *On Death and Dreams,* pp. 66–67.

125. Some evidence suggests that LSD may interfere with the transfer of oxygen on the enzymatic level. Anoxia, or diminished levels of oxygen in the bodily tissues, is also found in dying patients as well as in conjunction with certain yogic techniques involving breath control. Thus, anoxia may activate transpersonal matrices in the unconscious, giving rise to experiences associated with near-death experiences, certain yogic states, and LSD sessions. See Grof and Halifax, *The Human Encounter with Death,* pp. 183ff; and Thomas J. Riedlinger and June R. Riedlinger, "Psychedelic and Entactogenic Drugs in the Treatment of Depression," *Journal of Psychoactive Drugs* 26, no. 1 (1994): 41–55.

126. Stanislav Grof, *Realms of the Human Unconscious: Observations from LSD Research* (New York: E. P. Dutton, 1976). See also Robert B. Millman and Ann Bordwine Beeder, "The New Psychedelic Culture: LSD, Ecstasy,

'Rave' Parties, and the Grateful Dead," *Psychiatric Annals* 24, no. 3 (1994): 148–150; and Susanna Prepeliczay, "Socio-Cultural and Psychological Aspects of Contemporary LSD Use in Germany," *Journal of Drug Issues* 32, no. 2 (2002): 431–458.

127. See Stanislav Grof, *LSD Psychotherapy* (Pomona, Calif.: Hunter House, 1980), pp. 252ff; Grof and Halifax, *The Human Encounter with Death,* pp. 16ff; and Peter Stafford, *Psychedelics Encyclopedia* (Berkeley, Calif.: And/Or Press, 1977), pp. 23–39.

128. Grof and Halifax, *The Human Encounter with Death,* pp. 120–121.

129. Stanislav Grof and Christina Grof, *Beyond Death: The Gates of Consciousness* (New York: Thames & Hudson, 1980), p. 24.

130. David M. Wulff, "Mystical Experience," in *Varieties of Anomalous Experience: Examining the Scientific Evidence,* ed. Etzel Cardeña, Steven Jay Lynn, and Stanley Krippner (Washington, D.C.: American Psychological Association, 2000), pp. 397–440.

131. Stanislav Grof and Joan Halifax, "Psychedelics and the Experience of Dying," in *Life After Death,* ed. Arnold Toynbee and others (New York: McGraw-Hill, 1976), pp. 192–193.

132. Grof, *LSD Psychotherapy,* p. 294. See also, by Grof, *Psychology of the Future: Lessons from Modern Consciousness Research* (Albany: State University of New York, 2000).

133. Grimes, *Deeply into the Bone,* p. 237.

134. Herman Feifel, *The Meaning of Death* (New York: McGraw-Hill, 1959), p. xiv.

135. International Work Group on Death, Dying, and Bereavement, "Assumptions and Principles of Spiritual Care," *Death Studies* 14, no. 1 (1990): 75–81.

136. See Thomas Attig, "Respecting the Spiritual Beliefs of the Dying and the Bereaved," in *Dying, Death, and Bereavement: A Challenge for Living,* 2nd ed., ed. Inge Corless, Barbara B. Germino, and Mary A. Pittman (New York: Springer, 2003), pp. 61–75.

137. Clyde M. Nabe, "'Seeing As': Death As Door or Wall," in *Priorities in Death Education and Counseling,* ed. Richard A. Pacholski and Charles A. Corr (Arlington, Va.: Forum for Death Education and Counseling, 1982), pp. 161–169.

CHAPTER *15*

1. Allan B. Chinen, "The Mortal King," in *The Path Ahead: Readings in Death and Dying,* ed. Lynne Ann DeSpelder and Albert Lee Strickland, 335–336 (Mountain View, Calif.: Mayfield, 1995).

2. Donald Keene, *The Pleasures of Japanese Literature* (New York: Columbia University Press, 1988), p. 86.

3. David Clark, ed., *The Sociology of Death: Theory, Culture, Practice* (Cambridge, Mass.: Blackwell, 1993), p. 3.

4. Thomas Attig, "Coping with Mortality: An Essay on Self-Mourning," in *The Path Ahead,* ed. DeSpelder and Strickland, pp. 337–341. See also Herman Feifel and Steven Strack, "Thanatologists View Death: A 15-Year Perspective," *Omega: Journal of Death and Dying* 43, no. 2 (2001): 97–111; and, in the same issue, Jeanne Quint Benoliel, "Commentary: Thanatologists View Death" (117–118).

5. Darrell Crase, "Black People Do Die, Don't They?" *Death Studies* 11, no. 3 (1987): 221–228. The role of gender in shaping attitudes and behaviors relative to dying and death is similarly underrepresented; see, for example, Felicity Allen, "Where Are the Women in End-of-Life Research?" *Behaviour Change* 19, no. 1 (2002): 39–51.

6. Ronald K. Barrett, "Contemporary African-American Funeral Rites and Traditions," in *The Path Ahead,* ed. DeSpelder and Strickland, pp. 80–92.

7. Ronald K. Barrett, "Sociocultural Considerations for Working with Blacks Experiencing Loss and Grief," in Kenneth Doka and Joyce D. Davidson, eds., *Living with Grief: Who We Are, How We Grieve,* 83–96 (Philadelphia: Brunner/Mazel, 1998), pp. 88–91; and Lynne Ann DeSpelder and Ronald K. Barrett, "Developing Multicultural Competence," *The Director* 64 (December 1997): 66–68; esp. p. 68.

8. Elizabeth J. Clark, "The Future of Social Work in End-of-Life Care: A Call to Action," in Joan Berzoff and Phyllis R. Silverman, *Living with Dying: A Handbook for End-of-Life Care Practitioners* (New York: Columbia University Press, 2004), pp. 838–847; quote p. 841. See also Rita Chi-Ying Chung and Fred Bemak, "The Relationship of Culture and Empathy in Cross-Cultural Counseling," *Journal of Counseling and Development* 80, no. 2 (2002): 154–159; Irene Papadopoulos and Shelley Lees, "Developing Culturally Competent Researchers," *Journal of Advanced Nursing* 37, no. 3 (2002): 258–264; and Jeanne-Marie R. Stacciarini, "Experiencing Cultural Differences: Reflections on Cultural Diversity," *Journal of Professional Nursing* 18, no. 6 (2002): 346–349.

9. Lynne Ann DeSpelder and Albert Lee Strickland, "Culture, Socialization, and Death Education," in *Handbook of Thanatology,* 2nd ed., ed. David K. Meagher and David E. Balk, 323–331 (New York: Routledge, 2013), pp. 323, 324–325, 331.

10. DeSpelder and Barrett, "Developing Multicultural Competence."

11. Wolfgang Stroebe and Margaret Stroebe, "Is Grief Universal? Cultural Variations in the Emotional Reaction to Loss," in *Death and Identity,* 3rd ed., ed. Robert Fulton and Robert Bendiksen, 177–209 (Philadelphia: Charles Press, 1993), p. 201.

12. Fritz Roth, *Einmal Jenseits und Zurück: Ein Koffer für die Letzte Reise* (Gütersloh: Gütersloher Verlagshaus, 2006).

13. Sinéad Donnelly, "Give Me Your Hands, or *Meitheal,*" *Mortality* 10 (Suppl., September, 2005): 24.

14. Dolores M. Dooley, "End-of-Life Decision Making: An Irish Perspective," in *Handbook of Thanatology,* 2nd ed., ed. David K. Meagher and David E. Balk, 111–118 (New York: Routledge, 2013), p. 111.

15. Amy Chow, Cecilia Chan, and Samuel Ho, "Social Sharing of Bereavement Experience by Chinese Bereaved Persons in Hong Kong," *Death Studies* 31, no. 7 (2007): 601–618.

16. Isa Fonnegra de Jaramillo, *Morir Bien: Un Compromiso Personal* [Dying Well: A Personal Commitment] (Barcelona: Planeta, 2006).

17. Alfons Deeken, "Evolving Japanese Perspectives on Death and Dying," *Budhi* (1999): 215–232. Published by Office of Research and Publications School of Arts and Sciences, Ateneo de Manila University, Philippines. See also Lynne Ann DeSpelder, "Desu Edyukesyon no Shimei [The Mission of Death Education]," trans. Keiji Takeuchi, in *Otono no Inochi no Kyoiku* [The Death Education for Adults], edited by Shigeaki Hinohara, Alfons Deeken, and Jitaro Mizuno (Tokyo: Kawadeshobo Shinsha, 2006).

18. K. Takeuchi, Reitaku University, Chiba, personal communication, January, 2006.

19. Lynne Ann DeSpelder, "A World View: International Thanatology," *The Forum: Newsletter of the Association for Death Education and Counseling* 34, no. 1 (2008): 1, 3–4.

20. Robert Kastenbaum, "Theory, Research, and Application: Some Critical Issues for Thanatology," *Omega: Journal of Death and Dying* 18, no. 4 (1987–1988): 397–410; quote p. 408.

21. Myra Bluebond-Langner, "Wither Thou Goest?" *Omega: Journal of Death and Dying* 18, no. 4 (1987–1988): 257–263. See also James A. Thorson, "Qualitative Thanatology," *Mortality* 1, no. 2 (1996).

22. Robert A. Neimeuyer and Darcy L. Harris, "Building Bridges in Bereavement Research and Practice: Some Concluding Reflections," in *Grief and Bereavement in Contemporary Society: Bridging Research and Practice,* ed. Robert A. Neimeyer, Darcy L. Harris, Howard R. Winokuer, and Gordon Thornton, 403–418 (New York: Routledge, 2011), pp. 404–405 (slightly edited).

23. See Bridging Work Group, "Bridging the Gap Between Research and Practice in Bereavement: Report from the Center for the Advancement of Health," *Death Studies* 29 (2005): 93–122.

24. John R. Jordan, "Research That Matters: Bridging the Gap Between Research and Practice in Thanatology," *Death Studies* 24 (2000): 457–467; quote pp. 461, 463.

25. David E. Balk, "Scholarship, Students, and Practitioners: Bringing Scholarship into the Expectations of Practitioners," *Death Studies* 29 (2005): 123–144.

26. Allan Kellehear, *Compassionate Cities: Public Health and End of Life Care* (New York: Routledge, 2005), p. x.

27. Helen Youngelson-Neal, Arthur G. Neal, and Jacob Fried, "Global and Local Culture in the 21st Century," *Journal of American and Comparative Cultures* 24, nos. 3–4 (Fall 2001): 31–36, esp. 33–35.

28. Youngelson-Neal, Neal, and Field, "Global and Local Culture."

29. Kellehear, *Compassionate Cities,* p. x.

30. Ira Byock, *The Best Care Possible: A Physician's Quest to Transform Care Through the End of Life* (New York: Avery, 2012), pp. 250–271.

31. Kellehear, *Compassionate Cities,* p. 16.

32. Kellehear, *Compassionate Cities,* p. 162.

33. See Phyllis Silverman and others, "The 2004 Tucson IWG (International Work Group) Charter for the Normalization of Dying, Death, and Loss," *Omega: Journal of Death and Dying* 50 (2004–2005): 331–336, esp. 332.

34. Silverman and others, p. 46.

35. Allan Kellehear, "Public Health Approaches to Palliative Care: Developments in Australia," *Rikkyo Social Work Review* 23 (2003): 27–35; quote p. 32.

36. See http://webpages.scu.edu/ftp/fow/pages/fowcourseindex.html.

37. Robert E. Goss and Dennis Klass, *Dead but Not Lost: Grief Narratives in Religious Traditions* (Walnut Creek, Calif.: AltaMira Press, 2005), p. 279.

38. Ronald L. Grimes, *Deeply into the Bone: Re-Inventing Rites of Passage* (Berkeley: University of California Press, 2000), p. 221.

39. Herman Feifel, "Psychology and Death: Meaningful Rediscovery," in *The Path Ahead,* ed. DeSpelder and Strickland, pp. 19–28; quote p. 27.

40. Feifel, "Psychology and Death: Meaningful Rediscovery," p. 28.

41. Robert Fulton and Greg Owen, "Death and Society in Twentieth-Century America," *Omega: Journal of Death and Dying* 18, no. 4 (1987–1988): 390. On the many key contributions by women to both clinical and academic approaches in the field, see the special issue focusing on "Women in Thanatology," edited by Inge B. Corless, in *Illness, Crisis & Loss* 9, no. 1 (2001), which includes articles by Jeanne Quint Benoliel, David Clark (on Cicely Saunders), Thelma Bates, Zelda Foster, Catherine Sanders, Doris A. Howell, Ida M. Martinson, Sandra Bertman, Hannelore Wass, Phyllis R. Silverman, and Mary L. S. Vachon.

42. Alfred G. Killilea, "The Politics of Being Mortal," in *The Path Ahead,* ed. DeSpelder and Strickland, pp. 342–347.

43. J. Eugene Knott and Richard W. Prull, "Death Education: Accountable to Whom? For What?" *Omega: Journal of Death and Dying* 7, no. 2 (1976): 178; see also Joseph A. Durlak, "Changing Death Attitudes Through Death Education," in *Death Anxiety Handbook: Research, Instrumentation, and Application,* ed. Robert A. Neimeyer (Washington, D.C.: Taylor & Francis, 1993), pp. 243–259.

44. Christopher Alexander, Sara Ishikawa, and Murray Silverstein, *A Pattern Language: Towns, Building, Construction* (New York: Oxford University Press, 1977), p. 354.

45. See Daniel Callahan, "Defining a Peaceful Death," in *The Troubled Dream of Life: Living with Mortality* (New York: Simon & Schuster, 1993), pp. 195–196.

46. Allan Kellehear, *A Social History of Dying* (New York: Cambridge University Press, 2007), p. 232.

47. Grimes, *Deeply into the Bone,* p. 223.

48. Vernon Reynolds and Ralph Tanner, *The Social Ecology of Religion* (New York: Oxford University Press, 1995), p. 204. For an engaging account of how individuals sustained this concept of a good death despite distressing and unusual circumstances, see Drew Gilin Faust, "The Civil War Soldier and the Art of Dying," *Journal of Southern History* 67, no. 1 (2001): 3–38.

49. Robert Kastenbaum, *On Our Way: The Final Passage Through Life and Death* (Berkeley: University of California Press, 2004), pp. 131–135.

50. Stu Farber, Thomas Egnew, and Annalu Farber, "What is a Respectful Death?" in *Living with Dying: A Handbook for End-of-Life Care Practitioners,* ed. Joan Berzoff and Phyllis R. Silverman (New York: Columbia University Press, 2004), pp. 102–127; quote p. 103.

51. Avery Weisman, *On Dying and Denying: A Psychiatric Study of Terminality* (New York: Behavioral Publications, 1972), pp. 39–40; see also, by Weisman, *The Coping Capacity: On the Nature of Being Mortal* (New York: Human Sciences, 1984).

52. Edwin Shneidman, "Criteria for a Good Death," *Suicide and Life-Threatening Behavior* 37, no. 3 (2007): 245–247; quote p. 247.

53. This account of Lindbergh's death draws from various sources, including a description by Dr. Milton H. Howell, one of Lindbergh's physicians, reported by Ernest H. Rosenbaum, "The Doctor and the Cancer Patient," in *A Hospice Handbook,* ed. Michael P. Hamilton and Helen F. Reid (Grand Rapids, Mich.: Eerdmans, 1980), pp. 19–43.

54. Yoshida Kenkō, quoted by Donald Keene, "Kenkō: Essays in Idleness (*Tsurezureguswa*)," in *Approaches to the Asian Classics,* edited by Wm. Theodore de Bary and Irene Bloom (New York: Columbia University Press, 1990), p. 313.

55. Sharon R. Kaufman, *And a Time to Die: How American Hospitals Shape the End of Life* (New York: Scribner, 2005), p. 323.

56. Stephen S. Hall, "On Beyond 100," *National Geographic* 223, no. 5 (May 2013): 28–49; p. 46.

57. Elizabeth Arias, Melonie Heron, and Betzaida Tejada-Vera, "United States Life Tables Eliminating Certain Causes of Death, 1999–2001," *National Vital Statistics Report* 61, no. 9 (2013).

58. Kaufman, *And a Time to Die,* p. 324.

59. "Resident Population Projections by Sex and Age: 2010 to 2050," *Statistical Abstract of the United States: 2009,* 128th ed. (Washington, D.C.: Government Printing Office, 2008), p. 14.

60. Stewart Brand, *Whole Earth Discipline: An Ecopragmatist Manifesto* (New York: Viking, 2009), p. 61.

61. Ron Crocombe, *The South Pacific: An Introduction* (Auckland, New Zealand: Longman Paul, 1983).

62. Crocombe, *South Pacific,* p. 73.

63. See Carla J. Sofka, "Social Support 'Internetworks,' Caskets for Sale, and More: Thanatology and the Information Superhighway," *Death Studies* 21, no. 6 (1997): 553–574.

64. Damon Knight, "Masks," in *A Pocketful of Stars,* ed. Knight (New York: Doubleday, 1971).

65. Reported in Dick Teresi, *The Undead: Organ Harvesting, the Ice-Water Test, Beating-Heart Cadavers—How Medicine is Blurring the Line Between Life and Death* (New York: Pantheon, 2012), p. 173.

66. Clifford Simak, "Death Scene," in *The Worlds of Clifford Simak* (New York: Simon & Schuster, 1960); Robert A. Heinlein, "Life-Line," in *The Man Who Sold the Moon: Harriman and the Escape from the Earth to the Moon!* ed. Heinlein (New York: Shasta, 1950).

67. Kit Reed, "Golden Acres," in *Social Problems Through Science Fiction,* ed. John W. Miestead and others (New York: St. Martin's, 1975).

68. Sten Odenwald, *Back to the Astronomy Café* (Boulder, Colo.: Westview, 2003), p. 39.

69. Odenwald, *Back to the Astronomy Cafe,* p. 88.

70. Gary Snyder, *The Practice of the Wild: Essays* (San Francisco: North Point Press, 1990), p. 176.

71. Sandra L. Bertman, "Bearing the Unbearable: From Loss, the Gain," in *The Path Ahead,* ed. DeSpelder and Strickland, pp. 348–354; quote p. 353.

72. Doris M. Schoenhoff, *The Barefoot Expert: The Interface of Computerized Knowledge Systems and Indigenous Knowledge Systems* (Westport, Conn.: Greenwood, 1993), p. 100.

Credits and Sources

Prologue and Epilogue: Copyright © 1982 by David Gordon. Used by permission.

Pages 4, 101, & 276: Courtesy of the Center for Creative Photography. Used by permission.

Page 10: *Language Log Blog,* "Kim Jong Il: Did he "die" or "pass away?," blog entry by Harlow Wilcox, December 20, 2011; http://languagelog.ldc.upenn.edu/nll/?p=3643.

Page 17: From Jean Lipman-Blumen, "Our Existential Vulnerability to Toxic Leaders"; *Death and Denial: Interdisciplinary Perspectives on the Legacy of Ernest Becker,* ed. Daniel Liechty, 161–172; Praeger, 2002, p. 162. John O'Hara's *Appointment in Samarra* was published in 1982.

Page 19: Quote by Suse Lowenstein from Ann F. de Jong Hodgson, "Interviews and Issues: Dark Elegy," *Illness, Crises and Loss* 4, nos. 3–4 (1995): 18–38; quote, p. 21.

Pages 21, 24, 79, 169, 202, 254, 294, 325, 329, 343, 349, 427, 429, 443, 549 & 568: Courtesy of Albert Lee Strickland. Used by permission.

Page 25: From *The Kitchen Chronicles: 1001 Lunches with J. Krishnamurti* by Michael Krohnen; Edwin House, 1997, p. 292.

Pages 30, 52, 193: Courtesy of Nick Downes. Used by permission.

Page 35: From "Death in Cades Cove" by A. Crosby, in *Appalachia: When Yesterday Is Today,* ed. students at the University of Tennessee, Knoxville, 1965, pp. 1–3; quoted in *Death and Dying in Central Appalachia: Changing Attitudes and Practices* by James K. Crissman; University of Illinois Press, 1994.

Pages 36 & 37: U.S. Census Bureau, *Historical Statistics of the United States, Colonial Times to 1970;* Washington, D.C.: Government Printing Office, 1975, pp. 55, 59; and Donna L. Hoyert and Jiaquan Xu, "Deaths: Preliminary Data for 2011," *National Vital Statistics Reports* 61, no. 6; Hyattsville, Md.: National Center for Health Statistics, 2012, pp. 1, 26.

Page 38: Donna L. Hoyert and Jiaquan Xu, "Deaths: Preliminary Data for 2011," *National Vital Statistics Reports* 61, no. 6; Hyattsville, Md.: National Center for Health Statistics, 2012, p. 4.

Page 40: From the *Los Angeles Times* (December 21, 1990).

Pages 45, 152 & 304: Courtesy of Edward C. and Gail R. Johnson.

Pages 48, 320 & 575: Courtesy of Robin Van Doren, Open Doors.

Pages 54 & 277: From *Mortality* by Christopher Hitchens; Twelve, 2012, pp. 6, 101.

Page 55: Based on Erik H. Erikson, *Childhood and Society,* 2nd ed.; Norton, 1964, pp. 247–274.

Page 58: Tammy Maas, *Reader's Digest* (July 2009), p. 57.

Pages 60, 335, 336 & 398: Used with permission of Joe Allen, Brooks Allen, and Janice Laurent.

Pages 61, 138, 197, 250, 258, 582 & 591: Courtesy of Carol A. Foote. Used by permission.

Page 72: Courtesy of William M. Lamers, Jr., "The Little Sounds of Grief: Poetry and Grief," a presentation to the 21st International Death, Grief, and Bereavement Conference, University of Wisconsin, LaCross, May 28, 2003.

Page 73: From *Journeys Through Bookland,* Vol. 1, ed. Charles H. Sylvester; Bellows-Reeve Company, Publishers, Chicago, 1922.

Page 74: Courtesy of Christine DeVault. Used by permission.

Page 81: From *Shifting Interludes: Selected Essays* by Willie Morris, edited by Jack Bales; University Press of Mississippi, 2002, p. 173.

Pages 88, 126, & 136: Courtesy of Patrick Dean. Used by permission.

Page 93: Illustration copyright © 1982 by Eric Mathes. Courtesy of Eric Mathes.

Page 93 (bottom): From *Death Customs* by E. Bendann; Knopf, 1930.

Page 94: "When Hare Heard of Death" excerpted from pp. 23–24 of *The Road of Life and Death: A Ritual Drama of the American Indians* by Paul Radin, Bollingen Series V. Copyright © 1945, renewed 1973, by Princeton University Press. Reprinted by permission of Princeton University Press and Doris Woodward Radin.

Page 95: Aesop's "Eros and Death" reworked by Steve Sanfield, from *Death: An Anthology of Ancient Texts, Songs, Prayers, and Stories,* ed. David Meltzer; North Point Press, 1984.

Pages 96–97: Based on *A Social History of Dying* by Allan Kellehear; Cambridge University Press, 2007. Used with permission.

Page 100: From *Strange Facts About Death* by Webb Garrison. Copyright © 1978 by Webb Garrison. Used by permission of the publisher, Abingdon Press.

Page 110: Papago song by Juana Manwell. By permission of Smithsonian Institution Press from *Papago Music* by Frances Densmore;

Bureau of American Ethnology Bulletin 90; Smithsonian Institution, Washington, D.C. 1929.

Page 110: Dakota song from *The Primal Mind: Vision and Reality in Indian America* by Jamake Highwater; Harper and Row, 1981.

Page 111: Burial oration (Wintu) from "Wintu Ethnography" by Cora Du Bois, in *University of California Publications in American Archaeology and Ethnology* 36 (1935). Reprinted by permission of the University of California Press.

Page 113: From *Religions of Africa: A Pilgrimage into Traditional Religions* by Noel Q. King; Harper and Row, 1970.

Page 121: Courtesy of Shmuel Thaler. Used by permission.

Page 122: Reprinted from *Phnom Penh Post* (October 21, 2001). From *Under the Dragon: California's New Culture* by Lonny Shavelson and Fred Setterberg; co-published by Heyday Books and the Oakland Museum of California, p. 120.

Page 124: From *Chuang Tzu: Basic Writings,* trans. Burton Watson; Columbia University Press, 1964, p. 113.

Page 127: From *The Four Seasons: Japanese Haiku Second Series,* trans. Peter Beilenson. Copyright © 1958 by The Peter Pauper Press.

Page 128: Courtesy of Andy Hau Yan Ho. Used by permission.

Page 145: Courtesy of David Rodriguez. Used by permission.

Page 146: Adapted from "Low-Tech Autopsies in the Era of HighTech Medicine: Continued Value for Quality Assurance and Patient Safety" by George D. Lundberg; *JAMA* 280, no. 14 (October 14, 1998), pp. 1273–1274.

Pages 149, 205, 252, 285, 354 & 596: The New Yorker Collection drawings from The Cartoon Bank. All Rights Reserved.

Page 153: Used by permission of Elizabeth Bradbury.

Page 155: From "Clarifying the Paradigm for the Ethics of Donation and Transplantation: Was 'Dead' Really So Clear Before Organ Donation?" by Sam D. Shemie; *Philosophy, Ethics, and Humanities in Medicine* 2 (August 24, 2007), p. 18.

Page 158: From *Mystics, Magicians, and Medicine People: Tales of a Wanderer* by Doug Boyd. Copyright © 1989 by Doug Boyd. Reprinted by permission of Paragon House.

Page 161: From "Dying As a Social Relationship: A Sociological Review of Debates on the Determination of Death" by Allan Kellehear; *Social Science & Medicine* 66 (2008), pp. 1533, 1544.

Page 162: President's Commission for the Study of Ethical Problems in Medicine and Biomedical and Behavioral Research, *Defining Death: A Report on the Medical, Legal, and Ethical Issues in the Determination of Death;* Washington, D.C.: Government Printing Office, 1981, p. 73.

Page 170: From *Postmortem: How Medical Examiners Explain Suspicious Deaths* by Stefan Timmermans; University of Chicago Press, p.103.

Page 177: From *Dying and Death: A Clinical Guide for Caregivers,* ed. David Barton; Williams & Wilkins, 1977, p. 181.

Page 178: Adapted from *Taming the Beloved Beast: How Medical Techinology Costs are Destroying Our Health Care System* by Daniel Callahan; Princeton University Press, 2009, pp. 47–48.

Page 180: From *The Week* (June 26, 2009), p. 3.

Page 182: From the Honolulu *Star-Bulletin* (October 20, 1985).

Page 184: From "Dying Words: How Should Doctors Deliver Bad News?" by Jerome Groopman; *New Yorker* (October 28, 2002), p. 62–70; quote, p. 66.

Page 186: Reprinted with permission of Simon & Schuster from *To Live Until We Say Good-Bye,* text by Elisabeth Kübler-Ross and photographs by Mal Warshaw. Copyright © 1978 by Ross Medical Associates, S.C., and Mal Warshaw. Photograph copyright © 1978 by Mal Warshaw.

Page 187: From "Medicine and the Question of Suffering" by Richard B. Gunderman; *Second Opinion: Health, Faith, and Ethics* 14 (July 1990).

Page 189: Adapted from "Referring a Patient and Family to High-Quality Palliative Care at the Close of Life," by Joan M. Teno and Stephen R. Connor; *JAMA* 301, no. 6 (February 11, 2009): 651–659; p. 653.

Page 190: Provided courtesy of Maurizio Marinelli by Fondazione Hospice MariaTeresa Chiantore Seràgnoli Onlus, Bologna, Italy.

Pages 199 & 422: From *You Don't Miss Your Water* by Cornelius Eady, © 1995 by Cornelius Eady; Henry Holt, 1995; first published in *Pequod,* no. 35 (1993), p. 114. Reprinted by permission of the author and Henry Holt and Co.

Page 201: Adapted from *Our Aging Parents: A Practical Guide to Eldercare,* ed. Colette Browne and Roberta Onzuka-Anderson; University of Hawaii Press, 1985, pp. 204–209.

Page 203: From *On Fire: A Personal Account of Life and Death and Choices* by Larry Brown; Algonquin, 1994, pp. 47–48.

Page 206: From *Passing On: The Social Organization of Dying* by David Sudnow; Prentice-Hall, 1967.

Page 209: From *A Gradual Awakening* by Stephen Levine. Copyright © 1979 by Stephen Levine. Reprinted by permission of Doubleday & Company, Inc.
Page 216: President's Commission for the Study of Ethical Problems in Medicine and Biomedical and Behavioral Research, *Making Health Care Decisions, A Report on the Ethical and Legal Implications of the Patient-Practitioner Relationship;* Washington, D.C.: Government Printing Office, 1982, pp. 64–65.
Page 220: From *Care of the Dying* by Richard Lamerton; Technomic Publishing, 1976.
Page 223: Adapted from *Connect Core Concepts in Health,* 13th ed., by Paul M. Insel and Walton T. Roth; McGraw-Hill, 2013, p. 446.
Page 225: From *Journeys* (July 2006), Hospice Foundation of America, p. 3.
Page 240: James Scott, e-mail message to authors, July 11, 2013.
Page 241: From *To A God Unknown* by John Steinbeck; R. O. Ballou, 1933.
Page 245: From *News from Native California* 4 (August–October 1990).
Pages 246–247: Will of Tomás Antonio Yorba, trans. H. Noya [HM26653]. Reproduced by permission of The Huntington Library, San Marino, California.
Page 255: From the *Honolulu Star-Bulletin & Advertiser* (August 26, 1990).
Page 262: From *Enjoy Every Sandwich: Living Each Day As If It Were Your Last* by Lee Lipsenthal; Crown Archetype, 2012, page 14.
Page 263: Adapted from "A Task-Based Approach to Coping with Dying," by Charles A. Corr; *Omega: Journal of Death and Dying* 24, no. 2 (1991–1992): 81–94.
Page 265: "But You Look So Good" from *No Pain, No Gain.* Reprinted by permission of Judith L. Ellsworth.
Page 267: Adapted from "Coping with Life-Threatening Illness: A Task Model," by Kenneth J. Doka; *Omega: Journal of Death and Dying* 32, no. 2 (1995–1996): 111–122.
Page 268: From the *Register-Pajaronian,* Watsonville, Calif. (March 11, 1981).
Page 270: Used by permission of Joan J. Conn.
Page 271: From "Love Bade Me Welcome" by Christian Wiman in *The Best American Spiritual Writing 2008;* Houghton Mifflin, 2008. Originally published in *The American Scholar* (Summer 2007).
Pages 274–275: Adapted from *Living with Cancer* by Ernest H. Rosenbaum; The Mosby Medical Library series, The C. V. Mosby Company, St. Louis, 1982. Used with permission of The C. V. Mosby Company.
Page 279: From *There is a Rainbow Behind Every Dark Cloud,* The Center for Attitudinal Healing; Celestial Arts, 1978, p. 71.
Page 283: From "Pain Management on Trial" by Maureen Cushing; *American Journal of Nursing* 7 (February 1992): 21–22.
Page 287: Adapted from *Living Well at the End of Life* by Joanne Lynn and David M. Adamson; RAND, 2003, p. 8.
Page 288: Adapted from "Preparing for the Death of a Loved One," *American Journal of Hospice and Palliative Care* 9, no. 4 (1992): 14–16; *The Merck Manual of Medical Information: Home Edition,* ed. Robert Berkow, Merck Research Laboratories, 1997, p. 21; and "The Last Few Days," by Robert E. Enck, *American Journal of Hospice and Palliative Care* 9, no. 4 (1992): 11–13.
Page 292: From *The End of Life Advisor: Personal, Legal, and Medical Considerations for a Peaceful, Dignified Death* by Susan Dolan and Audrey Vizzard; Kaplan, 2009, p. 75.
Page 299 (bottom): From *The County Journal,* Bayfield County, Cable, Wis. (April 25, 1991).
Page 303: Used by permission of Edgar N. Jackson.
Page 306: From "Take Only As Directed" by Wayne Delk; *U. S. Gospel News* (September 1999). Reprinted by permission of the author.
Page 314: Adapted from General Price List Survey, National Funeral Directors Association.
Page 316: Athenaeum of Philadelphia Collection.
Page 321: From *The History of American Funeral Directing* by Robert W. Habenstein and William M. Lamers; Bulfin Printers, Milwaukee, 1962.
Pages 327 & 561: Courtesy of P. S. Mueller. Used by permission.
Page 331: From *Traversing the Minefield—Best Practice: Reducing Risk in Funeral-Cremation Service* by Michael Kubasak and William M. Lamers, Jr.; LMG Publishing, 2007, p. 233.
Page 332 (bottom): Adapted from "Dying to Be Green," by Neil Shea, *National Geographic* (July 2008).
Page 333: From *The Secret Cemetery* by Doris Francis, Leonie Kellaher, and Georgina Neophytou; Oxford: Berg, 2005, p. 1.
Page 338: Courtesy of Fritz and Inge Roth, Pütz-Roth, Bergisch Gladbach, Germany.
Page 342: From *Living Your Dying* by Stanley Keleman; Random House, 1974.
Page 344: From *Playboy* interview by Eric Spitznagel (October 16, 2012).

Page 347: From *A Death in the Sanchez Family* by Oscar Lewis; Random House, 1969.

Page 349 (left): From *Victorian Cemetery Art* by Edward V. Gillon, Jr.; Dover, 1972. Reproduced by permission of Edward V. Gillon, Jr.

Page 352: Adapted from "The Two-Track Model of Bereavement: Overview, Retrospect, and Prospect," by Simon Shimshon Rubin, *Death Studies* 23 (1999): 681–714, p. 685; and "The Two-Track Model of Bereavement Questionnaire (TTBQ): Development and Validation of a Relational Measure," by Simon Shimson Rubin and others, *Death Studies* 33 (2009): 305–333, p. 309.

Page 361: Reprinted from "Mourning and Meaning," by Robert A. Neimeyer, Holly G. Prigerson, and Betty Davies; *American Behavioral Scientist* 46, no. 2 (October 2002): 235–251, p. 244.

Page 364: From *Class: A View from Middle England* by Jilly Cooper; Methuen, 1979.

Page 368: From *A Harvest Yet to Reap: A History of Prairie Women* by Linda Rasmussen and others; Women's Press, Toronto, Ontario, 1976.

Page 378: From *Ethical Practice in Grief Counseling,* by Louis A. Gamino and R. Hal Ritter, Jr.; Springer, 2009, p. 213.

Page 382: "Anguish of Loss," "Sharing the Grief," and "Collapsing" from *The Anguish of Loss,* 2nd ed. Copyright © 1992 by Julie Fritsch and Sherokee Ilse. Photographs by Paul Schraub. Reprinted by permission of Wintergreen Press and Julie Fritsch.

Page 389 (bottom): Drawing by Dominic Horath created in Mrs. Bronwyn Luffman's classroom at Salesian Sisters School and provided by Linda DaValle. Reprinted by permission of Mary and Frank Horath.

Pages 394 & 449: From *Never the Same: Coming to Terms with the Death of a Parent* by Donna Schuurman; St. Martin's Press, 2003.

Page 395: Used with permission of Christine and Donovan Longaker.

Page 396: Courtesy of Karen Saltzman. Used by permission.

Page 400: Adapted from *Approaching Death: Improvimg Care at the End of Life,* ed. Marilyn J. Field and Christine K. Cassel; National Academy Press, 1997, p. 65.

Page 408: "Peanuts" reprinted by permission of United Features Syndicate, Inc.

Page 410: From *A Tropical Childhood and Other Poems* by Edward Lucie-Smith. Copyright © Oxford University Press, 1961. Reprinted by permission of Oxford University Press.

Page 411: Courtesy of Francesco and Sofia Campione.

Page 414: Caption to cartoon by E. H. Shepard, ©Punch/Rothco. Reprinted by permission of Rothco Cartoons, Inc.

Page 418: From "Scream of Consciousness" by Ruth Kramer Ziony; *Neworld* (1977).

Page 425: From *The Undertaking: Life Studies from the Dismal Trade* by Thomas Lynch; W. W. Norton, 1997, pp. 82–83, 51.

Page 431: From *The Journey Through Grief and Loss: Helping Yourself and Your Child When Grief Is Shared* by Robert Zucker; St. Martins Griffin, 2009, p.70.

Page 433: Transcribed by the authors from an inscription at the National Civil Rights Museum in Memphis, Tennessee.

Page 440: From *The Warming of Winter* by Maxine Dowd Jensen; Abingdon Press, 1977.

Page 441: Adapted from *Last Chapters: A Sociology of Aging and Dying,* by Victor W. Marshall; Brooks/Cole, 1980, pp. 169–177.

Page 444: From *Chipping Bone: Collected Poems* by Maude Meehan; Embers Press, 1985. Courtesy of Maude Meehan.

Page 448: From (a) *Merriam-Webster's Collegiate Dictionary,* Eleventh Edition, © 2003 by Merriam-Webster, Inc., publisher of the Merriam-Webster® Dictionaries; used by permission. (b) *Pathways to Suicide: A Survey of Self-Destructive Behaviors,* by Ronald W. Maris, Johns Hopkins University Press, 1981, p. 290. (c) *Suicide,* by Jean Baechler, Basic, 1979, p. 11. (d) *Death: Current Perspectives,* 2nd ed., ed. Edwin S. Shneidman, Mayfield, 1980, p. 416.

Page 451: Adapted from "Procedures and Problems in Conducting a Psychological Autopsy," by Thomas J. Young; *International Journal of Offender Therapy and Comparative Criminology* 36, no. 1 (Spring 1992): 43–52.

Page 452: Adapted from "Psychological Autopsy: Clinical and Legal Perspectives," by James R. P. Ogloff and Randy K. Otto, *Saint Louis University Law Journal* 37, no. 3 (Spring 1993): 610–614; and "Procedures and Problems in Conducting a Psychological Autopsy," by Thomas J. Young, *International Journal of Offender Therapy and Comparative Criminology* 36, no. 1 (Spring 1992): 47–48.

Pages 456, 464, 468, 472 & 480: Suicide notes courtesy of Edwin S. Shneidman.

Page 458: Edwin Arlington Robinson, "Richard Cory," in *The Children of the Night;* Charles Scribner's Sons, 1897. Copyright under the Berne Convention. Reprinted with the permission of Charles Scribner's Sons.
Page 460: Adapted from *Death, Society, and Human Experience,* 2nd ed., by Robert J. Kastenbaum; The C. V. Mosby Company, St. Louis, 1981. Used with permission of The C. V. Mosby Company and Robert J. Kastenbaum.
Page 462: Kim Bridgeford, Department of English, Fairfield University, Fairfield, Conn.
Page 465: Adapted from *Deaths of Man* by Edwin S. Shneidman; Quadrangle Books, 1973, pp, 82–90. Courtesy of Edwin S. Shneidman.
Page 467: Adapted from "Suicide: The Ultimate Escape" by Brian Barry; *Death Studies* 13, no. 2 (1989): 185–190.
Page 474: From *The Savage God: A Study of Suicide* by A. Alvarez; Random House, 1972.
Pages 477–478: Courtesy of Magaret Macro.
Page 478: "Resume" by Dorothy Parker, from *The Portable Dorothy Parker,* revised and enlarged edition, ed. Brendan Gill. Copyright 1926 by Dorothy Parker. Reprinted by permission of Viking Penguin, Inc., and from *The Collected Dorothy Parker* by permission of Gerald Duckworth, Ltd.
Page 479: From *The Suicide Index: Putting My Father's Death in Order* by Joan Wickersham; Harcourt, 2008, p. 303.
Page 484: Used by permission of Maude Meehan.
Page 490: From *Life in the Fast Lane: Selected Works of Stephen St. Croix,* by Stephen St. Croix; Mix Books, 2008, p. 210. Originally published in *Mix* (December 2003), p. 22.
Page 493: From "Groundfall" by William G. Higgins; *Sierra* (November–December 1979).
Page 497: Drawing by Haruna Sato, age 7. Used by permission of Mie Sato. Reprinted from the book, *Tsunami: The Complete Essays by Children from the Disaster Areas* edited by Ken Mori. Courtesy of Ken Mori and Bungeishunju Ltd., Chiyoda, Tokyo, 2012, published by Yasushi Toriyama (www.bunshun, co.jp). With thanks to Makiko Matsumoto and Jitaro Mizuno, as well as to Mie Sato and her daughter Haruna.
Page 499: From *Salvage the Bones,* by Jesmyn Ward; Bloomsbury, 2011, pp. 216–217.
Page 501: From *Life, Sex, and Ideas: The Good Life Without God,* by A. C. Grayling; Oxford University Press, 2003, p. 125.
Page 506: Adapted from *The Psychology of Death: Concise Edition,* by Robert Kastenbaum and Ruth Aisenberg; Springer, 1976, pp. 291–294.
Page 509: From "Down at the Cross: Letter from a Region in My Mind," by James Baldwin, in *The Fire Next Time,* © 1963 James Baldwin, Vintage Press. Reprinted in James Baldwin, *Collected Essays;* Library of America, 1998, p. 330.
Page 513: From *A Journal for Jordan: A Story of Love and Honor* by Dana Canedy; Crown, 2008, p. 247.
Page 516: Adapted from *Faces of the Enemy: Reflections of the Hostile Imagination* by Sam Keen; Harper and Row, 1986.
Page 520: Courtesy of Carla Sofka, Ph.D., the New York State Museum History Collection, and the World Trade Center Relief Fund. Acquisition number 202.25.184 (cover). All rights reserved.
Page 522: Adapted from *Understanding Terrorism: Challenges, Perspectives, and Issues,* 3rd ed., by Gus Martin; Sage, 2010, p. 6.
Page 528: From "Back to a Future: One Man's AIDS Tale Shows How Quickly Epidemic Has Turned" by David Sanford; *The Wall Street Journal* (November 8, 1996).
Page 536: Courtesy of Barbara J. Paul, Ph.D. All rights reserved.
Page 541: From "Go Down Death—A Funeral Sermon," in *God's Trombones* by James Weldon Johnson. Copyright 1927 by Viking Press, Inc. Copyright renewed 1955 by Grace Nail Johnson. Reprinted by Permission of Viking Penguin Inc.
Page 542: From *Religious Encounters with Death: Insights from the History and Anthropology of Religions,* ed. Frank E. Reynolds and Earle H. Waugh; Pennsylvania State University Press, 1977.
Page 546: From Mahabharata, 3.314.118, W. S. Merwin's translation, from J. Moussaieff Masson, "Introduction," in *Sanskrit Love Poetry,* trans. W. S. Merwin and J. Moussaieff Masson; Columbia University Press, 1977, p. 20.
Page 547: From *Zen Mind, Beginner's Mind* by Shunryu Suzuki; 1970. Reprinted by permission of John Weatherhill, Inc.
Page 548: Courtesy of Bodhidharma Inc.
Page 565: From *The Gospel at Colonus.* Music by Bob Telson, lyrics by Lee Breuer.
Page 577: From *Einmal Jenseits und Zurück: Ein Koffer für die Letzte Reise,* by Fritz Roth;

Gütersloher Verlagshaus, 2006, pp. 84–85. Courtesy of Pütz-Roth.

Page 580: From *At the Edge of the Body* by Erica Jong. Copyright © 1979 by Erica Mann Jong. Reprinted by permission of the poet.

Page 583: From an advertisement for *Sex Money Kiss* by Gene Simmons in *Publishers Weekly* (April 28, 2003).

Page 585: Courtesy of *Rolling Stone* magazine.

Page 586: Reprinted by permission. Advertising agency: Robaire and Hogshead, Venice, Calif. Photography: Michael Ruppert Studios, Los Angeles, Calif.

Page 588: Adapted from "In Search of a Good Death: Observations of Patients, Families, and Providers," by Karen E. Steinhauser and others; *Annals of Internal Medicine* 132, no. 10 (2002): 825–832.

Page 590: Adapted from "Criteria for a Good Death," by Edwin Shneidman; *Suicide and Life-Threatening Behavior* 37, no. 3 (2007): 245–247.

Pages 592–593: From *Big Winds, Glass Mornings, Shadows Cast by Stars: Poems 1972–80* by Morton Marcus; Jazz Press, Los Angeles, 1981. Copyright © by Morton Marcus. Used by permission of Morton Marcus.

Name Index

Subject Index